D0023044

A CENTENNIAL BOOK

One hundred books
published between 1990 and 1995
bear this special imprint of
the University of California Press.
We have chosen each Centennial Book
as an example of the Press's finest
publishing and bookmaking traditions
as we celebrate the beginning of
our second century.

UNIVERSITY OF CALIFORNIA PRESS

Founded in 1893

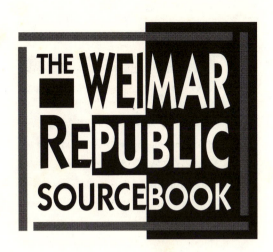

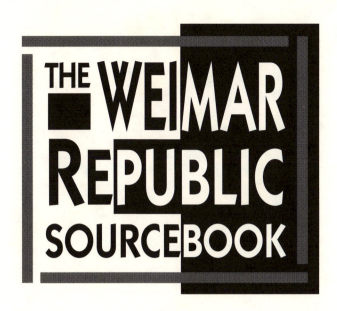

THE WEIMAR REPUBLIC SOURCEBOOK

EDITED BY

ANTON KAES

MARTIN JAY

EDWARD DIMENDBERG

UNIVERSITY OF CALIFORNIA PRESS

BERKELEY   LOS ANGELES   LONDON

Published with the assistance of the Getty Grant Program.

The Press would also like to acknowledge support of grants from the National Endowment of the Humanities, an independent federal agency, the Siemens Corporation, the Associates of the University of California Press, the Center for German and European Studies at the University of California, Berkeley, and Henry J. Bruman.

Acknowledgments to reprint previously published material can be found on page 789.

Front endsheet: German soldiers returning home from WWI. (Landesbildstelle Berlin)

Back endsheet: Hitler marches at Braunschweig Parteitag rally, October 1931. (Landesbildstelle Berlin)

University of California Press
Berkeley and Los Angeles, California
University of California Press
London, England
Copyright © 1994 by
The Regents of the University of California
Printed in the United States of America
1 2 3 4 5 6 7 8 9

Library of Congress Cataloging-in-Publication Data
The Weimar Republic sourcebook / edited by Anton Kaes, Martin Jay, Edward Dimendberg.
     p. cm. — (Weimar and now ; 3)
    Includes bibliographical references and index.
    ISBN 0-520-06774-6
    1. Germany—Politics and government—1918–1933—Sources.
2. Germany—Social conditions—1918–1933—Sources.   3. Germany—
Social life and customs—20th century—Sources.   4. National socialism—
Germany—Sources.   5. Government, Resistance to—Germany—History—
20th century—Sources.   I. Kaes, Anton.   II. Jay, Martin, 1944–   .
III. Dimendberg, Edward.   IV. Series.
DD240.W3927   1994
943.085—dc20   93-42108

The paper used in this publication meets the minimum requirements of American National Standard for Information Sciences—Permanence of Paper for Printed Library Materials, ANSI Z39.48-1984 ⊗

Contents

PRESSURE POINTS OF SOCIAL LIFE

Preface

TRADITIONAL NARRATIVES of German history typically describe the Weimar Republic as a troubled interlude between two eras of greater and more sinister importance: the Wilhelmine *Kaiserreich,* which created a unified Germany, and the Third Reich, which destroyed it. In these accounts, Weimar is seen as a desperate and grudging experiment in democracy whose decisive failure had consequences not only for Germany but the world. Its cultural innovations, varied and controversial, are said to have matured only in the cruel exile forced by the Nazi regime. Its political legacy has been understood almost entirely in negative terms; as the advocates of the Federal Republic, founded after World War II, were fond of saying: "Bonn is not Weimar!"

In recent years, however, many historians have become skeptical about straightforward, univocal narratives that assign events and eras a simple place in a coherent story. They have returned to an insight articulated by two of Weimar's most insightful intellectuals, Ernst Bloch and Siegfried Kracauer: history is composed of many threads that can be interwoven only with difficulty, if at all, into a single tapestry. What Bloch called "non-synchronicity" or "non-contemporaneity" (*Ungleichzeitigkeit*) and Kracauer the "heterogeneity of the historical universe" acknowledges the multiple temporal strands that rarely, if ever, cohere in any historical period. Some are residues of past eras, others are anticipations of future ones; the significance depends on the larger narrative in which they figure.

The turbulent fourteen years of the Weimar Republic confound any attempt to fashion one wholly integrated story. Instead, the historian must recognize the variety of radically different stories that can be wrested from the debris of Weimar. What appeared to some who lived at the time as the birth of modernity and the dawn of a modern technological age, seemed to others the epitome of alienation and decadence. If a master narrative of Weimar history with collapse and horror as its telos is no longer viable, the principle of montage suggests itself as a more appropriate strategy for comprehending the fragments of an untotalizable whole. Indeed, the multiperspectivism of montage was often praised during the period itself as a technique that challenges synthesis and closure.

The legacy of Weimar continues to haunt the political and cultural imagery of the twentieth century. As a reunited Germany struggles to master demons long thought dead, the lessons of Weimar—however they are drawn—appear uncannily relevant. A laboratory for modernity, the Weimar period offered a panoply of political, economic, social, and cultural models, some of which blended imperceptibly into the Nazi ideology while others survived in exile after 1933. Political blueprints, practical and utopian; cultural experiments, elitist and popular; social initiatives, progressive and reactionary—all circulated among a populace still in shock from the loss of a four-year war and a nearly fifty-year-old imperial identity.

The result was a frantic kaleidoscopic shuffling of the fragments of a nascent modernity and the remnants of a persistent past. Odd combinations of progressive traditionalism and reactionary modernism vied with the seemingly more appropriate alliances of avant-garde or conservative political, social, and cultural ideology. Innocent expressions of radical hope struggled against a mood of resigned world-weariness. What one Weimar survivor, Theodor W. Adorno, dubbed the "jargon of authenticity" competed with what a later German commentator, Peter Sloterdijk, called the corrosive triumph of "cynical reason." The categories of "high" and "low," whether applied to politics, culture or social relations, no longer seemed relevant.

We have sought to make the rich legacy of Weimar come alive by assembling a wide variety of original documents and presenting them in thirty chapters that juxtapose politics with culture, philosophy, social thought, and anecdotal material from everyday life. Even though hierarchical determinations of importance and influence unavoidably affect any process of selection and arrangement, we have endeavored to question these assumptions as frequently as possible. Although the documents are chronologically organized and contextualized in chapter introductions (for the benefit of those unfamiliar with the general contours of the period), the texts themselves will no doubt interact for every reader in ways that undermine any predetermined order or pattern. Along with the obvious figures and dominant themes, we have included many pieces that will be unfamiliar to even the most learned of Weimar scholars.

Our major selection criteria were the specificity of a document to the Weimar era and its relevance and resonance for us today. We are painfully aware of the many texts that could not be included because of restrictions of space. We also regret that we needed to shorten a number of texts for the same reason. At the same time we are heartened by the hope that it may well be these gaps and omissions that will stimulate further forays into one of the most creative and troubling periods of the twentieth century.

A few words are in order about the editorial principles of the book. All documents were selected from writings originally published during the Weimar period. These include government records and reports; political fliers, speeches, and manifestoes; party programs; daily newspapers and popular magazines; cultural and political journals; trade publications; literary and film reviews; artists' statements; exhibition catalogs; pamphlets and books. Since we focused on texts that publicly circulated between 9 November 1918 and

30 January 1933, we omitted, with a few exceptions, unpublished materials and correspondence as well as retrospective interviews and autobiographies. In some cases we included documents composed before the end of the Weimar Republic but published shortly after its demise. We favored texts that ignited debates, spawned controversy, or articulated an issue particularly well. Predominantly fictional works—poems, plays, short stories, and novels—were excluded. We strongly believe, however, that literary works, as well as other cultural productions of the period, will resonate more dynamically once positioned in the contexts reconstructed here. In the tradition of the "history of everyday life" (the *Alltagsgeschichte* only recently discovered by German historians), we have incorporated writings that lend a voice to the private fears and anxieties, wishes and aspirations of the period. Material that might strike some readers as "cultural plankton" is meant to convey a sense of daily life that is so often missing in purely political and (high-)cultural histories of the Weimar Republic.

Generally, document headings translate the original title of articles or books. In the rare case of texts published without a title or taken from larger works, we have provided our own titles within square brackets. We also have supplied annotations in footnotes when they seemed helpful. All of our own editorial interventions—explanatory information and omissions—are indicated by square brackets. Most of the texts presented here are translated for the first time. Those that appeared previously in English, some dating as far back as the Weimar Republic, are reprinted in their original wording. Variations in style and expression among the different translations are therefore inevitable. As a matter of principle, we sought to preserve the documents' historical patina and phrasing, even at the cost of retaining an occasional opaque passage and instances of offensive racist and sexist language.

Publication of this book would not have been possible without the assistance and support of many individuals and organizations. To the large number of friends, colleagues, and donors, who provided encouragement and concrete help, we offer our sincere gratitude. Sander L. Gilman, Andreas Huyssen, and Helmut Kreuzer were early advocates of the project. Charles W. Haxthausen suggested selections for the art section and provided assistance with translations. Iain Boyd Whyte was equally helpful with the chapters on architecture. Margaret Anderson, Ulrike Bauriedel, Bruce Campbell, Albrecht Dümling, Gerald Feldman, Peter Jelavich, Barbara Kosta, Helmut Lethen, Thomas Levin, Cornelia Levine, Hans Mommsen, Sigrid Müller, Eric Rentschler, Wolfgang Theis, Karl Toepfer, and John Willett shared their expertise and recommended texts which found their way into the book. Participants in NEH summer seminars conducted by Anton Kaes in Berkeley and Berlin, which dealt with Weimar culture and modernity, offered challenging feedback about the analytical dimension of the project and propelled it forward by their sheer enthusiasm.

Nancy P. Nenno, the principal research assistant in the last phase of the book, unsparingly gave her time and provided invaluable editorial help. We are especially grateful for her expert work on the political chronology and biographies, as well as her careful reading of the manuscript. Leslie A. Pahl also helped with research and editing. We thank Don Reneau, who translated the majority of the documents. We also were fortunate to enjoy the assistance of Benedikt Burkard, Fred Dewey, Enno Hoppe, Noah Isenberg, Bettina Lemke, David Levin, Felix Najer, Karen Nissen, and Millie Zinck.

For financial support of this project, we are indebted to the Getty Grant Program, the Guggenheim Foundation, the National Endowment for the Humanities, the Siemens Corporation, the Associates of the University of California Press, Henry J. Bruman, and the Center for German and European Studies at the University of California, Berkeley. Richard Buxbaum, director of this Center, was especially supportive and generous, as were Deborah Marrow of the Getty Grant Program, and Hans Decker of the Siemens Corporation. Kurt Forster, Thomas Reese, and Herbert Hymans of the Getty Center for the History of Art and the Humanities provided a stimulating environment for exploring the multidisciplinary nature of Weimar culture. The good will of an untold number of librarians was put to the test at the University of California at Berkeley and Los Angeles, Columbia University, the Leo Baeck Institute in New York, the New York Public Library, the Staatsbibliothek in Berlin, and the Deutsches Literaturarchiv in Marbach. Within the University of California Press, William J. McClung was an early and forceful advocate. We are grateful to James H. Clark, the director of the Press, for his unflagging enthusiasm. Dan Dixon, Stephanie Emerson, Diana Feinberg, Rebecca Frazier, Stanley Holwitz, Deborah Kirshman, and Lynne Withey provided invaluable help while the book was being produced. For its original design, we are indebted to Sandy Drooker. Finally, we wish to thank the many publishers and copyright holders for their permission to reprint material.

Far longer in preparation than its editors anticipated, *The Weimar Republic Sourcebook* tried the patience of all those connected with it, none more than that of our families and friends. We therefore owe a special debt of thanks to Christine Kaes, Catherine Gallagher, and Ardath Grant. Although he did not live to see its publication, Leo Löwenthal, embodiment par excellence of the Weimar spirit, was an invaluable source of inspiration. His friendship and counsel will be sorely missed. We dedicate the book to his memory.

Berkeley, October 16, 1993

Anton Kaes
Martin Jay
Edward Dimendberg

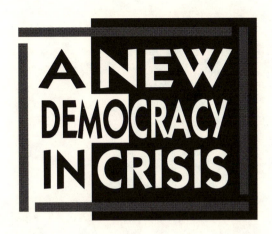

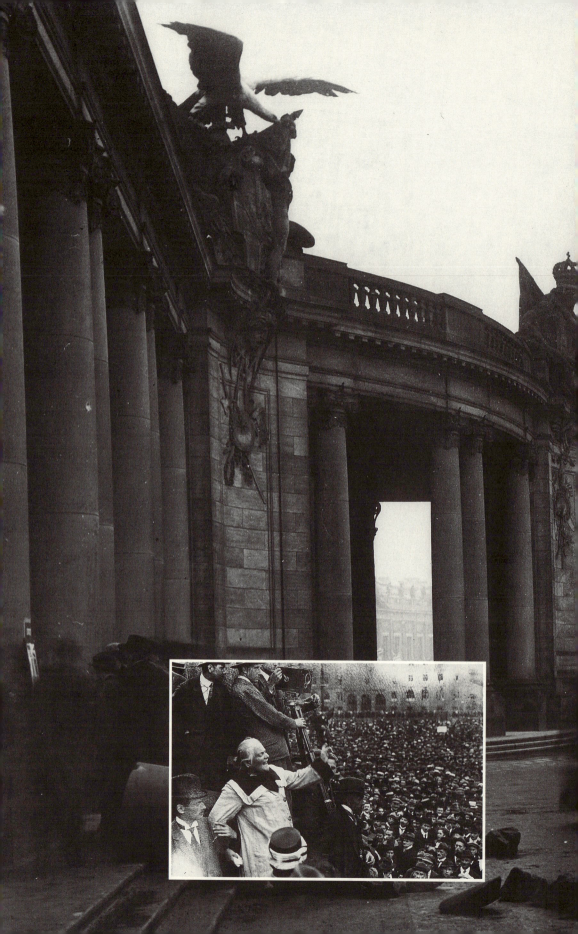

*Damages to the Kaiser Wilhelm I Memorial after the Revolution in Berlin,
December 24, 1918. (Landesbildstelle Berlin.) Inset: Clara Zetkin speaking at KPD
political demonstration against the murder of Matthias Erzberger, August 31, 1921.
(Landesbildstelle Berlin.) First announcement of Mein Kampf by Adolf Hitler, 1924.
(Landesbildstelle Berlin.)*

1
The Legacy of the War

FROM THE BEGINNING, the Weimar Republic was burdened by its unexpected and, in many quarters, unwelcome birth in the bitter aftermath of a lost war. When the armistice ending World War I was signed on November 11, 1918, some two million German soldiers were dead—more than those of any other combatant—over four million more were disabled, physically and psychologically, and the German economy was in shambles. The Allied blockade remained in effect until the peace treaty was signed at Versailles on June 28, 1919, and the clamor for punitive reparations continued among the victors for years to come. The harsh legacy of defeat was especially hard to bear for some because the German armies surrendered while still occupying foreign soil. Complete demobilization was hindered by the need to fight internal battles over Germany's political future, as well as by the reluctance of some who had fought to unlearn the brutal lessons they had learned in the trenches. In its short and tumultuous existence, the Weimar Republic never had the opportunity to work through the legacy of the war and come to terms with its defeat. The physical wounds of those who survived may have healed, but their psychological traumas, whose severity was recognized by psychoanalysts like Ernst Simmel as early as 1918, continued to fester for years to come.

The treaty ending the war, signed reluctantly and under pressure, was quickly dubbed the *Diktat* of Versailles. Political figures blamed for accepting the "Carthaginian Peace" it imposed on Germany were discredited or worse, as demonstrated by the assassination of the Catholic Center Party's Matthias Erzberger in 1921. Among the more controversial clauses were those attributing war guilt to Germany and demanding extensive compensation, which had been vigorously, but vainly resisted by the German delegation to the conference. Even more devastating were the significant losses of territory to France, Poland, Denmark, Lithuania, and Belgium, suffered either outright or after plebiscites, and the radical reduction of the armed forces and demilitarization of the Rhineland.

Hostility to the peace treaty was often accompanied by a search for scapegoats for the defeat, leading to the "stab in the back legend" promulgated by unrepentant military leaders like General Paul von Hindenburg in his testimony to the constitutional assembly's investigative committee on the war in November 1919. Even more moderate defenders of the new republic, such as

5

the philosopher and theologian Ernst Troeltsch, resisted accepting Germany's responsibility for its plight, however much they may have also faulted the aggressive war policies of the general staff. Voices such as that of Willi Wolfradt, who claimed in *Die Weltbühne* in 1922 that the army *should* have been stabbed in the back, were a distinct minority. Indeed, it might be argued that not until the debate unleashed by the revisionist historian Fritz Fischer's *Germany's Aims in the First World War* in 1961 did the Germans attain a more even-handed, if still often contested, assessment of the war's origins.

During the Weimar Republic, feelings about the war ran too deep to allow any such dispassionate analysis. Not only was the justice of the war's goals still widely maintained, but also the devastating experience of trench warfare could be given a romantic gloss in the writings of veterans such as Ernst Jünger. The postwar exploits of the Freikorps, the still-mobilized veterans used by the government to crush leftist revolts, were subject to even greater glorification in the memoirs of participants, such as Ernst von Salomon's *The Outlaws.* Here the celebration of violence, a yearning for charismatic leadership, and communal fantasies of male bonding that were to have so sinister an outcome in post-Weimar German politics can be easily discerned.

Yet at least once the republic was successfully defended against these forces of reaction, as the failure of the Kapp Putsch, a rightist coup attempt led by Wolfgang Kapp, an East Prussian politician, and Hermann Ehrhardt, leader of the most notorious Freikorps brigade, demonstrates. Calling for a general strike on March 13, 1920, the German left, in a rare display of unity, mobilized nearly 100,000 workers and civil servants.

There were, to be sure, some German voices opposed to the glorification of war and the politics of belligerent resentment to which it led. A decade after hostilities began, Kurt Tucholsky, the independent leftist journalist associated with *Die Weltbühne,* mocked the current nostalgia for the chauvinist "spirit of 1914." But as the storm generated in 1929 by Erich Maria Remarque's novel *All Quiet on the Western Front* and the film made from it demonstrates, the wounds of the war festered until they helped bring about the death of the republic itself. As for the prospects of another war, even pacifist intellectuals like Albert Einstein and Sigmund Freud could offer little hope that it might be averted, as evinced in the grim letters they exchanged in 1932.

1

ERNST SIMMEL

War Neuroses and "Psychic Trauma"

First published in *Kriegs-Neurosen und "Psychisches Trauma"* (Munich and Leipzig: Otto Nemnich, 1918), 5–6, 82–84.

When I speak about the war as an event, as the cause of illness, I anticipate something which has revealed itself in my experiences—namely that it is not only the bloody war which leaves such devastating traces in those who took part in it. Rather, it is also the difficult conflict in which the personality finds itself, confronted with a world changed by the war and with which it must struggle, a struggle in which the victim of war neurosis succumbs in silent, often unrecognized, torment.

He can leave the war without physical illness, his physical wounds, if any, already healed. Nevertheless he departs from the arena of war as one branded with a so-called "functional" illness, war neurosis. The damage which the war neurotic carries home with him as a result of his fighting on the lines can befall a single organ, or it may encompass the entire person. [. . .]

Wherever the neurosis is the result of a single debilitation of the personality complex that occurred in a particular war experience, we are able, by means of suggestion, temporarily to interpolate our own healthy ego that acts as a catalyst and thereby reestablish the unity of the fractured personality. These are the cases in which a single session is enough to bring about a cure.

If however, we are unable to cure a war neurosis by means of suggestive hypnosis then, being aware of the particular psychic cause, we can no longer abandon the patient to his fate and send him home untreated, i.e. permanently crippled. Rather we must tell ourselves that we have not yet touched upon the real reason, the psychic cause of his suffering. We must pursue every aspect of psychoanalytic work and thereby effect a cure which impedes the unnecessary increase of the large number of men who were crippled by the war.

However, in my opinion we must be very careful in our application of suggestive hypnosis to those forms of neurosis that manifest themselves in hyper-sensitivity—from spasticity to convulsions.

If we keep in mind that this physical sensitivity is merely the external symptom of an internal, strongly repressed affect, it then becomes clear that suggesting away such a symptom does nothing more than eliminate a safety valve which the organism had created to compensate for an inordinate amount of internal psychic pressure.

If such a cure lasts, which in my experience is frequently not the case, it obviously conceals certain dangers for the patient. Namely, the release may violently take a different tack; I have often observed unmotivated outbursts of rage or other forms of "hysterical attacks" as a result of suggestion-cures. Consideration of the possibility of strongly repressed affects is essential as well for assessing the meaning of these patients' disciplinary infractions.

However, as the reader will realize at the end of this discussion, the self-assertion of the organism as it articulates itself in neurosis ultimately signifies self-protection in the face of the threat of psychosis.

Whatever in a person's experience is too powerful or horrible for his conscious mind to grasp and work through filters down to the unconscious levels of his psyche. There it lies like a mine, waiting to explode the entire psychic structure. And only the self-protective mechanism, with its release of waves of affect, and its attachment to an individual organ, to external symptoms, and to symptomatic actions prevents a permanent disturbance of the psychic balance.

In this way, according to the work of Freud and his followers, a boundary thought by medical science to be stable is shown to be in flux. We recognize that functional psychoses are merely gradual intensifications of functional neuroses.

We gladly abstain from diagnoses out of desperation, by which we previously accorded a psychosis the status "hysterical" in order to believe it curable; instead, we hope that, through a corresponding elaboration of psychoanalytic-hypnotic methodology, we are on the way to healing all emotional illnesses that are not based in organic damage.

Today we may already recognize the time in which—by releasing people from mental institutions—we participate in a part of the human economy that has become necessary because of the waste of human life during the war years and for the preservation of all nations.

2

The Treaty of Versailles: The Reparations Clauses

First published in *The Treaty of Peace Between the Allied and Associated Powers and Germany* (London: His Majesty's Stationery Office, 1919).

PART VIII: REPARATION

Section I: General Provisions

Article 231. The Allied and Associated Governments affirm and Germany accepts the responsibility of Germany and her allies for causing all the loss and damage to which the Allied and Associated Governments and their nationals have been subjected as a consequence of the war imposed upon them by the aggression of Germany and her allies.

Article 232. The Allied and Associated Governments recognize that the resources of Germany are not adequate, after taking into account permanent diminutions of such resources which will result from other provisions of the present Treaty, to make complete reparation for all such loss and damage.

The Allied and Associated Governments, however, require, and Germany undertakes, that she will make compensation for all damage done to the civilian population of the Allied and Associated Powers and to their property during the period of the belligerency of each as an Allied or Associated Power against Germany by such aggression by land, by sea and from the air, and in general all damage as defined in Annex I hereto.

In accordance with Germany's pledges, already given, as to complete restoration for Belgium, Germany undertakes, in addition to the compensation for damage elsewhere in this Part provided for, as a consequence of the violation of the Treaty of 1839,[1] to make reimbursement of all sums which Belgium has borrowed from the Allied and Associated Governments up to November 11, 1918, together with interest at the rate of five percent

---

1. The general European treaty that guaranteed Belgian independence and neutrality.

(5%) per annum on such sums. This amount shall be determined by the Reparation Commission, and the German Government undertakes thereupon forthwith to make a special issue of bearer bonds to an equivalent amount payable in marks gold, on May 1, 1926, or, at the option of the German Government, on May 1 in any year up to 1926. Subject to the foregoing, the form of such bonds shall be determined by the Reparation Commission. [. . .]

Article 233. The amount of the above damage for which compensation is to be made by Germany shall be determined by an Inter-Allied Commission, to be called the Reparation Commission and constituted in the form and with the powers set forth hereunder and in Annexes 2 to 7 inclusive hereto.

This Commission shall consider the claims and give to the German Government a just opportunity to be heard.

The findings of the Commission as to the amount of damage defined as above shall be concluded and notified to the German Government on or before May 1, 1921, as representing the extent of that Government's obligations. [. . .]

Article 235. In order to enable the Allied and Associated Powers to proceed at once in the restoration of their industrial and economic life, pending the full determination of their claims, Germany shall pay in such installments and in such manner (whether in gold, commodities, ships, securities or otherwise) as the Reparation Commission may fix, during 1919, 1920 and the first four months of 1921, the equivalent of 20,000,000,000 gold marks. Out of this sum the expenses of the armies of occupation subsequent to the Armistice of November 11, 1918, shall first be met, and such supplies of food and raw materials as may be judged by the Governments of the Principal Allied and Associated Powers to be essential to enable Germany to meet her obligations for reparation may also, with the approval of the said Governments, be paid for out of the above sum. The balance shall be reckoned towards liquidation of the amounts due for reparation. [. . .]

Article 236. Germany further agrees to the direct application of her economic resources to reparation as specified in Annexes 3, 4, 5, and 6 relating respectively to merchant shipping, to physical restoration, to coal and derivatives of coal, and to dye-stuffs and other chemical products; provided always that the value of the property transferred and any services rendered by her under these Annexes, assessed in the manner therein prescribed, shall be credited to her towards liquidation of her obligations under the above Articles.

3

COUNT ULRICH VON BROCKDORFF-RANTZAU

Speech of the German Delegation, Versailles, May 7, 1919

First published as "Ansprache des Reichsaußenministers Grafen Brockdorff-Rantzau bei Überreichung des Friedensvertrags-Entwurfs durch die Alliierten und Assoziierten Mächte," in Graf Brockdorff-Rantzau, *Dokumente* (Charlottenburg: Deutsche Verlagsgesellschaft für Politik und Geschichte, 1920), 113ff.

Gentlemen, we are deeply impressed with the great mission that has brought us here to give to the world forthwith a lasting peace. We are under no illusions as to the extent of our defeat and the degree of our powerlessness. We know that the strength of the German arms is broken. We know the intensity of the hatred which meets us, and we have heard the victor's passionate demand that as the vanquished we shall be made to pay, and as the guilty we shall be punished.

The demand is made that we shall acknowledge that we alone are guilty of having caused the war. Such a confession in my mouth would be a lie. We are far from seeking to escape from any responsibility for this world war, and for its having been waged as it has. The attitude of the former German government at the Hague peace conferences, its actions and its omissions in the tragic twelve days of July may have contributed to the catastrophe, but we emphatically deny that the people of Germany, who were convinced that they were waging a war of defense, should be burdened with the sole guilt of that war.

Nobody would wish to contend that the catastrophe goes back merely to the fateful moment when the successor to the throne of Austria-Hungary fell a victim to murderous hands. In the past fifty years the imperialism of all European states has constantly poisoned the international situation. The policy of retaliation, the policy of expansion, and a disregard of the right of national self-determination have played their part in that illness of Europe which came to its crisis in the world war. The Russian mobilization made it impossible for statesmen to find a remedy, and threw the final decision into the hands of military power.

Public opinion in every enemy country is echoing the crimes Germany is said to have committed in the war. Here, too, we are ready to admit that unjust things have been done. We have not come here to diminish the responsibility of the men who have waged the war politically and economically, and to deny that breaches of the law of nations have been committed. We repeat the declaration which was made in the German Reichstag at the beginning of the war: injustice has been done to Belgium and we shall make reparations.

But in the manner of waging war, Germany was not the only one that erred. Every European nation knows of deeds and of individuals which the best of their people remember only with regret. I do not want to respond to reproaches with reproaches, but, if we alone are asked to do penance, one should remember the Armistice. Six weeks went by before we obtained an armistice, and six months before we came to know your conditions of peace. Crimes in war may not be excusable, but they are committed in the struggle for victory, when we think only of maintaining our national existence, and are in such passion as makes the conscience of peoples blunt. The hundreds of thousands of noncombatants who have perished since November 11 because of the blockade were destroyed coolly and deliberately after our opponents had won a certain and assured victory. Remember that, when you speak of guilt and atonement.

The measure of guilt of all those who have taken part can be established only by an impartial inquiry, a neutral commission before which all the principals in the tragedy are allowed to speak, and to which all archives are open. We have asked for such an inquiry and we ask for it once more.

At this conference, where we alone and without our allies are facing our many opponents, we are not without protection. You yourself have brought us an ally: that justice which was guaranteed us in the agreement as to what should be the principles governing the treaty of peace. In the days between October 5 and November 5, 1918, the Allied and Associated governments swore that there would be no peace of violence, and inscribed on their knightly banners a peace of justice. On October 5 the German government proposed that the basis of peace should be the principles set forth by the President of the United

States of America, and on November 5 their Secretary of State, Mr. [Robert] Lansing, declared that the Allied and Associated Powers had accepted this basis with two definite reservations. The principles of President Wilson thus became binding for both parties to the war, for you as well as for us, and also for our former allies.

Certain of the foregoing principles call upon us to make heavy national and economic sacrifices. But by such a treaty, the sacred and fundamental rights of all peoples would be protected. The conscience of the world would be behind it, and no nation that violated it would go unpunished.

Upon that basis you will find us ready to examine the preliminary peace which you have submitted to us, with the firm intention of joining with you in rebuilding that which has been destroyed, in making good whatever wrong has been committed, above all the injustice to Belgium, and in showing mankind new goals of political and social progress. Considering the confusing number of problems which arise, we ought, as soon as possible, to have the principal problems examined by special commissions of experts, on the basis of the treaty which you have submitted to us. Our principal problem will be to restore the broken strength of all the nations which took part in the war, and do it by providing international protection for the welfare, health, and freedom of the working classes.

I believe we should then proceed to restore those parts of Belgium and Northern France which we occupied and which have been destroyed by the war. We have taken upon ourselves the solemn obligation to do so, and we are resolved to execute it to the extent which has been agreed upon between us. In this we are dependent upon the cooperation of our former opponents. We cannot accomplish it without the technical and financial participation of the victor nations, and they could accomplish it only with our cooperation. Impoverished Europe must desire to bring about this reconstruction as successfully, but at the same time at as little cost as possible. Such a project could be carried out only by means of a clear and businesslike understanding as to the best methods to be employed. To continue to have this done by German prisoners of war would be the worst of methods. Unquestionably such work can be done cheaply. But it would cost the world dear if hatred and despair should overcome the German people, forced to think of their sons, brothers, and fathers still held prisoners, and languishing as if in penal servitude. We cannot arrive at a lasting peace without an immediate solution of this problem, a problem which has already been postponed too long.

Experts on both sides will have to give thought as to how the German people can best meet the financial obligations called for by such reparations, without collapsing under the weight of their burden. A financial breakdown would take from those who have a right to reparations the advantages which are theirs by right, and would throw into irreparable disorder the whole European economic system. The victors as well as the vanquished must guard themselves against this menacing danger and its incalculable consequences. There is only one means of removing it: belief without reservation in the economic and social solidarity of all nations, and in a free and all-inclusive League of Nations.

Gentlemen, the sublime idea of deriving from the most terrible catastrophe in history the greatest of forward movements in the development of mankind, by means of the League of Nations, has been put forth and will make its way. But only by opening the gates of the League of Nations to all who are of good will can the goal be attained, and only by doing so will it be that those who have died in this war shall not have died in vain.

In their hearts, the German people will resign themselves to their hard lot if the bases of the peace, as mutually agreed upon, are not destroyed. A peace which cannot be defended before the world as a peace of justice would always evoke new resistance. No one could sign it with a clear conscience, for it could not be carried out. No one could venture to guarantee its execution, though this obligation is implied in the signing of the treaty.

We shall, with every good intention, study the document submitted to us, in the hope that our meeting may finally result in something that can be signed by us all.

4
ERNST TROELTSCH
The Dogma of Guilt

First published as "Das Schulddogma (June 19, 1919)," *Spektatorbriefe. Aufsätze über die deutsche Revolution und die Weltpolitik 1918–1922*, ed. Hans Baron (Tübingen: J. C. B. Mohr, 1924), 314–321.

What emerges with considerable clarity from the peace at Versailles is the enormous importance of the question of guilt. This kind of peace was possible because of the formal German declaration of war and its invasion of neutral Belgium, thus making Germany exclusively responsible for the war. This peace, while presenting itself as a court of inquisition, is also an imperialist monstrosity made possible by the deceit of the Fourteen Points and by Germany's voluntary disarmament. It is reminiscent of the way Rome once proceeded against Carthage. The German counterproposals to this peace acknowledged the legitimate demands for reconstruction assistance for severely damaged France and Belgium. But the holy alliance, just about as holy as the one of a hundred years ago and with exactly as much right to moral sloganeering, did not accept these proposals. Instead, the response to them was: the heretic is to be burned. Profound political, sociological, national, psychological, and technical justifications underlie the peace, which themselves suffice to show that this division of the world and the expropriation of land was produced by a court of inquisition.

The belief in German guilt and German responsibility for a war made inevitable by this same guilt fed the world's prejudice, which gained inestimably in its effect on all neutral and small states due to that fateful act of German politics and military conduct, the invasion of Belgium, although the latter, as Bethmann-Hollweg's book [*Reflections on the World War*] details with utter clarity, was demonstrably *not* the reason for the English declaration of war. The invasion made it possible for the governments to draw their respective antiwar citizenries into war hysteria and to maintain their positions even in the face of the most monstrous atrocities. The heretic was neither to be trusted nor to be believed; to show him the slightest consideration was a crime against humanity. In accordance with such sentiments, idealism was whipped into a fury, especially among the Americans; they were persuaded of the intimate relationship of this German crime against culture and the outmoded German autocracy, while every attempt at German self-defense, every German counterplea, was kept from America because England was granted surveillance of the German post. But this was only a part of the series of events we are addressing here. To the extent that Germany's actions were represented as criminal, its entire military undertaking and the ensuing destruction took on the character of wanton brutality and crime, prompted not by participation in a just war, as with the [Triple] Entente, but through rapacious and godless atrocities which served solely to reveal and further confirm the nature of the German enterprise as a whole. It was the fate of

Germany's early successes in Belgium and northern France that they resulted in its undoing: the deplorable suffering that did in fact occur was represented not as the consequence of war but as the consequence of German madness and wantonness; every atrocity and all destruction not absolutely necessary multiplied in significance.

Nor was it different with regard to the submarine war, a German military tactic unforeseen in previous agreements on the rights of peoples. In comparison to the slow and undramatic effects of the blockade, submarine warfare was much more visible and stimulated the imagination through its destruction of goods and people, which, by its nature, struck friend and enemy alike. It was therefore an extremely severe and questionable tool of war. Still, it was not represented as a political mistake and an act of self-defense against the hunger blockade, but as wanton murder, as an insane destruction of goods, as an inevitable product of the German military spirit, and this representation is a strategic decision of world-destroying proportions.

Nor was it any different with regard to zeppelins and long-range artillery. The course of the war only amplified the accusations of guilt. And as these accusations continued they were also applied to the new revolutionary government—which was in no way responsible for the "imperial" administration—as well as to the fully debilitated Germany of the cease-fire period. Thus it was possible to refuse every negotiation, to mistrust, "in principle," to this day every explanation and every policy, to prepare the peace in complete secrecy, despite all "democratic ideals," and to impose it upon the Germans without any negotiation. The victors could then demand whatever they wanted, partly as "punishment," partly as "obligatory reparations," and partly as "security" against such a horribly dangerous people. This is precisely the reason for their further demand, which, in practical terms was utter nonsense and was otherwise unheard of—the extradition of the "guilty"—because that, along with their condemnation, put the seal on the theory of German guilt, without which the enemies could not have endured the war and could not have designed this peace. At the same time, the theory of German guilt allayed the doubts gradually awakened among the victors' own ranks, where workers and liberals were beginning to sense the monstrosity of this peace. It was just as much the ambition of the enemy to rob German socialism of its dangerous powers of infection, for it was characterized as the spiritual heir and unchanged continuation of the old government which was simultaneously to be fettered or even strangled through the "terms of punishment."

Finally, the guilt implies a period of atonement and rectification during which Germany remains excluded from "national alliances" and the Entente can go about dividing the world undisturbed. The confusing repercussions on the German people of this whole moralistic polemic, the mutilation of its belief in itself, the exacting of German acknowledgments of guilt (by which weak spirits hope to lighten their fate)—all of this is merely a secondary issue, albeit an important one. Exacting acknowledgments of guilt as a condition of milder punishment in was a measure similar to the incentives for voluntary disarmament given in the promise of Wilson's Fourteen Points. [. . .]

But how was the establishment of such a dogma possible? This is not a purely historical question. It was possible through Germany's political mistake of making a formal declaration of war out of fear of falling behind militarily and thus losing important advantages. We might just as well have let the cannons go off by themselves, an inevitability, as we now know from [Russian] General [Pavel von] Rennenkampf's orders to the army. Military authorities certify that such patient waiting would have been possible. The second point is the fateful German invasion of Belgium, which seemed to have become necessary given the nature of the only elaborated war plan of the years 1913–1914. Earlier there would have been several contingency plans. [. . .]

But that alone would not have won the accusers their dominance. The real precondition was that the whole world was eager to believe the accusations. Germans were already hated to such a degree that the worst appeared plausible and required no authentic proof whatever. Max Scheler supplied the particular reasons for this hatred of the Germans in his well-known book, [*Why the Germans are Hated* (1917)], which suffers only from underestimating the effect of the Kaiser's senseless exhortations in his speeches, of the Pan-German writings, of the Navy League, and of the Bülow-Tirpitz policy in intensifying this hatred. And particular note must be taken of the Anglo-Saxon spirit, which does nothing without moral grounding and never pursues its own interests without being conscious simultaneously of its moral superiority. The habit stems from the heritage of the old Puritan spirit, which applies boundless rigor to the emphasis of its own purported moral right, and which serves to provide it with a good conscience for the sake of profit and the exercise of power. [. . .] Calvinistic self-righteousness is not simply hypocrisy. Among the Anglo-Saxons it is combined—relatively honestly, although subjectively, and, above all, extremely effectively in terms of national psychology—with an astounding sense for business and power, which could be learned from the book by Troeltsch, *The Social Teachings of the Christian Churches.*[1] But how many among the Germans think, in their enlightenment, to take such spiritual things seriously and even to regard them as important?

The worst and most unfortunate, however, was the German war policy itself. Seduced by its initial successes and later renewed by further successes in critical situations, the policy-makers allowed themselves to surpass the original goals of maintaining the status quo and pure defense. The General Staff policy had existed since [Erich von] Falkenhayn and [Erich] Ludendorff; the economic associations and the masses, misled by journalism, demanded ever greater gains. Weapons now became many times more destructive than would have been necessary. Humanity and justice began to be sentimentalized, and support for a settlement was viewed as defeatism. The political leadership was powerless and ambivalent, ultimately wholly discredited by the General Staff. The Kaiser never kept politics and the military mutually coherent and in balance, and at this critical moment he failed more than ever before. The nation was divided. It became very easy for the Entente through its tireless campaign of innuendo to prove Germany's desire for world conquest, its war guilt, and its violation of accepted military conduct. Nor may one forget that our moral powers, both internal and external, so declined that the experience of German occupation on the eastern and western fronts everywhere awakened hatred for Germany. For the occupation and the treatment of occupied areas, our dominant class had not the slightest talent. All of this allowed the dogma of guilt to take such firm root that the enemy finally could dare to reject with a sneer even the demand for international, nonpartisan confirmation. The dogma of German guilt is as endemic to the modern court of inquisition as it was to the inquisition of the Middle Ages. For what could calling the dogma of the devil's existence into question represent other than an unheard of impudence?

And still a final factor came into play: the techniques of journalism. As surely as the technological delirium of this war killed all sense and understanding, elevating acts of war, comprehensible in and of themselves, to the level of sheer insanity, so have the techniques of belief and opinion-making, as developed by the countries with democratic election

---

1. This essay was published under the pseudonym "Spectator," which allowed Troeltsch to refer to himself in the third person.

campaigns, celebrated monstrous and unprecedented triumphs. [. . .] The enemies have understood incomparably better the techniques of journalism. And, as no one dare forget, through arrogance, spiritlessness, and incautious and reckless prattling of secret wishes and thoughts, we gave them inexhaustible stores of raw material. We no longer believed in the power of morality, nor in its function as a weapon of war, and thereby played into their hands, whether they themselves were dirty or not.

One must understand such things, if one wants to comprehend the peace conditions.

5

PAUL VON HINDENBURG

The Stab in the Back

First published in *Stenographischer Bericht über die öffentlichen Verhandlungen des 15. Untersuchungsausschusses der verfassunggebenden Nationalversammlung*, testimony delivered on November 18, 1919, vol. 2 (Berlin, 1920), 700–701.

General Field Marshall v. Hindenburg: History will render the final judgment on that about which I may give no further details here. At the time we still hoped that the *will to victory* would dominate everything else. When we assumed our post, we made a series of proposals to the Reich leadership which aimed at combining all forces at the nation's disposal for a quick and favorable conclusion to the war; at the same time, they demonstrated to the government its enormous tasks. What finally became of our proposals, once again partially because of the influence of the parties, is known. I wanted forceful and cheerful cooperation and instead encountered failure and weakness.

Chairman: That, too, is a value judgment, against which I must enter a definite protest.

von Hindenburg: The concern as to whether the homeland would remain resolute until the war was won, from this moment on, never left us. We often raised a warning voice to the Reich government. At this time, the secret *intentional mutilation of the fleet and the army* began as a continuation of similar occurrences in peace time. The effects of these endeavors were not concealed from the supreme army command during the last year of the war. The obedient troops who remained immune to revolutionary attrition suffered greatly from the behavior, in violation of duty, of their revolutionary comrades; they had to carry the battle the whole time.

(Chairman's bell. Commotion and shouting.)

Chairman: Please continue, General Field Marshall.

von Hindenburg: The intentions of the command could no longer be executed. Our repeated proposals for strict discipline and strict legislation were not adopted. Thus did our operations necessarily miscarry; the *collapse* was inevitable; the revolution only provided the keystone.

(Commotion and shouting.)

An English general said with justice: "The German army was stabbed in the back." No guilt applies to the good core of the army. Its achievements are just as admirable as those of the officer corps. Where the guilt lies has clearly been demonstrated. If it needed more proof, then it would be found in the quoted statement of the English general and in the boundless astonishment of our enemies at their victory.

That is the general trajectory of the tragic development of the war for Germany, after a series of brilliant, unsurpassed successes on many fronts, following an accomplishment by the army and the people for which no praise is high enough. This trajectory had to be established so that the military measures for which we are responsible could be correctly evaluated.

6

SOCIAL DEMOCRATIC PARTY (SPD)

Appeal of the Social Democratic Party for a General Strike

First published as "Aufruf der sozialdemokratischen Mitglieder der Reichsregierung und des Parteivorstandes der SPD zum Generalstreik" in Karl Brammer (ed.), *Fünf Tage Militärdiktatur* (Berlin: Verlag für Politik und Wissenschaft, 1920), 65.

The military putsch is here. Ehrhardt's marine division is marching toward Berlin to force a transformation of the government. The Freikorps members who fear disbandment want to install reactionaries in high government positions. We refuse to buckle under to this military pressure. We did not make the revolution so as once again to legitimize the bloody Freikorps regiment. We will not sign a pact with the Baltic criminals.

Workers, comrades! We would be ashamed before you, if we were to behave otherwise. We say no and no once more! You must confirm our belief that we have acted in your interest. Use every means possible to negate the return of bloody reactionary politics. Go on strike, put down your work, and stop the military dictatorship. Fight with every means for the preservation of the republic. Forget your divisiveness. There is only one way to prevent the return of Wilhelm II: Shut down the economy! No one should work. No proletarian should assist the military dictatorship! A general strike all the way! Proletarians unite!

> The Social Democrat Members of the Government:
> Ebert, Noske, Schlicke, Schmidt, David, Müller
> The Executive Committee of the Social Democratic Party of Germany, Wels

7

WILLI WOLFRADT

The Stab-in-the-Back Legend?

First published as "Dolchstoß-Legende?" *Die Weltbühne* 18, no. 24 (June 15, 1922), 592–594.

A discussion is going on in Germany for and against the "stab in the back." A stab in the back from the rebellious homeland caused the army to collapse—no, the preponderance of enemy forces and severe mistakes on the part of the leadership were to blame. Recently the tireless propagators of the stab-in-the-back legend have caused Franz Oppenheimer to reflect that proof that a sharpened dagger was drawn does not suffice to shift the blame, nor even is it proof of a stab aimed at the homeland; perhaps what the dagger struck was already mortally wounded by the enemy. But to resort to such argumentation, as irrefutable as it is, betrays the ideals of the peace and denies the true facts. This betrayal is occurring today generally in regard to this important issue. That a stab in the back was responsible for the collapse of the military forces is contested by many, and it has not in fact been proven. But the blameworthiness of a stab in the back causing the collapse—no one dares dispute that. No one has the courage required to own up to the heroic, saving act of a stab in the back.

When I hear that someone has been stabbed, I want to know: was it murder or self-defense? That is, after all, critical for any evaluation of the act. This stab in the back, if it did occur, was self-defense, the desperate act of a people in mortal danger. Those capable of denying its justification in this way are only those who have either entirely forgotten or never saw the terrible distress, the steady increase in mortal agony, and the torment to which one's conscience was subjected during the war. Capable of denying its sacred right are only those for whom the carnage did not last long enough. By dismissing the stab in the back as a "legend," one abandons one's feelings at the time, abandons our bitter resolve in favor of peace in the present. And one concedes at the same time that sabotaging the war was a crime. One legitimates the war in retrospect and arms the next one by dulling the only real weapon we have against it: the consciousness of people that war must not be—must not be.

The dagger: that is the will of the masses to prevent by all means the formation of an army prepared for war. Because the dagger lies sharpened and ready, it is effective. The duller it becomes, the more imminent becomes the danger of a new war. If the point is broken off, the war is no longer to be stopped. The tactic of renouncing the stab in the back, instead of exalting it as a saving act of desperation, will soon have completely broken off the point. To choose this tactic, instead of showing one's true colors, is hardly clever. And those who argue for other than tactical reasons about who deserves the blame—they are not to be counted on. They have failed to recognize the insanity and transgression of war; they will consent to the next one.

How does it happen that there are so many people currently at pains to dispel the stab-in-the-back legend who at the time, either in their convictions or practically, contributed proudly and courageously to the destruction of the war spirit? It comes today from the success of propaganda claims that an unarmed Germany will be annihilated by the victors. The lie that peace has increased misery, instead of ending it, prevails. If it were generally assumed that peace had decreased misery, then everyone would bless the peace and not ask how it came about. By declaring the stab in the back to have been a crime—whether or not one admits that it took place—one gives up the argument that peace, even achieved in such an extraordinary way, could be more fruitful than war. By denying one's involvement, instead of expressing one's pride in it, one lends credence to the fraud that the peace has increased the German people's misery; one appears to be trying to shift the responsibility for a perpetrated wrong from oneself. Thereby the feeling is nourished that Germany has gone from the frying pan into the fire, which is the cause of our general paralysis and joylessness and renders the completion of the peace impossible. It was quickly forgotten: Things have not only gotten better with the revolution—it marked the return, despite everything, from a thousand deaths into life. How that is so, how that came to be might be bitterly disillusioning. Nevertheless, it is life and the gift of all its potential!

Who was it who was stabbed? Not the German people, but its most terrible enemy: German military power. How many were destroyed by the catastrophe of the arduous peace? Thousands certainly! That is not many if one remembers that every day of war destroyed as many. A small sacrifice considering what hellish nonsense, what a dreadful misuse of people, has finally been brought to an end.

8

ERNST JÜNGER

Fire

First published as "Feuer" in *Der Kampf als inneres Erlebnis* (Berlin: Verlag Mittler, 1922), 72–76.

We have known one another for a long time as bold adventurers, have met on many a hot day beneath the smoke-filled sky of a battlefield where it is simply the spirit of the hour that always brings those similar together. We know we are the select embodiments of a powerful masculinity and take pride in this awareness. Just yesterday we sat together following the old tradition of a final drink and felt how the will to battle, that peculiar lust to cross the front again and again, to leap where volunteers are needed, would not have lost its familiar intensity and this time, too, would cast us into danger. Yes, if only it were time; we are a race that rises to the challenge.

Nevertheless, this discontent, this unyielding chill from the inside out, these portentous thoughts tearing across our horizon like vague, tattered traces of clouds, were not to be banished; not even once we had taken a long, slow drink of cognac. It is stronger than we are. A fog that lies within us and, in such hours, spreads its mysterious nature across the troubled waters of the soul. Not fear—fear we can stare sharply, disdainfully, in the eye and frighten into its cave—but an unknown realm in which the boundaries of our capacity to feel melt away. That is where one first notices how little one is at home in oneself. From deep within, something slumbering, drowned out by restless dailiness, rises and, before quite taking form, dissolves into a dull sadness.

Of what help is it that for three long weeks a man has steeled himself for this hour, until he believes himself to be hard and free of weaknesses. Of what help is it that he says to himself, "Death? Ha, what's that? A transition that can't be avoided anyway." All that is of no help whatever, for suddenly, from having been a thinking being, he becomes a feeling one, a plaything of phantoms against which even the sharpest reason is a powerless weapon. Those are factors we take care to deny because they are unreliable. But in the moment of experience all denial is futile; then every unknown is possessed of a higher and more convincing reality than all the familiar phenomena of a midday sun.

We have reached the most advanced line and are seeing to the final preparations. We are eager and precise, for we sense a pressure to be active, to fill the time, to escape from ourselves. Time, which had racked us so in the trenches, a concept that comprehends all conceivable torment, a chain that only death can break. Perhaps in the coming minutes. I know it to be a conscious experience, the quiet flow of an ebbing life into the sea of eternity; I have already stood at times on the border. It is a slow, deep sinking with a ringing in the ear, peaceful and familiar like the sound of Easter bells at home. One should avoid such ponderings, such a readiness to pounce upon mysteries that will never be explained. Everything comes in its own time. Head high, let the thoughts scatter to the winds. Die with dignity—that we can do; we can stride into the ominous dark with a warrior's cunning and bold vitality. Do not be shaken, smile to the last, even if the smile is only a mask to hide from yourself: that itself is something. A human is incapable of anything greater than mastering oneself in death. Even the immortal gods must envy him that.

We are well armed for our journey, loaded with weapons, explosives, and lighting and signaling instruments, a proper, fighting, shock troop, up to the supreme challenges of modern warfare. Not only up to it through joyful dare-devilry and brutal force. Seeing the people this way in the twilight, slender, haggard, most of them almost children, one has little inclination to trust them. But their faces in the shadow of their steel helmets are sharp, fearless, and smart. I know, they do not waver from the danger for an instant; they pounce on it, fast, sinewy, and smooth. They combine ardent courage with cool intelligence; they are the men who clear a severely jammed shell with a steady hand amidst a maelstrom of annihilation, who fire a smoking grenade back at the enemy, who, locked in a struggle for life and death, read the intentions in the enemy's eyes. They are men forged of steel, whose eagle eyes peer straight over the propeller's whir, studying the clouds ahead, who, captive within the motorized din of the tanks, dare the hellish journey through the roar of shell-pitted fields, who, for days on end, approaching a certain death, crouch in encircled nests heaped with corpses, only half alive beneath glowing machine guns. They are the best of the modern battlefield, suffused with the reckless spirit of the warrior, whose iron will discharges in clenched, well-aimed bursts of energy.

When I observe how they silently cut lanes through the tangles of barbed wire, dig stepped assault trenches, compare their luminescent watches, and orient themselves towards north by the stars, then I am overcome with recognition: this is the new man, the storm pioneer, the elite of Central Europe. A whole new race, smart, strong, and filled with will. What reveals itself here as a vision will tomorrow be the axis around which life revolves still faster and faster. The path will not always, as here, have to be forged through shell craters, fire, and steel; but the double-quick step with which events are prosecuted here, the tempo accustomed to iron, that will remain the same. The glowing twilight of a declining age is at once a dawn in which one arms oneself for new, for harder battles. Far behind, the gigantic cities, the hosts of machines, the empires, whose inner bonds have been rent in the storm, await the new men, the cunning, battle-tested men who are ruthless toward themselves and others. This war is not the end but the prelude to violence. It is the forge in which the new world will be hammered into new borders and new communities. New forms want to be filled with blood, and power will be wielded with a hard fist. The war is a great school, and the new man will bear our stamp.

Yes, it is now in its element, my old shock troop. The deed, the stroke of the fist, has torn away the fog. Already there comes a quiet joke across the shoulder of the trench. It is perhaps not tasteful to ask: "Well, fatso, are you up to your slaughter weight?" Nevertheless—they laugh, and fatso most of all. Just don't be moved. The festival is about to begin, and we are its princes.

It is a pity nonetheless. If the advance troops fail to penetrate, if just *one* machine gun remains intact on the other side, these splendid men will be cut down like a herd of deer. That is war. The best and most worthy, the highest embodiment of life, is just good enough to be cast into its insatiable maw. One machine gun, just a second's gliding of the cartridge belt, and these twenty-five men—one could cultivate a sizeable island with them—will hang in tattered bundles from the wire, left slowly to decompose. They are students, cadets with proud old names, mechanics, heirs to fertile estates, saucy big city sorts, and high school students, from whose eyes the Sleeping Beauty dream of some kind of ancient nest has not entirely drifted away. Peasant sons, grown up beneath the lonely thatched roofs of Westphalia or the Lüneberger Heide, ringed by the primeval oaks planted by their forebears around the surrounding fence of stone.

In the neighboring regiment on the left there bursts a storm of fire. It is a feinting maneuver, to confuse and split enemy artillery. It is just about time. Now the task is to gather oneself. Yes, it is perhaps a pity. Perhaps as well we are sacrificing ourselves for something inessential. But no one can rob us of *our* value. Essential is not *what* we are fighting for, but *how* we fight. Onward toward the goal, until we triumph or are left behind. The warriors' spirit, the exposure of oneself to risk, even for the tiniest idea, weighs more heavily in the scale than all the brooding about good and evil. That is what gives even the knight of the rueful countenance his awe-inspiring aura. We want to show what we have in us; then, if we fall, we will truly have lived to the full.

9

KURT TUCHOLSKY
The Spirit of 1914

First published as "Der Geist von 1914," *Die Weltbühne* 20, no. 32 (August 7, 1924), 204–209.

The wave of drunkenness which overtook the country ten years ago has left behind many hung-over people who know no other cure for their hangover than to become drunk again. They have learned nothing.

Today the spiritual foundation on which Germany rests is no different from that when it was founded. No spiritual experience has touched the country, for the war was none. It changed bodies into cadavers, but it left the spirit completely untouched. 1879–1914–1924: the years differ only in their terminology. 1914 is the logical consequence of the founding years of the Wilhelmine Reich. Nothing has changed. [. . .]

After the cease-fire, of which the center parties in their endless folly were themselves signatories—over there, [General Ferdinand] Foch, here in Germany [Matthias] Erzberger—came the horrible fear for the purse. And that finished everything.

The all-but-childish dread of a bolshevism that could never have lasted in Germany— that indeed was not intellectually prepared in the slightest here, and could not ever have won a place for itself in a country with such a high level of civilization—this fear was ultimately the most profound expression of the unalterability of the old way of thinking. It was the old spirit of 1914. And it had its firm principles, which were valid in 1875, were valid during the war, and remain just as valid today. These principles are, among others:

One need not be anything—one must become something. Superiors are always right. If you earn money, look around at the same time for a suitable philosophy that makes you "right." You never have to wonder how anyone else is feeling; act as if you were the only one in the world. It's all not so bad. Authority conveys rights, not duties.

This catechism can be expanded at will; it characterizes the horrible type of the subordinate, those sadomasochistic soldiers in the Stahlhelm, a sad product of the last years of civilization, equipped with an entire vocabulary of medieval concepts. Karl Kraus was probably the first to have drawn attention to this condensed nonsense: "Ever since someone pressed a halberd into the hands of the merchant, we've known what a hero looks like." The contractors do the business; [Richard] Wagner and Wilhelm II were there for the poetry.

Nothing in this spirit has changed.

The foray into romantic nationalism seems to have ended; every day that slips by represents deprivation, because nothing happened and because the stock exchange is spinning the enchanted forest grey with its deadly web. What is coming next is much more dangerous. It is the wholly unromantic form of the mercantile German.

The day of the profiteer as a type is over. He never really existed: the harmless picture-book figure who distracted the scorn of the streets onto something else is an excellent invention. The real one looked quite different. That was a fellow of flesh and blood: robust, heavy, not altogether inelegant in style with his hairnet on his head in the morning; not disinclined toward a good car ride, a good glass of wine, and already an entertaining book. Mix up foreign words—? The concepts were fixed, and that sufficed. They were: say yes, have success, and be less scrupulous, more brutal, alert, and shrewd than the others—and as much as possible at their expense. He did well for himself.

These characters are all good nationalists. Even in Jewish circles (of which a portion would still vote German-National today, were the party not so stupid as to trade in anti-Semitism) and even in merchant circles, this way of thinking prevails. Do business, pay a little taxes, recognize the state pro forma—it can be useful. Otherwise, *nationalist* signifies a group-perpetrated crudeness that beats everything. Not many would have murdered Erzberger: everyone would have hid the murderers. That these murderers did not come before a German court is good: that way we were spared a new desecration of the name Fechenbach.[1]

And thus does Germany view the world with its near-sighted eyes through glasses:

We didn't lose the war—you merely won it. No one was conquered, least of all us. We have goodwill enough to want to do business with you again—if it has to be, we will crawl after you a bit, but not much. You have to understand, of course, that "tactical considerations" make it necessary and useful for us to rain extravagant abuse upon the whole world every time we dedicate a memorial—we believe ourselves in part. In bank accounts we are international. Our words to ourselves are true or untrue, all depending on what we find useful. We are, incidentally, the center of the world!

And then they wonder when they get a reaction over there, which also happened in France. That can be explained above all by one motive: France is afraid. And this fear is justified.

---

1. Matthias Erzberger, one of the signatories of the peace treaty, was murdered by two former officers of the Ehrhardt Brigade on August 12, 1921. They fled to Hungary, which did not extradite them. Felix Fechenbach, formerly secretary to the murdered Kurt Eisner, was sentenced by the Bavarian People's Court to no less than eleven years imprisonment for alleged high treason in 1922—a wholly politically motivated sentence generally acknowledged as a miscarriage of justice.

Elsewhere the world goes on. It is, by God, not so much better, but rather different. Here too time passes: here too the economic activity of the individual is worlds away from its effects. (That seems to me the most outstanding trait of our time, that we no longer see, like the weavers of old, the actual effect of our actions. [Oswald] Spengler specifies as the most important feature the abstraction of property through paper currency—but the former aspect appears still worse to me, and more grievous.) Elsewhere as well industry hides behind the state when it wants something and unfurls flags where petroleum is meant. But all of them make it without that troublemaker, Germany.

Meanwhile, the country conducts politics after its fashion. One must just once, just one time, leaf through the German press to see who it is that has a voice, who is allowed to speak. Prophets whose credibility has been eroded by constant failures in the art of prediction; the oldest left-overs of departed liberalism; cautious tacticians who find no more subscribers but do not offend the advertisers; educators of youth who have taught young people the most dreadful jargon of rigidity and abstraction—those are the leaders of a herd that scarcely turns their heads toward the one who leads them. It is just so indifferent. [. . .] All day long they invent something old. At the moment they are busy opening up the "war guilt question." But not a single person has asked; rather, the whole world has long since answered. They pour over fat white books; there is probably even a periodical devoted to this purpose. Today after ten years—after so many files have disappeared, been stolen, removed—today they come up with this chess move that seems so terribly diplomatic to them. And no one is listening, except the readers of the *Süddeutsche Monatshefte,* and they like it just fine.

On August 3 there was one of those kitschy "memorial days," or whatever it is called in the official thieves' Latin. Mr. [Karl] Jarres, the German interior minister, arranged it, and that's why it turned out so well. The *Reichswehr* marched out, the associations, the bureaucrats, among them—unfortunately not in robes—what passes here in this country for judges. [. . .] And all were of one spirit, a genuine fatherland spirit.

But today, after these ten years, adult Germans gather together and speak of the poor, pointlessly fallen victims of the slaughter without the burning desire: "How can we avoid the next one? How? How?" Not one, without exception, not one of these influential German men musters the moral courage to turn his back on these advertisements for war. Not a single person can speak about war other than to proclaim, in a more or less skillfully veiled way, a cry of vengeance for a new massacre. That all this is possible should suffice to justify my calling it a disgrace.

Not a glimmer of understanding for what happened; no heartbeat in the rhythm of this time; anachronisms in tophats or an obsolete uniform; a lazy and insipid bourgeoisie that understands the meaning of what one deserves in only one sense, and not two: a defeated and—not without its share of responsibility—broken-down working class; the bowling-club chairmen from the parties; and—not to forget!—the German woman, with her colors so pleasing to the eye, and not only the eye: this is you, Germany—?

Damn you. And bless you, because you are changing.

10

CARL ZUCKMAYER

Erich Maria Remarque's *All Quiet on the Western Front*

First published as "Erich Maria Remarque, *Im Westen nichts Neues*," *Berliner Illustrirte Zeitung* (January 1929).

There is now a book, written by a man named Erich Maria Remarque, which was lived by millions and will be read by millions too, now and for all time, and not read as one reads books—rather like one succumbs to one's fate, to the inescapable in one's time and existence, like one lays hold of it and like one is laid hold of, like one bleeds, like one struggles, like one dies.

This book belongs in the schoolrooms, the reading halls, the universities, in all the newspapers, all the broadcast stations, and all that is not yet enough. For it is not concerned with a good thing, as are many war-and-peace novels of the present; it is concerned with the fundamental fact of our life and future being, with the primal stratum, and with the cellular core of centuries. This is the war as we experienced it at the front—we, a very definite generation formed in only a few years, who had had no life before the war, no form, and no content, who were born of the war and crushed by it, and who—along with its dead—live on beyond the war as a singular new beginning.

All Quiet on the Western Front. An eternally recurring statement from the German military reports. I want, for those born later, to show in a trifling personal example how it was. One evening in Freiburg, where my brother lay in the army hospital, my parents sat in the dining room of a small hotel. A lady entered with the special printing of the daily military report, which had just come out. My mother asked what news there might be. The lady said, "Nothing new, there is still nothing going on. South of the Somme, an insignificant, bullet-riddled village that no one knows has fallen: Chilly." My mother knew, however, that I had been emplaced in this village for weeks. For her the unknown village Chilly meant more than if the entire western front had been breached, Strasbourg conquered, Paris conquered, the czar murdered, and England in collapse. It was September 4, 1916. Nothing new.

Nothing new. Except that for a few hundred thousand people the world was collapsing, along with everything that until then had fulfilled and enlivened them; except that they did not know whether it was now the void, the end, a complete dissolution that would swallow them up—or the whirlpool and obscurity of a new creation. Yes, that they did not even ask, nor had any idea whether they were the plow or the earth, the axe or the wood, seed grain or a rotting carcass.

That is what Remarque offers here, for the first time clearly and indelibly: what went on in these people, what happened inside, in the mines and sap of the soul, in the blood, in the tissue; and that is why it is the first war book that offers truth. We have all repeatedly experienced the impossibility of saying anything about the war. There is nothing more miserable than to hear someone tell his war experiences. So we fall silent and wait. But we do not forget. And it is hardly to be believed and borders on the miraculous that this book has already been written: one always thought two more decades would have to pass before someone could do it. Everything that has been created out of this time until now is patchwork by comparison. And there have already been a few war books that mean much to us: but they derive their momentary value and their present significance precisely from their misrepresentation, exaggeration, or distortion. *The Fire* by [Henri] Barbusse, the novellas by Leonhard Frank, they were so near, were created so much in the middle of it all that they could offer only flashes of light and shadows. And Leonhard Frank's most mature and finest novella, *Karl and Anna,* entirely outgrows the war and enters the timelessly human. Then came books that reported and documented: *Soldier Suhren* and *War* by Ludwig Renn, *1902* by [Ernst] Glaeser. But here, from Remarque, fate itself has become the protagonist for the first time. The whole. That which was behind it, which burned beneath it—that which remained.

And so written, so created, so lived that it becomes more than reality: truth, pure valid truth. The writer preceded the book with a statement: "This book is intended to be neither indictment nor confession. It is intended only as an attempt to report on a generation that was destroyed by the war—even if they escaped the grenades."

The book fulfills this prefatory statement fully and completely.

But it does still more. It draws everyone into the fate of this generation. It shows, without saying it in one word, how it lives, along with its dead, how it raises its head, gathers its scattered limbs, slowly, gropingly, unsteadily, stumbling, and how step by step, inexorably, unbreakably, it begins to march. How it retrieves its face from shadows, insane lights, fog, and masks, then retrieves its cheek, its will, which it will force upon the century. We are the ones whose lives began with the knowledge of the ultimate and greatest things of earthly existence—of the most terrible, the mortal abandonment of man, and the highest, comradeship.

11

ERNST VON SALOMON
The Outlawed

First published in *Die Geächteten* (Gütersloh: Bertelsmann, 1929), 48–49.

Slowly, some twenty men assembled. They recognized each other by a look, a word, a smile. They knew they belonged together.

But they were not loyal to the government. By God, they were not loyal to the government, anything but that. They could not respect the man and the orders they had obeyed up to then, and the order they had created seemed to them no longer to make sense.

They were troublemakers in their companies. The war had not yet discharged them. The war had formed them, it had let their most secret passions break through the crust like sparks, it had given their lives a meaning and hallowed their engagement. They were the unruly and the untamed, outcasts from the world of civil norms, stragglers who re-grouped themselves in small bunches in order to seek their own front line. There were many banners around which they could gather—which waved most proudly in the wind? There were still many castles left to storm, many enemy bands were still camped in the fields. They were the *Landsknechte*—but where was the land which they served? They had recognized the greatest swindle of this peace, they did not want to take part in it. They did not want to participate in the wholesome order, which was praised to them in a slimy way. They had remained under arms according to an infallible instinct. They shot things up all over because the banging was fun, they marched through the land hither and thither because the smell of tart adventure waved to them everywhere. And yet each of them sought something else and gave different reasons for their search, for the word had not yet been given to them. They sensed the word, yes, they even spoke it out loud and were ashamed of its washed-out sound; they turned it over, tested it in secret fear, and left it out of the interplay of manifold conversations, and yet it stood over them. The word stood wrapped in deep gloom, weather-beaten, beckoning, full of secrets, beaming magical powers, felt and not yet recognized, loved and not yet bidden to them. And the word was Germany.

Where was Germany? In Weimar? In Berlin? Once it had been on the front line, but the front fell apart. Then it was supposed to be at home, but home deceived. It was sung in song and speech, but the note was false. They spoke of fatherland and motherland, but even the niggers had that. Where was Germany? Was it in the people? But they cried for bread and voted for the fat-bellied ones. Was it in the state? But the state sought its form garrulously and found it in renunciation.

Germany burned darkly in daring brains. Germany was there where it was being fought for, it showed itself where armored hands reached out for its very existence, it beamed dazzlingly where those possessed of its spirit dared the final sacrifice for the sake of Germany. Germany was on the border. The articles of the Treaty of Versailles told us where Germany was.

We had been recruited for the border. Orders held us in Weimar. We protected rustling constructions of paragraphs, and the border burned. We lay in maggoty quarters, but French columns marched in the Rhineland. We shot it out with daring sailors, but in the east the Poles lay waste with fire and sword. We drilled and formed honor guards for umbrellas and soft felt hats, but for the first time in the Baltic, German battalions formed for an advance.

On April 1, 1919, Bismarck's birthday—the right-wing parties held patriotic celebrations—we left Weimar and our unit without resignation or orders, twenty-eight men, Lieutenant Kay at the head, went to the Baltic.

12

ALBERT EINSTEIN AND SIGMUND FREUD

Why War?

First published as *Warum Krieg?* (Paris: International Institute of Intellectual Co-operation, League of Nations, 1933).

Caputh near Potsdam, 30th July, 1932.

Dear Professor Freud,

The proposal of the League of Nations and its International Institute of Intellectual Co-operation at Paris that I should invite a person, to be chosen by myself, to a frank exchange of views on any problem that I might select affords me a very welcome opportunity of conferring with you upon a question which, as things now are, seems the most insistent of all the problems civilization has to face. This is the problem: Is there any way of delivering humanity from the menace of war? It is common knowledge that, with the advance of modern science, this issue has come to mean a matter of life and death for civilization as we know it; nevertheless, for all the zeal displayed, every attempt at its solution has ended in a lamentable breakdown.

I believe, moreover, that those whose duty it is to tackle the problem professionally and practically are growing only too aware of their impotence to deal with it, and have now a very lively desire to learn the views of men who, absorbed in the pursuit of science, can see world problems in the perspective distance lends. As for me, the normal objective of my thought affords no insight into the dark places of human will and feeling. Thus, in the enquiry now proposed, I can do little more than seek to clarify the question at issue and, clearing the ground of the more obvious solutions, enable you to bring the light of your far-reaching knowledge of man's instinctive life to bear upon the problem. There are certain psychological obstacles whose existence a layman in the mental sciences may dimly surmise, but whose interrelations and vagaries he is incompetent to fathom; you, I am convinced, will be able to suggest educative methods, lying more or less outside the scope of politics, which will eliminate these obstacles.

As one immune from nationalist bias, I personally see a simple way of dealing with the superficial (i.e. administrative) aspect of the problem: the setting up, by international consent, of a legislative and judicial body to settle every conflict arising between nations. Each nation would undertake to abide by the orders issued by this legislative body, to invoke its decision in every dispute, to accept its judgments unreservedly and to carry out every measure the tribunal deems necessary for the execution of its decrees. But here, at the outset, I come up against a difficulty; a tribunal is a human institution which, in proportion as the power at its disposal is inadequate to enforce its verdicts, is all the more prone to suffer these to be deflected by extrajudicial pressure. This is a fact with which we have to reckon; law and might inevitably go hand in hand, and juridical decisions approach more nearly the ideal justice demanded by the community (in whose name and interests these verdicts are pronounced) in so far as the community has effective power to compel respect of its juridical ideal. But at present we are far from possessing any supranational organization competent to render verdicts of incontestable authority and enforce absolute submission to the execution of its verdicts. Thus I am led to my first axiom: the quest of international security involves the unconditional surrender by every nation, in a certain measure, of its liberty of action, its sovereignty that is to say, and it is clear beyond all doubt that no other road can lead to such security.

The ill-success, despite their obvious sincerity, of all the efforts made during the last decade to reach this goal leaves us no room to doubt that strong psychological factors are at work, which paralyze these efforts. Some of these factors are not far to seek. The craving for power which characterizes the governing class in every nation is hostile to any limitation of the national sovereignty. This political power-hunger is wont to batten on the activities of another group, whose aspirations are on purely mercenary, economic lines. I have especially in mind that small but determined group, active in every nation, composed of individuals who, indifferent to social considerations and restraints, regard warfare, the manufacture and sale of arms, simply as an occasion to advance their personal interests and enlarge their personal authority.

But recognition of this obvious fact is merely the first step towards an appreciation of the actual state of affairs. Another question follows hard upon it: How is it possible for this small clique to bend the will of the majority, who stand to lose and suffer by a state of war, to the service of their ambitions? (In speaking of the majority, I do not exclude soldiers of every rank who have chosen war as their profession, in the belief that they are serving to defend the highest interests of their race, and that attack is often the best method of defense.) An obvious answer to this question would seem to be that the minority, the ruling class at present, has the schools and press, usually the Church as well, under its thumb. This enables it to organize and sway the emotions of the masses, and make its tool of them.

Yet even this answer does not provide a complete solution. Another question arises from it: How is it these devices succeed so well in rousing people to such wild enthusiasm, even to sacrifice their lives? Only one answer is possible. Because people have within them a lust for hatred and destruction. In normal times this passion exists in a latent state, it emerges only in unusual circumstances; but it is a comparatively easy task to call it into play and raise it to the power of a collective psychosis. Here lies, perhaps, the crux of all the complex of factors we are considering, an enigma that only the expert in the lore of human instincts can resolve.

And so we come to our last question. Is it possible to control human mental evolution so that people can resist the psychoses of hate and destructiveness? Here I am thinking by no means only of the so-called uncultured masses. Experience proves that it is rather the so-called "intelligentsia" that is most apt to yield to these disastrous collective suggestions, since the intellectual has no direct contact with life in the raw, but encounters it in its easiest, synthetic form—upon the printed page.

To conclude: I have so far been speaking only of wars between nations; what are known as international conflicts. But I am well aware that the aggressive instinct operates under other forms and in other circumstances. (I am thinking of civil wars, for instance, due in earlier days to religious zeal, but nowadays to social factors; or, again, the persecution of racial minorities.) But my insistence on what is the most typical, most cruel and extravagant form of conflict between man and man was deliberate, for here we have the best occasion of discovering ways and means to render all armed conflicts impossible.

I know that in your writings we may find answers, explicit or implied, to all the issues of this urgent and absorbing problem. But it would be of the greatest service to us all were you to present the problem of world peace in the light of your most recent discoveries, for such a presentation well might blaze the trail for new and fruitful modes of action.

Yours very sincerely,
A. Einstein.

Vienna, September, 1932.

Dear Professor Einstein,

When I learned of your intention to invite me to a mutual exchange of views upon a subject which not only interested you personally but seemed deserving, too, of public interest, I cordially assented. I expected you to choose a problem lying on the borderland of the knowable, as it stands today, a theme which each of us, physicist and psychologist, might approach from his own angle, to meet at last on common ground, though setting out from different premises. Thus the question which you put me—what is to be done to rid mankind of the war-menace?—took me by surprise. And, next, I was dumbfounded by the thought of my (of our, I almost wrote) incompetence; for this struck me as being a matter of practical politics, the statesman's proper study. But then I realized that you did not raise the question in your capacity as scientist or physicist, but as a lover of his fellow men, who responded to the call of the League of Nations much as Fridtjof Nansen, the Polar explorer, took on himself the task of succouring homeless and starving victims of the World War. And, next, I reminded myself that I was not being called on to formulate practical proposals, but, rather, to explain how this question of preventing wars strikes a psychologist.

But here, too, you have stated the gist of the matter in your letter—and taken the wind out of my sails! Still, I will gladly follow in your wake and content myself with endorsing your conclusions, which, however, I propose to amplify to the best of my knowledge or surmise.

You begin with the relations between Might and Right, and this is assuredly the proper starting-point for our enquiry. But, for the term "might," I would substitute a tougher and more telling word: "violence." In right and violence we have today an obvious antinomy. It is easy to prove that one has evolved from the other and, when we go back to origins and examine primitive conditions, the solution of the problem follows easily enough. I must crave your indulgence if in what follows I speak of well-known, admitted facts as though they were new data; the context necessitates this method.

Conflicts of interest between people are resolved, in principle, by recourse to violence. It is the same in the animal kingdom, from which humanity cannot claim exclusion; nevertheless people are also prone to conflicts of opinion, touching, on occasion, the loftiest peaks of abstract thought, which seem to call for settlement by quite another method. This refinement is, however, a late development. To start with, brute force was the factor which, in small communities, decided points of ownership and the question of whose will was to prevail. Very soon physical force was implemented, then replaced, by the use of various adjuncts; he proved the victor whose weapon was the better, or handled the more skilfully. Now, for the first time, with the coming of weapons, superior brains began to oust brute force, but the object of the conflict remained the same: one party was to be constrained, by injury or impairment of strength, to retract a claim or a refusal. This end is most effectively gained when the opponent is definitively put out of action—in other words, is killed. This procedure has two advantages; the enemy cannot renew hostilities, and, secondly, this fate deters others from following the example. Moreover, the slaughter of a foe gratifies an instinctive craving—a point to which we shall revert hereafter. However, another consideration may be set off against this will to kill: the possibility of using enemies for servile tasks if their spirits be broken and their lives spared. Here violence finds an outlet not in slaughter but in subjugation. Hence springs the practice of showing mercy; but the victor, having from now on to reckon with the craving for revenge that rankles in the victim, forfeits some personal security.

Thus, under primitive conditions, it is superior force—brute violence, or violence backed by arms—that lords it everywhere. We know that in the course of evolution this state of things was modified, a path was traced that led away from violence to law. But what was this path? Surely it issued from a single verity; that the superiority of one strong man can be overborne by an alliance of many weaklings, that *l'union fait la force*. Brute force is overcome by union, the allied might of scattered units makes good its right against the isolated giant. Thus we may define "right" (i.e. law) as the might of a community. Yet it, too, is nothing else than violence, quick to attack whatever individual stands in its path, and it employs the self-same methods, follows like ends, with but one difference; it is the communal, not individual, violence that has its way. But, for the transition from crude violence to the reign of law, a certain psychological condition must first obtain. The union of the majority must be stable and enduring. If its sole *raison d'être* be to fight some powerful individual, after whose downfall it would be dissolved, it leads to nothing. Someone else trusting to superior power, will seek to reinstate the rule of violence and the cycle will repeat itself unendingly. Thus, the union of the people must be permanent and well organized; it must enact rules to meet the risk of possible revolts; must set up machinery ensuring that its rules—the laws—are observed and that such acts of violence as the laws demand are duly carried out. This recognition of a community of interests engenders among the members of the group a sentiment of unity and fraternal solidarity which constitutes its real strength.

So far I have set out what seems to me the kernel of the matter: the suppression of brute force by the transfer of power to a larger combination, founded on the community of sentiments linking up its members. All the rest is mere tautology and glosses. Now the position is simple enough so long as the community consists of a number of equally strong individuals. The laws of such a group can determine to what extent the individual must forfeit personal freedom, the right of using personal force as an instrument of violence, to ensure the safety of the group. But such a combination is only theoretically possible; in practice the situation is always complicated by the fact that, from the outset, the group includes elements of unequal power, men and women, elders and children, and, very soon, as a result of war and conquest, victors and the vanquished—i.e. masters and slaves—as well. From this time on the common law takes notice of these inequalities of power, laws are made by and for the rulers, giving the servile classes fewer rights. Thenceforward there exist within the state two factors making for legal instability, but legislative evolution, too: first, the attempts by members of the ruling class to set themselves above the law's restrictions and, secondly, the constant struggle of the ruled to extend their rights and see each gain embodied in the code, replacing legal disabilities by equal laws for all. The second of these tendencies will be particularly marked when there takes place a positive mutation of the balance of power within the community, the frequent outcome of certain historical conditions. In such cases the laws may gradually be adjusted to the changed conditions or (as more usually ensues) the ruling class is loath to reckon with the new developments, the result being insurrections and civil wars, a period when law is in abeyance and force once more the arbiter, followed by a new regime of law. There is another factor of constitutional change, which operates in a wholly pacific manner, viz: the cultural evolution of the mass of the community; this factor, however, is of a different order and can only be dealt with later.

Thus we see that, even within the group itself, the exercise of violence cannot be avoided when conflicting interests are at stake. But the common needs and habits of men who live in fellowship under the same "sky" favor a speedy issue of such conflicts and, this being so, the possibilities of peaceful solutions make steady progress. Yet the most casual glance at world history will show an unending series of conflicts between one community and another or a group of others, between larger and smaller units, between cities, countries, races, tribes and kingdoms, almost all of which were settled by the ordeal of war. Such wars end either in pillage or in conquest and its fruits, the downfall of the loser. No single all-embracing judgment can be passed on these wars of aggrandizement. Some, like the war between the Mongols and the Turks, have led to unmitigated misery; others, however, have furthered the transition from violence to law, since they brought larger units into being, within whose limits a recourse to violence was banned and a new regime determined all disputes. Thus the Roman conquests brought that boon, the pax romana, to the Mediterranean lands. The French kings' lust for aggrandizement created a new France, flourishing in peace and unity. Paradoxical as it sounds, we must admit that warfare well might serve to pave the way to that unbroken peace we so desire, for it is war that brings vast empires into being, within whose frontiers all warfare is proscribed by a strong central power. In practice, however, this end is not attained, for as a rule the fruits of victory are but short-lived, the new-created unit falls asunder once again, generally because there can be no true cohesion between the parts that violence has welded. Hitherto, moreover, such conquests have only led to aggregations which, for all their magnitude, had limits, and disputes between these units could be resolved only by recourse to arms. For humanity at large the sole result of all these military enterprises was that, instead of frequent not to say incessant little wars, they had now to face great wars which, for all they came less often, were so much the more destructive.

Regarding the world of today the same conclusion holds good, and you, too, have reached it, though by a shorter path. There is but one sure way of ending war and that is the establishment, by common consent, of a central control which shall have the last word in every conflict of interests. For this, two things are needed: first, the creation of such a supreme court of judicature; secondly, its investment with adequate executive force. Unless this second requirement be fulfilled, the first is unavailing. Obviously the League of Nations, acting as a Supreme Court, fulfils the first condition; it does not fulfil the second. It has no force at its disposal and can only get it if the members of the new body, its constituent nations, furnish it. And, as things are, this is a forlorn hope. Still we should be taking a very short-sighted view of the League of Nations were we to ignore the fact that here is an experiment the like of which has rarely—never before, perhaps, on such a scale—been attempted in the course of history. It is an attempt to acquire the authority (in other words, coercive influence), which hitherto reposed exclusively on the possession of power, by calling into play certain idealistic attitudes of mind. We have seen that there are two factors of cohesion in a community: violent compulsion and ties of sentiment ("identifications," in technical parlance) between the members of the group. If one of these factors becomes inoperative, the other may still suffice to hold the group together. Obviously such notions as these can only be significant when they are the expression of a deeply rooted sense of unity, shared by all. It is necessary, therefore, to gauge the efficacy of such sentiments. History tells us that, on occasion, they have been effective. For example, the Panhellenic conception, the Greeks' awareness of superiority over their barbarian neighbors, which found expression in the Amphictyonies, the Oracles and Games, was strong enough to humanize the methods of warfare as between Greeks, though inevitably it failed to prevent conflicts between different elements of the Hellenic race or even to deter a city or group of cities from joining forces with their racial foe, the Persians, for the defeat of a rival. The solidarity of Christendom in the Renaissance age was no more effective, despite its vast authority, in hindering Christian nations, large and small alike, from calling in the Sultan to their aid. And, in our times, we look in vain for some such unifying notion whose authority would be unquestioned. It is all too clear that the nationalistic ideas, paramount today in every country, operate in quite a contrary direction. There are some who hold that the Bolshevik conceptions may make an end of war, but, as things are, that goal lies very far away and, perhaps, could only be attained after a spell of brutal internecine warfare. Thus it would seem that any effort to replace brute force by the might of an ideal is, under present conditions, doomed to fail. Our logic is at fault if we ignore the fact that right is founded on brute force and even today needs violence to maintain it.

I now can comment on another of your statements. You are amazed that it is so easy to infect men with the war-fever, and you surmise that man has in him an active instinct for hatred and destruction, amenable to such stimulations. I entirely agree with you. I believe in the existence of this instinct and have been recently at pains to study its manifestations. In this connexion may I set out a fragment of that knowledge of the instincts, which we psychoanalysts, after so many tentative essays and gropings in the dark, have compassed? We assume that human instincts are of two kinds: those that conserve and unify, which we call "erotic" (in the meaning Plato gives to Eros in his Symposium), or else "sexual" (explicitly extending the popular connotation of "sex"); and, secondly, the instincts to destroy and kill, which we assimilate as the aggressive or destructive instincts. These are, as you perceive, the well-known opposites, Love and Hate, transformed into theoretical entities; they are, perhaps, another aspect of those eternal polarities, attraction and repulsion, which fall within your province. But we must be wary of passing over-hastily to the notions of good and evil. Each of these instincts is every bit as indispensable as its opposite and all the phenomena of life derive from their activity, whether they work in concert or in opposition. It seems that an instinct of either category can operate but rarely in isolation; it is always blended ("alloyed," as we say) with a certain dosage of its opposite, which modifies its aim or even, in certain circumstances, is a prime condition of its attainment. Thus the instinct of self-preservation is certainly of an erotic nature, but to gain its ends this very instinct necessitates aggressive action. In the same way the love-instinct, when directed to a specific object, calls for an admixture of the acquisitive instinct if it is to enter into effective possession of that object. It is the difficulty of isolating the two kinds of instinct in their manifestations that has so long prevented us from recognizing them.

If you will travel with me a little further on this road, you will find that human affairs are complicated in yet another way. Only exceptionally does an action follow on the stimulus of a single instinct, which is per se a blend of Eros and destructiveness. As a rule several motives of similar composition concur to bring about the act. This fact was duly noted by a colleague of yours, Professor G. C. Lichtenberg, sometime Professor of Physics at Göttingen; he was perhaps even more eminent as a psychologist than as a physical scientist. He evolved the notion of a "Compasscard of Motives" and wrote: "The efficient motives impelling man to act can be classified like the 32 Winds, and described in the same manner; e.g. Food-Food-Fame or Fame-Fame-Food." Thus, when a nation is summoned to engage in war, a whole gamut of human motives may respond to this appeal; high and low motives, some openly avowed, others slurred over. The lust for aggression and destruction is certainly included; the innumerable cruelties of history and daily life confirm its prevalence and strength. The stimulation of these destructive impulses by appeals to idealism and the erotic instinct naturally facilitates their release. Musing on the atrocities recorded on history's page, we feel that the ideal motive has often served as a camouflage for the lust of destruction; sometimes, as with the cruelties of the Inquisition, it seems that, while the ideal motives occupied the foreground of consciousness, they drew their strength from the destructive instincts submerged in the unconscious. Both interpretations are feasible.

You are interested, I know, in the prevention of war, not in our theories, and I keep this fact in mind. Yet I would like to dwell a little longer on this destructive instinct which is seldom given the attention that its importance warrants. With the least of speculative efforts we are led to conclude that this instinct functions in every living being, striving to work its ruin and reduce life to its primal state of inert matter. Indeed it might well be called the "death-instinct"; whereas the erotic instincts vouch for the struggle to live on. The death instinct becomes an impulse to destruction when, with the aid of certain organs, it directs its action outwards, against external objects. The living being, that is to say, defends its own existence by destroying foreign bodies. But, in one of its activities, the death instinct is operative within the living being and we have sought to trace back a number of normal and pathological phenomena to this introversion of the destructive instinct. We have even committed the heresy of explaining the origin of human conscience by some such "turning inward" of the aggressive impulse. Obviously when this internal tendency operates on too large a scale, it is no trivial matter, rather a positively morbid state of things; whereas the diversion of the destructive impulse towards the external world must have beneficial effects. Here is then the biological justification for all those vile, pernicious propensities which we now are combating. We can but own that they are really more akin to nature than this our stand against them, which, in fact, remains to be accounted for.

All this may give you the impression that our theories amount to a species of mythology and a gloomy one at that! But does not every natural science lead ultimately to this—a sort of mythology? Is it otherwise today with your physical science?

The upshot of these observations, as bearing on the subject in hand, is that there is no likelihood of our being able to suppress humanity's aggressive tendencies. In some happy corners of the earth, they say, where nature brings forth abundantly whatever people desire, there flourish races whose lives go gently by, unknowing of aggression or constraint. This I can hardly credit; I would like further details about these happy folk. The Bolsheviks, too, aspire to do away with human aggressiveness by ensuring the satisfaction of material needs and enforcing equality between people. To me this hope seems vain. Meanwhile they busily perfect their armaments, and their hatred of outsiders is not the least of the factors of cohesion amongst themselves. In any case, as you too have observed, complete suppression of aggressive tendencies is not at issue; what we may try is to divert it into a channel other than that of warfare.

From our "mythology" of the instincts we may easily deduce a formula for an indirect method of eliminating war. If the propensity for war be due to the destructive instinct, we have always its counter-agent, Eros, to our hand. All that produces ties of sentiment between man and man must serve us as war's antidote. These ties are of two kinds. First, such relations as those towards a beloved object, void though they be of sexual intent. The psychoanalyst need feel no compunction in mentioning "love" in this connection; religion uses the same language: Love thy neighbour as thyself. A pious injunction easy to proclaim, but hard to carry out! The other bond of sentiment is by way of identification. All that brings out the significant resemblances between people calls into play this feeling of community, identification, whereon is founded, in large measure, the whole edifice of human society.

In your strictures on the abuse of authority I find another suggestion for an indirect attack on the war-impulse. That people are divided into leaders and the led is but another manifestation of their inborn and irremediable inequality. The second class constitutes the vast majority; they need a high command to make decisions for them, to which decisions they usually bow without demur. In this context we would point out that people should be at greater pains than heretofore to form a superior class of independent thinkers, unamenable to intimidation and fervent in the quest of truth, whose function it would be to guide the masses dependent on their lead. There is no need to point out how little the rule of politicians and the Church's ban on liberty of thought encourage such a new creation. The ideal conditions would obviously be found in a community where everyone subordinated instinctive life to the dictates of reason. Nothing less than this could bring about so thorough and so durable a union between people, even if this involved the severance of mutual ties of sentiment. But surely such a hope is utterly utopian, as things are. The other indirect methods of preventing war are certainly more feasible, but entail no quick results. They conjure up an ugly picture of mills that grind so slowly that, before the flour is ready, people are dead of hunger.

As you see, little good comes of consulting a theoretician, aloof from worldly contacts, on practical and urgent problems! Better it were to tackle each successive crisis with means that we have ready to our hands. However, I would like to deal with a question which, though it is not mooted in your letter, interests me greatly. Why do we, you and I and many an other, protest so vehemently against war, instead of just accepting it as another of life's odious importunities? For it seems a natural thing enough, biologically sound and practically unavoidable. I trust you will not be shocked by my raising such a question. For the better conduct of an inquiry it may be well to don a mask of feigned aloofness. The answer to my query may run as follows: because every people has a right over their own lives and war destroys lives that were full of promise; it forces the individual into situations that shame humanity, obliging them to murder fellow human beings against their will; it ravages material amenities, the fruits of human toil, and much besides. Moreover wars, as now conducted, afford no scope for acts of heroism according to the old ideals and, given the high perfection of modern arms, war today would mean the sheer extermination of one of the combatants, if not of both. This is so true, so obvious, that we can but wonder why the conduct of war is not banned by general consent. Doubtless either of the points I have just made is open to debate. It may be asked if the community, in its turn, cannot claim a right over the individual lives of its members. Moreover, all forms of war cannot be indiscriminately condemned; so long as there are nations and empires, each prepared callously to exterminate its rival, all alike must be equipped for war. But we will not dwell on any of these problems; they lie outside the debate to which you have invited me. I pass on to another point, the basis, as it strikes me, of our common hatred of war. It is this: we cannot do otherwise than hate it. Pacifists we are, since our organic nature wills us thus to be. Hence it comes easy to us to find arguments that justify our standpoint.

This point, however, calls for elucidation. Here is the way in which I see it. The cultural development of mankind (some, I know, prefer to call it civilization) has been in progress since immemorial antiquity. To this processus we owe all that is best in our composition, but also much that makes for human suffering. Its origins and causes are obscure, its issue is uncertain, but some of its characteristics are easy to perceive. It well may lead to the extinction of humanity for it impairs the sexual function in more than one respect, and even today the uncivilized races and the backward classes of all nations are multiplying more rapidly than "the cultured elements." This process may, perhaps, be likened to the effects of domestication on certain animals—it clearly involves physical changes of structure—but the view that cultural development is an "organic" process of this order has not yet become generally familiar. The psychic changes which accompany this process of cultural change are striking, and not to be gainsaid. They consist in the progressive rejection of instinctive ends and a scaling down of instinctive reactions. Sensations which delighted our forefathers have become neutral or unbearable to us; and, if our ethical and aesthetic ideals have undergone a change, the causes of this are "ultimately organic." On the psychological side two of the most important phenomena of culture are, firstly, a strengthening of the intellect, which tends to master our instinctive life, and, secondly, an introversion of the aggressive impulse, with all its consequent benefits and perils. Now war runs most emphatically counter to the psychic disposition imposed on us by the growth of culture; we are therefore bound to resent war, to find it utterly intolerable. With pacifists like us it is not merely an intellectual and affective repulsion, but a constitutional intolerance, an idiosyncrasy in its most drastic form. And it would seem that the aesthetic ignominies of warfare play almost as large a part in this repugnance as war's atrocities.

How long have we to wait before the remainder of humanity turns pacifist? Impossible to say, and yet perhaps our hope that these two factors—people's cultural disposition and a well-founded dread of the form that future wars will take—may serve to put an end to war in the near future, is not chimerical. But by what ways or by-ways this will come about, we cannot guess. Meanwhile we may rest on the assurance that whatever makes for cultural development is working also against war.

With kindest regards and, should this exposé prove a disappointment to you, my sincere regrets,

Yours,
Sigmund Freud

2
Revolution and the Birth of the Republic

KAISER WILHELM II, already in Dutch exile, formally abdicated his imperial throne on November 28, 1918, and with it the crown of Prussia. The republic, however, had already been proclaimed on November 9 by the Social Democratic Party leader Philipp Scheidemann to forestall a similar declaration by the more radical Spartacist Party. On the previous day a separate republic had been announced in Bavaria by the Independent Socialist Party leader Kurt Eisner. The sudden dissolution of autocratic power, following the unexpected collapse of the German armies in the field, left a political vacuum, which intellectuals like Heinrich Mann rushed to fill.

Although soon dubbed the November Revolution, the events surrounding the new republic's origin were anything but the product of a triumphant mass movement. As one of the republic's shrewdest observers, Count Harry von Kessler, noted two months later, only a small minority of the population associated with the splinter socialist faction known—in homage to the leader of a Roman slave revolt—as the Spartacists really had a radical agenda. In fact, on the day after Scheidemann's proclamation, the new chancellor, Friedrich Ebert, another "majority" Social Democrat who had been named to the position by his predecessor, Max von Baden, concluded a fateful agreement with the chief of staff of the German army, Wilhelm Groener. The army was put at the new republic's command in return for the assurance that it would be used to suppress bolshevik rebellion. Ebert's fragile leftist coalition survived only until the end of December, when the Independent Socialists (USPD) joined the Spartacists in opposition. With the creation of the German Communist Party (KPD), whose founding congress took place from December 30, 1918, to January 1, 1919, the splits on the left became permanent. They were if anything deepened after the collapse of the Spartacist movement and the murders of its leaders Rosa Luxemburg and Karl Liebknecht on January 15, 1919. Mourned as martyrs by many on the left, they were coldly dismissed by more skeptical observers of the revolution, such as the aristocratic former foreign minister, Bernhard Prince von Bülow, whose memoirs were published a decade later.

Despite the continuing turmoil in the streets of Berlin and elsewhere, a national election to select delegates to a constitutional convention was held on January 19, 1919. It was convened in the small city of Weimar, historically associated with the enlightened eighteenth-century court of Karl August, whose cultural tone was set by Goethe and Schiller. Not only did Weimar symbolize a very different Germany from the martial *Obrigkeitsstaat* (authoritarian state) epitomized by Prussian Berlin, it was also a far less vulnerable location than the still-unsettled capital. The 421-seat assembly was dominated by the Social Democrats (163 delegates), the Catholic Center Party (88 delegates) and the newly formed Democratic Party (75 delegates). After electing Ebert the provisional president—his swearing-in ceremony in August was mordantly recorded in Count Harry Kessler's diary—the assembly set out to write a new constitution, providing legal status to the shift from autocracy to popular sovereignty.

The Democratic politician Hugo Preuss was the assembly's intellectual leader and was largely responsible for the constitution adopted on August 11, 1919. For the first time women were given the vote, and the unequal franchise that elected the powerful Prussian *Landtag* (Assembly) during the Wilhelmine era was abolished. Among the Weimar constitution's more salient provisions were Articles 17 and 22, which introduced proportional representation both in the states (now called by the less-exalted title of *Länder* rather than *Staaten*) and the Reich government; Article 41, which stipulated direct presidential elections every seven years; and Article 48, which granted the Reich president emergency powers to suspend certain sections of the constitution under exceptional, but ill-defined, circumstances.

Proportional representation meant that voters selected party lists rather than individual candidates, making those elected less representatives of their districts than of their parties. It also led to the splintering of the party system throughout the republic, helping to prevent the consolidation of a strong centrist consensus. During the republic's short existence, more than fifteen parties vied for support, leading to increased polarization towards the extremes of right and left by its end. Article 48 was invoked in July 1930 by Chancellor Heinrich Brüning to deal with the crisis produced by the growing inability to form a parliamentary majority coalition. Here the autocratic residues in the constitution came to the "rescue" of its more radically democratic innovations. When government by presidential decree was finally lifted in January 1933, the result was even worse, as a new parliamentary coalition including, for the first time, the National Socialists came to power. Knowing this outcome, it is hard to read without a sense of bitter irony the defense of German democracy written by Theodor Heuss for the tenth anniversary of the constitution he did so much to forge.

13

[Spartacus Manifesto]

First published as "Richtlinien für die Arbeiter—und Soldatenräte Deutschlands" in *Die Rote Fahne* (November 26, 1918).

PROLETARIANS! MEN AND WOMEN OF LABOR! COMRADES!

The revolution has made its entry into Germany. The masses of the soldiers, who for four years were driven to the slaughterhouse for the sake of capitalistic profits, and the masses of workers, who for four years were exploited, crushed, and starved, have revolted. That fearful tool of oppression—Prussian militarism, that scourge of humanity—lies broken on the ground. Its most noticeable representatives, and therewith the most noticeable of those guilty of this war, the Kaiser and the Crown Prince, have fled from the country. Workers' and soldiers' councils have been formed everywhere.

Proletarians of all countries, we do not say that in Germany all the power has really been lodged in the hands of the working people, that the complete triumph of the proletarian revolution has already been attained. There still sit in the government all those socialists who in August 1914 abandoned our most precious possession, the [Second] International [Workingmen's Association], who for four years betrayed the German working class and at the same time the International.

But, proletarians of all countries, now the German proletarians are speaking to you. We believe we have the right to appeal before your forum in their name. From the first day of this war we endeavored to do our international duty by fighting that criminal government with all our power, and by branding it as the one really guilty of the war.

Now, at this moment, we are justified before history, before the International, and before the German proletariat. The masses agree with us enthusiastically; constantly widening circles of the proletariat share the knowledge that the hour has struck for a settlement with capitalist class rule.

But this great task cannot be accomplished by the German proletariat alone: it can fight and triumph only by appealing to the solidarity of the proletarians of the whole world.

Comrades of the belligerent countries, we are aware of your situation. We know very well that your governments, since they have won the victory, are dazzling the eyes of many strata of the people with the external brilliance of this triumph. We know that they thus succeed through the success of the murdering in making its causes and aims forgotten. [...]

The imperialism of all countries knows no "understanding"; it knows only one right—capital's profits; it knows only one language—the sword; it knows only one method—violence. And if it is now talking in all countries, in yours as well as ours, about the "League of Nations," "disarmament," "rights of small nations," "self-determination of the peoples," it is merely using the customary lying phrases of the rulers for the purpose of lulling to sleep the watchfulness of the proletariat.

Proletarians of all countries! This must be the last war! We owe that to the twelve million murdered victims; we owe that to our children; we owe that to humanity.

Europe has been ruined through the infamous international murder. Twelve million bodies cover the gruesome scenes of the imperialistic crime. The flower of youth and the best men of the nations have been mowed down. Uncounted productive forces have been annihilated. Humanity is almost ready to bleed to death from the bloodletting. Victors and vanquished stand at the edge of the abyss. Humanity is threatened with the most dreadful famine, a halting of the entire mechanism of production, plagues, and degeneration.

The great criminals of this fearful anarchy, of this chaos let loose—the ruling classes—are not able to control their own creation. The beast of capital that conjured up the hell of the world war is not capable of banishing it again, of restoring real order, of insuring bread and work, peace and civilization, and justice and liberty to tortured humanity.

What is being prepared by the ruling classes as peace and justice is only a new work of brutal force from which the hydra of oppression, hatred, and fresh bloody wars raises its thousand heads.

Socialism alone is in a position to complete the great work of permanent peace, to heal the thousand wounds from which humanity is bleeding, to transform the plains of Europe, trampled down by the apocryphal horsemen of war, into blossoming gardens, to conjure up ten productive forces for every one destroyed, to awaken all the physical and moral energies of humanity, and to replace hatred and dissension with fraternal solidarity, harmony, and respect for every human being. [. . .]

Proletarians of all countries, when we now summon you to a common struggle, it is not done for the sake of the German capitalists who, under the label of "German nation," are trying to escape the consequences of their own crimes; it is being done for our sake as well as yours. Remember that your victorious capitalists stand ready to suppress in blood our revolution, which they fear as their own. You yourselves have not become any freer through the "victory," you have only become still more enslaved. If your ruling classes succeed in throttling the proletarian revolution in Germany, as well as in Russia, then they will turn against you with redoubled violence. Your capitalists hope that victory over us and over revolutionary Russia will give them the power to scourge you with a whip of scorpions and to erect the thousand-year empire of exploitation upon the grave of socialism.

Therefore the proletariat of Germany is looking toward you in this hour. Germany is pregnant with the social revolution, but socialism can be realized only by the proletariat of the world.

And therefore we call to you: "Arise for the struggle! Arise for action! The time for empty manifestoes, platonic resolutions, and high-sounding words has passed! The hour of action has struck for the International!" We ask you to elect workers' and soldiers' councils everywhere that will seize political power and, together with us, will restore peace.

Not David Lloyd George and [Raymond] Poincaré, not [Sidney] Sonnino, [Woodrow] Wilson, and [Matthias] Erzberger or [Philipp] Scheidemann; these must not be allowed to make peace. Peace is to be concluded under the waving banner of the socialist world revolution.

Proletarians of all countries! We call upon you to complete the work of socialist liberation, to give a human aspect to the disfigured world, and to make true those words with which we often greeted each other in the old days and which we sang as we parted: "And the International shall be the human race."

14

HEINRICH MANN

The Meaning and Idea of the Revolution

Address to the Political Council of Intellectual Workers, Munich. First published as "Sinn und Idee der Revolution. Ansprache im Politischen Rat geistiger Arbeiter, München," *Münchner Neueste Nachrichten*, no. 607 (December 1, 1918).

Like the present time itself, with its new institutions and men, our association is the product of need. A victorious outcome of the war would never have occasioned a German revolution, and even a timely peace accord would have prevented it. Today we all are children of defeat. Is it not, however, natural that a defeated land would be more loved by its children than a triumphant one? Triumph exposes much ugliness. For too long have we seen it exposed in Germany. We are much happier to call ourselves German today. That is why above all we are concerned to say that we love Germany wholeheartedly and that we wish to serve it according to our views and our abilities.

We are far from desiring that the victory of our enemies become their misfortune as our old victories have finally become ours. Rather, we hope and desire that the moral earnestness a beaten country [France] gained fifty years ago thanks to its defeat may survive the greatest threat, its present victory. Now, however, we want to gain this moral earnestness ourselves. Are there not at this hour some who feel what they never would have believed it necessary to feel—how greatly we had lost ourselves in the enduring glow of our earlier victories, and that only now, on this journey through dust and our first eclipse, we have the hope of coming to terms with ourselves once again.

"Don't be too upright!" the cry, already, of [Friedrich Gottlieb] Klopstock to his Germans; and such a thought was, speaking morally, the beginning of the end. We cannot be upright enough. Every departure from absolute uprightness immediately occasions the most monstrous effects in the outside world; the rape of small provinces causes, even decades later, the collapse of great empires. More terrible, however, are the disturbances in our inner world once we have allowed injustice to enter. The falsification of our entire national character with boasting, provocation, lies, and self-deceit becomes our daily bread. Rapacity as the only drive of life; this was the imperial Germany that now lies happily behind us. And this is all that it could be, because under its rule, inwardly and outwardly, might took precedence over right.

Might instead of right means war directed externally, and that is what it means internally as well. Uprightness has long demanded the extensive realization of socialism. Now it should put socialism into practice. We are by its side—not only with our reason but also with our hearts. We desire the material happiness of our compatriots as honestly as we desire our own. They will perhaps understand if we consider their spiritual well-being as well. Spiritual well-being is more important, for the fate of mankind is more determined by its way of feeling and thinking than by economic rules. Think righteously, bourgeois! Should you ever have the majority in any sort of legislative assembly, do not succumb to the fateful error of believing you could banish from the world, by voting them down, the justified claims of the socialists. But you too must think righteously, socialists! Should you wish to attribute socialization to the chance circumstance of your power, rather than the insight and conscience of the majority, you will have won nothing. Dictatorship, even the most progressive, remains dictatorship and ends in catastrophe. The abuse of power bears the same fatal countenance everywhere.

One should not pretend that the socialization of even the last aspect of human activity represents the most radical deed to be done. There is a radicalism that supersedes all economic transformations: the radicalization of the mind. Whoever wants to be righteous to humanity must not be afraid. Those who love justice dare the most. We see a man who in his intellectual boldness has surpassed the most reckless of all the Russian dictators: Wilson,[1] who, despite enormous pressure from the victors and untouched by the temptations of unprecedented power, perseveres in that which his judgment calls right.

---

1. Woodrow Wilson (1856–1924), American president from 1913–1921, who in 1918 formulated the famous Fourteen Points that he thought would make the world "safe for democracy."

In this council, which wants only to counsel for the good, judgment can never be passed on a German revolution even when it commits excesses, because its worst excesses would never equal the crimes of the old regime. The revolutionary fanatics of today have only too many excuses. They get them from those pan-German fanatics, who until yesterday held the floor and who are waiting only to reclaim it in order, if possible, to depopulate the country once again, to demoralize it, and once again to reduce it to ruin. Where then are the revolutionaries who have come to power supposed to have learned uprightness? They grew up under the imperial regime. They might indeed say they would not think of giving up their power voluntarily, an imperial phrase. Whoever speaks it still has virtually everything to learn about the laws of a truly liberated world.

We are here to do our part in the introduction of the moral laws of a liberated world into German politics. We want our republic, even though the accidental gift of defeat, to be served by republicans. And in republicans we see neither bourgeois nor socialists, untenable distinctions in the face of a higher principle. Republicans we call people to whom the idea is superior to advantage, the individual superior to power. Among republicans, the condemnation of innocents can instigate battles of conscience that are so unrestrained as to threaten the commerce, the domestic peace, even the security of the nation—even were their republic to be merely a so-called rentier republic. An imperial regime, however, even a socially minded one, will never know such battles of conscience.

Our Germany will become as righteous, free, and true as some of us have striven for and demanded in its darkest days—fortified in our belief in the future of the German mind by its great past. In this country, come what may, the mind will finally rule. It will conquer Germany and the world; it is the only real victor of the world war. Those who resist it are lost. Those who accept it join the equal fraternity of all. Our reconciliation with the world will transpire in the name of eternal ideas, which we are finally sharing with it once again. We intellectual workers want to have the merit of being among the first to reconcile Germany with the world.

15

ROSA LUXEMBURG

Founding Manifesto of the Communist Party of Germany (KPD)

First published as "Konstituierung der Kommunistischen Partei," *Die rote Fahne,* no. 45 (December 31, 1918).

Comrades! Our task today is to discuss and adopt a program. In undertaking this task we are not actuated solely by the consideration that yesterday we founded a new party and that a new party must formulate a program. Great historical movements have been the determining causes of today's deliberations. The time has arrived when the entire socialist program of the proletariat has to be established upon a new foundation. We are faced with a position similar to that which was faced by Marx and Engels when they wrote the *Communist Manifesto* seventy years ago. As you all know, the *Communist Manifesto* dealt with socialism, with the realization of the aims of socialism, as the immediate task of the proletarian revolution. This was the idea represented by Marx and Engels in the Revolution of 1848; it was thus, likewise, that they conceived the basis for proletarian action in the international field. In common with all the leading spirits in the working-class movement, both Marx and Engels then believed that the immediate introduction of socialism was at hand. All that was necessary was to bring about a political revolution and to seize the political power of the state, and socialism would then immediately pass from the realm of thought to the realm of flesh and blood.

Subsequently, as you are aware, Marx and Engels undertook a thoroughgoing revision of this outlook. In the joint preface to the reissue of the *Communist Manifesto* in the year 1872, we find the following passage: "No special stress is laid on the revolutionary measures proposed at the end of section two. That passage would, in many respects, be differently worded today. In view of the gigantic strides of modern industry during the last twenty-five years and of the accompanying improved and extended organization of the working class, in view of the practical experience gained, first in the February Revolution and then, still more, in the Paris Commune where the proletariat for the first time held political power for two whole months, this program has in some details become antiquated. One thing especially was proved by the Commune, viz., that the 'working class cannot simply lay hold of the ready-made state machinery and wield it for its own purposes.'"

What is the actual wording of the passage thus declared to be out of date? It runs as follows:

The proletariat will use its political supremacy: to wrest by degrees all capital from the bourgeoisie; to centralize all instruments of production in the hands of the state, i.e., of the proletariat organized as the ruling class; and to increase the total of productive forces as rapidly as possible.

Of course, in the beginning, this cannot be effected except by means of despotic inroads on the rights of property, and on the conditions of bourgeois production; by measures therefore which appear economically insufficient and untenable, but which, in the course of the movement, outstrip themselves, necessitate further inroads upon the old social order, and are unavoidable as a means of entirely revolutionizing the mode of production.

The measures will, of course, be different in different countries.

Nevertheless, in the most advanced countries, the following will be pretty generally applicable:

1. Abolition of property in land and application of all land rents to public purposes.
2. A heavy progressive or graduated income tax.
3. Abolition of the right of inheritance.
4. Confiscation of the property of all emigrants and rebels.
5. Centralization of credit in the hands of the state by means of a national bank with state capital and an exclusive monopoly.
6. Centralization of the means of communication and transport in the hands of the state.
7. Extension of factories and instruments of production owned by the state: the bringing of wastelands into cultivation and the improvement of the soil generally in accordance with a concerted plan.

8. Equal obligation upon all to labor. Establishment of industrial armies, especially for agriculture.
9. Coordination of agriculture with manufacturing industries: gradual abolition of the distinction between town and country by a more equal distribution of the population throughout the rural areas.
10. Free education for all children in public schools. Abolition of children's factory labor in its present form. Combination of education with industrial production, etc., etc.

With a few trifling variations, these, as you know, are the tasks that confront us today. It is by such measures that we shall have to realize socialism. Between the day when the above program was formulated and the present hour, seventy years of capitalist development have intervened, and the historical evolutionary process has brought us back to the standpoint which Marx and Engels had abandoned in 1872 as erroneous. [. . .] It has become our urgent duty today to replace our program upon the foundations laid by Marx and Engels in 1848. In view of the changes effected since then by the historical process of development, it is incumbent upon us to undertake a deliberate revision of the views that guided the German social democracy down to the collapse of August 4. Upon such a revision we are officially engaged today.

How did Engels envisage the question in that celebrated preface to the *Class Struggles in France,* composed in 1895, twelve years after the death of Marx? First of all, looking back upon the year 1848, he showed the belief in the imminence of the socialist revolution to be obsolete.

Engels appends a detailed criticism of the illusion that, under modern capitalist conditions, the proletariat can possibly expect to effect anything for the revolution by street fighting. It seems to me, however, seeing that today we are in the midst of a revolution, a revolution characterized by street fighting and all that this entails, that it is time to shake ourselves free of the views that have guided the official policy of the German social democracy down to our own day, of the views that share responsibility for what happened on August 4, 1914. (Hear! Hear!)

I do not mean to imply that on account of these utterances Engels must share personal responsibility for the whole course of socialist evolution in Germany. I merely draw your attention to one of the classical pieces of evidence of the opinions prevailing in the German social democracy—opinions that proved fatal to the movement. In this preface Engels, as an expert in military science, demonstrated that it was a pure illusion to believe that the workers could, in the existing state of military technique and of industry, and in view of the characteristics of the great towns of today, successfully bring about a revolution by street fighting. Two important conclusions were drawn from this reasoning. In the first place, the parliamentary struggle was counterposed to direct revolutionary action by the proletariat, and the former was indicated as the only practical way of carrying on the class struggle. Parliamentarism, and nothing but parliamentarism, was the logical outcome of this criticism.

In the second, the whole military machine, the most powerful organization in the class state, the entire body of proletarians in military uniform, was declared on a priori grounds to be absolutely inaccessible to socialist influences. [. . .]

I must remind you of the well-known fact that the preface in question was written by Engels under strong pressure on the part of the parliamentary group. At that time in Germany, during the early 1890s after the antisocialist law had been annulled, there was a strong movement towards the left, the movement of those who wished to save the party from becoming completely absorbed in the parliamentary struggle. [August] Bebel and his associates wished for convincing arguments, backed up by Engels's great authority; they wished for an utterance which would help them to keep a tight rein upon the revolutionary elements.

It was characteristic of party conditions at the time that the socialist parliamentarians should have the decisive word in theory and in practice alike. They assured Engels, who lived abroad and naturally accepted the assurance at face value, that it was absolutely essential to safeguard the German labor movement from a lapse into anarchism, and in this way they constrained him to write in the tone they wished. From then on the tactics expounded by Engels in 1895 guided the German social democrats in everything they did and in everything they left undone, down to the appropriate finish of August 4, 1914. The preface was the formal proclamation of the nothing-but-parliamentarism tactic.

The fourth of August did not come like thunder out of a clear sky; what happened on the fourth of August was not a chance turn of affairs, but was the logical outcome of all that the German socialists had been doing day after day for many years. (Hear! hear!) Engels and Marx, had it been possible for them to live on into our own time, would, I am convinced, have protested with the utmost energy and would have used all the forces at their disposal to keep the party from hurling itself into the abyss. But after Engels's death in 1895, in the theoretical field the leadership of the party passed into the hands of Karl Kautsky. The upshot of this change was that at every annual congress the energetic protests of the left wing against a purely parliamentarist policy, its urgent warnings against the sterility and the danger of such a policy, were stigmatized as anarchism, anarchizing socialism, or at least anti-Marxism. What passed officially for Marxism became a cloak for all possible kinds of opportunism, for persistent shirking of the revolutionary class struggle, for every conceivable half measure. Thus the German social democracy, the labor movement, and the trade-union movement as well were condemned to pine away within the framework of capitalist society. No longer did German socialists and trade unionists make any serious attempt to overthrow capitalist institutions or to put the capitalist machine out of gear.

But we have now reached the point, comrades, where we are able to say that we have rejoined Marx, that we are once more advancing under his flag. If today we declare that the immediate task of the proletariat is to make socialism a living reality and to destroy capitalism root and branch, in saying this we take our stand upon the ground occupied by Marx and Engels in 1848; we adopt a position from which in principle they never moved. [. . .]

A study of the existing situation enables us to predict with certainty that in whatever country, after Germany, the proletarian revolution may next break out, the first step will be the formation of workers' and soldiers' councils. (Murmurs of assent.)

Herein is to be found the tie that unites our movement internationally. This is the motto that distinguishes our revolution utterly from all earlier revolutions, bourgeois revolutions. On November 9, the first cry of the revolution, as instinctive as the cry of a newborn child, was for workers' and soldiers' councils. This was our common rallying cry, and it is through the councils alone that we can hope to realize socialism. But it is characteristic of the contradictory aspects of our revolution, characteristic of the contradictions which attend every revolution, that at the very time when this great, stirring, and instinctive cry was being uttered, the revolution was so inadequate, so feeble, so devoid of initiative, so lacking in clearness as to its own aims, that on November 10 our revolutionists allowed nearly half the instruments of power they had seized on November 9 to slip from their grasp. We learn from this, on the one hand, that our revolution is subject to the prepotent law of historical determinism, a law which guarantees that, despite all difficulties and complications and notwithstanding all our own errors, we shall nevertheless advance step by step towards our goal. On the other hand, we have to recognize, comparing this splendid battle cry with the paucity of the results practically achieved, we have to recognize that these were no more than the first childish and faltering footsteps of the revolution, which has many arduous tasks to perform and a long road to travel before the promise of the first watchwords can be fully realized.

The weeks that have elapsed between November 9 and the present day have been weeks filled with multiform illusions. The primary illusion of the workers and soldiers who made the revolution was their belief in the possibility of unity under the banner of what passes by the name of socialism. What could be more characteristic of the internal weakness of the revolution of November 9 than the fact that at the very outset the leadership passed in no small part into the hands of persons who, a few hours before the revolution broke out, had regarded it as their chief duty to issue warnings against revolution—(hear! hear!)—to attempt to make revolution impossible—into the hands of such as Ebert, Scheidemann, and [Hugo] Haase. One of the leading ideas of the revolution of November 9 was that of uniting the various socialist trends. The union was to be effected by acclamation. This was an illusion that had to be bloodily avenged, and the events of the last few days have brought a bitter awakening from our dreams; but the self-deception was universal, affecting the Ebert and Scheidemann groups and affecting the bourgeoisie no less than ourselves.

Another illusion was that affecting the bourgeoisie during this opening act of the revolution. They believed that by means of the Ebert–Haase combination, by means of the so-called socialist government, they would really be able to bridle the proletarian masses and to strangle the socialist revolution. Yet another illusion was that from which the members of the Ebert–Scheidemann government suffered when they believed that with the aid of the soldiers returned from the front they would be able to hold down the workers and curb all manifestations of the socialist class struggle. Such were the multifarious illusions that explain recent occurrences. One and all, they have now been dissipated. It has been proven plainly that the union between Haase and Ebert–Scheidemann under the banner of socialism serves merely as a fig leaf for the decent veiling of a counterrevolutionary policy. We ourselves, as always happens in revolutions, have been cured of our self-deceptions.

There is a definite revolutionary procedure whereby the popular mind can be freed from illusion, but unfortunately the cure requires that the people must be bled. In revolutionary Germany events have followed the course characteristic of all revolutions. The bloodshed in Chaussee Street on December 6 and the massacre of December 24 brought the truth home to the broad masses of the people. Through these occurrences they came to realize that what passes by the name of a socialist government is a government representing the counterrevolution. They came to realize that anyone who continues to tolerate such a state of affairs is working against the proletariat and against socialism. (Applause.)

Vanished likewise is the illusion cherished by Messrs. Ebert, Scheidemann & Co., that with the aid of soldiers from the front they will be able to keep the workers in subjection forever. What has been the effect of the experiences of December 6 and 24? Of late, a profound disillusionment among the soldiers has been obvious.

The workers have completely lost the illusion that had led them to believe that a union between Haase and Ebert–Scheidemann would amount to a socialist government. Ebert and Scheidemann have lost the illusion that had led them to imagine that, with the aid of proletarians in military uniform, they could permanently keep down proletarians in civilian dress. The members of the middle class have lost the illusion that, through the instrumentality of Ebert, Scheidemann and Haase, they can humbug the entire socialist revolution of Germany as to the ends it desires. [. . .]

It was typical of the first period of the revolution down to December 24 that the revolution remained exclusively political. Hence the infantile character, the inadequacy, the halfheartedness, and the aimlessness of this revolution. Such was the first stage of a revolutionary transformation whose main objective lies in the economic field, whose main purpose it is to secure a fundamental change in economic conditions. Its steps were as uncertain as those of a child groping its way without knowing where it is going; for at this stage, I repeat, the revolution had a purely political stamp. But within the last two or three weeks a number of strikes have broken out quite spontaneously. Now, I regard it as the very essence of this revolution that strikes will become more and more extensive, until they at last become the focus of the revolution. (Applause.) Thus we shall have an economic revolution and therewith a socialist revolution. [. . .]

The inevitable consequence of this will be that the struggle in the economic field will be enormously intensified. The revolution will therewith assume aspects that will be no joke to the bourgeoisie. The members of the capitalist class are quite agreeable to mystifications in the political domain where masquerades are still possible, where such creatures as Ebert and Scheidemann can pose as socialists; but they are horror-struck as soon as profits are touched.

To the Ebert–Scheidemann government, therefore, the capitalists will present these alternatives. Either, they will say, you must put an end to the strikes, you must stop this strike movement that threatens to destroy us, or else we have no more use for you. Indeed I believe that the government has already damned itself pretty thoroughly by its political measures. Ebert and Scheidemann are distressed to find that the bourgeoisie no longer possesses confidence in them. The capitalists will think twice before they decide to cloak in ermine the rough upstart, Ebert. If matters go so far that a monarch is needed, they will say: "It does not suffice a king to have blood upon his hand; he must also have blue blood in his veins." [. . .]

It is far from easy to say what will happen to the National Assembly during the second act of the revolution. Perhaps, should the assembly come into existence, it may prove a new school of education for the working class. But it seems just as likely that the National Assembly will never come into existence. [. . .]

We refuse to stake everything upon the belief that the National Assembly will never come into existence. We wish to be prepared for all possibilities, including the possibility of utilizing the National Assembly for revolutionary purposes should the assembly ever come into being. Whether it comes into being or not is a matter of indifference, for whatever happens, the success of the revolution is assured. [. . .]

What general tactical considerations must we deduce from this? How can we best deal with the situation with which we are likely to be confronted in the immediate future? Your first conclusion will doubtless be a hope that the fall of the Ebert–Scheidemann government is at hand, and that in its place a socialist, proletarian, revolutionary government will be declared. For my part, I would ask you to direct your attention, not to the apex but to the base. We must not fall again into the illusion of the first phase of the revolution, that of November 9; we must not think that in our wish to bring about a socialist revolution it will suffice to overthrow the capitalist government and to set up another in its place. There is only one way of achieving the victory of the proletarian revolution.

We must begin by undermining the Ebert–Scheidemann government by destroying its foundations through a revolutionary mass struggle on the part of the proletariat. [. . .]

First and foremost, we must extend the system of workers' councils in all directions. What we have taken over from November 9 are mere weak beginnings, and we have not wholly taken over even these. During the first phase of the revolution we actually lost extensive forces that were acquired at the very outset. You are aware that the counter-revolution has been engaged in the systematic destruction of the system of workers' and soldiers' councils. In Hesse, these councils have been definitely abolished by the counterrevolutionary government; elsewhere power has been wrenched from their hands. Not merely then must we develop the system of workers' and soldiers' councils, but we must induce the agricultural laborers and the poorer peasants to adopt this system. [. . .]

We must make the masses realize that the workers' and soldiers' council has to be the central feature of the machinery of state, that it must concentrate all power within itself, and that it must utilize all powers for the one great purpose of bringing about the socialist revolution. Those workers who are already organized to form workers' and soldiers' councils are still very far from having adopted such an outlook, and only isolated proletarian minorities are as yet clear as to the tasks that devolve upon them. But there is no reason to complain of this, for it is a normal state of affairs. The masses must learn how to use power—by using power. There is no other way. We have, happily, advanced since the days when it was proposed to "educate" the proletariat socialistically. Marxists of Kautsky's school are, it would seem, still living in those vanished days. To educate the proletarian masses socialistically meant to deliver lectures to them and to circulate leaflets and pamphlets among them. But it is not by such means that the proletarians will be schooled. Today the workers will learn in the school of action.

16

The Constitution of the German Republic

Published in *Die Verfassung des Deutschen Reiches vom 11. August 1919*, 7th ed. (Leipzig, 1930).

Preamble

The German people, united in all their racial elements and inspired by the will to renew and strengthen their Reich in liberty and justice, to preserve peace at home and abroad, and to foster social progress, have established the following constitution:

CHAPTER I: STRUCTURE AND FUNCTIONS OF THE REICH

Section 1. Reich and States

Article 1. The German Reich is a republic. Political authority emanates from the people.

Article 2. The territory of the Reich consists of the territories of the German member states. [. . .]

Article 3. The Reich colors are black, red, and gold. The merchant flag is black, white, and red, with the Reich colors in the upper inside corner.

Article 4. The generally accepted rules of international law are to be considered as binding integral parts of the German Reich.

Article 5. Political authority is exercised in national affairs by the national government in accordance with the constitution of the Reich, and in state affairs by the state governments in accordance with state constitutions. [. . .]

Article 12. Insofar as the Reich does not exercise its jurisdiction, such jurisdiction remains with the states [. . .] with the exception of cases in which the Reich possesses exclusive jurisdiction. [. . .]

Article 17. Every state must have a republican constitution. The representatives of the people must be elected by universal, equal, direct, and secret suffrage of all German citizens, both men and women, in accordance with the principles of proportional representation.

Section 2. The *Reichstag*

Article 20. The Reichstag is composed of the delegates of the German people.

Article 21. The delegates are representatives of the whole people. They are subject only to their own conscience and are not bound by any instructions.

Article 22. The delegates are elected by universal, equal, direct, and secret suffrage by men and women over twenty years of age, according to the principle of proportional representation. Election day must be a Sunday or a public holiday.

Article 23. The Reichstag is elected for four years. New elections must take place at the latest on the sixtieth day after this term has run its course. [. . .]

Article 32. For decisions of the Reichstag a simple majority vote is necessary, unless the constitution prescribes another proportion of votes. [. . .]

Article 33. The Reichstag and its committees may require the presence of the Reich chancellor and every Reich minister. [. . .]

Section 3: The Reich President and the Reich Cabinet

Article 41. The Reich president is elected by the whole German people. Every German who has completed his thirty-fifth year is eligible for election. [. . .]

Article 42. On assuming office, the Reich president shall take the following oath before the Reichstag:

> I swear to devote my energies to the well-being of the German people, to further their interests, to guard them from injury, to maintain the constitution and the laws of the Reich, to fulfill my duties conscientiously, and to administer justice for all.

It is permissible to add a religious affirmation.

Article 43. The term of office of the Reich president is seven years. Re-election is permissible.

Before the expiration of his term, the Reich president, upon motion of the Reichstag, may be recalled by a popular vote. The decision of the Reichstag shall be by a two-thirds majority. Through such decision the Reich president is denied any further exercise of his office. The rejection of the recall motion by the popular referendum counts as a new election and results in the dissolution of the Reichstag. [. . .]

Article 48. If any state does not fulfill the duties imposed upon it by the constitution or the laws of the Reich, the Reich president may enforce such duties with the aid of the armed forces.

In the event that the public order and security are seriously disturbed or endangered, the Reich president may take the measures necessary for their restoration, intervening, if necessary, with the aid of the armed forces. For this purpose he may temporarily abrogate, wholly or in part, the fundamental principles laid down in Articles 114, 115, 117, 118, 123, 124, and 153.

The Reich president must without delay inform the Reichstag of all measures taken under Paragraph 1 or Paragraph 2 of this article. These measures may be rescinded on demand of the Reichstag. [. . .]

Article 50. All orders and decrees of the Reich president, including those relating to the armed forces, must, in order to be valid, be countersigned by the Reich chancellor or by the appropriate Reich minister. Responsibility is assumed through the countersignature. [. . .]

Article 52. The Reich cabinet consists of the Reich chancellor and the Reich ministers.

Article 53. The Reich chancellor and, on his recommendation, the Reich ministers, are appointed and dismissed by the Reich president.

Article 54. The Reich chancellor and the Reich ministers require for the exercise of their office the confidence of the Reichstag. Any one of them must resign if the Reichstag by formal resolution withdraws its confidence.

Article 55. The Reich chancellor presides over the government of the Reich and conducts its affairs according to the rules of procedure laid down by the government of the Reich and approved by the Reich president.

Article 56. The Reich chancellor determines the political program of the Reich and assumes responsibility to the Reichstag. Within this general policy each Reich minister conducts independently the office entrusted to him and is held individually responsible to the Reichstag. [. . .]

Section 4: The *Reichsrat*

Article 60. A Reichsrat is formed to give the German states representation in the lawmaking and administration of the Reich.

Article 61. Each state has at least one vote in the Reichsrat. In the case of the larger states one vote shall be assigned for every million inhabitants.[1] [. . .] No single state shall have more than two fifths of the total number of votes. [. . .]

---

1. Amended by law of March 24, 1921, to "every 700,000 inhabitants."

Article 63. The states shall be represented in the Reichsrat by members of their governments. [. . .]

Section 5: Reich Legislation

Article 68. Bills are introduced by the Reich cabinet, with the concurrence of the Reichsrat, or by members of the Reichstag. Reich laws shall be enacted by the Reichstag. [. . .]

Article 73. A law of the Reichstag must be submitted to popular referendum before its proclamation, if the Reich president, within one month of its passage, so decides. [. . .]

Article 74. The Reichsrat may protest against laws passed by the Reichstag. In case of such protest, the law is returned to the Reichstag, which may override the objection by a two-thirds majority. The Reich president must either promulgate the law within three months or call for a referendum. [. . .]

Article 76. The constitution may be amended by law, but acts . . . amending the constitution can only take effect if two thirds of the legal number of members are present and at least two thirds of those present consent. [. . .]

Section 6: The Reich Administration

[Articles 78–101 cover the jurisdiction of the Reich administration in such matters as foreign affairs, national defense, colonial policies, customs, national budgets, postal and telegraph services, railroads, and waterways.]

Section 7: Administration of Justice

[Articles 102–108 provide for a hierarchy of Reich and state courts, with judges appointed by the Reich president for life.]

CHAPTER II: FUNDAMENTAL RIGHTS AND DUTIES OF THE GERMANS

Section 1: The Individual

Article 109. All Germans are equal before the law. Men and women have the same fundamental civil rights and duties. Public legal privileges or disadvantages of birth or of rank are abolished. Titles of nobility [. . .] may be bestowed no longer. [. . .] Orders and decorations shall not be conferred by the state. No German shall accept titles or orders from a foreign government.

Article 110. Citizenship of the Reich and the states is acquired in accordance with the provisions of a Reich law. [. . .]

Article 111. All Germans shall enjoy liberty of travel and residence throughout the whole Reich. [. . .]

Article 112. Every German is permitted to emigrate to a foreign country. [. . .]

Article 114. Personal liberty is inviolable. Curtailment or deprivation of personal liberty by a public authority is permissible only by authority of law.

Persons who have been deprived of their liberty must be informed at the latest on the following day by whose authority and for what reasons they have been held. They shall receive the opportunity without delay of submitting objections to their deprivation of liberty.

Article 115. The house of every German is his sanctuary and is inviolable. Exceptions are permitted only by authority of law. [. . .]

Article 117. The secrecy of letters and all postal, telegraph, and telephone communications is inviolable. Exceptions are inadmissible except by national law.

Article 118. Every German has the right, within the limits of the general laws, to express his opinion freely by word, in writing, in print, in picture form, or in any other way. [. . .] Censorship is forbidden. [. . .]

Section 2. The General Welfare

Article 123. All Germans have the right to assembly peacefully and unarmed without giving notice and without special permission. [. . .]

Article 124. All Germans have the right to form associations and societies for purposes not contrary to the criminal law. [. . .]

Article 126. Every German has the right to petition. [. . .]

Section 3: Religion and Religious Societies

Article 135. All inhabitants of the Reich enjoy full religious freedom and freedom of conscience. The free exercise of religion is guaranteed by the Constitution and is under public protection. [. . .]

Article 137. There is no state church. [. . .]

Section 4: Education and the Schools

Article 142. Art, science, and the teaching thereof are free. [. . .]

Article 143. The education of the young is to be provided for by means of public institutions. [. . .]

Article 144. The entire school system is under the supervision of the state. [. . .]

Article 145. Attendance at school is compulsory. [. . .]

Section 5: Economic Life

Article 151. The regulation of economic life must be compatible with the principles of justice, with the aim of attaining humane conditions of existence for all. Within these limits the economic liberty of the individual is assured. [. . .]

Article 152. Freedom of contract prevails. [. . .] in accordance with the laws. [. . .]

Article 153. The right of private property is guaranteed by the Constitution. [. . .] Expropriation of property may take place [. . .] by due process of law. [. . .]

Article 159. Freedom of association for the preservation and promotion of labor and economic conditions is guaranteed to everyone and to all vocations. All agreements and measures attempting to restrict or restrain this freedom is unlawful. [. . .]

Article 161. The Reich shall organize a comprehensive system of [social] insurance. [. . .]

Article 165. Workers and employees are called upon to cooperate, on an equal footing, with employers in the regulation of wages and of the conditions of labor, as well as in the general development of the productive forces. [. . .]

Concluding Provisions

Article 181. [. . .] The German people have passed and adopted this constitution through their National Assembly. It comes into force with the date of its proclamation.

Schwarzburg, August 11, 1919.

The Reich president
EBERT
The Reich cabinet
BAUER
ERZBERGER   HERMANN MÜLLER   DR. DAVID
NOSKE   SCHMIDT
SCHLICKE   GIESBERTS   DR. BAYER
DR. BELL

17

COUNT HARRY KESSLER
[On Ebert and the Revolution]

Diary entry, August 21, 1919.

Thursday, 21 August 1919
Weimar

At five o'clock this afternoon Ebert's swearing-in at the National Assembly. The stage was festively decorated with the new German colors and plants, gladioli and chrysanthemums placed on a floor covering which in its day has obviously been the mossy turf of *A Midsummer Night's Dream.* The organ played and everyone in their black jackets crowded between the plants like guests at a better-class wedding. The house was crowded except for the seats belonging to the Nationalists and Independents, which remained ostentatiously empty. A number of secretaries and shorthand-writers spread across the Nationalists' seats.

After an organ prelude, Ebert appeared on the stage in a frock-coat, small, broad-shouldered, with gold-rimmed spectacles. He was followed by Bauer, the hobbling Chancellor, and the whole government, all of them in solemn black too. Ullstein's *Berliner Illustrierte* saw fit to publish today a photograph of Ebert and Noske in bathing trunks. The memory of the picture haunted the ceremony.

When Ebert was supposed to take the oath, the text was found to be missing. A search was instituted and, the organ having stopped playing, a fidgety interval ensued. Finally someone pushed their way through the frock-coats to the front with the piece of paper.

Ebert spoke the words of the oath in quite a pleasing, clear voice. Fehrenbach pronounced the official welcome. Ebert made a speech. All very decorous but lacking go, like a confirmation in a decent middle-class home. The republic should avoid ceremonies; they are not suited to this type of government. It is like a governess dancing a ballet. All the same, the whole occasion had something touching and, above all, tragic about it. This petty drama as conclusion to the tremendous events of the war and the revolution! Pondering the deeper significance of it can bring tears very close.

18

WILHELM HAUSENSTEIN

Remembering Eisner

First published as "Erinnerungen an Eisner," *Der neue Merkur* 3 (1919–1920), 56–57.

[Kurt Eisner's] life was guided by this problem: to find a transition from the Prussian north to the German south.

He was born between the wars of 1866 and 1870 in Berlin. Into the first decade of the new century he was surrounded by the black and white of the twice-victorious Prussians. Prussian hubris was a magnet for his hate. Like [Franz] Mehring, Eisner found his way from bourgeois to socialist journalism, to fight them—the Hohenzollern, feudal, militarist Prussians. His instrument was the newspaper *Vorwärts*. Eisner's time was the classical period of *Vorwärts*. A trial for insulting the monarch—which heralded the era of the Socialist Laws and proved Plötzensee [a prison near Berlin] once again to be a foreign branch of the Peter-Paul Fortress [a prison in St. Petersburg]—landed the good gladiator in prison. This was where Eisner first began to learn that between the candid word, particularly the refined word, and solid majorities there was no connection. Conscience makes a statement, and prison is the response. This profound discrepancy between thought and effect became the tragic leitmotif of his life. The one side offended the Prussian prosecutor; the other side offended conventional radicalism. In these vexatious conditions Eisner was relieved of his editorship by party comrades who suspected him of insufficient intransigence. Eisner experienced this event as another bit of Prussian history. It was the essence of resistance to differentiation, to standards, to the humane. It was to him the paradigm of a political biology incapable of combining emphasis and subtlety, which thinks instead that only the crude gesture can vouchsafe reliability.

Assailed from the right and the left, Eisner turned south. He took his leave of Prussia with a work that was to become a formidable pamphlet, the most formidable text ever written against Prussia. It bore the sensational title—for Eisner always remained enough of a journalist not to slight the sensational where it coincided with irony and deeper meaning—*The End of the Reich*. It dealt with the collapse of post-Frederician Prussia in the year 1806 and was full of suggestive remarks on the eternally Prussian as well as on the misfortune of German history. [. . .]

Eisner's point of departure was the system of workers' councils. He considered it the core of the revolution. But it corresponded to his all-around and plainly humanitarian, indeed poetic, concept of society that he attempted to build a state directly onto the revolutionary people. As this became impossible, the revolution's prospects lay increasingly in the permanence of the councils. Now the task became clear: to find the only decisive way out of the contract between the councils and parliamentarism in the intensity of revolution. The task was doubly difficult because Eisner's politics were completely directed toward the ideal of the bloodless revolution. It remained this man's greatest happiness to have been able to forge the first decision of the night of November 7 without the spilling of blood. It remained his greatest sorrow that, in the course of his term as prime minister, citizen stood armed against citizen and one caused the other's blood to flow. It was not that he had over-sensitive nerves that could not endure the blood. No one has the right to reproach this man, who proved the depth of his personal courage, with some sort of weakness. More important were his concepts of revolution and of the political as such, his belief that only weapon in the civic struggle was the energetic spirit that enjoys the good fortune of being able to ascend to its sources: to the poets of Weimar, to Kantian and Fichtean philosophy, to [Ferdinand] Lassalle and [Karl] Marx. It appears that Eisner, just before the feudal–clerical thug fired the shot that cut him down, had decided to abandon the dissolution of the contract between the councils and parliamentarism, in favor of the latter. But this is not the only meaning of the declaration by which he wished to put his presidency back into the hands of the parliament. It would be wrong to believe that this action would have meant a capitulation to parliamentarism. On the contrary. Rather it would have spelt opposition to parliamentarism and to those who could conceive of civic life only according to the divisive mechanics of parliamentarism. No. There can scarcely be any doubt that Eisner saw in the councils, which were born of the productive anarchy of the revolutionary moment, the creation of revolutionary spontaneity, the living tools, the true vessels of the new epoch. It was his plan to use the councils to revitalize socialism as a whole, to take up the feud against the parliamentary system—which he recognized as the historical ideal of the state in the bourgeois epoch—resolutely from atop the councils, and along this path to prepare the entire community of socialists for a new, more fundamental, and decisive revolution. Not only the socialists but all those whose political visions were stirred by the seventh of November. The peasants, whom he recognized as the actual substance of the Bavarian people, were not the least in his thoughts.

19

THEODOR HEUSS

Democracy and Parliamentarism: Their History, Their Enemies, and Their Future

First published as "Demokratie und Parlamentarismus: ihre Geschichte, ihre Gegner, und ihre Zukunft," in *Zehn Jahre deutsche Republik. Ein Handbuch für republikanische Politik,* ed. Anton Erklenz (Berlin: Sieben-Stäbe Verlag, 1928), 98–117.

Democracy and parliamentarism do not represent prophecies of salvation, nor do they provide an absolute prescription against the ailments of this world. They are historical forms of state deliberation, conditioned historically essentially through the pedagogical force of the self-imposed responsibility that is specific to them. They have had to accept attacks on their theoretical and historical position. The standpoint of the attack varies. Peculiar to most fundamental discussions is that they determine democracy to be a child of "Western rationalism" whose time is past. They confront it, a time-bound intellectual form, with the claims of an absolute valuation, in the process overlooking the circumstance that every extension of their theoretical antitheses into concrete demands brings them into the realm of corporate ideologies of fascist or some other salvational form, which, in turn, leads into a labyrinth of a typically irrationalist stamp.

In this connection, Germany has become infatuated with a couple of catchwords. Democracy "atomizes" the people by turning the individual, as a fundamental elector cut off from any social estate and heritage, into a political factor. This *homo politicus,* pronounced sovereign on voting days, is regarded as a fiction; a person is not a citizen *per se,* but a member of a society of manifold stratifications, which is now being leveled by force of doctrine. And so on. Weimar, so goes the claim, merely copied foreign models; the fragmentation of the German spirit was already so severe that no reference was made to the basic constituents of corporate estates and legal forms as they existed in German history. For a time much mischief was made with this incantation of the particular character of the German state. Estate stratification–it is necessary here to repeat a frequently rehearsed chain of thought–was never, as romantic legend would have it, specific to the German essence, but was rather an aspect of an historical epoch; it was not "leveled" by the rationalism of the democratic idea, but broken down by the absolutist territorial state equipped with a bureaucracy. Nor does the attempt to revitalize it theoretically and transpose it into the essence of a new "corporate estate system" derive from the labor of a specifically German spirit—its first classical representative was the Genevan [Jean Charles] Sismondi, who is considered part of the French world. One will recall that this idea acquired political significance when, in a strange to and fro of motives, it served to strip the council idea of political offshoots: at the time a corporatist ideology had been grafted onto it in political economic form. The gardeners and botanists are still not entirely sure whether the tree will bear nourishing fruit in the hothouse of the national economic council. But here we may let it rest at that.

The emphasis remains as always on the side of political ideas. The parties are social organs of struggle based on persuasion and publicity, with fluid boundaries, whose power is subject to changing conditions, often determined by purely tactical tendencies that do not derive from the matter at hand. Would legislation and the allocation of powers not be more stable if public affairs were based on integrated corporate groupings? Then there would be no more demagogy freed from the obligations of expert knowledge, then the professional politicians would no longer make decisions that affect them very little but to which the economy reacts very sensitively; instead of the negative votes of power politics or the search for compromise, a synthesis of objective consensus would result. And in such a political order, since all are equal in their properly designated circles true democracy would come into being. The representation of the hierarchical corporate state belongs among the stirring simplifications of speculative thinking—but is it not a misjudgment? Is there a very realistic set of economic organizations, associations, leagues, and unions not behind this idea? Is it not a simple matter of legitimizing a given situation of power and interests, that it might become the structure of the state?

Certainly the facts of power are at hand; but just because it revolves around power, the picture in which the order and the procedures are so finely drawn falls apart. There simply is no formula by which the proper ratios among economic groupings can be expressed. And today nearly everyone agrees that *expert* is in most cases merely a charming substitute for *vested interest*—by which nothing is said against the latter's rights, but only against a misconstrual of the state that declares itself a battlefield of vested interests. One need imagine only for a moment a foreign and cultural policy meant to operate on such a basis—it would necessarily succumb to the friction. We will not even mention the complex structure of present-day society, the inescapable fact that such a system would have to produce a new, completely independent type of professional politician. The construction overlooks the circumstance that political life does not rest on a static integration of corporate identities but oscillates within the dynamic of a multiplicitous, colorful, changing, and even contradictory, set of political wills.

From a different corner came and comes the purely politically formed resistance against the world of ideas and realities contained in democracy. It objects to the "right" of the majority; historical decisions have always been—this is the ideological point of departure— the work of minorities that knew what they wanted, that did not talk, persuade, negotiate, and vote, but did that what they held to be right and necessary. In this view, democracy and parliament are either sentimentalities or falsehoods, which must allow themselves to be pronounced wrong by virtue of the success of an alternative path. What, incidentally, is the meaning of "allowed"? Moral inquiry is perhaps the concern of political journalists, reasoning historians, but not that of political actors. Even if the latter take it as a technical exigency that they hoist the flags of moral objection!

One can find the embodiment of this way of thinking both in Russian bolshevism and Italian fascism. Reference has frequently been made to their intellectual historical context: they can be traced back to Marx's counterpart in the First International, Mikhail Bakunin, to the antiparliamentary mutation of French syndicalism, which had systematized the lessons of the *action directe*, the extraparliamentary methods of proletarian class struggle. The particular historical situation as well as the nature of those decisively involved made it possible for the inheritors to appear as exponents of opposed tendencies, one focusing on the state and the other on the economy. They did in fact become that to a certain extent, though in assessing their worth one must not neglect completely the common source of their fundamental view. Whether Lenin or Mussolini, the political accomplishment in its uniqueness is significant enough—but the theoretical music that accompanied it, which they composed themselves or had composed, is equally paltry. The Lenin legend, done up brilliantly in propagandistic terms, might do justice to the tactician, but his theoretical writings are more clever than profound. And Mussolini's pronouncement that he embodies a new concept of the state is simply a rhetorical lantern he flashes along his path, which, however, errs in the direction of the trivial wherever it does not apply strictly to the particular situation he has created in contemporary Italy.

The dictatorship of the proletariat remains, in intellectual terms, an artificial construction laid over the domination of a party machine in order to mask it; but the construction is too transparent and soon the question assumes its proper form: Who has the dictatorship over the proletariat? Then it is no longer a theoretical affair but a personal one: To what extent can intellect, will, the power of suggestion, and disposal over a military apparatus be regarded as a substitute for the legitimacy of dynastic absolutism? To try to make of Caesar and Napoleon a systematic method of state formation and political guidance represents a supreme misunderstanding of history and politics; the failed Napoleons lurking like apparitions and slowly gathering dust on the edges of the postrevolutionary years offer distressing documentation. The state must under no circumstances fail to appreciate what dangers can arise from the romanticism of illegitimacy—we have, after all, a few experiments behind us. Nor will it be overlooked how injurious the intellectual disavowal of the inner binding force of majority-based laws and ordinances is to the necessary growth of free and secure sentiment in the nation. That is the concern of politics and education. But in principle the antithesis to its democratic existence has worn thin; it has not succeeded in expounding a clear concept of a legitimate state. The mistakes and defects of difficult, unromantic, and unillusioned politics alone are insufficient to nurture it as a force of its own.

When democracy entered into the history of our epoch, it proclaimed, via the fiction of natural right, the right of the dominated to participate in the exercise of power and to possess it. The internal problematic of state formation seemed to be its essential focus. But the course of things soon enough shifted the emphasis. Now the securing of individual rights, which taken together would result in collective rights, no longer demanded an answer; rather, this collectivity presented itself as a greater and comprehensive individual right; in the struggles of democracy for political legitimacy the nation-state was born. It is absolutely inconceivable without democracy. There have always been peoples, but democracy opened their mouths so that they could find and form the essence of their political consciousness. The idea of the nation-state grew out of democracy—it was the great leitmotif of European history in the nineteenth century.

In recent years, the recognition of this connection has, if only hesitantly, also become established among those who reject democracy who want to represent the nation in a particularly emphatic sense. In their embarrassment they have found a way out: democracy might well conform to the closed regions of the European West, they claim, but not to the central and eastern areas. As if an intellectual idea and a moral claim, once they have taken root in the peoples, have to find out beforehand if the two conform to each other. The overthrow of the Hapsburg and Ottoman empires are the effects of this intellectual–political process. But the Paris peace accords of 1919, rather than providing a respite, have merely perpetuated the tensions by denying or destroying the preconditions of democracy, while they invoke democratic ideology propagandistically.

It is utterly trivial to dream of the Pan–European idea or to hold in reserve some other fashionable plan for the salvation of the world, through world parliaments and similar institutions, as long as this situation is overlooked. Democracy is neither pacifistic nor militaristic in its essence; it can be both, with its intellectual attitude determined by the degree of tension or consensus pertaining in popular life and state structure. Democracy has not resolved the problem of the coexistence of nations, nor rendered it harmless, nor resolved its hostility; democracy, rather, has awakened in it the evil spirit of self-assurance. That is precisely what makes politics so intricate, dangerous, and portentous on a densely populated continent marked by endless reciprocity. But this situation may only be mentioned; to pursue it further exceeds the scope of this work.

20

BERNHARD PRINCE VON BÜLOW

[Revolution in Berlin]

First published in Bernhard Fürst von Bülow, *Denkwürdigkeiten* (Berlin: Ullstein, 1931), 305–312.

In Berlin on November 9, I witnessed the beginnings of revolution. Alas, she did not come, as Ferdinand Lassalle had envisaged her in his moments of giddiest ambition, in the shape of a radiant goddess, her hair flowing in the wind, and shod with sandals of iron. She was like an old hag, toothless and bald, her great feet slipshod and down at the heel. The German revolution was drearily philistine, lacking in all fire or inspiration. It revealed no such figures as the Danton whose statue in bronze stands on the Paris boulevard: erect, with clenched fist, to the left of his plinth a *sans-culotte* with fixed bayonet, to his right a tambour, beating up the *levée en masse*. Our revolution brought us no Gambetta to proclaim war to the knife and prolong our resistance by five months, not even a Delescluse, to get himself killed at the barricades. I have never in my life seen anything more brutally vulgar than those straggling lines of tanks and lorries manned by drunken sailors and deserters from reserve formations which trailed through the Berlin streets on November 9. That afternoon, from the window of my suite at the Adlon, I had a view both of the Linden [street] and the Pariserplatz. I have seldom witnessed anything so nauseating, so maddeningly revolting and base, as the spectacle of half-grown louts, tricked out with the red armlets of social democracy, who, in bands of several at a time, came creeping up behind any officer wearing the Iron Cross or the order *Pour le mérite,* to pin down his elbows at his side and tear off his epaulettes.

When young Captain Bonaparte stood watching the attack on the Tuileries of August 10, 1792, the sight inspired his well-known exclamation: "*Avec un bataillon on balayerait toute cette canaille,*" and there can be no possible doubt that on November 9, 1918, the Berlin streets could easily have been cleared with a few battalions of storm troops. Such battalions would have been easy enough to form from the troops and officers of Berlin, who were positively itching for such an order. With a few machine guns set in position simultaneously at the Brandenburger Tor, in the Schlossplatz, and the Alexanderplatz; a few tanks, each with a crew of sharpshooters, sent through the streets of the town, the Berlin *canaille* would soon have scuttled back to their holes. But for this, not an authorization but the formal order to fire with ball ammunition would have been necessary. Prince Max had not the courage to give this order, especially since he feared it might disqualify him from succeeding to the Baden throne.

While the populace gained possession of Berlin's streets, endless telephone conversations were in progress between Berlin and Spa, Spa and Berlin. At the Berlin mouthpiece sat Privy Councillor Wahnschaffe, at Spa, von Grünau, the Councillor of Legation; Wahnschaffe, as a rule a sound official, had managed to lose his head completely under the enervating influence of Prince Max. As for Grünau, he had no head to lose. He was a young and very callow diplomat with neither knowledge nor practical experience, utterly ignorant of the questions of civil law to be decided. The fruit of a morganatic marriage between a Prince von Löwenstein and a governess, he was on fairly intimate terms with the Court at Karlsruhe, and therefore in the confidence of Prince Max, who had attached him to the emperor's person at Spa. In this hour of deadly peril to his dynasty, a tragic fate had given the King of Prussia, as his sole adviser, a young man, possibly endowed with every talent, but not, in any case as yet, a prudent and vigilant guardian of the glorious and menaced Prussian throne. The result of all this ringing of telephone bells was that Prince Max began to placard every kiosk and street corner in Berlin with the official announcement to Berliners that their emperor and king had abdicated. The truth, as it later was established, was that William II had only wished to divest himself of his imperial dignities, while at the same time remaining King of Prussia. The announcement was either hysterical or a blunder—but, in either case, entirely characteristic of this last chancellor whom the emperor had seen fit to appoint. Prince Max, without consulting any of his colleagues or those military chiefs who for the last twenty-four hours had been longing for their orders to intervene, wrote off to the Socialist leader, Fritz Ebert, into whose hands he gave the affairs of the empire, relinquishing to the Socialist party the business of forming another government.

Ebert assumed the title of People's Commissar, which he further bestowed on several of his revolutionary friends, the Socialist leaders of Berlin, and began to govern. The energy which they all, especially Gustav Noske, displayed in the next few days in keeping down the Spartacists, grown too insolent, might have served as an example to Prince Max. But, careless of what happened in Berlin, the prince was on his way to Baden, whose dynastic interests seemed to him far more important than all the destinies of the empire. Whomever Kaiser Wilhelm II had cared to select, in that fatal October 1918—general, diplomat, civil servant, or deputy—none could have served him worse at the critical moment than this neurasthenic prince whose egotism and family interests entirely outweighed his sense of duty. Prince Max, however, had miscalculated in supposing that he could save himself or his house. He lives today as a private citizen on Lake Constance.

But our new masters were equally unfit to govern. Most characteristic of their mentality was the speech from the Reichstag steps, delivered by Scheidemann, an ex-imperial state secretary, who, in proclaiming the Republic, began his oration with the following: "The German people have won all along the line." A stupid lie! And a very cruel piece of self-deception! No, alas, the German people had not "won"—it had been conquered, overpowered by a host of enemies, wretchedly misled politically, reduced by famine, and stabbed in the back!

To any unbiased spectator of these events, to whoever watched it all in the one hope that the German nation might not perish, these first days of our republic were days of the return to chaos. Children could scarcely have done worse. The new regime was so constituted that the Council of People's Commissaries (*Rat der Volksbeauftragten*) gave an equal number of seats to the Majority and Independent Socialists—the SPD and USPD. Two mandates, therefore two executives! Such a system had never been seen, since the two quæstors, two consuls, of ancient Rome, which certainly did not resemble modern Germany! And above the Council of People's Commissaries reigned the Executive Committee of Workers' and Soldiers' Councils, in whose hands lay the real power. In modern art, as it is called, there was for a time a certain vogue for dadaism, whose aim was a complete return to the lispings and gurglings of sucklings. The beginnings of the German Republic were a kind of political dadaism. Such phenomena as [Hermann] Müller made their appearance. Müller had been nicknamed "corpse-Müller" for declaring that there should be no more Reichstag elections, unless they were held over his dead body. Herr Müller is today in the best of health, yet since he spoke his memorable words there has been more than one election to the Reichstag.

The socialist left was all for suppressing the Reichstag out of hand and replacing it by workers' and soldiers' councils, though even this suggestion was not original but a miserable, servile copy of Bolshevik Russia. [Theobald von] Bethmann[-Holweg] from the very start had given an antitsarist turn to our war propaganda, and every fool had applauded him. Now our own people, like apes, could only try to imitate forms of government set up in Russia by the Bolsheviks, and unworkable even there on such a passive herd as the Russians.

In Prussia there were two ministers for each department: the one majority (SPD) and the other (USPD) Independent Socialist. Konrad Hänisch and Adolf Hoffman were the simultaneous ministers of education. The first had risen from the ranks by becoming *cavaliere servente* to Rosa Luxemburg, then he had sloughed off his communist skin and by degrees emerged a moderate socialist. He was moderate when I made his acquaintance.

He seemed not a bad sort of fellow, jovial and very good-natured, the usual dyed-in-the-wool Bohemian, certainly without wide and delicate culture, and still less with any profundity of thought—the ordinary half-educated mind. His political Siamese twin, the Berlin publican Adolf Hoffman, was at least what Countess Terzky in Schiller's *Wallenstein* desires her stepbrother to become, that is, a truly self-integrated personality, since he never cared to bother about such trifles as bad grammar in a Reichstag speech. On the premature termination of his ministerial activities, Hoffman became the spokesman of revolution on the Municipal Council of Berlin, and for years he set the tone of that assembly. The Berlin city leaders hurled invectives; at moments they even came to blows, while from every tribune there were catcalls, stink bombs, and similar intellectual weapons of the young republic. [. . .]

The republic that emerged from our revolution was, as I have said, flatly amenable. It was petit-bourgeois and philistine; its leaders the perfection of mediocrity. But at least there were no serious disorders. [. . .]

The elements which, in Berlin in these first months, gave revolution its own peculiar character, were mostly callow, half-grown youths. At that time we were still at the Hotel Adlon. A self-styled republican commissar forced his way into our suite. I had been asked to a bachelor dinner and was out. The 'commissar' enquired of my wife whether we had any officers in hiding. Had I brought my uniform to the Adlon? Did I keep a revolver about me? My wife insisted politely that she knew nothing at all of any such antirepublican plots and secret armings, and the embarrassed 'commissar' made his excuses and departed. Another day, as we walked down the long corridor, a youth of not more than seventeen emerged from the lift and pursued us, in either hand a revolver. My wife asked why he wanted to shoot us, and he answered in a piping treble: "You must excuse me, Madame, but we are all so terribly nervy and strung-up. We have the republic to defend and the least you can carry is a revolver. But we don't mean you any harm. If you like even come out with you for walks and we will protect you." With a smile of thanks I declined this republican guard of honor. [. . .]

It seemed likely that there would be fighting in the Pariserplatz and the proprietor of the Adlon asked me to vacate our suite. He feared for the precious glass of his windows and wanted to keep the shutters closed. I decided to change my hotel. [. . .]

A few days after our arrival there I noticed some uniforms in the corridor and learned that the general staff of the cavalry division of the guard had been transferred to our hotel. Next morning we were told that during the night Liebknecht and Rosa Luxemburg had been summoned before the court-martial of this division. Liebknecht had tried to escape into the Tiergarten on their way to the hotel, and had been shot. Rosa Luxemburg had begun to scream sedition at the top of her voice and a soldier had cracked her skull with a rifle butt. But we had noticed nothing of all this.

3
Economic Upheaval: Rationalization, Inflation, and Depression

THE GERMAN ECONOMY, the most powerful in Europe before the war, was severely damaged by defeat. The loss of important resources in Alsace and Lorraine, uncertainty about the effects of punitive reparations, and the after-effects of financing the war by loans rather than taxation created a crisis that manifested itself in several ways. One was the ruthless concentration of German industry, already begun before the war, in such vital sectors as iron manufacturing. Another was the rapid devaluation of the German currency which soon produced the most devastating inflation in history. The government fanned the flames by continuing to borrow and print money in order to wipe out its international debt. Claiming Germany was trying to default on its loans, the French government occupied the Ruhr in January 1923. The result was widespread nationalist indignation, even on the left. In November 1923, with the mark virtually worthless at 4,200,000,000 to the dollar (and the debt nearly "paid off"), the government acted to halt the inflation. Abandoning its passive resistance to the French occupation of the Ruhr and agreeing to a reparations settlement, it introduced a new currency, the so-called *Rentenmark,* which was nominally backed by all of Germany's land and real estate.

The human cost of the inflation was extraordinarily high. Observers like Friedrich Kroner detailed the psychological traumas while others like Hans Ostwald wrote of the pressure it put on ethical behavior. Although fortunes were made by unscrupulous businessmen like Hugo Stinnes, who bought up bankrupt firms for a fraction of their real worth, the majority of middle- and lower-class Germans suffered the total loss of their savings.

The six years from 1923 to 1929 were comparatively prosperous as foreign loans, primarily from the United States, offset the reparations payments that were leaving Germany according to the schedule set by the Dawes Plan in August 1924. During this period, industry continued its concentration into large-scale concerns, as the number of national and international cartels increased. Even the entertainment and publishing industries came under the control of giant concerns, such as that owned by the right-wing politician Alfred Hugenberg. At the same time, new techniques of scientific management, derived in part from the older European "science of work" and the newer American techniques of Taylorization (named after Frederick Winslow Taylor) helped to "rationalize" methods of production. The result was what the Social Democratic economist and finance minister (in 1923 and 1928–1929) Rudolf Hilferding called "organized capitalism."

The international capitalist system began, however, to dissolve rapidly after the collapse of the American stock market in October 1929. The withdrawal of credit had a ripple effect on the European banking system, which was graphically noted by the writer B. Traven. In 1932, Chancellor Franz von Papen reported to the Lausanne conference on the radical changes that ensued throughout the economy. The conference led to the suspension of Germany's remaining reparations payments, but by then the situation was desperate. As Heinrich Hauser observed, unemployment had reached catastrophic proportions, with over six million Germans out of work in 1932. The resulting desperation helps explain the appeal of National Socialism even among members of the working class.

21

DAS TAGEBUCH

[On the Occupation of the Ruhr]

First published as an editorial in *Das Tagebuch* 4 (January 27, 1923), 124–125.

The result of passive resistance in the Ruhr district will in any case be this: that the spirit of brutality and force—which rules the imperialistic military machine of France as much as any other, which was able for years to hide from the blinded eyes of the uninvolved world behind agreeably peaceful words and gestures—that this infamous spirit will be quickly and radically exposed for what it is. This success alone would merit extreme sacrifice; by itself it would suffice to justify Germany's position. Meanwhile whatever material solution will ultimately issue from moves and countermoves in an increasingly confusing situation is a question that no longer lies on the moral but on the economic plane, a question which, insofar as we are able to judge, will be determined by the following factors.

First, will the mechanism of occupation actually be capable of blocking the export of coal from the Ruhr district to unoccupied Germany? Until now there have been no serious attempts to block the land routes, though water transport has admittedly been almost completely stopped. This raises the question of whether customs border stations and the like can achieve the same success on land as has been achieved on water.

Second, if the coal blockade operates effectively and stored reserves are consumed in at most four weeks, will it be possible for Germany to supply its needs, roughly four million tons per month, from England, Czechoslovakia, and America? Expenditures here would run to approximately six million pounds (equivalent to approximately 600 billion paper marks). Such payments would only be possible, if at all, over a considerable period without causing great damage to the currency as long as relatively long-term foreign credits could be secured. It was said recently that Mr. Stinnes had been granted a coal credit of two million pounds, raising the question of whether the German government or prominent private persons have received substantially more generous assurances.

Third, if the coal supply from foreign sources succeeds but the resistance in the Ruhr district itself, after an intensification of French pressure, can be carried out only through comprehensive strikes, will it be possible to pay the workers' wages from Germany and thus save them from being compelled by hunger to give in? Strike funds are being gathered and the forty-five billion which is necessary for roughly 450,000 workers on a monthly basis (not counting white-collar workers) could ultimately (in the worst case) be delivered from the printing press. The question is whether the French can so tightly seal the occupied border with Germany that the transfer of money into the Ruhr district would become impossible, or whether the compulsory introduction of francs or a new Ruhr currency could create a situation that would make strike payments in marks illusory.

Fourth, if, over time, the needs of the strikers can be met by Germany just as successfully as Germany can be supplied by foreign sources, will France find the stoppage of production from the Ruhr so devastating to its own interests, will the maintenance of vitality in the Ruhr be so necessary in regard to France's own needs that it will resolve in the foreseeable future that it is better to go to Canossa and once again withdraw its troops than to continue to endure the loss of Ruhr products? France's need for coal is secured at present from domestic sources, with the reparation coal being sold primarily to foreign buyers anyway.

This raises the question of whether it can replace the coke it gets from the Ruhr, which it needs for smelting ore, with coke from somewhere else, and whether it is not necessary perhaps to shut down the Lothrigen foundries and see who can hold out longer.

Four sober, economic problems: the material shape they take will determine, given the present correlation of forces and without regard to moral consequences, the success of the passive resistance! Neither side has as yet implemented measures that could be regarded as decisive solutions to these four problems.

One thing, incidentally, should not be forgotten: that the entire resistance in the Ruhr would be impossible without the participation of the workers. The main goal of the occupation forces has always been to win the workers over to their side; all efforts of this sort so far have worked by appeal to ego. They could, however, be met with the answer that in Germany the social rights of the working population are much more extensive than in France, that in Germany the workers have an entirely different social status than over there. Suddenly, gentlemen, the modest policy of economic democracy, which until now has been so often and fiercely attacked as ruinous, is bearing fruit! Suddenly it appears fortunate that in the factory councils we possess organizational centers for the individual plant personnel. Had you succeeded, as many of you wanted, in taking from the workers their factory councils, their humane working hours, and the rest of their political influence, the outcome of the present situation would have been doubtful!

22

FRIEDRICH KRONER

Overwrought Nerves

First published as "Überreizte Nerven," *Berliner Illustrirte Zeitung (August 26, 1923).*

There is not much to add. It pounds daily on the nerves: the insanity of numbers, the uncertain future, today, and tomorrow become doubtful once more overnight. An epidemic of fear, naked need: lines of shoppers, long since an unaccustomed sight, once more form in front of shops, first in front of one, then in front of all. No disease is as contagious as this one. The lines have something suggestive about them: the women's glances, their hastily donned kitchen dresses, their careworn, patient faces. The lines always send the same signal: the city, the big stone city will be shopped empty again. Rice, 80,000 marks a pound yesterday, costs 160,000 marks today, and tomorrow perhaps twice as much; the day after, the man behind the counter will shrug his shoulders, "No more rice." Well then, noodles! "No more noodles." Barley, groats, beans, lentils—always the same, buy, buy, buy. The piece of paper, the spanking brand-new bank note, still moist from the printers, paid out today as a weekly wage, shrinks in value on the way to the grocer's shop. The zeros, *the multiplying zeros!* "Well, zero, zero ain't nothing."

They rise with the dollar, hate, desperation, and need—daily emotions like daily rates of exchange. The rising dollar brings mockery and laughter: "Cheaper butter! Instead of 1,600,000 marks, just 1,400,000 marks." This is no joke; this is reality written seriously with a pencil, hung in the shop window, and seriously read.

It rises with the dollar, the haste to turn that piece of paper into something one can swallow, something filling. The weekend markets overflow with people. City police regulate traffic. The lines consume the produce stands. "I'll have two dozen turnips." "There's only one dozen." Once packed away and the money counted into the hand like at the train ticket window, the next pushes forward from behind: "Two dozen turnips." "There's only one. . . . Next!"

Somewhere patience explodes. Resignation breaks. Not at the turnip man, who is a big fellow. One also swallows the butcher's biting remark, that all cows have to have bones. One pays and staggers off. But then the girl in the dairy store, the one whose face is always pinched, whose way of speaking becomes ever more finicky the fuller her store—this nervous milk maid—she issues regulations: how one is to behave as a customer, that shoving is rude, that everyone should not shout at once. Otherwise she can not concentrate on the scale. "Come on, when am I finally going to get my butter?" screams a woman. "Your butter? It is not your butter by a long shot. By the time you get to the front of the line, your butter will be all gone." And then comes the umbrella handle, a response crashing through the glass cover on the cream cheese. And the cop standing watch outside pulls a sobbing woman from the store. And there is an uproar. And charges are filed.

23

The Dawes Committee Report

First published as "Text of the Dawes Committee Report," *World Peace Foundation Pamphlets* 7, no. 5 (1924), 364–385.

We have approached our task as business leaders anxious to obtain effective results. We have been concerned with the technical, and not the political, aspects of the problem presented to us. We have recognized indeed that political considerations necessarily set certain limits within which a solution must be found if it is to have any chance of acceptance. To this extent and to this extent only, we have borne them in mind. [. . .]

The Committee has had to consider to what extent the balancing of the budget and the stabilization of the currency could be re-established permanently in Germany in her present state with limitations on her fiscal and economic rights over part of her area.

We should say at the outset that we have been unable to find any practical means of ensuring permanent stability in budget and currency under these conditions, and we think it unlikely that such means exist. The solution of the double problem submitted to us implies indeed the restoration of Germany's credit both externally and internally, and it has appeared to us impossible to provide for this restoration under the conditions mentioned. We have therefore been compelled to make the assumption that the fiscal and economic unity of the Reich will be restored, and our whole report is based on this hypothesis. [. . .]

The task [of the committee] would be hopeless if the present situation of Germany accurately reflected her potential capacity; in that case the proceeds from Germany's national production could not enable her both to meet the national needs and to ensure the payment of her foreign debts.

But Germany's growing and industrious population; her great technical skill; the wealth of her material resources; the development of her agriculture on progressive lines; her eminence in industrial science; all these factors enable us to be hopeful with regard to her future production.

Further, ever since 1919 the country has been improving its plant and equipment; the experts specially appointed to examine the railways have shown in their report that expense has not been spared in improving the German railway system; telephone and telegraph communications have been assured with the help of the most modern appliances; harbors and canals have likewise been developed; lastly, the industrialists have been enabled further to increase an entirely modern plant which is now adapted in many industries to produce a greater output than before the war.

Germany is therefore well equipped with resources; she possesses the means for exploiting them on a large scale; when the present credit shortage has been overcome, she will be able to resume a favored position in the activity of a world where normal conditions of exchange are gradually being restored.

Without undue optimism, it may be anticipated that Germany's production will enable her to satisfy her own requirements and raise the amounts contemplated in this plan for reparation obligations. The restoration of her financial situation and of her currency, as well as the world's return to a sound economic position, seem to us essential but adequate conditions for obtaining this result.

We propose to deal in the first place with the currency problem. [. . .] By means of the *Rentenmark,* stability has been attained for a few months, but on a basis which, in the absence of other measures, can only be temporary.

The Committee proposes the establishment of a new bank of issue in Germany, or, alternatively, a reorganization of the Reichsbank, as an essential agency for creating in Germany a unified and stable currency. Such a currency, the Committee believes, is necessary for the rehabilitation of Germany's finances, the balancing of her budget and the restoration of her foreign credit. [. . .]

The new bank will have a capital of four hundred million (400,000,000) gold marks, part to be subscribed in Germany and part abroad. It is to be administered by a German president and a German managing board, which can have the assistance, as in the case of the Reichsbank, of a consultative committee. Alongside this German managing board there is to be another board, called the General Board, which will consist of seven Germans and seven foreigners, one each of the following nationalities: British, French, Italian, Belgian, American, Dutch and Swiss. This General Board will be given broad powers in such matters of bank organization and operation as might affect the interests of the creditor nations. [. . .]

We repudiate, of course, the view that Germany's full domestic demands constitute a first charge on her resources and that what is available for her obligations to the peace treaty is merely the surplus revenue that she may be willing to realize. But at the same time, if the prior obligation for reparation that is fixed for Germany to pay, together with an irreducible minimum for her own domestic expenditure, make up in a given year a sum beyond her taxable capacity, then budget instability at once ensues and currency stability is also probably involved. In that event, an adjustment of the annual treaty obligations is obviously the only course possible. The amount that can safely be fixed for reparation purposes tends therefore to be the difference between the maximum revenue and minimum expenditure for Germany's own needs. [. . .]

We fully recognize both the necessity and the justice of maintaining the principle embodied in the treaty that Germany's payments should increase with what may prove to be the increase in her future capacity.

We also recognize that an estimate now made once and for all might well underestimate this, and that it is both just and practicable that the Allies should share in any increased prosperity. All that we regard as essential as a condition of stabilization is that any such increased demands to correspond with increasing capacity should be determined by a method which is clearly defined in the original settlement and which is capable of automatic, or at least professional, impartial, and practically indisputable application.

This requirement we have tried to meet, as will be seen, by providing that, in addition to a fixed annual payment, there shall be a variable addition dependent upon a composite index figure [the index of prosperity] designed to reflect Germany's increasing capacity. [. . .]

After a short period of recovery we believe that the financial and economic situation of Germany will have returned to a normal state, after which time the index will begin to operate. [. . .]

There has been a tendency in the past to confuse two distinct though related questions, i.e., first, the amount of revenue that Germany can raise and make available for reparation account, and second, the amount that can be transferred to foreign countries. The funds raised and transferred to the Allies on reparation account cannot, in the long run, exceed the sums that the balance of payments makes it possible to transfer, without currency and budget instability ensuing. But it is quite obvious that the amount of budget surplus that can be raised by taxation is not limited by the entirely distinct question of the conditions of external transfer. We propose to distinguish sharply between the two problems and to deal first with the problem of the maximum budget surplus and afterwards with the problem of payment to the Allies. In the past, the varying conclusions formed as to Germany's "capacity" have often depended upon which of these two methods has been chosen.

As a first method of approach the budgetary criterion has obvious advantages and attractions. Reparation must first be provided for as an item in the budget. [. . .]

But the limits set by the economic balance, if impossible to determine exactly, are real. For the stability of a country's currency to be permanently maintained, not only must her budget be balanced, but her earnings from abroad must be equal to the payments she must make abroad, including not only payments for the goods she imports but the sums paid in reparation. Nor can the balance of the budget itself be permanently maintained except on the same conditions. Loan operations may disguise the position—or postpone its practical results—but they cannot alter it. If reparation can, and must, be provided by means of the inclusion of an item in the budget—i.e., by the collection of taxes in excess of internal expenditure—it can only be paid abroad by means of an economic surplus in the country's activities.

We have, it will be seen, attempted to give effect to both these sets of considerations by a method we believe to be both logical and practical. We estimate the amount which we think Germany can pay in gold marks by consideration of her budget possibilities; but we propose safeguards against such transfers of these mark payments into foreign exchange as would destroy stabilization and thereby endanger future reparation. [. . .]

Above all, we recommend our proposal for these reasons: it adjusts itself automatically to realities; the burden which should rest upon the German taxpayer should in justice so obviously be commensurate with that borne by the Allied taxpayer that, in our view, nothing but the most compelling and proved necessity should operate to make it lighter. It would be both speculative and unjust to attempt to forecast the possibilities of the future exchange position and to determine Germany's burden in advance with reference to a problematic estimate of it. Experience, and experience alone, can show what transfer into foreign currencies can in practice be made. Our system provides in the meantime for a proper charge upon the German taxpayer, and a corresponding deposit in gold marks to the Allies' account; and then secures the maximum conversion of these mark deposits into foreign currencies which the actual capacity of the exchange position at any given time renders possible.

With these principles in mind, we recommend that Germany should make payment from the following sources:

(a) From her ordinary budget.
(b) From railway bonds and transport tax.
(c) From industrial debentures. [. . .]

The committee has been impressed with the fairness and desirability of requiring as a contribution to reparation payments from German industry a sum of not less than five billion gold marks to be represented by first mortgage bonds bearing five per cent interest and one per cent sinking fund per annum. This amount of bonds is less than the total debt of industrial undertakings in Germany before the war. Such indebtedness has for the most part been discharged by nominal payments in depreciated currency or practically extinguished. In addition the industrial concerns have profited in many ways through the depreciated currency, such as the long-delayed payment of taxes, by subsidies granted and advances made by the German government, and by depreciation of emergency money that they have issued. On the other hand it is incontestably true that losses have also resulted in many instances through the depreciation of currency, from the sale of output at fixed prices, and in other ways. [. . .]

Realizing the depletion of the liquid-capital supply in Germany, and that a period should be provided for its recuperation, we recommend that the interest on the five billion in debentures referred to above be waived entirely during the first year, that the interest during the second year be 2½ per cent, during the third year five per cent, and thereafter five per cent plus one per cent sinking fund.

24

ERNST NECKARSULMER

[Hugo Stinnes]

First published in *Der alte und der neue Reichtum* (Berlin: Fontane Verlag, 1925), 58–61.

No man who has emerged in the postwar period has been written and spoken about as much as Hugo Stinnes, the greatest master of the capital market that Germany has yet produced. And if the coinage "industrial dukedom" dates from 1919, then it does not apply to Hugo Stinnes to the extent that his industrial realm signifies not a dukedom but a royal kingdom, if not an empire. Death in April 1924 prepared an early end for him, and had he not been ripped so suddenly from his plans and projects the Stinnes empire would in all probability have continued to become larger and more powerful. For of this man, fifty-four years old at his death, nothing would be less accurate than the claim that he was sated. In this he stood in sharp contrast to most other industrial leaders, whose ambitions in their declining years were directed exclusively toward keeping, if possible, what they had inherited or made for themselves in the years or decades past.

It was completely different with Hugo Stinnes, whose goals were of a wholly different sort. With [Gustav von] Krupp, [August] Thyssen, [Franz] Haniel, [Emil] Kirdorf, their strivings did not extend beyond the mining and steel industries, nor generally the range of their own provinces, nor above all the national boundaries of the German fatherland. One or the other, to be sure, might have secured for himself certain footholds abroad for purely technical, manufacturing reasons, or acquired ore works in French Lorraine, Normandy, Sweden, or Spain, but for the most part they restricted themselves to Germany. These industrial dukes did indeed have the desire to expand their dukedoms as opportunities allowed, but they were no emperors setting out to conquer foreign lands. Hugo Stinnes knew no geographical boundaries and his ambition sought to create for itself an empire on which the sun never set.

His successes were also of a quite different sort from those of all other major German industrialists. As the war broke out, Hugo Stinnes's fortune amounted to about thirty million marks. The Krupp fortune was roughly ten times as large; Count Henckel von Donnersmarck was likewise about ten times as rich; Privy Councillor Haniel was at least twice as rich; among other Western industrialists, the families Stumm, Hoesch, and von Guilleaume were approximately equal and some of the Silesian magnates were many times superior to Stinnes in capital; and towering above everyone was the the lord of Landsberg Castle, August Thyssen. When Hugo Stinnes died not quite ten years later, he had far outstripped them all. He stood at the top towering over Krupp, Haniel, Thyssen, and Donnersmarck. All the others began the decade subject to the same conditions—or for some decidedly better ones because of their greater capital reserves—but still lost major shares of their property. In a tragic period for the economy and prosperity of Germany, Stinnes alone understood how to increase his fortune, indeed to multiply it. All of the other big industrialists look back on more or less considerable material losses; many millions, once in their firm possession, dwindled, eaten away in those catastrophic months of 1923. Only a single one of them, Hugo Stinnes, knew how to master his economic fate and turn adverse conditions to his advantage. [. . .]

The magnitude of his property at the time of his death cannot be estimated even approximately. In any case, he ranked as the richest man Germany has ever known, and it is commonly assumed that the fortune he left behind far exceeded a billion in gold, indicating that his assets increased by a factor of more than thirty in the decade following 1914. Not even in the "land of unlimited possibilities," America, had a fortune ever grown so rapidly, and the multimillionaire most admired in this connection, the founder of the Vanderbilt dynasty, Cornelius Vanderbilt, needed fifteen years to accumulate a fortune of one hundred million dollars, an accomplishment considered scarcely conceivable at the time.

25

RUDOLF HILFERDING

[The Organized Economy]

First published as "Die Aufgaben der Sozialdemokratie in der Republik," in *Rede auf dem Parteitag des SPD zu Kiel* (Berlin: Volksblatt, 1927).

If we want to know what the present situation really is we must examine it much more closely and characterize it more precisely than is done by the phrase "late capitalism." The crucial point is that we find ourselves at present in the period of capitalism in which the era of free competition, during which capitalism was wholly under the sway of blind market laws, has been essentially superseded, and we are moving towards a capitalist organization of the economy; in short, from an economy regulated by the free play of forces to an organized economy.

The technological characteristics of the organized economy—briefly summarized—are that alongside steam and electrical power, synthetic chemicals now play an increasingly prominent role, after something like half a century of scientific development during which they were becoming ripe for technical application in manufacturing. This application of chemistry signifies something quite new in principle. It makes the capitalist economy independent of the supply of individual raw materials, since the aim is, in principle, to produce important raw materials artificially from inorganic substances which are everywhere readily available in large quantities. [. . .] A second aim of synthetic chemistry is to produce raw materials in such a form that they are far more suitable than natural materials for industrial use, or have quite new qualities. A third aim of this development is to produce costly organic materials out of cheap inorganic materials. Here I need only recall the enormous progress of artificial silk production which has made such inroads into the former realm of the textile industry. [. . .]

The second characteristic of the situation is that capitalist industry, reanimated by the vigorous and unprecedented influx of scientific knowledge, is wholly committed to utilizing the new opportunities in an organized way. It is significant that newly established industries are not only built upon a more complex technological base (as was already the case in the immediately preceding period) but at the same time are organizing themselves, so far as possible, on a worldwide scale. For example, the artificial silk industry is not only a monopoly industry in Germany, but fundamentally constitutes a single international capitalist concern which has close links with other trusts in Germany and England, and these in turn have connections with other concerns. Thus the development of cartels and trusts which has been successfully accomplished in industry is now the first word to be uttered by the new industries as they enter upon the world scene.

A third characteristic phenomenon is the internationalization of capitalist industry; the effort to unite the various national monopolies, trusts, and cartels at an international level. Anyone who comes into contact with capitalist business circles [. . .] is astonished at the eagerness with which these people, whose economic outlook before the war was confined to the national scene, now seek international connections and cultivate their foreign relations, and how vigorous this trend towards international organization has become. When the working class was first becoming organized and the trade unions formed the first organized economic element in capitalism, the entrepreneurs, helped by their greater class-consciousness and their smaller numbers, began to overtake our organizations. We must take care that this does not also happen in the international arena. [. . .]

The fourth point, which is not usually noticed and is only just beginning to be apparent is perhaps the most important of all. We all have the feeling nowadays that even those businesses carried on by a single entrepreneur have ceased to be simply a private affair of the entrepreneurs. Society has come to realize that it has an interest in raising productivity in every individual undertaking, and hence that the person responsible for economic management in each case should actually carry out his technical and organizing functions to increase productivity. I should remind you that bodies such as the *Kuratorium für Wirtschaftlichkeit,* and all those officially promoted efforts for greater rationalization which are designed to induce entrepreneurs to increase the output of their undertakings, are simply statements by society to the effect that the running of his business is no longer the private affair of the entrepreneur but a matter for society as a whole. The most important thing is this: the formation of combines, the concentration of increasing numbers of undertakings under a single head, means the elimination of competition so far as the individual business is concerned. It was the doctrine of capitalism that only the pressure of free competition can stimulate the economy and bring about the necessary technical innovations and advances. The principal argument against socialism has always been: you eliminate the private initiative of free competition and offer nothing in its place. Hence your economy will not work, because you fail to take into account the ambition and self-interest of the private owner of the means of production. It is most interesting to see how, in the development of modern business science, methods are being sought of replacing this free competition between private self-interests with scientific methods of planning. It is quite clear that the director of a combine has a great interest in being able to establish at any time whether any one company which forms part of his concern, but is not in competition with other similar undertakings in the combine, is operating at maximum efficiency. Very sophisticated methods have been developed in order to substitute for competition based on self-interest, a scientific method of competition. That is the very principle which we socialists would apply to our management of the economy. Capitalism itself thus abandons the principal objection which it can raise against socialism, and at the same time the last psychological objection to socialism collapses. In fact, therefore, organized capitalism means the theoretical replacement of the capitalist principle of free competition by the socialist principle of planned production. This planned and consciously directed economy supports to a much greater extent the possibility of the conscious action of society; that is to say, action by means of the only conscious organization in society equipped with coercive power, namely the state.

If this is the case, then the capitalist organization of the economy on one side and the state organization on the other confront each other, and the problem is how we want to shape their interpenetration. That simply means that our generation faces the problem of transforming—with the help of the state, which consciously regulates society—an economy organized and directed by the capitalists into one which is directed by the democratic state. It follows that the problem facing our generation can be none other than that of socialism. If we as a social democracy fought in an earlier period for political rights and for the initiation and extension of social policies, then as a result of economic development itself the question of socialism is now posed. [. . .]

I referred to the growing interpenetration of economy and state, of their reciprocal relation which becomes increasingly close as the economy becomes more organized. In this connection I draw attention to the fact that even during the period of free competition the influence of the state upon the economy already existed in certain spheres; for example, in the state control of the money market which has become very significant again in the last few days through the fact, unique in the history of stock-market crises, that a capitalist government artificially produced a panic on the stock market or in questions of fiscal policy and trade policy. Here, however, I have the impression that it is necessary to remind the mass of the people of the significance of trade policy. We have recently experienced an extraordinary rise in the price of cereals and it must be made clear to the people that the price of bread and the price of meat is not only an economic but also a political price that is determined by political power relations, and that it is a matter of urgency, if the people desire an improvement in this sphere, that they take the initiative themselves in implementing and supporting a policy capable of diminishing or eliminating this political factor in the economic price.

But what is new, and even more important, is state regulation in that area which directly affects the lot of the proletariat; namely, the labor market. Thanks to the revolution we now have unemployment insurance. This means a very specific regulation of supply and demand on the labor market. As a result of the system of wage agreements and courts of arbitration there is now a political regulation of wages and of working hours. The personal situation of the worker is determined by the policy carried out by the state. If we have been able, with more than two million unemployed, to maintain on the whole the level of real wages, this defense of the wage level has been possible above all because the political influence of the working class was great enough—through unemployment insurance, arbitration, and wage agreements—to prevent at least a reduction of wages. We must drum it into the head of every worker that the weekly wage is a political wage, that the size of the pay packet at the end of the week depends upon the strength of working-class representation in parliament, the strength of its organization, and the power relations in society outside parliament. And to working women in particular it must be said: When you vote, make your decision about bread and meat and about the level of wages at the same time. Of course, this is something new in the capitalist economy, an element of great economic, social, and political significance. Professor Cassel, that fossil from the laissez-faire era of capitalism who strangely enough is able to travel around as an international expert on the subject, is quite right when he says that this contradicts the nature of capitalism—that is, capitalism as he understands it. It is indeed incompatible with the principle of free competition. It is only possible because we have an organized economy, which is subject to ever-increasing conscious organization by society and by the state.

At this point I come to our position with regard to the state. Here I should like to invoke the best of all Marxists—history—which on this occasion too is in agreement with Karl Marx. What was our attitude to the state historically? There is no doubt that from the very beginning the labor movement, and in particular the socialist movement, has been the bearer of the idea of state influence on the economy, in opposition to liberalism. There is no doubt that—initially in the field of social policy—we have repeatedly demanded state intervention and an increase in state power, and that we now demand its extension from the sphere of social policy to that of economic policy and the management of the economy. To regard the management of industry and the economy as social concerns is the very principle of socialism, and society has no other organ through which it can consciously act than the state. So for the present no doubts regarding our position on the state are possible. But if that is the case historically, we have always been careful to avoid lapsing into the conceptions of the bourgeois, particularly the German, philosophy of the state. Marxist method requires that in dealing with all social phenomena we should dissolve the fetishism of appearance by an analysis of reality. The German philosophy of the state has absolutized and deified the state; it has taught that the state is the realization of freedom, morality, or some other metaphysical principle. The German philosophy of the state flourished all the more profusely the less state power we actually had. Only since 1870 have we had what can be called a state, and our philosophy of the state, which dates from the eighteenth and the beginning of the nineteenth centuries, is therefore unusable in understanding it. Marx undoubtedly indicated a crucial feature of the state when he said that it is not to be regarded only as a political body but also in terms of its social content, which means that the ruling class maintains its domination by means of state power. But this definition of the state by

Marx is on that account not a theory of the state because it is valid for all state formations since the beginning of class society; it is instead a matter of explaining the distinctive features in the development of the state.

The British, who have already had a state for such a long time, have never concerned themselves with mere philosophical conceptions of the state. The British literature on the subject does not deal at all with the state, but with government. For us, as socialists, it should be self-evident that an organization consists of its members, the leadership, and the apparatus of administration; this means, therefore, that the state—in political terms—is nothing but the government, the machinery of administration and the citizens who compose it. In another context this means that the essential element in every modern state is the parties because the individual can only make his will effective through the medium of his party. Consequently, all parties are necessary components of the state, just like the government and the administration. This also involves acknowledgment of the basis of the Marxist definition because the party struggle is no more than a reflection of the struggle between classes and hence the expression of class conflict.

If therefore the content of the struggle over the state is to gain influence over the management of the economy, only then does the full originality of an observation by Marx become clear; an observation which he considered so important that he included it not only in *Capital,* but also in his *Inaugural Address* [*to the International Workingmen's Association*]. There he speaks of the ten-hour working day and concludes: "Hence the Ten Hours Bill was not only a great practical success; it was the victory of a principle; it was the first time that in broad daylight the political economy of the middle class succumbed to the political economy of the working class." What this means is that the more capitalist society succumbs to the increasing influence of the working class, the more victorious is the political principle of the working class to use the state as a means for the management and the control of the economy in the interests of all.

26

ERICH SCHAIRER

[Alfred Hugenberg]

First published in *Mit anderen Augen. Jahrbuch der deutschen Sonntagszeitung* (Stuttgart: 1929), 18–21.

Hugenberg, a German National representative in parliament, is one of the most powerful men not only in the German National People's party, but in Germany altogether. What is the basis of his power?

In 1913, August Scherl informed the Reich chancellor Bethmann-Hollweg of his willingness to sell eight million marks worth of common shares in the Scherl Press; Rudolf Mosse offered him eleven and a half million marks—but he, Scherl, said he was prepared to sell the shares "to friends of the government" for ten million.

Bethmann negotiated with a few rich people—in vain. The danger that Rudolf Mosse or the Ullstein brothers might take over the Scherl Press became increasingly threatening. To fend off this "Jewish threat," which shook high, even the highest, offices in Berlin, the shares were ultimately purchased (don't laugh!) by Baron Alfred von Oppenheim and the Cologne financier Louis Hagen for eight million marks.

But then Alfred Hugenberg, chairman of the board of Krupp, intervened. He founded the German Press Association in Düsseldorf, and it bought out the Scherl Press over the course of the following years. Hugenberg simply turned to the Prussian government with the request that the German Press Association "be given an advance from some source unknown to us." Through a secret arrangement arranged by the Prussian interior minister, the Press Association received two payments of two-and-a-half million marks each in August 1914 and sometime in 1916. (That these five million marks have still not been repaid is not exactly to the credit of the republican administration in Prussia.)

Thus did Hugenberg acquire the Scherl Press, which now publishes a number of strictly German National newspapers (at the head of the list is the *Berliner Lokalanzeiger*), periodicals, magazines, and books.

Hugenberg, however, recognized that in Germany the provincial press is just as important as the Berlin press. Paris and London newspapers have a much larger circulation than those in Berlin because they are also read in the provinces. In Germany, in contrast, even the smallest provincial city has its own local paper, and most people, modest as they are, make do with the intellectual nourishment it offers.

Hugenberg put these channels to the people's brains to work for his interests. In 1922 he founded the Provincial Press Economic Bureau, which publishes a stereotypic news service. Following the inflation he purchased another one. These services send impressions of lead articles, news reports, incidental commentaries, novels, sports reports, etc., to provincial printers, who use a simple metal-casting machine to produce printing plates from the impressions. Pick up any provincial paper and, aside from the local news, everything in it (including complaints about Berlin's centralism) will have been created in Berlin. And the majority of provincial papers take their material from Hugenberg's workshops.

Such a service, however, can only supply newspapers with reports that it has gotten from somewhere; it is therefore dependent on the news bureaus. After the war, there was only a single news bureau of note in Germany: Wolff's Telegraph Bureau (WTB). It depended on the government for its domestic reporting (as the official news bureau), and for foreign reports on the English and French news organizations (Reuter's and Havas). So when a revolution broke out in Buenos Aires, the report went through the Reuter office and the WTB to the news-service offices. When the metal workers went on strike in Berlin, the WTB informed the Reuter office of the details, having appended the appropriate commentary, and Reuter sent the report on to newspapers in New York. How the story looked when it got there can only be imagined.

Hugenberg inserted himself into the process by acquiring and expanding the Telegraph Union (TU). He broke the domestic news monopoly WTB held by dispensation of the government and then got to work establishing his own news service outside the country: he concluded contracts with foreign news bureaus and founded his own affiliates. Now when a strike breaks out in Berlin, the TU gives the report with the appropriate commentary to United Press, and the latter must, by contract, distribute it unchanged to American newspapers. When a riot occurs in Prague, the Prague affiliate of the TU notifies Berlin where the news report is prepared and then sent on, partly over the telegraph, partly already in stereotype, to approximately 1,600 German newspapers. And not only to German National newspapers—no, Hugenberg also supplies news reports and lead articles to newspapers of the German People's party, even Center and Democratic papers. Naturally the reports have to be selected and "interpreted" (that is, provided with a commentary) according to the partisan position of the recipient newspaper. For this task

Hugenberg employs, aside from roughly 2,000 contributors, 500 to 600 permanent office workers and 90 editors.

To select, formulate, and comment on the news—that means to conduct news politics. And to conduct news politics at the level Hugenberg does it—that means to rule over people. Are foreigners correct when they call Hugenberg the *roi sans couronne,* the uncrowned king?

They are correct. They are correct ten times over, since Hugenberg is also trying to gain control over film and cinema. As early as 1916 he founded the German Moving Picture Company, which became the Deulig Film Corporation in 1920. And a year ago he acquired the studios and theaters of the largest German film enterprise, the Universal Film Company (UFA). No words need be wasted on the increase in power signified by this penetration of the film industry.

Where did Hugenberg get the money with which he acquired this power? Answer: first, from the Prussian government (see above); second, from heavy industry; third, from owners of large estates. There is, to be sure, one exception, and it is very telling in regard to the development and current power of the Hugenberg combine: Hugenberg acquired UFA entirely on his own without any donations of capital from industry or agriculture; that is, he absorbed it into his combine on the strength of reserves and normal commercial bank credits.

Thus has Alfred Hugenberg erected a structure over the last fourteen years that will not be easily toppled. For he knows people and has based his edifice on their taste for the mediocre, their lack of civic courage, their intellectual dullness, and their gullibility. And those are the most solid foundations.

27

B. TRAVEN
[Bank Failures]

First published in *Die weiße Rose* (Berlin: Büchergilde Gutenberg, 1929), 94–95.

Rushes on the banks are beginning. Savers have been seized by panic. They fear, no, they are certain that their money, for which they have saved and slaved, is lost. They stand as early as midnight in endless lines to be the first when the cash drawers open. The earlier one arrives the better the chances of still saving something. The ordered life of the banks is being torn apart. All personnel must be mobilized to disburse payments. No one makes deposits. All credit is being called in. Banks in other countries are receiving imploring cables to help out with fluid money and with checks. All the reserves of the national banking association are being called up. But the lines in front of the banks grow longer.

And then the banks begin to crash, because they cannot make the payments. The money has been leant out; for when the bank is not able to make loans then it cannot pay interest to its small savers. The little banks crash first. The larger ones still get by, limiting banking hours first to two hours, then to one. Then the larger banks begin to crash.

And behind all of this chaos is no sudden disappearance of a continent, no gigantic natural catastrophe that destroys values irretrievably. Behind this whole collapse of economic order and economic security, which is under constant threat by agitators, is nothing other than the disrupted notions of those who have something, the suddenly insecure hope of those who possess much, and of those who possess little. Everything that is now taking place on Wall Street is based on nothing but the fact that thoughts have suddenly, too suddenly, taken on unexpected turn. Mass hypnosis. Mass suggestion. The suggestion, the notion: "I can lose!" tears this beautiful economic system, willed by God, blessed by God, protected by God, to shreds. And nonetheless all values remain the same. Values have not changed. There is just as much cash in the world as before. All the money is still there, and not a single cent has fallen off the globe into space, where it cannot be fished back onto land. All the buildings are still standing. All the forests. All the waterfalls. All the oceans. The railroads and the ships all remain intact. And hundreds of thousands of strong and healthy people are willing to work and to produce and to increase the available wealth of the world. Not a single engineer has lost the ability to design new machines. No vein of coal has been hidden by the forces of nature. The sun rises bright and warm in the sky as always. It rains as always. The grain waves in the fields and ripens as always. The fields of cotton extend in splendor. Nothing has changed in the available value of earthly riches. People, seen as a whole, are just as wealthy as yesterday. And for the simple reason, and only the simple reason, that the property of individuals is in danger of changing and shifting does a catastrophe overtake humanity as a whole. [. . .]

An economic system, an economic order, created by people who claim to possess intelligence. People, however, who, despite all the highly developed technology they created, have still not overcome primitiveness as far as a studied and well-regulated economic system is concerned.

28

ERWIN KUPZYK

Postwar Concentration in the German Iron Industry

First published as "Die Konzentrationsbewegung in der deutschen Großeisenindustrie nach dem Kriege," *Wirtschaftsdienst* 4 (October 10, 1930), 1746–1752.

The idea of concentration is not at all a creation of the postwar period. Rather, in the decades before the war the German iron and steel industries already regarded the progressive integration of originally independent production units into large, powerful structures as a valuable means of increasing productivity. Nevertheless, the overwhelming postwar trend toward concentration, which has transformed the economic organization of the iron and steel industries with the aim of recovering and improving productivity, is distinguished by its unflagging tempo. A degree of concentration has been established in just a few years that would have required decades before the war: the preconditions and effects of the consolidation of economic forces have an entirely different character in the postwar period than in the years preceding the war.

The movement toward concentration that seized the German iron industry shortly following the war was caused by a shortage of raw materials. With the stroke of a pen, the Treaty of Versailles accomplished a structural change that put a whole new stamp on the German iron industry. The ties between the Rhineland and Westphalian works and the plants of Lorraine—expressed in the exchange of coal and coke from the Ruhr district for ore and rolling-mill products from Lorraine—were dissolved; in Upper Silesia the destruction caused by the redrawing of boundaries extended to operating relations between plants, so that the technological unity of previous years was torn apart. To regain the lost constellation, individual enterprises attempted especially to recreate or at least improve the common substructure of the combines. New connections therefore had to be created both in regard to the suppliers of raw materials and to the industries dedicated to further processing. Thus the steel works, in addition to coal mines, incorporated ore mines in Siegerland (which, however, did not adequately compensate the loss of ore from mines in Lorraine). [. . .]

Processing and refining industries, frequently even the manufacturing industry, were drawn into the consolidating movement. The most important example of this vertical formation of combines is the electromining combine, the Rhein-Elbe-Siemens-Schuckert Union founded under the direction of Hugo Stinnes. Due to the raw materials shortage, the mixed operation—the beginnings of which extend back before the war—came to predominance in the iron industry, and it quite likely belongs among the more valuable assets created by large industry in Germany since the war.

In general the formation of combines following the Treaty of Versailles was nothing other than a regrouping of the forces remaining in the German iron industry, whereby the difficulty lay in regaining the old style of organic cohesion among the various plants involved. If the structure of most combines was determined by considerations of production, then the hunger for real values that went hand in hand with the increasing currency devaluation also led to the formation of combines in which speculation played the dominant role. Commercial enterprises, favored by profit opportunities during and after the war and the Reichsbank credit policy in the inflationary period, were responsible in particular for forming this type of combine. The vertical concentration from blast furnaces to rolling mills, which was initiated by the steel industry, increasingly extended to both raw materials and manufacturing, and bore the unmistakable character of an organic development. On the other hand, the commercial combines which resulted from the purchase of stock packages simply because they came on the market at a favorable price generally lacked such economically coherent integration. [. . .]

In the first years following the war, the securing of raw materials played a critical role, but now raw materials were readily available. The increased need for sales urgently required a reduction in production costs for the sake of becoming competitive on the world market; it became apparent that the productive plant in the German iron and steel industries was backward to an extraordinary degree. The very considerable energy invested in the technical rationalization of individual plants proved insufficient for recapturing a secure position in foreign and domestic markets and therefore required extension; the enormous need for capital called up by the technical reorganization of plants also compelled an invigoration of underlying operational capacity through the consolidation of similar productive units, that is, horizontal combines. Across-the-board technical rationalization of all the existing sites of production, however, would ultimately have led to an unbridgeable gap between productivity and the potential for sales and thus would have raised the spectre of misguided investments on a grand scale. To avoid them, horizontal consolidation had to go hand in hand with a process of purposeful selection; precisely this aspect of rationalization was of a particularly decisive character and was responsible for the internal transformations in the iron industry that most obviously distinguish industry in Germany today from that prior to the war. The incorporation of similar productive sites gave the large combines the opportunity to consolidate production at the most favorable and best suited plants and to remove less promising plants from the production process by shutting them down. Thus through the most efficient possible exploitation of the operating units and the technological improvement of the production process, they achieved a reduction in production costs, thereby re-establishing profitability as well as lowering the price and improving the quality of the individual goods.

29

HANS OSTWALD

A Moral History of the Inflation

First published as *Sittengeschichte der Inflation. Ein Kulturdokument aus den Jahren des Marksturzes* (Berlin: Neufeld und Henius, 1931), 74–75.

Thinking back on the inflationary years an extravagant image of a hellish carnival appears before the eyes: plunderings and riots, demonstrations and confrontations, profiteering and smuggling, agonizing hunger and gluttonous feasts, sudden impoverishment and rapid enrichment, debauched, maniacal dancing, the horrific misery of children, naked dances, currency conjurers, hoarders of real value, amusement ecstasy—indulgence, materialist worldviews and religious decline, flourishing occultism and clairvoyance—gambling passion, speculation frenzy, an epidemic of divorce, women's independence, the early maturity of youth, Quaker food, student aid, raids and profiteering trials, jazz bands, narcotics.

Truly a dazzlingly colorful county fair of life!

One could probably list more catchwords and facts, happenings and circumstances. What novelty failed to appear! What a loud, boisterous battle for attention!

It was a time of intense revaluation—in the economy and culture, in material as well as psychological things. Rich people who could have afforded all the pleasures in the world were suddenly glad to have someone hand them a bowl of warm soup. Overnight little apprentices became powerful bank directors and possessed seemingly inexhaustible funds. Foreigners, some the most impoverished of pensioners at home, could suddenly step out in Germany like princes.

Everything seemed reversed.

The family, too, seemed to be in rapid decline. An ecstasy of eroticism cast the world into chaos. Many things that otherwise took place in secret appeared openly in the bright light of the public stage. Above all it was the women who in many respects completely transformed themselves. They asserted their demands, particularly their sexual demands, much more clearly. In every conceivable way they intensified their claim to the rights of life and a full range of experience. Amorous scandals came much more strongly to light. Some of them served as symbols of the time. Nudism was no longer confined to specific circles and to theatrical revues and cabarets. It permeated fashion throughout society: the pretty leg was discovered and gladly put on display. Beauty aids were everywhere. Developments continued. If during the war women were forced to take over many male jobs, they did not allow themselves afterward to be pushed quite all the way back into the home. That had its effect on relations between the sexes as well. And, as the last stage of development, there arose the female bachelor, the woman in charge of her own life, whether unmarried, divorced, or widowed.

To that was added our experience of the remarkable juvenescence of the woman's world. Grandmama, in a practically knee-length skirt and a bobbed hairdo, danced with young men in the clubs, hotels, and cafés—wherever the opportunity presented itself. And mama danced with friends. And youthful mademoiselles took the opportunity to dance along—and the children suffered their fears alone at home.

Postwar eroticism was nourished by the insecurities of life, by the rapid up and down of the economy. Nevertheless, the era produced new knowledge and developments in the erotic as well as in many other areas.

Despite the apparent collapse of all the values that had guided human life for centuries, indeed for millenia, they were transformed or newly defined only to a very small extent, with only some of them emended.

That became evident as the inflation came to an end.

The nightmare vanished.

The German people resurrected itself. It created a new currency—on its own. And with that it rebuilt its economy, which was possible only because they were a people of work. Only through attention to work, only through work could it create values that became the basis for a new life.

In a short time illicit trade and profiteering disappeared. This pestilence on the economy and on the entirety of the German people's intellectual and psychological life shriveled up and went away. And the whole noxious odor of exaggerated eroticism and of the crimes and conventions of the inflation flew away like clouds of dust in a purifying wind.

And we recognized that the broad masses of the German people were still intact. They had always been diligent and proper, and had remained so. The upright little man, the postman and the railroad engineer, the seamstress and the washerwoman, had always, just like other kinds of workers, fulfilled their duties. Doctors had treated the sick, scholars had advanced science, and inventors had developed and realized their ideas.

Everyone, no doubt, was visited frequently enough during the inflation by temptation. But the majority did not succumb; they overcame it.

And thus it was that such a healthy people could quickly rid themselves of the inflation and most of the consequences of that demoralizing time. The temporary symptoms, the crimes, the ecstasy, the damages, nearly all remained on the periphery, at the edges, on the surface!

Some things likely did change, were improved by new approaches and discoveries. But the great, good core remains.

30

ROLF WAGENFÜHR

[The Inflation Boom]

First published as "Die Industriewirtschaft: Entwicklungstendenzen der deutschen und internationalen Industrieproduktion, 1860–1932," *Vierteljahreshefte zur Konjunkturforschung*, Special Issue 31 (Berlin: Rainer Hobbing Verlag, 1932), 24.

German industrial production reached its low point in 1919. From 1919 to 1922 productive volume increased by more than ninety percent: if in 1919 production amounted to only about thirty-seven percent of the prewar level (within former national boundaries), in 1922 as much as seventy-one percent of prewar production had already been attained. [. . .]

In general the inflation had a favorable effect on entrepreneurial income, while the effect on workers' income was unfavorable. Neither wages nor salaries, especially since 1921, were able to keep pace with price increases. The wage bill in industry therefore fell proportionately farther and farther behind; an ever larger share of the net industrial product was not available for distribution. [. . .] Moreover, industry, like other economic sectors, was relieved of interest costs and amortization requirements by the progressive currency devaluation. The financial resources previously reserved for these purposes—which, under normal market conditions, was by no means certain to redound to the benefit of industry's physical plant—could from now on be invested in those plants directly.

In addition, the financial requirements of public bodies were met to an increasing extent by taxes levied at the source, which were less subject to currency devaluation than other taxes. Therefore the share of entrepreneurial income diverted to tax payments steadily declined; these unpaid taxes were also free for investment purposes.

Even if voluntary saving was steadily declining in significance, forced saving in connection with income fluctuations emerged increasingly into the foreground. "The bulk of the population no doubt devoted a greater share of its income to consumption purposes; but only a much smaller share of the total national income ever found its way into the hands of the consumers."

The rapid increase in investment activity was reflected on the side of production. If one takes 1919 as a starting point, then the number of ships built, for example, more than tripled by 1922, the number of newly built dwellings increased by a factor of 2.5; iron and steel production more than doubled and metalworks production enjoyed nearly an equal increase. The rise in production from 1919 to 1922 in the production-goods industry as a whole totaled approximately 100 percent.

The production of consumption goods did in fact rise between 1919 and 1922, but the increase here totaled only sixty-nine percent. Particularly small was the increase in the food and luxury industries, which were nearly completely dependent on the dwindling purchase power of the domestic market. The increase in textiles and the group of leather-processing industries was somewhat larger; but the proportion of such goods exported may have risen from year to year.

In general, developments in export during this phase of the inflation were relatively favorable. Compared with the prewar period, the cost of raw materials to industry rose less sharply in Germany than in France, Great Britain, or the United States of America. Even if the marginal difference decreased to Germany's disadvantage over the years, the low German price level continued to provide an important stimulus to export for a substantial period.

The export quota of German industry in 1921–1922 was even higher than in the year prior to the war.

In the autumn of 1922, there was a clear turn for the worse. The inflationary tempo picked up. With the increasing rate of monetary turnover, the turnover itself—calculated in gold—declined noticeably. In the course of 1923, cash reserves everywhere sank to an intolerable minimum.

At the same time, the hypertrophy of the commercial and banking apparatus become increasingly blatant. While the number of industrial workers had not yet reached its prewar level, the number of bank employees had tripled in comparison to 1913. The number of active accounts at the three big D-banks (Deutsche Bank, Dresdener Bank, and Darmstädter und Nationalbank) grew five-fold in the same period. Commercial enterprises and banks made up an increasing proportion of the existing stock companies (1919: sixteen percent; 1923: twenty-two percent). Industry was increasingly burdened by administrative costs because an ever greater number of employees were required to manage firm accounting chores.

That forced saving also began steadily to lose significance at this time was particularly disadvantageous for production. In 1920 and 1921 it had been possible to refinance continually industrial-commodity production through the effects of income fluctuations. To the extent, however, that all cost elements necessarily conformed to the currency devaluation (the transition to the gold standard), inflation no longer had a stimulating effect on commodity production. The stimulus was definitively lost as the workers then succeeded in bringing wage increases into conformity with the progressive currency devaluation. "From this moment on, there was no longer anyone onto whom the burden of the inflation, that is, the substantive loss it caused, could be transferred."

From autumn 1922 industrial unemployment, which had steadily declined up to that point began to rise again. Opportunities for temporary work also began to shrink considerably.

In the context of the rise in production costs, the cost advantage relative to other national economies slowly but surely eroded.

Up until autumn 1922 exports, compared to the corresponding periods of the previous year, rose steadily. Beginning in August 1922, however, a contraction began; by the summer of 1923, exports amounted to only slightly more than a third of the previous high point. [. . .]

Given the general regression—which necessarily accompanied inflationary developments—the results of the Ruhr invasion could only be catastrophic. One of the most highly-developed industrial sectors was removed from the overall structure of the national economy; exchange among the individual regions came to a complete stop. A portion of Ruhr industrial production was shut down entirely so that supplies of important raw materials (coal, iron, chemical products) to unoccupied Germany were threatened; conversely, goods otherwise sold in the Ruhr district (construction materials, wood, consumer goods, and agricultural products) encountered the predictable sales blockages.

As a whole the volume of production from 1922 to 1923 declined by a good third, returning it to a level below that of 1920. The production-goods industries were especially hard hit, with the decline in some areas amounting to as much as fifty percent. At the same time the production of consumer goods contracted by twenty-seven percent. The inflation boom had turned into a crisis.

31

FRANZ VON PAPEN

Speech to the Lausanne Conference, June 16–July 9, 1932

Published in *Documents on British Foreign Policy, 1919–1939,* First Series, vol. 3 (London: H.M. Stationery Office, 1960), 197–201.

Nothing can prove more clearly the catastrophic upheaval that has occurred during this period than a comparison between the world as it was, to all appearances at any rate, in 1929 and the situation today.

In those days there existed a system of international credit that appeared to function without friction and an active and fruitful exchange of capital from one country to another. Commercial relations between almost all countries seemed to be regulated on a solid basis by a clear and well-organized system of commercial treaties. Competent authorities, governments, parliaments, economic circles, and public opinion were unanimous in recognizing and condemning any policy of isolation as unreasonable. Every country was ready to welcome the goods of other countries in well-ordered exchanges. Industry worked at a profit. Agriculture, if not in Germany, at any rate in the majority of other countries, could live. The world opened itself wide to commerce. Banks evidenced a spirit of enterprise and granted credits to foreign countries. Investors were disposed to entrust their savings to foreign governments. In the majority of countries unemployment was still at that time an unknown problem. Those were the characteristic features of the period during which the Young Plan was conceived.

What an abyss between the glowing optimism of those days and the pessimism and despair of today! None of the promises of that period have been realized.

The desperate situation that prevails today is evidenced by the number of twenty-five million unemployed. [. . .] In Germany this state of things has most strongly shaken the confidence of the masses in the good functioning of the capitalist system.

A certain number of states have already found themselves obliged to suspend their payments abroad. This constitutes a grave warning not to delay taking the necessary measures in order that other great countries may not find themselves in the same position. I need not describe what the repercussions would be, the disastrous results on the world crisis of such further steps. In the present uncertainty there is no need to be surprised that the international circulation of capital and credit is, for the moment, almost entirely arrested. The capitalists of wealthy countries, far from collaborating in a reasonable distribution of such capital, think only of withdrawing as rapidly as possible the credits that they have granted, and do so even though in their own countries capital can no longer find remunerative investment. Employers are often obliged, in order to make up their losses, to live on their capital. The capital that is in existence, and is destined to form the basis of fresh prosperity, shrinks steadily.

On the other hand, as a consequence of the increase in the value of gold, or as a result of the fall in prices, debtors are obliged to pay from forty to fifty per cent more, and in this connection private debtors and debtor states are in exactly the same position. If an improvement of the situation does not speedily occur, we must expect a general adjustment of debts to become inevitable.

There remain two facts of a general character which I would also like to address.

The world has had to pass through crises in the past. [. . .] In one essential point, however, the present crisis differs from earlier ones. Formerly we had to deal with crises resulting from a lack of equilibrium between production and consumption, and a period of two to three years was generally sufficient to re-establish equilibrium. But upon the present crisis of international exchange has been superimposed a second crisis—an unprecedented crisis of credit. This credit crisis has causes peculiar to itself. The most important are the public international debts and political payments, which are contrary to all sound or reasonable economic principles. The crisis of international exchange will not be surmounted unless the credit crisis is also overcome, and the latter cannot be overcome unless the specific cause from which it results is ruthlessly swept aside. That is the first point.

The second point is this. Under the influence of political debts a complete displacement has taken place between debtor and creditor countries in the repartition of gold on the one hand and the exchange of merchandise on the other. Gold has accumulated in the two national economic systems that are creditors under the system of international debts, whereas Germany is today the only debtor country that is almost entirely lacking in gold. In the creditor countries gold has become sterile, and in Germany the absence of gold is causing a growing paralysis of the economic machinery.

On the other hand, the commercial balance of Germany has become favorable during the last two years, under the pressure of its external debt, which is closely linked to the political debts, whereas in former decades it was always unfavorable. In the same period a development in the opposite direction has taken place in the creditor countries. [. . .]

The German problem is the central problem of the entire world's difficulties.

The German situation is characterized by the following:

1. The high level of interest, which crushes agriculture and also industry;
2. The burden of taxation, which, in the opinion of the Special Advisory Committee, is so oppressive that it cannot be increased but has yet been increased in order to assure the very existence of the state by the imposition of fresh taxes within the last few days;
3. The external debt, the service of which becomes ever more difficult by reason of the progressive diminution of the surplus of exports; and
4. Unemployment, more widespread than in any other country, constitutes from twenty to twenty-five per cent of the population and is a burden on public funds.

What is particularly fatal is that an ever-growing number of young people have no possibility and no hope of finding employment and of earning their livelihood. Despair and the political radicalization of the youthful section of the population are the consequences of this state of things. [. . .]

The former reserves of the Reichsbank are exhausted. The reserves in gold and foreign currency of which the Reichsbank can freely dispose are no more than 390 million marks for a fiduciary circulation of 3,800 million marks, which means that the legal cover for the currency circulating in the country, which should be forty per cent, is now no more than about 10 per cent. If in the next few weeks we are to fulfill our obligations, this small cover will become even more insufficient.

The foreign trade of Germany closed in 1931 with an excess of some three billion marks. [. . .] The forced development of this favorable balance has led in all countries to protective measures against German imports, with the consequence that the excess of exports rapidly diminished in 1932.

In view of the fact that the prices of all goods have fallen by fifty percent as compared with the prices of 1928–1929, the loan charges on private German debts abroad have alone reached almost to the level of the normal annuity contemplated by the Dawes Plan.

Germany could not by herself arrest this development. No international decision has been taken up to now by the responsible statesmen to arrest this development. The very wise initiative of President Hoover in June 1931[1] was inspired by the idea of giving the world a respite so as to produce a solution to the most urgent economic problems. This goal, nevertheless, has not been reached. Sufficient account has not been taken of the reality of economic laws. [. . .]

1. A one-year moratorium on debt payments.

The external debt of Germany, with its very heavy interest charges, is, for the most part, attributable to the transfers of capital and the withdrawals of credits which have been the consequences of the execution of the Treaty of Versailles and of the reparations agreements. Thus, the Special Advisory Committee finds that the eighteen billion marks that were borrowed by Germany from other countries after the stabilization of her currency have been counterbalanced by an exodus of more than ten billion marks under the heading of reparation payments alone. At the present time, when we are beginning to convert into goods the value of money obligations, it is almost impossible to form an idea of the importance of the payments which have been made by Germany. I do not want to enter into a discussion of the question of what may have been the real value of those payments to the creditor countries that received them. It is natural that when goods to the value of several billion are thrown on the market, there is not only a fall in prices, but there is also a noneconomic utilization of those goods in the countries that receive them. Therefore the profit realized by those who receive the goods is considerably inferior to the loss suffered by those who provide them. [. . .]

It is often said that Germany would become a formidable competitor with other countries if she were freed from her political debts. I am firmly convinced that those fears are based on absolutely erroneous considerations. The lightening of the budget charges produced by inflation through the reduction of the service of internal debts only constitutes an apparent alleviation of the burden. Inflation has also destroyed private fortunes and savings; indeed, all the resources in capital which the German economic system had at its disposal. The lightening of the budgetary burden was therefore illusory. A comparison between the fiscal charges in Germany and in other countries is problematic, because such a complete confiscation of fortunes as has taken place in Germany has not occurred elsewhere.

Inflation has therefore lessened the capacity for competition of the entire German economic system. The state and private economy have lost their reserves. The destruction of those reserves of capital was followed by the contracting of fresh debts too rapidly and on too large a scale. The consequences became intolerable to the national economy. Agriculture and industry found themselves faced with the impossible task of meeting interest rates of ten percent and more for short-term credits, and only very little less for long-term credits. In addition, they are both crushed under the burden of taxation and fiscal charges. The present high level of public expenditure is to a large extent made necessary by social-service obligations. On the other hand, the economic depression has automatically confronted the state with obligations which formerly fell upon private shoulders. The state has only assumed those obligations in view of its duty to prevent social distress and violent disturbances of public order which such distress threatens to bring about. For all these reasons, the German government has gone to the very limit in the utilization of its resources and reserves. Today the public and private economies are once more at the point where they found themselves after the inflation, that is to say, they are devoid of any reserves and find themselves faced with an unemployment problem unprecedented in history. It is obvious that an industrial debtor country devoid of reserves, as Germany is now, could not constitute a menace to its competitors for a long time to come.

32

HEINRICH HAUSER

The Unemployed

First published as "Die Arbeitslosen," *Die Tat* 25, no. 1 (April 1933), 76–78.

An almost unbroken chain of homeless men extends the whole length of the great Hamburg-Berlin highway.

There are so many of them moving in both directions, impelled by the wind or making their way against it, that they could shout a message from Hamburg to Berlin by word of mouth.

It is the same scene for the entire two hundred miles, and the same scene repeats itself between Hamburg and Bremen, between Bremen and Kassel, between Kassel and Würzburg, between Würzburg and Munich. All the highways in Germany over which I traveled this year presented the same aspect.

The only people who shouted and waved at me and ran along beside my automobile hoping for a ride during their journey were the newcomers, the youngsters. They were recognizable at once. They still had shoes on their feet and carried knapsacks, like the *Wandervögel*. [. . .]

But most of the hikers paid no attention to me. They walked separately or in small groups with their eyes on the ground. And they had the queer, stumbling gait of barefoot people, for their shoes were slung over their shoulders. Some of them were guild members— carpenters with embroidered wallets, knee breeches, and broad felt hats; milkmen with striped red shirts, and bricklayers with tall black hats—but they were in a minority. Far more numerous were those to whom one could assign no special profession or craft— unskilled young people for the most part who had been unable to find a place for themselves in any city or town in Germany, and who had never had a job and never expected to have one. There was something else that had never been seen before—whole families that had piled all their goods into baby carriages and wheelbarrows that they were pushing along as they plodded forward in dumb despair. It was a whole nation on the march.

I saw them—and this was the strongest impression that the year 1932 left with me—I saw them, gathered into groups of fifty or a hundred men, attacking fields of potatoes. I saw them digging up the potatoes and throwing them into sacks while the farmer who owned the field watched them in despair and the local policeman looked on gloomily from the distance. I saw them staggering toward the lights of the city as night fell, with their sacks on their backs. What did it remind me of? Of the war, of the worst period of starvation in 1917 and 1918, but even then people paid for the potatoes. [. . .]

I entered the huge Berlin municipal lodging house in a northern quarter of the city. [. . .] Dreary barracks extended to the edge of the sidewalk and under their dripping roofs long lines of men were leaning against the wooden walls, waiting in silence and staring at a brick structure across the street.

This wall was the side of the lodging house and it seemed to blot out the entire sky. [. . .] There was an entrance arched by a brick vaulting, and a watchman sat in a little wooden sentry box. His white coat made him look like a doctor. We stood waiting in the corridor. Heavy steam rose from the men's clothes. Some of them sat down on the floor, pulled off their shoes, and unwound the rags that bound their feet. More people were constantly pouring in the door, and we stood closely packed together. Then another door opened. The crowd pushed forward, and people began forcing their way almost eagerly through this door, for it was warm in there. Without knowing it I had already caught the rhythm of the municipal lodging house. It means waiting, waiting, standing around, and then suddenly jumping up.

We now stand in a long hall. [. . .] There under yellow lamps that hang from the ceiling on long wires sit men in white smocks. We arrange ourselves in long lines, each leading up to one of these men, and the mill begins to grind. [. . .]

What does the man in the white smock want to know? All these fellows in white smocks belong to a very special type of official. The way they let the line flow by while they work so smoothly together is facile, lazy, almost elegant. The way they say "Mr." to the down-and-outers from the street is full of ironic politeness. [. . .] The whole impersonal manner of the officials makes them as incomprehensible as a cash register. [. . .]

Then come the questions. When and where were you born, and where have you come from? Name of your parents? Ever been in a municipal lodging house before? Where have you spent the last three nights? Where did you work last? Have you begged? The first impression that these questions and answers make on me is that it is just like the army. [. . .]

My second impression is the helplessness of the men on my side of the bar and the shocking ruthlessness with which the men on the other side of the bar insult this helplessness. Eight out of every ten men on my side of the bar are young fellows and about a third of these are mere boys. [. . .]

The official presses a white card into my hand and tells me to go to the desk of another clerk with the sign, "adjuster," over it. While waiting in line I look at my white card. It is divided into squares and has my name at the top and all kinds of mysterious symbols underneath. [. . .] I do not remember what the "adjuster" said to me—there was some inconsistency in my papers, I believe. [. . .] [Hauser was sent on to a police examiner, but eventually was cleared.]

When I come out I am holding a check that has been given me for a night's sleep and food in the lodging house. [. . .] The bare walls of the room that we have entered are lined with iron bedsteads. There are no windows but a sloping roof with skylights that reminds me of a factory. We sit down on the bedsteads along the middle of the room, closely packed together. A voice near me whispers, "What was the matter with you, buddy?"

"My papers."

"Say, you had luck to get out again. They kept the fellow that went in with you. He spent his dole of eighteen marks [about $4.30] in two days. Oh, boy, think of it! Eighteen marks! . . ."

I look at the clock again. Our reception ceremony lasted an hour and a half, and we now sit here another half hour, which makes two hours. They do not make it easy for you to get supper and a bed in a municipal lodging house.

4
Coming to Terms with Democracy

AFTER THE UNIFICATION of the Italian peninsula in 1870, a wise politician quipped, "Italy has been made; now is the time to make Italians." After the founding of the Weimar Republic, a similar task was at hand: the making of enthusiastic republicans from the disgruntled masses who resented the new system as a foreign importation thrust on them only by defeat in the war. Many leading intellectuals took it upon themselves to promote this transformation, even if they were convinced of its necessity more by their intellect than their heart. Dubbed *Vernunftrepublikaner* because they supported it on rational grounds, but not on emotional ones, they sought to convince the German public to accept the new order.

Some intellectuals, like the prominent historian Friedrich Meinecke, tried to persuade their compatriots that the authoritarian polity created by Bismarck had contained a hidden flaw from the beginning. Over time, that polity had grown brittle and unresponsive, needing only a small stimulus from without to topple it and permit the emergence of the democracy latent within. Others, like the novelist Heinrich Mann, stressed the need to infuse the republic with the spiritual energy it needed, claiming that the intellectuals had a special role in the reconciliation of *Geist* with politics. In a speech to the Council of Intellectual Workers in December 1918 [doc. 13], Mann exhorted his listeners to leave behind class conflict and considerations of power, and to replace them with higher values such as those inspiring Wilsonian democracy.

More sober observers, like the sociologist Max Weber, appealed to those who were called to political life to employ an "ethics of responsibility," sensitive to all the consequences of their actions, rather than "an ethics of intentions," in which any means could be justified in the name of an ultimate end. In his celebrated lecture at the University of Munich, "Politics as a Vocation," delivered only a short time before his death in 1920, Weber cautioned that a "polar night of icy darkness and severity" lay ahead, requiring heroic leadership with the patience to combine passion and judgment.

Still other advice came from the prominent theologian Ernst Troeltsch, who, in a speech of December 1918, reminded his listeners that democracy was not entirely alien to German tradition, as evidenced by the revolution of 1848. Drawing on the example of America, he also claimed that political democracy was perfectly compatible with social conservatism and need not be the prelude to more radical upheaval. An even more striking attempt to legitimate the republic in conservative terms by a recently converted *Vernunftrepublikaner* came in October 1922 when the novelist Thomas Mann unexpectedly made a plea for "The German Republic." Mann, unlike his brother Heinrich, had been a nationalist supporter of the war effort, which he had justified in the name of German *Kultur* in his mammoth *Reflections of a Nonpolitical Man* (1918). Now rejecting the mandarin stance of being "above politics," he sought to win his audience, which included the skeptical writer Gerhart Hauptmann, over to the life-affirming qualities of republican virtue. In so doing Mann anticipated his literary farewell to the lure of decadence and irrationality in his novel of 1924, *The Magic Mountain.*

Not all German intellectuals were as sanguine about the republic's chances or as inclined to be its supporters. Cynical about the residues of the old regime that remained in power, critics like Kurt Tucholsky, a leading member of the "homeless left" centered around the journal *Die Weltbühne,* refused to abandon their negative stance. In "We Nay-Sayers" written in March 1919, Tucholsky defiantly defended the intellectuals' obligation to forego mere realism in the name of more exacting standards of political decency. In 1924 Carl von Ossietzky, his *Weltbühne* colleague, voiced similar skepticism about defending the republic in its present hollow form. When Ossietzky was sentenced to prison for printing revelations about the illegal rearmament of the aviation industry in 1929, Tucholsky vigorously protested that his journal would continue to expose the truth about the republic no matter the consequences. Documented proof of the obstacles to democracy in the judicial system had been available as early as 1922 when the *Weltbühne* writer Emil J. Gumbel published his shocking survey of reactions to political murder, showing that the murders committed by the right, many more in number than those committed by the left, were given far more modest punishment. A year later the left-liberal journal *Das Tagebuch* bemoaned the collective amnesia following the assassination of no less a figure than the foreign minister, Walther Rathenau, who had been shot down scarcely a year before.

Still, with all of its flaws, the republic did have a functioning democratic system until it was suspended in 1930 by presidential decree. It was supported largely by three parties in the middle of the political spectrum, the so-called Weimar Coalition, consisting of the Social Democratic Party (SPD), the Catholic Center Party, and the German People's Party (DVP). Concluding this section are excerpts from their respective party platforms. Despite fundamental differences in outlook, they all shared a belief in the republic, a belief sadly lacking in parties further to their left and right.

33

FRIEDRICH MEINECKE

[On German History]

First published in *Deutsche Allgemeine Zeitung* (November 20, 1918).

Many may have thought in recent days of the catastrophe of 1807 when a new, freer state structure arose from the defeat of the old state system. Much is in fact similar today, yet again much is very different. We have experienced no Jena and no Prenzlau, but victory upon victory. The Prussian Germany created by Bismarck can retire from the field of battle with great honor and give up the now pointless struggle against a superior world power. The old system ended its days with a monumental show of strength. But this show of strength is not to be *exclusively* attributed to the old system. [. . .]

The Prussian Germany organized by Bismarck was indeed an advance over the Prussia of 1806, a legacy of Frederick the Great in that it was from the beginning more capable of allying with new forces in the life of the nation. This national life was itself dynamically superior in strength and richness to the narrow, still-semimedieval national existence of the period before 1806. For this expanded capacity to forge alliances, the Bismarckian system had its greater broad-mindedness to thank, as well as its liberal and democratic concessions and safety valves, its social reform and, in general, its ability to keep pace with certain modern needs and developments. [. . .] However, even the Bismarckian creation one day had to confront its majestic decline; its accumulated failings had to become so evident and severe that it could no longer be maintained; new forms of national integration would replace it. [. . .] Bismarck's system was for its time a miracle of integration of state and nation, old and new historical forces, but, because it remained in effect an authoritarian state, it fell short of the last and highest form of national coherence. It bore within a hidden fissure that Bismarck himself expanded by adopting the wrong tactic in his struggle against social democracy, by driving the masses out of the state. Bismarck, as Friedrich Engels expressed it in 1887, "did not understand the historical situation he himself produced." Bismarck was wrong in both his assessment and his treatment of the mass forces of modern social and economic life, whose development his own creation, the Bismarckian empire, served to foster. He had to admit to himself that even the modern war for existence, which he perceptively foresaw, would one day demand a different structure for the state than the one he bequeathed it. He had to admit to himself that the modern war all but automatically pressed toward democracy, because one cannot conduct a war over the long run with masses—both those who fight and those who work for the war in the factories—unless one also includes them, over the long run, in politics. The modern national war leads with necessary, unrelenting consistency to the national state. [. . .]

And thus did we experience in this war, with the one following quickly upon the other, the extreme heights and limitations of the capacities of the hitherto existing Prussian German military state. In the six months from spring to autumn 1918 everything came dramatically together, and our fate became linked with the name of Ludendorff. A powerful military dynamic, built and nourished by the forces of old Prussian Germany, raised itself to grandiose plans and deeds to gain the desired "peace through victory." At the same time it encompassed the world of the conquered east to create there political protectorates and dependencies, and in the process its power came to exceed the political leadership of the nation, to hinder—whether consciously or not is debatable—the democratization that the latter had begun. For, so it was said at the time, the dissolution of the chamber of deputies—the sole means then available for pushing through electoral reform in Prussia—was not to be advised during the western offensive. But this entire system of goals, intentions, and desires in the realm of power politics suddenly failed because it had the audacity to reach "beyond its authority," because it ignored that fissure that had existed in the national organism since Bismarck, because it failed to recognize that power politics requires giving notice of decisions and of internal political restructuring, and because it failed to note that a central European sphere of influence with a military and undemocratic structure could not long preserve itself as an island in the sea of a fully democratized world. [. . .] Could the precipitous fall of this system have been prevented? Would a peaceful, gradual reformation and modernization over the course of the last decades through farsighted, wise, and powerful statesmen have been possible? [. . .]

It is not, however, the time for answering the ultimate theoretical questions of this sort posed by our present situation. Our constitutional reform was possible in the fashion in which it transpired due to the pressure of the international situation, for which the old system was no longer fit. But that elements very capable of development, forward pointing, and ready for reform already existed in our now-bygone *ancien regime* is demonstrated by the fact that the constitutional transformation—the substance of which represents an enormous revolution—despite its abruptness, was completed with astounding calm, carried by the judgment and unanimity of all legislative elements. It therefore fell into the laps of the people like an overripe fruit.

34

ERNST TROELTSCH

The German Democracy

First published as "Die deutsche Demokratie (December 29, 1918)," in *Spektatorbriefe. Aufsätze über die deutsche Revolution und die Weltpolitik 1918–1922*, ed. Hans Baron (Tübingen: J. C. B. Mohr, 1924), 301–313.

Overnight we have become the most radical democracy in Europe, and are obliged as well to consider it the relatively moderate solution to the problem of our political life. On closer inspection, it did not, admittedly, happen overnight. Democracy is the natural consequence of modern population density, combined with the education of the population necessary to nurture it, with industrialization, mobilization, defense preparations, and politicization. Democracy has been suppressed in Prussia since 1848 by the constitution and the military system, but it struggled constantly and powerfully for supremacy against both. [. . .] It fell solely to the terrible world war to deliver democracy to victory, which moreover introduced the danger that the development will not stop at democracy because the "dictatorship of the proletariat" will assume the form of the terrorist domination by a minority.

Questions arise whether this socialist revolution was avoidable; whether the initiatives of Prince Max's government against the resistance of the old ruling strata were truly capable of being executed, including the doubtlessly great and sweeping social reforms;

or whether it would be in fact impossible to accomplish anything without the complete destruction of the old structure. It remains impossible today to answer these questions; perhaps it will never be possible. It is certain that the revolution broke the backbone of the Reich in the most terrible moment of its history, when it would have had greater need of such a structure than at any other time. It is certain furthermore that the genuine democraticization of the Reich through proletarian class domination, even if it remains mixed with the remnants of the old order, has been delayed. It is certain finally that an order capable of functioning in domestic and foreign affairs and of garnering recognition can be regained only by way of a decisive return to both the democratic principles of participation by and justice for all classes and to the democratic means of constitutional formation on the basis of honest majorities. [. . .]

It means principled antimilitaristic thinking and an approach based on the League of Nations as the sole means of maintaining our existence and rebuilding within the geographical borders at that time. [. . .] We have to adapt ourselves to a wholly new situation, which can *only* be secured externally through the idea of the League of Nations and internally through a new order renovated along democratic and social lines, if Germany is not to become a volcano of misery, ever subject to eruption, as well as a focus of civil wars and an endless slave rebellion against despots.

It means secondly that the Bismarckian creation of the Reich has been worn down to its foundations, and, since the latter ultimately rest on the military and bureaucratic state of old Prussia, that the entire political order and formation since the reorganization of the German territorial state through absolutism is undergoing dissolution or at least total transformation. [. . .] The Reich as a whole, as well as in its individual parts, must be rebuilt with a new administration and new constitution, the army newly organized with a social foundation—the German solution must be expanded into the pan-German solution. [. . .]

That means thirdly that democracy is no longer a pure question of political and moral principle, nor is it any longer the weapon of the aspiring classes who employ the moral element of the democratic idea to the advantage of their claims on state and society. It has departed completely from the sphere of doctrine and the doctrinaire and become a practical necessity. [. . .] Democracy can unite broad social strata to facilitate enormous productivity, can supply a foundation of love and affection for the common state, can bring into greater play the dignity and personality of each citizen, can root responsibility and initiative in individual will, and can effect a selection of fresh talents and will: all things of the highest ethical value and most fruitful political significance. At the same time it is of course threatened by the dangers of anarchy and leveling, of petty conflicts of interest, and of the artful spread of mediocrity that holds everything down. [Alexis de] Tocqueville already saw all of this in the third decade of the previous century and expressed it in his famous book, *Democracy in America*. He also drew the logical conclusion that the triumph of democracy is inevitable because it corresponds to modern society and that therefore its great and noble aspects must be advanced. Precisely that, however, is the issue here. *Ours is not to wish and imagine, but to act and shape.* And as acutely as one looks for the strains on democracy in the modern, overpopulated, and mobilized big cities does one gain a sense for the great and noble human meaning that it can contain, and so encourage the latter rather than frightening others with its dangers and defects. [. . .] We Germans have no talent for democracy, none at all for politics, or, what amounts to the same thing, we have not been trained for it by our history and are unprepared. The old Germany's cities and villages long ago possessed republican and democratic spirit enough; the detached parts in Switzerland and the Netherlands developed it quite strongly. We must be as capable of it as they, and must at all events learn it. We *will* learn it, even at the cost of suffering and pain and much confusion. [. . .]

But does this fundamental upheaval also imply an upheaval of German spirit and German culture? This is the question that will lie most heavily on the hearts of those who esteem German greatness in the achievements of the spirit more than anywhere else and for whom the path to our poets and thinkers, to romanticism and humanism, extends from the great German empire of the Middle Ages, as from the cities of the late Middle Ages, through Luther and the Reformation. Without this historical context and without a homeland for the soul in our history, so filled with sorrow and yet so full of soul, with all of its secret nooks and violent outbreaks—without this there is for us no German spirit and no future for the German soul. Is all that to decline with the old state and its glorious memories, to make room now for a new spirit? [. . .]

It is merely a matter of finding the actual points of reference in the first place, elaborating them, and lending them emotional and imaginative power, which, indeed, is an on-going process. Everywhere ideas of community and unity as well as ideas of personal dignity and responsibility, must be formed out of the nature of the thing, and these ideas will constantly seek and find points of contact with the particular, overall cultural spirit dominant at any given time. But the spirit and its cultural content is never exhausted by this achievement, indeed is not even primarily located within it. It appears so only in times of revolutionary struggle, when the political–social goal being pursued tends to become unified, adding the impetus of a universal, humanitarian dimension that carries everyone along with it. [. . .] In this respect the greatest and healthiest democracy in the world, North America, is thoroughly instructive in its antithesis. That democracy is conservative and lacking in any eternal dogma of revolution, in any welding of a revolutionary disposition in principle with a spiritual-ethical conviction. [. . .] Thus is a radical democracy united with the complete freedom of an extremely conservative customary practice and with a spiritual life that nourishes itself from its own sources and that moreover increasingly exploits the spiritual accomplishments of the entire world for its own purposes.

So will it and must it become in Germany. Our classical spiritual heritage also offers sufficient lines of connection to a spiritual-ethical conception of democracy. Otherwise, however, spirit and culture, the depth of the soul, continue to remain exactly what they were. [. . .] The relics of the German spirit in ethics, science, art, poetry, and music, its medieval and its classical magnificence: all of this remains for us a source and inspiration as before. And the more deeply the new German state is necessarily grounded in the life of the people, the more seriously will its spiritual life be obliged and able to strive for the force and plenitude, the dignity and capacity to adapt, the independence and formal security of the German spirit. [. . .]

As dark and difficult as this future might be, it can also become a reconstruction, and above all it is no break with the German spirit and its history. We want to ground ourselves anew in this history and draw from it its great treasures in order to stamp it with a new vitality and unity. In this respect we want to establish the ideal of a conservative democracy, since novelty will be sufficiently looked after on its own. And, contrary to the despondency and embitterment of so many, we side with the conclusion of Goethe's *Wilhelm Meister:* "We bid you to hope."

35

MAX WEBER

Politics as a Vocation

Published as "Politik als Beruf," in Max Weber, *Gesammelte politische Schriften* (Munich: Duncker und Humblot, 1921), 396–450. Speech delivered at Munich University, 1918.

What can politics as a vocation offer in the way of inner satisfaction, and which personal qualities does it presuppose in anyone who devotes himself to it?

Well, it offers first of all the sense of power. Even in positions which are, formally speaking, modest, the professional politician can feel himself elevated above the everyday level by the sense of exercising influence over men, of having a share in power over their lives, but above all by the sense of having a finger on the pulse of historically important events. But the question which he has to face is this: through which personal qualities can he hope to do justice to this power (however narrow its limits in his particular case) and so to the responsibility it lays on him? At this point we enter the domain of ethical questions; for it is in this domain that the question arises: what kind of man must one be to venture to lay hands on the spokes of the wheel of history?

Three qualities above all, it might be said, are of decisive importance for the politician: passion, a sense of responsibility, and judgment. By passion I mean *realistic* passion—a passionate commitment to a realistic cause, to the god or demon in whose domain it lies. I do not mean passion in the sense of that state of mind which my late friend Georg Simmel used to call "sterile excitement"—a state that is characteristic of a certain kind of intellectual, especially of Russian intellectuals (though perhaps not all of them!), and which now plays such a large part amongst our own intellectuals in this carnival that is dignified with the proud name of a revolution. It is a kind of 'romanticism of the intellectually interesting' which lacks any realistic sense of responsibility and runs away to nothing. For it is not enough merely to have the passion, however genuine. That alone does not make a politician, unless it is used to further some real cause and so makes a *sense of responsibility* towards this cause the ultimate guide of his behavior. And that requires the decisive psychological quality of the politician—*judgment*—the ability to contemplate things as they are with inner calm and composure before allowing them to affect one's actions, or, in other words, an attitude of *detachment* towards things and people. Lack of detachment is one of the mortal sins for every politician, and one of those qualities that would condemn our rising generation of intellectuals to political impotence if they were to cultivate it. The problem therefore is simply how hot passion and cool judgment can be made to combine within the same personality. Politics is made with the head, not with other parts of the body or mind. And dedication to politics can only be born from passion and nourished by it, if it is not to be a frivolous intellectual game but an authentic human activity. But that firm discipline of the personality which is the hallmark of the passionate politician and distinguishes him from the political dilettante who is merely possessed by sterile excitement is achievable only through the habit of detachment, in every sense of that word. The strength of a political personality is to be found above all in the possession of these qualities. [. . .]

It is undeniably true, indeed a fundamental truth of all history (though not one to be explored more closely here) that the final result of political activity often, nay regularly, bears very little relation to the original intention: often indeed it is quite the opposite of what was first intended. But, for this very reason, if the activity is to have any kind of inner balance, the intention of serving some real cause must be present. It is a matter for the politician's own fundamental beliefs what *form* this cause, for the sake of which he seeks power and uses power, should take. He can seek to promote national or universal, social-cum-ethical or cultural, secular or religious causes. He can be carried away by enthusiasm for 'progress' (in whatever sense) or he can coolly reject this sort of belief. He can insist on standing firm in the service of an ideal, or he can reject such pretensions on principle and choose to serve the more external goals of everyday life. At any rate, some belief or other must always be there. Otherwise, there will weigh on him in the event, it is perfectly correct to point out, the curse of futility to which all finite creatures are subject, even in what seem from the outside to be his greatest successes.

With what has just been said we have already begun to consider the last problem concerning us this evening: the ethos of politics as a cause. What sense of vocation can we find in the profession of politics itself, quite independently of any goals it may serve within the general moral economy of life? In which area of ethics, so to speak, is it at home? Here, to be sure, we find a confrontation of ultimate conceptions of life, between which in the end a choice must be made. [...]

But what is the nature of the real relation between ethics and politics? Have they, as has sometimes been said, nothing whatever to do with each other? Or, on the contrary, is it correct to say that the same ethical standards apply in political life as in every other area of activity? The view has sometimes been taken that these two propositions present us with mutually exclusive alternatives: either the one or the other is correct. But is it true that any ethical system in the world could impose identical rules of conduct on sexual, commercial, familial, and professional relationships; on one's relations with one's wife, greengrocer, son, competitor, friend, and defendant? Should it really matter so little, in deciding on the ethical standards required in politics, that the specific instrument of politics is power, backed up by *violence*? Don't we see that the bolshevik and Spartacist ideologues achieve exactly the same results as any military dictator you care to mention, precisely because they use this essential instrument of politics? What difference is there between domination by the workers' and soldiers' soviets and that by any ruler of the old regime, apart from the persons of the power holders and their dilettantism? What difference is there between the polemics of most representatives of the so-called new morality against the opponents whom they criticize and those of any demagogue you care to mention? Someone will say: the nobility of their intentions. Fine! But what we are talking about here is the means they use; and the opponents whom they attack claim likewise, with equal honesty from their point of view, that their ultimate intentions are noble. "They who take up the sword shall perish by the sword," and war is war wherever it is fought.

Well then, what about the ethics of the Sermon on the Mount? The Sermon on the Mount, or, in other words, the absolute ethics of the Gospel, is a more serious matter than it is believed to be by those who are nowadays so keen to quote it. It is not something to trifle with. What has been said about the scientific principle of causality holds as well for the Sermon: it is not a cab that one can hail at will, to get in or out of as one thinks fit. What it really means, if it is not to be reduced to a set of trivialities, is: all or nothing. [...]

Finally, the duty to tell the truth. For absolute ethics this is unconditional. The conclusion has therefore been drawn that all documents should be published, especially those that lay the blame on one's own country, and that, on the basis of this one-sided publication, guilt should be acknowledged unilaterally, unconditionally, and without regard for the consequences. The politician will find that the result of this is not that truth is advanced but rather that it is obscured by the misuses to which it is put and the passions which are unleashed; that the only approach that could be fruitful is for impartial umpires methodically to set out the evidence in a way that takes all sides into account. Every other procedure can have consequences for the nation that adopts it which would be impossible to make good even after several decades. But absolute ethics is not even concerned with consequences.

That is the decisive point. We must be clear that all activity that is governed by ethical standards can be subsumed under one of two maxims, which are fundamentally different from, and irreconcilably opposed to, each other. The ethical standards may either be based on intentions or on responsibility. Not that an ethic of intentions is the same as irresponsibility or an ethic of responsibility the same as indifference to intentions. Naturally, there is no question of either of these two things. But there is a profound antithesis between actions governed by the ethics of intention, where, to put it in religious language, "The Christian acts rightly and leaves the outcome to God," and actions governed by the ethics of responsibility, where one is answerable for the (foreseeable) consequences of one's actions. [. . .]

No system of ethics in the world can avoid facing the fact that "good" ends in many cases can be achieved only at the price of morally dubious or at least dangerous means and the possibility, or even the probability, of evil side effects. No system of ethics in the world can make it possible to decide when and to what extent the morally good end sanctifies the morally dangerous means and side effects.

For politics, the essential means is violence. The significance of the tension between means and ends from the ethical point of view can be judged from the fact that, as is well known, the revolutionary socialists of the Zimmerwald faction, even during the war, professed a principle that could be formulated in the following pregnant words: "If the choice that faces us is between several more years of war followed by revolution and immediate peace with no revolution, then we choose several more years of war!" [. . .]

It is of course simply ridiculous for those on this side to express moral revulsion for the power politicians of the old regime on account of their use of the same means—however completely justified the rejection of their ends may be.

It is on this very problem of the sanctification of the means by the end that the ethics of intention in general seems to have run aground. Indeed, the only logical course open to it is to repudiate all activity which involves the use of morally dangerous means. I repeat, this is the only logical course. [. . .]

The problem of political ethics is definitely not simply a modern phenomenon arising from the rejection of religious belief which originated in the hero cult of the Renaissance. All religions have grappled with it with very different degrees of success, and after what has been said it could not have been otherwise. It is the specific use by groups of human beings of the means of legitimate violence as such that determines the particular character of all ethical problems of politics.

Anyone who accepts the use of this means to whatever ends (and every politician does so) is thereby committed to accepting its specific consequences. This is particularly true of the warrior of faith—religious or revolutionary.

Anyone who wants to take up politics in general, and especially politics as a vocation, must be conscious of these ethical paradoxes and of his own responsibility for the changes that may be brought about in himself under pressure from them. I repeat, he is meddling with the infernal powers that lie in wait for him in every use of violence. The great virtuosi of other-worldly love of mankind and saintliness, whether from Nazareth, Assisi, or the castles of Indian kings, have not employed the instrument of politics, force. Their kingdom was "not of this world." [. . .]

It is true: politics is made with the head, but certainly not only with the head. In that respect those who advocate the ethics of intention are absolutely right. No one can tell anyone else whether they ought to act according to the ethics of intention or the ethics of responsibility, or when they should follow the one and when the other. One thing only can be said. In these days of an excitement which, in your opinion, is not "sterile" (though excitement is certainly not always the same thing as genuine passion), when suddenly the politicians of intention come forward en masse with the watchword, "It is the world that is stupid and vulgar, not me; the responsibility for the consequences doesn't concern me, it concerns the others whom I serve and whose stupidity and vulgarity I shall eradicate," then, I often think, we have to ask first how much inner strength lies behind this ethics of intention. I have the impression that, in nine cases out of ten, I have to do with windbags, who do not really feel what they profess to feel but are simply intoxicating themselves with romantic sensations. This does not interest me very much from the human point of view and impresses me not at all. But it is enormously impressive if a more mature man (whether old or young in years), who feels his responsibility for the consequences genuinely and with all his heart and acts according to the ethics of responsibility, says at whatever point it may be: "Here I stand: I can no other." That is an expression of authentic humanity and stirs one's feelings. For the possibility of this sort of situation occurring at some time or other must indeed exist for any one of us who is not inwardly dead. To that extent, the ethics of intention and the ethics of responsibility are not diametrically opposed but complementary: together they make the true man, the man who can have the "vocation of politics." [. . .]

It is not summer's bloom that lies before us, but first of all a polar night of icy darkness and severity, whichever group may be outwardly victorious at present. For where there is nothing, it is not only the Kaiser but the proletarian too who has lost his rights. When this night slowly begins to fade, who of those will be left still living whose spring has now, to all appearances, been clad in such luxuriant blossom? And what will by then have become of the inner lives of you all? Embitterment or philistinism, simple, apathetic acceptance of the world and of one's profession or, third and far from least common, mystical escapism in those who are gifted in that direction or, as is frequently and regrettably the case, who force themselves into it to follow the fashion? In every such case I shall conclude that such people were not suited to their field of activity, not able to cope with the world as it really is and with the routine of their daily lives. Objectively and factually, in their innermost hearts they did not have the vocation for politics which they thought they had. They would have done better to promote brotherly love between men in a simple, straightforward way; and for the rest to have worked in a purely down-to-earth way at their everyday tasks.

Politics is a matter of boring down strongly and slowly through hard boards with passion and judgment together. It is perfectly true and confirmed by all historical experience that the possible cannot be achieved without continually reaching out towards that which is impossible in this world. But to do that a man must be a leader and furthermore, in a very straightforward sense of the word, a hero. Even those who are not both must arm themselves with that stoutness of heart which is able to confront even the shipwreck of all their hopes, and they must do this now—otherwise they will not be in a position even to accomplish what is possible today. Only someone who is confident that he will not be shattered if the world, seen from his point of view, is too stupid or too vulgar for what he wants to offer it; someone who can say in spite of that, "but still!"—only he has the vocation for politics.

36

KURT TUCHOLSKY

We Nay-Sayers

First published as "Wir Negativen," *Die Weltbühne* 15, no. 12 (March 13, 1919), 279–285.

> *How gentle and tender it is here! It wills well-being, and quiet enjoyment, and mild pleasures for itself, for others, for all. This is the theme of Anacreon. Thus by allurement and flattery it works its way into life; but when it is in life, then misery introduces crime, and crime misery; horror and desolation fill the scene. This is the theme of Aeschylus.* SCHOPENHAUER[1]

We at the *Weltbühne* are always being reproached for saying no to everything and not being positive enough. We only reject and criticize and even foul our own German nest. And we have fought—this is taken to be the worst—hate with hate, violence with violence, fist with fist.

The people airing their views in this magazine are in fact always the same ones. And it bears pointing out for once how sincerely we all agree, even though we barely know each other. Some issues of the *Weltbühne* have every appearance of having been created in long editorial meetings, but the truth is that the editor produced them altogether on his own. It therefore seems to me that the reproach that we are negative applies to intellectually independent men, innocent of mutual influence. But are we negative? Are we really?

I want finally to pull out all the drawers of our German dresser to see what is to be found in them.

The revolution. If revolution means merely collapse, then it was one; but no one should expect the ruins to look any different from the old building. We have suffered failure and hunger, and those responsible just walked away. And the people remain: they had their old flags torn down, but had no new ones.

The bourgeois citizen. Citizenship is—how often this has been misunderstood!—a classification of the spirit; one is a citizen by virtue of predisposition not birth, and least of all on account of profession. These middle-class citizens of Germany are antidemocratic through and through—their like scarcely exist in any other country—and that is the seat of all misery. It simply is not true that they were oppressed before the revolution; it was their deepest need to look up from below, eyes true as a dog's, to submit to forcible correction and to feel the strong hand of God's guardians! Now the guardians are gone and the citizens are chilled by their sense that something is missing. The censor has been abolished; obedient, they continue to pray the old prayers, babbling anxiously as if nothing

---

1. Arthur Schopenhauer, *The World as Will and Representation,* vol. 2, trans. E. F. Payne (New York: Dover, 1966), 569.

had happened. They know no middle between patriarchal domination and the banditry of a degenerate bolshevism, for they are unfree. They accept everything so long as they are allowed to continue earning money. And to that we are supposed to say yes?

The officer. We have demonstrated in these pages why and to what extent the German officer failed in the war, and of what betrayal of his people he is guilty. It is not a matter of social status—attacks against a collective are always unjust—but a matter of the bad spirit that animates the status and has eaten its way deep into the citizenry. The lieutenant's and his—we still say it—spirit was a German ideal, and the reserve officer needed little time to grow into the uniform. It was the infernal desire to tread upon one's fellows without penalty, the German desire to appear to be more in service than one was in private life, the gratification of putting on airs for the wife or the lover; and down below grovels a human being. A certain devotion to duty (in a spirit that also characterized many of his subordinates) should not be denied, but duty was done, often enough, only on the basis of insatiability and the worst sort of avarice. The young gentlemen into whose character I acquired some insight during the war made no outstanding impression. But it is not, of course, a matter merely of individuals, and you can't expect improvement if no one says so now! Now, for later, it makes no sense; now, for later, once the new army is established, it would be superfluous to leaf once more through the sins of the old regime. It must be hammered into the Germans that it must never happen again, and the message must be given to all, for indeed it was not the sin of particular reactionary circles but of all: all were involved! The wretchedness of the soldier—and with it the wretchedness of all "underlings" in Germany—was not a consequence of political conviction: it was one of too little culture. The worst instincts were awakened in the unchained citizens of the middle class; the state filled them with the authority of a superior. They did not deserve it. And to that we should say yes?

The civil servant. What do you think of an administration in which the civil servant is more important than the procedures and the procedures more important than the thing in question? How the old apparatus creaks and how impressively it swaggers! What a bother it was with all those offices and little desk sitters! What rapture when one could give orders! Of all the other offices—and there really were so many—the sitter in this one was stifled: now for once he gets his chance! Meanwhile the thing itself drowned in regulations and decrees; the little cabals and the constant frictions took up entire human lives. And the taxpayer was defenseless against his own creation. And to that we should say yes?

The politician. Politics in this country can be defined as the accomplishment of economic goals by means of legislation. Politics here was a matter of venal office holding, not of the spirit. It was reeled off and pulled apart in precinct clubs, and, against the workers, everyone else stood as one. Forgotten was the spirit, the basis for arriving at proposals and laws; forgotten the underlying mentality that, stimulus and motive in one, was what made what one wanted understandable and explicable. The diplomat of the old school proved a poor manager; "he lacks a modern spirit," everyone said. Now the businessman is to take his place. But he lacks it too. There commenced a wild overestimation of the economic. Feudal remnants and traders tussled over influence in the state, which in reality was supposed to devolve upon each under the leadership of the intellectuals. And to that we should say yes?

The screeches of the middle-class citizen, to whom proper politics is nothing more than interference in business, do not surprise us. That intellectuals inveigh against us does.

Where is the knowledge of the intellect ultimately to lead if its carriers do not for once clamber down from the heights of wisdom to apply its results to daily life and attempt to form the latter in its image? Nothing is more embarrassing or hated among the Germans than intellectuality become concrete. You are permitted everything: to advance the most dangerous demands *in abstracto,* to foment theoretical revolutions, to depose dear God himself—but the tax laws, they would rather keep that to themselves. They have an uncannily delicate scent and the most reliable instinct for everything capable of disturbing their dreary industriousness; their mistrust is immense, their antipathy insurmountable. They literally smell whether your loves and hates get along with their colonial import shops. If they don't: God have mercy on you!

Here we have a case of will confronting will. No result, no goal on this earth is won according to the logic of proof *ex argumentis.* The goal favored by the emotions is everywhere established in advance; the arguments follow as apology to the mind, as a parlor game for the intellect. Never yet has one persuaded the other with logic. Will confronts will here: as to the goals, we are agreed with others of reasonable mind—I believe what they struggle against in us does not concern the struggle but the tactics.

But how should we approach low-browed louts and iron-hard farm hands except with clubs? That has been the great misery and distress of this country for centuries: that one presumed it possible to acquire unequivocal force with piercing intellect. If those of us who have peered behind the scenes, those of us who believe that the world as it is cannot be the ultimate goal of humanity, have no executor of our intellectual disposition, then we are damned eternally to live our lives with journeymen hawking their wares, where there remains to us only permission to stroll among our books, ink, and paper. It is so endlessly fruitless, if one wants to build, to believe it possible to forego the negative activity of tearing down. Let us be concrete. A speech by [Friedrich] Naumann in Weimar obligates us to absolutely nothing; the resolution of some local council reveals the citizen in all his nakedness.

The unqualified solidarity of all money-earners must be opposed by the equally unqualified solidarity of the intellectuals. It will not do to perform a theater of struggle before grinning citizens; such mere appearance prompts them only to pose their incessant questions: may we continue to haggle or may we not? May we go on profiteering in our cliques and coteries or may we not? Only the prompting will be heard, no metaphysical truth and no critical error.

Has everything already been forgotten? Are we already slipping back into our comfortable trot where peace and quiet is the first and final duty? Already the stale saying is everywhere stirring the air: "It could not have been that bad." "Your good husband has died from pneumonia?" says the man, "well, it could not have been that bad!"

It was that bad. And surely no one would attempt again to claim that the "pioneer work of the German businessman" will "get us out of it!" We are ridiculed the world over for having hidden our best talents deep in the countryside and for having sent our mediocre ones abroad. But already the voices make themselves heard, those trying to persuade the German that everything will set itself right, if he would only deliver cheap goods. That is not what we want! We no longer want to be used because our young people have underbid everyone else in foreign parts, and because everyone here toiled but did not work. We want to be respected for our own sake.

To be respected in the world we must first undertake a thorough cleaning at home. Are we fouling our own nest? But an Augean stable cannot be fouled, and it is nonsense to put an old hayloft on a crumbling roof and then sound the national anthem from above.

We should make positive proposals. But all the positive proposals in the world come to naught if a genuine honesty does not pervade the land. The reforms we have in mind are not to be achieved through regulations, nor through new national agencies from which everyone today, each within his own specialization, anticipates salvation. We do not believe it suffices to establish a great card catalogue and an extensive personnel and then work the field with it. We believe that what is essential in the world exists behind the scenes and that a decent cast of mind can come to terms with every regulation, even with the worst, and deal with it. Without it, however, nothing is accomplished.

What we need is this decent cast of mind.

We cannot yet say yes. We cannot reinforce a consciousness that forgets from on high the humanity in human beings. We cannot encourage a people to do its duty only because for every toiler a mirage of honor has been created that only hinders essential work. We cannot say yes to a people who remain today in the frame of mind that, had the war somehow come to a happier end, would have justified our worst fears. We cannot say yes to a country obsessed with collectives and for whom corporate bodies are elevated far above the individual. Collectives merely provide assistance to the individual. We cannot say yes to those whose fruits are now displayed by the younger generation: a lukewarm and vapid species infected with an infantile hunger for power at home and an indifference toward things abroad, more devoted to bars than to bravery, with unspeakable antipathy for all *Sturm und Drang*—no longer bearable today—without fire and without dash, without hate and without love. We are supposed to walk, but our legs are bound with cords. We cannot yet say yes.

Persons utterly devoid of appreciation for a will to rise above daily concerns—here in Germany one calls them *Realpolitiker*—oppose us because we see no salvation in compromise, because we see no salvation in new insignias and new documents of state. We know that ideals cannot be realized, but we also know that nothing has happened, nothing has changed, nothing has been achieved without the fire of ideals. And—precisely this, and correctly, seems a danger to our opponents—we do not believe that the flame of ideals is merely to glow decoratively among the stars. It must burn among us; it must burn in forgotten cellars where the wood louse lives, and burn on the palace rooftops of the rich, burn in the churches where rationalism is busy subverting the old miracles, and burn among the money changers who have made of their little stalls a temple.

We cannot yet say yes. We know only this: with brooms of iron, right now and today we must sweep away whatever in Germany is and has been rotten and born of evil. We will get nowhere hiding our heads in cloth of black, white, and red, whispering anxiously: later, my good sir, later! no fuss just now!

Now.

It is ridiculous to reproach a new movement, now four months old, with having failed to produce the same positive accomplishments of a tradition of three hundred years. We know that.

We confront a Germany full of unrivaled corruption, full of profiteers and sneaks, full of three hundred thousand devils among whom each assumes the right to secure his black self from the effects of revolution. But we mean him, precisely him, and only him.

And we have the opportunity of choice: do we fight him with love or do we fight him with hate? We want to fight with hate out of love. With hate against that fellow who has dared to drink the blood of his countrymen as one drinks wine, raising a glass to his own health and to that of his friends. With hate against the clique to which the disproportionate snatching up of property and the misery of cottage workers appears to be the will of God, which orders proofs from professors purchased for the task that it must be so, and which celebrates friendly idylls on the bent backs of others who languish. We fight in any case with hate. But we fight out of love for the oppressed, who are not always necessarily proletarians, and we love in humans the thought of humanity.

Negative? For four and a half years we have been hearing that terrible yes that called good everything that insolent arrogance ordered done. How delightful was the world! How everything worked, how all were *d'accord,* one heart and no soul; how the artificially adorned landscape moved with uniformed puppets to the glory of our masters! It was the theme of Anacreon. And with a thundering crash it all collapsed, what one earlier thought was iron wasn't even cast iron; the generals get started with their self-justifications, of which they have no need at all for no one wants to be reminded; and the revolutionaries, who came too late and were checked too early, are accused of having caused the misery on which in truth generations had been at work. Negative? Blood and misery and wounds and trampled humanity—it should at least not have been for nothing. Let us continue to say no when necessary. It is the theme of Aeschylus.

37

EMIL JULIUS GUMBEL

Four Years of Political Murder

First published in *Vier Jahre politischer Mord* (Berlin: Verlag der neuen Gesellschaft, 1922), 145–149.

The following lines report on the political murders that have occurred in Germany since November 9, 1918. The murders committed by the left and by the right are equally represented. A case has been taken up when it concerned a premeditated, illegal killing of a well-known German by another German for domestic political motives, whereby the incident is characterized not as mass action but as an individual deed. I have addressed only those cases in which the shooting party did not maintain that he had been attacked by the crowd and where it was not a matter of a lynching by a nameless crowd or some other form of mass action, but instead by a very definite perpetrator.

In the selection of cases I have proceeded much more cautiously in the murders by the right than of those by the left. I have therefore included several cases of the left which had more of the character of riots than of political murders.

I have exercised the greatest possible conscientiousness in regard to the exactness of allegations and attempted in all cases to achieve documentary precision. I have relied on court records, judgments, decisions to quash the proceedings, witness testimony, information from attorneys and from survivors, and, finally, newspaper notices. The court reports I have studied primarily in the right-wing newspapers. In all cases in which the materials were not precise I have written to the relatives and reporters. If the reports were still incomplete, then the cases in question were omitted. Thus I can document beyond question every contention offered here. In principle, I have taken up only those cases in which the victim's name was known to me. Where anonymous cases appear in the text they serve only to illustrate the proceedings in question. I have departed from this principle only in two places.

The status of the respective proceedings was the most difficult to ascertain. It is therefore possible that in cases where no proceedings were known to me that they are in fact pending or that the proceedings were already quashed. On the other hand, I believe that the number of imposed sentences I have listed is complete.

This book can make no claim of having presented all political murders that have occurred in recent years in Germany. I therefore request all readers who know of further cases to write to me in care of the Verlag der neuen Gesellschaft, Berlin-Fichtenau.

The present book is a continuation and expansion of my brochure, *Two Years of Murder*. I had advanced there the contention, among others, that the German judicial system had left over three hundred political murders unpunished and I expected that that could have only one of two effects. Either the judicial system would believe that I was speaking the truth, and then the murderers would be punished or it would believe that I am lying, and then I would be punished as a slanderer. In fact, something else totally unforeseen has occurred.

Although the brochure in no way went without notice, there has not been a single effort on the part of the authorities to dispute the correctness of my contentions. On the contrary, the highest responsible authority, the Reich minister of justice, expressly confirmed my contentions on more than one occasion. Nevertheless, not a single murderer has been punished.

Berlin, October 16, 1922

POLITICAL DIFFERENTIATION OF MURDER TECHNIQUES

How is the enormous difference between 354 murders by the right and 22 by the left to be explained? It would be false, in my judgment, simply to say, "Leftists are just morally superior." This cannot be concluded primarily because only a single type of crime has been researched. Thus property crimes, for example, have not been drawn into the compass of observation. Of them one could perhaps presume that, given the social structure, they are to be found more frequently in the leftist camp than in the rightist. Nor admittedly may it be forgotten that crimes against property, in contrast to crimes against the person, also have a social component, that they are for the most part produced by the fact of the present distribution of property. And in a social order that eases the individual's struggle for existence they would surely decrease considerably in number. That, however, crimes against property committed by the right are in no way rare can be seen from the numerous plunderings and robbings of the corpses. Thus, of 184 victims of fatal "accidents" in Munich, in 68 cases the corpses were plundered.

The genuine distinction between the two camps is in my judgment not a moral but a technical one. The adherents of leftist parties have gone through decades of training in the unions, which have preached to them that mass action is the sole effective means of struggle. For the leftist movement is based on the materialist conception of history, which emphasizes economic and technical aspects as the effective factors in history.

On the right there is no such union training. On the right it is a question of preserving the anarchistic economic order characterized for them by the words *peace and order*. And individual means correspond to this goal, whose effects are identical to those of the anarchist "propaganda of the deed." For the right adheres to the heroic conception of history, according to which the hero "makes" history. Correspondingly, the right is inclined to hope that it could annihilate the left opposition, which is carried by hopes for a radically different economic order, by defeating its leaders. And the right has done it: all of the leaders of the left who openly opposed the war and whom the workers trusted—Liebknecht, Luxemburg, Eisner, [Gustav] Landauer, [Leo] Jogisches, et al.—are dead. In recent times, as the assassinations of Erzberger, Auer, Scheidemann, and Rathenau demonstrate, they are also proceeding to murder the leaders of the moderate parties.

The effectiveness of this technique is for the moment indisputable. The left no longer has any significant leaders, no more people toward whom the masses have the feeling: he has suffered so much for us, dared so much for us that we can trust him blindly. The working-class movement has thereby doubtlessly been set back by years. This success is all the greater since in no case has punishment occurred.

That this method has become so widespread in the military (all of the murders by the right have been committed by officers or soldiers) naturally lies in the psychological brutalization of the war, in which the life of the individual was no longer allowed to count. In this regard the frequently spoken and unspoken order not to take prisoners has had an especially significant influence.

POLITICAL MURDERS THEN AND NOW

The indifference with which one greets political murders and the victims of turbulent street demonstrations today in Germany is to be explained by the fact that the war has numbed us to the value of human life.

The unbelievable leniency of the court is also quite well known to the perpetrators. Thus are the political murders of today in Germany to be distinguished from those common previously in other countries by two aspects: their great number and the fact that they go unpunished. Earlier a certain resolve was part of political murder. A certain heroism was not to be denied: the perpetrator risked life and limb. Flight was only possible given extraordinary effort. Today the perpetrator risks nothing at all. Powerful organizations with an extensive network of confidantes over the whole country provide him with shelter, protection, and material sustenance. "Right-minded" bureaucrats and police chiefs supply falsified papers for potentially necessary trips abroad. This technique has improved greatly since the time of Lieutenant Vogel. The beneficiaries live magnificently and happily in the best hotels. In short, political murder has gone from being a heroic deed, to becoming a daily act, an easy source of earnings for "impulsive customers."

THE COMPLICITY OF THE COURTS

These conditions would naturally be inconceivable without the perhaps unconscious assistance of the courts. This can even be proved geographically. In the occupied territory of the Rhineland the frequency of murder is much lower than in the rest of the nation. It is known that the Rhineland Commission would not share the interests and standpoint of the German judges. (If similar things occurred in their country, they would probably make the same judgments.) A further proof of the courts' unconscious complicity in the murders lies in the fact that the verbal call for the murder of well-known pacifists is in no way regarded as a crime. A fine of a few paper marks, and the one who issued the call can resume stirring up the seeds of hate. On the day following the murder of Erzberger there appeared in the *Spandauer Tageblatt:* "To the Scaffold! The Second Victim, Hello von Gerlach!" The author, Lehmann, received a two-hundred-mark fine from the second district criminal court.

This thesis of mine, that the mildness of the German courts is a precondition of political murders is also represented by most radical-right newspapers. One frequently reads sentences there like: "It is a pity that the traitor so-and-so (a pacifist, of whom not even the least of a criminal nature can even be said) lives not in Germany but in another country. There, unfortunately, the arm of punitive justice cannot reach him, as it did Erzberger." According to this, one cannot murder a political opponent who lives abroad, but not, for example, because it would be technically impossible (that is not the case) but because one would run the risk of being punished there.

Despite these horrendous facts I would not want to affirm unconditionally the assertion that German judges consciously bend the law. They did let over three hundred murders go with no punishment. But I would like to plead mitigating circumstances for them. They lack the consciousness of the culpability of their actions. Formerly, when today's economic system was unconditionally protected against attacks from without and when the members of the right-wing parties made up uncontestedly the upper strata, the thought that there could come from this caste a bunch of murderers and instigators of murders is unimaginable to them. That is why the murderers are set free.

In the main, public opinion, for understandable reasons given the underlying interests, takes the position: *Roma locuta, causa finita;* the courts released the ones charged with murder. They are nonpartisan. The matter is settled. Only a small fraction protested, and indeed in essence always only the fellow party members of those who were murdered. This fiction of the nonpartisan nature of the German courts, incidentally, also has an extra-political origin: regarding the [Triple] Entente all doubt that just measures are being instituted against war criminals in Germany itself is to be banished.

THE TECHNIQUE OF ACQUITTAL

Virtually all of the relatively small number of assassinations of reactionaries have been atoned for through severe penalties; of the very numerous assassinations of men of the left, on the other hand, not one has been atoned. Credulousness, wrongly understood orders, or actual or purported insanity were always the bases of the defense to the extent that trials even took place. Most of the proceedings were quashed either by the prosecutor's office or the criminal court.

When the murderer and the course of the crime are known precisely then the following judicial comedy develops. An officer gave an order that could have been understood to mean that Spartacists were to be shot. The subordinate shoots people whom he takes to be Spartacists, and is acquitted because he could have believed himself to be acting on orders. He is, therefore, released on account of "putative Spartacism." Just like Lieutenant Forster in his time was released because of putative self-defense. Nothing, however, is undertaken against the officer. For either that was not what the order meant or, if that is what it meant, then it simply was not an official order. Naturally, the "Spartacist" is dead. The guilt lies with . . . the scapegoat. Thus do the proceedings before the prosecutor end. This process is most interesting when the treasury, in a civil proceeding being pursued simultaneously, is made to pay compensation because of a murder committed by a soldier or officer. For then it is acknowledged by a court that the killing was illegal. Nevertheless, nothing happens to the perpetrator.

Public opinion in general approves of this procedure. For clever propaganda has taught it that every enemy of militarism is a Spartacist, therefore an enemy of humanity, therefore open game.

If a member of a leftist party is murdered by the right, even the judge is instinctively incapable of ridding himself of the notion that the murdered person was his enemy, and because of his, the victim's, beliefs deserved a severe penalty. Thus the murderer really only preceded criminal justice. And for that reason should be treated with lenience. Thus it frequently occurs that in the court proceedings it is not the murderer but the murdered who stands morally before the judge. The murderer comes from the same social strata, from the same life as the judge. Countless social bonds connect the murderer–officer with the judge who will acquit him, to the prosecutor who will quash the proceeding, and to the witness who depicts in detail the "attempted flight." They are flesh of their flesh, blood of their blood. The judge understands their language, their feelings, their thinking. Underneath the heavy mask of formalism, his soul resonates tenderly with the murderer. The murderer is set free.

Woe, however, to the murderer who is on the left. The judge, who himself belongs to the former upper classes, has an age-old familiarity with the thought that this economic order must be defended. His own position, after all, rests upon it. And every opponent of this economic order is reprehensible. The accused is capable of any crime. And even if he can only be nominally convicted, the most severe punishment is his certain lot.

I am not optimistic enough to believe that my work will cause even one of the murderers to be punished or that political murders will cease. Should, however, my lines have contributed at least to the atonement of the coming political murders, then I will regard my task as having been fulfilled.

38

GERMAN CENTER PARTY

Program

Accepted at the Deutsche Zentrumspartei Congress on January 16, 1922. Published in *Handbuch des öffentlichen Lebens,* ed. Maximilian Müller-Jabusch (Leipzig: Verlag von K. F. Koehler, 1931), 441–444.

As a Christian party of the people: the national community of Germans; the realization of Christian principles in the state, society, economy, and culture. Views the solidarity of the German peoples toward the outside world and the turning of its energies inward as the foundation of the international standing of Germany. Longings for self-determination and self-assertion should not be guided by selfish conceptions of power but by the moral idea of the nation. True Christian community as the highest ideal of world politics. A Christian conception of the state and the constitutional party. Rejection of violent overthrow, repudiation of the all-powerful state, opposition to the denunciation and dissolution of the idea of the state. The power of the state finds its limits in natural right and divine law.

Commitment to the German national state; self-government; the professional civil service as the backbone of government. The dominance of a class or caste is incompatible with the essence of the national state.

The independence of regional states within the frame of national unity. Strong central power secures the existence and free development of peoples and regional states; a centralized state structure does not correspond to the character of the German people.

Solidarity of all social strata and professions; rejection of class struggle and class domination.

The final goal of the economy is the individual and his higher duties; human dignity and the moral character of work may never be sacrificed to purely economic ends. The predominance of capital, alongside the attending political, social, and cultural dangers, is to be prevented. The goal of the economy is an increase in the production of goods, whereby, however, a just distribution of goods is to be maintained, which is also the guarantee of free participation in cultural values. Recognition of private property; striving for a steady increase in the number of property owners. Recognition of the economic significance of free entrepreneurial activity and the desire for personal gain; equally meaningful, however, is the promotion of joy in labor and the productivity of wage-earners; for that reason, the securing of a role for the latter in the administration of business, of the possibility of sharing in profits and owning property. The goal of social policy is to defend and promote the professions. A just distribution of public burdens and the active support of the economically weak.

Safeguarding of freedom of conscience, religious freedom, and the freedom of education, and the free development of vital religious energies as provided for in the constitution. The freedom and independence of ecclesiastical communities and the safeguarding of their influence on the life of the people. The cooperation of state and church without violation of their mutual independence. Popular morality as the source of the people's health and the fertile foundation for the forces responsible for the creation of culture. Tending the health of the family as the basic cell of human community.

Recognition of the role of the state in the education of the young, while rejecting a state monopoly on schools and insisting on the right of the church to the religious education of the young. Support for the natural right of parents to the education of their children; confessional schools.

39

THOMAS MANN

The German Republic

First published as "Von deutscher Republik: Aus einem Vortrag," *Berliner Tageblatt,* no. 469 (October 17, 1922).

You were among my listeners, Gerhart Hauptmann—may I remind you?—when I was privileged to speak one day before the University of Frankfurt during the Goethe celebrations. My subject was culture and cultural loyalties. In other words, my subject was our humane tradition. You sat in the front row, and behind you the tiers of seats rose almost to the ceiling, crowded with German youth. That was excellent; so may it be again today. Once more, though today only thanks to my imagination, I see you before me as you then sat and I speak to you upon your birthday. And raising my head a little higher, I see the hosts of German youth there too, pricking up their ears; for it is to them that I am speaking today, above your head, it is to them I have something to say, with them that I have, perhaps—in the sense of the common phrase—a bone to pick. [. . .]

I will persevere to the end, for I have set my heart and my mind on winning you over. German youth must be won over, so much is fact; and they are to be won, that must be a fact too, since they are not bad but only a little stiff-necked and defiant and prone to shuffle their feet. [. . .]

War is romantic. No one has ever denied the mystic and poetic element residing in it. But today only the insensible would deny that it is utterly debased romanticism, an utter distortion of the poetic. To save our national feeling from falling into disrepute, to keep it from becoming a curse, we must learn to understand that a warlike and brawling spirit is not its whole content but more and more absolutely a cult of peace in accord with the mysticism and poetry in its nature. (Here shufflings.)

I must beg you, young men, not to take this tone. I am no pacifist, of either the unctuous or the ecstatic school. Pacifism is not to my taste, whether as a soporific for the soul or as a middle-class rationalization of the good life. It was not Goethe's, either, or would not have been; yet he was a man of peace. I am no Goethe; yet a little, distantly related somehow or other, as Adalbert Stifter put it, I "belong to his family." The side of peace is my side too, as being the side of culture, art, and thought, whereas in a war vulgarity triumphs . . . not alone, not alone, I know, so be quiet!—but as things now are in the world, and as the human being is, war is not much else today. The peoples of the world are old and sophisticated, their epic and heroic stage lies far in the past, any attempt to return to it involves a desperate revolt against the decree of time and constitutes a spiritual insincerity. War is a lie, its issues are a lie; whatever honorable emotion the individual may bring to it, war itself is today stripped of all honor, and to any straight and clear-eyed vision reveals itself as the triumph of all that is brutal and vulgar in the soul of the race, as the archfoe of culture and thought, as a blood orgy of egoism, corruption, and vileness. [. . .]

My aim, which I express quite candidly, is to win you—as far as that is needed—to the side of the republic; to the side of what is called democracy, and what I call humanity, because of a distaste I share with you for the meretricious overtones of the other word. I would plead with you for it, in the sight of this man and poet here before me, whose genuine popularity rests upon the loftiest union of folk and human elements. For I could wish that the face of Germany, now so sadly drawn and distorted, might once more show lineaments like his, this poet's face, which still displays so many traits of that high trustworthiness which we connect with the German name. [. . .]

Our students, our student associations, by no means lack democratic tradition. There have been times when the national idea was far from coinciding with the monarchical and dynastic; when they were in irreconcilable opposition. Patriotism and republic, so far from being opposed, have sometimes appeared as one and the same thing; and the cause of freedom and the fatherland had the passionate support of the noblest youth. Today the young, or at least considerable and important sections of them, seem to have sworn eternal hatred to the republic and forgotten what might have been once upon a time—for remembering must have exercised a restraining effect upon such hatred. [. . .]

The republic is our fate; the only correct attitude to which is *amor fati,* none too solemn a phrase for the content, for it is no light fate. Freedom, so called, is no joke, I do not say that. Its other name is responsibility; the word makes it only too clear that freedom is truly a heavy burden, most of all for the intellectual.

[. . .] The State has become our business; a situation profoundly hated by considerable sections of citizens and young people who will simply have none of it because, forsooth, it did not come to birth in triumph and the exercise of free choice but in defeat and collapse, making it seem bound up forever with weakness, shame, and foreign domination. "We are not the republic," these patriots tell me, averting their faces. "The republic is foreign domination—insofar (why cannot we too quote Novalis?) as weakness is only the other side of foreign power, taking the upper hand, controlling, setting its mark." True, true. But in the first place it is also true, as the poet says, that "a man can ennoble everything, make it worthy of himself, by dint of willing it"—a very true saying, very fine, and almost sly in the bargain, a shrewd expression of aptitude for life. In the second place, it is not true, and I deliberately repeat that it is utterly and entirely untrue, that the republic as an inner fact (I am not now referring to established public law) is the creation of defeat and humiliation. It is the issue of honor and exaltation. [. . .]

Students and citizens, your resistance to the republic and the democracy is simply a fear of words. You shy at them like restive horses; you fall into unreasoning panic at the sound of them. But they are just words: relativities, time-conditioned forms, necessary instruments; to think they must refer to some outlandish kind of foreign humbug is mere childishness. The republic—as though it were not still and always Germany! Democracy! As though one could not be more at home in that home than in any flashing and dashing and crashing empire! Have you heard the *Meistersinger von Nürnberg* lately? Nietzsche made the scintillating remark about it that it was "directed against civilization" and incited "the Germans against the French." But meanwhile it is democratic through and through, as pronouncedly and exemplarily as Shakespeare's *Coriolanus* is aristocratic. It is, I repeat, German democracy; its honest-hearted pomp and circumstance, its fervid romanticism, are evidence that the expression *German democracy*, so far from being an offence to nature or a logical impossibility, is as a compound organically correct, as correct as perhaps only one other combination could be—I mean *the German people*. [. . .] There is no ground in the world for imagining the republic to be a concern of keen-witted young Jews. Do not leave it to them! Take the wind out of their sails, in the popular political phrase—the republican wind! [. . .]

Of course, it is advisable for the republicans to take the wind out of the monarchists' (that is, the national) sails and not let them sail with it alone; they must not leave to them alone the deciding voice when honor and dishonor, love and anger are in the scales. They must take the words out of their mouths, as Father Ebert has just now done so frankly and shrewdly in his Constitution Day decree. He took "Deutschland über alles" out of the mouth of the "*völkisch*" and told them plainly it was not their song any more than it was his; and now he strikes up with it full-throated. A new sort of singing competition, this, and a capital one! For of course the nationalists will not stop singing it; and when everybody with one voice is singing "Deutschland über alles" then we shall have the republic, and "smooth seas and a prosperous voyage." [. . .]

And I have got the impression, which I invite you to share with me, that it is possible for democracy to be more German than imperial grand opera. [. . .]

What you will answer me now, I very well know. You will say: "No, no—that is precisely what it is not. What has the German soul to do with democracy, republic, socialism, let us boldly say Marxism? All this economic materialism, this fine talk about the 'ideological superstructure' and the rest of the nineteenth-century twaddle, all this is simply childish now. It would be unfortunate if it came to be realized in fact at a time when it had become intellectually defunct! And is not the same true of the other fine things for which you are most surprisingly trying to stir up the enthusiasm of German youth? Do you see the stars above us? Do you know and revere our gods? Do you know who were the heralds of our

German future—Goethe and Nietzsche, were they liberals, pray? [Friedrich von] Hölderlin and [Stefan] George—is it your notion that they were democratic spirits?"—No, they were not. Of course, of course, you are right. My dear friends, you behold me crestfallen. I was not thinking of Goethe and Nietzsche, Hölderlin and George. Or, rather, I was thinking of them to myself, and asking myself which is the more absurd notion: to plead for the republic in their name, or to preach the restoration in their name as well. [. . .]

Now you are angry; if the presence of certain highly placed personages did not restrain you, you would shout at me: "And what about your book? What about your antipolitical, antidemocratic meditations of the year 1918? Renegade, turncoat! You are eating your own words, you are riding for a fall! Come down from the platform, and stop having the effrontery to think that the words of an unprincipled apostate can win us over!"

My dear friends, I am still here. I have still something to say that seems to me good and important. As for the fall and the betrayal, that is not quite a fair way to look at it. I retract nothing. I take back nothing essential. I told the truth and tell it today. [. . .]

I am in fact a conservative; that my natural occupation in this world is to preserve not to destroy—in the sense that Novalis defined in an aphorism, with both delicacy and force:

> It may be at certain times needful that everything should fall into a fluid state, to bring about new and necessary mixtures and produce a fresh and purer crystallization. But it is just as indispensable to moderate the crisis and prevent total liquefaction. A stock must remain, a kernel for the new mass to gather round and shape itself into new and beautiful forms. Then let what is solid concentrate even more firmly, thus preventing an excess of caloric, the crumbling of the bony structure, the wearing out of the essential fabric.

Well, just such a concentration of the solid, such a provision against the destruction of the essential fabric, was this book of mine, in just such a way did it seek to conserve. It was conservative, not in the service of the past and reaction but in the service of the future. Its concern was the preservation of that stock, that kernel around which the new might crystallize in beautiful forms. The fever of revolution, inevitable and indispensable as it always is, must not be thought of as an end in itself, a condition to be perpetuated; and the statement applies no less to the solidification of the next stage, which seems to be hostile to the future but must at the right time be fluid enough to permit the fixed and the flowing coming together to form a just peace for the sake of life and the new form. [. . .]

Let met just interpolate here my opinion of [Oswald] Spengler's work—this seems a suitable place. His *Decline of the West* is the product of enormous power and strength of purpose; scientific, rich in *aperçus;* a high-brow romance, vastly entertaining and reminiscent of Schopenhauer's *World as Will and Idea* not only in the musicianly method of its composition. That is to rate the book very high. At the same time, I have my own democratic opinion about it: I find its attitude false, arrogant, and "convenient" to the point of extreme inhumanity. It would be different if this attitude were a cloak for irony, as I at first supposed; if its prophesying were a polemical technique. Certainly one can prophesy about a thing like civilization—according to Spengler the inevitable, biological end-condition of every culture, including the present Occidental one—but not that it may come to pass, no, in order that it may not come to pass; to anticipate and prevent it as a sort of mental exorcism. I thought that was the case here. But when I found out that this man wanted his prophecies of death and petrifation taken in sober earnest; that he was instructing the young not to waste their emotions and passions on culture, art, poetry, and such things but to hold fast to what must inevitably be the future, which they must will in order to will anything at all, to technique and mechanics, administration, perhaps politics; when I perceived that the hand this man reached out towards the yearnings and wishes of the human being was actually just the old, natural Satanic claw, then I averted my own face from so much inhuman hate and put the book out of my sight, lest I find myself admiring so harmful and deadly a work. [. . .]

Between the Calamus songs and [Novalis's] "Hymns to the Night" lies the difference between life and death—or, if Goethe's definition is the right one, between the classic and the romantic. "Sympathy with death": such a formula does not of course comprehend the whole strange shimmering complex of romanticism, but it does define its heights and depths. [. . .]

No spiritual metamorphosis is more familiar to us than that where sympathy with death stands at the beginning and resolve to live and serve, at the end. The history of European decadence and aestheticism is rich in examples of this thrust through to the positive, to the people, to the state—particularly in the Latin countries. [. . .]

Let us drop this question of the French. A people who had the wit to invent nationalism would have enough to abandon its invention. As for us, we shall do well to be concerned with ourselves and with our own—yes, let us with modest satisfaction use the word—our own national concern. I will call it again by its name—an old-fashioned one, yet today bright with youthful allure: humanity. It is the mean between aesthetic isolation and undignified leveling of the individual to the general; between mysticism and ethics; between inwardness and the state; between a death-bound negation of ethical and civic values and a purely ethical philistine rationalism; it is truly the German mean, the Beautiful and Human, of which our finest spirits have dreamed. We are honoring its explicit, legal form, whose meaning and aim we take to be the unification of our political and national life, when we yield our still-stiff and unaccustomed tongues to utter the cry: "Long live the republic!"

40

DAS TAGEBUCH

[On the Anniversary of the Death of Walther Rathenau]

First published as an editorial in *Das Tagebuch* 24 (June 16, 1923), 837–838.

The anniversary of the day on which Walther Rathenau was murdered is now approaching. A year? To those who live all too quickly, he is deeply buried, but we would be a people without a future if fast living, actually not-at-all-living, defined our essence. A people without memory—that also means a people without hope. He who lacks ties to the past, how will he be tomorrow? Internal apathy is the worst of all deaths and occasionally it seems that this horrible fate is our lot. When hired killers shot down Rathenau, a cry burst from the soul of Germany. A short cry. The little, dumb hangers-on of the murderous gang were captured; the murderers themselves and, worse, their princely employers escaped the judge. (It is said advisedly here: the princely employers.) The darkness surrounding Organization C has still not been illuminated. In spite of the republic defense law. Incidentally: Rathenau's murder was nevertheless the last in the series. How many more would have been killed without the defense law? The series of murders had just begun. This question is being posed for the consideration of good democrats in the stamp of [Carl] Siemens and [Wilhelm] Koch. A more active people than the Germans could perhaps have done without a defense law, because an elemental movement from among the people themselves would have put a stop to the murders. But elemental movements endure oh so briefly among the Germans. We lack the doggedness of the English, the rage of the French; we quickly recapture our equanimity, return too quickly to comfort. How was it possible that the wound opened by Rathenau's murder was so quickly scarred over and the scar no longer burns today? Was it that we instantly found a successor for him? Do we not miss him every day we have to negotiate with Europe? Where is the German who represents us in the international concert? Did Rathenau's sobriety not spare us war over the Ruhr? Was Rathenau not the counterpart to the monarchist [Hugo] Stinnes, who since 1915 (first through [Walther] Nikolai, [Max] Bauer, and [Erich] Ludendorff, now through Hugenberg, Siemens, and [Carl] Becker) rules Germany? And nevertheless, although we miss him every day, Rathenau is not merely dead for Germany, but deeply buried. Oh, on some dreary days one asks oneself with a shudder, growing conscious of this extinction of the German soul, whether Germany itself is not more dead than Walther Rathenau.

41

CARL VON OSSIETZKY

Defending the Republic: The Great Fashion

First published as "Schutz der Republik—die große Mode," *Das Tagebuch* 37 (September 13, 1924), 1,291–1,293.

Things have changed somewhat in these last few months in Germany. People who want to defend the republic have become visible. They have created an organization that today already embraces the entire country. [Otto] Hörsing's formation of the Reichsbanner Black-Red-Gold [ex-servicemen's association], was epoch–making with surprising speed. A useful and necessary act. The state was not able to defend itself, had disgraced itself in compromises with reaction. It was the duty of the citizens to step in. The recognition came a little late, but nevertheless . . .

The Reichsbanner contested the right to the streets of the thugs of the right-wing parties, showed the colors of the republic in public, and confronted the German Days [imperial holidays] with the Republican Days [republican holidays]. In present circumstances that is a fine show. But the Reichsbanner also displays a troubling tendency to let it rest at that. And here a critique is in order. Whoever has learned from the events of the past five years knows that it is not the nationalists, the monarchists, who represent the real danger but the absence of substantive content and ideas in the concept of the German republic, and that no one will succeed in vitalizing that concept. Defense of the republic is good. It is better to go beyond that to an understanding of what in the republic is worth defending and what should not be retained. This question escapes the Reichsbanner; more precisely, it has probably not yet recognized that such a question even exists.

Our republic is not yet an object of mass consciousness but a constitutional document and a governmental administration. When the people want to see the republic, they are shown Wilhelmstrasse. And then one wonders why they return home somewhat shamed. Nothing is there to make the heart beat faster. Around this state, lacking any ideas and with an eternally guilty conscience, there are grouped a couple of so-called constitutional parties, likewise lacking an idea and with no better conscience, which are not led but administered. Administered by a bureaucratic caste that is responsible for the misery of recent years in domestic and foreign affairs and that smothers all signs of fresh life with a cold hand. If the Reichsbanner does not find within itself the idea, the inspiring idea, and the youth does not finally storm the gates, then it will not become the avant-garde of the republic, but the cudgel-guard of the partycrats, and their interests will be defended foremost, not the republic.

The Reichsbanner produces an association newspaper. This organ is worth a shameful glance. Along with long-ago-postmarked essays from sometimes forgotten personalities, there is a list of items available from the Magdeburg shopping center. It begins with a unity windbreaker and moves on to "posters, oak leaf border with eagle and text: 'Hail Freedom,' 'Long Live the Republic,' 'Welcome!'" One section is headed: "Shell Splinter," another: "In the Canteen." That, dear comrades, is body and soul the style of the justly slandered, old, army newspaper. Is it really not possible for you to improve on such copy? Do you have such an irresistible longing for oak leaves and eagles, and does one have to have the feeling in the republic of being in the canteen?

Great energy threatens to be squandered in trivialities. The unossified elements in the left-wing parties felt the need for an arena in which to work. Their activity was in fact on the verge of making off with the bars on the party dungeon. It was therefore necessary to change course, a little camouflage was in order. So they were given their own precinct, which was cautiously bounded. A thing which should have been a matter of the intellect was made into the business of caps and uniforms, thus the business of an unadulterated war association. Thus was the party rebellion channeled along preapproved lines, and instead of creating a new republican type, the old subordinate officer type was painted in new colors. And a broad, hopeful movement turned into a fashion—not a conviction, but a fashion. This time, for a change: Defense of the republic! Moody, flexible, like all fashions.

And the effect? The Reichsbanner honors the constitution with festivals; the Reichsbanner goose steps; the Reichsbanner drapes Potsdam in black-red-gold; the Reichsbanner scraps with the communists—and [Felix] Fechenbach sits in the penitentiary. That is the joke of it. But if the Reichsbanner had as many determined fellows among its members as Captain [Hermann] Erhardt, then Fechenbach would no longer be sitting in the penitentiary today. French democrats rescued their Spanish brothers in the cause, whom they did not even know by sight, from the claws of the dictator. The thought of an injustice committed somewhere in the world kept them from sleeping. The German democrats and socialists are more solidly organized. It is not at all true that they are as weak-kneed as is always believed; it is just that they have such a terribly thick skin. Besides, they are faithful to the law and to the constitution. To rescue someone from prison—that would mean acting against the law! God forbid! And Fechenbach sits in the penitentiary.

Meanwhile, however, unity windbreakers will continue to be sold and army haversacks and satin scarves, basic model; better model, lined; silk moiré, with gold fringe (see the association newspaper). Hail Freedom! Whoever has gambled on the eternal corporal in the German character has never yet gambled badly. Stahlhelm and the Bismarck League also sold cockades and haversacks.

Between black-white-red and black-red-gold a world is supposed to lie. Really, really?! Variations on a German theme.

42

SOCIAL DEMOCRATIC PARTY (SPD)

Program

Accepted at the Heidelberg Sozialdemokratische Partei Deutschlands Congress on September 18, 1925. Published in *Handbuch des öffentlichen Lebens,* ed. Maximilian Müller-Jabusch (Leipzig: Verlag von K. F. Koehler, 1931), 432–434.

The democratic republic offers the most favorable ground for the liberation of the working class and therefore for the development of socialism. For this reason, the Social Democratic Party defends the republic and is committed to its full development. The Party demands the following:

The Reich is to be transformed into a unified republic on the basis of decentralized self-government. Upon the organically reorganized substructure of regional and state administration will rise a strong national authority possessed of the powers necessary for unified leadership and the maintenance of national unity.

Extension of direct national administration to the judiciary: all courts are to become national courts. The security police is to be subjected to unified principles established by legislation. A unified, national, criminal police force is to be created.

Protection against all monarchical and militarist strivings. Transformation of the armed forces of the Reich into a reliable organ of the republic.

The complete extension of constitutional equality to all citizens, without regard to distinctions of gender, national origin, religion, or property.

ADMINISTRATION

The goal of Social Democratic policy is the replacement of the police-state executive carried over from the authoritarian state structure through an administrative organization that invests the responsibilities of government in the people on the basis of democratic self-government. [. . .]

JUDICIARY

The Social Democratic Party opposes all forms of class and partisan bias in the judiciary and supports a legal order and judicial system informed by a social spirit and based on the critical participation of selected lay judges in all branches and on all levels of the judiciary.

In particular it demands:

In civil law, the subordination of property rights to the rights of the society at large, the facilitation of divorce, the granting to women of equal rights with men, and the equalization of children born out of wedlock to those born within.

In criminal law, greater protection of individual and social rights, the replacement of the principle of vengeance by the principle of rehabilitation of the individual and the protection of society. Repeal of the death penalty.

In criminal proceedings, the reintroduction of trial by jury and the extension of its jurisdiction in particular to political trials and those involving the press; the right to appeal in all criminal cases; the abolition of all regulations that infringe upon the right to a just defense.

In pretrial proceedings, the protection of detainees against encroachment by the authorities; arrest, except in cases of apprehension in the act, only on the basis of judicial warrant and oral hearings concerning appeals against such warrants.

In the execution of sentences, constitutional regulation in the spirit of humanity and in accord with the principle of rehabilitation.

SOCIAL POLICY

The defense of workers, white-collar employees, and civil-service employees and the elevation of living standards for the broad masses demands:

Defense of the freedom of association and the right to strike. Equal rights for women in the workplace. The prohibition of the employment of school–age children.

The legal codification of a working day of a maximum of eight hours and the reduction of this maximum for the youth and in occupations posing an increased risk to health and life. Restriction of night work. Weekly, uninterrupted respites from work of at least forty-two hours. Annual vacations with no interruption of wages.

The responsibility for the disposal of unemployment relief is reserved exclusively for the trade unions.

Control of abuses in cottage industries with the goal of eliminating it entirely, with due attention to the welfare of those affected.

Supervision of all plants and enterprises by means of a system of industrial inspection, which is to be expanded into a nationwide institution based upon the participation of workers and white-collar employees in the capacity of civil servants and shop stewards.

Securing the legal validity of wage agreements and assistance payments through their conclusion by mediation authorities.

Independent labor courts outside the network of regular jurisdiction.

Unified labor law.

The standardization of social insurance to the point of its restructuring into a general system of social welfare. Inclusion of those unfit for work and the unemployed.

Comprehensive, preventive, enlightening, and effective measures in the area of the popular welfare, in particular as regards education, health, and economic concerns; the national regulation of welfare support, organized so as to ensure the participation of the working class in its execution.

Promotion of international agreements and legislation.

CULTURAL AND EDUCATIONAL POLICY

The Social Democratic Party is striving for the abolition of the educational privileges of the propertied classes.

Education, schooling, and research are public matters; their operation is to be secured through public institutions and the expenditure of public funds. The provision of instruction and instructional materials free of charge. Economic support for pupils and students.

The public institutions of education, schooling, culture, and research are secular. All legally grounded interference in these institutions by churches and religious or ideological communities is to be opposed. Separation of church and state. Separation of church and schools. Secular technical and occupational schools and institutions of higher education. No expenditure of public monies for ecclesiastical or religious purposes.

The unified structuring of the school system. The creation of the closest possible relations between practical and intellectual labor on all levels.

The common education of both sexes by both sexes.

Standardized training of teachers in colleges and universities. [. . .]

ECONOMIC POLICY

In the struggle against the capitalist system, the Social Democratic Party demands:

Land, property, mineral resources, and natural sources of energy supplies are to be withdrawn from the system of capitalist exploitation and transferred to the service of the whole community.

Developing the system of economic councils to implement the right of codetermination by the working class of the organization of the economy with the continuation of close cooperation with the trade unions.

National control over capitalist special-interest associations, cartels, and trusts.

Promotion of increased productivity in industry and agriculture.

Support for the system of land settlement.

Abolition of the protective tariff system through long-term trade contracts in the name of the free exchange of goods and the economic integration of nations.

Expansion of the operations of the nation, states, and public bodies while simultaneously avoiding bureaucratization.

Promotion of nonprofit cooperatives and enterprises devoted to the common good.

Promotion of residential construction in the public interest. The official codification of rental law and opposition to construction profiteers.

INTERNATIONAL POLICY

As a member of the Socialist Workers' International, the Social Democratic Party of Germany struggles together with the workers of all nations against imperialist and fascist advances and for the realization of socialism.

It confronts every intensification of conflict between peoples and every threat to the peace with its most energetic opposition.

It demands the peaceful resolution of international conflicts and insists that they be brought before obligatory courts of arbitration.

It is committed to the right of self-determination of peoples and to the right of minorities to democratic and national self-government.

It opposes the exploitation of colonial peoples and the violent destruction of their traditional economic arrangements and their culture.

It demands international disarmament.

It is committed to the creation of European economic unity, now made pressing by economic circumstances, for the formation of a United States of Europe, in order thereby to achieve a solidarity of interests among the peoples of all continents.

It demands the democratization of the League of Nations and its further development into an effective instrument of peace.

43

GERMAN PEOPLE'S PARTY (DVP)

Program

Published in *Handbuch des öffentlichen Lebens,* ed. Maximilian Müller-Jabusch (Leipzig: Verlag von K. F. Koehler, 1931), 447–448.

1. FATHERLAND AND FREEDOM

Fatherland. All of our thoughts, our burning desires, and our struggles are dedicated to the greatness and freedom of the fatherland. A people, whose *Lebensraum* has been brutally cut down, whose freedom to live has been cast into chains through senseless treaties, whose economic power has been crippled by subjection to a system of utterly extravagant tributes, can only wrestle its way back up through the strength of its love for the fatherland and national solidarity. Over many years Marxism has been breeding a sickly international and pacifist romanticism in the place of a resolute will devoted to the fatherland. In its surrender to the fatherland, in the passion of its national will, the German People's Party stands steadfast at the most advanced front. An unwavering belief in the forces still present in the German people provides it with the foundation of all its effectiveness. The spirit of the national community of the German people is its supreme law.

Freedom. Our faith and our view of life is rooted in the spiritual soil created in the times of Bismarck and [Rudolf von] Bennigsen and before them the great minds of German idealism. The freedom of the individual is for us the point of departure for all political and cultural strivings. Freedom without moral responsibility, however, means the corruption of the community grounded in the state. The freedom of the days of revolution is caprice and destruction. The freedom that we mean is that of the morally responsible individual. All moral responsibility, however, is rooted in faith and religiosity. Revolution and socialism have bred a desolate materialism, the struggle of classes against one another, envy, and ill will, because they have no knowledge of the religious forces in the life of the people. This spiritual and moral pauperization of the people leads those who are mistaken and unsure along the path of desperation. In contrast to mass mania and the herd mentality, we are fighting for the recognition of the rights of the free individual grounded in religion and morality. Only when the moral concept of freedom has regained universal recognition will, as in our great past so forevermore in the future, German national community be able to develop.

2. STATE, ECONOMY, AND CULTURE

State. We are fighting against the caricature of a dictatorial state that enslaves the free life of national forces. We demand an organically structured state, the essence of which must be the liberation and development of the living forces in the national community. State socialism is an economically utopian system of compulsion that will lead the whole people into financial impoverishment. That is why we are fighting to regain spiritual, economic, and moral freedom for the forces of the national community now fettered by the chains of state power.

It is our task to fill the state of today with the truly free spirit of the fatherland, which will lend the state the inner force it requires and once again make its citizens proud to be members of a healthy state organism. Respect for the symbols of the state is for us an obvious truth.

Constitution. Everything in constitutional life that is un-German and alien to our nature, everything that places the rule of the masses in the place of the rule of achievement, must be overcome. Only that constitution is enduring in which the concept of the rule of the people is juxtaposed on equal terms with the concept of leadership and authority. Mass rule leads to partisan caprice and to the corruption of the civil service.

We are opposed to the exaggeration of parliamentarianism. Therefore we demand: *a second chamber.* To the Reichstag must be joined an equal chamber, consisting of representatives of the regional states, representatives of the economy, and leading figures in spiritual and public life, who are to be called to service by the president on the basis of nominations of the churches and institutions of higher learning in particular.

Reform of the Reich. The following are bitter necessities: the unified gathering of the national will in the supreme instance; the implementation of this will down through the last and least of the civil service! Economic and financial considerations as well as cultural and political necessities demand that the task of reform be taken in hand without further hesitation. Experts from the German People's Party have elaborated proposals for a strictly structured, unified German Reich.

We are taking a first, decisive step along the path to reform of the Reich by demanding that the president of the Reich henceforth also become the chief official of the Prussian state. The president of the Reich will appoint, like the chancellor and ministers of the Reich, the Prussian prime minister and the Prussian minister of state. That will simultaneously achieve the *strengthening of the power of the president of the Reich and the authority of the state.*

The government called by the president of the Reich should not be permanently subject to dismissal by an arbitrary vote of an incidental majority. The national government is obligated to resign only when the majority of the elected members of the Reichstag casts an explicit vote of no confidence. Against the over-hasty resolutions of parliament, the president of the Reich should have a suspensive power of veto.

The question of voting rights is a matter of dispute. The formation of political will in the people does not depend exclusively on the electoral system. Therefore the question of the electoral system must be removed from the Reich constitution. Above all, we demand that the franchise be restricted once again to those 25 years of age and older.

44

KURT TUCHOLSKY

For Carl von Ossietzky

First published as "Für Carl v. Ossietzky: Generalquittung von Kurt Tucholsky," *Die Weltbühne* 28, no. 20 (May 17, 1932), 734–736.

Carl von Ossietzky is going to jail for eighteen months because the government wants to avenge itself on the *Weltbühne* for what it has been doing for years. Ossietzky is not going to jail for the contributor who wrote the incriminating article. He is going to jail for all of his contributors. This judgment is a demand for payment in full.

The witch-hunt was conducted in spite of serious difficulties.

To prevent Ossietzky from launching a timely counterattack, the original indictment included a charge of military espionage, a crime which did not exist. The applicable paragraph, however, stipulates, as in a case before the Westphalian imperial court or a trial of the Inquisition, that the public may not even be informed that charges have been raised. Ossietzky therefore had no chance whatever of defending himself before the trial.

The trial took place behind closed doors. The defendants had nothing to fear from publicity, the government everything. The defendants had a good conscience. The government did not.

A strict order of silence was imposed upon the accused and their defenders. There was a prohibition on the publication of anything having to do with the proceedings, even after the judgment was entered. It is now a question of tactics and temperament whether one should abide by it.

Ossietzky has not only abided by all aspects of the order of silence but he has made himself subordinate to the matter at issue in a practically heroic fashion. From the very first moment until today, there has been no statement either written or spoken by this man in which he complained, extolled, or explained himself. As the judgment came down, Ossietzky forbade me, in a fashion equally friendly and firm, "to sing his praises." I could not, therefore, say at the time what all participants have long since known: how during the trial he attempted to use himself to shield the writer of the article; how he attempted to take all of the guilt upon himself; and how he endured this horrible waiting period quietly and without giving in to the temptations of rhetoric. Not to know what is going to become of oneself tomorrow—and continue to do one's work: that is not easy. Ossietzky has done so for approximately two and a half years.

The attempt has now been made to obtain a remission of the sentence or a suspension of the prison term to house arrest through an appeal to mercy. On this attempt, we wish to say the following:

Ossietzky, while these efforts were in progress, has continually attacked not only, obviously, [Wilhelm] Groener but also the man who has final authority to decide on the appeal to mercy. He has written against Hindenburg, that is, he has done precisely the opposite of what one could characterize as opportunism. He has signed these attacks with his own name.

Reason enough, following certain notions of German chivalry, to argue: "But he has attacked us—why should one pardon such a man?"

A spark of chivalry was perhaps to be expected from the official side. I never expected it, and it did not spark. The "old man" sees no frivolity in military affairs, nor does the

Weltbühne, and Ossietzky is going to prison. The majority of the appeals for mercy did not even reach the office of the German president.

I summarize on the basis of the foreign press:

The alleged facts are true: the German War Ministry is deranged.

Nothing was betrayed, and for the simple reason that the alleged facts were already known, especially among the French. From the standpoint of the military of the German Republic, therefore, no damage was done. It is not the exposure that did damage; the facts did the damage.

The hostile press behaves as if Ossietzky sought exceptional treatment. That is untrue.

The appeal for mercy seeks only to mitigate a past injustice, nothing more. For here a severe injustice has been done. To impose this punishment on such a man as Ossietzky for this crime, which was none, is a disgrace. To take it upon oneself is not.

The punishment is and remains nothing but the exploitation of a formal occasion to deal a blow to a group of writers with which the government is very uncomfortable. The contributors and readers of the *Weltbühne* have in fact done something that stings the fascist enemy to the quick: they have laughed at him in these pages. Here a laugh, while others thundered. Here they have not been taken seriously. They can do much, but one thing they cannot do. They cannot force a person to speak to them other than from a position of superiority. In the intellectual struggle they will continue to get their due, and that must have hurt. If not, they would not have become so enraged and would not have pushed it further and further. It will not help them.

Vigorous words of parting seem to me inconceivable for a comrade so quiet and so non-pathetic as my friend Ossietzky; we are not the chairmen of a club. In the name of all of his friends, I wish that he come through his imprisonment in good health.

All properly sympathetic people will demand a pardon. Truncheons are not arguments. Nor is this judgment anything more.

The magazine, however, borne by the powerful lift given it by Ossietzky, will remain what it has always been.

A year and a half in prison for delivering a good product—that can be certified. Deliveries will continue.

5
The Rise of Nazism

OFTEN ACCOMPANYING the radical right's hostility to liberalism, internationalism, socialism and capitalism was the demonization of the Jews as their
promoters and beneficiaries. For no faction within it, however, was anti-
Semitism as obsessive a concern as it was for the National Socialist German
Workers' Party (NSDAP), founded in 1920. A characteristic expression of
their hatred can be seen in the work of the Nazi literary publicist Adolf Bartels,
who had been the leader of the *Deutschvölkischer Schriftstellerverband* (German
Völkisch Writers Union) since 1910. Published in its organ, *Deutsches Schrifttum,* in January 1920, Bartels's "The Struggle of the Age" demonstrates the
appeal of anti-Semitism to resentful intellectuals who transferred their hostility towards "international plutocracy" onto the Jews.

Paradoxical as it may seem, the Jews could also be identified with the
bolshevik version of anticapitalism. In February 1919, Alfred Rosenberg, later
notorious as the Nazi's official "philosopher," contributed an essay on "The
Russian Jewish Revolution" to Dietrich Eckart's journal *Auf gut Deutsch.*
Predicting the failure of the revolution due to Russian anti-Semitism, he
chillingly claimed that it would lead to either the annihilation of the Jews or
their forced exile to a Germany that would also know what to do with them.

As their initial party platform of 1920 demonstrates, however, the Nazis
also drew on many other resentments to attract as wide a spectrum of the
discontented as possible. Thus, alongside calls to reverse the outcome of World
War I, expand Germany's living space, and institute governmental control of
the press, it included demands to nationalize trusts, share profits from wholesale trade, and abolish incomes unearned by labor. What can be called the left
wing of the Nazi Party, led by Otto and Gregor Strasser, took the socialist
elements in its platform seriously. In 1926, Joseph Goebbels, who at that time
shared their thinking, appealed to his "dear friends on the left" to shift their
allegiance from bolshevism to Nazism, arguing that all it would require was
the substitution of nationalist for internationalist sympathies. As late as 1930
Goebbels was still promoting a non-Marxist, anti-Semitic, vaguely defined
socialism as the answer to the "social question."

For Hitler, however, the socialist dimension of Nazism was little more than
a slogan. Realizing the costs of antagonizing Germany's industrial elite, he
sought to reassure them of his intentions in a talk to the Düsseldorf Indus-

trieklub in January 1932 arranged by the steel magnate Fritz Thyssen. Stressing the need for a powerful, expansionist state to pave the way for a flourishing economy, he ignored the redistributive imperative in the Party's platform as well as its appeal to petit-bourgeois antimodernism. Although historians continue to debate the extent of big-business support for Nazism before its takeover of power, Hitler's speech accurately reflected the hollowness of National Socialism's name. As a 1932 election pamphlet directed at farmers demonstrates, Nazism promised a vague "third way" between capitalism and socialism.

It would, however, be inadequate to credit the success of Nazism to a rational appeal to economic interests, or even a mélange of political resentments. Realizing the importance of cultural issues, in 1932 the NSDAP established a Fighting League for German Culture (Kampfbund für deutsche Kultur) with its own journal, *German Culture Watch* (*Deutsche Kultur-Wacht*), in the hope of attracting nationalist intellectuals and artists to its cause. Vulgarized notions of eugenic breeding, like the "blood and soil" theories of R. W. Darré, gave the movement a pseudoscientific rationale. Its careful manipulation of symbols, typified by the "Horst Wessel Song" dedicated to one of the party's "martyrs," was also remarkably effective in mobilizing support. So too, of course, was the personality of its leader, for whom the concept of charisma, developed by Max Weber only a few years earlier, seemed invented. Many intellectuals were also mesmerized by Hitler's power, as Count Kessler ruefully noted after his visit in August 1932 to the Nietzsche Archives in Weimar. That Hitler himself cannily understood his charismatic appeal and even brazenly admitted his manipulation of it to political effect is shown by passages in his 1925 autobiography, *Mein Kampf,* where he extolled the power of the spoken over the written word to seduce the masses. Ironically, his insight was grimly borne out as the premonitions of horrible deeds contained in *Mein Kampf* itself—including the gassing of Jews—were blithely ignored by many Germans and non-Germans alike.

45

ALFRED ROSENBERG

The Russian Jewish Revolution

First published as "Die russisch-jüdische Revolution," in *Auf gut Deutsch,* nos. 14–15 (May 24, 1919), 218–227.

"Does it not occur to you that the Jews, even without your help, are citizens of a state mightier and more powerful than any of yours, and that if you in addition give them citizenship in your own states, they will trample your other citizens under foot?" With this warning, based on deep historic insight, [Johann Gottlieb] Fichte addressed the German nation a hundred years ago. His words were in vain: ignoring the potential force possessed by a homogeneous race, bemused by the slogans of human equality, all parliaments adopted the dogma of infinite tolerance. Tolerance toward the alien, the hostile, and the aggressive was seen as a highly humanitarian achievement, but was, as the history of the nineteenth and especially of our present century shows, merely an ever-greater abandoning of ourselves.

The gullible European has only too credulously listened to these temptations, sung to the lyrics of the sirens' song—freedom, justice, brotherhood. The fruits of this subversion are apparent today. They are so nakedly apparent that even the most unbiased person, a person who has no idea of the necessary historical relationships, must become aware that he has placed his confidence in crafty and glib leaders, who intended not his good, but the *destruction of all laboriously acquired civilization, all culture.* The proof, grown to a bloody reality, can be found in the Russian revolution, which has been passed over in silence by the liberal or Jewish papers in striking contrast to their other doings. And during the war the newspapers of the right suppressed the clear facts of the matter in order to protect their inner front. This resoluteness came too late; in Germany too the Jews had become the leading enemies of the Germanic ideal.

Let us turn to the *facts* of the Russian revolution.

There can be no doubt that the entire Russian people longed for the end of Tsarist rule. Anyone who has witnessed this form of government must acknowledge that it discouraged by every means any kind of independent activity—economic, communal, or intellectual; that the rule of a rotten civil service was a repressive one. Thus all of Russia felt as if relieved from a nightmare when the news of the fall of the Tsar spread from the Baltic to the Pacific. The suppressed self-confidence of the citizen reappeared everywhere with a vigor that one would never have believed possible, and the leaders had every reason to look ahead optimistically and to hope to be able to solve their new problems peacefully.

But soon *centrifugal* forces set in *in the form of the Soldiers' Soviets* (!!)

The soldiers, who during March of 1917 had all promised to continue the war in Russia's defense until victory, came under the influence of manipulative agitators who aimed at aggravating discord and loosening discipline. The Soldiers' Soviets and the workers were first led by a couple of Georgians, Chkheidze and Tseretelli, who thought the time had come to apply socialism to politics, although they set aside economic and social demands. But very soon they were pushed aside, pushed aside by Jews, who flocked from all corners of Russia and from abroad. By energetic agitation, aimed at the egotism of each individual, they soon managed to be popular with the mob.

Taking note of the strong and widespread mood, they at first pretended to be moderates; thus the party spokesmen and representatives [M. I.] Kogan-Bernstein, [Mark] Liber, [Fedor] Dan, and [Abram] Gotz acted loyal to the state, but secretly hindered the government, in the name of freedom, from taking steps against the rapidly growing bolshevik movement.

The soul of this movement was the well-known [Lev] Bronstein, alias Trotsky, a Jew from the Ekaterinoslav Province, and his blood brother [Grigorii] Apfelbaum, called Zinoviev. The Jewish spirit, with all its energy, fastened on these two, together with the Russo-Tatar V. I. Lenin. In the streets, in the barracks and military hospitals, in meetings and at the front, it was the Jews who promised peace, freedom, and bread to everybody, demanded a general fraternization with the Germans, in short, tried to disorganize the state with deliberate lies.

In July 1917, the Kronstadt sailors (!!), led by the infamous [Simon] Roschal, a Jewish student from the technical college of Riga, tried to overthrow the [Alexander] Kerensky administration. The revolt failed and the Bolshevik leaders, the Jews Bronstein (Trotsky), [Lev] Rosenblum (pseud. Kamenev), [Alexandra] Kollontai and others, were taken prisoners. But not for long. Thanks to the energy of Liber and Dan they were released by the weak Kerensky. Dan and Liber, of course, justified their demand in the name of freedom. After all, the Bolsheviks had only fought for their ideals, and these convictions ought to be honored! Which goes to show that it is good to have one's brothers at work in many parties.

Now the agitation began in earnest. The soldiers were told that they were too tired to go on with this war, that the slaughter had to end, and so forth. Their moral resistance had of course been worn down by three years of war and so it is no wonder that they yielded to the seductions of peace and threw away their arms when they were supposed to attack. Kerensky (by the way no Jew) wavered between his socialist principles and the national will; his hysterical speeches did not succeed in stemming the attrition, and in October 1917 a soldiers' congress appealed to all the armies, over the heads of their governments, to lay down their arms.

The history of this congress is informative and typical. It was supposed to discuss all social and political questions, but most of the Russian armies, in the face of the threatening military situation, refused to engage in political disputes for the time being. This hindered the zealous Bolsheviks not at all: they gathered all their representatives together; the Jew [Nikolai] Abraham (Krylenko) took the chair and, incompetent and unauthorized, issued proclamations and decrees in the name of the entire Russian army, in the name of the entire Russian people. Kerensky's attempt to suppress this impudence failed miserably: the Petersburg garrison, demoralized by idleness and provided with money by a mysterious source (people were sure it was German, since the Jew Fürstenberg-Genezky had evidently transferred large sums from Stockholm to the Petersburg Soldiers' Soviet), sided with its patrons, and overthrew the last Russian government in the beginning of November 1917. It is also characteristic that during the last sessions of the constituent assembly no Russian spoke against the government, only Jews.

In this way the victory of the Bolsheviks was decided, and now the Jews showed no restraint. They removed their masks and established an almost purely Jewish "Russian" government.

Lenin is the only non-Jew among the peoples' commissars; he is, so to speak, the Russian storefront of a Jewish business. Who were the others? The names to be given here will completely reveal a rule of Jews which can no longer be denied. [. . .]

But one can observe, and all recent news confirms it, that the hatred against the Jews in Russia is constantly spreading despite all terror. The most tenderhearted and tolerant Russians are now as full of this hatred as a Tsarist bureaucrat used to be. If the present government falls, no Jew will remain alive in Russia; one can say with certainty that what is not killed will be driven out. Where to? The Poles are already keeping them at bay, and so they will all come into old Germany, where we love the Jews so much and keep the warmest seats ready for them.

46

ADOLF BARTELS

The Struggle of the Age

First published as "Der Kampf der Zeit," *Deutsches Schrifttum* 10 (January 1920), 1–2.

According to its spokesmen, the revolution has put an end to the monarchy and the class domination that went with it and founded a people's state in which pure democracy rules. We from the other side see things a bit differently. According to our view, with the revolution internationalism triumphed over nationalism or, put more precisely, Judaism over the Germans. Democracy or, more correctly, absolute parliamentary rule, the supposed foundation of the perfected people's state, is for us only a mask behind which the domination of the international plutocracy conceals itself. With the fall of the Empire, the destruction of the Bismarckian constitutional order means to us the ruin of the state corresponding to the German national character; what has taken its place is in no way a German people's state, but a cosmopolitan formation that can only lead the German people to its final ruin. Even before the collapse, the political, ethical, and social development of the "West"—that is, England, France, and America—was held up to us Germans as a model. But, however highly we must estimate the national feeling of peoples hostile to us, we are easily justified, more than ever after the experiences of the peace, in designating them inferior socially and ethically and declaring even in purely political terms our old monarchy, born of the spirit of Prussia, that is, of a concentration of the German national character, as a higher form. The conditions in present-day Germany, which basically can probably only get worse, offer some proof of the conclusion that we are in severe need of relearning our lessons.

We are obviously of the opinion that the struggle between internationalism and nationalism is in no way decided with the German revolution and the constitutional order born of it, that the struggle will continue and can in consequence produce events of another nature. For us it is the great struggle of the age, which must be fought out not only in politics, but in all areas of life and culture. The internationalists or, let us say clearly, the Jews and the comrades of the Jews, have long maintained the practice of posing as the only true representatives of culture and, if words were deeds, so would the new rulers be, in fact, its most faithful servants. But we Germans who are conscious of our national character, those of us who have not yet lost the habit of thinking, did not fall for Wilhelm II's empty talk of culture and even less for that of the new rulers. Wilhelm II, who may have been a bad ruler from a German point of view, still stood at least somewhat in the

Prussian and German tradition; the *homines novi* have spiritually nothing and are spiritually nothing, as is shown in the currently fashionable fixation on the allegedly universal humanism of classical Weimar, which was much more German than even the average scholar of today realizes. No, dear gentlemen, we are just as little taken in by the hazy idealism with which democracy has done its hawking for a hundred years as by the business culture of the international Jew. We want to save, maintain, and fortify our German national character, make it the firm foundation of all state and existential forms; we want back the Germany of Bismarck, but we also want to open it up to new possibilities of development, especially in the area of culture. We have use for neither Karl Marx nor [Ferdinand] Lassalle, neither August Bebel nor Hugo Preuss for this development; indeed, however, we do have use for Ernst Moritz Arndt and Friedrich Ludwig Jahn (of whom you have not even a proper knowledge), indeed for Jeremias Gotthelf and Friedrich Hebbel, Heinrich von Treitschke and Paul de Lagarde. These are no Jewish sophists, but German thinkers, no phrasemongers, but German fighters.

We see with particular clarity the area of German literature. There do exist German fools who still declare Heinrich Heine a great writer, the greatest lyric poet next to Goethe, who have our most recent writing culminate in someone like Hugo von Hofmannsthal. But we no longer let them annoy us; long have we learned to laugh at them. Even the most modest artist of the homeland, if he simply comprehends life faithfully and lends it honest form, is dearer to us than the greatest Jewish artist of momentary fashion. We also foresee for the former a greater future: he will at least continue to be loved and read in his homeland, while the Jewish virtuoso will amount to nothing more than a curiosity for literary researchers. Perhaps there is no truly great German today, but there is no lack of capable writers, and their help suffices to advance us in the struggle of the age, the struggle for our national character. What we need most immediately is an authentic German literature of indictment—everywhere and without consideration, the truth must be spoken. Then perhaps a literature of renewal will arise, one with new ideas, new forms, new voices, perhaps new people. Expressionism, of course, seeks something like this as well. But in its Jewish disfigurement, it elevates the puny individual to the measure of all things, while that role of course can only be played by national character, something large. The German national character, is what we, proud and modest, wish to serve.

47

GERMAN WORKERS' PARTY (DAP)

The Twenty-five Points

First announced on February 25, 1920 in Munich. Published in *Das Programm der NSDAP und seine weltanschaulichen Grundgedanken* (Munich: Franz Eher Nachfolger, 1932), 15–19.

The program of the German Workers' Party[1] is limited as to period. The leaders have no intention, once the aims announced in it have been achieved, of setting up fresh ones, merely in order artificially to increase the discontent of the masses, and so ensure the continued existence of the party.

1. The name of the German Workers' Party was changed to the National Socialist German Workers' Party (NSDAP) in August 1920.

1. We demand the union of all Germans to form a Great Germany on the basis of the right of self-determination enjoyed by nations.
2. We demand equality of rights for the German people in its dealings with other nations and abolition of the peace treaties of Versailles and Saint-Germain.
3. We demand land and territory (colonies) for the nourishment of our people and for settling our excess population.
4. None but members of the nation may be citizens of the state. None but those of German blood, whatever their creed, may be members of the nation. No Jew therefore may be a member of the nation.
5. Anyone who is not a citizen of the state may live in Germany only as a guest and must be regarded as being subject to foreign laws.
6. The right of voting on the leadership and legislation is to be enjoyed by the state alone. We demand therefore that all official appointments, of whatever kind, whether in the Reich, in the country, or in the smaller localities, shall be granted to citizens of the state alone. We oppose Parliament's corrupting custom of filling posts merely with a view to party considerations and without reference to character or capacity.
7. We demand that the state shall make it its first duty to promote the industry and livelihood of citizens of the state. If it is not possible to nourish the entire population of the state, foreign nationals (noncitizens of the state) must be excluded from the Reich.
8. All non-German immigration must be prevented. [. . .]
9. All citizens of the state shall be equal as regards rights and duties.
10. It must be the first duty of each citizen of the state to work with his mind or with his body. The activities of the individual may not clash with the interests of the whole, but must proceed within the frame of the community and be for the general good.

We demand therefore:

11. Abolition of incomes unearned by work.
12. In view of the enormous sacrifice of life and property demanded of a nation by every war, personal enrichment due to a war must be regarded as a crime against the nation. We demand therefore ruthless confiscation of all war gains.
13. We demand nationalization of all businesses (trusts). [. . .]
14. We demand that the profits from wholesale trade shall be shared.
15. We demand extensive development of security for old age.
16. We demand creation and maintenance of a healthy middle class, immediate communalization of wholesale business premises, and their lease at a cheap rate to small traders, and that extreme consideration shall be shown to all small purveyors to the state, district authorities, and smaller localities.
17. We demand land reform suitable to our national requirements. [. . .]
18. We demand ruthless prosecution of those whose activities are injurious to the common interest. Sordid criminals against the nation, usurers, profiteers, etc., must be punished with death, whatever their creed or race.
19. We demand that the Roman Law, which serves the materialistic world order, shall be replaced by a legal system for all Germany.

20. With the aim of opening to every capable and industrious German the possibility of higher education and of thus obtaining advancement, the state must consider a thorough reconstruction of our national system of education. [. . .]

21. The state must see to raising the standard of health in the nation by protecting mothers and infants, prohibiting child labor, increasing bodily efficiency by obligatory gymnastics and sports laid down by law, and by extensive support of clubs engaged in the bodily development of the young.

22. We demand abolition of a paid army and formation of a national army.

23. We demand legal warfare against conscious political lying and its dissemination in the press. In order to facilitate creation of a German national press we demand:

a) that all editors and their assistants of newspapers employing the German language must be members of the nation;

b) that special permission from the state shall be necessary before non-German newspapers may appear. These are not necessarily printed in the German language;

c) that non-Germans shall be prohibited by law from participation financially in or influencing German newspapers. [. . .]

It must be forbidden to publish papers which do not promote the national welfare. We demand legal prosecution of all tendencies in art and literature of a kind likely to disintegrate our life as a nation, and the suppression of institutions which militate against the requirements mentioned above.

24. We demand liberty for all religious denominations in the state, so far as they are not a danger to it and do not militate against the moral feelings of the German race.

The party as such stands for positive Christianity, but does not bind itself in the matter of creed to any particular confession. It combats the Jewish-materialist spirit within us and outside of us. [. . .]

25. That all the foregoing may be realized, we demand the creation of a strong central power of the state. Unquestioned authority of the politically centralized Parliament over the entire Reich and its organizations, and formation of chambers for classes and occupations for the purpose of carrying out the general laws promulgated by the Reich in the various states of the confederation.

The leaders of the party swear to go straight forward—if necessary, to sacrifice their lives—in securing fulfillment of the foregoing points.

48

JOSEPH GOEBBELS

National Socialism or Bolshevism?

First published as "Nationalsozialismus oder Bolschewismus?" *NS-Briefe* (October 25, 1925).

My dear friend from the Left,

Not as *captatio benevolentiae,* but straight out and without reservations, I confess I liked you, you are a fine fellow! Yesterday evening I could have gone on debating with you for hours before the thousand of our flock who were listening because I had the feeling that the central question of our likenesses and our differences was here being raised in the forum of the German workers, whom it in the last analysis concerns. And out of the same feeling I am writing you these lines.

You have clearly realized what it's all about. We agreed about the causes. No honest-thinking person today would want to deny the justification of the workers' movements. The important thing is the performance and the formulation of the final goal of these movements. Grown out of need and misery, they stand before us today as living witnesses to our disunity and impotence, to our lack of national courage and will for the future. We no longer need to discuss whether the demand of the German employee for social compensation is justified, just as we don't need to discuss whether or not the disenfranchised fourth estate may or must live.

National or international in path and goal, that is the issue. We are both fighting honestly and resolutely for freedom and only for freedom; we want as final fulfillment peace and community, you that of the world, I that of the people. That this fulfillment cannot be attained in this system is entirely clear and evident to both of us. To talk of calm today is to make the cemetery one's home; to be peaceful under this government is to be pacifist and cowardly. You and I, we both know that a government, a system that is inwardly thoroughly mendacious, is meant to be overthrown; that therefore one must sacrifice and fight for the new state. Yesterday we both could have written the same thing in this respect in the album of the bourgeois coward of black–red–gold Social Democracy.

So far we would have agreed.

I do not have to emphasize for you that for me people and nation means something different than they do for the talkative gentleman with the belly and the golden watch chain stretched across it, who unctuously recapitulates the diluted phrases of [Gustav] Stresemann and [Oskar] Hergt like a phonograph. People, that is, we, you and I, the thousand who yesterday sat attentively before us, the millions who are of the same spirit and the same blood as we. Nation is the organic union of these millions in a community of need, bread, and fate. A longing for the nation is alive in the people. To form the nation as a community of need, bread, and fate is our first goal. The second goal follows from this first one necessarily and as if of its own accord: the freedom of the nation. For this freedom the people will have to fight, and will be impelled to fight when they have become a nation. That is our way. Nothing new, nothing shocking for those in the know, an ancient, historical, causal chain. The history of peoples is nothing other than a single consequence of the will to build the nation and of the energetic movement of nations toward freedom. Never has a people been redeemed by another people, whether out of goodness, love, or philanthropy; it achieved redemption always by its own will for freedom alone, which found help from the neighboring people only if the will for power and existence shared the same direction.

You praise Russia as the country of international solidarity and admit yourself that today Russia is more Russian than ever. What you call the bolshevik internationalism of Moscow is pan-Slavism in its clearest and most pronounced form. I wouldn't think of singing along with the choir of middle-class liars and ignoramuses. Russia, Russian bolshevism, are not about to collapse. But the Russian soviet system does not endure because it is bolshevik, because it is Marxist, because it is international, but because it is national, because it is Russian. No tsar ever grasped the Russian people in its depths, in its passion, in its national instincts as Lenin has. He gave the Russian peasant what bolshevism always meant to the peasant: freedom and property. In this way he made the most indigenous group, the peasants, into the real supporters of the new system. The more the Russian peasant hates the Jew, especially the Soviet Jew, the more passionately is he a follower of agrarian reform, the more ardently does he love his country, his land, and his soil. "Down with the Jewish Soviets, long live the Leninist agrarian reform!" This slogan characterizes most strikingly the attitude of the Russian peasant toward the new system in Russia.

The German Communist sees bolshevism just as the capitalist Jew of the West would wish: ideological, theoretical, with an infernal hatred for the enemies of his idea; impractical, without understanding of true reality, even as idea without regard for the possibility of its practical completion. Not for nothing is he a child of the people of poets and thinkers. He sees in Russia the seed of the Marxist world state, while in reality it is only the seed of a new national organization of the states of Europe.

To recapitulate: Lenin sacrificed Marx and instead gave Russia freedom. You want to sacrifice German freedom for Marx.

Even the Bolshevik Jew has clearly recognized the compelling necessity of the Russian national state and has early and wisely adjusted himself to it. Whether for tactical reasons, whether with ulterior motives, who knows? Probably! In any case, today he has to sing with the rest of the chorus. And that spoils the harmony for the capitalist Jews in the West. Therefore the brooding hatred of the West for Soviet Russia. The stock exchange cannot and will not tolerate a national state, and the bolshevik-international Jew is not enough security against a national-bolshevik Russia.

Yesterday you beat about the bush on the Jewish question. I know why. Please don't object. We don't want to deceive each other. You are an anti-Semite as I am. You don't yet want to admit this to yourself. The Jew can at best exist in communism. The Jew in a national-bolshevik state is an absurdity. He himself knows that best. But he is tactically clever. With refined calculation he adjusts to the forces that are stronger than he is. He adjusts to the national instincts of a people, which he sees and takes into account earlier than we do, because he is not bound to them with his heart but at best observes them as an interested spectator. The Jewish question in bolshevism too is more complicated than one might think. It will probably not be that the capitalist and the Bolshevik Jew are one and the same. Perhaps in the final effect but never in present practice. Perhaps they both want the same in the end: You shall devour all peoples! But they are too intelligent to offer resistance at the wrong places to those forces that are stronger than their merchant instincts. One such force is the national will for creation, which in Russia today is more awake than ever.

For the German burgher bolshevism begins with the demand for personal sacrifice. To him everything, everything is bolshevism that in any way lays a hand on his wallet. For him the only thing that is politically right and true, that is, not bolshevik, is the guarantee of his possessions and his complacent, philistine peace. I see you smile: yes, there we can scold him together. That is common, base, disgusting, and in the true sense of the word nationally irresponsible. You and I don't give a hoot for national phrases behind which there is no will for sacrifice. Bolshevism only begins with the preparation of international mush. It has nothing, absolutely nothing to do with the size of the sacrifice demanded of the possessors. We can and must demand everything, everything, if the freedom of the nation requires it.

What you said yesterday about international fraternization, my friend, that is nonsense, and you certainly know that as well as I do. Do you really believe that the Russian people want solidarity? Has it never occurred to you that Russia stands on the side of the German proletariat because it sees in it the first and most important factor in the stabilization of its national existence? There is not a single ruble working in German communism on which the word *Russia* is not written as a program.

Never has an oppressed class freed itself by international protests, but always by the national will for the future. The French bourgeois at the end of the eighteenth century did not wait for the solidarity of the German and English bourgeoisie. He shook off his chains alone, with his own strength, at the moment when they became unbearable for him. The powers of the old system tried to break his spirit, but he defended himself and victoriously carried his idea, liberalism, throughout the entire world. The same today. The German worker will be free only if he frees himself, with his own strength, and he will do that when he can no longer bear the chains of slavery.

You rave about the International without having understood it in its deepest meaning. The more corrupt a system, the more international its relations. Your and our most bitter enemy, democracy, money, is international. It tries to swindle the fighters for freedom with this International, because it knows that it will then be eternally invincible.

The path to freedom leads through the nation. The more united this nation, the stronger and more fervent the will for freedom. To set in motion this passionate will for freedom in the nation, that is the task of National Socialism. We want freedom, as you do, but with other means, with means that lead to the goal. International solidarity is your program; the solidarity of the nation, the community of the people is ours. I noticed one thing yesterday with joy: You now believe me that our community of the people is not the pacifistic mush that Mr. [Wilhelm] Marx and Mr. Stresemann mean. The community of the people today is nothing but the struggle for the rights of the people for the sake of the nation. We want this struggle because it alone can bring freedom.

There must be fighting for the future. You and I, we fight each other without really being enemies. In this way we splinter our forces, and we never reach our goal. Perhaps the most extreme need will bring us together. Perhaps!

Do not shake your head! This question is a matter of Germany's future, and more, of Europe's future. The new state or the decline of the West, both lie in our hands.

We young men, you and I, we are the bearers of the fate of generations.

Let us never forget that!

I greet you!

                                                                Dr. Goebbels

49

ADOLF HITLER

Mein Kampf

First published in *Mein Kampf,* vol. 2 (Munich: Verlag Franz Eher Nachfolger, 1927), 525–536, 771–772.

All great, world-shaking events have been brought about not by written matter but by the spoken word. [. . .]

The bourgeois intelligentsia protest against such a view only because they themselves obviously lack the power and ability to influence the masses by the spoken word, since they have thrown themselves more and more into purely literary activity and renounced the real agitational activity of the spoken word. Such habits necessarily lead in time to what distinguishes our bourgeoisie today; that is, the loss of the psychological instinct for mass effect and mass influence.

While the speaker gets a continuous correction of his speech from the crowd he is addressing—since he can always see in the faces of his listeners to what extent they can follow his arguments with understanding and whether the impression and the effect of his words lead to the desired goal—the writer does not know his readers at all. Therefore, to begin with, he will not aim at a definite mass before his eyes but will keep his arguments entirely general. By this to a certain degree he loses psychological subtlety and in consequence suppleness. And so by and large a brilliant speaker will be able to write better than a brilliant writer can speak, unless he continuously practices this art. On top of this there is the fact that the mass of people as such is lazy; that they remain inertly in the spirit of their old habits and, left to themselves, will take up a piece of written matter only reluctantly if it is not in agreement with what they themselves believe and does not bring them what they had hoped for. Therefore, an article with a definite tendency is for the most part read only by people who can already be reckoned to this tendency. At most a leaflet or a poster can, by its brevity, count on getting a moment's attention from someone who thinks differently. The picture in all its forms up to the film has greater possibilities. Here a man needs to use his brains even less; it suffices to look, or at most to read extremely brief texts, and thus many will more readily accept a pictorial presentation than read an article of any length. The picture brings them in a much briefer time, I might almost say at one stroke, the enlightenment that they obtain from written matter only after arduous reading.

The essential point, however, is that a piece of literature never knows into what hands it will fall, and yet it must retain its definite form. In general the effect will be the greater, the more this form corresponds to the intellectual level and nature of those very people who will be its readers. A book that is destined for the broad masses must therefore attempt from the very beginning to have an effect, both in style and elevation, different from a work intended for higher intellectual classes.

Only by this kind of adaptability does written matter approach the spoken word. To my mind, the speaker can treat the same theme as the book; he will, if he is a brilliant popular orator, not be likely to repeat the same reproach and the same substance twice in the same form. He will always let himself be borne by the great masses in such a way that instinctively the very words come to his lips that he needs to speak to the hearts of his audience. And if he errs, even in the slightest, he has the living correction before him.

As I have said, he can read from the facial expression of his audience whether, firstly, they understand what he is saying, whether, secondly, they can follow the speech as a whole, and to what extent, thirdly, he has convinced them of the soundness of what he has said. If firstly he sees that they do not understand him, he will become so primitive and clear in his explanations that even the last member of his audience has to understand him; if he feels secondly that they cannot follow him, he will construct his ideas so cautiously and slowly that even the weakest member of the audience is not left behind, and he will thirdly if he suspects that they do not seem convinced of the soundness of his argument, repeat it over and over in constantly new examples. He himself will utter their objections, which he senses though unspoken, and go on confuting them and exploding them until at length even the last group of an opposition, by its very bearing and facial expression, enables him to recognize its capitulation to his arguments.

Here again it is often a question of overcoming prejudices that are not based on reason, but, for the most part unconsciously, are supported only by sentiment. To overcome this barrier of instinctive aversion, of emotional hatred, of prejudiced rejection, is a thousand times harder than to correct a faulty or erroneous scientific opinion. False concepts and poor knowledge can be eliminated by instruction, the resistance of the emotions never. Here only an appeal to these mysterious powers themselves can be effective; and the writer can hardly ever accomplish this, but almost exclusively the orator can. [. . .]

Let no one reply (as a big German national newspaper in Berlin tried to do) that Marxism itself, by its writings, especially by the effect of the great basic work of Karl Marx, provides proof counter to this assertion. Seldom has anyone made a more superficial attempt to support an erroneous view. What gave Marxism its astonishing power over the great masses is by no means the formal written work of the Jewish intellectual world, but rather the enormous wave of oratorical propaganda that took possession of the great masses over the course of years. Of a hundred thousand German workers, not a hundred on the average know this work, which has always been studied by a thousand times more intellectuals and especially Jews than by real adherents of this movement from the great lower classes. And this work was not written for the great masses, but exclusively for the intellectual leadership of that Jewish machine for world conquest; it was stoked subsequently with an entirely different fuel: the press. For that is what distinguishes the Marxist press from our bourgeois press. The Marxist press is written by agitators, and the bourgeois press would like to carry on agitation by means of writers. The Social Democratic, yellow journalist, who almost always goes from the meeting hall to the newspaper office, knows his public like no one else. But the bourgeois scribbler who comes out of his study to confront the great masses is nauseated by their very fumes and faces them helplessly with the written word.

What has won the millions of workers for Marxism is less the literary style of the Marxist church fathers than the indefatigable and truly enormous propaganda work of tens of thousands of untiring agitators, from the great agitator down to the small trade-union official, the shop steward, and discussion speaker; this work consisted of the hundreds of thousands of meetings at which, standing on the table in smoky taverns, these people's orators hammered at the masses and thus were able to acquire a marvelous knowledge of this human material which really put them in a position of choosing the best weapons with which to attack the fortress of public opinion. And it consisted furthermore in the gigantic mass demonstrations, these parades of hundreds of thousands of men, which burned into the small, wretched individual the proud conviction that, paltry worm as he was, he was nevertheless a part of a great dragon, beneath whose burning breath the hated bourgeois world would some day go up in flame and the proletarian dictatorship would celebrate its ultimate final victory.

Such propaganda produced the people who were ready and prepared to read a Social Democratic press, however a press which in turn is not written, but spoken. For, while in the bourgeois camp professors and scholars, theoreticians and writers of all sorts, occasionally attempt to speak, in the Marxist movement the speakers occasionally try to write. And precisely the Jew, who is especially to be considered in this connection, will in general, thanks to his lying dialectical skill and suppleness, even as a writer be more of an agitational orator than a literary creator. [. . .]

Important as the movement's literature may be, in our present position it will be more important for the equal and uniform training of the upper and lower leaders than for the winning of the hostile masses. Only in the rarest cases will a convinced Social Democrat or a fanatical Communist condescend to acquire a National Socialist pamphlet, let alone a book, to read it and from it gain an insight into our conception of life or to study the critique of his own. Even a newspaper will be read but very seldom if it does not bear the party stamp. Besides, this would be of little use; for the general aspect of a single copy of a newspaper is so chopped up and so divided in its effect that looking at it once cannot be expected to have any influence on the reader. We may and must expect no one for whom pennies count to subscribe steadily to an opposing newspaper merely from the urge for objective enlightenment. Scarcely one out of ten thousand will do this. Only a man who has already been won to the movement will steadily read the party organ, and he will read it as a running news service of his movement.

The case is quite different with the "spoken" leaflet! The man in the street will far sooner take it into his hands, especially if he gets it for nothing, and all the more if the headlines plastically treat a topic that at the moment is in everyone's mouth. By a more or less thorough perusal, it may be possible by such a leaflet to call his attention to new viewpoints and attitudes, even in fact to a new movement. But even in the most favorable case this will provide only a slight impetus, never an accomplished fact. For the leaflet too can only suggest or point to something, and its effect will only appear in combination with a subsequent, more thoroughgoing instruction and enlightenment of its readers. And this is and remains the mass meeting.

The mass meeting is also necessary for the reason that the individual, who at first, while becoming a supporter of a young movement, feels lonely and easily succumbs to the fear of being alone, for the first time gets the picture of a larger community, which in most people has a strengthening, encouraging effect. The same man, within a company or a battalion, surrounded by all his comrades, would set out on an attack with a lighter heart than if left entirely on his own. In the crowd he always feels somewhat sheltered, even if a thousand reasons actually argue against it.

But the community of the great demonstration not only strengthens the individual it also unites and helps to create an esprit de corps. The man who is exposed to grave tribulations, as the first advocate of a new doctrine in his factory or workshop, needs that strengthening that lies in the conviction of being a member and fighter in a great, comprehensive body. And he obtains an impression of this body for the first time in the mass demonstration. When from his little workshop or big factory, in which he feels very small, he steps for the first time into a mass meeting and has thousands and thousands of people of the same opinions around him; when as a seeker he is swept away by three or four thousand others into the mighty effect of suggestive intoxication and enthusiasm, when the visible success and agreement of thousands confirm to him the rightness of the new doctrine and for the first time arouse doubt in the truth of his previous conviction—then he himself has succumbed to the magic influence of what we designate as *mass suggestion*. The will, the longing, and also the power of thousands are accumulated in every individual. The man who enters such a meeting doubting and wavering leaves it inwardly reinforced: he has become a link in the community. [. . .]

No more than a hyena abandons carrion does a Marxist abandon treason. And don't annoy me, if you please, with the stupidest of all arguments, that, after all, so many workers bled for Germany. German workers, yes, but then they were no longer international Marxists. If in 1914 the German working class in their innermost convictions had still consisted of Marxists, the war would have been over in three weeks. Germany would have collapsed even before the first soldier set foot across the border. No, the fact that the German people was then still fighting proved that the Marxist delusion had not yet been able to gnaw its way into the bottommost depths. But in exact proportion as, over the course of the war, the German worker and the German soldier fell back into the hands of the Marxist leaders, in exactly that proportion he was lost to the fatherland. If at the beginning of the war and during the war twelve or fifteen thousand of these Hebrew corrupters of the people had been held under poison gas, as happened to hundreds of thousands of our very best German workers in the field, the sacrifice of millions at the front would not have been in vain. On the contrary: twelve thousand scoundrels eliminated in time might have saved the lives of a million real Germans, valuable for the future. But it just happened to be in the line of bourgeois "statesmanship" to subject millions to a bloody end on the battlefield without batting an eyelash, to regard ten or twelve thousand traitors, profiteers, usurers, and swindlers as a sacred national treasure and openly proclaim their inviolability.

50

R. W. DARRÉ

Marriage Laws and the Principles of Breeding

First published as "Die Grundgedanken der Zuchtaufgaben und die Ehegesetze," in *Neuadel aus Blut und Boden* (Munich: Lehmanns Verlag, 1930), 127–144.

> *The German Empire will not rise again until the good German blood rises again.*   RUEDOLF

"It annoys me to see how much trouble is taken to cultivate pineapples, bananas and other exotic plants in this rough climate, when so little care is given to the human race. Whatever people say, a human being is more valuable than all the pineapples in the world. He is the plant we must breed; he deserves all our trouble and care, for he is the ornament and the glory of the Fatherland" (Frederick the Great).

Doubtless if Frederick the Great had had the misfortune to be our contemporary, the host of his historic enemies would have been swelled by a group of Germans who would damn him utterly for his audacity in wanting to apply the laws of plant cultivation to the human race. For today it is part of the intellectual equipment of the complete idealist that he views the application to mankind of any breeding principles, learned from the world of plants or animals, as an expression of the worship of matter. He regards such things as materialism in the worst sense of the word.

This kind of negative attitude toward the application of principles of breeding to mankind is generally rooted in ideological considerations. Let me say something about that now, because one cannot very well create aristocracy without somehow subjecting it to principles of breeding.

The fact that today's German sees any effort to couple breeding questions with those of the public good as contrary to idealism is in itself a peculiarity in intellectual history. What these Germans now condemn was for centuries considered by our people to be an expression of custom and morality. It is perhaps even more peculiar that this is happening in a people who as recently as about a century ago would not permit an apprentice to become a master unless he could show proof of his unobjectionable descent; nor could he retain the rank of master if he chose a girl of unknown or undesired origin as his wife. In Germany until well into the nineteenth century, not only the nobility, but also groups of craftsmen and Germanic peasants very consciously pursued a policy of selective breeding. It is surprising to discover in the old traditions the extent to which German marriage laws were filled with wisdom about the interdependence of blood and culture, especially in those cases where the Germans intentionally erected a blood barrier, as for example toward the Slavs. Today our people seem to have lost all this wisdom, and we have carelessly gone so far that he who points out the need to pay attention to such things runs the risk of antagonizing some of the best of our people.

Today antagonism begins quite often with a certain excitement about the word *breeding*. But it is not so that the application of this term to human propagation would import something new from animal and plant breeding! No, in earlier times the word *breeding* was used for everything living; only later did the term nearly disappear in its application to mankind, while remaining in use for animals and plants. [. . .]

Züchtung [breeding] is applied knowledge of heredity. It is unimportant whether this knowledge of heredity has been gained by belief in a divine creation of the clan, or by belief in descent from an original ancestor, or by observation of human life, or by all of these together (as was obviously the case with our forefathers), or whether one uses modern instruments, like calipers, tape measure, magnifying glass, learned experiments and calculations, to establish that physical and mental abilities are indeed hereditary, that human beings are hereditarily different. The fact that until well into the nineteenth century the whole status system and social order of our people originated in equality of birth in marriage is enough to show clearly that our people had been inspired by the idea of breeding (in the earliest sense of the term) for one and a half millennia—and this in spite of Christianity, which circumstance is really the greatest peculiarity. Each rank consciously engaged in breeding: each rank *supervised its own procreation* by rejecting in marriage the next of kin and selecting from among other suitable girls. It does not matter whether the model for selection was firmly anchored in the consciousness, easily grasped, as it were, in material terms (and underlying racial evaluations, as is more or less clear in the case of the prescriptions against the Slavs), or whether it was only an indirect result of mental and physical merits of more immediate importance (such as might have come up, for example, in evaluating a girl as a housewife, etc.). In either case they understood the significance of the woman with her genetic inheritance for the ups and downs of the clan and tried to the best of their knowledge and ability to protect from harm the institution of marriage, which controls the direction of the clan's journey into the future, toward good or evil. If therefore until about a hundred years ago no journeyman—not to speak of noblemen or urban patricians—could become a master without having proved that he was born in "legal wedlock," and that for his four grandparents the same was true, it proves that for one and a half millennia German culture consciously built upon the concept of breeding: a concept of breeding which controlled the legal order and was itself conditioned by it, and which must be seen as the rock upon which the culture of the German people rested, as if created for eternity. It therefore shows either simple thoughtlessness or serious ignorance of the history of German culture and customs when Germans among us today attack the science of heredity by arguing that it is degrading to the German soul to use the word *breeding*—this concept of "animal" breeding—in any connection with Germans.

The old German marriage law, fused with the goals of breeding and with the prerogatives of rank, worked on the one hand as a filter that permitted complete procreation only to that blood which had been tested in constructive work; on the other hand as a safety device to protect the tested blood against the struggle of life sufficiently so that the founding of families and the number of children would not suffer. This old German marriage law was the wall that protected valuable German humanity, that kept subhumans outside the German social order and limited very considerably their opportunities to reproduce themselves, even sometimes making it impossible. It must be emphasized that the present victory of "subhumanity" (which caused the North American Lothrop Stoddard to write his well-known work, *The Cultural Revolution: The Threat of the Subhuman,* and has made our geneticists look for the cause of the population excess among the inferior and undesirable races, that is, those races that influence the German social order in an undesirable way) could only become a problem to the German people when, about a hundred years ago, [Prince Karl August von] Hardenberg adopted a course which necessarily had to end in the final dissolution of all marriage restrictions, a situation which has now been reached. Read what Freiherr [Karl] vom Stein, with his clear understanding of the causal interrelationships within the German people, prophesied as the result of these insane measures: it is easy to see that our present situation is solely the result of having at that time turned away from German views of marriage, thereby creating the foundation for a rank proliferation of inferiors of all colors. When today people talk about the "birthrate war among the races" as the cause of decline, they are confusing cause and effect.

Every legal order has not only an educational but also a breeding effect upon the whole of a people, even if this is not always apparent to the individual. The social order is the formal expression of the law, come alive. To use an analogy from natural science: the social order burns up as fuel the residual values of the people. It is less important that something is burned up than what is burned up. This "what" determines the "how" of the social order, which is directly dependent on the legal order. Therefore one can say that the legal order has *the* decisive significance for the fate of the hereditary values of a people, since it determines *which human values are furthered and which limited or even eliminated.*

The form of the law in turn is an expression of a certain world view. So we get the following chain of causes and effects: world view—legal order—social order—breeding—human physical characteristics. As applied to our people this means: Christianity and the late Roman Empire changed the world view of the Germanic peoples; hand in hand with this change went a change in legal concepts in an un-Germanic direction; it is therefore, as shown above, thoroughly logical that Germanic-German culture and the Germanic physical characteristics of Germans are being more and more displaced by an un-Germanic humanity. [. . .]

Thus we are facing the realization that questions of breeding are not trivial for political thought, but that they have to be at the center of all considerations, and that their answers must follow from the spiritual, from the ideological attitude of a people. We must even assert that a people can only reach spiritual and moral equilibrium if a well-conceived breeding plan stands at the very *center* of its culture. [. . .]

It has become apparent that what we call human culture and what "history" shows as its essential meaning were obviously dependent on some very specific races and still are. Thus the concept of race left the purely scientific realm and began to become an instrument of evaluating people in relation to culture and customs. This racial theory was developed by *ethnology;* today applied ethnology is already attempting to utilize the findings of ethnology for human society.

Actually the procedures of this evaluation should be very simple. If it can be established that this or that race is exclusively or predominantly responsible for creating a culture, and that the condition and persistence of this culture depend upon the race concerned, then basically the task is very easy: that race, upon which the culture to be sought or to be maintained depends, is to be preserved and furthered. But strangely enough this simple conclusion is drawn by only a few; even fewer are those who set forth demands based on it. A great proportion of ethnologists, together with a correspondingly large audience, want to transfer the scientist's objectivity toward natural phenomena to races and cultural questions as well. But we are evading life itself if we are unwilling, or no longer able, to express our opinion of life. [. . .]

Today we pursue only population increase, not breeding. We are surprised that German culture more and more disappears. But the general public in Germany is already too cowardly—for ultimately it is a question of cowardice!—to analyze these phenomena and find their *causes*. Or has the logical ability of the German people already diminished so much that it can no longer recognize the causes? *Population increase alone is of no use at all; the important thing is the heredity of the children.* But if we could ask our children what they have to say about this, they could only answer:

We are becoming fewer and fewer!

and:

We are becoming more and more inferior!

And thus our customs are condemned to death: they are useless! That is the truth! Let us at least have the courage to admit at last that it is the truth, and that fine speeches about our "belief in Germany's future" and similar subjects help matters not at all, even if made in frock coat, top hat, and officially; we are helped even less by sentimental, edifying discussions of the evils of modernity and the superiority of a pure and noble German soul.

Let us return to the customs of our forefathers: they sufficed to keep German culture alive for one and a half millennia. Let us re-educate our girls to a full understanding of the old German concept of *Züchtigkeit* [chastity]. For our ancestors it was not that bashful girl who had no knowledge of the facts of her sex who was *züchtig* [chaste], but she who consciously prepared herself to become a *mother* and as a *mother* to rule over a large number of children. Having children, for these women, was not exercising the right of self-determination but fulfilling their responsibility to the next generation; for them, service to the clan was still a guiding principle of life: their task was the preservation, furthering, and increase of their kind. These women knew about breeding and it was their pride. They did not feel degraded to a "brood-mare," as is the silly objection voiced today by those who apparently understand the highly praised "personal freedom" of the woman to mean only the freedom to taste all the joys of a "bedfellow" at their discretion and preferably without limit. Instead it was the pride of these women to become the ancestress of a noble clan and to receive the *confirmation of her own value in her noble son.* [. . .] If in our plan to create a new nobility the concept of marriage includes breeding, we are not thereby importing anything animal-like and unworthy of human beings. We are but resuming the best spiritual and moral traditions of our ancestors, while cleansing and clarifying them with the findings and researches of modern genetics. Thus we can thereby discredit any suspicion of "materialism."

51

JOSEPH GOEBBELS

Why Are We Enemies of the Jews?

Published as "Warum sind wir Judengegner?" in *Die verfluchten Hakenkreuzler. Etwas zum Nachdenken* (Munich: Franz Eher Nachfolger, 1930), 1–28.

We are NATIONALISTS because we see in the NATION the only possibility for the protection and the furtherance of our existence.

The NATION is the organic bond of a people for the protection and defense of their lives. He is nationally minded who understands this IN WORD AND IN DEED.

Today, in GERMANY, nationalism has degenerated into BOURGEOIS PATRIOTISM, and its power exhausts itself in tilting at windmills. It says GERMANY and means MONARCHY. It proclaims FREEDOM and means BLACK-WHITE-RED.

Young nationalism has its unconditional demands. BELIEF IN THE NATION is a matter of all the people, not for individuals of rank, a class, or an industrial clique. The eternal must be separated from the contemporary. The maintenance of a rotten industrial system has nothing to do with nationalism. I can love Germany and hate capitalism; not only CAN I do it, I also MUST do it. The germ of the rebirth of our people LIES ONLY IN THE DESTRUCTION OF THE SYSTEM OF PLUNDERING THE HEALTHY POWER OF THE PEOPLE.

WE ARE NATIONALISTS BECAUSE WE, AS GERMANS, LOVE GERMANY. And because we love Germany, we demand the protection of its national spirit and we battle against its destroyers.

WHY ARE WE SOCIALISTS?

We are SOCIALISTS because we see in SOCIALISM the only possibility for maintaining our racial existence and through it the reconquest of our political freedom and the rebirth of the German state. SOCIALISM has its peculiar form first of all through its comradeship in arms with the forward-driving energy of a newly awakened nationalism. Without nationalism it is nothing, a phantom, a theory, a vision of air, a book. With it, it is everything, THE FUTURE, FREEDOM, FATHERLAND!

It was a sin of the liberal bourgeoisie to overlook THE STATE-BUILDING POWER OF SOCIALISM. It was the sin of MARXISM to degrade SOCIALISM to a system of MONEY AND STOMACH.

We are SOCIALISTS because for us THE SOCIAL QUESTION IS A MATTER OF NECESSITY AND JUSTICE, and even beyond that A MATTER FOR THE VERY EXISTENCE OF OUR PEOPLE.

SOCIALISM IS POSSIBLE ONLY IN A STATE WHICH IS FREE INSIDE AND OUTSIDE.

DOWN WITH POLITICAL BOURGEOIS SENTIMENT: FOR REAL NATIONALISM!

DOWN WITH MARXISM: FOR TRUE SOCIALISM!

UP WITH THE STAMP OF THE FIRST GERMAN NATIONAL SOCIALIST STATE!

AT THE FRONT THE NATIONAL SOCIALIST GERMAN WORKERS' PARTY! [. . .]

WHY DO WE OPPOSE THE JEWS?

We are ENEMIES OF THE JEWS, because we are fighters for the freedom of the German people. THE JEW IS THE CAUSE AND THE BENEFICIARY OF OUR MISERY. He has used the social difficulties of the broad masses of our people to deepen the unholy split between Right and Left among our people. He has made two halves of Germany. He is the real cause for our loss of the Great War.

The Jew has no interest in the solution of Germany's fateful problems. He CANNOT have any. FOR HE LIVES ON THE FACT THAT THERE HAS BEEN NO SOLUTION. If we would make the German people a unified community and give them freedom before the world, then the Jew can have no place among us. He has the best trumps in his hands when a people lives in inner and outer slavery. THE JEW IS RESPONSIBLE FOR OUR MISERY AND HE LIVES ON IT.

That is the reason why we, AS NATIONALISTS and AS SOCIALISTS, oppose the Jew. HE HAS CORRUPTED OUR RACE, FOULED OUR MORALS, UNDERMINED OUR CUSTOMS, AND BROKEN OUR POWER.

THE JEW IS THE PLASTIC DEMON OF THE DECLINE OF MANKIND.

THE JEW IS UNCREATIVE. He produces nothing, HE ONLY HANDLES PRODUCTS. As long as he struggles against the state, HE IS A REVOLUTIONARY; as soon as he has power, he preaches QUIET AND ORDER so that he can consume his plunder at his convenience.

ANTI-SEMITISM IS UN-CHRISTIAN. That means, then, that he is a Christian who looks on while the Jew sews straps around our necks. TO BE A CHRISTIAN MEANS: LOVE THY NEIGHBOR.

52

ADOLF HITLER

Address to the Industry Club

First published in *Vortrag Adolf Hitlers vor westdeutschen Wirtschaftlern im Industrie-Klub zu Düsseldorf am 27. Januar 1932* (Munich: Verlag Franz Eher, 1932), 14ff.

Gentlemen, the development is clear for all to see: the crisis is very serious. It forces us to cut down expenses in every sphere. The most natural way of economizing is always to save in human labor-power. Industries will continuously be forced to ever greater rationalization, that means increase in achievement and reduction in the number of workmen employed. But if these workmen can no longer be given a place in newly started occupations, in newly developed industries, then that means that gradually three national banking accounts must be opened. The first account is called agriculture: from this national, basic account men were formerly economized to constitute the second account. This second account was handwork and later industrial production. Now an economy in manpower is being practiced on this second account and the men saved from this account are driven over into the third account—unemployment. With this word *unemployment* one is but shame-facedly seeking to put a better appearance upon hard facts: for the proper term is not *workless* but *existenceless* and therefore in truth "superfluous." It is the characteristic feature of our European nations that gradually a certain percentage of the population is statistically proved to be superfluous.

It is now quite clear that the necessity for supporting this third account thus falls upon the other two. That increases the pressure of taxation, and the consequence of that will be an enforced further rationalization of the method of production, further economy, and a still greater increase in the third account.

And to this must be added the fact that the fight which today all European nations wage for the world export market results naturally in a rise of prices which in its reaction compels men to practice further economies. The final result which today can hardly be foreseen will in any event prove decisive for the future or for the downfall of the white race, especially those peoples who in their narrow living space can establish economic autarchy only with very great difficulty. The further consequence will be that, for instance, England will carry through a reorganization with an eye to her internal market and for its protection will raise tariff barriers, high today and tomorrow still higher, and all other peoples, so far as they are in any way able to do so, will follow suit.

So far all those are in the right who regard the melancholy position of Germany as calling for special attention when considering our present distress, but they are wrong in seeking the cause of our distress in externals, for this position is certainly the result not merely of the external development but of our internal, I might almost say, aberration of spirit, our internal division, our internal collapse. [. . .]

Gentlemen, we know from our own experience that, through a mental aberration whose consequences you can in practice trace on every hand, Germany lost the war. Do you believe that when seven or eight million men for ten or twenty years have found themselves excluded from the national process of production that for these masses bolshevism could appear as anything but the logical theoretical complement of their actual, practical, economic situation? Do you really believe that the purely spiritual side of this catastrophe can be overlooked and that one day it will not transform itself into bitter reality—the evil curse following on the evil deed? [. . .]

The essential thing is to realize that at the present moment we find ourselves in a condition which has occurred several times before in the history of the world: already there have been times when the volume of certain products in the world exceeded the demand. Today we are experiencing the same thing on the largest possible scale: if all the motor factories in the world today were employed a hundred percent and worked a hundred percent, then one could replace the world's entire stocks of motors in four and a half or five years. If all the locomotive factories were employed a hundred percent, they could easily renew the entire locomotive material in the world in eight years. If all the rail-factories and rolling-mills of the world were employed a hundred percent, perhaps in ten to fifteen years one could put the whole system of railway lines at present in existence once more round the world. And that is true for nearly all industries. There has arisen such an increase in productive capacity that the current possible consumption market stands in no relation to this increased capacity. But if bolshevism as a world idea tears the Asiatic continent out of the human economic community, then the conditions for the employment of these industries which have developed on so gigantic a scale will be no longer even approximately realized. [. . .] When a politician or economist objects: that was, it is true, the case between Rome and Carthage, between England and Holland, or between England and France, but today the business world decides the matter, then I can only reply: that is not the spirit which formerly opened up the world for the white race, which for us Germans, too, opened the way into the economic life of the world. For it was not German business which conquered the world and led to the development of German power, but in our case, too, it was the power-state (*Machtstaat*) which created for the business world the general conditions for its subsequent prosperity. *In my view it is to put the cart before the horse when today people believe that by business methods they can, for instance, recover*

Germany's power-position instead of realizing that the power-position is also the condition for the improvement of the economic situation. That does not mean that one should not forthwith try to oppose the malady which has seized upon our economic life, although one cannot immediately attack the source of the malady. But it does mean that every such external solution ignores the kernel of the problem, since it fails to recognize that there is only one fundamental solution. That solution rests upon the realization that economic systems in collapse have always as their forerunner the collapse of the state and not vice versa—that there can be no flourishing economic life which has not before it and behind it the flourishing powerful state as its protection—that there was no Carthaginian economic life without the fleet of Carthage, and no Carthaginian trade without the army of Carthage— that it goes without saying that also in modern times—when blow is met by blow and the interests of peoples clash—*there can be no economic life unless behind this economic life there stands the determined political will of the nation absolutely ready to strike—and to strike hard.* [. . .]

And now behind us there lie twelve years of fighting. That fight has not been waged in theory alone and only by the party turned into practice: we are also ready to wage that fight on the larger scale. I cast my mind back to the time when with six other unknown men I founded this association, when I spoke before eleven, twelve, thirteen, fourteen, twenty, thirty, and fifty persons; when I recall how after a year I had won sixty-four members for the movement, how our small circle kept on growing, I must confess that what has today been created, when a stream of millions of our German fellow countrymen is flowing into our movement, represents something which is unique in German history. The bourgeois parties have had seventy years to work in; where, I ask you, is the organization which could be compared with ours? Where is the organization which can boast, as ours can, that at need it can summon 400,000 men into the street, men who are schooled to blind obedience and are ready to execute any order—provided that it does not violate the law? Where is the organization that in seventy years has achieved what we have achieved in barely twelve years?—and achieved with means which were of so improvised a character that one can hardly avoid a feeling of shame when one confesses to an opponent how poverty-stricken the birth and the growth of this great movement were in the early days.

Today we stand at the turning point of Germany's destiny. If the present development continues, Germany will one day of necessity land in bolshevik chaos, but if this development is broken, then our people must be taken into a school of iron discipline and gradually freed from the prejudices of both camps. A hard schooling, but one we cannot escape! [. . .]

People say to me so often: "You are only the drummer of national Germany." And supposing that I were only the drummer? It would today be a far more statesmanlike achievement to drum once more into this German people a new faith than gradually to squander the only faith they have. Take the case of a fortress, imagine that it is reduced to extreme privations: as long as the garrison sees a possible salvation, believes in it, hopes for it, then they can bear the reduced ration. But take from the hearts of men their last belief in the possibility of salvation, in a better future—take that completely from them, and you will see how these men suddenly regard their reduced rations as the most important thing in life. The more you bring it home to their consciousness that they are only objects for men to bargain with, that they are only prisoners of world politics, the more will they, like all prisoners, concentrate their thoughts on purely material interests. On the other hand, the more you bring the people back into the sphere of faith, of ideals, the more will it cease to regard material distress as the one and only thing which counts.

And the weightiest evidence for the truth of that statement is our own German people. We would not ever forget that the German people waged wars of religion for 150 years with prodigious devotion, that hundreds of thousands of men once left their plot of land, their property, and their belongings simply for an ideal, simply for a conviction. We would never forget that during those 150 years there was no trace of even an ounce of material interests. Then you will understand how mighty is the force of an idea, of an ideal. Only so can you comprehend how it is that in our movement today hundreds of thousands of young men are prepared at the risk of their lives to withstand our opponents. I know quite well, gentlemen, that when National Socialists march through the streets and suddenly in the evening a tumult and commotion arises, then the bourgeois draws back the window-curtain, looks out, and says: Once more my night's rest disturbed: no more sleep for me. Why must the Nazis always be so provocative and run about the place at night? Gentlemen, if everyone thought like that, then no one's sleep at night would be disturbed, it is true, but then the bourgeois today could not venture into the street. If everyone thought in that way, if these young folk had no ideal to move them and drive them forward, then certainly they would gladly be rid of these nocturnal fights. But remember that it means sacrifice when today many hundred thousands of SA and SS men of the National Socialist movement every day have to mount on their trucks, protect meetings, undertake marches, sacrifice themselves night after night, and then come back in the gray dawn either to workshop and factory or as unemployed to take the pittance of the dole: it means sacrifice when from the little which they possess they have further to buy their uniforms, their shirts, their badges, yes, and even pay their own fares. Believe me, there is already in all this the force of an ideal—a great ideal! And if the whole German nation today had the same faith in its vocation as these hundred thousands, if the whole nation possessed this idealism, Germany would stand in the eyes of the world otherwise than she stands now! For our situation in the world in its fatal effects is but the result of our own underestimate of German strength. Only when we have once more changed this fatal valuation of ourselves can Germany take advantage of the political possibilities which, if we look far enough into the future, can place German life once more upon a natural and secure basis—and that means either new living space (*Lebensraum*) and the development of a great internal market or protection of German economic life against the world without and utilization of all the concentrated strength of Germany. The labor resources of our people, the capacities, we have them already: no one can deny that we are industrious. [. . .]

And so in contrast to our own official government I cannot see any hope for the resurrection of Germany if we regard the foreign politics of Germany as the primary factor: the primary necessity is the restoration of a sound national German body politic armed to strike. In order to realize this end I founded thirteen years ago the National Socialist movement: that movement I have led during the last twelve years, *and I hope that one day it will accomplish this task and that, as the fairest result of its struggle, it will leave behind it a German body politic completely renewed internally, intolerant of anyone who sins against the nation and its interests, intolerant of anyone who will not acknowledge its vital interests or who opposes them, intolerant and pitiless against anyone who shall attempt once more to destroy or disintegrate this body politic, and yet ready for friendship and peace with anyone who has a wish for peace and friendship.*

53

German Farmer You Belong to Hitler! Why?

First published as National Socialist Campaign Pamphlet, 1932.

The German farmer stands between two great dangers today:

The one danger is the American economic system—Big capitalism!

  it means "world economic crisis"

  it means "eternalinterestslavery" . . .

  it means that the world is nothing more than a bag of booty for Jewish finance in
    Wall Street, New York, and Paris

  it enslaves man under the slogans of progress, technology, rationalization, stan-
    dardization, etc.

  it knows only profit and dividends

  it wants to make the world into a giant trust

  it puts the machine over man

  it annihilates the independent, earth-rooted farmer, and its final aim is the world
    dictatorship of Jewry [. . .]

  it achieves this in the political sphere through parliament and the swindle of
    democracy. In the economic sphere, through the control of credit, the mortgaging
    of land, the stock exchange and the market principle [. . .]

  The farmer's leagues, the Landvolk and the Bavarian Farmers' League all pay
    homage to this system.

The other danger is the Marxist economic system of bolshevism:

  it knows only the state economy

  it knows only one class, the proletariat

  it brings in the controlled economy

  it doesn't just annihilate the self-sufficient farmer economically—it roots him
    out [. . .]

  it brings the rule of the tractor

  it nationalizes the land and creates mammoth factory-farms

  it uproots and destroys man's soul, making him the powerless tool of the communist
    idea—or kills him

  it destroys the family, belief, and customs [. . .]

  it is anti-Christ, it desecrates the churches [. . .]

  its final aim is the world dictatorship of the proletariat, that means ultimately the
    world dictatorship of Jewry, for the Jew controls this powerless proletariat and
    uses it for his dark plans

  Big capitalism and bolshevism work hand in hand; they are born of Jewish thought
    and serve the master plan of world Jewry.

Who alone can rescue the farmer from these dangers?

NATIONAL SOCIALISM!

54

JOSEPH GOEBBELS

Fighting League for German Culture

First published as "Kampfbund für Deutsche Kultur," *Deutsche Kultur-Wacht* 1, no. 3 (1932), 17.

1. The Kampfbund für Deutsche Kultur (Fighting League for German Culture) assumes the task of leading the struggle in the greater Berlin district for German culture in all areas of art.

2. All artists and cultural workers, aside from educators, who are members of the party are therefore obligated to join the Kampfbund für Deutsche Kultur.

3. At events intended to represent the efficacy of German culture, all party offices are required to seek the advice of the appropriate specialists from the Kampfbund für Deutsche Kultur in both substantive and personnel matters, in accord with our basic principle of rejecting all limited, partisan artistic creations in an exclusive recognition, protection, and promotion of *German art and culture*.

4. The membership of the Kampfbund für Deutsche Kultur is composed of all creative and reproducing artists in the visual arts, architecture and technology, literature, the entertainment arts, and music. Party members employed as artists must in addition, for the protection of their legal and social-political interests, be enrolled in the National Socialist cell organization at their workplace. The department in charge of popular education in Central Department III encompasses all groups in education and the sciences that are *not* active in the cultural-artistic sphere, while the National Socialist Professional Association represents, in its engineering and technical department, the professional association protecting the economic interests of engineers and architects.

5. The official organ of the Kampfbund für Deutsche Kultur for the greater Berlin district, and thus the militant cultural–political publication due the support of the membership, is the *Deutsche Kultur-Wacht,* the national organ of the Kampfbund, which appears fortnightly in Berlin. Through special arrangement with the publisher it is available by subscription at a reduced price to members of the NSDAP and the Kampfbund für Deutsche Kultur.

District Administration for Greater Berlin, NSDAP
Dr. Goebbels

55

COUNT HARRY KESSLER

[On the Nietzsche Archive and the German Elections]

Diary entry, August 7, 1932.

Sunday, August 7, 1932
Weimar

In the afternoon visited Frau [Elisabeth] Förster-Nietzsche. The Nietzsche Archives are now, as she herself put it, "right in the center of politics." Emge, a Nazi professor of legal philosophy at Jena and a prospective Nazi minister in the Thuringian government, has been appointed chairman. Inside the Archives everyone, from the doorkeeper to the head, is a Nazi. Only she herself remains a nationalist.

She recounted how Hitler came to see her after the first night of Mussolini's play at the Weimar National Theatre. He had himself announced while she was talking to a number of Italian newspaper correspondents and, carrying an enormous bouquet, entered her box accompanied by his staff. Hitler, in the presence of the Italians, began a lively political discussion, expressing himself, in her view, rather incautiously about Austria and an *Anschluß*. He emphasized that he has no desire for this because Vienna is not a purely German city. She did not think it right that he should have said that in front of foreigners.

I asked her what impression Hitler made on her as a man. Is his a personality of any stature? Chiefly, she said, she noticed his eyes, which are fascinating and stare right through one. But he struck her as a religious rather than political leader and she did not feel him to be an outstanding politician.

Winifred Wagner, she told me, is a keen Nazi sympathizer. In fact this whole section of German intellectuals, whose background is really Goethe and the Romantic movement, is Nazi-contaminated without knowing why. The Nietzsche Archives have at least derived material advantage from their fascism: Mussolini sent them twenty thousand lire at the end of last year. "Empress" Hermine has announced her attendance at an Authors' Tea that Frau Foerster-Nietzsche gives next Thursday. Börries Münchhausen will read poems and Walter Bloem honor the occasion with his presence. It is enough to make one weep to see what has become of Nietzsche and the Nietzsche Archives!

As for the wife of the former emperor paying court to this eighty-six-year-old woman, the notion is almost grotesque when His Majesty's attitude towards Nietzsche in pre-1914 days is recalled! She added that the officers of the Reichswehr [Army] divisional staff headquarters include her in their official calls when they are posted here. What happened in my youth at Potsdam when Bernhard Stolberg, I, and our friends read Nietzsche? Stolberg was removed by his father and locked up with a priest for six months. At that time Nietzsche was reckoned as a revolutionary and almost as unpatriotic a fellow as the socialists.

We talked in the small parlor on the first floor. Through the connecting door I had a view of the sofa where Nietzsche sat, looking like an ailing eagle, the last time I saw him; our conversation made a deep impression on me. Mysterious, incomprehensible Germany.

6
The Struggle against Fascism

ALTHOUGH THE MENACE of Nazism was generally underestimated during the early years of the republic, isolated cries of alarm were made by a small number of prescient critics. For example, Ernst Bloch, a heterodox Marxist who appreciated the importance of myths, symbols, and utopian yearnings, cautioned the readers of *Das Tagebuch* against taking the threat lightly. His 1924 essay, "Hitler's Force," called Nazism the "ecstasy of bourgeois youth" and warned against discounting its revolutionary appeal, especially at a time when the Majority Socialists were obstructing a genuine revolution on the left.

After Hitler's success in the elections of 1930, the warnings grew louder and more frequent. The Marxist critic Walter Benjamin denounced the aestheticization of violence in fascist glorifications of World War I, an aestheticization he would later see as emblematic of the fascist approach to politics in general. The novelist Thomas Mann, whose unexpected endorsement of the republic is included in section 4, issued "An Appeal to Reason" in October 1930 at a meeting in Berlin, which only police protection prevented the Nazis from turning into a brawl. Proclaiming his allegiance to the cultural standards of the educated middle class (*Bildungsbürgertum*) and distancing himself from romantic irrationalism, Mann argued that the best hope of preserving German culture was the moderate SPD.

A few months later, another novelist, Lion Feuchtwanger, whose politics were further to the left than Mann's, expressed a more pessimistic view of the possibility of resistance. In *Welt am Abend* he posed the question "How Do We Struggle against a Third Reich?" and gloomily concluded as early as January 1931, that the battle was already all but lost. Berlin, he noted in despair, was a "city full of future emigrés." Heinrich Mann, Thomas's older brother and also an eminent novelist, darkly warned in late 1931 that Germany's moment of decision had come, and, were Hitler not stopped, blood was sure to flow. A similar note of desperation can be found in the appeal made by the KPD to working-class voters for National Socialism and members of the SA (*Sturmabteilung*) in an open letter in 1931.

If many intellectuals clearly recognized the mortal threat posed to culture and free intellectual inquiry by Nazism, others acknowledged its menace to traditional religion as well. The Austrian-born novelist Joseph Roth, a journalist for the *Frankfurter Zeitung* during most of the Weimar era, combined these two fears in his 1932 critique of the concept of "cultural bolshevism." Although of Jewish origin, Roth stressed the blasphemous implications of the Nazis' conflation of the cross and the swastika in their bastardized notion of a Christian-Germanic religion. The eminent theologian Paul Tillich directed an even more explicit appeal to Protestants to repudiate fascism in his 1932 "Ten Theses." Hoping to wean German Lutherans from their traditional obedience to temporal authority, Tillich insisted that, unless they actively opposed the Nazis, the future of Christianity itself was in jeopardy. A similar note was struck in the same year by the conservative Prussian Junker, Ewald von Kleist-Schmenzin, a jurist who was a member of the DNVP and the Stahlhelm.

All of these warnings proved, of course, to be in vain. Shortly after the Nazi seizure of power in January 1933, Bloch, the two Manns, Feuchtwanger, Roth, and Tillich joined thousands of other German intellectuals in exile who had struggled against fascism and lost. Benjamin committed suicide on the French-Spanish border after being turned back while attempting to leave for America in 1940. Kleist-Schmenzin remained in Germany and was beheaded for treason in the aftermath of the failed assassination plot against Hitler in 1944.

56

ERNST BLOCH

Hitler's Force

First published as "Hitlers Gewalt," *Das Tagebuch* 5 (April 12, 1924), 474–477.

At first we coldly ignored it. Shrugged our shoulders at the malicious pack that crawled forth. At the red posters with the driveling sentences, but the knuckledusters behind them. That which roughly stepped to our bedside early in the morning to demand our papers, stuck itself up as a party here. Jews are forbidden to enter the hall.

All this was able to sink back again. It was still too alien and had not penetrated deep enough, the old Munich was still alive. The animosity towards the war had matured earliest here; for a long time foreign beauty had been brought into the cityscape and flourished with it, became acclimatized. The grim recollection of 1919, of Eisner's[1] death and the entry of the White Guard could fade and the brutality withdraw into its shell, as if it had never been. The successful Kapp putsch[2] and the banishment of the socialist ministers admittedly indicated ruffled air again. But even this could still be understood as the reaction of a peasant province, a peasant city against very clumsy Communist dilettantisms. To Hitler this act seemed like a swan song; the further the soviet republic was left behind purely in temporal terms, the more certainly Bavaria seemed to assume its old aspect again.

Instead, as we know, the province became increasingly embittered. The peasants, the urban peasants, still exist here as a rabble: primitive, open to suggestion, dangerous, unpredictable. The same people who had blackened the streets at Eisner's funeral in countless processions hounded the leaders of yesterday to their death. From one day to the next the flag shops exchanged the soviet star for the swastika; from one day to the next the people's court, created by Eisner, put Leviné[3] up against the wall. The faithless rabble which all rulers have despised and used vacillated here, and it not merely vacillated, but certainly the hunting of animals and human beings proved to be its most characteristic nature. These were not only impoverished petite bourgeoisie, who grab at now this and now that means of assistance, nor were these an organized proletariat, not even a relatively organizable lumpenproletariat that could be kept up to scratch, but definitely mere riffraff, the vindictive, crucifying creatures of all ages. They were dazzled by the sham, by students in regalia, by the magic of processions, parades, and ringing spectacle; but Bavaria does not paint votive pictures any more. And the beaters are as ambiguous, unambiguous as the rabble, often even more contemptible than the latter. Baptized Hungarian Jews became spies for Hitler, bribed "democrats" from the stock of Balkan journalists filled the ranks. The genuine Thersites[4] and Vansens[5] did not want to be left out, gave the rabble its homogeneous head.

Nevertheless, he who no longer knows what to do knows nothing as yet of the whole. The case lies deeper, disgust and wit are now no longer the correct response alone. For

---

1. Kurt Eisner, 1867–1919, assassinated prime minister of the short-lived Munich Räterepublik (Soviet Republic).

2. Right-wing coup in March 1920 under Wolfgang Kapp.

3. Eugen Leviné, 1883–1919, prominent Communist leader who took part in the Munich Soviet Republic in 1919 and was condemned to death for his participation in it.

4. Thersites: the ugliest, most scurrilous man in the Greek army at Troy.

5. Vansen: a dissipated clerk and public agitator in Goethe's *Egmont*.

separate from the hideous gawpers and accomplices, new youth glows at the core, a very vigorous generation. Seventeen-year-olds are burning to respond to Hitler. Beery students of old, dreary, reveling in the happiness of the crease in their trousers, are no longer recognizable, their hearts are pounding. The old student fraternity member is arising again, Schill's[6] officers reborn, they find their brother in Schlageter,[7] heroic associations with all the signs of irrational conspiracy are gathering under a secret light. Hitler, their leader, did not deserve the indulgence of his judges and this farcical trial;[8] but even with the wit of Berlin lawyers there is no getting at him, and even Ludendorff, this brutally limited masculine symbol, does not live on the same level with him. Hitler the tribune is undoubtedly a highly suggestive type, unfortunately a great deal more vehement than the genuine revolutionaries who incited Germany in 1918. He gave the exhausted ideology of the fatherland an almost mysterious fire and has made a new aggressive sect, the germ of a strongly religious army, into a troop with a myth. Nor is the lasting power of Hitler's program explained by the fact that liberation from Jews, the stock market, the feudal tenancy of international capital, and the international Marxism hostile to the fatherland, is promised here along with similar, confused music for the ears of the undiscriminating petite bourgeoisie. But if the economy here moves to the periphery and the state ethos to the center, the music of the old unbourgeois discipline thereby rings out again at the same time, the secularized ethics of the chivalric orders.

Thus the extent to which Hitler has young people on his side should not be underrated. We should not underestimate our opponent but realize what is a psychological force for so many and inspires them. From this standpoint various connections with left-wing radicalism become clear, those of a demagogic, formal kind, if not with regard to content. Through this affinity (mostly only a opportunistic copy of socialism, tuned to primitive instincts) changing banners was made all that much easier for the Bavarian rabble. Among the Communists as among the National Socialists an appeal is made to able-bodied youth; in both cases the capitalist, parliamentary state is negated, in both cases a dictatorship of obedience and command, the virtue of decision, is demanded instead of the cowardly acts of the bourgeoisie, this eternally discussing class. It is above all the type of Hitler and of those who follow his example, who are in psychological terms strongly revolutionary. The goals and contents of this gang are also of course, despite all confusion, recognizably only the totally counterrevolutionary expression of the will of sinking strata and of their youth. The twenty thousand dollars of the industry of Nuremberg already indicate the way in which the bourgeoisie does not feel at all threatened here, how it faces the new state mysticism, apparently hostile to capital, without fear. Engels called anti-Semitism the socialism of the stupid mugs, whereby non-Jewish financial capital and above all original capital superbly prosper. The socialism of the cavalier—patriarchal, reactionary anticapitalism—is an even greater misconception or rather an open deception, in order to conceal by means of the mere contrast to financial capital the very much greater contrast to socialism. Folkish instead of international, romantic–reactionary state mysticism instead of the socialist will towards the atrophy of the state, faith in authority instead of the ultimate anarchy latent in all genuine socialism—these are incompatible contrasts of positive volition, stronger than the apparent affinities of form and of the common negation of the

6. Ferdinand von Schill, 1776–1809, Prussian officer who fought with his hussars against Napoleonic occupation.

7. Albert Leo Schlageter, 1894–1923, officer who actively resisted the occupation of the Ruhr. He was shot by the French.

8. Hitler's trial in 1924 for his role in the Nazi putsch of the previous year.

present state. Othmar Spann,[9] the Austrian sociologist, a small imitator of the Austrian state theologians of the Vormärz, sought in this way to create a definition for National Socialism; and what emerged was as different from socialism as the Romantic idolization of the state was from this sentence of the young Engels: "The essence of the state and of religion is humanity's fear of itself." The underling, whom the feudal pressure lasting for centuries has produced and left behind, races around and longs as a formal predator to return to stability. He churns up messianic dreams and perverts them with feudal ones, radicalizes the dull center in order to make them into ascetic rebels, and adopts the ideology of "rebellion" by the grace of Metternich,[10] the author of the Karlsbad decrees and guardian of the Holy Alliance.[11]

So to what lengths will this unrest yet lead? It divides into three elements, to be considered separately, and indeed treated in a very different tone of voice. *Below* runs the petit-bourgeois pack, which deserted from Red to White and is willingly open to malicious and mindless agitation. *Above* them stand the shock troops of Hitler and his officers, good vigorous youth, raw and infected by the hideous background of the camp followers, but on the whole with pure intentions: nauseated by the stock-market age, the depression of the lost war, the lack of ideals in this dull Republic. Hitler himself here ignited or at least fanned a thoroughly unbourgeois movement in bourgeois youth, and shaped a certain ascetic energy that differs by several degrees from the mindlessness of the first German enthusiasm for war, and also from the senior primary-school-teacher pathos of the former fatherland party. *Thirdly,* though, the National Socialist ideology and practice is very treacherous. It seeks to have the bourgeois ousted by the knight, but leaves the bourgeois feeling all the more protected and preserved by the young knights. And even the knight himself—he is admittedly more human than the bourgeois, but at the moment even more unreal than the latter, even more abstractly and even more unclearly preventing the breakthrough into reality. Hitler, Hitlerism, fascism is the ecstasy of bourgeois youth: this contradiction between strength and bourgeoisie, between ecstacy and the most lifeless nationalism makes the movement into a spectre. It does not become any more real through the feudal ghosts it carries with it, through the alliance of powerfully present enthusiasm with long-sunken chivalric dreams or Old Germanic folk royalty from the tenth century. All the same, the Hitler Youth sustains the only "revolutionary" movement in Germany at the moment, after the proletariat has been robbed by the majority socialist leaders of its own, of the solely valid, consistent revolution. One part of fascism in Germany is as it were the crooked governor of the revolution, an expression of the fact that the social situation is by no means static. But the genuine tribunes of the people are lacking or prove by themselves the shrewd saying of Babel:[12] "Banality is the counterrevolution."

9. Othmar Spann, 1878–1950, Austrian economist and philosopher who demanded a Christian corporate state. The Vörmarz refers to the era before the March, 1848 revolution.

10. Clemens Fürst von Metternich, 1773–1859, Austrian statesman; the Karlsbad decrees were issued under his influence in 1819 by the German governments against the National and Liberal movement.

11. Alliance between Tsar Alexander I, the Emperor of Austria, and the King of Prussia, 1815.

12. Isaac Babel, 1894–1941, Russian writer.

57

THOMAS MANN

An Appeal to Reason

First published as "Appell an die Vernunft," *Berliner Tageblatt* (October 18, 1930).

I do not know if I can reckon upon the understanding of my audience for the perhaps fantastic-seeming step that I have taken in asking you to come here to listen to me this evening. It may appear sheer presumptuous folly; it may seem that I wanted to play the *præceptor patriæ,* to assume the role of the new Fichte. We shall, if you please, put such ridiculous thoughts aside—I scarcely like even to have mentioned them. But the fact is that I am to give a reading in the Academy tomorrow from a new novel on which I am working; the occasion will probably be a pleasant one, from the artist's point of view: it will amuse a few people and encourage me blithely to go on in my self-appointed artistic enterprise. Well and good. And yet is it worthwhile, I ask myself, is it decent or defensible the way things stand today to come to Berlin to read a chapter from a novel, to pocket a little praise and a little blame—from an audience that cannot but give me a rather divided attention—and then to go home again?

I do not hold with the remorselessly social point of view that looks upon art—the beautiful and useless—as a private pastime of the individual, which in times like these may almost be relegated to the category of the reprehensible. There was a time—the epoch of æsthetic idealism—when Schiller could extol pure play as the highest state of man. But even though that day be past, yet we need not quite subscribe to the school of action that would put idealism on the level of frivolity. For form, be it ever so playful, is akin to the spirit, to that which leads one on to social betterment; and art is the sphere wherein the conflict between the social and the ideal is resolved.

And yet there are hours, there are moments of our common life, when art fails to justify itself in practice; when the inner urgency of the artist fails him; when the more immediate necessities of our existence choke back thought, when the general distress and crisis shake him too, in such a way that what we call art, the happy and impassioned preoccupation with eternally human values, comes to seem idle, ephemeral, a superfluous thing, a mental impossibility. So it was sixteen years ago when the war broke out that was to be for every conscious human being so much more than a war. So it was in the postwar years. So it was twelve years ago when Germany, after prolonged and criminal abuse of all her powers by those who called themselves her leaders, collapsed, and men who had never dreamed of such a task and would gladly have been relieved of it struggled and saved the Reich and Germany in the form which we inherited from our fathers. And so it is again today, after years in which the well-intentioned have tried to believe in recovery and a slow return to comfort and security—though all the while the world economic system, struck down and trodden upon by the war, was in no way healed nor could look forward to healing, but remained in a state of confusion rendered more acute by the blind and archaic policy of tribute adopted by the governments that dictated the peace. And now we are swept into a new economic crisis that stirs political passions afresh—for one need not be a materialistic socialist to understand that the masses' thinking and feeling are dictated by their economic condition and get translated into political opinion, much as though a sick philosopher were to erect his physiological draw-backs into a system without the corrective of the ideal.

Surely it is too much to demand sound political thought from an economically ailing people.

The national government has set up a plan of financial reform designed to effect economy in the administration. The plan is spoken of abroad as courageous and practical, even exemplary, and calculated to raise the credit of the Reich. That may be a consolation. But in Germany we feel that a financial program is after all not an economic one, and that this "proposal for the rehabilitation of the Reich and the restoration of sound economic conditions" has a right to only half the name it bears. What can the government's plans to set its house in order for the coming budget year give to those who are staring horror-struck into these next winter months of unemployment, lockouts, hunger, and ruin, months that threaten to fill the cup of misery for millions and display all the phenomena and all the consequences of a people's despair? Every person with any feeling is conscious of the state of things. Heavy as lead—as in the darkest years of the war—the weight lies on every breast and will not let us breathe. The strength of our common bond, our common destiny, remains; there can be no individual happiness where misery rules the hour. We are all drawn into the maelstrom of want and nervous exasperation; it seems no escape is possible. He who in brighter days happily preoccupied himself with *le superflu* feels paralyzed and distraught. For how can he behave with frank human confidence in the midst of a torn and divided people, where hatred—morbid fruit of want—robs every eye of ingenuous vision? Little wonder, then, that under such circumstances he is led to speak of these things—of which it can no longer be said that they are no affair of his, since they stare us all in the face—to the society, or rather to the stratum of society, which brought him forth, to which he belongs and feels himself spiritually akin. Almost as though he were talking to himself! I am a son of the German bourgeoisie, and never have I disowned the spiritual traditions which belong to my origin. My work has been sustained by the sympathy of the great educated middle class of Germany, by the moral support, that is, of the Germany that is still the decisive feature in any composite picture of the nation's intellectual life; and it is only to repay confidence with confidence if I turn with my distressed self-communings to that same middle class. Not as a class-conscious man—that I am not. And not as a member of any political economic group of interests—I belong to none. All I want is to stand with you upon that intellectual plane where the conception *the German citizen* is actually at home, and where, at least until yesterday, German middle-class habits of thought were still natural. How I should rejoice if any word of mine could contribute to bring about such a stopping to think as seems to me even now more German than the strident slogan that is uttered today for the saving and the uplifting of the fatherland—the slogan of fanaticism!

The result of the elections cannot be explained entirely on economic grounds. If I have seemed to express myself in that sense, I must correct the impression. Neither to the world outside Germany would it be wise or conformable to the facts to present such a picture of the situation. The German people are by nature not radical; and if the amount of radicalism we have seemed to display for the moment were purely a product of economic depression, it would account for an increase in the communist vote but not for the flight of the masses to a party which seems to combine the national ideal with the social in so militant and stridently effective a way. We may not present the political as simply a product of the economic. Rather, if we wish to interpret the astonishing state of mind that our people have revealed, we must refer it to political passions, or, more appositely put, to political pains. And though it would be neither wise nor dignified to be proud of the issue of September 14[1] and parade it before foreign countries, still, we may silently let it do its cautionary work: as a storm signal, a warning that one can at no time demand of a people, which has as much ground for self-esteem as any other, all that has in fact been demanded of Germany, without producing in it a state of feeling that may become a world menace.

This is not the moment to go into the particulars of that huge complex, material and spiritual, that ushered in the World War. Germany was led into that war by a system of government that—most naïvely from the historical point of view—put its own interest on a par with that of its people, and in the struggle to survive brought people and country to the last gasp. Against that system of government, which had made itself hated in the world, there reared itself ostensibly, but also in the popular mind, the warlike heroism of our antagonists: a democratic heroism with overwhelming resources of propaganda. To it, quite aside from all material superiority, the German power of resistance at length succumbed. The democratic morality, which during the war had used such large phrases, seeming to regard the war as an opportunity to create a newer and better world, when peace came kept only a fraction of its word; the after-effects of the war psychosis, the intoxication of victory, the hard reality of postwar conditions, were destructive to a degree that made it difficult for the German people to believe in the moral and historical significance of their defeat and the lofty calling of the other side to victory. The Treaty of Versailles was an instrument calculated to shackle the vital powers of one of the chief peoples of Europe for the duration of history; to regard this instrument as the continental Magna Carta, upon which future history must base itself, ran contrary to life and nature, and seems scarcely to possess an advocate in the world today. Life and reason themselves have already refuted the inviolability of this treaty; and when French nationalists complain—as one hears them complain—that after twelve years it is as full of holes as a sieve, they are only proving the impossibility of the impossible, only supporting the methods that have been applied on the German side to bring this inherent impossibility in evidence. That it is still far from being full of enough holes for the good of the world is in private scarcely disputed even outside of Germany; but the German people are not aware of such a point of view, they must stick by the facts which surround them, and they feel themselves sacrificed to the preposterousness of these facts. Already it is almost superfluous to say, and yet necessary to repeat: it is not a tenable position that Germany stands unarmed alone among peoples proud of their shining armor; so that the Pole in Posen, the Czech on the Wendelsplatz, can wreak their anger on her unabashed; so that the promise that German disarmament should be the prelude to a general disarmament is put off to the Greek kalends for fulfillment, and every expression of indignation on the part of Germans is regarded as a threat to be answered by new armaments. This is the first wrong that must be mentioned in an effort to understand the German state of mind, but it is only too easy to cite five or six others that cast a gloom over the spirit: the absurd frontier regulations in the east, the system of reparations erected on the principle of *vae victis* and beneficial to nobody at all; the utter inability of the Jacobinical statesman to understand German sensibilities in the minorities question; the problem of the Saar region, which should be no problem; and so on.

These are the burdens and irritants which affect the German mind from without. To them are added profound if vague and confused misgivings of a domestic nature: doubts whether the parliamentary system of western Europe, which Germany adopted after the collapse of the feudal system, is after all quite suited to her case; whether it does not in

---

1. Elections producing rise of Nazi representation in the Reichstag from 12 to 107 delegates.

some sense and to some extent warp and do violence to her political ethic. These troubles of a political ethic proper to her people are the more tormenting since nobody knows how to make concrete proposals for anything more adequate or suitable; so that for the present there seems no other conclusion than that, so long as Germany does not succeed in inventing some new and original political theory, we are driven to make the best and most personal use we can of the traditional and historical. Certainly no one who knows Germany doubts that other attempts, on the east and south, to prevail over democratic parliamentarism—the dictatorship of a class and the dictatorship of a Caesar-adventurer brought forth by democracy—are still more foreign to the blood of the German people than that against which, to some extent, its hand was raised on September 14.

One need not be a great psychologist to recognize in these trials, both foreign and domestic, the causes which, together with the bad economic situation, conditioned the sensational election results. The German people took advantage of a garish election poster, the so-called National Socialist, to give vent to its feelings. But National Socialism could never have attained the strength or scope it has shown as a manifestation of popular feeling had it not, unknown to the mass of its supporters, drawn from spiritual sources an element that, like everything born of the spirit of the times, possesses a pragmatic truth, legitimacy, and logical necessity, and by virtue of them lends reality to the popular movement. The economic decline of the middle classes was accompanied—or even preceded—by a feeling that amounted to an intellectual prophecy and a critique of the age: the sense that here was a crisis that heralded the end of the bourgeois epoch that entered with the French Revolution and the notions associated with it. A new mental attitude was proclaimed for all mankind, which should have nothing to do with bourgeois principles such as freedom, justice, culture, optimism, faith in progress. As art, it gave vent to expressionistic shrieks from the soul; as philosophy, it repudiated the reason and the mechanistic and ideological conceptions of bygone decades; it expressed itself as an irrational throwback, placing the conception *life* at the center of thought, and raised on its standard the powers of the unconscious, the dynamic, the darkly creative, which alone were life-giving. Mind, quite simply the intellectual, it put under a taboo as destructive of life, while it set up for homage as the true inwardness of life the Mother-Chthonic, the darkness of the soul, the holy procreative underworld. Much of this religion of nature, by its very essence inclining to the orgiastic and to bacchic excess, has gone into the nationalism of our day, differentiating it sharply from the nationalism of the nineteenth century with its bourgeois, strongly cosmopolitan, and humanitarian cast. It is distinguished in its character as a nature cult precisely by its absolute unrestraint, its orgiastic, radically antihumane, frenziedly dynamic character. But when one thinks what it has cost humanity through the ages to rise from orgiastic nature cults, from the service of Moloch, Baal, and Astarte, with the barbaric refinements of its gnosticism and the sexual excesses of its divinities, to the plane of a more spiritual worship, one stands amazed at the lighthearted way in which today we repudiate our gains and our liberations—while at the same time realizing how fluctuating and ephemeral, in a general sense how really meaningless, such a philosophical reaction must be.

It may seem daring to associate the radical nationalism of our day with these conceptions from a romanticizing philosophy. Yet the association is there, and it must be recognized by those concerned about gaining insight into the relations of things. And there is even more: there are other intellectual elements to strengthen this National Social political movement—a certain ideology, a Nordic creed, a Germanistic romanticism, from philological, academic, professorial spheres. It addresses the Germany of 1930 in a high-flown, wishy-washy jargon, full of mystical good feeling, with hyphenated prefixes like race- and folk- and fellowship-, and lends to the movement a fanatical cult-barbarism, more dangerous and estranging, with more power to clog and stupefy the brain, than even the lack of contact and the political romanticism which led us into the war.

Fed, then, by such intellectual and pseudo-intellectual currents as these, the movement that we sum up under the name of National Socialism and which has displayed such a power of enlisting recruits to its banner, mingles with the mighty wave—a wave of anomalous barbarism, of primitive popular vulgarity—that sweeps over the world today, assailing the nerves of mankind with wild, bewildering, stimulating, intoxicating sensations. The fantastic development, the triumphs and catastrophes of our technical progress, our sensational sports records, the frantic overpayment and adoration bestowed upon "stars," the prize-fights with million-mark purses and hordes of spectators—all these make up the composite picture of the time, together with the decline and disappearance of stern and civilizing conceptions such as culture, mind, art, ideas. Like boys let out of school humanity seems to have run away from the humanitarian, idealistic nineteenth century, from whose morality—if we can even speak of morality in this connection—our time represents a wide and wild reaction. Everything is possible, everything permitted as a weapon against human decency; if we have got rid of the idea of human freedom as a relic of the bourgeois state of mind—as though an idea so bound up with all European feeling, upon which Europe was founded, for which she has made such sacrifices, could ever be utterly lost—it comes back again, this cast-off conception, in a guise suited to the time: as demoralization, as a mockery of all human authority, as a free rein to instincts, as the emancipation of brutality, the dictatorship of force. In Poland the leaders of the opposition are arrested before the elections, and the president rails at Parliament in the language of a street arab. In Finland the Lapps kidnap and mishandle the contrary-minded; in Russia they think to still with the blood of counterrevolutionists the hunger of those whose food they have taken away to dump it, to the general confusion, on foreign markets. The secrets of Fascist prisons are not quite secrets: we have heard of the islands of compulsory residence and the methods used to Italianize the southern Tyrol—methods that could Italianize Munich today and Berlin tomorrow. In all this, violence demonstrates itself and demonstrates nothing but violence, and even that is unnecessary, for all other considerations have fallen away, man no longer believes in them, and so the road to vulgarity is unrestricted.

This fantastic state of mind, of a humanity that has out-run its ideas, is matched by a political scene in the grotesque style, with Salvation Army methods, hallelujahs and bell-ringing and dervishlike repetition of monotonous catchwords, until everybody foams at the mouth. Fanaticism turns into a means of salvation, enthusiasm into epileptic ecstasy, politics become an opiate for the masses, a proletarian eschatology; and reason veils her face.

Is all that German? Is there any deep stratum of the German soul where all that fanaticism, that bacchantic frenzy, that orgiastic denial of reason and human dignity is really at home? Do the heralds of radical nationalism perhaps plume themselves too much upon their success at the polls? Is National Socialism, regarded as a party, just possibly a colossus with feet of clay, whose prospects of endurance cannot compare with those of the Social-Democratic organization of the masses? It is being said that only fanaticism can put Germany on her feet again. In the Epilogue to "The Bell," Goethe describes the bearing of a great man in the face of a world in opposition; he speaks

> *"Von jenem Mut, der früber oder später*
> *Den Widerstand der stumpfen Welt besiegt,*

Von jenem Glauben, der sich stets erhöhter
Bald kühn hervordrängt, bald geduldig schmiegt,
Damit das Gute wirke, wachse, fromme,
Damit der Tag dem Edlen endlich komme."²

Would not this sort of courage better befit the German—whom the world sees as a picture of moderation, integrity, intellectual uprightness—than a berserker despair, than that fanaticism which today passes for the only German thing? Statesmen of the true German stamp, recognized and loved as such throughout the world, have displayed the courage that now presses boldly forward and now shrewdly submits, the courage that knows how to be patient and therewith to gain more than could possibly be gained by exposing to the wonder of the world the spectacle of an ecstatic nervous collapse.

Indeed, the moment has already come when militant nationalism displays itself less militantly for foreign than for domestic consumption. Already it is seeking to clothe its foreign policy with innocence and sweet reasonableness, declaring that Germany is powerless to carry on war and that under its guidance there will be no violent changes of foreign policy. This is to make itself possible in the eyes of the world. Its hatred is leveled not so much without as within; yes, actually its fanatical love of the fatherland appears chiefly as hatred not of the foreigner but of all Germans who do not believe in its methods, and whom it promises to destroy root and branch (even today that would be rather a large order); as hatred, in short, of everything that makes for the good name and intellectual renown of Germany in the world today. More and more it looks as though the chief goal were the inner purification of the country, the return of the German to the conception that radical nationalism has of him. But even supposing that such a return were desirable, is it any way possible? Can a people old and ripe and highly cultured, with many demands on life, with a long emotional and intellectual experience behind it; a people who possess a classical literature that is lofty and cosmopolitan, a romantic literature of the profoundest and most subtle; who have Goethe, Schopenhauer, Nietzsche, and in their blood the noble malady of the *Tristan* music—can such a people conform, even after ten thousand banishings and purificatory executions, to the wish image of a primitive, pure-blooded, blue-eyed simplicity, artless in mind and heart, which smiles and submits and clicks its heels together? Nationalism wants to blend fanaticism and dignity; but the dignity of a people like ours cannot be the dignity of simplicity but only the dignity of knowledge and mind, and that turns its face away from fanaticism.

But if radical ecstatics are in the nature of things impossible to the German burgher, how then shall he bear himself politically? If he is a Catholic, he is well provided, even politically—one says it with a certain envy—in the bosom of his Church. The spirit of that Church, universal and supranational as it is, has always sternly set its face against ethnic paganism, and is altogether on the side of the forces that are working to cure Europe of her disease of nationalism. For the German who calls himself its son, there is always available a synthesis of the contradiction—which should never have been allowed to become acute—between humanity and the nation. It is harder for the rest of us to find our right political path; I imagine I see—no, I am convinced that I see quite clearly—what phantom and national hobgoblin it is that stands in the way, that makes it so hard for the German citizen to find himself politically. It is a conception, a word—looked at quite

2. Of that courage that sooner or later conquers the resistance of the apathetic world / Of that belief which at times boldly presses forward, at times patiently yields / So that the good can flourish, grow, and take effect / So that the day finally comes to the noble.

calmly and quietly it seems today scarcely more than a word—of which a clever and injurious use is made to frighten the average citizen. I mean the word *Marxist*. Now, there is no sharper, profounder contrast, speaking from the point of view of parties, than that between the Social Democrat and the orthodox Marxist of the Moscow-communistic brand. The so-called Marxism of the Social Democratic Party consists today in a threefold program: firstly, it is at pains to protect and improve the social and economic position of the worker; secondly, it seeks to maintain the doubly threatened democratic form of government; and thirdly it strives to maintain the foreign policy of peace and mutual understanding which proceeds from its democratic theory. And these three categories of its program exhaust, as far as practice goes, the Marxism of the Social Democratic Party. It has shown a tenacity of purpose in advocating the interests of its economic class which was partly responsible for the dissolution of the last Reichstag, and which checked the cooperation between the middle class and the socialists, which had been set in motion by the political personality of Stresemann. Nobody can deny that our luxuriant development as a social and political state is an abnormality in an impoverished and debt-burdened people; it must give offence both at home and abroad. And the stubbornness with which the socialist leaders thought they could cling to the "conquests of the Revolution" can be explained but scarcely excused by the tactical compulsion under which they acted. But in the first place party egotism is not precisely the most telling feature of social democracy, by which it would stand or fall in German political life; and in the second place it is plain that even today it puts economic special interest second to the national policy of preserving the democracy, and is bent above all things on dealing with the danger which would result from a paralysis of parliamentary business and from letting the economic misery of the masses get the upper hand. We may consider it characteristic of the spirit of the German working classes that, in the recent conference for the adjustment of difficulties in the Berlin metal industry, the operators met the proposal of the managers for a fifteen per cent wage reduction with the counterproposal that the working week be shortened to forty hours and then, by the help of the savings thus effected, unemployed be taken on. Considering the brazen self-interest which is taken for granted in the economic field all over the world today, this proposal shows a common feeling and a readiness for sacrifice which is wholly admirable. And, en passant, it indicates one of the methods that might be used to mitigate the dangers of the coming months.

Just now I professed my bourgeois origins and the cultural traditions that go with them. I know, of course, the instinctive distaste, from the point of view of the world, of the German citizen for what one knows as Marxist tenets: the predominance of the class idea above that of the state, the people, and civilization; the economic materialism; I know all that is not intellectual enough for our tradition. It is true that our civic culture has intellectual roots, while the socialistic class idea cannot deny its economic origin. But it has long been time for us to recognize that the socialistic class idea looks with a far friendlier eye upon the things of the mind than does the educated middle class, which only too often betrays that it has lost touch with the living spirit and its demands. I have spoken of the unhealthy and dangerous tension that has been set up in the world between the state of knowledge actually arrived at and taken for granted at the apex of humanity, and what, in actual reality, is pos sible in the circumstances. But the workers, the socialist class, undeniably display a livelier goodwill towards the uprooting of this mortifying and dangerous discrepancy than their cultured other half, whether in legislation, the ratio-nalization of the life of the state, the in ternal constitution of Europe, or what you will. The socialist class is opposed to the cultured middle class of the nation in being anti-intellectual by economic theory, but in practice it is friendly to the intellect—and that, as things stand today, is the decisive factor.

One of those young officers of the Reichswehr who are now atoning for their errors of enthusiasm with penalties that take into consideration the time-distracted sincerity of their intentions, declared before the court that it was the working class and the youth of the land that fought and defeated separatism on the Rhine. But what is the working class if not social democracy? Every child knows that if the Rhineland had fallen at that time, it would not have stopped with the Rhineland. If the social-democratic attitude at this crisis was decisive for the defeat of separatism—and such is the historic fact—then social democracy saved the Reich, and not for the first time. When it came to extremes with us, when the reins of authority and self-control were dragging in the blood-stained dust, and nobody was there to seize them, it was social democracy that grasped those riderless reins, that took up the tragic and unutterably thankless task of the war settlements, and reduced to some kind of order the chaos in which a beaten and fugitive system had left the country. It gave the land a constitution, which no more needs to be the last word, the inviolable Magna Carta for Germany, than the Treaty of Versailles needs to be for Europe; but under it Germany has been able to live up to now and take the first steps towards liberation and rehabilitation. There is a phrase of reckless injustice, a perfectly conscienceless phrase: "the November criminals"; whoever lets it pass his lips or hears it without indignation is unworthy of the German name. Is it a crime to seize power when history forces your hand and there is no one else there? What else do the National Socialists want to do today? Anyhow, the Social Democrats, at a time when there was no right way for Germany, at least found a possible way. But whither National Socialism would lead us we do not know for the simple reason that it does not know itself; and we are daily strengthened in our doubts of its real will to power.

The German statesman whose work persuaded the outer world once more to couple greatness with the name of Germany—I mean Stresemann—performed his task with the support of the Social Democratic Party. Upon his own party he could not count. It never followed him with its convictions, and only the strength of his personality compelled its allegiance. The history of this extraordinary man belongs to all that is most remarkable and moving in German life. From a conservative middle-class circle, with the intellectual and political traditions of his origin in his blood, loyal to his class and country if also cultured above the average and making more intellectual demands upon life; a partisan of the policy of expansion and even in the war a convinced advocate of imperial conquest; he was, thanks to a lively and vigorous understanding still further sharpened by illness, led and driven by a plastic yielding to life which bore in itself the seeds of death. He grew out of and beyond all his origins, and more and more swiftly—for he was a man in the grip of the idea and he had not much time—into a world where he thought, believed, and acted for European solidarity in a way he could never have dreamed of in his youth. We know today, particularly from Lord D'Abernon's[3] journals, that the policy that led to Locarno and the liberation of the Rhineland was no prescription from abroad but the personal conception of the German statesman and was not understood abroad when he made his first tentative efforts to shape matters upon its lines. There was hesitation, fear of a trap, the opposition in Paris and London seemed insurmountable for months. It will always remain a question how he acquired the belief, the human sympathy, and the admiration of the world—he was no linguist, could not even speak French—a sympathy

---

3. British ambassador to Germany (1920–1926).

and admiration which at his death (and that was a truly German piece of ill luck; without it much would have been spared us) revealed a universality of regret, a convinced and convincing warmth of feeling. They are still felt. There was no speech in Geneva this autumn that did not begin with homage to the memory of the great German minister; and his successor in office still profits by the regard he enjoyed. In the assembly at Geneva, when the Rumanian presiding officer, in his Slavic French, announces the German minister, there is a silence; and old [Aristide] Briand,[4] old [Albert] Apponyi,[5] the Englishman, the Pole, the Italian, all take their ear pieces in order not to lose the utterances of the representative of the German nation. Then one sees and feels the change that has come to pass since the days when our delegates at Versailles were kept separate from the others as though they had the plague, and Clemenceau took off his pince-nez in spiteful astonishment if a German chanced to speak. "Stresemann," writes Lord D'Abernon, "may claim to have raised Germany from the position of a disarmed and stricken foe into that of a diplomatic equal, entitled to full consideration as a great power and enjoying international guarantees for the protection of her frontiers. To have accomplished this in a few years of power without the support of armed force is a feat worthy of those who have written their names most memorably on the scroll of fame."

The remarkable thing is that he won all this sympathy and admiration, this trust and authority, despite the fact that his colleagues, not excepting the French ones, perfectly knew—what was quite obvious—that Stresemann's policy was the policy of a German patriot and aimed at the very thing that one would have thought most obnoxious to the leaders of the former entente: namely, "to put holes into" the Versailles Treaty and to achieve the liberation and rehabilitation of Germany. They ought to have fought against any success in that direction, and the more he succeeded, the more they should have feared and hated him. If that was not the case, but quite the contrary, the reason is of course that his work for Germany was at the same time done in the interest of Europe, and that at his death, as Lord D'Abernon says, "he left Germany infinitely stronger than when he took the helm in 1923, and Europe comparably more peaceful."

And yet there still remains an unsolved puzzle and contradiction, which, if I may so express myself, seems to belong to Europe's psychology of the unconscious. The Treaty of Versailles is supposed to be sacrosanct, it is taboo, it is the foundation of the peace. That is the view abroad; it regulates the consciousness of the authors of the treaty. But perhaps there is something they do not know: that not only Germany but they themselves, that all Europe, in its heart, is longing to escape from the ban, and looks with secret hope and expectation towards Germany, towards this country, the object of so many conscious and unconscious hopes and expectations: will she have the wisdom, the subtlety, the political contrivance to spare the world by leading it up and away from the Treaty of Versailles? Paradoxical as it may sound, the extraordinary affection with which Stresemann was regarded in Europe and the general regret at his early death favor such a conjecture.

The goal of Stresemann's policy was and is the peaceful revision of the treaty, with the deliberate acquiescence of France, and a Franco-German alliance as the basis for a peaceful reconstruction of Europe. The German people, who even in the war never hated France, however things may have looked on a short view, are ready for such an alliance. I say this not because I wish it, nor because I am an admirer of French literature, nor on any other personal grounds, but simply because my German feeling says it to me. And Frenchmen

4. French diplomat.
5. Hungarian diplomat.

who know their nation as well as I imagine that I know mine hold the same view. In all the discussions upon the state of Europe, of course, in all the efforts to ease the rigors of the international situation, France puts in the foreground the thesis of security, the indisputably precious security of France. Now I am well aware that the walls of this hall have ears, and that perhaps even some Frenchmen, out of respect for the intellectual life of Germany, are listening to my words. And therefore I say that the best, the most realistic security for France is the mental health of the German people; and all the world sees that this health is upset by a general political and economic crisis, rendered for Germany more dangerously acute by the unwisdom of the peace conditions. Then let France ask herself what is fitting, as between civilized and reasonable peoples, upon the crucial points of a treaty born of a mental state that never could produce a genuine one, a treaty that from the beginning has worn its transient character on its forehead.

Every foreign policy corresponds to a domestic one that is its organic complement, together forming an indissoluble intellectual and moral whole. When I state my conviction—and I am so convinced that I am ready to set not only my pen but my person upon the issue—that the political place of the German citizen is today with the Social Democratic Party, I am using the word *political* in the sense of the foreign and domestic union of policy which I have defined. Marxism aside, it is precisely the intellectual tradition of the German citizen which shows him where his place is; for only to a foreign policy that envisages a Franco-German understanding can any domestic program correspond which has a chance of satisfying the claims of the German citizen to the blessings of freedom, culture, or intellectual well-being. Any other must result in a cramping and penury of the nation which would mean a frightful conflict between culture and the fatherland, and therewith calamity to us all.

Such a morbid and destructive struggle we must all abhor. Peace without is one with peace within. The last word of the lawyer in Leipzig in asking for the conviction of the young officers was: "I have no rancor against the accused." No, there must be today no question of rancor. The word full of love and sorrow which binds us together, which after years of lesser tension moves us today as it did in 1914 and 1918, setting free our hearts and our tongues, is for us all the same: Germany!

58

WALTER BENJAMIN

Theories of German Fascism

First published as "Theorien des deutschen Faschismus. Zu der Sammelschrift 'Krieg und Krieger.' herausgegeben von Ernst Jünger," *Die Gesellschaft* 7 vol. 2, (1930), 32–41.

Without approaching the surface of the significance of the economic causes of war, one may say that the harshest, most disastrous aspects of imperialist war are in part the result of the gaping discrepancy between the gigantic power of technology and the minuscule moral illumination it affords. Indeed, according to its economic nature, bourgeois society cannot help but insulate everything technological as much as possible from the so-called spiritual, and it cannot help but resolutely exclude technology's right of codetermination in the social order. Any future war will also be a slave revolt of technology.

Today factors such as these determine all questions of war and one would hardly expect to have to remind the authors of the present volume[1] of this, nor to remind them that these are questions of imperialist war. After all, they were themselves soldiers in the World War and, dispute what one may, they indisputably proceed from the experience of this war. It is therefore quite astonishing to find, and on the first page at that, the statement that "it is of secondary importance in which century, for which ideas, and with which weapons the fighting is done." What is most astonishing about this statement is that its author, Ernst Jünger, is thus adopting one of the principles of pacifism, and the most questionable and most abstract of all its principles at that. Though for him and his friends it is not so much some doctrinaire schema that lies behind this as it is a deep-rooted and—by all standards of male thought—a really rather depraved mysticism. But Jünger's mysticism of war and pacifism's clichéd ideal of peace have little to criticize each other for. Even the most consumptive pacifism has one thing over its epileptically frothing brother for the moment; a certain contact with reality, at least, some conception of the next war.

The authors like to speak—emphatically—of the "First World War." Yet how little their experience has come to grips with that war's realities—which they refer to in an alienated exaggeration as the "wordly-real"—is shown by the altogether thoughtless obtuseness with which they view the idea of future wars without any conception of them. These trailblazers of the *Wehrmacht* could almost give one the impression that the uniform represents their highest end, most desired by all their heartstrings, and that the circumstances under which one dons the uniform are of little importance by comparison. This attitude becomes more comprehensible when one realizes, in terms of the current level of European armaments, how anachronistic is their espoused ideology of war. These authors nowhere observe that the new warfare of technology and material (*Materialschlacht*) which appears to some of them as the highest revelation of existence, dispenses with all the wretched emblems of heroism that here and there have survived the World War. Gas warfare, in which the contributors to this book show conspicuously little interest, promises to give the war of the future a face that permanently displaces soldierly qualities by those of sports; all action will lose its military character and war will assume the countenance of record-setting. The most prominent strategic characteristic of such warfare consists in its being waged exclusively and most radically as an offensive war. And we know that there is no adequate defense against gas attacks from the air. Even individual protective devices, gas masks, are of no use against mustard gas and Levisit. Now and then one hears of something "reassuring" such as the invention of a sensitive listening device that registers the whir of propellers at great distances. And a few months later a soundless airplane is invented. Gas warfare will rest upon annihilation records, and will involve an absurd degree of risk. Whether its outbreak will occur within the bounds of international law—after prior declarations of war—is questionable; but its end will no longer be concerned with such limitations. Since gas warfare obviously eliminates the distinction between civilian and military personnel, the most important basis of international law is removed. The last war has already shown that the total disorganization imperialist war entails, and the manner in which it is waged, threaten to make it an endless war.

More than a curiosity, it is symptomatic that something written in 1930 about "war and warriors" overlooks all this. It is symptomatic that the same boyish rapture that leads to a cult, to an apotheosis of war, is here heralded particularly by [Wilhelm] von Schramm

---

1. *Krieg und Krieger,* ed. Ernst Jünger (Berlin, 1930).

and [Albrecht Erich] Günther. The most rabidly decadent origins of this new theory of war are emblazoned on their foreheads: it is nothing other than an uninhibited translation of the principles of *l'art pour l'art* to war itself. [. . .]

The point is this: War—the "eternal" war that they talk about so much here, as well as the most recent one—is said to be the highest manifestation of the German nation. It should be clear that behind their "eternal" war lies the idea of cultic war, just as behind the most recent war lies that of technological war, and it should also be clear that these authors have had little success in perceiving these relationships. But there is something rather special about this last war. It was not only one of material warfare but also a war that was lost. And in that special sense it was the German war. To have waged war out of their innermost existence is something that other peoples could claim to have done. But to have lost a war out of their innermost existence, this they cannot claim. What is special about the present and latest stage in the controversy over the war, which has convulsed Germany since 1919, is the novel assertion that it is precisely this loss of the war that is characteristically German. One can call this the latest stage because these attempts to come to terms with the loss of the war show a clear pattern. These attempts began with an effort to pervert the German defeat into an inner victory by means of confessions of guilt which were hysterically elevated to the universally human. This political position, which supplied the manifestoes for the course of the decline of the West, faithfully reflected the German "revolution" made by the expressionist avantgarde. Then came the attempt to forget the lost war. The bourgeoisie turned to snore on its other side—and what pillow could have been softer than the novel. The terrors endured in those years became the down filling in which every sleepyhead could easily leave his imprint. What finally distinguishes this latest effort from earlier ones in the process involved here is the tendency to take the loss of the war more seriously than the war itself. What does it mean to win or lose a war? How striking the double meaning is in both words! The first, manifest meaning, certainly refers to the outcome of the war, but the second meaning— which creates that peculiar hollow space, the sounding board in these words—refers to the totality of the war and suggests how the war's outcome also alters the enduring significance it holds for us. This meaning says, so to speak, the winner keeps the war in hand, it leaves the hands of the loser; it says, the winner conquers the war for himself, makes it his own property, the loser no longer possesses it and must live without it. And he must live not only without the war per se but without every one of its slightest ups and downs, every subtlest one of its chess moves, every one of its remotest actions. To win or lose a war reaches so deeply, if we follow the language, into the fabric of our existence that our whole lives become that much richer or poorer in symbols, images, and sources. And since we have lost one of the greatest wars in world history, one which involved the whole material and spiritual substance of a people, one can assess the significance of this loss.

Certainly one cannot accuse those around Jünger of not having taken this into account. But how did they approach it, monstrous as it was? They have not ended the battle yet. They continued to celebrate the cult of war when there was no longer any real enemy. They complied with the desires of the bourgeoisie, which longed for the decline of the West, the way a schoolboy longs for an inkblot in place of his wrong answer. They spread decline, preached decline wherever they went. Not even for a moment were they capable of holding up to view—instead of doggedly holding onto—what had been lost. They were always the first and the bitterest to oppose coming to one's senses. They ignored the great opportunity of the loser—which the Russians had taken advantage of—to shift the fight to another sphere until the moment had passed and the nations of Europe had sunk to being partners in trade agreements again. [. . .]

If at the beginning of the war supplies of idealism were provided by order of the state, the longer the war lasted the more the troops had to depend on requisitions. Their heroism turned more and more gloomy, fatal, and steel-gray; glory and ideals beckoned from ever more remote and nebulous spheres; and those who saw themselves less as the troops of the World War than as the executors of the postwar era took up the stance of obstinate rigor. Every third word in their speeches is *stance*. Who would deny that the soldier's position is one of stance? But language is the touchstone for each and every position taken, and not just, as is so often assumed, for that of the writer. But those who have conspired here do not pass the test. Jünger may echo the nobel dilettantes of the seventeenth century in saying that the German language is a primeval language, but he betrays what he means when he adds that as such it inspires an insurmountable distrust in civilization and in the cultivated world. Yet the world's distrust cannot equal that of his own countrymen when the war is presented to them as a "mighty revisor" that "feels the pulse" of the times, that forbids them "to do away with" "a tried and proven conclusion," and that calls on them to intensify their search for "ruins" "behind gleaming varnish." Far more shameful than these offenses, however, is the smooth style of these purportedly rough-hewn thoughts which could grace any newspaper editorial; and more distressing yet than the smooth style is the mediocre substance. "The dead," we are told, "went in their death from an imperfect reality to a perfect reality, from Germany in its temporal manifestation to the eternal Germany." This Germany "in its temporal manifestation" is of course notorious, but the eternal Germany would really be in a bad way if we had to depend on the testimony of those who so glibly invoke it. How cheaply they purchased their "solid feeling of immortality," their certainty that "the terrors of the last war have been frightfully exaggerated," and their symbolism of "blood boiling inwardly!" At best, they fought the war that they are celebrating here. However, we will not tolerate anyone who speaks of war, yet knows nothing but war. Radical in our own way, we will ask: Where do you come from? And what do you know of peace? Did you ever encounter peace in a child, a tree, an animal, the way you encountered a patrol in the field? And without waiting for you to answer, we can say No! It is not that you would then not be able to celebrate war, more passionately than now; but to celebrate it in the way you do would be impossible. [. . .]

These are professional freebooters speaking. Their horizon is fiery but very narrow. What do they see in their flames? They see—here we can entrust ourselves to Friedrich G. Jünger—a transformation: "lines of psychic decision cut across the war; transformations undergone by the war are paralleled by transformations undergone by those fighting it. These transformations become visible when one compares the vibrant, buoyant, enthusiastic faces of the soldiers of August 1914 with the fatally exhausted, haggard, implacably tensed faces of the 1918 veterans of machine warfare. Looming behind the all-too-sharply arched curve of this fight, their image appears, molded and moved by a forceful spiritual convulsion, by station after station along a path of suffering, battle after battle, each the hieroglyphic sign of a strenuously advancing work of destruction. Here we have the new type of soldier schooled in those hard, sober, bloody, and incessant campaigns of attrition. This is a soldier characterized by the tenacious hardness of the born fighter, by a manifest sense of solitary responsibility, of psychic abandonment. In this struggle, which proceeded on increasingly deeper levels, he proved his own mettle. The path he pursued was narrow and dangerous, but it was a path leading into the future." Wherever precise formulations, genuine accents, or solid reasoning are encountered in these pages, the reality portrayed is that of Ernst Jünger's "total mobilization" or Ernst von Salomon's "landscape of the front." A liberal journalist who recently tried to get at this new nationalism under the heading of "Heroism out of Boredom" fell, as one can see here, a bit short of the mark. This soldierly type is a reality, a surviving witness to the World War, and it was actually this "landscape of the front," his true home, that was being defended in the postwar era. This landscape demands further attention.

It should be said as bitterly as possible: in the face of this "landscape of total mobilization" the German feeling for nature has had an undreamed-of upsurge. The pioneers of peace, those sensuous settlers, were evacuated from these landscapes, and as far as anyone could see over the edge of the trench, the surroundings become a problem, every wire entanglement an antinomy, every barb a definition, every explosion a thesis; and by day the sky was the cosmic interior of the steel helmet and at night the moral law above. Etching the landscape with flaming banners and trenches, technology wanted to recreate the heroic features of German Idealism. It went astray. What is considered heroic were the features of Hippocrates, the features of death. Deeply imbued with its own depravity, technology gave shape to the apocalyptic face of nature and reduced nature to silence—even though this technology had the power to give nature its voice. Instead of using and illuminating the secrets of nature via a technology mediated by the human scheme of things, the new nationalists' metaphysical abstraction of war signifies nothing other than a mystical and unmediated application of technology to solve the mystery of an idealistically perceived nature. "Fate" and "hero" occupy these authors' minds like Gog and Magog,[1] yet they devour not only human children but (new ideas) as well. Everything sober, unblemished, naive, and humanistic ends up between the worn teeth of these Molochs who react with the belches of 42cm mortars. Linking heroism with machine warfare is sometimes a bit hard on the authors. But this is by no means true to all of them, and there is nothing more revealing than the whining digressions exposing their disappointment in the "form of the war" and in the "senselessly mechanical machine war" of which these noble fellows "had evidently grown bored." Yet when one or another of them attempts to look things squarely in the eye, it becomes obvious how very much their concept of the heroic has surreptitiously changed; we can see how much the virtues of hardness, reserve, and implacability they celebrate are in fact less those of the soldier than those of the proven class militant. What developed here, first in the guise of the World War volunteer and then in the mercenary of the postwar era, is in fact the dependable, fascist class warrior. And what these authors mean by nation is a ruling class supported by this caste, a ruling class—accountable to no one, and least of all to itself, enthroned on high—which bears the Sphinxlike countenance of the producer who very soon promises to be the sole consumer of his commodities. Sphinxlike in appearance, the fascists' nation thus takes its place as a new economic mystery of nature alongside the old. But this old mystery of nature, far from revealing itself to their technology, is exposing its most threatening feature. In the parallelogram of forces formed by these two—nature and nation—war is the diagonal.

It is understandable that the question of "governmental checks on war" arises in the best, most well-reasoned essay in this volume. For in this mystical theory of war, the state naturally plays more than a minor role. These checks should not for a moment be understood in a pacifist sense. Rather, what is demanded of the state is that its structure and its disposition adapt themselves to, and appear worthy of, the magical forces that the state itself must mobilize in the event of war. [. . .]

---

1. Biblical personifications of the nations that, under Satan, are to war against the Kingdom of God.

Until Germany has broken through the entanglement of such Medusalike beliefs that confront it in these essays, it cannot hope for a future. Perhaps the word loosened would be better than broken through, but this is not to say it should be done with kindly encouragement or with love, both of which are out of place here; nor should the way be smoothed for argumentation, for that wantonly persuasive rhetoric of debate. Instead, all the light that language and reason still afford should be focused upon that "primal experience" from whose barren gloom this mysticism crawls forth on its thousand unsightly conceptual feet. The war that this light exposes is as little the "eternal" one that these new Germans now worship as it is the "final" war that the pacifists carry on about. In reality that war is only this: the one, fearful, last chance to correct the incapacity of peoples to order their relationships to one another in accord with the relationship they posses to nature through their technology. If this corrective effort fails, millions of human bodies will indeed inevitably be chopped to pieces and chewed up by iron and gas. But even the habitués of the chthonic forces of terror, who carry their volumes of [Ludwig] Klages in their packs, will not learn one-tenth of what nature promises its less idly curious, but more sober children who possess in technology not a fetish of doom but a key to happiness. They will demonstrate this sobriety the moment they refuse to acknowledge the next war as an incisive, magical turning point, and instead discover in it the image of everyday actuality. And they will demonstrate it when they use this discovery to transform this war into civil war and thereby perform that Marxist trick that alone is a match for this sinister runic humbug.

59

HEINRICH MANN

The German Decision

First published as "Die deutsche Entscheidung," *Das Tagebuch* 12, no. 51 (December 19, 1931), 1,964–1,967.

Hitler's instructions for National Socialist speakers include the provision that gatherings are to be held exclusively in the evenings. It is easier to work the crowd and stupefy it then than during the day. Supposedly, people are already worn down by the struggle then, more likely to submit.

It is already evening in Germany, if not midnight. That gives Mr. Hitler his big chance, as he most likely knows. Were Germans able to examine their situation with a clear head, he would not win them over. The majority is still not thinking of giving in now. Nevertheless, they are losing a bit of their courage because the enemy no longer appears to have any doubts. In reality, he only acts confident. The republic is secure in the masses, and they own substantial portions of public life. The party laying siege to the state, but in particular its leaders, are seriously mistaken in this; they launch surprise attacks and they bluff, as is usual in war. Never forget that this is a mere war party! It is tailored to win with cunning and force. To make something useful with the victory afterward, aside from seizing booty—it does not even consider that.

I cannot imagine that it makes a great impression in other countries when Mr. Hitler sends his envoys as if the republic's legations were already being dismantled, or when he "receives" the foreign press. Elsewhere people do not feel threatened by him and can look him calmly in the eye, which is the eye of a basilisk only for many Germans; once they have peered into it, they are resigned to being gobbled up. The reason is that they have not overcome the war; it continues to rule them and, in their feelings, has never ended. They say, "It was different in peacetime," wholly forgetting when they are living. They have taken great pains to get used to a new peace, but circumstances have been stronger than they; war now seems to them a primal and permanent condition. Nearly everyone wanted peace; many had become pacifists. They were nonetheless tempted to attribute a greater chance to the one with a militarized mien. He had appearance on his side, the hard world in which one is obviously trapped, the nearly hopeless situation of the majority, the insecurity of property as well as of person. Most people would have been democratic and peaceful; they are that even now and will remain so. It is just that they do not find enough resistance in themselves against someone who employs the methods of war, wholly aside from the circumstance that the government of the republic itself never mounted any serious resistance of its own.

The condition of Germany is above all a psychological fact. All external facts pale in comparison. The collapse of the economy would have been nothing unusual. The economy is collapsing more or less everywhere, but only in Germany does the process achieve its maximum effect on the spirits. One recalls that the currency in all countries was threatened. Only in Germany did it succumb utterly to ruin; the Germans themselves let it become ruined, without any external necessity, for reasons of spirit, from a deficiency of inner resistance. Thus could it be that they now allow National Socialism to come to power because they are hearing once again the call of the abyss. The Germans hear it quite frequently. The question is whether this time they really will listen to the call of the abyss. The catastrophes they have previously suffered, after all, have taught them well. What speaks for that, and what against?

Speaking for the victory of National Socialism, above all, is the fact that in this country democracy has never been won in bloody battle. In one historical moment, after the defeat in the war, it appeared as a possible way out, compared to the disaster of the monarchy and the threat of bolshevism—only a way out, not a goal, much less a passionate experience. Had they been aware in 1918 of the nature of their enterprise, Germans would have taken the necessary steps to secure their democracy. All of those who have since had time to undermine the republic would have been prevented then for all time from perpetrating harm. Instead German democracy simply set itself up as if there remained no one in Germany who did not recognize the primacy of the ballot. They saw foreign democracies resting securely on majorities and took this arrangement to be inviolable. They had no idea of what must be paid for such an arrangement and what lessons the enemies of every lasting democracy have had to learn before they accepted it. German democracy was even proud of its nonviolence. Until today it has left the application of force to its enemies, who make the best use of their kind permission. The world might recognize how unfair it would be to take the Germans for worshipers of force. No, the majority lived the whole time according to the simple convention of the ballot and did not even allow the suspicion to arise that they could be defeated, plundered, and deprived of their rights despite the ballot. Probably no other people would have been capable of this innocence, this trust.

Now the majority is calling to the state for help—instead of helping itself. It has still not become clear to the majority that, for the most part, the state has already abandoned them, not that the contrary was ever even true. The judiciary was never republican. No one knows anything for certain about the military. Now one sees that the state is treating Hitler's private army not as a threat to its own existence but as a desirable increase in its own power. If that is so, where does the government stand? Not necessarily where the majority still assumes it to stand when it calls on the state for help. One of the state ministers declared that the government must not allow itself to be isolated from the body of the people. Did he mean the majority? Or a minority that just happens to be heavily armed?

Enough—these and other circumstances as well, including the power of money, speaks for the victory of National Socialism. More important, incomparably more important, is what speaks for its defeat and for the survival of democracy; for this must be clearly recognized, or it will never be fully exploited. Democracy is justified in placing its hopes in the people's instinct for self-preservation. Its vision is not unclouded and its spirit is terribly rent. But it must retain its sensitivity, as even animals do, to the approach of the slaughter bench. It is to be defeated internally, but then driven into further wars abroad: a people discerns that in advance. If it has long hesitated and allowed itself to be paralyzed, it will perhaps gather all its forces in the end after all. The proletariat, which is split only through the ideologies of its leaders, could unite. Moreover it is not yet certain that the means of state power, to the extent that they remain in republican hands, will be surrendered without a struggle. The outcome of that struggle would be at least uncertain. If the army should hold back, cautiously awaiting evidence as to who is stronger, then the majority will prove stronger, as soon as it wants unreservedly to be so.

The democratic majority's best trump card, however, remains the unmistakable dubiousness of its enemies' humane qualities and their questionable morality. The National Socialists and their leaders want to put themselves in the clover, to get their hands on power and nothing else. They steal the ideas of others who they nevertheless oppose. They are corruptible and were originally the paid defense force of a coterie of industrialists, before they got big enough to set themselves up as the saviors of Germany. This is all sensed by the many who know nothing. It is in particular no secret to Germans in the bottom of their hearts how little personal legitimacy Hitler and his sort bring with them to their arrogated role. Hitler is supposed to have "foamed at the mouth" while speaking his nonsense about France, and everyone says to himself that there is something in the former Austrian that is not right. Germany's "traditional enemy" just does not have that much to do with someone born to the east of Germany's borders. He must be a comedian. What, even, does Germany have to do with him? The Austrian comedian avails himself of a German vice, anti-Semitism—with what justification? How does he himself and those like him see that? One senses all this, and it is just this feeling that tips the scales. It would be very strange if their outer crudeness not their inner weaknesses, determined the future of National Socialism.

Assuming, however, that they win and set up their stupid dictatorship; for whom are they really ruling? For their creditors, a certain number of persons who call themselves "the economy" and who have twice brought the state to ruin through their influence over its affairs. They drove the first Reich into the war, the second into nationalism. Are they suddenly supposed to have run short of talent, so that they cannot drive the Third Reich into anything? The Third Reich will founder on its incompetence and its dependency. But then would come an extraordinarily bloody period in German history. The Reich of the pseudo-Germans and pseudosocialists will be established consciously by the shedding of blood, but that is nothing compared to the blood that will flow as it falls. Then democracy will make up for all that it missed, then it will be experienced—and, incidentally, it will then no longer be the incomplete democracy of a concluded epoch but a genuine democracy, the one the people have wanted.

60

LION FEUCHTWANGER

How Do We Struggle against a Third Reich?

First published as "Wie kämpfen wir gegen ein Drittes Reich?" *Welt am Abend* (January 21, 1931).

The war liberated the barbarian instincts of the individual and society to a degree that was previously unimaginable. National Socialism has skillfully organized the barbarity. Among the intellectuals it is called OBG: Organized Barbarity of Germany.

Anti-logical and anti-intellectual in its being and ideology, National Socialism strives to depose reason and install in its place emotion and drive—to be precise, barbarity. Just because intellect and art are transnational, National Socialism distrusts and hates them to the extreme. To gag the intellect and art is one of the most important points in its program, and since it proclaims that they can be accomplished with least danger, it is here that it has its greatest success.

As National Socialism has risen in influence, it has turned with particular fanaticism against everything intellectual and everything artistic.

Nearly without a struggle the liberal bourgeoisie has cleared all cultural positions for its advance. Aside from a couple of workers' theaters, no cinema nor theater dares any longer to portray material uncongenial to the National Socialists; writers who take positions unacceptable to the OBG (and that includes, with isolated exceptions, all German writers of rank) are overwhelmed with threatening letters. Not for a century has the mind in Germany been so unfree as it is today.

What the intellectuals and artists have therefore to expect once the Third Reich is definitely established is clear: extermination. And that is what the majority does expect. Those intellectuals who can do so are already preparing to emigrate. Anyone who moves among the intellectuals in Berlin gets the impression that Berlin is a city full of future emigrés.

It is therefore the demand of naked self-preservation that all intellectuals struggle with body and soul and all their abilities against the Third Reich. As long as there remains a single corner in Germany where art is allowed to open its mouth, we want to pronounce it unmistakably and hammer it through the skull: the Third Reich means the extermination of science, of art, and of the intellect.

61

COMMUNIST PARTY OF GERMANY

Open Letter of the KPD to the Working Voters of the NSDAP and the Members of the SA

First published as "Offener Brief der KPD an die werktätigen Wähler der NSDAP und die Mitglieder der Sturmabteilungen," *Die Rote Fahne* (November 1, 1931).

Working National Comrades!

The working people of Germany are suffering dire need! The capitalist plunderers of the people and their state are sucking the people dry. Wages are being reduced so that more dividends, bonuses, and higher directorial salaries can flow into the pockets of the rich. Millions of workers are being thrown out of the plants that are being shut down while the working people are deprived of the vital necessities of life.

Support for the unemployed and the pensions of the invalids of war and those injured in the workplace are being reduced so that the rentier class and wealthy princes can become even richer. We are experiencing the collapse of countless livelihoods on a daily basis. Finance capital and the marshals of the Brüning government[1] are stripping the middle class and the peasantry of their property.

Thus does the Brüning government, in the service of big capital, decree bitter need for the working people, while simultaneously giving away millions in subsidies to the big industrialists, the big banks, and the big agriculturalists.

Who is to blame for this need?

To blame are those who own the factories, the big banks, and the land. As long as [Alfons] Goldschmidt, [Albert] Vögler, [Fritz] Thyssen, [Gustav] Krupp, [Ernst von] Börsig, and [Carl] Siemens own the factories, the banks, and the land, Germany will not be governed differently.

The working people want bread, work, and freedom. That will not come to them from the hands of Krupp, Goldschmidt, Brüning & Co. The working people must struggle for it themselves.

You call for a people's war against poverty. A people's war against poverty can only be a people's war against the rich and the powerful who cut your wages, reduce your salaries, decrease your relief payments and pensions; who collect usurious interest through attachments, increase the price of bread and other important foodstuffs through usurious tariffs, and repress the freedom of speech, press, and assembly.

Those who honestly want to struggle against the plundering of the people and the enslavement of the Young Plan must, today and tomorrow, put all their energies at the disposal of the working people and organize mass resistance to the plundering and repression of the workers.

In the numerous strikes led of late by the revolutionary union opposition, National Socialist workers fought alongside Communist and Social Democratic workers against every penny of reduced wages while employers, social democratic union bosses, and leaders of the NSDAP issued their calls to break the strikes.

At some relief offices unemployed National Socialist workers, under the leadership of a committee of the unemployed, have fought together with Communist and Social Democratic workers against cuts in relief payments, for supplemental relief, and against compulsory unpaid work hours. As honest fighters against the hunger system, proletarian followers of the NSDAP have joined the United Front of the proletariat and done their revolutionary duty in committees of the unemployed. But the leaders of their party defended, in particular by rejecting Communist proposals in Parliament, the reduction of relief. They stood on the side of Brüning.

In numerous residential areas followers of the NSDAP have helped revolutionary workers mobilize the masses against the eviction of the unemployed.

In many villages members of the NSDAP, under Communist leadership, have prevented working peasants from having their cow seized or their small holding auctioned off.

---

1. Heinrich Brüning was chancellor from 1930 to 1932.

What did your leaders say about that? They forbade every self-help measure. They admonished you to remain within the law. You are supposed to starve legally.

Social liberation your leaders promised, but they joined together in Harzburg with the leaders of the big trusts and banks, promising them their faithful service. In Harzburg the SA marched in review for the millionaire [Alfred] Hugenberg, the finance princes, and trust lords.

In the economic council of the Brüning government, the big capitalists represented in Harzburg give their advice along with the Social Democratic union leaders on how the wool can be pulled most quickly over the eyes of the working people. And you are expected to help them! [. . .]

For us there is only one way out: socialism.

Socialism—the expropriation of the big capitalist and big agriculturalists!

The free worker and peasant lord of the factories, lord of the banks and the land—that is socialism!

Fight with us in the front of the revolutionary freedom army for bread, work, and freedom, for socialism!

> Communist Party of Germany
> District Administration for Berlin–Brandenburg–Lausitz–Grenzmark

62

JOSEPH ROTH

Cultural Bolshevism

First published as "Der Kulturbolschewismus," *Das Tagebuch* 13 (July 9, 1932), 1,050–1,057.

I

Among the excavations the new political archaeologists of Germany are starting to undertake in the desolate cemeteries of dead phrases, the first, as we know, was that long-since-decayed cry of "cultural bolshevism." At a time when corpses cheerfully go for strolls and even march, when mummies direct their own exhumations, and when ghosts exercise both the active and the passive right to vote, it is admittedly no wonder that the cadavers of the moralistic phrase also raise themselves up from the dead. There would be little value here in stepping back and explaining the logical and philological absurdity of the term cultural bolshevism. Nor do we want to deal in detail with the vague concept of culture, but will allow the banal meaning ordinarily attributed to it to pertain from the outset. We understand quite clearly what is meant by the words *cultural bolshevism:* the destruction of German culture. [. . .]

II

The author[1] sees a danger above all in the texts of the "pacifistically inclined" writers, those who "protest against the governmental leadership creating a reliable and adequate

---

1. Roth refers to Wilhelm Westecker, a contributor to a collection called *Der Feind im Land* (Berlin, 1932).

military. In doing so they prevent the state from actually becoming an authority. For they truly hate authority. They want to perpetuate the 'dominance of the inferior,' of the quick and nimble. For in an organic condition organized by authority, the intellectually adroit play no role. They attend only to people and the peace of the visible world and in doing so disavow all supernatural authority. This denial amounts to the systematic destruction of the feeling that no man belongs only to himself but to his family, his children, his people, and his God. Characteristic of this position are the frivolous statements of Alfred Kerr: 'Why should a woman who possesses very great beauty not give of it to two at once?' For these writers erotic freedom is merely an aspect of political freedom, as in Russia, and political freedom is above all a state of being free—from all duty toward the nation. For duty toward humanity rarely requires active confirmation. And even then personal ambition is usually stronger than idealism. But a rationalistic preference for abstract concepts is already dangerous—the socialization and materialization of the German soul. These writers' activism can only destroy, not build—an artistic nihilist, like Heinrich Mann—but not all Germans are silent, and then it is to be hoped that the loud ones will have crawled away."

Futile effort, the introduction of any semblance of order into this gibberish! One would like to seize not himself but the author by the head, if one could only figure out where he keeps it! What a whirlwind of paper, misunderstanding, desperation, bitterness, and character! A grown-up little boy flails about with a sword of printed pasteboard. Compared to this champion of the military valor of the nation, even a pacifist scorner of arms is a valiant knight and one of the "quick and nimble," a hero of iron and steel. Were the honesty not so visible amidst all the confusion, one could believe that the man out of pure egotism was wishing into being that condition "in which the intellectually adroit play no role." But just as certainly as he cannot be counted among the intellectually adroit, he seems to me to belong among the ranks of the honestly helpless who compromise the cause for which they want to fight. And, were I the commandant of the imperial army, I would not hesitate to take into protective custody the intellectually unadroit, who undermine my authority by coming to my defense, and to wrest from their hands the pasteboard swords with which they caricature my parades. [. . .]

It is pointless to go into more detail or to investigate other pamphlets by men who distinguish themselves so little from one another! This polymorphous phalanx of mummies, of corpses, of striplings, who display precisely as much senile debility in areas of intellectual concern as they do youthful prowess on the fields of sport and battle, is held together solely by a common dialect, a ghostly, two-dimensional shadow language; the phalanx advances inexorably, flooding the land. The cemeteries are open. The graves of old have ruptured. The muscular shadows of the putrified spread over the earth in brown shirts, and with living pistols they shoot the living dead. A fresh, free, cheerful host of pure Aryan corpses and ghosts calls to a land already wakeful that it might awake and look: the living follow the putrified, the day grows dark and imagines it ought to be night, because the night is brighter. Heathen skeletons equipped with muscles and cudgels of death rip the crosses from their own graves, bend them into swastikas, and cry out in the name of Christianity the blasphemous call to a "Christian–Germanic culture." They spread the lie that Jesus Christ died for us on the deformity of their twisted cross! "Bolsheviks"— the truest ones there have ever been (to speak in the language of the enemies of "cultural bolshevism"), namely stutterers, Germanic defilers of the German language, and subversives imagining themselves to be "builders"—degrade Germany by calling it balkanized, which it never was, and thereby subject even geography to falsification. "Destroyers," who desecrate the eternal law of language, logic, and national character with every word they fling from their crippled tongues, are allowed by a state preserved only by impotent authorities to be called legalized tenders of culture, and louts who have neither a notion of "culture" nor of "bolshevism" are allowed to coin a senseless, official phrase that becomes their sole program and that of a "Christian government." Authorities capable of certifying their authority only through their insistence that they are such are allowed to defend a cross supported by the caricaturing deformity of the swastika, which reviles the cross as never before in the two thousand years it has illumined the earth and the German land. Never has a Jew, never has a Russian Bolshevik so derided the symbol of European (and German) culture, as the movement that twists and deforms the cross into a swastika.

People who, supported by the swastika, fight against cultural bolshevism, appear to us to be worse than Bolsheviks. At least the Soviet star does not caricature the cross. The Soviet star is an enemy of the cross, to be sure. But the swastika is a sacrilege! More pressing than the struggle against cultural bolshevism seems to be the struggle of genuine conservatives against the paganism of the swastika, against the desecrators of the cross, and against the nationalistic, the true cultural bolshevism.

63

PAUL TILLICH

Ten Theses

First published as "Zehn Thesen," in *Die Kirche und das Dritte Reich. Fragen und Forderungen deutscher Theologen,* ed. Leopold Klotz (Gotha: Klotz, 1932), 126–128.

1. A Protestantism that is open to nationalism and repudiates socialism is on the verge of once again betraying its mission to the world.

2. Apparently in obedience to the principle that the Kingdom of God is not of this earth, it proves itself, as it often has in history, obedient to the victorious powers and their demonry.

3. To the extent that it justifies nationalism and the ideology of blood and race through a doctrine of the divine order of creation, it sacrifices its prophetic basis in favor of a new paganism, whether open or concealed, and betrays its mission to bear witness to the one God and the single humanity.

4. To the extent that it lends the capitalist–feudal form of domination, the protection of which National Socialism in fact serves, the consecration of divinely ordained authority, it helps to perpetuate the class struggle and betrays its mission of bearing witness against violence and for justice as the standard of all social order.

5. Protestantism is in the gravest danger of following this path that, over the long run, will ruin it. From its beginnings it has lacked a sustaining group independent of the earthly powers and national divisions. It lacks a socially critical principle grounded in prophecy. It lacks on Lutheran soil the will to form reality in the image of the Kingdom of God. In Germany it is now sustained sociologically nearly exclusively by the groups standing behind National Socialism, and is thereby bound to them ideologically and politically.

6. Official declarations of neutrality on the part of church authorities changes nothing in the actual attitude of the broadest Protestant circles, theologians, and laity. They become

completely worthless when the church at the same time institutes measures against socialist pastors and congregations and when theologians who oppose pagan National Socialism find no refuge whatever in the church.

7. It is for Protestantism to preserve its prophetic Christian character by opposing the paganism of the swastika with the Christianity of the cross. It must attest that the nation, race, blood, and sovereign authority are subjected in their sanctity to the cross and brought to judgment.

8. It is in the nature of Protestantism that it does not enjoy the possibility of representing itself in conformity with a specific political tendency. It must preserve freedom from itself by enabling Protestants to belong to any political party, even those that struggle against Protestantism in its institutional embodiment. It must, however, judge every party—as every human and indeed churchly deed—in accord with the hope of the original Christian prophecy of the kingdom of God on earth.

9. In this way it can inform the political aspirations of the groups comprising National Socialism with a true and just goal appropriate to their social needs, and liberate the movement from the nationally and universally destructive demonry to which it is subject today.

10. An open or clandestine alliance of the Protestant churches with the National Socialist Party for the repression of socialism and combating of Catholicism, given the present increase in the power of the churches, must lead to the future dissolution of German Protestantism.

64

EWALD VON KLEIST-SCHMENZIN

National Socialism: A Menace

First published in *Der Nationalsozialismus. Eine Gefahr* (Berlin: Verlag Neue Gesellschaft, 1932).

The impact of National Socialism is assuming dimensions that threaten our future. National Socialism has caused a complete change of attitude among a large number of people, particularly workers, who were originally just nationalistically minded. These people, who were unmoved by the socialistic demands and slogans of the Social Democrats, have adopted these same demands and slogans when they were offered in nationalistic wrappings. Now they are firmly convinced of their truth, and most of them turn with hatred against any kind of personal property. The ideal of nationalism pales into a slogan. The party is made an equivalent of the nation, and loyalty to the fatherland is transferred to the party. The intuitive contradiction between religion and fanatic hatred of private property is gradually leading to disdain and even fervent rejection of religion. The same is true of their attitudes toward monarchy, reverence, tradition, obedience outside of the party discipline, and so on. Mere mention of the word *religion* has caused eruptions of animalistic rage among the National Socialists. Basically dependable workers neglect their duties under the influence of National Socialism. It appears that this anti-establishment attitude is being passed on to children as well, in a way previously known only in the Communist districts of large cities. The discipline of the SA should not divert us from this fact. The indoctrinated belief in the unique salvation and redeeming qualities of National Socialism, and in Hitler personally, fosters an incredible intolerance. In villages where conservative Nationalists and Social Democrats once lived together tolerably, those Nationalists and National Socialists now often oppose each other like enemy nations. Similar destructive effects are evident among National Socialist farmers, notably the younger ones. Laborers, artisans, lesser job holders, and others might go Social Democratic in the foreseeable future, but they are more likely to join the Communists. Declining Marxism is reviving because of Hitler; that is the harvest of his dragon's seed.

The devastating effects of National Socialism are making themselves felt in every aspect of life. The fanatic Nazi followers are loyal only to their party. They undercut proper decision-making, even in nonpolitical organizations, and employees neglect their work. In short, everywhere the conditions for living together in human and governmental association are being destroyed.

The youth and educated classes who have succumbed to National Socialism are uprooted and constitute a threat to the future. In general it is no longer true except in isolated cases that National Socialism makes nationalism attractive to Marxists. Those Marxists whom the Nazis converted had already recognized the inadequacy of Marxism in the face of economic distress and would have abandoned it sooner or later. Some of these converts hope to foster the class struggle more successfully with nationalist slogans than with international ones. Others were ready for a genuine inner conversion and, attracted by nationalist slogans, are now hooked by the National Socialist ideology that forces them back to socialistic thinking.

These circumstances cannot necessarily be ascribed to all National Socialists, but generally things are developing thus and in fact have accelerated in the last few weeks. The National Socialist assault on the very foundation of human and political life is even more dangerous than that of the Social Democrats. Because of its misleading name and the deliberate duplicity of its leadership, people who would normally resist an open attack on their way of life succumb to National Socialism. Public National Socialist agitation is unprincipled and thorough, especially in small gatherings; but the propaganda on a personal level is even more ruthless. Even in this region, where the National Socialists still pretend to support conservative national views and behave somewhat peaceably, their agitation consists of an alarming amount of purely communistic hatemongering. This incitement to destruction persists and engulfs all the other professed national aspirations. One is constantly amazed how few people see, or want to see, this danger.

National Socialism would never have taken this dangerous upsurge if nationally minded groups had openly divorced themselves from it. The view tolerated in those groups, that National Socialism should be seen as a nationalist movement with just a few shortcomings, has produced danger for our future that can only be countered by the greatest of effort. During the second presidential election, the slogans of the *Reichslandbund,* the Crown Prince, the United Patriotic associations, and others . . . were so bereft of political instinct that they drove hundreds of thousands of nationalists over to Hitler and exposed them to spiritual corruption and brainwashing. There were also failings on the part of the German National People's Party. At the very least after the Harzburg Meeting [a demonstrative gathering of some conservatives and Nazis], or by the time that candidates were nominated for the first presidential ballot, it was clear that a workable coalition would never be possible with National Socialism and Hitler. After that, all the divisive and incriminating remarks of Hitler should have been used against the Nazis, with dignity but with ruthlessness, to expose the true nature of this party. But that occurred only partially and insufficiently. This weakness caused the loss of many nationalist adherents because they were left in confusion as to the nature and goals of National Socialism and Hitler.

The flow of followers to Hitler is largely a movement of fear and desperation. In fear of what may yet come, people flock to the National Socialist Party in senseless despair because they hope that the mass of voters, by casting like ballots, can avert the troubles threatening us and can above all spare the individual from personal involvement. Many of them put all their hopes in Hitler and do not want to see the shortcomings of National Socialism. Those who stick with the German National People's Party only do so because they believe that a counterbalance is still somehow necessary. No wonder there is such confusion of thought. If political action is to be successful for Germany's future, . . . our struggle against the aberrations of National Socialism must be waged promptly with dignity and earnestness, but with rigorous determination.

Religious attitudes are crucial in separating conservative thinking from National Socialism. The foundation of conservative policy is that obedience to God, and faith in Him, must determine the whole of public life. National Socialism is based on a fundamentally different point of view in which questions of faith must of course be dropped as irrelevant. Hitler actually recognizes race and its demands as the highest law of governmental action; if at times he says otherwise, that does not make any difference. His materialism cannot be reconciled with Christianity. According to Hitler, the state does not have the responsibility to foster creativity but only to guard the racial heritage! . . . Hitler is primarily interested in breeding healthy bodies; he stresses emphatically that building character is only of secondary importance. This conviction is unacceptable. . . . Inseparably connected with National Socialism are a superficial search for happiness and a streak of liberal rationalism that is expressed in its motto, group welfare has priority over individual desire. National Socialism leans increasingly toward the liberal conception of the greatest good of the greatest number. For us, the nation per se is not the ultimate measure but rather the will of God which obligates us to live for the nation. That is a fundamental difference.

It is difficult to tell how National Socialism officially views marriage and the family, but it is evident from numerous comments of well-known Nazis that they accept many views which we must resolutely reject.

It is certain that National Socialism does not favor monarchism and is definitely republican in conviction. The core of its domestic political program is synonymous with Social Democracy on economic, social, and tax policy, and largely also in agrarian proposals. Hitler is demanding continuation of the socialist policy that contributed to our economic collapse and harmed the workers as well. His excessive agitation against property and capital and his unscrupulous provocation of people to militancy, threaten to destroy every possibility of reconstruction by arousing instincts of envy that will not easily be controlled.

Hitler has declared that efforts to forge a united front are superfluous. How could an honest coalition be established with such a man?

The National Socialists said they were prepared to join a cabinet formed by Democrat Otto Gessler as chancellor and with Brüning as foreign minister. Where does that leave their loud campaign against the establishment with which they meant to catch the voters? Hitler has declared to a foreign correspondent that the Versailles Treaty cannot simply be torn up but must be replaced at a conference by a new one. Where does that leave the campaign he has hitherto fought against our foreign policy? Where does that put the slogan of a struggle for freedom? Hitler stated publicly in Lauenburg that he was not prepared to defend our borders against a Polish invasion as long as the present government was in power. This statement has been repeated and confirmed in writing by other National Socialists who were present. This declaration openly means abandonment of the German nation and actually encourages the Poles to invade. *Hitler and the party have publicly set themselves above the fatherland.* Given such an attitude, can one expect them to join a coalition government and conduct foreign policy in the national interest?

A glance at National Socialist newspapers, pamphlets, and other propaganda should convince anyone (who is still willing to look) of the unscrupulous dishonesty of the movement and its leaders. Their arguments can be cited both for and against almost any position. Since people are not aware of this duplicity, it is no wonder that they succumb to National Socialism in their ignorance. We can no longer tolerate the pretense that National Socialism is the one movement that can save the nation. This delusion must be destroyed together with the totally false image that the people have of Hitler. In light of the foregoing, I ask: have we conservatives anything left in common with National Socialism? Surely we must recognize that its essential assumptions are a menace to the nation and to unselfish patriotic convictions. The many respectable groups presently cooperating with National Socialism will progressively have less power to influence the nature of the movement. In the French Revolution, with its appeal to national striving for freedom and socialism, a vanguard of selfless and confused visionaries prepared the way for destruction; similarly under National Socialism the nationalist elements will involuntarily set the stage for a national disaster. A National Socialist government will inevitably end in chaos. Their rulers would soon be swept away by the unmanageable tide of upheaval they created. We conservative nationalists should no longer abet the destruction caused by Nazi slogans of national interest and by Hitler's romantic image.

Hopes for a coalition government are at the moment nonexistent, but even if one could assume the prospects were favorable, how promising would they be? We conservatives are united in our common determination to supplant the present democratic leaders. We only seek this change so that a different policy can be pursued, one which will save the nation. The National Socialists, however, want to overthrow the present governmental system in order to assume power themselves. Once arrived, they will do all they can to dissolve the coalition and would ally with any other faction if necessary. Considering their numerical strength, the National Socialists would certainly not leave the important offices to administration experts. We would achieve nothing but support of a policy that would be more disastrous than the previous one. It would be a fateful error to assume that National Socialism could ever abandon its ambitions for total control. These intentions are as determined as the claim of the Roman Catholic Church to absolute rule. Only in defeat can National Socialism be coerced to offer limited cooperation.

To summarize: it is the task of all conservative forces, like the German National People's Party and other patriotic organizations, resolutely to renounce cooperation with the politically fashionable Nazi disease; for the sake of Germany's future, we cannot tolerate the destruction of the remaining genuinely conservative principles that are a necessary part of the foundations of the new state. We must give up the mistaken belief that favorable political change can only be brought about by the enervating elections that characterize this parliamentary system. We must redouble our political action and bring it elsewhere to bear on the political process. The thought and action of the people must be focused on crucial matters. It is always just a few individuals who institute crucial and favorable political change. But behind them must stand dedicated men whose every thought and action is determined by unselfish patriotism, who are united by a deep inner communion and whose whole posture is determined by unshakeable faith.

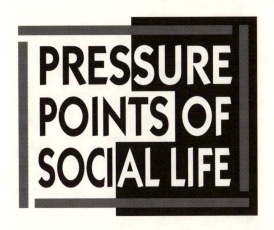

PRESSURE POINTS OF SOCIAL LIFE

Working class family in Berlin Kreuzberg district, 1920. (Landesbildstelle Berlin.) Inset: Otto Dix, "Portrait of Sylvia von Harden," 1926. (Copyright © 1993 ARS, New York/VG Bild Kunst, Bonn.) August Sander, Savings Bank Cashier, Cologne, 1928. (Collection of the J. Paul Getty Museum, Malibu, California. Print courtesy of the Museum.)

7
White-Collar Workers: *Mittelstand* or Middle Class?

THE RAPID BUT UNEVEN modernization of the German economy produced enormous opportunities for some, but critical problems for others. Among the most vulnerable to the changes were the growing number of white-collar workers (*die Angestellten*) sandwiched between organized labor and big business, which grew increasingly concentrated after the war. The white-collar workers were composed of an older stratum made up of the residues of a precapitalist artisanal economy and a newer one including salaried employees in commerce, governmental bureaucracy, and the new service industries that emerged during the Weimar Republic. Stubbornly identifying themselves as an estate status group (*Stand*) rather than a class, they vigorously retained a self-image of being superior to that of the workers (beneath them on the social scale), even though their economic situation was no longer better. Although they attempted to defend their common interests through a large number of ineffective organizations, many white-collar workers felt insecure economically and under enormous social pressure, especially during the inflation of the early 1920s and the depression that began at their end. The rationalization of the German economy—the enhancement of productivity by scientific management, the take-over of smaller units by larger ones, and technological advances in designing plants—only worked to increase their sense of alienation and anomie.

As a result, white-collar workers were the object of considerable political and social-scientific concern, with sociologists like Emil Lederer and Theodor Geiger probing their condition and analyzing their relations to the middle and working classes.

The crisis of their cultural identity also drew considerable attention, perhaps most tellingly in the classic 1929 study, *Die Angestellten,* by the critic Siegfried Kracauer, who pointed out the ominous implications of their "spiritual homelessness." But however much politicians and intellectuals sought to analyze and soothe their anxieties, they often remained the objects of a certain contempt as "little men" (as well as "little women"), more pathetic than powerful. It was no wonder that many harbored a resentment that would make them prone to the seductive rhetoric of radical movements on the right.

65

HANS GEORG

Our *Stand* at the Abyss

First published as "Unser Stand vor dem Abgrund," *Deutsche Handelswacht. Zeitschrift des deutschnationalen Handlungsgehilfen-Verbandes*, no. 3 (January 26, 1921).

White-collar employees used to belong to the *Mittelstand*. That the income of a white-collar employee was usually not much higher than a worker's, indeed often lagged behind it, does not refute this but only proves that the social position of an occupation does not absolutely and without exception depend upon its economic ranking. Who would seriously deny that the life-style of white-collar employees was not superior to that of the workers! White-collar employees dressed better, lived in nicer homes, possessed higher quality household goods, pursued educational opportunities, attended lectures, concerts, or theatrical performances, and read good books. Their standard of living approximated that of the propertied class, not perhaps in range and freedom but in type. The reasons for their proud appearance are neither beyond explanation nor solely a response to the demands of their occupation. It was a thoroughly justified expression of a deeper need, of a more refined intellectual and spiritual education. There is no denigration of the manual worker in this statement, though there is perhaps a reproach directed at the independent unionists and party socialists who, mistaking the facts, have subjected "white-collar proletarians" to ridicule.

These slanderers of the middle class were also wrong when they claimed that white-collar employees had merely invented the prized relationship between themselves and their superiors as that of being co-workers. Their appraisal of this relationship undoubtedly waned over time but never entirely disappeared. It remained significant in the legislation regulating firings of white-collar employees. While workers could be turned out of the factory from one day or one week to the next, white-collar employees could be dismissed only four times a year and, moreover, had to be given six weeks' notice. But even this limited right of dismissal was generally not invoked, even when a decline in business would clearly have made it tempting. The resulting existential security of white-collar employees once again contributed to their adoption of the ways of thinking and life-styles of the higher social classes. Workers were in fact exploited like machines, and they had no defense against being sacrificed to every economic downturn. They became depersonalized numbers, and generally nothing but need gave them any feeling of a connection to the factory in which they worked. They were genuine proletarians! White-collar employees instead were each valued as a distinct personality because of their smaller number and the variety of the functions they fulfilled; they were thus able, since they remained in continual contact with "their" business, to develop themselves along with it. To them, work did not appear as it did to workers, to be an unavoidable evil, but offered them psychological satisfaction. For that reason and despite gloomy experiences on an individual level, white-collar employees as a group were always able to feel, more or less, that they occupied the role of co-workers.

In terms of income undeniably closest to the proletariat, but, just as undeniably, most nearly related to the propertied class in life-style and mental habits—in this way the white-collar employees, along with small manufacturers, occupied the middle; thus the designation *Mittelstand*.

It is impossible to overestimate the value of these classes. The leading strata of the population and economy are replenished and renewed from their ranks. They are in turn renewed by the most capable recruits from the proletariat, which is consequently the particular significance of the latter. It is a permanent—note the word well—mediation between the bottom and the top. There is a naturally ordained, indispensable order in this arrangement. Whoever has doubts should check the biographies of former workers now functioning as county governors, mayors, city-council presidents, and state ministers. To the extent that they are any good at all in their offices they were previously white-collar employees, whether party secretaries, union officials, leaders of consumer cooperatives, or editors.

66

MARGOT STARKE
The Bank Clerk

First published as "Der Bankbeamte," *Der Querschnitt* 3 (1923), 138–139.

The bank clerk is, in comparison with Nietzsche's Superman [*Übermensch*], an underman, for there where human being stops the bank clerk begins; that is, there where humane feelings cannot function, he gets started. We have become accustomed to regarding him as if he were like other people, like, for example, art dealers, used-book sellers, and other merchants who often take on a more human form in their leisure hours; but we fool ourselves if we take the "as if" to be an absolute. For the bank clerk only acts as if he were a human being, but is not one; for if he were a human, he could not be a bank clerk. In reality, his head is a calculator, his arms respectively a pencil and a pen stand, his legs two rulers, and his body a ledger in which he writes most maliciously, unconscious of his degeneracy, "In God We Trust."

Should we examine his insides, a practice by preference anxiously avoided, we notice no such notions as love, friendship, desire, passion, or hate; we see only numbers, darkening the white pages like swarms of grasshoppers that greedily eat each other up. This greedy feast he calls *Debit* and *Credit,* words that he always capitalizes because they are the main words for him, fetishistically worshipped since they convey to him the single revelation of his life, namely that what is debit to one is credit to another. He kneels with special reverence before the credit. He is always expressing it in formal terms just as in earlier times officers were required to do in the presence of their superiors.

Since the vocabulary of a bank clerk is extremely limited, he finds himself forced to perform the purest tricks of magic with these two words that fill the entirety of his thoughts and endeavors. Playfully and lovingly he transforms the one into the other, so that sometimes credit means debit and debit means credit, two resounding organ tones in his wildly chromatic, contrapuntal symphony from hell. Whether we humans understand his gibberish does not concern the bank clerk at all. It is only important that he understands them himself in the very fibers of his nerves; he coils them tightly about the two words till they wriggle convulsively, threaten to rip, and then become calm and strong again, according to whether they have wrapped themselves around the debit or the credit—his

A-B, upon which follows no *C,* upon which follows nothing at all, for here he is at his end. Unless, that is, one counts as new words the other two he yet speaks, which, however, are the complete equivalents of debit and credit in meaning: *receipt* and *charge.*

Receipt! As a child one receives gifts, later one receives wisdom, visions—discrete things-in-themselves from heaven. Geniuses received invisible revelation; the Holy God. But the bank clerk can imagine nothing of this whatsoever; for when he says "receipt," to him that means pay, just like everything, everything that he contemplates, says, and bears within himself means pay. He pays when he receives; he pays when he charges. He pays when he says "credit"; he pays when he says "debit." By add, subtract, value, sign, and transfer, he means pay. And that is it! He has no access to further words and, finally, to none at all; he uses them only for the sake of concealment, to satisfy the sorriest propriety, or in place of a number. Should he once utter a complete sentence—like, "From me to you to them" (he is not capable of a better one)—it means threefold pay: Y pays, he pays, Z pays.

The bank clerk has no time to be tired; he is steadfast. In perpetual motion, by sunlight or in nightly dreams, the little two-times-two circles the big two-times-two, onto which he hangs many, many zeros to make them heavier. And should this circling suddenly stop then he has stopped being; then he would be dead. Or, he would not be dead at all, since another bank clerk exactly like the first would take his place. In consequence he lives eternally like immortal matter, unless Judgment Day—but unfortunately that takes so long to come! [. . .]

If one were, however, to assume that he was really dead, he cannot go to heaven, for he is spat from hell.

If one were further to assume that he did go to heaven, then would heaven not be heaven for a moment but the empty space his simple presence would make of the Elysian Fields, in which the bank clerk would restlessly revolve, rising through the spheres, using the gentle moon, the bright sun, and all the stars for adding machines until he reached that empty void which is himself.

67

FRITZ SCHRÖDER

The Labor Market for White-Collar Workers

First published as "Der Arbeitsmarkt für Angestellten," *Die Arbeit. Zeitschrift für Gewerkschaftspolitik und Wissenschaftskunde* 1, no. 6 (1924), 340–343.

Chronic unemployment can result from a wide variety of causes that lie in the over-crowding of the white-collar professions, such that no relief is gained from a period of economic prosperity. The social structure of the white-collar professions was fundamentally altered during and after the war. Male employees who were drafted into the war had to be replaced by others. Added demand was created by the military authorities and other economic organizations of military significance during the war. This demand was then met by an enormous increase in the number of working women and a return of retired persons to their previous occupations. An unprecedented increase in the number of white-collar employees followed the period of inflation, since the inflation destroyed the middle classes as a whole, forcing their members back to gainful employment. To a considerable degree they streamed into white-collar occupations. Banks, the insurance industry, commercial enterprises, loan offices, and public authorities were nearly incapable of managing the surplus of work created by the inflation, and continually increased the demand for white-collar employees. The house of cards collapsed when the implementation of constant-value wages and salaries left inflation devoid of meaning, since it was no longer possible to levy inflation like a tax.

A few statistics will illuminate the crisis in the white-collar labor market. The number of employees discharged from banks is estimated at about 200,000. In the insurance industry there is likewise a considerable number of layoffs. A December 1, 1918, survey by the Central Association of Insurance Associations indicated approximately 90,000 white-collar employees working in insurance; the number of insurance-industry employees presently working can be estimated at about 33,000. A similar process is evident among public employees. On January 1, 1923, public employees working on the national level numbered 93,903; on July 1, 1924, the number of working public employees amounted to 29,808. On October 1, 1919, there were roughly 40,000 white-collar jobs in public assistance offices; on October 1, 1924 the number was 767. In the provinces the decline in the number of white-collar workers employed in public offices can be estimated at about fifty percent, so that there as well tens of thousands of employees have been put out of work. In Prussian municipalities on October 1, 1923, 110,615 persons were employed in white-collar positions; of those an estimated 30,000 have lost their jobs. Social insurance agencies presently engage 4,000 to 5,000 fewer employees than at their high point. The number of sales personnel in merchandising has been reduced by an estimated twenty-five percent, in some places still more. Here too tens of thousands of white-collar employees have been discharged. If one adds to these figures the tens of thousands of laid-off employees in industry, it becomes possible to gauge the enormous pressure now being put on the white-collar labor market. . . .

Given such a hopeless situation in the labor market, there is naturally a blossoming of fraudulent job placement services. White-collar employees are promised every conceivable chance to earn some additional income at the cost of the last dimes they have in their pockets. It is possible to get some idea of the extent of such practices by considering the example of a job placement swindler in Hamburg, who took out an ad seeking engineers for work in South America—and received over 4,000 responses in a single day.

68

WILHELM KALVERAM

Rationalization in Business Management

First published as "Rationalisierung in der kaufmännischen Verwaltung," in Ludwig Elster, ed., *Handwörterbuch der Staatswissenschaften,* 4th ed. (Jena: G. Fischer Verlag, 1929), 803ff.

The rationalization of office operations results in serious social problems. Civil servants and white-collar employees of all sorts condemn rationalization as an important cause of unemployment. Even if the mechanization of office operations has driven numerous employees from their previous occupations, it does not follow that the machines should be rejected. We have become irrevocably integrated into the entire economy and, if we were to attempt to work with outmoded organizational methods, we would necessarily drop a rung on the cultural ladder. The rationalization of office operations, if it is carried out in the proper spirit, has to result in an increase in per capita productivity and the living standards of the general population, and therefore lead to new employment opportunities. Certainly, the fate of those temporarily hard hit by the transition must be monitored with all due responsibility, and the speed of mechanization tempered by social considerations.

Many of the effects of specialization in mass production are also ascribed to the mechanization of office operations, and the claim is made that it is monotonous, it kills interest, and it stresses the nerves. The mechanization of occupational tasks for workers is supposed to engender a mechanization of the conception of occupational roles among white-collar workers as well. With the mechanization of office work, however, there is no danger that work will decline in vitality, that people will be reduced to being slaves of the machine, even if the degree of mental stimulation is limited by the very narrow range of tasks. Machines require the full mental involvement of their operators. Machines do not run independently like the automated processes of production work, but instead take over the thoughts of those who use them, while easing the execution of tasks, that is, the mechanical aspect. To execute an entry with a complicated bookkeeping machine simultaneously on six to ten different forms with different texts requires considerable mental concentration. If a business transaction is entered falsely just once, all the corresponding accounting documents are wrong. It may be that the machine makes no mistakes, but if it is improperly set or wrongly operated, it cannot deliver accurate results. The mental capacities of the person working on it determine the correctness of the mechanically accomplished outcome. An assessment of mechanized work must further consider that the traditional division of labor in office operations also entails a multitude of dull, monotonous, and nearly automatic activities.

In another direction the social effect of office machines appears more worrisome. They are outfitted with many automatic-control mechanisms and function with a high degree of reliability, if they are reliably operated. They even indicate operator errors while in use by means of trouble signals, by blocking the mechanism, etc. These reduce human control to a minimum. The development of an automated system such as a machine in combination with independently operating controls reduces the possibility of errors or fraud being committed. The result can be that less significance is attributed to the general knowledge and absolute *trustworthiness* of the employees responsible for mechanized or routine tasks, and that the social status of business employees thereby decreases. For the execution of individual tasks in a mechanized operation it is not absolutely necessary for employees to have comprehensive knowledge of the commercial operation. It suffices if they understand how to carry out their specialized tasks. This exclusion of individual employees from the overall context of the work process, this narrowing of their areas of activity, and the reduction of the responsibilities with which they are entrusted through automation, means that they can be easily replaced, thereby increasing their dependence on their employers. Employees have no need of individual experience, of memory, because the processes run mechanically and someone else can quickly take their place. That hampers personal development along with the work and impedes the employees' full devotion to their assignments. The same is true for many preparatory and control tasks.

Despite this disadvantageous effect of rationalization, an attempt must be made to preserve the employees' feelings of duty and pleasure at work. The ultimate success of the enterprise, the enhancement of profitability, is just as much a result of the employees' attitude toward their occupation as it is of the employers' interest in business success.

Alongside the material factors of production—mechanical and human labor power—and the intellectual factors, which find expression in good organization and strict rationalization, psychological factors significantly influence profitability. In a rationalized operation a powerful distinction remains between what employees do reluctantly and what they achieve voluntarily in cheerful awareness of their responsibilities. The employees' unqualified devotion to their work is of inestimable significance as a factor in profitability.

Well-conceived labor legislation must offer a generally secure basis in a rationalized operation for making work satisfying. It must enable employees to participate in defining working conditions and can sharply reduce the tension between employees and employers. Now consider the relation between employee achievement and the problem of compensation. Higher wages can have a positive effect on profits and can raise the quality and rate of work if they relieve those involved of the pressure and concerns of daily life.

The question of wages is, however, in no way the sole determinant of a person's attitude toward work. Particularly important is that the employer adopt a psychologically appropriate approach to employees, which reflects an understanding of the latter's ways of thinking. The psychological significance of the human economy is not yet sufficiently appreciated. Extensive studies of the best ways to win buyers for a product have indeed been made based on careful psychological observation of their specific characteristics; but the knowledge of modern labor psychology should also be exploited to inspire the lively participation of employees in their work.

69

HILDE WALTER

The Misery of the "New *Mittelstand*"

First published as "Die Misere des 'neuen Mittelstands,'" *Die Weltbühne* 25, no. 4 (January 22, 1929), 130–134.

According to the occupational census of 1925, the number of employed persons increased by 28.5 percent since the year 1907. It grew twice as fast as the population, which in the same period increased by only 13.5 percent. The social and economic causes for this shift are known, but it is important to determine which occupations were most intensively involved in the absolute and relative increase in the employed population. For its congress in the fall of last year, the Allgemeine freie Angestelltenbund (AFA) published two books that are of extraordinary significance for these questions: an historical handbook on economic, social, and labor-union policy, *Die Angestelltenbewegung* [*Employees Movement*] *1925–1928,* and a brochure with a plenitude of interesting data, *Die Angestellten in der Wirtschaft* [*The Employees in the Economy*].

Without the complicated specialized counts by the AFA, the occupational census processed by the state statistical office would not have allowed us to determine the social stratification of employed persons with sufficient precision because the state statisticians combine white-collar employees and civil servants. The AFA with official help and consent, undertook to separate out the white-collar employees so the data published in the two books can be regarded the best material currently available on these questions. Obviously the main contingent of employed persons is made up of blue-collar workers. If one includes domestic workers, then according to the census of 1927 workers comprise

49.2 percent of employed persons, that is, approximately half, while white-collar employees (excluding civil servants) represent only 11.2 percent of the employed population. These ratios refer, as indicated, to the employed population as a whole and therefore include entrepreneurs, the self-employed, and the family members who assist the latter. The picture changes sharply if one looks at the distribution solely among the occupations of persons employed by others. In 1925 workers, including those employed at home and those occupied in domestic services, comprised 76 percent, the white-collar workers, excluding those in supervisory positions, 17 percent, and civil servants, excluding those in supervisory positions, 7 percent of the employed population. The social stratification of employed persons was also determined for the census years 1892, 1895, 1907, and 1925, and the number of white-collar employees and civil servants constantly increased at the expense of the self-employed and the assisting family members, as well as blue-collar and domestic workers. Just in the period from 1907 to 1925 the number of white-collar employees (excluding civil servants) more than doubled, while concurrently the number of blue-collar workers increased by only 22 percent. The cause of this increase of white-collar employees is not only the entry of previously non-working elements into the labor force, whose first jobs are frequently white-collar; it is also the structural transformations of the economy itself, of certain forms of rationalization, and of the typical increase in the apparatus of distribution in all regions which has prompted this development. Trade unionists often term this "a very significant social reshuffling of the proletariat," while bourgeois parties of all shades are especially fond of proclaiming the rise of "the new middle class" [*Mittelstand*]. Unfortunately the apostles of the new middle class are not able to deliver to the bearers of this enticing title even a fraction of the economic basis that was previously the essential characteristic of the old middle class, which was statistically very considerable and has now largely disappeared.

An illustration of the social structure of the German people (then 54 million) presented by Gustav Schmoller in 1897 to the eighth Evangelical Social Congress in Leipzig now has the effect of an ancient fairy tale:

Aristocracy and wealthy:	0.25 million families
Upper middle class:	2.75 million families
Lower middle class:	3.75 million families
Wage Workers:	5.25 million families

At that time the most important characteristic of the lower middle class was a fundamentally secured existence, a combination of capital owned and income from work. The question of education or culture arose only as a secondary or tertiary factor and played scarcely any role in the delimitation downward, in distinction to the unsecured life of those who earn wages exclusively. How differently the living conditions of the new middle class, which is being courted from both sides, appear today! There is hardly any reliable documentation of the white-collar workers' true income situation because there are no statistics on salaries actually paid. Other sources, however, offer clues: of the subscribers to the national insurance plan for white-collar employees, two-thirds of those insured paid premiums in income categories under 200 marks. The Institut für Konjunkturforschung [Economic Research Institute] calculated the average salaried income of white-collar employees at 159.50 marks in January 1927 and 170.96 marks in June 1927. Since the calculated average includes higher income levels as well, one can imagine that a large number of salaried employees have to get by on much less than the average wage. Of these amounts, 18.70 marks in January went for taxes and social security, 20.40 marks in June. In Berlin and other cities most people have to allow a further 10 marks per month for transportation. There remains then as an average income (still including the highest figures) 130.80 and 140.50 marks per month respectively! It is probably unnecessary to compare the purchasing power of these sums with that of 1913 to verify the dreariness of such an income level. Shrewd old capitalists are fond of telling us about the extraordinary improvement in the situation of white-collar employees thanks to the eight-hour day; in so doing they forget to mention that the enormous intensification and mechanization of white-collar work results in a doubling of the energy output required, and that no one likes to hire employees over forty years old any longer, with the possible exception of expressly confidential positions. The needs of the white-collar employees who have lost their jobs far exceed the capacities of unemployment provisions. In April 1928 official publications counted a total of 183,371 white-collar workers seeking employment; of those approximately 62,000 received insurance payments and approximately 31,500 received emergency provisions; therefore 90,000 unemployed white-collar workers were without unemployment support and, in the best of cases, received small payments from social welfare for the poor. Those receiving emergency support, that is, one-third of all those supported, had already been unemployed for over six months, and therefore in many cases drew only about one-third of their salaries for over half a year.

Thus appear the living conditions of a social stratum, which in the wishful dreams of bourgeois ideologues is destined to be the embodiment of small capitalist enterprises. It should be assumed that to those immediately involved the clear similarity of their own position with that of the proletariat would make them think and that the model of the organized worker would have to inspire imitation. Obviously this comparison has not yet taken hold among the majority of white-collar employees, for out of a total of 3,500,000 only 1,300,000 are members of professional associations of any sort; the overwhelming majority lives without relying on an organization that could represent their interests.

70

SIEGFRIED KRACAUER

Shelter for the Homeless

First published as "Asyl für Obdachlose," in *Die Angestellten* (Frankfurt: Societäts-Verlag, 1930), 91–101.

The average worker, upon whom the minor white-collar employee sometimes likes to look down, often enjoys not only a material but also an existential superiority over the latter. His life as a class-conscious proletarian proceeds beneath the protective cover of vulgar Marxist concepts, which nonetheless have the merit of informing him as to his meaning. Today the cover is a very imperfect one.

The mass of white-collar employees distinguishes itself from the working-class proletariat by being intellectually homeless. For the moment they are incapable of finding their way to their comrades, and the house of bourgeois ideas and feelings in which they previously lived has collapsed due to the erosion of its foundations, brought on by economic development. They are living at present without a doctrine to which they can look up, without a goal to guide them. They live, therefore, in the fear of looking up and dissolving in a welter of questions.

Nothing so characterizes this life, which can be termed a life only in a restricted sense, as the various ways in which it has access to higher things. It perceives these higher things not as substance but as glitter, the result not of a gathering but of a dispersion. "Why do people spend so much time in bars?" asked a white-collar employee of my acquaintance. "Quite likely because it is so miserable at home and they want to experience some excitement." It is to be understood, incidentally, that "at home" encompasses daily as well as residential life, as charted by advertisements in magazines for white-collar employees. They concern, in the main: pens; Kohinoor pencils; hemorrhoids; hair loss; beds; crepe soles; white teeth; rejuvenation treatments; coffee consumption habits; dictaphones; writer's cramps; trembling, particularly in the presence of others; quality pianos on weekly installments; etc. A stenotypist inclined to reflection expressed herself similarly to the employee mentioned above: "The girls come mostly from modest circumstances and get seduced by the glamor." Then she explained in a quite remarkable way that the girls in general avoid serious conversations. "Serious conversations," she said, "are just distractions, shifting attention away from the surroundings they would like to enjoy." When serious conversation is ascribed a distracting effect, then the matter of distraction has come to a serious pass. [. . .]

Confrontations between white-collar employees and their role models are astonishingly obvious. Often an unintentional brush with society suffices to awaken slumbering desires in the employees. This easy excitability, among other things, is evidenced by the observations of a white-collar employee in industry. If in any one of the departments in his office even just a couple of employees happened to have dealings with customers, the elegant behavior of these advanced social watchguards began immediately to rub off on the other personnel. Imperceptible signals are constantly offering superfluous guidance to the employees' desires. Thus in the display windows of a prestigious department store mannequins, dressed in cheap ready-to-wear, strike proud poses among fancy orchids; thus does a race track in Luna Park create for lower-level salaried employees the pleasure of being allowed to feel like gentlemen drivers. Minor effects, major causes.

In relation to the masses, the gentle language of signs does not suffice. Where they throng together, as they do in Berlin, their own kind of shelters come into being. Shelters in a literal sense are those gigantic clubs in which, as a chatterbox once put it in a Berlin daily, "one can feel the wide world for little money." The Fatherland House, meant more for the provincials; Resi (the residential casino), which likewise aims for those with higher salaries; the Moka-Efti enterprise on Friedrichstraße—they and their like have called into being an infallible instinct to still the hunger of big-city dwellers for glamor and distraction. From the office mill into the amusement mill is their unspoken motto. [. . .]

All events relating to the unorganized masses of white-collar employees, and no less so all the movements undertaken by these masses themselves, are ambivalent today. A secondary meaning is attached to them, which often distances them from their original determination. Under the pressure of the dominant society, they become homeless shelters in a metaphorical sense. Aside from their immediate purpose, they have another as well: to keep white-collar employees in the place assigned them by the elite and to distract them from critical questions to which, incidentally, they are scarcely drawn in the first place. As for contemporary film, I demonstrated in two essays published in the *Frankfurter Zeitung* ("The Little Shopgirls Go to the Movies" and "Contemporary Film and its Audience") that nearly all the industry's productions work to legitimate the existing state of affairs by failing to examine either its excesses or its basic foundations. They numb the people with the pseudoglamor of counterfeit social heights, just as hypnotists use shining objects to put their mediums to sleep. The same applies to the illustrated newspapers and the majority of magazines. A closer examination would presumably show that the constantly recurring pictorial motifs function like magical incantations to plunge certain substantive matters forever into the abyss of pictureless amnesia—those matters that are not comprehended within the design of our social existence but that rather bracket this existence itself. The flight of images is the flight from the revolution and death.

If pictorial magic assails the masses from without, then sport—in fact, the whole of body culture, which has also led to the custom of the weekend—is one of the central forms of their existence. The systematic training of the body no doubt fulfills the mission of producing a vitally necessary counterbalance to the burgeoning demands of the modern economy. The question, however, is whether the contemporary sports industry is exclusively concerned with this necessary training, whether or not sport is ultimately attributed such an outstanding place in the hierarchy of social values because it offers the masses the welcome opportunity of a distraction, which they fully exploit. [. . .]

The popularization of sports does not resolve complexes, but it is a symptom of repression on a grand scale; it does not promote the reformation of social relations, but is a major means of depoliticization. This does not mean sport cannot also be the expression of a revolutionary mass desire for natural right that could be invoked against the harms of civilization.

71

THEODOR GEIGER

[The Old and New Middle Classes]

First published in *Die soziale Schichtung des deutschen Volkes* (Stuttgart: F. Enke, 1932), 84–87, 103–105.

The culture of the early capitalist epoch derived from the "old middle classes." It continues to live, despite all modern influences, in parts of this demographic grouping—a relic whose resistance and moral force should not be underestimated.

In this demographic segment we have an example of, borrowing from geological terminology, a "social historical fault": structures that appear in social historical succession and, dispersed among various demographic segments, find themselves located next to each other in the historical present. Thus in the old middle classes the social strata of the early capitalist epoch show the residual effect of differentiations across social categories; class-based customs and conceptions of life have been preserved and resist the historical realization of developed capitalism with tenacity. This is true of peasants and artisans to a greater degree than of merchants; peasants alone represent more than half of the entire old middle classes, and the independent artisans, including former artisans living in retirement as landlords, may be estimated as an additional 750,000 to 1,000,000 people.

The economic mode of existence of these demographic groupings, in particular that of the peasantry, is characterized by the high number of immediate relatives involved in the family enterprise; the family thus continues to be a thoroughly viable production unit. This characteristic, which is so important in regard to social mentality, has once again become even more marked in recent times, particularly in handicrafts and commerce; the number of family members primarily employed in family enterprises has increased from 3.77 million (1907) to 5.44 million (1925). In handicrafts and commerce the number has nearly doubled.

Closely related of course is the circumstance that the family, as that which defines the contours of lived experience, has been most effective in resisting the disintegrating influences of modern life in the propertied middle class; therefore the culture of family and the home continues substantially to determine the way in which life as a whole is conducted, in both the best and the philistine sense. This traditionalism is expressed in particular in the continuing centrality among the old bourgeoisie of a religious attitude and church affiliation as conventional attributes.

The relatively least stable is the class of small merchants. Unlike handicrafts, commerce underwent an unstable and, as regards the national economy, coincidental increase in the number of smaller independent merchants, which is clearly manifest in the particularly large number of proletarian-like merchant livelihoods. This inflation in the number of independent merchants is, as is well known, encouraged by the fact that no expert knowledge of any sort is required to open up a shop and call oneself a merchant. Thus do we find one group of independent merchants who are thoroughly comparable to the group of unskilled occasional workers among the dependents. Here, however, we are discounting those designated as proletarian-like; the merchant middle class also encompasses a large number of livelihoods that are in no way to be included in the professional, but at most in the propertied class, and which have been deprived of their basis in the class customs and traditions that remain alive among artisans. Precisely this coincidence of conditions makes the smaller-merchant class particularly open to National Socialism. The need for defense against economic distress, which is largely caused by the irresponsible oversaturation of the occupational category (ungrounded livelihoods), and the lack of occupational expertise coincide with the lack of genuine class traditions guards against radical outbreaks just as much as the inferiority complex produced by the absence of solid professional moorings encourages them.

A transitional category has developed between those involved in handicrafts and those in commerce: the former artisan, who today has become a merchant of wares that were once time self-produced but are now produced in the factory, is no longer based in the workshop. These livelihoods, today very numerous, also tend to produce a mentality that is between positions.

The way of life of the peasantry has been described extensively and it would be pointless to offer a sketch in just a few pages. Only note that the peasants are to be distinguished from all other segments of the old middle classes by a particularly strong tie to their respective localities and by the fact that they are active as purchasing consumers within a much narrower radius. Their economic autarchy, as far as their meeting daily nutritional needs is concerned, raises their self-confidence in comparison to that of the city dweller and the nonagricultural population as a whole; the fact, however, that their own cash income in relation to their overall requirements is low inclines them to be prejudiced towards the economic condition of salary- and wage-earners; peasants overestimate their money income according to false standards. . . .

The category of white-collar employees as a social position defined by the presumption of estate entitlements poses a problem in itself. White-collar employees today represent a far larger percentage of the employed population than ever before. The number of second-generation occupants of this social position is estimated at twenty percent. The over-whelming majority are newcomers to the category through social mobility, either personal or generational. We do not know precisely in what proportion the other demographic groups contribute white-collar employees; we can only be certain that the primary con-tributors must be descendants of the urban bourgeoisie and the working class. Since 1895 the industrial working class has not been growing sufficiently to absorb their own offspring into their occupations; the number of openings in industry and commerce stagnated in absolute terms so that, given the good birth rate among these demographic groups, there must be a considerable surplus that finds employment in other occupations.

Since the investigation of the General Association of White-Collar Employees appeared, it has become common to regard its assertion that twenty-five percent of white-collar employees are descended from workers as generally valid. That is not acceptable. This figure was derived from a survey of 120,000 GAWE employees; its validity for all 330,000 members of the association is questionable. That it cannot be applied to the entire population of white-collar employees is beyond doubt. The GAWE, with its elite character and national–democratic political tendency, is an organization of white-collar employees who share quite specific common attitudes. It is clear that the family origins of white-collar employees, alongside other motives, play a considerable role in their choice of a professional association. If the proportion of children of workers is twenty-five percent in the GAWE, it is certainly much higher in the socialist General League of White-Collar Workers. In addition, it is significant that the GAWE counts very few foremen among its ranks. Therefore precisely the group of white-collar employees that is typically recruited from workers' circles, both generationally and individually, is quite weakly represented. It may be that the urban bourgeoisie, which is much smaller than the working class, contributes many more white-collar employees. Among new white-collar employees the descendants of the much more numerous working class would still be either equally or somewhat more heavily represented.

Whatever the case may be, white-collar employees—who, because of their sheer numbers represent a new element in the demographic structure—initially face the task of developing a mentality appropriate to their social position, requiring in part assimilation and in part the shedding of inherited mentalities. Now the much smaller group of commercial white-collar employees of the previous century justly considers itself the offspring of the professional category of independent merchants. Thus is estate mentality grounded in the history of the white-collar employees. In addition, there is the influence of a conservative factor: if a new demographic group is composed of many elements of differing heritage, then the inherited mentalities decay rapidly; if, however, the descen-dants of a particular stratum move in a block as a typical element of the new group, then they have the chance of collectively preserving the traditional mentality, for example, the descendants of the urban bourgeoisie in their transition into the class of white-collar employees. The estate element has preserved its mentality, which frequently erupts more passionately as resentment, the more painfully it is exposed as illusory and supplanted by a hopelessly dependent status.

A second consideration, however, is the complex of estate-specific cultural character-istics that everyone, including (perhaps especially) those white-collar employees with working-class backgrounds, have in common. [Siegfried] Kracauer sketched them, often in telling detail, in his report on white-collar employees [*Die Angestellten*], unfortunately with too much emphasis on surface details, and he probably judged them too impatiently. White-collar employees' professional activity, with the office as their occupational location, gives them a superficial affinity with civil servants; the concept of civil service includes the idea of an estate-specific education, to whose prestige white-collar employees lay claim in order to distance themselves from worker's status. The extension and leveling involved in so-called general education, the literary, feuilleton culture of our age, and a certain, even professionally requisite, minimum of conventional manners lend support to this claim. [. . .]

If the new middle classes represent a typical social position, then its members face the initial task of adjusting to and making themselves at home in it. [Joseph] Schumpeter provides the following prognosis. Until everything gets settled, a characteristic drama will unfold: demographic elements of diverse social backgrounds are transplanted into a new position in the social structure—whether through individual mobility or the movement of whole social subgroups (members of the liberal professions, employees of the traditional merchant class, etc.). They bring with them their own ideologies and manner of living, which were the organic product of their previous social position but now become inadequate in the new one. The trait typical of their stratum is therefore the ideological insecurity of a settler in new social territory. The mentality typical of the social position of the new middle classes remains insecure and fragmented, which, as has been established, is fertile soil for false ideologies. Examples include: academic arrogance, whereby academics no longer enjoy any acknowledged preferential social rank; the estate-specific need for validation that the son of a propertied bourgeois carries with him when he becomes an office employee; and what Kracauer caricatured as the spurious educational ambitions of the white-collar employee.

8
The Rise of the New Woman

WORLD WAR I and the advent of the republic significantly altered the role of women in German society. Although the Wilhelmine world of patriarchal domination classically portrayed in Theodor Fontane's novel *Effi Briest* was no longer intact, the so-called New Woman of Weimar was under considerable pressure to conform to traditional expectations. The war had placed many women in the workplace and opened the doors to higher education, the revolution had brought them to the polls, and Weimar voters would elect 111 women to the Reichstag. But the struggle for full equality on all fronts was by no means victorious, as many of the parties who paid lip service to women's rights failed to make good on various promises. Not even the SPD was ready to support equal pay for equal work. And despite the Communists' paeans to working women, they consistently subordinated gender to class considerations.

Ever since the pioneering efforts of Luise Otto-Peters in the 1860s, women themselves had been organizing to demand improvements in their situation. In 1894 the Bund deutscher Frauenvereine (League of German Women's Associations) became the umbrella for a wide variety of bourgeois women's organizations. By the eve of the war it had some 300,000 members. Led by Helene Langer and Gertrud Bäumer before the war, and Marianne Weber, Max Weber's wife, afterwards, the BDF emphasized educational reform, founded homes and recreational centers for unmarried working women, and established kindergartens.

The BDF was nevertheless relatively conservative in matters of family and sexual policy and grew increasingly nationalist during the war. Combating the "new morality" of Helene Stöcker's Bund für Mutterschutz (League for the Protection of Mothers) in the name of "spiritual motherhood," it rejected demands for both abortion rights and governmental support for unmarried mothers. The BDF was less radical politically (and also somewhat smaller in size) than the socialist women's movement which had been created in the wake of August Bebel's 1878 classic *Woman and Socialism* and was led by the revisionist Lily Braun. Rosa Luxemburg and Clara Zetkin countered Braun's position with a more class-oriented perspective on the plight of women in their newspaper *Die Kommunistin*. Typical of the BDF's attitude was Marianne Weber's 1918 plea in *Die Frau* for women to fulfill their special cultural

195

mission as moral reformers of society. Significantly, women were assigned a similar task a decade later by Max Brod in an essay on their relation to the New Objectivity. Here too they were asked to function as an antidote to the coldness and impersonality of a "masculine" style.

But the New Woman of Weimar seemed unwilling to play this role. She lived instead, according to Elsa Herrmann, for the present and according to her own desires. Like the fictional father and son whose conversation Alfred Polgar concocted in 1928, men too were themselves often confused about the behavior expected of them by changing times.

One of the most volatile issues for Weimar women was the prohibition of abortion, articulated in paragraphs 218 and 219 of the legal code. Sympathetic men like Manfred Georg, a writer for *Die Weltbühne*, argued strongly in 1922 against the state's right to control birth at a time when it had given up universal conscription, the right to control bodies after birth. (Paradoxically, he also argued for the discontinuation of suffrage for women because they seemed to be voting for the conservative parties of the right). Drawing upon the Gretchen story from *Faust*, Gabriele Tergit articulated the impact the increasingly stringent application of the law had upon women's lives. Nevertheless the anti-abortion laws remained on the books and in 1931 were invoked during the chancellorship of the Center Party's Heinrich Brüning in order to jail the Communist writer and physician Friedrich Wolf who advocated abortion in his play *Cyanide*, and Dr. Else Kienle who actually performed abortions.

The new role of women in the work force, which became especially contested during the Depression, was another critical issue. In 1931, Hilde Walter contemplated the "twilight of women" caused by resentment from all across the political spectrum at the perception that women had taken "men's jobs." The subsequent year Siegfried Kracauer followed his classic study, *Die Angestellten,* with a sobering analysis of the actual situation of working women, which he contrasted with the glittering media image of the New Woman.

Under these stresses—social, cultural, and political—women in the Weimar Republic were understandably ambivalent about the effects of their newly won freedoms. As Alice Rühle-Gerstel noted toward the end of the republic, the woman's movement had run out of steam. Many women in fact voted for conservative, even radical, right-wing parties because these promised a restoration of order through traditional roles. Once in power, the Nazis carried out a ruthless reversal of all the gains women had made during the republic. Sadly, a few former members of the BDF, formally dissolved in 1933, found ways to accommodate themselves, if uneasily, to the new order. In this way, Gertrud Bäumer was able to continue publication of *Die Frau* until 1943.

72

MARIANNE WEBER

The Special Cultural Mission of Women

First published as "Die besonderen kulturellen Aufgaben der Frau," in *Frauenfragen und Frauengedanken. Gesammelte Aufsätze* (Tübingen: J. C. B. Mohr, 1919), 238–261.

In order to master the devastating effects of this terrible war, still scarcely estimated in their magnitude, we are in need of unflagging moral energies and great faith. Long periods of privation have taught us an extraordinary amount about the measure and soundness of human nature. We have learned that heroism, the unconditional willingness to surrender the self to the whole, just as much as the overwhelming flood of sacrificial love, represents an uncommon soaring of the human soul, the heights of which the average person is incapable of sustaining for long. In any case, the extraordinary, intensified demands to which our moral bearing has been subjected, alongside the incomparably great achievements to which they compelled us, have resulted in an equally extraordinary relapse into wickedness, into uncommon acts of baseness. How the years of living rootlessly, homelessly in foxholes and trenches, in the wet and filth, in ghastly spiritual uniformity, how the experience and commission of unspeakable things have stamped the souls of our male compatriots, is difficult to measure. We can only hope that their inner natures were protected by some kind of immunity to poisonous influences. But it is clear that the long deprivation of regular work, of the home and its order and cleanliness, of the quiet pleasures of life, and, above all, the suspension of family life, are not to be endured without departures from the path of culture. In the struggle for life and death, the form-giving power of civilization is nullified. One can only hope that the millions of men who had to withstand the years of inconceivable hardships have not lost their desire for it. But as difficult as it was for countless men to conform to military discipline and the terrible deprivation of all life's blessings, it will now be just as difficult for them to reintegrate themselves into home life and its uniform rhythm, especially since civic existence for millions must be established wholly anew and under more difficult circumstances. Cultural habits have been cast off, sexual needs have perhaps had to be satisfied in completely heartless, even bestial ways—all of this engraves deep traces upon yet impressionable natures, traces that can be effaced only with great difficulty. This is why many women and mothers, awaiting their husbands and sons with tremendous longing and secret fears, are facing the immediate prospect of continued hard times.

73

DIE KOMMUNISTIN   *Lady Communist*

[Manifesto for International Women's Day]

First published as "Zum internationalen Frauentag. An alle werktätigen Frauen!" *Die Kommunistin* 6 (March 25, 1921).

workers

TO ALL WORKING WOMEN!

Working women, employed women of all kinds in city and countryside, small-property holders, mothers of the proletariat and the dispossessed.

Come out for International Women's Day!

It must become your day!

Your lives and deeds are dominated by exorbitant price increases with which small and medium incomes cannot keep pace. Exorbitant prices deplete your bread and season it with the bitterest of worries and scalding tears. They tear the shirt from the backs of your children and rob them of their rosy cheeks and happy smiles. Uncounted numbers of you are massed in stifling back rooms, in dark and airless courtyard apartments, in damp, moldy cellars and drafty garrets. Unmanageable fees and taxes increase the burden of your worries and add to your privations.

Those who still have work and earnings appear happy. In front of the employment agencies and factory gates, troops of unemployed men and women gather together. That means people without bread, often the homeless too, and those without a country. Millions are no longer earning enough to salt their bread, and they tremble in fear that tomorrow unemployment will be their fate. Among all these unfortunates are countless women. As long as the men were being misused in the trenches as cannon fodder for the rich, *you women* were drawn by the hundreds of thousands into the factories as machine fodder for scant pay, used as exalted "emergency assistants" in banks, department stores, offices, and schoolrooms. Now you are pocketing the promised "gratitude of the fatherland."

Since distant millionaires and billionaires cannot pit you against the men to suppress wages and salaries, you have the doors to the places of work and employment slammed in your faces. It is *the family* you should tend to, *which you don't have* or for which you would need bread. Think of the mass graves in which flourishing male life lies moldering, the endless lines of war cripples and invalids. Of what concern is it to the factory owner, merchant, stock company, local government, state, or nation how you prolong your troubled existence? The spirit of mammon, of exploitative capitalism, is their master. That is why you are cast into the streets as prostitutes, even those half-grown children in need of protection among you!

The house they talk about, *what is it?* The exploitative capitalist economy transforms it from a home—a place of rest, peace, and happiness—into a treadmill whose operation mercilessly crushes you, body and soul. Hard, growing burdens of work and duty press you to the floor; condemned to stay inside your narrow four walls, your *spirit is numbed* into a backwardness alien to our times. It stunts your humanity. But because you cannot be whole, cannot be free persons, neither are you capable of being understanding, helpful comrades to your husbands, nor mothers, raising your children to be beautiful, proud human beings.

And what a mockery of your fate! You and yours are ground down by toil and drudgery, you and yours starve and suffer. Next to you, however, usurers, racketeers, speculators, profiteers of war and revolution, capitalist exploiters of every type and color squander and waste immeasurable riches in absurd, disgusting sensual frenzies. People, many of whom have never lifted a finger in productive work, harvest where you and yours have plowed and sowed. *Working women, is this injustice, this insanity to last forever?*

The political equality of the female sex, the democracy of the new Germany, will overcome this insanity, put an end to this injustice. Do you not hear this chorus daily, working women? Yes, in the new Germany you may vote for democracy. Yes, you may even be voted for. But, despite everything, is not the *equality of women* in political as well as public life, just *on paper?* Does it count that a few a women in official positions shape the social conditions of women, make decisions about affairs of inherent concern to women? Just recently the majority of the Reichstag decided on an empty pretext to delay still further the day when women may act as jurors. In reality, teachers, women civil servants on the whole, still remain condemned to celibacy if they do not want to lose their positions.

But above all, working women, employed women, housewives of the dispossessed and those of scant means, *who among you has been made full, free, and happy by the right to vote and be elected?* The economic power of the capitalists to exploit, to take advantage of, and to oppress you and yours persists. The democracy of the bourgeois order offers you the drudgery of work without its fruits—poverty and unfreedom. It defends idleness and excess for some. It has prison and bullets for others. It has *prison and bullets for you, too, working women,* if you "no longer want the lazy belly to squander what diligent hands have earned." [. . .]

You working women, you who make demands and struggle, count in the millions. International Women's Day proves it. In all countries where, demanding their rights, the disinherited surge forward under the sign of communism against the exploiting and subjugating power of capital, on International Women's Day mothers filled with pain, housewives bent with worry, exhausted working women, clerical workers, teachers, and small-property holders flow together. The same need forces the same demands to their lips. Their shared understanding lends them to the common struggle. Across borders, over mountains and seas, they are of a single will. *The demands of the working women of Germany are also the demands of their sisters in Switzerland, in Austria, in Holland, in France and other countries. They are the international demands of women.* The women communists, proletarians, and small-property holders in Russia are taking the lead, setting an example for the women struggling here. The revolution in Russia is also their immortal work. With it demands for rights were fulfilled for which women in other countries must still struggle hard. Your Women's Day can call the manual and mental laborers to work on the construction of the communist order. *Working women, in a front with these gallant ones, with the rising, fighting proletarians of the whole world!*

74

MANFRED GEORG
The Right to Abortion

First published as "Das Recht auf Abtreibung," *Die Weltbühne* 18, no. 1 (January 5, 1922), 7–9.

It was to be expected that a short while after the conclusion of the peace and the establishment of the German republic the issue of population policy would lay greater claim to the public's interest. Just as the nationalists are finding insufficient new blood for their sacrifices to Moloch, so must the major progressive parties confront the issue of the nation's fertility. For these parties the main question has been whether they should move against previously existing legal interpretations and findings to support a deliberate population policy or whether they should proceed without a plan. Thus is the alternative between the right to abortion or lack of it once again on the agenda.

The proposals of both social democratic parties in the Reichstag indicate that the Majority Social Democrats want to grant immunity from prosecution under paragraphs 218 and 219 of the criminal code, if the abortion "is ordered by the pregnant woman or a legally recognized (certified) doctor within the first three months." The Independent Social Democrats instead demand the complete repeal of both paragraphs. It is obvious that, in a country as intellectually and culturally diverse as Germany, political unanimity on the question of abortion can never be achieved. Nevertheless the proposals of both social democratic parties have been subjected to so much criticism and hostility, by their own ranks and from circles supporting the content of the proposals, that it might well be worthwhile to take a look at the actual views of the democratic socialist segment of the population.

Astonishingly, the whole phalanx of well-intended critics gets mired in a tangle of technical questions before the question has even been properly posed. As much can at least be said of the Berlin university professor [Alfred] Grotjahn, who points to the danger of national population decline, and, as a doctor, fears the rise of a sordid and surreptitious practice on the part of inferior members of the profession. Professor Rudolf Lennhoff also foresees difficulties for doctors, fearing that they will suffer a conflict of conscience if they are expected "to undertake a physical procedure on a person in perfect physical health which cannot be justified in medical terms." He also denies that welfare doctors have any obligation to perform the operation (a position of the greatest significance given the enormous future significance of welfare), since welfare represents an insurance only against illnesses; he too fears the rise of a malevolent group of specialists. [Gustav] Radbruch, the majority socialist minister of justice, fails entirely to address the core of the matter in his criticism, instead supporting his party's proposal for juridical reasons; he regards a law that is obviously class based and that moreover will be successfully circumvented in ninety out of a hundred cases, as little more than a means to subvert the true supremacy of law.

In a free state that has renounced its right to require a fixed term of military service— that is, the obligation of its subjects to allow themselves to be killed for the state—the rights over one's own body should be incontestable. At birth, a child becomes a legal subject and the mother no longer controls the fate of the newborn. For it to be otherwise would completely contradict the essence of the community ideal of a purely socialist state, since, upon separation from the mother, the infant becomes a member of this community. Nevertheless it is wishful thinking to expect that people will discuss whether a fetus conceived in a necessarily organic process—conception is a drive, but birth need not be one—must be carried to term under all circumstances. For many today the fact of a child poses a severe physical and social problem. The continued assertion of a public right to intervene in this area, since the repeal of obligatory military service (which alone would have justified it logically), entails an intolerable condescension toward the individual. Likewise, just as today the responsibility for self-inflicted injury is left to the individual, and attempted suicide is no longer punishable, so must the physical and social responsibility for the destruction of a fetus not carried to term be left to the individual. Obviously, given the concept of marriage as a life partnership which is mutually entered into, the man must have the right to claim abortion as immediate grounds for divorce. Such a stipulation as this would also punish abortion for criminal motives, such as inheritance fraud and the like.

Considerable inroads into the understanding of this issue could be made if we could understand why today's women have abortions. There are those highly developed, thoughtful persons who are mature enough to recognize that the fact of a child is a circumstance that would ruinously impede or even destroy the development of themselves or their marital partnership; they are mature enough to refuse to subject themselves frivolously to an operation that, given the danger of infection and residual effects, always represents an enormous risk. Immunity from prosecution for an abortion for this category is probably clear to everyone. The second category of women who have abortions are those who do so in the knowledge that having a child under present economic conditions would result in the ruin or worsening of the economic existence of their family, especially if it is the third or fourth child. Frequently in such cases, if the abortion is not undertaken, severe daily strain causes the eventual break-up of the marriage. In these cases too, where economic need compels the operation, one would hardly want to punish the unfortunate woman further. There remains the third category of women who act for reasons of vanity, love of pleasure, or personal convenience. Why should they be punished? It cannot be said that human society depends either upon these women or their children, and when they risk an operation, which, aside from the risk of sterility, can entail the worst of consequences, then they should in God's name be left alone. Who benefits, who is hurt here by the punishment?

It is evident that in the end both social-democratic and public criticism approach the issue of abortion from the completely wrong angle. It is not a matter of whether and how the perpetrator of this act should be punished, but of how—and here only the numerically largest category (number two, abortion from need) is relevant—the perpetrator is to be protected from the consequences of the act; the issue of abortion is an issue of protecting birth, a population policy that is willing to take its cue directly from the needs of the fetus. Of what use to the state is the equal franchise, insurance for invalids, health care, and socialization of the mining industry, if it does not begin to understand that all this comes to nothing as compared with a general application of force to secure the generation of the nation in the mother's womb! Basically all the hitherto-existing regulations of maternity care and the like are rubbish, paltry moment-to-moment assistance that has failed to help a single mother relieve more than the crudest of her needs. With all that, nothing is done. The construction of a new merchant fleet is not as necessary as a generous system genuinely devoted to infant care. So generous that, for the mother, it starts at the beginning of pregnancy and then does not cease. It is necessary to guarantee comprehensive care to the nation's mothers: a peaceful pregnancy, a hygienic delivery, and complete psychological equanimity as to the fate of the child—this latter provision, even to the extent that, upon

the request of the mother, the state will take over the raising of its new citizen unconditionally. Indeed, the mother must even be assured that she can reclaim her child from
state care at any time.

The care of children is the only area in which a country should not strive to be
economical. To ensure this a good five dozen of all so-called current plans and problems
could be abandoned and redefined. Only such a course would make it possible to create
a new generation of human beings, and as a result, it would also diffuse other issues. For
then the right to abortion would be used only in very essential, or very nonessential, cases.
Such a state policy would simultaneously entail an additional and very important advance,
namely the general recognition of the difference between the sexes alongside their equality;
in short, the repeal of the current and ultimately ridiculous right of women to vote. This
is not to say that the influence of women would thereby be reduced. On the contrary it
would become much greater, but would be confined to the areas for which women and
mothers are responsible. A "mother's chamber" thus suggests itself, a state body upon
which, along with other legislative bodies, the decisions over the life of a people would
devolve, that is, the decision over their sons and daughters, the decision to go to war,
including veto power against it. Such a happy "republic of mothers" would suffer no more
wars.

75

GABRIELE TERGIT

Paragraph 218: A Modern Gretchen Tragedy

First published as "Moderne Gretchentragödie," *Berliner Tageblatt* (November 5, 1926).

Yesterday negotiations over Paragraph 218 lasted from morning late into the evening; but
then, it is a matter of human beings.[1]

The defendants: the girl; the lover; the doctor; the midwife. The girl's testimony
contradicts that of the others. She is on one side, alone, fighting the last fight about and
against the man. She is a robust, big girl with broad hips; she has a broad, red face, was
originally a playful, innocent thing, capable and quick; comes from a good home, the foster
child of academics. Her name is Lotte and she calls herself Mara. Her family name is Hister,
her parents' Hilmer; she calls herself Hister-Hilmer. She is a mere teenage girl, who must
now suffer the eternally constant, bitter fate of woman.

In 1923, barely seventeen, she met "him" in a cafe, a beautiful, blond boy. First they
became friends, then "it" happened. The consequence is visible. She would like to keep
it. "I will marry you, if the consequence disappears," says he, "otherwise it's over." And
so begins the path, more bitter than any pill, to the doctors and women. Finally, one is
found. She tells her parents she's taking a trip to Silesin. To make it believable, she travels
to Frankfurt on the Oder to mail a card from the train station. It cost the two of them
thirty marks for the postcard. She arrived, says the girl, completely healthy at the doctor's;

1. Paragraph 218—which remains a contested legal provision even today in Germany—was adopted in 1871;
it decreed a five-year jail sentence for aborting a fetus. The number of women (almost all of whom were working
class) prosecuted for its violation rose from 2,450 in 1920 to 60,000 in 1933.

eight days later she arrived back home, sick and ruined for life. And as she lies in a fever, the lover comes and says it has to end, he has to marry a rich girl. She wants to kill herself. Then he sends a friend to her with a love letter, to check whether she is still alive. Meanwhile the parents have taken it all in and so the poor father delivers an ultimatum. All right, then, they will become engaged. The guests have already been invited when he refuses a second time, over the telephone: "I don't love you anymore." And so the poor father goes there again and asks, and the girl begs, and the young man condescends—not to marriage, but to continued friendship. He is no longer welcome at the house, but she loves him and agrees.

Meanwhile, she has lost her good position at the bank because of her illness. Times have gotten harder; she winds up in a lowly bar, degrades herself. After another year it is finally over. A girlfriend registered the complaint.

He had absolutely no notion what was supposed to happen at the doctor's. He thought it was an illness, otherwise he would never have allowed it. But he nevertheless paid for the illness!

But then the girlfriend came forward, the one who made the complaint. Stenotypist; she has left her parents.

Judge: "Why did you register the complaint?"
Witness: "Lotte wanted it herself." General surprise.
Defendant: "I must confess. I wasn't sober and was so desperate, away from home, in the bar, my life ruined. I can't love anyone else. Kurt shouldn't just get away with it, I thought. It wasn't thought out."

The girlfriend warned her. She is full of life and insolent to the judge and prosecutor; beautiful, wrapped in an expensive fur.

And the way the two girls stand there, they are the two poles of womanhood. The one cool, clever, superior, and skeptical; love does not happen to her: "She was just crazy," she says of the other one. Lovely, smiling, and elegant, the born mistress, the victor. And the other, warm, foolish, impulsive, and gullible, who can only love one and wants it that way, her whole life; not pretty, ruined by tears, broken.

We will not speak of the medical aspects. The girls' allegations certainly had an internal plausibility; the doctor's statements on the other hand were unclear. But both Professor Strauch and the medical commissioner Dyrenfurth pronounced a *non liquet* [not proven].

The prosecutor demanded a six-month term for each of the defendants, three months for the midwife.

The girl remained true to her testimony: "I am guilty," she said, "and I want to pay the penalty. But I have spoken the truth."

The court, too, essentially believed her.

The guilt of the doctor and the midwife could not be proven; they were therefore released. The contempt anyone with proper sensitivities has to feel for the shabby behavior of the young man was expressed in the young judge's verdict and reasoning.

The girl did it because she was promised marriage if she did. But the man consciously put her life at risk. The court is of the opinion that he only wanted to avoid the alimony. The girl was punished with a two weeks' sentence, suspended to probation.

The man got two months in jail, which will be served.

76

ALFRED POLGAR

The Defenseless: A Conversation between Men

First published as "Die Schutzlose. Ein Gespräch zwischen Männern," *Uhu* 5, no. 3 (1928), 56–60.

My son, I noted with some discomfort that you keep your seat on the streetcar, instead of offering it to one of the women who otherwise must stand. Does it count as modern to be a boor?

Father, you have slept through some new developments. The women of your time acknowledged their weaknesses as a claim to all manner of protection and consideration, as the weak are owed by the strong. This obligation grew out of the circumstance that they didn't share the rights that men had; in so-called gallantry male compassion for female powerlessness found its refined expression. That has changed. It was the women themselves, due to an easily understood hunger for air and life, who shattered the bell jar in which they were vegetating. They have become comrades in work and play, in pleasure and struggle, and among comrades everything is equal. They've acquired better nerves and stronger muscles; they've emancipated themselves from the signs of slavery: the long skirt, the long hair; they've made a place for themselves where they wanted it and dismissed us from the necessity of offering a place of our choosing, in life as in the streetcar. If you do it anyway, then you risk a retort: "Thank you! I am not yet so infirm with age that I cannot stand!"

My son, certainly women no longer live today so much in the shadow and from the mercies of men, as they did in earlier times. [. . .] But the pelvis of a woman is still broader and heavier than our own; they still bear the children and the changing moon still demands from them its tribute—or has something changed in this respect as well?

Father, these particulars certainly still exist, but women wish that little be made of them; they probably fear that emphasizing them could justify viewing women as creatures of lesser value and usefulness in life, creatures of a second order. Gender, father, has become a secondary human characteristic. A man of contemporary thought distinguishes in his behavior as little between man and woman as, for example, between Christian and Jew.

My son, if things were as you say, then I would not so much blame the women, that no more chivalry or gallantry or whatever you want to call it is shown them, as the men who no longer show it. You have bypassed something very lovely if women awake in you at most desire, but no more longing to take care and protect. You have become very poor if that blessed joy in a woman is no longer vital which continually awakens in you the wish to thank them, merely for being.

As long as a man is still in love with love . . . he will offer his seat in a streetcar to a woman who otherwise has to stand. The missing links between that great cause and this small effect you can fill in easily yourself. Or is it that you no longer see love, my son, through your strong spectacles? Old man that I am, I still see it with my failing eyes.

Father! It is just a passing fog.

77

MAX BROD

Women and the New Objectivity

First published as "Die Frau und die neue Sachlichkeit," *Die Frau von Morgen, wie wir sie wünschen,* ed. Friedrich M. Huebner (Leipzig: E. A. Seemann, 1929), 38–48.

Recent literature has taken on an increasingly hard, cold, masculine tone. Exactly the same as modern music, which sounds antiromantic, antisentimental. It is unacceptable either to sing or to speak of love. It is incompatible with "objectivity," the supreme postulate of the present. This remarkable change of mind is a consequence of the following: since the beginning of the nineteenth century the times have assumed a hard and mechanical form, but writers have adopted a position of protest. Flaubert certainly recognized the mercilessly sober mechanical nature of our epoch, but his heroes (Bovary, like the sentimental Frédéric) grate against the time, for they cannot make themselves conform to the machine. This was in essence the fundamental posture of the writer for decades. He secretly remained the enemy of modern development, of Americanism. The problem arises: have the new writers submitted to it? Have they given up their struggle in the name of the spirit? Has the sober era triumphed once and for all over the last remaining protest?

Love, the desire for love, used to mean a glimpse into the deeper meaning of existence. The passion of a woman magically illuminated interactions that lifted them above the duller senses of simply egoistic relations among people. (What is said here of love applies to all noble passions of the heart, those that strive to surpass daily routine.) As a result of the war, the younger generation justifiably learned to mistrust everything that partook of passions of the heart. Behind so much of what appeared to be lofty passion, behind the beautiful colors of patriotism, *ver sacrum,* nationalist and erotic flights, lay nothing but phrases, lay vexation worse than phrases: the base interests of war profiteers, capitalists conducting politics! It is then understandable that a generation grows up to be disillusioned. Once one has seen with [Erich Maria] Remarque and [Ernst] Glaeser how everything can be reduced to the common denominator of mortal fear and roast goose, once one has experienced such need and the unforgettable degradation of the human creature, then one certainly has the right to regard everything as a swindle—with the single exception of the drive to secure humanity from such abominable fortune in the future.

In a situation so reduced to elemental defense, love and woman and heart and soul have in fact no place. Youth only defends itself; experiences of the heart were always raids of conquest into unknown territory—according to today's writers then, these experiences were luxury, distraction from the essential goal.

The young writers see only the quotidian—the document, the photograph, the report— objectivity, beyond which there is nothing to conquer, behind which there is no meaning to be sought. Religious interpretation of any kind appears to them an illusion. (Thus the clear distance between the New Objectivity and the older realism of, for example, Gerhart Hauptmann.) Modern authors fear nothing like they fear illusions. Through illusions we were dragged into war. To abstain from an affirmation of daily life, to see it in its utter hideousness, chaos, immorality—such a posture seems to carry the force of a law. From daily life, regarded as the only reality, behind which there is nothing more real, more benevolent, more loving (more womanly), one can seek distance only through humor and irony. Accordingly, irony becomes the single artistic tool of the youngest generation. In writing as in music. [. . .]

Insofar as the content of the New Objectivity includes the destruction of false glorification, it should fulfill its function to the utmost. For from this perspective it is a new impetus and a true beginning, a justified protest of the young against the war makers and despots who remain at the helm, the outcry and last hope of humanity. But if objectivity means Americanization, a refusal of the heart, of problems, of love, then it is not a protest against war but rather against its result, its continuation and, finally (see the recent German production of Maxwell Anderson's *What Price Glory?*), its approbation. It will be the task of the woman of tomorrow, full of instinct and cleverness, to distinguish the good components of the New Objectivity from the bad. In this task I see her significance, not simply for man and the masculine spirit (which, for the moment, is racing up a dead-end street with its masculine writing), but for the development of a genuine society, one no longer based on exploitation, but rather a true community of nations.

78

ELSA HERRMANN

This is the New Woman

First published as *So ist die neue Frau* (Hellerau: Avalon Verlag, 1929), 32–43.

To all appearances, the distinction between women in our day and those of previous times is to be sought only in formal terms because the modern woman refuses to lead the life of a lady and a housewife, preferring to depart from the ordained path and go her own way. In fact, however, the attitude of the new woman toward traditional customs is the expression of a worldview that decisively influences the direction of her entire life. The difference between the way women conceived of their lives today as distinguished from yesterday is most clearly visible in the objectives of this life.

The woman of yesterday lived exclusively for and geared her actions toward the future. Already as a half-grown child, she toiled and stocked her hope chest for her future dowry. In the first years of marriage she did as much of the household work as possible herself to save on expenses, thereby laying the foundation for future prosperity, or at least a worry-free old age. In pursuit of these goals she helped her husband in his business or professional activities. She frequently accomplished incredible things by combining her work in the household with this professional work of her own, the success of which she could constantly observe and measure by the progress of their mutual prosperity. She believed she had fulfilled her life's purpose when income deriving from well-placed investments or from one or more houses allowed her and her husband to retire from business. Beyond this, the assets saved and accumulated were valued as the expression of her concern for the future of her children.

The woman of yesterday pursued the same goal of securing the future in all social spheres, varied only according to her specific conditions. The woman defined exclusively by her status as a lady determined the occasions when she would allow herself to be seen in public by considering the possible advantages to herself and her family, a standpoint that would often determine the selection of the places she would frequent and where she would vacation. Less well-off women often kept a so-called "big house." They invited guests and took part in social functions to give the impression in their milieu that all the financial and social requisites for their husbands' career advancement were at hand. For every genuine woman of yesterday it was quite natural to make all manner of sacrifices in a completely selfless fashion, provided they served to advance the social ascent of the family or one of its members.

Her primary task, however, she naturally saw to be caring for the well-being of her children, the ultimate carriers of her thoughts on the future. Thus the purpose of her existence was in principle fulfilled once the existence of these children had been secured, that is, when she had settled the son in his work and gotten the daughter married. Then she collapsed completely, like a good racehorse collapses when it has maintained its exertions up to the very last minute. She changed quickly, succumbing to various physical ailments whose symptoms she had never before noticed or given any mind.

The woman of yesterday was intent on the future; the woman of the day before yesterday was focused on the *past*. For the latter, in other words, there was no higher goal than honoring the achievements of the "good old days." In their name she strove to ward off everything that could somehow have disturbed her accepted and recognized way of life.

In stark contrast, the woman of today is oriented exclusively toward the present. That which is is decisive for her, not that which should be or should have been according to tradition.

She refuses to be regarded as a physically weak being in need of assistance—the role the woman of yesterday continued to adopt artificially—and therefore no longer lives by means supplied to her from elsewhere, whether income from her parents or her husband. For the sake of her economic independence, the necessary precondition for the development of a self-reliant personality, she seeks to support herself through gainful employment. It is only too obvious that, in contrast to earlier times, this conception of life necessarily involves a fundamental change in the orientation of women toward men which acquires its basic tone from concerns of equality and comradeship.

The new woman has set herself the goal of proving in her work and deeds that the representatives of the female sex are not second-class persons existing only in dependence and obedience but are fully capable of satisfying the demands of their positions in life. The proof of her personal value and the proof of the value of her sex are therefore the maxims ruling the life of every single woman of our times, for the sake of herself and the sake of the whole. [. . .]

The people of yesterday are strongly inclined to characterize the modern woman as unfeminine because she is no longer wrapped up in kitchen work and the chores that have to be done around the house. Such a conception is less informative about the object of the judgment than the ones making it, who have adopted a view about the essence of the sexes based upon various accidental, external features. The concepts *female* and *male* have their ultimate origin in the erotic sphere and do not refer to the ways in which people might engage in activity. A woman is not female because she wields a cooking spoon and turns everything upside down while cleaning, but because she manifests characteristics that the man finds desirable, because she is kind, soft, understanding, appealing in her appearance, and so on. [. . .]

Despite the fact that every war from time immemorial has entailed the liberation of an intellectually, spiritually, or physically fettered social group, the war and postwar period of our recent past has brought women nothing extraordinary in the slightest but only awakened them from their lethargy and laid upon them the responsibility for their own fate. Moreover, the activity of women in our recent time of need represented something new neither to themselves nor to the population as a whole, since people had long been theorizing the independence and equality of woman in her relationship to man.

The new woman is therefore no artificially conjured phenomenon, consciously conceived in opposition to an existing system; rather, she is organically bound up with the economic and cultural developments of the last few decades. Her task is to clear the way for equal rights for women in all areas of life. That does not mean that she stands for the complete equality of the representatives of both sexes. Her goal is much more to achieve recognition for the complete legitimacy of women as human beings, according to each the right to have her particular physical constitution and her accomplishments respected and, where necessary, protected.

79

TEXTILE WORKERS

My Workday, My Weekend

First published in *Mein Arbeitstag, Mein Wochenende. 150 Berichte von Textilarbeiterinnen,* ed. Deutscher Textilarbeiterverband (Berlin: Textilpraxis Verlag, 1930), 187–189.

As far as I'm concerned, the work at home would be enough. . . . The workday begins at 4:45. Make the beds, comb my hair, feed Mizzi and the rabbits, drink something warm, and the clock reads 5:30. It is time to go to the factory. Lunch box and coffee thermos in hand, and it's off to the work bench. 6:00 start, year in, year out. I do my work standing. We work nine and a half hours a day. 8:30 to 9:00 in the morning we have a break to eat. In this half hour I usually have a lot of socks with me to darn, because the time at home is short. Back to work at 9:00 until 12:00. From 12:00 to 1:00 in the afternoon is lunchtime. I usually have some mending to do; sometimes a letter to write as well. At 1:00 it starts up again until 5:00 or 5:30—after twelve hours away, back home!

Without a rest it's off to the stove to prepare lunch for the coming day. Then washing, drying, a bit of dinner, finishing by 9:00 in the evening at the latest. Then I'm finished too and want nothing but some peace.

Thursday evenings the wash is usually put in to soak. Friday evening it's washed, Saturday morning hung out to dry. Afterwards it's off to the factory till 12:00. Sunday morning is for ironing, often for baking too, but always for cooking for Sunday and Monday. Sunday afternoon (usually in the winter) I mend the linen and clean up. At 4:00 I can rest a little.

My view is that if a housewife and mother could be at home, then the household and children would be better served. In France, Alsace, and Saxony the women do not work in the factory and their life is easier than in Bavaria. In Bavaria the poor women live like slaves, so to speak. (Housewife, mother, factory worker.) The way of life is rugged and hard, as is the weather. But there are also women who have been used to the factory since they were fourteen and don't want to have it any better. *As far as I'm concerned, the work at home would be enough,* because my health isn't all that it could be. How could it be otherwise when you have to work in an overheated environment?

Six days of vacation once a year, but that's no relaxation, just the opposite. That's when the apartment gets whitewashed and painted, big washes get done, and spring cleaning. And these days are over in no time without an hour of real relaxation. That's how the life of a woman working in the factory goes all year round. Not even at night do you really feel calm, because your nerves are so agitated.

If a co-worker tells you differently, then she is at best still young and dumb. Or maybe she lets some things go that should get done. Or she could have her old mother with her who does the housework for her. But I am alone with my husband and two sons, sixteen and seventeen.

That is my work time and my weekend.

I would be happy if I could properly provide for my household and children. . . . Up—it is 4:30 in the morning; it's still like I'm wiped out. No wonder, after work last night I washed until midnight and I often think in the morning, if it were only quitting time again right now. But this is no time for idle thoughts, instead it's hurry to wash, get dressed, make food for the whole day, because my husband and I work away from home and at 5:45 the train leaves and it doesn't wait. When I'm far enough along I wake my husband and *then comes the hardest work, waking and dressing the children. Everybody knows that a three-year-old child is still sleepy at 5:00 in the morning and it cries when I take it to the babysitter, and then usually I have to jump to get to the train on time.* At 6:00 we're in G., where I work; we don't start working until 7:00. You spend *another whole hour shivering in the waiting room.* What you couldn't get done in this time at home! At 7:00 work begins; I work in the weaving mill on two looms. On one loom I have ottomans, where, with the heavy woof used there, the spool runs out every minute, and on the other one there is such a sticky chain I can't move from the spot and have to lean over the loom the whole day and pull in threads. *How that wears you out, outsiders can't even imagine, and especially if, like me, you're pregnant.* 8:30 is the breakfast break; fifteen minutes, but only on Saturdays, because we work straight through on that day until 12:45. The other weekdays we work until 11:30, then a half hour for lunch and then it continues until 4:00 without interruption. *There is no breakfast or afternoon break. The worker always has to swallow his skimpy little bit of schmalz or butter bread while he's working. I often think he has it worse than livestock, because they at least get to eat in peace.* At 12:45 the machinery shuts down. Then it's time to clean. That is probably the most disgusting work for every weaver, for the amount of filth and glue and starch dust you swallow is incredible. And how you sweat! In a half hour two looms have to be cleaned and then the overseer comes and whoever hasn't finished gets scolded and has to begin again. *12:45 is quitting time, because it's the weekend.* I have to wait again until 1:30 for the train. *Then you have to stand in the crowded train, squeezed in like a sardine. I think sometimes I'm going to fall down, I'm always so tired.* When I get home, I first have to sit down and rest for fifteen minutes. *Often I sit there and howl like a child, for no reason; I'm so tired, my nerves just go.* But I always have to pull myself together again. First it's time to pick up my son. I take the opportunity to shop at the same time and then it's time to get on with the work at home: cleaning, washing, and everything a working woman has to do on a Saturday evening. *A cleaning lady is too expensive for me, for of the 25 marks average earnings a week 1.50 marks already goes for transportation, 6 marks for childcare, and what it otherwise costs for you to be out of the house all day—which means Saturdays and every night is spent washing.*

If I'm finished with the housework on Saturdays around 9:00 or 9:30, I'm usually too tired to give the child a bath which means I have to start up again Sunday morning. *But that doesn't matter because I don't even know a Sunday and holiday like they prescribe so nicely in the church!* Then there are things to mend, and everything else that didn't get done during the week; that has to be taken care of on Sundays. *So those are the famous weekend joys of a working woman. Isn't it understandable that I often wonder what I live for, and why everything is so unequal.*

80

HILDE WALTER

Twilight for Women?

First published as "Frauendämmerung?" *Die Weltbühne*, no. 27 (July 7, 1931), 24–26.

Women have become unpopular. That is not good news because it touches on things that cannot be explained by reason alone. An uncomfortable atmosphere is gathering around all working women. A perhaps unorganized but very powerful countermovement is taking aim at all of them; individual women will be feeling its effects sooner or later.

Along the entire spectrum from left to right the meaning of women's employment and their right to it are suddenly being questioned, more or less directly. At the moment it is not even the old discussion over so-called "equal rights," over "equal pay for equal work" that occupies the foreground. Suddenly we are obliged to counter the most primitive arguments against the gainful employment of women.

We are unfortunately not entirely blameless for the strength of this new wave of hostility: the phenomenon of working women in general is being twisted to meet the needs of a variety of propagandistic goals. Perhaps only the hard-working proletarian woman, whose way of life is subject to no optimistic renderings of any kind, is being exempted from the general rage for falsification and rosy distortions. When people speak of "women's work," they are not usually thinking of the figures in Käthe Kollwitz's pictures. For years now it has been much more the case that every type of women's work has been proclaimed, photographed, and trivialized as an "accomplishment," has been drenched in the sweet sauce of the eternal march of prosperity. The victory cry of the unlimited potential of women's "abilities," of the steady conquest of new positions in the work force, has issued in part from the representatives of newly–acquired female professions. Anxiety and fear has gripped male colleagues who have necessarily experienced the brilliant sheen of the new and unusual, possibly intensified by feminine charms, as unfair competition.

In addition, all the consumer-goods industries geared to female customers were very quick to recognize the attractiveness of such catchwords and make full use of them in their advertisements. Even the most poorly paid saleswoman or typist is an effective billboard; in a provocative get-up she becomes the very emblem of endless weekend amusements and the eternal freshness of youth. Women's moderate professional successes, often deficiently compensated, are glorified in annuals and wall calendars, if possible under the heading "Women for Women." When was a machinist, ranking tenth on the income scale, ever portrayed to the world building a locomotive for his dear gender compatriots?

In the long run, that had to get on men's nerves. Only on such a basis could the superstition have developed that the exclusion of women from the work place would remedy mass unemployment. To argue against this objectively is like whistling into the wind. In vain has nearly every newspaper left of the D. A. Z. [*Deutsche Allgemeine Zeitung*]—in the service of clarification and instruction—published the familiar figures from the occupational census proving without a doubt that the elimination of married women, for example, from the labor market would accomplish nothing. Fruitlessly have the independent trade unions repeatedly declared that the overwhelming majority of the 11.5 million working women are employed to mass produce those consumer goods that were produced in earlier times by women in the household; that 2.5 million married women work in family-owned agricultural and commercial enterprises; and that two million women of marriageable age would be left altogether unprovided for were they to be without work.

A mass psychosis cannot be exorcized by such reasonable, sober arguments, nor can they now stamp out the nearly mythical idea of the economic detriment caused by working women. Psychologists must discover the sources from which this male emotional disturbance is constantly renewed. They could perhaps investigate the extent to which an unknown sexual fear prevents the majority of men from seeing economic facts objectively and clearly. An elucidation of the misrepresented social state of affairs, however, can only be accomplished by women themselves if they resolve to speak just as openly about their occupational fate as they do about their love life.

There is the successful upper stratum of our much-celebrated pioneers who, as representatives and higher civil servants, as leaders of large occupational groups, can count on an economically secure old age. They might wish to report on how old they were when they entered the economic competition, how much money had to be invested in their rise until, in the critical years, they were no longer dependent on superiors and co-workers who refused employment to every woman getting on in years. There are the young academicians, who got their positions as research assistants only because they could also type. The host of female white-collar workers who, to keep their positions, have to maintain a standard of living corresponding to 250 marks a month on an income of 150. Additional duties in some form or other are usually an implicit part of their job.

Working women in general are also blamed quite often for accidents in the work place. If the daily rhythm of work is ever broken by the time-consuming effects of affairs of the heart, it seems to scream for the elimination of the disturbing female element. As if private emotional complications are not equally capable of interfering with male performance at work. Unfortunately, management science has not yet ascertained how much working women can enhance productivity by combining profession and love.

The truth about the living and working conditions of the contemporary woman is to be found in part in the publications of occupational associations. A new survey entitled *Working on Typewriters* determined that most stenographers and typists are completely exhausted after ten or fifteen years in the profession. But the best studies and most valuable monographs do not receive as much publicity as the eternal optimism that is always gushing forth from prominent positions in the name of the gender as a whole. When, for example, the public-speaking trainees of Madame von Kardorff take the stage as the new female youth to rediscover "women's grand political mission," then the appropriate male reaction can scarcely come as any surprise.

It is high time to do away with the fiction of the united front of all working women. All the propaganda for the vague concept of women's work as such is distressingly mixed up with the victory cry for gains long since accomplished and works only to destroy the good will of the other side. If women would quietly invest the same intensity in encouraging their colleagues of both genders within individual occupations, better working conditions could probably be achieved for everyone.

81

Women's Work and the Economic Crisis

First published as "Frauenarbeit and Wirtschaftskrise. Erklärung des Bundes deutscher Frauenvereine,"
Frankfurter Zeitung (April 29, 1931), 404.

The prejudices, still not overcome, against women having full-time occupations are finding
fresh impetus in the population due to the unemployment of millions of men. The demand
that women act to relieve the overburdened labor market meets with broad emotional
support.

According to the most recent occupational census the number of working women in
Germany is 11.5 million. In the last two decades the participation of women in the work
force has risen from 30.5 to 35 percent of all employed persons. Of these women,
approximately 5 million work in agriculture, 3 million in industry, 1.5 million in commerce
and trade, about 300,000 in administration and the liberal professions, approximately the
same number in health-care and welfare services, and 1.5 million in domestic service. Of
all these women, about 1 million are self-employed, 1.5 million are white-collar workers
and civil servants, 3.5 million working class, and 5.5 million either work in family-owned
enterprises or are domestic servants.

The areas in which female competition is primarily being attacked are those of
white-collar employees and workers.

As for women workers in industry, the need of industry for female labor power, much
more than the need of women for work, is responsible for the increased number of women
industrial workers. The rationalization of recent years, motivated purely by considerations
of profit, has steadily replaced male labor power with female—a development for which
women are not to blame and the dangers of which the Bund deutscher Frauenvereine
appreciates to the fullest. This organization shares the view that it is healthier for families
to be maintained by male labor and wages to be paid to men. Among white-collar
employees the situation is quite similar, since, due to the restructuring of enterprises, the
need for more workers in this category has risen dramatically.

Moreover, no one familiar with contemporary economic conditions can ignore the fact
that the average young woman seeks employment prior to marriage and that families are
not in the position of supporting daughters who are capable of working until they are
married. For those women to whom the possibility of marriage is closed because of the
numerical imbalance of women of marriageable age to men, independent gainful employment is a matter of course.

For both economic and personal reasons, it is necessary that these women be integrated
into occupational life in accordance with their abilities. It is neither desirable for economic
reasons nor just to the individual women to attempt to exclude them from employment
in areas suited to their abilities. For these reasons the educational and occupational
freedoms won by women and guaranteed them in the constitution must be unconditionally
upheld. There is the danger that the pressure of the economic situation will result in a
setback for women striving for more satisfying accomplishments and integration into the
national economy as befits their individual natures.

As a rule, caring for the family should be regarded as a full-time female occupation.
The increasing number of women employed outside the home, however, indicates that it
is not personal choice but economic necessity that determines their actual decision to seek
employment. In evaluating whether married women represent an unavoidable burden on

the labor market, one must consider both their economic position as well as the type and degree of their potential.

We are far from rejecting experimental labor-market policies that suggest making an adjustment favoring families in which no one is gainfully employed at the cost of other families in which several members have work. That the livelihood of considerable segments of the working population depends upon the employment of women outside the household, however, must not be overlooked. [. . .] It must moreover be required that, in the judgment of their right to work, the objective potential of women, the quality and specific type of their work, be evaluated exactly as it is for men. And, finally, any such temporary emergency measures must not be framed in such a way as to undermine, in principle, women's hard-won, constitutionally guaranteed legal status.

82

ELSE KIENLE

The Kienle Case

First published as "Der Fall Kienle," *Die Weltbühne*, no. 15 (April 14, 1931), 535–539.

There has been so much written about Paragraph 218 in reference to the case involving Friedrich Wolf and myself that I do not want to comment on it today. Just like Friedrich Wolf and every other sensitive human being, I am against so-called abortion, and am instead an advocate of birth control. It is perhaps of some import that I emphasize that my colleague Wolf is the father of four children. In countless lectures I have indicated my clear awareness of what the termination of a pregnancy means to every woman: it is an enormous invasion of her entire physical and psychological being. Aside from a few snobbish exceptions, it is incorrect to say that the modern woman no longer wants to have children for reasons of convenience or because she lacks maternal feelings. The notion of *disgrace*—in earlier times the prevailing response in bourgeois circles to unmarried pregnant women—is of far less practical concern today than the fear on the part of young women of losing their positions as clerks, teachers, or workers. Eighty percent of all patients who go to a doctor to have their pregnancy terminated are women who have already had several children. They have become modern, but only in the sense of an awakened awareness of responsibility. Where four people sleep in the same bed and experience it as a rare event when together they can afford thirty cents for a bit of ham—in such conditions a fifth being simply has no right to exist. Hunger and love have been and remain the primal drives of human beings, and love is quite likely the only diversion a family of workers can afford in 1931. When such a woman comes to a doctor's office with a new pregnancy, one need not inquire directly into the reasons for her coming. Her timid entrance, her face, alternately flushed and pale, her careworn, hardened appearance tell the whole sorrowful tale. I would go so far as to maintain that it is wholly inappropriate to treat such a woman in terms of such notions as social factors. If one understands a doctor in the higher sense of the word, as one who lends help to suffering people and not the practitioner of a trade, then the idea of social factors is a given. It seems to me a disgrace when one, from the allegedly lofty standpoint of science, demands that a wretched, oppressed, and emaciated body should bear new life. Whoever is a doctor in an ethical sense must be willing and able to help in these cases before the woman, exhausted by need and resolved to do whatever is necessary, goes to a quack or lays hands on herself.

In my case, I was denounced by a colleague, who, permanently employed by a hospital and receiving his salary on the first of every month, probably has no idea of the need of the poor and the poorest. That was quite likely the reason it was so easy for him, from his lofty position, to anonymously denounce a female colleague whose socially-conscious opinions were known throughout the community of working people.

Fifteen minutes later, I learned that his denunciation had already been made by the middle of December 1930. Only eight weeks later my card index and all of my case files were confiscated. In these eight weeks I spoke openly with doctors and lawyers about my situation. I was repeatedly advised to make sure that the materials "implicating" me disappear. But I did not change or remove the file of a single patient. During this time I continued my work and, despite the fact that the denunciation had already been lodged, noted each new case by name, date, and physical complaint. It was completely apparent to me, especially in Württemberg, a state known for its conservative and strict administration of justice, that I was to be made an example. There was not a single case in which I terminated a pregnancy without undertaking a thorough and complete examination of the patient. Every woman I saw whose chance of recuperation allowed for the possibility that the pregnancy might be carried to term, I turned away, albeit with a deep feeling of pain. Those cases in which the most conscientious examination of all relevant circumstances made it apparent to me that a termination of the pregnancy was the only and last remaining way to avoid severe danger to the health and life of the mother, I sent the patient to a second doctor, who, without knowledge of my findings, examined her and determined whether a termination of the pregnancy appeared necessary or not. I did not perform a single termination without the certification of a second doctor. Among the materials confiscated by the police, incidentally, was also the entire collection of physicians' certifications. The fact that fifty or sixty of them came from my colleague Friedrich Wolf is solely due to the similarity of our socially-minded activity and the similarity of our practices.

Without either Wolf or myself having been given a hearing, we were arrested for the crime of performing abortions for pay.

For myself, just as for Friedrich Wolf, the time of arrest was set for the late evening hours. It happened that precisely on this evening I had to give a lecture on Paragraph 218 at the Free Thinkers' Association. I was on my way to the lecture when, going out the door into the garden, I saw the police officers coming up the steps. They, however, failed to find the feared criminal they were seeking, who, a few minutes later and still affected by the sight of the officers, was delivering a passionate lecture against Paragraph 218. During the night I was informed of Friedrich Wolf's arrest. I immediately packed my little suitcase, in order to prepare myself appropriately for an early-morning visit by officers of the court, and so as not to forget anything one might need for such exceptional circumstances. Punctually, at the appointed hour, the righteous brotherhood arrived and I drove with them to the prison.

After my arrest such a wave of smut washed over me that even one of my defense attorneys believed that it would be years before I saw the light of day. In Stuttgart I was generally abandoned; only a very few people stood by me. No public opinion in my favor existed. I had no opportunity to defend myself against all that was being said about me from official and private quarters. At my arraignment, during which I still retained a certain belief in law and justice, I was thrown back into jail on devastating charges. The sole ray of hope was that Friedrich Wolf had been released.

I sat once again in my cell. Ripped out of my practice. The Württemberg Physicians' Council, covering for the denouncer, emphatically disavowed us. Six weeks later, however, after I had regained my freedom, the Council returned just as emphatically to our side. The court physician, without any kind of expert inquiry, did what was expected of him: he entered his notorious provisional report according to which I had acted contrary to the law in more than three hundred cases. The director of the court press office in Stuttgart made allusions to the inferiority of my person, thinking less about the fate of a defenseless detainee than of the retrospective justification of the blunder made by the judicial authorities. In the end, rather than devoting themselves to a serious study of the adjudication of Paragraph 218, members of the Stuttgart prosecutor's office recommended that the cases of Wolf and Kienle be less vigorously pursued, and so on.

I took consolation in Horace, my favorite poet. During one sleepless night the meaning of the ode, "Aequam memento rebus in ardius," suddenly revealed itself to me: "Preserve equanimity in difficult circumstances!" I resolved to assist the examining magistrate in clarifying the matter through calm, expert discussion. In the following weeks I was interrogated six to eight hours a day about a total of two hundred and ten cases. I gave them all the details necessary for a complete clarification of every single case. I cautiously gave the magistrate a daily course of lectures on the issues raised by Paragraph 218 of which he was ignorant, then I carefully went through each case with him, one by one, supported by my good memory. I trust it is no indiscretion to reveal that, while the lawyer in him took pains to continue thinking formally, from under the formal exterior there gradually emerged a human being who was astonished to notice the edifice of accusations beginning to totter. I had myself requested that my defense attorneys delay their appeals to the judgment of the preliminary hearing until after my interrogation was completed. I was amused by the thought of my Stuttgart colleagues, who might face the prospect of landing in the same situation and confronting an examining magistrate who, as a result of my lessons, was now an expert.

The criminal court denied my appeal, although it was forced to recognize that I had accepted quite moderate honoraria and that only nineteen cases remained suspect.

My interrogation was approaching its end. Shortly before its conclusion, the case was suddenly broadened to include out-patients. I protested, giving assurances on my word of honor, that I had never performed a termination of pregnancy on an out-patient, but for that purpose had always kept patients a few days in my clinic. Fifty new cases were unexpectedly named for investigation, meaning that fifty women and girls were to be subjected to the inquisition of the police authorities, meaning that numerous families were to suffer through anxious days and sleepless nights worrying about the uncertainty of their fate.

Contrary to the promises made to me, I was to be kept in detention.

Since I had meanwhile learned what it means when the judicial system sharpens its teeth, especially when it does not know how to extricate itself from an impasse, I resolved to begin a hunger strike. I would have been more inclined to fight on objective legal grounds, but self-defense, the instinct for self-preservation, and in particular the feeling of having a mission to fulfill, caused me to choose the demonstrative strategy of a hunger strike. Wolf and I declared in solidarity that we would refuse to give any further testimony.

Fasting for three or four days is a small matter for a well-trained body, perhaps even a kind of recuperation. It is only from the fourth day on that one has any feeling at all of hunger. Every drop of water in an empty stomach feels like water poured on red-hot iron. Then, given even the best physical training, one begins to suffer a general loss of vigor, and intellectual acuity begins to lapse; a condition of failing physical and mental balance sets in, gradually joined by a growing sense of apathy. Up to the seventh day I was still able to keep myself more or less erect. On the morning of that day the court physician was still of the opinion that I was completely fit for detention. That afternoon I began experiencing episodes of severe weakness, so that I considered the time to have arrived for me to make my final arrangements. My last thought was of Paragraph 218 and the unspeakable suffering it had brought to so many thousands of women and now upon myself as well. Meanwhile, an ambulance had been standing by the door to the women's prison for three hours, with four men waiting with a stretcher to take me to the hospital. With the last of my strength I protested against these measures, declaring that I would continue to refuse any kind of nourishment in the hospital as well. After a hard struggle, I was left in my prison cell. On Sunday the twenty-eighth of March, 1931, at four o'clock in the afternoon, I was awakened from a sleep similar to unconsciousness to be informed that my detention had been interrupted because my health would no longer bear it.

How our trial will turn out I cannot say. For Friedrich Wolf and myself the struggle is not about whether or not we are pronounced guilty. People are transient and paragraphs can be changed. But there is a law that stands above all paragraphs, and that is the law of human dignity and women's dignity.

83

SIEGFRIED KRACAUER

Working Women

First published as "Mädchen im Beruf," *Der Querschnitt* 12, no. 4 (April 1932), 238–243.

To the extent that working women have appeared at all in popular film, they have usually, until very recently, been cheerful young private secretaries or typists who take dictation for the fun of it and do a little typing. They are pretty because they have time to take care of themselves; they sing a hit tune to the rhythm of their work, which has none, and, at the end, they marry the boss or a rich American. There is always a happy ending, which is not only the dream of many girls but also a tested means of transforming them into compliant instruments. Even were the last bank to fail, it would presumably remain the task of the imaginary bank directors in film to fulfill the double task of binding these girls to the system as workers and as wives.

Nevertheless the tension between reality and the illusions created in film has become so marked that the majority of working women are no longer so easily enchanted. I am acquainted personally with a sufficient number of young working women who speak disparagingly about the swindle on the screen. They are literally worn down by physical reality and impregnated with experiences that do not disappear. Meanwhile, the steady increase in the supply of enlightening literature continues, which, in contrast to the usual belles lettres and misleading films, attempts to make employed women (and men) conscious of their real situation. Rudolf Braune, *Das Mädchen an der Orga Privat;* Josef Breitbach, *Rot gegen Rot;* Christa Anita Brück, *Schicksal hinter Schreibmaschinen;* Otto Roeld, *Malenski auf der Tour*—these are a few of the books belonging in that category. The public discussion of the issue of white-collar employees was considerably stimulated by my own book, *Die Angestellten,* the findings of which were also presented in the play *Die Mausefalle.* Of academic publications I will name yet another: the small, very useful text by Susanne Suhr, *Die weiblichen Angestellten,* which analyzes the results of a survey by the General Association of White-Collar Employees.

How many female white-collar employees are there in Germany today? Approximately 1.4 million, meaning that about one-third of all white-collar employees are women. The influx of women into white-collar occupations, which in recent years has grown steadily, is to be explained by the circumstance that both women who were previously employed in other areas as well as those belonging to the impoverished middle classes have increasingly sought entrance to these occupations; furthermore, this increase may be traced to a certain shift from male to female white-collar workers, which clearly derives less from an increase in female than from a sharp decline in available male workers. The majority of employed women (in particular those of the new generation) come from the working class, and the majority of them are single (the number of those with husbands is estimated at 7 to 11 percent). In terms of compensation, they are paid roughly 10 to 15 percent less than men. [. . .]

Everyone knows women employed in white-collar jobs, or believes he does. But do people who have contact with them only at work, or who have even once made friends with a sales girl, really know them? These girls parade much of a superficial nature. Of course, they find their amusements where they can, rowing, making love, giving themselves either mechanically or romantically because they have nothing else; this overpublicized distraction industry, however, neither blends with the daily life of a white-collar employee nor is it characteristic of the overwhelming majority. The industry's existence testifies to the triviality of the bourgeoisie and the emptiness of an employee's life.

That daily work life for employed women can rise to the level of so-called meaningful life content is sufficiently assured only in the rarest of cases. For the most part, white-collar workers (male and female) raise themselves above the level of skilled workers only because they are paid in the form of a salary. Otherwise—excepting those who hold white-collar jobs in which mechanization plays a minor role—their life conditions are approximately the same. Both enjoy only negligible chances for advancement and both live in the fear of cutbacks, with a gigantic reserve army of replacements looming in the background. The nature of occupational life depends, naturally, on the type of occupation in question.

A specifically female occupation is that of the *stenotypist,* since here ninety-nine of every one-hundred employees are women. Half of them suffer from nervous afflictions, which almost qualify as a new occupational illness. These nervous problems are not caused solely by the immediate strains of the job, by the din of all the machines in the room, by the exaggerated tempo of work, etc., but also by disturbances to the psychological balance, which appear just as frequently under the pressure of the same conditions in other occupations. [. . .] Those who do not find a husband—and there are many—have nothing to expect from the future and are therefore especially prone to suffer health problems. (See in this connection the survey conducted by the General Association of White-Collar Employees concerning work at the typewriter.) Contemporary medicine continues, in complete harmony with the capitalist world view, to conceive all illnesses as symptoms attached to the individual; ultimately, it will have to learn to observe the collective body instead of the body of a single individual, and to trace the connection between individual illness and those of the society at large. [. . .]

And away from work? It is not difficult to calculate what can be done on the typical average salary, although very few people go to the trouble of doing so. Precisely because their income levels are low, the bulk of the girls live with their families. They are frequently required to support their parents and only one-third of them have their own room. [. . .]

I have intentionally kept silent on the political and social ideas of working girls. Naturally, the false consciousness shared by most male employees concerning their class status—a consciousness primarily characterized by its fixation on economic proletarian-ization—is not so strongly marked in the life of female employees. Still, for many, much of their ambition is invested in not being mistaken for a proletarian woman, believing, now as before, that members of higher social strata dwell in higher spheres.

84

ALICE RÜHLE-GERSTEL

Back to the Good Old Days?

First published as "Zurück zur guten alten Zeit?" *Die literarische Welt* 9, no. 4 (January 27, 1933), 5–6.

It began with a slight uneasiness; with a feeling that something was not right, was no longer right. About two or three years ago. Just at the time, incidentally, when the world crisis was first making itself known with the same slight, uneasy feeling. Gradually a few timid women's emancipationists retreated into the ranks of the opponents of women's eman-cipation, into the ranks of those who had always—already in 1870, already in 1920—said "that's as far as it can go" with the so-called liberation of women. It began, that is, as women began to cut an entirely new figure. A new economic figure who went out into public economic life as an independent worker or wage-earner entering the free market that had up until then been free only for men. A new political figure who appeared in the parties and parliaments, at demonstrations and gatherings. A new physical figure who not only cut her hair and shortened her skirts but began to emancipate herself altogether from the physical limitations of being female. Finally, a new intellectual-psychological figure who fought her way out of the fog of sentimental ideologies and strove toward a clear, objective knowledge of the world and the self.

This new figure never became average, never became the mass female. There was no time for that. Until today this new figure has remained a pioneer, the standard-bearer—no, the female standard-bearer—of something that had yet to develop. But before she could evolve into a type and expand into an average, she once again ran up against barriers. Her old womanly fate—motherhood, love, family—trailed after her into the spheres of the new womanliness, which immediately presented itself as a new objectivity. And she therefore found herself not liberated, as she had naively assumed, but now doubly bound: conflicts between work and marriage now appeared, between uninhibited drives and inhibited mores, conflicts between the public and private aspects of her life, which could not be synthesized. There remained only the compromise: lukewarm and listless for herself and for those affected or a decisive break with everything up to the previous generation that had signified woman's fate and woman's nature. It easily appeared as if the new freedom for women had achieved nothing. For those who saw only a small segment of our present, with no perspective on the past and future, they were justified in their view of the new woman in missing the nice balance of the modest mother, the sublime femininity of the tender of the hearth, the expression of a harmony complete within itself.

Women themselves missed it too: both as an attribute of gender as well as an ideological marker of womanliness—and above all, as the emotional content of life. For, with a little work, one can probably learn to think in perspective; but to feel in perspective, for that one needs to be embedded in vital currents of life, to be carried along by the steady flow of the future. The emancipated woman, having emerged from the muddy pond (or, if you will, the clear lake) of her previous state, found herself on a bleak shore, surrounded here and there by skyscrapers that blocked her view. She simply noted: I have less time than my mother had; I have less money, less joy, less hope, less consolation. And thus did she too, with quiet disillusion defiantly concealed, begin her cautious return to the ranks of the backward-looking. *prior to WWI.*

Among the young girls and women of today there is a strong tendency toward marriage, toward motherhood, indeed, even toward cooking, a weariness of the "freedom" experienced as futile, an emptiness in the present which only a few experience as provisional, only a few are capable of filling with a future. The pioneers have grown tired because they see that they cannot storm the bastions alone and because they have had to wait too long for help, for a push from society at large. That is why they seize upon it when the past, the good old days, beckon enticingly, paraded before them by good and bad advertising artists of all ages and both sexes. Bobbed hairdos and short skirts have beaten a retreat; economic conditions have done away with the office chair and the teacher's desk and closed the door in women's faces. And the ideology of the new womanliness hangs in the present vacuum, flat as yesterday's balloon.

Literature is able to demonstrate what transpires only after the fact. As long as it is happening, it is too unconscious to be seen. Thus the appearance of war books ten years after the war, and thus the well-intentioned books summoning women to go "back" a few years after they have begun to withdraw on their own; because they knew or because they had had enough of staying in front, where no one wanted to follow, or because they did not dare go farther.

1932 - 2 pres. elections
2 Reichstag elections

conservatives looking back.

Voted for R wing party.

Nazi's
flat out told
women to stay home—
women voted for them

secretary =
secret keeper

9
Forging a Proletarian Culture

DURING THE WILHELMINE ERA the working class developed its own cultural institutions, iconography, and rituals. Although designed to prefigure the socialist society of the future and provide what the Italian Marxist Antonio Gramsci would have called a "counter-hegemonic" challenge to the dominant culture, the impact of these cultural innovations was ambiguous. Some historians have in fact called the inadvertent effect of this alternative culture the "negative integration" of the proletariat into German society. During the Weimar period efforts continued, nonetheless, to foster an autonomous working-class culture. These were now complicated, however, by the fracturing of the proletarian movement, not merely between Socialists and Communists but also among factions within each group.

Typical of those who called for a radical break with the legacy of bourgeois culture was the author of a 1920 essay in *Die Aktion* who was identified only by the initials "A. R." Others like the ultraleftist Otto Rühle sought to harness the rebellious energies of the youth movement to overthrow authority. Sport, contended the gymnast Fritz Wildung, should be a weapon in the class struggle. So too should art, proclaimed the communist playwright and physician Friedrich Wolf. To this end a League of Proletarian–Revolutionary German Writers was founded in 1928, with its tasks spelled out by the former expressionist poet Johannes R. Becher.

By the end of the decade, supporters of a purely proletarian culture could boast only modest successes. The difficulties in encouraging new poetry were reflected in the answers given to a questionnaire in *Die literarische Welt* in 1929. Two years later, the League's journal *Die Linkskurve* reported only partial success in generating a market for proletarian literature sold door-to-door. Similar problems were encountered in the creation of a workers' music movement, despite the optimism of militant composers like Hanns Eisler. "Red" mass novels were also distributed cheaply by communist publishing houses and promoted by critics like Yugoslavian-born Otto Biha. But their tendency to mimic the reportage of everyday life aroused the ire of Marxist aestheticians like Georg Lukács, who denounced Willi Bredel for failing to show the dialectical movement of society as a whole. Although considerable enthusiasm remained for working-class cultural initiatives, such as the proletarian films called for by the communist propaganda chief Willi Münzenberg in 1931 or the radical agitprop theater, the evidence of a successful overcoming of the bourgeois cultural legacy in Weimar is negligible.

Material pressures in particular were responsible for distracting workers from the cultural tasks assigned them by socialist leaders. In the Berlin workers' quarter, to take a salient example, housing was crowded, families often broken, and unemployment a persistent threat; not surprisingly the type of cultural activity most favored was sports or the cinema rather than concerts or the theater. An even bleaker picture was painted of a small working-class town in the region near Hamburg by a visiting Soviet journalist, Larissa Reissner, in 1923. Her portrayal of a communist heroine may seem idealized, but her account of the lot of female factory workers still commands respect.

85

A. R.

On Proletarian Culture

First published as "Zur proletarischen Kultur," *Die Aktion* 10, nos. 35–36 (September 4, 1920), 492–494.

The decline of bourgeois ideology began long before the collapse of bourgeois society. Bourgeois ideology was finished the moment the bourgeoisie became a ruling class. As a class based on exploitation, conquest, and competition, its cultural leaders preach freedom, peace, and humanity. They teach Kant and live off the interest.

The closer the bourgeoisie came to the pinnacle of its power, the crasser this contradiction became.

To the rising social class, the proletariat, the bourgeoisie left a bad heritage. In the area of culture the proletariat confronts a fundamental task. It must have the courage to cast off all bourgeois concepts of culture, morality, ethics, and aesthetics.

With sure instincts, the bourgeoisie turns up its nose at technology. It suspects that technology is the means by which capitalist society can be overcome and communist society constructed. Bourgeois culture views technology as something profane, something with which one can indeed make money and create comforts, but which otherwise is a matter of business.

To recognize and accept the moral and aesthetic value of culture—that is what confronts the proletariat. To apply ethics as an organizational principle and to accept ethical considerations as the standard of human relations, which is to say, as the standard of work—that is the proletariat's great task.

The victory of the proletariat transcends humanity's millenia-old dichotomy between good and evil. For every ruling class until now, good was what was evil for those ruled. The concepts of good and evil are inborn, and only because the classes that have ruled until now could not apply them as a principle without giving up their privileges has it been necessary to write a thousand complicated books about them. In reality good and evil can be organized just like cold and warm. The communist social order, which will be constructed without personal and class privilege, will not view the doctrine of good and evil as a mystical affair only accessible through revelation by higher beings (called professors), but will regard it as a regulator and teach about it. Schoolbooks will no longer teach "Do not torment animals, because they feel pain just like you do," but "It is evil to exploit another human being." This imperative alone is capable of illustrating the "profound philosophical" concept of good and evil, to show what good and evil are. People will endeavor to simplify all the complicated nuances in order to be able to apply them. Whether one should be good or evil (which is a contentious question in bourgeois society!) will, in communist society, be equivalent to the question, must one be cold?

The task of the coming revolution is not to introduce culture—the heritage taken over from the bourgeoisie will not allow it; rather the task is to clear the way for real culture. And only then, only later, *only in a truly communist society will a culture become possible* that provides a basis for the complicated, abstract, individualistic affairs of humanity. It will develop and promote the ethical and aesthetic needs of human beings and elevate them to a higher plane.

The proletariat will inject a new element into both ethics and aesthetics: *the collective moment.* It is easiest to trace the historical development of collectivism in art. The first artworks in history bore the character of a cult of the person: castles, palaces—buildings of whatever sort erected for one person or a family. Later, as the concept of ethics spread somewhat, as early as the rise of religions, we see artworks for an expanded community: churches, then museums, buildings of state, etc., all the way to warehouses—which, however, continue to represent authority based on the might of a preferential community. *Artworks expressive of the collective can and will be created only by the proletariat.*

The whole of laboring humanity is now excluded from the enjoyment of art. Even more effectively than a thousand chains, the lack of free time bars them from it. And, still worse, the "art" forced upon them by industry over the last hundred years has spoiled their sense and taste. Big-city buildings that violate all the dictates of harmony and natural law and whose construction has been guided solely by the principle of exploitation; convertible sofas; the utterly cheap plunder of modern industry geared exclusively to sales; the pictures and drawings disseminated by the thousands in magazines and journals—all of this has corrupted and destroyed the natural instincts of the overwhelming majority in the "cultured" civilization of our time.

Proletarian culture must begin here. Not with monuments and art collections, but *in the proletariat's own environs.* This is impossible in a capitalist society based on the labor of others. Scarcely has technology freed a number of people from work than new "needs" are invented in rapid-fire succession; every instance of technological perfection frees so-and-so many workers' hands for yet more intensive exploitation. The principle of capitalist society is not work but exploitation.

The defenders of the capitalist system fear that when this exploitive regulator disappears, the initiative for raising the level of industry will also decline. But this declining initiative would be a blessing for humanity. There will remain sufficient drive toward creative work. Freed from the forced grind of drudgery, new talents, now lost as productive forces to the struggle for bread, will arise a thousandfold. The curtailment of work for its own sake is the proletariat's most important cultural task.

86

OTTO RÜHLE

The Psyche of the Proletarian Child

First published as *Die Seele des proletarischen Kindes* (Dresden: Verlag am anderen Ufer, 1925), 203–205.

Proletarian youth challenged the principle of authority for the first time in June 1919 when a number of young workers abandoned Free Socialist Youth in order not to oppose from within an authoritarian organization (which was an appendage of the parties) but to adopt a new position of their own. "Where are the leaders of the young," ran a manifesto of these young people on this occasion, "who have not run their heads up against 'fatherly benevolence' and the 'well-intentioned advice' of older men? It is high time that an end be put to the fairy tale of disinterested and selfless friendship of age to youth."

This youth—anarchistic youth, as they called themselves—refused utterly, decisively, and consistently all membership in any sort of party or union and all tutelage of whatever form by any organization of adults. Indeed when the syndicalists—an organization with a federal basis—mistakenly passed a resolution that obligated "all organizations and executive committees to initiate syndicalist youth groups everywhere," the young proletarian anarchists made a great commotion rebelling against it. "Just as you struggle against the thought that socialism can be initiated centrally from the top down by decree," they called out to the syndicalists in their publication, "we reject the idea that a youth movement be initiated by a congress resolution and by older people." This led to conflicts in which the old struggle between fathers and sons was identically repeated—conflicts in which the profound leaning toward a mentality anchored in authoritarianism of even the best and purest among the syndicalist champions was betrayed. Their threat that the rebellion of the young would force them to apply "the whole of their authority as fathers" was the most embarrassing unmasking, for behind the masks of the nicest socialist language there peered out for an instant the face of an extreme bourgeois despotism. The syndicalists still enjoyed the success of having an anarcho-syndicalist youth organization come into being, a fatal success for this appendage of the syndicalist union is the weakest, most powerless, final offshoot of the authoritarian youth movement born of the instinct for power and the drive for domination, which, in its deepest foundations, has nothing to do with socialism.

Socialism is precisely community, and community is the antipode to domination, authority, and violence. To hold authority as distant as possible means to be closest to socialism. That is why the anarchist youth groups—isolated, not very strong, but unshakable in their fundamentally nonauthoritarian attitude—which have joined together in a revolutionary community as "free youth," as well as the youth groups of the General Workers' Union, are today the vanguard and apex of the proletarian march toward the socialist goal. By virtue of their mental disposition, it is they who are most clearly called to the new work, they who are the chosen ones.

87

LARISSA REISSNER

Schiffbek

First published in *Hamburg auf den Barrikaden. Erlebtes und Erhörtes aus dem Hamburger Aufstand 1923* (Berlin: Neuer Deutscher Verlag, 1925), 45–52.

Lying a little way out of Hamburg where a dreary line of telegraph poles marches off in the direction of flat, denuded, sandy Prussia is a small working-class town by the name of Schiffbek. It ranges out between the Bille brook, murky and smooth as tinplate, and hills on which grow sparse trees that have run bareheaded and tousled into the wind and also assorted little two-storey houses of a workers' settlement.

In the center the evangelical church stands empty like a rusty umbrella stuck into the ground to dry out after the rain and forgotten there forever. Not believing in God, the cosmopolitan population of this working-class town does not visit it. Today, after the battles, it stands there with a black eye, without windowpanes or doors—a priest who has strayed and ended up in someone else's fight.

A large chemical factory stands on a little island on the far side of the Bille: cold, venomous, and full of crystals that are deposited into the icy, black water, naphthaline and green poisons that seem to cover the riverbed with a film of fresh, vitriolic moss. Some thousand workers are employed there.

Inside the kilns that never cool off, fire that is as dense as the molten planets is poured out. It is observed through tiny windows. Sometimes the white heat is coated with a light, coaly haze but more often it is as white and still as blindness. Naked to the waist, workers charge away from the blazing kilns out into the frost, snow or rain to escape an atmosphere in which the one-time gigantic mare's-tails and warm swamps that are now stacked in the corners as heaps of coal might have grown and revelled.

Along either side of a narrow stone corridor lies a steam mill and a huge iron-rolling works. On Christmas Eve its chimney, higher than all the others, is like a sullen smoker left suddenly without tobacco.

Tin shacks are spread out along the fringe of the now-frozen, white waste patches. This factory has one long, legless body pressing its belly against the ground and seven equally tall chimneys set in a row like minarets from which every morning a shrill muezzin of labor sounds.

Work at this factory is extremely damaging to the lungs. The toughest cannot stand more than four years of it. You have to be like S., a hero of the Hamburg Rising, to emerge unharmed after working several years in the inferno. But then S. is a giant of whose build all Schiffbek is proud.

Ask any little urchin and he will tell you that S. can lift on his shoulder six men clinging to an iron crowbar, that his hands are much bigger and can hold much more than the purses that the good housewives of Schiffbek take to market, and that in the morning when he swings his extraordinary legs out of bed the whole tenement creaks and shakes so much that neighbors without watches know it is time to wake their husbands for work. So then as we have said, since S. is such a colossus, a bold spirit, a bolshevik, and generally devilish, the tin shacks have not done him too much harm. But little C. came out of them with a leg seared to the bone, K. with red spittle wrapped up in his dirty handkerchief.

Further up the Bille stand the smoky towers of Jute, one of Hamburg's largest manufacturing plants. It is predominantly women who work here, poorly remunerated and poorly organized, for whom the party has year after year conducted a bitter struggle against the menshevik trade unions, the women's remarkably clamorous, inflammable, but easily intimidated inertness, the employer, and the priest.

The Jute women doggedly resisted any stable organization. Where possible they would moan about their wages and after the first few days of a strike would go whining to make peace with the manager, first smashing the office windows and then informing on the instigators. However, the factory, in the course of its normal capitalist business, is itself combing out of this tangled, unexacting, conveniently exploitable, female mass the first strands of a strong proletarian solidarity. Amenable as the women might have been, their wages still slipped down and down. First one department and then another was subjected to the frantic inflationary race of prices and wages. Yet within the bounds of their own homes, their own housekeeping, and their own factory the women remain as united as they are indifferent to political movements that go beyond those bounds. They may not take any notice of a general strike but they will never let their workmates down in the next section. Thus, for over a year now, the basically peaceable Jute has, thank goodness, worked no more than three days out of six: the rest of the time the factory is out in the street supporting the section on strike at that particular time.

"O, ha!" (that is a pet expression of every true Hamburger).

"O, ha!" say the workers who have been conducting propaganda at the Jute factory for months and years, "Hunger is making good communists of them."

Here is one of the astonishing women to have come out of the Jute. Let's call her Elfriede and say that she is the daughter of a Schiffbek night watchman. Father was well known about the town as an orthodox menshevik and the owner of a superb carbine with which he maintained order and tranquillity in the derelict areas and buildings in his care called *Hundebuden* (dog kennels) by the workers. And so it was.

But if the watchman faithfully upheld the law of private property with his carbine, then Elfriede in every way overturned and trampled down those sacred bastions with her amazing beauty.

Elfriede was not only a perfect communist, an excellent workmate, and a heroic girl who fought at the barricades—taking out, while under fire, hot coffee and fresh cartridges fastened around her slim waist to the marksmen in the trenches and raising Schiffbek's entire female population to its feet to set up field kitchens—with her own hands she put her old man under lock and key adding his old-fashioned rifle to the party's scanty war material and was finally caught by the police in the heat of her criminal activity, namely while cleaning potatoes for the insurgents with her sleeves rolled up amid piles of fresh peelings; not only was she a courageous active woman forever dedicated to the party but also perhaps one of the first examples of a new brave type so unsuccessfully faked in the pages of the neoproletarian novel and the homilies of armchair revolutionaries.

There came with her into the poverty-stricken district of Schiffbek the spirit of destruction and liberty. Elfriede refused to become anyone's wife. Her name evoked the timid respect and furious hatred of legal wives whose husbands she would take away for a day, a year, or for life, of fathers, and of lovers.

She would conquer whomever she chose, make love for as long as there were no lies in that loving, and then haughtily return her captive to freedom. But she asked no one for a name, a shield, or aid for herself or her child. Never, neither in weakness nor in sickness, did she seek support in the law that all her life she had despised.

From the bench she went to jail.

But first a scene, an astonishing scene that actually took place in a corridor of the Hamburg City Hall from whose balcony [Independent Socialist Heinrich] Laufenberg was carefully thrown in 1918 and where arrested communists were brought on October 23 [after the failure of the Hamburg Workers' Council].

On that dreadful day there stood in the forecourt of Schiffbek police station in rows of three, four, or five, lorries loaded with captured workers lying on their backs, heaped on top of each other.

The rebels! They had fought in open battle according to all the rules of honest warfare, pitting life against life with an adversary a hundred times stronger, yet still sparing prisoners and letting the wounded go. After the defeat they were of course treated like hunted ruffians, renegades standing outside the law. The police pounded their feet on those rows of bloody, gasping bodies heaped upon each other. Dying men crushed by their comrades on top lay underneath with faces squashed against the coal-smeared boards while above the *Wachtmeister* (sergeants) of the Reichswehr tugged hair out and with their rifle butts cracked the napes of the immobilized men who then lost consciousness.

Three men were overwhelmed there. S., that oak among men, a superman in his astounding physical strength, spewed blood and lost his senses. K. was dying, and agile little L. beneath his pacifier's boot was ready to leap out of his crushed existence just as an eye slips from its socket full of fire and tears. About all this later: I don't wish to start on Schiffbek with the phase of police atrocities. They are merely a bloody and dirty epilogue to three days of the Rising that cannot be stamped out by a soldier's boot from the history of a new working-class humanity. For indeed how unattainable is the shining peak on which stands the struggle of Hamburg labor above the bloody filth of police-station floors, the vile courtroom offices where the proceedings were written out and torn up, torn up and rewritten, the reeking stifling lavatories of that now illustrious City Hall where the arrested were forced to wash and even take a shower so that members of the city government, and socialist deputies who had come to be convinced of the police's kind and humane treatment of its prisoners of war, did not become queasy at the sight of blood smeared everywhere or the smell of the clothes of an adolescent member of the Hamburg Young Communists, beaten until he had lost control of his physiological functions.

So it was that in that long, white corridor where the drunken soldiery drove the living piece of revolution that had fallen back through the lines into its hands, men cowered by the walls under the lash and it smelt of rubber and blood, in that corridor Elfriede who had so zealously and laboriously upheld her lonely dignified life free from the prop of any official morality, yet as pure and as straight as an arrow, in that corridor she was swamped with the foulest, filthiest abuse and mockery.

Every quarter of an hour a new group of Reichswehr burst into the hall, picked up off the floor those who had already collapsed, beat up again those who had already been beaten up, revived those who had fainted so as to knock them down again and then each of those gangs started once again on her standing as if naked among wild beasts.

"Communist slut," they shouted.

"Whore," they shouted.

"You're not a German woman but an animal," they shouted.

And in that ghastly interminable torture chamber that lasted a day, a night, and another day, this girl recalled: yes, there had been a great German woman, as great as a marble statue, and nothing since her ghastly death had been quite so fine and wise in the German revolution.

And what's more, she had left behind a small book of letters. A white cover with red lettering. Letters from prison.

Rosa Luxemburg.

Elfriede stood in that satanic corridor and cried out about Rosa Luxemburg until she was heard. When a girl arms herself with Rosa's name she is as powerful and as dangerous as an armed man—she is a warrior and no one will dare touch her.

It is impossible to pick up what she said and how or what her words were.

But some noncommissioned officer made an apology.

One of the gangs went off with tails between their legs saying that "they hadn't known." Perhaps this interval was used to get one of the injured men away from the soldiers and drag him out of the scrum by the arm.

That is the tale of Elfriede from Schiffbek.

88

WILLI MÜNZENBERG

Conquer Film!

First published as "Erobert den Film!" in *Winke aus der Praxis für die Praxis proletarischer Filmpropaganda* (Berlin: Neuer Deutscher Verlag, 1925), 1–28.

Ferdinand Lassalle characterized the press as a new major power. The same can be said today of film. Indeed, in a few countries film has perhaps already achieved a greater significance than the press. The number of film-goers in America, England, and France might well already be greater today than the number of newspaper readers in these countries. The number of persons attending the cinema in America in 1924 is estimated at 16 million. Even if more people read newspapers than watch films, it ought not to be forgotten that film, through visual images, has a much stronger and penetrating effect on the viewer than the written word does on the newspaper reader. The doubts about using film, raised broadly in academic and intellectual circles in the early years, have completely disappeared today. The constant progress in technical improvements has persuaded even the remaining die-hard opponents of film about the possibility of its exploitation. [. . .]

Just a glance at the development of film, from its initial appearance at annual fairs in the 1890s to today's deluxe theaters outfitted with all the refinements, conveys the extent to which film will dominate the world in coming decades. The revolutionary workers' movement therefore has a paramount interest in devoting the greatest attention to this exceedingly important problem, and to search for the ways and means of enlisting this effective, vital means of propaganda and agitation into its service.

"We must," said Clara Zetkin,

develop in a revolutionary sense the great cultural potential reposing in the cinema. In a revolutionary sense—that naturally does not mean that we simply run the bourgeois film with reversed premises, the bourgeois as devil, the proletarian as angel. Film should reflect social reality instead of the lies and fairy tales about it with which the bourgeois mass cinema deludes and defrauds the working people. Social reality, however, will be lent form through the class contradiction between the proletariat and the bourgeoisie and through the effects of this class contradiction.

The film with revolutionary content must therefore convey knowledge of the class situation of the proletariat, develop proletarian class consciousness, awaken and strengthen resolve and the willingness to sacrifice for the revolutionary struggle. It should present to the exploited the transforming, constructive, creative life that begins to arise and blossom wherever the proletariat, as in Soviet Russia, has crushed the state power of the propertied classes.

As is so often the case, it is the workers' organizations that are the last and the most timid in their attempts to turn this technologically important innovation to their own purposes. Indeed, the time was not so distant when socialist leaders—not unlike, incidentally, the ideologues of bourgeois society—proposed in all seriousness that film should be denounced in principle and opposed. It was common in the first years to see in the (admittedly often inadequate) film versions of literary works the danger that artistic offerings would be turned into kitsch and tastes would be leveled and to fear the competition that film posed to the theater. We recall a discussion carried out by the workers' movement in Zurich in 1912 on the potential uses of cinematography in which well-known leaders proposed that film be boycotted and that workers and workers' families be discouraged from attending any film presentation at all, even those of an educational nature. Only after the war did there appear within the workers' movement the first timid initiatives to place film at the service of working-class propaganda. [. . .]

One of the main problems characterizing efforts to present socialist and revolutionary films in earlier years was the fact that none existed. The European and American film industry is firmly in the hands of small, self-contained film concerns, most of which depend on big banking institutions; they either produce directly for nationalistic, bourgeois propaganda purposes or exploit the need for sensation on the part of broad petit-bourgeois strata and present worthless, sensational, cinematic kitsch. It may be stated without exaggeration that today the whole of American and European film production is created from one or the other of these points of view. A change for the better in this regard is not to be expected. Like the capitalist press, film too will be used quite consciously by big capital for purposes of advertising and brainwashing the broad masses. In the struggle against the bourgeois press, it was easier for the working class to establish its own because producing a newspaper is relatively simple and inexpensive. More difficult, nearly impossible, is the production of anticapitalist and antibourgeois films in capitalist countries because for a good film—and only good ones have a chance of exercising a mass effect—the necessary sums are so large that no workers' organization is capable of financing them. A good film with mass scenes and with the necessary technical sophistication costs several hundred thousand gold marks today, with bigger films running from a half-million to a million gold marks. Opposing antiproletarian and bourgeois kitsch films would be altogether impossible were it not that the victory of the proletarian revolution in Soviet Russia changed at least the issue of film production and, with the establishment of the Soviet state, made possible the production of proletarian revolutionary films. In Soviet Russia the film industry, except for small vestiges, is all state operated and engaged in communist enlightenment and propaganda. The Russian cinematic industry, however, has the additional advantage, among others, of producing for a country and a population that alone nearly suffices to absorb and finance its production. The sphere of Soviet state influence today comprises one-seventh of the habitable surface of the globe, 120 million people. Not surprisingly, the Russian film industry suffered the severest setbacks from the war and later from the civil war and the period of War Communism. It is understandable that the state, during the war and while the economy was in complete disarray, would concern itself primarily with grain, coal, food, etc., and that film and the like would have to be pushed aside. But with the gradual strengthening of the Russian economy in recent years, the film industry has been recovering and undergoing steady development. Since 1923 the Russian film industry has once again begun to produce its own films and put them on the market. The most important Russian film producers are the Kinoburo in Kiev for the Ukraine, the Northwest Kinoburo in Leningrad, and the film companies Mezhrabpom-Russ and ProletKino in Moscow. Aside from a number of films serving direct educational purposes, nearly all the films produced in Russia in recent years concern themselves with the problems of the workers' movement, the proletarian revolution, and the fate of individual workers in the movement and revolution.

89

FRIEDRICH WOLF

Art is a Weapon!

First published as "Kunst ist Waffe!" in *Broschüre des Arbeiter-Theater-Bundes Deutschland* (Berlin, 1928), 105–108.

The writer as the conscience of the age!

The writer as prophet! Ever since Cassandra's political prediction of the fall of Troy, the writer's "voice of Cassandra" has usually been made light of and derided. "Writer," comes the response, "stick to your pen!"

Over and over, whenever the ashes of a historical turning point have glowed, whenever politics have become a manifest part of life, writers have joined in and put their shoulders to the wheel. In the states of North America it was a woman writer whose work securely guided the people through a sharp turn, who called forth a great political act with a literary work: Harriet Beecher Stowe! With her world-stirring *Uncle Tom's Cabin*! It was she who summoned public opinion in the northern states to oppose the slaveholding despotism of the South, who issued the first demand for the equality of the Negroes. It came to a battle and to the victory of the northern states, from which the United States emerged. [. . .]

Nor today can genuine dramatists continue to work in airless rooms or in the museum of the past; for them too "the scene becomes a tribunal!" [. . .] The stage becomes the court and conscience of the age! [. . .]

Or, as a well-known theatrical director recently put it in his playbill:

A lack of imagination leaves most people unable to experience even their own lives, not to mention their world. If it were otherwise, reading just a single page in the newspaper would cause humanity to rise up in revolt! So stronger tools are needed. One of them is [. . .] theater!

The newspaper? As the material for a drama? The art dignitaries turn up their noses.

They do not know, or do not want to know what official statistics tell us: that of 510,219 schoolchildren under fourteen years of age in the state of Saxony, 93,936, or nearly 20 percent, are already working; that certain packaging factories enforce working hours for school children of "as long as eleven hours"; that in the Annaberg inspectoral district "children from eight years (!) on were found in the plants." They do not know that every year there are 20,000 certified cases in Germany in which mothers die in the dingy rooms of abortionists as the insane result of Paragraph 218; that none other than the Forty-fifth Conference of German Doctors, meeting in Eisenach in 1925, estimated the annual number of illegal abortions in Germany to be 800,000! How dire must be these women's need! They do not know that, according to the 1922 report of the municipal welfare office in Berlin, 34 percent of those suffering from tuberculosis have no bed of their own—that is, every third coughing tuberculosis patient has to sleep in the same bed with a healthy person for reasons of need! Please do not turn away in disgust and flee to [Goethe's play] *Iphigenia* or to the sublimity of a Gothic cathedral! The average number of inhabitants of a building in London is eight persons; in Paris it is thirty-eight, in Berlin, seventy-six! [. . .]

In all "eternity" there is only one tangible moment: that is the present! The writer who does not see the tragic conflicts of today on our streets, who is not seized by them and overpowered—he has no blood in his veins! He sees the world from his writer's studio or through the dusty windows of the church; but he does not forge ahead into hard, wild, crusty, unadorned life, of which art *today* is a part!

The writer of our present day, who brings to the stage the misery, the struggles, the faith, and defeat of the people on the street, in back houses, factories, and mines—he cannot pull in his claws and offer up sweet promises of the beyond; his thoughts will necessarily take the offensive, his words will be weapons! He will not flee into the past and speak of Charlemagne or the apostle Paul; he will present us with the tragedy of an unemployed worker, the desperate act of a sick, weakened mother carrying her seventh child, the oppression by the Western powers of the awakening colonial peoples, the new arms race in the struggle for oil; or the utter farce of the Lukutate swindle, the grotesque comedy of industrial espionage, the film projects of a high naval office. "Motifs" in masses!

Certainly, it falls far short of workers' theater to deliver steadfast cries of "Long live the world revolution!" to have the actors sing the "Internationale," and to have Lenin make repeated personal appearances on the stage. That is at most "the same old stuff" that very quickly bores workers in particular. A workers' play, precisely a workers' play must also be crafted! It must, in a word, be *good!* No well-intentioned, sensational shocker, but as vital and well-crafted a work as [Sergei] Eisenstein's *Potemkin.* Such a work bowls even its enemies over, opens a path to the future as wide as a house! [. . .]

We have tremendous work before us! Shame on the "writers" for having sung of fantastic little blue blossoms and Charlemagne, while the fellows with shriveled lungs in the mines used to have to dig eight hours beneath the ground and were allowed an average longevity of only forty years. The other twenty to thirty years of life were flatly denied them. No one asked about them. [. . .]

But *art* is neither a means for edification in the hands of pedagogues, headmasters, and bearded scholars imposed upon manual workers "starving for education," nor is it a luxury, caviar or opium that makes us forget the ugly details of "dismal daily life."

Art *today* is a floodlight and a weapon! Just as much a weapon as it was two thousand years ago at the time of Aristophanes's comedies, as much a weapon and an instrument of power as five hundred years ago when the Renaissance popes intimidated the people with paintings of Christ's descent into hell by Raphael and Michelangelo, and built St. Peter's to advertise their earthly power! [. . .]

You writers, you who feel the simple, unmythical misery of our time, give us short works that understand a locksmith, an errand girl, a streetcar conductor, or a washer-woman! Art is always only for the few? Humbug! The greatness of Greek, African, Indian art, the greatness of the words of Christ lies in their being understood by every man.

You workers, come in to the Workers' Theater League, to the Proletarian Fighting Troupe, to the Workers' Megaphone, and, above all, to the People's Film Association! *Film* in particular proves how clearly art is a weapon today! It was certainly not because of its artistic value or its beauty that the industrial magnate [Alfred] Hugenberg bought UFA, the largest of all German film companies. It was suffering severe losses at that time. But Hugenberg saw the potential profits! He recognized the tremendous power represented today by film, since millions go to UFA theaters every day. Film as the invisible weapon in the class struggle, as the tasteless and odorless gas that befogs and stupefies the people with kitsch, with smarmy Rheingold films, pale Nibelungs, and Fausts! [. . .]

What a genuine workers' theater, a film production company of the workers' own, could mean for the dissemination, development, and the fighting power of the socialist idea is unimaginable!

A flag, a sword, a power, a weapon!

90

WALTER BENJAMIN

Program for a Proletarian Children's Theater

Programm eines proletarischen Kindertheaters, written in 1928, posthumously published.

Every proletarian movement, once it breaks away from the pattern of parliamentary discussion, sees the power of the new generation, among the many forces which it suddenly faces unprepared, as the strongest, yet also the most dangerous. The self-complacency of parliamentary stupidity comes from the fact that the adults keep to themselves. In contrast, mere phrases have no power over children. In a year, one can get the children throughout a country to mimic these phrases. But the real question is how to insure that in ten or twenty years the party program will be the basis for action. And mere phrases are incapable of accomplishing this.

Proletarian education must be built from the party program, or to be more exact, it must be built out of class consciousness. However, the party program is not itself the instrument of a class-conscious education because the ideology, although extremely important, reaches the child only as empty words. We ask very simply, but we shall not stop asking, what the instruments for a class-conscious education of proletarian children are. We will not be concerned here with their advanced scholarly training, since children can, indeed must, be taught in a proletarian fashion (in technical science, class history, rhetoric, etc.) at a much younger age. We begin at age four.

The bourgeois education of younger children is unsystematic, and this corresponds to the class situation of the bourgeoisie. Of course the bourgeoisie has its educational system. The inhumanity of its contents betrays itself precisely in the fact that it fails in early childhood. Only that which is true can be effective with children of this age. The proletarian education of small children must first of all distinguish itself from bourgeois education through its system. System here, however, means a frame. It would be a completely unbearable situation for the proletariat if, as in bourgeois kindergartens, a new method with the latest psychological refinements were introduced into its pedagogic system every six months. Everywhere, and pedagogics is no exception, interest in the method is an essentially bourgeois attitude; it is the ideology of laziness, of muddling along in the same direction. First and foremost, then, proletarian education needs a frame, a relevant area *within* which the child is educated. Not, as with the bourgeoisie, an idea to which he is educated.

We shall now show why the frame of proletarian education from age four to fourteen is the proletarian children's theater.

The education of the child requires that *his total life be affected*.

Proletarian education requires that *the child be educated in a circumscribed area*.

That is the positive dialectic of the question. Only on the stage does all life in its unlimited fullness appear framed and as a circumscribed area; therefore, the proletarian children's theater is the dialectically determined place of education for the proletarian child. [. . .]

The children's theater has nothing in common with that of the present-day bourgeoisie. The theater of the present-day bourgeoisie is economically determined by profit; sociologically, both on and off the stage, it is first and foremost an instrument of sensationalism. Not so the proletarian children's theater. Just as the first act of the Bolsheviks was to raise the red flag so their first instinct was to organize the children. In this organization, the proletarian children's theater developed as the center, the basic motif of bolshevik education. This fact can be tested by its opposite. The proof checks out: there is nothing that the bourgeoisie considers so dangerous for children as the theater. This is not just a carry-over from the old bourgeois bugaboo that traveling actors steal children. Far more, the intimidated bourgeois consciousness struggles here against perceiving the most powerful force of the future summoned up in children by the theater. And this consciousness demands that bourgeois educators put a ban on children's theater. [. . .]

In order to have a fruitful effect, proletarian children's theaters relentlessly demand a collective as their audience. In other words, the class. Just as conversely only the working class possesses an unerring eye for the existence of collectives. Such collectives are the people's assembly, the army, the factory. But the child is also such a collective. And the working class is privileged in having the most open eyes for seeing the children's collective that the bourgeoisie can never discern. This collective radiates not only the most forceful powers but also the most current ones. Indeed, the topicality of children's patterns and behavior is unparalleled. (We refer to the well-known exhibitions of the latest children's drawings.)

By putting a cold stop to the "moral personage" within the director, enormous forces are set free for the real genius of education: observation. This alone is the heart of unsentimental love. In nine-tenths of all cases of knowing better and wanting to do the right thing, the teacher's love is good for nothing because there is no observation of the child's life, and this stifles the child's very spirit and desire. Such love is sentimental and vain. To the observer, however, (and this is where education begins) every action and gesture of the child becomes a signal. These are not so much, as psychologists like to think, signals of the unconscious, of latent powers, repressions, or censors; instead they proceed out of a world in which the child lives and gives commands. The new knowledge of children which has been developed in the Soviet children's clubs has led to the thesis that the child lives in his world as dictator. Hence a "theory of signals" is no mere figure of speech. Almost every child's gesture is command and signal in a realm which, only occasionally, extremely gifted men have revealed. The foremost of these was [the Romantic poet and novelist] Jean Paul.

It is the task of the director to rescue the children's signals out of the dangerous magic realm of mere fantasy and to bring them to bear on the material. [. . .]

Every child's gesture is a creative impulse that corresponds exactly to the receptive one. The developing of these gestures into various forms of expression, such as the production of theatrical props, paintings, recitation, dance, and improvisation, falls to the separate sections.

In all of these, improvisation is central; for in the final analysis the performance is merely their improvised synthesis. Improvisation rules; it is the condition from which the signals, the signal-giving gestures, arise. And that is precisely why performance or theater must be the synthesis of these gestures, for it alone has the unintended, one-time-only particularity in which the child's gesture finds its true place. What is tortured out of children as an outright "performance" can never compare to the genuineness of improvisation. [. . .]

The inferiority of bourgeois education and of the young bourgeois generation has recently given vent to the movement for "youth culture." The conflict which this new tendency is determined to conceal lies in the claims that bourgeois society (like all political societies) makes on the energies of youth, which can never be excited in an immediately political manner. Especially the energies of children. Youth culture is presently attempting a hopeless compromise. It empties youthful enthusiasm by means of idealistic self-reflection so that, imperceptibly, the formal ideologies of German idealism can be replenished with bourgeois class contents. The proletariat cannot pass its class interests onto the young generation through the unfair means of an ideology which is geared to suppress the child's suggestibility. The discipline which the bourgeoisie demands from its children is its stigma. The proletariat disciplines only the maturing proletarians; its ideological class education begins with puberty. Proletarian education proves its superiority by guaranteeing to children the fulfillment of their childhood. The space in which this education takes place does not thereby need to be isolated from the area of class struggle. Modes of play can, indeed perhaps must, find space for the contents and symbols of class struggle. However, these cannot exert real control over the child. Nor is this required. For the proletariat does not need all the thousands of little words by which the bourgeoisie masks class struggles in its own pedagogy. The "unprejudiced," "understanding," "empathetic" bourgeois practices, the "child-loving" teachers—these we can do without.

The performance is the great creative pause in the educational enterprise. It is in the realm of children what the carnival was to the ancient cults. Everything is turned upside down, and just as master served slave during the Roman Saturnalia, so during the performance, children stand on stage and teach and educate their attentive educators. [. . .]

In this children's theater lies a power that will overthrow the pseudorevolutionary behavior of the recent bourgeois theater. For what is truly revolutionary in effect is not the propaganda of ideas that here and there excites actions that cannot be consummated, and which are dismissed at the theater exit in the first sober moment of reflection. What is truly revolutionary in effect is the *secret signal* of what will come to be, which speaks from the gesture of children.

91

JOHANNES R. BECHER

Our Front

First published as "Unsere Front," *Die Linkskurve* 1, no. 1 (August 1928), 1–3.

Once our front has become what it could be and for which, in our view, the necessary forces are at hand, then the moment of our gathering here will not only carry significance for all of proletarian revolutionary literature but will be a decisive event in the history of the working-class movement.

The front did not arise from mere theory, it is not the design of somebody's brain; it was not founded the way so much is founded. No—back when our works and our comrades were being persecuted by class justice, we banded together under the pressure and remained banded together: and the front was there. What we have to do today is to confirm this fact, to say that the way it happened was good, and to go a step farther.

A host of tasks immediately faces a front of proletarian revolutionary writers.

Our front is above all the practical statement, the living proof, of the existence of a proletarian revolutionary literature. It is there and cannot be denied. You are all aware that the possibility of its existence has been disputed not only in the bourgeois camp but also well within revolutionary circles. We believe in this "literature from below," and our primary effort is devoted to its development. We hope that it will be the sharpest and most useful artistic–literary weapon in the class struggle; it—not the bourgeois radical intellectuals—represents the first front. We cannot simply wait for our literature, sit there with folded arms and moan that it has not yet emerged with the glory of a masterpiece. Those who would put their wagers only on such finished results prove definitively that they understand nothing of growth and development. It is not possible to wait for the literature from below; it must be stimulated and carefully cultivated. We must apply all of our energies to the encouragement of a powerful new generation of writers, writers who have learned from our mistakes and who succeed in lending simple, persuasive form to the unambiguous content of class struggle. We need young proletarian writers who eschew all formal games and dilettantism, who are immune to ideological vagueness and the exaltation of feeling and thought. This literary generation is there. It wants to grow. With it we stand or fall. This young generation is the glue holding our front together.

Now, our front, if it wants to be viable and fulfill the tasks confronting it, may neither indulge in the celebration of names nor tolerate namelessness. Here in our ranks everyone must be devoted to learning. The central characteristic of the proletarian revolutionary writer is precisely his modesty, the knowledge that he is nothing more than an organizer of the experiences of others. The proletarian revolutionary writer does not live for himself; he is in service to his class and therefore to humanity. Thousands, uncounted hundreds of thousands, are collaborators in his work, and he—what he does is voice and expound that which happens all around him, is felt and thought through him.

The times are not such that we need fear being inundated. These are not times in which revolutionary parasites will infiltrate our ranks to skim off the cream. We are not living in the fat years of the revolution; we are living in times that are lean and bitter for every revolutionary. This fact in particular offers us the security that those who are with us today will remain with us, tomorrow and the day after, when it is once again do or die. And I believe I am speaking for everyone when I say that just as we, as members of the front, are prepared today to fight for our cause with our pens, so will we also be prepared when it becomes necessary to fight not only with the weapon of the pen.

I see a further task of the front in the need for self-clarification. Marxist theory has advanced to a high degree of perfection in regard to politics and the economy. The application of Marxism to literature, Marxist criticism, Marxist aesthetics, remains in essential aspects an unresearched area in which there is still much to be done.

You will agree with me when I designate as one of the front's tasks an openly critical confrontation with ourselves. In contrast to the poets and writers of the Soviet Union, we are not in the position of organizing mass criticism, for example, by having books discussed in a cell and listening to authors speak and answer questions. We are in the desperate position that nothing like creative criticism exists at all in Germany today. Not even on our own side is there any such edifying criticism as that which Franz Mehring pursued in exemplary fashion. We also pass much too quickly and uncritically over the most important events. The enervated, squanderous atmosphere created by the bourgeois practice of literature—we are subject to that as well and its notorious apathy eats its way into us. We pass by each other, over each other, function at cross purposes. The potential for learning from each other, elevating each other, is minimized by this lack of mutuality. We want to become a collective, although not one in which our names are merely listed one after the other and we, as individuals, have fundamentally nothing to do with each other. A collective cannot be conjured into existence, it must be achieved by effort. The front is an initial step, the modest beginning of such a collective—we are struggling toward the same goal, permeated by the same world view. Our paths might not be entirely the same, but we are all willing to take the shortest and quickest path that leads to our common goal.

In such a front it will also be possible to achieve what must be closest to our hearts as poets and writers: the discussion of questions of craft. The techniques of writing and composition, linguistic problems, and formal organization, are matters that we must treat effectively to create effective and powerful works. Particularly in recent years, manifold problems of this sort have arisen, without them having been discussed, even cursorily, before a larger group.

It goes without saying that our front must take up the struggle against all forms of bourgeois literature, and even against a certain type of so-called working-class writing. The precondition of such a struggle is knowledge of the literature from the opposing camp. Investigations will have to be undertaken to see whether there are elements in the literature of the past and present from which we can learn or which we, having made the necessary corrections, should adopt. We must break out of isolation, take leave of our wallflower existence. There remains something to be said—for some a primary concern—about presses, newspapers, magazines, about the chances given to us as prole-tarian revolutionary writers to put our works before the public. I am sure that this topic will be so abundantly treated in our future meetings that I need not speak further about it today.

The range of our tasks is therefore extensive—is immense, for we must make up for past omissions. We need a certain degree of discipline and organizational caution to accomplish what we must. If we do not move rashly, but approach our work calmly and soberly, we will succeed.

Who is a revolutionary proletarian writer? One who sees the world from the standpoint of the revolutionary proletariat and lends it form.

Here I continue in the words of Maxim Gorky:

You ask me, "What are the marks of a true proletarian writer?" I do not believe that there are very many. Among them belongs the writer's active hatred of everything that oppresses the people from without, and also from within, of what-ever hinders the free development and growth of human abilities; a relentless hatred of laziness and all types of parasites, of triviality, of hypocrites and do-nothings. . . . The best of all the theories thought up by sincere or clever prophets is the theory of evolution, of the slow, gradual development of the form of civic life. But sincerity and cleverness are all the same in the end. You already know that the "evolution" of capitalist society led to four years of bloody carnage in which many of the healthiest people were destroyed, and that the socialists who put their faith in the deliverance of "evolution" were pulled into the carnage, that this war turned "civilized" Europe unbelievably savage, that the number of scoundrels feeding off the blood multiplied enormously—that this "evolution" is now threatening with a new, even more terrible carnage. And you know that the plan for general disar-mament proposed by the Soviet Union has been rejected by those "cultured" men of Europe who believe in the redeeming theory of evolution. You must understand and constantly keep before your eyes the fact that the disgraceful cowardice of the League of Nations represents nothing other than the final bankruptcy of European culture and class society, which has revealed its antihumanitarian essence. And if you want to be honest people, you must be revolutionaries . . .

In 1905 Maxim Gorky cried: "Go to the people! Struggle with them! Help them rise up from their knees!"

Today in 1928 we can cry: "Go with the proletariat! Join the class struggle! Struggle alongside it in things great and small! Use your art as a weapon! Declare war on war!"

Our front should form a comradely bond between writers. It should create a tie between ourselves and the masses. The struggle of the working class is our vital element; we want to sink our roots ever deeper into proletarian soil. And the front should bind us yet more firmly to the cause we serve, to the great cause of the social revolution, which is the best cause in the world.

The more firmly we bind ourselves in this way, the freer we become. We have recognized the essence of bourgeois freedom, which is a freedom of the individual at the cost of bestial unfreedom for the majority of people. We embrace the freedom of socialism, which is a freedom of people not against one another, but a freedom of people together. We embrace the struggle for this freedom, the revolutionary class struggle . . .

I spoke at the beginning of how this moment can become a decisive event in the history of the working-class movement.

I want to say openly in conclusion what I believe: the realization of our goal lies with us and only with us.

To work in this spirit!

92

A Survey on Proletarian Writing

First published as "Eine Rundfrage über proletarische Dichtung," *Die literarische Welt* 5, no. 28 (July 12, 1929), 3–4.

I

Proletarian writers (in the artistic–revolutionary sense as represented more than 150 years ago, following the emancipatory movement of the bourgeois classes, by the bourgeois writers of the *Sturm und Drang* era) have not yet been produced by German literature. This is not meant to deny that already before the social revolution there were writings whose social convictions quite clearly touched upon—or even recorded—the proletarian milieu. But even if I were to list these few writers by name, recognizing Heinrich Heine, [Georg] Herwegh, Georg Büchner, [Ferdinand] Freiligrath, Gerhart Hauptmann, Heinrich Mann, and Richard Dehmel as the leading figures, I would nevertheless not be justified in concealing the fact that all of them, more or less intensively, represent products and adherents (as well as suppliers) of the bourgeois-capitalist world. Nor is this statement altered in the slightest by the observation that the works created by these writers have been recognized as valuable by the proletariat and its affective milieu and made into staple items in its heritage. [. . .]

II

But it still has nothing to do with proletarian writing if members of socialist parties (or their well-disposed neighbors and the like) have adopted the words *factory, mine shaft, machine, barricades,* and *revolution* as their setting and against such backgrounds executed political fireworks crackling with journalistic depictions and social criticism in the style of bad bourgeois literary works. As admirable as the public aesthetic profession of socialist convictions might be, and although it might even possess a suggestive power capable of drumming the half-hearted and sluggish inhabitants of the same proletarian misery to the wakefulness of a decisive act, literature devoted merely to milieu and convictions has nothing in common with the manifestation of an active, new, proletarian aesthetic will.

III

Nevertheless, there must emerge from the economic and intellectual struggle for proletarian independence a proletarian aesthetic will into which flow all the elements responsible in a historical–sociological sense for lending form and content to a work of art. Critical here will not be the pertinent words but, much more, the proletarian ethic, where the single individual disappears self-sacrificially and without objection into the great fiery arch of the universal community. Only from the active, collective consciousness and sense of being-in-the-world, that is, will proletarian writers be able to derive the artistic power capable of raising them to the status of creative shapers of universal, proletarian revolutionary feeling. [. . .]

Rudolf Braune writes:

You ask me whether the seeds of a coming culture are forming within the German working class, that is in a certain sense, islands are forming that some time later will merge together in a great proletarian continent.

You depart from a false assumption. The German worker has no desire for a coming culture. He wants a roof over his head and respectable work in respectable conditions for a just wage; he wants to have enough to sate himself and his family. And he wants to have time to be able to look at the things he doesn't care a bit about now: theater, art, museums, and concert halls. How that is supposed to come about, he doesn't know. He has only a vague idea that all these things won't be as they are now. But that is also just one thing. His interest today is justifiably focused on more important things: his wages and the length of the workday. He doesn't want to be tricked and does want to take up his own cause. You see, the German worker thinks in just these simple, plebeian terms. He can imagine nothing of a coming culture. He therefore regards vegetarians with some pity, immigrants with great distrust, and intellectuals with scorn. With justice. That is why an intellectual who has examined the matter and understood the motivating forces at work is far from having to "betray the mind for the masses" (as someone recently put it so nicely). If an intellectual worker joins the ranks, doesn't command, doesn't prattle nice little speeches, and just keeps his trap shut, no worker is going to look at him askance. The German worker needs comrades and fellow fighters, not pretty talkers painting the future utopia in brilliant colors.

I'm speaking here of the skilled core of the German working class. Seeds of a coming culture? These seeds are forming in the organizations of political struggle. For example, in its weekend schools, instructional courses, and basic knowledge circles, the prohibited but vital Red Front Fighting League is accomplishing enormous cultural work that remains invisible to outsiders. Workers learn there how to speak, how to express themselves; they learn how to think, how to think dialectically. In these small courses the thrust into the future is being prepared.

Reading matter? Our workers reach hungrily for everything, often reaching wrongly. Fortunately, at least, the shooting-gallery figures of so-called working-class writers, who neither can nor want to conceal their assimilation, or the attitude of the proletarian aristocracy, are largely unknown to the German working class. Aside from these heroes, however, the circle of proletarian revolutionary German writers that is just now developing is tinged with the unhealthy clichés of the bourgeois novelist. Content with reversed emblems and slogans isn't enough. A clear, rounded form that meets the workers' imaginative power and sense of class half-way, such a form that distances itself consciously from the style of the literary papas, we haven't yet found in the German novel (though we likely have in the poetry of [Johannes] Becher and [Oskar] Kanehl).

And because the workers sense this vacuum, they do the only thing possible. They read (alongside real trash that can't do them much harm) the daily newspaper, union papers, plant papers, and political brochures. They study theory. The popular editions of Marx, Engels, [Nikolai] Bukharin, and Lenin have attained printings in recent years that compete with even the best bestsellers.

There in the unknown territory, in the hearts of the workers, in solidarity actions, in the factories, in the secret work of the cells, in the grandiose struggle in the Ruhr district at the end of 1928, in this month's lockout of the Silesian weavers, in the fourteen-week strike of the Henningsdorf steel-mill workers, there where theory is being tested in practice, where literature is a trifle and the class front is everything, that is where innovative elements are forming.

93

OTTO BIHA

The Proletarian Mass Novel

First published as "Der proletarische Massenroman. Eine neue Eine-Mark-Serie des 'Internationalen Arbeiterverlages,'" *Die Rote Fahne*, no. 178 (August 2, 1930).

Literary activity must become a constituent element of organized, planned, unified Party work.

LENIN

The fight for the conquest of the majority of the working class will doubtlessly be fought on the cultural front as well as elsewhere. Along this front, literature is one of the most important means by which the ruling class maintains its power. It influences the masses by the millions and contributes to their development. Reactionary literary trash more than anything else exercises a devastating influence on the consciousness of the masses.

Gigantic editions, millions of books, and a tower of printed paper issue daily from the world's printing presses. Ready-made wares for the mind which penetrate the pores of social life with startling speed and stubborn persistance. On their assembly lines of the mind, Scherl and Ullstein [publishers] produce ideology for the world, extremely dangerous poisonous gas deployed on the cultural front.

In overcrowded waiting rooms, on the morning subway, the imaginations of millions in industrial centers everywhere follow romanticized reports on the fate of the self-made man, of the little man who achieved success, of the upright fellow who amounts to something, while the readers continue their daily race on the treadmill of a cheerless reality. This romanticism accompanies them home to their miserable quarters and conjures the dream of luxury and reality on the grey walls of their lives. It fills the lending libraries in working-class neighborhoods; it resides in the coat pockets of the unemployed in the relief lines; it pursues those no longer eligible for aid into homeless shelters and the sick into hospitals.

These mass novels of the classless idyll and economic peace parade their slogans: The way is clear for the diligent! All for patience and order, for love of the fatherland and humility, for the sanctity of property! They are more dangerous than the so-called great literature of the bourgeoisie.

In its struggle for the masses, the party must repel this literature. The *red mass novel* will help it to do so. The novel that, instead of depicting personal conflicts and private passions, gives shape to the conflicts of our time and the *struggle of the masses* by depicting the fate of individuals in their actual interactions inside the class struggle in society. No less gripping and entertaining but aglow with the *fighting will of the working class,* the red novel has to carry the ideology of revolutionary consciousness to oppressed people of all sorts.

Thus far in its forward advance, proletarian revolutionary literature has primarily taken note of the supreme achievements of bourgeois literature. This is a mistake that has only recently been rectified. It is necessary to repel the literature of the class enemy in its entirety: from the leading works to [Hedwig] Courths-Mahler and, beyond this, to the countless examples of contaminating literary trash.

Here is where the proletarian one-mark novel, which will begin to appear from the International Workers' Press in the next few days, should and will intervene.

The first books in this series—Hans Marchwitza's *Assault on Essen,* the novel of a revolutionary coalminer; Klaus Neukrantz's *Barricades in Wedding,* the novel of Bloody May [Day] in 1929; Willy Bredel's *N & K Machine-works,* a report on proletarian daily life—as well as a series of other novels (which will be extensively reviewed when they appear) will breach the lines of enemy literature. These novels are born of the political reality of our time; they depict life in the factories, pits, and rental blocks—the life of the proletariat. The plan calls for high-quality literature filled with class spirit, and the red mass novel begins its march. It must truly become the red novel of the masses.

94

HANNS EISLER

Progress in the Workers' Music Movement

First published as "Fortschritte in der Arbeitermusikbewegung," *Kampfmusik* 4 (1931), 113–115.

The workers' music movement has now entered a new phase of planned experiment. It is significant that this new and fruitful phase, which is already showing some theoretical and practical results, appears at a moment when the *Deutscher Arbeitersängerbund* (DASB-German Workers' Choral Society), the chief organization of the workers' music movement, has formed a vigorous revolutionary opposition to the narrow-minded reformist leadership within its ranks.

The obstacle to progress lies mainly in the false ideas about music and the difficulty in combating them. The anarchic bourgeois music business produces a kind of music fetishism with the result that broad masses of the people are only able to take in music in its stupidest, most dangerous, but above all its most acceptable, soporific form. Moreover, technical devices—the record player and radio—are organizing this flight from reality on a mass scale. The reformists have no desire to change things in this respect, they only endeavor to clothe the narcotic possibilities in a more noble mantle, on the principle that the farther removed from reality the nobler.

The progress achieved stems mainly from the revolutionary opposition in the DASB. A circle was formed spontaneously at the Marxist School for Workers after a course on an historical–materialist approach to music, where, in addition to working-class officials a number of left-wing musicologists and music theoreticians took part, and this circle is attempting to apply the method of dialectical materialism to music. A number of specialists from the bourgeois camp have also come over to the side of the revolutionary workers. Together with Karl Rankl, composers and conductors like Josef Schmidt, Vladimir Vogel, Karl Vollmer, Ernst Hermann Meyer, and others should be mentioned.

With regard to progress, experience has taught us that we must make a difference between music to listen to and music to perform. In arriving at this formulation we had to break with conventional opinions on choral singing. For us it was no longer enough for a piece to have an effect on the listeners because it was well sung by a choir: we had to find methods to revolutionize the singers as well, not to regard them simply as interpreters. We were forced to broach the question of revolutionizing the working-class singers because for years and years they of the DASB had been singing a number of revolutionary songs yet remained reformists in political life. One contribution to a solution of this question was [Bertolt Brecht's play] *Die Massnahme* [Measures Taken].

The activities of the agit-prop groups brought to light the great contradictions between the "serious" songs of choirs and the topical fighting songs. We are now trying to change the extraordinary situation in which the workers' choral movement has not produced a single fighting song for the mass movement during the last ten years. Because of this their audiences are forced into the same position as concert listeners; in the agit-prop groups it is different. Yet we are well aware that it is wrong only to listen to a fighting song; that the activating purpose of a fighting song can only be achieved if the people sing it themselves. Unemployed workers from the Fichte organization spontaneously formed a small agit-prop choir and taught new fighting songs to the audiences at mass meetings.

Concerning the style of revolutionary music, we formulated the following: the style, that is, the method of organizing the tones, should vary according to the purpose of the music. A song of struggle to be sung by the people in the audience must be constructed differently from a choral work with a theoretical content. So our aesthetic standards are not inflexible, but when composing we take into consideration the revolutionary purpose for which we are writing.

Further experience induced us to reject the concert form. The concert form arose in the epoch of the bourgeoisie and is useless for the purposes of the revolutionary working class. It can only offer noncommitted pleasure and make the listener passive. In the next few years it will be our task to develop further the ideas of the didactic play in practical experiment.

Summarizing, we can say that all the attempts made and the progress achieved were and are only possible in close association with the militant working class. First we must never forget that those cultural organizations which sever their connections with the political organizations of the working class will necessarily become shallow and petit-bourgeois.

We must not become too easy-going or be satisfied with the usual effects of music, but must aspire to something more than that, examining and improving our methods again and again so that the wonderful tasks that the class struggle places before music can be accomplished.

95

GEORG LUKÁCS

Willi Bredel's Novels

First published as "Über Willi Bredels Romane," *Die Linkskurve* 3, no. 11 (November 1931), 23–27.

I. FOR DIALECTICS AS A LITERARY PRINCIPLE

Bredel's two novels hold an important place in the development of proletarian revolutionary literature in Germany. With the happy combination of both genuine talent and militant class standpoint, Bredel has chosen themes that are not only central to the interest of every worker, but open up a new landscape for all readers. Neither of his subjects, the effects of the beginnings of rationalization on the working class, and the everyday life and struggle of a proletarian tenement block, have ever before been depicted in Germany from the proletarian class position.

This is no small thing. And yet it is by no means the whole of Bredel's achievement. In the organization of his subject-matter and the construction of his works, he shows a skilled hand, a sure political instinct and a militant combativeness. His first novel was already well constructed in this way, with its description of the preparation, outbreak and defeat of a strike in a factory. Here Bredel not only creates the outlines of a lively plot, through which the details of everyday working-class life are translated into elements and stages of the class struggle; over and above this, he shows that the entire action is only a single moment in the class war as a whole, which began before the novel opens, and will continue with undiminished vigor after the present battle is lost. This is undoubtedly a correct pattern for a proletarian novel. For it offers the possibility of fitting the whole significant class development within the factory (the struggle of the workers against the capitalists, the intervention of state power, the stratification of the workers, political divisions, the role of the social democrats and the trade union, the life of the Communist cells, etc.) into an artistic composition, which even though it forms a coherent narrative entity, still has no absolute beginning or end, but is portrayed as one part of the overall process.

The composition of the second novel marks a further step forward in this direction. Here Bredel extends still further the framework of his composition, setting himself the correct and important goal of depicting the life of the workers in concrete interaction with that of the other classes, in particular the petite bourgeoisie. Both politically and artistically this goal is absolutely correct, and an important development. For most works of our proletarian revolutionary literature suffer from the defect of taking as their theme either the contradiction between bosses and workers within the factory, or else that between the workers' state and the bourgeois state in a situation of acute class warfare—a narrowing of the field that sometimes even amounts to "economism." In this way, the political horizon is narrowed from one which, while "national in form," poses the question at an overall level, to the isolated emphasis on a single aspect, no matter how important this might be. And this inevitably leads also to narrowness, insufficiency and impoverishment from the artistic standpoint as well. It is against this tendency that Bredel stands out with such boldness and vigor. The content of this novel is the life of a working-class tenement. Here both workers and petite bourgeoisie of the most varied levels and political tendencies, Communists, social democrats, Nazis, apolitical, etc., live closely together and come into contact with one another in the most varied of ways in the course of their everyday life. A rent strike, and at the close of the book the Hamburg elections, provide the nucleus of the story around which the most diverse episodes of proletarian and petit-bourgeois life are colorfully hung, both political (Nazi attacks, demonstrations, etc.), and private (an abortion tragedy, childbirth, the pawnshop, etc.). Here again, we have a picture that is correctly conceived from the standpoint of its content, and thus once again has genuine epic potential: once more the framework and pattern for a fine proletarian revolutionary novel.

Unfortunately, however, in both cases it is no more than a framework or pattern, an outline and no more. For Bredel's novels fail to develop far beyond the conception stage. To summarize the basic weakness in Bredel's artistic creation, we can say that there is an artistically unresolved contradiction between the broad narrative framework of his story, which includes everything that it essentially requires, and his manner of telling it, which is partly a kind of journalistic reportage, and partly a kind of public speech. The bare bones of the novel are correct, but there is nothing more than these bare bones. What is needed to make them come alive, i.e. living human beings, with living, changing and developing relationships between them, is as good as completely lacking. True, Bredel does provide sketches of his various characters, describing quite well, even, their external features, and emphasizing certain of their character traits, etc. But the whole thing still remains rigid. His characters fail to grow and develop. At most, they change suddenly overnight. Not that this is inherently impossible, but it works only if it is artistically prepared, if there is a transformation from quantity (i.e. small changes that might well remain unnoticed even for the people who undergo them) to quality, and not just a sudden pistol-shot. This unprepared and sudden transformation fails to ring true in its artistic effect even if it is abstractly possible. Bredel's characters, therefore, turn out to be little more than what in theatrical language used to be called '*Chargen*' [stereotypes]: they possess a fixed and characteristic feature (possibly more than one), which is repeated and underlined at every possible (and even impossible) opportunity. But in this way the characters fail to come alive, even if these features are observed correctly. A novel simply demands a different kind of characterization than a journalistic report: what may be good enough for the one is completely inadequate for the other. [. . .]

Many comrades will certainly think this criticism too hard. But its author is only applying the words that Comrade Stalin expressed in regard to another literary question: "Since when have Bolsheviks feared the truth?" Our proletarian revolutionary literature has had to fight for its existence, and has proved its right to exist in hard struggle. Our proletarian revolutionary writers are proven and devoted soldiers of their class. And now, when the tasks facing us on all fronts of the class struggle are greater than ever, they must not lag behind the general movement. On the contrary, they must confront their failings by unsparing self-criticism, unembellished exposure of this backwardness and its causes, and by setting themselves tasks that correspond to the general level of development of the revolutionary class struggle. By tenacious and deliberate work, by learning to deploy materialist dialectics in literary creation, they must eliminate these weaknesses as quickly as possible. [. . .]

96

LEAGUE OF PROLETARIAN-REVOLUTIONARY WRITERS

To All Proletarian-Revolutionary Writers, To All Workers' Correspondents

First published as "An alle proletarisch-revolutionäre Schriftsteller, an alle Arbeiterkorrespondenten," *Die Linkskurve* 3, no. 12 (December 1931), 12–13.

As long as a year ago, at gatherings with the revolutionary working class, at mass criticism evenings, and at meetings with the various proletarian culture organizations, we were met with the following reproach: although we could point to a certain success within the scope of the proletarian feuilleton (short stories, reportage, proletarian revolutionary poetry), we were still lacking any good, cheap proletarian novels (as a dam against the filth spread among the masses by Scherl, Ullstein, and hundreds of other bourgeois presses); still more important, we had neglected dime and twenty-cent collections of feuilleton material to counter the flood of disgusting detective novels, bittersweet, inflammatory missionary stories, and backstairs bourgeois kitsch. References were also made in this connection to precisely how important these dime and twenty-cent collections were: first because the proletariat really would buy them by the tens of thousands, for it is indeed already buying approximately 500,000 mass political brochures—not per year but per month; and second because such collections would far exceed the dissemination of mass political brochures, would extend into working-class circles that have not yet been reached by political propaganda.

We promised to create such a literature, but we have not kept our promise. To be sure, proletarian novels have appeared; approximately 300,000 have been distributed as one-mark novels. But the dime and twenty-penny collections are still lacking. Longer stories narrating the life of the working class have still not appeared. That represents a lacuna within the advance of proletarian literature that cannot be reproved sharply enough, and we must do everything to fill it in as quickly as possible. Why are they lacking? Certainly there are enough themes: stories of informers, lengthier reportages, biographical narratives, reports of on-going struggles (in Leuna, Hamburg, Essen, Munich), strike stories, back-alley narratives. The topics, then, are there—hundreds of topics. It is simply necessary that they be written down.

We are now entering the Month of the Proletarian Book for the third time. Workers will reproach us everywhere, and with the same justification as last year, that they will not be able to order good dime collections of feuilletons, in addition to other literature, and distribute them in plants, apartment blocks, and unemployment offices. Indeed, they will no doubt sharpen their reproaches; they will say to us that it is all but criminal, given the general campaign for the united front of the working masses against fascism, that we have not written and published stories to aid in the spread of our slogans to the farthest reaches of the working population. Let us therefore see to it that we can at least answer these reproaches with the claim that we are now at work creating this literature. But at the same time let us see to it that our proletarian dime collections do not become colportage in the bourgeois sense, that we do not, that is, begin where bourgeois colportage began in 1890—with backstairs romanticism—and where it remains today; for the bourgeoisie cares not that the colportage it floods upon the masses of workers and petite bourgeoisie is worth anything. Our dime collections have to be far above average in every respect. If we succeed in creating not simply an inexpensive literature but one that is valuable in literary terms, then we will have reached a new stage in the struggle for good proletarian literature, then we will have created—even more important in the moment—another useful weapon in the struggle of the revolutionary proletariat for bread and freedom!

Executive Committee
League of Proletarian, Revolutionary Writers

97

GÜNTHER D. DEHM

[Berlin Workers' District]

First published in *Proletarische Jugend. Lebensgestaltung und Gedankenwelt der großstädtischen Proletarierjugend* (Berlin: Fusche-Verlag, n.d.), 16–19.

The working-class district, residence to many civil servants and tolerably well-off members of the middle classes, is heavily bourgeois in the center but becomes increasingly proletarian as one proceeds outward. We are a pure workers' community, with 95 to 97 percent of the inhabitants proletarian in sociological terms. The remaining 3 to 5 percent is made up of low- and middle-level civil servants, merchants, and landlords. The landlords played a certain role earlier, as, so to speak, the bourgeois *pièce de résistance* in the swelling sea of the masses. There are still some Berlin landlords of the old stamp, broad-minded and eager for progress, thrifty and orderly (alongside, admittedly, the greedy and inconsiderate), but only a few. Many buildings belong to foreigners or companies. Members of the upper social classes do not live in our community. The highest civil-service category is that of a secretary. The dozen doctors living here are all Jewish. Two rectors have their official residences in our community. Scarcely three or four teachers live in this "bad" district. A consequence of the economic instability of recent years, one occasionally meets people here who used to be prosperous but have become impoverished. A number of business people are tolerably situated, but we lack a single rich or even just prosperous man in the community. The real mass of the population consists of a stratum of workers living in relatively stable conditions, most of whom work in the large factories nearby. Right in the neighborhood are big plants owned by General Electric [AEG] and Siemens, as well as a few machinist works: Ludwig Löwe, Freund, and Berlin-Anhalter, among others. We have no real lumpenproletariat. Prostitutes and pimps are scarcely to be found. There are a few transient lodgings. Most of the workers are in the metal trades; next in number come the host of unskilled laborers. Very many women and girls work in the Osram plant, which produces light bulbs. Skilled workers earn fifty to sixty marks a week, unskilled thirty to forty; women factory workers often get no more than fifteen to twenty marks. . . .

Economic crises are very noticeable here. Unemployment is a spectre constantly haunting the community. If a downturn lasts for a long time it causes severe economic hardship. Relief support is just barely sufficient to pay the rent and procure the essential foodstuffs. If the father has work, then the family more or less gets through it. Things are better if there are grown children who earn money. They usually pay only a very little for board, but mutual support is the rule in emergencies. In other aspects of life, the most important thing is having good clothes.

When people can afford it, they also eat rather well. Apartment conditions, however, are very bleak. The buildings are large blocks of rental flats from the 1880s and 1890s. There was some consideration taken then that the courtyards not be too small. Old Berlin is often much worse in this respect. But it is bad enough here. There are side- and cross-wings everywhere, occasionally even two or three. One cannot, of course, speak of courtyard lawns. Nor does one dare call the rear building the garden house. Most of the apartments have one room and a kitchen; the ones at the front are mostly two rooms and a kitchen. Three rooms are rare; four are found only in the few best buildings. A number of buildings have studios, that is, apartments that consist only of a single room. Sometimes clever landlords have gotten the idea of renting each room in an apartment individually, including the hallway. The poorest of the proletariat live there. But I have not yet encountered here the chalk-line system (two families in one room). There are no bath facilities anywhere. The common lavatory for the inhabitants of a floor (three to four families) is usually located down a half flight of stairs.

On the whole, one is continually amazed at how fundamentally peaceful and orderly the people who live here are. Of course there is a bar in every third building, and no shortage of customers in it. And of course there is the noise of drunks on the streets every evening. But one must consider how densely the area is settled. Our streets have fifty to seventy buildings and it takes only five to seven minutes to walk their length, and about 9,000 people are living in each one of them. It is easy to forget that the majority of these people live in quite modest circumstances and, despite all the disintegrating influences in the urban environment, still live relatively ordered lives.

The usual picture of family life is roughly like this: The father leaves the house early to go to work, which keeps him away ten to twelve hours, depending on how far he has to travel. The mother looks after the household, a chore often made more difficult by the fact that each of the grown children arrives home from work at a different time and requires a specially scheduled meal. The woman going regularly to the factory in addition to the man is an exception, on account of the unfavorable labor market. But she frequently does take in work at home, or she occasionally does washing or cleans outside of the home. Evenings the father takes care of this or that household chore (resoling boots, doing kitchen repairs, overseeing the small children's homework), then he reads his newspaper and goes to bed early. Only 25 to 30 percent of the workers, incidentally, reads the socialist press in the true sense. A small proportion of the people own a small house outside the city (relatively many among us, because we live near the city limits), which they visit regularly in the summer. Sundays the father and mother go out of the city with school-age children, if possible for the entire day. Sundays are also very popular for visiting relatives or having them over. Everyone knows people here. This was the reason for moving to Berlin. Among the adults, born Berliners are few. Most moved here from the eastern provinces, with East Prussians and Pomeranians the most numerous. A site of really popular entertainment is the cinema, also on weekdays. Theater and concerts are in comparison scarcely relevant. Sunday afternoon sports events are very popular. Masquerade balls and club festivities (there are countless country-home, savings, and entertainment clubs) play a certain role in the winter months.

It is characteristic of the proletarian district that the normal family (father, mother, and children from a single marriage) is often not the rule. There are very many premarital and extramarital children in the families. One also finds many foster children, or children being raised by their grandparents. Our poor district also has a lot of widows who have children and are obliged to work. In these families the social and moral perils of the working-class district are particularly evident.

The political attitude of the population is expressly oriented to the left. In elections the number of votes cast for the communist candidates is absolutely preponderant. The older workers in the big factories are mostly social democratic; so are the lower state and municipal civil servants. The petite bourgeoisie are German nationalists.

10
The Jewish Community: Renewal, Redefinition, Resistance

ALTHOUGH IT IS IMPOSSIBLE to avoid reading the history of Weimar Jewry through the lens of its ultimate fate, it would be equally mistaken to regard it solely in terms of an outcome that was by no means inevitable or even probable at the time. Most of the half million or so German Jews felt that they belonged to German society, were full participants in its cultural heritage, and could count on the majority of their compatriots to spurn the appeals of the anti-Semites in their midst. Still it was clear to many that what was often called "the Jewish question" remained as ominously open in Germany as elsewhere in Europe. Although during World War I some twelve thousand Jews lost their lives for the fatherland (a figure disparaged by the radical right), and Jewish officers were allowed for the first time in the army, by its end, allegations of Jewish war-profiteering and shirking of military duty contributed to the stab-in-the-back legend promulgated by self-serving leaders like General Hindenburg. Jewish organizations like the Fatherland Association of Jewish Front Soldiers were created to protest their patriotism. But when it appeared that a disproportionate number of Jews participated in the revolutionary events after the war, more fuel was added to the anti-Semitic fire.

The war also added to the complexity of the situation by forcing large numbers of Jews from eastern Europe (*Ostjuden*) to flee to Germany to escape Russian and Polish persecution; they congregated in places like the Scheunenviertel in Berlin. Less assimilated and modern than their German counterparts, they often aroused anxieties within the established Jewish community, which feared that any reminder of its ghettoized past would give credence to anti-Semitic stereotypes. Some commentators, however, like the novelist Joseph Roth, were able to portray the dilemma of the new arrivals with considerable sympathy. And a small number of German Jews like Arnold Zweig were even inspired by the communal solidarity and vibrant religious feeling they sensed among the Ostjuden, whom they first encountered on the eastern front during the war.

In fact, a revival of Jewish thought was stimulated in part by exposure to religious impulses no longer very evident among Orthodox let alone Reform Jews in Germany. Most notably, Franz Rosenzweig, Martin Buber, and their colleagues at the Frankfurt Lehrhaus rejected what they saw as the dessicated legalism of Orthodoxy and the modernist compromises of Reform.

Rosenzweig's "new thinking" was classically expressed in *The Star of Redemption,* written in the trenches during the war and published in 1921. It rejected the rationalist essentialism of philosophical idealism in the name of a religion based on the direct experience of God's spoken word. As the great scholar of the Kabbalah, Gershom Scholem, noted when the book appeared in a second edition nine years later, it had revivified the redemptive core of Jewish belief and challenged the lachrymose interpretation of Jewish history, thus opening the door for a more hopeful encounter with the divine. In a similar manner, Buber's dialogic philosophy of "I and Thou" drew on the resources of the Hasidic tradition of the Ostjuden, in particular their communitarian spirit and openness to the mystical teachings of the Kabbalah.

Still, the situation of German Jews was turbulent enough in the immediate postwar period for journals like *Das Tagebuch* to publish editorials defending their contribution to German culture and others like *Der neue Merkur* to devote articles to their mythic role in European culture as a whole. Within the Jewish community itself a variety of responses were forthcoming. They included appeals to support a Jewish state in Palestine, such as that delivered by Buber to the Twelfth Zionist Congress at Karlsbad in 1921, and to build strong Jewish bodies by the Bar Kochba Gymnastic and Sports Association of Hamburg in 1927. They also included expressions of self-doubt that reflected the internalization of many of the anti-Semitic stereotypes directed against them. This phenomenon of "Jewish self-hatred" was classically analyzed by the Hannover philosopher Theodor Lessing in his book of that name, published in 1930. Although by then a Zionist, Lessing had himself experienced the lure of self-hatred, having written vicious attacks on Ostjuden before the war from a culturally pessimistic perspective that invited comparison with Oswald Spengler's *Decline of the West*. Ironically, he was assassinated by Gestapo agents in Prague in 1933 because of his outspoken agitation against the Nazis.

Contrary to the reputation for naive complacency that has sometimes been attributed to Weimar Jewry, such agitation did not begin only after Hitler came to power. During the waning years of the republic, many among even the most assimilated Jews began to grow alarmed. Their major body, the Central Association of German Citizens of the Jewish Faith, engaged in a vigorous if ultimately fruitless campaign to appeal to Germans of good will. Gentile allies, such as Carl von Ossietzky, rightfully bemoaned the growing indifference in the early 1930s to anti-Semitism, even on the pro-republican left.

98

MARTIN BUBER

Nationalism

First published as "Nationalismus," in *Kampf um Israel* (Berlin: Schocken-Verlag, 1933), 225–242. (Delivered as an address during the Twelfth Zionist Congress at Karlsbad on September 5, 1921).

We have passed from the difficult period of the World War into a period which outwardly seems more tolerable, but on closer examination proves still more difficult, a period of inner confusion. It is characteristic of this period that truth and lies, right and wrong are mingled in various spiritual and political movements in an almost unprecedented fashion.

In the face of this monstrous and monstrously growing phenomenon, it is no longer enough to draw the usual distinctions according to general, currently accepted concepts. For in every such concept, the true and the false are now so intertwined, so tangled and meshed, that to apply them as heretofore, as though they were still homogeneous, would only give rise to greater error. If we are to pass out of confusion into new clarity, we must draw distinctions *within* each individual concept.

It is a well-known fact that, *sociologically* speaking, modern nationalism goes back to the French Revolution. The effects of the French Revolution were such that the old state systems which had weighed so heavily on the peoples of Europe were shaken and the subject nations were able to emerge from under the yoke. But as they emerged and grew aware of themselves, these nations became conscious of their own political insufficiencies, of their lack of independence, territorial unity, and outward solidarity. They strove to correct these insufficiencies, but their efforts did not lead them to the creation of new forms. They did not try to establish themselves *as peoples,* that is, as a new organic order growing out of the natural forms of the life of the people. All they wanted was to become just such states, just such powerful, mechanized, and centralized state apparatuses as those that had existed in the past. They looked back into past history rather than forward into a future nationally motivated in its very structure.

We shall understand this more readily if we review the *psychological* origin of modern nationalism. European man became more and more isolated in the centuries between the Reformation and the Revolution. United Christendom did not merely break in two; it was rent by numberless cracks, and human beings no longer stood on the solid ground of connectedness. The individual was deprived of the security of a closed, cosmic system. He grew more and more specialized and at the same time isolated, and found himself faced with the dizzy infinity of the new world image. In his desire for shelter, he reached out for a community structure which was just putting in an appearance, for nationality.

A great historian has asserted that power is evil. But this is not so. Power is intrinsically guiltless; it is the precondition for the actions of man. The problematic element is the will to power, greedy to seize and establish power, and not the effect of a power whose development was internal. A will to power, less concerned with being powerful than with being "more powerful than," becomes destructive. Not power but power hysteria is evil.

In the life of human beings, both as individuals and groups, self-assertion can be genuine as well as false, legitimate as well as illegitimate. [. . .]

Modern nationalism is in constant danger of slipping into hysteria, which disintegrates the responsibility to draw lines of demarcation. [. . .]

The distinction between the two kinds of nationalism I am concerned with depends entirely on the right understanding of this responsibility and this danger. But to arrive at this understanding, we must first analyze the phenomenon of nationalism and its relation to peoples and nations. Or to be more exact, we must define what "people" means. What, in this relation, is a nation? What is the significance of nationalism in relation to both people and nation?

The word "people" tends, above all, to evoke the idea of blood relationship. But kinship is not the sine qua non for the origin of a people. A people need not necessarily be the fusion of kindred stems; it can be the fusion of unrelated stems just as well. But the concept "people" always implies unity of fate. It presupposes that in a great creative hour throngs of human beings were shaped into a new entity by a great molding fate they experienced in common. [. . .]

A people becomes a nation to the degree that it grows aware that its existence differs from that of other peoples (a difference originally expressed in the sacral principle that determines endogamy), and acts on the basis of this awareness. So the term "nation" signifies the unit "people," from the point of view of conscious and active difference. Historically speaking, this consciousness is usually the result of some inner—social or political—transformation, through which the people comes to realize their own peculiar structure and actions, and sets them off from those of others. It is decisive activity and suffering, especially in an age of migrations and land conquests, which produces a people. A nation is produced when its acquired status undergoes a decisive inner change which is accepted as such in the people's self-consciousness. [. . .]

Original nationalism is the indication of a fundamental lack in the life of the nation, a lack of unity, freedom, and territorial security; it warns the nation to mend this situation. It is a demand upon the world for what it needs, a demand that the unwritten *droits de la nation* be applied to a people to enable it to realize its essence as a people and thus discharge its duty to mankind. Original nationalism inspires the people to struggle for what they lack to achieve this. But when nationalism transgresses its lawful limits, when it tries to do more than overcome a deficiency, it becomes guilty of what has been called hubris in the lives of historical personalities; it crosses the holy border and grows presumptuous. And now it no longer indicates disease, but is itself a grave and complicated disease. A people can win the rights for which it strove and yet fail to regain its health—because nationalism, turned false, eats at its marrow.

When this false nationalism, i.e., a nationalism that has exceeded the function it was destined to fulfill, and persists and acts beyond it, prevails not only in *one* people, but in an entire epoch of world history, it means that the life of mankind, pulsing in its stock of peoples, is very sick indeed. And that is the situation today. [. . .]

There is no scale of values for the function of peoples. One cannot be ranked above another. God wants to use what he created, as an aid in his work. In an hour of crisis true nationalism expresses the true self-awareness of a people and translates it into action.

He, on the other hand, who regards the nation as an end in itself will refuse to admit that there is a greater structure, unless it be the worldwide supremacy of his own particular nation. He tries to grapple with the problem of the cracked and shattered present by undermining it instead of by transcending it. He does not meet responsibility face to face. He considers the nation its own judge and responsible to no one but itself. An interpretation such as this converts the nation into a moloch which gulps the best of the people's youth.

National ideology, the *spirit* of nationalism, is fruitful just so long as it does not make the nation an end in itself; just so long as it remembers its part in the building of a greater structure. The moment national ideology makes the nation an end in itself, it annuls its own right to live, it grows sterile.

In this day and age, when false nationalism is on the rise, we are witness to the beginning of the decline of the national ideology which flowered in the nineteenth and early twentieth centuries. It goes without saying that it is perfectly possible for this decline to go hand in hand with increasing success of nationalistic politics. But we live in the hour when nationalism is about to annul itself spiritually. [. . .]

Judaism is not merely being a nation. It is being a nation, but because of its own peculiar connection with the quality of being a community of faith, it is more than that. Since Jewry has a character of its own and a life of its own, just like any other nation, it is entitled to claim the rights and privileges of a nation. But we must never forget that it is, nevertheless, a *res sui generis,* which in one very vital respect, goes beyond the classification it is supposed to fit.

A great event in their history molded the Jews into a people. It was when the Jewish tribes were freed from the bondage of Egypt. But it required a great inner transformation to make them into a nation. In the course of this inner change, the concept of the government of God took on a political form, final for the time being, that of the anointed kingdom, i.e., the kingdom as the representative of God.

From the very beginning of the Diaspora, the uniqueness of Judaism became apparent in a very special way. In other nations the national powers in themselves vouch for the survival of the people. In Judaism, this guarantee is given by another power which, as I have said, makes the Jews more than a nation: the membership in a community of faith. From the French Revolution on, this inner bond grew more and more insecure. Jewish religion was uprooted, and this is at the core of the disease indicated by the rise of Jewish nationalism around the middle of the nineteenth century. Over and over this nationalism lapses into trends toward "secularization" and thus mistakes its purpose. For Israel cannot be healed, and its welfare cannot be achieved by severing the concepts of people and community of faith, but only by setting up a new order including both as organic and renewed parts.

A Jewish national community in Palestine, a desideratum toward which Jewish nationalism must logically strive, is a station in this healing process. We must not however forget that in the thousands of years of its exile Jewry yearned for the Land of Israel, not as a nation like others, but as Judaism (*res sui generis*), and with motives and intentions which cannot be derived wholly from the category "nation." That original yearning is behind all the disguises which modern national Judaism has borrowed from the modern nationalism of the West. To forget one's own peculiar character and to accept the slogans and paroles of a nationalism that has nothing to do with the category of faith means national assimilation. [. . .]

And what part does Jewish nationalism play at the present time? We—and by that I mean the group of persons I have belonged to since my youth, that group which has tried and will continue to try to do its share in educating the people—we have summoned the people to turn, and not to conceit, to be healed, and not to self-righteousness. We have equipped Jewish nationalism with an armor we did not weld, with the awareness of a unique history, a unique situation, a unique obligation, which can be conceived only from the supernational standpoint and which—whenever it is taken seriously—must point to a supernational sphere.

In this way we hoped to save Jewish nationalism from the error of making an idol of the people. We have not succeeded. Jewish nationalism is largely concerned with being "like unto all the nations," with affirming itself in the face of the world without affirming the world's reciprocal power. It too has frequently yielded to the delusion of regarding the horizon visible from one's own station as the whole sky. It too is guilty of offending against the words of that table of laws that has been set up above all nations: that all sovereignty becomes false and vain when in the struggle for power it fails to remain subject to the Sovereign of the world, who is the Sovereign of my rival, and my enemy's Sovereign, as well as mine. [. . .] The supernatural task of the Jewish nation cannot be properly accomplished unless—under its aegis—natural life is reconquered. In that formal nationalism disclaims the nation's being based on and conditioned by this more than national task; in that it has grown overconscious and dares to disengage Judaism from its connection with the world and to isolate it; in that it proclaims the nation as an end in itself, instead of comprehending that it is an element, formal nationalism sanctions a group egoism which disclaims responsibility. [. . .]

The nationalistic crisis in Judaism is in sharp, perhaps too sharp, relief in the pattern of the nationalistic crises of current world history. In our case, more clearly than in any other, the decision between life and death has assumed the form of deciding between legitimate and arbitrary nationalism.

99

EFRAIM FRISCH

Jewish Sketches

First published as "Jüdische Aufzeichnungen," *Der neue Merkur* 5 (1921–1922), 297–317.

The final myth Europe still possesses is—the Jew. And it obviously does not want to see it destroyed. It is much more the case that a kind of science, which usually destroys myth, is continually occupied with keeping it alive, with translating the demonization of the Jew as formulated by the medieval church into a modern idiom. Given a more precise inspection, the towering stack of literature about Jews and Judaism is mainly nothing but the scholasticism and exegesis of an established belief that may not be doubted, a speculative dogma resting on myth. Therefore it betrays that lack of impartiality, trust, and sincerity, that chicanery that can prove whatever it pleases, that venom and veiled hostility proper only to religious conflicts which has characterized the pro and con of the Jewish question since the beginning. This is even more the case as the power of the myth has succeeded in actually transforming certain suitably disposed Jews to conform to the image of this belief, as the belief in witchcraft created the witches. In the *ressentiment* Jew, in the Jew plagued by self-hatred, in the cynical Jew and his various mutations, the demonology persists in its effects. Thus has the Jewish question (for the Jews a question in a quite different sense than for those who pose it) grown into an impassable undergrowth of the most tangled sort, causing pure and sensitive people to keep their distance. [. . .]

The speculations of racial philosophy concerning the nature, worth, and worthlessness of Jews are significant only as documents in the psychology of prejudices formed by majorities toward minorities of a different nature—in whatever scientific garb they might appear. Otherness is postulated in order to divert hostility along more comfortable channels. That which is mutual, which runs parallel, disappears somewhere in an abyss; or the given hostility is taken as the point of departure to prove the alien nature, the otherness. Germans can find plenty of instructive examples of this maneuver in various works of French or English war literature that take as their object the German nation, culture, and history in order to prove to the world, with no little display of scientificity, the inferiority of their enemy. In reference to the Jews there is practically nothing but war literature. And, under the pressure of the defensive posture that has been eternally forced upon them, the Jews, primarily in the West, have long since forfeited all manner of impartiality. Their position oscillates between the sharpest oppositions: beginning with an emphatic just-so nationalism (of both colors) all the way to playing dead out of social awkwardness. Not that it should be forgotten that it was never a confrontation among equals nor a harmless theoretical conflict, but that behind the "questions" of majorities lurked boycotts, expulsion, the funeral pyre, the pogrom. [. . .]

Anti-Semitism has always proved itself incapable of answering the question it allegedly poses. Obviously, because it is not seeking an answer. Divided within itself, it indeed lives from myth, but even as a defensive movement it proves itself so bereft of instincts that it accepts any allies, even Jewish ones. It has to receive the cross breed, indeed even every convert keen to put on a chummy display. It is incapable of even hinting at the boundaries of Jewishness, indeed sniffs it everywhere, but nevertheless is unable to recognize it whenever it fails to confront him with the crudest symbols. It practices realpolitik to the point of characterlessness, but then is finally to be judged as only an occasional inciter of pogroms. A discussion with it remains just as fruitless as itself. But even where it is recognized that in this world crisis the Jewish fate cannot be conceived as something passively bestowed exclusively upon the Jews, and where an exchange is attempted in good faith, the two parties talk past each other. The essential preconditions are lacking: knowledge of Jewish reality, where it is Jewish and real at once; knowledge of the sources of Jewish religiosity and the Jewish view of life, admittedly not easy to come by. [. . .]

An end should finally be put to speculations about such abstractions as Jews and Judaism, to the fight against a preconceived phantom, in favor of acquaintance with the concrete "exceptions." (As is characteristic of anti-Semitism, everyone knows the few "respectable" Jews; only those one does not know are the "bad" ones.) The admission of Jews to Europe (half-way, completely, three-quarters, or even only on the paper of constitutions) is in some places still less than one hundred years old. The results are provisional and various, depending on the respective characters of the nations. It is altogether impossible for Jews as a whole to give an answer to the Jewish question in this sense. (Solidarity exists only among those suffering oppression together and those in whom there is sufficient clarity concerning the meaning of the fate of the Jewish people. There is no inner connection binding the Jews of the Western nations together.) A response to the question is much more incumbent upon the peoples who have admitted them. Among the Germans the relative absence of national homogeneity and the consequent frailty of its constitution have an unfavorable effect in this regard. It seems as if Germany exhausted its power to assimilate during the early colonization of eastern Europe, and it manifests this weakness everywhere it meets with cultures of a different nature and stamp, not only in the case of Jews. It is not, however, encapsulation that is helpful here but opening; in particular since Jews, even those well to the east, have been assisted in their Europeanization by the German spirit and German culture. [. . .]

In the whirlwind of recent world events and in view of the shifting of boundaries to the east, beyond the areas including mass Jewish settlements, the question of the legal status of Jews and their integration into new state structures has obviously become acute. But there is no occasion, no deep-seated reason, for the drive to make the so-called Jewish question current in Germany, as has been evident from a certain side for the last two years. It makes the impression of an underhanded diversionary tactic, as if the point were to distract attention from the essential questions, those bearing profoundly and immediately on the future of the people; and that is the terrible danger of this turbulent anti-Semitism, that by way of it and its empty industriousness the people will be prevented from searching within themselves for substantive goals so sorely lacking. With that political naïveté that must cause all well-informed people to shake their heads, the people are saying: Yes, but what we need right now is a sense of the national, we need it desperately! It is of no avail when the feeling is only intensified by the repulsion of the Jews. Now the answer is probably simple enough: the national sense that is lacking cannot be negative, and it helps nothing to choose here the path of least resistance, having nothing but this mythical *consensus omnium* for the sake of being unified at least on one issue. This consensus will not be capable of replacing the deficiency of inner connectedness. It is also of little aid that in all questions of social togetherness mutual enmity has been raised to such a pitch that civil war has already been made into a self-evident *ultima ratio,* as war was in earlier times. Such a tactic of deportation will finally take its vengeance, since someone is going to recall that revolutions and democracies existed for a long time before a Jewish minority participated in public and political life. If capitalism is Jewish, and socialism and even imperialism (I read somewhere: the Jewish idea, Berlin–Bagdad), then the "German Spirit" called up in opposition will evaporate into an empty ideology with nothing to contribute, although it should be working on the reconstruction of real things.

The critical significance of Protestantism in particular to the development of modern capitalism has been definitively revealed by Max Weber. The most powerful private capitalist holdings were gathered on the American continent, far from any Jewish influence, long before mass Jewish immigration. The sons of the Pilgrim fathers are creating the models of great capitalist organization with the aid of the political system. The Rothschild family has long since become an anachronism. But the temptation arises to move beyond this negative defense, which has little difficulty showing of what the Jews are not guilty, over to a characterization of those guilty ones who have a vital interest in promoting this new round of venom.

100

ARNOLD ZWEIG

The Countenance of Eastern European Jews

First published as preface to *Das ostjüdische Antlitz* (Berlin: Welt–Verlag, 1922) 2d ed., 9–11.

This book about the eastern Jews is written by someone who attempted to see them. In the days in which the plan occurred to him, a year ago in a Lithuanian–Jewish city, one might have expected much to happen concerning the fate of these our brothers, and nothing would be easy. For then it appeared as if the anti-Jewish hand of the Junkers and merchants would continue to float over the east like a cloud. We certainly thought it was very bad.

But what came instead was the reign of plunder, of the whip and the club, of executions and murder, of disappearances without a trace and ruination in prisons—we did not suspect the rule of the Poles.

We spoke with our brothers and sisters, while we were still in the uniform of German soldiers. They said, "Your system is disgusting. You regiment and play tricks as much as you can, you beat innocent people in interrogations, you confiscate and steal, and you outrage us with your disdain. Your forced labor battalions are a good imitation of Siberia in the middle of the country; your decrees aim at letting the weak among us starve and die in epidemics we did not have here before. It was better under the tsars than under you, and if only the Russians would return!

"But we will manage with the Lithuanians and White Russians, and even with you. Just do not abandon us to the Poles. For then we are all dead."

Poles and pogroms have befallen the eastern Jewish people who live piled together in the big cities and scattered through towns and villages. From the big cities comes shocking news, but the towns and villages, without railroads, without telegraph offices, have long been mute. Slowly one hears what is happening there: murder and massacre.

I do not believe a word of all the disavowals being composed, spread, or trickled out by the ruling Poles. One needs only to have been in Lithuania two months to be forced to think this way.

The Jews in the east want to live in their Jewish manner, in the confines of their own culture, their own faith, and their own language. Yiddish is a language in itself, like Dutch and English—which assimilated Jews in Poland as well as here would traitorously like to deny.

I know that there are Poles of refined thinking. It is only that, unfortunately, they can not restore our brothers to life.

We ascribe these murders and torments to the Polish people so that the better among them might blush with shame when they see a Jew. For it is not a matter of being better but of putting a stop to it; to do that they are too few and too weak.

We say here and now what Europe and America could say today as well if they were not infected by the delirious fear of all socialism: the murdered Jews, to the extent they were socialists, were not murdered on account of their "bolshevism."

To begin the futile struggle against socialism where it belongs, in one's own house, and to provide convincing doctrines and deeds—is that too much to ask? Perhaps it is today, when Europe, excited by the smell of blood and greed for plunder, is scurrying wildly down the trail to decline.

For that reason we predict that the Polish people themselves will avenge our brothers—by way of Polish socialism.

May Israel think of the Polish deeds as the deeds of Amalek, who is not yet forgiven after three thousand years, how he, after countless murders and the disasters of epidemics, war, and hunger, produced the murder of national hatred, the cowardly murder by the armed of the unarmed, upon our brothers.

Admittedly we are not capable of rushing to your aid. And every word we speak for you will be deemed lies and German politics among those who could help.

You are dying of a cowardly, murderous, and profit-hungry time in Europe. What does it help all of us that later generations will shame themselves for the sake of your murdered souls? It is all quite futile.

Nevertheless a single person's testimony does not die. Thus do we bear witness for you and leave it to those in the know to intuit when just one of us speaks and when it is both.

May the taste of blood on the tongue of the man-eating bull of Europe soon disappear.

"Do you think that I find liking in the death of the godless," says the Lord God, "and not much more that he mend his ways and live?"

Summer 1919
In the month of Ab 5679 — Jewish Calendar
Hermann Struck   Arnold Zweig

101

S. STEINBERG

What We Strive For

First published as "Was wir erstreben," *Zeitschrift des Vaterländischen Bundes jüdischer Frontsoldaten* 1, no. 1 (March 1922), 1–2.

COMRADES!

Like a wave driven by an ocean storm, there surges a fanatical hatred against Judaism. We are being summoned by our honorable duty to defend our precious heritage during these passionate, agitated times, to repulse the hateful attacks that are threatening our property, the product of centuries of arduous struggle. With the devotion of former German front soldiers we stand firmly shoulder to shoulder to uphold our highest sacred treasure: *fatherland and faith to the last breath.* Our magazine arose permeated by this spirit of the fatherland; we foster the unshakable certainty that it will not only lend effective support to our aspirations but will also substantially promote the spiritual union of all Jewish front soldiers. As the towering lighthouse on the ocean shore points a secure way through storm and danger, filling the anxiety-ridden sea voyager with new confidence, so fortified by hope do we gaze into the deep, medieval gloom of our fatherland torn by base passions and gaze up at the bright rays of light in the sky above our homeland. The day is coming when sunlit understanding will tear the dark cloud of religious hatred, and the anti-Semitic attacks directed at us will be recognized by all as a disgrace inflicted upon true Germanness. Until then, comrades, we will stand firm and unwavering in our sense of duty and honor, as we have proven it as faithful German soldiers fighting the external enemy. Every Jewish front soldier is honor-bound to join our association for the fatherland, and, as much as he is able, to seek to advance the one exalted goal to which we all, in love for our fatherland, are dedicated!

May the newly founded magazine develop into a broadly shining symbol of true cooperation and provide refuge for the heart of every comrade suffering the oppression of anti-Semitic hatred.

WHAT WE STRIVE FOR

A horrible fate has destroyed the proud edifice of our fatherland, demolished its intellectual, spiritual, and economic accomplishments. Shaken to the bone, our severely tested people stand before the ruins of their ethical and material possessions. Everything that cheered their souls and moved their hearts perished in the devastating storm. Of all our nation's comrades the citizens of the Jewish faith suffer the most painfully from the unspeakable misfortune of their fatherland. Hate-filled agitators see in the national tragedy a propitious opportunity for a shameless assault on their Germanness, to the defense of which they sacrificed themselves in times of need and peril. The agitators are venturing an outrageous violation of this heritage of their forefathers, won over centuries of struggle at the cost of many victims. Filled with a sense of duty, arisen in response to the shameful course of events, the Fatherland Association of Jewish Front Soldiers confronts this hateful deportment; those who marched off enthusiastically in the defense of our common fatherland, who fought and suffered shoulder to shoulder without distinction with their Christian comrades, are compelled to preserve their honorable engagement against lies and slander. If the consciousness of duty faithfully fulfilled remains the most secure defense against malice and baseness, there nevertheless burns in the soul of the Jewish front soldiers a seering pain that a medieval hatred seeks to tarnish their military honor. Every truth-loving comrade, no matter which congregation he belongs to, who endured with his Jewish comrades-in-arms the common fate of the enemy's annihilating fire, knows that in the moment of death every distinction born of human superstition vanishes without a trace and the enemy bullet makes no distinctions as to which breast it penetrates. *One God—One Fatherland—One Faith!*—thus did they all think, our thousands of comrades who in the prime of their lives suffered death for the fatherland and, as testimony to sacred duty, slumber in foreign ground. In the spirit of our faithful comrades-in-arms, we want to preserve their honorable sacrifice as our supreme legacy, to strive for the one common goal free of any deviation, to stride straight ahead on the path which alone leads to the welfare of all, to the blessing of our German people. Filled with the sense of duty and love, we want to contribute to the new construction of our dear fatherland, in the blissful certainty that the freedom of faith offers all human ideals a secure abode.

102

DAS TAGEBUCH

The German Spirit

First published as "Der deutsche Geist," editorial in *Das Tagebuch*, no. 8 (February 23, 1924), 234–235.

Those who complain about the increasing influence of Judaism on the German spirit are obliged to ask themselves the question: what would the German world look like without the electrifying element of the Jews? An ultra-German writer, the Silesian seer of the soul, Hermann Stehr, recently celebrated his sixtieth birthday. Who celebrated with the demure writer? The *Deutsche Zeitung* of February 15 gives the answer:

> Whoever was present at the celebration of Hermann Stehr's sixtieth birthday in Berlin's Beethoven Hall must have noticed with astonishment that it was mainly

Jews who felt themselves called to honor this native son of Germany with their attendance. Even among the honorary guests there were many Jewish names. Of the representatives of German literature and literary criticism, nearly all those named were Jewish. Yet the prominence of Judaism in the celebration itself was even more unpleasant; the succession of lectures, at least insofar as the celebration proceeded according to plan, was delivered mainly by Jews.

Every sensitive German present, however, could not help but be pained by the repetition of the same spectacle we witnessed in the case of Gerhart Hauptmann. Hermann Stehr, who comes from the manufacturing middle class—his father was a saddlemaker in a small provincial town in Glatz province—Hermann Stehr, the teacher of German youth in numerous Silesian villages, this man of solid and upright German values (his movements and his words proved this as he expressed his thanks for the celebration), was honored primarily by Jews and allowed himself to be honored by them.

But German literary and artistic circles can certainly not be spared the reproach that here too, given a little attentiveness and some *willingness to sacrifice,* the mistake of turning over the tribute to Hermann Stehr almost exclusively to Jews could have been avoided.

The grieving lads of German nationalism could have listed still other examples besides Hauptmann and Stehr to prove that without German Jews the best minds of our nation would have gone without a hearing. For twenty years Friedrich Nietzsche produced one book after the other. He had the books printed at his own cost by a small press in Saxony. He waited for an echo, but the Germans paid him no attention—indeed the German nationalists who knew him from the Richard Wagner circle were silent as a tomb. Then Georg Brandes, a Jew, wrote an essay, "Aristocratic Radicalism," for the *Deutscher Rundschau,* which still existed at that time and was directed by Julius Rodenberg, another Jew, and that was the day Nietzsche was discovered for the Germans. The grieving lads of the *Deutsche Zeitung* hit on the sorest spot of the nationalist system. Certainly, Felix Dan, Rudolf Herzog, Euphemia von Ballestrem bloomed from the German soil without a Jewish echo. But as soon as a German mind outgrew the realm of normal mediocrity, it was the German Jews who first took note and applauded. The world of the German spirit, robbed of the Jews, would become sleepy and dull.

103

FRANZ ROSENZWEIG

The New Thinking

First published as "Das neue Denken," *Der Morgen* 1, no. 4, (October, 1925), 426–451.

Philosophy has always inquired into the essence of things. This is the concern that marks it off from the unphilosophical thinking of sound common sense, which never bothers to ask what a thing actually is. Common sense is content to know that a chair is a chair, and is unconcerned with the possibility that it may actually be something quite different. It is just this possibility that philosophy pursues in its inquiry into the essence of things. Philosophy refuses to accept the world as world, God as God, man as man! All these must actually be quite different from what they seem, for if they were not, if they were really only what they are, then philosophy—God forbid!—would be utterly super-fluous. [. . .]

The question as to the essence of things can produce nothing but tautological answers. Burrow down and still further down, and God will still be only godly, man only human, and the world only worldly. And this holds equally for all three terms. The concept of God is by no means an exception. God as a concept is no more remote than the concepts of man and of the world. On the other hand, the essence of man and the essence of the world are no easier to understand than the essence of God. We know equally much—or equally little—about each of them; we know everything and nothing. [. . .]

Where are such forms [*Gestalten*] that have essence, yet lack truth, life, or reality, to be found? Where is there a God who is not the true one, and not real, a world not living and not true, and human beings neither real nor alive; forms, each of which does not know and does not want to know anything about the other two? In other words, forms that do not occupy the same space with what we call our reality, our truth, our life, and yet hover over everything that goes on within that space? If the reader will recall his Spengler, he can give his own answer. Spengler's Apollonian culture is concerned with just those gods, worlds, and men that we are speaking of. Spengler's concept of the Euclidean accurately designates the separation in essence, the transcendence with relation to one another, which we have here described. Only that Spengler, as always, interprets falsely what he sees correctly. [. . .]

What the new philosophy, the new thinking, actually does is to employ the method of sound common sense as a method of scientific thinking. How is this sound common sense distinguished from the unsound that gets its teeth into something and will not let go until it has gulped the something in its entirety, in the same way as the old philosophy? Common sense waits, goes on living; it has no fixed idea; it knows: all in due time! [. . .]

The new thinking, like the age-old thinking of sound common sense, knows that it cannot have cognition independent of time—though heretofore one of philosophy's boasts has been that it is able to do this very thing. [. . .]

Thus the tenses of reality cannot be interchanged. Just like every single happening, so reality as a whole has its present, its past, and its future, without which it cannot be, or—at any rate—cannot be properly known. Reality too has its past and its future, an everlasting past and an eternal future. To have cognition of God, the world, and man is to know what they do or what is done to them in these tenses of reality, and to know what they do to one another or what is done to them by one another. [. . .]

In the new thinking, the method of speech replaces the method of thinking maintained in all earlier philosophies. Thinking is timeless and wants to be timeless. With one stroke it would establish thousands of connections. It regards the last, the goal, as the first. Speech is bound to time and nourished by time, and it neither can nor wants to abandon this element. It does not know in advance just where it will end. It takes its cues from others. In fact, it lives by virtue of another's life, whether that other is the one who listens to a story, answers in the course of a dialogue, or joins in a chorus; while thinking is always a solitary business, even when it is done in common by several who philosophize together. For even then, the other is only raising the objections I should raise myself, and this is the reason why the great majority of philosophic dialogues—including most of Plato's—are so tedious. In actual conversation, something happens. [. . .]

I use the term *speaking thinker* for the new thinking. Speaking thought is, of course, still a form of thinking, just as the old thinking that depended solely on thinking could not go on without inner speech. The difference between the old and the new, the "logical" and the "grammatical" thinking, does not lie in the fact that one is silent while the other is audible, but in the fact that the latter needs another person and takes time seriously— actually, these two things are identical. In the old philosophy, "thinking" means thinking for no one else and speaking to no one else (and here, if you prefer, you may substitute "everyone" or the well-known "all the world" for "no one"). But "speaking" means speaking to someone and thinking for someone. And this someone is always a quite definite someone, and he has not merely ears, like "all the world," but also a mouth.

Whatever the *Star of Redemption* can do to renew our ways of thinking is concentrated in this method. Ludwig Feuerbach was the first to discover it. Hermann Cohen's post-humous work reintroduced it to philosophy, though the author himself was not aware of its iconoclastic power. When I wrote the *Star of Redemption,* I was already familiar with the pertinent passages in Cohen's book, but their influence was not decisive for the genesis of my own work. The main influence was Eugen Rosenstock; a full year and a half before I began to write I had seen the rough draft of his now-published *Applied Psychology.* [. . .]

Martin Buber in his *I and Thou,* and Ferdinand Ebner in *The Word and Spiritual Realities,* written at exactly the same time as my book, approached the heart of the new thinking. [. . .] The notes to my [translation of] Judah ha-Levi give instructive examples of the practical application of the new thinking. The epochal, largely unpublished works of Florens Christian Rang are founded in a precise and profound knowledge of all this.

With all these men, theological concerns have assisted the new thinking in coming to the fore. But this does not mean that the new thinking itself is theological, at least not in the sense in which the term has been used up to now, either with respect to the end or the means. The new thinking does not center on the so-called religious problems, which it treats side by side with, or rather together with, the problems of logic, ethics, and aesthetics; nor has it anything in common with the attitude characteristic of thinking along theological lines, an attitude made up of attack and defense and never quietly concentrated on the matter in hand. If this is theology, it is at any rate no less new as theology than as philosophy. [. . .] Theology must not debase philosophy to play the part of a handmaid, yet the role of charwoman which philosophy has recently assigned to theology is just as humiliating. The true relationship of these two regenerated sciences is a sisterly one, and this must necessarily lead to the personal union of those who deal with them. Theological problems must be translated into human terms, and human problems brought into the pale of theology. [. . .]

In the *Star of Redemption* the picture of Judaism and Christianity is determined above all by the quest for an eternity that exists, hence by the task of fighting the danger of interpreting the new thinking in the sense (or rather non-sense) of tendencies directed toward a "philosophy of life" or other irrational goals. In our day and age, all those who are clever enough to avoid the jaws of the Scylla of idealism seem to be drawn into the dark whirlpool of this Charybdis. In both cases, Judaism and Christianity, the picture is not beholden to the ways in which they interpret themselves; in Judaism it does not proceed from law, in Christianity it does not proceed from faith: but in both, from the external, visible forms by whose means they wrest their eternity from time; in Judaism from the fact of the Jewish people, in Christianity from the event on which the Christian community is founded, and only through these do law and faith become visible. And so here Judaism and Christianity are set both side by side and in contrast on a sociological basis. [. . .]

There still exists the belief that all philosophy should begin with considerations that are part and parcel of a theory of knowledge. Actually it may end with them. [. . .]

If something is to come out of knowledge, it means that—exactly as in the case of a cake—something has to be put into it. What was put into the *Star of Redemption* was first of all the experience of factuality that precedes all facts of real experience, factuality that forces thinking to employ (instead of its favorite term "actually") the little word "and" the basic word of all experience, the word the philosopher's tongue is not used to. God and the world and man! This "and" was the beginning of experience and so it must recur in the ultimate aspect of truth. For there must be an "and" within truth itself, within ultimate truth that can only be one. Unlike the truth of the philosophers, which is not allowed to know anything but itself, this truth must be truth for some one. If it is to be the one truth, it can be one only for the One, God. And that is why our truth must of necessity become manifold, and why the truth must be converted into our truth. Thus truth ceases to be what "is" true and becomes a verity that wants to be verified, realized in active life. This becomes the fundamental concept of this new theory of knowledge. This theory replaces the old theories of noncontradiction and objects and introduces a dynamic for the old static concept of objectivity.

104

EDGAR MARX

Ideological Self-determination of Bar Kochba: The New Year of the Jewish Gymnastics and Sports Association Bar Kochba

First published as "Ideologische Selbstbestimmung des Bar Kochba: Das neue Jahr des jüdischen Turn-und Sportvereins Bar Kochba," *Gemeindeblatt der Deutsch-Israelitischen Gemeinde zu Hamburg* (November 10, 1927), 6–7.

Work and success—that is what the leaders of Bar Kochba anticipate from the coming year, both in the sense of greater external, athletic activity and success and in the other sense of more internal, that is, pedagogical work with the Jewish youth of Hamburg entrusted to us. We are aware of the responsibility vested in us and do not take it lightly, but we also believe ourselves, without undue modesty, justified in answering the question of whether we have achieved something in both areas with "yes." Our athletic successes and, naturally, our occasional failures are known and can be read about in the newspaper, if, as we unfortunately have to add, more frequently by the general reader interested in sports than by the Jewish community to which we belong. I can only regret that, in contrast to conditions in other large congregations in Germany, there is no widespread interest within the Hamburg congregation in the matches and achievements of Bar Kochba, at least not any that would be expressed by a corresponding attendance at our events. That is regrettable for many reasons. For one, the match with the frequently not-very-friendly opponent is easier if one knows oneself to be surrounded by well-meaning friends. Moreover, others can form an idea of the fitness achieved through gymnastic and athletic activity only if they themselves occasionally witness our ability to perform. And only in this way can our activities be publicized among broader Jewish circles. And one more reason why we so desire visitors at our athletic events: that for which we struggle is more than victory, the amount of goals scored, or the number of points, for every match which our team with the Star of David on their chests plays is a match of the Jewish association and in some way becomes a Jewish matter. Every single member of the team, especially the youngest, feels very clearly that it is not merely a matter of victory for you, your team, your association, but that it is much more—a matter of victory to increase Jewish prestige, to prove the Jewish ability to perform in the area of gymnastics and sports as well. And that nothing can more quickly, nicely, and objectively constrain anti-Semitism—about that there is no discussion. Just as little do we, at least those of us in Bar Kochba, doubt that this goal can be achieved only in purely Jewish associations.

With the points just addressed we enter the area that I designated above as the internal work, the pedagogical. In this we are working more quietly, but all the more diligently. It is our established belief that athletic successes are particularly frequent when our pedagogical work in the sense of creating a conscious sense of Jewish collective identity is properly understood. We scarcely need mention that for us, even as we involve ourselves in physically training young Jews, it is not a question of training as such, of the creation of an unspiritual or even antispiritual "Judaism of the muscles." We Jews are already much more subject to the danger of being too one-sided in spirit, so that a balance through physical training is usually quite desirable. But even with this training we want more than mere balance; we strive for higher goals and challenges, as the Maccabi World Association [International Jewish Sports Federation], to which we belong, poses them to us. For one thing we certainly do believe: without the sustaining and invigorating ardor of a great, gripping idea it will not be easy to keep young Jewish people together over the long run in gymnastic squads and soccer teams.

105

JOSEPH ROTH

Wandering Jews

First published in *Juden auf Wanderschaft: Berichte aus der Wirklichkeit*, vol. 4, ed. Eduard Trautner (Berlin: Verlag Die Schmiede, 1927), 65–74.

I

No eastern Jews come to Berlin voluntarily. Who in the whole world comes voluntarily to Berlin?

Berlin is a way station where pressing circumstances force people to stay on. Berlin has no ghetto. It has a Jewish quarter. Emigrants come here wanting to travel on to Hamburg and Amsterdam to America. They often get stuck. They have too little money. Or their papers are not in order.

(Of course: their papers! Half a Jewish life slips by in a fruitless struggle over papers.)

The eastern Jews who come to Berlin often have a transit visa authorizing them to stay two to three days in Germany. There are already some who arrived with only a transit visa and have stayed on two to three years in Berlin.

Of the eastern Jews who have been settled in Berlin for a long time, the majority came before the war. Relatives followed. Refugees from the occupied territories came to Berlin. Jews who performed services for the German occupation army in Russia, in the Ukraine, in Poland, in Lithuania were forced to return to Germany with the German army.

There are also criminals among the eastern Jews in Berlin. Pickpockets, marriage swindlers, con men, counterfeiters, inflation profiteers. Almost no burglars. No murderers, no violent thieves.

An eastern Jew is freed from the struggle over papers only when he undertakes to struggle against society by criminal means. The eastern Jewish criminal was usually a criminal in his homeland. He comes to Germany either without papers or with false ones. He does not register with the police.

Only the honest eastern Jew (he is not only honest but fearful) registers with the police. That is considerably more difficult in Prussia than in Austria. The Berlin police have the habit of checking up on people in their houses. They also check for papers on the street. This happened frequently during the inflation.

Trade in old clothing is not prohibited, but it is also not permitted. No one who does not have a business license is allowed to buy my old pants. Nor is he allowed to sell them.

Nevertheless, he buys them. He sells them too.

He stands on Joachimsthalerstraße or on the corner of Joachimsthalerstraße and Kurfürstendamm and acts like he is doing nothing at all. He has to see in the passers-by first whether they have old clothes to sell and second whether they need money.

The clothes bought are sold the next morning at the clothing market.

There are status distinctions among peddlers too. There are rich, powerful peddlers and smaller ones who look up to them quite humbly. The richer a peddler is, the more he earns. He does not go out on the streets. He does not need to. Indeed, I am not even sure I should call him a peddler. Actually, he has a shop with old clothes and a business license. And if it is not his own business license, then it belongs to one of the settled immigrants, to a citizen of Berlin, who understands nothing of the clothing trade but has a percentage share in the business.

Mornings, the shop owners and peddlers gather at the clothes market. They bring their yield from the previous day, all the old skirts and dresses. In the spring there is a boom in summer and sports suits. In the fall, the boom is in cutaways, tuxedos, and striped pants. Whoever comes in the fall with summer and linen suits does not understand the business.

The clothes that the peddlers have bought for a ridiculously small sum from passersby they sell to the shop owners for a ridiculously small profit. The latter have the clothes ironed, freshened up, and mended. Then they hang them in front of their shop sign and let them flutter in the wind.

Those who are good at selling old clothes are soon able to sell new ones. They will open a store instead of a shop. Someday they will become department store owners. In Berlin even a peddler can have a career. They will assimilate more quickly than their equals in Vienna. Berlin smooths out the differences and cancels particularities. That is why there is no large ghetto in Berlin.

There are only a couple of small Jewish streets, around the Warschauer Bridge and in the Scheunenviertel. The most Jewish of all Berlin streets is the sad Hirtenstraße.

II

No street in the world is as sad. Hirtenstraße does not even have the hopeless cheerfulness of mere dirt. Hirtenstraße is a Berlin street made less harsh by eastern Jewish residents, but unchanged. There are no streetcars running along it. No buses. Rarely an automobile. Always trucks, carts, the plebians among vehicles. There are little taverns stuck in walls. Down at the bottom of steps. Narrow, dirty, worn-out steps. Like the hollowed-out landings. There is rubbish in the hallways. Including rubbish that has been collected, bought. Rubbish as an object of trade. Old newspapers. Torn stockings. Soles of shoes. Shoestrings. Apron strings. Hirtenstraße is boringly suburban. It does not have the character of a small-town street. It is new, cheap, already used up, damaged goods. A little department-store street. A cheap department-store street. It has a few empty display windows. Jewish baked goods, poppy-seed bagels, rolls, black bread lie in the windows. An oil can, flypaper covered with sweat.

Otherwise, of course, there are Jewish Talmud schools and synagogues. One sees Hebrew letters. They seem alien on these walls. One sees the spines of books through half-covered windows.

One sees Jews with prayer shawls under their arms. They are leaving the synagogue going toward the shops. One sees sick children, old women. Attempts to turn this boring Berlin street, kept as clean as circumstances permit, into a ghetto are always gaining strength. Always, Berlin is stronger. The inhabitants are fighting a futile fight. They want to spread their influence a bit? Berlin pushes them together.

III

I enter one of the small taverns. In the back room a couple of guests sit waiting for lunch. They have their hats on their heads. The proprietress stands between the kitchen and the bar. Behind the counter is the husband. He has a beard like red twine. He is fearful.

Why should he not to be fearful? Do the police not enter this place? Were they not already here a few times? The proprietor extends his hand to me anyway. And he says, "Oh, there's a guest! You've not been here for such a long time." A cordial greeting never hurts. One drinks the Jewish national drink: mead. That is the alcohol with which they can intoxicate themselves. They love heavy, dark brown mead; it is sweet, bitter, and powerful.

IV

Sometimes Salomon's Temple comes to Berlin. A Mr. Frohmann from Drohobycz produced it faithfully from the details in the Bible, out of spruce wood, papier-mâché, and gold paint. Not at all of cedar and real gold like the great King Salomon's.

Frohmann claims he worked seven years building this miniature temple. I believe it. To rebuild a temple precisely according to the details in the Bible requires just as much time as love.

It has every curtain, every courtyard, the smallest points of every tower, every sacred instrument. The temple sits on a table in the backroom of a tavern which smells of Jewish onion-stuffed fish. Very few guests take a look. The old ones already know the temple and the young ones want to go to Palestine to build streets, not temples.

And Frohmann travels from one ghetto to the other, from Jew to Jew, showing them his artwork. Frohmann, the defender of tradition and the single great architectonic work the Jews ever created, which consequently they will never forget. I believe that Frohmann is the expression of this desire, the desire of an entire people. I saw an old Jew standing before the miniature temple. He was just like his brothers who stand crying and praying before the only remaining, sacred wall of the destroyed temple.

V

I found the cabaret by accident, one bright evening as I wandered through the dark streets, glancing through the windowpanes of small synagogues, which were nothing but simple shops by day and houses of God mornings and evenings. Such is the proximity of heaven and gainful work to the Jews of the east: for their holy service they need nothing but ten adult (that means, over thirteen years old) fellow believers, a cantor, and knowledge of their geographical situation, to know where east is, *misrach,* the Holy Land, the Orient from which the light is supposed to come. Here everything is improvised: the temple by virtue of their having come together, trade by virtue of their standing still in the middle of the street. It is still the exodus out of Egypt, going on already for millenia. They must always be prepared, carry everything with them, bread and an onion in one pocket, their *tefillin* [prayer-shawl fringe] in the other. Who knows if they will not have to resume their wanderings at any hour? The theater pops up suddenly as well.

The theater was set up in the courtyard of an old and dirty tavern. It was a square courtyard open to the sky. Halls and corridors with glass windows hung on the walls concealed the various intimacies of domesticity, beds, shirts, and buckets. An old, misplaced linden tree stood in the middle, representing nature. Through a couple of lighted windows I could see the insides of a typical tavern kitchen. Steam rose from the boiling pots; a fat woman swung a spoon, her fat arms half exposed. Directly in front of the window and placed so that it covered half of it stood a stage from which one could go straight into the restaurant hallway. In front of the stage were the musicians—a choir of six men, said to be brothers, the sons of the great musician Mendel from Bericzew, whom the oldest Jews from the east could yet remember and whose violin playing was so splendid that no one could forget it, neither in Lithuania, nor in Volynka, nor in Galicia.

The acting troupe that was supposed to appear here shortly called itself the Troupe Surokin. Surokin was the manager, director, and cashier—a fat, clean-shaven gentleman from Kovno who had already sung in America, cantor and tenor, hero of the synagogue and opera, spoiled, proud, and condescending, businessman and comrade in equal parts. The audience sat at small tables, eating bread and sausages and drinking beer, collecting their food themselves from the restaurant, conversing, screaming, laughing. They were petty merchants and their families, no longer orthodox but "enlightened," which is what people in the east call Jews who shave (even if only once a week) and wear European clothes. These Jews observe religious customs more from piety than religious need: they think of God only when they need him, and such is their fortune that they need him often. Among them there are cynics and superstitious sorts, but all of them become sentimental in certain situations and are moved in the way they are being moved. In business matters they are ruthless toward themselves and strangers—and yet one need only touch upon a certain hidden chord to make them generous, kind, and humane. And yes they can cry, especially in such an open-air theater as this one was.

The troupe consisted of two women and three men—and the attempt to describe what they performed on the stage leaves me at a loss for words. The whole program was improvised. First came a short, thin man, his nose sitting on his face like an alien creature, an astonished one; it was an impertinent, intrusively questioning and yet touching, ridiculous nose, more Slavic than Jewish, broad and with a surprisingly pointed end. The man with this nose was playing music, a foolish–wise jester; he played old songs, teasingly appending surprising, funny, nonsensical points on the end. Then the two women sang an old song, an actor told a humorous story of Scholem Alechem, and, in conclusion, the honorable director Surokin recited modern Hebrew and Yiddish poems of living and recently deceased Jewish authors. He pronounced the Hebrew verses, followed immediately by Yiddish translations, and occasionally he began to sing two or three lines quietly, as if he were singing to himself in his room, and it became dead silent and the petty merchants' eyes grew large, their chins resting on their fists, and one could hear the rustle of the linden leaves.

I do not know if you are familiar with all of the Jewish melodies from the east and I want to try to give you an idea of this music. I think I will have characterized it most clearly by calling it a mix of Russia and Jerusalem, of folk song and psalm. This music has the pathos of the synagogue and the naiveté of folklore. The text seems, if one only reads it, to require cheerful, lively music. But if one hears it sung, it reveals itself to be a painful song, one that "smiles beneath the tears." Once one has heard it, it echoes for weeks; the contradiction was only an apparent one, for in reality this text *can* be sung to no other melody.

It goes:

> Ynter die griene Beimelach
> sizzen die Mojschelach, Schlojmelach,
> Eugen wie gliehende Keulalach . . . [1]

They sit! It is not that they romp about under the green trees. If they were to romp about, the rhythm of these lines would be as lively as it appears to be on first glance. But they do not romp about, the little Jewish lads.

I listened to that old song that Jerusalem the city sings, so melancholy that its pain floats over all of Europe, floats far into the east, floats over Spain, Germany, France, Holland, all along the whole bitter way of the Jews. Jerusalem sings:

> Kim, kim Jisruleki I aheim
> in dein teuers Land arain . . . [2]

All the merchants understood this singing. The little people drank no more beer and ate no more sausages. Thus were they prepared for the beautiful, serious, even difficult and sometimes abstract poetry of the great Hebrew poet [Chaim Nachman] Bialik, whose songs have been translated into nearly all civilized languages and who is expected to spur a reinvigoration of literary Hebrew, finally making it a living language. This poet has the scorn of the old prophets and the sweet voice of a rejoicing child.

---

1. "Under the little green tree / sit the Moishes, the Shlomos, eyes like glowing coals."
2. "Come, come home, Jisruleki / to your dear land."

106

THEODOR LESSING
Jewish Self-Hatred

First published as *Der jüdische Selbsthaß* (Berlin: Jüdischer Verlag, 1930), 9–17.

I

On the day I began writing this book on self-hatred, the Jews in the east groan under the burden of oppressive news. In Jerusalem, in the area of the Haram, a religious war has broken out before the Wailing Wall. It began as all wars in history have begun: because overwrought people cast senseless words at one other until from the senseless words there came forth senseless deeds. But a hatred stored up for a long time was released in these deeds. It can threaten the endeavor of the Jewish people.

"The endeavor of the Jewish people": the resurrection of our homeland seemed to have been secured! For even the sober experts—who in no way dream of an exodus of Israel to Palestine but consider themselves German, French, English, Italian, or whatever—had been won over to the thoughts of Zionism to the extent that they founded an executive organization, the so-called Jewish Agency, for the solution of the insoluble Jewish question. But then there transpired what could easily transpire again in the future: the villages and farms newly constructed, wrung with sorrowful pains from the malarial land; the plantings in which every tree embodied the life of a *chaluz* [pioneer]; and the fields fertilized with sweat and tears went up in flames.

Artuf burned. Ataroth burned. Moza burned. Bands of Arabs set fire to the Jewish suburb of Talpioth and laid waste to the house of the poet [Shmuel Yosef] Agnon. The famous yeshiva in Hebron, the Talmudic school from Lithuanian Slobodka, was attacked. Unarmed young students, led by the son of the rabbi, fled into the oratory where they were slain one after the other as they pronounced their final prayer. And all of this happened under the eyes of the British Mandate authorities.

What does the world expect us Jews to do?

For thirty years and longer, since the Bilu movement of 1882, our noble elite has worked on the solution to the nationality question. Tired of ever-fresh outbreaks of mass hysteria, which no nobility of deed, of decorum, or of the heart has ever been able to reconcile; tired of the eternal either–or (either you give yourselves up or you get out of the country); tired of the centuries of reprimands, relocations, and regimentation—whether born of caprice or mercy; tired of all the insecurity and uncertainty, the oldest of all the peoples of the earth attempted to take its fate into its own hands.

It was said: "You are parasites on the property of others"—then we tore ourselves from the chosen homeland. It was said: "You are the middlemen among the peoples." Then we raised our children to be gardeners and peasants. It was said: "You are degenerating and will become cowardly weaklings." Then we went to battle and supplied the best soldiers. It was said, "You are only tolerated wherever you are." We responded: "We know no deeper desire than to escape from toleration."

But when we established ourselves on our own, we heard once again: "Have you still not learned that the tenacious self-preservation of the chosen people is a betrayal of the wealth of the universal human, of *trans*national values?" We answered, after a hundred deaths and wounds, by silently dissolving the Jewish Legion. We renounced self-defense and placed our due right under the protection of the European conscience. What is the answer?

Today, September 6, 1929, the answer seems to be: "Live or work however you can, you will be tolerated as long as you can be used." "Business people!" the Jews will be called. But when there is no more business to be done with the Jews, they will be dropped. The power most maniacally bent on exploiting the earth, the English–American, will also sacrifice Judaism for the next enterprise of colonial expansionism that comes along. Woe, however, to the defenseless: *"Niflad kidra al kefla, weile kidra. Niflad kefla al kidra, weila kidra. Wenkach, unwenkach, weile kidra!"* "If the pot falls on the stone, woe to the pot. If the stone falls on the pot, woe to the pot. Always, always, woe to the pot!"

What should the Jew do? The question is not to be answered. And because it is not to be answered, there arises a difficulty for one's conscience. How does one allay those difficulties?

They are allayed only in rare cases by confessing: "I am guilty." By far the majority of cases, however, attempt to attribute the *guilt* for the insufferable situation to the involuntary author of the condition. This is the law of "lending sense in retrospect." The fundamental law of all of history![1]

II

The events of human history, this endless chain of accidental transfers of power and acts of caprice, this ocean of blood, bile, and sweat, would be unbearable if it were not possible for people to read a meaning into all of these blind occurrences. They are not at all satisfied to discover the *original* meaning for all that happens; much more they want to find the *sensible* reason. And when they ask: "What is *responsible* for that?" they are already making a *moral* judgment.

Even if therefore the fate of peoples were "accidental" and if everything could also have come about differently, people would still, once it came about *as it did,* always undertake *to interpret* what happened in terms of its sense and ethics!

However, this *making sense* of all senselessness and nonsense can (as we already suggested) transpire in *two* ways. Either by attributing guilt to the "other" or by seeking the guilt in oneself.

Now it is one of the most profound and secure realizations of national psychology that among all peoples the Jewish people were the first, indeed perhaps the only people who have sought this responsibility for world events solely *in themselves.*

To the question "Why are we not loved?" Jewish doctrine has answered since ancient times: *"Because we are guilty."* There have been great Jewish thinkers who have discovered in this formula, "Because we are guilty," and in the experience of the collective attribution of guilt and collective responsibility of the people of Israel, the innermost core of the Jewish doctrine.

We may not go into more detail here concerning the significance of this religious collective guilt, but it is important that the reader sense that in this acknowledgment of guilt, emphasized in the mighty Judeo-Christian ethic, is also the key to the *pathology* of our national soul.

Very deep inside of every Jewish person there is a tendency to comprehend a misfortune that befalls him as atonement for a sin. If the reader should ask why this is so, I could

1. Theodor Lessing, *Geschichte als Sinngebung des Sinnlosen,* 2nd ed. (Munich, 1921), 211–252.

only point here to the terrible fact that Jewish history over nearly three thousand years has been solely a *history of suffering*. And, indeed, a history of hopeless, irredeemable suffering.

To make sense and be bearable, however, such a condition of suffering permits only a single emergency exit: the person must believe that fate exercises a particular intention toward him. "God disciplines those he loves." With this understanding of his suffering as a *penalty,* the beginnings of the phenomenon of self-hatred are clearly given.

It is, however, different among the happy and victorious peoples. They have had no occasion, in self-analysis and self-torment, to endanger the healthy emotional relation to life and natural self-esteem. To the question: "Why does misfortune happen to us?" they answer with a forceful accusation against those who, in their opinion, are the "*cause* of the misfortune."

The situation of the Jewish person was thereby doubly endangered. Once because he himself responded to the question "Why are we not loved?" with the answer "Because we are guilty." Then, however, because now the other people could likewise respond to the question, "Why is the Jew unloved?" with the answer, "He says so himself. He is guilty."

Behind the sociological phenomenon designated as anti-Semitism (whereby an entire national type was characterized as *odium generis humani*), there is not merely bad will, the national egotism, or the envy and hate of the competition of peoples. There is a law behind it. A law of "lending sense to the *senseless.*" And this law of history arises out of an ultimate depth.

It is the same law that also sows discord into many an individual fate and leads to sundry enmities. For how often is it not the case that brothers and sisters, lovers, and friends estrange themselves forever because no one wants to look into himself and acknowledge *his* guilt, and instead everyone travels the easiest and most natural path: "Wherever I must introduce suffering into the life of another, I justify my action by the nature of the *other.*" A few examples will suffice to illuminate the great significance of this simple fact.

III

All of us, in order to be able to live at all as people have to assume some guilt onto ourselves. We have, for example, to exterminate a world of animals, wonderful, perfect in itself, and originally superior to us. When we destroy the big beasts of prey, lions and leopards, then we conduct ourselves very badly. Therefore we say that the animal of prey is bad. When we exterminate the big snakes, we use much cunning in the task; therefore we say that snakes are cunning.

If I have ever cherished bad thoughts against another, then I have to *justify* these bad thoughts to myself precisely by way of the bad qualities in the other.

Whoever has once said, "God punish England," or "Germany must be humbled," from now on unconsciously cherishes an inclination to gather together and value highly whatever is expedient in the justification of his unfavorable prejudice. Ultimately it could even be that we do not hate something bad at all because it is bad; but rather that which we hate and must hate we *call* bad.

This procedure by which the hated is made hateful is further intensified when a secret feeling of sympathy has to be stifled and deadened. One finds this in such cases where a love or friendship is transformed into hate and persecution.

If I have esteemed or loved a person highly and feel disappointed and disillusioned, then as a rule I experience the disappearance of the old feelings in no way as my fault or as my error; rather I supply the motivation for the transformation of my emotions by saying that the other has changed. That is usually self-deception. It is not the other who has changed, but my inner attitude. But wherever people have to bear the weight of conscience and take responsibility for their actions, there we find beautiful words and ideals as well, in the name of which we can also recast our injustice as our good right.

Now to apply this universal law to the Jewish question:

The Jewish people have without a doubt been wrongly injured. Their unworthy being would have become a reproach to every one of the healthy peoples, among whom the sick people continue to vegetate, if there had been no historical formula thanks to which the wrong exercised upon the Jewish people had not been justified as a wrong, that is, as a *right*. To the Jews as well as to the non-Jews such sense-lending formulae were *necessary*. If one wants to exploit us in the future, then one will justify it with the insight that we were the exploiters of others. If one wants to push us out and reduce the vitality of our lives, then one will adduce everything that justifies exceptional determinations and particular laws. There is no wrong in history that cannot in retrospect be proven to have been justified or otherwise necessary. Wherever a group of people has been condemned to bear its cross on its back, there it will always be said: "They nailed the Savior to the cross."

What researcher into the human soul knows, however, whether the diminishing of souls over centuries does not actually transform the nature of those diminished as well, so that in the final reckoning all the wrongs of history actually become proven wrongs, that is, *become* true? For to change human beings into dogs, one only needs to shout at them long enough, "You dog!"

107

GERSHOM SCHOLEM

On the 1930 Edition of Rosenzweig's *Star of Redemption*

First published in *Frankfurter Israelitisches Gemeindeblatt* 10 (1931), 15–17.

Hardly ever had there been a Jewish theology of such vacuity and insignificance as existed in the decades before World War I. The inability to penetrate religious reality with rigorous concepts as well as the lack of readiness to perceive the religious world of Judaism in its totality were apparent equally in all the movements. [. . .]

Since the collapse of the Kabbalah and the last efforts to describe the reality of Judaism from this point of view—attempts such as those of Solomon Plessner and Elijah Benamozegh only showed the complete decay of this movement—orthodox theology has suffered from what one might call "Kabbalah-phobia." [. . .]

This decision had most disastrous and destructive results in the theology of Samson Raphael Hirsch who—a classical instance of the frustrated mystic—preferred to construct a highly questionable and nearly coarse symbolism of his own design just to avoid any reference back to the world which he had forbidden himself: the world of the Kabbalah. And what healthy chunks the liberal theologians took out of Judaism! For the sake of an abstraction they had more or less to eliminate the realities of language, land, and peoplehood from their theories. [. . .]

Finally, Zionism with its seemingly secularizing tendencies was as yet unable to contribute to a theology that on account of its weakness was incapable of recognizing, let alone of grasping, the religious problematics, only incompletely and ineffectually concealed by that secularization.

Given this situation, we found in Rosenzweig's work something new which in an unanticipated way addressed us from the center of our hopes for renewal. [. . .]

It was obtained by philosophical penetration into the order of a world that would be able to survive the catastrophic collapse of [German] idealism as the structural principle of the world—which would in fact grow out of this catastrophe. The seductive illusion of man's moral autonomy determined the theology of Jewish liberalism, which had its origins essentially in idealism. From here no path lay open, except for a radical reversal in direction, back toward the mysteries of revelation that constituted the basis of Rosenzweig's new world, which turned out to be the most ancient world of all. [. . .]

By his use of the doctrine of the anticipation of redemption in Jewish life, a concept as fascinating as it is problematic, Rosenzweig took a decided and hostile stand against the one open door in the otherwise very neatly ordered house of Judaism. He opposed the theory of catastrophes contained in messianic apocalypticism which might be considered the point at which even today theocratic and bourgeois modes of life stand irreconcilably opposed. The deep-seated tendency to remove the apocalyptic thorn from the organism of Judaism makes Rosenzweig the last and certainly one of the most vigorous exponents of a very old and very powerful movement in Judaism, which crystallized in a variety of forms. This tendency is probably also responsible for the strangely churchlike aspect that Judaism unexpectedly sometimes takes on here. Apocalypticism, as a doubtlessly anarchic element, provided some fresh air in the house of Judaism. [. . .] A thinker of Rosenzweig's rank could never remain oblivious to the truth that redemption possesses not only a liberating but also a destructive force. [. . .] If it be true that the lightning of redemption directs the universe of Judaism, then in Rosenzweig's work the life of the Jew must be seen as the lightning rod whose task it is to render harmless its destructive power. [. . .]

Only when the enchanting beauty of its language will have worn off and the figure of the martyr, which for us contemporaries is inseparably part of it, will have withdrawn to cast an aura of its own—only then shall this testimony to God be able to assert itself in its undisguised intent.

108

CENTRAL ASSOCIATION OF GERMAN CITIZENS OF THE JEWISH FAITH, HAMBURG CHAPTER

Flyer

First published as "Flugblatt des Central-Verein deutscher Staatsbürger jüdischen Glaubens, Ortsgruppe Hamburg" (April, 1932).

GERMAN MEN AND WOMEN!

We publicly are turning to all the men, women, and young people of Germany. For the falsehoods, insults, and slanderous remarks concerning Judaism and Jewish people—

disseminated in gatherings by the thousands where entry is refused us, in newspapers that completely lack responsibility, and in pamphlets in unheard-of numbers—can no longer be tolerated. With all the passion of our hearts we reject it. Despite everything we trust in your sense of uprightness and your truthful conscience. We expect you to listen not only to the one side but also to our side.

Read what we have to say here! Think it over! Consider it!

For each of our responses the proof is available, accessible to all. It is a question of race and stock, they tell you, claiming that the Jews are of inferior blood. What they do not tell you, however, is what science has to offer: that today there scarcely exist on earth any more races in pure form; that all the peoples of modern history are mixed of the most various races; that the German people in particular is especially strongly mixed of many races.

Even self-annointed, nationalistic race researchers therefore admit the truth: "If it were a question of race, the German people would fall to pieces." A backward development of today's cultural groupings into races is impossible, just as it is impossible for an adult to return to childhood.

The Jews too are a group of people mixed of the most diverse races. There are just as many blond, blue-eyed, and tall Jews as there are dark-haired, brown-eyed, and short non-Jews. They are "Jews" because they and their ancestors before them, from whom they come, have carried and continue collectively to preserve a distinct spiritual identity—Judaism—through a history of several millenia.

Ignorant people slander Judaism as a *secret teaching*. But you all know that it is no secret, that it is open to everyone, accessible to everyone. It is the spirit of the Bible, which promotes love of one's neighbor, forbids killing, forbids the bearing of false witness, commands respect for the honor and property of others, gives to people the gift of the Sabbath, and created the ethical foundation of all of humanity in the Ten Commandments.

Does one dare to represent as inferior those people who brought this to the world? Consider that there are in many countries narrow-minded people who claim all virtues as their own and attribute everything ugly, that which the slanderers say about "the Jews," to people elsewhere whom they hate.

The accusers point to the Talmud and the codex of a Jewish scholar, called *Schulchan Aruch!* However, these writings are not secret, but available to anyone. The Talmud is a collection of books in which the thoughts and meditations of many generations on the meaning of the word of God are written. Statements from all times on questions of the holy writ and on all matters of life are to be found there. A few fantasizing zealots, who are mostly not able even to read the Hebrew alphabet let alone understand the words, bring you alleged quotations, statements, and sayings from the work, which have nearly all been exposed as falsifications and distortions. Should there really be in fact, in the endlessly expansive writings of biblical and postbiblical times, isolated statements taken to be expressed in rage or grief or bitterness over the offenses and persecutions suffered—no one knows them today! They have no meaning for the whole! But we ask you, have you ever thought of taking responsibility if one of your ancestors, in times long since past, had said or done something you do not understand today?

You would laugh at anyone who wanted to reproach you today for what occurred, let's say, in the times of torture!

Why do you tolerate it when ill-intentioned and ignorant people are allowed to behave like that toward Jews?

Why do you tolerate it at all when, in the context of serious political and economic matters, you are presented with such a bogeyman as "the Jew," as he appears in the generalizations of the hatemongers? Everywhere you are confronted with "the Jew."

Wherever he is, he is supposed "to dominate" you! He is supposed to be responsible for whatever comes up, even the most contradictory things: capitalism and bolshevism, finance capital and Marxism.

How is it possible? The clear numbers and facts tell you the truth.

Not even one in a hundred Germans is a Jew. Is it really possible that one would prevail against a hundred of you?

"The Jews" are supposed to be "rich." Count the rich and you will see that it is always only an isolated few who possess riches, an isolated few among the Jews, exactly as among the non-Jews. The majority of Jews work like you do; they toil and trouble for their daily bread just like you!

In reality the Jews, in accord with their economic and social status, belong to the political parties that correspond to their social situation. Thus does one find a few Jewish financiers and big businessmen in the parties of the right; thus does one find most of the Jews, those belonging to the middle class, in the middle-class parties; and one thus finds Jews in the working-class parties of all tendencies. They do not, however, belong to these parties in their quality as Jews, but as people like you—as people of their respective economic and social situations and political disposition.

Thus it is a shameless falsification to act as if there were a unified Jewish tendency. The Jews are in every conceivable manner just as divided in various directions as any other group in Germany. If isolated Jews have capital and exercise influence, that does not mean "the Jews" created capitalism or that "Jewish finance capital" exists. If isolated Jews are active in visible positions in the working-class parties, that does not mean "the Jews" created socialism or bolshevism or Marxism.

This nonsense reaches its pinnacle in the cliché of a "Jewish" Marxism.

Karl Marx did come from a Jewish family, but he had nothing to do with Judaism or the Jewish community and wanted nothing to do with them. His conception of history derived from the theoretical construction of the most German of all philosophers, *Hegel*. What is taken today for socialism and communism does originate in Marx's theoretical writings but is a completely different movement created by men who were not Jews, men like Engels, Bebel, Lenin.

So is it too with the outcry about the so-called Jewish press. Count them! Among approximately 1,500 political newspapers in 1927 nearly three-quarters, that is, 1,148 are right-wing, and only 362 are left-wing papers.

In comparison, there are today 1,200 papers in Germany which are explicitly directed *against the Jews*.

The "Jewish press" is simply what the hatemongers call all newspapers whose line does not appeal to them. For the majority have no Jewish publishers at all, and only among the very few are there individual Jewish editors.

Who produces the newspapers today?

The newspapers are run today primarily by a host of nationalistic journalists who are completely irresponsible and usually take refuge behind the immunity of representatives.

The largest news bureaus are in the hands of right-wing organizations. These, and nearly the whole news service for the provincial press are almost exclusively in the hands of Hugenberg and his concern.

Just as empty as the talk about the "Jewish press" are the constant lamentations over the allegedly disproportional representation of Jews in the intellectual vocations. Does it really appear so surprising that people would turn more to intellectual vocations who for centuries on end were forcibly kept away from all professions having to do with manual labor and so were forced to occupy themselves intellectually, as the Jews have done through the generations with their teaching? If all vocations but commerce are closed to a person, is it then so surprising that many Jews are engaged in commerce?

Do you not know that wherever vocations involving manual labor are open to Jews, Jews are found in them? For example, that the dockworkers in southern Russia and Greece are Jews, that almost all craftsmen in the Polish settlement area and thousands of the industrial workers there are "Jews?" That in Germany, too, Jews make up a host of employees and workers and, now, unemployed people?

Do you know that until just before the war there were hardly any Jewish civil servants? That hatemongers of the same stamp as those today, but from a hundred years ago—when the Jews did not even have equal rights and therefore were never and could never become civil servants at all and, God knows, didn't govern—called the government of the time a "Jewish government"?

Do you understand now that to the hatemongers "Jews" are always the ones they want to get out of the way, that they designate as "Jewish" whatever it is they do not like? And why do they want them out of the way?

Because the hatemongers believe themselves able to reap where the Jewish person comes to economic ruin as a result of this squandrous and evil sowing. Therefore the brazenness of the call to open and secret boycotts: "Don't buy from Jews!" "Don't go to Jewish doctors and lawyers!" And however else the calls might go.

In all times people from all circles, high or low, have also turned to Jewish doctors or lawyers. Did they do so because these professionals were "worse" or perhaps because they—as the hatemongers would like you to believe—being of a "different race" could not help them or could not help them properly? No, one went to them because one had trust in them, because they made their living through good and conscientious work.

Alongside these examples of those who worked faithfully and modestly in their daily lives, should the merits of others be forgotten, of all those who achieved high merits for German culture and German prestige in the world—[Albert] Ballin, [Walther] Rathenau, Max Liebermann, [Fritz] Haber, [Heinrich] Caro, and [Albert] Einstein, to mention just a few? Should it be forgotten that fifteen of the twenty-five German Nobel prizewinners are Jews?

You too had trust in those Jewish people when you went to them. What forces you to turn away from this trust? Do you want to allow yourselves to be led by a mentality of hate based on error, delusion, indeed, on malicious lies?

Consider that a hundred thousand Jewish men stood next to their comrades on the front in the Great War. Among them twelve thousand died for the fatherland.

Our slanderers and hatemongers have gone so far as to desecrate the dead. Over 150 desecrations of Jewish cemeteries and memorials have occurred in the last few years, committed mostly by young people led astray by this disgraceful provocation.

Brutality, acts of violence, and barbarism everywhere are the signs of this abominable provocation! Political murders, abuse of peaceful people, hateful licentiousness in thought, word, and deed mark their path!

109

CARL VON OSSIETZKY

Anti-Semites

First published as "Antisemiten," *Die Weltbühne,* 28, no. 29 (July 19, 1932), 88–97.

One of those matters which the republican left rarely mentions any more is anti-Semitism. Newspapers are content to recognize its existence without going very closely into its manifestations. For them it is enough, from time to time, to deprecate some overly offensive excess. On the whole they are ready to sacrifice Israel quietly along with so many other things. But now the human and civil rights of the Jews, although nobody can impeach them, have again become a subject of lively controversy. Again counterrevolution has succeeded in forcing the play. It has taken the initiative, and the democracy is trying to create the impression that the entire argument is nonexistent by keeping out of it.

Anti-Semitism is akin to nationalism and its best ally. They are of a kind because a nation that, without territory or state power, has wandered through two thousand years of world history is a living refutation of the whole nationalist ideology that derives the concept of a nation exclusively from factors of power politics. Anti-Semitism has never had roots among workers. It has always been a middle-class and small-peasant affair. Today, when these classes face their greatest crisis, it has become to them a kind of religion, or at least a substitute for religion. Nationalism and anti-Semitism dominate the German domestic political picture. They are the barrel organs of fascism, whose pseudorevolutionary shrieks drown out the softer tremolo of social reaction.

The anti-Semitic wave begun by Court Chaplain Adolf Stöcker ebbed about twenty-five years ago. The attitude and influence of the Anti-Semitic party then in the Reichstag roughly resembled those of the Economic Party of today. Anti-Semitic violence was the monopoly of the notorious Count Pückler-Tschirine, who represented nothing but his own muddled head. This worthy went down in general laughter when he tangled with a Jewish traveling salesman in a hotel lobby and took a terrific beating.

Intellectual anti-Semitism was the special prerogative of Houston Stewart Chamberlain, who, in *The Foundations of the Nineteenth Century,* concretized the fantasies of Count Arthur de Gobineau, which had penetrated to Bayreuth. He translated them from the language of harmless snobbery into that of a modernized, seductive mysticism. Arthur Moeller van den Bruck, a writer on art, was an offshoot of this tendency. In his book *The Germans,* which is still worth reading, he attempted to define the Germanic type. His book *The Third Reich,* although an unpolitical, monotonous lament rather than an agitational shriek, gave a slogan to the movement.

Contemporary literary anti-Semitism has covered itself by abandoning racial theories long since recognized as invalid and by ceasing to make a great fuss about Aryanism and Nordicism. Gobineau claimed to be a descendant of Hakon Jarl, and the parvenus of Bayreuth tried to trace their pedigrees back to the Vikings. Today only minor yellow journalists have the effrontery to publish stuff of that sort.

Contemporary anti-Semitic literature, insofar as it is not simple, crude Jew-baiting, in so far as it claims intellectual consideration, is satisfied to postulate an imposing Teutonism which, examined critically, dissolves into thin air like a beautiful Epicurean god. The word *blood* plays a large part in its phraseology. Blood, the immutable substance, determines the fate of nations and men. Because of the secret laws of blood, Germans and Jews will never be able to mix, must be mutually antagonistic until doomsday.

This is romantic, but hardly deep. No real science of nationalities can be based on such flimsy premises. For *German* and *Jewish* are not fixed categories established once and for all in some mystic prehistoric age but rather flexible concepts which change their content with spiritual and economic changes dependent on the general dynamics of history. What has the German of [Albrecht] Dürer's time in common with the German of the rococo period? What does the Americanized Stalinist of the Russian five-year plan have to do with the sluggish Oblomov [a character in Ivan Goncharov's novel of the same name] of the 1860s. Every notion of literary anti-Semitism is nebulous and fuzzy. Its confusion is no different from that of neoconservatism or the national romanticism so much the vogue today.

In the following pages we shall discuss several of these anti-Semitic documents, not because we consider them important performances but because, like the famous hospital horse, they embody all the diseases of the species, and some of their formulations are rapidly gaining currency and creating mischief.

If my own indignation does not suffice for the purpose of cursing a Jewish tailor who has overcharged me, the contents of a Nazi pamphlet will. But if I want to find out just why my neighbor, the elderly Jewish eye doctor generally regarded as a public benefactor, is in reality a public enemy, I have to get hold of a certain volume by Hans Blüher. This is what has happened to the prophet of the *Wandervögel*, the exponent of the creative force of youth organization, an author of really fruitful ideas! It requires a real effort to get through his book, *The Revolt of Israel against Christian Values*. It has often been said of Charles Maurras, the sabre-rattling Bayard of French royalism, that somewhere inside him is hidden a joker. I wonder whether here too a capricious satirist is not thumbing his nose at wiseacres. Certainly one is entitled to doubt a little Blüher's sincerity when he bellows like any ultraroyalist, a very Jacobite of Scotland, a noble of the Vendée. [. . .]

Of what does Blüher accuse Jewry? Let us summarize: Jewry consumes the German substance. It can assume the guise of a nation other than itself. Jewish flesh has an "organic–plastic talent for mimicry. It has something important to hide." Blüher wants nothing to do with political or economic anti-Semitism. The "Jewish mission" of which he drivels, and to establish which he relies on medieval parchments, is exclusively religious. Hence there is no real reconciliation:

> While Jews of top quality rise to the top, those of inferior quality are pushed to the bottom. The informed Jew will admit that the nadir to which his people may sink is substantially lower than that of other nations, and that any middle class, as one might call it, is lacking. Ten damned tribes and only two blessed ones! In our daily life we run into the damned, while the blessed manage the politics of the Kingdom of Judah against our interests. There can be sincere controversy only with the latter; they alone are our real enemy. This state of affairs explains sufficiently how stupid anti-Semitism is to declare that there are also decent Jews and that they are not included.

Here we have again the wisdom of the Grand Inquisitor: "Kill them all; God knows his own." Thus the pious can in all conscience raise his hand even against the best Jews. It therefore seems to be neither logical nor courageous when Blüher, having mercilessly banished all notion of reconciliation, is still rather perplexed and fails to tell us what should be done practically.

Nor do we get an answer from an author whom Blüher calls one of the few "genuine anti-Semites" extant in Germany, one Dr. Wilhelm Stapel, who has collected in a pamphlet, *Anti-Semitism and Anti-Germanism,* some articles previously published in his magazine. Whereas Blüher, despite all his prejudices, remains a strange and often-moving example of a misguided intellectual in a critical epoch—a servant of darkness to be sure, but a Paracelsus at heart—Stapel is simply the dull, narrow-minded pedagogue gone haywire and posing as a prophet.

Admirers consider Stapel the finest pen on the right, and I admit that he has rich forms of expression. Of course, he would be a much better writer if his style were less rhetorical and if he did not display his learning so pretentiously. Like a speaker spoiled by his audience, he pauses when he expects applause. He offers an unusual quotation ceremoniously, as a waiter serves an especially expensive dish, with two new, shiny, white napkins. He dances in front of his telling points with fluttering coattails, like David in front of the Ark of the Covenant. A writer should take himself seriously, yes—but not so damned seriously.

Stapel, too, rejects anti-Semitism on economic grounds. Nor does he seek to deprive the Jews of the rights of citizens. But a gulf must be established. For instance, Jews should not mix in politics. Good faith on both sides should decide borderline cases. Sometimes, of course, a clash is unavoidable:

> The Jew speaks of the sturdy knighthood of anti-Semitism using "brute force." We value intellect higher than physique. But intellect is not always with the "intellectuals." It is often with the upright and honest man who uses the God-given power of his arms in the interests of his higher feelings, for whose justification he need not first consult a philosopher. I am not inclined to give moral preference under all circumstances to a talented spiller of ink just because he works in a safe place with "intellect," as against an upright warrior who, after all, exposes life and limb to danger.

It has never yet happened that in a pogrom—that is the name given to certain "discussions" held with Jewish fellow citizens—the aggressors exposed their lives and limbs to danger. These upright and honest lads have usually used the God-given power of their arms only collectively, i.e., when they have been fifty against five. [. . .]

All these anti-Semites who are so much concerned about the welfare of the fatherland recall the tale of the princess and the pea. Why are they so upset by a few Jews? There is only one Jew to a hundred Germans, as Stapel says himself. I do not think so badly of Germany as does this fervent patriot. Germany is not so thin or colorless that her very character is endangered by some strange chemical. If Jews are relatively strongly represented in the academic professions, and if they occupy a few leading cultural positions, then I ask who has a right to complain? What did Germany do during her greatest prosperity, the period of the empire, to select her talented youth among the poor? Jews, even in bad times, contrived to spend money on children worthy of advancement. But the German proletarian youngster had to go in early youth either onto a farm or into a factory; he was a force which did not rise. The only ladder upward offered by the class–state was the school for noncommissioned officers. As a matter of fact, in many countries competition among people of different origins is considered stimulating, and certainly not troublesome. In the English press and letters, for instance, the flexible Celtic mind is dominant. And we were taught in school to admire the wisdom of the great Elector because he admitted French refugees into Prussia. Of course, that energetic Hohenzollern did not suffer from the inferiority complex of present-day German nationalism.

Stapel is constantly repeating the words *folkdom* and *folk*. These words, mystically adorned, save him the trouble of much proof. Like Blüher, Stapel refuses to operate with the concept of *race*. He knows that here he can win no laurels. But things are no less nebulous when he persistently compares Jewish with German folkdom. Here, too, bothersome economics plays a part. The folkdom of a small Jewish employee is not the same as that of his Jewish boss who has two cars in the garage. Of course the folkdom of the Jewish proletarian will awaken when some swastika scamps try to test the God-given power of their arms on him. Whether the same conscience will move within him when his boss is so treated, we cannot say.

Another error of nationalist theory is to assume that all day long we run around as Germans, Jews, and whatnot. The contemporary man with his specialized activities is made up altogether differently. In general, *folkdom* is a term with which little can be done. The state and economy determine the individual's fate, while daily social life fixes the general forms of thought and existence.

Folkdom cannot be applied to a nation of several score millions; it is a term restricted to a region and pervaded by peasant memories. There is no German folkdom, but one for each of the German tribes, for Thuringia, for the Rhine, for Bavaria. There is no British, no French, no Spanish folkdom, but those of Scotland, Normandy, Biscay. There is not even a standardized German–Jewish type. The Swabian Jew is different from the Jew of Hamburg or Lübeck—not because Jews are peculiarly adaptable, but because the influence of environment has always proved more effective than imported traditions.

> Mankind is not a sum of individual men, but of nations. The strange entity "nation" is not an unreal concept nor is it a creation of human beings, like societies and the state. It is a natural, organic growth, like a tree, a coral reef, a swarm of bees.

Wrong, wrong, and once again wrong. Only the individual is a natural growth; the nation is not. The nation is a human scheme of organization. Nature produces trees but not boundary stones. Nature's scheme of things includes animals, but not the cages in which they are locked by men. Nature does not care whether man houses himself in a coconut tree or a mail-order mansion. Nature is indifferent.

Stapel's ingenious researches would, of course, be incomplete without a word about Jewish penetration into literature.

> As [Gotthold Ephraim] Lessing once resisted the French, so we are right in opposing the Jews today.

Stop! Even if the equation of French and Jews were acceptable without reservation, it should be recalled that Lessing was justified by history. He helped the rise of youthful German letters. Moreover, Lessing fought not only *against* Voltaire but *for* another foreigner, Shakespeare. For a century suspicious *littérateurs* have observed the alleged Jewish domination of our literature. For a century, every notable author has had to undergo a physical examination by foolhardy foreskin experts. And what has been the result? What did that antiquated Jew-sniffer, Adolf Bartels, who has been drooling onto his bib for two generations, achieve by his denunciations? For decades they have been throwing mud on every recognized poet for being a Jew or a half-Jew. Has all that smoothed the path of a single valuable poet of unimpeachably German blood? Have these gentlemen discovered a single one? Let them name him!

Stapel senses a Jewish accent in the works of Karl Marx—"very distinctly." It never struck me that the *Communist Manifesto* sounded like Yiddish. But the economist Ferdinand Fried scents similar things. According to him Friedrich Engels, "son of a patrician from the Wupperthal," was the true founder of scientific socialism; he unfortunately let himself be overshadowed by Marx, the Jew.

And when Stapel gets on to Heinrich Heine, it is a circus. In order to show Jewish elements in Heine's lyrics he applies a procedure that, having nothing in common with philology, seems to be adapted from scientific criminology. Stapel subjects the poor "Lorelei" to a linguistic analysis just about the way a detective would. Of course the result bears out his thesis. True, he admits that Heine was a great artist with words, but as an "intellectual" he was unable to write a German folk song. Stapel presents his results with the moral satisfaction of an ill-mannered police doctor who, though unable to establish that a certain disreputable slut is guilty of picking pockets, has at least found symptoms of gonorrhea. [. . .]

There is much darkness, much hurly-burly, and still more unintended fun in this sort of intellectual anti-Semitism. I want to assure the learned doctor that although I laughed cruelly at his bold synthesis of literary criticism and criminology, my pleasure did not equal my regret that it has become necessary to handle such rubbish. Stapel, of course, is just a whining rhetorician, a sort of ladies'-club lecturer. But even a man of greater intelligence could not elaborate an anti-Semitism of really intellectual character. To be sure, intellect is not as gentle as a lamb and can quite well be reconciled to force. But intellect is incompatible with the oppression of a minority that can be blamed only of being suspected of differing. Anti-Semitism will never find any symbol except the blackjack.

Both Hans Blüher and Wilhelm Stapel swear emphatically that they advocate neither physical nor intellectual maltreatment of the Jews nor a denial of their civil rights. These gentlemen forget the background of the times and the echoes they may arouse. Today the cowardly scribbler need not stir himself. A well-directed word is sufficient to produce action. Today there is a strong smell of blood in the air. Literary anti-Semitism forges the moral weapon for murder. Sturdy and honest lads will take care of the rest. [. . .]

These literary anti-Semites must find themselves in an awful dilemma. They are always skirting the edge of a pogrom, they "eat of it on the sly," but they hesitate to become as active as those contemporaries who are intellectually less burdened. Why so shy, gentlemen? Step out, express the vulgarity which is part of every anti-Semite. Pick up the manure, throw it in the face of your Jewish fellow citizens, yell "Jewish swine!" You will find this a relief, and, since we live in Germany, there will be a court to express appreciation for the provoked condition of your soul. A little exertion of that kind would liberate you from an ugly, dirty atavism and exempt you from the disagreeable obligation of writing books whose personal sincerity is beyond question but whose distortions must intensify the prevalent national mendacity. Instead, Stapel finds heart-rending words that recall the famous proclamation of that neo-Hebrew classicist, Erich Ludendorff—"To the Jews of Poland." "Jewish fellow-citizens," shouts Stapel, "never forget where God has set the boundary!" Stapel, leave God out of this!

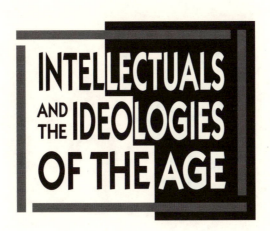

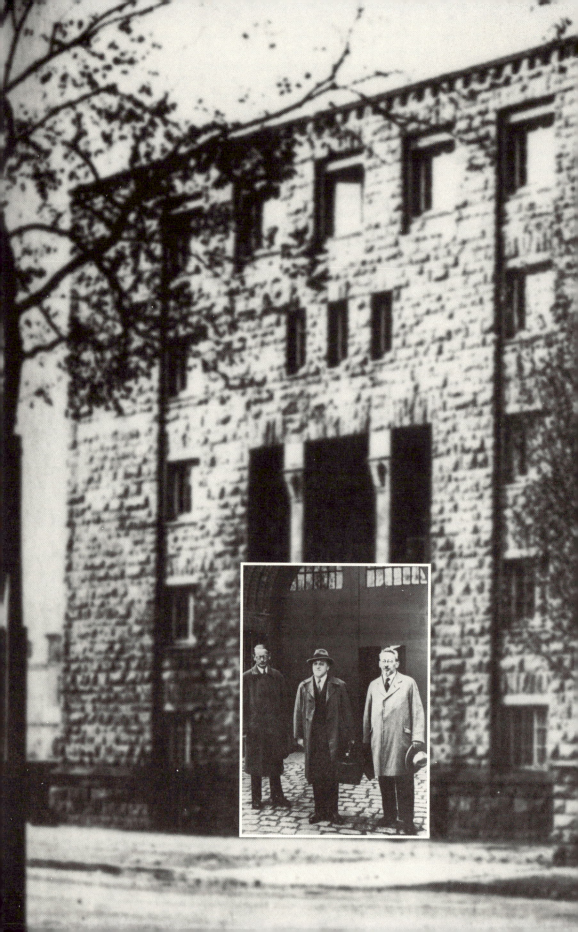

Institute for Social Research, University of Frankfurt, 1924. Inset: Carl von Ossietzky and his supporters outside of Tegel Prison, May 1932. Carl Schmitt. (Landesbildstelle Berlin.)

11
Redefining the Role of the Intellectuals

THE TURBULENT SOCIAL CHANGES of the Weimar era combined with the rapid transformation of German culture to produce an unprecedented self-consciousness among intellectuals, who began to worry about their status and function. No longer able to play the role of state-supported mandarins, yet still often arrogating to themselves the role of universal spokesmen, many intellectuals sought to redefine their position in radically new ways. The pressures of making a living in the marketplace, especially severe during the hyper-inflation, forced some of them to consider themselves proletarianized. In 1923 Alfred Weber wrote of the "predicament of intellectual workers," and eight years later Siegfried Kracauer remarked that writers were in danger of losing their exalted status and being turned into journalists because of economic exigencies.

But if some intellectuals were aware of the threats to their traditional role, others doggedly maintained their special claim to speak for the whole. In 1921 the novelist Alfred Döblin appealed for a renewed relationship between state and writer in which the former would provide support and the latter would act responsibly to give the new republic spiritual legitimacy. A decade later, writing from a more Marxist perspective, the critic Walter Benjamin exhorted radical intellectuals to lose the "left melancholy" that paralyzed them in the wake of the failed revolutions of the early Weimar years. Charging that writers like Erich Kästner, Walter Mehring, and Kurt Tucholsky, leading figures of the so-called homeless left, were ineffectual critics of the status quo, Benjamin implied that only allegiance to an active proletarian party would realize the intellectuals' true mission.

From the other side of the political spectrum, the editor of *Die Tat,* Hans Zehrer, bemoaned the cultural vacuum he perceived in the Weimar Republic and connected it to a failure to realize a viable concept of freedom. Only the intellectuals, he argued in 1929, could provide the inspiration for a spiritual revolution, precisely because they can stand above the fray. A similar argument appeared in the classic sociological study *Ideology and Utopia* published by the Hungarian-born scholar Karl Mannheim in the same year. Acknowledging the subjective limits on knowledge produced by the particular social status of every knower, he nonetheless held out hope for a totalizing synthesis of different points of view. Borrowing a term from Alfred Weber, Mannheim claimed that the "free-floating intelligentsia" beyond class affiliation was best equipped to bring about such a synthesis based on a scientific political sociology. Mannheim's so-called "relationist" solution to the threat of relativism was, to be sure, highly controversial. One of the most important critiques came from a young philosopher, who was very much influenced by Martin Heidegger, Hannah Arendt. In her review of *Ideology and Utopia*, Arendt attacked the very possibility of resolving disputes over truth by sociological means, claiming that this reduced ontological questions to mere "ontic" ones (as Heidegger called everything not concerned with Being). Thus, for Arendt, the role of intellectuals was to transcend their social situation and think about ultimate questions rather than merely to synthesize socially determined points of view.

Such exalted views of the tasks of the intellectual were not, however, universally shared during the republic. Suspicions of theoretically abstract, power-hungry, elitist intellectuals were evident on the left as early as Marx's quarrels with figures like Wilhelm Weitling and Mikhail Bakunin. During the Weimar era they still provoked vigorous polemics, such as that between Franz Seiwert and Franz Pfemfert in 1923. In certain other quarters the very word *intellectual* became an unequivocal term of opprobrium. In 1919, the feminist leader Gertrud Bäumer expressed her disdain for the arrogance of men of culture estranged from the people. The link between anti-intellectualism and antiliberal individualism was made even more explicit in Ernst von Salomon's 1930 diatribe "We and the Intellectuals." With such sentiments so prevalent during the Weimar period, the Nazis' infamous burning of books a few years later becomes easier to understand. So too does the retreat from public commitment evident in the poet Günter Eich's plea for a withdrawal into lyrical self-absorption as a way to escape politics. Here the so-called "inner emigration" of certain artists and intellectuals during the Nazi era was implicitly prefigured.

110

GERTRUD BÄUMER

The "Intellectuals"

First published as "Die Intellektuellen," *Die Hilfe* 25, no. 28 (July 10, 1919).

The arrogant and unreasonable demands of one of today's many special interest groups were being discussed at a conference. A cabinet secretary asked, "And who was the representative?" Answer: "An intellectual." The cabinet secretary replied, "Of course!"

Who are the intellectuals? Their "mentality" (this is their word) is as difficult to describe as it is characteristic of our time. The term is apparently meant to establish a cultural vantage point from which to present the facts and views of life in a way that is attached to their intellectual and spiritual side. At the same time this concept implies something incomplete, insufficient; both of these—in terms of the relationship to outer and inner reality—are rooted in each individual's own being.

The "intellectual" marks a failure of culture. These cultured and learned persons are to be found wherever the power of emotion, the energy of actions, and factual sense do not keep up with the intellect's brisk pace; these people want nothing more than to appropriate the most interesting problems that arise from all that is happening around them. But the kind of intelligence that is not rooted in a strong, simple nature, in an unwaveringly clear high-mindedness, and in a relationship to reality that is respectful and competent is a power more ruinous than many other less-refined vital energies. The influence of this sort of intelligence, boundless and treacherous, is undeniably the principal destiny of a faltering age.

Two things characterize these intellectuals: first, their conviction that they are the salt of the earth, born leaders who appoint themselves the mass movement's interpreters and commentators; second, their timidity in the realm of ideas. Alienated from nature and removed from powerful emotions, these are shallow human beings who take their in-spiration from ideals, from intellectualism as a sport or game. This is the only way for them to be enthusiastic and excited, to become enthralled by something, even to be touched by madness. But all of this occurs, as it were, not out of the spring-fresh powers of the soul but in the realm of mere "cultural experiences." People of culture are such complicated pieces of work that all of their primal feelings are also articulated on an artificial and literary level—a secondhand level. They experience themselves as if in the theater or in a novel, playing a role, and scarcely knowing anymore what is authentic, what is their own. This is complicated by the fact that such people are even able consciously to imitate what they lack: faith, warmth, instinct, simplicity. Their intellectuality is a self-reflexive pleasure that they cultivate by declaring war on themselves, dissolutely intoxicating themselves with instincts and passion they lack. "He dreams of a palm tree . . ."

How we are to rid ourselves of this type of person is a question we ask in despair. All young people of the educated class have to find their way through this tangled mass of "patched-together half-beings," and the more gifted they are the harder they have to struggle to find their way back to their own upright, simple, logical self. They are not helped in the least by the stifling epicurean desire that asphalt has for nature and earth, a desire that vents itself in an amazingly malleable advocacy of a certain type of con-temporary spiritual creed. The only thing that does assist them is life itself; that is, if they are still healthy, innocent, and principled enough to submit themselves to it—to the actual business at hand, the true, formative work that seizes the day, the power of clarity over the cheapness of all ideals that are *not* forged in the hard battle of everyday reality.

This counterfeit, irresponsible, grandiloquent intellectuality of the "intellectuals" lies like an impure cloud over the terrible inner battle being waged by our apprehensive and despairing people. They do not shrink back from radicalism of any kind because they have never endured, never traveled down, the quotidian path of ideals; they outdo each other in terms of "progress" because what should be the tension between the goal of tomorrow and what exists today is nothing more to them than a mental exercise. They always seize upon extremes because they can then justify their contempt for those who are conscientious, patient, and honest; they are the heroes of the unconditional demand because they delight in moral indignation. They are revolutionary at all costs because they can find no more appreciative forum for their aversion toward reality and their conscious and unconscious posturings.

At one point in German development it was necessary to denounce the philistine. Today there is no more vile yet more characteristic type than this sort of "intellectual" who was unknown in the past. Or was he? Goethe speaks prophetically in *Wilhelm Meister* about these bunglers who afflict us today like a spiritual plague: "They have no secrets and no power, their doctrine is like baked bread, tasty and satisfying for a day; but flour cannot be sown, and the fruits of the harvest are not to be milled."

111

ALFRED DÖBLIN

The Writer and the State

First published as "Der Schriftsteller und der Staat," *Die Glocke* 7, no. 7 (March 16, 1921), 177–182, and no. 8 (May 23, 1921), 207–211.

The task of the writer in this newly forming state is large; optimal aesthetic conditions are given to him. If he does not attain stature from them, if he fails now to achieve a new dignity in the state, he is ruined, and we will never see a German writer.

What is demanded of writers at this moment? Nothing and everything: responsibility. Perhaps the writer's severe economic distress hinders his achieving the dignity due him in popular life as disseminator of knowledge and suggestions, as animator of ethical impulses. These difficulties may not be allowed to become so insurmountable that he does not overcome them. Every animal struggles for its life, though the life of the writer is his mind. Whoever does not feel that is not, or is not yet, a writer. Whoever values warmer domesticity or greater ostentation more than hardness of mind has nothing to do with us. Whoever does not wage the struggle against the crude economic subordination of the mind, the struggle for the mind that is also for the state, is inferior to the animal. The responsible writer stands emotionally by his people as one of them once stood by a woman of whom he said: you were to me in past days sister, mother, child, and bride. As tenderly as toward a child, solicitously and respectfully as toward a mother, lovingly and with the resolute guidance of a man. The responsibility that must be demanded of the German writer at present, which are critical both for him and for the state, should inspire him to all conceivable strictness toward himself. His passion is there. But a writer's passion serves his knowledge. There are voices that say the position of the intellectual is hopeless; he can achieve nothing of importance in the state; the great driving forces of industry, technology, and commerce are omnipotent. Against these forces no idea of any consequence can thrive; the writer and the poet will soon be lackeys, decor, ornaments for the festivals of the parvenues. The writer is to be warned about these voices. Perhaps they speak truthfully of the past, but we speak of the present and the future. Industry, technology, and commerce are strong, but they are not qualified to build the state or, indeed, to maintain and advance humanity. A state that gives itself over without leadership to the elementary forces of industry and technology sooner or later will race along the way like a bolted team and be smashed against a stone. There is, however, yet another elementary force in man besides the force developed by industry and technology, and that is this: solidarity with the people, tending the community, feeling that the ethical drive is incomparably important. And this force is stronger, more elemental than any other. It is this force alone that makes up the genuine essence of man. And that is our sphere, the sphere of responsible people and the disseminators of knowledge.

Writers should not get discouraged. They should know what great tasks await them in today's state. One is justified, however, in saying that the desperate commotion inside Germany is greatly attributable to the deficit economy of a helpless and fevered mind. Instead of insights, one suggestive image after another is being hurled into the world and disseminated by writers. There are new forms and solutions being found for everything conceivable. Enraged battles erupt over banalities, so that many are already resigning themselves with a sigh: there is too much boorishness about, the Germans are far too immature for political freedom. In this time of incipient freedom movements—with their chaos of programs, their thousandfold ambitions and prejudices, their childish dogmatisms—writers must maintain the strictest reliance on themselves, knowing what a fine and dangerous instrument they possess in language. Even in peaceful times writers have observed there is something rather awkwardly self-willed contained in words: one believes oneself to be writing and is being written instead; the writer must constantly be on guard to assert themselves in relation to language, must deal with it like a tamer of wild animals. It is quite dangerous in agitated times for the writer to lose his composure, to fail to master his instrument, and to subordinate himself to suggestive images that are at home with bad, unclear words. And this defeat of the writer, this failure in the face of his own words, is now apparent a hundred times over. This defeat puts the writer on a par with the little man inspired to excess by speeches bellowed in the streets. [. . .]

I would like to point out in particular to lyricists, epic poets, and dramatists that previously existing conditions have caused them to produce for a homogeneous social stratum, for people who were fundamentally always the same. Things are different now. It must be recognized that the enormous mass of the so-called lowly people want to participate henceforth and that they must participate. The worries, passions, temptations, and vices of a single stratum will hardly suffice as the writer's representational objects in the future. He will accomplish the great task appropriate to his standing in the state when he learns to feel with the people who are looking to him, when he allows the people to enliven his work, and when he uses it to awaken them. The time will soon come when we must become much simpler, more understandable, and therefore more full of life than we now are.

Now I want to speak of the attitude that the state must adopt in regard to its writers. We know that the European states have insufficient feeling for what responsible writers mean to them and will come to mean again. The states must learn that all the industry and all the expansion of commerce in the world does not halt the decline of peoples once they have been robbed of their spirit. Indeed, it is impossible to repress the thought that the high value placed on economics for the sake of the state as well as on the reckless progress of industry and technology has already demonstrated its legacy in a decline in the force responsible for state building, in an anemia of the state. The writers and the poets, as those who preserve and fan the flames of the peoples, should be protected most carefully by the state. I do not have to speak of financial support designed to relieve the writer's economic struggle, to hinder his fall into the abyss of mammonism.

This is a large issue at the moment, and requires its particular spokesmen. I want to indicate the spiritual obligation of the state in relation to the writer.

Prevailing conditions, especially in Germany, are intolerable and nearly unbelievable. It can be taken as a notorious fact that, with very few exceptions, German statesmen, bureaucrats, and judges, are now as ever out of touch with all that concerns German education, especially living education. Among the men who represent the German state— this is known of the old Reich with utter certainty—one would search in vain for a pervasive, continually felt thread of universal education. Indeed, the representatives of earlier epochs have been all but proud of their ignorance of us, and Goethe and Schiller were only matters with which their daughters occupied themselves. Thus today the great culture of the German people floats freely and loosely around the state; what our great cultural figures have accomplished appears scarcely or not at all among officials of state. The poet should not become politicized, but the state must—this is our demand—become humanized and cultivated to the greatest degree. It owes this to itself; the youth are to be educated toward this end. This the state owes to the writers, if they are not to work for nothing and degenerate. [. . .]

What we demand of the writer in relation to the state: responsibility, overview, calm. These will win him a new dignity in the state. What we demand of the state in its spiritual attitude toward the writer: participation in cultural life, insight into the development of a new feeling of responsibility, more latitude toward spiritual forces, respect for the accomplishments of writers who are conscious of their responsibility.

And this is the core of what I am saying: amidst the droning of the factory, amidst the display windows enticing and unsettling the people, amidst the political brawling, I wanted, without resignation and full of hope, to address the writers. Let them not take part in the agitation and desperation of this time. Let the old merits of intellectuals remain with them, their unfading knowledge of the genuine, ideal goods of life, these goods that will once again appear as the fixed stars of our confused occident. This knowledge will obligate writers to the strictest cultivation of the self. The state will receive them. And they will achieve the dignity in the state that their works deserve in the sphere of human culture.

112

FRANZ W. SEIWERT AND FRANZ PFEMFERT

The Function of Intellectuals in Society and Their Task in the Proletarian Revolution

First published as "Die Funktion der Intellektuellen in der Gesellschaft und ihre Aufgabe in der proletarischen Revolution," *Die Aktion* 13, nos. 21–22 (June 14, 1923), 281–285.

FRANZ W. SEIWERT

The exploited class breaks down into two groups: the one that supplies the thinking and the other that does the work and for which the thinking is supplied. The functioning of both is restricted by the exploiting class's desire for profit. The group that supplies the thinking—the intellectuals—not only performs the mental work that generates profit via the manual labor of the proletariat but apparently is also the head of the exploiting class, which receives from it its countenance, its culture, and its life. But only apparently, for in reality it is not capable of thinking a thought that is not determined within the frame of the exploiting class, that does not, transformed by the labor of the proletariat, generate profits. Intellectuals cannot perform any mental work that is independent of the exploiters' interests. They are dependents, exploited like the proletariat, who can only—even in their own garden allotments—perform work that functions in the exploiters' interest. The difference is solely that the ruling class allows intellectuals the illusion of belonging to it because their work is so enormously important for the further existence of such a society. For it is not only that the intellectuals can perform mental work exclusively for the ruling class, but that they also interfere with the development of the mental capacity of the manual worker by allowing as teachers, journalists, and engineers, through an extremely refined and clever system, only as much of their mental labor to reach the class of manual workers as is necessary for the latter to perform their work in a profit-generating manner. To render any independent thought among the working class impossible, they have already created their own language, their own analytical method, which becomes increasingly incomprehensible to the working class. Because, however, mental labor, like all labor in human society, can only be performed collectively and is built upon the experiences of previous generations, the working class is excluded from this collective mental labor because the language and method has become incomprehensible to it; at the same time the working class is denied the knowledge of preceding generations, which, after all, could likewise be conveyed only in the language and method that have become incomprehensible. That which is conveyed to the working class is falsified in the sense that it maintains the worker in the status of a willing beast of burden and legitimates a society devoted to profit.

The goal is set! It may be that it has not yet been attained today and that the hope exists that, as a result of the internal contradictions of the profit society, it will never be attained. But it will not be attained only if, in this regard as well as in the struggle over production, the proletariat turns the internal contradictions in society to its own advantage, becomes clear as to its goal, understands its role in society, and gears its actions accordingly. The goal is set, which means that, if social development continues upon its present course, the whole of humanity will be split into two species differing essentially from each other in all respects. The one will develop a giant head swollen in thought as its most essential element; the other will consist essentially only of hands. Mutually dependent, both will function according to the overall will of a third species, which, headless and handless like a mollusk, encompasses the two and fills its own belly with the fruits of their labors. With that, humanity will have become incapable of fulfilling its mission of changing the earth and the world, and nature will have to give birth to new forces in order to rid itself of the pest of humanity and begin the changing of the world.

"Divide and conquer"—that is the principle that secures for the ruling class its rule over the slaves. It divides the exploited class into a great number of small groups, which it plays off one against the another. [. . .]

The classless society, just as it must transcend the division of humanity into exploited and exploiter, must also transcend the precondition of exploitation, the division into the knowing and unknowing. [. . .]

It may be that the impossibility of a classless society has until now been determined by economic and historical conditions. Today, however, economic relations all but demand the transcendence of classes and the profit society based upon them. The historical task of intellectuals who are disposed to the proletariat in thought would be to press the phenomenological relativity identified by the bourgeois cultural system to the point where it finds its source in the absolutism of the individual and his relationship to the whole. Those standpoints that lie outside the sphere of my essence as confirmed by my actions must be given up.

Intellectuals disposed to the proletariat have something of supreme importance to accomplish: to give themselves up, just as the proletariat brings about its own disappearance through its revolution.

Because of the many sins committed against the proletariat by the intellectual in bourgeois society—as teacher, scholar, engineer, priest, doctor, judge, party leader, and artist, where the intellectual has always been the defender and legitimator of the society that produces and sustains him—a few factory organizations have barred intellectuals from taking direct part in their organization. This forces workers to refrain from having someone working or thinking for them and instead to attend to their own cause. However, the workers in the factories are thoroughly dependent on the collaboration of intellectuals. Of primary importance is the subversive work of communist intellectuals in the sense mentioned above, which can accomplish the destruction of existing society. But workers need intellectuals as well to transform the capitalist economy and society along proletarian lines for, in the current situation, it is only the intellectuals who are knowledgeable about social relations and expert in the finely tuned mechanics of capitalist economics and production. [. . .]

The point would be to bring together all intellectuals disposed toward the proletariat: to organize political economists, engineers, and artists. We call on all who are dedicated to advancing the revolution, rather than the creation of positions and formation of a caste of prominent figures, on all who are not merely seeking leadership roles in the proletarian movement, to join together in pursuit of this work that is barred to us individually by the current organization of society.

FRANZ PFEMFERT

Comrade Franz W. Seiwert demands, on the one hand, for all "intellectuals who are disposed toward the proletariat" to give themselves up; on the other, he takes the union of "all intellectuals disposed toward the proletariat" to be absolutely necessary. I would consider both demands wrong, even if they were not mutually exclusive.

The union of all "proletarian-thinking intellectuals"—that would be roughly the contrary of those factory organizations that seek to exclude intellectuals from actively participating in the social revolution.

The separation of mental from manual workers has, from the side of the exploiting class, been systematically instituted in the interest of the rule of capitalism; indeed, the types—exclusively mental and exclusively manual workers—only arose in the context of class society. One of the first and most vital acts of the approaching storm of social transformation must be to tear down the wall separating them and to *unify* all exploited persons in the service of the new, communist order—not the mobilization of the manual proletarians against the mental proletarians!

The distrust of proletarians awakening to class consciousness toward their previous "leaders" is thoroughly understandable, and in the thirteen years of its existence, *Die Aktion* has appealed over and over to this mistrust. Nowhere has the struggle against the prosperity hyenas been conducted more relentlessly than here. And, in particular, it was the parasites from the camp of intellectuals who have been pilloried and pilloried. But precisely for that reason I am justified and obligated in saying here: the way Comrade Franz W. Seiwert and the way all of the comrades in the factory organizations pose the question and attempt to answer it is not how it must be posed and not where an answer is to be sought if the victory of the revolution is not to be delayed and altogether endangered!

It is not proletarian but petit-bourgeois to treat the intellectuals themselves, the mental workers themselves as inferior beings! Because scoundrels, corruptible creatures, unprincipled *lumpen,* climbers, toadies, and shameless revolutionary careerists are to be found in abundance among the intellectuals? Because the majority of the mental workers are still in the camp of the exploiters?

Take a look, if you will, among the ranks of the traitorous leadership before you venture to cast stones (or filth) at the intellectuals themselves. Spartacus, Christ, Florian Geyer, Voltaire, Buddha, Marx, Engels, Bakunin, Liebknecht, Rosa Luxemburg, and Lenin were intellectuals; [Gustav] Landauer, [Leo] Jogisches, and [Eugen] Leviné were intellectuals; Erich Mühsam is an intellectual, and Max Hölz! *Proletarians, workers,* however, are [Friedrich] Ebert, [Philipp] Scheidemann, [Gustav] Noske, [Carl] Severing, [Otto] Bauer, [Carl] Legien, [Heinrich] Brandler, *et al.* [Otto Emil] Runge, the murderer of Liebknecht, was a *worker;* the mercenaries who put themselves voluntarily in the service of Noske's bloody work in November 1918 were primarily *workers.* Manual workers, exploited wage slaves, continue to form the *primary line of defense of the bourgeoisie* against the revolutionary proletariat.

To the extent that intellectuals have not recognized (or willfully refuse to accept) that they are also among the exploited in the present social order, that they are wage slaves just like the manual worker, and that intellectuals remain in the camp of the class enemy, they are to be judged like the manual workers who still stand on the other side of the barricades. *But*—and this is the decisive point—*not because they are intellectuals, but because they are on the other side!* We should be trying to awaken them to class consciousness, precisely as we do with manual workers who remain captive to bourgeois ideologies.

If, however, mental workers have come to acknowledge their class position, *if* they have freed themselves of the bonds of capitalist thinking, if they wish to join the struggle against the exploiting class—should they then be treated as second-class soldiers? Why? Because they have occupied themselves with intellectual things? Because they know how to think methodically? Because, as engineers, scholars, doctors, writers, mathematicians, etc., they have distanced themselves from the parasitic class, generally having burned more bridges in doing so than the manual worker who has arrived at the conviction of his class mission—for that, degradation? *Desecrate intellect?*

The communist social order for which we are struggling will be founded upon the absolute *equality* of duties and rights *for all working people*—or it will not be.

113

ALFRED WEBER

The Predicament of Intellectual Workers

First published in *Die Not der geistigen Arbeiter* (Munich and Leipzig: Duncker und Humblot, 1923), 12f.

There is a rigid and abstract quality to capitalist-mechanistic society, which has to a certain extent become invisible to unrefined examination. The personal organization that was socially visible and became most vivid in the salons and courts of the ancien régime has collapsed; all that remains is the anonymous public, which, indeed, was already there in the background—the public of newspapers, magazines, books, theater, concert halls, exhibitions, and museums—out of which the actual constituent elements were only occasionally brought together by means of various loose organizations or lectures, concerts, and the like. These constituent elements are nonetheless there, each as something with its own life. The high capitalism of the prewar period even recreated for them a unique, new form of integration into society. It operated in a twofold fashion on the educated elite which survived the collapse of court society as landed aristocrats, urban patricians, and a secular and ecclesiastical bourgeoisie with civil service appointments. Those segments of the elite already situated closer to practical life and more interwoven into it were cast by prewar capitalism into the ups and downs of its crises and booms, transforming landed aristocrats into large-scale agriculturalists and patricians into *haute bourgeoisie,* denuding both in cultural terms by thoroughly economizing them and subjecting them to the hectic tempo of modern business life. In the intellectually satiated atmosphere of the patrician household of "debit and credit," the modern big industrialist who, forced by circumstances, hangs on the telephone from morning to night, is stuck in conferences and therefore scarcely has the chance for any intellectual content beyond his ledger the pietist and romantically enthralled Junkers of the time of Bismarck's youthful letters became the agriculturalists fighting over prices and grain duties in the period since the 1870s and 1880s. This depletion of the intellectual, which results from the dynamic of the new economy and the new tempo of life, has, as if via a kind of contagion, spread to the greater part of the higher civil service employees: the privy councillor who sits from nine o'clock in the morning to eight o'clock at night over his files (there are even supposed to be ministers of this sort in Germany) cannot possibly remain productive culturally to any degree as a recipient of works, or amount to a strong intellectual factor at all. I choose not to speak at all of the currently desiccated pastorate.

That is the one side. High capitalism, which in those places where it took vigorous hold caused the old, educated elite to wither, created, on the other hand, sites for intellectual refuge. It separated off from the second and third generation of the ascendant *haute bourgeoisie* a monied stratum that was generally no longer active in business life, but on the whole related to it only in the capacity of rentiers (one thinks of the character Tonio Kröger [in Thomas Mann's novella of 1903]). From this monied stratum was generated a new elite typified by its cultural and idealist concerns: the modern intellectuals.

The category of the modern intellectual is almost exclusively made up of rentier intellectuals. It possesses small or moderate liquid funds, not generally of a magnitude that spares it the necessity of a profession and income, but such that these funds as a whole comprise the background that makes it possible to get through the lengthy period of preparation and qualification to the point of earning a full income from intellectual activity. Insofar as the private funds later supplement the earned income, they simultaneously form the basis of this elite's freedom in relation to the tyranny of the position occupied or the particular job undertaken.

114

HANS ZEHRER

The Revolution of the Intelligentsia

First published as "Die Revolution der Intelligenz," *Die Tat* 21, no. 7 (October 1929), 486–507.

FRAGMENTS OF A FUTURE POLITICS

To those who consciously breathed the air of the imperial regime, who yet continue to bear resentment against the royal Prussian police, the Junkers, and the military, it may seem paradoxical to declare that no air could be more stifling than today's.

To those who believed themselves, at least emotionally and in their imaginations, to be experiencing a revolution in 1918, it might seem just as ridiculous to declare that we have never been farther from freedom than we are today.

Those, however, who shake their heads in incomprehension no longer count. They are satisfied either because they already possess power or because they consider themselves contenders for power. They are old, and therefore one can no longer demand that they break with an ideology that has become dear to them, that offers them security. Or they are young, and therefore they are merely mediocre individuals eager to conform, whose way is clear along paths that the independent intelligentsia cannot travel for reasons of conviction. They might be strong in numbers, but their qualitative, intellectual potency is slight. Whoever enjoys success today is either part of an average too lacking in individuality to have convictions to protect, or succeeds at the expense of his convictions. Neither species, however, is capable of establishing a new beginning, a new authority on the basis of the power they are striving for or already hold.

Freedom! Clear the way! The German people—and this might again sound paradoxical to many—has had its great experience of freedom. It has also had its revolution. The revolution began in August 1914; it ended in November 1918. As the fire slowly burned out, as the bloodlust drew to a close, no one was concerned with power. War is always one step closer to metaphysics than revolution is. Internal power fell into the hands of those who were there to pick it up because those who shed blood in the name of freedom fought only for external power. The tragic situation is this: the war consumed all the concentrated energies, it released all the tensions, it squandered all the forces of revolution. What came after it was the revolt. Only in Russia where the revolution possessed the technical experience of decades, the intellectual foundation of half a century, and an inestimable psychological tradition could the war not destroy it. Central Europe, however, dispensed with revolutionary transformation; it chose the path of evolution. The profiteers began their work with a conservative act: they quashed the carriers of revolt.

This fact became profoundly symbolic for further development. At the time of its founding, today's pseudorevolutionary state had to do without all of those energies from which revolutionary states up to now have drawn their best and most loyal forces. It could not cast the slogan of freedom among the masses and let itself be carried along by the energies thus unleashed. These energies had been exhausted in four years of war—freedom, however, had dissolved into chaos to such an extent that its place was taken over by weariness and the urge for restraint. [. . .]

Freedom today has become an empty concept. It hangs like a rain-soaked flag in the room, but the winds do not blow. Instead we have the rule of hypocrisy and pretense. Instead we have the rule of a silent, reactionary censorship, which is much more effective than open prohibitions. Weighing down upon the vital forces are the blocks of the old parties, the tedious uniformity of the bureaucracy, the stony power of the factories.

The question of freedom has been posed. Today it is beginning to stir among the masses. The future of the state will be filled with it. And at this moment it is important to approach the present with this question: From which side will this question be posed? What will be the resistance to it? What chances does it have? And where is the soil in which it can plant the ideas originating from its camp?

THE CONCEPT OF THE INTELLIGENTSIA

From which side will the question of freedom be posed? That it will be posed at all might seem absurd to those who have not freed themselves of the illusion of 1918. This illusion began with the slogan "Clear the way for the able," with which freedom seemed to be adequately grounded. It had found its anchor in the national constitution. If, however, the question of freedom is to be posed anyway, this fact alone demonstrates that it cannot be fully realized within present conditions.

Now who is posing this question? Despite all the assurances of Marxism to the contrary, it will always be in the first instance *an intellectual question;* that is, it will be posed by a stratum that can be designated a priori as the revolutionary element in a state, in a community. "All previous historical movements were movements of minorities or in the interest of minorities," says the *Communist Manifesto.* This sentence must be defined more pointedly: all movements were first of all intellectual movements of intelligent, qualified minorities, whose initiative sprang from the discrepancy between what is and what should be. Other characteristics appear only secondarily to the first: the muzzling of the free expression of opinion, the impossibility of free, unimpeded work, and the obstacles confronting productive activity. Then come as a third moment the strivings of this stratum to convey their ideas to the masses, to point out the social tensions, to bring them to consciousness and give them a direction—in order, together with the masses, to do away with the obstacles that stand in the way of a rectification of existing power relations in the sense of an already apparent intellectual necessity. Revolutions always have first of all intellectual and only then political or economic origins. That it appears to be the other way around lies first in the circumstance that it is usually the same forces limiting the freedom of the intellect that exercise real political and economic effects. Secondly, the intellect itself does not advance by demanding, "Sire, give me freedom of thought!" Instead it needs experiences of concrete power for its realization. It must therefore wear masks and don disguises; it must give itself over to concrete forces and incite them against the concrete instances of power. It cannot, however, accomplish this by hammering into these oppressed forces metaphysical or philosophical principles; rather it can count on success only if it makes these forces conscious of their respective situations, taking up the tensions that lie within them.

Thus the following has been asserted: There is at all times and in every community a stratum with a greater degree of internal independence from given conditions and the values of the time, a stratum that achieves an overview of the contours of the time within a larger intellectual context and that pushes for the objectivization of its latent tendencies. This stratum acts to a certain extent as a mechanism of self-correction in the *Zeitgeist*. The degree of security for the continued existence of an age, a state, or a community can only be measured according to the intensity of the tensions within its intellectual stratum, for it is at the same time the stratum that will pose the question of freedom; it poses the question for all the other sites of political or economic tension and provides their carriers with the material with which to establish themselves in their particularity.

115

KARL MANNHEIM

Ideology and Utopia

First published as *Ideologie und Utopie* (Bonn: Cohen, 1929), 121–130.

How are we to conceive of the social and political bearers of whatever synthesis there is? What political interest will undertake the problem of synthesis as its task and who will strive to realize it in society?

Just as at an earlier period we should have slipped back into a static intellectualism if instead of aiming at a dynamic relative synthesis we had leaped into a supertemporal absolute one, similarly here we are in danger of losing sight of the hitherto constantly emphasized interest-bound nature of political thought and of assuming that the synthesis will come from a source outside the political arena. If it be once granted that political thought is always bound up with a position in the social order, it is only consistent to suppose that the tendency towards a total synthesis must be embodied in the will of some social group.

And indeed a glance at the history of political thought shows that the exponents of synthesis have always represented definite social strata, mainly classes who feel threatened from above and below and who, out of social necessity, seek a middle way out. But this search for a compromise from the very beginning assumes both a static as well as a dynamic form. The social position of the group with which the carriers of the synthesis are affiliated determines largely which of these two alternatives will be emphasized.

The static form of mediation of the extremes was attempted first by the victorious bourgeoisie, especially in the period of the bourgeois monarchy in France where it was expressed in the principle of the *juste milieu*. This catch phrase, however, is only a caricature of a true synthesis rather than a true solution, which can only be a dynamic one. For that reason it may serve to show what errors a solution must avoid.

A true synthesis is not an arithmetic average of all the diverse aspirations of the existing groups in society. If it were such, it would tend merely to stabilize the status quo to the advantage of those who have just acceded to power and who wish to protect their gains from the attacks of the right as well as the left. On the contrary a valid synthesis must be based on a political position which will constitute a progressive development in the sense that it will retain and utilize much of the accumulated cultural acquisitions and social energies of the previous epoch. At the same time the new order must permeate the broadest ranges of social life, must take natural root in society in order to bring its transforming power into play. This position calls for a peculiar alertness towards the historical reality of the present. The spatial "here" and the temporal "now" in every situation must be considered in the historical and social sense and must always be kept in mind in order to determine from case to case what is no longer necessary and what is not yet possible.

Such an experimental outlook, unceasingly sensitive to the dynamic nature of society and to its wholeness, is not likely to be developed by a class occupying a middle position but only by a relatively classless stratum which is not too firmly situated in the social order. The study of history with reference to this question will yield a rather pregnant suggestion.

This unanchored, relatively classless stratum is, to use Alfred Weber's terminology, the "socially unattached intelligentsia" (*freischwebende Intelligenz*). It is impossible in this connection to give even the sketchiest outline of the difficult sociological problem raised by the existence of the intellectual. But the problems we are considering could not be adequately formulated, much less solved, without touching upon certain phases of the position of the intellectuals. A sociology which is oriented only with reference to socio-economic classes will never adequately understand this phenomenon. According to this theory, the intellectuals constitute either a class or at least an appendage to a class. Thus it might describe correctly certain determinants and components of this unattached social body, but never the essential quality of the whole. It is, of course, true that a large body of our intellectuals come from rentier strata, whose income is derived directly or indirectly from rents and interest on investments. But for that matter certain groups of the officials and the so-called liberal professions are also members of the intelligentsia. A closer examination, however, of the social basis of these strata will show them to be less clearly identified with one class than those who participate more directly in the economic process.

If this sociological cross-section is completed by an historical view, further heterogeneity among the intellectuals will be disclosed. Changes in class relationships at different times affect some of these groups favorably, others unfavorably. Consequently it cannot be maintained that they are homogeneously determined. Although they are too differentiated to be regarded as a single class, there is one unifying sociological bond between all groups of intellectuals, namely education, which binds them together in a striking way. Participation in a common educational heritage progressively tends to suppress differences of birth, status, profession, and wealth, and to unite individual educated people on the basis of the education they have received.

In my opinion nothing could be more wrong than to misinterpret this view and maintain that the class and status ties of the individual disappear completely by virtue of this. It is, however, peculiarly characteristic of this new basis of association that it preserves the multiplicity of the component elements in all their variety by creating a homogeneous medium within which the conflicting parties can measure their strength. Modern education from its inception is a living struggle, a replica on a small scale of the conflicting purposes and tendencies which rage in society at large. Accordingly, the intellectual horizon of the educated person is determined in a variety of ways. This acquired educational heritage subjects that person to the influence of opposing tendencies in social reality, while the person who is not oriented toward the whole through his education, but rather participates directly in the social process of production, merely tends to absorb the world view of that particular group and to act exclusively under the influence of the conditions imposed by his immediate social situation.

One of the most impressive facts about modern life is that in it, unlike in preceding cultures, intellectual activity is not carried on exclusively by a socially rigidly defined class, such as a priesthood, but rather by a social stratum that is to a large degree unattached to any social class and that is recruited from an increasingly inclusive area of social life. This sociological fact determines essentially the uniqueness of the modern mind, which is characteristically not based upon the authority of a priesthood, which is not closed and finished, but which is rather dynamic, elastic, in a constant state of flux, and perpetually confronted by new problems. Even humanism was already largely the expression of such a more or less socially emancipated stratum, and where the nobility became the bearer of culture it broke through the fixedness of a class-bound mentality in many respects. But not until we come to the period of bourgeois ascendancy does the level of cultural life become increasingly detached from a given class.

The modern bourgeoisie had from the beginning a twofold social root—on the one hand the owners of capital, on the other, those individuals whose only capital was their education. It was common therefore to speak of the propertied and educated class, the educated class, the educated element being, however, by no means ideologically in agreement with the property-owning element.

There arises, then, in the midst of this society, which is deeply divided by class cleavages, a stratum that a sociology oriented solely in terms of class can only slightly comprehend. Nevertheless, the specific social position of this stratum can be quite adequately characterized. Although situated between classes, it does not form a middle class. Not, of course, that it is suspended in a vacuum into which social interests do not penetrate; on the contrary, it subsumes in itself all those interests with which social life is permeated. With the increase in the number and variety of the classes and strata from which the individual groups of intellectuals are recruited, there comes greater multiformity and contrast in the tendencies operating on the intellectual level which tie them to one another. The individual, then, more or less takes a part in the mass of mutually conflicting tendencies.

While those who participate directly in the process of production—the worker and the entrepreneur—being bound to a particular class and mode of life, have their outlooks and activities directly and exclusively determined by their specific social situations, the intellectuals, besides undoubtedly bearing the imprint of their specific class affinity, are also determined in their outlook by this intellectual medium that contains all those contradictory points of view. This social situation always provided the potential energy that enabled the more outstanding intellectuals to develop the social sensibility that was essential for becoming attuned to the dynamically conflicting forces. Every point of view was examined constantly as to its relevance to the present situation. Furthermore, precisely through the cultural attachments of this group, there was achieved such an intimate grasp of the total situation, that the tendency towards a dynamic synthesis constantly reappeared, despite the temporary distortions with which we have yet to deal.

Hitherto the negative side of the "unattachedness" of the intellectuals, their social instability, and the predominantly deliberate character of their mentality has been emphasized almost exclusively. It was especially the politically extreme groups who, demanding a definite declaration of sympathies, branded this as "lack of character." It remains to be asked, however, whether in the political sphere a decision in favor of a dynamic mediation may not be just as much a decision as the ruthless espousal of yesterday's theories or the one-sided emphasis on tomorrow's.

There are two courses of action that the unattached intellectuals have actually taken as ways out of this middle-of-the-road position: first, what amounts to a largely voluntary affiliation with one or the other of the various antagonistic classes; second, scrutiny of their own social moorings and the quest for the fulfillment of their mission as the predestined advocate of the intellectual interests of the whole. [. . .]

The first way, then, out of the predicament of the intellectuals, namely the direct affiliation with classes and parties, shows a tendency, even though it is unconscious, towards a dynamic synthesis. It was usually the class in need of intellectual development which received their support. It was primarily the conflict of intellectuals which transformed the conflict of interests into a conflict of ideas. This attempt to lift the conflict of interests to a spiritual plane has two aspects: on the one hand it meant the empty glorification of naked interests by means of the tissues of lies spun by apologists; on the other hand, in a more positive sense, it meant the infusion of certain intellectual demands into practical politics. In return for their collaboration with parties and classes, the intellectuals were able to leave this imprint upon them. If they had no other achievement to their credit, this alone would have been a significant accomplishment. Their function is to penetrate into the ranks of the conflicting parties in order to compel them to accept their demands. This activity, viewed historically, has amply shown wherein the sociological peculiarity and the mission of this unattached social stratum lie.

The second way out of the dilemma of the intellectuals consists precisely in their becoming aware of their own social position and the mission implicit in it. When this is achieved, political affiliation or opposition will be decided on the basis of a conscious orientation in society and in accordance with the demands of the intellectual life.

One of the basic tendencies in the contemporary world is the gradual awakening of class-consciousness in all classes. If this is so, it follows that even the intellectuals will arrive at a consciousness—though not a class-consciousness—of their own general social position and the problems and opportunities it involves. This attempt to comprehend the sociological phenomenon of the intellectuals, and the attempt, on the basis of this, to take an attitude towards politics have traditions of their own quite as much as has the tendency to become assimilated into other parties.

116

HANNAH ARENDT

Philosophy and Sociology: On Karl Mannheim's *Ideology and Utopia*

First published as "Philosophie und Soziologie. Zur Karl Mannheims *Ideologie und Utopie*," *Die Gesellschaft* 7 (1930), 163–176.

We are concerned here solely with the fundamental philosophical question. We presuppose thereby the knowledge contained in Mannheim's book, the significance of which lies in pointing out the general dubiousness of modern intellectuality given an historical understanding. What does this proof of dubiousness purport for philosophy? How is the problematic that emerges here constituted, such that it can disquiet philosophy?

The reason it can do so is based in Mannheim's demonstration that every intellectual expression is bound up with the concrete position, even political position, of the thinker in life; but he makes the claim without himself having adopted one of these positions—except in his reflexive inquiry as to the social situation from which such "positionlessness" remains possible in the first place. Only in this respect does sociology extend to the philosophical problematic and have something to say to the latter. [. . .]

Mannheim inquires first of all into the reality, that is, into the possible authentic origin of the intellectual. Secondly he understands *all* positions with radical relativity, and considers the fate of all "interpretations of being" as orientations in a particular, historically given world. [. . .]

In a philosophical formulation, the problem at the foundation of Mannheimian sociology is the dubious nature of the relation of the ontic to the ontological. If philosophy inquires into the "being of existence" (*Sein des Seienden;* Heidegger) or into the self-understanding of "existence" removed from the quotidian ([Karl] Jaspers), then sociology inquires, precisely the other way around, into the existence at the basis of this "interpretation of being," into that which philosophy maintains is irrelevant to it. [. . .]

Philosophy is therefore not merely not transcendent of quotidian reality in principle; philosophy arises out of it even in its vital motivation: reality is the *conditio per quam.* Philosophy from a sociological point of view is no longer an answer to the question of the "being of existence," but is itself now taken to be enmeshed and entangled in the world of the existent and its motivational possibilities, to be an existent among existents. Philosophy itself is doubted here in its absolute reality, in that it is derived from an original reality that it has forgotten; indeed, its transcendence is assessed as a simple instance of having forgotten: its claim to nondetermination rests on a forgetting of its historical rootedness. With this, however, not only is the claim to absoluteness of every philosophy destroyed, but it is also made questionable in its specific momentary actuality. Sociology allows the (likewise) philosophical question as to the meaning of philosophy to arise. [. . .]

The sociologist does not inquire into "being in the world" as a formal structure of existence as such, but into the particular historically determinant world in which the person lives. This delimitation of sociology is apparently harmless, as if it were simply delineating the boundaries of its competence. It begins to threaten philosophy only when it maintains that the world cannot in principle be disclosed as a formal structure of human being, but only as the determinant content of the particular world of a particular life. This claim disputes the possibility of an *ontological* understanding of being as such. The ontological structures of human being in the world, to the extent that they remain indisputably the same—roughly, hunger and sex—are precisely the inessential, that which is of no concern to us. In every attempt to give an account of our own being, we are directed to the ever-changing ontic, which exists as the true *reality* in relation to the "theories" of the philosophers. To the intellect, however—if never explicitly in Mannheim's book—is attributed, as a point of departure in principle, no reality.

Everything spiritual is understood either as ideology or utopia. Both "transcend actual existence" and spring from a consciousness "that is incongruous with the state of reality in which it occurs." The *mistrust* of the intellect, which is evident in sociology and its attempt at destruction, originates in the homelessness to which the intellect is condemned in our society. The homelessness and apparent rootlessness ("socially unattached intelligentsia") makes everything intellectual suspect from the outset; a search is undertaken for a reality that is prior to the intellect itself, and all testimony of the intellect is to be interpreted in reference to it, which is to say, destroyed. Destruction here does not mean demolition as such, but a reduction of claims of validity to the particular situation from which they originated. [. . .]

Sociology itself has an historically bounded position, without which it could never have arisen: it is located where a justified mistrust of intellect was awakened out of the homelessness of intellect. It thereby acquires, as an historical science, a quite definite boundary to its historical *competence*. Interpretation of the intellectual as critique aimed at ideology or utopia first becomes legitimate where economics have become so predominant that the intellect *in fact* can and must develop into an ideological superstructure. The priority of the reality of the determinant economic structure itself has a history and is a part of the history of the modern intellect. [. . .]

Only here does the question of *meaning* arise, which is born of the dubiousness of one's own situation. Only when the individual is allotted his place in the world via economic affiliation and not through tradition does he become homeless. And only in this homelessness, finally, can the question as to the right and meaning of the *position* come up. This question of meaning, however, is older than capitalism because it derives from a historically prior experience of human insecurity in the world: from Christianity. The concept of ideology, indeed, the fact of ideological thinking, itself refers further to a *positivum,* to the question of meaning. The destruction of this question of meaning through reference to the "more originary" reality of economics only becomes possible once the world and life of the human being are primarily determined economically. Reality, to which the intellect is bound, will thereby have become alien in principle to intellect and meaning, which it originally (in contrast to the reality concept in psychoanalysis) was not. Prior to Mannheim's question as to the social and historical location of the sociological formulation is the question as to the ontological circumstance in which sociological analyses are historically justified.

117

ERNST VON SALOMON

We and the Intellectuals

First published as "Wir und die Intellektuellen," *Die Kommenden* 5, no. 18 (May 2, 1930), 206–207.

The intellectual speaks and writes "I." He feels no connectedness. He causes disintegration, the disintegration of the mass of individual beings into the particularized individual being, who henceforth stands not under and not over the people, but at their side. The means by which this is accomplished is the misunderstood concept of "education." Education in the German sense (*Bildung*) means giving form, both inner and outer. Form, however, can only be given where there is content, and content comes only from an idea. An idea always manifests a connectedness. A thought stands alone and is produced in a brain. An idea is something mutual. It grows out of the tensions between one individual and another. Where there is tension, there is also connectedness. For the intellectual, education is at most a highly developed acrobatics of thought and always only the property of the "I." The arrogance attached to the concept of education could only have arisen in the intellectual's conception, and this conception could only flourish in the empty space in which the intellectual lives.

The emphatic "we" of the new generation is a clear renunciation of intellectualism. The "we" of the young, nationalistic generation comes about consciously. We—that is the still small group of men and, in the broad sense, masculine youth—have gone beyond mere renunciation to establish values in place of the old ones or in the empty space. We have no intellectuals—we say it with pride; we say it because we are reproached for this alleged failing. What is intellectual in nationalism is of a different sort than the intellectual of the past historical period. It is tied to blood. It knows no dialectic and where it seeks new interconnections it does so in the sense of responsibility for the whole. The intellectual content of misconceived education knows no whole and has its goal and its zenith in prominence. We know a mutuality, from which we draw force, and this mutuality is rooted not in the word but in the deed and in the readiness to commit the deed. The individuals who come from our ranks, and whom we prize, do not in consequence stand aside, for they drew their force from the consciousness of connectedness with the community, and they are, in the most heightened moment, never dissolved from us but over us, before us; they are leaders. Knowing about the unconditioned nature of leadership and the purification of this concept of all base superfluousness—that is what primarily distinguishes us from liberalism. The liberal system knows no leadership. Instead of leaders it has intellectuals. Marxism knows no leadership. Its first guides and masters were racially alien intellectuals and what it then, uneasily, bore in the way of "leaders"—those were philistines selected and thrown up from below; Marxists themselves call them "bosses." The system that collapsed in November of 1918 had "representatives" who derived their leadership solely from "tradition." The system was completely liberal and collapsed for one reason—because the ruling forces, who stood invisibly behind events waiting for the failure of those in charge, either wanted the collapse, or possessed, in their merchant's mentality, no notion of leadership, or—and this is a special chapter—saw in every form of leadership a danger that could spoil business for them.

Whatever the case may be, we are now confronting a new situation. The structure of our movement is a particular one. It is rooted in the people. Every movement must be, and not only every movement, but every inspired thing that seeks to grow straight. But we draw conclusions from our commitment to the people. That only those who are conscious of their nationality can be part of the German people, that is one conclusion. That all ideas by which one lives must in turn exclusively serve the nation, that is another. That all the phenomena of our multifaceted life are to be recognized, tested, and embraced or repudiated according to the values by which we live, that is a third. Intellectualism we repudiate. It has been weighed and found too light. Our "we" grows out of our will and our service. And our will and our service belong, to the point of ultimate fanaticism, to the German people. Since we have in anguish become persuaded that it is different with others, we use this "we."

118

WALTER BENJAMIN

Left-Wing Melancholy

First published as "Linke Melancholie. Zu Erich Kästners neuem Gedichtbuch," *Die Gesellschaft* 8, no. 1 (1931), 181–184.

Today [Erich] Kästner's poems are already available in three imposing volumes.[1] However, anyone wishing to study the character of these strophes is advised to stick to the form in which they originally appeared. In books they are too crowded and somewhat stifling, but they dart through the daily papers like fish in water. If this water is not always the cleanest and has quite a lot of refuse floating in it, all the better for the author, whose poetic minnows can fatten themselves thereon.

The popularity of these poems is linked to the rise of a stratum which took unveiled possession of its economic power positions and prided itself as none other on the nakedness, the unmasked character of its economic physiognomy. This is not to say that this stratum, whose only aim was success, which recognized nothing else, had now conquered the strongest positions. Its ideal was too asthmatic for that. It was the ideal of childless agents, parvenus of insignificant origin, who did not, like financial magnates, provide for their families over decades, but only for themselves, and that hardly beyond the end of the season. Who cannot see them—their dreamy baby eyes behind horn-rimmed spectacles, their broad, pale cheeks, their drawling voices, their fatalism in gesture and mode of thought? From the beginning, it is to this stratum and to this stratum alone that the poet has something to say, this stratum that he flatters, insofar as from dawn to dusk he holds up a mirror to them, or rather holds it against them. The gaps between his stanzas are the folds of fat in their necks, his rhymes their thick lips, his caesurae dimples in their flesh, his full stops pupils in their eyes. Subject matter and effect remain restricted to this stratum, and Kästner is as incapable of striking the dispossessed with his rebellious accents as he is of touching the industrialists with his irony. This is because, despite appearances, this lyricism protects above all the status interests of the middle stratum—agents, journalists, heads of departments. The hatred it proclaims meanwhile towards the petite bourgeoisie has itself an all-too-intimate petit-bourgeois flavor. On the other hand, it clearly abandons any striking power against the big bourgeoisie and betrays its yearning for patronage at last in the heartfelt sigh: "If only there were a dozen wise men with a great deal of money." No wonder Kästner, in settling accounts with the bankers in a "Hymn," is as obliquely familial as he is obliquely economic when he presents the night thoughts of a proletarian woman under the title "A Mother Strikes the Balance." Ultimately home and income remain the leading strings by which a better-off class leads the mewling poet.

1. Erich Kästner (1899–1974), best-known for the children's book *Emil and the Detectives* (1928), was a well-regarded poet, novelist, and journalist in the Weimar Republic. His mostly ironic light verse in the detached mode of New Objectivity appealed to middle-class readers of the late 1920s. A selection of Kästner's poetry is available in English translation: *Let's Face It,* ed. Patrick Bridgwater (London: Jonathan Cape, 1963).

This poet is dissatisfied, indeed heavy-hearted. But this heaviness of heart derives from routine. For to be in a routine means to have sacrificed one's idiosyncrasies, to have forfeited the gift of distaste. And that makes one heavy-hearted. It is this circumstance that gives this case a certain similarity with that of Heine. The notes with which Kästner indents his poems, to give these shiny children's balls the appearance of rugby balls, are routine. And nothing is more routine than the irony which, like baking powder, helps to raise the kneaded dough of private opinion. It is only unfortunate that his impertinence is as much out of all proportion to the ideological forces at his disposal as it is to the political ones. Not least does the grotesque underestimation of the opponent that underlies these provocations betray how much the position of this left, radical intelligentsia is a lost one. It has little to do with the labor movement. Rather, as a phenomenon of bourgeois dissolution, it is a counterpart to the mimicry of feudalism that the *Kaiserreich* admired in the reserve lieutenant. Left radical publicists of the stamp of Kästner, Mehring, and Tucholsky are the decayed bourgeoisie's mimicry of the proletariat. Their function is to give rise politically speaking not to parties but to cliques, literarily speaking not to schools but to fashions, economically speaking not to producers but to agents. And indeed, for the last fifteen years this left-wing intelligentsia has been continually the agent of all spiritual conjunctures, from Activism,[2] via expressionism to New Objectivity. However, its political significance was exhausted by the transposition of revolutionary reflexes, insofar as they arose in the bourgeoisie, into objects of distraction, of amusement, which can be supplied for consumption.

Thus was Activism able to impose the face of a quasi-classless, sound common sense on the revolutionary dialectic. It was in some sense the sale week of this intelligentsia's department store. Expressionism exhibited the revolutionary gesture, the raised arm, the clenched fist in papier-mâché. After this advertising campaign, New Objectivity, from which Kästner's poems spring, was added to the catalogue. What then does the "spiritual elite" discover as it begins to take stock of its feelings? Those feelings themselves? They have long since been remaindered. What is left is the empty spaces where, in dusty heart-shaped velvet trays, the feelings—nature and love, enthusiasm and humanity—once rested. Now the hollow forms are absentmindedly caressed. A know-all irony thinks it has much more in these supposed stereotypes than in the things themselves, it makes a great display of its poverty and turns the yawning emptiness into a celebration. For this is what is new about this objectivity—it takes as much pride in the traces of former spiritual goods as the bourgeois do in their material goods. Never have such comfortable arrangements been made in such an uncomfortable situation.

In short, this left-wing radicalism is precisely the attitude to which there is no longer in general any corresponding political action. It is to the left not of this or that tendency, but simply to the left of what is in general possible. For from the beginning all it has in mind is to enjoy itself in a negativistic quiet. The metamorphosis of political struggle from a compulsory decision into an object of pleasure, from a means of production into an article of consumption—that is this literature's latest hit. Kästner, who is a considerable talent, has all its means at his fingertips. By far the most important of these is an attitude expressed even in the titles of many of his poems. Among them are an "Elegy with Egg," a "Chemically Purified Christmas Carol," "Suicide in the Mixed Bathing," the "Fate of a Stylised Negro," etc. Why these dislocations? Because criticism and knowledge are ready

---

2. Activism was a movement dating back to the war years; it called for the elite, i.e. intellectuals and artists, to engage actively in a new kind of spiritual politics.

to intervene; but they would be spoil-sports and should on no condition be allowed to speak. So the poet must gag them, and their desperate convulsions now have the same effect as the tricks of a contortionist, ie, they amuse a wide public, insecure in its taste. In [Christian] Morgenstern, nonsense was only the obverse of a flight into theosophy. But Kästner's nihilism conceals nothing, as little as a mouth that cannot close for yawning.

Poets early became acquainted with a curious variety of despair: tortured stupidity. For the truly political poetry of the last decades has for the most part hurried on ahead of things as a harbinger. It was in 1912 and 1913 that Georg Heym's poems anticipated the then inconceivable constitution of the masses that came into the open in August 1914, in repellent descriptions of never-glimpsed collectivities: of suicides, of prisoners, of the sick, of sailors or of the insane. In his lines the earth armed itself for its submergence in the red deluge. And long before the Ararat of the Goldmark was the only peak sticking up above the flood, every inch of it besieged by Feeding-Trough, Belly-Liner and Sweet-Tooth, Alfred Lichtenstein, who fell in the first days of the War, had brought into view the sad and flabby figures for which Kästner has found the stereotypes. Now what distinguishes the bourgeois in this early, still pre-expressionist version from the later, post-expressionist one, is his eccentricity. Not in vain did Lichtenstein dedicate one of his poems to a clown. The clowning of despair was still deep in the bones of his bourgeois. They had not yet shifted eccentricity outside themselves as an object of urban amusement. They were not yet so totally satiated, nor had they so totally become agents that they did not feel their obscure solidarity with a commodity whose sales crisis is already on the horizon. Then came peace—the collapse of the market for the human commodity with which we have become familiar as unemployment. And the suicide for which Lichtenstein's poems are propaganda is like dumping, the disposal of a commodity at ruinous prices. Kästner's strophes have forgotten all this. Their beat very precisely follows the notes according to which poor rich folk play the blues; they correspond to the mournfulness of the satiated man who can no longer devote all his money to his stomach. Tortured stupidity: this the latest of two millenia of metamorphoses of melancholy.

Kästner's poems are for the higher-income bracket, those mournful, melancholy dummies who trample anything or anyone in their path. With the rigidity of their armor, the slowness of their advance, the blindness of their action, they are the rendezvous that tank and bedbug have made in people. These poems teem with them like a city café after the stock exchange closes. Is it surprising that their function is to reconcile this type to himself and to establish that identity of professional and private life which these men understand by the name *humanity,* but which is in truth the genuinely bestial since authentic humanity—under the present conditions—can only arise from a tension between these two poles? In this tension, consciousness and deed are formed, to create it is the task of all political lyricism, and today this task is most strictly fulfilled by [Bertolt] Brecht's poems. In Kästner it has to give way to complacency and fatalism. This is the fatalism of those who are most remote from the process of production and whose obscure courting of the state of the market is comparable to the attitude of a man who yields himself up entirely to the inscrutable accidents of his digestion. The rumbling in these lines certainly has more to do with flatulence than with subversion. Constipation and melancholy have always gone together. But since the juices began to dry up in the body social, stuffiness meets us at every turn. Kästner's poems do not improve the atmosphere.

119

SIEGFRIED KRACAUER

On the Writer

First published as "Über den Schriftsteller," *Die neue Rundschau* 42, no. 6 (June 1931), 860–862.

As remarkable as it sounds, under the pressure of economic and social conditions, journalists and writers are almost exchanging roles. Not that the journalist has been seized more than usually by an ambition to produce works comparable to literature; but, insofar as he is a bourgeois journalist, he has been noticeably relieved of his function of exercising a substantive effect on conditions. It may be that the representatives of capital feel seriously threatened; it may only be that they have become particularly sensitive: in any case, the chances for the free expression of journalistic opinion in the bourgeois press today are almost more limited than they were under imperial military rule. It is not for nothing that the press that depends on capital is displaying a growing tendency toward neutrality, giving more space to information than to commentary, not to mention fundamental critique. At a time when the economic crisis has become a crisis of the system as a whole, it can scarcely behave otherwise. By virtue of the passivity that has been forced upon them, however, journalists have been robbed of the air to breathe. They find themselves shunted off onto a sidetrack, having generally to satisfy themselves with observing events as spectators and softening them, instead of using them to constitute instructive examples. To the same degree as the genuine journalist is being eliminated, there is emerging, it seems to me, a *new type of writer* whose endeavor it is to fill the vacated place—a type that does not feel itself called to serve the "absolute," but sees its assignment in rendering for itself (and the public at large) an account of our present situation. I am thinking of the [few] journalists who have joined the writers in order to fulfill their journalistic duty (whereas some writers in the official sense of the word are welcome guests in the newspaper columns without thereby being journalists); thinking of the many documentary texts of recent years aimed at making us aware of our social conditions; and thinking of those novels that, in fact, are descriptions of conditions and concern themselves with the plight of the unemployed, the white-collar workers, the parties, etc. The artistic value of this output might be slight; its producers, however, have not made artistry their primary goal.

If the writer in the new sense is in no way identical with the journalist, they do have one thing in common that fundamentally distinguishes the contemporary writer from writers of the old stamp: the new writer fundamentally disavows the "transcendent layer of existence." In this regard, he adopts an attitude that could be nicely legitimized by the materialist dialectic, and, in a few cases, is quite likely based upon it in fact. According to this doctrine, which I will introduce here only to the extent required by the context, so-called transcendent determinations are not admissible objects of observation. Reality appears solely to a mode of thought that actively advances the social process that is moving in the direction of a classless society. I am not maintaining that all the modern writers to whom I refer here have made dialectical materialism their own, but I believe nevertheless that, in their rejection of the absolute, they have become subject to it. A theory need not dominate to have its effect, and, should it be fortified a hundredfold by conditions, it acquires life for many who do not otherwise know it. The disinterest of these writers in idealistic values is, in any case, no less marked than their need to descend into this-worldly social realities—the recent "topical dramas" (*Zeitstück*) also derive from this intention.

Instead of contemplatively, they behave politically; instead of seeking the general through the particular, they find the general in the process of the particular; instead of pursuing development, they strive after discontinuities. This says nothing about the value or expediency of their publications; I am concerned only with a summary indication of an attitude that is becoming prevalent in contemporary writing.

The Russian writer S. M. Tretyakov recently spoke to an audience of intellectuals in Berlin about a "new type of writer." Since he was insufficiently acquainted with the situation in Germany, his much-too-general attacks against professional writers missed their mark. Certainly the planned collectivization of writers in Russia today in the interest of socialist construction is a significant experiment that might lead to significant results. In a country like Germany, however, the conditions for such an approach do not exist. Economic anarchy, the potential for the resistance of outdated ideologies, and the social-structural rigidity of the intellectual class are for the moment maintaining the writer in *isolation*. Only as individuals (or, in the best of cases, in collaboration with like-minded others) can they, for the time being, destroy false consciousness, prepare a correct one, and fulfill all the other critical functions incumbent upon them in contemporary society.

12
Critical Theory and the Search for a New Left

DURING THE WILHELMINE ERA, the German socialist movement was united in the SPD, whose internal tensions rarely produced irreversible fissures. Even Eduard Bernstein weathered the crisis produced by his revisionist critique of Marxist orthodoxy and remained within the party. The year 1914 and the fateful decision by the party's parliamentary delegation to vote for the war credits shattered this unity and split the SPD. The Independent Socialists (USPD), a cross-section of different tendencies sharing only a hostility to the war, and the Spartacists, who hoped to turn the war into a civil war between classes, were the most prominent dissident groups. But there were also Independent Socialists and anarchists like Gustav Landauer and the writer Kurt Eisner, who briefly led the Bavarian government during its short-lived revolution in 1919. Eisner's hostility to Prussian domination and pacifist inclinations and faith in workers' councils, recalled in the memoir included in section 2 by Wilhelm Hausenstein written shortly after Eisner's murder by Count Anton Arco-Valley on February 21, 1919, exemplifies one impulse on the left that favored decentralization and control from below.

A very different position was represented by the newly-formed Communist Party (KPD), which came into being in December 1918, modeling itself after the successful Bolshevik Party in the Soviet Union. The KPD was an outgrowth of the Spartacists and was joined by the left wing of the USPD when it dissolved in 1922. At the KPD's founding convention, Rosa Luxemburg, soon to share Eisner's martyrdom, echoed his enthusiasm for the councils and advocated the use of mass strikes to bring down the Majority Socialist government. But shortly after her murder (and that of her colleague Karl Liebknecht) in January 1919, the KPD began to adopt less drastic measures and abandon its hopes for immediate revolution. By 1923, after a series of abortive upheavals, its leadership adopted the tactic of the "united front from below," which advocated alliances with other proletarian groups but not their reformist leadership in the hope of forming a "workers' government." Within the KPD itself, only the most disciplined centralization was to prevail in the struggle against all deviations from its Leninist line.

On occasion, the Communists' search for broad appeal led it into strange alliances. In 1923, following the death of the German soldier Albert Leo Schlageter during the French occupation of the Ruhr, Karl Radek, the Soviet communist delegate to the KPD, exhorted the Party to harness nationalist resentment against the Entente for its own radical purposes. In considering this option, the KPD showed its cynical willingness to adopt symbols that were also those of the radical right-wing opposition to the Weimar Republic (Schlageter was one of the Nazis' main heroes). In so doing, it tacitly approached the "national bolshevism" advocated by fringe figures like Ernst Niekisch. By 1929, in fact, the party had abandoned its semiconciliatory stance towards other progressive forces and, following a directive from the Comintern, began to attack the SPD as "social fascists." By directing its main blow against the socialists, it fatally weakened whatever common action the left might have taken against the Nazi threat. Appeals like those made by the Berlin Iron Front, a loose union of democratically minded groups supporting Hindenburg against Hitler for president in April 1932, fell on deaf ears.

Outside of the major leftist parties, a number of radical thinkers who were disenchanted with their policies began to rethink the theoretical basis of Marxism. Along with the Hungarian Marxist Georg Lukács and the Italian Antonio Gramsci, they were among the founding fathers of what later became known as Western Marxism. Anxious to rekindle the utopian and redemptive fires of Marxism and wean it from its reliance on science and economics, they often redirected attention to the philosophical roots of Marx's own ideas, anticipating the recovery of his 1844 *Economic and Philosophical Manuscripts* in the late 1920s. Among the first to reemphasize the Hegelian sources of Marxist theory was Karl Korsch, who broke with the KPD in 1926 to join the leftist opposition. In *Marxism and Philosophy* (1923), he sought to vindicate the critical, activist, praxis-oriented dimension of Marxism by establishing its philosophical rather than sociological credentials. Along with Lukács's *History and Class Consciousness* (1923), it moved Marxist theory away from the scientism and economism of the Second International's leading theorists.

Following their lead, others, like the philosopher Max Horkheimer, employed both concrete analyses of everyday life and theoretical treatises in the effort to criticize bourgeois society. In his aphorisms written before 1933, pseudonymously published as *Dawn and Decline* a year later, Horkheimer reflected on, among other things, the impotence of the working class to resolve its internal conflicts. In the programmatic statement written when he assumed the directorship of the Frankfurt Institute of Social Research in 1930, he proposed a theoretically informed, collective research enterprise that would later become celebrated as the Frankfurt School.

Among its other members were the philosopher Herbert Marcuse and the sociologist of literature Leo Löwenthal, who integrated the critique of art and mass culture into the institute's critical theory. In the Frankfurt School's rethinking of Marxist theory, the contribution of psychoanalysis, initially as interpreted by Erich Fromm, played a crucial role. It was equally influential in the work of another heterodox leftist, Wilhelm Reich, who was a member of the KPD until his expulsion in 1932. Reich's theoretical work was matched by his practical efforts, both as an analyst and a sponsor of so-called Sex-Pol clinics, which attempted to politicize the sexual problems of youth.

120

KARL RADEK

Leo Schlageter: The Wanderer in the Void

First published as "Leo Schlageter: Der Wanderer ins Nichts," *Die Rote Fahne*, no. 144 (June 26, 1923).

We have heard the far-reaching and deeply penetrating report of Comrade [Clara] Zetkin on international fascism, on this hammer that is to fall crushingly on the head of the proletariat, which will have its first effects on the petit-bourgeois strata, who wield it in the interests of big capital. I can neither expand upon nor complete this speech of our venerable leader. I could not even follow it properly because continually before my eyes was the corpse of the German fascist, our class enemy, who has been sentenced to death and shot by the executors of French imperialism, that powerful organization of another section of our class enemy. During the entire speech of Comrade Zetkin on the contradictions of fascism, the name Schlageter and his tragic fate buzzed in my head. We want to be mindful of it here as we take a political position on German fascism. The fate of the martyrs of German nationalism should not be passed over in silence nor should they be dispatched with a dismissive phrase. They have much to say to us, much to say to the German people.

We are no sentimental romantics who forget enmity at the funeral nor are we diplomats who say, speak nicely over the grave or be still. Schlageter, the brave soldier of the counterrevolution, deserves to be appreciated honestly, man-to-man. His comrade in thought, [Friedrich] Freska, published a novel in 1920 that depicted the life of an officer who fell in a battle against Spartacus. Freska titled the novel *The Wanderer in the Void*. If those German fascists who honestly want to serve the German people do not understand the meaning of Schlageter's fate, then Schlageter has fallen in vain and they should write on his memorial: The Wanderer in the Void.

Germany lay on the ground, defeated. Only fools believed that the victorious capitalist Entente would treat the German people differently than victorious German capital treated the Russian and the Rumanian people. Only fools or cowards afraid of the truth could believe the promises of [Woodrow] Wilson, the declarations that only the Kaiser, not the German people, would have to pay for the defeat. In the east a people still in battle—hungry and freezing—struggled against the Entente on fourteen fronts: Soviet Russia. One of these fronts consisted of German officers and German soldiers. Schlageter fought in the Freikorps Medem, which stormed Riga. We do not know whether the young officer understood the meaning of his act. The German administrative commissar of the time, the social democrat [August] Winnig, and General [Rüdiger] von der Goltz, the Baltic commander, knew what they were doing. They wanted, with their military engagement against the Russian people, to win the goodwill of the Entente. So that the conquered German bourgeoisie would not have to pay tribute to the victors, it took a lease on young German blood, so far spared from the bullets of the world war, offering them as mercenaries for the Entente against the Russian people. We do not know Schlageter's thoughts about this time. His leader, Medem, realized later that he wandered through the Baltic states into the void. Did all German nationalists understand that? General Ludendorff spoke at Schlageter's funeral in Munich, the same Ludendorff who continues today to offer himself to England as well as to France as commander in the crusade against Russia. Schlageter was mourned by the Stinnes press. Stinnes then became the partner in the Alpina Montana of Schneider-Creusot, the supplier of armaments to the murderers of Schlageter. Against whom did the German nationalist want to fight, against the capital of the Entente or against the Russian people? With whom did they want to ally? With the Russian workers and peasants in the mutual shaking off the yoke of Entente capital, or with Entente capital in the enslavement of the Russian and German people?

Schlageter is dead. He cannot answer the question. On his grave his comrades-in-arms swore to continue his struggle. They have to answer the questions: Against whom? On whose side?

Schlageter left the provinces of the Baltic for the industrial district of the Ruhr, not in 1923 but already in the year 1920. Do you know what that means? He participated in the ambush of German capital on the Ruhr workers; he fought in the ranks of the troops who were to subjugate the coal miners of the Ruhr to the kings of iron and coal. [Oskar von] Watter's troops, among whom he fought, fired the same bullets with which General [Jean-Marie-Joseph] Degoutte pacified the Ruhr workers. We have no reason to assume that Schlageter helped to quell the starving coal miners for egoistic reasons.

His choice of the path of mortal danger speaks and testifies for him, says that he was convinced of his service to the German people. But Schlageter believed himself to be serving the people best in helping to establish the domination of the classes that had until now led the German people and had conducted them into this unspeakable misfortune. Schlageter saw in the working class a rabble that had to be governed. And he most certainly shared the opinion of Count [Ernst] Reventlow, who calmly pronounced that all struggle against the Entente was impossible as long as the internal enemy is not quashed. But the internal enemy was for Schlageter the revolutionary working class. Schlageter was able to see with his own eyes the results of this policy when he arrived in the Ruhr Valley in 1923 during the occupation. He could see that, even if the workers stood united against French imperialism, a struggle of a unified people on the Ruhr was neither underway nor possible. He could see the workers' deep mistrust of the German government, of the German bourgeoisie. He could see how the deep rift in the nation crippled its capacity for defense. He could see more. His comrades in thought bemoaned the passivity of the German people. How can a defeated working class be active? How can a working class be active if it has been disarmed? If one demands that it let itself be exploited by profiteers and speculators? Or should the activity of the German working class be replaced by the activity of the German bourgeoisie? Schlageter read in the newspaper how the same people who came forward as protectors of the nationalist movement exported capital to impoverish the Reich while enriching themselves. Schlageter certainly placed no hope in these parasites, and he was spared reading in the newspapers about representatives of the German bourgeoisie, such as Dr. [Johann Anton] Lutterbeck, who turned to his hangmen with the request that they allow the kings of steel and iron to use machine guns to scatter the starving sons of the German people, the men responsible for the resistance on the Ruhr.

Now, as the German resistance has become a mockery—through the villainy of Dr. Lutterbeck and still more through the economic policy of the propertied classes—we ask the honest, patriotic masses who wanted to fight against the imperialist invasion of the French: How do you want to fight? From whom do you want support? The struggle against the imperialism of the Entente is war, even when the cannons are silent. One cannot conduct a war on the front when the hinterland is in revolt. A minority in the hinterland can be suppressed. The majority of the German nation consists of working people, who have to struggle against need and misery brought down upon them by the German bourgeoisie. If the patriots of Germany do not decide to adopt the cause of this national majority, thereby establishing a front against the capital of the Entente and of Germany, then Schlageter was a wanderer in the void. Then would Germany, because of the foreign invasion and because of the constant danger posed by the victors, become a field of bloody internal struggles, and it will be easy for the enemy to crush and dismember it. [. . .]

The Communist Party of Germany must say openly to the nationalistic petit-bourgeois masses: whoever, in the service of the profiteers, the speculators, or the masters of iron and coal, wants to try to enslave the German people, to plunge it into ill-sought adventures, will confront the opposition of the communist workers of Germany. They will answer violence with violence. Whoever through misunderstanding seeks to ally himself with the mercenaries of capital will be fought with all means at our disposal. But we believe that the great majority of the nationalistically-inclined masses belong not to the camp of capital but to the camp of labor. We are determined to find the way to these masses. We will do everything to see that men like Schlageter who were prepared to meet death in the service of a common cause, become not wanderers in the void but wanderers toward a better future for all mankind, that they do not shed their hot, unselfish blood for the profits of the barons of coal and iron but in the cause of the great working people of Germany, which is a part of the family of peoples struggling for emancipation. The Communist Party of Germany will speak this truth to the broadest masses of the German people, for it is not the party of struggle for a bit of bread for the industrial workers alone but the party of the fighting proletarians, which fights for their emancipation—an emancipation that is identical with the freedom of the whole people, with the freedom of all who work and suffer in Germany. Schlageter can no longer hear the truth. We are certain that hundreds of Schlageters will hear it and understand it.

121

KARL KORSCH

Marxism and Philosophy

First published as "Marxismus und Philosophie," *Archiv für die Geschichte des Sozialismus und der Arbeiterbewegung* 2 (1923), 74–121.

The translation of dialectics from its mystification by Hegel to the "rational form" of Marx's materialist dialectic essentially means that it has become the guiding principle of a single theoretical–practical and critical–revolutionary activity. It is a "method that is by its very nature critical and revolutionary." Even in Hegel "the theoretical was essentially contained in the practical." "One must not imagine that man thinks on the one hand and wills on the other, that he has thought in one pocket and will in another; this would be a vacuous notion." For Hegel the practical task of the concept in its "thinking activity" (in other words, philosophy) does not lie in the domain of ordinary "practical human and sensuous activity" (Marx). It is rather "to grasp what is, for that which is, is reason." By contrast, Marx concludes the self-clarification of his own dialectical method with the eleventh *Thesis on Feuerbach*: "The philosophers have only *interpreted* the world, it is now a question of *changing* it." This does not mean, as the epigones imagine, that all philosophy is shown to be mere fantasy. It only expresses a categorical rejection of all theory, philosophical or scientific, that is not *at the same time* practice—real, terrestrial, immanent, human, and sensuous practice—and not the speculative activity of the philosophical idea that basically does nothing but comprehend itself. Theoretical criticism and practical subversion are here inseparable activities, not in any abstract sense but as a concrete and real alteration of the concrete and real world of bourgeois society. Such is the most precise expression of the new materialist principle of the scientific socialism of Marx and Engels.

We have now shown the real consequences of the dialectical materialist principle for a Marxist conception of the relationship of consciousness to reality. By the same token we have shown the error of all abstract and undialectical conceptions found among various kinds of vulgar Marxists in their theoretical and practical attitudes to so-called intellectual reality. Marx's dictum is true not just of forms of economic consciousness in the narrower sense, but of all forms of social consciousness: they are not mere chimeras, but "highly objective and highly practical" social realities and consequently "must be abolished in a practical and objective manner." The naïvely metaphysical standpoint of sound, bourgeois common sense considers thought independent of being and defines truth as the correspondence of thought to an object that is external to it and mirrored by it. It is only this outlook that can sustain the view that all forms of economic consciousness (the economic conceptions of a prescientific and unscientific consciousness, as well as scientific economics itself) have an objective meaning because they correspond to a reality (the material relations of production which they comprehend)—whereas all higher forms of representation are merely objectless fantasies that will automatically dissolve into their essential nullity after the overthrow of the economic structure of society, and the abolition of its juridical and political superstructure. Economic ideas themselves only *appear* to be related to the material relations of production of bourgeois society in the way an image is related to the object it reflects. In fact they are related to them in the way that a specific, particularly defined part of a whole is related to the other parts of this whole. Bourgeois economics belongs with the material relations of production to bourgeois society as a totality. This totality also contains political and legal representations and their apparent objects, which bourgeois politicians and jurists—the "ideologues of private property" (Marx)—treat in an ideologically inverted manner as autonomous essences. Finally it also includes the higher ideologies of the art, religion, and philosophy of bourgeois society. If it seems that there are no objects which these representations can reflect, correctly or incorrectly, this is because economic, political, or legal representations do not have particular objects that exist independently either, isolated from the other phenomena of bourgeois society. To counterpose such objects to these representations is an abstract and ideological bourgeois procedure. They merely express bourgeois society as a totality in a particular way, just as do art, religion, and philosophy. Their ensemble forms the *spiritual structure* of bourgeois society, which corresponds to its economic structure, just as its legal and political superstructure corresponds to this same basis. All these forms must be subjected to the revolutionary social criticism of scientific socialism, which embraces the whole of social reality. They must be criticized in theory and overthrown in practice, together and at the same time with the economic, legal, and political structures of society. Just as political action is not rendered unnecessary by the economic action of a revolutionary class, so intellectual action is not rendered unnecessary by either political or economic action. On the contrary, it must be carried through to the end in theory and practice, as revolutionary scientific criticism and agitational work before the seizure of state power by the working class, and as scientific organization and ideological dictatorship after the seizure of state power. If this is valid for intellectual action against the forms of consciousness that define bourgeois society in general, it is especially true of philosophical action. Bourgeois consciousness necessarily sees itself as apart from the world and independent of it, as pure critical philosophy and impartial science, just as the bourgeois state and bourgeois law appear to be above society. This consciousness must be philosophically fought by the revolutionary materialistic dialectic, which is the philosophy of the working class. This struggle will only end when the whole of existing society and its economic basis have been totally overthrown in practice, and this consciousness has been totally surpassed and abolished in theory. "Philosophy cannot be abolished without being realized."

122

MAX HORKHEIMER

The Impotence of the German Working Class

Written in 1927. First published under the name Heinrich Regius, as "Die Ohnmacht der deutschen Arbeiterklasse," in *Dämmerung: Notizen in Deutschland* (Zürich: Opprecht und Hebling, 1934).

Marx showed that there is a tendency in the capitalist economic process for the number of workers to decrease as more machinery is introduced. An increasingly smaller percentage of the proletariat is really employed. This decrease also modifies the reciprocal relations of the various strata of the proletariat. The more the temporary not to mention the permanent and rewarding employment of an individual becomes the rare exception, the more the life and consciousness of the respectable employed worker will come to differ from those of the regularly unemployed strata. As a consequence, the solidarity of the proletariat, the community of shared interests shrinks more and more. [. . .]

Today the term proletariat to designate a class that experiences the negative side of the present order, the wretchedness, in its own existence applies to its components so unevenly that revolution may easily seem an individual concern. For the employed workers whose wages and long-term membership in unions and associations assure a certain, albeit small, security for the future, all political acts involve the danger of a tremendous loss. They, the regularly employed, do not have the same interests as those who even today have nothing to lose but their chains. Today the gulf between the employed and those who only work sporadically or not at all is as wide as that between the entire working class and the lumpenproletariat of an earlier period. Today wretchedness weighs even more exclusively on a social stratum whose members society has condemned to utter hopelessness. Work and misery no longer come together, people no longer experience both. This does not mean that the workers are well off, that economic relations change their brutal character toward them, or that the existence of the reserve army no longer depresses wages. Not at all! The misery of the employed continues to be the condition for and basis of this form of society. But the employed worker is no longer typical of those who most urgently need change. Instead, the misery and the restlessness of the existing order bears ever more exclusively on a certain lower segment of the working class, one part of the proletariat. But unlike the prewar proletariat, these unemployed who are most directly interested in revolution lack the capacities for education and organization, the class consciousness and the dependability of those who are more or less integrated into the capitalist enterprise. This mass wavers; there is not much to be done with it from an organizational point of view. The younger men who were never part of the work process have faith but no understanding of theory.

The capitalist process of production has thus driven a wedge between the interest in socialism and the human qualities necessary for its implementation. That is the new element. From our present perspective its development can of course be traced back to the inception of capitalism. Even today the realization of a socialist order would be better for all proletarians than capitalism would be, but the difference between the present circumstances of the regularly employed and their personal life under socialism seems less certain, hazier, than the danger of dismissal, misery, penitentiary, and death to which they can look forward were they to participate in a revolutionary uprising or possibly just a strike. The life of the unemployed, however, is torment. The two revolutionary elements, the direct interest in socialism and a clear theoretical consciousness, are no longer the common property of the proletariat but are now found among different, important segments of it. This is a result of the economic process. In contemporary Germany it expresses itself through the existence of two workers' parties and the wavering of sizable segments of the unemployed between the Communist and the National Socialist parties. It dooms the workers to practical impotence.

The impatience of the unemployed finds theoretical expression in the mere repetition of the slogans of the Communist party. The quantity of material worked through does not give principles a relevant form but leads to their being undialectically preserved. Political practice therefore fails to exploit all available possibilities for strengthening political positions and often exhausts itself in pointless commands or moral reprimands to the disobedient or faithless. The certainty of sinking into the misery of unemployment keeps nearly all who still work from obeying communist strike calls. Even the unemployed become hopeless and resigned as they face the fearful power apparatus which, though no longer a danger for an external enemy, is merely waiting to be used within, anxious to test all weapons from truncheon and machine gun to the most effective poison gas in a brisk, certainly riskless civil war. For these reasons party orders often become meaningless, and this cannot fail to have a markedly negative influence on the make-up and condition of its leadership. The disinclination to merely restate fundamentals may therefore have a significance conditions justify, even where that refusal extends to remote intellectual spheres such as sociology and philosophy; it rebels against its own futility.

In contrast to communism, the reformist wing of the workers' movement no longer knows that human conditions cannot be effectively improved under capitalism. It has lost its grasp of all theoretical elements, and its leadership is a precise image of the most secure members. Many try with all available means, even the renunciation of ordinary loyalty, to keep their jobs. The fear of losing them gradually becomes the only explanation of their acts. The need to suppress what remains of their better consciousness explains the constant readiness of these reformist German politicians angrily to dismiss Marxism as an outdated error. Their hatred of any precise theoretical point of view is greater than that of the bourgeoisie. [. . .] These ideologues of reformist practical politics turn out to be the successors of the bourgeois positivism they themselves combatted: they oppose theory and plead for an acceptance of facts. But because they even relativize our understanding of those facts and know no absolutes other than this activity of relativizing and questioning, they strike the outsider as people who merely run everything down. The life of the unemployed is hell, their apathy is the night whereas the present existence of the working population is the grey everyday. The philosophy that reflects its life therefore seems impartial and free of illusions. As a way of reconciling itself to the bad state of affairs, it tends to combine resignation here on earth with a vague belief in an entirely hazy, transcendental, or religious principle. It replaces causal explanation by the search for analogies. To the extent that it does not wholly reject Marxist concepts, it formalizes them or makes them academically respectable. [. . .] They do not organize that material by consciously taking sides in the historical struggle, for they believe they can float above it.

Just as both the positive capacities workers acquire through their integration in the capitalist production process, and the entire inhumanity of that process are presently the experiences of different social groups, so the two elements of the dialectical method—factual knowledge and clarity concerning fundamentals—do not coexist among intellectuals of the left, from political functionaries all the way to the theoreticians of the workers' movement. Loyalty to materialist doctrine threatens to become a mindless and contentless cult of literalism and personality unless a radical turn soon occurs. At the same time, the materialist content, which means knowledge of the real world, is the possession of those who have become disloyal to Marxism. It is therefore also about to lose its only distinguishing characteristic, its existence as knowledge. Without the materialist principle, facts become blind signs or enter the domain of the ideological forces that control intellectual life. There are those who recognize existing society as bad, but they lack the knowledge to prepare practically and theoretically the revolution. The others might be able to produce that knowledge but lack the fundamental experience of the urgent need for change. The social democrats therefore have altogether too many reasons for quarreling among themselves. They painstakingly take all circumstances into account, thus paying their respect to truth and objectivity, and shaming their ignorant opponents by multiplying the possible points of view. The Communists lack sufficient reasons, in fact they frequently don't advance reasons but refer to authority. Convinced as they are of being the sole possessors of the truth, they are not sticklers for particular truths and use moral and, if necessary, physical force to make their better informed opponents see reason.

To overcome this state of affairs in theoretical questions, good will can do little toward the elimination of the fragmentation of the working class which underlies it. The economic process that denies employment to a large part of the population from birth on, and dooms it to a hopeless existence, necessarily produces and reproduces it. There is no point in becoming condescending when one notes these intellectual symptoms nor in pretending that the person who becomes aware of this condition could escape its consequences. In both parties there exist some of the forces on which the future of humanity depends.

123

MAX HORKHEIMER

The State of Contemporary Social Philosophy and the Tasks of an Institute for Social Research

First published as *Die gegenwärtige Lage der Sozialphilosophie und die Aufgaben eines Instituts für Sozialforschung* (Frankfurt am Main: Englert and Schlosser, 1931), 3–16.

Although social philosophy is the focus of general philosophical concern, it is in no better shape today than most philosophical, indeed most fundamentally intellectual, efforts. One is unable to find a substantive conception of social philosophy that could be considered everywhere as binding. Given the present situation in the sciences, in which the traditional boundaries between disciplines are in question and we do not yet know where they might be drawn in the future, the attempt to give ultimate definitions for academic domains seems rather untimely. Nevertheless one can reduce the general views of social philosophy to one brief idea: The final goal of social philosophy is the philosophical interpretation of human fate—insofar as humans are not mere individuals but members of a community. Social philosophy must therefore primarily concern itself with those phenomena that can be interpreted only in the context of the social existence of humans, such as the state, law, economy, religion: in short, with all of the material and spiritual culture of humanity.

Social philosophy, thus understood, became in the history of classical German Idealism the decisive philosophical task. Its most brilliant achievements are the most powerful aspects of Hegel's system. [. . .]

For Hegel, the structure of objective spirit (*Geist*), which realizes in history the cultural artifacts of the absolute spirit (i.e., art, religion, philosophy), is not discerned any longer from a critical analysis of personality (*Persönlichkeit*) but rather from universal dialectical logic. The development and the works of the objective spirit are not arrived at by the free decisions of a subject but by the spirit of the dominant peoples that succeed each other on the battlefields of history. The destiny of the particular fulfills itself in the fate of the universal. The essence, the substantial content, of the individual is not revealed in personal actions but in the life of the totality to which it belongs. Thus Hegel's idealism has in its constitutive parts become social philosophy: the philosophical understanding of the collective whole, in which we live and which serves as the foundation for all creations of absolute culture, is now simultaneously knowledge of the meaning of our own being, its true worth and content.

Let me remain for a moment with this Hegelian conception. From its dissolution and the impossibility of recreating it in thought without falling behind the present state of knowledge, one is in principle able to explicate the present state of social philosophy. Hegel assigned the realization of the goal of reason to the objective spirit, in the last instance to the world-spirit. The development of this spirit is shown in the conflict of the "concrete ideas," the "spirit of the peoples," out of which "as signs and ornaments of its grandeur" the world-historical kingdoms emerge in necessary sequence. This development happens whether individuals in their historical actions know of it and will it; the development has its own law. Nevertheless, as with the French Enlightenment and English liberalism, Hegel does accept the drives and passions of human beings as real motive powers. [. . .]

But if history and the state are created eternally out of the "medley of arbitrariness," if therefore the historian has to deal with a chain of pain and death, of stupidity and baseness, and if finite being perishes in indescribable agony and history can be seen in Hegel's term as the "slaughterbench on which the happiness of peoples, the wisdom of states, and the virtue of individuals are being sacrificed," then philosophy transcends the viewpoint of the empirical observer. Because "what is called reality," he teaches in the *Philosophy of History,*

> is seen by philosophy only as something rotten, which seems to exist but is not real in and of itself. This insight, one might say, is consolation against the conception of absolute disaster, the madness of all that has come to pass. Consolation, however, is only a substitute for the misfortune that should never have happened, and makes its home in the finite world. Philosophy is therefore not a consolation; it is more: it reconciles, it transfigures a reality that appears to be unjust, making it appear rational. It exhibits it as such, shows it to be grounded in the idea itself, as that with which reason is supposed to be satisfied.

The "transfiguration" of which Hegel speaks is precisely attained by that theory according to which the true essence of human beings does not exist in mere inwardness and the actual fate of finite individuals but asserts itself in the lives of peoples and is realized in the state. With the thought that the material essence, the idea, is preserved in world history, the destruction of the individual seems to carry no philosophical weight. [. . .]

According to Hegel, the finite individual being can attain the conceptual consciousness of its freedom within the state only through idealist speculative thinking. He essentially saw in this mediating function the achievement of his philosophy, and thus of philosophy as such. Philosophy is to him identical with the transfiguration of the real "that appears unjust." When the esteem of his system waned in Germany around the middle of the last century, a future-oriented, individualistic society believing in progress replaced the metaphysics of the objective spirit with an unmediated belief in the prestabilized harmony of individual interests. It seemed as if what was needed to mediate between the empirical existence of the individual and the consciousness of its freedom in the social totality was not philosophy but steady progress in the positive sciences, technology, and industry. But as the disappointment in that belief grew, a scorned metaphysics took its revenge. Deserted by the philosophical conviction that the divine idea existing within the totality is its true reality, the individual experienced the world as a "medley of arbitrariness" and itself as the mere "price of existence and transitoriness." The sober glance directed towards the particular and the immediate was no longer capable of discerning "the cunning of reason" behind the surface of warring individual wills, perpetual need, the indignities of the everyday world, and the terror of history. And so Hegel's greatest enemy, [Arthur] Schopenhauer, saw the dawn of his antihistorical, pessimistic, and consolatory philosophy.

The conviction that all by virtue of their association with a historical unity and its own characteristic laws, which forms the dialectic of world history, partakes of the eternal life of the spirit—this notion ensuring the salvation of the individual from the infamous chain of becoming and perishing—disappeared with objective idealism. The suffering and the death of individuals threatened to appear in their naked meaninglessness—the last fact of an age enthralled by facts. With the deepening of the contradiction in the principle of individualistic life form (that is, the contradiction between the unbroken progress of the happiness of the individuals within a given social context on the one hand and the prospects of their actual situation on the other), philosophy, and especially social philosophy, was called more and more urgently to play again the role that Hegel had assigned to it. And social philosophy has heeded that call. [. . .]

All of these projects of contemporary social philosophy seem to provide individual human beings with access to a suprapersonal sphere that is more invested with being, more meaningful, more substantial than their own existence. They therefore accomplish the task of transfiguration prescribed by Hegel. Further, in Heidegger's *Sein und Zeit* [Being and Time]—the only modern philosophical work that radically rejects social philosophy and that discovers real being only in the interior of individually existing human beings—care (*Sorge*) is the focal point. This philosophy of individual human existence is in its simple contents not transfiguration in Hegel's sense. Human existence is in it only a being-unto-death, a sheer finitude. It is a melancholy philosophy. If it is acceptable at this point to put the matter bluntly, one might say that today social philosophy meets the desire of a life hindered in its own individual pursuit of happiness with a new statement of meaning. Social philosophy appears to be part of the philosophical and religious efforts to plant the hopeless individual existence back into the womb, or to put it, in [Werner] Sombart's term, in the "golden ground" of meaningful totalities.

But, ladies and gentlemen, having confronted this situation of social philosophy, let us now turn to delineate its deficiency. Social philosophy today, as we have seen, has taken a generally polemical stand against positivism. Positivism, it is charged, sees only the particular and thus in the realm of society sees only the individual and the relations between individuals; all is exhausted by facts. That there are facts that can be ascertained by means of analytical science philosophy does not dispute. But philosophy posits against these facts more or less constructively, more or less in its own philosophizing, ideas, essences, totalities, independent spheres of objective spirit, units of meaning, spirit of peoples that it considers to be "more original" or even "genuine" elements of being. [. . .]

This view presupposes a conception of philosophy that is no longer tenable. However one might want to draw the boundaries between the particular disciplines of sociology and social philosophy, which, I believe, would necessitate a high degree of arbitrariness, one thing is certain: If sociophilosophical thought about the relationship of the individual to society, the meaning of culture, the formation of communities, or the overall status of social life—in short, about the great, principal questions—should be left behind as the sediment in the reservoir of social-scientific problems after those problems that can be advanced in concrete investigations have been drained off, then social philosophy can still perform a social function (e.g., that of transfiguration), but its intellectual fruitfulness would be destroyed. The relationship between the philosophical and the empirical disciplines should not be conceptualized as if it were philosophy that treated the essential problems, constructing theories that cannot be attacked by the empirical sciences, its own conceptions of reality and systems embracing the totality, while in contrast empirical science comes out of its long, boring studies fragmented into a thousand individual questions in order only to end up in the chaos of specialization. This view, according to which the empirical scientist has to regard philosophy as a beautiful yet scientifically fruitless enterprise, and the philosopher in contrast emancipates himself from the empirical scientist because the former assumes that he cannot wait for the latter in his far-reaching quest, is presently being superseded by the thought of an ongoing dialectical permeation and evolution of philosophical theory and empirical scientific praxis. [. . .]

The correction of the deficiency in the situation of social philosophy hinted at above seems to us to lie neither in a profession of faith to a more or less constructive interpretation of cultural life, nor in positing a new meaning for society, state, law, and what have you. Today on the contrary, and I am surely not alone in this opinion, everything depends on organizing research around current philosophical problematics in which philosophers, sociologists, political economists, historians, and psychologists engage by joining enduring research groups in order to do together what in other areas one is able to do alone in the laboratory and what all true scientists have always done: namely, to pursue their philosophical questions directed at the big picture with the finest scientific methods, to transform and to fine-tune these questions as the work progresses, to find new methods, and yet to never lose sight of the whole. In this way no positive or negative answers to philosophical questions can be given. Instead, the philosophical questions themselves are dialectically integrated into the empirical scientific process; that is to say, their answers are to be found in the progress of substantive knowledge which also effects the form. This approach to the science of society cannot be mastered by one person alone—given the vast subject matter as well as the variety of indispensable scientific methods whose assistance is called for. Despite the gigantic effort on his part, even Max Scheler has failed in this regard.

Given this situation, one has to view the transformation of the chair of this university for the directorship of the Institute of Social Research into a chair for social philosophy and its relocation to the department of philosophy as highly legitimate. Carl Grünberg held this chair as a lecturer in political economy in the department of political science. With the new, difficult, and decisive task of employing a grand empirical scientific apparatus in the service of social philosophy, with my appointment I have felt the immeasurable gap separating a great scientist, whose name is mentioned with great respect and thankfulness all over the world wherever work in his discipline is done, from the young, unknown man who was designated as his successor. His long illness belongs to those senseless facts in the lives of individuals that put philosophical transfiguration to shame. According to his own deeply-rooted and precisely-defined interests, as determined by the historical school of political economy, he emphasized first and foremost the history of the labor movement. In doing so, his all-encompassing knowledge of the relevant sources in the world has made possible the acquisition of archival material and especially of a unique special library now containing approximately fifty thousand volumes; this library is now being put to good use, not just by students at our university but also by many scholars both in and outside of Germany. The series of writings from the Institute, edited by him, contains only works that have been recognized by relevant authorities of diverse political viewpoints as exceptional scientific achievements.

Having set myself the task of directing the work of the Institute towards a new goal following the prolonged illness of its director, I am able to draw not only on the experience of its associates and its collected library treasures, but on the Institute's charter, defined in an important way by its director. According to this charter the director, designated by the minister, is independent "with respect both to the educational administration and the founders" to the point where there exists, as Grunberg used to say, in place of a council charter "the dictatorship of the director." Because of it, it will be possible for me to use what has been created by him in order to erect with my colleagues, at least on a small scale, a dictatorship of the planned work over the coexistence of philosophical construction and empirical research in the theory of society.

124

WILHELM REICH

Politicizing the Sexual Problems of Youth

First published as "Politisierung der sexuellen Probleme der Jugend," in *Der sexuelle Kampf der Jugend* (Vienna: Sexpol Verlag, 1932), 10ff.

We must be quite clear in our minds about the possibilities open to working youth in a capitalist society. Since the Young Communist League is adopting the clear political line of social revolution, it should aim at being the leader of youth in the field of sexual problems, too. And working youth would recognize it as such if only its approach to this question—this urgent and delicate question—were the right one of ruthless candor; if only they could feel that the YCL really understands their plight, and is defending their cause.

We must practice genuine self-criticism. We must ask ourselves why it is that, on this of all problems, we have until now been so mealy-mouthed, why we have not dared to consider the only opportunities open to working youth. As a first step, we must admit that on this question of sex we have behaved like the man asleep who keeps trying to chase a fly away by vainly flapping a hand in its direction.

It has been pointed out again and again in the revolutionary youth organizations that the "sex question" disturbs and impedes the struggle for revolution. And the conclusion has been drawn, again and again, that we must leave the sex question aside, because we have no time to deal with it and because we have more important things to do. But if the issue has come up again and again, more and more urgently, more and more pressingly, if, as a matter of fact, many youth organizations have collapsed, owing to the sexual difficulties of their members (a fact we must openly admit), then we must ask ourselves why the question is so disturbing, and we must not, just because it is disturbing, declare that we have no time for it and have more urgent things to do, that sex life is a private affair, etc. Sex life is not a private affair if it preoccupies you, and in the form in which it has existed hitherto, it interferes with the political struggle.

What other problem that causes similar difficulties would we dismiss in the same way? What would we say to such an attitude toward any other issue? We should rightly say that it was an evasive attitude. We should rightly condemn anyone who resorted to such excuses. We ought to be consistent with ourselves. Our view should be that for Bolsheviks there is no such thing as an insurmountable difficulty—and therefore, the attitude that I have described is a bourgeois and opportunist one.

When such problems arise they do not fall from the sky, but come out of the very real contradictions of our social system; and, as such, they demand an answer. We have found time in our class struggle to deal with sport, the theater, religion, the radio. Why are we not equally consistent when it comes to the sexual problem of youth? However, if we agree that we have been evading the issue, we must become clear about why this is so.

A superficial reason is the fact that by ignoring the problem of sex we hope to be able to devote ourselves entirely to revolutionary work, thus emphasizing the difference between us and the bourgeois types whose interest is centered on the problem of sex and who do nothing but chatter about it. This has led us into serious error. Many of us have wanted to dismiss sexuality altogether, as something inessential or even "bourgeois." We were wrong: that is the lesson of reality. We must solve the sex problem in a revolutionary way, by evolving a clear sexual-political theory; proceeding from it to a sexual-revolutionary praxis; and integrating both these in the proletarian movement as a whole. That, we are convinced, is the right way toward a definitive solution.

Many comrades justify their negative attitude by invoking Lenin's conversation with Clara Zetkin in which he sharply criticized the discussions and debates on sex taking place in workers' and youth associations and said that there were more important things to be done. We completely endorse the point of view which Lenin adopted at the time. He was attacking superficial, woolly chatter about sex which merely took people's minds off more essential things, and we, too, are against that. These "sex discussions" are generally nothing more than a substitute for sexual activity, intellectual masturbation of the most common kind. But we shall understand at once how the problem ought to be treated if, at the same time, we quote a second remark of Lenin's made in the course of the same conversation with Clara Zetkin: "Communism will not bring asceticism, but joy of life, power of life, and a satisfied love life will help to do that." If communism is to bring about the enjoyment of sexual life, surely this has to be fought for.

The point of the matter, therefore, is this: we must not indulge in empty discussions about sex, but neither must we ignore the sex problem. Without talking about it we cannot solve it. What is left for us to do? We must talk about it politically. Then we shall be discussing it in the right way and taking the right action as a result. However, before we go into further detail and produce evidence to show that this is the only possible way out, we must still define the deeper reason for our avoidance of this question.

Where were we all brought up? Under what conditions did we grow up? We grew up in families, and were brought up under the capitalist system. The objection will be raised that there is a great difference between proletarian and bourgeois families. But it isn't as simple as that. We don't have to think for very long before coming up with a response; we need only consider some of the elements of our way of thinking and living.

Have we freed ourselves from the bourgeois ideology concerning property? Yes, to a considerable extent, for there is a marked difference between bourgeois and working-class families as regards property relations. Have we completely freed ourselves from religion? Here things are no longer as simple. There are many thousands of proletarian families that are religious. The further we penetrate into the petit-bourgeois proletariat, the more deep-seated we find religion to be. And what about sexual morality? Isn't it rooted in the very nature of the family—which proletarians, too, are forced to maintain, because of the conditions of life under capitalism?

Doesn't sexual oppression and the implanting of bourgeois morality form part and parcel of bourgeois marriage and the bourgeois family? Of course, the contradictions between the worker's way of life and bourgeois family morality are very great. The contradictions are different too in the middle and upper bourgeoisie. But bourgeois sexual morality nevertheless exists in the proletariat; and of all bourgeois ideologies it is the most deeply anchored because it is the most strongly implanted from earliest childhood. It is one of the bourgeoisie's strongest ideological props within the oppressed class.

We see all the time that even class-conscious youth find it very difficult to liberate themselves from this. Bourgeois sexual morality—whose most essential feature is that it does not view sexual life as natural, self-evident, and also connected with the particular social order of the time, but denies it and is afraid of it—is more deeply embedded in the very marrow of us Communists than we all realize. We should not allow ourselves to be deceived, either, by sexual showing-off, which is the counterpart of sexual timidity. This is simply the same bourgeois sexuality, with a different mathematical sign in front of it. Lenin was perfectly right, therefore, when he described the "glass of water" theory as a "good bourgeois theory."

What matters are the sexual deformations that every one of us bears inside himself as a result of sexual oppression and that are connected with unconscious repressed attitudes, so that in our sex life we are not quite masters of ourselves. These are the deeper reasons for our reluctance to deal openly and consistently with the problem of sex—the reasons why all of us without exception, even those who have the best insight into the problem, do not dare to include sexual liberation slogans in the rest of our propaganda. We must learn to understand why so many Communists get that funny smile and start pulling that special face as soon as sex is mentioned. We must seriously put an end to all that, however hard it will be for us to overcome our own inhibitions. [. . .]

In capitalist society there can be no sexual liberation of youth, no healthy, satisfying sex life; if you want to be rid of your sexual troubles, fight for socialism. Only through socialism can you achieve sexual *joie de vivre*. Pay no attention to the opinions of people who do not know anything about sex. Socialism will put an end to the power of those who gaze up toward heaven as they speak of love while they crush and destroy the sexuality of youth.

125

LEO LÖWENTHAL
On the Sociology of Literature

First published as "Zur Literatursoziologie," *Zeitschrift für Sozialforschung* 1, no. 1 (1932), 85–102.

The history of literature is in a unique way subject to the difficulties that arise with every historical effort. Not only is it implicated in all theoretical discussions concerning the conceptual meaning and material structure of history but in addition its object of study falls into the realm of numerous scientific disciplines. Beyond the techniques involved in the critical analysis of sources, numerous disciplines step forward with a variety of claims, among them philosophy, aesthetics, psychology, pedagogy, philology, and even statistics. When we turn to daily practice, however, we find that literary studies have become scientific jetsam. Everybody, from the "naïve reader" to the presumably legitimate teacher with special expertise, is prepared to launch interpretations of literary texts in the most arbitrary and capricious ways. Knowledge of a language combined with the conviction that an adequate technical terminology can be dispensed with are considered sufficient prerequisites to engage in such ventures. Academics, however, have so far not developed methods of research and analysis which would do justice to the complexity of their object of study. This is not a wholesale indictment of every single specialized work; rather, what I am concerned with here are the prevailing principles underlying the contemporary study of literary history and literary criticism.

Virtually all of the scholars who contributed to the collection of essays *Die Philosophie der Literaturwissenschaft* (The Philosophy of Literary Studies) are in agreement that a "scientific" approach to the history of literature would lead nowhere. Not only do they believe—and rightly so—that each literary work contains some nonrational elements, they also consider any rational approach inadequate because of the very nature of the object under investigation. Consequently, the study of literature as it was founded in the nineteenth century is condemned and rejected as "historical pragmatism," as "historicizing psychologism," and as "positivistic method." [. . .]

This rigid and irrational stance on the part of those representing literary scholarship today presumes its legitimation insofar as the "methods of the natural sciences" analyze their object into bits and pieces, and when attempting to define its "vital poetic soul" these methods cannot help but entirely miss its "secret." The significance of these statements is hard to grasp. For nobody has ever demonstrated why and to what extent an object would be harmed or distorted by a rational approach. Any study of a phenomenon can be mindful of its wholeness, its gestalt, while being conscious of a selective methodology. Admittedly such an analysis will only yield the elements of a mosaic whose sum never represents the whole. But where on earth does scientific analysis exhaust itself in nothing but a summation of fractured parts? And are the methods of the natural sciences exclusively atomistic in nature? Certainly not, and neither do methods of literary analysis have to be, if they are inappropriate to a specific task. [. . .]

Inasmuch as these fashionable literary scholars point to the pitfalls involved in seeking to understand the relationship of author and work through, for instance, mere philological data analysis, I have no quarrel with this antipositivistic attitude. But when it comes to an evaluation of a work of art and its qualitative aspects, an understanding of its intrinsic merit and its authenticity—questions so much at the center of the concerns of these scholars—their methods reveal their utter inadequacy. The question of whether and to what extent the literary artist consciously applies conventions of form can only be explored by rational means. But the metaphysical mystification so prevalent in contemporary literary studies impedes any sober reflection and scholarship. Its tasks are not only historical in nature; I would like to refer to [Wilhelm] Dilthey's concept of understanding (*Verstehen*) and its particular emphasis on the relationship between the author and his work. Admittedly the demystification of investigative approaches to literature cannot be achieved by means of a formal poetics alone. What is needed above all is a psychology of art, i.e., a study of the psychological interaction between artist, artistic creation, and reception. [. . .]

In contrast to the vague declamatory statements so characteristic of Jungian psychology, the classical Freudian model of psychoanalysis has already made important theoretical contributions to a psychology of art. Some of its proponents have discussed central questions of literature, particularly those dealing with the psychic conditions under which great works of art originate, specifically the origins and structure of artistic imagination, and last but not least, the question of the relationship between the artistic work and its reception which so far has been ignored or at least insufficiently explored. Admittedly, some of these psychoanalytic propositions are not yet polished and refined enough and remain somewhat schematic. But to reject the assistance of scientific psychology in the study of art and literature does not provide protection from "a barbarian assault of conquerors," as one contemporary literary mandarin put it, but rather is a "barbarian" argument itself!

Coupled with the condemnation of "historicizing psychologism," which cannot explore the secret of the "authentic poetic soul," is the repudiation of accepted historical methodology and particularly of any theory of historical causality, in short, what in modern literary scholarship is anathematized as "positivistic materialism." [. . .]

By no means do causal questions require infinite regress; clearly stated they can be precisely answered, even if new questions might be posed by this answer. An investigation of the reasons for Goethe's move to Weimar does not require an investigation of the history of urban development in Germany! [. . .]

In fact, it is possible to conceive of a theoretical approach to literature that remains faithful to "knowledge and learning" and interprets literary works historically and sociologically, avoiding the pitfalls of both descriptive positivism and mere metaphysical speculation.

Such concern with the historical and sociological dimensions of literature requires a theory of history and society. This is not to say that one is limited to vague theorizing about the relationships between literature and society in general, nor that it is necessary to speak in generalities about social conditions that are required for the emergence of literature. Rather the historical explanation of literature has to address the extent to which particular social structures find expression in individual literary works, and what function these works perform in society. Man is involved in specific relations of production throughout his history. These relations present themselves socially as classes in struggle with each other, and the development of their relationship forms the real basis for the various cultural spheres. The specific structure of production (i.e., the economy) is the independent explanatory variable not only for the legal forms of property and organization of state and government but at the same time for the shape and quality of human life in each historical epoch. It is illusory to assume an autonomy of the social superstructure, and this is not altered through the use of a scientific terminology claiming such autonomy. As long as literary history is exclusively conceived as *Geistesgeschichte* [the history of spirit or mind], it will remain powerless to make cogent statements, even though in practice the talent and sensibilities of a literary historian may have produced something of interest. A genuine, explanatory history of literature must proceed on materialistic principles. That is to say, it must investigate the economic structures as they present themselves in literature as well as the impact that the materialistically interpreted work of art has in the economically determined society. [. . .]

Contrary to common assertions, this theory neither postulates that culture in its entirety can be explained in terms of economic relations nor that specific cultural or psychological phenomena are nothing but reflections of the social substructure. Rather a materialistic theory places its emphasis on mediation: the mediating processes between a mode of production and the modes of cultural life including literature. Psychology must be considered as one of the principal mediating processes, particularly in the field of literary studies, since it describes the psychic processes by means of which the cultural functions of a work of art reproduce the structures of the societal base. Inasmuch as the basis of each society can be seen as the relationship between ruling and ruled classes and is in fact a metabolic process between society and nature, literature—like all other cultural phenomena—will make this relationship transparent. For that reason the concept of ideology will be decisive for the social explanation of all phenomena of the superstructure from legal institutions to the arts. Ideology is false consciousness of social contradictions and attempts to replace them with the illusions of social harmony. Indeed, literary studies are largely an investigation of ideologies. [. . .]

It has always been of great interest to me why a task as important as the study of the reception of literature among various social groups has been so utterly neglected even though a vast pool of research material is available in journals and newspapers, in letters and memoirs. A materialistic history of literature, unhampered by the anxious protection of the literary arts by its self-styled guardians, and without fear of getting stranded in a quagmire of routine philology or mindless data collection, is well prepared to tackle this task.

126

ERNST THÄLMANN

[The SPD and NSDAP Are Twins]

First published in *Der revolutionäre Ausweg und die KPD* (Speech to the plenary session of the Central Committee of the Communist Party of Germany, February 19, 1932), 25, 36, 37, 60, 61.

What is the relation between the politics of the Hitler party and social democracy? The eleventh plenum has already spoken of the entanglement of these two factors in the service of finance capital. Already in 1924 Comrade Stalin characterized the role of these two wings most clearly when he spoke of them as twins that complement each other.

This development is currently displayed unmistakably in Germany. [. . .]

As for the organization of terror, the SPD increasingly imitates Hitler's fascism. One needs only think of the flag-defense formations or more recently of the so-called Hammer Units of the Iron Front, which are to be deployed as aids of the dictatorship of capital in defense of the capitalist system against the revolutionary proletariat.

Above all, however, it is the Prussian government of the SPD and the General Association of German Trade Unions which completely and fully confirm the role of social democracy as the most active factor in the fascist transformation of Germany.

Whereas social democracy thus increasingly approaches Hitler's fascism, the latter from the opposite direction stresses its legality and openly mounts of late the platform of Brüning's foreign policy. [. . .]

All of these points display the extensive similarities between the SPD and the National Socialist policies on fascist transformation. [. . .]

WHY MUST WE DIRECT OUR MAIN BLOW AGAINST SOCIAL DEMOCRACY?

Our strategy directs the main blow against social democracy, without thereby weakening the struggle against Hitler's fascism; our strategy creates the very preconditions of an effective opposition to Hitler's fascism precisely in its direction of the main blow against social democracy. This strategy is only to be understood once one has understood clearly the role of the proletariat as the only class that will carry the revolution through to the end. [. . .]

The practical application of this strategy in Germany demands that the main blow be struck against social democracy. With its leftist affiliates it supplies the most dangerous props for enemies of the revolution. It is the primary social basis of the bourgeoisie; it is the most active factor in fascist transformation, as the eleventh plenum pronounced quite correctly; and at the same time it knows in the most dangerous fashion, as the "moderate wing of fascism," how to use deceitful maneuvers to win the masses for the dictatorship of the bourgeoisie and its fascist methods.

The defeat of social democracy is equivalent to the conquest of the majority of the proletariat and the creation of the most important preconditions of the proletarian revolution. [. . .]

WHAT IS THE REVOLUTIONARY UNITED FRONT POLICY?

To carry out the revolutionary United Front policy means to pursue a relentless struggle against social fascists of all shadings, above all against the leftist varieties of social fascism that are the most dangerous: against the SAPD [Socialist Workers Party of Germany], against the [Heinrich] Brandler group [moderate Communists], and against similar cliques and tendencies.

To pursue the revolutionary United Front policy means to mobilize the masses for the struggle truly from below, in the factories and at the unemployment offices.

The revolutionary United Front policy demands the systematic, patient, and comradely persuasion of the Social Democratic, Christian and even National Socialist workers to forsake their traitorous leaders.

The United Front cannot be achieved through parliamentary negotiations. It cannot be achieved through agreements with other parties or groups, but must grow out of the mass movement and, carried by this movement, must represent a truly vital fighting front.

Joint negotiations between the KPD and the SPD, the SAPD, or the Brandler group— there are none! There will be none!

127

SOCIAL DEMOCRATIC PARTY (SPD)
The Iron Front for a United Front!

First published as "Eiserne Front für Einheitsfront!" *Vorwärts* (June 18, 1932).

The Leadership of the Iron Front (Berlin) gives the following answer:

[. . .] the organizations united in the Iron Front are absolutely convinced that a unification of the proletariat is more essential than ever before. The fascist danger demands this unity. The danger of fascism, however, can only be countered when a *genuine* common will to unity is present. At the demonstration of the Iron Front on June 9, comrades Künstler and Aufhäser referred to the possibility of all proletarian organizations joining together to fight fascism. As a precondition for this we demanded that the attacks of the communist party against our organizations and leaders should stop. You refer in your letter of June 16 to the call published in the *Rote Fahne* on the same day. This proclamation includes, in contrast to your offer of forming a united front, a whole series of unjust and damaging attacks upon our organizations, our functionaries and our leadership, attacks which hardly point to an honest desire to join a common struggle against fascism.

We agree with you that the ban on demonstrations must be lifted. We have already taken our petition to the relevant authorities. But you have made it impossible to pursue the necessary united front against fascism because of your year-long attempts to subvert and dismember strong workers' organizations, your common cause with the fascists both inside and outside parliament, your attempts to cripple the trade-union movement through the revolutionary trade unions, and your slogans, "Severing—the same as Hitler" and "Social Democracy—the real enemy."

When you have honestly met the necessary preconditions as set out above, the Iron Front sees no reason why a united front should not be forged.

13
Revolution from the Right

IF THE WEIMAR REPUBLIC can justly be called a laboratory for leftist political theory and practice, it was no less of one for the right. Despite the existence of some residual nostalgia for the Wilhelmine system, most conservatives recognized the need for new solutions to the problems of political order and legitimacy. The old Conservative and Free Conservative parties reconstituted themselves as the Deutschnationale Volkspartei (DNVP) in November 1918. Although initially hoping for a monarchical restoration, its leaders grudgingly proclaimed their willingness to work within the new electoral system. As its platform of 1931 shows, the DNVP was progressively drawn to the more radical, antirepublican tenets of *völkisch* thought, especially after their leadership passed from Count Kuno Westarp to the powerful media magnate Alfred Hugenberg in 1928. There were in fact some seventy-five *völkisch* groups in Weimar, advocating racial and cultural purity as well as the restoration of hometown (*heimat*) communalism.

Other rightist theorists were impatient with all the existing parties and sought a more radical solution to the ills of not merely the new political order but modern life as a whole. Seeking respite from a despair that was as much cultural as political, they entertained fantasies of redemption through violence and upheaval, which brought them on occasion into proximity with the extreme left. The communist Karl Radek's attempt to exploit nationalist sentiments was mirrored in the "national bolshevism" of right-wing ideologues like Ernst Niekisch, who attempted to portray Germany as a "proletarian nation." What the poet and playwright Hugo von Hofmannsthal later popularized as "the conservative revolution" and the sociologist Hans Freyer dubbed the "revolution from the right" attracted many intellectuals such as the disenchanted aesthete Arthur Moeller van den Bruck. His 1922 diatribe, *Das Dritte Reich,* translated as *Germany's Third Empire,* provided a sinister myth whose future success he did not live to witness (he committed suicide in 1924.) Others, including the jurist and political theorist Edgar J. Jung, who, like Spengler and Moeller was a member of the elitist *Herrenklub,* trumpeted the same ideology until the Nazis took them at their word and then, in many cases, eliminated them soon after (Jung was killed in the Roehm purge in 1934).

Metapolitical fantasies like Moeller's and Jung's were actively supported by figures like the novelist and Freikorps leader Ernst von Salomon, whose impatient contempt for the political caution of traditional nationalists—those still beholden to the Second Reich of the Wilhelmine era or cautious *Vernunftrepublikaner* like Thomas Mann—was shared by many who had been brutalized by the war. They joined antirepublican organizations of veterans, like the Bund der Frontsoldaten founded by Franz Seldte, which became known as the Stahlhelm. As much a paramilitary force as a political pressure group, they had little difficulty in being integrated into the Nazi SA (Sturm Abteilung, or Storm Troops) in 1933.

The Weimar right also contained more substantial intellectual figures such as the legal and political theorist Carl Schmitt. Although later a member of the Nazi Party, whose "crown jurist" he was to become from 1933 to 1936, Schmitt published several controversial analyses of Weimar politics and the assumptions underlying it, which drew the attention, and often the respect, of many on the left as well as the right. In *The Crisis of Parliamentary Democracy,* first published in 1923, with in a second edition in 1926, he attempted to drive a wedge between liberalism and democracy and undercut the assumption that rational discourse and legal formalism could be the basis of political legitimacy. In *The Concept of the Political,* published in 1928, he claimed that genuine politics was irreducible to socio-economic conflicts and unconstrained by normative considerations. The "political" was grounded instead in an existential conflict between friend and foe. Schmitt's defenders have argued that these works show a certain distance from the *völkisch* tenets of the conservative revolution, but they certainly provided no obstacle to Schmitt's opportunistic embrace of Nazism.

The radical right's struggle against liberalism permeated all spheres of culture. As the 1931 appeal for a nationalist theater by the former expressionist playwright Arnolt Bronnen demonstrates, the desire for a mythic and cultic rather than a rational public sphere was very strong. The nineteenth-century composer Richard Wagner's celebrated call for the renewal of German culture through the restitution of an irrational festival of communal de-individuation found its echo in Weimar and its realization in the Nazi spectacles of the 1930s. Although it would be wrong to reduce the spectrum of right-wing theory and practice in Weimar to a mere prolegomenon to Nazism, as the later conservative resistance to its rule makes clear, hatred for the republic and yearning for metapolitical redemption were widespread enough to help prepare the ground for its triumph.

128

ARTHUR MOELLER VAN DEN BRUCK
The Third Empire

First published in *Das Dritte Reich* (Berlin: Ring Verlag, 1923), ii–iv.

The attempt this book makes was not possible from any party standpoint; it ranges over all our political problems, from the extreme Left to the extreme Right. It is written from the standpoint of a third party, which is already in being. Only such an attempt could address itself to the nation while attacking all the parties; could reveal the disorder and discord into which the parties have long since fatefully fallen and which has spread from them through our whole political life; could reach that lofty spiritual plane of political philosophy that the parties have forsaken, but which must for the nation's sake be maintained, which the conservative must preserve and which the revolutionary must take by storm.

Instead of government by party we offer the ideal of the third empire. It is an old German conception and a great one. It arose when our first empire fell; it was early quickened by the thought of a millennium; but its underlying thought has always been a future that should be not the end of all things but the dawn of a German age in which the German people would for the first time fulfill their destiny on earth.

In the years that followed the collapse of our second empire we have had experience of Germans; we have seen that the nation's worst enemy is herself: her trustfulness, her casualness, her credulity, her inborn, fate-fraught, apparently unshakable optimism. The German people were scarcely defeated—as never a people was defeated before in history—when the mood asserted itself: "We shall arise again all right!" We heard German fools saying: "We have no fears for Germany!" We saw German dreamers nod their heads in assent: "Nothing can happen to me!"

We must be careful to remember that the thought of the third empire is a philosophical idea; that the conceptions which the words *third empire* arouse—and the book that bears the title—are misty, indeterminate, charged with feeling; not of this world but of the next. Germans are only too prone to abandon themselves to self-deception. The thought of a third empire might well be the most fatal of all the illusions to which they have ever yielded; it would be thoroughly German if they contented themselves with daydreaming about it. Germany might perish from her third-empire dream.

Let us be perfectly explicit: the thought of the third empire—to which we must cling as our last and highest philosophy—can only bear fruit if it is translated into concrete reality. It must quit the world of dreams and step into the political world. It must be as realist as the problems of our constitutional and national life; it must be as skeptical and pessimistic as befits the times.

There are Germans who assure us that the empire that rose out of the ruins on the ninth of November is already the third empire: democratic, republican, logically complete. These are our opportunists and eudaemonists. There are other Germans who confess their disappointment but trust to the "reasonableness" of history. These are our rationalists and pacifists. They all draw their conclusions from the premises of their party–political or utopian wishes, but not from the premises of the reality that surrounds us. They will not realize that we are a fettered and maltreated nation, perhaps on the very verge of dissolution. Our reality connotes the triumph of all the nations of the earth over the German nation; the primacy in our country of parliamentarism after the Western model—and party rule. If the third empire is ever to come it will not beneficently fall from heaven.

If the third empire is to put an end to strife it will not be born in a peace of philosophic dreaming. The third empire will be an empire of organization in the midst of European chaos. The occupation of the Ruhr and its consequences worked a change in the minds of people. It was the first thing that made the nation think. It opened up the possibility of liberation for a betrayed people. It seemed about to put an end to the "policy of fulfillment" that had been merely party politics disguised as foreign policy. It threw us back on our own power of decision. It restored our will. Parliamentarism has become an institution of our public life, whose chief function would appear to be—in the name of the people—to enfeeble all political demands and all national passions.

When the revolution overwhelmed the war, burying all prospects and all hopes, we asked ourselves the inner meaning of these events. Amidst all the insanity we found a meaning in the thought that the German nation would be driven into becoming politically minded: now, at last, belatedly. [. . .]

Today we call this resolution not conservative but nationalist.

This nationalist will desires to conserve all that in Germany is worth conserving. It wills to preserve Germany for Germany's sake, and it knows what it wills.

The nationalist does not say, as the patriot does, that Germany is worth preserving because she is German. For him the nation is not an end in itself.

The nationalist's dreams are of the future. He is a conservative because he knows that there can be no future that does not have its roots in the past. He is also a politician because he knows that past and future can only be secure if the nation is secure in the present.

But his thoughts range beyond the present. If we concentrate exclusively on the past, we might easily imagine that German history is closed. It is nowhere written that a people has a right to life eternal. For every people the hour at length strikes when they perish either by murder or by suicide. No more glorious end could be conceived for a great people than to perish in a world war where a world in arms overcame one single country.

German nationalism is in its way an expression of German universalism, and turns its thought to Europe as a whole, not in order—as Goethe in his middle period expressed it—to "lose itself in generalities" but to maintain the nation as a thing apart. The German instinct of self-preservation is penetrated by the experience to which Goethe in his age confessed that art and science alone are "poor comfort" and no substitute for the "proud consciousness" of "belonging to a strong people, respected at once and feared." Roman nationalism thinks only of itself. German nationalism thinks of itself in relation to other things. The German nationalist wants to preserve Germany not merely because she is Germany, which might easily mean simply to preserve the past. He wants to preserve Germany as a country arising out of the revolutionary upheavals and changes of a new age. He wants to preserve Germany because she holds a central position from which alone the equilibrium of Europe can be maintained. The center, not the west as [Rudolf] Pannwitz thought and not the east as Spengler too rashly anticipated, is the creative focus of our hemisphere. The German nationalist wants to preserve German nationhood, not to exchange it for the "supernational culture" of a [Friedrich Wilhelm] Foerster—in whom the bastardization of German idealism reached its zenith—but to preserve Germany in the consciousness that the Germans have a task in the world which no other people can take from them. [. . .]

Nationalism seeks to secure for the nation a democratic participation in which the proletariat shall also have a share.

The ideals of a nationalist movement differ as greatly from the ideals of a merely formal democracy as from the ideals of a class-conscious proletariat—above all in this: that it is a movement from above and not from below. Participation implies consciousness of the values that are to be shared. This consciousness can never be imparted unless a movement of ready acceptance comes from below; it must, however, be imparted from above.

The democrat, who always leans towards cosmopolitan points of view, and still more the proletarian who hankers after international trains of thought, both like to toy with the thought that there exists a neutral sphere in which the differences between the values of one people and of another vanish. The nationalist instead holds that its own peculiar values are the most characteristic and precious possession of a nation, the very breath of its being. These give a nation form and personality; they cannot be transferred or interchanged. [. . .]

129

CARL SCHMITT

[On the Contradiction between Parliamentarism and Democracy]

First published as Preface to the 1926 edition of *Die geistesgeschichtliche Lage des heutigen Parlamentarismus*, (Berlin: Duncker und Humblot, 1926), 10–23.

The situation of parliamentarism is critical today because the development of modern mass democracy has made public discussion an empty formality. Many norms of contemporary parliamentary law, above all provisions concerning the independence of representatives and the openness of sessions, as a result function like a superfluous decoration, useless and even embarrassing, as though someone had painted the radiator of a modern central-heating system with red flames in order to give the appearance of a blazing fire. The parties (which according to the text of the written constitution officially do not exist) do not face each other today discussing opinions, but as social or economic power groups calculating their mutual interests and opportunities for power, and they actually agree on compromises and coalitions on this basis. The masses are won over through a propaganda apparatus whose maximum effect relies on an appeal to immediate interests and passions. Argument, in the real sense that is characteristic for genuine discussion, ceases. In its place there appears a conscious reckoning of interests and chances for power in the parties' negotiations; in the treatment of the masses, posterlike, insistent suggestion or—as Walter Lippmann says in his very shrewd, although too psychological, American book *Public Opinion*—the "symbol" appears. The literature on the psychology, technique, and critique of public opinion today is very large. One may therefore assume as is well known today that it is no longer a question of persuading one's opponent of the truth or justice of an opinion but rather of winning a majority in order to govern with it. What [Camillo di] Cavour identified as the great distinction between absolutism and constitutional regimes, that in an absolute regime a minister gives orders whereas in a constitutional one he persuades all those who should obey, must today be meaningless. Cavour says explicitly: I (as constitutional minister) persuade that I am right, and it is only in this connection that his famous saying is meant: "The worst chamber is still preferable to the best antechamber." Today parliament itself appears a gigantic antechamber in front of the bureaus or committees of invisible rulers. It is like a satire if one quotes [Jeremy] Bentham today: "In Parliament ideas meet, and contact between ideas gives off sparks and leads to evidence." Who still remembers the time when [Lucien-Anatole] Prévost-Paradol saw the value of parliamentarism over the "personal regime" of Napoléon III in that through the transfer of real power it forced the true holders of power to reveal themselves, so that government, as a result of this, always represents the strongest power in a "wonderful" coordination of appearance and reality? Who still believes in this kind of openness? And in parliament as its greatest platform?

The arguments of [Edmund] Burke, Bentham, [François] Guizot, and John Stuart Mill are thus antiquated today. The numerous definitions of parliamentarism which one still finds today in Anglo-Saxon and French writings and which are apparently little known in Germany, definitions in which parliamentarism appears as essentially "government by discussion," must accordingly also count as moldy. Never mind. If someone still believes in parliamentarism, that person will at least have to offer new arguments for it. A reference to Friedrich Naumann, Hugo Preuss, and Max Weber is no longer sufficient. With all due respect to these men, no one today would share their hope that parliament alone guarantees the education of a political elite. Such convictions have in fact been shaken and they can only remain standing today as an idealistic belief so long as they can bind themselves to belief in discussion and openness. [. . .]

The belief in parliamentarism, in government by discussion, belongs to the intellectual world of liberalism. It does not belong to democracy. Both liberalism and democracy have to be distinguished from one another so that the patchwork picture that makes up modern mass democracy can be recognized.

Every actual democracy rests on the principle that not only are equals equal but unequals will not be treated equally. Democracy requires therefore first homogeneity and second—if the need arises—elimination or eradication of heterogeneity. To illustrate this principle it is sufficient to name two different examples of modern democracy: contemporary Turkey, with its radical expulsion of the Greeks and its reckless Turkish nationalization of the country, and the Australian commonwealth, which restricts unwanted entrants through its immigration laws and like other dominions only takes immigrants who conform to the notion of a "right type of settler." A democracy demonstrates its political power by knowing how to refuse or keep at bay something foreign and unequal that threatens its homogeneity. The question of equality is precisely not one of abstract, logical, arithmetical games. It is about the substance of equality. It can be found in certain physical and moral qualities, for example, in civic virtue, in *arete*, the classical democracy of *vertus (vertu)*. In the democracy of English sects during the seventeenth century, equality was based on a consensus of religious convictions. Since the nineteenth century it has existed above all in membership in a particular nation, in national homogeneity. Equality is only interesting and valuable politically so long as it has substance, and for that reason at least the possibility and the risk of inequality. There may be isolated examples perhaps for the idyllic case of a community in which relationship itself is sufficient, where each of its inhabitants possesses this happy independence equally and each one is so similar to every other one physically, psychically, morally, and economically that a homogeneity without heterogeneity exists, something that was possible in primitive agrarian democracies or for a long time in the colonial states. Finally one has to say that a democracy—because inequality always belongs to equality—can exclude one part of those governed without ceasing to be a democracy, that until now people who in some way were completely or partially without rights and who were restricted from the exercise of political power, let them be called barbarians, uncivilized, atheists, aristocrats, counterrevolutionaries, or even slaves, have belonged to a democracy. Neither in the Athenian city democracy nor in the British Empire are all inhabitants of the state territory politically equal. Of the more than four hundred million inhabitants of the British Empire more than three hundred million are not British citizens. If English democracy, universal suffrage, or universal equality is spoken of, then these hundreds of millions in English democracy are just as unquestionably ignored as were slaves in Athenian democracy. Modern imperialism has created countless new governmental forms, conforming to economic and technical developments, which extend themselves to the same degree that democracy develops within the motherland. Colonies, protectorates, mandates, intervention treaties, and similar forms of dependence make it possible today for a democracy to govern a heterogeneous population without making them citizens, making them dependent upon a democratic state, and at the same time held apart from this state. [. . .]

Until now there has never been a democracy that did not recognize the concept *foreign* and that could have realized the equality of all men. If one were serious about a democracy of mankind and really wanted to make every person the political equal of every other person, it would be an equality in which every person took part as a consequence of birth or age and nothing else. Equality would have been robbed of its value and substance, because the specific meaning that it has as political equality, economic equality, and so forth—in short as equality in a particular sphere—would have been taken away. Every sphere has its specific equality and inequalities in fact. However great an injustice it would be not to respect the human worth of every individual, it would nevertheless be an irresponsible stupidity, leading to the worst chaos and therefore to even worse injustice, if the specific characteristics of various spheres were not recognized. In the domain of the political, people do not face each other as abstractions but as politically interested and politically determined persons, as citizens, governors or governed, politically allied or opponents—in any case, therefore, in political categories. In the sphere of the political, one cannot abstract out what is political, leaving only universal human equality; the same applies in the realm of economics, where people are not conceived as such, but as producers, consumers, and so forth, that is, in specifically economic categories.

An absolute human equality, then, would be an equality understood only in terms of itself and without risk; it would be an equality without the necessary correlate of inequality, and as a result conceptually and practically meaningless, an indifferent equality. Now such an equality certainly does not exist anywhere, so long as the various states of the earth, as was said above, distinguish their citizens politically from other persons and exclude politically dependent populations that are unwanted on whatever grounds by combining dependence in international law with the definition of such populations as alien in public law. In contrast it appears that, at least inside the different modern democratic states, universal human equality has been established; although there is of course no absolute equality of all persons, since foreigners and aliens remain excluded, there is nevertheless a relatively far-reaching human equality among the citizenry. But it must be noted that in this case national homogeneity is usually that much more strongly emphasized, and that general human equality is once again neutralized through the definitive exclusion of all those who do not belong to the state, of those who remain outside it. [. . .]

The equality of all persons as persons is not democracy but a certain kind of liberalism, not a state form but an individualistic, humanitarian ethic and Weltanschauung. Modern mass democracy rests on the confused combination of both. Despite all the work on [Jean-Jacques] Rousseau and despite the correct realization that Rousseau stands at the beginning of modern democracy, it still seems to have gone unnoticed that the theory of the state set out in *The Social Contract* contains these two different elements incoherently next to each other. The facade is liberal: the state's legitimacy is justified by a free contract.

But the subsequent depiction and the development of the central concept, the "general will," demonstrates that a true state, according to Rousseau, only exists where the people are so homogeneous that there is essentially unanimity. [. . .]

A popular presentation sees parliamentarism in the middle today, threatened from both sides by bolshevism and fascism. That is a simple but superficial constellation. The crisis of the parliamentary system and of parliamentary institutions in fact springs from the circumstances of modern mass democracy. These lead first of all to a crisis of democracy itself because the problem of a substantial equality and homogeneity, which is necessary to democracy, cannot be resolved by the general equality of mankind. It leads further to a crisis of parliamentarism that must certainly be distinguished from the crisis of democracy. Both crises have appeared today at the same time and each one aggravates the other, but they are conceptually and in reality different. As democracy, modern mass democracy attempts to realize an identity of governed and governing, and thus it confronts parliament as an inconceivable and outmoded institution. If democratic identity is taken seriously, then in an emergency no other constitutional institution can withstand the sole criterion of the people's will, however it is expressed. Against the will of the people especially an institution based on discussion by independent representatives has no autonomous justification for its existence, even less so because the belief in discussion is not democratic but originally liberal. Today one can distinguish three crises: the crisis of democracy (M. J. Bonn directs his attention to this without noticing the contradiction between liberal notions of human equality and democratic homogeneity); further, a crisis of the modern state (Alfred Weber); and finally a crisis of parliamentarism. The crisis of parliamentarism presented here rests on the fact that democracy and liberalism could be allied to each other for a time, just as socialism and democracy have been allied; but as soon as it achieves power, liberal democracy must decide between its elements, just as social democracy, which is finally in fact a social, liberal democracy inasmuch as modern mass democracy contains essentially liberal elements, must also decide. In democracy there is only the equality of equals, and the will of those who belong to the equals. All other institutions transform themselves into insubstantial social-technical expedients that are not in a position to oppose the will of the people, however expressed, with their own values and their own principles. The crisis of the modern state arises from the fact that no state can realize a mass democracy, a democracy of all people not even a democratic state.

Bolshevism and fascism by contrast are, like all dictatorships, certainly antiliberal but not necessarily antidemocratic. [. . .]

Even if bolshevism is suppressed and fascism held at bay, the crisis of contemporary parliamentarism would not be overcome in the least. For it has not appeared as a result of the appearance of those two opponents; it was there before them and will persist after them. Rather the crisis springs from the consequences of modern mass democracy and in the final analysis from the contradiction of a liberal individualism burdened by moral pathos and a democratic sentiment governed essentially by political ideals. A century of historical alliance and common struggle against royal absolutism has obscured the awareness of this contradiction. But the crisis unfolds today ever more strikingly, and no cosmopolitan rhetoric can prevent or eliminate it. It is, in its depths, the inescapable contradiction of liberal individualism and democratic homogeneity.

130

ERNST NIEKISCH
Where We Stand

First published as "Unser Standort," *Widerstand* 1, no. 2 (August 1926), 17–18.

A warning against *Widerstand* has been directed at workers—and how might we have expected anything else?—suggesting that it fosters "nationalistic obscurantism" in the consciousness of the working class with the aim of winning that class over to the socially reactionary aims of the bourgeoisie. Reference has been made to certain terminological similarities as if they offered proof of such assertions; we have made use, it was said, of some expressions that one also hears from social reactionaries. Such terminological similarities might in fact be present; it cannot be helped that such persons also speak of vital national necessities for whom it is more a matter of the pocketbook than a serious consideration of these necessities. Naturally we presume that those who have "identified" these terminological similarities seek intentionally to misunderstand us. For it truly does not take much to grasp the essential tendencies that inform our position. We are wholly rooted in the vital feelings and sentiments of the working people of Germany; their needs and their instincts are our own. We do not want to lead them astray, do not want to betray them; we are flesh of their flesh, blood of their blood; our thoughts, feelings, and aspirations issue exclusively from the ground of their being and the current circumstances of their fate. What moved us most profoundly was this: that the burden of the tributes to which Germany has been subjected weigh most heavily on the working people; that it is the living conditions of precisely the German worker which have been called into question by the collapse of German status in the world. Here the challenges of the German nation coincide with the law of self-preservation of the working class. That to be sure can be truly understood only by those who are more than mere literary figures. So many such literary sorts are busy insinuating to workers what they are supposed to think that they have already diverted workers from many a good course of action.

We speak justifiably of the proletarian situation of Germany: the nation is oppressed and dependent; it slaves for others and lives hand-to-mouth. That signifies the historical moment in which the worker, the personification of a proletarian situation as such, has a national mission to fulfill: he turns against the ultimate causes of his social oppression, the victorious states of the Treaty of Versailles, he also rises up against the chains by which the nation is shackled. Is it not strange that social democracy, which has vainly set itself the goal of "liberating the working class," continually conceals from the worker the social effects of the policy of acceding to the treaty demands? He is not supposed to know of them. How is that to be explained? Social democracy is vaguely aware that the moment the working class becomes conscious of the equivalence between its social struggle for liberation and the national struggle for liberation, it will become such an elemental, vehement, and vitally progressive force that no little party secretary will be capable of controlling it and no rootless literary type of interpreting it. Therefore it is silent on the question of the nation's task! Therefore if resistance to the yoke of social oppression must necessarily take on a national coloration, better that there be no resistance at all, better that the workers patiently resign themselves to the social yoke. We will have no part in lulling the worker to sleep—that is what characterizes us. This, however, does not convict us of a sin against the worker's livelihood. It is his freedom that we want, even if Mr. [Aristide]

Briand and Mr. [Austen] Chamberlain turn up their noses. To us, contrary to many social-democratic writers, the freedom of the German worker is more important than the welfare of Briand and Chamberlain. To chase after their welfare—that is truly not the substance of socialism.

That is why we are very far from being national socialists in the usual sense of the term. What distinguishes us above all from the latter is this: they are, similar to social democracy, driven almost exclusively by the point of view of domestic politics. They think too much of "hanging the criminals of November"; their intentions are too much dominated by hate, revenge, retaliation. Those are not the means by which one pulls a people together in a struggle for liberation. We are less destructive and negative. We affirm everything that increases the political power of the German people; we are concerned solely with the question of how it can be raised to its highest level. Those who want to hang the "November criminals" *partout,* will afterward probably have to let the French go free; they will scarcely have sufficient force in reserve to inflict upon the latter the justice they deserve.

131

Berlin Stahlhelm Manifesto

First published in *Stahlhelm und Staat* (May 8, 1927).

Stahlhelm, the union of battle-tested German soldiers returned undefeated from the front and the German cadets trained by them in the spirit of valor, announces on the eighth annual memorial to the Reich's soldiers of the front in the capital city of the Reich the political goals, to struggle for which it and all its comrades accept anew as their duty:

Stahlhelm proclaims the battle against all softness and cowardice, which seek to weaken and destroy the consciousness of honor of the German people through renunciation of the right of defense and will to defense.

Stahlhelm declares that it does not recognize the state of affairs created by the Treaty of Versailles and its later supplements. It therefore demands the recognition of the national state for all Germans, the restoration of the German right of defense, the effective revocation of the extorted acknowledgment of war guilt, and the regulation and reparation of war damages on the basis of the collective liability of all peoples responsible for the world war. These goals may not be abandoned in the execution of the rights stipulated in the treaty in the premature clearing of the occupied territories and in the adjustment of the eastern borders.

Stahlhelm demands the renewed recognition of the national colors: black, white, and red. Under this flag the German Reich conducted the period of its incomparably heroic struggle against a world of enemies.

The economic and social want of our people is caused by the deficiency of *Lebensraum* [living space] and the territory in which to work. Stahlhelm supports the foreign policy that opens up settlement and work territories for the German population surplus and that maintains vital cultural, economic, and political ties between these territories and the core motherland. Stahlhelm does not want the German people, driven by want to desperation, to become the victim and storm center of bolshevism.

Stahlhelm embraces the conviction that the destiny of the German people may be determined only by a strong leadership able and willing to bear responsibility for it.

Therefore Stahlhelm demands an increase in the competency of the president of the Reich; the securing of the welfare of the nation and people against the caprice of parliamentary emergency agreements and contingencies; and the creation of an electoral right the results of which guarantee both the correspondence with the true will of the people and the possibility of genuine administrative responsibility.

Stahlhelm does not want to form or become a new party. But it does want to represent the civic will of the former front soldiers. It wants for its members to acquire the possibility and the right of decisive participation in all positions of public service and popular representation, from the local community to the national government. The right of the front soldiers to this participation is based on the special aptitude that they gained through the closest connection between personal accomplishment and the most severe struggle of the German people for its rights and its future. [. . .]

True to its origins and its history, Stahlhelm opposes all efforts and conceptions that seek to divide the German people. It esteems highly the experience of old comradeship at the front and unity and wants to develop out of it a national sense of unity. It denies the validity of the materialist conception of history and the Marxist doctrine. It opposes the idea of class struggle. And in full recognition of the value and the vital unity among enterprise, entrepreneur, and fellow workers, Stahlhelm will not hinder an honest and decisive settlement of natural conflicts of interests. It demands, however, the maintenance and preservation of the transcending interest of the German community.

Stahlhelm looks with concern on the increasing separation of healthy popular forces from the native soil which accompanies increasing industrialization, and demands an agrarian policy that makes settlements possible. Interior colonization and a settlement policy for the strengthening of German Austria by filling the border area with German peasant villages are weapons in the struggle for national preservation in the employment of which Stahlhelm is able and willing to assist.

Stahlhelm demands that measures be taken against the increased foreign influence in our political, economic, and cultural life since the revolution and against the degeneration of ethical views.

Stahlhelm demands the recognition and achievement of its goals by the constitutional representatives of the German people in the administration and parliaments. It has firmly decided to struggle for its goals only through the employment of just and legal means together with all parliamentary and extraparliamentary forces among the German people that desire to maintain community with it for work and struggle.

This is the path and the will of Stahlhelm for the internal and external liberation of Germany.

Hail to the Front!

Stahlhelm, Union of Front Soldiers

Franz Seldte
First Union Director

Theodor Duesterberg
Second Union Director

Countersigned, Czetteritz

132

HUGO VON HOFMANNSTHAL

Literature as the Spiritual Space of the Nation

First published as "Literatur als geistiger Raum der Nation," *Die neue Rundschau* 38, no. 2 (1927), 25–26.

Like no other generation before, this one, as well as the next, already to be seen rising among us, knows itself to be confronting the totality of life, and knows it in a stricter sense than the Romantic generation was able even to anticipate. All dualities into which life has been spiritually polarized are to be overcome in spirit, to be transformed into spiritual unity; everything in the rent world of exteriority must be drawn into the interiority of each and there composed into one, making a unity of the exterior, for only to those who are whole in themselves will the world become a unity. Here the isolated, titanically searching ego, abandoned to its own devices, breaks through to supreme community by uniting in itself that which for centuries has split a people lacking in the common bond of a culture. Here will the isolated become allies and dispersed, worthless individuals become the core of the nation. For, rising from synthesis to synthesis, charged with true religious responsibility, omitting nothing, never straying aside, leaping over nothing—such a coiled striving as this, where elsewhere the genius of the nation does not foresake it, must attain this supreme end: that spirit becomes life and life spirit; in other words becomes the political comprehension of the spiritual and the spiritual of the political, becomes the formation of a genuine nation.

In this fundamental attitude is anticipated the securing of the spiritual space, as the dissipation of the space was contained in the Romantic attitude and its narrowing in that of the cultural philistines.

What this spirit seeking after synthesis accomplishes (such that here, even within the individual breast, accomplishments can be spoken of at all) amounts to points projected into chaos, between which the connections would yield the outline of this spiritual space.

I am speaking of a process in whose midst we are, a synthesis as slow and grandiose, were one capable of observing it from without, as it is ominous and searching to one dwelling within it. We are quite justified in terming it long and grandiose when we consider that even the lengthy period of development from the first flickers of the age of enlightenment to our own constitutes no more than a moment within it, when we consider that it, in fact, has arisen as a countermovement to the spiritual upheaval of the nineteenth century, which we are accustomed to calling, in its two aspects, renaissance and reformation. The process of which I am speaking is nothing other than a conservative revolution of a scope unknown to European history. Its goal is form, a new German reality in which the entire nation participates.

133

CARL SCHMITT

The Concept of the Political

First published as "Der Begriff des Politischen," *Heidelberger Archiv für Sozialwissenschaft und Sozialpolitik* 58, no. 1 (August 1927), 1–33.

The specific political distinction to which political actions and motives can be reduced is that between friend and enemy. This provides a definition in the sense of a criterion and not as an exhaustive definition or one indicative of substantial content. Insofar as it is not derived from other criteria, the antithesis of friend and enemy corresponds to the relatively independent criteria of other antitheses: good and evil in the moral sphere, beautiful and ugly in the aesthetic sphere, and so on. In any event it is independent, not in the sense of a distinct new domain but in that it can neither be based on any one antithesis or any combination of other antitheses, nor can it be traced to these. If the antithesis of good and evil is not simply identical with that of beautiful and ugly, profitable and unprofitable, and cannot be directly reduced to the others, then the antithesis of friend and enemy must even less be confused with or mistaken for the others. The distinction of friend and enemy denotes the utmost degree of intensity of a union or separation, of an association or dissociation. It can exist theoretically and practically without having simultaneously to draw upon all those moral, aesthetic, economic, or other distinctions. The political enemy need not be morally evil or aesthetically ugly; he need not appear as an economic competitor, and it may even be advantageous to engage with him in business transactions. But he is nevertheless the other, the stranger; and it is sufficient for his nature that he is, in a specially intense way, existentially something different and alien, so that in the extreme case conflicts with him are possible. These can neither be decided by a previously determined general norm nor by the judgment of a disinterested and therefore neutral third party.

Only the actual participants can correctly recognize, understand, and judge the concrete situation and settle the extreme case of conflict. Each participant is in a position to judge whether the adversary intends to negate his opponent's way of life and therefore must be repulsed or fought in order to preserve one's own form of existence. Emotionally the enemy is easily treated as being evil and ugly, because every distinction, most of all the political, as the strongest and most intense of the distinctions and categorizations, draws upon other distinctions for support. This does not alter the autonomy of such distinctions. Consequently the reverse is also true: the morally evil, aesthetically ugly, or economically damaging need not necessarily be the enemy; the morally good, aesthetically beautiful, and economically profitable need not necessarily become the friend in the specifically political sense of the word. Thereby the inherently objective nature and autonomy of the political becomes evident by virtue of its being able to treat, distinguish, and comprehend the friend–enemy antithesis independently of other antitheses.

The friend and enemy concepts are to be understood in their concrete and existential sense, not as metaphors or symbols, not mixed and weakened by economic, moral, and other conceptions, least of all in a private–individualistic sense as a psychological expression of private emotions and tendencies. They are neither normative nor pure spiritual antitheses. [. . .]

The enemy is not merely any competitor or just any partner of a conflict in general. He is also not the private adversary whom one hates. An enemy exists only when, at least potentially, one fighting collectivity of people confronts a similar collectivity. The enemy is solely the public enemy, because everything that has a relationship to such a collectivity of men, particularly to a whole nation, becomes public by virtue of such a relationship. The enemy is *hostis,* not *inimicus* in the broader sense; πολέμιος, not ἐχθρός. As German and other languages do not distinguish between the private and political enemy, many misconceptions and falsifications are possible. The often-quoted "Love your enemies" (Matt. 5:44; Luke 6:27) reads *diligite inimicos vestros,* ἀγαπᾶτε τοὺς ἐχθροὺς ὑμῶν, and not *diligite hostes vestros.* No mention is made of the political enemy. Never in the thousand-year struggle between Christians and Muslims did it occur to a Christian to surrender rather than defend Europe out of love toward the Saracens or Turks. The enemy in the political sense need not be hated personally, and only in the private sphere does it make sense to love one's enemy, i.e., one's adversary. The biblical quotation touches the political antithesis even less than it intends to dissolve, for example, the antithesis of good and evil or beautiful and ugly. It certainly does not mean that one should love and support the enemies of one's own people.

The political is the most intense and extreme antagonism, and every concrete antagonism becomes that much more political the closer it approaches the most extreme point, that of the friend–enemy grouping. In its entirety the state as an organized political entity decides for itself the friend-enemy distinction. [. . .]

The ever-present possibility of conflict must always be kept in mind. If one wants to speak of politics in the context of the primacy of internal politics, then this conflict no longer refers to war between organized nations but to civil war.

For to the enemy concept belongs the ever-present possibility of combat. All peripherals must be left aside from this term including military details and the development of weapons technology. War is armed combat between organized political entities; civil war is armed combat within an organized unit. A self-laceration endangers the survival of the latter. The essence of a weapon is that it is a means of physically killing human beings. Just as the term *enemy,* the word *combat,* too, is to be understood in its original existential sense. It does not mean competition, nor does it mean pure intellectual controversy nor symbolic wrestlings in which, after all, every human being is somehow always involved, for it is a fact that the entire life of a human being is a struggle and every human being symbolically a combatant. The friend, enemy, and combat concepts receive their real meaning precisely because they refer to the real possibility of physical killing. War follows from enmity. War is the existential negation of the enemy. It is the most extreme consequence of enmity. It does not have to be common, normal, something ideal, or desirable. But it must nevertheless remain a real possibility for as long as the concept of the enemy remains valid.

It is by no means as though the political signifies nothing but devastating war and every political deed a military action, by no means as though every nation would be uninterruptedly faced with the friend–enemy alternative vis-à-vis every other nation. And, after all, could not the politically reasonable course reside in avoiding war? The definition of the political suggested here neither favors war nor militarism, neither imperialism nor pacifism. Nor is it an attempt to idealize the victorious war or the successful revolution as a "social ideal," since neither war nor revolution is something social or something ideal. The military battle itself is not the "continuation of politics by other means" as the famous term of [Carl von] Clausewitz is generally incorrectly cited.[1] War has its own strategic,

---

1. Carl von Clausewitz (*Vom Kriege,* 2nd ed. [Berlin: Ferd. Dümmlers Verlagsbuchhandlung, 1853], vol. III, part III, p. 120). "War is nothing but a continuation of political intercourse with a mixture of other means."

tactical, and other rules and points of view, but they all presuppose that the political decision has already been made as to who the enemy is. In war the adversaries most often confront each other openly; normally they are identifiable by a uniform, and the distinction of friend and enemy is therefore no longer a political problem which the fighting soldier has to solve. A British diplomat correctly stated in this context that the politician is better schooled for the battle than the soldier because the politician fights his whole life whereas the soldier does so only in exceptional circumstances. War is neither the aim nor the purpose nor even the very content of politics. But as an ever-present possibility it is the leading presupposition that determines in a characteristic way human action and thinking and thereby creates a specifically political behavior. [. . .]

A world in which the possibility of war is utterly eliminated, a completely pacified globe, would be a world without the distinction of friend and enemy and hence a world without politics. It is conceivable that such a world might contain many very interesting antitheses and contrasts, competitions and intrigues of every kind, but there would not be a mean-ingful antithesis whereby men could be required to sacrifice life, authorized to shed blood, and kill other human beings. For the definition of the political, it is here even irrelevant whether such a world without politics is desirable as an ideal situation. The phenomenon of the political can be understood only in the context of the ever-present possibility of the friend-and-enemy grouping, regardless of the aspects which this possibility implies for morality, aesthetics, and economics.

War as the most extreme political means discloses the possibility that underlies every political idea, namely, the distinction of friend and enemy. This makes sense only as long as this distinction in mankind is actually present or at least potentially possible. On the other hand, it would be senseless to wage war for purely religious, purely moral, purely juristic, or purely economic motives. The friend-and-enemy grouping and therefore also war cannot be derived from these specific antitheses of human endeavor. A war need be neither something religious nor something morally good nor something lucrative. War today is in all likelihood none of these. This obvious point is mostly confused by the fact that religious, moral, and other antitheses can intensify to political ones and can bring about the decisive friend-or-enemy constellation. If in fact this occurs, then the relevant antithesis is no longer purely religious, moral, or economic but political. The sole remaining question then is always whether such a friend-and-enemy grouping is really at hand, regardless of which human motives are sufficiently strong to have brought it about.

Nothing can escape this logical conclusion of the political. If pacifist hostility toward war were so strong as to drive pacifists into a war against nonpacifists, in a war against war, that would prove that pacifism truly possesses political energy because it is sufficiently strong to group men according to friend and enemy. If, in fact, the will to abolish war is so strong that it no longer shuns war, then it has become a political motive, i.e., it affirms, even if only as an extreme possibility, war and even the reason for war. At present, this appears to be a peculiar way of justifying wars. The war is then considered to constitute the absolute last war of humanity. Such a war is necessarily unusually intense and inhuman

War is for him a "mere instrument of politics." This cannot be denied, but its meaning for the understanding of the essence of politics is thereby still not exhausted. To be precise, war, for Clausewitz, is not merely one of many instruments, but the ultima ratio of the friend-and-enemy grouping. War has its own grammar (i.e., special military-technical laws), but politics remains its brain. It does not have its own logic. This can only be derived from the friend-and-enemy concept, and the sentence on page 121 reveals this core of politics: "If war belongs to politics, it will thereby assume its character. The more grandiose and powerful it becomes, so will also the war, and this may be carried to the point at which war reaches its absolute form. . . ."

because, by transcending the limits of the political framework, it simultaneously degrades the enemy into moral and other categories and is forced to make of him a monster that must not only be defeated but also utterly destroyed. In other words, he is an enemy who no longer must be compelled to retreat into his borders only. The feasibility of such war is particularly illustrative of the fact that war as a real possibility is still present today, and this fact is crucial for the friend-and-enemy antithesis and for the recognition of politics.

134

ARNOLT BRONNEN

German Nationalism, German Theater

First published as "Deutscher Nationalismus—Deutsches Theater," *Münchner Neueste Nachrichten*, no. 97 (April 11, 1931).

Theater in this country is the child of a liberal epoch. It lives in buildings simulating the baroque, and it works its effects through gestures that drive toward the liberation of the instincts. Should an actor want to produce particularly loud applause, he has only to throw out the word *freedom*. It is to this extent also the playground of contented people (for only the contented demand freedom). Should, however, a malcontent chance to enter these buildings, where the stucco façades of pride and arrogance are decaying into pitiless nakedness, he hears, through the vapors of the satiated crowd and through the thickest of walls, the sharp wind whistling scornfully outside around the dome.

This sharp wind is first of all only a harbinger. A harbinger of nationalism.

The struggle has not yet broken out, the front lines are not yet clearly visible. The institution, consecrated by a single great name—if desecrated by many small ones—wards off the movement with an indolent hand. And nevertheless there will be a battle on this spot; nevertheless social trends, as well as cultural and national trends, push for the confrontation of enemies precisely on this spiritual terrain.

Theater has always styled itself the center of all the arts, and in fact nowhere does the lever of artistic creation work more powerfully than here. But just as powerfully it has attracted to itself the instincts associated with social displacement and moral libertinage. [. . .]

Should a creative power like nationalism arise once again in opposition to all this, should a movement comprehending the totality of our existence raise itself once more in opposition, then it is not merely struggle that will eventuate, but annihilation. The origins of German theater coincide with the liberalism of Frederick the Great. Frederick could afford to be liberal in a state consisting in essence of the most disciplined army in the world, but the theater displayed from the start its serviceability to the overall tendencies of decay.

One need not begin with the public, although the most annihilating critique of German theater would be the public; one need only consider the theatrical repertory in the big cities to recognize that there is no longer all that much that nationalism will have to annihilate. The trifling vestiges of native production capable of holding its own in the midst of abundant foreign vegetation cling anxiously to the present; their only chance lies in photographic treatments of the problematic of daily life on the level of commentary, at best of the feuilleton. What is there here to be destroyed? Nothing but the administration. [. . .]

The seven years' peace and the late capitalist period of reparations are national crises the likes of which other nations do not suffer in their entire histories. Everything with the slightest connection to national life is trembling, fevered, locked in struggle. Not the theater. It keeps its distance. In thirteen years of reparations there were three or four plays in which the peasant was cast as wrath, the worker as outrage, the middle-class citizen as national will. But the nation has 350 stages on which approximately a thousand plays a year can be performed. Of thirteen thousand plays, three or four made reference to misery, to need, to the struggle of the nation—in a time of misery, need, and struggle.

It seems that such an institution would have forfeited its existence, even had it proven its usefulness. Useless as it is, the coming epoch will all the more certainly destroy it. No cure is of help here, nor any dictatorial stipulation of repertory. Neither from the side of production nor of performance can this situation be changed in which antinational tendencies and destructive instincts have established themselves as essential elements. Were there honest, manly, national plays, then there would be no actors to act in them. Even were there actors to act in them, then there is no tradition in which they might find expression. Even where the word remained unspoiled, the air in which it appeared would spoil it anew.

These are the reasons why all theatrical plays serving the national purpose remain without effect. The plays which were presented by the nationalist Experimental Theater failed not only due to a lack of tradition and actors, but also from a confusion, not always excusable, of national will and national ability. [. . .] But plays such as Gerhard Menzel's *Bork* and [Hans Henning Freiherr] Grote's *Stein* have to fail, because existing producers either squeeze the life out of them or if not, reinterpret them. How little of national will was left to plays such as [Fred Antoine] Angermayer's *Flieg, roter Adler von Tirol* where the primacy of the theater was left completely untouched.

This primacy is the first thing that must fall. Nationalism knows only one primacy: the people. And the new theater can arise anew only on the basis of the people. But what, within the organic totality of the people, can theater still be today? If from the outset one excludes the ideas of amusement and relaxation—for the only relaxation known to the hero is activity—what remains of an institution that is not inflamed in the face of battle and does not pour its blood into the process of creation? Nothing exceeds the authenticity of the cult.

Nationalism recognizes the theater only as a site of cultic rites. With this it prescribes for itself a difficult task, one that can only begin in the void. Only in long stages stretched over many years can work proceed which creates once again a cultic theater for this people—a theater of ideas and godly service. Neither schools for actors, dramaturgical assignments, nor set ateliers lie along this path. Rather education in the image, education to the word, spiritual obedience, and the dissolution of corporeal bounds: transubstantiation.

Already the troops of young believers are marching, losing their way among the streets, through the nation. They are searching for God. They will find him.

135

HANS FREYER

Revolution from the Right

First published in *Revolution von rechts* (Jena: Eugen Diedrichs Verlag, 1931), 5–7.

A new front is taking shape on the battlefields of bourgeois society: the revolution from the right. With the magnetic force inherent in a watchword of the future before it is pronounced, it draws from all camps the hardest, the most alert, the most contemporary of people into its ranks. It is still gathering its forces, but it will strike. Its movement is still a mere assembly of minds, without consciousness, without symbols, without leadership. But overnight the front will be established. It will undermine the old parties, their stagnated programs and their antiquated ideologies. It will successfully dispute not the reality of the tangled class contradictions of a society become everywhere petit-bourgeois but the arrogance of the claim that they can be politically productive. It will clear away the remnants of the nineteenth century where they persist and free the way for the history of the twentieth.

Those who think in the day-before-yesterday terms of bourgeoisie and proletariat, of class struggle and economic peace, of progress and reaction, who see nothing in the world but problems of distribution and insurance premiums for the have-nots, nothing but opposing interests and a state that mediates among them, they naturally fail to see that since yesterday there has been a regrouping of goals and forces underway. They confuse the revolution from the right with all sorts of honest but harmless troublemakers and eccentrics from the old world: with nationalist romantics, with counterrevolutionary activism, with an idealistically embellished *juste milieu,* or with the splendid notion of a state above the parties. They think that fascism is being imitated here, bottled *Action Française* [French right-wing nationalist movement] in Germany, or a Soviet Germany, made enticing to romantics too through the assistance of certain reminiscences from German legal history. That which unites us with these is that, despite their confusions, they themselves have a troubled conscience. In the end they sense merely that something incomprehensible is drumming on their blinders from outside. In this, insofar as they are involved, they have hit upon the truth.

But even those in whom the new will is vital are mostly only semiconscious of what is happening. When they want to explain themselves they speak in the cramped language of a bygone radicalism. Or they do not dare to acknowledge that, with their eyes pointed forward, things look different than they have for a century. As promising as it is that the revolution from the right, without attempting to prove, legitimate, or promote itself, has, within the old society, silently given form to a new one, so has the time arrived for the new reality to gain an initial conception of itself.

It is not a matter of persuading the doubtful, encouraging the hesitant, attracting the resistant, or disengaging the complacent. And it is certainly not a matter of offering the kind of proof that no movement believes it can do without today: that world history has simply been waiting for it and everything before it has aimed in its direction. It is solely a matter of establishing a few facts, of lifting into consciousness a few future-oriented developments, and of laying before those concerned the decisions implicit in them.

Otherwise all has been long since underway. The movement needs no stimulus and no awakening. However, it quite likely will eventually require a consciousness of what is at issue and how far we have come. Opportunities can always be missed, forces misdirected. At a certain moment autonomous development must be transformed into willed action, events into resolve, and readiness raised to the potency of a front. Only the most pitiless clear-sightedness toward the self will rescue the revolution, already underway, from the political forces of the old right, which continue to burden it in so many ways, and free it from the danger of using some sort of monarchical, big capitalist, or petit-bourgeois cart for the lead team. Only the most pitiless clear-sightedness toward the self will protect it from confusing itself with itself, that is, identifying itself ultimately with one of the waves that it has produced on the surface of the present.

Social reality—before our eyes, beneath our hands, indeed even in our heads—has reshuffled itself, unnoticed but unmistakably. Let us therefore open our eyes, reach with our hands, make order in our heads, and also reshuffle our ideas concerning social reality. We are still thinking as if we were of the nineteenth century, but the major thoughts, the key thoughts of that century have long since run aground, and the rocks of its faith have drifted away like sand. The idealists of its progress are the true reactionaries of today. That century's ideas of history, the present, and fulfillment have themselves become history overnight. Let us accept them as such; let us keep them from turning our heads, instead mummifying them as the classical testaments of a bygone epoch.

Meanwhile, the new reality is working in thousands and many more thousands of senses. It cuts right through us, for who is wholly of the present? But all of us are in its grasp. What it needs in the way of ideals, values, illusions, it will itself produce as part of its actuality. To anticipate its ideas would be an empty indulgence of prophecy. Historical movements cannot be prepared like theatrical performances, for there is no text according to which it should play; only in that it transpires does it find its language.

But one thing can be done: inscribe the front that is presently taking shape into the map of time; without undue anticipation but with a feel for the dynamic of the present; without *pronunziamento* but with confidence; without a belief in historical miracles but merely establishing what is.

136

GERMAN NATIONAL PEOPLE'S PARTY (DNVP)
Program

Published in *Handbuch des öffentlichen Lebens,* ed. Maximilian Müller-Jabusch (Leipzig: Verlag K. F. Koehler, 1931), 442–445.

I. THE LIFE OF THE NATION AND STATE

The liberation of Germany. The liberation of the German people from foreign domination is the precondition of national rebirth. For that reason we are committed to a revision of the Treaty of Versailles, the re-establishment of German unity, and the restoration of the colonies necessary for our economic development.

The German population abroad and in border areas. We are inseparably linked to our fellow Germans living beyond the borders that have been forced upon us. The defense of German nationality in the lost and occupied territories and the defense of German nationals on foreign soil are an essential focus of national policy. A keen awareness of our national community ties us to Germans living abroad, in particular with German Austria, and we pledge our support for its right to self-determination.

Foreign policy. We demand a strong and steady foreign policy defined exclusively from a German point of view, a worthy, firm, and skilled representation of German interests, and the utilization of our economic power in the service of Germany's foreign-policy goals. Appointments to the foreign office are to be made solely on the basis of ability, preparation, and reliable German national convictions and to be kept free of considerations of partisan domestic politics.

Monarchy. The monarchical form of government corresponds to the uniqueness and historical development of Germany. Standing above the parties, the monarchy offers the best guarantee of national unity, the defense of minorities, the constancy of state operations, and the incorruptibility of public administration. The German states should enjoy a free choice over the form of their individual governments; for the nation, we are committed to the renewal of the German empire as established under the Hohenzollerns.

Essence of the nation. A solidly unified German nation provides the most important foundation for German greatness. The independence of the individual states and the uniqueness befitting their racial origins are to be preserved and cultivated for the sake of national unity. The interest of Germany as a whole requires an unpartitioned Prussia with no reduction in its holdings and rights; in the reconstruction of the nation we cannot do without its state formative power.

Popular representation. On the soil of the constitutional development of our political conditions we represent the organic idea of the state. The popular representation issuing from general, equal, direct, and secret elections by both sexes is entitled to a critical voice in legislation and effective supervision over politics and administration. Alongside this parliament, we demand a representational body structured according to professional rankings in the economic and cultural spheres.

Administration and justice. The strong state needed by our people requires, especially given the current parliamentary form of government, a powerful executive branch and a firmly articulated, systematic administrative structure. To this belongs a professional civil service free of party influences and the preservation of its proven self-definition as a profession. Judicial independence is to be maintained. Justice and administration are to be carried out with exclusive reference to objective considerations. Administration is to be simplified and conducted in a social spirit; in place of the waste of public monies prevalent since the revolution, strict economies must be reintroduced. The established self-government of municipalities and municipal associations is to be preserved.

Civil service. Civil service law is to be recast as appropriate to the times. Civil service commissions and professional organizations should have an active role in the regulation of the conditions of service. We demand for all civil servants the preservation of permanent appointments and full freedom in exercising their rights as citizens. Teachers and municipal civil servants should be made the equals of state civil servants in respect to legal and economic conditions. For promotions within the civil service, not only educational preparation but also knowledge and ability should be decisive. For the preservation of a reliable, dutiful, incorruptible civil service, its economic security is to be effected through an organization of compensation corresponding to social position and geared to the cost of living. Any restructuring of compensation must have an appropriate effect on the income of survivors and those who receive partial pay and pensions, whose legal situation as a whole is in urgent need of reorganization.

Armed forces. We are committed to compulsory, equal military service and want to preserve among the people a vital memory of Germany's rise in international affairs and educational values, for both of which they have the national armed forces and its leadership, in times of war and peace, to thank. The defense of our native coasts and the political and economic position of the nation call for the re-creation of the German navy. Care for the invalids of war and the survivors of fallen soldiers, the legal and economic security of active and discharged military personnel, of pensioners and their survivors is the honorable duty of the nation and people.

Equal rights of women. The German woman, as the guardian of the moral and religious foundations of family and national life, is indispensable. Participation in public life on an equal footing is her due. The rights of women, who are responsible for the education of the future generation and in professional and family life, are to be elaborated. The irreplaceable values created through the work of housewives and mothers deserve due social and economic recognition.

Nationality. Only a strong German nationality that consciously preserves its nature and essence and keeps itself free of foreign influence can provide the foundation for a strong German state. For that reason we resist the undermining, un-German spirit in all forms, whether it stems from Jewish or other circles. We are emphatically opposed to the prevalence of Judaism in the government and public life, which has emerged ever more ominously since the revolution. The flow of foreigners across our borders is to be prohibited.

National health. We will support all measures that serve the reconstruction of national vitality and the cultivation of national health. We are committed to the improvement of our nutritional conditions, to the care of mothers and children, and to the struggle against infant mortality, tuberculosis, and venereal diseases, all of which eat away at the quality of the people. We demand the promulgation of a physician's policy, the legal regulation of care for the insane, the development of the apothecary system, a modern law on midwifery, and improvement in the education as well as the protection of all medical personnel. The masses are to be educated about the dangers of a low birth rate; in legislative matters, families with many children are to receive special consideration on principle.

II. SPIRITUAL LIFE

Religion. From a deepening of Christian awareness we expect the moral rebirth of our people, which is a fundamental condition of its political resurgence. Religion is a national issue. The vital absorption of Christian energies depend upon the purity of the family, the development of the youth, the reconciliation of social contradictions, and the health of the state. A nation without religion is deprived of its moral footing and thereby its power of resistance against the anxieties and privations of the time. We are fighting for the purity of German spiritual life, for a stronger emphasis on moral values in economics and politics. We are fighting against filth and trash in all manner of representation, against the spirit of easy pleasures and effortless acquisition, against dishonesty and corruptibility.

Equality of all faiths. Religious communities and their institutions as well as all genuine religious convictions have the right to respect, consideration, and defense by the state, given that they do not contradict state law. The equalization of independent churches and independent religious communities with religious organizations that already enjoy public recognition as legal entities is to be implemented.

Ecclesiastical freedom. With the separation of the church from the state, the state services grounded in law, contract, or particular legal titles, as well as other justly acquired rights of the church and its servants are to be secured. Every attempt to encroach upon the freedom of the churches to organize themselves independently and administer their internal affairs is to be resolutely resisted. For spiritual care in the military, in hospitals, and in prisons, state financial support is to be provided.

Education. Education should lead to the spiritual unity of the nation. With greater intensity than before, we must form the character and will of the people in the service of conscious German identity and a vital intellectual commitment to the state. The strongest foundation for the formation of will and character is vital, truly Christian religious instruction and historical instruction filled with the spirit of the fatherland, which can only be effective when the schools bear the stamp of a unified world view. For that reason the parochial school is to be preferred in principle over the nondenominational school. For the success of the educational system, full freedom of conscience for teachers and others certified in the educational field is a precondition.

The school system. It remains the inalienable right of parents to determine the type of school to which they wish to send their children. For that reason, the free development of private schools is also to be secured. For education in the first school years, a common primary school is to be established. On this basis other types of schools are to be developed, which will be organized into a school system internally unified through appropriate approaches to the issues of transitions and promotions through the various levels. In this sense, we are committed to the standardized primary school. Arrangements are to be made that extend the advantages for promotion enjoyed by the large cities, including continuing education and the technical school system, to the countryside and the smaller cities. This restructuring of the school system must not be allowed to lead to a leveling in our educational system, to a degradation of educational goals, or to the sacrifice of the uniqueness of our institutions of higher education.

Teacher education and school supervision. All teachers should receive their general education at one of the institutions for higher education. In the education of the coming generation women will participate as equal members of the national community. State supervision of the schools is a matter for experts.

Colleges and universities. The unique, historically evolved position of the institutions of higher education, in particular the unlimited freedom granted to the teachers, is to be maintained. The right of self-administration on the part of docents and students is to be preserved on the basis of traditional academic freedom. Educational goals and entrance requirements should not be lowered. Students with German citizenship or of German ancestry have a prior entitlement to these educational facilities. The institutions of popular higher education should devote themselves mind and soul to the deepening and enrichment of the German way and the German nature.

Care of the youth. More intensely than before, we want to be certain of the cultivation in our youth of the tempering of the body and the strengthening of German and patriotic sentiments. For that reason the care of the youth is to be promoted more strenuously than before and every freedom extended to the movement for healthy youth.

Art. Genuine art grows in the soil of a vital nationalism. The people see themselves in their art and becomes conscious of their true nature. Art should be accessible to all segments of the population and become a fruitful contributor to the education of the nation.

137
EDGAR J. JUNG
Germany and the Conservative Revolution

First published as "Deutschland und die Konservative Revolution," in *Deutsche über Deutschland* (Munich: Albert Langen, 1932), 369–382.

We currently find ourselves in the midst of a German revolution that can scarcely be expected to manifest itself in such forms as the French did through the storming of the Bastille. It will be protracted, like the Reformation, but it will still leave its mark all the more fundamentally on the countenance of humanity. It will prompt a ruthless revision of all human values and dissolve all mechanical forms. It will oppose the driving intellectual forces, the formulas, and the goals born of the French Revolution. It will be the great conservative revolution that puts an end to the decline of occidental humanity, founding a new order, a new ethos, and a new unity in the West under German leadership. However, just as the new leadership within state and society is based not on force but on the voluntary compliance with the noble authority of those persons who are prepared to assume responsibility, so will the new leadership of Europe lie beyond the conceptual world denoted by conquest, imperialism, militarism, or denationalization. As the French Revolution shifted the center of European gravity to the west, so will the German allow the heart of Europe, its center, to come back into its own. However obstinately France might press its will for the "order" of Versailles, that nation will not be preserved from the bitter realization that issued from the world war and has inclined France today toward a politics of pure power: the realization that, biologically, the most powerful people in Europe are the Germans. [. . .]

By "conservative revolution" we mean the return to respect for all of those elementary laws and values without which the individual is alienated from nature and God and left incapable of establishing any true order. In the place of equality comes the inner value of the individual; in the place of socialist convictions, the just integration of people into their place in a society of rank; in place of mechanical selection, the organic growth of leadership; in place of bureaucratic compulsion, the inner responsibility of genuine self-governance; in place of mass happiness, the rights of the personality formed by the nation.

The fundamental attitude of the new individual who will be responsible for establishing this order—which recreates the inherent particularity of personality by setting the latter into a humble relationship to the whole, by blending together microcosmic value and macrocosmic preeminence—is a religious one. The present examination will venture neither into the philosophy of religion nor even into theological concerns. It seeks solely to make clear that the humble individual, who can assume the role of the master for precisely the reason that he feels himself to be the tool of God, will be the carrier of the coming new order. I measure the fitness of an individual to be the pathbreaker of the German revolution by his degree of personal humility, which is proportional to his unbroken pride in relation to the mass tendencies of our age. The great divide that is looming does not concern moral values, social attitudes, or nationalist conviction. It concerns who is a true master because he is capable of being a servant. It concerns the question of the extent to which the individual—independently of the external force of law—establishes laws for himself. The horrible moral degeneration of our time is, in the first instance, not at all to be explained on the plane of ecclesiastical faith, obedience to state law, or any other superficial code of honor. The chaos stems much more from the absence of a "caste" that unfailingly establishes laws for itself, which are also unfailingly carried out. That is the one side. The other is equal standards for all. Who can wonder, given the current predominance of these equal standards, that the "sense of honor" of the rabble will ultimately destroy that of the elite? What can a word of honor still mean in a time when words of honor are strewn about by a streetwalker? Who can wonder at disappointments over presumed friends in a time when even the worst blood forces its way without reservation into social strata that are simply incompatible with the conceptual world of such illegitimate upstarts? Who can greet the general lack of honor with astonishment, given that there no longer exists a stratum that enforces an iron discipline upon itself to keep its ranks pure? And what, finally, has happened to that dynamic model without which it is impossible for a social ethos to influence the broad masses, such as English society succeeds in imprinting its message upon the simple man?

Humility toward higher things, freely accepted responsibility, and, for that, a claim to dominion—such is the expression of the fundamental religious attitude that only individuals of good breeding are able to muster. From this attitude, this new faith, a compelling religious world of forms will mature. When it was said above that the conservative revolution was in all ways the opposite of the French Revolution, this opinion also comprehended the hope that the conservative revolution will erect a new altar to God, as the French erected one to the goddess of reason.

The Third Reich therefore cannot be a continuation of the great process of secularization but only its termination. It will be Germanically Christian or not at all. It encompasses in itself the turn away from the secular forms of the nation-state, from the constrictions of a misdirected nationalism. The new nationalism is a religious–cultural concept because it presses toward totality and tolerates no restriction to the purely political. The language of the German revolution will be—despite and precisely because of this fundamentally nationalistic attitude—a world language. In the struggle for our self-preservation we will, for the first time, speak a language that captures the hearts of other peoples. For the German cause will become the cause of all the peoples who do not want, like France, to constrain the course of history by attempting to constitute themselves and their culture as the crowning summit of all time. Thereby the moment of international liberation is already embraced within the voluntary assumption of the German revolution as the task of Europe as a whole. Revolution signifies the domination of a new principle of social value. Every revolution must therefore be a world revolution, though its specific form might remain confined within boundaries drawn by national character. But should we dream about our little place in the sun, merely proclaim our right to existence? Or should we, frankly and freely, go before the world and say to it that, failing our contribution, the face of humanity would display no ordered spiritual features? Should we, the people of Luther, Kant, Beethoven, and Goethe, should we be denied decisive participation as well in the new political ordering of the world?

German cannot easily be used as a world language of the spirit, a statement that is not meant philologically. The language of a Hegel, a Marx, a Nietzsche has indeed acquired political vitality in the world. People in Italy, in France, and in other nations do indeed strain to hear the voices of Germany's conservative revolution. However, much more notice is being given to the mighty mass protest represented by National Socialism. It professes its commitment to the Third Reich, but whether in that profound, comprehensive sense with which it is being cultivated by the men who have reinvigorated the idea of the holy Reich remains an open question. It is possible to maintain that it is necessary for National Socialism to be permeated by the spiritual renaissance with which Germany has been blessed in the last decade. Yet it is also permissible to attribute a more limited historical task to National Socialism, the destruction of a rotten world and the preparation of the great field upon which the new seed is to be sewn. This much is certain: the longing of all the masses making sacrifices today for National Socialism springs from the great conservative genetic inheritance that stirs within them and compels them to such action. Whether—to continue in the language of racial hygiene—the phenomenal form of this longing, which goes today under the name of National Socialism, predominantly bears the traits of the conservative revolution or of the liquidation of liberalism will remain unanswered here. The mighty energies that pulse through the awakening German people are indestructible. Prophets, enemies, and friends might passionately debate the future of National Socialism; they might proclaim its rapid fulfillment or temporary setbacks. Those of us who carry the coming Reich and the will to achieve it steadfastly in our hearts will not be diverted from our fundamental course either by setbacks or the tumultuous success of the masses.

We are reproached for proceeding alongside or behind active political forces, for being romantics who fail to see reality and who indulge in dreams of an ideology of the Reich that turns toward the past. But form and formlessness represent eternal social principles, like the struggle between the microcosm and the macrocosm endures in the eternal swing of the pendulum. The phenomenal forms that mature in time are always new, but the great principles of order (mechanical or organic) always remain the same. Therefore if we look to the Middle Ages for guidance, finding there the great form, we are not only not mistaking the present time but apprehending it more concretely as an age that is itself incapable of seeing behind the scenes. A romantic is one who presents historical models that run counter to the laws of an age. The romantics of the nineteenth century painted such model images and failed to recognize that the wave of liberalism had not yet broken. When, however, they attempted from the depths of their souls to give life to a new reality in opposition to the apparent reality of the liberal world model, they were not divorced from reality. Their reality was a greater and more profound one because their perceptual senses were more finely developed.

For us things are different. The time has come, since the dissolution is complete, since the reality of the liberal conception of the world has revealed itself as illusory, since it has proved impossible to gain mastery over life through abstraction and the rule of the understanding. We once again see the world as it is because we are ourselves not only of *this* world, but because we have an immediate sense of the metaphysical and feel its presence within us as a cosmic law. That is why our hour has come: the hour of the German revolution.

14
Cultural Pessimism: Diagnoses of Decline

Even before the defeat in the war, German intellectuals often pondered with alarm what they saw as the crisis of Western culture. At least since Nietzsche's *Untimely Meditations,* written in the disappointing aftermath of German unification in 1871, pessimistic appraisals of the outcome of that crisis were rife in a Germany struggling to accommodate rapid economic, technological, and political change. For every Nietzsche or Jacob Burckhardt, the great historian of ancient Greece and the Renaissance, there were a dozen lesser figures, like Paul de Lagarde and Julius Langbehn, who disseminated in vulgarized form the message of cultural despair. The ground was thus well prepared for the apocalyptic philosophies of culture which blossomed during the Weimar period, an era, as the novelist Hermann Hesse put it, "longing for a worldview."

Perhaps none had the widespread impact of Oswald Spengler's *The Decline of the West,* a metahistorical meditation on the melancholy fate of all cultures, which appeared in the summer of 1918. Spengler's pseudoscientific morphology of inevitable decay, his appropriation of the culture–civilization opposition so beloved by German mandarins, and his claim that the "Faustian West" had reached a point of no return all struck a chord, especially on the right. Spengler's defense of Caesarist authoritarianism against "decadent" democracy and his hostility to the leveling in mass society appealed to "conservative revolutionaries" like Moeller van den Bruck, whose myth of a Third Reich nonetheless sought to reverse the former's pessimism, at least so far as Germany and Russia were concerned. More cosmopolitan philosophers of life, such as Count Hermann Keyserling, the director of the School of Wisdom in Darmstadt, were inspired by Spengler's elitist diatribe against the "soft" materialism of modern, mass society, which they saw leading to "negro" laziness. Even liberal writers like the sociologist Max Weber were affected by the apocalyptic climate. Although he had no use for Spengler's ideological misuse of history and obscurantist critique of science, Weber shared Spengler's sense that a profound cultural crisis had placed the West in an "iron cage" of modernization from which escape was all but impossible.

In the thinking of the novelist, war veteran, and political nihilist Ernst Jünger, the bourgeois craving for order and security had to be undermined in the name of heroic self-sacrifice. Rather than bemoaning the loss of cultural confidence, Jünger welcomed the increase in danger that it betokened as an opportunity to test the mettle of postbourgeois warriors. In the "total mobilization" of the working masses advocated in his influential 1932 book, *The Worker: Domination and Form*, Jünger prophesied the overcoming of decadent bourgeois culture through violent struggle. His spiritualization of technology in the service of an authoritarian domination of nature earned Jünger the reputation as one of Weimar's premier "reactionary modernists."

Close to Jünger in many respects, although certainly the more philosophically creative thinker, was Martin Heidegger. In his enormously influential *Being and Time* of 1927 Heidegger interwove reflections on the most cosmic of questions with observations about the decay of modern life. One of his most revealing passages lamented the ways in which an overvaluation of curiosity had led to a cult of distraction and idle chatter, which led people away from the more fundamental questions of their existence and being in general. The poet Gottfried Benn was likewise convinced that the current age was one of profound nihilism, which he blamed on an excess of "cerebration." His solution was to push beyond nihilism to a vaguely articulated state of formal aesthetic beauty in which primordial energies would somehow once again be unleashed.

Far more cautious in his recipe for a solution to the cultural crisis was the existentialist philosopher Karl Jaspers, who probed the "spiritual situation of the age" in a widely discussed 1931 work translated as *Man in the Modern Age*. For Jaspers, man in a postreligious era, bereft of any metaphysical consolation, deprived of any certain beliefs, needed to learn to live with his existential isolation rather than succumb to false alternatives. Unable to transcend the mandarin tradition from which he came, Jaspers ignored socio-economic matters in favor of intellectual history, expressed little positive interest in political democracy and mass society, and advocated instead personal decisions for authentic selfhood.

Others sought to harness the healing powers of religion for more directly political purposes. In 1924, Willy Hellpach, the president and cultural minister of Baden, argued for a Catholic cultural offensive that would be commensurate with the Center Party's pivotal role in the Weimar coalition. Others like Chancellor Franz von Papen, writing in October 1932, drew on the rhetoric of Lutheranism to excoriate "cultural bolshevism" and to demand the return of authoritarian Christianity. Not surprisingly, liberal observers like Ludwig Bauer could deplore the potential restoration of medieval anti-individualism.

No less protective of the individual menaced by the mass was the modernist novelist Alfred Döblin, best known for his 1929 masterpiece *Berlin Alex-anderplatz*. Although close to the Social Democrats and a frequent contributer to leftist journals like *Die Weltbühne,* Döblin, in an essay entitled "May the Individual Not be Stunted by the Masses," pleaded for the defense of a non-egoistical self impermeable to the pressures of conformity.

138

OSWALD SPENGLER

The Decline of the West

First published as Introduction to *Der Untergang des Abendlandes* (Vienna: Wilhelm Braumüller, 1918), 3, 21–22, 31–32, 36–37, 44.

Is there a logic of history? Is there, beyond all the casual and incalculable elements of the separate events, something that we may call a metaphysical structure of historic humanity, something that is essentially independent of the outward forms—social, spiritual and political—which we see so clearly? Are not these actualities indeed secondary or derived from that something? Does world-history present to the seeing eye certain grand traits, again and again, with sufficient constancy to justify certain conclusions? And if so, what are the limits to which reasoning from such premises may be pushed?

Is it possible to find in life itself—for human history is the sum of mighty life-courses which already have had to be endowed with ego and personality, in customary thought and expression, by predicating entities of a higher order like "the Classical" or "the Chinese Culture," "Modern Civilization"—a series of stages which must be traversed, and traversed moreover in an ordered and obligatory sequence? For everything organic, the notions of birth, death, youth, age, lifetime are fundamental—may not these notions, in this sphere also, possess a rigorous meaning which no one has as yet extracted? In short, is all history founded upon general biographic archetypes?

The decline of the West, which at first sight may appear, like the corresponding decline of the Classical Culture, a phenomenon limited in time and space, we now perceive to be a philosophical problem that, when comprehended in all its gravity, includes within itself every great question of Being. [. . .]

We know it to be true of every organism that the rhythm, form, and duration of its life, and all the expression-details of that life as well, are determined by the properties of its species. No one, looking at the oak, with its millennial life, dare say that it is at this moment, now, about to start on its true and proper course. No one as he sees a caterpillar grow day by day expects that it will go on doing so for two or three years. In these cases we feel, with an unqualified certainty, a limit, and this sense of the limit is identical with our sense of the inward form. In the case of higher human history, on the contrary, we take our ideas as to the course of the future from an unbridled optimism that sets at naught all historical, i.e., organic, experience, and everyone therefore sets himself to discover in the accidental present terms that he can expand into some striking progression-series, the existence of which rests not on scientific proof but on predilection. He works upon unlimited possibilities—never a natural end—and from the momentary top-course of his bricks plans artlessly the continuation of his structure.

"Mankind," however, has no aim, no idea, no plan, any more than the family of butterflies or orchids. "Mankind" is a zoological expression, or an empty word.[1] But conjure away the phantom, break the magic circle, and at once there emerges an astonishing wealth of actual forms—the Living with all its immense fullness, depth and movement—hitherto veiled by a catchword, a dry-as-dust scheme, and a set of personal "ideals." I see, in place of that empty figment of one linear history which can only be kept

---

1. "Mankind? It is an abstraction. There are, always have been, and always will be, men and only men." (Goethe to Luden.)

up by shutting one's eyes to the overwhelming multitude of the facts, the drama of a number of mighty Cultures, each springing with primitive strength from the soil of a mother-region to which it remains firmly bound throughout its whole life-cycle; each stamping its material, its mankind, in its own image; each having its own idea, its own passions, its own life, will and feeling, its own death. Here indeed are colors, lights, movements, that no intellectual eye has yet discovered. Here the cultures, peoples, languages, truths, gods, landscapes bloom and age as the oaks and the stone-pines, the blossoms, twigs and leaves—but there is no aging "Mankind." Each culture has its own new possibilities of self-expression which arise, ripen, decay, and never return. There is not one sculpture, one painting, one mathematics, one physics, but many, each in its deepest essence different from the others, each limited in duration and self-contained, just as each species of plant has its peculiar blossom or fruit, its special type of growth and decline. These cultures, sublimated life-essences, grow with the same superb aimlessness as the flowers of the field. They belong, like the plants and the animals, to the living Nature of Goethe, and not to the dead Nature of Newton. I see world history as a picture of endless formations and transformations, of the marvelous waxing and waning of organic forms. The professional historian, on the contrary, sees it as a sort of tapeworm industriously adding on to itself one epoch after another. [. . .]

The "Decline of the West" comprises nothing less than the problem of Civilization. We have before us one of the fundamental questions of all higher history. What is civilization, understood as the organic-logical sequel, fulfillment and finale of a culture?

For every culture has its own civilization. In this work, for the first time the two words, hitherto used to express an indefinite, more or less ethical, distinction, are used in a periodic sense, to express a strict and necessary organic succession. The civilization is the inevitable destiny of the culture, and in this principle we obtain the viewpoint from which the deepest and gravest problems of historical morphology become capable of solution. Civilizations are the most external and artificial states of which a species of developed humanity is capable. They are a conclusion, the thing-become succeeding the thing-becoming, death following life, rigidity following expansion, intellectual age and the stone-built, petrifying world-city following mother-earth and the spiritual childhood of Doric and Gothic. They are an end, irrevocable, yet by inward necessity reached again and again.

So, for the first time, we are able to understand the Romans as the successors of the Greeks, and light is projected into the deepest secrets of the late-classical period. What, but this, can be the meaning of the fact—which can only be disputed by vain phrases—that the Romans were barbarians who did not precede but closed a great development? Unspiritual, unphilosophical, devoid of art, clannish to the point of brutality, aiming relentlessly at tangible successes, they stand between the Hellenic culture and nothingness. An imagination directed purely to practical objects—they had religious laws governing relations with the gods as they had other laws governing human relations, but there was no specifically Roman saga of gods—was something which is not found at all in Athens. In a word, Greek soul–Roman intellect; and this antithesis is the differentia between culture and civilization. Nor is it only to the Classical that it applies. Again and again there appears this type of strong-minded, completely non-metaphysical man, and in the hands of this type lies the intellectual and material destiny of each and every "late" period. Such are the men who carried through the Babylonian, the Egyptian, the Indian, the Chinese, the Roman civilizations, and in such periods do Buddhism, Stoicism, Socialism ripen into definitive world-conceptions which enable a moribund humanity to be attacked and reformed in its intimate structure. Pure civilization, as a historical process, consists in a progressive taking down of forms that have become inorganic or dead.

The transition from culture to civilization was accomplished for the Classical world in the 4th, for the Western in the 19th Century. From these periods onward the great intellectual decisions take place, not as in the days of the Orpheus-movement or the Reformation in the "whole world" where no hamlet is too small to be unimportant, but in three or four world-cities that have absorbed into themselves the whole content of History, while the old wide landscape of the culture, become merely provincial, serves only to feed the cities with what remains of its higher mankind. [. . .]

Imperialism, of which petrifacts such as the Egyptian empire, the Roman, the Chinese, the Indian may continue to exist for hundreds or thousands of years—dead bodies, amorphous and dispirited masses of men, scrap-material from a great history—is to be taken as the typical symbol of the passing away. Imperialism is civilization unadulterated. In this phenomenal form the destiny of the West is now irrevocably set. The energy of culture-man is directed inwards, that of civilization-man outwards. And thus I see in Cecil Rhodes the first man of a new age. He stands for the political style of a far-ranging, Western, Teutonic and especially German future, and his phrase "expansion is everything" is the Napoleonic reassertion of the indwelling tendency of every Civilization that has fully ripened—Roman, Arab or Chinese. It is not a matter of choice—it is not the conscious will of individuals, or even that of whole classes or peoples that decides. The expansive tendency is a doom, something demonic and immense, which grips, forces into service, and uses up the late mankind of the world-city stage, willy-nilly, aware or unaware. Life is the process of effecting possibilities, and for the brain-man there are only extensive possibilities. Hard as the half-developed socialism of today is fighting against expansion, one day it will become arch-expansionist with all the vehemence of destiny. Here the form-language of politics, as the direct intellectual expression of a certain type of humanity, touches on a deep metaphysical problem—on the fact, affirmed in the grant of unconditional validity to the causality-principle, that the soul is the complement of its extension. [. . .]

A century of purely extensive effectiveness, excluding big artistic and metaphysical production—let us say frankly an irreligious time which coincides exactly with the idea of the world-city—is a time of decline. True. But we have not chosen this time. We cannot help it if we are born as men of the early winter of full civilization, instead of on the golden summit of a ripe culture, in a Phidias or a Mozart time. Everything depends on our seeing our own position, our destiny, clearly, on our realizing that though we may lie to ourselves about it we cannot evade it. He who does not acknowledge this in his heart ceases to be counted among the men of his generation, and remains either a simpleton, a charlatan, or a pedant.

139

COUNT HERMANN KEYSERLING
The Culture of Making It Easy for Oneself

First published as "Die Kultur des Sich-leicht-Machens," *Das Tagebuch* 20 (May 29, 1920), 662–664.

It is said with increasing frequency that the West is in decline: the title of Spengler's massive narrative of the spirit has become a catchword. No less eagerly do people repeat comparisons of our time with the era of mass migrations or prophesy inexorable barbarization. And thus does there grow among the so-called educated people a peculiar consciousness perhaps most accurately characterized as the right to a mood of failure. The latter is expressed less in the impulse toward *carpe diem* of late antiquity, which at least knew how to enjoy itself fully, than in a wish, perhaps never altogether present or directed purely at the object, for a thoroughgoing liquidation. On the whole spending is indulged just as boundlessly, albeit joylessly, as the Puritan fathers of capitalism accumulated their wealth. And this applies no less to the intellectual than to the material sphere.

How so intellectually? Much of what is referred to as progress in truth means liquidation. The West is liquidating intellectually to the extent that its most recent cultural will aims at one thing above all: to make it easy for oneself.

Many still feel themselves obligated to complain about the cinema, but when it comes to attending film presentations nearly all do and do so fondly. Psychologists and aestheticians have investigated the causes of its triumphal rise and discovered in the process that the moving light pictures truly and absolutely relax the viewers. Reading the stupidest book one must think just a little bit; every picture show draws the participant into its three-dimensional force field. The cinema nearly completely switches off the activation of the self; one's experience there does not differ greatly from a dream. Now absolute relaxation admittedly has its good side. The relatively high quality of English politics is based in part on the ability of its leaders to relax to a degree unknown on the continent. Nor do I doubt that it is possible to create meaning within the frame of artistic conventions most particular to cinematography, as within any other that is properly conceived and practiced. This consideration alone changes nothing of the circumstance that the cinema renders thinking superfluous to an unheard-of degree. Reading Chinese letters without working mentally in the process is out of the question because the understanding of the sense of a combination of ideograms is what makes their external absorption possible in the first place; every book requires that one bring something of oneself to it. But no film does. A company recently asked me whether I wanted to have a film made of my travel diary. I was tempted to say yes, being curious as to how such an intention could be realized. The sense of it enlightened me in an instant: the point was to make the absorption of this book, which interests many, easier.

Democracy everywhere is considering the introduction of a purely phonetic orthography. Why should one make it difficult for oneself by bringing to mind, in addition to the sound, the sense and history of a word? The Greek example should indeed set one to thinking; if I am correctly informed, the modern Greeks, given the extraordinary tension between their written language and pronunciation, considered a plan to introduce a new alphabet, but then immediately let it drop. It was not taken to heart. Bolshevik Russia already writes in accord with an, as it were, tempered ear, and things might soon develop similarly everywhere. In actual fact, why should one make it difficult for oneself? For the same reasons, the English language is now triumphing over the entire globe. Not indeed the English of Shakespeare but that of the colonialists, whose vocabulary is not much richer than that of the Hawaiians and which can be learned in two weeks by anyone with roughly normal talents. The French, for their part, still believe in the potential of cultural imperialism: here as well they completely mistake the signs of the times. French as such stands and falls with a strict and purified form; it must be properly learned and thoroughly mastered. Therefore its spirit is absolutely contradicted by that of the present epoch of liquidation, which neither the cult of the soldier's idiom nor [Paul] Claudel's Germanization nor other enemies of Latin can change in any way. For our time wants above all else to make things easy for itself.

Today the mighty consider popular higher education, although of course this is never admitted, as the ideal of higher education altogether. Nothing should, or may, be withheld from the great masses. This good intention is inexorably turned into deed. Now, however, it turns out differently: to speak clearly to the unprepared, those responsible for teaching must not only set ever lower standards but strive to meet them as well. So they have to set ever lower standards for themselves. The result is that it is not the masses that are elevated, but the other way around: they pull the teachers down to their level. Popular higher education simply does not recognize the distinction in capacity between the prepared and the unprepared, departs from the presumption that everyone is equally ready for the highest levels of knowledge, as, according to Rousseau, all people are supposed to be equally good originally. Therefore no strenuous preparation is needed: one should just make it easy on oneself. As with popular education, so it is with all art calculated for the people. As wonderful as the creation of the popular spirit might sometimes be, those who take their orientation directly from the masses necessarily flatten the work or render it crude. That is why, and not for external reasons of imitation, Europe increasingly converges with America in its most modern aspects. The accomplishments of Max Reinhardt's Großes Schauspielhaus cannot help but work, as if separated by an ocean from the best of his pieces, for more intimate theater. Those who aim to make things easy have to produce something different from those who positively value making things hard.

140

WILLY HELLPACH

The Catholic Cultural Offensive and Political Catholicism

First published as "Die katholische Kulturoffensive und der politische Katholizismus," *Der neue Merkur* 8, no. 1 (1924–1925), 363–367.

An old prophecy is supposed to have said: "*Pius Decimus pontifex ultimus!* [Pius X will be the last pope!]" As one sees, it was no more accurate than most prophecies. But there would perhaps be a kernel of truth to be gained from it after all were one to insert the words *sui generis* in the middle. Pius X may in fact turn out to be the last pope of his particular type for the foreseeable future: one marked by that dogmatic stubbornness we recall from his encyclical *Pascendi dominici* [1907 attack on modernist heresy] and the battle over the modernist oath. The paths of his two successors in the Holy See are completely different. Under them, at least with their tolerance and probably with their support, Catholicism has left the position of rejecting without discussion the life of the modern mind in favor of a comprehensive confrontation with it. That which a scant generation before—in the inferiority conflict, in Hermann Schell's passionate struggle, in Karl Muth's *Veremundus* pamphlets and his founding of [the journal] *Hochland,* in Julius Bachem's *Heraus aus dem Turm*—trickled like a tiny brook of new Catholic thought and work is now flooding the Western world like a powerful torrent of Catholicism. This torrent's forces are now being directed to that place where they should be able to develop best, to the most resolute of the always clearly aimed minds in the Society of Jesus.

The "return from exile" is what one Catholic writer recently called this extraordinary turn in Catholicism, a thoroughly appropriate designation. Into all the spheres of contemporary life and its expression, away from all separation and isolation—this is the formula that is becoming real in a thousand different forms. And not into life merely as sentries, as watchful and penetrating observers and spies! Such a role as this becomes the Catholic Church today just as little as ever. With all the caution and discipline won in a thousand years of schooling, Catholicism in this most recent turn is also thoroughly activist: it seeks out confrontation, in order to persuade, to influence, to convert, and to overcome. Confrontation admittedly demands a recognition of psychological facts. It is not to be had through audacious provocation and the rigid assertion of theses toward the presumptuous aim of subjugation. Rather it must first of all accept the souls of others as they are, must begin with their "mentality," their standpoints, their questions and ways of getting answers, their interests, and their curiosities. Thus we see the essence of Catholicism in this perhaps boldest of all the missions ever dared by Christianity, defined with such generality that it must suggest to millions of non-Catholics that in principle they too could, indeed must, be Catholics. As one reads, for example, in the lead article of the June issue of *Stimmen der Zeit,* a periodical written exclusively by Jesuit fathers:

> Catholicism means the whole, the totality. The Catholic seeks always to be a person of wholeness, one who strives to lend form to the whole of his humanity. To live a Catholic life means, indeed, to grow to approximate the great central and original value of all things: God, in whom the plenitude of being is the highest perfection of the most vital reality. It therefore means to put all the positive forces in people and in the world into these great ideas and fill them with their spirit. It means to strive for an ever more God-like existence.

There is, in other words, absolutely no mention of tenets of faith here. Here Catholicism appears in a definite, partly ethical (fulfilling oneself as a human being), partly mystical (fulfilling oneself in God) spiritual attitude. One believes silently that this path nevertheless coincides with the recognition of dogma. Whoever has heard with their own ears how a dogmatist of the caliber of Engelbert Krebs arrives at the essence of the trinity by way of simple, common experiences of daily life, whoever has been present at the lectures of [Romano] Guardini, the sensitive interpreter of mystery and symbol, or of [Peter] Lippert, S.J., the most daring patrol commander in the Catholic cultural offensive—such a listener achieves a better understanding of the particularity of the new apologetic and missionary method, the success of which we must reckon in decades, than could be gained by the most lengthy of discussions. The new method is active in all areas—science, philosophy, the arts, economic and social life, education and sociality; indeed it takes up even simple entertainment with the same enthusiasm. It is almost superfluous to add that it encompasses tolerance to a degree that was wholly alien to the essential nature of a Pius X. Precisely in relation to the Protestant mentality, Catholicism has taken visible steps in the direction of forbearance, indeed, of understanding; perhaps never before, except in the age of Josephinism[1] (which was, however, of a wholly different internal nature), has there been such a frank discussion of Protestantism as once was devoted to the "other Christian

---

1. Reform Catholicism initiated in the 1780s by Habsburg Emperor Joseph II.

confession." One likewise hears the new tone resound across the entire register when, in Baden's legislature negotiations concerning the terms of a loan favorable to the Lutheran church, an important Catholic functionary approves an act beginning with the words, "The Lutheran church is in dire need," and draws all the appropriate conclusions as to the obligation of his own church to render aid.

What this mighty movement, which will doubtless develop its full potential only among the coming generations of Catholics, will mean for the Catholic church itself, for non-Catholic Christianity, and, beyond that, for the whole of Western culture, is not to be examined here and is presumably in no way foreseeable in this first phase. What, however, is the relation of *political Catholicism* in Germany to this movement? Will it, and how will it, assert itself in relation to the movement? These questions are of the most immediate relevance and not to be put off; for it is possible that the answers will contribute decisively to the shaping of the whole future of the German state.

It is even probable, indeed as good as certain. The collapse of the German state in 1918 created a position of power for the political party of Catholicism, the Center Party, which has exceeded everything that the clever preparations in the age since the *Kulturkampf* could have hoped for or counted on. Put more fairly, the Center Party created its position of power through its statesmanlike behavior following the collapse of 1918. It stepped resolutely onto the ground of the new reality without pressing its claims in a doctrinaire fashion. It is no reproach if, alongside pure love for the fatherland, it was also critically motivated by a desire to put the Catholic cause into the saddle. For what is "pure" love for the fatherland? No serious political party can do anything other than want to shape the fatherland in the way its overall view identifies as ideal; every party carries within itself the idea of the best fatherland, which it attempts at every opportunity to transform into reality; otherwise, it would be a mere collection of prattlers. It was the historical destiny of the National Liberals that they tired prematurely in the process of liberalizing the new Reich and failed in the fateful hour of 1877. It is self-evident that the Center Party would take pains to secure for the Reich, which it helped to save, a more marked Catholic configuration than the Germany of the "evangelical empire" would have permitted. That changes nothing on the question of credit for having helped to save the Reich. And this credit bears a quite crucial character. It is unlikely that the chaos of the winter of 1918–1919 could have resulted in the beginnings of a new political order if the forces of socialist and bourgeois democracy had been required to accomplish it on their own and if the Center Party had taken the position of fundamental opposition against the new, or had even simply crossed its arms and assumed the role of a spectator. For it brought to its contributory role in reconstruction not only a resolute conviction, but also a set of qualities, which could only have been supplied by the German–Democratic partner of the old coalition in this degree and form, and not at all from the socialist partner.

These qualities contributed by the Center Party were the old capacities of the Roman church in a new form: a traditional shrewdness that occasionally extends to the point of cunning; an extraordinary knowledge of human nature and motivation; an absence of commitment to short-term, temporal values ("second values," as contemporary Catholicism likes to say, while our liberal bourgeoisie quarrels, sometimes disastrously, over second, third, fourth, and tenth values); an astounding ability to wait, bound to the greatest of all virtues of practical Catholicism: a readiness for genuine responsibility. Perhaps the last named was the critical one. We observe this willingness in such figures as [Matthias] Erzberger, [Joseph] Wirth, and [Wilhelm] Marx. It is that which in past years most conspicuously distinguished clericalism from socialism, which, for its part, preferred to avoid formal responsibility, thereby believing itself able to minimize its actual responsibility. The chancellorship of Marx, the so-called "ideal, typical" Center politician, demonstrates these qualities with extraordinary clarity.

In this way the Center Party has made itself indispensible in all the phases of the last six years—and that is the critical point, for politics knows nothing of gratitude for something accomplished in the past. There soon will be no one in Germany who can raise the courage to attempt to do without this party. And if he did? The breach between that which is right and left of the center will remain for a long time to come so unbridgable that a coalition between right and left without the Center Party or even against it is utterly inconceivable; a lasting coalition, rather in the manner of the former grand coalition in Baden, has become as good as hopeless in the Reich and in all the states that could in any way be considered for it. Whoever takes the rudder, whether of the right or of the left, will have to form a coalition with the Center Party. The two southwestern states, Baden and Württemberg, in the one of which the left, in the other the right, rules together with the Center Party, are textbook examples lying right before our eyes.

The Center Party, however, is political Catholicism, now and for all foreseeable times. Every wager on a "deconfessionalization" of this party has been lost. The Center Party might take this or that positive, feudal, Christian–socialist Protestant into its ranks; that does not change the fact that it draws the force of its convictions from Catholic *soil* and its mass force from the Catholic population. And that is why the spirit assumed and expressed by Catholicism is of the greatest, and certainly immediate, political significance for the spirit of the Center Party.

141

HERMANN HESSE

The Longing of Our Time for a Worldview

First published as "Die Sehnsucht unser Zeit nach einer Weltanschauung," *Uhu* 2 (1926), 3–14.

The new image of the earth's surface, completely transformed and recast in just a few decades, and the enormous changes manifest in every city and every landscape of the world since industrialization, correspond to an upheaval in the human mind and soul. This development has so accelerated in the years since the outbreak of the world war that one can already, without exaggeration, identify the death and dismantling of the culture into which the elder among were raised as children and which then seemed to us eternal and indestructible. If the individual has not himself changed (he can do this within two generations no more than any animal species could), then at least the ideals and fictions, the wishes and dreams, and the mythologies and theories that rule our intellectual life have; they have changed utterly and completely. Irreplaceable things have been lost and destroyed forever; new, unheard-of things are being imagined in their place. Destroyed and lost for the greater part of the civilized world are, beyond all else, the two universal foundations of life, culture and morality: religion and customary morals. Our life is lacking in morals, in a traditional, sacred, unwritten understanding about what is proper and becoming between people.

One need only undertake a short journey to be able to observe in living examples the decay of morals. Wherever industrialization is still in its beginnings, wherever peasant and small-town traditions are still stronger than the modern forms of transportation and work, there the influence and emotional power of the church is quite essentially stronger as well. And in all of these places we continue to come across, more or less intact, that which were once called morals. In such backward regions one still finds forms of interaction—greeting, entertainment, festivals, and games—which have long since been lost to modern life. As a weak substitute for lost morals, the modern individual has fashion. Changing from season to season, it supplies him with the most indispensible prescriptions for social life, tosses off the requisite phrases, catchwords, dances, melodies—better than nothing, but still a mere gathering of the transitory values of the day. No more popular festivals, but the fashionable entertainment of the season. No more popular ballads, but the hit tune of the current month.

Now, what morals are to the exterior shaping of a life, the agreeable and comfortable guidance of tradition and convention, religion and philosophy are to more profound human needs. The individual has not only the need—in customs and morals, dress and entertainment, sports and conversation—to be ruled and guided by a valid model by some kind of ideal, be it merely the daily ideal of fashion. He has as well in the deeper recesses of his being the need to see meaning attached to all that he does and strives for, to his existence, his life, and the inevitability of death. This religious or metaphysical need, as old and as important as the need for food, love, and shelter, is satisfied in calm, culturally secure times by the churches and the systems of itinerant thinkers. In times like the present a general impatience and disillusion with both received religious creeds and scholarly philosophies grow; the demand for new formulations, new interpretations, new symbols, new explanations is infinitely great. These are the signs of the mental life of our times: a weakening of received systems, a wild searching for new interpretations of human life, a flourishing of popular sects, prophets, communities, and a blossoming of the most fantastic superstitions. For even those who are superficial, not at all spiritual, and disinclined to thought still have the primal need to know that there is meaning to their lives. And when they are no longer able to find a meaning, morals decay, and private life is ruled by wildly intensified selfishness and an increased fear of death. All of these signs of the time are clearly legible, for those who care to see, in every sanatorium, in every asylum, and in the material reported everyday by psychoanalysts.

But our life is an uninterrupted fabric of up and down, decay and regeneration, demise and resurrection. Thus are all the dismal and lamentable signs of cultural decline matched by other, brighter signs that point to a reawakening of metaphysical needs, to the formation of a new intellectuality, and to a passionate concern for the creation of new meaning for our lives. Modern literature is full of these signs, modern art no less so. Making itself felt with particular urgency, however, is the need for a replacement for the values of the vanishing culture, for new forms of religiosity and community. That there is no shortage of tasteless, silly, even dangerous and bad substitute candidates is obvious. We are teeming with seers and founders; charlatans and quacks are mistaken for saints; vanity and greed leap at this new, promising area—but we must not allow these facts alone to fool us. In itself this awakening of the soul, this burning resurgence of longings for the divine, this fever heightened by war and distress, is a phenomenon of marvelous power and intensity that cannot be taken seriously enough. That there lurks alongside this mighty current of desire flowing through the souls of all the peoples a crowd of industrious entrepreneurs making a business of religion must not be allowed to confuse us as to the greatness, dignity, and importance of the movement. In a thousand different forms and degrees, from a naïve belief in ghosts to genuine philosophical speculation, from primitive county-fair ersatz religion to the presentiment of truly new interpretations of life, a gigantic wave is surging over the earth; it encompasses American Christian Science and English theosophy, Mazdaznan [neo-Zoroastrian cult] and neo-Sufism [Muslim sect], [Rudolf] Steiner's anthroposophy, and a hundred similar creeds; it takes Count Keyserling around the world and leads him to his Darmstadt experiments [a spiritual School of Wisdom], supplies him with such a serious and important collaborator as Richard Wilhelm, and concurrently gives rise to a whole host of necromancers, sharpers, and clowns. I do not dare draw the line between that which is worthy of discussion and the utterly farcical. But, aside from the dubious promoters of modern secret orders, lodges, and fraternities, the unabashed superficiality of fashionable American religions, and the ignorance of unflinching spiritualists, there are other, sometimes supremely worthy phenomena, like [Karl Eugen] Neumann's [1922] translation and dissemination of sacred Buddhist texts, Wilhelm's translations of the great Chinese thinkers; there is the great and splendid return of Lao Tse, who, unknown for centuries in Europe, has appeared within three decades in countless translations in nearly all European languages, and conquered a place in European thought. Just as there arose within the chaos and irritating bustle of the German revolution a few pure, noble, unforgettable figures, like Gustav Landauer and Rosa Luxemburg, likewise there stands amid the raging, murky flood of modern attempts at religion a number both noble and pure: theologians like the Swiss pastor Ragaz; figures like Frederik van Eeden, who returned to Catholicism in old age; men, quite singular in Germany, like Hugo Ball, once a dramaturge and one of the founders of dadaism, then unabashed opponent of the war and critic of the German war mentality, then recluse and author of the wonderful book, *Byzantinisches Christentum;* and, so as not to forget the Jews, Martin Buber, who points modern Judaism toward profounder goals and has reacquainted us with the piety of the Hasidim, one of the most charming of all the blossoms in the garden of religions.

"And now," some readers will ask, "where is it all leading? What will be the result, the final destination? What might we expect of it in general? Has one of the new sects the prospect of becoming a new world religion? Will one of the new thinkers be able to put forward a new, broad-minded philosophy?"

In some circles these questions will be answered in the affirmative. Among some adherents of the new doctrines, in particular the young, the happy mood of devotees confident of victory reigns, as if our epoch were destined to give birth to the savior, to give the world new certainties, new faiths, and new moral orientations for a new period of culture. That black mood of decline of some older, disillusioned critics of our time corresponds to this youthful credulity of the newly converted as its antipode. And still these youthful voices resound more pleasantly than those of the ill-humored and old. Nevertheless, these believers might be in error.

It is proper that we meet the longing of our time—this yearning search, these experiments, some blinded with passion, others coolly bold—with respect. Even if they are all condemned to failure, they nonetheless remain serious concerns with supreme goals; should none at all of them survive our time, they fulfill an essential function while they live. All of these fictions, these religious elaborations, these new doctrines of faith help people live, help them not only to endure this difficult, questionable life but to value it highly and hold it sacred. And if they were nothing but a lovely stimulus or a sweet anesthesia, then even that perhaps would not be so little. But they are more, infinitely more. They are the schools through which the intellectual elite of our times must pass. For every intellectualism and culture has a twofold task: first to give security and encouragement to the many, to console them, and to bestow meaning on their lives and second the more secret but no less important task for the few, for the great minds of tomorrow and the day after: to make it possible for them to mature, to lend protection and care to their beginnings, to give them air to breathe.

The intellectualism of our time is infinitely different from the one that our elders once took up as our heritage. It is more turbulent, wilder, and poorer in tradition; it is less well schooled and has little in the way of method. But all in all, this contemporary intellectualism, including its powerful bent for mysticism, is certainly in no way worse off than the better trained, more learned, richer in traditional heritage, although less powerful intellectualism of that time in which aged liberalism and youthful monism were the leading tendencies. To me personally even the intellectualism in today's leading currents, from Steiner to Keyserling, remains a few degrees too rational, too little bold, too little prepared to enter upon the chaos, upon the underworld, there to overhear from the "mothers" of Faust the longed-for occult doctrine of the new humanity. None of today's leaders, however enthusiastic or clever they might be, has the breadth and the significance of Nietzsche, whose true inheritors we have not yet learned to be. The thousand intersecting voices and paths of our time, however, have this one valuable thing in common: a coiled desire, a will born of the need to surrender. And these are the preconditions of all greatness.

142

MARTIN HEIDEGGER

Being and Time

First published in *Sein und Zeit* (Halle: Max Niemeyer Verlag, 1927), 172–173.

Which existential state of Dasein will become intelligible in the phenomenon of curiosity?

Being-in-the-world is proximally absorbed in the world of concern. This concern is guided by circumspection, which discovers the ready-to-hand and preserves it as thus discovered. Whenever we have something to contribute or perform, circumspection gives us the route for proceeding with it, the means of carrying it out, the right opportunity, the appropriate moment. Concern may come to rest in the sense of one's interrupting the performance and taking a rest, or it can do so by getting it finished. In rest, concern does not disappear; circumspection, however, becomes free and is no longer bound to the world of work. When we take a rest, care subsides into circumspection that has been set free. In the world of work circumspective discovering has de-severing as the character of its Being. When circumspection has been set free, there is no longer anything ready-to-hand which we must concern ourselves with bringing close. But, as essentially de-severant, this circumspection provides itself with new possibilities of de-severing. This means that it tends away from what is most closely ready-to-hand and into a far and alien world. Care becomes concern with the possibilities of seeing the "world" merely as it looks while one tarries and takes a rest. Dasein seeks what is far away simply in order to bring it close to itself in the way it looks. Dasein lets itself be carried along (*mitnehmen*) solely by the looks of the world; in this kind of Being, it concerns itself with becoming rid of itself as being-in-the-world and rid of its Being alongside that which, in the closest everyday manner, is ready-to-hand.

When curiosity has become free, however, it concerns itself with seeing, not in order to understand what is seen (that is, to come into a Being towards it) but just in order to see. It seeks novelty only in order to leap from it anew to another novelty. In this kind of seeing, that which is an issue for care does not lie in grasping something and being knowingly in the truth; it lies rather in its possibilities of abandoning itself to the world. Therefore curiosity is characterized by a specific way of not tarrying alongside what is closest. Consequently it does not seek the leisure of tarrying observantly, but rather seeks restlessness and the excitement of continual novelty and changing encounters. In not tarrying, curiosity is concerned with the constant possibility of distraction. Curiosity has nothing to do with observing entities and marvelling at them—θαυμάζειν. To be amazed to the point of not understanding is something in which it has no interest. Rather it concerns itself with a kind of knowing, but just in order to have known. Both this not tarrying in the environment with which one concerns oneself, and this distraction by new possibilities, are constitutive items for curiosity; and upon these is founded the third essential characteristic of this phenomenon, which we call the character of "newer dwelling anywhere" (*Aufenthaltslosigkeit*). Curiosity is everywhere and nowhere. This mode of Being-in-the-world reveals a new kind of Being of everyday Dasein—a kind in which Dasein is constantly uprooting itself.

Idle talk controls even the ways in which one may be curious. It says what one "must" have read and seen. In being everywhere and nowhere, curiosity is delivered over to idle talk. These two everyday modes of Being for discourse and sight are not just present-at-hand side by side in their tendency to uproot, but either of these ways-to-be drags the other one with it. Curiosity, for which nothing is closed off, and idle talk, for which there is nothing that is not understood, provide themselves (that is, the Dasein which is in this manner [*dem so seienden Dasein*]) with the guarantee of a "life" which, supposedly, is genuinely "lively." But with this supposition a third phenomenon now shows itself, by which the disclosedness of everyday Dasein is characterized.

143

ERNST JÜNGER

On Danger

First published as "Über die Gefahr," in *Der gefährliche Augenblick. Eine Sammlung von Bildern und Berichten,* ed. Ferdinand Bucholtz (Berlin: Junker und Dünnhaupt Verlag, 1931), 11–16.

Among the signs of the epoch we have now entered belongs the increased intrusion of danger into daily life. There is no accident concealing itself behind this fact but a comprehensive change of the inner and outer world.

We see this clearly when we remember what an important role was assigned to the concept of security in the bourgeois epoch just past. The bourgeois person is perhaps best characterized as one who places security among the highest of values and conducts his life accordingly. His arrangements and systems are dedicated to securing his space against the danger that at times, when scarcely a cloud appears to darken the sky, has faded into the distance. However, it is always there: it seeks with elemental constancy to break through the dams with which order has surrounded itself.

The peculiarity of the bourgeois' relation to danger lies in his perception of it as an irresolvable contradiction to order, that is, as senseless. In this he marks himself off from other figures, for example, the warrior, the artist, and the criminal, who are given a lofty or base relation to the elemental. Thus battle, in the eyes of the warrior, is a process that completes itself in a higher order; the tragic conflict, for the writer, is a condition in which the deeper sense of life is to be comprehended very clearly; and a burning city or one beset by insurrection is a field of intensified activity for the criminal. In turn bourgeois values possess just as little validity for the believing person, for the gods appear in the elements, as in the burning bush unconsumed by the flames. Through misfortune and danger, fate draws the mortal into the superior sphere of a higher order.

The supreme power through which the bourgeois sees security guaranteed is reason. The closer he finds himself to the center of reason, the more the dark shadows in which danger conceals itself disperse, and the ideal condition which it is the task of progress to achieve consists of the world domination of reason through which the wellsprings of the dangerous are not merely to be minimized but ultimately to be dried up altogether. The dangerous reveals itself in the light of reason to be senseless and relinquishes its claim on reality. In this world all depends on the perception of the dangerous as the senseless; then in the same moment it is overcome, it appears in the mirror of reason as an error.

This can be demonstrated everywhere and in detail within the intellectual and actual arrangements of the bourgeois world. It reveals itself at large in the endeavor to see the state, which rests on hierarchy, as society, with equality as its fundamental principle and which is founded through an act of reason. It reveals itself in the comprehensive establishment of an insurance system, through which not only the risk of foreign and domestic politics but also that of private life is to be uniformly distributed and thus subordinated to reason. It reveals itself further in the many and very entangled efforts to understand the life of the soul as a series of causes and effects and thus to remove it from an unpredictable into a predictable condition, therefore to include it within the sphere in which consciousness holds sway.

In this sense the securing of life against fate, that great mother of danger, appears as the truly bourgeois problem, which is then made subject to the most diverse economic or humanitarian solutions. All formulations of questions at present, whether aesthetic, scientific, or political in nature, move in the direction of the claim that conflict is avoidable. Should conflict nevertheless arise, as cannot, for example, be overlooked in regard to the permanent fact of war or criminality, then all depends upon proving it to be an error whose repetition is to be avoided through education or enlightenment. These errors appear for the sole reason that the factors of that great equation—the result of which has the population of the globe becoming a unified, fundamentally good as well as fundamentally rational, and therefore also fundamentally secure humanity—have not yet achieved general recognition. Faith in the persuasive force of these views is one of the reasons that enlightenment tends to overestimate the powers given to it.

One of the best objections that has been raised against this valuation is that under such circumstances life would be intolerably boring. This objection has never been of a purely theoretical nature but was applied practically by those young persons who, in the foggy dark of night, left their parental home to pursue danger in America, on the sea, or in the French Foreign Legion. It is a sign of the domination of bourgeois values that danger slips into the distance, "far away in Turkey," in those lands where pepper grows, or wherever the bourgeois likes to deplore everyone not conforming to his standards. For these values to disappear entirely, however, will never be possible, not just because they are always present but above all because the human heart is in need not only of security but of danger too. Yet this desire is capable of revealing itself in bourgeois society only as protest, and it indeed does appear, in the form of romantic protest. The bourgeois has nearly succeeded in persuading the adventurous heart that the dangerous is not present at all. Thus do figures become possible who scarcely dare to speak their own superior language, whether that of the poet, who compares himself to the albatross, whose powerful wings are nothing more than the object of a tedious curiosity in a foreign and windless environment, or that of the born warrior, who appears to be a ne'er-do-well because the life of a shopkeeper fills him with disgust. Countless examples could show how in an era of great security any profitable life will depart for the distances symbolized by strange lands, intoxication, or death.

In this sense the world war appears as the great, red balance line under the bourgeois era, the spirit of which explained—that is, believed itself capable of invalidating—the jubilation of the volunteer who welcomed the war by attributing to him either a patriotic error or a suspect lust for adventure. Fundamentally, however, this jubilation was a revolutionary protest against the values of the bourgeois world; it was a recognition of fate as the expression of the supreme power. In this jubilation a revaluation of all values, which had been prophesied by exalted spirits, was completed: after an era that sought to subordinate fate to reason, another followed which saw reason as the servant of fate. From that moment on, danger was no longer the goal of a romantic opposition; it was rather reality, and the task of the bourgeois was once again to withdraw from this reality and escape into the utopia of security. From this moment on, the words *peace and order* became a slogan to which a weaker morale resorted.

This was a war that not only nations but two epochs conducted against each other. As a consequence, both victors and vanquished exist here in Germany. Victors are those who, like salamanders, have gone through the school of danger. Only these will hold their own in a time when danger, not security, will determine the order of life.

Precisely for this reason, however, the tasks that order must accomplish have become much more comprehensive than before; these tasks have to be performed where danger is not the exception, but is constantly present. As an example, the police force might be mentioned. It has transformed itself from a group of civil servants into a formation that already greatly resembles a military unit. Likewise the various large parties acknowledge the need to adopt means of power that express the fact that the battle of opinions will not be decided solely through votes and programs but also by the stalwarts committed to march in support of those programs. Such facts are in no way to be isolated and regarded as a temporary or transient change in the political landscape. Nor can the inclination to danger be overlooked in intellectual endeavors, and it is unmistakable that new forms of the volcanic spirit are at work. Phenomena like modern atomic theory, glacial cosmogony, the introduction of the concept of mutation into zoology all point clearly, completely apart from their truth content, to how strongly the spirit is beginning to partake of explosive events. The history of inventions also raises ever more clearly the question of whether a space of absolute comfort or a space of absolute danger is the final aim concealed in technology. Completely apart from the circumstance that scarcely a machine, scarcely a science has ever existed which did not fulfill, directly or indirectly, dangerous functions in war, inventions like the automobile engine have already resulted in greater losses than any war, however bloody.

What especially characterizes the era in which we find ourselves, into which we enter more deeply with every passing day, is the close relationship that exists between danger and order. It may be expressed in this way: danger appears merely as the other side of our order. The whole is more or less equivalent to our image of the atom, which is utterly mobile and utterly constant. The secret concealed within is a new and different return to nature; it is the fact that we are simultaneously civilized and barbaric, that we have approached the elemental without having sacrificed the acuity of our consciousness. Thus does the path through which danger has penetrated our life present itself as twofold. It has intruded upon us first of all out of an arena in which nature is still more vital. Things, "the likes of which were only possible in South America," are now familiar to us. The distinction is that danger, from a romantic dimension, has in this way become real. Secondly, however, we are sending danger back out over the globe in a new form.

This new form of danger appears in the closest connection having been made between elemental events and consciousness. The elemental is eternal: as people have always found themselves in passionate struggle with things, animals, or other people, as is the case today. The particular characteristic of our era, however, is precisely that all this transpires in the presence of the most acute consciousness. This finds expression above all in the circumstance that in all of these conflicts the most powerful servant of consciousness, the machine, is always present. Thus does humanity's eternal struggle with the elemental nature of the sea present itself in the temporal form of a supremely complicated mechanical contrivance. Thus does the battle appear as a process during which the armored engine moves fighting men through the sea, over land, or into the air. Thus does the daily accident itself, with which our newspapers are filled, appear nearly exclusively as a catastrophe of a technological type.

Beyond all this the wonder of our world, at once sober and dangerous, is the registration of the moment in which the danger transpires—a registration that is moreover accomplished whenever it does not capture human consciousness immediately, by means of machines. One needs no prophetic talent to predict that soon any given event will be there to see or to hear in any given place. Already today there is hardly an event of human significance toward which the artificial eye of civilization, the photographic lens, is not directed. The result is often pictures of demoniacal precision through which humanity's new relation to danger becomes visible in an exceptional fashion. One has to recognize that it is a question here much less of the peculiarity of new tools than of a new style that makes use of technological tools. The change becomes illuminating in the investigation of the change in tools that have long been at our disposal, such as language. Although our time produces little in the way of literature in the old sense, much of significance is accomplished through objective reports of experience. Our time is prompted by human need—which explains, among other things, the success of war literature. We already possess a new style of language, one which gradually becomes visible from underneath the language of the bourgeois epoch. The same, however, is true of our style altogether; it is reminiscent of the fact that the automobile was for a long time constructed in the form of a horse-drawn coach, or that a wholly different society has already long since established itself beneath the surface of bourgeois society. As during the inflation, we continue for a time to spend the usual coins, without sensing that the rate of exchange is no longer the same.

In this sense, it may be said that we have already plunged deeply into new, more dangerous realms, without our being conscious of them.

144

KARL JASPERS

The Spiritual Situation of the Age

First published in *Die geistige Situation der Zeit* (Berlin: de Gruyter, 1931), 5–6, 13–14, 145–147.

For more than a century, the problem concerning the situation of humanity has been growing ever more urgent, and each generation has endeavored to solve that problem according to its own lights. But whereas in former days only a few were anxiously considering the dangers to which our mental world is exposed, since the war the gravity of the peril has become manifest to everyone.

The topic, however, is not merely inexhaustible but insusceptible of fixed definition, inasmuch as it is modified by the very act of concentrating attention on it. Past situations can be regarded as finished, as having had the curtain rung down on them, as having had their day and ceased to be; whereas the stimulating characteristic of a present situation is that thinking about it helps to determine what will become of it.

Everyone knows that the world situation in which we live is not a final one.

There were periods in which man felt his world to be durable, an unchanging intermediate between the vanished Golden Age and the end that would come in due course when the Almighty's purposes were fulfilled. Man accommodated himself to life as he found it, without wishing to change it. His activities were limited to an endeavor to better his own position amid environing circumstances deemed to be substantially unalterable. Within these circumstances he had safe harborage, linked as he was both with heaven and with earth. The world was his own world, even though it was of no account, because for him true being existed only in a transcendental realm.

As compared with man in those eras, man today has been uprooted, having become aware that he exists in what is but a historically determined and changing situation. It is as if the foundations of being had been shattered. How self-evident seemed the unity of life and knowledge to the man of old has become plain to us now that we realize that the life of our fellows in the past was spent under conditions in which reality was, as it were, veiled. We, however, have become able to see things as they really are, and that is why the foundations of life quake beneath our feet; for, now that the identity of thought and being (hitherto unchallenged) has ceased to exist for us, we see only on the one hand life and on the other our own and our companions' awareness of that life. We do not, as did our forefathers, think merely of the world. We ponder how it is to be comprehended, doubting the validity of every interpretation; and behind every apparent unity of life and the consciousness of life there looms the distinction between the real world and the world as we know it. That is why we live in a movement, a flux, a process, in virtue of which changing knowledge enforces a change in life; and, in turn, changing life enforces a change in the consciousness of the knower. This movement, this flux, this process, sweeps us into the whirlpool of unceasing conquest and creation, of loss and gain, in which we painfully circle, subject to the power of the current but able now and then to exert ourselves within a restricted sphere of influence. For we do not only live in a situation proper to humanity but we experience this situation as it presents itself in specific historical circumstances, issuing out of a previous situation and progressing towards a subsequent one. [. . .]

Before and during the Great War were penned the two most outstanding mirrors of our time: [Walther] Rathenau's *Critique of the Age* (1912) and [Oswald] Spengler's *The Decline of the West* (1918). Rathenau's book is a searching analysis of the mechanization of modern life; Spengler's work is a philosophy of history furnished with a wealth of observations and attempting to demonstrate that the decay of the Western world is the outcome of the operation of natural laws. The novel features of these two books are their material actuality, the way in which the ideas they put forward are sustained by positive data, the wide circulation they have achieved, and the increasing emphasis of their insistence that mankind stands face to face with Nothingness. Still, [Søren] Kierkegaard and Nietzsche remain the leaders in this field—though Kierkegaard has found no disciples to sustain his advocacy of primitive Christianity, and Nietzsche's Zarathustrian philosophy has not been generally adopted. Since, however, both of them revealed the trend towards annihilation, it was only to be expected that the war should draw unprecedented attention to their doctrines.

Without question there is a widespread conviction that human activities are unavailing; everything has become questionable; nothing in human life holds good; existence is no more than an unceasing maelstrom of reciprocal deception and self-deception by ideologies. Thus the epochal consciousness becomes detached from being and is concerned only with itself. One who holds such a view cannot but be inspired with a consciousness of his own nullity. His awareness of the end as annihilation is simultaneously the awareness that his own existence is null. The epochal consciousness has turned a somersault in the void. [. . .]

More urgent than ever has become the problem concerning the present situation of humanity as the upshot of past developments and in view of the possibilities of the future. On the one hand we see possibilities of decay and destruction and on the other hand we see possibilities that a truly human life is now about to begin, but as between these conflicting alternatives, the prospect is obscure. [. . .]

The novelty of our century, the changes whose completion will set it so utterly apart from the past, are not, however, exhaustively comprised within the limits of the despiritualization of the world and its subjection to a regime of advanced technique. Even those who lack clear knowledge of the subject are becoming decisively aware that they are living in an epoch when the world is undergoing a change so vast as to be hardly comparable to any of the great changes of past millennia. The mental situation of our day is pregnant with immense dangers and immense possibilities; and it is one which, if we are inadequate to the tasks which await us, will herald the failure of humanity.

Is it an end that draws near, or a beginning? Is it perhaps a beginning as significant as that when man first became man, but now enriched by newly acquired means, and the capacity for experience upon a new and higher level? [. . .]

Existence-philosophy is the way of thought by means of which man seeks to become himself; it makes use of expert knowledge while at the same time going beyond it. This way of thought does not cognize objects but elucidates and makes actual the being of the thinker. Brought into a state of suspense by having transcended the cognitions of the world (as the adoption of a philosophical attitude towards the world) that fixate being, it appeals to its own freedom (as the elucidation of existence) and gains space for its own unconditioned activity through conjuring up transcendence (as metaphysics).

This existence philosophy cannot be rounded off in any particular work, nor can it acquire definitive perfection as the life of any particular thinker. It was in modern times originated by Kierkegaard, and through him procured widespread diffusion. [. . .]

Existence philosophy cannot discover any solution, but can only become real in the multiplicity of thought proceeding from extant origins in the communication from one to another. It is timely, but is already more obvious in its failures than in its successes, and has already succumbed to the premature tumultuousness with which everything significant that enters the contemporary world is greeted.

Existence philosophy would be instantly lost if it were once more to imply a belief that we know what man is. It would again provide outlines for the study of the types of human and animal life, would again become anthropology, psychology, sociology. It can only have a possible significance so long as the objects at which it is to direct its attention are not laid down and limited exclusively. It awakens what it does not itself know; it elucidates and gives impetus, but it does not fixate. For the man who is on the right road it is the expression thanks to which he is enabled to maintain his direction; it is the instrument whereby he is empowered to safeguard his sublime moments of realization throughout life.

Existence philosophy may lapse into pure subjectivity. Then selfhood is misunderstood as the being of the ego, which solipsistically circumscribes itself as life that wishes to be nothing more. But genuine existence philosophy is that appealing questioning in which today man is again seeking to come to his true self. Obviously, therefore, it is found only where people wrestle on its behalf. Out of a chance medley with sociological, psychological, and anthropological thought, it may degenerate into a sophistical masquerade. Now censured as individualism, now used as a justification for personal shamelessness, it becomes the perilous foundation of a hysterical philosophy. But where it remains genuine, where it remains true to itself, it is uniquely effective in promoting all that makes man genuinely human. [. . .]

The basic problem of our time is whether an independent human being in his self-comprehended destiny is still possible. Indeed, it has become a general problem whether man can be free—and this is a problem which, as clearly formulated and understood, tends to annul itself; for only he who is capable of being free can sincerely and comprehendingly moot the problem of freedom.

145

ERNST JÜNGER

The Worker: Domination and Form

First published in *Der Arbeiter: Herrschaft und Gestalt* (Hamburg: Hanseatische Verlags-Anstalt, 1932), 197–201.

The world we live in displays on the one hand positive similarities to a workshop and on the other, to a museum. The distinction between these two landscapes, from the point of view of the demands they imply, is that no one is forced to see in a workshop more than simply a workshop whereas over the museum landscape there reigns a grotesquely proportioned spirit of edification. We have risen to a level of historical fetishism that stands in a direct relation to our deficiency in productive energy. Therefore the dismal thought occurs that some sort of secret correspondence causes the pace of our accumulation and preservation of so-called cultural goods to be matched only by the grandiose scale on which we simultaneously create instruments of destruction.

These goods, that is, the art, culture, and the education industry, have so come to permeate our emotional and aesthetic environment that the need to lighten our load can scarcely be imagined in sufficiently fundamental and comprehensive terms. It is not the worst that around the most out-of-the-way little hovel that life has ever forced the body to endure a circle of experts, collectors, snoopers, and curators gathers. Such was ultimately, albeit on a more modest scale, always the case.

More dubious is the issue of all this industriousness in a network of stereotyped values behind which is concealed utter mortification. At play here are only the shadows of things, with advertisements being made for a concept of culture that is alien to all manner of primal strength. This is happening at a time in which the elemental has regained its strength, a time in which it penetrates our environment and poses unambiguous challenges. While the state faces more original and pressing tasks than ever in history, effort is instead expended attempting to attract a new generation of administrators and cultural bureaucrats and to cultivate a perverse feeling for the "true greatness" of the people. Regardless of how far one might wish to look back, it would be difficult to hit upon such a distressing blend of banality and arrogance as has become common in the inevitable invocations of German culture in the official state language. What our fathers had to say about progress was in comparison truly golden.

The question arises, how, in a time so filled with things of burning importance, those presently transpiring and those yet to come, such a veneer of pale idealism and infused romanticism is possible in the first place. The answer that no one is capable of doing better may well be naïve, but it is also apt. The museum industry represents nothing other than one of the last oases of bourgeois security. It supplies the seemingly most plausible pretext upon which one can evade the political decision. This is an activity the world is happy to catch the Germans undertaking. As soon as it became apparent that the "workers' representatives" in Weimar in 1919 had their *Faust* in their knapsacks, it was possible to predict that the bourgeois world had been saved for a reasonable time to come. The flatness with which cultural propaganda was practiced in Germany during the war developed afterward literally into a system, and there is scarcely a postage stamp, scarcely a banknote on which one does not run across the same things. All of these things have won for us the reproach, unfortunately mistaken, of being perfidious. It is a matter here, however, not of perfidy, but of the bourgeois absence of instinct in questions of value.

This absence is a kind of opium that veils danger and summons up the deceitful consciousness of order. That, however, is an intolerable luxury at a moment that demands one not speak of traditions but create them. We are living at a moment in history when all depends on an enormous mobilization and concentration of the forces at hand. Our fathers had perhaps the time to occupy themselves with the ideals of an objective science and an art existing for its own sake. We in contrast find ourselves quite clearly in a position in which not this or that but the totality of our life is in question.

This makes imperative the act of total mobilization. Its task is to pose to every phenomenon, both human and material, the brutal question of its necessity. Instead, in the years since the war, the state has occupied itself with things that are not just superfluous to an endangered existence but harmful, and it has neglected other things that are critical to survival. The image one ought to have of the state today resembles not a convivial passenger steamer but a warship ruled by extreme simplicity and economy on which every motion is made with an instinctive sense of confidence.

What ought to inspire respect in foreigners visiting Germany are not façades preserved of past times, not ceremonial speeches made during the centenary celebrations of classic artists, and not the concerns from which novels and plays derive their themes; it is rather the virtues of poverty, work, and diligence which today represent cultivation much more profoundly than the bourgeois ideal can even dream.

Do people not know that our entire so-called culture is incapable of preventing even the smallest neighboring country from violating our territory? Do they not know that it is, on the contrary, enormously important for the world to know that the defense of the nation will enlist even children, women, and the aged in its cause? And that, just as individuals renounced the pleasures of their private existence, so would the government not hesitate for a second to sell the art treasures in all the museums to the highest bidder, if this defense required it?

Such expressions of the highest form of tradition, namely, the vital, living form, obviously presuppose a supreme sense of responsibility, a sense to which it is clear that the point now is not our responsibility to images but to the primal strength to which these images bear witness. That requires, to be sure, a genuine greatness of another kind. Let us however be persuaded: if there still exists among us genuine greatness, if somewhere a poet, an artist, a believer is hidden, then it is this sense of responsibility and their need to make themselves useful that will make them recognizable.

It requires no prophetic gift to predict that we are standing not at the beginning of a golden age but before great and difficult changes. There is no optimism capable of obscuring the fact that great conflicts are more numerous and more serious than ever. The point is to match the stature of these conflicts by creating orders that are unshakable.

The situation in which we find ourselves, however, is that of an anarchy concealed behind the delusion cast by values become obsolete. This situation is necessary insofar as it guarantees the decay of those old orders whose fighting strength has proved insufficient. The strength that one finds in the depths of the people, in contrast to the creative soil of the state, has preserved itself in unsuspected ways.

Already today we are justified in saying that exhaustion has been essentially overcome—that we possess a youth that knows its responsibility and whose core was invulnerable to anarchy. It is inconceivable that Germany would ever lack good people. How grateful is this youth for every sacrifice asked of it. The critical point, however, is lending this willing and ready issue of nature a form corresponding to its essence. This task poses the greatest and most significant challenges to our productive energies.

But what can be the spiritual nature of minds that fail to comprehend that there is no more profound or knowing spirit than that of any given soldier who fell somewhere on the Somme or in Flanders?

That is the standard that we need.

146

FRANZ VON PAPEN

German Cultural Policy

First published as "Deutsche Kulturpolitik," *Der Türmer* 35, no. 1 (October 1932), 1–3.

The fundamental task of a conservative policy of renewal consists of seeing to it that the supremacy of state power is once again raised above the conflict of parties and interest groups to resume its status as an inviolable bulwark of legitimacy.

But the power of the state is neither an end in itself nor is it omnipotent. It is the symbol of the orderly autocracy and self-discipline of a healthy and manly people. It is at the same time an expression of the ever-present divine will of creation, which preserves the immutable orderings of human life from degeneration. For this reason the power of the state serves not only the economic well-being of the people, but also the cultivation of their inner vitality. It preserves and promotes their traditional culture and uniqueness. It steels their will to freedom with an education in voluntary obedience and subordination to the interests of the nation as a whole. Through the state's political leadership, it maintains the spirit of the people in a wakeful condition and pulls their energies together for the sake of coordinated creation, for the sake of collective service, which inclines the people living in the present to goals beyond themselves and binds them to the happiness of coming generations.

It is also said that political leadership cannot give rise to culture, but can only protect it and maintain its vitality. In times when the people are secure in themselves and, conscious of their traditions, put themselves to the test in daily acts of preservation, the tasks of cultural policy are easy to accomplish. In such times it is enough to prevent aberrations and remedy abuses in a timely fashion. In times like these, however—when the people threaten to succumb to inner strife because they have been beset and torn apart by alien spirits, when the people have lost trace of the true sources of their heritage and are seeking to find them anew—then there devolves upon the power of the state the high office of leading the people along the path of inner renewal, systematically examining and separating out the spirits, gathering the healthy forces, and ridding itself of the sick.

The leadership of the state must once again, as it did 120 years ago in Prussia, offer an immediate representation of the self-consciousness and self-knowledge of the whole people. It therefore does not suffice for the government to lead the people silently along the path of reason, merely to undertake measures and pronounce decrees answering to the necessities of a difficult economic situation. A people in the midst of a spiritual turn are never able to live by such reason through such harshness. All sacrifices lead to embitterment when hope cannot be awakened, when the spirit and faith of the nation is not summoned to action. That is why the current bearers of state power must have the courage to name by name the enemy of the people and proscribe it, and not just its political but also its spiritual enemy so that the decision itself can incline the people, in their will for renewal, to compose themselves internally and clearly conceive its goal.

This enemy is cultural bolshevism in whatever form it takes and wherever it works to subvert the spiritual foundation of our existence, loyalty to our people, as well as faith in the eternal truths of Christianity. Among the followers of this enemy must be counted all individuals who do not love the arduous fate of the German people as their own and assume their part in bearing it.

True cultural policy today is a systematic struggle for the inner recuperation of the people, for the preservation of its best force and inherited values, a struggle that admittedly cannot be conducted by means of laws and regulations alone. What I have detailed elsewhere is valid here as well: the meaning of conservative state leadership lies in the task of constructing with only a few laws a framework in which the forces of the nation can develop freely. The culture of the German people is infinitely rich; it will tolerate no regimentation and no centralized experimentation. History has left us the Reich as a form of government that not only allows freedom and individual responsibility but demands them. A strong Reich has therefore no need to prescribe to the people its convictions and inner life. I reject emphatically any imposition of uniformity on German culture, any violation of it by force, no matter whether it is attempted from the standpoint of a Marxist, a liberal, or for that matter a nationalist ideology. It will never be possible to press the German people into the uniformity of the Latin or Slavic nations. They owe themselves and their European mission the preservation of the uniqueness of their cultural heritage in the manifold array of its particularities. Unity must be maintained where necessary; and what is necessary will be determined by the requirements of an ordered national community and the fundamental rules of German culture. Beyond that, however, even in education, freedom may reign.

The constitution expressly protects the freedom of those authorized to give instruction. But it presupposes that the educators remain conscious of the duties imposed upon them by the historical heritage of the German people. The fundamental error of the encyclopaedists and the liberal era was the proclamation of unlimited freedom of thought, that freedom which destroys before it has constructed anything, that freedom which, molding public opinion, reproduces itself daily by the thousands, yet conveys to the people nothing but the corrosive poison of negative criticism and spiritual abnegation. Never yet has anyone grown into a mature person without experiencing the limits imposed by authority and learning to serve responsibility. Never yet have a people become great and independent who have not held fast to the legacy of their history and measured their own accomplishments against it. This legacy obligates. Schools and teachers who deny this obligation have no warrant to give instruction. Families and religious societies are authorized to teach according to the constitution but the parties are not. A state that is supposed to supervise education can accept no binding tasks from the parties. It represented a political abuse of state power, for example, when the ruling coalition parties in Prussia managed educational policy through four different ministers according to their respective party points of view. Schools, exactly like the administration of the state, should gather together the forces of the people and not promote fragmentation within the national community.

It is therefore the most noble task of a cultural policy to call especially upon those involved both in the education of the youth and in the further development of German culture in science, literature, and art to supply every assurance that their concern for the national community is predominant over any particular social interest. It is not the modest achievements of one or the other private world view, which nourishes itself by shredding tradition to tatters and then collapses, that can aid the state in the education of the nation. The eternal sources of faith must again be opened to education. The doctrines of Christianity, which have already trained and watched over the European peoples for over a thousand years and to which the spiritual life of the German people in particular is inextricably bound, are more vital to us today than ever. They alone will be able to heal the enormous injuries arising from a century of overestimation of intellectual education. The division between the enlightened academics and the working people will not be closed by bringing academic education to the people and commending to them the cast-off garb of an academic elite. An education that is not capable of furthering the spiritual development of the various branchings and strata of our people in their autonomous particularity, that no longer has any consciousness of the fact that a people consists not of the sum of individual intelligences, but of families and natural, organically evolved communities based on landscape and occupation, surrounded and suffused by the supernatural community of the church—such an education will lead the people into anarchy. The artificial blossoms of an indifferent urban culture have never been the signs of renewal in a people but signs of the end and decay.

This pseudoculture must once again be put down by the simple principles offered by a conservative knowledge of human nature. The goal of education should be to cultivate believing Christians, faithful members of the people, and able citizens who once again recognize service to the fatherland as their highest task. Higher education too must recall its duty to educate people, not in an intellectuality alien to the nation but into leaders who remain spiritually connected to their people.

That a consciousness of a true national community, however, be awakened by speeches and theories is by no means the most pressing requirement. That alone can do nothing. Crucial above all is striding along the practical path that need has revealed to us. The promising sites of a new national education, which have come spontaneously to life in the work place and in occupational associations and leagues, appear to me valuable schools of renewal. I would have every possible means of support dedicated to them once they have integrated themselves consciously into the state federation.

A German cultural policy that carefully tends, in a conservative spirit, to the treasures of German culture and defends them relentlessly against all destructive attempts can only be carried out successfully by an independent state power. Nothing is less salutary for the growth of a genuine spiritual life than when partisan powers strive to subject it to their arrogated rule. So that the German people can once again work in freedom on the education of their children and the fulfillment of their German mission, so that it will not be disturbed in this work by the constant shifting of party coalitions, it is inescapable that the authority of state power be established as the model for a truly ordered life. I will struggle for that in the consciousness that all authority, even that of the state, has its origin solely in God.

147

GOTTFRIED BENN
After Nihilism

First published in *Nach dem Nihilismus* (Berlin: Gustav Kiepenheuer, 1932), 7–17.

In the following essays and speeches (which do not systematically deal with a common theme because they are the response to the most various occasions and the outgrowth of all sorts of moods) two concepts nevertheless assume a foreground position, due to the constant and rather specifically directed thrust of the author's philosophical preference. The two concepts are progressive cerebration and nihilism, and they are juxtaposed, in several places, with the concept of constructive intelligence, an expression for those forces and efforts that seek to counteract the lethargizing influence of the former. Do we still have the strength, asks the author, to oppose the scientific-deterministic world view with a self that is grounded in creative freedom? Do we still have a strength drawn from the power of traditional Western thought, not from economic chiliasms and political myth-ologems, to break through the materialistic-mechanical form-world and to design the images of deeper worlds out of an ideality that posits itself as such, and in a measure that sets its own limits? A constructive intelligence, then, as an emphatic and conscious principle of far-reaching liberation from materialisms of every stripe—psychological, evolutionist, physical, not to mention the sociological variety—constructive intelligence as the essentially anthropological style, as the essential hominid substance which, through its mythopoetical unfolding, its eternal metaphorical irradiation, would fulfill human destiny in the unreality of light, in the phantasmic nature of all things, and pour itself out among the stars, their space, and their infinity in a kind of far-flung play, commingling the genii in one's own breast with vast swarms of creative spirits in their heavens and their hells.

As for the two initial concepts, they are inseparable, connected both by content and chronology, both of them having risen into the European consciousness in the last century, the first one very recently indeed. This concept of progressive cerebration originated from a combination of anthropology and the study of the brain and was established by [Konstantin] von Economo in Vienna. According to this idea, humanity has experienced a clearly perceptible, irresistible increase of intellectualization, has, in short, become more brainy. [. . .]

As for nihilism, it is a fairly well-known phenomenon, and I have contributed some observations concerning its genesis in "Goethe and Natural Science." In this essay I demonstrate that the seventeenth and eighteenth centuries appear to have been an age when the German nation's creative life occurred in a closed spiritual space that remained undisrupted even by the internal struggles of generations and ideologies, because there was *one* faith, *one* feeling that remained untouched throughout all the changes; and that the end of this age coincided approximately with Goethe's death. The faith or feeling that prevailed at the beginning of this epoch was called God, and the feeling or faith prevailing at the end was called Nature. But a conception of nature that had been formed under the influence of Leibniz and Spinoza. Nature: a pantheistic universe, already atomized, or rather divided into monads, since the concept of the atom did not exist before [John] Dalton's chemical investigations of 1805; but the topmost monad was still called God. In Goethe, we still frequently find this expression, but even more frequently the impersonally universalistic expression, *Nature,* which is really his characteristic expression: a Nature that is still experienced in a purely irrational manner, is lyrically greeted in stanzas to the moon; Nature again in her ancient veiled maternal form; explanations are not to be stripped off her body, he says; she is everything, I entrust myself to her, let her do with me as she will, I shall praise her in all her works—and these lines from the hymn to Nature published in the journal of the Tiefurter Gesellschaft in 1782 are in a sense Western civilization's farewell to a world which for two thousand years, for example, since the mythological age of Greece, had been felt to be permeated with spirit, its trees and creatures given to man but ensouled by the presence of gods.

The dissolution of this feeling began around the time of Goethe's death. A worldview developed that lacked any relationship to a beyond, any obligation to an extrahuman existence. Man became the crown of creation and the ape his favorite beast, providing him with his phylogenetic confirmation, a glory which he had attained by the excellence of his metabolism. Two dates are of special importance in this development, for they provide the chronological basis of the new age and the supposed solidity of its truth. The first date is July 23, 1847, the date of the meeting of the Physical Society of Berlin in which [Hermann] Helmholtz supplied the mechanical proof of Robert Mayer's thesis of the conservation of energy and computed it as a general law of nature. That day marks the beginning of the idea of the world's complete comprehensibility, of its comprehensibility as a mechanism, and it is just as epochally significant as an earlier date that lives among us with post- and ante-. Consider that until that day the world could not be comprehended, only experienced; that it was not approached and computed with physics and mathematics but was felt and experienced as a gift of creation, as the expression of a supraterrestrial order. To make it very clear, Goethe said: "Man finds himself quite satisfactorily part of the world by his experience, there's no need to surpass it conceptually." Now began the conceptual surpassing, the beginning of modern physics.

The second date is 1859, when [Charles] Darwin's theory was published. A time of racial boom, inextricable conglomerations of enormous population growth, Wall Street intervening in the money market, a frenzy of colonizations, continent-wide intensifications of instinct and luxury, ascension of groups fit and ready for usurious expansion, economic strangleholds, imperial proclamations and debacles, and now this theory of the animal race's attainment of fitness and of the reward accruing in struggle and victory to the strong. These two dates gave Europe a new impetus; they provided the source material for a new human type, the materialistically organized commodity type, the montage character, optimistic and shallow-layered, cynically emancipated from any conception of human fatality—minimal pain for the individual and maximal comfort for all, wasn't that the gist of [Auguste] Comte's philosophical welcome to the new age?

The age began with the doctrine of man's essential goodness. [. . .]

Man is good, his nature is rational, and all his sufferings are hygienic and socially controllable—this on the one hand and creation itself on the other. Both were supposed to be accessible to science. From both these ideas came the dissolution of all the old bonds, the destruction of the substance, the leveling of all values; from them came the inner situation that produced that atmosphere in which we all live, from which we all drank to the bitter dregs: nihilism.

This concept took shape in Germany in 1885 and 1886, the years when [Nietzsche's] *The Will to Power* had been partly conceived and partly written, the first part of which bears the subtitle: "European Nihilism." But this book already contains a critique of this concept and designs for overcoming it. If we wish to trace its earlier history, if we wish to determine where and when this fateful concept first appeared as a word and as a spiritual experience, we must, as is well known, turn to Russia. The hour of its birth was in March 1862, the month when Ivan Turgenev's novel *Fathers and Sons* was published. That's as far back as anyone, even Russian historians, can trace it. But the hero of this novel, named Bazarov, is already a full-fledged nihilist, and Turgenev introduces him by that name. This name then became popular with great rapidity. In his afterword to the novel, the author tells how the word was already in everyone's mouth when he returned to St. Petersburg two months later, in May. It was the time of the great incendiaries, the burning of the Apraxin court, and people cried out to him: "Look at your nihilists, they're setting St. Petersburg on fire." It is of great interest, in this context, that this Bazarov's nihilism was not an absolute form of nihilism at all, was not negativism pure and simple but a fanatical faith in progress, a radical positivism with regard to natural science and sociology. He is, for the first time in European literature, the mechanist confident of victory, the plucky materialist, whose somewhat dubious grandsons we can still see engaged in lively activity among us. [. . .]

Yes, even dadaism, whose recent appearance in Zurich and Berlin was found so interesting by our times, can be found in a novel of the 1860s, *What Is to Be Done,* by [Nicholas] Chernyshevsky: art, we read there, means moving two pianos into a drawing room, seating a lady in front of each instrument, letting a half chorus form around each, and having every participant sing or play a different song simultaneously and very loudly. This was called the melody of revolution and the orgy of liberty. So we can see that the intellectual effects of the materialistic philosophy of history begin in the 1860s and are therefore at least eighty years old, so that strictly speaking it is they that are old and reactionary. Strictly speaking, and here we are pushing ahead into the future, all materialism is reactionary, whether as a philosophy of history or as a political faith: namely, backward-looking, backward-acting, for we are already faced with a completely different kind of man and a completely different goal. A goal before which man as a being purely dedicated to drives and pleasures already represents a quite crepuscular theory. Engineering the soul, spare parts for a so-called collective or normative humanity, that's no more nor less than stale rococo. All these attacks against the higher man we've had to listen to for the past eighty years, and that includes [George Bernard] Shaw's farces, are all downright old-fashioned by now, flat and intellectually poverty stricken. There is only the higher, that is to say, the tragically struggling man; he is history's only subject; only he is anthropologically in possession of all his senses, which is more than can be said for the instinctual complexes. So it will have to be the superman after all who overcomes nihilism, though it won't be the type Nietzsche described in a pure nineteenth-century spirit. He describes him as a new, biologically more valuable, racially improved, vitalistically stronger, eugenically perfected type, justified by a greater capacity for survival and preservation of the species; he sees him as biologically positive—that was Darwinism. Since then we have studied the bionegative values, which are rather more harmful and dangerous to the race but are a part of the mind's differentiation: art, genius, the disintegrative motifs of religion, degeneration; in short, all the attributes of creativity. So today we do not posit the mind as partaking of biological health, nor do we include it in the rising curve of positivism, nor, for that matter, do we see it in tragic, eternally languishing conflict with life; rather we posit the mind as superordinate to life, constructively superior to it; as a formative and formal principle: intensification and concentration—that seems to be its law. This entirely transcendent attitude may result in an overcoming, namely, an artistic exploitation of nihilism; it could teach us to look at it dialectically, that is to say, provocatively. To let all the lost values remain lost; to let all the expired motifs of the deistic epoch remain finished and gone; to put all the force of nihilistic feeling, all the tragedy of nihilistic experience at the disposal of the mind's formal and constructive powers; to generate and cultivate a morality and a metaphysics of form that would be completely new for Germany. There are more than a few indications that we are on the verge of a decisive anthropological turning point. A banal way to put it: displacement from inside to outside, a surging forth of our last specific substance in formative activity, translation of powers into structure. Modern technology and modern architecture point in this direction: space is no longer philosophic-conceptual, as it was in the Kantian epoch, but dynamic-expressive; spatial feeling is no longer in-drawn in lyrical lonesomeness but projected, extruded, metallically realized. There are numerous signs, such as expressionism, surrealism, psychoanalysis, that suggest we are advancing biologically toward a reawakening of myth, and cortically toward a build-up by means of discharge mechanisms and pure expression. Our resistances against the purely epical, against any influx of external matter, against rationalizations, psychological glue-jobs, causality, milieu development, contrasted with our urge for direct contact, for cutting, for arrangement, for pure behavior, suggest the same. The last specific substance wants expression, leaps over all ideological interpositions, and assumes naked and immediate control of technology at the same time that civilization in its inward content turns back to myth—that appears to be the final stage. Primordial, eternal man, the primal monist, catches fire in the glow of his ultimate image, an image under the golden helmet: how many rays still fall through the runes, how much radiance still on the shadows' edge, how multifarious: tied to frenzies and eugenics, to the tension of departure toward the finale, with the elemental synthesis of creation in memory and the progrediently cerebralized analysis of his historical mission in the brain, throwing aside Europe's normalized masses, brushing past the Yucatan's white crumbled rock and the Easter Islands' transcendent colossi, he ponders his ancestors, aboriginal man, proselenic man, ponders his incalculably ancient but unrelentingly murderous, antidualistic, anti-analytic struggle and rouses himself once again to a final formula: constructive intelligence.

"An antimetaphysical world view, fine—but in that case, let it be artistic." This sentence from *The Will to Power* would then acquire a truly final meaning. It would acquire for the German, as an indication of a last escape from his lost values, his addictions, his riotings, his wild enigmas, a quality of tremendous seriousness: the goal, the faith, the overcoming would then be called the law of form. It would acquire for him the character of an obligation to his people, to struggle, to fight the fight of his life, in an effort to work his way close to those things that are really in essence unconquerable, the possession of which accrued to older and more fortunate peoples from their endowments, their limits, their skies and their seas when they were still young: a sense of space, proportion, magic of realization, adherence to a style. Does this imply aesthetic values in Germany, artistry in a country so given over to dreams and obfuscation? Yes, the cultivated absoluteness of form, whose degrees of linear purity and stylistic immaculateness must by all means be equal to the degrees of perfection in content achieved by earlier cultural epochs, including the degrees marked by the cup of hemlock and the cross. Indeed, only out of the ultimate tensions of the formal, only from the utmost intensification of the spirit of construction, pushed to the limits of immateriality, could a new ethical reality take shape—*after* nihilism!

148

LUDWIG BAUER

The Middle Ages, 1932

First published as "Mittelalter, 1932," *Das Tagebuch* 13, no. 1 (January 2, 1932), 10–13.

The train of development is racing at a speed that can only be experienced, and therefore not imagined, straight into a new Middle Ages. The whole of humanity has booked a round-trip ticket. The nineteenth century is being tossed on the rubbish heap; Mussolini has discovered the eighteenth to have been the dumbest of them all. And now the German Mussolini substitute, with all his haughty and anti-intellectual professors, has taken up the Italian's abusive lead. For in the last century humanity strode the path of general progress, from "we" to "I"; it discovered the individual as an end in himself, the state to be a necessary evil, and it lighted the torch of human rights, now threatening to go out in a dense intellectual fog. Today we are thirsting to be unburdened of our "I," are born right into a uniform; we unburden ourselves of our soul and submit to the mass. Tolerance is replaced by fanaticism, a smile by inflexibility.

The individual is being rebound.

Whether Hitlerism or fascism, whether *Heimwehren* [paramilitary organizations] or *Camelots du roi* [Action Française thugs] all of them turn away from the clarity of understanding to mysticism and self-idolization. The meaning of existence is no longer the happiness and freedom of the individual but a massing together in race, class, and state. Thus develops that species that loves to stand in rank and file, that finds happiness only in mass faith. Disdainfully, it casts the glorious achievements of the Enlightenment aside; Voltaire never lived. From the confusions of a humanity fleeing from itself was born this generation, which has no use for human dignity, freedom of thought, and tolerance; and what the best have heroically conquered over centuries appears to it indifferent or harmful. They take over dogmas—one must, one should—until one is finally no longer allowed to think; everything has already been determined, and whoever denies, doubts, or opposes it is a rebel and a heretic. Such narrowness and dullness is typically medieval, and—in that the Enlightenment is being trampled underfoot, dismissed as a mere mistake—it is only logical that the Middle Ages, with all its strictness, its base, dogged exclusiveness, would be proclaimed a lost paradise. And all of this repeats itself in the economy; we are leaving the world economy behind, smashing the ties between peoples, reinvigorating the old guilds, desiring ever more compulsion and commandment. We shun responsibility, want to be unburdened by a doctrine of salvation that directs and orders everything. Third Reich? Dear people, it existed for a long time and was a most gloomy period. Everyone born into and predetermined by his fate. Enterprise neutralized, thoughts sinful, dirt inside and out. Humanity a ghetto of stupidity, hatred, and superstition. The godsend and consolation of the oppressed that they were allowed to oppress others. Division: the one ordered to flog, the other to be flogged. Small and narrow the world, the distant dangerous.

That is where we are going again. Only now it is 1932 and we are plunging into it with the speed of a race car. A sign of the plunge is that the machine works inexorably to the advantage of regression. Because we were unable to master it, it defeats us. So we seek protection in concentrations of violence and invent for ourselves a new romanticism. Class or race proclaims itself the new nobility. Do they not laugh at the vain French glancing self-admiringly at the little red ribbon in their buttonholes? They, that is, who themselves grace the entirety of their people with the superiority of Nordic nobility. What must be sacrificed for that: freedom, goodness, peace, human dignity—everything for which the best have fought and suffered. But in exchange the masses are justified, even duty-bound, in their arrogance. The old state was not able to tame the unfettered machine. The new one, which in truth is the oldest, can do so just as little; but it is able to compensate by leading us into a darkness where misery becomes infinitely more comprehensive and no longer visible in consequence. A strangely frightening spectacle:

The I is disappearing.

Individuals count only as a part of the whole; they become the tool of a fighting sect, and soviets, fascists, Nazis, Camelots du roi have the impudence to prescribe for them the meaning of their existence. They do not have the right themselves to determine their own measure, define their happiness; they are returned to immaturity with others doing these things for them, and the only obligation they are spared is that of being allowed to choose their own fate. Such a repression of the personality is only possible by virtue of the epoch's mechanized tools of assimilation; newspapers, film, and radio educate the people, erode differentiations, and authorize and promote the cultivation of the mass soul. It is grotesque that a humanity more uniform than ever is divided by the deepest of rifts, entrenches itself behind magical lines drawn in the air: the borders. Everyman is increasingly a mere part and no longer whole, and thus has he ever less need of tolerance, respect, and personal dignity. And what for anyway, since he is actually only there in appearance? Everything is transferred onto fetishes, onto class, race, party, and state. Whether we listen to the verdicts of a judge in Leipzig, which call to mind a modern witch trial, or whether we hear the

Prince of Wales admonish his people to buy only English goods, it remains everywhere the same: the new Middle Ages. All the drawbridges are being raised; in medieval castles and behind city walls, starved and greedy for booty, the enemy awaits his foreign prey. And all have become the enemy of all. Not only every foreign citizen but also the bales of cloth, the heaps of coal, the bushels of wheat of the other are the enemy. [. . .]

Middle Ages, 1932—a Middle Ages that wants to believe, but in truth no longer can. Forced into union, it is more and more divided by the day. Will it be merely an episode? Even such as that could, in haste, destroy more than more clever centuries have built. The air smells of dullness and stupidity. It is time to read Voltaire. It is time, even more so, to live Voltaire.

149

ALFRED DÖBLIN

May the Individual Not Be Stunted by the Masses

First published as "Daß der Einzelne unter dem Einfluß der Masse nicht verkrüppelt," *Uhu* 8, no. 6 (1932), 7–8.

You have to protect yourself from the masses. They are the calamity of the day and the genuine obstacle to being really human. They are arrogant troublemakers, and more than anything they are indestructible despots and absolutists. Whether they openly call themselves emperor or secretively, the public or the collective, do not let yourself be fooled. They all have the same thing in mind; they want to swallow you up.

Have you ever heard of a house that demands of you that you should and must live in it and should and must conform and subordinate yourself to it? You would say no. If you do not like a house, you move out, and, if you prefer, you do not live in any house at all. Have you ever heard of someone giving you clothes and telling you to put them on then, if they do not fit, to get fat or thin so they do fit? Organizations and the collective are just such houses and clothes. They have already been produced and you call it an honor to change yourself accordingly.

Why is the glorification and idolization of this arrangement dangerous? Because they lead each of us astray from our obligation to being. But no one can relieve the individual of his responsibility for his life. There is no court that can rise up and take from us our responsibility for our conduct. No church, no priest can do that. The door to the ultimate court that does exist is so constructed, so narrow, that only individuals ever pass through it. Even the priest himself passes through it without his robes; the judge has no bench there; the self goes alone, without help, without adherents.

Whoever wants to take from the self, from the individual, the single person, his obligation to his being, the responsibility for his life, whoever even has the cheek to maintain that the self first becomes the self in these collectives and these arrangements, is first fulfilled as self and need not be concerned—whoever does that is engaged in a wicked maneuver of trickery and fraud.

We are not alone, we cannot get along one without the other, men and women without each other. Children cannot get along without their parents and guardians. There are friendships. We have projects in common. We cannot build our houses alone; doctors must care for the sick. We have conflicts; they must be put right. What is all this? Is it the public realm, the party, the collective? It is the most basic nature of every one of us. Granted only existence and health, the individual has this love for man or woman, the tie to children or parents, has friendships, has the will and inclination to work together with others. Buildings and bridges must be built. Doctors want to go to the sick; the sick are in need of help. This is not how the collective, the public realm, the party is; this is how every person is. When institutions are set down upon individuals, both the individuals and the mutual ties among them wither. In the strictest states one finds the loneliest people. Where the realm of the public begins, there begins fragmentation. Where the public realm leaves off, things order themselves and natural relations resume. Individuals come to themselves, and when they come to themselves, they come to community.

None of this has anything to do with individualism pursued egotistically by the isolated being. Egotism is the effect of the bad society itself, which has exceeded and canceled the connection between individuals. The forcibly egotistic society creates egotists. In it are to be found only hoarders for the family, pseudo-individuals and go-getters, human cripples and weeds.

Paul Citroen, "City." Photomontage from around 1922. (Copyright © Paul Citroen/
VAGA, New York 1994.)

15

Imagining America: Fordism and Technology

CHARLIE CHAPLIN, jazz, boxing, Henry Ford, chewing gum, Chicago gangsters: American culture and life-styles captured (or colonized?) the German imagination from the inception of the republic. At once Germany's victor on the battlefield and the impetus for wide-ranging economic and social change in its aftermath, the United States was seldom absent from the mirror that politicians and writers of all persuasions regularly held up to the republic. Economic assistance, a regular diet of Hollywood films and popular music, and the influence of ideologies such as Taylorism and Fordism led many to discern "Americanism" everywhere and to posit it as a characteristic Weimar phenomenon. Typically, as in Rudolf Kayser's essay, it is described in the language of pre-1914 vitalist philosophy, as a new type of culture unburdened by history and directly related to nature and the body. Such idealization of sports and the trim physique of the athlete quickly became incorporated into the aesthetic of the New Objectivity. Equally revealing is Kayser's opposition of America and Russia, a dialectic of civilizational forms that presents Germany and Europe as privileged terms of synthesis. Yet such an image is deceptive. For while the America cult never reached the apogee in Britain or France that it reached in Germany, enthusiasm for "American objectivity" and technological prowess remained potent in the Soviet Union throughout the 1920s.

While such commentators as Felix Stössinger openly acknowledged Americanism as a European construction, most brought less methodological self-consciousness to their ruminations. Simplistic oppositions between an imaginary organic totality of European culture and a mechanistic, profit-driven "Yankee civilization" were frequently drawn by conservatives. Adolf Halfeld's excoriation of America as a land of mass civilization, cultural sterility, and rationalized uniformity typifies the hostility of many traditionalists to Americanism. More than a few observers discerned a powerful economic subtext to such debates, especially evident after the infusion of American capital from the 1924 Dawes Plan. While already employed before the war in the factories of such large concerns as Bosch and Daimler-Benz, rationalized production techniques greatly expanded during the years 1926–1928, as Otto Bauer notes. The German publication in November 1923 of Henry Ford's autobiography boosted public awareness of Fordism and Taylorism, and a year later the first automobile rolled off the assembly line at the newly constructed Ford plant in Cologne. While Taylorism favored time and motion studies and the segmentation of the assembly line production process to increase worker efficiency, Fordism promoted set work norms, higher wages, employee loyalty, and a leisure ethic. Both doctrines eventually integrated the ideas of a more psychologically oriented prewar science of work (*Arbeitswissenschaft*) into a uniquely German theory of scientific management. While Bauer, a Marxist, criticized rationalizing practices for leading to unemployment, the conservative industrial spokesman Friedrich von Gottl-Ottlilienfeld praised Fordism for its efficiency and elimination of labor conflict. Others raised concerns about psychological and social consequences. In his 1923 Marxist analysis, *History and Class Consciousness,* Georg Lukács attacked rationalization for fragmenting the personality of the worker, while pointing to its growing omnipresence throughout capitalist society. Liberal critics advanced the now familiar theses of industrial psychology, while noting the danger for office workers of the disappearance of the soul (*Entseelung*) through work, a loss of individual experience (*Erfahrung*), which forms a recurrent motif in German philosophy from Wilhelm Dilthey to Walter Benjamin.

This potential for the mechanization and standardization of individual experience represented everything most worrying about Americanism. Popular curiosity about technology remained palpable during the Weimar Republic, as evidenced by the success of Fritz Lang's 1926 film, *Metropolis*. Yet many feared the machine and a reduction of all values to quantities (brilliantly parodied in Friedrich Sieburg's description of a Taylorized American beauty pageant). In his noted essay, "The Mass Ornament," Siegfried Kracauer discerns in the movements of the Tiller Girls, a popular chorus-girl ensemble, "the aesthetic reflex of the rationality aspired to by the prevailing economic system." Transformed into a de-eroticized spectacle suggestive of later Busby Berkeley films, the Tiller Girls raise the spectre of a world marching toward total rationalization. A similar cry of despair is evident in Stefan Zweig's essay "The Monotonization of the World." Prefiguring the critique of inauthentic existence Heidegger would develop two years later in *Being and Time,* Zweig's attack on the homogeneity of media environments in the 1920s hints at themes subsequently developed in Marshall McLuhan's theory of the global village.

150

RUDOLF KAYSER

Americanism

First published as "Amerikanismus," *Vossische Zeitung,* no. 458 (September 27, 1925).

Americanism is the new European catchword. It suffers the usual fate of catchwords: the more it is used, the less one knows what it means. It is certain that in this case the range of meanings is enormously broad, far exceeding particular minor phenomena, and that it applies to the fundamental character of our time. So the remarkable situation has arisen in which, for the designation of a truly radical change in the inner and outer forms of our life over the last few decades, we have no expression other than the name of a foreign continent that previously appeared to us infinitely far away, and not only in the geographical sense.

What is it then with Americanism?

Certainly it has nothing or only little to do with the American, whom we, after all, know less than any other national type. As a literary type, the American is also much less familiar to us than that of the European or the Oriental. The French citizen, the English lord, the Russian peasant, the Eastern sage—they have become palpable realities to us through their literatures, offering perspectives on the spiritual and social structures of their nations. There are those who say we do possess the figure of the American in literature. But what do we know of their writings? Who in Germany reads [Joseph] Hergesheimer, [Theodore] Dreiser, Sinclair Lewis, [H. L.] Mencken . . . ? In Eugene O'Neill we became acquainted with our first American dramatist, and—let us be honest—he left us cold.

But we have other things: trusts, highrises, traffic officers, film, technical wonders, jazz bands, boxing, magazines, and management. Is that America? Perhaps. Since I have never been there, I can make no judgment. But I do know that the images of these things come to us from America. But does all this then amount to Americanism? Are these phenomena not much more than the external and revealed symptoms of a more secret, spiritual, soulful essence? Is Americanism not a new orientation to being, grown out of and formed in our European destiny? This is a question that the Viennese writer (who died a year ago) Robert Müller first raised and answered: "Americanism is therefore either a method or a fanaticism." And with this we come much closer to its character and its Europeanness.

In fact, Americanism is a new European method. The extent to which this method was itself influenced by America seems to me quite unimportant. It is a method of the concrete and of energy, and is completely attuned to spiritual and material reality. The European's new (Americanized) appearance corresponds to it too: beardless with a sharp profile, a resolute look in the eyes, and a steely, thin body; and the new female type (explained only minimally by sexology alone): boyish, linear, and ruled by lively movement, by her step, and by her leg. It is altogether fitting to the method of Americanism that it expresses itself very strongly in the corporal, that it possesses body-soul. This in no way implies superficiality, only a clear turn away from abstraction and sentimentality and a transformation of even our noblest capacities into the concreteness and wakeful liveliness best revealed by the body. (Sport is therefore but one symptom of this new inner split.) Concrete and unsentimental, thus in a positive sense naïve—such is the method of Americanism, in the life of the soul and the spirit as in practical affairs. No burden of culture weighs this method down. It is young, barbaric, uncultivated, willful. It has that free and strong breath we sense in the poems of Walt Whitman and which already enchanted Baudelaire. It follows no abstract or historical ideal, but instead follows life. Americanism is fanaticism for life, for its worldliness and its present-day forms.

Americanism thus appears as the strongest opponent of romanticism, which sought to flee worldliness. It is the natural enemy of all distraction from the present, whether through a backward-looking conception of history, through the mystical, or through intellectualism. Americanism is very northern, clear, and secure; it billows with a seawind. It has a strong and exact relation not only to the exactness of a machine, organization, economy but also to nature. It does not experience nature as a symbol of subjective feelings or as a Rousseauian idyll but as the mightiest and most extravagent reality, which people do not face, but in which and with which they live. This new experience of nature reverberates most strongly in the books by Knut Hamsun, as in the Scandinavian character in general—one thinks too of Johannes V. Jensen—he is very close to Americanism (which Robert Müller likewise emphasized). But it is Prussian in its sober technical methods and reaches down into the Latin countries insofar as clarity of form and rationalism are at issue. Nothing, however, is more foreign and bygone to Americanism than the old Russian East, its fatigue and passivity. Americanism hates unfruitful passions, the unplumbable depths of the soul, and a stifling, deadening religiosity. Only in the world of reality does it find a worthy test for humanity.

Marcel Proust's declaration, "Toute action de l'esprit est aisée, s'il n'est pas soumise au réel,"[1] is easily understood by Americanism (and, incidentally, understood in the sense of the American philosophy of pragmatism). But Paul Valéry's elevation of architecture to an ideal—not in the sense of classical laws of form but by virtue of the experience of building and statics—also contains a recognition, despite the writer's formal strictness and musicality, of reality. Perhaps, though, the proximity of these two Frenchmen to Americanism is controversial. Its literary inroads become clearer in cases of writers who consciously turn away from tradition in their desire to create a new world in a new form out of the radical experience of the immediate present, for example, the epic writers Alfred Döblin and Ilya Ehrenburg. Their novels are carried by the experience of collectivism; they are visions bursting with vitality and monumental legends of the present. Electrical centers explode into action and send their energy waves through the mechanized world. In the most recent Parisian literary fashion, Surrealism, the attempt is made to reduce this new experience of reality—a near total opposite of the old biological–romantic naturalism—to a theoretical formula.

But literature follows Americanism only minimally at first. Its vitality is still too overpowering and uncultivated, so that it is still sensed as nearly antiliterary. Its intellectual potential is still problematic. Perhaps it marks an end or an intermission in the cultural history of Europe; but perhaps as early as tomorrow we will find ourselves confronting a surprisingly new flowering. It would be fruitless to pose and solve puzzles here. On the other hand, it would be wrong to want to recognize the epoch only in the external phenomena of economy and exchange, thereby passing over the new orientations of the spirit. The present clings to reality as the most powerful creative substance, as energy, as mastery of the world.

Now should we complain or rejoice over Americanism? Neither. We sense its vitality and should not measure its manifestations against false standards.

---

1. "All action of the spirit is easy, if it is not subordinated to the real."

The jazz band, too, is force and sound, magical in the wild brilliance of its rhythm. But why, as we listen to the pounding of its instruments, speak of classical music?

151

STEFAN ZWEIG

The Monotonization of the World

First published as "Die Monotonisierung der Welt," *Berliner Börsen-Courier* (February 1, 1925).

Monotonization of the World. The most potent intellectual impression, despite the particular satisfactions enjoyed, of every journey in recent years is a slight horror in the face of the monotonization of the world. Everything is becoming more uniform in its outward manifestations, everything leveled into a uniform cultural schema. The characteristic habits of individual peoples are being worn away, native dress giving way to uniforms, customs becoming international. Countries seem increasingly to have slipped simultaneously into each other; people's activity and vitality follows a single schema; cities grow increasingly similar in appearance. Paris has been three-quarters Americanized, Vienna Budapested: more and more the fine aroma of the particular in cultures is evaporating, their colorful foliage being stripped with ever-increasing speed, rendering the steel-grey pistons of mechanical operation, of the modern world machine, visible beneath the cracked veneer.

This process has been underway for a long time: before the war [Walther] Rathenau prophesized this mechanization of existence, the dominance of technology, would be the most important aspect of our epoch. But never have the outward manifestations of our ways of life plunged so precipitously, so moodily into uniformity as in the last few years. Let us be clear about it! It is probably the most urgent, the most critical phenomenon of our time.

Symptoms. One could, to make the problem distinct, list hundreds. I will quickly select just a few of the most familiar, uncompromising examples, to show how greatly customs and habits have been monotonized and sterilized in the last decade.

The most conspicuous is dance. Two or three decades ago dance was still specific to nations and to the personal inclinations of the individual. One waltzed in Vienna, danced the csardas in Hungary, the bolero in Spain, all to the tune of countless different rhythms and melodies in which both the genius of an artist and the spirit of the nation took obvious form. Today millions of people, from Capetown to Stockholm, from Buenos Aires to Calcutta, dance the same dance to the same short-winded, impersonal melodies. They begin at the same hour. Like the muezzin in an oriental country call tens of thousands to a single prayer at sundown—like those twenty words, so now twenty beats at five in the afternoon call the whole of occidental humanity to the same ritual. Never, except in certain ecclesiastical formulas and forms, have two hundred million people hit upon such expressive simultaneity and uniformity as in the style of dance practiced by the modern white race of America, Europe, and the colonies.

A second example is fashion. Never before has such a striking uniformity developed in all countries as during our age. Once it took years for a fashion from Paris to reach other big cities, or to penetrate the countryside. A certain boundary protected people and their customs from its tyrannical demands. Today its dictatorship becomes universal in a heartbeat. New York decrees short hair for women: within a month, as if cut by the same scythe, 50 or 100 million female manes fall to the floor. No emperor, no khan in the history of the world ever experienced a similar power, no spiritual commandment a similar speed. Christianity and socialism required centuries and decades to win their followings, to enforce their commandments on as many people as a modern Parisian tailor enslaves in eight days.

A third example: cinema. Once again utter simultaneity in all countries and languages, the cultivation of the same performance, the same taste (or lack of it) in masses by the hundreds of millions. The complete cancellation of any individuality, though the manufacturers gloriously extol their films as national: the *Nibelungen* triumphs in Italy and Max Linder from Paris in the most German, most nationalistic constituencies. Here, too, the mass instinct is stronger and more authoritarian than the thought. Jackie Coogan's triumphal appearance was a more powerful experience for our day than was Tolstoy's death twenty years ago.

A fourth example is radio. All of these inventions have a single meaning: simultaneity. Londoners, Parisians, and Viennese listen at the same second to the same thing, and the supernatural proportions of this simultaneity, of this uniformity, are intoxicating. There is an intoxication, a stimulus for the masses, in all of these new technological miracles, and simultaneously an enormous sobriety of the soul, a dangerous seduction of the individual into passivity. Here too, as in dance, fashion, and the cinema, the individual acquiesces to a herdlike taste that is everywhere the same, no longer making choices that accord with internal being but ones that conform to the opinion of a world.

One could infinitely multiply these symptoms, and they multiply themselves from day to day on their own. The sense of autonomy in matters of pleasure is flooding the times. It will soon be harder to list the particularities of nations and cultures than the features they share in common.

Consequences. The complete end of individuality. It is not with impunity that everyone can dress the same, that all women can go out in the same clothes, the same makeup: monotony necessarily penetrates beneath the surface. Faces become increasingly similar through the influence of the same passions, bodies more similar to each other through the practice of the same sports, minds more similar for sharing the same interests. An equivalence of souls unconsciously arises, a mass soul created by the growing drive toward uniformity, an atrophy of nerves in favor of muscles, the extinction of the individual in favor of the type. Conversation, the art of speaking, is danced and sported away, theater brutalized into cinema; literature becomes the practice of momentary fashions, the "success of the season." Already, as in England, books are no longer produced for people, but increasingly as the "book of the season"; as in radio an instantaneous form of success is spreading which is announced simultaneously from all European stations, and annulled a second later. And since everything is geared to the shortest units of time, consumption increases: thus does genuine education—the patient accumulation of meaning over the course of a lifetime—become a quite rare phenomenon in our time, just like everything else that can be achieved only by individual exertion.

Origin. What is the source of this terrible wave threatening to wash all the color, everything particular out of life? Everyone who has ever been there knows: America. The historians of the future will one day mark the page following the great European war as the beginning of the conquest of Europe by America. Or, more accurately, the conquest is already rippingly underway, and we simply fail to notice it (conquered peoples are always too-slow thinkers). The European countries still find the receipt of a credit in dollars a cause for celebration. We continue to flatter ourselves with illusions of America's philanthropic and economic goals. In reality we are becoming colonies of its life, its way of life, slaves to an idea profoundly foreign to Europe: the mechanical idea.

But our economic obedience seems to me minor compared to the spiritual danger. The colonization of Europe would not be so terrible politically; to servile souls all slavery is mild and the free always know how to preserve their freedom. The genuine danger to Europe seems to me to be a matter of the spirit, of the importation of American boredom, of that dreadful, quite specific boredom that rises over there from every stone and every house on all the numbered streets. The boredom that does not, like the earlier European variety, come from calmness, from sitting on the park bench playing dominoes and smoking a pipe—a lazy waste of time indeed, but not dangerous. American boredom is restless, nervous, and aggressive; it outruns itself in its frantic haste, seeks numbness in sports and sensations. It has lost its playfulness, scurries along instead in the rabid frenzy of an eternal flight from time. It is always inventing new artifices for itself, like cinema and radio, to feed its hungry senses with nourishment for the masses, and it transforms this common interest in enjoyment into concerns as massive as its banks and trusts.

America is the source of that terrible wave of uniformity that gives everyone the same: the same overalls on the skin, the same book in the hand, the same pen between the fingers, the same conversation on the lips, and the same automobile instead of feet. From the other side of our world, from Russia, the same will to monotony presses ominously in a different form: the will to the compartmentalization of the individual, to uniformity in world views, the same dreadful will to monotony. Europe remains the last bulwark of individualism and, perhaps, of the overly taut cramp of peoples—our vigorous nationalism, despite all its senselessness, represents to some extent a fevered, unconscious rebellion, a last, desperate effort to defend ourselves against leveling. But precisely that cramped form of resistance betrays our weakness. Rome, the genius of sobriety, is already underway to wipe Europe, the last Greece in history, from the table of time.

Defense. What to do now? Storm the capitol, summon the people: "To the trenches, the barbarians are coming to destroy our world!" Cry out once more in Caesar's words, this time more earnestly: "People of Europe, preserve your most sacred possessions!" No, we are no longer gullible enough to believe that with associations, with books and proclamations, we can rise up against a world-encompassing movement of such a monstrous sort and defeat the drive to monotonization. Whatever one might write, it remains a piece of paper cast against a gale. Whatever we might write, it does not reach the soccer players and the shimmy dancers, and if it did, they would no longer understand it. In all of these things, of which I am mentioning only a few, in the cinema, in radio, in dance, in all of these new means for mechanizing humanity there is an enormous power that is not to be overcome. For they all fulfill the highest ideal of the average: to offer amusement without demanding exertion. And their insurmountable strength lies in the fact that they are unprecedentedly comfortable. The new dance can be learned by the dumbest servant girl in three hours; the cinema delights the illiterate and demands of them not a grain of education; to enjoy radio one need only take the earpiece from the table and hang it on one's head, and already there is a waltz ringing in the ear—against such comfort even the gods would fight in vain. Whoever demands only a minimum of intellectual, physical, and moral exertion is bound to triumph among the masses, for the majority is passionately in favor of such; whoever continues to demand autonomy, independence of judgment, personality—even in entertainment—would appear ridiculous against such an enormously superior power. If humanity is now letting itself be increasingly bored and monotonized, then that is really nothing other than its deepest desire. Autonomy in the conduct of one's life and even in the enjoyment of life has by now become a goal for so few people that most no longer feel how they are becoming particles, atoms in the wash of a gigantic power. So they bathe in the warm stream that is carrying them off to the trivial. As Caesar said: *ruere in servitium,* to rush into servitude—this passion for self-dissolution has destroyed every nation. Now it is Europe's turn: the world war was the first phase, Americanization is the second.

152

FRIEDRICH VON GOTTL-OTTLILIENFELD

Fordism

First published in *Fordismus. Über Industrie und technische Vernunft* (Jena: Verlag von Gustav Fischer, 1926), 6, 13, 16–18.

While the creativity of Fordist methods is manifest on the level of immense systems of plants taken together, the Taylor system is meant for exclusive application to single plants that have already been established and organized. The goal of the latter is to improve plant operations in a single, one-sided fashion—namely, through technical refinements in the way work is performed, that is, in the execution of jobs in the plant. The basic idea of the system derives from its focus on regular drudge work: loading iron ingots, shoveling ore, etc. The story of Schmidt, the valiant ore shoveler, continues to circulate through the world making propaganda for the Taylor system.

For [Frederick Winslow] Taylor, the point of departure lies in plant management. That is always an important matter. A plant can be organized in this way or that and as a consequence be capable of greater or lesser productive potential, since everything finally depends on how able the directors and employees are in getting something out of it; or, more precisely, on what the administration and the workforce are able to wring from the plant once they seriously get down to work. That obviously depends on the output potential of human action, on how it is integrated in its manifold types and forms into the chain of effects represented by the plant. Now Taylor attempts to get the most out of it from the outset by aiming at the highest possible performance, toward which end those involved are expected to give their best. Maximum performance, however, is a goal that can be pursued in a wide variety of ways. The Taylor system represents only one of them! This striving for maximum performance, a very significant goal, I have called Taylorism, and it has filled the soul of every capable plant manager since long before Taylor. Taylor, however, has worked more effectively in its favor than anyone before; above all he has sharpened the critical eye focused on plant operations and preached the necessity of a regular stock-taking to management. No one but he, that is, can claim to have cultivated a science of work, the promotion of which is incumbent upon those branches of scientific research where the forms of expertise associated with the discipline intersect. [. . .]

Maximum performance reaches its peak in the plants of the Ford Motor Company. I do not mean so much the mathematical success that can be measured in the output potential of the individual worker, which may still be subject to increase by Taylorism. But the completely different approach adopted by Ford is infinitely more fruitful in terms of overall success. Here that "supreme individual potential," of which Count [Ferdinand] Degenfeld-Schonburg speaks in his instructive book,[1] is transmitted to the whole plant; it is transmitted down from the top—which in this case is Henry Ford. [Hugo] Münsterberg's representation of the "spirit of individual initiative at the margins" as one of the characteristic features of Americanism is well known; and the Ford plants themselves do in fact "Americanize" their numerous acquisitions, or they get rid of them—both principles quite contrary to Taylorism. But what radiates more strongly from the top—in absolute contrast to Taylorism—is the vital spirit of the personality! It blows through the whole gigantic operation and draws every last worker into its wake.

There are, for example, no departments at Ford, nor any permanent, titled positions. Someone needs only to deliver the proof that he, in some way or another beneficial to the indefatigable completion of the whole, knows how to produce a result, and he has obtained a position for himself and will be better paid for it. Departmental responsibilities do not exist; no one, however, not even the last drudge worker, is deprived of the purely human responsibility for what he does and does not do. There is no coordination of the lines of command of any kind, not a trace of the drab horror of a conventional office; a personnel office serves as the registry for the plant and that is all. Only the top management has a staff, such as the executive general staff for the really big issues. The only ones who hold their own up there are those who do not turn into narrow-minded experts; for what Ford wants to say, wants to believe, is this: that people already have the best solutions for everything in their heads. Nor could a more unpardonable offense to the spirit of the Ford plant be conceived. Nothing is already or ever will be fully developed and perfect in Henry Ford's eyes! He is dynamism personified. It is truly as if this most American of all industrial organizations were the intellectual embodiment of activism, of, strictly speaking, the meliorism of William James. [. . .]

It is no mere distance but a profound and purely intellectual contradiction that separates Ford from Taylor! What Taylor accomplishes through his ingeniously thought-out system of management Ford achieves as well, but through the completely different, thrilling verve of leadership. To judge by the many interesting examples Ford cites from the concrete world of his plants, the output potential of a Ford worker is scarcely inferior to that of a Taylor worker. It is only that this amounts to the whole of Taylor's success, with the question remaining of how much his direction detracts from it. Meanwhile it represents only a partial success for Ford when his workers owe the plant nothing in the way of honest performance, and this concerning a plant to which he lends such grandiose form quite independently of questions of individual output! For Ford plays not only the role of the watchmaker simply "mending" the flaws in plant operations; he is also the mighty forger who hammers the plant into shape in the red-hot glow of stormy transformations.

I scarcely believe that anyone would have to struggle harder than myself against the temptation of following in Ford's footsteps precisely in the context of his incomparable example of the administration of technical reason. I will content myself with a single example, which, however, is equally singular in kind. This example, incidentally, also blesses

1. Ferdinand Graf von Degenfeld-Schonburg, *Die Lohntheorien von Adam Smith, David Ricardo, John Stuart Mill und Karl Marx,* (Munich and Leipzig: Duncker und Humblot, 1914).

the quite numerous family of my *Principles of Technical Reason* with a new member: it falls, namely, under the principle of the "unitary linkage of all processes through intersecting pathways"—a highly gifted offspring of my principle of "properly linked execution"!

Every Ford automobile is composed of more than 5,000 parts, all of them interchangeable, so that each part would fit in its assigned place on every car. Even though this number naturally includes many of the same parts, and even though the numerous machines devoted to their manufacture operate in concert (accomplishing much while demanding little in the way of operator movements, little in the way of labor), about 8,000 different functions still result.

Every worker is devoted to only one function, but the same function is often assigned to several and even many workers, for in all Ford employs not 8,000 but 50,000 workers, the majority of whom are continually occupied operating machines. Ford calculates that it would take 2,000,000 trained workers, specialists of all sorts, if one were to match the production of his plants by traditional toolmakers' means; he is obviously presupposing optimum organization and the highest level of desire on the part of the workers, so that given production in artisanal style these millions would have to be further multiplied. In any case, it is necessary to distribute properly in space not only the workers but also the machines they are to operate. Expressed more precisely, the various processes themselves, which are at the same time the specific acts in the production process, must be arranged properly in space. For that there is only one law: that productive functions be organized into an ideal succession; and this ideal of a closed, unified production process—for the processes in fact are accomplished in separate locations—simultaneously generates an ideal arrangement of processes, that is, of machines and workers. For a product as complex as an automobile does not result from a linear process, but from the coordinated march of interwoven tasks. At first they march separately, that is, the parts are conducted through to completion individually from station to station; then they are put together one after the other, that is, "assembled" (in that, for example, a wheel is made up of a rim, hub, and spokes); likewise must the chassis be put together, and the motor, and finally the automobile as a whole. It is also always necessary to conceive of these assembly procedures as a succession of operations, so that here too an organized march results: from the basic part, for example, a wheel rim—to which the spokes are attached one after the other and then the latter connected in succession to the hub—to the point of final completion.

153

FRIEDRICH SIEBURG

Worshipping Elevators

First published as "Anbetung von Fahrstühlen," *Die literarische Welt* 2, no. 30 (July 23, 1926), 8.

Everyday the resort towns on the California coast hold beauty pageants. Seventy-five virgins clad in scanty tricot show what God gave them. They arrive in long chains, lay their hands on one another's shoulders, and march through the market square or along the boardwalk. Once the photographers have finished, powerful, square-shouldered men approach to fasten banners around the girls' bellies, with numbers visible from a distance. The police maintain order (keeping special watch over the fiends on whom the display has some kind of effect) as a commission put together of film directors, girl traffickers, ministers, artists, and other specialists works to assess the limbs in particular and the overall impression in general. The Taylor system is used here too. One concerns himself only with the legs, the other with the line of the back, the third takes the face into account, a fourth measures bottoms, so that the result is achieved rather quickly. It turns out that Miss Williams from Salt Lake City wins first prize. The biggest of the square-shouldered men comes forward to wrap a starred banner around her middle, so that the tempting stomach muscles are no longer visible. The band picks up a patriotic tune. Old people who still remember the Civil War wipe away a tear. The minister congratulates the dear girl and entreats her to continue to bring her parents joy.

A man emerges from the crowd and pinches her on the fanny—the least he could do—and is seized by the indignant crowd, tarred, feathered, and thrown into the water.

Meanwhile, lyricists of all ages in Europe are writing their excited homages to the American tempo, how it finds its supreme expression in elevators, and to the American spirit, how it primarily appears in a quickly resolved attack and the lightning-quick conclusion of agreements. Moved, they celebrate the speedy performance of tasks in New York hotels—for example, when one sends a pair of pants away to be ironed. Almost sobbing, they praise the way traffic is managed and toss the old German God determinedly overboard from the decks of smooth-running Hudson River boats.

The American businessman, who dispatches several wagons loaded with cornmeal or railroad ties over the telephone, has worked a profound effect on German literature. He is characterized as "cold, hard, and unbending"; one idiot even speaks of Napoleon's American traits. Because one does not understand these people's language, because one sees that they do not wear moustaches, that they do not speak Yiddish, one believes them to be Caesars. Their dialogue as they discuss freight instructions is taken for economical, their padded shoulders appear monumental, their uniform faces, six of one, a half-dozen of the other, seem to be masks of iron. In short, in view of their own lachrymose sentimentality, verbosity, and inability to master a shipping schedule, writers import the American face into literature.

This is a disgraceful reaction to the alleged failure of the European tradition. For how does America represent itself in its own statements, to the extent that they even reach Europe? How does it present itself in its films, in its reporting, in its novels, in its politics, and in its illustration industry? Its relation to God is known from the Scopes Monkey Trial, its relation to women from films and novels, in which sexual intercourse can only appear in the form of a rape in the untamed forest or a bad neighborhood. The middle-class American brings his children into the world with a fade-out or by closing the chapter with an enticing "to be continued." Then one day the children are suddenly there, and, late in an evening, the husband stops to knock on his wife's bedroom door to discuss the household budget or announce the acquisition of a new automobile. On hot days women drive through the city streets of Chicago in bathing suits—one learns by watching that a contest for the prettiest legs is somehow bound up with the trip—but should the sight cause anyone to have impure thoughts, a policeman reads it on his face and drags him into court. As compensation the young men in films beat one another's faces bloody with their fists while the pure young lady stands quivering in the background. The one who gets knocked out is, of course, the one who attempted a rape, because one day he had seen the young lady ride her bicycle down the street in a bathing suit. The victor takes her off to a minister, and, in some mysterious way in the intermission between the fifth and sixth acts, a child appears who will later grow up to be one hundred percent American—anti-Semite, football player, and virtuous husband.

What America produces in the way of artistic and moral values comes from the pariahs of the country, the Negroes, Jews, and Germans. They are persecuted and oppressed, and deprived, with justice, of the title of a one-hundred-percent American.

What in the world drives a portion of Berlin's literati to admire these people, to write millionaire dramas, to adorn boxers with halos, to depict Canadian lumber traders, to worship elevators, to prattle on about steel rhythms, to kneel before the General Motors Company? A writer nearly burst into tears because he heard a song on a gramophone in which the singers said "Tyenaseee" instead of Tennessee. Why is this? What does he say when he hears "Laipzch" instead of Leipzig? Is a new romanticism being born here? Should [Peter] Rosegger or [Arthur] Achleitner be repressed?[1] Perhaps country boys and girls are putting on airs, and maybe the tuxedo no longer suggests a contrast. This is how we begin now: "McCormick reached for the telephone and, with an iron expression on his face, ordered the twelve train cars with wheat for Ohio off onto dead-end tracks." I do not see the alternatives being between an ideology that throws a certain human type—the peasant—into relief and opens the way to general admiration and one which idealizes motors, elevators, and businessmen at the expense of other human and figurative values. Without denying that a skyscraper and a forest both have their aesthetic value, I still do not agree that they are particularly to be recommended as ideal symbols. The so-called Americanization of the world is certainly not yet an established fact.

Such unfamiliarity with the world is expressed in this engineer romanticism, which does not understand the workings of a carburetor and therefore hears the breath of our time in the pounding of six cylinders. Where one once wore velvet skirts and loose neckties, one now goes around in a leather jacket. I see no difference. It is astounding that a writer of animal stories, Charles Robert, is celebrated and by exactly the same people who make fun of [Hermann] Löns, who is certainly no worse. Germany will soon make a place for the stories of [Thomas Henry] Marshal and [James Oliver] Curwood in which disillusioned amateur hunters gather up virginal daughters of millionaires, drape them over their horses, and gallop off to the preacher. And they will be taken seriously for the reason that they take place in New Brunswick and not on the Luneberg heath.

The machine need not be an enemy, nor should it be an object of worship. It has released other powers, but has created no new ones. The machine can be understood and, to the mechanic, is not a mystical object. Why then for the writers? How can something learnable inspire reverence? One looks with regret at the replacement of Hölderlin's Greece by America just because some people do not know what happens on the wheat exchange in Chicago or inside an electrical power plant.

154

SIEGFRIED KRACAUER

The Mass Ornament

First published as "Das Ornament der Masse," *Frankfurter Zeitung,* no. 420 (June 9, 1927).

The position that an epoch occupies in the historical process can be determined more strikingly through an analysis of its inconspicuous surface-level expressions than from that epoch's judgments about itself. Since these judgments are expressions of the tendencies of a particular era, they do not offer conclusive testimony about its overall constitution. The

---

1. Peter Rosegger (1843–1918) and Arthur Achleitner (1858–1927) were rural poets in Southern Germany.

surface-level expressions, however, by virtue of their unconscious nature, provide unmediated access to the fundamental substance of the state of things. Conversely, knowledge of this state of things depends on the interpretation of these surface-level expressions. The fundamental substance of an epoch and its unheeded impulses illuminate one another reciprocally.

In the domain of body culture, which also covers the illustrated newspapers, a change in taste has been quietly taking place. It began with the *Tiller Girls*. These products of American distraction factories are no longer individual girls, but indissoluble girl clusters whose movements are demonstrations of mathematics. As they condense into figures in the revues, performances of the same geometrical exactitude are taking place in what is always the same packed *stadium,* be it in Australia or India, not to mention America. The tiniest village, which they have not yet reached, learns about them through the weekly newsreels. One need only glance at the screen to learn that the ornaments are comprised of thousands of bodies, sexless bodies in bathing suits. The regularity of their patterns is cheered by the masses, themselves arranged by the stands in tier upon ordered tier.

These extravagant spectacles, which are not only staged by girls and stadium dwellers, have long since become an established form. They have gained *international* stature and are the focus of aesthetic interest.

The bearer of the ornaments is the *mass* and not the people, for whenever the people form figures, the latter do not hover in mid-air but arise out of a community. A current of organic life surges from these communal groups—who share a common destiny—to their ornaments, endowing these ornaments with a magic force and so burdening them with meaning that they cannot be reduced to a pure assemblage of lines. Those who have withdrawn from the community and consider themselves to be unique personalities with their own individual souls also fail when it comes to forming these new patterns. Were they to take part in such a performance, the ornament would not transcend them. It would be a colorful composition which could not be worked out to its logical conclusion since its points—like prongs of a rake—would be implanted in the intermediate strata of the soul, a residue of which would survive. The patterns seen in the stadiums and cabarets betray no such origins. They are composed of elements which are mere building blocks and nothing more. The construction of the edifice depends on the size of the stones and their number. It is the mass that is employed here. Only as parts of a mass, not as individuals who believe themselves to be formed from within, do people become fractions of a figure.

The ornament is an *end in itself.* Earlier ballet also used to yield ornaments, which arose in kaleidoscopic fashion. But even after discarding their ritual meaning, these remained the plastic expression of erotic life, an erotic life that both gave rise to them and determined their traits. The mass movements of the girls, by contrast, take place in a vacuum; they are a linear system that no longer has any erotic meaning but at best points to the locus of the erotic. Moreover, the meaning of the living star formations in the stadiums is not that of military evolutions. No matter how regular the latter may turn out to be, that regularity was considered a means to an end; the parade march arose out of patriotic feelings and in turn aroused them in soldiers and subjects. The star formations, however, have no meaning beyond themselves, and the masses above whom they rise are not a moral unit like a company of soldiers. One cannot even describe the figures as the decorative frills of gymnastic discipline. Rather, the girl-units drill in order to produce an immense number of parallel lines, the goal being to train the broadest mass of people in order to create a pattern of undreamt-of dimensions. The end result is the ornament, whose closure is brought about by emptying all the substantial constructs of their contents.

Although the masses give rise to the ornament, they are not involved in thinking it through. As linear as it may be, there is no line that extends from the small sections of the mass to the entire figure. The ornament resembles the *aerial photographs* of landscapes and cities in that it does not emerge out of the interior of the given conditions, but rather appears above them. Actors too do not grasp the stage setting in its totality, yet they consciously take part in its construction; and even in the case of ballet figurines, the figure is still subject to the influence of its performers. The more the coherence of the figure is relinquished in favor of a mere linearity, the further it becomes removed from the immanent consciousness of those constituting it. Yet this does not lead to its being scrutinized by a more incisive gaze. In fact, nobody would notice the figure at all if the crowd of spectators, who have an aesthetic relation to the ornament and do not represent anyone, were not sitting in front of it.

The ornament, detached from its bearers, must be understood *rationally*. It consists of lines and circles like those found in textbooks of Euclidean geometry, and also incorporates the elementary components of physics, such as waves and spirals. Both the proliferations of organic forms and the radiations of spiritual life remain excluded. The *Tiller Girls* can no longer be reassembled into human beings after the fact, their mass gymnastics are never performed by the fully preserved bodies whose contortions defy rational understanding. Arms, thighs, and other segments are the smallest component parts of the composition.

The structure of the mass ornament reflects that of the entire contemporary situation. Since the principle of the *capitalist production process* does not arise purely out of nature, it must destroy the natural organisms that it regards either as means or as resistance. Community and personality perish when what is demanded is calculability; it is only as a tiny piece of the mass that the individual can clamber up charts and service machines without any friction. A system oblivious to differences in form leads on its own to the blurring of national characteristics and to the production of worker masses that can be employed equally well at any point on the globe.

Like the mass ornament, the capitalist production process is an end in itself. The commodities that it spews forth are not actually produced to be possessed, but rather for the sake of a profit that knows no limit. Its growth is tied to that of business. The producer does not labor for private gains whose benefits he can only enjoy to a limited extent—in America the surplus profits are directed to spiritual shelters such as libraries, universities, etc., which cultivate intellectuals whose later endeavors repay with interest the previously advanced capital. No: the producer labors in order to expand the business. The production of value is not for the sake of value. Though labor may well have once served to produce and consume values up to a certain point, these have now become side effects in the service of the production process. The activities subsumed by that process have divested themselves of their substantial contents. The production process runs its secret course in public. Everyone does their task on the conveyor belt, performing a partial function without grasping the totality. Like the pattern in the stadium, the organization stands above the masses, a monstrous figure whose creator withdraws it from the eyes of its bearers, and barely even observes it himself. It is conceived according to rational principles which the Taylor system only pushes to their ultimate conclusion. The hands in the factory correspond to the legs of the *Tiller Girls*. Going beyond merely manual capacities, psycho-technical aptitude tests attempt to calculate dispositions of the soul as well. The mass ornament is the aesthetic reflex of the rationality aspired to by the prevailing economic system.

Educated people—who are never completely lacking—have taken offense at the emergence of the *Tiller Girls* and the stadium images. They judge anything that entertains the crowd to be a distraction of that crowd. Contrary to their opinion, the *aesthetic* pleasure gained from the ornamental mass movements is *legitimate*. They are in fact among the rare creations of the age that bestow form upon a given material. The masses organized in these movements come from the offices and factories; the formal principle according to which they are molded determines them in reality as well. When significant components of reality become invisible in our world, art must make do with what is left, for an aesthetic presentation is all the more real the less it dispenses with the reality outside the aesthetic sphere. No matter how low one gauges the value of the mass ornament, its degree of reality is still higher than that of artistic productions which cultivate outdated noble sentiments in obsolete forms—even if it means nothing more than that.

155

ADOLF HALFELD

America and the New Objectivity

First published as "Amerika und die neue Sachlichkeit," *Der Diedrichs-Löwe* 2 no. 4 (1928), 244–248.

We speak of Americanization, New Objectivity, nationalization, and chauffeur people with an absolutism, as if that was also enough to satisfy the cultural needs of a civilized people. We underscore the observation that the American worker in some branches produces two to three times the number of goods as a German worker in a given period of time, all the while failing to ask whether the American worker also lays claim to three times as much inspiration and beauty. We rave about American bustle and traffic and attempt foolishly to forget how productive Germany is in its leisure. What is the meaning of three-floor apartment houses if the people who have to live in them are ten thousand floors farther from the sun and the spirit?

The content of Americanism reaches its peak not in cultural values but in the idea of success. Work only rarely means something for its own sake to Americans. The creative will has perished. Visual beauty counts only insofar as it serves that abstraction called profitability. There is no heritage of craftsmanship in America because it never had any place for the love and attention that crafts born of the soil and tradition lavished on single objects. They are unprofitable because they cannot be transformed into mass-consumption goods.

Thus arises the grotesque reversal of the American conception of work in the new world: not its objective, social utility but what it weighs in hard cash determines the value of creativity. It remained for Americanism to imbue its youth with a kind of new idealism, which, as "business idealism," produced the extraordinary trinity of God, money-making, and bourgeois virtues. In this peculiar order of moral values it can happen that shrewd real estate speculators and stock traders, blessed with a little luck, become the idols of ability and moral veneration, while pure creativity in all forms not immediately concerned with success assumes the status of a social wallflower.

This world-historical experiment of the American crossbreed, this grandly singular attempt to bring forth from a thousand resistant strains a new political order in the space of a few decades, has as its precondition an unprecedented simplification of all vital principles. Rooted here is the civilization of the mass individual in the most profound sense. If in other cultures the variety of interests, heritage, and character propels people along different paths, the American always departs from a single question that guides all thinking and overshadows all activity: how can I get rich the quickest? That is the origin of the undeniable monotony of American life, which does not become the less obvious for all the bustle in the streets, which permeates the theaters, churches, and schools, and which does not stop at the gates to the cultured world. For the principle of success exerts a dictatorship over the people that imperceptibly alters the face, extinguishes psychological differentiation, and deadens the inner sense for the refined sides of life.

What, however, have we European peoples, so near to each other in a deeper human sense and yet so evolved as individual nations, so vital in the creative interactions of our particular aspects and yet so fatefully rooted in the mythical underground of original tribes—what, I ask, have we in common with an America that, in order to meld Japanese with German or English with Negroes into an accidental, abstract nation, had to transplant the much-reviled militarism of the barracks into life itself? Californian fruit growers have succeeded in raising pineapples, melons, and grapefruit that far exceed their natural size—but they also robbed them of their heaven-sent fragrance and aroma. And thus it is everywhere in this instrumental culture.

It is the European community's world of symbols and ideas itself which the historically rootless normative ideal of Americanism opposes. They are essentially alien to each other and mutually exclusive: Americanism cannot be imported, and the new—even the unlimited and general—can only be sewn on living national soil. [. . .]

As a geographical unit America is a bounded continent; as a national unit it is planned; and it is based culturally in the intellectual world of the Puritans. What results from that is its independence from foreign as well as historical influences, while the people have become accustomed, in a long historical process, to guide their lives by a certain standard set of norms. American children are drilled "like the rest of them"; their judgment will be regulated to the grave by platitudes the sheer multitude of which would astound us.

For this reason, mass civilization could develop there more purely than anywhere else. From the start America was the land of regulated happiness. The guidance of the masses in the sense of an ordered, rational life is the idea upon which the rational state is based. Scarcely modern therefore is this "new, American objectivity," and hardly the logical result of the economic turn toward mass operations.

If then one speaks of the American principle of the collective, one does so with good reason. But it would be overhasty as well to prescribe, as a general cure, this new, supraindividual objectivity to the highly complicated soul of the European continent.

156

FELIX STÖSSINGER

The Anglicization of Germany

First published as "Die Anglisierung Deutschlands," *Sozialistische Monatshefte*, no. 35 (August 1929), 695–707.

Germany today offers the following spectacle: while the body of the Reich is being enchained by the Anglo-Saxons, its spirit is all but ecstatic in its thirst for anglicization.

Filled with the spirit of Anglo-Saxonism, the press and public opinion proudly and boastfully fancy to themselves and all the world that Germany is the most "American" of the European countries and for that reason obviously the leader of all of non-Anglo-Saxon humanity. And, as if seeking confirmation of this affirmation, the public grabs greedily and lustily at every scrap of Anglo-Saxonism it can have; it decorates itself with all kinds of linguistic thingamajigs, with the tinsel, fads, and absurdities of the Anglo-Saxon habitat, to cover the nakedness of its poor Europeanness in shame. Germany actually is adopting more and more of the manners and external appearance of a newly won English colony; it looks down like a parvenu on all the peoples who refuse to allow themselves to be anglicized, and considers this state of affairs to be Americanism. Whatever catchword one might choose to designate this process, it is important to establish that the anglicization sweeping over us like a storm is not, as is so often asserted, the course of the world in general against which it would be senseless to rise up, but that it is we who are diligently applying this new Indian coloration to ourselves. From out of the Anglo-Saxon psychosis of German foreign policy there has emerged as reflex and consequence an Anglo-Saxon psychosis of the mind, and thereby an endangerment of Germany and Europe. For the complacent abandonment of the mind and creativity to Anglo-Saxonism will inescapably work its reciprocal effect on foreign policy, and the anglicization of the spirit stemming from a false foreign policy will hasten and approve the further mistakes of such a policy. [. . .]

In no other nation is the inferiority complex in relation to Anglo-Saxonism as pathologically immense as in Germany. The material superiority of America has simply overpowered us. Is, however, American material superiority really the same as intellectual superiority? [. . .]

In its desire to anglicize itself, Germany has moved beyond the reach of reason; it works with all its might, by anglicizing its youth, to have its false image of the world prevail. In every branch of higher education the French language has either been supplanted entirely by the English or is in a clearly subordinate position. Schools are vigorously doing everything possible to prevent the new generation from fulfilling its continental European mission. That amounts to a slap in the face of the meaning of school and education. For all education ultimately has the obligation of making people capable of performing specific tasks. It is scarcely possible to conceive a case in which the anglicization of the mind as an act of political will would be any clearer than in the following. The German schools were anglicized in an act of senseless rage, of the senseless embitterment of the German Reich toward France. Although this is beyond dispute, I was just recently forced to witness how a figure close to the school system, who himself finds the matter worrisome, wrongly and naïvely expressed the usual view that the anglicization of the youth is the consequence of economic necessity. Today it has already been forgotten that during the war over the Ruhr things French were displaced by things English, and that this was a symbol of passive resistance against France. As Freud says, one forgets whatever one wishes not to know. [. . .]

The Anglo-Saxon psychosis has also left its mark on German literature. But even with the best of intentions, our writers could borrow nothing truly valuable from Anglo-Saxon literature, which, in a German version, would have retained its Anglo-Saxon effect. We therefore invent a super-Anglo-Saxonism, a super-Americanism, which does not exist at all over there, since the ideology of so-called Americanism is a product of our own mind. As a result, a rhythm is unleashed here, a Broadway-ism, that would thoroughly frighten a New Yorker. What is not English is given an English title. Thus the ballads of François Villon from the French Middle Ages are published here as "songs"; it cannot be done any other way. And what disappointment there will be one day in Germany when it becomes apparent that the famous New York tempo is largely a fantasy from Breslau and Prague. The best and most insightful letter about America, written by Ferrucio Busoni to the *Vossische Zeitung* on July 21, 1915, which the paper did not dare publish until twelve years later, rightly identifies "the slowness and old-fashionedness" of America. But something like that passes by German newspaper readers without leaving a trace. The Kurfürstendamm in Berlin does not want to be robbed of its America. Someday it will have to accept the fact that the "furious" American tempo has nothing to do with America but instead with large, unified economic regions, and that our tempo will leave America's behind as soon as the European continent has unified itself economically. That is why we demand the correct Americanism instead of the false one, that is, the transfer of the foundations of the American achievement, along with all of the consequences that have resulted from it, to Germany, to Europe.

157

OTTO BAUER

[Rationalization and the Social Order]

First published in *Kapitalismus und Sozialismus nach dem Weltkrieg,* vol. 1, *Rationalisierung, Fehlrationalisierung* (Berlin: Büchergilde Gutenberg, 1931), 161–163.

THE ESSENCE OF RATIONALIZATION

We now have sufficient facts for an overview, which will make us aware of the essence and meaning of rationalization. The word rationalization is used in various ways.

It is used chiefly to designate a *unique historical process*. When the German nation returned to a stable currency after the catastrophic inflation of 1923, and when, with the currency stabilization, the German economy suffered an over-supply crisis, German industry was forced to adjust to the changed market conditions. German entrepreneurs and their industrial bureaucracies took up the chant: "Our plants are obsolete! We are not competitive! We have to rationalize our plants!" German industry had to catch up with the technological development the United States had been undergoing since 1914. And hand in hand with the technological renovation of the German production apparatus went the development of industrial cooperation, the introduction of new practices aimed at the rationalization and intensification of labor, and the standardization of plant management on a scientific basis. This whole process of swiftly adapting German industry to the new conditions was completed between 1924 and 1929, and came to be summarized as rationalization. This usage was also taken over by other nations whose economies were in need of a similar process of conversion.

Rationalization created its own market. Since the whole of German industry was being renovated technologically, since new plants were being installed and the old reorganized, and new machines were being put to work, the demand for building materials, machines, tools, and steel was very high. The branches of industry specializing in the means of production experienced brisk sales. Since they employed more workers at better wages, the market for those industries producing consumer goods also expanded. Thus was the economic crisis following the stabilization of the mark overcome in 1926. The years 1926 to 1928 were the years of the great *rationalization boom*. That was when German capitalism believed it possible quickly to overcome the economic effects of the war and Germany's defeat through rationalization; when general economic optimism made it easier for German workers and employees to achieve significant increases in wages and salaries; when living standards in Germany rose rapidly; when German democracy was consolidated; and when the German people were eager supporters of [Gustav] Stresemann's peaceful foreign policy.

But the rationalization boom necessarily came to a speedy end. As soon as the majority of enterprises were finished renovating their plant technologically, the process of technological adaptation had to proceed more slowly. The slowing caused the demand for manufactured goods to fall, confronting the industries with stagnation. In turn, the layoff of large numbers of workers led to a downturn in the consumer-goods industry. Thus in 1929 a severe economic crisis set in. Following the rationalization boom came the *rationalization crisis*. The enterprises that had expanded their plant capacity so dramatically from 1924 to 1928 now saw that they could not sell the quantity of goods they were able to produce and could not adequately exploit the new plant and machinery they had installed. The optimism inspired by rationalization dwindled. People began to complain that there had been too much rationalization and it had been undertaken too hastily, that it was in many cases a "false rationalization." The belief that it was possible to overcome the effects of the war through rationalization diminished. The ensuing disillusion turned against democracy, which was supposedly unable to restore the economy, against the working class, whose wages had allegedly become too high, against the policy of negotiation, which seemed to have meekly ceded a high tribute paid out of the product of German labor to the victorious powers. A wave of nationalistic, antidemocratic reaction washed over the nation in 1930. In a similar way, the enthusiasm for rationalization faded in other countries as well. If the United States had proclaimed its belief in the triumph of rationalization by electing Herbert Hoover, the creator of the rationalization organization, to the presidency, his popularity began to decline in the fall of 1929 as the rationalization boom there also gave way to the rationalization crisis.

16
Berlin and the Countryside

RAPID URBANIZATION in the years after the founding of the Reich in 1871 touched every area of German life. From economic development to social attitudes to the flowering of important cultural and intellectual trends, the growth of the modern metropolis (evoked in the term *Die Großstadt*) was a pervasive force the significance of which cannot be emphasized enough. Yet the popular (and largely correct) view of the Weimar Republic as a cultural enterprise dominated by cities risks becoming myopic if not contextualized within the demographic figures of the time. Of the sixty-three million inhabitants counted in the 1925 German census, only 27 percent lived in the forty-five cities of more than 100,000. Another 27 percent lived in cities of between 5,000 and 100,000 dwellers. And, perhaps most revealingly, 46 percent of the population lived in communities of under 5,000 residents. Despite the dramatic, long-term trend toward urbanization in Germany (in 1871 76 percent of the population had lived in towns with fewer than 5,000 inhabitants), the populace of the Weimar Republic was primarily rural, living mostly in small villages and towns.

Unlike France, where centralization traditionally maintained Paris as the focal point of culture, no single German city during the Weimar Republic monopolized control of artistic and intellectual life. Theater, music, architecture, art, literature, and scholarship thrived in Dresden, Munich, Hamburg, Frankfurt am Main, Stuttgart, Leipzig, and Hannover. By the end of the republic, fifty-five German cities contained more than 50,000 people, and ten contained over 500,000. Yet no German metropolis enjoyed the cosmopolitan mythos of Berlin, which in the eyes of many seemed synonymous with all that was most hopeful and exciting—or alternately troubling and dysfunctional—about Weimar culture. With 4.3 million inhabitants by the early 1930s, it was nearly four times the size of the next largest metropolis, Hamburg. Unquestionably the most international of German cities, Berlin was home to many foreigners, one of whom, the British diplomat and historian Harold Nicolson, who was also the husband of Vita Sackville-West, wrote of his affection for it.

Prominent figures in culture, business, and politics resided in or frequently visited Berlin, whose status as film and media center of the republic insured that its fashions and sensations would capture attention throughout the world.

Already renowned as the gathering spot for the generation of expressionist writers before World War I, the Romanic Café was home to many Berlin celebrities and eccentrics, a mingling ground for a cross-section of German society, as Matheo Quinz suggests. A different face of the city is explored by Franz Hessel, a close friend of Walter Benjamin (with whom he translated Proust into German). Appropriating the rich literary legacy of the flaneur, the urban stroller invoked by Baudelaire and other chroniclers of urban modernity, Hessel recounts his walks through old and out-of-the-way neighborhoods.

Writing under the pseudonym Ignaz Wrobel, Kurt Tucholsky surveyed the mutual suspicions between Berliners and country dwellers. Finding little support for republican principles in rural Germany, he urged fellow intellectuals to nurture democratic and progressive tendencies in the provinces. Tucholsky also exploded the myth of Berlin as a haven of tolerance, claiming that only its size thwarted the forces of conservative reaction, thus reminding his readers of the difference between cultural prestige and political power. A graphic example of conservative anti-urban reaction is contained in Wilhelm Stapel's essay in which he combines invective against cultural modernity with a racist fear of the Jewish and East European "other." Less impassioned but still suspicious of Berlin, Ludwig Finckh viewed the atmosphere during the January 1919 upheavals from the perspective of the Swabian hinterland and underscored the political distance between the capital and the rest of Germany. The philosopher Martin Heidegger offered his own defense of the countryside in a radio talk he broadcast and then published as an explanation of his refusal to leave the Black Forest to accept an academic post in Berlin. Recalling the philosophical categories of idle talk and authenticity he developed in *Being and Time* (1927), Heidegger criticized urban life for its superficiality and absence of solitude. His valorization of the peasantry and its traditional values, while free of racial ideology, implied a rejection of the cosmopolitan view of the metropolis that suggests the end of Weimar and the onset of National Socialism.

158

LUDWIG FINCKH

The Spirit of Berlin

First published as "Der Geist von Berlin," *Schwäbischer Merkur*, no. 14 (January 10, 1919).

Berlin, once the capital of the nation, seat of war associations and encampment of war-making governments, has become a symbol. Once a symbol of power and splendor, it is now one of decay. Everything is topsy-turvy there; guns go off on their on, wolves have been turned into deer.

A small minority in Berlin keeps the German people in suspense. What do they want? At bottom, nothing other than what the pacifists and the cosmopolitans want: the world-wide brotherhood of peoples. The Savior was their refined brother. He sought brotherhood through love. But they seek it through violence, through revolution, through murder and homicide; and that is why they are as distant from the Savior as the fallen angel Satan is from heaven. They are, to put it very mildly, visionaries, dreamers, and adventurers. But they are on the wrong path; they live in a delusion, and they carry beneath their overcoats what must fear the light. They will never accomplish their dream. They want to overthrow all the governments of the world to make a single brotherhood of peoples on earth. Wonderful! Only it is a pity that once again the German has let himself in for it and allows patches to be cut from his skin for the others. The French, the English, the Italians laugh up their sleeves; it does not even occur to them to join in and be magnanimously international. The scent it leaves is not enticing. The dumb Germans will just devour themselves.

Standing opposed to this, however, are the Social Democrats, the government. They want no violence, but they are not saviors either. In loathing they look at their offspring and descendants, the spoiled sons who gnaw at their roots. They teach respect for every opinion and thereby cast themselves into chains. Bound hand and foot, they must observe the mutiny raging on all sides. The rebellion avenges itself on them. Germany, be on your guard! The spirit of Berlin is a demon. In the national elections the middle classes will rise from a sobering sleep to triumph, as happened in Baden, and will put the train back on track. One could very well imagine Germany as a republic with a trustworthy prince as president at the top—Württemberg with the King, Baden with Prince Max—and one would be in agreement with a leading Social Democratic paper from Württemberg, which already suggested this years ago. Until November 9, 1918, the German, above all the Swabian, was true to the crown; he discovered his republican heart only in the course of the revolution. One could also imagine, under the name of national democracy, an assembly of all faithful royalist elements with an inclination toward progress almost equal to that of social democracy to atone for all innocently committed injustice and to cure the blinded people of their delusion. But the fallen angels will try to prevent it, tomorrow as today, with violence, through murder and homicide, for they know no law. What then? In the name of God *they must be forced back within their bounds* and finally called to account. For that one needs *power,* not impotence.

The fatherland is not served by a national defense force that is now nothing more than a deformation, that is not even master of its own troops, to say nothing of foreign enemies. An army that is to be of some worth must have iron discipline; no qualified officer will want to command troops lacking in obedience and the capacity for sacrifice. But today's regiment of guards moves aside as soon as violence rears its head; the regiment opens the gates it is supposed to close and defend. It is not worth a charge of powder. *That is the spirit of Berlin.* Wherever it finds a mass of people, it becomes vital. For the rabid, the screamer, the seducer, the man of the wild word is correct among the masses. In Würt-temberg as in other states, two factories made the revolution, led by alien, un-Swabian elements that rule over the Swabian constitution at their discretion. Were they called to that position, those consisting predominantly of persons exempt from military service, those who, secure from the enemy, earned great sums of money? Was it not much more a matter of attacking the soldiers from the rear? Four weeks too soon! Four weeks of patience, then our position today would have been different! For I know, and everyone still of sound sense knows in the bottom of his heart: *the Entente is wrong,* more wrong than we, although we are defeated, defeated by an internal enemy. Siegfried was slain by Hagen.

As peasants in their villages do not look beyond their district, become selfish, and conduct a politics of the church steeple, so the Berliner is trapped within his four walls, dictating, setting the tone, believing that his and the German horizon are one. *But Berlin is not Germany.* Berlin is not even Prussia. There are many good Prussians who want nothing to do with it. We in southern Germany will no longer go along with it. We want to have a nation. But now Berlin has forfeited the right to be the capital of the nation and to represent us; it has shown itself unworthy of leading. We must draw a line between Berlin and ourselves, and leave it to its quarrels and its fate. In Berlin there is place enough for a republic of its own. The new nation must have a *new capital,* not in another big city, not in a city that has unmasked itself, where before long the old circumstances will reign anew. As in past times princes called settlements into being through the commanding word of their will and had flowering communities sprout from the earth—and who would want to do without them—Karlsruhe, Ludwigsburg, Potsdam, Kassel? Princes too have some-times accomplished something everlasting—thus today the idea of founding a new city. I welcome it. Somewhere in the heart of Germany, in a forest, on a heath, the new buildings should rise, in which a *better* national leadership will dwell. The spirit of the nation must renew itself. Building would follow a definite plan; authorities, settlements, and agricul-tural estates would find their places. Factories should be tolerated only within a restricted compass, as model plants, like all other operations.

To the spirit of Berlin another must be opposed, *the spirit of Germany!*

159

MATHEO QUINZ

The Romanic Café

First published as "Das Romanische Café," *Der Querschnitt* 6, no. 8 (1926), 608–610.

Only the painter John Höxter really knows the Romanic Café. He has outlasted the generations, which here as in the earlier spots, come and go and play at being bohemians. With the tragic demeanor of one who is eternally doomed, he has probed the subtlest swings of their artist souls and wallets, registered them in categories from half a mark to two, and, through steadfast borrowings over decades, turned this knowledge into money. He will survive this generation, too, and thus secure from Berlin's *soi-disant* Bohemia the right to his reputation and existence as long as he exists.

The Romanic Café is conspicuously divided, like a large bathing establishment with a big pool for swimmers and a small one for nonswimmers. The visitors to the respective sections scarcely have anything to do with one another. Where the revolving door divides the pools, two worlds are separated. Here stands Nietz, the doorkeeper, the most important person after Höxter. He regulates the traffic with a superior air, having adopted the objective, restrained yet energetic tone one otherwise finds only in warders of the insane. Only those guests whom Herr Nietz knows personally, knows by name so that he can summon them to the telephone without shouting loudly through the club, count as recognized guests, whether artists or otherwise. Most are advertising agents. Artists whom Nietz does not know simply do not exist.

The nonswimmers' pool is populated mainly by Egon Erwin Kisch, who has the astounding capacity of conducting excited conversations at all the tables at the same time, reading all the newspapers as well, without neglecting the fascinating gaze he reserves for all the women passing by the pool. If Kisch is not in Berlin, the pool depopulates itself noticeably.

In two corners of the nonswimmers' pool, the Romanic's Communist faction convenes its daily sessions, nightly too; the good old Talmud scholars occupy one table every day; at this table even a truly existing God was once invented. Located among the nonswimmers is also [Alfred] Flechtheim's table, and, overseeing everyone at the front of the club, the psychiatrist Dr. Emanuel observes his dear patients, and seeks out others who could yet join their number. Surgeons and the like are not to be found in the café; the speciality of the family doctors most frequently present, Dr. [Gottfried] Benn and Dr. Döhmann, should discreetly not be named but looked up in the directory.

The circle that encompasses the nonswimmers' pool is enormous. Journalists are there from the *Rote Fahne* all the way to the *Kreuzzeitung*. The district attorney Caspary sits next to the two-years-for-murder [Emil] Gumbel; [Arnolt] Bronnen and Leonhard Frank drink their coffee shoulder to shoulder with Arthur Rebner. The art dealers are there, from Flechtheim to the world's most significant woman art dealer. Valeska Gert and Celly de Rheidt, [Leopold] Jeßner and the director of the lovers' theater in Groß-Salze; nearly all the painters: Otto Dix, Mopp, Krauskopf, Lederer. One painter even answers to the name Feigel. All of the painters, incidentally, have suffered for some time now from chronic Dolbin disease.[1] They draw each other reciprocally with fantastic dexterity.

In the nonswimmers' pool there are also guests who never sit at a table—aside from Höxter who of course, for business reasons, has to see to all the tables. There is one man, a mathematician who possesses the additional ability of eating earthworms and throwing boomerangs, and who wears white pants and a monocle through which he carefully eyes the whole pool on average once every hour. Stefan Großmann also wanders through the rooms, always in the evenings, before he goes to sleep.

Between the two pools, at the port of entry for those who have arrived, is the dignitaries' table; geographically clearly in the swimmers' area. [Max] Slevogt reigns here in dignity with Bruno Cassirer. Only a few are allowed to assume a seat here, but to these few the dining hour at their regular table has become a life's goal. Here the art trainer [Karl] Scheffler from the Cassirer stables daily speaks one thousand words of art (Cassirer's trotter

1. Reference to work of Benedikt Fred Dolbin (1883–1971), German caricaturist and illustrator.

trainer does not frequent *this* club). Here, between two gatherings to tea and four dinners, [Emil] Orlik demonstrates how it is possible to draw with the right and the left hand at the same time without being an [Adolf von] Menzel. It was here that Großmann invented the sport of drawing without looking at the paper, a skill long since surpassed by Orlik, who draws on a sheet of paper in his pants pocket. The dignitaries' splendor lasts daily until nine o'clock. At that time Slevogt, whether he wants to or not, must leave the table, for then the proprietor consumes his schnitzel here. Even Orlik is powerless against that.

In the swimming pool seats are taken by people who have money, or at least act as if they do—film people, discharged theater producers, procurers of advertisements, cigarette salesmen, and the poet Oskar Kanehl. The guests in this section, namely the *filmiers,* are highly regarded by the waiters, and drink mostly mocha. On this side sits capital, in addition, to be sure, to those of sporadic appearance who evade paying the bill and get their overcoats confused. (It has been expressly determined that these gentlemen are to be counted among the swimmers; among the nonswimmers the noble, open loan dominates, the only motive that can drive an enraged guest of the little pool into the big one.) Here in the sun of capital sit the little girls as well. They have pretty names: Joa, the infanta of the Romanic; Bibiana; Biberl, who is old enough to have been educated by Peter Altenberg; Anja, whom the painter [Ludwig] Meidner was determined to teach to pray; the little Moth, of whom the tale is told that she once utterly ruined a man (the man does not frequent the Romanic). They all take the greatest pains to make their appearance as great ladies. Some will perhaps yet succeed, as Takka-Takka learned to or like Nadya, the much painted and much loved Nadya, who is to be seen only very rarely, between little trips to Cairo or Biarritz. It is impossible to determine who among the little women has a liaison with whom, or who was just married to whom or divorced. These intimacies are known only by the cafe's attorney with the Roman head, and he has refused comment on these things for twenty years. There are only a few among the the regular visitors, however, who have not been divorced with tact and successfully by Hans Braun, and scarcely one of the little girls who has not served at least once as a ground for the divorce.

The life of the café lasts from five o'clock in the afternoon to one o'clock in the morning. Otherwise it is lonely, and only a couple of utterly refined people, like [Richard] Huelsenbeck, the ex-dadaist, eat their schnitzel, or a couple of utterly poor devils wait for the patron who will see to the check. Only on Sunday afternoon does all hell break loose: everything that is distributed over ten hours on a weekday takes its bourgeois Sunday afternoon stroll through the Romanic.

And in the morning hours from eight to ten there is an infernal atmosphere: cold smoke, rancid powder, floor polish, and dust. This is when the gamblers from the countless little *tripots* [gambling dens] of the West take their breakfast, and in come the pairs of lovers, or at least the halves of them, from the awful hourly rate hotels around the zoo. These are rumpled and crumpled breakfast guests, but welcomed by the waiters: they do not sit eight to ten hours over a cup of coffee, as is otherwise the custom in the Romanic, but eat quietly and peacefully their two coddled eggs; they do not grumble, but after half an hour depart obedient and tired for home or work. Meanwhile the others make a ruckus when they leave and are obliged to interrupt their important discourses on Picasso, Sarotti,[2] and Mussolini, their professions, art works, and ventures. They all do seem so important to themselves, almost as important as Herr Meier, who thinks the world will stand still if he ever forsakes his regular table at the corner bar.

---

2. Reference to a brand of German chocolate popular at the time.

160

KURT TUCHOLSKY

Berlin and the Provinces

First published under the name Ignaz Wrobel as "Berlin und die Provinz," *Die Weltbühne* 24 (March 13, 1928), 405–408.

When journalists in Berlin speak of Germany, they are fond of using the ready expression, "out there in the countryside," which signifies a grotesque overestimation of the capital. For the basis and foundation of Germany, the source of its standards, lie "out there in the countryside"—and the extent to which Berlin is merely an exponent of provincial values remains to be seen.

As for the republican idea (in the attenuated form in which it is produced in Germany), it must be said that it is to be found only spottily out there in the countryside. East of the Elbe things look bad in this regard; west of the Oder things are worse. One has to read the minutes of a meeting of the Republican Press Association to comprehend the extent to which republicans are merely tolerated. A public assessor in Arnsberg inclines to the *Reichsbanner*[1] and therefore is not allowed to eat with the others at the "officials' table" in the clubroom. He complains and gets replaced; he gets replaced, not the governor. The good will and difficult position of the Prussian interior minister should not be mistaken: the tradition of [Carl] Severing's good days is still there.[2] But the republicans are almost always on the defensive; their appearances in public are frequently so timid that they give the impression of excusing themselves for their existence in the world. That not only signals, as they always contend, a shortage of the right kind of people—it is a lack of force, of courage, of strength.

Entirely aside from politics, however, the question arises to what degree Berlin influences the provinces and how they would actually look with or without Berlin.

As far as a single individual can say, I would contend that, in many minor and a few major areas of superficial civilization, Berlin influences the provinces quite strongly; at least the development of the capital city and the provincial cities runs parallel in this respect. Bars, stupid revue theaters, amusement centers; the whole "get-up"—all of that is prevalent in the larger provincial cities, and they are very proud of it too. But what about the individuality of the states?

It certainly is there, but I think that the civilizing process is rapidly progressing on a deeper level as well. A mechanization, an automation of life, has set in, against which the federalist idea signifies regression and a somewhat dangerous romanticism. That which F. W. Foerster,[3] for example, wants to reconstruct is dead—he overlooks the fact that the invigoration of small communities does not entail the invigoration of culture but supplies a pretext for localist vanity and a cover behind which what little constitutionality exists can be sabotaged yet more effectively than is already happening, for example, in Bavaria. Better a single Prussia than twenty-six, although it has also been noted by the major French press that Prussia is today one of the freest of the provincial states and no longer the seat of reactionary tendencies.

---

1. *Reichsbanner* was a defense of the Republic led by the SPD.

2. Carl Severing, Social Democrat, was Minister of the Interior 1920–1926 and 1930–1932.

3. Friedrich Wilhelm Foerster (1869–1966), influential pedagogue who wrote on political ethics, (*Politische Ethik*, 1925).

Berlin, however, vastly overestimates itself in believing that it is the core and heart of the country. Berlin journalists would do well to travel incognito to a large estate in Silesia or East Prussia, or to a Pomeranian town—that would be an experience for them. The farcical figures, Kaiser Wilhelm memorial top hats, centenary frock coats, and traditional forester beards spewed toward Berlin on the Hindenburg Day of old was only a small sample offering: the warehouses are to be found well-stocked in the small towns and can be viewed any time, if not always without danger. Not without danger whenever a "Berliner" has made an energetic attempt to shut down the terror, dictatorship, and insolence of the ruling local bourgeoisie. One will find no court to provide support there, no administrative officials, no newspaper. One is lost and has no choice but to forsake the field.

Does it look better in the culture of the provinces? Hardly.

The crisis of the Dessau Bauhaus recently demonstrated how things stand there. First they drove that black-red-gold[4] Jewish architecture out of Weimar; then a slander crusade lasting years got underway in Dessau as well; and now they have run the leader, Mr. [Walter] Gropius, quite completely into the ground. The facts are these:

The moment an artistic institution becomes dependent on municipal or state officials in the provinces it is lost: it falls helplessly into the reactionary mire of narrow-minded philistines; liberal men are fired, thrown out, overcome with disgust, and because one only occasionally finds a free-thinking local aristocrat, who has so often been the creator of rural culture, the provincial philistine rules absolutely. There are, of course, exceptions in the larger provincial cities.

The exceptions, however, are usually powerless. Opposition camps do exist in literally every provincial city, but they have a very difficult time and we in Berlin fail to support them adequately. Shocking letters prove this, as well as brochures and articles in little newspapers no one reads—consider, for example, the informative pamphlet "Würzburg—A Provincial City?" (from the press of the Würzburg Working Group, 1927). How they struggle, how they attempt to adopt the good from without while preserving their own. And how hopeless it all is, how fragmented, how permeated by romanticism, empty talk, and surreptitious Catholicism (which is more dangerous than the open variety). These small, impotent groups are bled to death by the municipal and provincial powers.

The provincial bourgeois press is not responsible for this, as the credulous zealots would like to believe; it is only a symptom and expression of the ruling caste, which uses all available means—boycotts, firings of editors, withdrawals of advertising—to make the newspapers what they are: a nearly invulnerable bulwark of reaction. A truly grave responsibility falls on the provincial Social Democratic press. Aside from a few exceptions (for example, in Zwickau), they are all busy emulating *Vorwärts* [the paper of the Social Democratic Party]. No problem is thought through to the end; nothing appears there without qualification. All too rarely do these papers break out of the narrow party tracks, with the result, just as in Berlin, that the local equivalent of the *Morgenpost* gets the masses and social democracy is left behind. Bellowing "keep bourgeois papers out of the house!" is of no use; as long as the workers' papers do not appeal to the youth and the women, without whom success is inconceivable, then the others will simply remain ahead.

Now, however, all the panels, nearly without exception, are artistically reactionary: those made up of city representatives, party secretaries, or members of regional committees or citizens' boards. Whether it is a question of art or culture, these pompous conferees will

---

4. Black-red-gold were the colors of the Republic.

always decide against the intellect. They can do so because they have power. The egg dances of these "intendants," as the city theater directors are fond of calling themselves today, the compromises forced upon liberal experimenters, amply testify to this. So does Berlin signify freedom? That would be a severely mistaken impression.

Berlin is merely a big city. And in a big city the individual disappears; groups are able to work with less interference, because here those involved number in the tens of thousands, while in Cologne they encompass only eighty or a hundred people; everything is simply multiplied by a hundred. Nor does it amount to more than that. For as considerable as negative freedom is in Berlin ("Here you can do what you want and ignore the rest"), the positive is just as limited. One need only go to where power is truly exercised—to the building authorities, to court, to schools—and there, with the exception of numerous enclaves of freedom, one confronts the provincial swamp, prejudices of a nearly diluvial sort, unlikely sorts who have been co-opted into the governing bodies and flourish there. You all went to school with a sour, rather humorless, not so well-washed fellow, usually to be found among the top ten—and you could swear that he sits there today and runs the show. His is the illegible signature on official decrees; he commits all the nearly incomprehensible chicanery in the administration; he and none other. In Berlin as well.

The provincial reproach that the tumult of Berlin is not Germany is justified to the extent that the prestige of large democratic newspapers, of artists, and of liberal associations in fact bears no relation to their actual power. On the other hand, the power of reaction— always there and working more skilfully and, above all, less respectfully—functions almost silently. It is supported by the pious wishes of the stock market and the merchant class, who lend their applause to those innocuous performances at the Berlin premieres.

But in the provinces, in a hundred different places, our people continue the struggle: for light and air and freedom. I do not believe that a new "National Association for . . ." can help them. If there were, however, an intellectual *Reichsbanner,* then they would be helped. As long as there is no such thing, it seems to me a duty and the commandment of good sense for everyone who holds a position of power in Berlin to radiate energy into the provinces instead of patting them on the back. To the outcry of the provinces against their own capital, there is only one answer: Speak out with the power of Berlin, which is light, to the provinces, where it is dark.

161

FRANZ HESSEL

The Suspicious Character

First published as "Der Verdächtige," in *Spazieren in Berlin* (Leipzig and Vienna: Verlag Hans Epstein, 1929), 7–12.

To walk slowly down lively streets is a special pleasure. To be left behind by the rush of the others—this is a bath in the surf. But my dear fellow Berliners do not make it easy, however gracefully one might move out of their way. I always receive suspicious looks whenever I try to stroll as a flaneur between the shops. I think they take me for a pickpocket.

Whenever my gaze lingers on their sailing shoulders and floating cheeks, the speedy, erect young women of the city with the insatiably open mouths become indignant. Not as if they have anything at all against being looked at. But the slow-motion gaze of the harmless spectator unnerves them. They realize that, in my case, there is nothing behind it.

No, there is nothing behind it. I would like to linger with the first glance. I would like to gain or rediscover my first glance at the city in which I live. [. . .]

In the quieter districts on the outskirts of the city I am not, incidentally, any less unpleasantly conspicuous. Toward the north there is a square with wooden scaffolding, the skeleton of a market, and right next to it the produce shop run by the widow Kohlmann, who also has rags; and on the slatted veranda, above the bundles of old paper, the rubbish bins, and skins, she has geranium pots. Geraniums, throbbing red in a sluggishly grey world, into which I simply have to gaze for a long time. The widow throws nasty looks my way. She does not dare complain, perhaps thinking me an informer and fearing that her papers are not entirely in order. Meanwhile I wish her nothing but good; I would love to ask her about business and her views on life. Now she sees me finally going away, to the other side where the cross street heads up the hill; I examine the backs of the knees of the children playing ball against the building—long-legged girls, enchanting to look at. They return the ball alternately with their hands, head, and chest, spinning round in the process, and the bend of their knees seems to me to be the center of their movements and the spot where it all starts up. I can feel the produce widow craning her neck behind me. Will she let the cop know what sort of character I am? The suspicious role of the spectator!

When the sun begins to set, women young and old lean out the windows cushioning their arms on pillows. What psychologists name with words like empathy happens to me with them. But they will not allow me to wait next to them and with them for what does not come, just to wait with no object.

Street merchants screaming out their wares have nothing against someone standing there with them. But I would prefer to stand next to the woman with so much hair from the last century on her head, who is slowly spreading her needlework out on blue paper and silently anticipating customers. And that does not suit her—she can hardly assume that I will buy something from her.

Sometimes I like to go into the courtyards. In old Berlin life around the courtyards off the street becomes denser and more heartfelt, which makes them rich, the poor courtyards with the bit of grass in the corner, the stands for beating rugs, the garbage cans, and the wells left over from days before the water system was installed. I manage it in the morning hours, when singers and fiddlers appear, or the organ grinder who adds to his music a tune whistled on a couple of free fingers, or the astonishing man playing two drums at once, one in front and one on his back. (He has a hook on his right ankle and a string from there to the kettledrum on his back with bells attached to it; when he stamps his foot, a drumstick strikes the drum and the bells clang together.) There I can stand next to the old woman doorkeeper—more likely she is the mother of the building porters, so old does she look, so habituated is she to sitting there on her camp stool. She takes no offense at my presence, and I am allowed to look up at the courtyard windows where the stenographers and seamstresses from the offices and shops crowd to get a view of the concert. Blissfully pacified, they pause until some tedious boss comes along and they have to slip back to their work. The windows are all bare. Only one in the second-to-last story has curtains; a bird cage hangs in that one, and when the fiddler sobs of broken hearts and the organ-grinder drones his lament, a canary begins to sing, the only voice from the mute stare of the windows. That is nice. But I would also like to have my share of evenings in these courtyards, the last game of the children being repeatedly called up to bed, and experience the young girls coming home and wanting to leave again. Alone, I have neither the courage nor an excuse for intruding; my status as trespasser is too easily seen.

Fortunately I can report that a compassionate girlfriend sometimes allows me to accompany her on her errands—to the stocking clinic, for example, where there is a sign above the door: "Runs Repaired." In this gloomy mezzanine a hunchback slips through her musty, woolly room, which has been brightened by the addition of shiny new wallpaper. Wares and sewing tools lie on tables and stands around little porcelain slippers, ceramic cupids, and bronze busts of little girls, like herd animals gathered around old wells and ruins. And I can carefully inspect it all while the women discuss their business.

Or I am taken along to the tailor, who lives on the groundfloor in the rear of a building on Kurfürstenstrasse. A curtain that does not quite reach the floor separates the work area from his bedroom. On a fringed cloth hanging over the curtain there is a colorful depiction of Kaiser Friedrich as crown prince. "That's how he came back from San Remo," says the tailor, following my gaze; then he shows me the rest of his faithful monarchical treasures: the last Wilhelm with his daughter on his knee, photographed and lavishly framed, and the famous picture of the old Kaiser with children, grandchildren, and great-grandchildren. He will be happy to tailor the green jacket for my republican girlfriend, but in his heart, he says, as long as the Republic provides only for the young, he stands "with the old authorities." I do not try to change his mind. With all those objects around him, my political views do not have a chance. He is very friendly to my girlfriend's dog, who is sniffing around at everything, curious and always on the trail of something, just like me.

I like to go on walks with the little terrier. Then we are both lost in thought; and he gives me a reason for lingering in one spot, which would otherwise be forbidden such a suspicious person as myself.

Recently, however, things went badly for us. I picked him up at a house neither of us knew. We went down one flight of stairs. An elevator enclosed with grating had been installed, a gloomy intruder in the once coolly expansive staircase. And the puffy ladies-in-waiting in the colorful windows looked crazily at the traveling dungeon, and the jewels and royal emblems loosened in their hands. Certainly it also smelled quite odd in this ensemble of various epochs, which so distracted my companion from the present and customary practices that, on the first step of the steep staircase leading down from the ground floor to the base of the elevator, he forgot himself! Such a thing, my girlfriend later assured me, could have happened to such a perfectly house-trained creature only in my company. I accepted that gladly. I was hit harder by the reproach made at the time of the embarrassing event by the doorman, who unfortunately had stuck his nose out of his box just as we forgot ourselves. In correct recognition of my complicity he turned not to the dog but to me. He pointed with a venerably ominous finger at the site of the crime and addressed me imperiously: "Huh? And you think you got culture?"

162

EGON ERWIN KISCH

We Go to a Café Because . . .

First published as "Wir gehen ins Café, weil . . ." in *Hamburger Illustrierte Zeitung* no. 11 (March 15, 1930), 5.

Of course, we in Europe can answer this question with ease, since we have the beloved coffee house, without which, in my opinion, one cannot live. If one is in a German city, one needs to telephone friends, with whom one makes an appointment in a coffee house, and thus the wheel of intellectual or social conversation comes full circle. The coffee house spares us from an apartment, which one does not necessarily need to have, if there is a coffee house. That is what we Europeans miss so much when we go over to America.

163

WILHELM STAPEL

The Intellectual and His People

First published as "Der Geistige und sein Volk," *Deutsches Volkstum* 12, no. 1 (1930), 5–8.

All around Berlin there still lie broad stretches of barbarian territory filled with German peasants and upright citizens, with villages and old princely seats. Out there are indigenous cities, still with their so-called "artistic life," and large centers of culture still infused with the ancient spirits of their clans. Should they stay that way? It is finally time to clean up all this rubbish that needs to be cleaned up. What an ironic goal!

Once the intellectuals get themselves established in Berlin, they get busy establishing themselves in the German provinces as well. Everything must be Berlinerized. Only then would one have the assurance that nowhere in the German landscape does there grow a dangerously healthy and self-confident form of life so that one day the German people, could become obviously not intellectually superior, but *genuinely* superior to the commotion in Berlin. The intellectual cloaca of Berlin must therefore be channeled everywhere through the country so that the *sentina republicae* [cesspool of the republic], the spoiler of all noble and healthy life, has a chance to expand. [. . .]

Living in the surrounding cities are people who hunger and thirst for Berlin. They would like every little rathole in all of Germany to become not only a metropolis but a microcosm of Berlin. [. . .] The German landscape marches in spite of itself toward provincialization. One feels elevated when Main Street smells a little like Kurfürstendamm, or when in the otherwise faithful weekly there appears the hundred-and-first reprint of Heinrich Mann or some advance copy from Stefan Zweig's soon-to-appear, newest, very weighty book.

Under the sign of liberalism many forces are at work on the provincialization of the remaining concentrations of German clan culture and German cities. Indeed, the people, who remain in truth one people, opposes it everywhere, but the intermediaries are blinded by Berlin. They do not see what the people want; they see only what Berlin puts before them and believe themselves obligated to imitate it. In the theater it is palpable: the people reject the Berlin tendencies straightaway; the theater directors nevertheless attempt to force Berlin upon them. [. . .] In other areas as well the German landscape reduces itself to a province.

A new major assault on the German landscape is just now beginning: the Berlin novel. A newspaper in Frankfurt, it is true, suffered a bloody defeat with Döblin's *Alexanderplatz,* but with importunity and intellectual superiority they will eventually achieve their goal. The republicanizing intellectuals work according to the French model. Berlin would and must become for Germany what Paris is for France. A "new cultural era begins" in which Germany becomes a slave to Berlin. The Germanic becomes the Berlinic. We are confronting a saucy future; just between us—simply nifty.

As Berlin began to become an intellectual authority for the west and south of Germany following the founding of the state, the sensibilities and cultural life of the people rose repeatedly in opposition. The success of books like [Julius] Langbehn's *Rembrandt as Educator* [1890] or Rudolf Huch's *More Goethe!* [1899], as well as the success of the journal *Kunstwart,* is largely to be explained by this general German mood of opposition to Berlin. [Friedrich] Lienhard's polemic, *Against the Predominance of Berlin* [1900], points its finger at what one does not want. All opposition of this sort concerns itself not only with the struggle against the metropolitan as such, against *deracination;* but in particular with the struggle against the spirit of *this* metropolis. [. . .] All too many Slavs and all too many altogether uninhibited East European Jews have been mixed into the population of Berlin. It is an embarrassing mixture; it determines through sheer quantity the character of this city, which, not because of them, became so large. This virulent pretender society partook of the brilliance of the political accomplishment of the Prussian tradition, which it hated. [. . .] Educated people elsewhere in the nation did not feel the culture of Potsdam to be an enemy; they were pleased to recognize the Palace and the Brandenburg Gate, but New Berlin got on their nerves.[1] The enemy was: the lip; the saucy airs, more precisely, self-aggrandizement; the insolent self-righteousness and the endless cackle of irony; the snobbish imitation; the shrill prattle; and the extravagances of the freshly civilized immigrants, the balkanized Parisianisms. All of this first of all contrasted with *genuine* Berlin society and the court. But today it belongs to the nature of Berlin as such. And today this Berlin spirit has entirely different means of disseminating itself through the country than ever before.

It is today a decisive question for German culture whether the countryside will choose to tolerate the presumptions and impudence of Berlin intellectuality. [. . .] All of these worn-out ironies, all of these new objectivities, all of these reports—this agitated *cri de Berlin* is clearly nothing other than an *inability to master the problems of our time intellectually.* [. . .] What of the people, whose brains are schooled in Kant, whose sensibilities have stormed the depths with Faust, whose longings for God in the rites of the old church have gained eternal blessing and, in Lutheran faith, an iron resolve? A people of such heritage will not be impressed by Berlin intellectuality in pan-European style. Those faithful to Berlin among the theater producers, newspaper editors, and radio directors, who are voluntarily reducing their countryside to provinces, will achieve nothing but general contempt for their "new," and they will finally end in deserved economic ruin. [. . .]

As the peasant of the German countryside begins to rebel against all that is going on in Berlin, so will educated Germany oppose what the Berlin intellectuals propagandize.

---

1. Potsdam, the seat of Frederick the Great, became the symbol of Prussian-German militarism.

The spirit of the German people rises against the spirit of Berlin. The demand of the day can be summarized like this: the rebellion of the countryside against Berlin.

164

HAROLD NICOLSON
The Charm of Berlin

First published (in English) as "The Charm of Berlin," *Der Querschnitt* 9, no. 5 (1932), 345–346.

My bedroom in Berlin looks out upon the elevated railway. It looks at it diagonally, across and aslant a triangle of loose-soiled garden. The garden contains a green bench, a long rectangle of red carpet which has hung for eight months upon a cord, a golden ball of glass on a green pole, and a large china statue of a bulldog. The bulldog turns his tail upon the trains as they rattle or thunder above him, but the glass ball reflects them very quickly. I have seldom seen any motion so quick and so continuous as the flashing reflection of the trains that skim around the golden ball. When I tie my tie in the morning, I stand by the window and look at the trains. The local electric trains jingle past me, like virgins going to school, like kingfishers or canaries darting across the shadow of a pool. For my garden is a pool. The great European trains flap up from the main stations like storks or herons, lumbering along so slow at starting, the black vans that terminate their scarlet Mitropa bodies, trailing cumbersomely backwards like the black legs of a heron or a stork. For they are off to the smell of leather which greets one at Eydkühnen, or to the smell which greets one at Bentheim of a proximate and salted sea. At night, when I tie my white tie for the evening (a symbol of bondage) the gold ball and the bulldog are no longer visible. There are no intermediaries between me and the Reichsbahn. The electric trains soar upwards as they pass me, they are chariots of gold, they are the rockets which carry people, who have been to tea at Rummelsburg, back to supper at Charlottenburg, they are the comets on which the intellectuals of Wilmersdorf are borne enchanted to the no less cultured homes at Weißensee. I look up at them and see a blur of light, the mist upon the windows, a man leaning outwards against the pane. They look down at me and see an English diplomatist (stout and amiable) tying his white tie. They think, if they have time to think "That man is a foreigner and as we passed him he was tying a white tie." They think, if they have time to think, "What is it that prevents us Germans from being able to tie a white tie?" But I, for my part, who am by then putting on my waistcoat, I think only, "What on earth is it which gives this town its charm?"

Movement in the first place. There is no city in the world so restless as Berlin. Everything moves. The traffic lights change restlessly from red to gold and then to green. The lighted advertisements flash with the pathetic iteration of coastal lighthouses. The trams swing and jingle. The jaguar in the zoo paces feverishly all night: the planetarium when closed flings revolving planets upon its ceiling: the directors of the museums pace their corridors alone at midnight. They are showing the Luca Signorelli by the light of an electric torch; they are explaining to a photographer from Holland the importance of the Turkestan frescos: they are merely unable to sleep. In the Tiergarten the little lamps flicker among the little trees, and the grass is starred with the fireflies of a thousand cigarettes. Trains dash through the entrails of the city and thread their way among the tiaras with which it is crowned. The jaguar at the zoo, who had thought it was really time to go to bed, rises again and paces in its cell. For in the night air, which makes even the spires of the Gedächtniskirche flicker with excitement, there is a throbbing sense of expectancy. Everybody knows that every night Berlin wakes to a new adventure. Everybody feels that it would be a pity to go to bed before the expected, or the unexpected, happens. Everybody knows that next morning, whatever happens, they will feel reborn.

This physical and luminous movement finds its parallel in the dynamics of the brain. At 3 A. M. the people of Berlin will light another cigar and embark afresh and refreshed upon discussions regarding Proust, or Rilke, or the new penal code, or whether human shyness comes from narcissism, or whether it would be a wise or a foolish thing to turn the Pariser Platz into a stadium. The eyes that in London or in Paris would already have drooped in sleep are busy in Berlin, inquisitive, acquisitive, searching, even at 4 A. M., for some new experience or idea. The mouths that in Paris or London would next morning be parched for bromoseltzer, in Berlin are already munching sandwiches on their way to the bank.

Second to movement comes frankness. London is an old lady in black lace and diamonds who guards her secrets with dignity and to whom one would not tell those secrets of which one was ashamed. Paris is a woman in the prime of life to whom one would only tell those secrets that one desires to be repeated. But Berlin is a girl in a pullover, not much powder on her face, Hölderlin in her pocket, thighs like those of Atalanta, an undigested education, a heart that is almost too ready to sympathize, and a breadth of view that charms one's repressions from their poison, and shames one's correctitude. One walks with her among the lights and in the shadows. And after an hour or so one is hand-in-hand.

Movement and frankness. The maximum irritant for the nerves corrected by the maximum sedative. Berlin stimulates like arsenic, and then when one's nerves are all ajingle she comes with her hot milk of human kindness; and in the end, for an hour and a half, one is able, gratefully, to go to sleep.

165

MARTIN HEIDEGGER

Creative Landscape: Why Do We Stay in the Provinces?

First published as "Schöpferische Landschaft. Warum bleiben wir in der Provinz?" First complete publication in *Der Alemanne* no. 1 (March 7, 1934), 1. (Previously broadcast over Berlin radio in autumn 1933.)

On the steep slope of a wide mountain valley in the southern Black Forest, at an elevation of 1,150 meters, there stands a small ski hut. The floor plan measures six meters by seven. The low-hanging roof covers three rooms: the kitchen that is also the living room, a bedroom and a study. Scattered at wide intervals throughout the narrow base of the valley and on the equally steep slope opposite lie the farmhouses with their large overhanging roofs. Higher up the slope the meadows and pastures lead to the woods with its dark fir trees, old and towering. Over everything there stands a clear summer sky, and in its radiant expanse two hawks glide around in wide circles.

This is my work world—seen with the eye of an observer: the guest or summer vacationer. Strictly speaking I myself never observe the landscape. I experience its hourly changes, day and night, in the great comings and goings of the seasons. The gravity of the mountains and the hardness of their primeval rock, the slow and deliberate growth of the fir trees, the brilliant, simple splendor of the meadows in bloom, the rush of the mountain brook in the long autumn night, the stern simplicity of the flatlands covered with snow—all of this moves and flows through and penetrates daily existence up there, and not in forced moments of "aesthetic" immersion or artificial empathy, but only when one's own existence stands in its work. It is the work alone that opens up space for the reality that is these mountains. The course of the work remains embedded in what happens in the region.

On a deep winter's night when a wild, pounding snowstorm rages around the cabin and veils and covers everything, that is the perfect time for philosophy. Then its questions must become simple and essential. Working through each thought can only be tough and rigorous. The struggle to mold something into language is like the resistance of the towering firs against the storm.

And this philosophical work does not take its course like the aloof studies of some eccentric. It belongs right in the midst of the peasants' work. When the young farmboy drags his heavy sled up the slope and guides it, piled high with beech logs, down the dangerous descent to his house, when the herdsman, lost in thought and slow of step, drives his cattle up the slope, when the farmer in his shed gets the countless shingles ready for his roof, my work is of the same sort. It is intimately rooted in and related to the life of the peasants.

A city dweller thinks he has gone "out among the people" as soon as he condescends to have a long conversation with a peasant. But in the evening during a work break, when I sit with the peasants by the fire or at the table in the Lord's corner, we mostly say nothing at all. We smoke our pipes in silence. Now and again someone might say that the woodcutting in the forest is finishing up, that a marten broke into the hen-house last night, that one of the cows will probably calf in the morning, that someone's uncle suffered a stroke, that the weather will soon turn. The inner relationship of my own work to the Black Forest and its people comes from a centuries-long and irreplaceable rootedness in the Alemannian-Swabian soil.

At most, a city dweller gets "stimulated" by a so-called stay in the country. But my whole work is sustained and guided by the world of these mountains and their people. Lately from time to time my work up there is interrupted for long stretches by conferences, lecture trips, committee meetings, and my teaching work down here in Freiburg. But as soon as I go back up there, even in the first few hours of being at the cabin, the whole world of previous questions forces itself upon me in the very form in which I left it. I simply am transported into the work's own rhythm, and in a fundamental sense I am not at all in command of its hidden law. People in the city often wonder whether one gets lonely up in the mountains among the peasants for such long and monotonous periods of time. But it is not loneliness, it is solitude. In large cities one can easily be as lonely as almost nowhere else. But one can never be in solitude there. Solitude has the peculiar and original power not of isolating us but of projecting our whole existence out into the vast nearness of the presence (*Wesen*) of all things.

In the public world one can be made a celebrity overnight by the newspapers and journals. That always remains the surest way to have one's ownmost intentions get misinterpreted and quickly and thoroughly forgotten.

In contrast, the memory of the peasant has its simple and sure fidelity which never forgets. Recently an old peasant woman up there was approaching death. She liked to chat with me frequently, and she told me many old stories of the village. In her robust language, full of images, she still preserved many old words and various sayings which have become unintelligible to the village youth today and hence are lost to the spoken language. Very often in the past year when I lived alone in the cabin for weeks on end, this peasant woman with her 83 years would still come climbing up the slope to visit me. She wanted to look in from time to time, as she put it, to see whether I was still there or whether "someone" had stolen me off unawares. She spent the night of her death in conversation with her family. Just an hour and a half before the end she sent her greetings to the "Professor." Such a memory is worth incomparably more than the most astute report by any international newspaper about my alleged philosophy.

The world of the city runs the risk of falling into a destructive error. A very loud and very active and very fashionable obtrusiveness often passes itself off as concern for the world and existence of the peasant. But this goes exactly contrary to the one and only thing that now needs to be done, namely, to keep one's distance from the life of the peasant, to leave their existence more than ever to its own law, to keep hands off lest it be dragged into the literati's dishonest chatter about "folk character" and "rootedness in the soil." The peasant does not need and does not want this citified officiousness. What he needs and wants is quiet reserve with regard to his own way of being and its independence. But nowadays many people from the city, the kind who "know their way around" and not least of all the skiers, often behave in the village or at a farmer's house in the same way they "have fun" at their recreation centers in the city. Such goings-on destroy more in one evening than centuries of scholarly teaching about folk character and folklore could ever hope to promote.

Let us stop all this condescending familiarity and sham concern for folk character and let us learn to take seriously that simple, rough existence up there. Only then will it speak to us once more.

Recently I got a second invitation to teach at the University of Berlin. On that occasion I left Freiburg and withdrew to the cabin. I listened to what the mountains and the forest and the farmlands were saying, and I went to see an old friend of mine, a 75-year-old farmer. He had read about the call to Berlin in the newspapers. What would he say? Slowly he fixed the sure gaze of his clear eyes on mine, and keeping his mouth tightly shut, he thoughtfully put his faithful hand on my shoulder. Ever so slightly he shook his head. That meant: absolutely no!

17

Designing the New World: Modern Architecture and the Bauhaus

THE DEVELOPMENT OF modern architecture in Germany began well before the Weimar Republic. In 1907 Hermann Muthesius founded the German Werkbund, an association of architects, designers, and industrialists dedicated to increasing the competitiveness of German products on the world market. Germany's dearth of natural resources also helped to rally government support for vocational training in the applied arts and to foster awareness of the economic significance of high design standards. The discussions of standardization and machine production presided over by Muthesius influenced the design philosophy of many modern German architects. Some, such as Peter Behrens, chief designer for the electric company AEG and early employer of Walter Gropius, Ludwig Mies van der Rohe, and Le Corbusier, had already incorporated geometric simplicity or restrained historicism into prewar buildings. This rejection of Victorian stylistic eclecticism soon emerged as a favorite theme in the writings of many Weimar builders and designers. At the 1914 Cologne Werkbund Exhibition, Bruno Taut's Glass Pavilion and Walter Gropius's and Adolf Meyer's Fagus Factory drew attention to the expressive features of glass and steel, which also rapidly became associated with the new style.

The devastation of the war helped to bring about a newly politicized concept of architecture as a vehicle for revolutionary social transformation. Taut's architectural program for the Work Council of Art (Arbeitsrat für Kunst) vividly expresses a widely prevalent conception of building as a unifying activity among the arts leading to a politically motivated *Gesamtkunstwerk*. Such yearnings were to remain largely unfulfilled until after 1924 when the economic situation had sufficiently stabilized to permit new construction. Writing in that same year, well after the revolutionary atmosphere had already subsided, Mies van der Rohe, a member of the November Group who would become the director of the Berlin Bauhaus, defined architecture as the spatial expression of the spirit of the age. Building would remain a socially and politically charged activity throughout the republic.

One short-lived manifestation of the years between 1918 and 1923 was the development of expressionist (or utopian or fantastic) architecture associated with both the work of Hans Poelzig and the early-1920s designs of Mies, Gropius, Taut, and Erich Mendelsohn. Buildings such as Mendelsohn's Einstein Observatory (1920–1921) and Poelzig's Großes Schauspielhaus (1919) captured both the popular and the architectural imagination of their day. Mendelsohn's dedication speech for his Nuremberg branch of the Schocken department store conveys an excitement about machine technology and a dynamism evocative of futurism. While architectural expressionism dissipated after the early 1920s, its formal legacy and innovative choice of materials (colored glass, windowed surfaces, reinforced concrete, brightly painted walls) decisively influenced the evolution of Weimar architecture.

"Four years of the Bauhaus reflect not only a period of art history but a history of the times, too, because the disintegration of a nation and of an era is also reflected in it," wrote Oskar Schlemmer, director of the Bauhaus theater, in 1923. No other institution in Germany, or anywhere else during the twentieth century, came to be more closely identified with modern architecture. The Bauhaus was established by Gropius in 1919 as the amalgamation of the Weimar Academy of Fine Art and the Weimar School of Arts and Crafts. This merger produced a structural rift that created tension, albeit sometimes productive, between the artists and craftspeople on its faculty. At once an alternative to the traditional art-school curriculum and a program to enable artists to become socially useful, the return to the crafts advocated in the "First Bauhaus Manifesto" defined its early educational philosophy. Subsumed within the *Gesamtkunstwerk* of architecture, painting and sculpture would enjoy no privilege over the applied arts. All first-year pupils (there were neither professors nor students at the early Bauhaus, only masters and apprentices) began their studies with the famous *Vorkurs* (preliminary course). Taught by Johannes Itten (and, following his departure in 1923, by Paul Klee, Wassily Kandinsky, Joseph Albers, and Laszlo Moholy-Nagy), it sought to release creativity. After their individual talents and abilities had become manifest, apprentices would specialize in a specific craft. Around 1923 the Bauhaus gradually shifted its emphasis from training craftspeople to the education of a new breed of artist–designer capable of responding to the challenges of machine production. From having once objected to the standardization urged by Muthesius, Gropius now viewed the design and fabrication of standardized building components and products as vital architectural and political tasks. His 1926 article for the popular magazine *Uhu* concisely presents his thoughts on standardization and tenacious insistence that it need not lead to uniformity or loss of individuality. Beginning in 1926, Marcel Breuer, an apprentice later appointed master in charge of the furniture workshop, produced tubular aluminum chairs and interior objects whose relation to modern spatiality he describes in "Metal Furniture and Modern Spatiality." Gradually, a functionalist orientation came to influence the school, finally dominating it in 1928 after the Marxist architect Hannes Meyer replaced Gropius as its director. Meyer's views on modern science and industrial standardization exemplify a worldview colored by the New Objectivity and shared by many Weimar intellectuals, and suggest just how far the Bauhaus would depart from the mystical and intuitive teachings promoted by Itten during its early years.

Despite increasing critical recognition enjoyed by the Bauhaus, conservative attacks against it were so common that Gropius once claimed he spent most of his time defending the school. Conservatives such as Paul Schultze-Naumburg faulted its designs for leading to cultural and racial decline and decried the replacement of the traditional German home by a mechanical "dwelling machine." Opposition from the conservative Thuringian government and generous financial support from the city of Dessau prompted the Bauhaus to move there in 1925. Here Gropius designed the building with which the school became identified, enthusiastically described by Rudolf Arnheim after a visit in 1927. Growing political pressure forced the Bauhaus to move again, this time to Berlin in 1932. A year later the Nazis closed its doors for good and forced its participants into exile. Many of them enjoyed a second professional life as influential architects, designers, and teachers in the United States.

166

BRUNO TAUT

A Program for Architecture

First published in "Ein Architektur-Programm," *Mitteilungen des Deutschen Werkbundes,* no. 4 (1918), 16–18.

Art—that is one single thing, when it exists! Today there is no art. The various disrupted tendencies can find their way back to a single unity only under the wings of a new architecture, so that every individual discipline will play its part in building. Then there will be no frontiers between the applied arts and sculpture or painting. Everything will be one thing: architecture.

The direct carrier of the spiritual forces, molder of the sensibilities of the general public, which today are slumbering and tomorrow will awake, is architecture. Only a complete revolution in the spiritual realm will create this architecture. But this revolution, this architecture will not come of themselves. Both must be willed—today's architects must prepare the way for tomorrow's buildings. Their work on the future must receive public assistance to make it possible.

Therefore:

I. Support and gathering together of the ideal forces among architects

    a. Support for architectural ideas which, above and beyond the purely formal aspect, strive for the concentration of all the national energies in the symbol of the building belonging to a better future and which demonstrate the cosmic character of architecture, its religious foundations, so-called Utopias. The provision of public funds in the form of grants to radically inclined architects to enable them to carry out such projects. Financial assistance towards the publication of written material, the construction of models and

    b. for a well-situated experimental site (e.g., in Berlin: the Tempelhofer Feld), on which architects can erect large-scale models of their ideas. Here, too, new architectural effects (e.g., glass as a building material) shall be tried out, perfected, and exhibited to the masses in full-scale temporary constructions or individual parts of a building. The layman, the woman, and the child will lead the architect farther than the inhibited specialist. Expenses could be met by melting down public monuments, breaking down triumphal avenues, etc., as well as by the participation of industries connected with the experimental buildings. Workshops with colonies of craftsmen and artists on the experimental site.

    c. Decision on the distribution of financial aid by a council made up half of creative architects, half of radically minded laymen. If agreement cannot be reached, the final decision will be taken by a layman chosen from the council.

II. People's houses

    a. Beginning of large-scale people's housing estates not inside the towns but in the open country in connection with settlements, groups of buildings for theater and music with lodging houses and the like, culminating in the religious building. Prospect of a prolonged period of construction, hence the beginning should be made according to a grandiose plan with limited means.

    b. Architects to be chosen not by competition but in accordance with I(c).

    c. If building is halted it should be given new incentives during the pauses by means of planned extensions and new ideas in accordance with I(a)–(c).

    d. These buildings should be the first attempt at unifying the energies of the people and of artists, the preliminaries for developing a culture. They cannot stand in the metropolis because the latter, being rotten in itself, will disappear along with the old power. The future lies on the newly developed land, which will feed itself (not "on the water").

III. Estates

    a. Unitary direction in the sense that one architect will establish overall principles according to which he will examine all projects and buildings, without thereby impeding personal freedom. This architect to have the right of veto.

    b. As II(b).

    c. Formal elements to be reduced radically to second place after agricultural and practical considerations. No fear of extreme simplicity, but also not of color.

IV. Other buildings

    a. For street development and, according to circumstances, for whole urban districts the same thing applies as for III(a) and (b).

    b. No distinction between public and private buildings. As long as there are freelance architects there will be *only* freelance architects. Until there are state potters there need not be state architects. Public and private buildings may be built by anyone; commissions in line with I(c) or through competitions that are not anonymous, whose participants are invited by a council in accordance with I(c) and awarded prizes; no unpaid designs. Unknown architects will apply for invitation to the council. Anonymity is rendered valueless by the recognizable artistic handwriting of successful architects. No majority decisions by the jury; in the event of no unanimity, each member of the jury is individually responsible for his vote. Best of all a single adjudicator. Final selection possibly by plebiscite.

    c. Building officials, such as municipal building advisers and the like, to be concerned only with the control of local building, demolition, and financial supervision, with purely technical functions. The intermediate fields, such as town planning, to be under the supervision of an advisory council of architects and gardeners.

d. *No* titles and dignities for architects (doctor, professor, councillor, excellency, etc.).

e. In everything, preference to be given to the creative; no control over the architect once he has been commissioned.

f. In the event of public contradiction, decision by a council in accordance with I(c) which can be established by an architects' corporation.

g. Only such architects' corporations are to have authority in this and other matters and are to be recognized by the State. These corporations are to exercise to the limit the principle of *mutual aid*. They are to bring their influence to bear on the police responsible for enforcing building regulations. Mutual aid alone makes an association fruitful and active. It is more important than the number of votes, which means nothing without social concord. It excludes inartistic and hence unfair competition.

V. The education of architects

a. Corporations in accordance with IV(g) have the decision as to the building, constitution, and supervision of technical schools; teachers to be selected in collaboration with the students. Practical work on the building site and in the workshop like an apprentice in a craft.

b. In the trade schools no artistic, but only technical tuition. Technical primary schools.

c. The artistic education in the offices of practicing architects, according to the choice of the young people and the architects themselves.

d. General education according to inclination and previous knowledge in people's colleges and universities.

VI. Architecture and the other arts

a. Designing of exhibitions by architects in cheerful shapes; lightweight buildings in busy public squares and parks, on popular lines, almost like a fair.

b. Extensive employment of painters and sculptors on all buildings in order to draw them away from salon art; the arousal of mutual interest between architect and "artist."

c. In accordance with this principle, also introduction of architectural students into the creative "new arts." That architect is alone significant who has a conspectus of the whole domain of art and understands the radical endeavors of painting and sculpture. He alone will help to bring about the unity of the whole.

Increased importance of the architect in public life through his holding important posts and the like will result automatically from the implementation of this program.

167

WALTER GROPIUS

Program of the Staatliches Bauhaus in Weimar

First published as "Programm des Staatlichen Bauhauses" (April 1919).

The ultimate aim of all visual arts is the complete building! To embellish buildings was once the noblest function of the fine arts; they were the indispensable components of great architecture. Today the arts exist in isolation, from which they can be rescued only through the conscious, cooperative effort of all craftsmen. Architects, painters, and sculptors must recognize anew and learn to grasp the composite character of a building both as an entity and in its separate parts. Only then will their work be imbued with the architectonic spirit that it has lost as "salon art."

The old schools of art were unable to produce this unity; how could they, since art cannot be taught. They must be merged once more with the workshop. The mere drawing and painting world of the pattern designer and the applied artist must become a world that builds again. When young people who take a joy in artistic creation once more begin their life's work by learning a trade, then the unproductive 'artist' will no longer be condemned to deficient artistry, for their skill will now be preserved for the crafts, in which they will be able to achieve excellence.

Architects, sculptors, painters, we all must return to the crafts! For art is not a "profession." There is no essential difference between the artist and the craftsman. The artist is an exalted craftsman. In rare moments of inspiration, transcending the consciousness of his will, the grace of heaven may cause his work to blossom into art. But proficiency in a craft is essential to every artist. Therein lies the prime source of creative imagination. Let us then create a new guild of craftsmen without the class distinctions that raise an arrogant barrier between craftsman and artist! Together let us desire, conceive, and create the new structure of the future, which will embrace architecture and sculpture and painting in one unity and which will one day rise toward heaven from the hands of a million workers like the crystal symbol of a new faith.

Walter Gropius

PROGRAM OF THE STAATLICHES BAUHAUS IN WEIMAR

The Staatliches Bauhaus resulted from the merger of the former Grand-Ducal Saxon Academy of Art with the former Grand-Ducal Saxon School of Arts and Crafts in conjunction with a newly affiliated department of architecture.

AIMS OF THE BAUHAUS

The Bauhaus strives to bring together all creative effort into one whole, to reunify all the disciplines of practical art—sculpture, painting, handicrafts, and the crafts—as inseparable components of a new architecture. The ultimate, if distant, aim of the Bauhaus is the unified work of art—the great structure—in which there is no distinction between monumental and decorative art.

The Bauhaus wants to educate architects, painters, and sculptors of all levels, according to their capabilities, to become competent craftsmen or independent creative artists and to form a working community of leading and future artist-craftsmen. These men, of kindred spirit, will know how to design buildings harmoniously in their entirety—structure, finishing, ornamentation, and furnishing.

PRINCIPLES OF THE BAUHAUS

Art rises above all methods; in itself it cannot be taught, but the crafts certainly can be. Architects, painters, and sculptors are craftsmen in the true sense of the word: hence a thorough training in the crafts, acquired in workshops and on experimental and practical sites, is required of all students as the indispensable basis for all artistic production. Our own workshops are to be gradually built up, and apprenticeship agreements with outside workshops will be concluded.

The school is the servant of the workshop and will one day be absorbed into it. Therefore there will be no teachers or pupils in the Bauhaus but masters, journeymen, and apprentices.

The manner of teaching arises from the character of the workshop:

Organic forms developed from manual skills.

Avoidance of all rigidity; priority of creativity; freedom of individuality, but strict study discipline.

Master and journeyman examinations, according to the Guild Statutes, held before the Council of Masters of the Bauhaus or before outside masters.

Collaboration by the students in the work of the masters.

Securing of commissions, also for students.

Mutual planning of extensive, utopian structural designs—public buildings and buildings for worship—aimed at the future. Collaboration of all masters and students—architects, painters, sculptors—on these designs with the object of gradually achieving a harmony of all the component elements and parts that make up architecture.

Constant contact with the leaders of the crafts and industries of the country.

Contact with public life, with the people, through exhibitions and other activities.

New research into the nature of the exhibitions, to solve the problem of displaying visual work and sculpture within the framework of architecture.

Encouragement of friendly relations between masters and students outside of work; therefore plays, lectures, poetry, music, fancy-dress parties. Establishment of a cheerful ceremonial at these gatherings.

RANGE OF INSTRUCTION

Instruction at the Bauhaus includes all practical and scientific areas of creative work.

1. Architecture,
2. Painting,
3. Sculpture, including all branches of the crafts.

Students are trained in a craft (1) as well as in drawing and painting (2) and science and theory (3).

1. Craft training—either in our own, gradually enlarging workshops or in outside workshops to which the student is bound by apprenticeship agreement—includes:

   a) sculptors, stonemasons, stucco workers, woodcarvers, ceramic workers, plaster casters;
   b) blacksmiths, locksmiths, founders, metal turners;
   c) cabinetmakers;
   d) scene painters, glass painters, mosaic workers, enamelers;
   e) etchers, wood engravers, lithographers, art printers, enchasers;
   f) weavers.
   Craft training forms the basis of all teaching at the Bauhaus. Every student must learn a craft.

2. Training in drawing and painting includes:

   a) free-hand sketching from memory and imagination;
   b) drawing and painting of heads, live models, and animals;
   c) drawing and painting of landscapes, figures, plants, and still lifes;
   d) composition;
   e) execution of murals, panel pictures, and religious shrines;
   f) design of ornaments;
   g) lettering;
   h) construction and projection drawing;
   i) design of exteriors, gardens, and interiors
   j) design of furniture and practical articles.

3. Training in science and theory includes:

   a) art history—not presented in the sense of a history of styles, but rather to further active understanding of historical working methods and techniques;
   b) science of materials;
   c) anatomy—from the living model;
   d) physical and chemical theory of color;
   e) rational painting methods;
   f) basic concepts of bookkeeping, contract negotiations, personnel;
   g) individual lectures on subjects of general interest in all areas of art and science.

DIVISIONS OF INSTRUCTION

The training is divided into three courses of instruction:

   1. course for apprentices;
   2. course for journeymen;
   3. course for junior masters.

The instruction of the individual is left to the discretion of each master within the framework of the general program and the work schedule, which is revised every semester. In order to give the students as versatile and comprehensive a technical and artistic training as possible the work schedule will be so arranged that every architect-, painter-, and sculptor-to-be is able to participate in part of the other courses.

ADMISSION

Any person of good repute, without regard to age or sex, whose previous education is deemed adequate by the Council of Masters will be admitted, as far as space permits. The tuition fee is 180 marks per year (it will gradually disappear entirely with increasing earnings of the Bauhaus). A non-recurring admission fee of 20 marks is also to be paid. Foreign students pay double fees. Address enquiries to the secretariat of the Staatliches Bauhaus in Weimar.

April 1919
The Administration of the Staatliches Bauhaus in Weimar
Walter Gropius

168

LUDWIG MIES VAN DER ROHE

Architecture and the Will of the Age

First published as "Baukunst und Zeitwille," *Der Querschnitt* 4, no. 1 (1924), 31–32.

It is not architectural achievement that makes the structures of earlier times seem to us so full of significance but the circumstance that antique temples, Roman basilicas, and even the cathedrals of the Middle Ages are not the works of single personalities but creations of entire epochs. In the face of such structures, who asks after names and what can be the significance of the chance personality of their builder? These structures are in their essence wholly impersonal. They are the pure carriers of the will of an age. Only as such could they have become symbols of their time.

Architecture is always the will of the age conceived as space, nothing else. Until this simple truth is clearly recognized the struggle over the foundation of a new architecture confident in its aims and powerful in its impact cannot be realized; until then it is destined to remain a chaos of uncoordinated forces. That is why the question of the essence of architecture is of decisive importance. It must be understood that every architecture is bound to its time and manifests itself only in vital tasks and through the materials of its age. It has never been otherwise.

Therefore it is a hopeless endeavor to make the form and content of earlier architectural epochs usable for our time; in this even the strongest artistic talent must fail. We see repeatedly how the outstanding builders fail to achieve an effect because their work does not serve the will of the age. They are ultimately dilettantes, despite their great talent, for it makes no difference with what elan one commits a falsehood. The essential is key. One cannot make forward strides looking to the rear, nor can one be the carrier of the will of an age while living in the past. It is the old sophism of distanced observers to hold that the age is responsible for the tragedy of such cases.

The tendency of our time is wholly oriented toward the secular. The efforts of the mystics will remain episodes. Despite a deepening of our conceptions of life, we will build no cathedrals. Nor do the grand gestures of the Romantics have any meaning for us, for we sense the emptiness of form behind them. Our time is not lofty; we do not value great soaring leaps but reason and the real.

The demands of the time for objectivity and functionality must be fulfilled. If that clearly happens, then the buildings of our day will convey the greatness of which the age is capable, and only a fool will maintain that they lack it.

Questions of a general nature are at the center of our concern. The individual declines increasingly in significance; his fate no longer interests us. The decisive achievements in all areas are objective in nature, and their originators are usually unknown. Here the great anonymous tendency of our age becomes evident. Our engineering projects supply the typical example. Gigantic dams, huge industrial installations, and important bridges arise as a matter of course, without their creators becoming known. These structures also demonstrate the technical means of which we will have to make use in the future.

If one compares the mammoth heaviness of a Roman aqueduct with the spider-web delicacy of the power system of modern iron cranes—massive arch constructions with the streamlined lightness of iron and concrete structures—then one senses how greatly the form and expression of our structures will distinguish themselves from those of earlier times. And industrial production methods will also exert an influence on them. The objection that it is only a matter of functional structures remains without significance.

If one renounces all Romanticism in one's way of seeing, then engineering achievements of unexampled cleverness become evident, too, in the stone structures of antiquity, in Roman brick and concrete constructions, as well as in the cathedrals of the Middle Ages. And it may be assumed with certainty that the first Gothic structures were perceived as foreign bodies in their Roman surroundings.

Our utilitarian structures will mature into architecture only when, through their fulfillment of function, they become carriers of the will of the age.

169

WALTER GROPIUS AND PAUL SCHULTZE-NAUMBURG

Who is Right? Traditional Architecture or Building in New Forms

First published as "Wer hat Recht? Traditionelle Baukunst oder Bauen in neuen Formen," *Uhu,* no. 7 (April 1926), 30–40.

WALTER GROPIUS

The pleasure taken in building, in lending form to our architectural structures and cities, is growing throughout the population. The complete change in the technological means of construction, which over two generations has entailed transformations surpassing perhaps the entire preceding millenium, has posed the world of building with such a multitude of new problems that, in practice, we are not yet fulfilling even the smallest fraction of what is possible.

Technical problems, the inspiration just a short while ago for utopian dreams, have been solved with the aid of newly-discovered forces—steam and electricity—with the result that the methods of our traditional way of life have been declared outmoded and left far behind. The natural inertia of the human heart hinders any quick adaptation to these recent advances. At first only a small portion of our needs will be met through the exploitation of the newly harnessed natural forces and their tool, the machine. But building in particular, that vast complex of heterogeneous crafts, still operates with the artisanal methods of the Middle Ages; the incorporation into this area of mechanical forces has just begun to cast off traditional materials, designs, and forms. The new materials—iron, concrete, glass—were available either not at all or only minimally to earlier generations. Their use today is beginning to give architecture a completely new, unexpected face. Just as we can identify a complete formal transformation of individual aspects of our surroundings, such as heating and lighting due to the application of industrial methods of production, the forms buildings take are beginning to change fundamentally.

This change becomes apparent first of all in buildings devoted to the new arrangements of space dictated by modern needs, such as factories, train stations, and bridges. These structures quite logically supplied architecture with a source of inspiration, for new inventions today, as always, are necessarily of critical significance for the development of architecture.

But ominously erroneous ideas interfere with the extension of these foregone conclusions to the great mass of other types of architectural design.

The decline of medieval handicrafts was accompanied by the rise of an academic concept of craft, and the custodians of architecture, architects, lost their natural connection to the technical advances spurred by the discovery of new materials and designs. They consequently became stuck in academic aestheticism, grew tired, gave in to convention, and ultimately let the formal vitality of dwellings and cities slip from their grasp. For the generation just prior to our own, the art of building declined into an enfeebled sentimentalism that saw its purpose in the formalistic employment of motifs, ornaments, and profiles attached to the body of buildings, so that the latter became, instead of living organisms, the carriers of dead, extrinsic, decorative forms.

The leaders of the modern movement in building took the field in decisive opposition to the exhausted and dying practice of a derivative, decorative architecture. In this technological epoch it cannot but seem senseless for people to surround themselves with imitations of past times—Gothic, Rococo, Renaissance, Baroque—so utterly different in structure from our own. Previous epochs never thought of imitating the past; they were proud to lend their own expression to their life. The effect of imitating past styles for both the interior and exterior of our buildings is just as silly as if we were to wander about our streets in the clothing and hairdos of those times. Modern individuals of 1926 need cities, buildings, dwellings, and appliances from their own time, the clear results in form and technology of the means and methods that *our* intellectual achievements have made available.

The subjection of all aspects of building for our needs to industry and the economy, to their precision and efficient exploitation of space and material, will determine the form of our creations. A resolute consideration of all modern methods in the erection of our buildings must be promoted, even if the resulting forms in diverging from the traditional appear strange and surprising. For the ability to make a building "beautiful" is founded on the mastery of the entire array of economic, technical, and formal preconditions, the result of which is the architectural organism. The way in which the builder orders the masses, materials, and colors of the building creates its characteristic face. Its cultural value lies in the proportions of this ordering not in the external application of decorative profiles and ornamentations. Such things disturb the clear contours of a building as soon as they are not functionally justified, which is to say, justified in a technical and spatial sense.

The new architecture articulates its affirmative manifesto as follows:

The formal development of things organically from the point of view of laws appropriate to the present, without romantic prettification and cuteness.

The exclusive use of typical fundamental forms and colors that are understandable to everyone.

Simplicity in multiplicity; the efficient exploitation of space, material, time, and money. The affirmation of the living environment of machines and vehicles, of their tempo and rhythm.

The mastery of increasingly daring formal devices to overcome the earth-bound inertia of buildings with the effect and appearance of suspension.

Tied to the enormous expenditure of technical and material means, development only haltingly pursues the rapidly advancing idea. Since building is collective work, its vitality depends not on individual interest but on the interest of the whole. A positive inclination for building must be promoted. Our overwhelming need for residential dwellings supplies us with a natural pretext for doing so.

How can we create *cheap,* good dwellings appropriate to our time? Generally applicable answers appropriate to this time have not yet been discovered because the problem of residential building as such has never been grasped in all its sociological, economic, technical, and formal aspects, much less adequately solved from the ground up in a fashion subject to responsible planning. A strategic general plan, the "how we want to live" as the universally valid result of thought geared to the intellectual and material possibilities of the present, does not yet exist. Does it correspond to our contemporary way of life that every individual has a domicile that differs fundamentally from everyone else's? We all wear the same modern garments, which nevertheless leave latitude to every individual; why do we not build our houses likewise?

The *economic issue* towers in the foreground. Attempts to economize traditional handicraft methods of residential construction through more rational operating procedures have brought only slight improvement. The problem was not attacked at the roots. The new goal is *dry-assembly construction, that is, the mass prefabrication of residential buildings to be constructed not at the building site but for the most part in assembly-ready units by special factories. That would mean something like a full-sized set of building blocks that would make it possible to order a house from the factory inventory as one orders a pair of shoes.*

Experts estimate the savings to be expected from constructing houses in this way at 50 percent or more compared to traditional methods. The reduction in the cost of our daily-consumption items resulted from an increase in the use of mechanical forces—steam and electricity—in comparison to individual manufacture by hand; the reduction in the cost of housing construction likewise depends on the exploitation of mechanical forces.

The majority of inhabitants of civilized countries have similar residential and daily needs. It is therefore not clear why the residential dwellings we create for ourselves cannot exhibit the same unitary concision as our clothes, shoes, suitcases, and automobiles. There is no justification for the fact that every house in our new outlying developments displays a different floor plan, a different exterior appearance, a different construction style, and different construction materials. On the contrary, such variety exhibits senseless waste and the uncultivated formlessness of a parvenu. The old peasant house in the north and south and the urban dwelling of the eighteenth century display a unified, nearly uniform arrangement of floor plan and overall structure in all European countries. However, making houses completely uniform must be avoided, for the violation of individuality is always short-sighted and wrong.

The planned construction methods must therefore aim at standardization and industrial reproduction of *structural elements,* not entire buildings, so that they can be used to construct various types of houses. Inventory planning would extend to the production in various special factories of all the structural elements required for construction, so that they could be delivered to the site as needed, as well as to tested assembly plans for various types and sizes of houses. Since the parts will be produced mechanically to standard specifications and always fit together, assembly will be possible following precise assembly instructions, in part by unskilled laborers, in the shortest time, with the least expenditure of labor power, and regardless of season and weather.

Practical approaches to the execution of prefabricated serial construction have already been tried in Germany and other countries.

The new construction procedures must be affirmed from an artistic point of view. The assumption that the industrialization of housing construction entails a decline in aesthetic values is erroneous. On the contrary, the standardization of structural elements will have the wholesome result of lending a common character to new residential buildings and neighborhoods. Monotony is not to be feared as long as the basic demand is met that only the *structural elements* are standardized while the contours of the buildings so built will vary. Well-manufactured materials and the clear, simple design of these mass-produced elements will guarantee the unified "beauty" of the resulting buildings, rather than something like aesthetic, decorative forms and profiles that are not determined by function and material. The satisfying form of the individual buildings depends on the builder's gift for working creatively with space; builders will maintain the individual latitude we all desire in their use of the structural elements. The reappearance of individual elements and the same material in various buildings will have an orderly and calming effect on us, as does the uniformity of our clothing, which nevertheless does not violate individuality.

The comprehensive goal of industrializing residential construction can only be achieved through an outlay of specifically dedicated public funds. We are lacking in points at which what has already been achieved is brought together and developed in a planned fashion according to a unified conception. *We need publicly funded experimental building sites.* For just as the form of an object intended for industrial manufacture is systematically developed over the course of countless experiments involving the salesman, the technical expert, and the artist before its formal type is constituted as a norm, so is the manufacture of standardized structural elements possible only through the large-scale cooperation of representatives from the realms of industry, the economy, and art.

Such a thoroughgoing transformation of the construction economy will clearly be achieved only gradually. But despite whatever objections can be raised, it is not to be stopped. A major product of the industry of the future will be *the massive residential building ready-made from inventory.* Only once the comprehensive goals of modern architecture have been achieved will our epoch have defined a style of its own!

DR. SCHULTZE-NAUMBURG

I

Those who have assimilated an image of our country and its buildings carefully and with their eyes open for its physiognomy will not have difficulty recognizing the following categories:

There is first of all a stock of buildings that can probably best be summarized as stemming from earlier times, even if they were constructed over many centuries, extending roughly to the Wars of Independence or the Congress [of Vienna] Period.

Then there has been an ever more rapid growth of buildings of all sorts that, as such, are obvious products of the modern period. In blunt contrast to the earlier stock, which displays clear, extremely memorable forms—so that together the buildings make the impression of a collection of splendidly hewn busts of knotty peasants, manly artisans, delicate scholars, and gallant aristocrats—we are suddenly confronted with a chaos of forms, more precisely of formlessness, such as if we were to find ourselves at a market square filled only with the dregs of a people. Everything here bears the marks of artificiality; the materials are artificial, so is the historical style—like a threadbare evening dress thrown on over shabby, soiled undergarments; artificial is the attitude that is constantly trying to appear as something other, if possible something "finer" than that which it actually signifies. This modern stock is utterly helpless even to offer a reasonable fulfillment of purely objective requirements—not to mention lending them an artistic and clearly defined form; it is dreary and sullen in its expression.

Then, at the end of the 1890s, a new movement suddenly began to halt the disaster spreading across the landscape like a gigantic malignancy. Initially it attempted to clear the table, to identify the actual needs of the time and to formulate them into a clear program on which building can be based. In form it did not want artificially to conserve bygone developmental stages that have disappeared from our purview, but it did seek to preserve our vital treasure of capacities and knowledge, which no single individual can ever conjure out of nothing since they are the fruits of long cultural epochs. Thus should new buildings acknowledge their origins in our northern culture and continue the tradition to precisely the point where it can be developed consistently and healthily until—for reasons that cannot be examined here—it arrives at a dead end. This new movement sought to contain the interregnum of the great style masquerade and allow it to decay.

The movement soon gained ground, gradually grew stronger and stronger and was accepted in various shadings by all serious and well-trained representatives of the architectural profession, even if it was not possible for us to emerge overnight from a period of utter confusion into a new epoch secure in its tradition.

II

Alongside this development, interrupted to be sure by the war, there have recently appeared attempts to break radically with our entire past. Buildings are being recommended to us that have nothing in common with our German spirit and German landscape.

At issue here is quite obviously a clear separation of spirits: on the one side, those who consciously gather together in the northern culture they cannot do without; and on the other those who intentionally eschew what is dear to the German heart, contending that they are drawn to it neither intellectually nor emotionally. We have no choice but to believe them.

Since all of this is not the product of a single school but represents the appearance of quite various, often conflicting forces, it is necessary to attempt to separate out what has been thrown together and look at each one individually.

III

Without doubt the range of architectural tasks has grown immeasurably over the course of the nineteenth and especially the twentieth century, and our architectural tradition can no longer serve as the only guide. Steamships, automobiles, and airplanes, though they are so often presented as model examples, can scarcely be counted as architectonic tasks. Their job is more to lend expression to the functions of a machine, even if their formal definition derives not only from the solution of mathematical design problems but is also the result of an artistic process. Still the architectural traditions at issue here are quite certainly inappropriate for application to railway stations, industrial plants, and various other things.

Under the pressure of these new needs there has arisen (more correctly, is still in the process of arising) a wholly new architectural sub-branch, the aim of which is to find appropriate architectonic expression for the rich variety of technological advances made in recent decades. The time when a smokestack was simply crowned with a Corinthian capital or when an electrical plant dressed in Gothic forms is past, leaving one scarcely able to comprehend how such conceptual errors could ever have been made.

IV

But one commits exactly the same error today in attempting to force upon the German residential dwelling, which has a very long and distinguished ancestral heritage, forms deriving from an utterly alien functional context, namely that of the machine and technology. Human beings are constantly creating for themselves more and better tools, and the more forcefully the utilitarian functions involved come to palpable expression the better those functions will be. Now, however, the ancient forms of human life, as they come to expression in household functions, have little in common with what has transpired in technology, and to seek in industrial forms a tuning fork for this aspect of life, not to mention machines, is neither particularly clever nor correctly felt on an instinctual level. Eating, drinking, sleeping, sociability, and cosy togetherness are extremely conservative things. And if it is admitted that nation, race, culture, and developmental stage also play a momentous role in forms of human life, they manifest an even higher degree of constancy, as becomes immediately evident by comparison to, say, the evolution of our systems of transportation or other specifically technological developments. One would find, for example, no great transformation in the eating styles of people of similar social status between the years 1825 and 1925, but there is a great difference in the way they might have traveled from Leipzig to Berlin. Or the way in which a cosmopolitan lady of the last century received guests in her salon is distinguished from the same procedure today by all manner of nuance, but is scarcely a different world.

Indeed, there even exists a general tendency to set domestic life into *conscious* opposition to the tumult of public life and the environment into which so many people are forced every day by work and habit. The industrialist experiences it as a blessing to forget his factory at the end of the day, and even the scientist, though he sees in technology not only a means of earning one's daily bread but the object of his passion, clearly wants to maintain a boundary between his laboratory and his living room.

Even in those areas in which technology is an integral part of our household life, such as in heating the home and supplying it with water, electricity, a telephone, and the like, the clear effort to make these things as *invisible* as possible is evident everywhere. One wants to be served, but the presence of the servant should not be allowed to make us feel uncomfortable.

V

A particularly German characteristic is the granting of such great influence to alien forms that we are not only capable of penetrating deeply into other cultures but we become carried away by a desire to adopt the alien forms ourselves. No doubt this inclination played a central role as the heritage of classical cultures was taken over so comprehensively during the Renaissance. Yet one should not overlook the fact that the Renaissance was undertaken by people with very closely related bloodlines. If one now characterizes it somewhat harshly, though not altogether unjustly, as theater when someone builds an Italian palace under our northern skies—despite the plethora of climatic contradictions that thereby arise—what kind of theater is being indulged when one recommends to Germans dwellings whose models are clearly seen in East Asian, Indian, or even Negro art?

VI

Alongside these hybridizations, often the cause of strange bloomings indeed, others occur of much greater magnitude when one makes the vulgar assumption of a genuine blood relation between Germans and peoples utterly alien to them.

Since the German national body represents a universal mingling in which Mongoloid, Negroid, and several other bloodlines play a considerable role, it should not be surprising that aesthetic instincts sometimes diverge quite sharply as well, for they are a matter not so much of education as of inheritance. There will therefore occasionally appear personalities who, without necessarily knowing it, do not feel themselves drawn by blood to the world of our Nordic forms but who are commanded by their blood to separate themselves from it.

170

HANNES MEYER

The New World

First published as "Die neue Welt," *Das Werk* 13, no. 7 (1926), 205–224.

The North Pole voyage of the *Norge,* the Zeiss Planetarium in Jena, and [Anton] Flettner's propeller ship are the most recent heralds of the step-by-step mechanization of our planet. As fruits of conceptual precision of the highest degree, they offer visible proof of the ongoing permeation of the world around us by science. Thus does the diagram of the present everywhere display, amid the tangled web of its social and economic force fields, the straight lines of mechanical and scientific provenance. They offer palpable proof of the victory of human consciousness over amorphous nature. This knowledge shakes the foundations of existing values and alters their form. It decisively shapes our new world.

Automobiles storm the streets: in the evenings from six to eight o'clock on the pedestrian island of the Champs Élysées in Paris, we are surrounded by the grandest possible fortissimo of the metropolitan dynamic. Ford and Rolls-Royce burst the confines of the city center, nullify distance, and efface the boundaries between city and countryside. Airplanes glide through the air: "Fokker" and "Farman" increase our mobility and distance us from earth; disrespectful of national borders, they overcome the separation between one people and another. Neon lights glow, loudspeakers screech, sirens scream, billboards advertise, display windows shine: the simultaneity of events expands our concepts of time and space out of all proportion; it enriches our lives. We live faster and therefore longer. Our sense of speed is sharper than ever, with speed records signifying indirect winnings for all. Glider flights, parachute experiments, and Vaudevillian acrobatics refine our sense of balance. The precise division of hours in the plant and at the office and the minute-by-minute regulation of travel schedules impel us to live more consciously. With the swimming pool, sanitarium, and public lavatory, hygiene bursts onto the local scene, creating a new generation of sanitary pottery in water closets and Faenza sinks and tubs. Fordson tractors and Von Meyenburg rotary hoes displace residential settlements, accelerate the tilling of the soil, and intensify the cultivation of the fields. Burrough's calculating machine frees the brain, the parlograph, our hands; Ford's motor unsettles our sense of the stationary and Handley-Page[1] liberates our earthbound spirit. The radio, Marconigram, and telephoto release us from national differentiation into the community of the world. Gramophone, microphone, orchestrion, and pianola accustom our ear to the sound of impersonal, mechanized rhythms: His Master's Voice, Vox, and Brunswick regulate the musical needs of millions of our countrymen. Psychoanalysis explodes the all-too-narrow edifice of the soul, and graphology exposes the essence of individual being. Mazdaznan,[2] [Émile] Coué,[3] Die Schönheit[4] are heralds of the will for renovation breaking out everywhere. Dress gives way to fashion and the outer masculinization of woman manifests the inner equality of the sexes. Biology, psychoanalysis, relativity theory, and entomology are becoming the common intellectual property of all: [Anatole] France, Einstein, Freud, and [Alfred] Fabre are the saints of recent times. Our dwellings become more mobile than ever: mass apartment blocks, sleeping cars, residential yachts, and the Transatlantique undermine the local concept of the homeland. The fatherland fades away. We learn Esperanto. *We become citizens of the world.*

The steady improvement of graphic, photographic, and cinematographic processes makes it possible to reproduce the world ever more precisely. Our visual image of the landscape today is more polymorphic than ever: hangars and dynamo halls are the cathedrals raised to the spirit of our age. The impression they make derives its overwhelming power from the specific forms, lights, and colors of their up-to-the-minute elements: from radio antennas, storage dams, and iron trussing from the parabola of the airship, the triangle

1. Reference to long-range civil aircraft and multi-engined bombers designed by British aviation engineer Sir Frederick Handley-Page (1885–1962).

2. Mazdaznan was a Zoroastrian spiritual practice introduced to the Bauhaus by Johannes Itten.

3. Reference to Émile Coué (1857–1926), French hypnotist and founder of a school of psychotherapy based on autosuggestion.

4. *Die Schönheit* (Beauty) was a popular magazine.

of the automotive warning sign, the circle of the railway signal, and the rectangle of the billboard; from the linearity of the lines of force in telephone cables, aerial trolley wires, and high-tension lines; and from broadcast towers, concrete pylons, flashing lights, and gasoline stations. Our children are already belittling the puffing steam locomotive, cool and measured in their confidence in the miracle of electrical power. [Gret] Palucca's dances, [Rudolf] von Laban's motion choirs, and [Bess] Mensendieck's functional gymnastics outstrip the aesthetic eroticism of painted nudes. The stadium vanquishes the art museum, and bodily reality replaces beautiful illusion. Sport unifies the individual with the masses. Sport is becoming the advanced school of collective feeling: hundreds of thousands were disappointed by Suzanne Lenglen's cancellation.[5] Hundreds of thousands were shaken by [Hans] Breitensträter's defeat.[6] Hundreds of thousands followed [Paavo] Nurmi's ten-thousand-meter run on the cinder track. The standardization of our needs is manifest: the derby hat, the bobbed hairdo, the tango, jazz, co-op products, presized stationery, and Liebig's meat extracts. The typecasting of intellectual fare is illustrated by our rush to Harold Lloyd, Douglas Fairbanks, and Jackie Coogan. Charlot,[7] Grock, and the three Fratellinis forge the masses—beyond distinctions of class and race—into a community of fate. Unions, cooperatives, Co., Inc., cartels, trusts, and the League of Nations are the expressive forms of modern social agglomerations, radio and rotary presses their instruments of information. Cooperation rules all the world. *Community rules over individual being.*

Every epoch demands its own form. Our task is to lend new form to our world by modern means. However, the burden of our knowledge of the past weighs upon us, and our institutions of higher education betray the tragedy of obstacles strewn along our path to the new. The unrestrained affirmation of the modern leads to a reckless denial of the past. The institutions of our elders become obsolete, the gymnasia and academies. City theaters and museums lose their audiences. The nervous perplexity of the applied arts is proverbial. Freed of the ballast of classical airs, artistic conceptual confusion, or the need for a decorative wrapping, the witnesses of a new epoch rise in their place: trade fair, grain silo, music hall, airport, office chair, standard ware. All of these things are products of the formula, function times economy. They are not artworks; art is composition, while purpose is function. The idea of the composition of a harbor strikes us as nonsense; the composition, however, of a city layout, an apartment house . . . ? ? But building is a technical not an aesthetic process, and the purposeful function of a building always contradicts artistic composition. Lent ideal and elementary form, *our apartment house becomes a residence machine.* Heating, sunning, natural and artificial light, hygiene, weatherproofing, garaging, cooking, radio reception, optimum convenience for the housewife, sex and family life, etc., are all the path-breaking force vectors, the components of which are built into the house. (Homeyness and status are not leitmotifs of apartment construction: the first resides in the human heart and not in a Persian rug, the second, in the personal attitude of the occupant and not on the apartment walls!) Modernity puts new building materials at the disposal of our new housing construction: panels, rods, and rungs of aluminum and duralumin, eubolite, rubberoid, torfoleum, eternite, rolled glass, triplex plates, reinforced concrete, glass bricks, Faenza pottery, steel frames, concrete slabs and pillars, troilite, galalite, cellon, ripoline, inanthracene colors. We organize these building elements, in conformity to purpose and the principle of economy, into a constructive unity. Architecture as the further

5. Suzanne Lenglen was a French tennis champion.
6. Hans Breitensträter was a German boxing champion.
7. Charlie Chaplin.

development of tradition or the creation of effect is no more. Individual form and overall contours as well as material colors and surface structure emerge automatically, and this functional understanding of building of all kinds leads to pure construction. *Pure construction is the mark of the new world of forms.* The constructivist form knows no fatherland; it is stateless and the expression of an internationalized way of thought. Internationalism is one of the virtues of our age.

The constructivist principle runs through all domains of our contemporary culture of expression. That it more clearly and directly prevails wherever the Greeks and Louis XIV have left no trace is to be explained by the law of human inertia: in the advertising industry, mechanical typography, light shows, and photographic processes. The new poster displays in a striking organization poster text and goods or trademarks. It is not a poster-art work, but a visual-sensation work. In the new display window, lighting is used to exploit the tensions of modern materials to psychological ends. Display window organization instead of display window decoration. It appeals to the vast differentiation in the modern person's feel for materials and exercises its effect across the range of expressive possibilities: FORTISSIMO = tennis shoes to Havana cigars to stain remover to chocolate with nuts! MEZZOFORTE = glass (as bottle) to wood (as crate) to paper (as wrapping) to tinplate (as box)! PIANISSIMO = silk pajama to batiste shirt to Valenciennes lace to "L'Origan de Coty"!

In Esperanto, following the law of least resistance, we are designing an international language in the standardized stenography of a traditionless script. The critical thing is the constructivist approach to city planning. As long as we fail to approach the city-planning problem with the lack of prejudice of a plant engineer, we suffocate the elegant life of the modern city in a cult of ruins and received notions of traffic axes and lines of sight. The city is the most manifold biological agglomeration that people have to master consciously and constructively form. The demands we make of modern life, either in general or by respective social standing, are of the same sort. The truest mark of community is the gratification of such needs by equivalent means. The result of such collective demands is the standard product. Typical standard wares of international origin and uniformity are: the folding chair, the rolltop desk, the light bulb, the bathtub, the portable gramophone. They are the instruments of mechanization in our daily life. Their standardized form is impersonal. Their manufacture proceeds serially. As serial item, serial equipment, serial component, serial house. The standardized cultural product is the hit tune. To the semi-nomad of contemporary economic life the standardization of residential, clothing, nutritional, and cultural requirements affords the vital quotient of mobility, economy, simplicity, and ease. *The degree of standardization is the index of our collective economy.*

Art's right to exist is uncontested, to the extent that the speculative spirit of the individual retains a need for a graphic-colored, plastic-constructivist, musical-kinetic expression of his worldview. (Advisedly, we do not speak in this context of "isms," of the specific attempts of individual artists; the best of whom, Piet Mondrian, recently termed what has already been achieved the surrogate of a yet-to-be-achieved better achievement.) New form can only come about on the ground of our time and with the tools of our time. Yesterday is dead: dead, the bohemian; dead, the mood and the value, the glaze and the brushstrokes of the accidental. Dead, the novel: we lack belief and time to read. Dead, painting and sculpture as a likeness of the empirical world: in the age of film and photography they seem to us a waste of effort, and the constant "embellishment" of our existing surroundings with interpretations by the "artist" is impudent. Dead, the artwork as a "thing in itself," as "L'art pour l'art": our collective consciousness tolerates no individualistic excess.

The artist's atelier becomes a scientific laboratory, and the artist's works are the product of mental acuity and the power of invention. The artwork of today, like every time-bound product, is subordinate to the conditions of life in our epoch, and the result of our speculative confrontation with the world can only be recorded in exact form. *The new artwork is a totality,* not a detail, not an impression. *The new artwork is formed elementarily through the application of primary means.* [. . .] *The new artwork is a collective work and intended for all;* it is neither a prize for the collector nor an individual's private privilege.

171

ADOLF BEHNE AND PAUL WESTHEIM

The Aesthetics of the Flat Roof

First published as "Zur Ästhetik des flachen Daches," *Das neue Frankfurt,* no. 7 (1926–1927), 163–164.

ADOLF BEHNE

The peaked roof has its beauty, in instances where it combines with the body of the house into a clear and simple form. The rows of workers' and middle-class houses in old cities, which are uniform in the angle of inclination, uniform in style, uniform in roofing material, and reflective of the tight knit of medieval life, are always pleasing to the eye.

But in later times people began to make the roof "interesting," until finally—when, that is, its forms were no longer motivated—the roof became an architectonic motif.

Slope and dormers are so easily misused, and when the little tower, the small cupola, the attics were added, and the most frequent variation of materials possible, and then even a touch of falsely understood "homeland," the roof chaos pointing restlessly toward the sky over residential areas for the past few decades could and had to result.

What all could be made out of a "roof"!

The building often seemed only a modest column for the architecture of the roof.

What a service that the new architects have put a rather radical stop to this nonsense.

The catchword "flat roof" signifies only that the conscience has once more become alert to the originally healthy meaning of the roof.

Others will speak about the economic and technical aspects of the flat roof. Artistically, the flat roof presents no fewer possibilities than the peaked roof. It obliges us to return to a view of the building as a unified body; it answers our desire for clear definition of appearance—and even if it had no other merit than to put a decisive end to the atmospheric roof still life, its aesthetic advantage would be very considerable.

PAUL WESTHEIM

I am in the habit of looking at houses, even residential settlements, from the perspective of the floor plan. Façades and the façade attitude are in any case our woe, and not only in architecture. It seems to me important that we produce mass residential dwellings that are habitable, in which one can live humanely. For people who finally do acquire a proper dwelling, one that is serviceable for people today, it is likely unimportant what kind of roof—whether flat or peaked—they have over their heads, so long as it does not leak.

For a cubic block—which is a technical term, since the residential cells of which a house is constructed are after all cubes—the flat roof sets natural aesthetic bounds. For the rest, the question of the flat roof is a purely expedient one. It should also be considered that the flat roof has long since been proven in practice. In his book, *Wie baut Amerika?* [How Does America Build?], which is well worth reading, [Richard] Neutra speaks of "the customary flat roofs" as of something self-evident. And whoever chances to look down on Berlin from an airplane will be able to confirm that for the last hundred years at least sixty percent of buildings in Berlin are covered with a flat roof. From the perspective of the street, that has just always been concealed. It is not surprising that an emotional and temperamental tradition reacts first of all negatively to the flat roof. At first it was also believed that it was necessary to decorate iron beams with acanthus ornaments. Today there is no longer any emotional, any temperamental reaction against naked iron beams conforming to their technical design. On the contrary, the forms of technical design are perceived as beauty. In architecture the law of inertia still holds sway. Inertia represents an impediment, but it need not be allowed to proliferate to the extent that it becomes a block.

172

RUDOLF ARNHEIM

The Bauhaus in Dessau

First published as "Das Bauhaus in Dessau," *Die Weltbühne* 23, no. 22 (May 31, 1927), 920–921.

Separated by the railway from the thick nest of dusty, peak-roofed, small-town houses and so already isolated in their exterior setting, sit two gigantic, blindingly white blocks, the one vertical, the other perpendicular to the first. A pair of balcony doors and a large glass window break the surfaces; otherwise the whole is bare and smooth and in no way suggests classification as a house. Rather it is more as if a synoptic exhibition model were being used to demonstrate how much 32,000 cubic meters of reconstructed space is—a cubic measure of a given quantity of people and working material. Like the smallest consumer article made in the Bauhaus workshop, this largest is put together out of a pair of the simplest spatial forms. Thus one senses from a brass ashtray all the way to an apartment house, the completely new, very intelligible unity of man-made things, which is independent of dimension and stands in contrast to all of nature.

The will to cleanness, clarity, and boldness in design has won a victory here. Already from outside one sees through the large windows the private life indoors, a person working down to his fingertips or one resting. Every single thing shows its design: no screw is hidden, no decorative carved work to conceal which raw material has been processed there. One is solely tempted to evaluate this honesty also in moral terms.

A house of pure function. Work is done constructively, not as before with the aim of accomplishing the most individual plenitude of visual impressions; this constructivism produces visual gratification of its own. The point is made here more clearly than ever that the practical really is at the same time the beautiful. It is also pleasing from the standpoint of aesthetic composition to see how banisters, chair legs, doorknobs, and teapots are all constructed of the same metal pipe. The old theme of unity in diversity, formerly applied only to buildings, statues, and paintings, receives a new meaning here: a house containing a thousand different things can be perceived as a structured totality.

And still a great deal must be decided by feeling, because it is not immediately dictated by function. What should be the color? Where on the door should the room number be positioned? For the problems everyone knows from wanting to hang a picture correctly in one's own home multiply themselves enormously when the living space and all the furnishings have such simply coherent proportions that everything depends on how one thing relates to another. In a room hung with diagonal curtains, in which a sofa sits obliquely to the corner and ten different, fully loaded little tables are set up every which way, there is hardly any reason why a new floor lamp should be placed here rather than there. But the position of everything in a Bauhaus room can be decided with nearly lawlike precision. One will soon learn to understand theoretically that it is not a question here of subjective taste, but that such feelings are a very secure and generally valid psychological phenomenon that leads to very similar results from different people. That is why one can speak even in the case of such problems as these of "objectively determined solutions."

Certainly the Bauhaus has not yet come so far as to be able to supply industry with conclusively standard patterns. Certainly it is not altogether innocent of affectation and pretentiousness. But the idea of breaking the tie to tradition and departing afresh from the two fundamental factors—the requirements of practical life and the conditions set by the raw materials—is so good that, for the moment, nothing else is important.

173

ERICH MENDELSOHN

Why This Architecture?

First published as "Warum diese Architektur?" *Die literarische Welt* 4, no. 10 (March 9, 1928), 1.

On the opening of the Schocken
Department Store in Nuremberg

Think back just one hundred years:
Crinoline and wigs
Tallow light and spinning wheels
General stores and craftsmen's guilds—
Then think of us, now, think of what surrounds you:
Bare knees and a sporty 'do
Radio and film
Automobile and aeroplane
Specialty shops and department stores.
Don't think they're superficialities—
the deeper meaning is in them.
A hundred years ago—as now.
Certainly man remains man and the heavens are broad as ever,
But the world around you is enormously alive, cities of millions,
    skyscrapers, eight-hour flights from Moscow to Berlin.

Napoleon needed months for that, and met his ruin there.

And you ask, what is this architecture for?

So, no wonder, but a product of life itself, our life, our times.

Not to be somehow against our Beautiful Fountain or impious to
  Saint Sebaldus.

Not to throw a stone in the Nuremberg Museum.

Only to be sincere.

You do demand sincerity? From your friends, from everyone? But
  you want to be tricked by the things around you, by your
  house, your builders?

Are those somehow things that do not belong to you—your electric
  stove and razor?

So efficient, so simple, so obvious.

And impossible to think away.

So, to want to disavow our life is self-deception, is miserable
  and cowardly.

Even wanting to repress developments is self-sacrifice, foolish
  and pointless.

Therefore be brave, be smart.

Grab life by the hair, right there where its best heart beats, in
  the middle of life, the middle of technology, traffic, and
  trade.

Accept it just as it is, accept its tasks as it poses them, to
  you, today, to all of us.

For each challenge demands efficiency, clarity, simplicity.

Each must be efficient because all labor is too valuable to be
  wasted senselessly.

Clear because not just the select but everyone must understand
  it.

Simple because precisely the best achievement is always the
  simplest as well.

Never has a powerful time trusted another more than itself.

And here we architects are supposed to lag behind and wear wigs,
  we engineers and construction chiefs who build your houses,
  your cities, the whole tangible world?

Don't be talked into anything; only one who cannot forget has no
  free mind. Only one who cannot invent is unfruitful. Only
  one who does not live dies before his time.

Only one who has no rhythm in the body—do not think of jazz, be
  serious—does not understand the metallic swing of the
  machine, the humming of propellers, the enormous new vitality
  that stimulates, blesses, and makes us creative.

You say there are no builders? Here they are!

However, palatial façades, decorative pomp, and tiny ornamental
  windows are far behind.

Into the room, the masses layered, out of the floorplan, the room
  conjured in the air.

Here are the stairs, here the entrance, here the rows of windows
  above the shelves.

Stairs, entrance, windows in with the rhythm of racing autos, of
   high-speed traffic.
Don't let yourselves be rushed; master time.
Don't let yourselves be fooled; you are the masters.
Be creators, architects, shape your time.
Those are your duties, out with your responsibility, be leaders.
Therefore this architecture.

174

MARCEL BREUER

Metal Furniture and Modern Spatiality

First published as "Metallmöbel und moderne Räumlichkeit," *Das neue Frankfurt* no. 1 (1928), 11.

Metal furniture is part of a modern space. It is styleless, for it should express no intentional
form beyond its function and the design its function requires. The new space should not
represent a self-portrait of the architect nor from the outset the composure of the soul of
its individual user.

Since the external world affects us today with the most intense and various impressions,
we change the form of our lives in more rapid succession than in earlier times. It is only
logical that our surroundings must undergo corresponding changes. We are approaching
furnishings, spaces, and buildings which, to the greatest possible extent, are alterable,
mobile, and accessible to various combinations. Furniture, even the walls of the space, are
no longer massive, monumental, apparently permanently rooted, or in fact permanently
installed. They are much more injected with air, drawn, so to speak, in space; it hinders
neither movement nor the view through space. The space is no longer a composition, no
rounded-off whole, since after all its dimensions and elements are subject to essential
changes. One comes to the conclusion that any correct, usable object fits in the space in
which it is needed, similar to how a living being fits in nature: a person or a flower. The
reproductions show metal furniture of the same characteristic form, determined by the type
of design, in the most various spaces: in the theater, auditorium, atelier, dining room, and
living room.

I have specifically chosen metal for these pieces of furniture to achieve the characteristics
of modern spatial elements just described. The heavy, pretentious upholstery of a comfortable armchair has been replaced by tightly stretched fabric surfaces and a few easily
dimensioned, springy, cylindrical brackets. The steel used, and particularly the aluminum,
manifest conspicuously little weight given the large static demands made (the tensile stress
of the fabric). The slit form increases mobility. All of the various types are constructed of
the same standardized, elementary parts that can be disassembled and interchanged at any
time.

These pieces of metal furniture should be nothing more than necessary instruments of
contemporary life.

18
Housing for the Masses

FROM THE PERIOD shortly before the war continuing through the early years of the republic, living conditions in German cities were among the worst in Europe. Cramped and unsanitary apartments often housed more than one family, while some resided in dwellings judged uninhabitable even by the lax standards of local housing codes. With its sprawling neighborhoods of concrete blocks, often dating from the end of the nineteenth century and popularly known as *Mietkaserne* (rental barracks), the situation in Berlin was especially dire. Few apartments were built during the war and this fact, combined with rising energy and materials costs and the influx of veterans to large cities after 1918, transformed what had long been a problem into a public crisis. By 1929 some estimated the apartment shortage in Berlin as high as 200,000 units.

Recognition of the housing predicament was included in the Weimar constitution, whose Article 153 announced that "Possession creates responsibility: use of the land must serve the common good." Even more boldly, Article 155 proclaimed the right of everyone to shelter and the state's responsibility for insuring its construction. Weimar architects, builders, politicians, and social activists proposed diverse solutions to the housing problem. While their efforts never resulted in sufficient new building to eliminate the apartment shortage, such agitation did lead to tax reforms, low-interest loans, and land grants that made possible many public housing projects.

Expressing the utopian idealism of the 1918 revolution as well as the influence of the fantasy writer Paul Scheerbart, the architect Bruno Taut espoused a return to the land and the construction of decentralized settlements combining industry and agriculture. While few architects and city planners shared such anti-urban sentiments (which Taut himself soon renounced), his exhortation to live in greater proximity to nature did find some resonance in the garden-city movement. Among the more remarkable interventions in the housing crisis were the construction projects initiated by public-interest building associations. Generally founded by Social Democrats and funded by unions, banks, and building trade groups, these associations combined social idealism, political activism, and architectural innovation in their efforts to provide affordable housing for workers and the middle class. Low-cost, publicly owned land facilitated the success of these projects, as did the cooperation of the socialized building trade unions described by Martin Wagner.

An early leader of the movement, Wagner was director of the government building administration in Berlin from 1927 and a founder in 1924 of GEHAG, an acronym of the Public Benefit Homestead, Savings, and Building Association. Best known for two garden settlements, Hufeisen in Britz and the Waldsiedlung in Zehlendorf, both designed for suburban Berlin by its chief architect, Taut, GEHAG constructed 9,300 housing units between 1924 and 1932. A typical inhabitant of the new housing projects is sketched by Otto Steinicke.

To publicize new architectural solutions to the housing shortage, the German Werkbund, a professional organization of industrialists and architects, organized the Weissenhofsiedlung exhibition in Stuttgart. Presenting single-family homes by leading European architects, the exhibition drew up to 20,000 visitors a day between July and October 1927. Ludwig Mies van der Rohe, the head architect of the exhibition, conceived it as a demonstration of how recent advances in design and engineering such as prefabricated building components could produce economical housing of high aesthetic standards. Standardization of building types, he maintained, did not imply uniformity and loss of individuality, an assertion easily borne out by the distinctive structures on display at the Weissenhofsiedlung. While the exhibition's great success consolidated the acceptance of modern architecture in Germany, particularly the austere style commonly identified with the New Objectivity, many remained skeptical about the architectural merits of individual buildings. Some commentators praised the Weissenhofsiedlung architects for creating domestic environments suitable for the new style of life, while others faulted the impracticality of their sumptuous furnishings and interior designs. Writing in the Werkbund journal, *Die Form,* Marie-Elisabeth Lüders considered the building by Mies van der Rohe poorly equipped to serve the needs of families. The usual complaint that modern architecture is overly intellectual and unsuited to the lives of ordinary people found early expression in Edgar Wedepohl's review of the buildings by Le Corbusier, Pierre Jeanneret, and Gropius at the Weissenhofsiedlung. Organizations such as the Werkbund and the journal *Das neue Frankfurt* publicized labor-saving innovations in home and appliance design, many of which were intended to ease the workload of women, as the essay by Grete Lihotzky suggests. A similar direction is evident in Taut's influential book, *The New Dwelling: The Woman as Creator,* which approached the domestic environment with language similar to the discourse of industrial management. No longer the exclusive province of industry, rationalization and increased efficiency had come to the modern home.

175

BRUNO TAUT

The Earth is a Good Dwelling

First published as "Die Erde eine gute Wohnung," *Die Volkswohnung. Zeitschrift für Wohnungsbau und Siedlungswesen* 1, no. 4 (February 24, 1919), 45–48.

"People were not made to scurry around in anthills but to spread out over the land that they were meant to build upon. Fragility of the body and vices of the soul are the inevitable consequences of excessive crowding. Of all the animals the one least fit to be a herd animal is the human; people who have been cooped up like sheep soon die. The breath of man is deadly to his own kind."

Thus wrote Jean-Jacques Rousseau long ago in his *Émile*. People heard his call and did not follow. Today the call is being issued again, but quietly and shyly—will they follow him now, or at least take one step along the designated path? In the early days of the revolution there was talk of how the land was now free, the great estates and state-owned territories divided up, and of the people returning to mother earth through freely distributed small holdings and gardens. But what happened? Endless discussions in meetings and newspapers, a pro and con of theories, and not one step toward action. Why this failure of the will? Do people sense that every step in that direction represents a death blow to the heart of the city, signals the beginnings of the dissolution of the city and the total upheaval of our entire culture? The socialist papers cry: "Workers! Leave the mass grave of the city!" But where is the path? Where is the program for settling the countryside?

The position that adheres to what exists, to established fact, is all too rigid and tenacious. It fears giving up a state structure based on the centralization of industry, the division of labor, the separation of city and countryside, and large urban concentrations. It is hardly worthwhile speaking of the symptoms of urban dissolution—they are so evident, and already were before the war. Thorough studies had already established the increasing economic instability in real estate as a consequence of property speculation; voices had increasingly been raised in an attempt to deflect attention from the prevailing course of world trade and push the maintenance of the nation through the domestic economy into the foreground. If before the war the material interests of specific groups, particularly industrialists, merchants, and large landowners, resisted the change in emphasis, during the war material need forced the transition from demands to action (such as was possible) and lent the demands new vigor. And today as a result of the war there is no choice: the nation must be able to feed every inhabitant from its own supplies. According to L. Migge,[1] a 1,200-square-foot garden would suffice to supply a family of five with fruits and vegetables without any reliance on the market; according to Franz Oppenheimer, twelve acres suffices for a small peasant holding, and the same scholar proves that such an allocation would allow forty million people to settle in the German countryside, instead of the seventeen million living there today. That would result in an enormous relief for industry, which would be freed from its participation in exports and world trade; industry could devote itself almost exclusively to the needs of the nation and do without the reserve army of unemployed—which it requires in boom times but just as quickly condemns to misery when a crisis arrives. Theories and interests notwithstanding, one thing is certain: given the sound and complete utilization of its land, Germany could feed its population.

1. *Jedermann Selbstversorger* (Jena, 1918).

For the prewar population figure of seventy million inhabitants there would be approximately two acres of land per person, while in Belgium—which, according to [Peter] Kropotkin, lives off of its own agricultural product—there is only a little less than one acre per person. Considering the obvious efforts of industry to settle as much as possible on the outskirts of cities (assuming, of course, access to good transport routes), as well as the frequent practice by large factories of purchasing land for cultivation by their workers, the beginning of the dissolution of the cities is clearly evident. The division of labor, with all its grievous effects, is beginning to be surpassed, and perhaps a wholly new understanding of the Taylor System is at hand, which would not base performance evaluations exclusively on hand and arm movements judged in isolation but much more on how a worker's energies could best be extended. The point would be to make the worker more valuable by preserving body and soul in harmonious interaction with the machine for half a day, with the other half spent cultivating the soil of the earth. Kropotkin's book, *Fields, Factories and Workshops,* offers us a strictly scientific investigation proving how industry is slowly moving away from monopoly consolidation and centralization, how it is spreading over the entire globe, and how the time will come when the industrial production of every nation will allow it to subsist nearly without imports and exports. Industry will then have completed its merger with agriculture; Kropotkin identifies the beginnings of this process and points out the ceaseless movement toward the transcendence of the division of labor, the fusion of city and countryside, and the establishment of a new way of life. In his book *Return to the Soil,* Jules Méline likewise comes to the conclusion that the old idea of nations specializing in particular branches of production is now completely out of date.

Theories and facts, experiences of the war and the present confront one another and pose unyielding challenges. And what happens? In the great French Revolution, 1792 glowed with the golden hope of rising to Rousseau's challenge; today we are a few steps farther and our revolution inspires the same hope. Is it to remain just as vain a hope now, 126 years later?

If a revolution contents itself just with a change of regimes and the implementation of reforms, it does not deserve the name. Then it has stopped short of revolutionizing the human spirit, which, not so easily satisfied, is thunderously demanding a fundamental transformation—one going to the roots of the matter and therefore genuinely "radical" for the first time—a transformation of conditions that have become unbearable. One day that step will be taken, and it would be regrettable if the opportunity offered by the present liberalization of social relations were ignored and the chance to make the transition into a new state of affairs neglected—before that step is forced upon us as a necessity. Well-founded and firmly anchored hopes might fall silent for a while, but they do not die. And this hope, which lives as the deepest desire of humanity and which Rousseau and countless others after him proclaimed (I mention only Tolstoy, Scheerbart, [Sir Henry] Campbell-Bannermann, and [Arthur] Posadowsky-Wehner), must not be allowed to die. Only on the surface is the desire for opening up the land a material one. And it may be that the government's recognition of the ultimate consequences is what allows it to shrink from beginning the journey—for then there is no more return. And it might be that the bourgeois strata, mesmerized by the "threat" of urban dissolution, will divert the stream into small channels.

There is, however, no point in sticking our heads in the sand like ostriches. We are already experiencing the disintegration of the city, and following it—even if only after another 126 years, as we slowly come to the end of the second millenium—comes dissolution. We must direct our gaze freely into the future and, so as not to wander aimlessly in all directions, set our sights firmly upon the distant goal on the horizon. This, the greatest of humanity's revolutions, will overturn countless values; how many have not already been lost in the world war! But it will be the less, the sooner all have set their sights on this goal.

"Dissolution of the cities"—that is a negation, but fundamentally it is much more an affirmation. Humanity will reclaim the earth; no longer content merely to stroll about on its surface, humanity will inhabit it. It may be that this new state of affairs, still lying in the future, appears at the outset only as the fulfillment of a material desire promising a healthier life and better nutrition, but it conceals much more within itself: a new culture from top to bottom with a completely different nature than the one we know today and from the past.

What is happiness? To this question Tolstoy gives the answer: Happiness is living in and with nature. So we city dwellers today are all unhappy. For the enjoyment of nature is happiness just as little as the enjoyment of art is happiness; happiness is achieved only by living in nature. Once humans find their happiness, their inner peace, through a connection to the earth, then their soul will once more be fulfilled; it will be at peace in the world, in God. Then Europe, after a long, long time, will once again have a religion. "The steps of religion," says Fechner in his daily column, "are large but slow. It requires millenia for one step. The raised foot of religion is hovering in the air, already on its way down. When will religion put it down?" Religion will take another step once humanity has rediscovered its dwelling on the earth. And with that, humanity will acquire content, and "where there is content, form comes along on its own" (Tolstoy). A new culture blossoms, a true culture.

Ideas are signposts, and the image of a distant future must light the way of our strivings. This image cannot be displayed to people often enough, so that they grow tired of the present and press ever more vehemently for its fulfillment. Am I as an architect not working against my own art when I demand the dissolution of the cities? The greatest buildings have risen, after all, from city landscapes, and I have myself, in *Crown of the City,*[2] attempted to describe the crowning achievement of a future city. The greatest buildings of all time, the gigantic temples of Asia, Angkor Wat and Borobudur, are solitary structures; and in my *Crown of the City,* I also wanted to describe the isolation of the architectural structure in the midst of an expansive settlement, primarily to awaken the sense of an isolated building.

We are determined to keep a vision of the new countenance of the earth before our eyes: large estates, like we have today, but organized as cooperatives and operated so that more people than today cultivate and live from them; wastelands dotted with small holdings and gardens, in between, woods, meadows, and lakes. Then expansive settlements strewn about with small houses, cottages, and gardens. Industry adheres to this image of itself: it is also scattered among many workshops so that it can most easily satisfy the demand for its products. The process will be accelerated by new forms of transportation: large railroad lines will recede; a tightly knit network of light roads for power vehicles will replace them. Raw materials will be supplied nearly exclusively by river and canal traffic. Markets will be all but superfluous since the population will supply its needs almost on its own, living from a natural exchange of its own products. The power of money will recede, even disappear: who needs to buy much in the countryside! People will live in

2. *Die Stadtkrone* (Jena: Eugen Diederichs, 1919), with contributions by Paul Scheerbart, Erich Baton, and Adolf Behne.

nature, work in nature, and conduct a harmonious way of life in a healthy balance between manual and mental activity, between the workshop and the land. Vacation trips will cease and, since people live harmoniously, they will experience solitude as an intensified to-getherness with others, whom they will seek out only when an inner need, the need to communicate after a period of development, impels them to do so. Then they will be guests of the others for a few days, and also have the room at home to take others in. And people will gather as a whole only where they have forever gathered together: in places of worship. That will be the only occasion for travel, and there will be places there to spend the night. Otherwise, traveling will no longer make any sense. (Although those who want to see a distant land can make use of air travel.) The development of airplanes will greatly accelerate this movement. The rarity of trips will make them truly valuable for the first time, and, for the rest, Scheerbart's words will be the rule: "Travel at home!"

But wait! The architectonic image of cities—what happened to it? Let us not complain about that. A wholly new one will arise. In the settlements the urban landscape will completely disappear, and individual buildings will acquire a completely different mean-ing, as will the isolated large building. If we rise above the earth in a balloon, what we will see below are houses strewn about like grains of sand, by now arranged in rows as well. The grains of sand will join together and the higher we rise the more they will appear like a fog, now thicker, now thinner, spreading over the green countryside. And in this fog, a few glistening spots sparkle, smaller and larger, like stars in the sky. It is the places of worship, erected in glass, illuminating the night. Everything has been loosened up; people now have their first profound understanding of the necessary isolation of archi-tectonic works of art, and they bloom here and there like rare and precious flowers. The stars in the sky and the stars on earth greet each other.

All of the great religious prophets—Buddha under the Bo tree and Christ in the desert—found God in solitude. And the new prophet and the new people will find him in the same way. A new bond will unite humanity. Where will anyone want to draw boundaries when the earth looks like I have described it? Boundaries will be impossible, and a whole new form of union will become necessary. States will disappear and with them the violence of states; in their place will arise a new form of human relationship, which is supremely prophylactic but no longer organizational and dictatorial. There will be institutions only of a voluntary sort and effect. The city is the symbol of state power, and the state and all that accompanies it—politics and wars—will never disappear before the city disappears. If this is what currently inhibits the colonization of the countryside, then we must revolutionize the human spirit by all possible means. For what we want is love, not hate. "The raised foot of religion is hovering in the air, already on its way down. When will religion put it down?" Will the new messiah be able to come at the beginning of the third millenium?

176

MARTIN WAGNER

Path and Goal

First published as "Weg und Ziel," *Soziale Bauwirtschaft* (November 9, 1920), 34–35.

The men in the construction industry do not want to occupy the lowest echelon. Building is their trade. They went to work with the spirit of true pioneers as the revolution made the first crack in the capitalist economic structure. With laudable farsightedness, the construction workers placed themselves at the head of a movement that seeks to transfer the German construction industry out of the capitalistic economic system of private ownership. As the first German union the Association of German Construction Workers has made itself the leader and bearer of this movement. The other unions in the construction trade—the Confederation of Technical Employees and Civil Servants, the Association of Factory Workers, the Central Association of Carpenters, the Central Association of Roofers, the Central Association of Potters, the Association of Painters, the Central Association of Machinists, the Association of Masons, and the Central Association of Asphalt Workers, among others—have joined the Association of German Construction Workers and put their well-established organizations at the fore of the incipient cells of a new general union in the construction trades to protect and strengthen it. They have created an Association of Social Construction Firms, whose task is to promote the development of the many new social construction firms that have appeared since the revolution and to make them strong and productive in the service of the general good. Beyond this, however, to the Association of Social Construction Firms accrues the great and responsible task of gathering the popular forces pushing for a collective economy into a unified movement and marking out the paths it should follow and goals for which it should strive.

As long as socialism was fighting for the recognition of its ethical goals, it could content itself with programs and principles laid down by its political representatives in the struggle against capitalism. Today, when socialism is supposed to be put into practice, these generally conceived programs no longer suffice. [. . .]

Readers will ask us why we have to create a new publication to pursue the goals mentioned above. We have a daily press that is active in the service of socialism; we have union papers devoted to narrower professional interests; and we have technical journals to promote the interests of the construction trade. That is certainly correct, but can these publications accomplish our task?

We refuse to make ourselves the servants of any particular party because we hope and wish that members of all parties will join hands in the construction of a new social construction industry. We cannot, however, leave the promotion of social construction firms to the many union papers, which necessarily represent particular professional interests, as long as the liberation of the mental and manual workers in the construction industry from the yoke of private capital is incomplete. It is utterly impossible to expect the technical journals (most of which are controlled by private capital) to pursue a social policy in the construction industry. Has it not already happened that technical journals like *Construction World* have been threatened by their advertisers with cancellations when they hosted an objective discussion of the socialization of the construction trades? Even if these difficulties did not exist, our publication would still have its own tasks to pursue and duties to assume, for which there is no organ at present.

Socialist Construction strives to be the central organ for all socialization endeavors in the building trades. It will follow the entire construction industry in order to illuminate the dark paths of private capital for a sure-sighted offensive by the pioneers of a new collective economy in the building trades.

In this sense it will be a fighting organ against the selfish profit interests of private capitalist enterprises and their professional associations.

Socialist Construction will become a counselor to all circles with a vital interest in having their construction needs met by trustee enterprises. It will disseminate materials and proposals for collective economic options among the legislative bodies—national, state, and local—in whose hands nearly ninety percent of all construction activity is concentrated today, and energetically support their struggle against the housing shortage. Drawing on practical experiences of life in the construction industry, it will in particular offer local building authorities its intensive assistance in all branches of the collective construction economy.

Socialist Construction will also be a consulting organ for the professional representatives of tenants, of construction guilds, building societies, and housing societies. Hundreds of millions of marks pass through the hands of these organizations yearly for housing construction and maintenance, and they are therefore, for better or worse, dependent on the profit interest of private capitalist enterprises.

Socialist Construction also wants to take up the struggle for the liberation of mental and manual workers in the building trades from the servile yoke of private capital. It strives to prepare and educate the active creative forces in the building trades for their new sphere of action in a free community of labor.

177

BRUNO TAUT

The New Dwelling: The Woman as Creator

First published in *Die neue Wohnung. Die Frau als Schöpferin* (Leipzig: Verlag von Klinkhardt und Biermann, 1924), 64–70.

[New dwellings will provide] the woman with a way to improve her performance. She will adopt a new organization for her work and, with due consideration to the given circumstances, arrange to perform individual chores—tending the children, cooking, serving meals, washing up, cleaning, laundry, shopping, etc.—according to a plan. Sufficient time for going on walks and sleeping will be calculated into it, as the new home economics teaches, which amounts to the application of the Taylor System to the household. All the members of the household, the man and the children, will contribute to making the beds, cleaning the washstand, etc., as necessary. The simplification of bedding plays a further role here, which begins by replacing cumbersome featherbeds with blankets or, when necessary in winter, by down blankets.

These changes will create a constant order in the dwelling, which will do away with the useless formality of having a parlor—because no one will need to feel embarrassed by unexpected visitors. The most important reason for that is disappearing anyway: previously, and to some extent today, people turned up their noses at any dwelling that was not overflowing with all kinds of odds and ends. A sparse household was disdained by society and its inhabitants shunned. This convention persists more or less unchanged at present. But that will change entirely in no more than a decade: "smart" will be what the new fashion is called, and everything in the way of knick-knacks, unnecessary items, and little pictures lying, standing, and hanging around the dwelling will be the reason for upturned noses and counsel against incautious contact with the peculiar inhabitants.

It is worthwhile to design and build new dwellings only on the basis of these presuppositions. What is the direction in which the arrangement of spaces and their furnishings should develop? The nerve center of the dwelling is the kitchen, where the housewife's main work in a small household takes place. The small or middle-sized dwelling plays the central role in our considerations because of its prevalence; but what is right for it is easily applied to the large dwelling, leading to a better solution to the problem of servants, which is equally difficult the world over. For what the housewife accomplishes in the small dwelling is done in larger households by the cook, the chambermaid, etc., and precisely in the latter case is the most straightforward organization a substantial financial concern. [. . .]

Instead of falling back into the error of old ways, residential habits should be observed and gradually improved so that family life can proceed without the slightest friction and disturbance. What is the easiest way for meals to be prepared and served, then the table cleared and the dishes washed and put away? The easiest way to deal with the process of going to bed and getting up, with daily washing, with the use of the bath and closet space? And the best way to store clothing, laundry, etc? Answers to these and other questions will result in new interior arrangements, in increased spaciousness in rooms, and therefore in savings in construction costs; for it actually is possible to satisfy the same needs better and in a more spacious manner while simultaneously reducing the overall size of the dwelling.

178

GRETE LIHOTZKY

Rationalization in the Household

First published as "Rationalisierung im Haushalt," *Das neue Frankfurt*, no. 5 (1926–1927), 120–123.

Every thinking woman must be aware of the backwardness of current methods of household management and see in them a severe impediment to her own development and therefore to the development of the family as a whole. Today's hectic urban life-style imposes demands on women far exceeding those of the calmer conditions of eighty years ago, yet today's woman is nevertheless condemned to manage her household (aside from the relief offered by a few exceptions) just like her grandmother did.

The problem of finding a more rational organization of the housewife's work is of nearly equal significance for all levels of society. Both the middle-class woman, who often has to run the house without help of any kind, and the working-class woman, who frequently has to pursue an occupation outside the home, are so over-worked that over the long run it cannot but have a negative effect on the general health of the whole population.

For more than a decade women leaders have recognized the importance of relieving the housewife of unnecessary burdens and have spoken out for the central management of residential buildings, that is, for the establishment of centralized cooking facilities. They said: Why should twenty women have to shop for groceries when one can do the same for all of them? Why should twenty women make a fire in twenty stoves when food could be prepared on one for everyone? Why should twenty women cook for twenty families when the proper organization would allow four or five persons to do the same work for twenty families? Such considerations are illuminating for every reasonable person, and they have had their effect. Buildings with centralized kitchens were constructed.

Soon, however, it became apparent that it is not possible simply to unite twenty families into one household. Aside from personal quarrels and conflicts, sharp variations in the material conditions of the respective inhabitants are unavoidable, which is why the merging of several families necessarily leads to conflicts. For workers and private employees, who are subject to unemployment at relatively short notice, the centralized kitchen arrangement is out of the question from the start, because it prevents them from lowering their standard of living to the necessary extent once they become unemployed. The problem of rationalizing the household, therefore, cannot be solved in isolation, but must go hand-in-hand with associated social considerations.

We recognize from past experience that the single-family dwelling is here to stay, but that it must also be organized as rationally as possible. The question is how to improve the traditional methods of household management, which waste both energy and time. What we can do is transfer the principles of labor-saving management developed in factories and offices, which have led to unsuspected increases in productivity, to the household. We must recognize that there is a best and simplest way to approach every task, which is therefore the least tiring as well. The three main working groups involved—housewives, manufacturers, and architects—face the important and highly responsible job of working together to discover and make feasible the simplest way of executing every household chore.

Among housewives the woman with some intellectual training is always going to work more rationally. Supported by the appropriate devices and appliances, and given that her dwelling is correctly arranged, she will quickly find the most efficient way to do her work.

Among manufacturers (with the exception of furniture builders) there are already a considerable number who have accepted the new requirements of our time and are putting labor-saving devices and appliances on the market. The greatest backwardness, however, continues to be represented in the way dwellings are furnished. Years of effort on the part of the German Werkbund and individual architects, countless articles and lectures demanding clarity, simplicity, and efficiency in furnishings, as well as a turn away from the traditional kitsch of the last fifty years, have had almost no effect whatever.

When we enter dwellings we still find the old knick-knacks and the usual inappropriate "decor." That all the efforts to the contrary had so little practical success is primarily the fault of women, who are remarkably uninterested in the new ideas. The furniture dealers say that the customers keep on wanting the old stuff. And women would prefer to take on the extra work in order to have a "snug and cozy" home. *The majority still takes simple and efficient to mean the same thing as dull.*

The Frankfurt housing office attempted to convince people of the contrary by displaying a completely furnished model building as a part of the exhibition, "The New Dwelling and Its Interior Structure," at the local trades fair. The point is to prove that simplicity and efficiency are not merely labor-saving but, executed with good materials and the correct form and color, represent clarity and beauty as well.

The Frankfurt Housewives' Association had its own display at the exhibition and it illustrated the importance of household rationalization particularly well. This part of the exhibition, called "The Modern Household," was primarily concerned with the problem of the labor-saving kitchen. Displayed first of all was a completely furnished dining-car kitchen and sideboard, which offered a particularly instructive example of how steps and other unnecessary movements can be saved. Three more fully equipped kitchens with built-in furniture (of which the first two have been exhibited about three thousand times in Frankfurt) show how effort can be saved by proper layout and furniture arrangement. Here the three different kinds of kitchen operations were taken into account: (1) house-holds without a maid (with annual incomes up to about 5,000 marks); (2) households with one maid (with annual incomes of up to 10,000 marks); and (3) households with two maids (with annual incomes over 10,000 marks).

Aside from wooden kitchen furnishings, the display also included a small cooking corner made of metal for bachelor apartments and a kitchen made of washable bricks; these last two kitchens represent attempts to find appropriate new materials that are less affected by external influences than wood. All of the kitchens are small, to save effort, and can be separated off completely from the dwelling's living area. The old style of combining kitchen and living space seems to have been superseded. Also exhibited were examples of free-standing kitchen furniture that is already on the market and contributes considerably to easing household work. Good and bad household and kitchen appliances—labor-wasting and labor-saving, hard and easy to clean—were identified by signs of different colors. Drying racks for bowls, plates, and cups, which save the work of drying the chinaware, and flour hoppers that dispense a specific, measured amount of flour into the bowl, represent devices that have been tried and approved by women in other countries for some time.

The exhibition devoted particular attention to electrical devices and appliances. Although not yet practical for lower income levels, we know that the not-too-distant future belongs to the electrical kitchen. The centralized electrical laundry facilities that had to be installed in the larger housing blocks should provide women with an example of the labor that can be saved, and encourage them to have smaller laundry rooms, which are already a reasonable investment for lower-income families, in their own homes. In a central washing facility in Frankfurt, the renters requested that manually operated washing machines be installed in addition to the electric ones. Now, after a year, the manually operated machines go unused, since all of the women want to do their wash in the other ones.

"The smallest bath in the smallest space," about five feet by four, proves that the demand "a bath for every dwelling" no longer represents an unrealizable ideal. A 1:10 model of a flat demonstrates the possibility of saving room by slipping a "wash and shower stall" between two bedrooms as well as by installing a shower room requiring only five and a half square feet. The constant flow of water makes a more thorough cleansing possible than can be had in a tub.

The extensive use of natural gas in the household is illustrated by a model of a one-family house fully supplied with gas. The exhibition took special pains to investigate the important topic of good lighting in the home. How much money can be saved solely through the choice of a wallpaper designed to enhance illumination! How important it is for the health of the family that women, who represent the majority of the buyers, be directed to the correct and technically satisfactory work lamps, so that they do not keep on thoughtlessly buying the small, ornate floor lamps with dust-gathering silk shades.

It is often for the silliest reasons that we are expected to surround ourselves with badly designed things. There is, for example, a large lamp factory whose stock consists exclusively of tasteless and impractical lamps. It produces inferior models because they are needed for large-scale export to India, while the small domestic turnover in new, good models makes their production unprofitable.

Are we supposed to spend our money on these bad lamps and ruin our eyes so that local lamps can be sent to the Indian colonies?

Here, as in all things, it must be a general principle, in particular for women, not to accept thoughtlessly whatever comes on the market, not to choose things that seem pretty at the moment, but to check for appropriateness and faultless technical quality.

This exhibition should sharpen the eye for that task.

179

DR. N.

A Contemporary Garden City

First published as "Eine neuzeitliche Gartenstadt," *Kommunalpolitische Blätter* 17 (1927), 172.

The words *residential development* are on practically everybody's lips today and development issues are at the center of all city-planning discussions. This is an expression of the longing of uprooted big-city dwellers for their own homes, the powerful drive to return from the unhealthy sea of houses in the modern industrial city to nature, to Mother Earth. This longing, as a well-known senior state-works supervisor recently put it, is comparable to the longing of a lost child for its mother. The garden-city movement derives from this longing, and is, at least in its core idea, deserving of the utmost appreciation. How the ideal of a garden city is to be more or less realized in practice is manifest in the city of Grünberg in Silesia, which has won the reputation of a garden city in its model residential and development projects. The city's administrative report (1923) on the projects contains the following interesting details:

The city of Grünberg, which has been surrounded since early times by a wreath of blooming gardens and vineyards, has gradually turned into an industrial city and displays a wealth of developmental possibilities in that direction. In order to fend off, or at least mitigate, the disadvantages necessarily associated with an industrial city, Grünberg pursues a *well-planned and far-sighted residential and development policy.* The city administration is gradually providing all of the non-property-owning inhabitants of the city with a garden, which if possible is located not more than one kilometer from their dwellings. To this end a green belt consisting not merely of parks but primarily of small gardens is to be laid around the city. For the practical execution of this plan, industry and the city administration have cooperated in founding the City Land Cultivation Society of Grünberg and a Small-Garden Producers Cooperative.

The Society concerns itself with the green belt as a whole and is attempting primarily to popularize the project's goals by means of a technical-management model and experimental garden and through enlightening and instructive lectures on garden cultivation, vegetable growing, etc. The society also ensures that garbage and sewage wastes are treated with maximum efficiency for the production of high-quality manure, which is passed on to the gardeners at cost. The Small-Garden Producers Cooperative includes everyone who would like to have a garden or who has already been allotted one. On a nonprofit basis, it acts as the general lessee for all of the land the city is gradually making available, concludes the individual leases with the tenants, sees to the collective acquisition of manure, water, planting seed, and arranges for the availability of whatever technical assistance is required. The lease price for a garden varies from roughly fifty to seventy-five pounds of grain per acre.

A gardening workshop in the schools is designed to foster an understanding of the small-garden concept as well as a love for being active in nature. Each schoolchild is assigned a small piece of land to be worked independently under the guidance of the teacher.

The construction of homes in the garden area has been conceived as the final goal of the green belt movement. The city projects in this regard are noteworthy primarily because, rather than being mere chimeras, they have been based in principle on the thorough calculation of economic factors.

180

EDGAR WEDEPOHL

The Weissenhof Settlement

First published as "Die Weissenhof-Siedlung der Werkbundausstellung, 'Die Wohnung,' Stuttgart 1927," *Wasmuths Monatshefte für Baukunst* 11, no. 10 (1927), 391–402.

LE CORBUSIER AND PIERRE JEANNERET

The two buildings Le Corbusier built with Pierre Jeanneret are, among the structures in the development, the ones that inspire the most thought about residential customs. The directors of the Werkbund exhibit deserve particular thanks for having invited the famous creator of the "coming architecture," so that he will be able to display a practical example of his innovative architectural thoughts in Germany as well as elsewhere. The positioning of Le Corbusier's buildings on the outermost wing of the Weissenhof development has a nearly symbolic effect. In comparison with all the others, these buildings represent something completely novel.

Le Corbusier and Jeanneret recently published a list of the five points of modern architecture, which they consider a fundamentally new aesthetic, in *Baugilde* (no. 15, [1927]).

1. Columns, on which the building rests instead of foundations and walls.
2. Rooftop gardens, which make the surfaces occupied by the building available for residential purposes, while protecting the reinforced concrete from the variability of exterior temperatures.

3. Floorplan-design flexibility, which is made possible by the absence of interior bearing walls.
4. Tall windows, with the possibility of superior illumination.
5. Flexible façade design, gained by projecting the concrete roofs out over the support columns.

RESIDENTIAL MACHINISTS

If dwelling type is supposed to correspond to the type of the person inhabiting it, then one can only imagine the inhabitant of Le Corbusier's houses as a certain kind of intellectual. It is the eccentric, unconcerned by sentiment, free to roam as he likes, and homeless, who can easily shed himself of all historical ballast, perhaps preferring to live in such a nomad's tent of concrete and glass. Though constructed of hard materials, his house has not grown out of the earth, is not rooted weightily to it, not solid, but appears to have condescended to land for a moment on earth like a colorful butterfly. One confronts this international type of the intellectual, this extreme form of the rootless city dweller, everywhere—especially, however, where it smells of book paper and newsprint. Certainly, the intellectual represents one form of contemporary human being. But is he *the* type, whose expectations and needs ought to determine the form of an apartment house, the furnishing of it with mass-produced goods and its devotion to the gratification of mass needs?

It is not everyone's desire over the long run to have a sleeping spot for the night and fold his bed away come morning, as in Le Corbusier's houses. Some people still want a closed-off bedroom in which one can not only rest and dream but make love, conceive, give birth, and die as well. It is not everyone's desire to enter the house and find the central heater's fiery furnace in the hall closet. One would be reluctant to put away one's things in a room dirtied by coal dust. And living in a room in which eating, dressing, sleeping, washing and bathing all go on, with only a head-high concrete partition to separate them, might well require a fundamental reorientation of the residential customs of most people. Certainly, the single room with the head-high partitions or movable walls creates a more dramatic and visually more interesting spatial effect, but it comes at the cost of certain amenities and comforts that many would be reluctant to give up. It is interesting to imagine somewhat large people in hallways only twenty-four inches wide, but washing at a sink installed in such a narrow passage cannot be particularly effective.

GROPIUS

Gropius likewise erected two structures, with one of them made of prefabricated structural elements that can be assembled in a dry process requiring no water. Thus he has set about solving a problem that is doubtless of economic importance because it aims to decrease the time required for construction and to allow dwellings to be inhabited more quickly. The system chosen seems to be subject in certain respects to simplification, and the use of nondomestic construction materials is particularly undesirable from an economic stand-point. The iron framework of Gropius's house is latticed with cork slabs (an import article), covered outside with asbestos slate, and covered inside with Enso plating (an import article from Finland). The second house is massively constructed out of cinder blocks covered by stucco. (The use of water on the exterior does not pose such an impediment.) Instead of interior plaster, which would contain disadvantageous amounts of water, a dry-wall covering is used. The interior walls and ceilings are made of a criss-cross wood construction.

The floor plans are efficiently and systematically thought through, but not unusual. Notable is the washing, drying, and ironing room on the upper floor, which displays several advantages. It is doubtful that machine-made furnishings would be within the means of most of the inhabitants. Some of the design details are not entirely persuasive, as, for example, the wobbly railings on the iron staircases, through which children could easily fall. It should also be assessed whether plywood exterior doors on the weathered side of the building will be sure to last.

The doctrinaire design characteristic of the Bauhaus gives the houses a strangely dry, pedantic flavor and at the same time something provisional and barracks-like, which robs them of cheerfulness and charm. That is also evident in the metal chairs by Breuer, which although not uncomfortable nevertheless produce the effect of sitting machines rather than chairs and are somewhat disturbingly mechanical.

181

MARIE-ELISABETH LÜDERS

A Construction, Not a Dwelling

First published as "Baukörper ohne Wohnung," *Die Form* (October 1927), 316.

Whoever has carefully examined the houses in the Weissenhof development is forced to pose the astonishing question of whether the majority of them have not been designed and executed in complete ignorance of all the things a family needs to make a dwelling a home. One asks if the builders know nothing about the daily requirements of running a household. Just a couple of examples: There are houses there (built by Mies van der Rohe) with gigantic casement windows on the staircases, going all the way down to ground level, which when opened completely block the landings and represent an unheard-of danger to children in the house. In front of one of these windows there is even a deck extending over the front door—without a railing. The windows themselves have three horizontal bars at the level of the landing, which, however, are set so far apart that children six years old and older can very easily climb through them. Inhabitants of two- and three-room apartments generally do not have nannies to conduct each child carefully down the stairs or to get scooters, sleds, etc. past the ground-level windows.

Following the motto "Bring the landscape into the house," various apartments also have windows extending all the way down to the ground. Some of the walls are made completely of glass—to the north and the south in the same room. In such rooms there is a constant draft over the floor, a cause for no little concern when small children are present. These rooms, whose windows cannot be outfitted with shutters because they are too big and set too high, are burning hot in the summer, and the light is so blinding that small children in the daytime and somewhat older children in early evening hours cannot sleep in them. In some of the apartments the landscape has been brought into the larder as well. The window, except for a very narrow socle at the bottom, takes up the entire wall, and the larders are facing south!! If the builders are perhaps assuming that man lives by curdled milk alone in the summertime, they are mistaken.

In another place the same sense for natural beauty has bestowed its beneficence on the kitchen, likewise facing south, and in a third on the bathroom. There can be no dispute as to the temperature of the former in summer. This kitchen, however, suffers from a further serious error: the gas stove—quite small for the number of people intended for the apartment—is located opposite the window against a narrow wall between two doors arranged at right angles to each other. First of all, one turns one's back to the light while cooking; second, every time one of the doors is opened the gas flame is disrupted; and, third, it is a miracle if everyone who goes through the door does not knock a pot off the stove or come too close to the flame. Since the kitchen has the advantage of a southern exposure on the ground floor, the two bedrooms, the larger of which serves two people, are half buried underground and facing north!!

In the bathroom of one of the houses there is, in addition to others, a large window located behind the tub that cannot be opened. Since the rim of the tub is right under the window, the question remains how one is supposed to clean the window, which is on the second floor. From inside one would have to put a ladder in the tub, which could not be done, and from outside one would have to call for professional window cleaners.

In various houses one notes the complete absence of a place for storing wet coats, galoshes, or umbrellas—and these are supposed to be family houses; instead, there is a terrace of approximately sixty square feet. The same apartments had beautiful furniture as well as well-designed and executed artworks, but, unfortunately, not a single washstand among the furnishings and in a very small bathroom in one of the apartments only a very small sink; even this was lacking in the second apartment. When apartments are shown fully furnished, as is universally the case in the Weissenhof development, it seems to us that the goal should not be to display beautiful furniture (which, incidentally, would certainly be too expensive for the inhabitants of these houses); rather the visitors should be taught something about the practical possibilities for furnishing their homes; they should be trained in the tasteful satisfaction of daily needs, as things are and not as they are imagined in a vacuum by the aesthetic sense of Mr. So-and-So. The kitchen in the same apartment has been executed with remarkably little care and left quite insufficient. In other kitchens, which are otherwise well dimensioned, practically arranged, etc., one nevertheless finds windows which are set so high above such a broad kitchen table that any normal-sized woman would have to stand on a stool to open them.

182

The Stuttgart Werkbund Houses

First published as "Die Stuttgarter Werkbundhäuser," in *Mit anderen Augen. Jahrbuch der deutschen Sonntagszeitung,* ed. Erich Schairer (Stuttgart: Verlag der Sonntagszeitung, 1929), 236–238.

Do not let anyone say anything to me against the old houses. I grew up in one of them; I have spent pleasant hours in old rural parsonages and small-town homes.

What they had of magnificent, large rooms, of mighty, bright staircases with a comfortable incline, of giant corridors (channels, we called them), of endless platforms (attics, you called them), two, three on top of each other, of eerie, deep, good cellars! *Room* is what we had in the old houses! Admittedly, there were also cross beams and nooks, dark alcoves, stuffy chambers, bad-smelling toilets. But that did not matter; no one needed to spend much time there. In good weather you stayed outdoors a lot. There was a yard next to the house, and to the woods or the water it was only five or ten minutes. Bathroom, no, there was none. But you made do. You did not bathe so often back then. It was not thought as necessary as it is today.

Those dwellings made for much work, true, especially in winter when it had to be cozy inside. You needed maids, and they had little leisure. On Saturdays, cleaning days, you were happy to get out of the way; for the big fall and spring cleanings it was best to take a trip. But the housewives and the maids knew no different, and, remarkably, still had time to raise a half-dozen or a dozen children, to cook wonderfully, to bake, to put up preserves, to sew, to mend, to wash, and in between to arrange visits for coffee, broth, and fabulous bowls of punch. You had *time* in the old houses.

Today we live differently from how we did back then. We do not have time anymore, and we are piled like lumps on top of each other in the big cities; we do not have any room anymore. A yard by the house, work outdoors, walks in the woods after quitting time, children tumbling in the grass in the evening or sitting around the big table: who knows that anymore? To a third of us, soon it will be half, this is the stuff of fairy tales. Regret it as much as you like, it *is* so. And that is why we need other houses.

The city and suburban houses and apartments we have contrived in the last thirty years are stunted, ugly, and misplaced attempts to maintain the old residential form and construction method. The present big-city dwelling is a deformation of the old rural dwelling. The large rooms have become small ones, the corridor a dark hallway, the cellar and attic each a mere compartment, the veranda or balcony a bird cage, the yards behind the house a flower stand with house plants. Remaining intact are chambers, nooks, lightless rooms; and remaining is the father's or grandfather's furniture, stuffed into the narrow apartment because it seems to be indispensable. To the extent that it is not actually left over, such furniture is reproduced by a diligent industry, only with a considerable decline in quality and a loss in taste and practicality compared to that delivered earlier by honest handicraft. The average "middle-class" city apartment of today is unbearable for all the second-hand stuff, the dust catchers, draperies, ghastly wallpaper, and impossible furniture and pictures.

For those of us who feel this way, and the number is gradually becoming considerable, the Werkbund development on the Weissenhof near Stuttgart was built. Thirty-three houses, some single-family, some duplexes and row houses, and a proper block of "rental barracks" (*Mietkaserne*) as well. The builders are a group of more- or less-famous modern architects: [Hans] Poelzig, both of the Tauts, [Peter] Behrens, and others; foreigners are among them too; a Swiss French, a Belgian, two Dutch are there.

This display, although one might find much to take exception to in its details, is an act of redemption for which the Werkbund and the city of Stuttgart are due thanks and recognition. Here it becomes apparent that we are finally at the point of producing houses and apartments for our time in which the people of today can feel good. They are houses made of new materials (wood and brick give way to concrete, iron, and artificial stone) and with new, unaccustomed forms (all of them with flat roofs). They have windows that are numerous and large, small but bright rooms with movable walls, few adjoining rooms, no attics (platforms), built-in closets; they have no wallpaper, no door curtains, no superfluous furniture; everything is smooth, simple, practical, easy to clean, and close together. The atrocious concept of room decor no longer exists; in its place the color on the walls comes into its own (about which grey-haired philistines shake their heads with particular vigor). If I am saying all this so summarily, I ask the reader not to think that all of the houses are of *one* type. They are quite varied, from the nearly old-fashioned Behrens to the revolutionary Le Corbusier; from the very small row houses, the most outstanding example of which is by the Rotterdam architect [J.J.P.] Oud, to the nearly pompous one-family homes of an [Adolf] Schneck or Gropius.

Public opinion and the press, as one can imagine, confront the display rather unappreciatively. The experts use all their fingers counting the mistakes that plague this or that solution. Naturally they are right. It teems with mistakes; there are fundamental and weighty issues, too—such as heating, protection from weather and water, maintenance—that have in no way been persuasively or ultimately resolved. But now that is impossible; years, decades of experience will be necessary. And one-sidedness and exaggerations, as one knows, are never avoidable in propaganda.

183

OTTO STEINICKE

A Visit to a New Apartment

First published as "Besuch in einer Neubauwohnung," *Magazin für Alle* 4, no. 7 (July 1929), 22.

The building in which Mrs. Müller lives is a gigantic new housing block divided into 160 separate rental units. The foundation walls are made of polished yellow sandstone. On top rise four storeys of red brick. The apartment block has a flat roof. Airplanes could land on it. The brick façades are covered with a coat of cement roughly textured with pebbles.

To visit Mrs. Müller one has to go through one of the imposing arched gates. Passing by the stairs to the apartments facing the street, one enters the expansive central courtyard. Air and light flood in through the rectangular opening at the top, brightening up every corner of the courtyard. In eight different places there are disposal facilities for kitchen refuse, built in the shape of tall hexagons and lined up straight as an arrow with small spaces between them, like Prussian soldiers on the parade ground. Plots of grass and playgrounds for the children have been marked off neatly and cleanly. The back wings here have nothing of the sad and shabby significance of the old rental blocks. No more stuffy air, no more semidark hallways and stink. Every bit of waste water flows away immediately in an underground drainage system; even the rain disappears into the ground through a gutter, leaving no puddles anywhere on the ground, no mud.

For hygienic reasons, the inhabitants of this new residential block are prohibited from hanging their wash out the windows to dry; nor are they allowed to shake dust out the windows. Those who want to clean make their way, after having settled an appointment with the porter, to a specific area of the courtyard. There, for three hours before noon, one can get rid of dust and beat rugs as much as one likes. There are large communal laundry rooms. They are available to all the renters on days specified for each unit. The entrances and stairways in the rear wings are in no way different from those in the front. Each of the staircases have been outfitted with carpet runners all the way up to the fifth floor.

Mrs. Müller's apartment is located through entrance five on the fourth floor in the back. I rang. A ten-year-old child opened the door: his mother is not yet home, but, being an acquaintance, I am let in. I immediately take a look around the new apartment.

For Mrs. Müller and her husband, a railroad worker, it was the luck of winning a lottery that landed them here. Five years the family waited, all the while listed at the housing office for an apartment in a new building. They were repeatedly put off. Finally their name was taken from the usual list and added to the other Müllers on the one marked "urgent"; then, two years later, to the "especially urgent" list. After another two years, this one Müller out of thousands had the pleasure of receiving a two-and-a-half-room apartment. And it is truly marvelous. Not at all comparable to the miserable holes for rent in the center, north, and east of the city. The main room, flooded with daylight, is seventy-five square feet. The walls are dry, if not thick enough to keep out noise. Only the old, poor-quality furniture does not go with the room. It was brought from the old apartment: a chaise lounge, an extension table, six chairs, and a buffet. The petit-bourgeois unculture, the so-called knick-knacks, are no longer visible. On the table is a large crystal vase with flowers. The wallpaper is brightly colored and covered over with elaborate decorative flourishes.

The bedroom measures sixty square feet, with a double bed and two children's beds, and a brand-new linen cabinet bought on credit from a warehouse. This room gets sunlight in the mornings. Then there is a bathroom with a built-in tub, hot and cold running water—very narrow so that only one person can move around in it at a time. The toilet is in the bathroom.

The kitchen looks nearly luxurious, with built-in furnishings attached to the walls. The stove is half electrified, with the other half working with gas. An electric iron is there for Mrs. Müller to use on the wash. The entire apartment is centrally heated with radiators. Otherwise, the apartment has a narrow hallway, about forty square feet, and a tiny so-called children's room.

I take a look at the husband's library, displayed on three boards against the wall in the main room. He is a unionized, politically neutral proletarian, an Independent Social Democrat until 1921. After the party split, he joined neither the Communists nor the old Social Democratic Party. Since then he has been more active in the union and sports clubs. Railroad worker Müller is 43 years old; he has lived with his wife since he was 22. The family has four children, of whom the oldest is now 18.

The library of this union man contains about 150 books collected over years of saving. One can find there all of the protocols of the Social Democratic party congresses, from 1905 to 1921: the prewar writings of [August] Bebel and [Karl] Kautsky and Rosa Luxemburg's *Accumulation of Capital;* Eduard Bernstein's pamphlets next to Lenin's *State and Revolution;* from [Maxim] Gorky there are the plays and the novel *The Informer;* from Tolstoy *War and Peace;* [Stijn] Streuvels' peasant novel from the Universal Library. There is one volume of Jack London's *Call of the Wild.* Much room is taken up by the writings of bourgeois philosophers. Ernst Häckel is represented alongside Kant and Nietzsche. A bunch of recent, typically German, entertaining literary kitsch is there as well. Collected among the brochures is everything the reformist union leadership published in recent years in opposition to the communists. But next to these pamphlets one comes upon the protocols of the R.G.I. Congress,[1] a small text by [Mikhail] Tomsky, a speech delivered to the international workers' delegates. Just now I have Larissa Reissner's book, *In Hindenburg's*

1. The Rote Gewerkschaftsinternationale (Red Trade Union International) was a revolutionary world labor organization founded in Moscow in July 1921.

Country, in my hand, and the woman of the house arrives home to make her excuses and welcome me.

At five in the afternoon her work in the factory ends. Mrs. Müller stamps tin products, more precisely, reaches for them with her hand on the conveyor belt. It takes her a full hour to get to her apartment after work. When I explain now that I have had a look at the new apartment on my own, we sit down in the table with a cup of coffee. Her husband sends his apologies: he had to rush off to meet his union associates for a few words in a bar. "You see," says Mrs. Müller, "here's our new apartment. You can imagine how happy we are to be out of the old hole." I ask about the rent. "Ninety marks a month, still quite cheap," asserts Mrs. Müller, "and only because this whole block was built with public funds and we were on the list for a long time did we even get in. My whole wage, four times a month, goes just for the rent. I make 30 cents an hour—9 hours times 30 cents! That doesn't quite make it in the end and our oldest boy has to add a little from his earnings so we can get it paid on time. My husband earns 44 marks and 73 cents a week by contract. We just get by with the family on that and we're all finally very happy to have a healthy place to live."

Mrs. Müller is nevertheless dissatisfied. She has a lot of worries with the two youngest children, now old enough for school, who need new clothing and school supplies every quarter year. "We can't afford anything extravagant. Now and then we go to the cinema, sometimes to a bar, sometimes to a concert. Our favorite thing, though, is seeing Russian films."

19
From Dada to the New Objectivity: Art and Politics

NOTWITHSTANDING THE painters and sculptors who continued to work much as they had since the late nineteenth century, artistic life in Germany between the wars witnessed an explosion of forms, subject matter, and ideologies. Perhaps most remarkable about Weimar art was its syncretism, a propensity for blurring styles and genres which was as ubiquitous as the hyperbole of its manifestos. No less notable was the internationalism of its aesthetic horizons. Western European developments such as the Italian Pittura Metafisca and Dutch De Stijl enjoyed positive receptions in Germany, while the evolving aesthetics of suprematism and constructivism led many to view developments in the East with equal interest, as Adolf Behne's enthusiastic account of the 1922 Russian art exhibition in Berlin suggests. Disillusioned with political events in Hungary and the Soviet Union, Eastern Europeans such as Laszlo Moholy-Nagy and Wassily Kandinsky settled in Germany in the early 1920s. They contributed to the vitality of Weimar art through their association with the Bauhaus. For many artists born around 1890, the carnage of World War I catalyzed opposition to German conservative politics and militarism, which had been growing among educated segments of the population since the turn of the century, and led them to a broad rejection of previous artistic traditions. While some dadaists denied the legitimacy of art and championed its negation, others turned to social and political criticism and sought, in the memorable phrase of Carl Einstein, to "aim the exploding kitsch of the present matter-of-factly in the faces of their contemporaries." Many artists—among them Hannah Höch, Raoul Hausmann, and Kurt Schwitters—explored the rich possibilities of such new media as collage, photomontage and performance art and produced work that challenged existing divisions between high art and mass culture.

Between the end of the war and the signing of the Weimar Constitution, artists and intellectuals viewed Germany's future with anxiety and expectation. The recent success of the Russian Revolution loomed large, and many initially placed their hopes in artists' and workers' councils. Founded in late 1918 and named after the month of the sailors' insurrection in Kiel, the November Group was among the earliest artists' associations, its members including Max Pechstein and Rudolf Belling. Its founding manifesto argued for moral and artistic reconstruction, a similar position to that proposed in the

Work Council for Art manifesto of March 1919. Both groups advocated the reintegration of the visual arts as a means of achieving a new progressive political and social order. Reforms in German art education, already underway since about 1900 at schools in Düsseldorf and Breslau, formed a key demand of the Work Council program, soon to be reflected in the tenets of the Bauhaus. By 1919 the belief that expressionism had run its course was widely shared by many on all sides of the artistic spectrum. For the critic Wilhelm Hausenstein, its collapse marked a crisis in representation and a loss of the painterly object, which led to nihilism and a devitalized art. In his influential 1925 book, *Post-Expressionism,* the art historian Franz Roh demarcated the spheres of the old and new artistic tendencies, listing their respective attributes in a chart.

The death of subjectivity bemoaned by Hausenstein was celebrated by the dadaists in a flood of manifestos, publications, performances, and, despite their dismissive views on art, poems, paintings, collages, and sculpture. German dada was most warmly received in Berlin, where its most successful entrepreneur, Richard Huelsenbeck, engaged in a series of scandalous performances with Hausmann, Johannes Baader, Wieland Herzfelde, and his brother, John Heartfield, whose fascination with America inspired him to anglicize his name. The two brothers and George Grosz are perhaps best known for the publications of Herzfelde's Malik Verlag, which Grosz and Heartfield frequently designed and illustrated. The dadaist contempt for the traditional function of art in bourgeois society is evident in Grosz's and Herzfelde's "The Art Scab" and Hausmann's "The German Philistine Gets Upset."

New artistic tendencies and controversial theories about the social vocation of art frequently elicited hostile responses and censorship. In 1925 a vivid painting of the wartime trenches by Otto Dix was removed from the Wallraf-Richartz Museum. George Grosz was prosecuted and fined for defaming the military, corrupting public morals, and commiting blasphemy in 1920, 1923, and 1928. Opponents of these artists and of modern art in general were plentiful. Paul Schultze-Naumburg, a conservative critic, advocated the reappearance of the "Nordic type" in German art to replace the degenerate symbols of "the idiot, the prostitute, and the sagging breast" that he saw despoiling contemporary painting and sculpture. Drawing on a nineteenth-century discourse of degeneration, the relation of art and race he articulated would later find growing acceptance in the Third Reich, most notably in the famous Degenerate Art exhibition organized in Munich in 1937.

Commonly viewed as the coinage of Gustav Hartlaub, the phrase *Neue Sachlichkeit* (New Objectivity) was already used by Hermann Muthesius, founder of the German Werkbund, in his writings on functional architecture around the turn of the century. As early as 1913 the painter Ludwig Meidner urged artists to select their themes from daily life and the metropolis, a theme echoed by one of the precursors of the new sensibility, Max Beckmann, in his essay of 1920. Rather than a consistent artistic style, the New Objectivity meant a shared mode of seeing that was rooted in a common rejection of expressionism. It received major attention after the exhibition that Hartlaub organized in Mannheim in 1925. A dramatic public success, it presented paintings by Beckmann, Dix, Grosz, Carl Mense, Rudolf Schlichter, and Georg Schrimpf. Yet even before the opening, its organizer expressed doubts about what he termed the "new verism." In his exhibition catalog essay, Hartlaub drew the influential distinction between the politically engaged "left-wing" verists and the "classicists" searching for the object of timeless validity. The sharp images, static compositions, and sober engagement with technology and daily life in the paintings of the New Objectivity encouraged many to invest them with allegorical and social significance. For the left-wing critic Carl Einstein, the unrelenting mockery of the bourgeoisie in the work of Dix constituted a vital artistic and political achievement. The heightened symbolism of Magical Realism, related stylistically to both the New Objectivity and to French surrealism, was defended by Misch Orend. Few documents on Weimar art may be as despairing as Grosz's 1931 essay in which his grim observations of a German art and society on the precipice of embracing National Socialism form a dramatic counterpart to the optimism of many artists a decade earlier. Two years later Grosz emigrated to America.

184

November Group Circular

First published as *Novembergruppe Rundschreiben vom* 13. Dezember 1918 (Berlin, 1918).

Dear Sirs:

The future of art and the gravity of the present moment force all of us revolutionaries of the spirit (expressionists, cubists, futurists) into mutual agreement and close association.

Therefore we are directing an urgent summons to all artists who have broken with old forms in art that they declare their membership in the November Group.

The elaboration and realization of a broadly conceived program—to be carried out in the various art centers by trusted associates—should achieve the closest possible relationship between the people and art.

Renewed contact with like-minded people of all countries is our duty. Our creative instinct already united us years ago as brothers. As the first sign that we have joined together, a common exhibition is being planned. The same should be demonstrated in all of the larger German cities and later elsewhere in Europe.

> *The Planning Committee:*
> M. Pechstein, C. Klein, G. Tappert,
> Richter-Berlin, M. Melzer, B. Krauskopf,
> R. Bauer, R. Belling, H. Steiner, W. Schmid.

185

November Group Manifesto

Published as "Manifest der Novembristen," *Zehn Jahre Novembergruppe: Zeitschrift für Kunst und Literatur* 3, nos. 1–3 (1928). First published in 1918.

We stand on the fertile ground of the revolution.

Our campaign slogan is:

FREEDOM, EQUALITY, FRATERNITY!

Our joining together is the result of the equivalence of a humane and an artistic way of thinking.

We regard it as our highest duty to devote our best energies to the moral cultivation of a young, free Germany.

We plead for excellence in every respect and dedicate all means at our disposal to the support of this way of thinking.

We demand that this view be lent unqualified expression and that one publicly declare one's position toward it.

We consider it our particular duty to gather together all abilities of value in the artistic sphere and to guide them toward the common good.

We are neither a party nor a class as such, but human beings—human beings who undertake to perform their work tirelessly from the places allotted to them by nature. Like any other kind of work that is to serve the common good, it must take account of general public interest and receive the respect and recognition of the whole.

186

Work Council for Art Manifesto

First published as "Arbeitsrat für Kunst-Flugblatt" (March 1919).

In the conviction that the political revolution must be used to liberate art from decades of regimentation, a group of artists and art lovers united by a common outlook has been formed in Berlin. It strives for the gathering together of all scattered and divided energies which, over and above the protection of one-sided professional interests, wish to work resolutely together for the rebuilding of our whole artistic life. In close contact with associations with similar objectives in other parts of Germany, the Arbeitsrat für Kunst hopes in the not-too-distant future to be able to push through its aims, which are outlined in the following program.

In the forefront stands the guiding principle:

Art and people must form a unity.
Art shall no longer be the enjoyment of the few but the life and happiness of the masses.
The aim is alliance of the arts under the wing of a great architecture.

On this basis six preliminary demands are made:

1. Recognition of the public character of all building activity, both state and private. Removal of all privileges accorded to civil servants. Unified supervision of whole urban districts, streets, and residential estates without curtailment of freedom over detail. New tasks: people's housing as a means of bringing all the arts to the people. Permanent experimental sites for testing and perfecting new architectural effects.

2. Dissolution of the Academy of Arts, the Academy of Building, and the Prussian Provincial Art Commission in their existing form. Replacement of these bodies, accompanied by a redefining of their territories, by others drawn from the ranks of productive artists themselves and free from state interference. The changing of privileged art exhibitions into exhibitions to which entry is free.

3. Freeing of all training in architecture, sculpture, painting, and handicrafts from state supervision. Transformation of all instruction in the arts and handicrafts from top to bottom. State funds to be made available for this purpose and for the training of master craftsmen in training workshops.

4. Enlivenment of the museums as educational establishments for the people. Mounting of constantly changing exhibitions made to serve the interests of the people by means of lectures and conducted tours. Separation of scientific material in specially-constructed buildings. Establishment of specially-arranged collections for study by workers in the arts and crafts. Just distribution of state funds for the acquisition of old and new works.

5. Destruction of artistically valueless monuments as well as of all buildings whose artistic value is out of proportion to the value of their material which could be put to other uses. Prevention of prematurely planned war memorials and immediate cessation of work on the war museums proposed for Berlin and the Reich.

6. Establishment of a national center to ensure the fostering of the arts within the framework of future lawmaking.

187

WILHELM HAUSENSTEIN

Art at this Moment

First published as "Die Kunst in diesem Augenblick," *Der neue Merkur* (1919–1920), 119–127.

To the point. Once again, what is the point? Who belongs to it? What is expressionism? Who is an expressionist?

That no one is an expressionist can be asserted just about as easily as that everyone is, or a few are: because what constitutes expressionism has not been established. There is something like a signature of expressionism, perhaps a schema underlying it. One could define it roughly like this: form from deformation. That is put negatively. Positively, one could say: form from imagination. [. . .] Obvious, too, the significance of procedure. Obvious, all too obvious, however, a vagueness over the long run; a by now, after a decade, terrible vagueness—gradually, for some, long since profoundly unsatisfying. Where does that come from?

Let me attempt an answer. Impressionism was from the beginning based on a kind of relativity. Therefore it is impossible to demand from it the absolutism that expressionism claims for itself, wants to offer us. But at the same time a peculiar reversal has obviously transpired: Impressionism has left us a body of absolute art. Acquiescence to relativism produced in that case an absolute. In expressionism, the claim to the absolute has yielded merely the relative.

We, precisely those of us who once expected everything from it, are not being spared the admission that, after having expended enormous effort, we are sinking back into bankruptcy. Ten or fifteen years ago, in some places even earlier, we correctly proclaimed the bankruptcy of impressionism. There is nothing for us to do today, following a period of passionate exertion, but confirm the collapse of expressionism. We have moved from the end of one thing into the end of another.

The end of Impressionism came as it began to demand too little from itself. Expressionism tested the saying: *qui trop embrasse mal étreint.*[1] It embraced the universe. It strove to embrace God and the heavens. It wanted more than it was capable of. But this would have merely been a tragedy; and that would have been no cause for shame because we are human. The misery began since the catastrophe, in which the best shed blood and it settled for the mannerism of the all-too-late and the all-too-much. Expressionism has long since spread to the arts and crafts. The lack of feeling for finer professional obligations that

1. Grasp all, lose all.

resulted from it—not even just in the case of the expressionist masses and mediocrity—corrupted the expressions, the setting, and particularly the dance expected of us by a multitude of dilettantes who are expressive at all costs but not at all experimental. Expressionism now has its crystal palace. It has its salon. No cigarette billboard, no bar can make it today without expressionism. It is disgusting. Those responsible really ought to have their skulls fractured. They are playing fast and loose with catastrophe. With the catastrophe—with our catastrophe. Expressionism is the ideal realm of the catastrophe; the fanciful flight of the catastrophe; its attempt to be positive, indeed optimistic. It has, however, secretly become the catastrophe of the catastrophe. We are living today—we who consciously experienced expressionism, who loved it, who lent it our support—with the consuming feeling of having arrived *vis-à-vis de rien*. [. . .]

Expressionism has two poles, the metaphysical and the formal.

Expressionist art can be traced historically in purely formal terms. It is not so difficult to follow the emergence—through all manner of intensification, concentration, consolidation, and sublimation—of expressionist devices from impressionist ones—in the extreme case through dialectical contrasts. The sublimation and overcoming of impressionist devices ultimately meant an overbreeding of the formal essence. Thus did the formalistic esoteric arise in expressionism. Along with the purely historical formal development—which possessed a kind of spontaneous movement, an incomprehensible but illuminating objectivity of the process—went a transformation of the motive. To the at least subjectively (out of the psyche of expressionism) growing strain of the formal concept there came a migration away from the continent of sensory objectivities over the ocean of the nonsensory to unknown shores. The moment was given various names. There was talk of the subordination of the object. There was talk of objectless art, of the destruction of the objective, of the autonomous dynamism of the absolute device—so many designations, so many errors. The nonobjective was solely relative: measured more or less by [Gustave] Courbet's *Hammock* or by [Wilhelm] Leibl. As to the rest, it was full of latent objectivity. Was there not even the expressionists' hatred of the beautiful painting of, for example, Munich of the 1870s? In expressionism someone like [Girolamo] Savonarola rose up against something like the Renaissance. That was only possible because expressionism was bound in another direction by self-imposed objective obligations. A purely formal aversion to beautiful painting would not have sufficed for that. Thus it was in fact. In expressionism a new objectivity rose up—roughly as in past times when the figure rose up against the ornament, the landscape against the figure, the still life against historical themes. The sole difficulty lay in the circumstance that expressionist objectivity failed to identify itself. What was it? Here lay the question.

Kandinsky said: "the spiritual." Picasso painted hieroglyphics of spatial melancholies in positive, a decomposition of visibility in negative. Others took up the historical as parable and painted, or modeled the gothic. The Bible was read (or not read): there were paintings of God, Mary, Jesus, the angels, the pious, and the saints. One was suspect to oneself, and thus did a desperate subjectivity—which possessed neither a friend nor God, neither a beloved nor a dog, nor even a bit of woods or a flower pot—spin off and into the vortex of nothingness. Or one fell into the mill of tradition, was pulverized between [Hans von] Marées, [Paul] Cézanne, [Eugène] Delacroix. To others, the first and the last, there remained perhaps a bit of nature, a chain of masks, a picture book, an atelier. They amassed themselves there: the pick of the time and history, unprecedentedly talented all in all but unredeemed; critical of the masses, nothing less than eclectic, but neither encouraged by the epoch nor themselves focused on a goal, master and slave in one, happily unconfined with such an infinite prospect and desperate because of so little determination in what remained such a narrow world. If anyone remained, he painted music or psychology. Who can say today whether an art that still now appears to us as a hyperbole of painting freed from the gravity of the objective will not one day appear as the hyperbole of a psychologistic naturalism? A naturalism that has simply transferred the object from being externally perceptible to being internal? That has merely pulled down the shades against green and sunlight, to observe and paint colors, intestinal convolutions, nerves, and blood vessels? (For which music perhaps would be the driving experience as compared to travel, or love, or the aroma of the atelier.) [. . .]

Expressionism is dead. The individuals who distinguish themselves from each other and from the movement—even if they have come from each other and from the movement—are alive. Their arts are absolute. The category no longer expresses anything. It has fulfilled its purpose. It can go. The selection has been made. The rest will pass away. [. . .]

The objectlessness of expressionism was ultimately no accident. The thing disappeared from painting as it disappeared from the world, and the subjugation of the object wanted to make a virtue of necessity. As long as things exist, art has no reason to ignore or subjugate them. But precisely this was fate, was—put most emphatically—the misery of the epoch, that it possessed neither people nor things. That painting is wrong because the gentleman depicted grew his eyes on his mouth, his ears on his nose? The objection—oh, he comes from a time when there were still faces. But take a look at how they have been growing for years now: crooked all around, horribly deformed, cross-eyed, loutish, mangled, sick, displaced. The painters only represented what was. There is no reason to reproach them. They painted their time. Instead of things the sons of the twentieth century had surrogates. The surrogates had their engineers. The increasing popularity of the artists engendered an ideology of its own. From Richard Strauss to [Lyonel] Feininger or Picasso, the technical ingenuity of the epoch has become art. The destruction of horizontal perspective by the airplane was the ideal precondition of expressionist painting in a moment when no concrete detail yet fortified this transformation individually in particular relationships. [. . .]

The issue today is art or cinema. Expressionism, in its last bursts of speed, its last spasms and contortions, had already assumed the fragmented and flat profile of cinematography. Will the calm of nature rise up in opposition—or will art strike a compromise with cinematography, which would signify one last naturalistic grimace? At stake is no more and no less than art. If the cinema is victorious, then art is done with. If nature triumphs, then the cinema is done with and art will have gained some latitude. [. . .]

Socialism, which once promised salvation, has entered into bankruptcy with the revolution. The proletariat is losing its nobility.

Is there nothing more than individuals? Than islands? Is there no end to the misery of being an island?

So it seems. But one must hold fast to the last of what is. There are a few artists. There are a few people. All around them there are cinemas and grocery prices. No, there are the old ones. There is Bach, Händel, Haydn, Gluck, and above all Mozart; there are the painters of past times whose summits were called Grünewald and Marées. There is the Bible and *Don Quixote*. There still are—if one is lucky—even mountains, plains, lakes, and seas. Magnificent things—magnificent temptations. The point would be not to become eclectic on their account and, in a time when there are no more objects, to remain one's own subject. It is bleak enough that a rational justification is needed for it. Hail the moment that would need no rational justification; for that moment would have a genuine existence and therefore art.

We are waiting, individuals, allied, the lovers of the last things yet on earth—and shiver with the thought that one day there could again be what always was and bore art like fruit: nature and God. This would be first, and would be so important that art would be unimportant in comparison. But for precisely that reason art would arise again. Its deepest essence is that it is incidental, not purposeful. We would truly become used to the thought of being without art for a while, if only we were certain, once again, of having heaven and earth.

188

RAOUL HAUSMANN

The German Philistine Gets Upset

First published as "Der deutsche Spießer ärgert sich," *Der Dada,* no. 2 (1919), 2.

Why? Who is the German philistine that he should be upset by dadaism? It is the German writer, the German intellectual who explodes with rage because his formally perfect schmalz-bread soul has been left to bake in the sun of ridicule, who fumes because he has suffered a direct hit to the brain, which in his case is located where he sits—and now he has nothing to sit on! No, do not attack us, gentlemen, we are already our own enemies and know better than you where we are vulnerable. Understand at last that your positions are a matter of utter indifference to us, that we have other things to worry about. Use your energies to beat only the drum of your own intellectual business, pound about fiercely only on your own bellies, until a god takes pity on the sound—we have long since cast this old drum aside. We play, squeak, curse, laugh our irony:

Dada! For we are—anti-dadaists!

There you have it! Spare yourselves your fingers worked to the bone and stitch up your torn traps. You have done it all for nothing! That you could not put us up against the wall, we take solemn note of that. It makes us want to wash out your intestines and present you with the balance of your solemn values.

After an enormous thinning of vital feeling in aesthetic abstractions and moral-ethical farces, there rises from the European soup the expressionism of the German patriot, who took a respectable movement started by the French, Russians, and Italians and fabricated a small, profitable war industry in an endlessly plump enthusiasm. The hurdy-gurdy of pure literature, painting, and music is being played in Germany on an extremely fit business footing. But this pseudotheosophic, Germanic coffee klatsch, which got as far as achieving recognition among East Prussian Junkers, should be a matter of indifference to us here, just like the businessman's machinations of Mr. [Herwarth] Walden, a typical German philistine who believes it necessary to wrap his transactions in a Buddhistic-bombastic little cloak. To the honor of his business genius, but send his aesthetic and his artistic Prussianism back to where they came from, the office of the shady lawyer. Were Walden and his writers' school revolutionary in the slightest, they would first have to comprehend that art cannot be the aesthetic harmonization of bourgeois notions of property.

Oh my gentlemen philistines, you say that art is in danger? Yes, do you not know then that art is a beautiful female form without clothes, that she counts on being taken to bed, or that she instigates the action herself? No, gentlemen, art is not in danger—art no longer exists! It is dead. It was the development of all things, it wrapped even the tuberous nose and piggish lips of Sebastian Müller with beauty. It was a beautiful appearance, departing from a sunny cheerful feeling for life—and now nothing elevates us any longer, nothing!

Give up sexual romanticism, my gentlemen writers—we are no longer in the mood; better you should show your beautifully tatooed bellies, spit words, splash some geometry in colors and call it abstract art—that is just as acceptable to us as your tightrope walk all around expressionism! The absolute incapacity to say something, to grasp a thing, to play with it—that is expressionism, an intellectual Preißnitz compress for decayed entrails, some jello putrid from the start and the cause of a solemn stomachache. The writing or painting philistine appears to himself properly sacred in the process; he finally expands somehow beyond himself into an indefinite, general blah-blah—oh expressionism, you universal turn in the romantic capacity for lies! But it is only the Activists that made the farce unbearable, who wanted to bring the spirit and the art that they perceived in expressionism to the people. These feeble minds, who somehow once read Tolstoy and of course did not understand him, are now dripping with an ethic one can approach only with a dung fork. These fools, who are incapable of engaging in politics, have invented this etheristic Activist marmalade to expand the market for itself, in this case among the proletariat. But the proletarian, if you will forgive me, is not nearly so stupid as not to recognize a fruitless tempest in a teapot. Art to him is something that comes from the bourgeoisie. And we are anti-dadaists to such an extent that when some fellow among us wants to exhibit something beautiful or aesthetic—a securely bounded good little feeling—we will knock his well-smeared sandwich out of his hand into the garbage. For us the world today has no deep meaning but that of the most unfathomable nonsense; we want nothing to do with spirit or art. Science is silly—quite likely the sun today still revolves around the earth. We advance no ethics, which always remain ideal (a swindle)— but that is why we do not want to tolerate the bourgeoisie, who hang their moneybag over the existential possibility of man like Geßler does his hat. We wish to organize the economy and sexuality rationally, and we do not give a hoot for culture, which was no tangible affair. We wish an end to it and with it an end to the philistine writer, the manufacturer of ideals that were nothing but its excrement. We wish the world moved and movable, disorderly instead of orderly—away with all the chairs, away with feelings and noble gestures! And we are anti-dadaists because for us the dadaist still possesses too much feeling and aesthetics. We have the right to every amusement, whether in words, in forms, colors, noises; all of this, however, is splendid idiocy, which we consciously love and manufacture—an enormous irony like life itself: the precise technique of nonsense definitively conceived as the meaning of the world!

Down with the German philistine!

189

JOHN HEARTFIELD AND GEORGE GROSZ

The Art Scab

First published as "Der Kunstlump," *Der Gegner* 1, nos. 10–12 (Berlin: Malik Verlag, 1920), 48–56.

What is the worker supposed to do with the spirit of poets and philosophers, who, in the face of everything that constricts his life breath, feel no duty to take up battle against the exploiters?

Yes, what is the worker supposed to do with art? Have painters given their works the appropriate content for the working people's struggle for liberation, the content that would teach them to free themselves from the yoke of a thousand years of oppression?

No, despite this disgrace they have painted the world in a calming light. The beauty of nature, the forest with the twitter of birds and evening twilight! Do they show that the forest is in the oily hands of the profiteer, who declares it far and wide to be his private property, over which he alone disposes, who chops it down when his wallet requires it, but fences it in, so that freezing people cannot fetch wood.

Yet art remains detached. Look and see! [. . .]

That is why in works of art they preach escape for feelings and thoughts, away from the unbearable conditions of the earth, to the moon and stars, into heaven, vouchsafed by the machine guns of democracy, whose purpose is to send the dispossessed on a journey into the purer Beyond. That is why a weakling like the poet Rainer Maria Rilke, supported by the perfumed do-nothings, writes: "Poverty is a great radiance from within" [*Book of Hours*].

Workers! By presenting to you the ideas of the Christian churches, they wish to disarm you, in order to deliver you more easily to the state machine.

Workers! By representing things in their paintings that the bourgeois can cling to, things that give you a reflection of beauty and happiness, they sabotage your class consciousness, your will to power.

By directing you to art with the cry: "Art to the People," they wish to seduce you into believing in a common possession that you share with your oppressors, for the love of which you should cease the most just struggle the world has ever known. They once again wish to use the "spiritual" to make you submissive and to instill in you the awareness of your own smallness in relation to the wondrous works of the human spirit.

A swindle! A swindle!

The vilest betrayal!

No, art belongs in the museums, to be goggled at on the walking tours of petit-bourgeois tourists; art belongs in the palaces of the blood hounds, in front of the safes. [. . .]

Workers, you, who continually create the surplus value that allows the exploiters to hang their walls with this "aesthetic" luxury, you who thereby guarantee the livelihood of artists, which is nearly always more affluent than your own; workers, now listen how such an artist regards you and your struggle.

After the Kapp Putsch, in which you armed yourselves, to the irritation of the antimilitarists and pacifists [. . .] during these days a little art chap by the name of Oskar Kokoschka, republican Professor at the Dresden Art Academy, displaying the traditional cowardice of the intellectuals, directed the following pithy manifesto to the inhabitants of Dresden:

> I urgently request all those who intend to use firearms in order to promote their political theories, whether of the radical left, the radical right or the radical center, to be kind enough henceforth to hold their combat exercises away from the Gemäldegalerie [art gallery] of the Zwinger—on the shooting ranges of the heath, for example, where works of human culture will not be in danger. On Monday, the 15th of March, a masterwork of Rubens was damaged by a bullet. [. . .] Certainly the German people will later find more joy and meaning in these preserved pictures than in the collected views of the politicized Germans of today. I do not venture to hope that my alternative proposal will find favor, whereby in the German Republic, as

in classical times, feuds should be resolved by single combat between the respective political leaders—in the circus, perhaps—with the effect enhanced by the Homeric scorn of their parties. This would be less harmful and confused than current methods.

Oskar Kokoschka
*Professor at the Academy
of Fine Arts in Dresden*

We urgently request all who have not yet become such complete imbeciles as to concur with the snobbish statement of this art scab to oppose it publicly. We exhort everyone to whom it is inconsequential that bullets damage masterworks, since they tear human beings to pieces, to rescue themselves from the fangs of the bloodsuckers. [. . .]

The people would welcome it if, following the examples of Vienna, these pictures would be offered to the allies in exchange for food supplies. That would be doing more for the "poor people of the future" than leaving them the opportunity of standing, their legs crippled by rickets, in front of the unblemished masterpieces in the galleries. [. . .] The struggles of "the collected views of the politicized Germans of today" are the logical outcome of the will to survive and offer future generations conditions of existence other than those which make it possible only for the divinely illumined Kokoschka to eat his fill and wisecrack about the hungry. Sated people naturally need quiet for their digestion. [. . .] He who wishes his business with the brush to be regarded as a divine mission is a scab. Today the cleaning of a gun by a Red soldier is of greater significance than the entire metaphysical output of all the painters. The concepts of art and artist are an invention of the bourgeoisie and their position in the state can only be on the side of the those who rule, i. e. the bourgeois caste.

The title "artist" is an insult.

The designation "art" is an annulment of human equality.

The deification of the artist is equivalent to self-deification.

The artist does not stand above his milieu and the society of those who approve of him. For his little head does not produce the content of his creation, but processes (as a sausagemaker does meat) the worldview of his public.

[. . .]

Kokoschka's statements are a typical expression of the attitude of the bourgeoisie. The bourgeoisie places a culture and its art higher than the life of the working class. This, too, leads to the conclusion that there can be no reconciliation between the bourgeoisie, its approach to life, and the proletariat.

Workers, we see the attempts of the Independents [the Independent Socialists or USPD] to preserve this culture and its mendacious views on art for the proletarian reconstruction of the world. We expect very shortly from Herr Comrade Felix Stössinger [editor of the USPD weekly newspaper *Freie Welt*], that he will soon illustrate for you works by the important painter Oskar Kokoschka and demonstrate to you their significance for the proletariat, just as he introduced to you the churchly rubbish of the Isenheim Altar [the work of Matthias Grünewald] or the individualistic artistic torments of a Van Gogh. Egocentric individualism went hand-in-hand with the development of capital and must fall with it.

With joy we welcome the news that the bullets are whistling through the galleries and palaces, into the masterpieces of Rubens, instead of into the houses of the poor in the working-class neighborhoods!

We welcome it if the open struggle between capital and labor takes place in the domain of this disgraceful culture and art, which consistently served to suppress the poor while edifying the bourgeois on Sunday, so that on Monday he could all the more calmly resume . . . his exploitation! [. . .]

We summon all to oppose the masochistic reverence for historical values, to oppose culture and art! [. . .]

We know, workers, that you will create your workers' culture entirely alone just as you have created your own organization for the class struggle.

190
RICHARD HUELSENBECK
Dada Tours

First published as "Dada Tourneen," in *En avant dada. Die Geschichte des Dadaismus* (Hannover: Paul Steegemann, 1920).

Dada enjoyed its greatest successes in Germany. We dadaists quickly formed a company that terrorized the population and to which, aside from myself, Messrs. Raoul Hausmann, George Grosz, John Heartfield, Wieland Herzfelde, Walter Mehring, and a certain [Johannes] Baader belonged. In 1919 we organized various large soirées in Berlin. In the beginning of December we gave (through no fault of our own in that institute of socialist hypocrisy, the "Tribune") two Sunday matinees, which yielded the dual success of a filled purse and the melancholy, reluctant recognition of the critic Alfred Kerr—very famous and recognized a century ago but now a complete invalid and severely arterio-sclerotic—in the form of an article in the *Berliner Tageblatt*. With Hausmann the dadasoph (to whom I attached myself quite closely on account of his unselfish cleverness) and the Baader who has already been mentioned several times, I undertook a dada tour in February of 1920. It was welcomed at the outset—in Leipzig on February 24 we performed in the Central Theater before approximately 2,000 people—with a ta da! (*bruit*) that shocked this old, fragile globe to its foundations. We began in Leipzig since we departed from the correct idea that all Germans are Saxons, with which, it seems to me, enough is said. We then traveled to Bohemia, where on February 26 we appeared before an audience of fools and curiosity-seekers. The same evening we drank ourselves senseless after we, in a final gesture of sobriety, had named the most intelligent inhabitant of Teplitz, Dr. Hugo Dux, the chief of all Czechoslovak dadaists.

Baader, who is nearly fifty years old and as far as I know already a grandfather, then went to the classical Roman bordello where he indulged his appetites with a bout of drink, food, and women, and conceived, at the expense of Hausmann and myself, a criminal plan that in his estimation was to cost us our lives on March 1 in Prague. For on March 1 we wanted to perform as a trio in the produce market, which holds nearly 2,500 people. Now the situation in Prague is a bit peculiar. We were threatened with violence from all sides. The Czechs wanted to beat us up because unfortunately we were Germans; the Germans believed that we were bolsheviks; and the socialists threatened us with death and annihilation because they took us for debauched reactionaries.

Weeks before our arrival the newspapers had published dada monster ads, and the level of anticipation could not have been higher. People obviously believed that live cows were going to fall from the sky—on the street they formed cordons behind us and rhythmically bellowed "dada"; on the editorial pages we were politely shown the revolvers with which circumstances permitting, people were thinking about shooting at us on the evening of March 1. All of this had a powerful impact on Baader's brain. The poor pietist had imagined the dada tour ending rather completely differently. He hoped to return to his bride and his children with a bit of money in his pocket to reap interest from dada and, having completed his marital obligation, to be able to dream gently of his heroic deeds while smoking a pipe of Germania ersatz tobacco.

Now he was supposed to lay down his dear life; now there was the possibility that his poetic career would end in a Prague mortuary. In his fear he wanted to assume responsibility for everything; he was willing to bear any shame if only his cousin, the old Jewish God with whom he had so often fraternized, would preserve him this time from the dissolution of his pseudobardic individuality. *Dum vita superest, bene est.* [While there is life, all is well.] The performance in the produce market was to begin at eight o'clock. Around half past I asked Hausmann about Baader. "He left me a note saying he was going off to the post office one more time." He allowed us to believe that he was coming back in order to keep us from changing the program and thus so as to deliver us the more securely to the rage of the audience.

The whole city was up in arms. Thousands crowded around the entrances of the produce market. They were already hanging by the dozens on the window bars, sitting on the piano, and bellowing and blustering for all they were worth. Hausmann and I were standing nervously in the adjoining room that had been set up as the artists' "dressing room" and where the windowpanes had already begun to rattle. It was twenty after eight—Baader was not there. We were just beginning to understand what was afoot. Hausmann remembered having seen a letter "To Hausmann and Huelsenbeck" among his clothes. We understood that Baader had left us sitting and that this time we would have to do the hocus-pocus, as best as we were able, on our own. The situation was as unfavorable as possible—the only way to get to the podium (a makeshift platform made of boards) was through the thronging masses, and Baader on the lam with half of the script. It was now or never. *Hic Rhodus!*

Respected readers, with the help of God and our routine, the first of March in Prague was a great success for dada. And on March 2 Hausmann and I appeared before a smaller audience in the Mozarteum, again with great success. On March 5 we were in Karlsbad where we were able to conclude to our satisfaction that dada is eternal and will achieve everlasting fame.

191

MAX BECKMANN

Creative Credo

First published in *Tribune der Zeit und Kunst. Eine Schriften-Sammlung,* ed. Kasimir Edschmid, vol. 13, *Schöpferische Konfession* (Berlin: Erich Reiß Verlag, 1920), 61–67.

My form is painting and I am quite satisfied with it, for I am actually taciturn by nature and only a burning interest in something can force me through the torment of getting the words out.

These days, when I frequently have the chance of observing eloquent painters with some astonishment, I have sometimes felt a bit uneasy that my poor mouth is not at all capable of capturing in beautiful and lofty words my inner enthusiasm and burning passion for the objects of the visible world. But ultimately I put my mind at rest about it and am now actually quite satisfied in that I say to myself, you are a painter, practice your craft and let those speak who are able to. I believe that the real reason I love painting is that it forces one to be objective. I hate nothing so much as sentimentality. The stronger and more intense my will to capture the unspeakable things in life, the more fiercely and deeply my emotions concerning our existence burn within me, then the more reticent my mouth becomes, the colder my will to get hold of this terrible convulsive monster of vitality and constrain it, subdue it, strangle it in lines and surfaces as sharp and clear as glass.

I do not cry. Tears are anathema to me and a sign of slavery. I always think only of the object.

I think of a leg, an arm, of the puncturing of the plane through the wonderful feeling of foreshortening, of the distribution of space, of the combination of straight lines with crooked ones; of the amusing juxtaposition of small, multiple-legged volumes to the straightnesses and flatnesses of adjoining walls; and of the depths of table surfaces, wooden criss-crosses, or building façades. To me the most important is volume, captured in height and breadth. The volume in the plane, the depth in the feeling of a surface, the architecture of the picture.

Piety! God? Oh, beautiful, much abused word. I will be both, once I will have done my work in such a way that I can finally die. A painted or sketched face, a grinning or weeping face—that is my testament of faith; if I have felt something of life, then it is to be found there.

The war is now coming to its sad end. It has changed nothing in my ideas about life; it has only confirmed them. We are probably approaching a difficult time. But just now I have the need, almost more than before the war, to remain among people. In the city. That is our place now. We must take part in all the misery that will come. We must sacrifice our hearts and our nerves to the terrible cry of pain of the poor, deluded people. Just now we must place ourselves as close to people as possible. That is the only thing that can lend some measure of meaning to our actually quite superfluous and egoistic existence. That we give people a picture of their fate—one can only do that if one loves them.

Actually we know it is senseless to love people, that pile of egoism (to which one oneself belongs). But I do it anyway. I love them with all their pettiness and banality. With their stupidity and cheap complacency and their oh-so-rare heroism. And nevertheless every day each person is to me a new event, as if each one had just fallen from Orion. Where can I gratify this feeling more intensely than in the city? In the country they say that the wind blows more purely and temptation beckons less powerfully. It is my view that the filth is the same everywhere, that purity resides in the will. Peasants and countryside are no doubt beautiful as well and sometimes the occasion for wonderful relaxation. But the big human orchestra is still the city.

That was what was unhealthy and loathsome in the period before the war, when the social rush and the mania for success and influence worked their sickly effect on every one of us. Now we have looked horror square in the face every day for four years. Perhaps it has penetrated some of us. Provided of course there was even the slightest predisposition for it there.

Complete withdrawal, to achieve personal purification and that famous immersion in God, remains for now too bloodless and also too loveless for me. One may do that only after one has accomplished one's work, and our work is painting.

We hope we have gotten rid of a lot of what was there before. Emerging from a thoughtless imitation of the visible, from a feeble, archaic deterioration into empty decoration, and from a false and sentimental, tumorous mysticism, we are hopefully arriving at a *transcendental objectivity,* which can issue from a deeper love for nature and people, as is evident in [Gabriel] Mäleßkircher, [Matthias] Grünewald, and [Peter] Bruegel, in [Paul] Cézanne and [Vincent] Van Gogh.

Perhaps through a less enterprising spirit, perhaps even—what I scarcely dare to hope—through a stronger communist principle, love for things for their own sake will become greater again. Only in that do I see the possibility of recapturing a great and general feel for style.

That is my crazy hope, which I cannot give up and despite everything is stronger in me than ever. Some time to build buildings along with my paintings. To build a tower in which people can scream out all of their rage and despair, all of their poor hopes, joys, and wild desires. A new church.

Perhaps the times will help me.

192

ADOLF BEHNE

[On the 1922 Russian Art Exhibition in Berlin]

First published as "Der Staatsanwalt schützt das Bild," *Die Weltbühne* no. 47 (November 23, 1922), 545–548.

The Russian exhibit in the Lutz Gallery[1] provides an excellent documentation of the transcendence of the image. That Kandinsky's paintings have been hung on the final wall is probably a concession to (mistaken) German exhibits of modern Russian art. In no sense is Kandinsky's abstract canvas the last word in Russian painting. The leading role has not been played by Kandinsky, still less by [Marc] Chagall (who has a very weak painting on display here), but by the constructivists, the splendidly represented [Kasimir] Malevich, [Alexander] Rodchenko, [El] Lissitzky, and [Vladimir] Tatlin, [Nathan] Altman, and [Naum] Gabo. The question is no longer whether the suprematist image is a better or more beautiful image than the impressionist image; rather the question is whether the image as such can continue to supply us with an accepted, fruitful area of work. The image itself is in crisis—not because a couple of painters thought this up but because the modern individual has experienced changes in intellectual structure that alienate one from the image. The image is an aesthetic matter whereas what the radical artists of all nations want is to lend immediate form to reality itself (the Russians call it production art). Soviet Russia was the first to recognize the possibilities inherent in this great new goal and give it free rein; the German "art lover" instead remains stubbornly closed to it (no salon has yet exhibited the German constructivists). This exhibit, the most audacious and richest in productive artistic work that Berlin has seen in a long time—and under what conditions!—is an official exhibit of the People's Commissariat for the Arts and Sciences in Moscow. The Commissariat charged the painter [David] Sterenberg with putting the show together (his works, incidentally, are among the most interesting on display). It is utterly inconceivable that even in a hundred years an official German exhibition would so frankly

1. At the time of the exhibition, the Lutz Gallery had not yet changed owners and was known as the Van Diemen Gallery.

embrace art, the times, and all that is of current vitality. "We hope," Sterenberg writes in the catalogue, "that our Western comrades, whom we would very much like to see in Moscow and Petrograd, will not keep us waiting long." I can imagine what will be sent to Russia (if anything at all) to represent artistic work in Germany. It will be at least ten years behind the times.

193

CARL EINSTEIN

Otto Dix

First published as "Otto Dix," *Das Kunstblatt* 7, no. 3 (March 1923), 97–102.

One has had quite enough of the color-soaked rural in-laws [Paul] Gauguin and [Vincent] Van Gogh; the officious, respectable nephews of [Henri] Matisse should withdraw to the provinces among the portly philistines. It was quickly over; may these trivial efforts stir up a little excitement in remote servants' quarters or gather dust in back hallways of middlebrow clothiers. Perhaps the frames should be saved; the materials are worth something.

The poles of contemporary art are stretched apart to the breaking point. Constructors, abstractionists established the dictatorship of form; others, like Grosz, Dix, and [Rudolf] Schlichter, demolish the real with pithy objectivity, unmask this era, and force it into self-irony. Painting, a medium of cool execution; observation an instrument of relentless attack. Such a recusant attitude disregards affable painting with a social conscience; it treats the latter the way revolutionaries value Wilhelmine pension plans. Bourgeois reality— droning performance, mercurial swindle, and choking philistinism—is a laughable anach- ronism; this society is a treatment plant for nausea. There is naturally no shortage of plumply aging pupils still turning out vacuous, formulaic imitations of the master who today, passionately and belatedly, disavows his pets. The time for conciliators may well be over; instead of portraits, servilely rendered and expensively framed, formal innovation or provocative uprightness is the order of the day. If a German wants to represent reality, he no longer thinks of spring, flowerpots, and the chattily ordinary salon. Spring forces not only the still lifes of the charmingly marketable; bedsores, abortion, and multiplying venereal diseases work best of all; sweet spring satirizes malicious plots, outrages, and budgetary details; winter gets soiled by wet feet, black-market galoshes, overheated houses of fornication, and murderous price increases—these simply routine tidbits of the stinking panorama.

Dix gives this era—which is only the caricature of one—a resolute and technically sound kick in its swollen belly, wrings confessions of vileness from it, and produces an upright depiction of its people, their sly faces grinning an array of stolen mugs. A great, old painter lives in Paris—[Georges] Rouault—who spits on the present in a similar fashion: bridal wreaths, shirtfronts, and medals. These painters are waging civil war; their repulsive subject matter draws opposition, whether opponents refuse and demolish it as adherents of objectlessness or as observers. Both are now expedient.

A sloganeering attack against these ridiculous times, iconoclasm. Painters wage war, whether they invent forms or ruin them through representation, reacting with a carefully structured counterattack on the peripheral charm of objects and individuals (a defect). They aim the exploding kitsch of the present matter-of-factly in the faces of their contemporaries.

Dix's pictures are an assault, sober, without the improper assertion of a beloved, false personality that always sells smirking Calembourg[1] instead of fact. Personality that accumulates in jokes and sly anecdotes is a defect and a sellout of the bankrupt. Whoever paints like Dix could easily turn into Meggendorf. Dix dares to produce a suitable kitsch, namely, the ridiculous world of the cleverly stupid bourgeois splashing properly about in stifling ordinariness.

Dix began with a dangerously literary approach; the picture did not yet absorb the insight. At first he stimulated his painting with banging sensations. Grosz and Schlichter began similarly; Georg, of course, discovered the spatial composition of the grotesque at the outset. Dix initially starts with shooting galleries and sexual murders. He is very talented, but somewhat oppressed by this mixture. Romanticism of the local section of the paper; somewhat childish journalism. Soon enough he dispensed with the literary and found among the sensations the bearer of his work: that disgusting element of permanently vacuous ordinariness. The anecdote was overcome. Now Dix paints heads, penetratingly and convincingly, flesh in action with inflated muscles. He discovered the arrogantly disgusting creature that squats on every chair, deceives in stupid philistine sentences, and defends a shaky situation with a rear end hot with cash; he gives kitsch to kitsch. He puts the gang in the place it deserves, negative and smeared, airless and with a narrowing background of bricks and nothingness. Dix rightly recognizes that it is not the accidental murderer who is especially dangerous; tripping and bone-breaking, the ladies and gentlemen glide along the proper path of legitimate baseness. So, instead of laboriously profound anecdotes, ceaselessly choking shabbiness, Dix renders permanent fact and principled point-of-view with exquisite painterly skills. These paintings are not caricatures—impossible since the whole noble breed sweats caricature in itself. That is where Dix, the forthright, self-trained observer, strikes. To him a rundown apartment house, an overstuffed chair, an irrigator, and a prosthesis become nature. He paints too well to be a [Eduard Ritter von] Grützner from the left like the liberally sensitive [Fritz] von Uhde. Dix sets craft and objectivity against sham and a sordid sensibility. The bourgeois gets kitsch back from him in sharp focus; he can do it because he paints very well, so well that his painting aborts kitsch, executes it. The time of the inoffensive portrait of wealthy gangsters and swindlers is over. Dix paints what is current and thereby knocks it down without the swollen solemnity of a prettifying dolt. Painting as a critical statement.

194

GUSTAV HARTLAUB

Introduction to "New Objectivity": German Painting since Expressionism

First published as "Zum Geleit," in *Ausstellung "Neue Sachlichkeit": Deutsche Malerei seit dem Expressionismus* (Mannheim: Städtische Kunsthalle, 1925).

On the threshold of this exhibition of the most recent German painting, it is important to avoid a dangerous mistake. Simply because evidence is displayed here of artistic

1. A word game.

endeavors that became recognizable *after* expressionism, and which, in a certain sense, appear to represent a reaction against the latter, does *not* mean that a position is being taken against expressionism and the generation of artists adhering to it. It is very doubtful that expressionism is dead—further developments by its best representatives in the most recent period is cause for thought. If, however, it truly is supposed to have been "overcome" as a "tendency," as a world view, and as an artistic signature, then that still says nothing against the achievements and *values* that produced it or against the particular persons who embodied it.

Every tendency is tied to a generation, fades along with it into the background, and becomes outmoded in order perhaps to reappear later under a new aspect. But what is a tendency other than the sharing of specifically artistic articulations within the general state of consciousness of a generation as a whole, within the range of its desires and reactions? What is it other than simply the new, not yet exhausted, still supple springboard from which a new generation of artists takes the leap into art? All depends finally not on the springboard, but on the *height* of the leap achieved by the individual through the force of talent and character. The standards by which the height is measured remain the same; they are *timeless.* And the higher an individual has leapt, the more certainly he has surpassed spatial and temporal specificity to make contact with the realm of free and timeless values.

And let us not forget that the designation of a tendency, of an -ism, is essentially the product of a retrospective historical construction dependent on the particular point of view of the observer! Thus may one concede that a few of the painters in our exhibition, in the manner of their approach to the things characteristic of our most immediate reality, have diverged sharply from the nonrepresentational, nearly supersensual expressive innovations of certain "expressionists." If, however, one sees the unbridled *intensity* with which the one projects his inner visions, the other his outer substantiations, or if one attends to the *constructional* bent, which the representational art of today emphasizes no less than the cubism or futurism of yesterday, then one finds much that they have in *common,* which could just as easily have been reduced to the lowest common denominator of an -ism. Just now—ourselves wholly under the influence of extremely dramatic transformations and variations in our lives and values—we see the distinctions more clearly: the timely, coldly verificational bent of a few, and the emphasis on that which is objective and the technical attention to detail on the part of all of them. It will soon become apparent that the germ of the new art was already present in the old and that much of the visionary fantasy of the old is preserved even in the verism of today.

The exhibition is not intended to provide a *cross-section* of all the artistic endeavors of the post-expressionists. It leaves aside the art of abstract, constructivist tendencies; these efforts, in which the new will to objectivity is proclaimed in a completely different way, are to be reserved for a separate exhibition. What we are displaying here is distinguished by the—in itself purely external—characteristic of the *objectivity* with which the artists express themselves. It is easy to identify two different *groups.* The first—one almost wants to speak of a "left-wing"—tears the objective from the world of contemporary facts and projects current experience in its tempo and fevered temperature. The other searches more for the object of *timeless* validity to embody the eternal laws of existence in the artistic sphere. The former have been called verists; classicists one could almost call the latter. But both designations are only *half* right, since they fail to focus the material sharply and could easily lead to a new domination of the aesthetic *concept* over the concrete plenitude of works. We do not want to commit ourselves to the new catchwords. What we are showing is solely *that art is still there,* that it is striving after the new and unexpressed, and that it is fighting for the rights of the new and unexpressed. That it is *alive,* despite a cultural situation that seems hostile to the essence of art as other epochs have rarely been. That artists—disillusioned, sobered, often resigned to the point of cynicism having nearly given up on themselves after a moment of unbounded, nearly apocalyptic hope—that artists in the midst of the catastrophe have begun to ponder what is most immediate, certain, and durable: truth and craft.

195

FRANZ ROH

Post-Expressionist Schema

First published as *Nach-Expressionismus, Magischer Realismus. Probleme der neuesten europäischen Malerei* (Leipzig: Klinkhardt und Biermann, 1925), 119.

Expressionism	*Post-Expressionism*
ecstatic objects	plain objects
many religious themes	few religious themes
the stifled object	the explanatory object
rhythmic	representative
arousing	engrossing
excessive	rather strict, purist
dynamic	static
loud	quiet
summary	sustained
obvious	obvious and enigmatic
close-range image	close- and long-range image
forward moving	also flowing backward
large size	large size and many-columned
monumental	miniature
warm	cool to cold
thick coloration	thin layer of color
roughened	smoothed, dislodged
like uncut stone	like polished metal
work process preserved	work process effaced
leaving traces	pure objectification
expressive deformation of objects	harmonic cleansing of objects
rich in diagonals	rectangular to the frame
often acute-angled	parallel
working against edges of image	fixed within edges of image
primitive	civilized

196

MISCH OREND

Magical Realism

First published as "Der magische Realismus," *Klingsohr. Siebenbürgische Zeitschrift* 5 (January 1928), 25–27.

The great cry is fading. Expressionism seeks to assume a form—and has already found a new form. From the subjectivist commotion that distorted and burst apart all things, a new look, a new way of seeing is emerging. The commotion ebbs and things reappear to the eyes, to people, in a new reality. They are once again becoming objects, becoming things.

And yet they are not the things nor the objects that they were before expressionism. One has to go back a long way to find a similar art, a similar way of seeing, and a similar attitude toward things. It is the echo following upon the great commotion of expressionism that defines the new people and their art.

This art has been given the names *New Objectivity*, which conveys a sense of being very cool and reserved, and more recently, *Magical Realism*, which indicates something essential in the new art, something that the first name fails to capture. The demon that blinds all eyes retreats a step, enters into communication with things, surrounds them in its sea, bestows on them the power borne by every symbol that stands for something incomprehensibly essential.

It is not a form of mysticism that denies the existence of things, disdains them, and seeks to stimulate the sense of some beyond. It is not a romantic infinity in which all individual being acquires value only by becoming part of the infinite. The thing stands there in its unqualified autonomy, with all the weight of its unique existence, whether it is a tree, a human being, or an animal. The unspeakable loneliness that seizes every being cognizant of its uniqueness now surrounds the thing—the distress, the tension, and the energy with which it asserts its singular existence.

And yet each thing has only a small share of the force, the tension that all things bear within themselves, that holds the earth, the world, together—but it *does* have a share of this small force.

That is why the deadest, most useless thing is capable of suddenly emanating this great force lying within it, of making it palpable while remaining nonetheless the dead and useless thing that it was. Here any given stone or a scarecrow can have the same relation to universal being as a human being or an animal. Suddenly all concepts of value are shifted by this single one; for every thing is filled with the essential force, precisely because it is a thing.

The magic that things emanate from the base of their singular existence and that we see in them is not a naive magic striving to move beyond a utilitarian existence into a higher one, striving to force upon a person his own pre-existing judgments. This new magic is the visible existence of the things themselves as they preserve it in themselves without reference to the human world. It is their uniqueness—and therefore infinity—with the uncanny calm that surrounds them.

This art is tragic and serious, for everything unique and singular lives within an enormous loneliness; no second being can replace the first existence, for the first is referred to no purpose. This art is heroic, for it disdains all compassion, knowing that no second being can lighten a singular existence.

There is no purpose to ornament and embellishment in this austere art, for they were there after all precisely to conceal the great weight of the tensions, to mitigate, to simulate sweetness and cheerfulness in order to avoid shocking a tender disposition. Thus has architectural ornament become frivolous, worthy only to be cast away in favor of the free and open representation of the original weight of the mass. All things rapturous and mushy betray a kind of childishness and effeminacy; to make everything rosy and to shut one's eyes in the face of the plenitude infusing every thing is a sign of senility.

This art has the courage to represent all beings in the nakedness of their primal origins. That is why it lacks the forbearance to observe the other side of things human with humor and an understanding smile; rather, it demolishes and condemns; the light it casts is harsh so that it might kill quickly. But it is not for the sake of killing and annihilating that it demolishes; it is for the sake of truth and reality, for the sake of this magical reality—which is just barely possible in a time as severely infected as ours with stale, old knowledge and crude prejudices.

Thus biting ridicule is a necessary part of this austere, strict, and heroic art. For where the most unpretentious thing overflows with the coiled force inhering in all things and holding the world together, people in full consciousness remain blind, endeavoring to escape this force by giving in to their delusions and closing their eyes. Ridicule, however, wants to open the eyes.

This art can best be compared to the realism of the Gothic period. Then, too, everything represented the likeness of the one, the true, and the real. The whole human being was fulfilled; there was no breach separating reason from the experience of things, no doubt to cripple one's ability to surrender to life, even if surrender was only preparatory and transitional to the *other* life.

Today's art knows no beyond; it lacks that joyful optimism, that childish faith—but it also lacks the breach between this world and the beyond, between above and below. All the values associated with the beyond have migrated into things; things do not strive to exceed, to get out of themselves but to go inside, to fill, and to intensify their being. They seek no dissolution from themselves!

And here is the fundamental distinction and here I see the first step, which will be taken by many, into the land of the spirit, of experience, and of interiority. From antiquity through the Middle Ages, the way is being paved to the Third Reich. Expressionism was the birth, magical realism is the first attempt to walk—the step is firm and heavy. Pure reason must abdicate its tyrannical throne. The air, which reason had made so thin, will once again be filled with fragrance, and the active life will regain the fullness and depth of meaning, because it is anchored in the ineffable to which every thing is linked. All the disunities that have built up in conscious knowledge will succumb to the kind of unity that has animated all energetic races down to the deepest of their foundations. Every great deed has issued forth from this unity.

Whoever pursues the course of such a spiritual life in Europe—the visible expression of which has always been art—will not be astonished to find that the story is not one of years but of decades and centuries. Such a life has never proceeded in a straight line but in loops and curves; it moves forward, then backward, until it has encompassed all the strata of humanity and fulfilled its task.

We are still at the beginning. And only those who have surrendered themselves without reservation to the journey can measure the struggles and shocks this beginning has cost. But never yet has such a struggle been waged without reward.

197

PAUL SCHULTZE-NAUMBURG

Art and Race

First published in *Kunst und Rasse* (Munich: J. F. Lehmanns Verlag, 1928), 1–3, 86–88, 101–104.

It is a matter of daily observation that works of art are subject to judgments differing from one another to such an extent, indeed contradicting each other so thoroughly, that one would scarcely believe such an emotional divergence possible. The customary explanation, that tastes simply do not agree, is hardly satisfying. For the emotional orientation from which the artistic judgment derives cannot be purely accidental, falling now this way, now that, but must have as its basis a regularity that can be exposed and recognized, at least in broad terms. Should it be possible to prove that every artistic judgment is at least in part bound to race, then we will have made a good start on overcoming the torment of apparently unfounded and therefore incomprehensible contradictions.

To this end, it will be initially demonstrated how the relation between the physicality of the artist and his work is one of inextricable dependence, and how impossible it is for him to surpass the conditions of his own corporeality. A recognition, however, of this close relation simultaneously establishes the contrary procedure, which allows us to draw inferences from the artwork (or the judgment of such) to the artist (or the one making the judgment). Thus is it possible to gain information about the racial basis of the population not only from works of the past; rather in regard to the present, too, it is possible to arrive at interpretations of artistic products which explain certain things that would otherwise remain enigmatic.

My own observations of this sort have their beginnings nearly thirty years ago. By changing my place of residence and settling in the countryside, I became subject to a series of perceptions explainable by noting that a certain type of behavior, certain judgments and capacities, must somehow be tied to the specific population groupings. The groups were clearly distinct from one another in physical appearance, though they occupied more or less the same geographical location. Little of ethnology was known at that time so I could be guided only by that which clearly and unmistakably appeared to my own eyes: that there were two different kinds of people living there, which I identified according to the historical origins of the locality as the Sorbs (Wends) and the Franks. The former were the original inhabitants of the area and were subordinated by the Franks, who pressed in upon them from the south and the west. This process of colonization was well established everywhere. I was only a little astonished that the physical and mental characteristics of these two populations, despite a thousand years of living together, had been maintained to such an extent that they continue to this day to be clearly distinct. Having found my investigation of the particularities of each of these two groups to be extraordinarily instructive, I turned my attention to ethnology, the development of which was being powerfully stimulated at the time by modern biology.

My fascination with ethnological studies has stayed with me. It became truly fruitful, however, only as I supplemented it with the doctrine of heredity, without which these observations would lack a proper context. From a phenomenon so clearly observed and understood in context, there then developed the designation of the *homo alpinus* and the *homo nordicus,* the representatives of which confronted me as Wends and Franks. Numerous measurements demonstrated to my satisfaction that, at least in regard to predominant type, it remains possible today to distinguish those with rounded from those with elongated heads, even if considerable intermixing has substantially effaced the distinction. (As, in general, the length-versus-breadth index cannot legitimately claim the importance still commonly attributed to it. It is certainly one of the many indications of race, but not *the* indication.) It is of course not without aesthetic significance that the narrow face of the northern type corresponds to the elongated skull, as likewise the alpine habitat harmonizes with the broad skull.

Racial interpretations became so familiar to me over time that I could not avoid relating them to my work as a specialist. The original plan, however, of devoting a chapter of a new edition of my *Cultural Investigations* (1922) to these racial observations had to be abandoned, since the topic had come to exceed by far the range of a single chapter. A separate volume would not have fit into the structure of that work, which was complete in itself, and thus I was happy to accept the proposal of the Lehmanns Verlag and have it appear independently as a book.

For it to be useful by itself, it was necessary to supply it with a rather short introduction to the central problems of ethnology and the law of heredity, as well as the basic features of racial hygiene. Perhaps those already familiar with these doctrines will nevertheless be interested in the treatment of the relevant questions from the point of view of art, while taking into account that one cannot assume even in educated circles a knowledge of the basic doctrines.

This lack of knowledge is most clearly evidenced by the fact that many people tend to fly into a passion even at the mere mention of the racial idea. And the less knowledge they have, the more bitterly they quarrel and fight. There is, however, no better means of subduing and reconciling the conflict than an honest attempt to become acquainted with the problem as a whole. The result is that a question previously answered on the basis of belief and opinion becomes subject to natural scientific examination, thus allowing at least those who make an honest attempt to find a common ground for discussion. [. . .]

Art, however, offers us instruction not only concerning the races that make up a people and, through a process of internal variation, more or less change its essential type; it also yields information concerning higher or lower instances within races or racial mixtures. The attempt will be made in the next chapter to depict how and under what circumstances changes in the body of the nation have appeared over the last hundred years and how they may be recognized in art. Let us take as a given the presupposition that this downward selection has taken place to a considerable degree—here on the basis of the otherwise unerring testimony of art. The question remains as to the reasons a people could, over a relatively short period of time, cease to venerate a highly evolved and noble human type to which an earlier time had willingly subjected itself, even if not all of the individuals composing the people were able to emulate the somewhat alien type in their own lives.

It is very instructive to wander through the art of the present with this idea in mind. For this purpose the form of customary art criticism, which is usually concerned with examining and determining the intensity and clarity of expression, is inappropriate. The extent to which contemporary artistic activity can be considered a genuine cross-section of our entire culture and the population underlying it will be left undecided for the moment. But if we assume that art is in fact to be regarded as a summarizing expression of our time, it is difficult to overlook the extraordinarily significant conclusions it suggests.

The most important problem is always the human type: how it confronts us in the paintings and sculptures not only as predominant but as dominant. As the central characteristic it is evident that the representation of the Nordic type in German art today can be found only as a very rare exception, and then as a rule only in lower instances. In matters of human representation, exotic foreign characteristics prevail. Within the latter type, however, it is noteworthy that there is a strong inclination not to represent the nobler instances of the type, but unmistakably those that approximate primitive humans, extending all the way to the grinning mugs of animal-like cave-dwellers. Moreover, we see a preference for and an emphasis on the symptoms of degeneration, as they are known to us from the multitude of the downfallen, the sick, and the physically deformed.

The activities chosen for representation in contemporary art, and which in every art are extremely characteristic of an era, refer more or less to a physical and moral nadir as well. Were one to name the symbols that find expression in the majority of the paintings and sculptures of our period, they would be the idiot, the prostitute, and the sagging breast. One has to call things by their right name. Spreading out here before us is a genuine hell of inferior human beings, and one sighs in relief upon leaving this atmosphere for the pure air of other cultures—in particular that of antiquity and the early Renaissance in which a noble race struggled to express its own longings in art. It is necessary to assume that the reader is acquainted with the representations filling today's art exhibits and the horror chambers of museums, those works about which the master advertisers are always crying "unheard of, unheard of." This book can do no more than refresh the memory with a few small illustrations and evoke an idea of the world into which the creators of these pictures are attempting to lead us. [. . .]

Should one search for an overall impression of contemporary art, it is above all that of utter chaos, of a planless and rootless mess, of an uncreative groping for sensations, of an utter lack of genuine, unpretentious humanity, and the absence of truthfulness of any kind. To this belongs the somewhat childish preference for wholly removed stages of sociological development, the nearly perverse ogling of alien races and their behavior. Whoever walks through an art exhibit these days has occasion enough to ask himself whether the Negro admixture about which the paintings literally boast is really based on an actual mixing of blood, or only on the outrageous renunciation of the painter's own racial instinct. Genuine Negro art can naturally be of great moment and give us remarkable glimpses into the process by which human culture developed, even if it cannot satisfy the longings of those belonging wholly to another race. Artificial Western imitations of Negro art, however, vacillate between the silly and the disgraceful.

Wherever a race degenerates, racial feeling has to disappear as well, and wherever racial feeling disappears, the ideal type rooted in every genuine race is also lost. If any further proof were needed of how the population living within our borders is now experiencing an unsuspected racial decline, it would have to be the atrophy of the feeling for physical beauty in art.

We are confronted with the fate of a people to whom a large share of Nordic blood was entrusted, with the question of whether they are going to live or die.

There are indeed sufficient numbers of human ostriches with their heads deep in the sand thinking, oh, it won't be that bad. Every era has regarded changes as dangerous and threatening, and it is not likely to be any different with us. If those with their heads in the sand were to take the trouble of acknowledging the many observable historical cases of the rapid decay of great cultures and empires, they would draw an entirely different conclusion. The fate of the Roman Empire, a consequence of its own racial degeneration, may be taken as the clearest warning. Many of those who are conscious of the magnitude of the tragedy merely hinted at here will perhaps be inclined to regard them as inevitable, against which human will is powerless. It is of course impossible to know whether the culture and art of the race to which one is devoted are approaching their decline. There has been no shortage of gloomy prophets willing to predict it. In this regard, however, everything depends on which race is threatened with such a fate. It is in the soft nature of one to submit passively to its doom, whereas the mightily inspiring ethos of another dictates that it rise in Promethean defiance of the gods. Since our people remain sufficiently endowed with this heroic blood, they must, from the deepest reach of their being, ask the question: how can I avoid this fate? And is there any possibility at all of putting a spoke in the wheel of world history?

The sociological point of view discloses that a developmental stage has been reached in which much that has been hidden in obscure drives has now crossed the threshold into consciousness. Thought has succeeded in raising to some extent the veil concealing the secrets of the renewal of the human race, and it is becoming possible to sense that something other than mere accident determines the rise and fall of nations and will determine what kind of race is one day to inhabit the planet.

198

GEORGE GROSZ

Among Other Things, a Word for German Tradition

First published as "Unter anderem ein Wort für die deutsche Tradition," *Das Kunstblatt* 15, no. 3 (1931), 79–84.

Certainly we live in a transitional period. All ideas have gradually become dubious and have begun to totter, and dusk falls on a superannuated liberalism. No one knows anymore what to do with the "freedom" that dates from 1793. Everywhere reorientation and determined reaction appear toward what was universally valid the day before yesterday.

Right and left become ever more sharply divided in preparation for the final battle for power. Both have the common will to receive commands en masse from above and to snap to attention when the order is called.

How quickly it moves! After the war—I believe—not a single person was willing to think of uniforms, standing at attention, and such.

Whatever the case may be, I regard Germany now as the most interesting and most puzzling country in Europe. I have the feeling that our country has been called, as if by fate, to play a great role. It often seems to me as if we are living in an epoch similar to that of the closing Middle Ages. Then, too, there was tremendous pressure on everyone. Nevertheless that terrible time feared its artists; [Hieronymous] Bosch and [Peter] Bruegel painted their cosmogonies, which are unrivaled in the history of painting.

Perhaps we are now facing a new Middle Ages. Who knows? In any case, humanistic ideas seem to me to be in the process of dying out, just as no one any longer places much value on the human rights announced so ecstatically a century ago. Civilization is instead marching ahead on all fronts with a healthy disdain for human life. This makes no sense in the context of the socialism we apply to nearly everything and even carry out practically. But it is so.

The masses and the little man are trump. Frequently encountered at the top is his counterpart, a former worker—proclaiming to the man below the miracle of his rise. The purest materialism reigns. Work, work, work . . . the alpha and omega of the operation. The dream is romantically offered and endlessly propagandized: life in comfort, bathtubs, sports, mass-produced automobiles, and when things are good, a weekend with cocktails and a beauty queen.

America led the way; we—set back a bit by the war—and by nature a little slow—follow surely after. In Marxist Russia, America is also the model and hotly desired goal. Goal means the rationalized exploitation of all raw materials to create comfort for the little man on the basis of mechanized mass production.

The precondition of culture, raising the standard, eating, sports, clothes, no more unemployed . . . culture then comes along on its own . . . from out of the working classes. So say the official theoreticians. America might present a different picture, but nevertheless.

I do not much believe in the official savants who can prove and disprove everything with economic statistics and tables. One thing is true: we lack today order and a plan.

Hundreds of thousands who would like to work find no employment. Every new machine pensions off so-and-so-many from their work. Eventually it all becomes too stupid even for the most self-satisfied capitalists, and they bust their thick-necked heads about how to overcome the evil. The talk of dictatorship is making the rounds. But will that make them master of the machine, which everyone knows is endlessly voracious? I have my modest doubts. As always, needs are blithely cultivated just so the beast does not stop. For that would mean death to production and prosperity. It is impossible to conceive . . . that tomorrow no more forests would be turned into paper, impossible to imagine a civilization without artificial silk stockings and sweaters. No. Needs have to be culti-vated—always go after the masses. Comfort in the name of progress. Raising the standards before all else. It is funneled into us daily through a thousand press channels. To live without a vacuum cleaner and a car . . . is not worth living. Then one takes a look at American magazines. True documents of unchecked civilization. Three-quarters adver-tisements; ever-new needs. Scattered among bits of a novel, in which thinly-veiled pro-paganda, even to the point of surfeit, is made for this doubtful life of comfort. Ceaselessly the machine swallows and spits . . . ready-made goods, more and more. It will not rest until the North Pole is artificially thawed and the Eskimos bound to an assembly line.

The big city, real water on the brain: trade city, sales city, marketplace. After work, doubtful amusements . . . rushed, noisy . . . fake sparkle, to rev up tired businessmen for a couple of hours. Just do not think . . . money, women, champagne. Cheap theater. Not to be had for anything serious outside their nerve-grating businesses. A revue and the endlessly cute, predigested cinema pictures. The women, made-up, manicured, high-heeled, and neglected, with gigolos in the hotels and at the tea dance. What life?

The crowning achievement: a big villa in a safe place, stuffed full of ancient artworks as financial investments . . . expensive cars and a storehouse of fancy shirts. Ghastly materialism and boredom.

The palaces of our time: office highrises with seven floors, warehouse cathedrals, radio palaces, cinema temples . . . consecrated to the unknown deities of senseless production.

The mighty of the earth glued to money. Their fate: sales and the purchasing power of the little man.

Work scientifically organized to the last detail. What is the meaning of craftsmanship in that? Cheapen . . . cheapen. Tackle that job. A few hours more and even the dullest fellow will get it . . . and become part of the production process. Tighten his screw from early to late. Faster, faster; as grotesque as it sounds, of all the junk the machines mass produce, there is still far too little. Frantically the people compete and produce against each other. Frenzied race for markets. Cheapen . . . Raising domestic purchasing power . . . the catchwords. That all of this rubbish from pressed metal, enamel, . . . pressed glass, and reinforced pasteboard is utterly superfluous to life occurs to no one.

Endless wage battles. Apparently inescapable eternal circulation. The workers banded together in mighty organizations. Union popes ascended from below and became almost more powerful than kings. Pompous union palaces in the latest style; statues symbolizing power on display in the vestibules . . . heralds of splendor and progress. Mile-long resort facilities and vacation colonies on the sea. Who would have suspected all this in 1830 as simpletons in prophetic transport were destroying the first English machines? . . . But it is real progress, is it not?

So it is in 1931, in the age of socialism.

Artists are scattered, leftover crumbs of a past time.

Isolated from the people. The best of them lost in an intellectual fog. Only formal problems, frenzied abstracts. Objects the property of photography. Formal problems that the average mortal lacking special empathy or snobbism can scarcely comprehend. Ascendancy of an equally boring take-anything photomania. The ivory-tower dwellers shunned and frightened behind locked doors, eavesdropping on their mathematical ego. T-square and compass ready for abstraction. Speculating oddballs and superstitious sorts at every turn. Driveling art historians. Stereoscopic novelties, new material as well as magical, mechanical catchwords. Sometimes under the banner of the proletariat and so on. Today, however, less than yesterday. Boom in peculiarities. Psychoanalysis and other patent medicines have to bear the brunt. A great divide between art of this sort (avant-garde) and the people. Only a few moody, rich people with bad habits retain an interest today in artists' experiments. And this great love is usually exposed afterward as the stale speculation of undercover art dealers. What a *juste milieu;* what a deterioration of art in contrast to the truly dark Middle Ages. Eyes to the rear, not ahead.

Now no medieval artist preached praise of ready-mades, of keep smiling; standard concepts and comfort were unknown to him. Making money was not valorized, celebrated, nor painted. Compass and ruler, in a correct hierarchy of values, led a subordinate existence.

Today, the best painters are estranged from the people. Occasionally there comes a simple man from the people, a dilettante who suddenly has everything the elite, intellectual avant-garde lacks: simplicity, soul, and feeling. Characteristics, incidentally, that the elegant art snobs and enemies of the people since Henri Rousseau have been discovering and claiming for themselves.

The art of our time is pale. A child with an overgrown head and horned-rim glasses. Anemic and very contemplative . . . a proper big-city stay-at-home. It is obvious from his looks that he broods a lot. Estranged from nature and reality, he creates from within himself exact circles and mathematical-looking figures. And takes all of this terribly seriously. Observers from a later time will smirk in genuine astonishment at what today's clever propaganda has passed off to the gullible people as the "latest" art.

There was even a certain Malevich back then, who (he was dead serious about it) once exhibited a painting, an empty white square. Praised, likewise dead-seriously, by a critic as the "deed of the epoch."

One can certainly no longer live today as an old "Dutch master." But in this faithless and materialistic time one should use paper and slates to show people the devilish mug concealed in their own faces. Let us tear down the storehouse of ready-mades and all the manufactured junk and show the ghostly nothing behind them. Political convulsions will influence us powerfully. Do not fear looking back to your ancestors. Look at them, [Hans] Multscher, Bosch, Bruegel, and Mäleßkircher, [Wolfgang] Huber, and [Albrecht] Alt-dorfer. Why then the usual pilgrimage to the philistine French Mecca? Why not return to our ancestors and set forth a German tradition?

Just among ourselves, better to be ranked second class but at least to have expressed a little of our national community. And besides, the French are not at all interested in followers of their three schools.

Naturally, no Matisse is going to prosper in Outer Pomerania or Berlin. But what's the difference! The air and everything is hard, a little unpleasant and graphic. It is easy to get sniffles and cold feet . . . this is not the tempered, calm soil of the south.

Now, in order not to be misunderstood, I in no way mean here an art program à la Schultze-Naumburg. [. . .] When I say "German," I do not mean those neat little painters, devoted more or less to kitsch and pleasing the public, who are always parading their softly agreeable, pathetically vague way of dressing things up as "German." These salon painter sorts, incidentally, are to be found wherever painting is done.

I am only saying quite modestly: we should devote more reflection to our good and not inconsiderable tradition of painting and drawing. I consider a return to the formal power of the great medieval masters to be precisely as appropriate . . . as what the French do, training their people and cultivating their tradition by drawing inspiration from old Neapolitan frescoes, from Oriental tapestries, from [Jean Auguste Dominique] Ingres or African sculpture or Bushman paintings. Ugh! I have spoken.

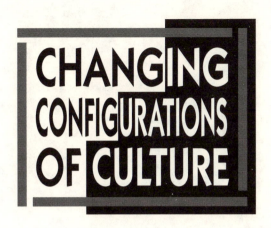

CHANGING CONFIGURATIONS OF CULTURE

Marlene Dietrich in Josef von Sternberg's film, The Blue Angel, 1930. Inset: Ringl + Pit,
"Bertolt Brecht," 1931. (Copyright © Ringl + Pit, Courtesy of Robert Mann Gallery.)

20
Literature: High and Low

AT THE END OF WORLD WAR I more than the territorial borders were redrawn. The boundaries of the literary province itself, traditionally associated in Germany with humanistic education (*Bildung*) and privilege, came under dispute as new political and social realities called for a democratization of all culture. A swiftly expanding urban mass culture of film, radio, illustrated press, sports, and entertainment challenged the notion of a literary domain isolated from public life. Reacting as much to the expressionist avant-garde elite as to the German classical tradition, literature in the Weimar Republic expanded its borders and renewed relations (in the tradition of preclassical German literature) with the political sphere, journalism, and, above all, "low" culture. At stake was a redefinition of the function and status of literature within an urban environment shaped by industrialization and modernization.

Both Franz Kafka and Thomas Mann stand out against this background. Kafka's early death in 1924 at age forty-one coincided with the beginning of a literary trend that took its cue from the New Objectivity movement in the arts; his death signaled the end of a mode of writing intimately linked to the private existence of the author. Although Max Brod may have exaggerated the now-prevailing image of Kafka as a self-absorbed artist, Kafka's uniquely enigmatic parables and allegories did indeed shun mass appeal and were almost unknown; furthermore, they seemed to belong to an earlier period. Similarly, Thomas Mann's novel *The Magic Mountain* (*Der Zauberberg*), which also appeared in 1924, was judged by Hermann von Wedderkop, editor of the voguish magazine *Der Querschnitt,* to be curiously out-of-step with the times. Of course, Thomas Mann himself had already ironically introduced his expansive portrait of prewar Europe as an illumination of a bygone era. Despite their subsequent fame, neither Kafka nor Thomas Mann was at the center of literary debates in the 1920s.

Most discussions about literature in the Weimar Republic focused on the various degrees to which literature should and could be used for social and political causes. Alfred Döblin, for instance, demanded that the poet no longer stand apart from the political life of the new republic, while Walter Benjamin pleaded for an "alternation between action and writing." Egon Erwin Kisch's detached eyewitness accounts (*Reportagen*), with their rejection of all personal, "lyrical" sentiments, defined the type of hard-boiled literature that was deemed thoroughly modern in its affinity to the tenets of the New Objectivity. Subjective distortion and expressionistic pathos were no longer in fashion; fiction and fantasy yielded to sober and rational prose that was seen as both "democratic" and "international." The ultimate mark of quality for a literary "product" was its usefulness; even poetry adhered to this philosophy, as the usable poetry (*Gebrauchslyrik*) of Bertolt Brecht's *Hauspostille* [Household Homilies] (1927) or Erich Kästner's *Herz auf Taille* (1929) demonstrated. Kurt Pinthus labeled this literature "masculine" because of its lack of emotion, sobriety, and matter-of-factness. Not surprisingly, the demands for a New Objectivity in literature evoked strong reactions both from the political right wing, which opposed the leftist leanings of this "modern," prosaic literature, and from the avant-garde proper, which criticized the collectivist ideology associated with politically engaged literature. Gottfried Benn's vitriolic attack on Russian collectivist art was directed, of course, primarily against the German writers who literally sat at the feet of Sergei Tretyakov during his visit to Berlin in 1930. Benn's fervent hope for a renewed belief in the individual has ominous overtones in view of his early (and short-lived) infatuation with the Nazi regime.

By the mid-1920s a new reading public had emerged whose demands were met by innovative marketing and distribution strategies. Book clubs, originally formed to keep books affordable during the inflation years, grew in size and created a fairly stable readership organized around ideological affiliations. Monthly bestseller lists were introduced in 1927 to orient the reader in a rapidly expanding marketplace. No fewer than 24,866 new books (4,000 of them literary) were published in Germany in 1927—twice as many as in the United States or France in the same year. New strategies were found to advertise literature: writers held readings in department stores, poets recorded their work on gramophone, and publishers dispensed paperbacks in vending machines; writers also increasingly branched out to work for radio and film. Popular genre fiction such as the detective and the war novel, as well as the serialized newspaper novel, created and organized a fairly predictable and large readership which was not easily won over to "modern" literature. Novelist Gina Kaus persuasively argued for the recognition of a distinct women's literature.

Alfred Döblin's 1929 novel *Berlin Alexanderplatz*, generally regarded as the novel most representative of the late 1920s, expressed in subject and style not only the experience of urban modernity but also the crisis of the novel as genre. In keeping with the anti-aesthetics of New Objectivity, *Berlin Alexanderplatz* cleverly undercut its own high-modernist, elitist experimentalism by using a half-criminal lower-class milieu, the Berlin dialect, and a pastiche of direct quotations from the collective semi-literary discourse such as advertising slogans, weather reports, proverbs, and songs. Inspired in part by James Joyce's *Ulysses,* which had appeared in German translation in 1928—see Döblin's review of it—*Berlin Alexanderplatz* is a stylistic patchwork emulating the proliferation of voices and signs in a modern metropolis such as Berlin.

By the end of the Weimar Republic, the calculated modernity of the New Objectivity and the political appropriation of literature were contested issues. In 1932, a young lyrical poet, Günter Eich, reinvoked the argument for a genuine poetry without any use value. This flight into the nonpolitical sphere foreshadowed the survival strategy of what later during the Third Reich would be called "inner emigration." Quietly writing poetry and radio plays throughout the period, Eich stayed in Germany. After the war he embodied the myth of the "zero hour" (*Stunde Null*), a term that would suggest a drastic and clean caesura in 1945. Eich himself disproved this myth by his career which followed a not uncommon trajectory: from critic of modernism during the Weimar Republic to inner emigré under Hitler to celebrated poet in West Germany.

199

MAX BROD

Franz Kafka's Posthumous Writings

First published as "Franz Kafkas Nachlaß," *Die Weltbühne* 20 (July 17, 1924), 106–109.

In June 1924 one of the greatest writers and finest people of all time passed away in Franz Kafka—a judgment in which, I believe, friendly exaggeration on my part plays not the slightest role; a judgment that already appears self-evident to the small circle of people to whom Kafka meant a great deal or everything. It is a judgment that will be shared in the not-too-distant future by everyone devoted to art, indeed by all humane people.

Nor is the pain of his passing responsible for the directness of my judgment. For while Kafka was still alive I spoke and wrote in my essay "The Writer Franz Kafka" (*Neue Rundschau*) with the same directness.

Franz Kafka was, to be sure, of a different opinion. We quarreled frequently about precisely this point, because Franz, in my view, severely underestimated his works. Everything he published I extracted from him with cunning, the arts of persuasion, and force. This is not contradicted by the fact that often for long stretches of time he drew much happiness from his writing. (He, of course, spoke constantly of his "scribbling.") Those who were privileged to hear him read his own prose in an intimate setting, with fiery excitement, with a rhythm whose vitality no actor will ever equal, received an immediate sensation of the tremendous creative drive and passion that stands behind his work. That he nevertheless repudiated it is to be explained first of all by certain sad experiences that inclined him to self-sabotage and therefore to nihilism in regard to his own work; and independently of that it is explained by the fact that he held his work (if without ever having said it) to the highest religious standards, which it, wrested from torment and doubt, could never satisfy. It could not mean anything to Kafka that his work was a great aid to the many striving for faith, toward nature, and toward the realization of psychic health. He had to counsel not others but himself first of all as he pursued with relentless earnestness his search for the proper path.

This is my personal interpretation of Kafka's negative attitude toward his own work. He often spoke of the "false hands stretched out to one in the process of writing," and also of how what he had already written or published distracted him from further work. Much resistance had to be overcome before a volume by Kafka appeared. Nonetheless he took proper joy in the finished books and occasionally in the effect they had on readers. And there were times when he would grace both himself and his work with equally benevolent looks, never entirely without irony but with a friendly irony—that concealed the enormous pathos of someone striving uncompromisingly for the absolute.

Franz Kafka left no testament. Under many other papers in his desk there lay a folded note written in ink and addressed to me. The content of the note is as follows:

> My dearest Max,
>
>   My final request: that everything among my papers (in book boxes, the linen cupboard, desk, at home, and in the office, or wherever else anything at all might have ended up and you see it) in the way of diaries, manuscripts, letters (from others and from me), drawings, and so on be burned in its entirety and without being read, likewise everything written or drawn in your possession or in other's, whom I ask

you to request to do the same. Those who have letters they do not want to give you should at least promise to burn them themselves.

Yours,
Franz Kafka

A more extensive search turned up another note, written in pencil, yellowed, and obviously old. It says:

Dear Max,

Perhaps this time I will not recover. After a month of pulmonary fever the onset of pneumonia is likely enough, and not even writing it down will ward it off, although the writing has a certain power.

For this eventuality, therefore, here is my last will in regard to everything written:

Of everything I have written only the books count: *The Judgment, America, The Metamorphosis, The Penal Colony, A Country Doctor,* and the story, "A Hunger Artist." (The few copies of "Investigations" can remain. I do not want to cause anyone the trouble of pulping them; but nothing in them may be printed.) When I say that only those five books and the story count, I do not mean that I want them to be reprinted and preserved for future times. On the contrary, they are to be lost entirely, in accord with my true desire. It is only that I will not hinder anyone, since they are already there, from keeping them if he wishes.

On the other hand, everything else I have written (printed in periodicals and in the way of manuscripts and letters) is without exception, to the extent that it is accessible or can be obtained by request to the addressees (you know most of the addressees)—all of this is without exception, preferably unread (though I will not prevent you from taking a look; my preference, however, is that you do not and in any case no one else is to be allowed to see it.)—all of this is without exception to be burned, and I ask you to do this as soon as possible.

Franz

If in regard to these instructions so categorically expressed I nevertheless refuse to carry out this Herostratian task demanded of me by my friend, I have the most profound reasons for doing so.

A few of them are inappropriate for public discussion. But those that I can convey are in my judgment completely sufficient to explain my decision.

The primary reason: when I changed my profession in 1921, I told my friend that I had written my testament, in which I requested him to destroy one thing and the other, to look through something else, and so on. Thereupon Kafka showed me the note written in ink, which was later found in his desk, from the outside and said, "My testament will be very simple—a request for you to burn everything." I still recall quite precisely my response to him at the time: "In case you might seriously ask me to do such a thing, I am telling you now that I will not fulfill your request." The whole discussion was carried out in our usual jocular tone, nevertheless with the secret seriousness we always expected of each other. Convinced of the earnestness of my refusal, Franz would have had to name another executor had his own instruction been his absolute and final will.

200

HERMANN VON WEDDERKOP

Thomas Mann's *Magic Mountain*

First published as "Thomas Manns Zauberberg," *Der Querschnitt* 5, no. 12 (1925), 1078.

There are still people who walk around the world, and, especially in the north, the loving and genial practice of handicrafts is still routine. And there are still novels of two volumes in which the protagonist develops little by little. Put modestly, this novel is an enormous accomplishment: who manages to say so much with so little color and with Lübeck setting the major mood?

Such novels are not otherwise written anymore, novels of such breadth, put together with proven elements like those of [Gottfried] Keller or [Theodor] Storm. If it had appeared in 1900, it would have been possible to classify it as a document of its time. As it is, it achieves with its old tools the effect of an incredible anachronism.

This, however, has its advantages: in this way Thomas Mann has cleanly slept through the horrid age of German expressionism. It is thoroughly to the credit of this novel that nothing of all the trickery, of so-called tempo, of pseudohumor and pseudocoarseness, of the bad-smelling rubbish with which our epoch masks its lack of talent is to be found in it.

The novel is doubtlessly sound; it is harder than *Buddenbrooks,* more biting in its humor, and, as if nothing else were to be expected, a work of genius in its individual observations. That it busies itself with worldviews on the side is a mistake; that is, it is a mistake on the part of Lübeck, for which it is unsuited. Moreover, worldviews concern morality and have, like the latter, nothing to do with talent, if they are not sooner injurious to talent. As grandly as it drapes the world, just as coldly does it leave us. Its effects are anything but genial, which (see the nice, regular life in the sanitarium) is ultimately Thomas Mann's element and his true worldview. It is just as cold and just as contrary to geniality as when the devil drives the author into political terrain, which results in official esteem for the intellectual patron saint of the republic and intellectual convergence with Gerhart Hauptmann.

201

EGON ERWIN KISCH

Preface to *The Racing Reporter*

First published as "Vorwort," *Der rasende Reporter* (Berlin: Erich Reiss, 1925), vii–viii.

This book may justifiably claim significance without requiring praise for its author. On the contrary:

> Quite unexceptional or dull people can produce very important books by virtue of the material they treat, if the same were accessible only to them—for example, descriptions of distant lands, rare phenomena of nature, one-time experiments,

stories of which they were witnesses or whose origins they have traced, or who have taken the time and trouble specifically to study them. [Arthur Schopenhauer, *Parerga and Paralipomena*]

The rare attempts that have been made to capture the present, to depict the times in which we live, suffer perhaps from the circumstance that their authors are precisely not the "quite unexceptional people" in the sense of the quotation from Schopenhauer. Their memoirs are justifications; their articles are tendentious; their books are written from their standpoint—that is, from a standpoint.

The reporter has no tendency to promote, has nothing to justify, and has no standpoint. He must be an unbiased witness and deliver unbiased testimony as reliably as testimony can possibly be given—particularly in such cases when testimony is more important (for clarification) than the ingenious speeches of the prosecutor or defense attorney.

Even the bad reporter—one who exaggerates or is unreliable—accomplishes useful work. He is dependent upon the facts; he has to turn them into information by being an eyewitness, by having a conversation, by making an observation, or by receiving a tip.

The good reporter requires the ability to practice the trade he loves. He would also experience what he has no need to report on. But he would not write without having experienced. He is no artist, no politician, no scholar—he is perhaps one of Schopenhauer's "dull people," and yet his work is very important "by virtue of the material."

The places and events he describes, the experiments he conducts, the stories he witnesses, and the origins he seeks out need not be so distant at all, so rare, or so difficult to trace when he devotes himself to his object in a world that is flooded with lies, in a world that wants to forget itself and therefore aims only at untruths. Nothing is more amazing than the simple truth, nothing is more exotic than our environment, nothing is more imaginative than objectivity.

And there is nothing in the world more sensational than the time in which we live!

202

WALTER BENJAMIN

Filling Station

First published as "Tankstelle," in *Einbahnstraße* (Berlin: Ernst Rowohlt, 1928), p. 7.

The construction of life is at present in the power of facts far more than of convictions, and of such facts as have scarcely ever become the basis of convictions. Under these circumstances true literary activity cannot aspire to take place within a literary framework—this is, rather, the habitual expression of its sterility. Significant literary work can only come into being in a strict alternation between action and writing; it must nurture the inconspicuous forms that better fit its influence in active communities than does the pretentious, universal gesture of the book—in leaflets, brochures, articles, and placards. Only this prompt language shows itself actively equal to the moment. Opinions are to the vast apparatus of social existence what oil is to machines: one does not go up to a turbine and pour machine oil over it; one applies a little to hidden spindles and joints that one has to know.

203

ALFRED DÖBLIN

Ulysses by Joyce

First published as "'Ulysses' von Joyce," *Das deutsche Buch,* nos. 3–4 (1928), 84–85.

There are still numerous authors in all nations—let us just say the solid majority—who put their sturdy books together and conjure up and reel off stories of larger and smaller scope, things with a proper beginning and a proper end, as if there were such a thing; who have never given a thought to this way of writing, way of thinking, or way of storytelling; and whose activity never strikes them as peculiar. For these authors are otherwise our age's private individuals, citizens who earn money, pay taxes, walk down the street, etc. It is necessary to know that art forms are systematically related to a particular manner of thinking and a general existential milieu. That is why forms are constantly being super-seded. Old novels entertain us; they activate our ability to combine and recombine new associations. They are otherwise expanded novellas, and novellas or expanded anecdotes and reduced aphorisms. These novels are more or less aphoristic. Meanwhile, let us say since [Goethe's] *Elective Affinities,* a development has taken place everywhere which opposes such aphoristic treatment and the isolation of a process of which neither authors nor the public have taken sufficient note. The cinema has penetrated the sphere of literature; newspapers must become the most important, most broadly disseminated form of written testimony, everybody's daily bread. To the experiential image of a person today also belongs the streets, the scenes changing by the second, the signboards, automobile traffic. The heroic, the importance altogether of the isolated event and the individual person, has receded substantially, overshadowed by the factors of state, parties, and the economic system. Much of this was already true, but now a person is truly no larger than the waves that carry him. A part of today's image is the disconnectedness of his activity, of his existence as such, the fleeting quality, the restlessness. The fabulating sense and its constructions have the effect here of the naïve. This is the core of the so-called crisis of today's novel. The mentality of the authors has not yet closed ranks with the age.

204

ERICH KNAUF

Book Clubs

First published as "Buchgemeinschaften," *Der Kulturwille,* no. 5 (May 1929), 99.

The German book market suffered severe losses from the war of 1914–1918. The image of the soldiers with *Faust* in their backpacks is so silly that it can be thrown away with the other war lies. The German book industry could not live from the few thousand old tomes that were read in the foxholes, barracks, and field hospitals.

The collapse was not only military and economic; the old ideological structure collapsed as well, leaving many "carriers of culture" lying like defective caryatids in the dust. The fiasco of the Wilhelmine era not only ripped the epaulettes from the officers' uniforms. Many a chief among the writers and many a prince of science lost his formerly seductive sheen. The time cried for other books, for works carrying no superfluous ballast. And these books did not appear right away. The dictatorship of the saber was succeeded by the rule of the moneybag. One economic crisis followed another and the hard struggle for existence forced books from the ranks occupied by the necessary articles of daily life.

In earlier decades the idea of a club was dismissed as "tedious leveling." Now, however, the outcast is being led to the altar of the fatherland with the speed of a wartime wedding. The marriage was very fruitful. Every year a new club has come into the world, but somehow all of the children got more of the father than the mother.

The first book clubs did not originate in the intention of clearing away the rubble of collapse and building a new world. They arose to put the rubble back together. Getting subscribers for cheap books, eliminating the retail trade, forging a direct connection between the publisher and the public—these ideas informed the founding of the first organizations. The goal was to lay hold of the former mainstays of book consumption, the middle-class readers who had now slipped down to the proletariat, and give them books that they otherwise would have had to do without because of the high price. The type of literature offered, the consumption of which was to be organized through the club, corresponded to the needs of these proletarianized readers who remained petit-bourgeois in their thinking. As little as these clubs had anything to do with the socially minded and cooperative economic enterprises of the class-conscious proletariat, their products displayed no more inclination to take into account the changed social structure nor to say to the consumers, the members of these clubs, what needed to be said. Some concessions were made to the "new spirit" regarded with so much mistrust and anxious hatred, but otherwise, under the tattered flag of political neutrality, they have been marching with diligent goose steps on the parade grounds of the "German spirit."

205

GINA KAUS

The Woman in Modern Literature

First published as "Die Frau in der modernen Literatur," *Die literarische Welt* 5, no. 11 (March 15, 1929), 1.

It has not been such a long time since the woman writer was regarded as a peculiar monster, a mongrel creature; she was the butt of jokes and characterized by inky fingers, eyeglasses, and erotic unavailability. [. . .] This intellectual mistrust and nearly physical aversion to women writers has persisted almost to the present—however, a radical stop has finally been put to gender prejudices whereby the most persuasive evidence comes from the fact that three of the living recipients of the Nobel Prize for literature are women. We meet women authors in all the publishers' catalogues, bookshop windows, newspapers, and magazines.

I cannot go into the question here of what is cause and what is effect, of whether women's increased productivity has vanquished mistrust or whether the general weakening of male resistance since the war has unleashed the productivity of women. There is simply more written today than ever before, which perhaps has to do with the difficulty of getting established in more stable professions but perhaps also simply with the decline in illiteracy.

Since women writers therefore no longer represent an abnormality, and also do not have the feeling that their activity sets them in opposition to their gender role, it is time to begin speaking of women's literature. The question of whether women's literature can be distinguished from men's literature is by itself sufficient justification for the topic; but perhaps such an investigation would also identify boundaries between the sexes, which otherwise so resemble one another today.

In my opinion, anyone who takes up any such investigation should first of all state what he wants to find; for no one approaches a topic without preconceived opinions, and it happens scarcely once in a century that anyone allows his hypothesis to be undermined by the results of an experiment. I would be one such rare exception were contemporary literary documents to persuade me that there are fundamental psychological or intellectual distinctions to be drawn between the sexes.

Let us begin with the novel, which represents the primary domain of female writers. Here, I believe, others of a different opinion would also find it difficult to draw boundaries, to the extent that they wish to use the words *male* and *female* in their customary meanings. Female, on the one hand, means—does it not?—subjectivity, sensitivity, and the primacy of emotion over understanding. Male, on the other hand means objectivity, formal command, breadth of intellectual range, etc. Now, among contemporary women authors there are no doubt those who are female in the sense given above including, indeed, examples along the whole qualitative continuum, up to Colette. But there are also male authors who could not be better characterized, including, once again, outstanding writers like Hermann Hesse. There are also to be found among women writers today some who know very well how to craft a powerful plot, like Selma Lagerlöf, Martha Ostenso, and Vicki Baum; women who can reconstruct an entire epoch in its historical context, like Sigrid Undset or Ricarda Huch; and others who maintain an extremely distanced objectivity toward their characters, like Rahel Sanzara. There are those with very logical, comic talents, like Sir Galahad or Mechthilde Lichnowsky. Then again, in her magnificent novel *Flamingo,* Mary Borden succeeds in depicting what transpires in the foreground between the characters against the backdrop of the deep sky of infinity, while simultaneously writing an outstanding political satire—that is, a novel worthy of being placed next to the works of her "most male" compatriot, [Joseph] Hergesheimer.

It would be utterly arbitrary to speak of exceptions. The frequency of borderline cases proves that here, where perhaps there once was a boundary, none exists today.

But maybe we will find it elsewhere. Maybe we will find typically "male" books in contemporary literature, if only we choose to give the word *male* a different meaning.

And there is indeed a species of the novel in which women authors might well not be represented at all (I say "might well" for the sake of caution, because ultimately I do not know all the books by women). That is the constructed novel, of which the detective novel represents a subgenre. It is the kind of novel, in other words, in which an artificial contrivance that determines the movement and direction of the plot takes the place of real life and its laws, takes the place of fate. In such novels (there are fine examples of this type by such writers as [H. G.] Wells), it goes without saying that no genuine people appear, only robots that function within the dynamic clockwork of the artificial mechanism and would immediately fall lifelessly to the ground were one to remove them from the contrivance and have them sit down, for example, to tea.

Such constructions with artificial contrivances are not women's forte but represent men's literature in the contemporary sense. Women are indeed able to navigate in a fantastic but not in a fictive world; that is why they are indisputably capable of writing sensational stories but not detective stories, why they are quite successful with the historical novel but not with utopias. And the explanation for why, given the extraordinary number of women novelists, there are not more women dramatists (at least not ones whose works are *performed*) than can be counted on one hand is also to be found here—not in the lack of formal command. There are plenty of characters created by women that could fill a stage with life, plenty of plots devised by women that could deliver an exciting evening—for books by women are occasionally dramatized to good effect and women display a particular aptitude for writing film scripts. Film is, namely, the counterpart of the novella and not the drama; and it is precisely the essence of drama that escapes women—the essence of the play.

This, however, is what continues to distinguish today's men from today's women: true playfulness. Whether they are flying kites with their sons on Sunday or playing cards among themselves, men are always able to give themselves over to a world that is artificial and fictive, in a word, a toy world. Just consider the sacred earnestness with which utterly unimaginative men, even dull businessmen, discuss the problems of a particular play in bridge or chess. Women play simply to pass the time or win some money; they would never be pursued by the problems of a game that has long since been won or lost. They are more serious than men, and for that reason frivolous things do not inspire their seriousness. There is no reproach in this.

And there is also nothing final about it. It has only been a short time since women have been allowed to consider the problems of reality (until recently they were either part of reality themselves or a fiction conceived by men). Like children faced with learning much too much at once, they do not dare take up the game. In twenty years this all might be different, and perhaps the next generation will bless us with what we most urgently need: a female Edgar Wallace.

206

ERICH KÄSTNER

Prosaic Digression

First published as "Prosaische Zwischenbemerkung," *Die literarische Welt* 5, nos. 13–14 (March 28, 1929), 6.

Although I write verse myself, I find many poets less likable than all the tenors together. Both in their lives and in the works they put out, poets spread the false message that the ability to write a poem is a divine concession; then they proceed to compromise their godly state of grace no less than certain other gentlemen from another privileged branch.

It is scarcely to be believed and yet it is so. The majority of contemporary poets continue to sing and declaim of the "love of my heart" and "blossoms in the meadow" and then maintain that the muses have kissed them directly on the mouth. [. . .]

Those poets with their brains fluttering freely in the breeze personally discredit poetry. They are responsible for the public's mistaken view that reading poetry has become an outmoded activity. These poets are the only thing outmoded. They should be painlessly done away with, and one of them put in a museum, if there is room for something like that in a museum.

Fortunately, there are one or two dozen poets—I have some hope of being among them—who are working to keep the poem alive. The public can read and hear their verses without falling asleep for the latter are suited to psychological application. They have been drawn from an acquaintance with the joys and pains of the present and are meant for everyone who has business with the present. A term has been invented for this type of poem: *usable poetry*—and the term proves how rare genuine poetry has been in recent times. For otherwise it would be superfluous to refer verbally to its usefulness. Verses that cannot be used in some fashion by contemporaries are rhyme games and nothing more. There are, of course, adept rhyme games and inept poems, but the latter are still to be preferred to the former. Tightrope-walking with language—that belongs in a variety show.

Now even people innocent of literature once again have verses that make their hearts pound or bring a happy smile to their lips while reading. Once again there are poets who experience feelings like natural people and, as surrogates, lend expression to these feelings and views and desires. And because they do not write merely for themselves or for the sake of their own half-penny originality, they forge a spiritual connection to their readers.

That someone expresses what moves and distresses him—along with others—is useful. Those who find this too simple can have the psychoanalysts explain it. It remains true nonetheless.

Poets once again have a purpose. Their activity is once again a calling. They are probably not as necessary as bakers and dentists, but only because stomach rumblings and teeth pullings require more explicit assistance than nonphysical ailments. The usable poets may nevertheless be a little glad that they rank immediately below the artisans.

207

KURT PINTHUS

Masculine Literature

First published as "Männliche Literatur," *Das Tagebuch* 10, no. 1 (June 1, 1929), 903–911.

"Masculine literature" stands here not only for the antithesis and opposite of feminine delicacy, with which all sorts of ephebi of various ages have attempted to create the appearance of poetry or poetry itself, but particularly for the antithesis and contrary of the expressionist writing of roughly 1910 to 1925 in which the adolescent, the screaming, demanding, rebellious adolescent, was the main character.

The adolescent: the representative type described in premonitions of decline in the prewar period. The representative type of the howling victim of the slaughter; the representative type of the humanitarian will to the future—this hyperbolic figure of the adolescent shouted out hyperbolic protests, demands, and ideas in hyperbolic language, whose form and formulation were so necessary and effective at the time. In poetry, drama, and narrative the adolescent was the central character; it was solely the adolescent's brilliance that brought the other figures to light. It appears that the fire and the rage of this adolescent type has now burned out . . . and from the ashes of the fallen arises triumphantly: the man.

The man or men, even if in age they are adolescents or boys, are the heroes of the books characteristic of the last few years. It is all a matter now not of adolescence but of becoming or being a man. The style of these books, whether the fruit of groping attempts or natural talent, is unpathetic, unsentimental, plain, and terse; some call this technique the New Objectivity. Why the "new" objectivity? It is objective, it is masculine, and it is the expressive form of man—if one does not understand by man the power quotient of the popular conception of masculinity, which itself, in its phony heroicization, is sentimental, overblown, and therefore unmasculine. This language—with no lyrical fat, with no intellectual listlessness, hard, tough, trained—is better compared to the body of a boxer.

While expressionism's adolescent worked with gaping emotion, the wrenching word, and the beckoning idea of the future, while he demolished reality, nature, and the cosmos to create a new world "from the spirit," current literature labors to capture things, events, and sensations in brief, sharp looks and words; the man satisfies himself with a clear, often artisanal act, with real effect in a small arena. Not the unattainable, distant, and eternal but the palpable, modest, and real is sought; the given is accepted so that it can be subdued. The phenomena of reality are neither exaggerated nor pushed to the point of explosion, but called by their correct names. The value of the idea is no longer driven to propagandistic overvaluation; rather the idea plays scarcely any role as a motive element: fact is the driving motivation of the artwork and simultaneously the object of literary technique. The functional abstractions "comprehend" and "compose" become synonymous with the concrete "grasp" and "contain."

Those who continue to harbor illusions get their ears boxed by fate in the new books—not only is their breath taken away but they also learn to breathe, now at home with and trusting in reality. Reportage lifts itself into the sphere of poetry and the report becomes an art form. This new masculine literature endeavors to work with the stylistic precision of scientific observation and formulation, while many a scientific work is nourished by the power of poetic intuition.

The arena of the so-called generally human and the social achieve their effects in the new books not through the revising and reviling of lamentations and accusations but through the immediate representation of the blatancy of conditions and events. This is not so much a literature of disillusion as one of anti-illusionism. The man who speaks does not cry and moan, but clarifies and defines—thus becoming clear and definitive himself. Admittedly it is less the spirit that speaks through him than the facts. And the objectivist's method of destruction appears to function not only more persuasively than that of the hyperbolic revolutionary but more constructively as well.

This is not to give the impression that these formulations are meant to represent and promote a programmatic theory; rather what has been said represents nothing but an extract from among a great number of works, a few of which may now be mentioned. Consider, for example, Joseph Roth's book, *Flight without End,* which is subtitled "A Report." It ends:

It was August 27, 1926, at four o'clock in the afternoon. . . . There stood my friend Tunda, thirty-two years old, healthy and alert, a strong young man of varied talents, on the square in front of the Madeleine in the center of the capital city of the world, not knowing what to do. He had no profession, no love, no lust, no hope, no ambition, not even any egotism.

In this book anti-illusionism is driven to the extreme of tempered hopelessness and indifference, the mark of many contemporary texts. [. . .]

An analysis of the most recent war books is simultaneously an explanation of their fantastic commercial success. [Erich Maria] Remarque and [Ludwig] Renn no longer provide visions, lamentations and accusations, and outcries and demands but objective factual reports, as far from heroicization as from outrage. A sun-drenched meadow and the most terrible military slaughter are presented in the same style and as objects of nearly equivalent gravity. This is no longer the adolescent rebelling against the experience of inhumanity, but the man, the common man, reporting all but indifferently from a distance, which alone conveys the hardening reality of the immediate. Remarque's poetry blossoms from the facts themselves; Renn's is coarse and sturdy; both lack the slightest glimmer of reconciliation. That such books, after people had supposedly "had enough of the war," are having a greater impact than the earlier, apparently more passionate war books is a symptom that this masculine war literature is not only literature or a literary fashion but a requirement and necessity of our time.

There is the potential objection that the authors of these "masculine" books are often still adolescents themselves, not yet having attained the age of man. Precisely this objection leads us to the root of the phenomenon. For the war and the postwar period destroyed the rising youth: children and adolescents became more clear-sighted and more discerning than the men who lived through the years of moaning as adolescents who remained, so to speak, adolescent. These young people were never young; they matured early. They had lost their illusions already as children. While the younger generation before the war lived through its developmental period, at least, with a certain financial security, embroiled only in introspective struggles, in struggles about ideas, and struggles against the grain of the time, this newest generation watched first as its family, then itself was drawn into a naked struggle for life and bread. "The struggle for existence" is not for it a scientific phrase, but raw fact. [. . .]

The works examined here have been chosen primarily from the genre of the narrative—because it is precisely among narratives that the best and most accomplished examples of masculine literature appears. Expressionism instead evidenced its characteristic accomplishments in the areas of poetry and drama.

Phenomenologists, however, will easily discover the masculine tendency in other branches of writing as well: in poetry, for example, which is otherwise relegated to the advertisement section of the newspaper; in the reemergence of the ballad and song; or in drama, now devoted all but entirely to the conditions of our time. Increasingly often in more recent plays the man takes over from the adolescent (note the programmatic title of Brecht's *A Man is a Man*). Investigators will be able to find the same masculinization, objectification in the related arts—in painting, architecture, and music—and also across the nation in the most popular reading material: biographies of men and adventure stories.

This attempt itself may be regarded as exemplary for the sphere of literary critical investigation. It sketches symptoms and material as proof of a stabilization amid the turbulence of our epoch and its art. It is possible that this stabilization in convictions, in the representation of events, and in style is fostering a further stabilization among the people, helping them to overcome their insecurity.

208

HEINRICH MANN

Detective Novels

First published as "Detektiv-Romane," *Die literarische Welt* 5, no. 34 (August 23, 1929), 1–2.

Every genre has its most successful representative; at the moment it is Edgar Wallace for the detective novel. His German language releases appear in editions that add up to nearly a million copies altogether. Statements from his readers impart not only recognition—every writer garners recognition, admiration, devotion. No, several of the letters attest directly to happiness, to absolute happiness over the simple fact that Wallace exists on earth. "It sometimes seems to me to be the thing that makes the world complete," confesses one.

Hence it is clear that these novels offer a considerable pleasure, indeed, a pleasure that produces a benevolent after-effect and inclines toward gratitude. What kind of pleasure is this? Entertainment with an effect as powerful as this is not easy to take. It makes use of certain human values and is not without social significance.

Life does not appear profound to most people. They find it laborious though familiar, even though the most remarkable things come true in the course of their individual existences. They were not greatly surprised by the war and have already forgotten it. But it is something altogether different when criminals lock an heiress in a dungeon. Such dread stimulates solely the imagination, and no reality can so easily promise the gentle lady reader the joy of turning a victim into an heiress—not even as a reward for the stay in the dungeon. The dungeon signifies deep mystery; the great inheritance is the embodiment of magical surprise. The reader longs for both, surprise and mystery. The pleasure taken in a detective novel rests on these two claims by our nature. We do not always like to see clearly what is coming. We are curious, but sometimes more for the process of discovery than for the simple truth; and once embarked upon this path we no longer want to be convinced but to be surprised.

Our unconsidered inclinations, which accompany us alongside the more rational ones, are often attached to a master of mysteries and dangers, to a deliverer from need. At present the public life of entire peoples fantasizes such a hero—why should he not appear in novels too? There he is called a detective. The sacrificial lamb he saves, the heiress, is almost always a typist. This confirms the general validity of a fantasy: at least 500,000 female employees of the most various enterprises have dreamt of themselves as the rescued heiress. In their own heightened imaginations they became classic romantic figures for as long as they were reading Wallace. They unexpectedly become the white, fully passive treasure in a *Rape of the Sabine Women*. The thieving brigands are dark brown and entirely active, at least in literature. In life, on the other hand, dependence and initiative are distributed fairly evenly among male and female employees. There is no talk of saving and being saved in the toil of daily life.

The need for the extraordinary increases the more laboriously we live. Only thus does the persistent success of the detective become comprehensible. When one reads, the experience should be an adventure that contrasts with everyday banality. Who remains able to see his own involvement in a much greater adventure novel, in the adventure of profits, of class struggle, of the secret war conducted within humanity between the two utterly hostile powers fighting over us?

209

ARNOLD ZWEIG

Is There a Newspaper Novel?

First published as "Gibt es einen Zeitungsroman?" in *Die Literatur* 32, no. 1 (October 1929), 2.

A good newspaper novel is the backbone of the interest that binds a large part of the readership to a newspaper. In essence, a newspaper really only establishes its relationship to a reader from one day to the next, only on the basis of the ceaseless flow of new events. A newspaper's continuing influence on a reader's assessment of events occurs behind the scenes, through the selection of what the paper will withhold or present to the reader.

Thus is the persistent tie of a reader to his newspaper also a subterranean one. Only in a novel, which many readers, especially women, await from day to day, is there any real moment of anticipation for the appearance of the paper. Already with that, the criteria of judgment for the newspaper novel is well prepared: it must be able to create suspense and for that reason must itself be suspenseful. A highly developed epic culture, like the English, French, or Russian, makes possible a kind of newspaper novel that can meet these requirements and convey high literary values. Both *Anna Karenina* and the novels of Charles Dickens or Guy de Maupassant first appeared in newspapers or similar publications. But in Germany the division of writing in two, half that counts as literature and half that is merely entertainment, has hurt the newspaper novel most of all. It is nearly without exception written by entertainers who work to satisfy very crude literary instincts. On the other side, newspapers often attempt to include in the entertainment section works of literary value, which, however, do not grow out of the novel form in their internal structure, are not suited to this attempt, and devalue both the genre and the effort. This is particularly bad because the newspaper novel provides an extraordinarily large readership with its only connection to the art of narrative and influences the world view of hundreds of thousands of women and adolescents much more decisively than great literature is able to do. That is why the average newspaper novel in Germany is an evil whereas the newspaper novel is a necessity and an extraordinarily important tool of mass influence. And when it succeeds, as it occasionally does, in making an epic work of art of uncontested literary value the object of passionate expectation and discussion for a large readership, in reaching into the inner life of the readers, making for them living companions, sometimes even from another time, of the invented characters whose fate daily enters the home in the form of installments, then a level of literary effect is achieved which continually enriches the newspaper, the readers, and the author as well.

210

GOTTFRIED BENN

The New Literary Season

First published as "Die neue literarische Saison," *Die Weltbühne* 27, no. 37 (September 15, 1931), 402–408.

Behind the purely seasonal literature that will capture the market this winter, there is also a genuine literary and intellectual war at hand. There is a problem that especially concerns the serious younger literature, and will doubtless concern it more than ever this coming winter, in view of the state of affairs today. If we try to formulate this problem briefly, it can be said to consist of the contrast between pure and collectivistic art. The question at stake is the following: in view of today's social and economic conditions, has man any right to feel and describe his own individual problems, or should there be only collective problems? Is the writer justified in taking his individuality as a starting point and giving it expression? Can he still expect his individuality to be taken seriously, or is he entirely reduced to his collective status, only worthy of attention or interest as a social being? Do all his inner difficulties become solved, or should they be solved, as soon as he helps in the construction of the social collectivity?

This circle of problems was discussed in a very shrewd and polemically fascinating lecture given this spring by the Russian writer Tretyakov, a lecture that was attended by the entire literary world of Berlin. Tretyakov, who is also known here as a playwright, is, as regards his exterior and the manner of his descriptions, a literary Cheka type—one who examines, judges, and sentences all unbelievers in Russia. It is worthwhile to scrutinize this burning question, which is so exciting for the young German writers of today. Tretyakov describes how in Russia, during the first two years of the Five-Year Plan, there still appeared a few psychological novels, against which the Writers' Soviet took preventive measures. To give an example, one novel showed how, in a house which had been expropriated from a bourgeois and subsequently requisitioned for a higher Soviet official, the latter began to drink, neglected his duties, deteriorated, so that, finally, the former owner of the house reoccupied his rooms. This was described in a Western psychological manner in the usual novel form, somewhat imaginatively and entirely unpolitically. Tretyakov ordered the author to appear before him. "Where did you experience this, Comrade?" he asked him. "In which city and in which street?" "I didn't experience it at all," answered the author, "it is just a novel." "Never mind," answered Tretyakov, "you have taken this from a reality that exists somewhere. Why didn't you report to the proper Soviet authorities that one of the officials, as a result of drunkenness, was carrying out his duties improperly, and that the bourgeois owner of the house had been reinstalled?" Again the author answered, "But I didn't see this in reality, I made this up, I just wrote a novel." Tretyakov: "Those are Western European, individual idiocies. You have acted in an irresponsible manner, with vanity, and as a counterrevolutionary. The plates of your book will be destroyed, and you will march to the factory." In this way, according to Tretyakov, all individual-psychological literature has been abolished in Russia, every belletristic attempt has been disposed of as ridiculous and bourgeois, the writer as a professional has disappeared, he works like everybody else in the factory, he helps in the social construction and the Five-Year Plan. And an entirely new type of literature is about to begin. Tretyakov brought a few examples along and exhibited them with great pride. They were books, or rather copybooks, each written by a dozen factory workers, under the direction of a former writer. Their titles, for instance, were: *Establishment of a Fruit Plantation near a Factory;* further, *How to Air the Dining Room in a Factory;* something particularly important, written by several foremen, *How to Get Raw Materials More Quickly to the Labor Centers.* This, then, is the new Russian literature, the new collective literature, the literature of the Five-Year Plan. German writers sat at Tretyakov's feet, and applauded enthusiastically. Tretyakov probably enjoyed this applause, perhaps he was also amused by it, this clever Russian who, of course, knew very well that he was developing here a propagandistic fragment for the new Russian imperialism while his simpleminded German colleagues accepted it as absolute truth. As what truth, I ask myself now? What psychology, I ask myself, is behind this Russian theory which finds so many disciples in Germany?

This Russian art theory, once you have studied it carefully, avers nothing more or less than that everything that exists in Occidental man as far as his inner life is concerned, in other words our crises, tragedies, our scission, our impulses, our enjoyment, is purely and simply a phenomenon of capitalistic decay, a capitalistic trick. And the artist moved by vanity and desire for glory, yea, Tretyakov added, with a truly infantile ignorance of conditions, especially by greed for money, works these "individual idiocies," as he called them, into his books and plays. According to Tretyakov's theory, however, as soon as man awakens to the Russian Revolution, all this falls from him, like the dew before the sun, and there stands before us the joyous collective being, wretched maybe, but clean and normal, without daemon or instinct, eager at last to be allowed to cooperate in social reconstruction, in the factory, especially in the strengthening of the Red Army, his chest swelling with joy. Into the dust with all enemies not only of Brandenburg but of Moscow!

I ask now, is this psychologically probable, or is it primitive? Is man, in the last analysis of his essence, rooted in a naturalistic, materialistic, economic condition, determined in his structure by hunger and clothes? Or is he the great involuntary being, as Goethe said, the invisible, the incalculable? Is he indissoluble despite all social and psychological analyses, does he also go through this epoch of materialistic philosophy and atomic biology on his destined way, closely bound to the earth and yet above the earth?

I read recently the following sentence by one of the leaders of the young German literature: "We loathe the eternally human." Since he said "we," he spoke, probably, in the name of a group of similarly minded people, perhaps in the name of the new German literature. He continued: "we" are for realities. "Let us organize life," he expounded, "let us leave the tragic problems to the 'profound' writers. So far as we are concerned, we want to live." This, I assume, is the Tretyakov group in Berlin, and it is against this group that I must maintain the thesis, old-fashioned and Western, that man is not changed in a fundamental way by the organization of his food and living conditions. By fundamentally I mean that he is not changed substantially in hereditary form or disposition. Even he who, not less radically than the official social writers, feels the destructive and almost incomprehensible character of our economic system cannot, in my opinion, fail to recognize that in all economic systems man remains the tragic being, the divided ego, whose abysses cannot be filled with bread and woolen vests, whose dissonances cannot be dissolved in the rhythms of the *Internationale*. He remains the suffering being, he who wore hair shirts for hundreds of thousands of years, during which he struggled not less deeply and sorrowfully for his humanity than today in buckskin and cheviot. Even if we could extinguish the entire epoch of individualism, the entire history of the soul from Hellenic days to expressionism, one experience would remain, opposite to the inner spatial void of this Tretyakov idea. It would remain a great truth through all epochs and all seasons, that he who would organize life will never create art, nor can he consider himself as belonging to art. To create art, whether it be Egyptian falcons or the novels of [Knut] Hamsun, means from the standpoint of the artist to exclude life, to narrow it down, yes, to combat it, in order to give it style. [. . .]

Out of a new sense of humanity the coming season will be made, but perhaps not this winter, and, as far as I can see, not in "literary" literature. But science takes our gaze ever farther back, to human races that lived on earth millions of years ago, races that at one time resembled the fish, at another the marsupials, and later the simians, but always remained the human being—creating dwelling places, creating tools, creating gods, creating age-long cultural relationships which again vanished in catastrophe beneath heavens as yet unstarred and moonless. I believe that from this viewpoint, and not from the flim-flam of littérateurs or from social theories, the new sense of humanity will develop, and the psychological and intellectual individualism of our time will be demolished.

The age-old, eternal man! The human race! Immortal within a creative system which is itself infinitely subject to mutations and expansions. What an endless epic! Luna, flooding bush and valley, is the fourth moon which we see. Not evolution but perpetuity will be the sense of humanity in the coming century. Let us wait quietly for it to approach—we shall probably find it outside of the literary season.

211

FRIEDRICH SIEBURG

Champagne: Notes on the Literature of High Society

First published as "Sekt. Noten zur mondänen Literatur," *Frankfurter Zeitung* (February 1, 1931).

One has only to open a German social novel to confront the tragedy of German literature. A way of life is conjured, but it immediately becomes apparent that it does not exist. A norm is assumed, but every line betrays a guilty conscience because it is only all too evident that the norm does not apply to us. If one were to draw conclusions from German literature (which, perhaps, is not permissible), then we do not even have an elite class about which novels could be written, except for the one to which luxury items are to be sold. Why are the advertisements for perfume, champagne, automobiles, and winter-sports resorts so fascinating in Germany? Because they do not only *seek* buyers, but try to *create* them. Whole sectors of German industry, and certainly not the worst albeit not the most essential, suffer from the German social structure. For expensive gratifications to establish themselves, not only are rich people required, who do exist in Germany, but also a society that has power over dispositions and that is completely secure in itself. Chattering on about the topic "What is the gentleman wearing this year?" does not create customers for the tailor; in a country where every gentleman knows what to wear, the fashion designer need not starve. Refined people must exist, but how does one get at them? [. . .]

Germany has many personalities and even more eccentrics, but it has no society—an old saw. The attempt to write a social novel must therefore lead to imitation of foreign models or to directionless wanderings among notions that are taken to be refined. On the right is the snob, on the left, the swindler, and in between a pure nothing full of striving. The depiction of customs remains a worthy task, but how is one to depict the customs of a class that does not exist because it has no customs in common? The chronicler of a class has to depend on a firm image of the world. To make himself understood, he must be able to rely on the recognition, at least by a *single* class, of certain arrangements and customs. The mood of class struggle in Germany must not be allowed to seduce writers into believing that the opposing classes possess a form, nor that there is such a thing as a tightly knit, self-conscious upper class. The split occurs much lower down. In England, where the propertied class has a sharply defined social function and is inexhaustible in its formal upper-class stock, no one has yet even discovered the class struggle, and perhaps no one ever will. In Germany, there is only one creative element: the masses. It would be a mistake to consider it amorphous, formless because it is a "mass." It is perhaps on the contrary the only social layer in Germany in which the force of social formation is inherent. Here is where *the tragedy of the German writer* begins. He has no influence; no one pays him any attention; no one fears him; all decisions of an intellectual and public sort are made without him. What to do? says Zeus, the world has been given away. Indeed, literature has developed itself so completely away from the *people,* that this, its creation, will not even notice. Happy France, where the writer is substantial and indispensable on a daily basis because he expresses the idea of his nation and confirms—even there where he destroys—France through his vital sensibility. Unhappy Germany, which so believes in its stupidity that it has no need of the writer and gives its writers nothing more than the taste of death and the will to immortality. The writing German belongs to no class, good! But nor does he find any social stratum that would offer him a structure for his ideas. The flight into the cosmos is the German way out. Unfortunately, it is usually for that reason insufficient. [. . .]

I believe that one day our anonymous Germany will create the forms necessary to depict the collective life of modern humanity when it is elegant. Meanwhile, it is all champagne, all a watery delirium of people who fear the maitre d'. Germany's stirring is elsewhere. In the dark. In pain.

212

LION FEUCHTWANGER

The Novel of Today Is International

First published as "Der Roman von heute ist international," *Berliner Tageblatt* (September 25, 1932).

It is obvious that the contemporary novel is international. Ever since economic and linguistic boundaries ceased to coincide, ever since the individual came to regard the planet rather than any politically bounded country as his homeland, native literature in the form of exclusively national writing has faced a difficult situation. Compared to the great writings of our time it looks like a Biedermeier display case filled with peasant knick-knacks next to a highrise outfitted with the most modern technology. Once a vital necessity, it has become a curiosity best suited to museums. Upon the invention of the rifle, the knight—and with him knightly literature—became senseless; Don Quixote took the place of Parsifal and Lancelot. Upon the invention of the railroad and the airplane, economic and political nationalism became senseless, and with it exclusively national literature. The last great writers who were intrinsically justified in devoting their writing exclusively to their homeland were Thomas Hardy, Gottfried Keller, and Knut Hamsun; the last who was intrinsically justified in devoting himself to national imperialism was Rudyard Kipling. Some works by Gabriele D'Annunzio and Maurice Barrès already have something caricaturelike about them, and as for our own nationalist authors, few critics ascribe to them any but local significance.

Certainly, contemporary writers of great novels choose their homeland as the object of their writing, yet they see it not only with the eyes of a local patriot but with the eyes of a citizen of the world. Thus is the Lübeck of Thomas and Heinrich Mann seen, thus John Galsworthy's London, [Alfred] Döblin's Berlin, and Sinclair Lewis's American Midwest.

To depict the expanded world, the modern novel needs forms other than those of its predecessor. Today's readers, due to the influence of film, have become quicker to understand and more agile in their perception of rapidly changing images and situations. The contemporary prose epic takes advantage of that. It has learned from film. Compared to earlier forms, it successfully dares to compress a much greater number of stories between two covers. The contemporary novel ventures to depict the boundless variety of the world in its simultaneity. It often delivers not one, two, or three plots, but twenty or fifty, without, however, thereby endangering the unity of its basic vision. Just as Elizabethan drama burst the unity of time and place, so the contemporary prose epic supersedes, very often successfully, the law of the unity of plot.

The second formal device to which the modern novel necessarily resorts to fulfill its purpose is objective depiction. Today's author must count on his readers knowing the outer structure of the world rather precisely, either from personal experience or the knowledge gained from film and radio. If he does not want seriously to imperil the illusion, he must awaken in the reader the impression that he is himself familiar with the things of which he speaks. Once the author's report on the exterior nature of his world ceases to be believable, then no reader will believe what he says about its interior constitution. It no longer suffices for an author to speak to the reader of his feelings, however honest these feelings might be. He must instead chart the contours of the things that inspired these feelings in him. Only in this way can he inspire the same feelings in the reader.

If you reread these last sentences carefully, you will immediately notice that they speak of the so-called New Objectivity. You will also notice, however, that I see in this notorious New Objectivity nothing like the purpose of the contemporary prose epic being fulfilled but solely a representational device. It is important to take every occasion to warn against the cheap parlor trick of attempting to present the New Objectivity as an end in itself when it is nothing other than a legitimate artistic device. Whoever proclaims that the contemporary novel endeavors to inform the reader about exterior matters of fact, about sociological or psychological issues—whoever proclaims this is a fraud. The contemporary novel is just as content as its predecessors to leave that to science and good journalism. The novel strives to affect the reader's emotions, not to appeal to his desire for knowledge—to be sure, without entering into conflict with the reader's logic and knowledge. Its goal is what has always been the goal of art: to convey to the reader the author's mode of feeling. It is only that today's author knows that he cannot do that if he has not fully absorbed the results of contemporary research.

Increasing barbarity since the war has caused immeasurable destruction in all areas of civilization, in all areas of literature as well. Theater, for example, has been made subject to the dictatorship of anti-intellectual governments that know nothing of art; likewise film and radio. These institutions are very frequently threatened by violent attacks by the stirred-up, idiotic masses. In response they have distanced themselves completely from literature and declined to the status of institutions of pure entertainment. The novel, on the other hand, has unexpectedly blossomed amid the general deterioration. The reason is probably that nationalism has been substantially incapable of working its ruinous influence on the novel. Not that the nationalists shrink from vilifying it, but those who are at home in the intellectual arena do not generally read nationalist newspapers, and those who read nationalist newspapers do not generally read books.

The German novel in particular has been surprisingly effective in establishing itself. If Gustav Freytag was justified declaring a half-century ago that every educated German could write a readable novel, then today, when representatives of the Reich and the mass electorate have difficulty delivering a proper German sentence at their most important public events, we can scarcely maintain the same. It is then with all the greater satisfaction that we can point to the worldwide impact of the esteemed German novel.

Certainly, the representatives of the German book lack the loud voice of the political charlatan and the military; but their word, even if they remain barred from radio, penetrates farther than the voice of the latter; it penetrates deeper, it stays. Our militarists and nationalists have squandered a great deal of German prestige in the world; our narrative literature has won back a major portion of Germany's respect.

213

GÜNTER EICH

Remarks on Lyric Poetry

First published as "Bemerkungen über Lyrik," *Die Kolonne* 3, no. 1 (1932), 3–4.

What is the essential aspect of a time? Quite likely not its outward manifestations, airplane and dynamo, but the change it occasions in human beings. But who among us knows today where the change is leading us? Who is capable of recognizing now the thoughts and things in which our time expresses itself most clearly? When one demands of lyric poetry that it embrace its time, what that means at most is that it should embrace Marxism or anthroposophy or psychoanalysis, for we are not at all certain which theoretical system or conception of life represents our time universally. We know only that every tendency and every movement raises that claim. [. . .]

A decision for the time, that is, for a partial manifestation of the time, interests the poet as poet not at all. (Which does not prevent him, as a private person, from embracing, for example, a particular political party.) The lyric poet decides for nothing, he is interested only in his ego; he does not create a you- and he-world, like the epic poet and dramatist; for him there exists nothing but the isolated ego outside community. And precisely because he decides for nothing, he gathers up the time in himself, causing it to reappear in the unclouded mirror of his ego. For the transformations of the ego are the essential aspect of a time. They cannot simply be read, as if in a newspaper, but those who know how to read poems (which can scarcely be learned) are able to sense that in them. Just as we experience [Joseph von] Eichendorff or [Eduard] Mörike as the expression of their time (without them using the current vocabulary of their respective times), in just this way can a contemporary, utterly private poem lend unmistakable expression to our time for those who come after us.

The transformations of the ego are the problem for the lyric poet. That carries with it the formal consequence that he will avoid, in general, the use of words that encompass a time-bound problem, that is, a problem that does not directly interest him. Indeed, I mean that the poet must use "old" words, which, having become unproblematic, acquire their new meaning only through the ego. Attached to words like "dynamo" or "telephone wire" are so many time-bound associations that they usually falsify the pure ego problematic of the poem through their own problematic. If such words can be employed at all in poetry, then it is at most as pure givens, as plain spatial objects, self-evident and unproblematic;

without, therefore, any "temporal" reference and meaning, only as an interpretive possibility of the ego, that is, just as incidentally as the poet says tree or moon, which interests him not at all as tree or moon. Only in the impersonal world of the epic do contemporary words have their place, for there the environment exists as such and no longer as a relation to the ego. There really do exist "prosaic" words. [. . .]

Poems have no intended utility, and if they do sometimes provide the meals on the "table of desire, which is never empty," then that, from the point of view of the poet, is an accident, for he does not have an effect of some kind as his goal. Certainly, things are different for the critic, who has to classify the poem in the array of human values and goals. He can confirm the effects of the lyric poem, but has to understand that these effects have meaning for the poem only in terms of cultural classification and utilization; that therefore his activity does not allow him to draw conclusions as to the essence and origin of the poems, or to demand of the creative process that it strive for any particular effect. One can say of the rain that it promotes the growth of plants, but it would occur to no one to say that that is the intention of the rain. The greatness of lyric poetry and all art, however, is that, although created by human beings, it has the intentionlessness of a natural phenomenon. Poems can exist when no one needs them, and perhaps there would be none if everyone desired them.

21
Theater, Politics, and the Public Sphere

As a communal art form fostering a common language and a shared sense of high moral values, theater has always been the most privileged literary genre within German culture. Heavily subsidized first by royal courts and later by the state, it has also been the most politically charged genre, compensating even for the lack of a unified nation state. It is within this powerful tradition that directors and critics after World War I expected the theater to lead a revolutionary fight for a new democratic state.

Elated by Germany's "rejuvenation" on November 9, 1918, Leopold Jessner, one of the major stage directors of the period, articulated his utopian dream of a new national theater, while Siegfried Jacobsohn, the influential theater critic and editor of *Die Schaubühne,* contended: "We might indeed have a German theater. But we have no German revolution." From the proletarian agitprop theater to Erwin Piscator's documentary multimedia spectacles, a strong left-activist streak runs through many theatrical productions in the Weimar Republic. Even Jessner's ground-breaking production in 1919 of Friedrich Schiller's classical play *Wilhelm Tell* was both celebrated and condemned as leftist because it dared to break with theatrical staging conventions. Departing from a naturalistic style of painted backdrops, Jessner reduced the set to nothing but huge stairs that spanned the entire stage. This design allowed the actors to move not only horizontally but also vertically, thus effectively expressing tensions between forces high up and those oppressed down below. Jessner radicalized Max Reinhardt's symbolic stage settings by paring down the mise-en-scène to quintessential forms. The combination of abstract sets and highly stylized acting revolutionized theater and stage design with reverberations that continue to be felt today. During the Weimar Republic classical plays by Shakespeare, Shaw, Molière, and others were reconceptualized in social terms, often reduced to an elemental political or moral conflict, and staged against a stark, highly symbolic backdrop. Brecht's plays (beginning in 1922 with his post-expressionist *Drums in the Night*) correspond to the principles of the new stagecraft in their emphasis on deceptive simplicity and stylized language as well as in their appeal to the audience's imagination. Herbert Jhering, one of the most influential theater critics of the time, was the first to recognize Brecht's potential as a radical innovator of a seemingly moribund art form. "Is the Drama Dying?" was the title of a survey conducted by the *Vossische Zeitung* in 1926, a time when growing competition from film, radio, gramophone, and sports events appeared to make theater obsolete. Brecht did not equivocate his position in this debate, stating: "A theater that makes no contact with the public is nonsense. Our theater is accordingly nonsense." It was precisely this new attitude toward the audience that distinguished his Epic Theater from the traditional naturalistic theater. Most of Brecht's plays in the 1920s acknowledged the audience's presence and often addressed it directly—thus emphasizing the specific quality of live theater that separates it from the medium of film.

This renewed focus on performance must have prompted Max Reinhardt, Germany's most innovative director between 1910 and 1930, to write an essay in praise of the actor and a theater that touched the emotions. Reinhardt's sumptuous productions at the Deutsches Theater drew less on contemporary writers than on Shakespeare, Shaw, Molière, Goethe and Schiller. Brecht disagreed with Reinhardt's apolitical concept of theater, setting it against his own notion of Epic Theater with its distancing devices, non sequitur jokes, banners and written messages, stylized acting and sets, and its hope for a detached and dialectically thinking audience. Lion Feuchtwanger, Brecht's fatherly mentor from his Munich days, succinctly summarized the main features of Epic Theater.

Piscator, Brecht's collaborator for a few years, translated the factual, documentary style of the New Objectivity onto the stage. He began experimenting in the mid-1920s—in the tradition of Russian constructivism—with the latest technical innovations such as slide and film projection, conveyor belt, radio, loudspeaker, and phonograph. Documentary usage of posters, photographs, newspaper quotations, original speeches, and historical figures turned his productions into high-tech revolutionary cabaret depicting the history of proletarian struggle from the rebellion of Spartacus to the Russian Revolution. Attended by relatively few workers, Piscator's productions became a favorite entertainment attraction for the Berlin bourgeoisie. Despite enormous critical successes between 1925 and 1929, Piscator's theater went bankrupt more than once, plagued by the inherent contradiction of having a proletarian, revolutionary theater for the educated middle class. In contrast, semiprofessional agitprop troupes reached working-class audiences in the streets, at demonstrations, and wherever political agitation and propaganda were needed. German agitprop groups incorporated new theater techniques inspired by the Russian Blue Blouses troupe that toured Germany in 1927. The result was an improvisational and topical street theater that commented on current political events from a revolutionary perspective.

Friedrich Wolf and Ernst Toller made a case for a topical theater (*Zeittheater*) that made no secret about its bias—its purpose was to effect social change. Brecht, for his part, wrote a few didactic plays in the agitprop mode, eschewing psychological characters and linear storyline to espouse an ideology that placed the interests of the Communist Party before those of the individual. *Die Rote Fahne,* its official newspaper, praised Brecht for heeding the precepts of Marxist revolutionary theory, but took him to task for his lack of revolutionary experience. The German Communist Party pursued a purist course at this time, engaging in ideological skirmishes with the left more readily than taking on the National Socialists on the far right who wanted to co-opt the theater for nationalistic purposes. Not unexpectedly, theater became a prime site of political conflict in the public sphere of the republic.

214

LEOPOLD JESSNER

To the Directors of the German Theater

First published as "An die deutsche Theaterleiter," *Berliner Tageblatt* (November 23, 1918).

At the dawn of Germany's rejuvenation, a new time has also come for the German stage, perhaps even *the* time.

If those at present called to lead the German theater want to remain at the helm, then now is the time for them to recognize the need of the moment and, free of all petty hesitations, to march purposefully to the beat of the new course. And it is only men with a real backbone who are capable of setting the course when the barometer points to storm.

Those for whom the theater as a national treasure has not become a worn-out phrase must feel that men whose primary interest is a positive balance sheet at year's end no longer have the right to occupy a leading position among those called to perform the highest cultural tasks.

The convulsive movement of recent weeks has overnight swept away things that appeared to be anchored for eternity—why should it remain utopian today to believe that the theater will now finally be allowed its true destiny and become an authentic general public good?

215

SIEGFRIED JACOBSOHN

Theater—and Revolution?

First published as "Theater—und Revolution?" in *Deutscher Revolutions-Almanach für das Jahr 1919 über die Ereignisse des Jahres 1918* (Hamburg and Berlin: Hofmann and Campe, 1919), 133–134.

Internally conflicted, like all of bourgeois Germany, theater, as the expressive organ of this world, regards the revolutionary bustle of the new age. Straining and groaning one decides to do without monarchical trash—although . . . why, then, since the dynasties remain rooted in every heart? And so we confront the misery.

The public that was capable, by virtue of its general education, literary knowledge, and receptiveness to artistic effects, of perceiving the revolution in writing—this public rejects it. The public, however, with fire in its blood is too little schooled; it makes do for the moment without the vital minimum of artistic pleasures, and longs for coarser fare, for the cinema and kitsch.

And, short and sweet or not so sweet: the task of setting theater and revolution in relation to each other escapes me. For we might indeed have a German theater. But we have no German revolution.

216
SIEGFRIED JACOBSOHN
Wilhelm Tell

First published as "Wilhelm Tell," *Die Weltbühne* 52 (1919), 797–798.

We know from Goethe how the drama was produced. Schiller pinned maps of Switzerland on the walls of his room, read travel descriptions and chronicles until he was intimately familiar with the roads and footpaths and with the history of the scene. And then began the torrent: he drank the fortification of black coffee and slept fully clothed every other night, sitting at his desk. The poet who was never in Switzerland is praised by the Swiss for having delivered as lively a portrayal of their country, its landscape, and its soul as any other. When the artist has seen with his inner eye, then the reader does too. Or the spectator. For Leopold Jessner has given us, as Schiller did himself, the picture of Switzerland. In a manner of speaking, he also pinned maps of Switzerland on the walls, instead of creating three-dimensional forms of mountains, lakes, valleys, alpine pastures, marketplaces, and [such sites as] Rütli and Hohle Gasse. The result deserves notice far and wide. [. . .]

A mighty green staircase fills the stage from left to right and from bottom to top. On both sides, shorter and lower steps lead up to vertical bridges, the arched gateways of which open onto Tell's house, or Stauffacher's, or wherever otherwise desirable. No limits are placed on the imagination. Abysses enclose us all around when two menacing black curtains intersect in sharp angles in the background. When the curtains do not come together there is room for the train of wedding celebrants to pass before the murder of the provincial governor, who—and this is no tragedy—cannot descend from his horse but rolls down the austerely structured incline into the beyond. For Attinghausen, two colorful, arched windows break the back wall of the hall invigoratingly in two. To depict Zwing-Uri, a brickwork construction towers like a cyclops. A fence extends diagonally and the presence of the eccentric Tell is separated from the company of others. [. . .]

Since no playwrights of substantial caliber have come along, the old ones suffice over and over. If we now, instead of ruckus-loving crooks, still had a public, we could have theatrical art in Germany despite the sorry condition of the world.

217
HERBERT JHERING
The Dramatist Bert Brecht

First published as "Der Dramatiker Bert Brecht," *Berliner Börsen-Courier* (October 5, 1922).

Never has the tension between the experience of an age and its expression been so great as it is at present. This unproductivity did not become a judgment upon the epoch as long as the slackening was the natural reaction to the tautened nerves of the war years. People cursed the emerging generation without realizing that they had had to fight harder than any generation for one hundred years. Not so much for their material existence. Not so much for their intellectual standing. They had to fight for something that had been denied to no generation except the one that came after the Thirty Years' War: experience itself. The horrors of the last few years were not the collapse of a nation, but the inability to experience the elemental things elementally. People's energy was so exhausted that they accepted apocalyptic events like everyday inconveniences. Pain is not the worst thing, lack of sensitivity to pain is.

It is only when we understand in this way the intellectual fate of the past few years that we can relate to contemporary drama. The writers of today can only be understood when we feel that the spectral character of today is due to the fact that it cannot hear its own sounds, nor see its own grimaces. The writers were isolated and attempted to project their language into the present, through areas pierced by no experience. This cramped situation was necessary and had to be resolved in that moment when the times themselves began to resolve.

There can be no doubt that this process of resolution is in preparation. It began in poetry and continued in the novel. And now the miracle commences. Nothing happens by chance. But even those who with their nerves felt that the times wanted to emerge from their unproductive stagnation; those who felt in [Arnolt] Bronnen the drive towards giving form and force to temperament; even these were overwhelmed by the intellectual change produced by the first deed of a genius. The twenty-four-year-old writer Bert Brecht has changed the poetic face of Germany overnight. Bert Brecht has brought a new tone, a new tune, a new vision to our times.

The artistic event is not that in his first play *Drums in the Night* Bert Brecht gives artistic form to contemporary events which were previously only talked about.

The event is that our times are the background, the atmosphere, even in those plays which are in no way contemporary in their theme. Brecht's nerves, Brecht's blood, are filled with the horror of the times. This horror exists as stale air and semilight surrounding people and places. It thickens in the intervals and the pauses between scenes. It releases the figures and swallows them again. The figures are phosphorescent.

Brecht physically feels the chaos and the putrefaction. This is the reason for the unparalleled pictorial strength of his language. This is a language that you feel in your tongue, your palate, your ears, your spine. It omits links and opens up perspectives. It is brutally sensual and melancholically tender. It contains sordidness and deepest mourning, grim humor and plaintive lyricism.

Brecht sees people, but always in their relation to others. None of his figures stands isolated. For long there has been no writer in Germany who without preliminaries realized the tragic necessity of showing how fates are linked, how people affect one another.

218

HANNS JOHST

The Drama and the National Idea

First published as "Das Drama und die nationale Idee," *Berliner Tageblatt* (October 25, 1922).

All genuine art is national, just like all genuine politics; and only genuine art and politics partake of greatness, only they are as imperishable as the peoples to whom they naturally belong. The present-day reality of international organizations is the attempt by human beings condemned to consciousness to resolve the situation brought upon themselves by capital and machines (products of consciousness!) in the materialist manner of shared interests. This intellectual hubris will be revealed as such; the catharsis will, as always, take hold on the plane of world history and solely from a national point of view. Put in literary terms, the Soviets will not escape Dostoyevsky.

We Germans have the misfortune of possessing neither a national godhead nor a godly nation, (but we do possess the desire for both). We Germans have prophets, and we Germans have great faith in the coming Reich. I personally value this obscure, unformed feeling more highly than all the intellectual programs by which the market offers its promises of immediate, practical aid. This intellectual life corresponds to the physical life to the extent that both require time and organs to come into being. We living today are not of critical importance to nature and its creations; we have value and meaning only if we devote ourselves obediently and fully to the service of merciful creation. This service presupposes faith. This faith is now growing in Germany!

The place, the sacred site of modernity where it is possible to work most popularly with the tools of language, of human culture, and of ideas, is the theater. Theater today has sunk to lower depths than ever. To despair of it, however, would be to despair of Germany, of the homeland. I already said that the tool of the homeland is art: therefore the writers of our day are duty-bound to dedicate themselves heart and soul to a vision of their people, their nation. If such service still remains thankless today, it is nevertheless the only service artists can consciously render to tomorrow.

Germany will have its national theater as Schiller saw it, for the nation needs it. Theater will increasingly become the public institution in which the struggle for the ideal unity of religious need and national desire will take place. Dramatic art will represent the vision, the message of man, who relinquishes his claim as an individual in order to be redeemed as part of the national whole. Only this path will release us from the nearly physiological methods by which dramas are produced today. The fashionable dramatists proclaimed the rights of estates and the grievances of classes; they illustrated the conditions of social life—they are marked, in short, by an international character. The tragedy of youth dedicates itself anew to the gigantic proportions of ancient tradition insofar as it sees in that tradition the tragic responsibility of literary power; it unites with the desire for national feeling such as it has already taken shape and form in the German language, and, in a transport of renewal, creates a Pentecostal faith in everything that Germany means.

219

BERTOLT BRECHT

More Good Sports

First published as "Mehr guten Sport," *Berliner Börsen-Courier* (February 6, 1926).

We pin our hopes on the sporting public.

Make no bones about it, we have our eye on those huge pans of concrete filled with 15,000 men and women of every variety of class and physiognomy, the fairest and shrewdest audience in the world. There you will find 15,000 persons paying high prices, and working things out on the basis of a sensible weighing of supply and demand. You cannot expect to get fair conduct on a sinking ship. The demoralization of our theater audiences springs from the fact that neither theater nor audience has any idea what is supposed to go on there. When people in sporting establishments buy their tickets they know exactly what is going to take place; and that is exactly what does take place once they are in their seats: viz. highly trained persons developing their peculiar powers in the way most suited to them with the greatest sense of responsibility yet in such a way as to make one feel that they are doing it primarily for their own fun. Against that the traditional theater nowadays is quite lacking in character.

There seems to be nothing to stop the theater having its own form of sport. If only someone could take those buildings designed for theatrical purposes, which are now standing eating their heads off in interest, and treat them as more-or-less empty spaces for the successful pursuit of sport, then they would be used in a way that might mean something to a contemporary public that earns real contemporary money and eats real contemporary beef.

It may be objected that there is also a section of the public that wants to see something other than sport in the theater. But we have never seen a single piece of evidence to prove that the public presently filling the theaters *wants* anything at all. The public's well-padded resistance to any attempt to make it give up those two old stalls that it inherited from grandpa should not be misinterpreted as a brand-new assertion of its will.

People are always telling us that we mustn't simply produce what the public demands. But I believe that an artist, even if he sits in strictest seclusion in the traditional garret working for future generations, is unlikely to produce anything without some wind in his sails. And this wind has to be the wind prevailing in his own period, and not some future wind. There is nothing to say that this wind must be used for travel in any particular direction (once one has a wind one can naturally sail against it; the only impossibility is to sail with no wind at all or with tomorrow's wind), and no doubt an artist will fall far short of achieving his maximum effectiveness today if he sails with today's wind. It would be quite wrong to judge a play's relevance or lack of relevance by its current effectiveness. Theaters don't work that way.

A theater that makes no contact with the public is nonsense. Our theater is accordingly a nonsense. The reason why the theater has at present no contact with the public is that it has no idea what is wanted of it. It can no longer do what it once could, and if it could do it, it would no longer wish to. But it stubbornly goes on doing what it no longer can do and what is no longer wanted. All those establishments with their excellent heating systems, their pretty lighting, their appetite for large sums of money, their imposing exteriors, together with the entire business that goes on inside them: all this doesn't contain five pennyworth of *fun*. There is no theater today that could invite one or two of those persons who are alleged to find fun in writing plays to one of its performances and expect them to feel an urge to write a play for it. They can see at a glance that there is no possible way of getting any *fun* out of this. No wind will go into anyone's sails here. There is no "sport."

Take the actors, for instance. I wouldn't like to say that we are worse off for talent than other periods seem to have been, but I doubt if there has ever been such an overworked, misused, panic-driven, artificially whipped-up band of actors as ours. And nobody who fails to get fun out of his activities can expect them to be fun for anybody else.

The people at the top naturally blame the people at the bottom, and the favorite scapegoat is the harmless garret. The people's wrath is directed against the garret; the plays are no good. To that it must be said that so long as they have been fun to write they are bound to be better than the theater that puts them on and the public that goes to see them. A play is simply unrecognizable once it has passed through this sausage-machine. If we come along and say that both we and the public had imagined things differently—that we are in favor, for instance, of elegance, lightness, dryness, objectivity—then the theater replies innocently: Those passions which you have singled out, my dear sir, do not beat beneath any dinner-jacket's manly chest. As if even a play like *Vatermord* [by Arnolt Bronnen] could not be performed in a simple, elegant and, as it were, classically rounded way!

Behind a feigned intensity you are offered a naked struggle in lieu of real competence. They no longer know how to stage anything remarkable, and therefore worth seeing. In his obscure anxiety not to let the audience get away the actor is immediately so steamed up that he makes it seem the most natural thing in the world to insult one's father. At the same time it can be seen that acting takes a tremendous lot out of him. And a man who strains himself on the stage is bound, if he is any good, to strain all the people sitting in the stalls.

I cannot agree with those who complain of no longer being in a position to prevent the imminent decline of the West. I believe that there is such a wealth of subjects worth seeing, characters worth admiring, and lessons worth learning that once a good sporting spirit sets in one would have to build theaters if they did not already exist. The most hopeful element, however, in the present-day theater is the people who pour out of both ends of the building after the performance. They are dissatisfied.

220

LEOPOLD JESSNER, BERTOLT BRECHT, AND FRITZ KORTNER
Is the Drama Dying?

First published as "Stirbt das Drama?" *Vossische Zeitung* (April 4, 1926).

We hear more and more that in their present form both drama and theater are in a state of decline or even demise. That our time is not capable of tragedy is an old contention. New is the charge that drama has outlived itself as an art form. Hasty eulogizers bury it to proclaim the cinema, radio, operetta, revue, or boxing match its successor. In the belief that this problem touches on a vital question of German culture, we have asked a number of professionals whether they too believe in the imminent decline of drama. Answers follow by artists whose names vouch for the honesty of their faith.

LEOPOLD JESSNER

The prophecy of the decline of the theater is by no means new; it is a periodically repeated bit of pessimism traceable back as far as the times of the great [eighteenth-century reformer Friedrich Ludwig] Schröder, of whom it was said that he magnified the chaos of theater.

If this prophecy today derives from the general change in the times, if one believes that the cinema, radio, operetta, revue, and boxing match are to be regarded as successors to theater, then it signifies an underestimation of the elemental drive underlying the theater, which has been deeply rooted in mankind for more than two thousand years.

Despite the cinema, despite radio broadcasting, despite all the inventions yet slumbering in the lap of nature, the theater's place will become ever more secure as long as the strivings after its perfection are pursued with passion.

Just as the art of painting rose to the heights from deep lows as photography emerged, so will all the competitors, those which are already apparent as well as those yet to come, cause genuine theater to arrive at its pure mission.

BERT BRECHT

If you ask a hundred-and-twenty-year-old whether life has any point at all, then he will tell you, particularly if he lived badly: little.

Times that drag about with such hideous rubbish as "art forms" (from yet other times) can bring about neither drama nor anything else artistic. It must be rather shameful for a generation when at its end the question arises of whether the work it did can have any value whatsoever. And we, we who do have considerable healthy appetite for theater, must admit (and make ourselves unloved in doing so) that such a cheap and tongue-tied thing as that plaster relief *Herodes und Mariamne* [by Friedrich Hebbel] can no longer satisfy us. That people of today will allow the whole of theater to be taken away from them altogether or be spoiled, is not very likely.

FRITZ KORTNER

The question of whether theater is being killed by the cinema, radio, boxing, etc., was posed a few weeks ago. Meanwhile the so-called tempo of our times has bestowed a quick-witted response: the theaters are doing well, the cinemas modestly so (they are trying out spoken inserts). Boxing is currently in the state that theater was in weeks ago, namely, K.O. Radio is not yet to be counted among the mature; it is therefore not yet allowed to decline. But cinema, radio, and boxing will also survive.

How could such a tough, ring-tested, inexterminable veteran of survival not continue to do what these infants of decline are already managing?

221

BERTOLT BRECHT
Difficulties of the Epic Theater

First published as "Schwierigkeiten des epischen Theaters," *Frankfurter Zeitung* (November 27, 1927).

Any theater that makes a serious attempt to stage one of the new plays risks being radically transformed. What the audience sees in fact is a battle between theater and play, an almost academic operation where, insofar as it takes any interest in the process of renovating the theater, all it has to do is observe whether the theater emerges as victor or vanquished from this murderous clash. (Roughly speaking, the theater can only emerge victorious over the play if it manages to avoid the risk of the play's transforming it completely—as at present it nearly always succeeds in doing.) It is not the play's effect on the audience but its effect on the theater that is decisive at this moment.

This situation will continue until our theaters have worked out the style of production that our plays need and encourage. It will not be an adequate answer if theaters invent some kind of special style for them, in the same way as the so-called Munich Shakespearean stage was invented, which could only be used for Shakespeare. It has to be a style that can lend new force to a whole section of the theatrical repertoire which is still capable of life today.

It is understood that the radical transformation of the theater cannot be the result of some artistic whim. It has simply to correspond to the whole radical transformation of the mentality of our time. The symptoms of this transformation are familiar enough, and so far they have been seen as symptoms of disease. There is some justification for this, for of course what one sees first of all are the signs of decline in whatever is old. But it would be wrong to see these phenomena, so-called *Amerikanismus* for instance, as anything but unhealthy changes stimulated by the operation of really new mental influences on our culture's aged body. And it would be wrong too to treat these new ideas as if they were not ideas and not mental phenomena at all, and to try to build up the theater against them as a kind of bastion of the mind. On the contrary it is precisely theater, art, and literature which have to form the ideological superstructure for a solid, practical rearrangement of our age's way of life.

In its works the new school of play writing lays down that the epic theater is the theatrical style of our time. To expound the principles of the epic theater in a few catch phrases is not possible. They still mostly need to be worked out in detail, and include representation by the actor, stage technique, dramaturgy, stage music, use of the film, and so on. The essential point of the epic theater is perhaps that it appeals less to the feelings than to the spectator's reason. Instead of sharing an experience the spectator must come to grips with things. At the same time it would be quite wrong to try and deny emotion to this kind of theater. It would be much the same thing as trying to deny emotion to modern science.

222

LION FEUCHTWANGER

Bertolt Brecht Presented to the British

First published as "Bertolt Brecht. Dargestellt für Engländer" *Die Weltbühne* 24, no. 36 (September 24, 1928), 372–376.

Bertolt Brecht has invented something he calls epic drama. He gets very angry if you ascribe this invention to his lack of a sense of construction. The content of this invention is that he rejects all tension in drama, that he regards the creation of antithesis and tension or any practically constructed plot as inartistic.

In fact Brecht's epic theater, in contrast to the French theater, destroys any tension by announcing in advance, naïvely and clearly, what is going to happen. According to Brecht the important thing is that the public should, for heaven's sake, not get involved. Any tendency on the part of the audience to participate vicariously in the fate and the life of another must, according to Brecht, be banished.

What is important, according to Brecht, is that the man in the theater should simply observe the events on the stage, craving knowledge, craving noise. The spectator should watch the course of a life. He should draw his conclusions, reject, agree, but, for heaven's sake, not have any sympathies. He should observe the mechanism of an event like the mechanism of a car. It is by no means necessary for the spectator to see a whole play. Since he is informed from the start about the various phases, he can decide for himself whether he wants to see how the hero behaves in this or that difficult and interesting situation, how he fights, how he changes himself or others, how he relates to the mass, either becoming absorbed in it or holding his own against it, how he swims with the stream or against it, how he dies.

The central point from which Brecht starts is probably the ballad. He has published a collection of ballads under the title *Household Homilies,* tales of life both great and small, presented in a popular and original manner, wild, impudent, bigoted, cynical. In these poems some persons and some feelings are seen for the first time and expressed for the first time.

It is probably not easy to convey the music of these verses in another language, but I believe that the character of this poetry is accessible to non-Germans; and I do not conceal my conviction that, apart from Kipling, Brecht is the leading ballad writer of our times.

Amongst Brecht's plays the comedy *Man is Man* is perhaps most easily comprehensible for wider circles. This play depicts the transformation of Galy Gay, a packer, into a soldier of the Indian Army. A machine-gun squad of an Indian regiment has lost its fourth member during a burglary, and in order to hush up the burglary has to get its fourth man back by hook or crook. For this purpose the three soldiers transform the harmless packer Galy Gay, a man who cannot say no, into their fourth man, Jeraiah Jip, soldier of the Indian Army. Working from the inside they rearrange Galy Gay the individual into a mass-person, and do it so that finally he really is no longer Galy Gay the packer but Jeraiah Jip; when the real Jeraiah Jip appears unexpectedly and belatedly, his substitute sends him to the devil.

The superficial circumstances of the plot are fantasy; the city of Kilkoa in which the action takes place is something invented in every respect by someone from Augsburg; the soldiers have been borrowed in a completely childlike way from Kipling; and a central role is played by an unusually silly joke about an artificial elephant. Nowhere is there a trace of apparent probability, every illusion is destroyed in a primitive manner. But the inner logic of the transformation of the man Galy Gay is convincing; when the live Galy Gay holds the funeral oration for the dead Galy Gay, I know of no scene by a living author which can equal it in greatness of grotesque-tragic invention and basic grasp.

The writer Bertolt Brecht has so far not been successful in Germany. Progressive theaters and large experimental provincial theaters present him, and he is a favorite subject for the literary world. It is not particularly easy to read your way into him, and to translate him is certainly very difficult. But I believe it is worthwhile.

223

FRIEDRICH WOLF

The Stage and Life

First published as "Bühne and Leben" *Arbeiter-Bühne* 16, no. 1 (January 1929), 7–8.

Every period possessing the courage of its convictions has created its own self-critique and its own theater that became a voice of the people, a people's court, a tribunal. Every page of the newspaper, if read properly, daily contains tragedies that cry out for the stage. It is shallowness, stupidity, mental indolence, and an artificial mania for education that presents *Faust* or *Wallenstein* to the forty-million working people of Germany, wanting to enthuse them with everything "good, beautiful, and true." *Faust,* with its focus completely on the beyond, with its redemptive ending through Mary, represents nothing more than lies and stultification for people today who can no longer believe in the devil incarnate. In this sense we do not want any artworks, even if they are precious stones. We want the truth of our time; we want the answers to the burning questions all around us. The Gretchen scene today must proceed from the problem of how the abused child of the people frees herself from the fruit of the dissolute student Faust by claiming the right to her body—not silence about this question and its apparent resolution through the cult of Mary! No! A clear position, in reference to Paragraph 218, on the problem: "Your body belongs to you." That is what we demand today.

Playwrights who do not avoid this issue have to be aware that they will not be writing a momentary box-office success; most of their dramas, in the hypocritical police state of today, in our present vacuum, can only be produced by very isolated theaters and the acting troupe of the Workers' Theater League.

After I had written the last scene of my *Kolonne Hund*—the gas attack by the Reichswehr troops on the workers of Bremen—it was clear to me that there was really no German theater at the moment that could perform the play. But I could not change it. However, Hamburg and Frankfurt dared to produce the piece, and since then *Kolonne Hund* has marched across seventeen national German stages. Precisely its unqualified avowal of the present and of the most biting side of life quite unexpectedly lent the piece persuasive force. None of the nine scenes is "invented." A hundred times we wore ourselves out fighting in our own ranks against discouragement, superficiality, betrayal, and relapses into considerations of personal self-interest, against the private feelings that separate the individual from the group. We were war casualties who had refused our pensions only to be left in the lurch by the unemployment relief department in the Ministry of Labor; we were manual and mental workers who dared for the first time to attempt to organize a communist cell in this isolated outpost. We know *today* that this attempt was destined to fail among the predominantly reformist workers; but we also know, precisely because of Karl Liebknecht, that these attempts are indispensable deeds . . . "from defeat to defeat to victory!" We have repeatedly experienced how the small, external victory was won in a rush of initial élan, but how the victory always went to the dogs because nothing is harder to maintain than . . . "the victory." That is why the last words of the Führer in *Kolonne Hund* is at the same time the question of whether the action must always end in defeat, of when the final victory would come: the victory? The victory is the hardest, for in victory you have to hold what you wanted. This piece of contemporary life in which we believed, for which we struggled and bled, in Bremen, in Kohlenpott, in Leuna and in Vogtland, in Berlin and in Düsseldorf, this piece of the present, flesh of our flesh, tried to hold the *Kolonne Hund* fast, tried to accentuate it so we would know ourselves . . . "and do it better the next time." This play, like every truly contemporary play, can and may not idealize nor show any already perfected state of the future or any already accomplished victory of the proletariat; in total, hard sincerity it must show the inner strife, the mistakes, the imperfections, the lack of faith, and yet the power of faith of the millions, to whom will belong not yet today but in years to come a more plain-spoken, less mendacious, and more just world.

224

ERWIN PISCATOR

The Documentary Play

First published in *Das politische Theater* (Berlin: Adalbert Schultz Verlag, 1929), pp. 63–71.

The first production in which the text and staging were based solely on political documents was *In Spite of Everything* (Großes Schauspielhaus, July 12, 1925).

The play grew out of a mammoth historical revue I was to put on in the spring of that year for the Workers' Cultural Union at a midsummer festival in the Gosen Hills [on the southern outskirts of Berlin]. The revue—I commissioned [Felix] Gasbarra to put the text together—was to show briefly the revolutionary highlights of the history of mankind from the Spartacus rebellion to the Russian Revolution, and to be a summary in instructive scenes of the whole development of historical materialism. We planned on a grand scale. There were to be 2,000 participants; twenty gigantic spotlights were to light up the natural arena, massive symbolic props would illustrate the various passages. (A sixty-five-foot battleship would represent British imperialism.) I had moved nearby to Schmöckwitz to be able to keep a constant eye on the work. The scenario had been worked out and the general outline of the music, again by Edmund Meisel, was ready, when the Cultural Union, prompted by Ernst Niekisch (who is after several changes of loyalty currently a pioneer of national "socialism"), suddenly had political reservations. While negotiations were still in progress, the German Communist Party asked us to put on a performance in the Großes Schau- spielhaus for their Berlin conference. The form and content of the thing had not been determined, but were to be worked out at a meeting at the central office the next day. The idea of having this performance stemmed from Ernst Torgler, a communist member of the Reichstag, and an old friend of ours from the days of the *Red Revue*.

I talked with Gasbarra about what we should do. To transfer our show from the Gosen Hills to the Großes Schauspielhaus was not feasible. On the other hand, we had gotten so used to thinking on a vast historical scale during the weeks of work on our revue, that the idea of using a ready-made play seemed unsatisfactory. Gasbarra suggested that we should take an extract from what we had already put together, perhaps turn the period between the outbreak of war and the murder of [Karl] Liebknecht and Rosa Luxemburg into a separate revue. The revue took as its title Liebknecht's phrase "In spite of everything" to show that the social revolution continued to take place, even after the terrible disaster of 1919. The plan caused head-shaking among senior party officials at the meeting because we intended to have figures like Liebknecht and Rosa Luxemburg portrayed on the stage.

Many felt that our plan to include members of the government in the revue (Ebert, Noske, Scheidemann, [Otto] Landsberg, etc.) was dangerous. They finally consented because nobody came up with a better suggestion, but remained skeptical—all the more so since we had barely three weeks left until the day of the performance.

The show was a collective effort. The separate tasks of writer, director, musical director, designer, and actor constantly overlapped. The scenery was built and the music composed as we wrote the script, and the script itself emerged gradually as the director worked with the group. Different scenes were put together simultaneously in different parts of the theater, sometimes even before a definite script had been worked out. Film was to be combined organically with live action on the stage for the first time. (As planned but not carried out in *Flags*.)

The way I combined apparently contrasting art forms features prominently in the critics' discussions and in the general public's appraisal of my work. For my part, I did not consider this aspect of the thing so important. The technique has been rejected out of hand, or praised to the skies, but rarely accurately appraised. The use of film clips followed along the same lines as the use of projections in *Flags*. (Not to mention the fact that the general idea of transforming the stage with film goes back to my time in Königsberg, though the stress then was still on the decorative possibilities.) All I did was to extend and refine the means; the aim stayed the same.

Later it was often maintained that I got the idea from the Russians. In fact I was quite ignorant of what was happening on the Soviet stage at this time—very little news about performances and so on came through to us. Even afterwards I never heard that the Russians had employed film with the same function I had had in mind. In any case the question of priority is irrelevant. It would merely prove that this was no superficial game with technical effects but a new, emergent form of theater based on the philosophy of historical materialism which we shared. After all, what do I consider the essential point of my whole work? Not the propagation of a view of life through formal clichés and billboard slogans but the presentation of solid proof that our philosophy and all that can be deduced from it is the one and only valid approach for our time. You can make all sorts of assertions, but repeating assertions does not make them more true or effective. Conclusive proof can be based only on scientific analysis of the material. This I can only do, in the language of the stage, if I can get beyond scenes from life, beyond the purely individual aspect of the characters and the fortuitous nature of their fates. And the way to do this is to show the link between events on the stage and the great forces active in history. It is not by chance that the factual substance becomes the main thing in each play. It is only from the facts themselves that the constraints and the constant mechanisms of life emerge, giving a deeper meaning to our private fates. For this I need some means of showing how human-superhuman factors interact with classes or individuals. One of the means was film. But it was no more than a means, and could be replaced tomorrow by some better means.

The film used in *In Spite of Everything* was documentary. From the archives of the Reich which were made available to us by one of our contacts we used authentic shots of the war, of the demobilization, of a parade of all the crowned heads of Europe, and the like. These shots brutally demonstrated the horror of war: flame-thrower attacks, piles of mutilated bodies, burning cities; war films had not yet come into "fashion," so these pictures were bound to have a more striking impact on the masses of the proletariat than a hundred lectures. I spread the film out through the whole play, and where that was not enough I projected stills.

For the basic stage I had a so-called *Praktikabel* built, a terraced structure of irregular shape with a raked platform on one side and steps and levels on the other. This structure stood on a revolving stage. I built the various acting areas into terraces, niches, and corridors. In this way the overall structure of the scenes was unified and the play could flow uninterrupted, like a single current sweeping everything along with it.

The abandonment of the decorative set was taken a stage further than in *Flags*. The predominant principle was that of a purely practical acting structure to support, clarify, and express the action. Freestanding structures, a self-contained world on the revolving stage, put an end to the peep-show world of the bourgeois theater. They can also be set up in the open. The squared stage area is merely an irritating limitation.

The whole performance was a montage of authentic speeches, essays, newspaper cuttings, appeals, pamphlets, photographs, and film of the war and the revolution, of historical persons and scenes. And all this was in the Großes Schauspielhaus that Max Reinhardt had once used to stage classical (bourgeois) theater. He, too, probably sensed that the masses had to be reached—but he came to them from the other side with foreign wares. *Lysistrata, Hamlet,* and even *Florian Geyer* and *Danton's Death* were no more than circus performances, blown up and coarsened. All Reinhardt did was to inflate the form. Actual involvement of the masses in the audience was not a conscious part of his program, and never amounted to more than a few ingenious touches from the director.

Nor did Karlheinz Martin's use of "expressionist movement" achieve this, either with classical drama or with [Ernst Toller's] *The Machine Wreckers*—it worked only in [Gerhart Hauptmann's] *The Weavers*. In our case arena and stage were fused into one. In this there was one decisive factor: Block bookings had been organized for the trade unions that summer. Class-conscious workers were sitting out front, and the storm broke. I had always been aware that we were not filling the house, and had wondered how we could actually reach this mass audience. Now I had them in my hand—and even today I still see that as the only real possibility for mass theater in Berlin.

For the first time we were confronted with the absolute reality we knew from experience. And it had exactly the same moments of tension and dramatic climaxes as literary drama and the same strong emotional impact. Provided, of course, that it was a political reality (political in the original sense: being of general concern).

I must admit that I myself was tense with apprehension as that evening approached. The tension was twofold: how would the interacting and interdependent elements onstage actually work, and would the effect that I was after come off to any degree?

The dress rehearsal was utter chaos. Two hundred people ran around shouting at one another. Meisel, whom we had just converted to Negro music, was conducting a loud, incomprehensible, fiendish concert with a twenty-man band, Gasbarra kept popping up with new scenes (until I put him in charge of the projectors), Heartfield stuck out his jaw and began to paint every single prop brown from top to bottom, none of the film clips came in on cue, the actors did not know where they were supposed to be half the time, and I myself began to be overwhelmed by the masses of material that still had to be fitted in. People sitting out in the auditorium during that rehearsal went home at 3:00 A.M. with no idea of what had happened on the stage. Even the scenes that were ready no longer pleased us. One thing was missing—the public.

On opening night there were thousands in the Großes Schauspielhaus. Every seat was taken; steps, aisles, entrances were full to bursting. The living masses were filled from the outset with wild excitement at being there to watch, and you could feel an incredible, willing receptivity out in the audience that you get only with the proletariat.

But this inner willingness quickly turned into active participation: the masses took over the direction. The people who filled the house had for the most part been actively involved in the period, and what we were showing them was in a true sense their own fate, their own tragedy being acted out before their eyes. Theater had become reality, and soon it was not a case of the stage confronting the audience, but one big assembly, one big battlefield, one massive demonstration. It was this unity that proved that evening that political theater could be effective agitation.

The drastic effect of using film clips showed beyond any theoretical consideration that they were not only right for presenting political and social mechanisms, that is, from the point of view of content, but also in a higher sense right from the formal point of view. The experience we had had with *Flags* repeated itself. The momentary surprise when we changed from live scenes to film was very effective. But the dramatic tension that live scene and film clip derived from one another was even stronger. They interacted and built up each other's power, and at intervals the action attained a furioso that I have seldom experienced in theater. For example, when the social-democratic vote on war loans (live) was followed by film showing the first dead, it not only made the political nature of the procedure clear, but also produced a shattering human effect, became art, in fact. What emerged was that the most effective political propaganda lay along the same lines as the highest artistic form.

225

MAX REINHARDT

On Actors

First published as "Über den Schauspieler," in *Max Reinhardt. 25 Jahre deutsches Theater,* ed. Franz Rothe (Munich: R. Piper, 1930), 9–12.

Theater is now fighting for its life, though not so much on account of economic need, which is general. It ails much more from the poverty of its own blood. It is to succored neither by literary nourishment, which is what it has been fed for a long time, nor by simpler, purely theatrical fare.

The present has tossed aside a wasteful abundance of strong actors. They remain wonderfully in their prime. But the sole vitalizing element of theatrical writing trickles thinly, and our truly dramatic times are only weakly mirrored in it. Human creative capacities flow now through other beds. For the moment. But we live in this moment.

Salvation can come only from the actor, for to him and him alone belongs the theater. All great dramatists were born actors, no matter whether they in fact pursued that profession.

Shakespeare is the greatest and utterly incomparable good fortune of the theater. He was writer, actor, and director at once. He painted landscapes and built architectures with his words. He came closest to equaling the Creator. He created an enchanted, complete world: the earth with all its flowers, the sea with all its storms, the light of the sun, the moon, the stars; fire with all its terrors; the air with all its spirits; and among them people. People with all their passions, people of elemental greatness as well as of the most vital truth. Shakespeare's omnipotence is infinite, incomprehensible. He was Hamlet and King

Claudius, Ophelia and Polonius in one person. Othello and Iago, Falstaff and Prince Hal, Shylock and Antonio, Zettel and Titania—the whole succession of lusty and sorrowful fools lived inside of him. They are all parts of his unfathomable being. He himself floated above them like a deity.

Theater can, if abandoned by all good spirits, be the saddest vocation, the most wretched prostitution. But the passion to see theater, to act in theater, is an elemental human drive. And this drive will always bring actor and audience together again and create that supreme theater that is the sole saving grace. For in every human being there lives, more or less consciously, the longing for metamorphosis.

We all bear within us the potential for all passions, for all fates, for all ways of life. "Nothing human is foreign to us." If that were not the case, we could not understand other people either in life or in art. But heredity, education, and individual experiences germinate and develop only a few of the thousand seeds in us. The others atrophy and slowly die out.

Bourgeois life is narrowly limited and poor in emotions. It has made a virtue of its poverty.

The normal person feels only one time in life the utter bliss of love, only once the jubilation of freedom; he hates one time fundamentally; he buries one time a beloved being and dies himself one time at the end. That is too little for our in-born capacities to love, to hate, to rejoice, to suffer.

We exercise daily to strengthen our muscles and our limbs so they do not shrivel up. But the organs of our soul, which are made after all for a lifetime of work, remain unneeded and therefore lose their capacities over time. Yet the health of our souls, our mental health, indeed even our physical health also depends on the undiminished function of these organs. We sense unmistakably how a hearty laugh can liberate us, a deep sob can relieve us, an outbreak of anger can release us. Indeed, we often seek such outbreaks with unconscious drives.

Our education admittedly works against this. Its first commandment is: you should conceal what is going on within. Thus we develop the sufficiently well-known repressions, the ailment of our times, hysteria, and ultimately that empty play-acting that fills life.

We have adapted to a series of generally valid forms of expression that belong to the armaments of society. These armaments are so stiff and narrow that there is hardly any room left for natural agitation. We have one or two cheap phrases for all occasions. We have ready-made faces for sympathy, joy, dignity, and that stereotypical grin of politeness. At weddings, baptisms, and burials a ghostly theater is made of hand shaking, bowing, brow furrowing, smiling—the emotional vacuity is terrifying. [. . .]

Today we can fly, hear, and see over the oceans. But the path to ourselves and those near to us is as distant as the stars. The actor is positioned along this path. With the light of the writer he sinks into the yet uncharted depths of the human soul, of his own soul, to transform himself secretly there and, hands, eyes, and mouth full of wounds, to rise once again to the surface.

He is the sculptor and sculpture at once; he is human on the most distant boundary between reality and dream; and he stands with both feet in both realms.

The actor is endowed with such autosuggestive power that he cannot only produce internal and psychological but also actual and external physical changes without resort to technical aids. And if one thinks of those much-discussed miracles that have occurred in all times and in many places, when simple people experience the Passion with such intense imaginative power that they manifest wounds on their hands and feet and cry genuinely bloody tears, then it becomes possible to gauge the mysterious depths which the art of acting can reveal. This is the same process Shakespeare describes when he says that the actor can visibly change his face, form, bearing, his whole being, and can cry over a distant or fictitious fate—and can make others cry with him.

226

DAS ROTE SPRACHROHR

How Does One Use Agitprop Theater?

First published as "Wie setzt man eine Agitpropgruppe ein?" in *Das rote Sprachrohr* 9 (1930).

Over the last few years the agitprop troupe has indisputably become our most effective means of struggle, publicity, and education. If nevertheless we are not yet fully exploiting the potential influence of the agitprop troupe, the reason lies for now in the fact that the agitprop functionaries do not yet realize how to create adequate preconditions for the effectiveness of our troupes.

That is the reason for these lines.

An agitprop troupe should not appear only on the stage; after the performance it should move through the premises for publicity purposes. It is necessary to use trained comrades for this. In these functions politically weak comrades who are not capable of discussing matters correctly, damage (unintentionally and unconsciously!!) the organization. A troupe that is not trained politically, however technically qualified it may be, will exert an inadequate or bad effect. Neither, of course, is a satisfactory political effect possible without appropriate artistic and technical qualifications. Therefore agitprop troupes should be assigned, to the extent that it is in any way possible, to trained, confident comrades, and they must devote intensive concentration through exercises, rehearsals, and courses to become qualified in their crafts.

But the agitprop troupes' field of activity is not confined solely to performances. They should appear at public swimming pools; at all of the recreation areas, parks, and fields used by the working population; at harvest festivals, annual fairs, and amusement parks; at demonstrations, meetings, and occasions for agitation in residential areas and courtyards. And they should be active with publicity work created particularly for that purpose (which can be seen and heard far and wide). The troupes must prepare themselves (for example, regarding their initial entrance marches) for this task as well. Here, too, appropriate qualifications are necessary!

Every agitprop functionary occupied with the potential influence and developmental conditions of an agitprop troupe—and that belongs absolutely among the functions of every agitprop director—will immediately recognize that an agitprop troupe will make the best use of limited financial resources if it is to carry out its work successfully. And here, concerning the issue of the box office, is where good, politically necessary collaboration usually falls to pieces. Either the troupe insists on a fixed price that seems too high for the event organizers—which with the tenacity of a cunning businessman they refuse to lower—or on the contrary, the comrade "organizers," who do indeed regard the troupe as an important "draw," attempt systematically to reduce its charge, likewise like a cunning businessman. (This happens especially in localities with several troupes where the one can be played off against the other.) The troupes that behave like a cunning businessman and shun the most important (the unpaid) aspects of their work, automatically remove themselves from the area of activity proper to an agitprop troupe and become no better than just any theater company. It must be mentioned in this connection that the method of playing off the individual troupes against each other regularly adopted by agitprop leaders (not least in regard to finances) has led to debt and thus frequently to the incapacitation and dissolution of serviceable troupes. It should be mentioned incidentally that some troupes were incapacitated because agreed-upon expenses frequently went unpaid or were never paid at all. [. . .]

Do not think, comrades, that "when one troupe goes under, we will just rely on another or even found a new one." That is false—the standards of the working class audience are continually on the rise. We need troupes with a potential for development to do justice to the continually rising political and artistic standards of the workers.

227

ALFRED KEMÉNYI

Measures Taken at the Großes Schauspielhaus

First published under the name Durus as "Die Maßnahme im großen Schauspielhaus," *Die rote Fahne* 16 (January 20, 1931).

The first performance in the Philharmonic inspired a lively discussion in our own camp. This innovative, formally outstanding work of art provokes an active political assessment from all sides, and it is not the least of its merits that it does not admit of a "merely aesthetic" reception.

We have to pronounce decisive approval of the second Berlin performance, although we are of the opinion that the overall conception of the text is contrived, since it has been developed not from the perspective of revolutionary practice but merely out of the mental elaboration of revolutionary theory.

We have to affirm the production politically because the positive, propagandistic merits of the overall effect largely compensate for the disadvantages caused by the lack of ideological clarity. The shooting of the young, undisciplined comrade by his theoretically clear but unscrupulous comrades (who repeatedly assign the young comrade difficult, illegal tasks) is not justified from the point of view of revolutionary practice.

But *Measures Taken* uses this overly intricate case to teach a positive, correct lesson that is critical for the revolutionary movement of all countries: the interests of the party are higher than the interests of the individual; however honest and enthusiastic a proletarian revolutionary may be emotionally, without the clarity of revolutionary theory he is only half a revolutionary.

To the author of *Measures Taken*, Bert Brecht, it must, however, be said that knowledge of the theory of Marxism-Leninism is not sufficient unto itself, that the ingenuity and well-read Marxism of a writer cannot replace revolutionary experience and detail work gained in the revolutionary movement.

Yet it is extraordinarily interesting and important to observe how the best bourgeois writers in Germany today are being affected by Marxism as a revolutionary theory. Now in order to comprehend revolutionary theory completely, the next step, submersion in *revolutionary practice,* is indispensible!

The performance of *Measures Taken* is of decisive significance from the standpoint of the workers' chorus movement. With this play, the most ideologically mature, most artistically accomplished, evening-filling choral work for working-class singers has appeared. This is no pointless musical freneticism. No sentimental industrial tumultuousness with leitmotifs like "poor proletarian!" but a call to revolutionary action! A decisive stand for revolutionary theory, for communism, for the party.

In terms of art, literature, and music, *Measures Taken* is epoch-making. It approaches the level of Marxist pedagogy found in the play *For Soviet Power,* performed by The Red Megaphone, without, to be sure, equalling the performance of that acting troupe ideologically and in the consistency of its creative work methods.

It is important that *Measures Taken* is formally innovative and compelling, works with contemporary tools of form and technique, and does not trumpet the aesthetic retrogression of "revolutionary virtue" (as did that earlier "proletarian" oratorio *Battleship Potemkin*).

There is a dialectical reciprocity between the artistic form and the social content of an artwork, and the yet half-anarchistic *Measures Taken* will certainly inspire many revolutionary working-class writers to more ideologically mature works.

22
The Roaring Twenties: Cabaret and Urban Entertainment

THE TREMORS OF WAR, revolution, and inflation shook the foundations of the Wilhelmine Empire and weakened the walls that kept German high culture protected from the onslaughts of the modern entertainment industry. The dadaists had begun as early as 1916 to poke fun at the humanistic ideals and institutional conventions of classical art and literature, arguing that the idealism of both German classicism and expressionism amounted to nothing when confronted with the inhumanity of the war. German culture, which has always felt superior toward Western civilization, suddenly seemed implicated in a cruel war that, ironically, had been fought to protect *Kultur* against the threat of *Zivilisation*. The early 1920s witnessed a Germany eagerly opening its borders to foreign influences that had been kept at bay during the war years. Trying to forget the past and enjoy the present, many intellectuals embraced American mass culture precisely because it represented the epitome of what conservative cultural critics called *Zivilisation*. As a radical countermodel to German culture—both classical and avant-garde—mass culture swept through the major cities, making traditional concepts of art appear isolated, elitist, and even undemocratic. For the growing urban population as well as for the younger generation of writers and intellectuals—and especially for Brecht and the Berlin avant-garde of the early 1920s—American mass culture promised to make German culture and life both modern and less aristocratic. Mass culture encompassed Charlie Chaplin, Josephine Baker, movies, jazz, and boxing, but, above all, it represented modernity and the ideal of living in the present. The infatuation with America implied a rejection of the recent German military past and disillusion with humanistic values. With the demise of the Kaiser's authoritarian rule all traditional aristocratic notions of culture inherent in the old political system were also called into question. German avant-garde writers and intellectuals understood American mass culture in its original sense as a modern folk culture that responded to the needs of large urban masses. America—more so than the Soviet Union—was consistently held up as the cultural model of the future.

The enthusiastic German reception of American jazz and American dances such as the Charleston and the Shimmy was fueled by the frenzy of those who had survived the bloodshed of the war and the "great collapse of the world and humanity," as Alice Gerstel put it in 1922. The Charleston, which by 1926 was the most popular dance in Germany, became an expression of "the mechanization and democratization of life." Showgirl troupes such as the Tiller Girls performed in elaborate revues to the applause of Berlin's intellectuals who saw in the synchronicity and exactness of the troupe's energetic movements a fitting symbol of the industrial process. German entrepreneurs such as Erik Charell, Hermann Haller, James Klein, and Rudolf Nelson developed their own revues into increasingly lavish Moulin Rouge-type shows featuring hundreds of nude female dancers (the so-called "girls"), singers, and musicians, as well as extravagant sets and costumes. By the mid-1920s revues had become the most popular form of live entertainment in Berlin. Consisting of a large variety of quick-paced numbers (songs, skits, dances), they had a structural affinity to the fragmented urban experience; their juxtaposition of sights and sounds seemed to express modernity more directly than classical theater ever could. During the 1926–1927 theater season Berlin offered no fewer than nine revues that were seen by a total of 11,000 spectators. The opulent productions tried to outdo each other in their technical perfection and their promise of visual pleasure—truly monuments to the giddy mass consumerism that took hold of Berlin in the 1920s. The American Revue Nègre— starring Josephine Baker—that toured Paris, London, and Berlin added a touch of the exotic to the amusement; its phenomenal success was seen by Ivan Goll as a challenge to Europe's drained and desiccated cultural identity. He reported from Paris in an article containing blatantly racial stereotypes prevalent at the time. Despite her enthusiastic reception in Europe, Baker did not escape being stereotyped as the embodiment of untamed and primitive (female) nature out to conquer Western civilization. The revue craze lasted as long as the prosperity did: from 1924 to 1929. By 1931, in the face of rising unemployment and social unrest, the popularity of revues had dropped noticeably. The Roaring Twenties were over.

Alongside the new America-inspired mass culture of movies, jazz concerts, and revues, the German tradition of the political-satirical cabaret continued to flourish in the Weimar Republic. Following the mixture of theatrical skits, recitations, music, songs, and comedy—first experimented with in Paris during the 1880s—the German cabarets tended to be literary, politically aggressive, and often mercilessly satirical. In 1919 Max Reinhardt once again started up his literary cabaret Schall und Rauch, which had enjoyed short-lived success back in 1901. It opened with a parody of Reinhardt's own production of Aeschylus's *Oresteia* at the Großes Schauspielhaus and ended in 1921 with Reinhardt's departure from Berlin. Numerous other cabarets—Rosa Valetti's Cabaret Größenwahn, Kurt Robitschek's Kabarett der Komiker, and Trude Hesterberg's Wilde Bühne, among others—featured biting lyrics by Kurt Tucholsky, Walter Mehring, and Erich Kästner. Friedrich Hollaender, one of the most prolific and popular songwriters and composers in the Weimar Republic, started his own cabaret, Tingeltangel, a proletarian version of the cabaret later immortalized in the film *The Blue Angel* in which Marlene Dietrich sang Hollaender's memorable tunes.

There were, of course, various types of cabaret. From 1921 to 1931, one of the most popular was Der Blaue Vogel. This folkloristic cabaret of Russian emigrés presented, in their own tongue, highly stylized, romantic, and amusing genre scenes from their homeland. Der Blaue Vogel easily found an audience among the 300,000 Russians who had been lured to Berlin by the strength of the ruble during the inflation. Berliners fell in love with the uncanny simplicity and naïveté of these performances. On a different artistic level, the Cabaret of the Nameless deserves mention as a forerunner of the American television "Gong Show," in which exhibitionists performed to the ridicule of an audience which enjoyed the obvious *lack* of talent. Kästner's description of this ostensibly humiliating show is flavored with the cynicism and high-strung chaos—he compares the show to a padded cell—that was typical for Berlin in the 1920s. Curt Moreck's guide to Berlin's nightlife is directed at tourists hungry for the thrills of the metropolis, which in the 1920s was justly called the amusement capital of the world. From the far right, Joseph Goebbels, commentator on the Berlin scene in his own periodical, *Der Angriff,* showed his contempt for such decadence and vowed to put an early end to what he saw as a dangerous disintegration of morals.

228

ALICE GERSTEL

Jazz Band

First published as "Jazzband," *Die Aktion* 12, nos. 4–5 (February 4, 1922), 90–91.

Every era has its expression. It could be many things: individual persons and books, warehouses, monasteries, or airplanes. But the deepest expression of any era is always its music.

What Palestrina was for the violently convulsed and yet radiant Catholicism of the fifteenth century, Bach for the heroic yet objective period of Luther, Wagner for a tinseled, theatrical, true-to-itself and profoundly mendacious epoch—is for the dying era of the bourgeoisie the jazz band. It unifies within itself everything that remains from the great collapse of the world and humanity, dances with it over the abyss, marking tangents (from tango with a capital T) on the charred edges with the easy caution and simple decadence of its pointed shoes. It has that desperate, burned-out, light, unscrupulous, gasping, yet liberating step. It has that exoticism of color that reigns—not by accident—over our desire. It has that rat-a-tat of the cannons they have been firing at the "enemy" for five long years and which have just recently been deployed in the conquest of Dachau near Munich. It has the trumpets that called the coalminers in Ostrau to arms, the drums that call exploited humanity to its last desperate revolt; and it has the festive sound reminiscent of the champagne they pour, at last permissible once more in noblest reconciliation with the international band of racketeers, down throats parched from so many lyrical cries.

A Negro sits behind the mystical instrument. It is a drum with trumpets, tambourines, bells, blocks, and straps attached like small but essential ornaments on the facade of a bank building. The Negro, half slave-driver, half juggler, holds two sticks in his hands. He beats them on the blocks. Sometimes it sounds like he is pounding nails into a coffin, then again as if his knife slipped while he was slicing salami. His thick lips press on the mouth of the trumpet; in his eyes he holds a sly and melancholy smile, meanwhile there is a drum roll, a blow on the tambourine, a stroke on the bell. Next to him a pale adventurer strums chords on a balalaika—the sound as monotonous as a debate in Parliament—and the violinist, the third in the devilish trio, occupies no fixed place but skips, fiddle under his chin, among the skipping couples, and plays sweet cantilenas for the ladies and rakish trills under their skirts. The dancing couples are under the spell of these rhythms, these colors and sounds, to which an English or German text can be nothing but a makeshift substitute for some sort of Dadaist, exotic howl and stammer. They slip in the wildest gyrations over the polished floor with a precision that suggests ultimately nothing other than a well-oiled automaton. The men stare fixedly, press their lips decisively together. Nothing can dissuade them from the secret of which they are certain: how dreadful is the wretchedness of this time, how there remains nothing for them to do but dance and the market runs itself and [Karel] Čapek's robots make the sewing needles and roll their cigarettes into ready-mades.[1] But the women are still as unaware as little animals. Half-charred, they still refuse to believe in fire. With half-open mouths and half-closed eyes they enjoy the drunken debauchery of this raving music, let the nails of the beat be driven into their masochistically lustful flesh, let them drift over the meadows of their dreams through glass flowers smelling lightly of Chypre and Fleur d'Orsay.

1. In Čapek's play *RUR-Rossum's Universal Robots,* 1920.

The halls are washed in an antique cubism, all the remnants of lost cultures celebrate inside them a last rendezvous, and it would not surprise us suddenly to see the daughter of Amenophis of Egypt dancing among the couples in the arms of Oscar Wilde. For here, here in the mood and in the jazz music what remains of the creative force of this sterile time unfolds: the genius of the eclectic, the cocktail mix of souls, the recklessness, the random toss and melding of complexes, the recklessness of puppets on a string, the passion of people condemned to death who want to eat one more blue and singing herring.

But sometimes out of the drumbeat whirlpool and the trumpet blasts comes the mighty rhythm of the *Internationale*: "Brothers, listen for the signal. . . ." And already massed in closed ranks behind the private boxes are the musical-instrument makers, the parquet polishers, the stokers, the electricians, and ditch diggers, the hundreds upon thousands of a menacing, unending, ultimate, mighty era!

229

FRANK WARSCHAUER

Berlin Revues

First published as "Berliner Revuen," *Die Weltbühne*, no. 51 (December 16, 1924), 920–921.

Theater makes itself autonomous in the revue; it emancipates itself from all convention, breeding, custom, and tradition and organizes its existence, so to speak, on its own. Free of the reins and bridle of literature, free too from the disruptive consistency of playwrights, it henceforth leads a life of magnificence and joy by entering into wild, truly wild marriages with the varieté, panopticon, cabaret, operetta, and even film—in short, with everything that could conceivably be thought to serve its purpose. It takes absolutely no more consideration of its family and forebears: it does quite simply what it pleases.

Armed with such idealistic speculations, the curious, pleasure-seeking Berliners make their first stop the theater in the Admiralpalast where a quite-marvelous revue—all revues are marvelous—is being performed. It is called *Noch und Noch*. Viewers have the right to feel like *roués* here, for they have already witnessed a fine show in this very place, created under the aegis of Emil Pirchan and displaying remarkable traces of this fine lineage. [. . .]

One of the chief people involved in this sort of thing is, of course, the set designer. In this case Haas-Heye. He offers little more than a thinly disguised, out-of-date version of the Metropol Theater. Otherwise the theater is also quite restrained in its extravagances. The girls on display behave themselves very nicely. The whole thing is downright boring.

In this respect Erik Charell got started much more cleverly in his revue, *An Alle,* for the Großes Schauspielhaus. It is clear to him that the mark of a good revue is above all variety and colorfulness. So he works not with one painter but with several; and the program puts together a wide variety of numbers, or, more precisely, arranges them in and over one another. Above all, Charell has a feel for how such a show has to be international, getting his people from widely diverse regions: from Russia, Scandinavia, England, France, and America. And from Berlin. In any case, one finds there a congenial chaos of languages, which gives the spectator the impression (or forces on him the illusion—I am not sure which) that we live in a truly cosmopolitan city.

Interspersed is the truly necessary touch of Berlin, created by Claire Waldoff with Oscar Sabo lending a hand. The collection of curiosities supplied by the theater-owner Bendow is nice and amusing.

All of this is stacked artlessly together with no sense for the rhythm of an evening in the theater and with just as little for the nerves of the audience. One is subjected to an unrelenting barrage of pleasures; it crackles and pops without interruption. One course follows the other with incredible speed—and everything, everything is dessert! The composition of the whole is still somewhat lacking.

So, these are your aberrations, o theater?! With mixed feelings, the sensitive and observant spectator leaves the site of this unleashed theater, this theater gone wild.

230

MAXIMILIAN SLADEK

Our Show

First published as "Unsere Schau," in Erik Charell, *An Alle* (Program Notes, 1924).

Life in the big city is a multiple interweaving of surfaces. But everyone wants an art in which one sees life reflected. This is how the cinema has become the expression of our time. What could be the point of opposing it? Nevertheless for the big-city dweller the true "mirror and abbreviated chronicle of the age" has always been the revue, that colorful, whirring, easy-going, incredibly mobile, suggestive replica of existence aswirl in a storm. In Paris, London, and New York, where the revue was born, this has long been recognized. Genuine theater holds itself a bit aloof in these cities, with the great show being offered by the one that pulls everything together into an incredible rhythm—dramatic art, varieté, music, fashion show—and defines the center of social life and social encounters. In the climate of advancing internationalization before the war, Berlin was also tending in this direction, but its isolation in the last decade has blocked further development. Now the revue has entered upon its triumphal march here as well, a triumph that can only be the greater since contemporary theater is in no position to capture the stirred-up life of the present. Ought one speak of symptoms of decay and recite the decline of the West? Cassandra did not change the fate of Troy, and the living demand their due.

That the revue, however, offers great developmental possibilities within its enlarged scope, and therefore need not be a merely mindless sensation, is not denied even by its opponents. And if the Großes Schauspielhaus is now opening its doors to our show, it has not sacrificed its lofty expectations. The advantage of this space—which like no other demands and encourages the grand movements and rhythm of the masses—allows for a complete exploitation of the full potential of gripping visual attractions. Beyond this, we hope in this show to have captured something of the more intimate pulse of our red-hot times.

231

FERDINAND HAGER

The Flight of the "Blue Bird"

First published as "Der Wanderflug des 'Blauen Vogels,'" *Baden-Badener Bühnenblatt* 26 (June 18, 1924).

Contrary to all other birds, the bluebird usually migrates in the summer. And I, its faithful friend and admirer, am sitting in the heat of Berlin, bent over foreign newspapers, following its proud flight. This year I followed the cabaret of Russian emigrés, The Blue Bird, through Austria, Hungary, Spain, Sweden, Denmark, Holland, all of Switzerland and the Bohemian spas, and everywhere I read of victories, triumphs, and cheers.

What is it that compels such a variety of people to a unanimous, nearly identical assessment and enthusiasm? There are, aside from religion, only two personal experiences capable of achieving such a result: that of genuine art and genuine humanity. And I believe it is just these two things that allow these minor entertainment arts from Russia to assume the proportions of a revelation for Europe and America. Perhaps it is wrong to speak of "minor arts" at all. It is major art in a minor key. It is modest: for a miniature, it sacrifices no less time, work, and spirit than would be required for an entire drama—and everything just to captivate the senses, to tune the soul for a few minutes through light, gesture, color, motion, and sound. The principles are: national flavor; resort to naïve popular painting in its sentimental and grotesque elements, treated here with a most modern audacity; an astounding pairing of expressionism and primitivism; and, in consequence, the introduction of expressionism to the stage. And, alongside sturdy folk art stand vital cross-sections from past epochs: the Rococo, the Renaissance, the Russian eighteenth and nineteenth centuries, the most modern Americanism, not mimicked, not caricatured but lived and raised to the level of overpowering effectiveness.

What the Russians have to offer is a cultivated art—not that *l'art pour l'art* understood only by those possessed of a superior aesthetic turn of mind but rather a bit of fantasy lent naïve form in which lifeless objects take on human essence or are filled with human essence; an art that glimpses in objects, in a machine or a toy, the smiling caricature of human actions and deeds.

It is no accident that it is precisely Russian art that we seek out and treasure today. It is somehow the expression of a deep longing for which we no longer find any resonance in Western European art. We expect of it the fulfillment of some kind of hope slumbering within us, unsuspected and inexplicable, and that is what unites all the different people over whose native lands the Blue Bird has made its summer migration.

For only in this way can one explain how all of these people listen for an entire evening to performances conducted in an utterly foreign language—and understand. That is where the Russians' achievement is manifest: they fill an entire evening using scarcely any of the words of the country in which they are performing, and one understands them anyway, as one rarely has understood anything. For the spectators do not consider what they have seen and heard might be—they simply experience it. [. . .]

But what is this remarkable thing that sweeps the audience along, that excites it, that causes this cold, spoiled audience of the European metropoles to give up their inner reserve and feel the feelings, join in the action on the stage? It is perhaps quite simply what the emcee does, with such cheerful and cordial directness, beyond all the limitations of distance, as if to every spectator personally: he speaks. All of these things and characters on the

Russians' stage speak. They do not declaim; they do not present something; they are not supposed to be works of art, they speak. They speak and we understand.

232

KATHARINA RATHAUS

Charleston: Every Age Has the Dance It Deserves

First published as "Charleston. Jede Zeit hat den Tanz, den sie verdient," *Uhu* 3 (1926), 120–121.

The waltz is dead—and all attempts to resuscitate it are failing and destined to fail. For the times have changed and with them, like a natural necessity, so must the dances. Today, when a new car rolls out of Ford's factory every minute, when "Valencia" and the latest hits are played simultaneously in major cities and the smallest provincial nests, when radio makes it possible for us and the deepest forest dwellers to check out simultaneously the applause earned by the closing Charleston in the Savoy Hotel in London, in Berlin's pace-setting Dance Palace, or in Paris—today the movement and rhythm of dance is different than it was in the cozy times of the blessed Strauss. They are creatures of the new mobility of life, of its whipped-up and racing tempo! They are full of the new spirit, and the new should not be judged, good or bad, too quickly! The notion of the "good old times" is marked by a fear of the new, and skepticism over the new dances usually goes along with an inability to dance them. And as the "new" is always the slogan of the young, so does the new generation fasten its excited grip on the new dances. It senses that the empty bowls of the old Europe will offer no new nourishment for the blood, that the burned-out temperament of the European centers of culture can convey to the body no unsuspected, electrifying rhythm. The mechanization and democratization of life force upon its members new and other movements. Instead of dancing dances in a strolling gait with the spirit of a bygone era, the younger generation takes its inspiration from the original motions of primitive peoples, from an unaffected return to the rhythmic, musical experiences of naïve souls. If such borrowed steps, perhaps movement fragments of savage peoples, end up melted together with the remnants of Western culture, tempered in the ovens of modern civilization, if they find their final form in the molds of a talented dancer's sense of style, to be cooled finally into social dances at parties and balls by the conventions of our democratic-bourgeois milieu—who would wonder then that hearts and legs fly, race to them, dance in exultation! For dance speaks to the blood and to the beat of the heart, not to reason! The associations of international dance teachers persist in their yearly efforts, in vain, "to invent" new dances. All "invented" dances are still-born children. They live a few fleeting days and hours. All the dance teachers in the world are incapable of forcing their artificial products on the dancing crowds, which instinctively defend themselves against the rape of their movement by affectation. On the contrary, the new, original dance; Terpsichore's modern face, made-up, powdered, and painted according to the current dictate of fashion; bobbed hair in the latest cut; crêpe de Chine streamers just to the knee—none of this needs advertising. This dance gets its own recruits, makes its own way, discharges itself (with occasional farcical misunderstandings) amid the thunder of a jazz band like a storm! It cleanses tradition of the dust of decades, inflames blasé dance fanatics anew, shows all those excited by dance the rhythm of their life, their feelings and thoughts. It answers to the name Charleston.

233

IVAN GOLL

The Negroes Are Conquering Europe

First published as "Die Neger erobern Europa," *Die literarische Welt* no. 2 (January 15, 1926), 3–4.

The Negroes are conquering Paris. They are conquering Berlin. They have already filled the whole continent with their howls, with their laughter. And we are not shocked, we are not amazed: on the contrary, the old world calls on its failing strength to applaud them.

Yesterday some of us were still saying, art is dead!—the terrible confession of a lifeless, enervated, hopeless age. Art dead? Then original art, superior art, lives again! The last art was: disintegration of the ego; disintegration of the world; despair over the world in the ego; the constant, mad revolution of the ego about itself. We experience that in all the twenty-year-old novelists finding fame in Paris just now—and there are dozens of them. Benn wrests the one bloody book in his life from his torment and calls it—still young— *Epilog*. That is almost more tragic than [Heinrich von] Kleist's suicide. And what otherwise is not the product of such pain remains precious and fin-de-siècle, thin and frivolous.

And yet, why complain? The Negroes are here. All of Europe is dancing to their banjo. It cannot help itself. Some say it is the rhythm of Sodom and Gomorrah. . . . Why should it not be from paradise? In this case, rise and fall are one.

The Revue Nègre, which is rousing the tired public in the Théâtre des Champs-Elysées to thrills and madness as otherwise only a boxing match can do, is symbolic.

Negroes dance with their senses. (While Europeans can only dance with their minds.) They dance with their legs, breasts, and bellies. This was the dance of the Egyptians, the whole of antiquity, the Orient. This is the dance of the Negroes. One can only envy them, for this is life, sun, primeval forests, the singing of birds and the roar of a leopard, earth. They never dance naked: and yet, how naked is the dance! They have put on clothes only to show that clothes do not exist for them.

Their revue is an unmitigated challenge to moral Europe. There are eight beautiful girls whose figures conjure up a stylized purity, reminiscent of deer and Greek youths. And at their head, the star, Josephine Baker. They have all oiled their curly hair smooth with a process just invented in New York. And on these rounded heads they don hats of manifold fashions, from 1830, 1900, or by the designer Lewis. This mix exudes a glowing irony. A belly dance is performed in a brocade dress by Poiret. In front of a church that could have been painted by Chagall, dressed in bourgeois skirts like women going to market, they dance around a white, bespectacled pastor strumming a banjo (American Negroes are pious and faithful Christians—you only have to listen to their modern songs to know that!). They dance a dance one might expect in a lunatic asylum.

It confronts us all, it confronts everything with the strange impression of a snarling parody. And it is a parody. They make fun of themselves when they perform the "Dance of the Savages" with the same mockery, wearing only the usual loin cloth and—a silk brassiere.

And here we see original art becoming one with the latest. These Negroes come out of the darkest parts of New York. There they were disdained, outlawed; these beautiful women might have been rescued from a miserable ghetto. These magnificent limbs bathed in rinse water. They do not come from the primeval forests at all. We do not want to fool ourselves. But they are a new, unspoiled race. They dance with their blood, with their life, with all the memories in their short history: memories of transport in stinking ships, of early slave labor in America, of much misfortune. Sentimentality breaks through. They become sentimental when they sing. "Swanee River" and "Give Me Just a Little Bit"— these universal hits in provincial jazz apply the rouge on civilization. Alas, these primeval people will be used up fast! Will they have the time to express what is in them in an art of their own making? It is doubtful.

The leader, director, and principal dancer of the troupe is Louis Douglas, the equal of the perfect Baker. He is the only one who wears a dark black mask, while all the others are nearly light brown. He has a gigantic white mouth. But his feet! They are what inspires the music. The orchestra takes its lead from them, not the other way around. He walks, he drags, he slips—and the beat rises from the floor, not from the flutes, which merely offer their accompaniment in secret. One number is called "My Feet Are Talking." And with his feet he tells us of his voyage from New York to Europe: the first day on the boat, the third in the storm, then the trip by railroad and a race at Longchamp.

The musicians play *with,* they do not merely play along! They are located left of the stage, then soon enough they are following after a dancer or tossing off their remarks in a song. They are genuine actors. They also help to emphasize the parody. They laugh continuously. Whom are they making fun of? No—they aren't making fun of anyone: they are just *enjoying,* the playing, the dancing, the beat. They enjoy themselves with their faces, with their legs, with their shoulders; everything shakes and plays its part. It often seems as if they had the leading roles.

But the leading role belongs to Negro blood. Its drops are slowly falling over Europe, a long-since dried-up land that can scarcely breathe. Is that perhaps the cloud that looks so black on the horizon but whose fearsome downpours are capable of so white a shine? [Claire Goll's] *The Negro Jupiter Robs Europe* [*Der Neger Jupiter raubt Europa*] is the name of a modern German novel just now coming out. The Negro question is pressing for our entire civilization. It runs like this: Do the Negroes need us? Or are we not sooner in need of them?

234

JOSEPH GOEBBELS

Around the Gedächtniskirche

First published as "Rund um die Gedächtniskirche," *Der Angriff* (January 23, 1928).

Thousands and thousands of electric lights spew illumination into the grey evening, so that brightness covers the Kurfürstendamm, as if by day. The bells on streetcars ring, buses clatter by honking their horns, stuffed full with people and more people; taxis and fancy private automobiles hum over the glassy asphalt. The red, yellow, and green signal lights regulate the stop and go of traffic; in the midst of all the bustle the green one stands high atop its post, releasing the black throng of people to their breakneck passage from one side of the street to the other. Squeals and squeaks so assault the ear that the novices run the constant risk of losing their calm disposition. In front of the huge cinemas the newest hits of the season shines forth in dazzling red: *Killed by Life, The Girl from Tauentzien Avenue, Just One Night.* The fragrance of heavy perfume floats by. Harlots smile from the artful pastels of fashionable women's faces; so-called men stroll to and fro, monocles glinting; fake and precious stones sparkle. All the languages of the world fall on the ear; there goes the yellow Indian next to the garrulous Saxon; an Englishman curses as he elbows his way through the crowd, and, resounding above the din, a frozen newspaper boy cries out the evening papers just off the press.

In the middle of this turmoil of the metropolis the Gedächtniskirche stretches its narrow steeples up into the grey evening. It is alien in this noisy life. Like an anachronism left behind, it mourns between the cafés and cabarets, condescends to the automobiles humming around its stoney body, and calmly announces the hour to the sin of corruption.

Walking around it are many people who perhaps have never gazed up at its towers. There is the snobby flaneur in a fur coat and patent leather; the worldly lady, *garçon* from head to toe with a monocle and smoking cigarette, taps on high heels across its walkways and disappears into one of the thousands of abodes of delirium and drugs that cast their screaming lights seductively into the evening air.

That is Berlin West: The heart turned to stone of this city. Here in the niches and corners of cafes, in the cabarets and bars, in the Soviet theaters and mezzanines, the spirit of the asphalt democracy is piled high. Here, here the politics of sixty-million diligent Germans is conducted. Here one gives and receives the latest market and theater tips. Here one trades in politics, pictures, stocks, love, film, theater, government, and the general welfare. The Gedächtniskirche is never lonely. Day plunges suddenly into night and night becomes day without there having been a moment of silence around it.

The eternal repetition of corruption and decay, of failing ingenuity and genuine creative power, of inner emptiness and despair, with the patina of a Zeitgeist sunk to the level of the most repulsive pseudoculture: that is what parades its essence, what does its mischief all around the Gedächtniskirche. One would so gladly believe that it is the national elite stealing day and night from the dear Lord on Tauentzien Avenue. It is only the Israelites.

The German people is alien and superfluous here. To speak in the national language is to be nearly conspicuous. Pan-Europe, the *Internationale,* jazz, France and Piscator— those are the watchwords.

"The *Girlfriend,* back issues only ten cents!" cries a resourceful hawker. It does not occur to a single passer-by that this is out of place. It is not out of place at all. The man knows the milieu.

Berlin West is the abscess on this gigantic city of diligence and industry. What they earn in the North they squander in the West. Four million make their daily bread in this stone desert, and over them sit a hundred-thousand drones who squander their diligence, turning it into sin, vice, and corruption.

The Kurfürstendamm raises a howl if anyone ever steps on the toes of these bloodsuckers; then humanity is in danger. The only one not seen suffering there is the professional. And a whole people is borne to the grave with a smile.

This is not the true Berlin. It is elsewhere waiting, hoping, struggling. It is beginning to recognize the Judas who is selling our people for thirty pieces of silver.

The other Berlin is lurking, ready to pounce. A few thousand are working days and nights on end so that sometime the day will arrive. And this day will demolish the abodes of corruption all around the Gedächtniskirche; it will transform them and give them over to a risen people.

The day of judgment! It will be the day of freedom!

235

ERICH KÄSTNER

The Cabaret of the Nameless

First published as "Kabarett der Namenlosen," *Magdeburger General-Anzeiger* (April 7, 1929).

The Cabaret of the Nameless designates the craziest institution one could possible conceive. Naturally it makes its home in Berlin and represents, as the producer of the cabaret (who is not inclined to embellish) boasts, one of the city's typical instances of tastelessness. He answers to the pseudonym Elow and his choleric leisure palace is only open Mondays. The rest of the week the space is given over to real cabaret performances. Only once a week do the artists seat themselves among the audience, from there contributing considerably to the "beautification" of the evening.

The first-time guest is in for a surprise. He expects to make the acquaintance of young talents who want to be discovered and to whom Elow has given the chance to try out their act on the boards. Whoever thinks that, however, discovers himself to be profoundly mistaken. The Cabaret of the Nameless serves a completely different purpose.

The more incompetent and ignorant the poor artist-to-be is, the more welcome he is to the producer. And the more hospitably Elow's public accepts him. For the whole point here in the Cabaret of the Nameless is to laugh oneself silly at stupid and pathological human beings.

The newcomer is seized with extravagant horror at this malicious amusement put on by a resourceful businessman for unhesitating enthusiasts. Sadists find ample nourishment here! Everyone wants to feed on the helpless imbecility of arrogant idiots. Here the public indulges the instincts it otherwise gratifies by visiting insane asylums and attending executions and bullfights. Nothing has changed since Roman gladiators took the field against slaves and Christians. Human beings are astonishingly constant when it comes to vices. The arena has become a cabaret. Armed conflict has turned into recitations. The bulls have become—oxen. Much changes, but the greed for sensation remains the same.

A single extenuating circumstance for this modern form of entertainment can be noted. And it nearly suffices to excuse the tastelessness of this undertaking: the nameless are for the most part such pig-headed beings that they are completely impervious to the ridicule and laughter of the audience. The reason for their immunity borders on the incomprehensible. Whoever has not been there cannot imagine the psychic lives of these victims. They are so occupied by their need to appear on the stage that they notice nothing of what is happening all around them. They recite the saddest stories one could possibly conceive and take no offense at the howling laughter from the audience because they quite simply do not hear it! They achieve a state of rapture that would cause every serious performer to envy them. With utterly vacant smiles playing on their lips they let the terrible merriment of the others completely pass them by, speak their nonsense or hop their dance steadfastly to the end, and are not even disturbed when Elow leaps onto the stage, bids them to pause, and lets the audience vote whether the "performer" should keep dancing or talking, or whether they have had enough. The ancient Romans turned their thumbs down when the vanquished was to be dealt the death blow. Here they scream: "Keep him up there, Elow! He's sooo good! Let him start over from the beginning!"

The less talented the artist in question, the more "natural" it is for the audience to press energetically for his performance to go on. While his face—in truth!—glows with happiness because he gets to be ridiculed again from the start.

Elow takes the stage to supply a kind of compensatory justice by reviling the audience in a fashion that would suffice anywhere else to sow mayhem and murder. Since those he honors with such insults are mostly regulars, no serious discord erupts. That is, unless there is a Bavarian in the audience who takes off his coat and threatens to pay Elow a visit on the stage. But peace is quickly restored—the guests after all are free to abuse the performers, which they do with impressive diligence.

The guests treat Elow roughly. Elow treats his guests roughly. Together they treat the "artists" roughly and take no offense whatever when the latter deliver extremely uninhibited responses. In short, people come here to pull out all the stops and let themselves go, to exempt themselves from internal constraints and behave as impossibly as possible. People unconsciously subject themselves to a psychoanalytic cure here. They are cured of the usual base instincts by allowing them free rein in safe surroundings. Elow is therefore a modern physician attending to Berlin's nervous disorders. . . . To hear him suddenly call oneself an "idiot" means nothing. It is already lucky that it was not much worse. The small room lined with tables from which wine and champagne are being drunk resounds with jokes, insults, and insolence of all sorts. People grow fangs by using them to bite, then return pacified to human society. This is a padded cell for the metropolis! One can rage, claw, and pound without hurting either oneself or others.

The metropolis in its natural form is an inhumane place to be and inhumane means are required for it to be endured. The main thing is that the nameless are as invulnerable as a sword swallower. So it is probably possible after all to absolve this cabaret, just like one excuses dreams in which murderous and shameful acts occur. Such dreams purify people for their doings by the light of day.

236

CURT MORECK

We Will Show You Berlin

First published as "Wir zeigen Ihnen Berlin," in *Führer durch das "lasterhafte" Berlin* (Leipzig: Verlag moderner Stadtführer, 1930).

Curiosity and a hunger for experience drive the people of our time from city to city, country to country, and continent to continent. For most work is obligatory and burdensome. Then they get into a car, board a train, or take their seat on an airplane and put miles between themselves and their everyday lives. They are trying to escape their obligations and recuperate and enjoy themselves.

Favored by the rapid development and perfection of transportation, an industry has put this drive to its own use. It sees in the traveler a welcome and useful object—sometimes to the point of exploitation. Big cities have established an extensive and complicated apparatus for organizing tourist traffic by creating their own visitors' bureaus. And provincial governments are already beginning to entrust tourism ministries with the organization of the tourist trade.

Both parties emerge the winners. For tourists, traveling is made easier, and the tourism industry gets the chance to offer its services. One day the visitors' bureau in Berlin issued the slogan, "A Visit to Berlin for Everyone." Modern advertising operates with the rigor of the categorical imperative. It has adopted a dictatorial tone, the effect of which is obvious. These days one receives commands as to which toothpaste, razor blades, fountain pen, brand of automobile, kind of beer, or holiday resort to choose, and one follows orders imparted with such suggestive power. There is no need to waste thoughts on incidentals. "A Visit to Berlin for Everyone!" The notion has something irresistible about it. Something enticing, promising, and fascinating hovers around the word *Berlin*.

The big questions arise only once one has left the train station. Then things become problematic. Big cities are indefinite promises. They are conglomerations of endless possibilities. They are labyrinths in which the most beautiful streets betray no hint of where they might lead. Tourists stumbling into a big city feel helpless, suddenly overtaken by the fear of passing up something they wanted to see, of missing something that promised an additional pleasure. The true essence of a city is not to be found on the big streets, on the surface, is not to be revealed easily and effortlessly. It wants to be sought after, sensed, dug up. Tourists have to dive into the turbulent whirlpool, surrender to it, but not without returning to themselves once the adventure is over. They have to take a wrong turn, but not without knowing the desired destination. They have to look around with the help of a guide. Without a guide they lose valuable time better devoted to enjoyment. They have, in short, to make use of the experience of others.

Every city has an official and an unofficial side, and it is superfluous to add that the latter is more interesting and more informative of the essence of a city. That which appears so clearly in the light of the arc lamps has a face more like a mask than a physiognomy. The smile it offers is more an appeal to the visitor's purse. It wears the makeup of the coquette, applied too thickly to permit the true features underneath to be recognized. Those who are looking for experiences, who long for adventure, who hope for sensations— they must go into the shadows.

Tourists seeking to travel with pleasure have to become acquainted with both sides of a city, have to coax it into showing its Janus-face. Such people may not content themselves with the surface, but have to venture into the depths. The depths are the more amusing side of life. Only surface and depth together produce the totality.

City officials offer travelers a guide that refers them to a tiring succession of representative sites and curries to the zeal of those who feel an irredeemable loss in passing unknowingly by a monument, building, or locality to which some kind of historical significance is attached. Oh, this historical significance! The landmark of boredom. It is a preservation of the past that amounts to mummified yesterdays. Traveling, however, means experiencing the present in all its intensity.

Intensity is to be experienced only at the vital sites of life, where polar opposites touch, where contradictions become one, where humanity is blended together like a piquant ragout, where the big world lives and the demimonde visits, or where the demimonde lives and the big world visits, and ultimately where the underworld is at home.

A visit to Berlin for everyone! Nighttime Berlin too. And the semi-official. The other side of the city, where the sights are not called out by the witty little comments of the tour-bus guide.

But one does need a guide here as well—here perhaps most of all. Theseus would never have ventured into the labyrinth without Ariadne's thread. And what was the labyrinth compared to Berlin at night, compared to the metropolis of pleasure, equally dazzling whether by light or dark?!

237

SIEGFRIED KRACAUER

Girls and Crisis

First published as "Girls und Krise," *Frankfurter Zeitung* (May 26, 1931).

A few days ago at the Scala I saw the Alfred Jackson Girls, who, the program indicated, had just returned from a foreign tour. It is not really sixteen girls that the troupe consists of (I may be mistaken in the number); rather every girl's leg is one thirty-secondth of a marvelously precise apparatus. Anyone who has ever taken a pleasure trip on a steamer has surely at some time or other leaned over the inside railing, his back to one or another sea, and looked down onto the ship's shining engines. The girls' poses recall the regular play of the pistons. They are not so much of military precision as they correspond in some other way to the ideal of the machine. A button is pressed and the girl contraption cranks into motion, performing impressively at thirty-two horsepower. All the parts begin to roll, the waves fall into their cycles. And while the machine stamps, shakes, and roars like a sawmill or a locomotive, a smile drips a steady supply of oil onto the joints so that the cogs do not suddenly fail. Finally an inaudible signal brings the mechanical action to a stop, and the dead whole automatically decomposes itself into its living parts. A process of destruction that leaves behind the sad feeling that the parts are wholly incapable of existing further on their own.

The effect achieved by these nice girls has to be termed ghostly. They seem like a remnant from long-lost years rising now at an inopportune time, their dances montages emptied of a former meaning. What is it that they, like an image become flesh, embody? The *functioning* of a flourishing economy. After the war, in that era in which prosperity appeared unlimited and one retained scarcely a memory of unemployment—in that era the girls were mass-produced in the USA and exported in waves to Europe. They were not merely American products but a demonstration at the same time of the vastness of American production. I clearly recall seeing such troupes in the season of their fame. When they formed themselves into an undulating snake, they delivered a radiant illustration of the virtues of the conveyer belt; when they stepped to a rapid beat, it sounded like "business, business"; when they raised their legs with mathematical precision above their heads, they joyfully affirmed the progress of rationalization; and when they continually repeated the same maneuver, never breaking ranks, one had visions of an unbroken chain of automobiles gliding from the factory into the world and the feeling of knowing that there was no end to prosperity. Their faces were made up with an optimism that nipped all resistance to economic development in the bud, and the little cries of pleasure, issued in a precisely calculated rhythm, gave ever renewed praise to the splendors of existence in such circumstances. They rolled uniformly over the boards, arousing just enough sensuousness to allow the audience to relax from the cares of business, exploiting with unflagging zeal the very boom they themselves were representing.

That has all changed today. One market crash after the other has rocked the economy, and the crisis has long since given the lie to one's faith in never-ending prosperity. One no longer believes them, the rosy Jackson Girls! They continue to attend just as meticulously to their abstract trade, but the happy dreams they are supposed to inspire have been revealed for years now as foolish illusions. And though they still swing their legs as energetically as before, they come, a phantom, from a yesterday dead and gone. Their smiles are those of a mask; their confidence a leftover from better days; their precision a mockery of the difficulties in which the very powers they call to mind now find themselves. Though they might continue to snake and wave as if nothing has happened—the crisis to which so many factories have fallen victim has also silently liquidated this machinery of girls.

238

FRIEDRICH HOLLAENDER

Cabaret

First published as "Cabaret," *Die Weltbühne* 28, no. 5 (February 2, 1932), 169–171.

The cabaret—which those terribly serious, bearded sorts are fond of dismissing as the undernourished half-sister of the verbal arts—is more like the happy child of an eleventh muse, conceived in an easy-going love affair with theater, variety shows, and political tribunals. Though no less serious than its three fathers whose sharpest criticism constantly reaffirms its mission, cabaret would nevertheless like to appear more lucid and less weighty but also more unruly. This might be explained by the fact that it often falls into the hands of unqualified pedagogues who from time to time, darken its path with their own frivolous behavior. Thus it happens that the cabaret is always being dragged down from its conquered heights, from its jovial perspective, and sometimes even descends to a level beneath that of the coasters under the beer glasses on the bar.

But we are speaking of restrained cabaret, which, true to its ironic mission, floats like a soap bubble above the things in our difficult-to-live life, reflecting them wickedly or tenderly, now using the distorting effects of color and light to render their value overwhelming, now screwing them back down to the diminutive status that is in truth their due. In Copenhagen "cabarets" mean the colorful bowls in the restaurants offering the hurried palate manifold stimuli in concentrated form. Where do connoisseurs begin? How can they secure for themselves a taste of all of them? And before they get to the enchanting taste of all these sophisticated little morsels, the bowls are empty, leaving behind, aside from a symphony of appetizing aromas, that splendid, not quite satisfied desire without which we would not be able to live.

That is the secret of the cabaret: the aphoristic novel, the burst of a short-lived drama, the two-minute song of our times, the sweetness of love, the heartbeat of unemployment, the bewilderment of politics, the standard-issue uniform of cheap amusement. All without the drain of five acts, three volumes, a thousand kilos of psychology—in the form of a pill, which might be bitter into the bargain. Who has ever seen enough of a fireworks display?

The laws inherent to this compressed form demand not only the rapid effect of the arresting word and the quickly understood gesture, they call imperiously for music that is provocative, short, revealing, essential; in its rhythm and coloring, in its melody and drama, the music must explode in a lightning flash and can permit itself no time to develop and build; the course of its burning away must be the moment of its birth. Its mood has to be present in the first beats. In the serious *chanson* the potential lies in the tightly arched bow of an instantaneous, dramatic flash; in the cheerful *chanson,* in the lethal precision of its pause (which must be one with the verbal joke), the way an arrow fired at the nearest target hits its mark. In taste it obediently follows the fashion of its time; the bourgeois romanticism proper to [Ernst von] Wolzogen's variety show would be too cheap for the modern political cabaret. The fashionable horror music played by the eleven hangmen in Wolzogen's time was enough to tighten the throats of the listeners, who were the delinquents of the piece, but now that music causes nothing but a tickle. Only one person from that time wrote music that would still be adequate for today's cabaret: [Jean] Bruyant in Paris, whose stomping, revolutionary rhythms excited the crowd to forsake song for action. For—and this should be a further law of the cabaret—within it there lies an aggressiveness that will forever distinguish it from all operatic, choral, and symphonic music. Cabaret that fails to take pleasure in the attack, that lacks the taste for battle, is not fit to live. It is the traditional battlefield on which the only proper weapons—sharp words and loaded music—are capable of beating into retreat those cast of iron. They are stronger and more successful than anything in the much-praised contemporary theater, that usually sober forum of dry theory that nearly always lacks the seductive magic of the ironic or forceful music needed to achieve a gratifying effect. The effect achieved by the contrasting moods in cabaret is truly not to be outdone; if one considers that eight-hundred people out of a thousand regard cabaret as an innocent amusement and attend it in this spirit, then it becomes possible to assess the healthy jolt to the psyche that a socially minded *chanson* fired off between two amusing parodies can occasion. Under the cover of an evening's relaxing entertainment, cabaret, like nothing else, suddenly dispenses a poison cookie. Suggestively administered and hastily swallowed, its effect reaches far beyond the harmless evening to make otherwise placid blood boil and inspire a sluggish brain to think. Music as seductress—it always succeeds whenever it has magic in its gut: as a hymn in church, as a military march before the campaign, as an indictment from the podium.

That is a profile of music in the cabaret. The joke is different, and a few words should be said about that. I do not mean the cheap shot as an end in itself, the musical chestnut that wrings a laugh from the listener who later recalls it in shame. I mean rather the regal joke, which, in affectionate derision of all-too-human frailties, returns the listener to a consciousness of his strength. That will make him happy on the journey home. Everyone who, in this age of fashions and the record book, has occasionally found himself being more snobbish than a snob, more knowing than an ignorant know-it-all, more beloved than Goethe's Werther, will see his hobby-horse put mercilessly through its paces—with himself in the saddle.

Now the music—if its caricatures of people, things, habits, and the commonplaces of daily life are to hit their mark with split-second timing—has to be superlative; that is, it has to bear within itself and bring to expression the sickest of the sick, the emptiest babble of the babbler, the most perverse of the perverse, the stingiest of the stingy. If it chooses, for example, the stingy Scot of popular anecdotes for its focus, it would best invent a model one-note melody. For a modish gigolo the musician ought to create an exaggerated tango, the supreme stylization of mock slow-motion. If a farcical Gandhi appears on the stage, the music must immediately become more Indian than real Indian music; once again, the most emancipated of the emancipated. To take the Gandhi example to its conclusion, one might conceive a contrapuntal battle between this "guaranteed genuine Indian hermit music" and the English national anthem. Those in the know will grin, and the others relish it just the same. But I am not talking here about unintelligent onomatopoeia. A satire of the automobile craze does not gain a musical dimension from a couple of cheap honking effects; the music must contain within it eighty miles per hour and high-test gasoline.

23
Music for Use: *Gebrauchsmusik* and Opera

MOST AVANT-GARDE ARTISTS of the 1920s felt the need to justify their activities vis-à-vis a society that was increasingly dominated by industrial production and its operating principles of rationality, practicability, and functionality. New Objectivity was the term given to a comprehensive realignment of all arts in relation to society. Music too experienced a legitimation crisis and was subjected to the litmus test of usefulness. *Gebrauchsmusik* refers to music with a practical purpose, such as compositions for film or radio and for dance halls, schools, or communities. "Utilitarian" music is, as Hanns Gutman hoped, only provisionally set against "artistic" music. Composers of the young generation, Kurt Weill, Ernst Krenek, and Paul Hindemith, addressed the "crisis of the opera" by closing the gap between light and serious music. Their notion of *Zeitoper* (topical, contemporary opera) was charged with the energies drawn from modern urban life; musically the new opera was influenced by American jazz, which became the secret center for musical innovation in the second half of the 1920s. American jazz orchestras (Sam Wooding's and Paul Whiteman's, among others) toured Germany during 1925–1926 and, thanks to phonograph and radio, American jazz could soon be heard across the republic.

In 1925, Alban Berg's opera *Wozzeck* marked a breakthrough in the history of opera in its renunciation of tonality and its social criticism; the production encountered strong resistance and nearly caused riots among opera-goers unaccustomed to atonality. Only a year or two later *Wozzeck* as well as numerous other operas with modern themes found wide acceptance. Max Brand's opera *Machinist Hopkins* explored technology, George Antheil's *Trans-Atlantic* was set on an oceanliner, and Krenek's 1927 jazz opera, *Jonny spielt auf* (Jonny Strikes up the Band) dealt with a love triangle between the black jazz violinist Jonny, the white composer Max, and the singer Anita. Although several of the modern operas were staged in Dresden, Leipzig, and Darmstadt, most premiered in Berlin's three opera houses where there was an abundance of talent. Ferruccio Busoni, Arnold Schoenberg, Franz Schreker, and Hindemith taught at the Music College, Wilhelm Furtwängler conducted the Berlin Philharmonic from 1922 on, and Otto Klemperer became director of the Oper am Platz der Republik, commonly known as the Kroll Oper. It was there between 1927 and 1931 that opera history was made.

According to a plan at once populist and avant-garde, season tickets to the opera were sold through the Volksbühne, a socialist theater, for performances that quickly acquired the reputation as brilliant not only in their modern reinterpretation of traditional works by Beethoven and Mozart, but also in their daring constructivist stagings of contemporary pieces that ranged from Igor Stravinsky's *L'Histoire du Soldat* to Schoenberg's *Erwartung* and *Die glückliche Hand*. The Kroll Oper became the target of constant right-wing attacks because of its radical experimentation, its social criticism, and its so-called cultural bolshevism. All major artists, Hindemith and Gropius among others, rallied in its support—in vain. It closed in 1931.

In an essay with the fashionable English title "Short Operas," the music critic H. H. Stuckenschmidt argued in 1928 for a concentrated form of opera that would be more in tune with the short attention span of contemporary audiences. The essay, referring to the Festival of German Chamber Music at Baden-Baden in 1927, discussed the four one-act chamber operas by Weill, Hindemith, Darius Milhaud, and Ernst Toch, which were performed for the first time. Other works presented at this festival included Hindemith's accompaniment to *Krazy Kat at the Circus,* an animated cartoon film. This was genuine Gebrauchsmusik not only in its practical use as film music, but also in its disregard of traditional barriers between high and low culture. Gebrauchsmusik, as Hanns Eisler argued in 1932, also occupied a central role in proletarian culture as an impetus for fighting songs and choral pieces sung by a collective.

The question of the public loomed large in all discussions about the social functions of modern music, as the tone of resignation in Schoenberg's statement of 1930 about his audience illustrates. In contrast, Kurt Weill managed to score both a critical and popular success with the music he composed for Brecht's *The Threepenny Opera,* which had its premiere in 1928. As Theodor W. Adorno remarked later, the popularity of *The Threepenny Opera* rested on a misunderstanding—assuming, of course, that mass appeal and avant-garde music are mutually exclusive. Still, as an "opera for beggars," *The Threepenny Opera* provided an example of an art form that was no longer elitist in its subject matter or its implied audience. And as a satire about capitalism's hypocritical use and reversal of all traditional bourgeois values (love, friendship, trust, religion, justice, and so on), it captured the hard-boiled and alluring street-smart cynicism that today is often associated with the Weimar Republic.

When Brecht collaborated with Weill in 1930 on another, even more radical epic opera, entitled *The Rise and Fall of the City of Mahagonny,* the reaction to its anticapitalist ideology and against the "cultural bolshevism" of its avant-garde aesthetics turned violent. Riots orchestrated by Nazis broke out during its March 4, 1930, premiere at the Leipzig Opera and during subsequent performances in Frankfurt and Berlin. Adorno, not yet associated with the Frankfurt Institute of Social Research, wrote an exhaustive review of *Mahagonny*'s radical aesthetics, which also illustrates the high level of music criticism in the Weimar Republic.

239

FRANK WARSCHAUER

Jazz: On Whiteman's Berlin Concerts

First published as "Jazz. Zu Whitemans Berliner Konzerten," *Vossische Zeitung* (June 19, 1926).

Jazz: the most entertaining and vital phenomenon in contemporary music. Moreover, the only musical mass movement. Not only in America but everywhere. This might be regretted by those who oppose it in principle, but it is not to be denied.

Whatever is current and vital just now often defines a new category. The old standards are not adequate to assess it. Thus it is with film and also with jazz (it is no accident that they have to be mentioned together). The same question always arises: whether it is art or could some day become art. Answer: the question either cannot be answered at all or at least not immediately. It is rather the last thing that can be determined. It bears repeating that the method usually applied in Germany is pernicious: to point a pistol at every new phenomenon with the demand that it reveal its ultimate aim and pass the test of whether it can be designated art!

In any case, Paul Whiteman, the most prominent figure in American jazz, tends quite clearly to take jazz into the sphere of its own established absolute values, that is, into the sphere of art. He is the first to have liberated jazz from its functional and utilitarian meaning. The external symbol of this change is that he has taken it out of hotels and dance halls and introduced it into concert halls. In the winter of 1924, Whiteman made this leap with the first great jazz concert, in New York at Aeolian Hall and then repeated in many other cities. His success, first in America and England, showed him that the presentation of jazz in the concert hall is capable of impressing a great many people who could not otherwise be reached.

Whiteman's real creation is his orchestra. He has cultivated, refined, and expanded the jazz orchestra in a way unknown until now. To the familiar sound of a conventional dance orchestra he added a full-scale string ensemble, thereby paving the way for the development of jazz symphonic forms on the one hand and jazz operas and jazz ballets on the other. Such works have in fact been produced recently in America.

If the intention of forging a connection to prestigious European musical forms is evident here, it is also true that the figures primarily responsible for both the origins of jazz and the boldest departures within it (which are defined by their own internal laws and independent of prior models) are the American Negroes. They have an extraordinarily original sense of rhythm, anchored deep in their nature, but also, remarkably, of melody. This combination also stimulates formal development intensively, which proceeds in jazz from an angle altogether unfamiliar to the European: namely, the angle of rhythm instead of harmony and melody, the dual basis of all European musical forms for hundreds of years. To appreciate this one must listen to a Negro orchestra; despite the presence of a strong reciprocal influence, Negroes and whites never play together—they remain strictly separated by American racial prejudices.

Jazz in America has become its own branch of music. There are a great many orchestras, some—a characteristic fact—under the directorship of amateurs. The number of saxophone players alone supposedly totals 400,000! There are also many schools and textbooks devoted to innovative musical techniques for playing jazz on every kind of appropriate instrument. Thus, for example, Zez Confrey, the composer of very important piano pieces (such as "Kitten on the Keys"), has defined in a textbook devoted to the characteristic forms of jazz piano the figurations making for embellishment and variation, the so-called breaks, the way bass strings should be played, and more; he also supplied an introduction to the corresponding variations. For this belongs among the most interesting facts of this new musical world: that it not only gives every individual musician a great deal of freedom, but actually demands ingenuity and creativity.

Whiteman once wrote that jazz is Henry Ford and the Ku Klux Klan and the skyscrapers and prohibition and *Babbitt*—the whole of contemporary American reality. It is more than that: it is a piece of the present of all countries and perhaps the one that is most characteristic. Jazz, filled with the youthful energy of America, is the pregnant outburst of a changed, untragic feel for life, and what it sings is a different *Lied von der Erde,* the song of a new generation.

240

KURT WEILL

Zeitoper

First published as "Zeitoper" in *Melos* 7 (March 1928), 106–108.

Most Respected Professor:

You ask me to take a position concerning the concept of Zeitoper from the standpoint of the opera composer, and I am able to respond to this invitation because you added that you find this concept embodied "most thoroughly" in my most recent works. For only thus does the clear "one-sidedness" of my point of view excuse itself.

This word Zeitoper has also had to suffer the unfortunate transformation from concept to slogan. It was just as hastily coined as it was incorrectly employed. This hasty, premature, incorrect use of a concept is not absolutely detrimental; it is perhaps necessary because it might allow a subsequent application to appear with the kind of naturalness that creates the correct conditions for its public acceptance. The Zeitstück, as we have come to know it in recent years, moved superficial manifestations of life in our time onto center stage. People took the "tempo of the twentieth century," combined it with the much-praised "rhythm of our time," and, for the rest, limited themselves to the representation of sentiments of past generations. The powerful stimuli that the process of transplanting accompanying phenomena of daily life to the stage conceals should not be underestimated. But they are stimuli, nothing more. Man in our time looks different, and what drives him outwardly and motivates him inwardly should not be so portrayed for the mere purpose of being current at any price or in the interest of topicality that is valid only for the narrowest time span of its creation.

In recent years the task of Zeittheater, with which most of us have been concerned in one form or another, has been to technicalize the stage and to broaden theater in its form, process, and sentiments. This task has been realized, and the means have quickly been made into an end in themselves. Only now, after the hitherto existing Zeittheater has freed the material, have we reached the unintentionality, the self-evident level where we can represent the world view that we see—each perhaps in his own way—no longer as a photograph but as a mirror reflection. In most cases it will be a concave or convex mirror, which reproduces life in a magnification or reduction proportionate to how it appears in reality.

You will ask whether this definition of Zeitoper in terms of Zeitspiegel (mirror of the times) does not bring with it a limitation in choice of subjects. But note that the intellectual (*geistigen*) and emotional (*seelischen*) matrices that music can depict are quite narrowly restricted already and have remained fundamentally the same for centuries. Only the object and the methods of application have changed. The human quality that music can articulate has remained the same. But man has changed: he reacts differently to external influences, events, and emotions.

The new type of man emerging on all fronts today does not accept much of what appeared significant to preceding generations as a given. Therefore the proportions between man and the things within and around him must also appear to shift in art that aims at a presentation of this type. However, this new type of man whom we see results in the possibility of again basing opera upon great, comprehensive, generally valid themes that no longer deal with private ideas and emotions but with larger relationships. In that context the intellectual and human fundamentals of the new type of man may make use of any major theme. Stravinsky's *Oedipus Rex* is no less a mirror of our time than, for example, Chaplin's *The Gold Rush*. But I am convinced that our era can also articulate major themes if one views it from the standpoint of a certain attitude. Yet the pure theater of opinion can find its application for opera (likewise for drama) only if it does not appear as proclamation of a trend, but if it instead gives the reflection of a world-picture from the viewpoint of an encompassing, enduring idea. Without a doubt, opera's treatment of great ideas of our time can result initially only from the collaboration of a musician with one of the representatives of literature who has at least an equivalent standing. The often expressed fear that such a collaboration with worthy literary figures could bring music into a dependent, subservient, or only equal relationship to the text is completely unfounded. For the more powerful the writer, the more he is able to adapt himself to music, and so much the more is he stimulated to create genuine poetry for music. (May I inform you that I have found in my present close collaboration with Brecht the feasibility of constructing a libretto whose total plan and scenario has been worked out together in all details, word for word, according to musical considerations.) In other respects, I believe that the collective conception that is entering the theater today, especially in opera, in which it always played a role, will become more prominent again.

In opera great subjects demand a great form for their representation. The broader and more significant the occasions for making music become, the greater the possibilities for the development of music in opera. The new operatic theater that is being generated today has epic character. It does not propose to describe but to report. It no longer proposes to form its plot according to moments of suspenseful tension but to tell about man, his actions, and what compels him to commit them. Music in the new operatic theater renounces pumping up the action from within, glazing over the transitions, supplying the background for events, and stirring up passions. It goes its own vast, peaceful way; it begins only at the static moments of the plot, and it can therefore preserve its absolute *concertante* character (if it hits upon the right subject matter). Since the narrative form never permits the spectator to be in suspense or uncertainty over the stage events, music can reserve for itself its own independent, purely musical effect. The sole prerequisite for such an uninhibited musical realization in opera is that music must naturally be "theater music" (in the Mozartean sense) in its innermost essence in order to be able to achieve a complete liberation from the stresses of the stage.

As we have seen, this altered fundamental attitude can lead to a junction with the form of the oratorio. It can also fundamentally recreate the genre of opera. But then it must fall in line with that development evident in all artistic areas which today proclaims the end of the socially exclusive, "aristocratic" art. And if through our work we ourselves thoroughly project the form of our audience, then we see the simple, naïve, unassuming and traditionless listeners who, trained by work, sport, and technical skill, bring along their healthy sense of fun and seriousness, good and bad, old and new.

Yours truly,
Kurt Weill

241

H. H. STUCKENSCHMIDT

Short Operas

First published as "Short Operas," *Musikblätter des Anbruch* 10, no. 6 (June–July 1928), 204–207.

I

The twentieth-century way of life displays a tendency toward pressure in all areas, a tendency to economize space, time, and nerves. Conciseness is the spice not only of wit; we have, as every child knows, no time to waste. Telegraph, telephone, automobile, subways all see to it that not a minute is squandered. But do they in fact? Or is the economy they suggest only a hint, a momentary thrill of superiority over temporary obstacles? No matter; savings are made everywhere. Our existence is split more and more into tiny and still tinier units of time, punctiliously filled up and made to serve their assigned purpose. We no longer manage the kind of concentration our parents devoted to endless intellectual pleasures; we count not in years but in quarter hours. Tempo, tempo! (Ah, the mind is still more nimble than a radio wave!) We work to get ahead of the succession of hours.

The press was the first to recognize this psychological tendency. In the evening it floods us with the following day's morning news; we can die on the thirty-first with the newspaper from the first in our pocket. It was also the press that first understood the necessity of not occupying our minds for longer than five minutes with any single bit of material. It invented, in America of course, the ingenious principle of the thirty-line feuilleton and short stories. The note, the shorthand memo, the gloss triumphant!

But we wanted to speak of short operas. [. . .]

II

It is difficult for the contemporary listener to endure an opera longer than three hours. One has to know a considerable amount about the musical details of something like *Parsifal* or the *Rheingold* to be able to enjoy it without getting tired.

Consider the kinds of art that have achieved the greatest popularity today. The operetta seems meanwhile to have been exhausted; it has been years since a product of this type has won worldwide acclaim. Notable on the contrary is the increasing favor bestowed upon the revue—not indeed a product of recent times as an art form, but it achieved its ultimate form in our day. And what are its formal characteristics? Change, a plenitude of plots, short scenes! The same principles dictate the structure of another modern art form: the film. Here we have the distinct antithesis to Wagner's ideology. And it is precisely the concrete formulations of this antithesis that draw the masses in, fill the box-office coffers, and have monopolized the world's attention.

(Let us not fool ourselves. Theater, even operatic theater, is a business. Opera knows only a single dogma, that of the effect!)

III

Theatrical directors harbor a traditional aversion to one-act plays. It was still justified a few years ago. But it appears that here as well taste is changing, that it has quite likely already changed.

The first short operas of world-renown were created more than thirty years ago. [Pietro] Mascagni wrote *Cavalleria* in 1890; two years later [Ruggiero] Leoncavallo wrote *Bajazzo*. Aside from [Giacomo] Puccini, no one has written any more successful operas. Richard Strauss's *Salome* and *Electra* (one-act, though still requiring an entire evening) are not really typical examples. Nevertheless, there is still Leo Blech and his much-performed *Versiegelt* that might be mentioned.

The moderns were the first to begin seriously to cultivate the principle of the short opera. Here as well Arnold Schoenberg's prophetic genius foresaw what the future would demand. His only two operas, the one-act *Erwartung* and *Die glückliche Hand,* were written in 1910. Schoenberg regarded the brevity of such operas as a psychological and artistic challenge. In *Erwartung,* the challenge was the representation of psychic states, how they inspire extremes of excitation—therefore dilation, the analysis of a moment. In *Die glückliche Hand* it was just the opposite: the compression of a person's fate into a couple of decisive moments that amount to a synthetic depiction of a life.

Stravinsky, in *Histoire du Soldat* and *Renard,* created a new formal type standing between revue, opera, and ballet, the style of which is defined by its incorporation of brevity and rapid-fire repartee.

Those, then, were the experiments. What remained was their full realization: the genuine short opera that is exclusively opera, that is, the successful compression of lively action into the most concise time frame without any sacrifice of effect. Then there appeared Paul Hindemith's three one-act operas: *Sancta Susanna; Mörder, Hoffnung der Frauen;* and *Das Nusch-Nuschi.* Success, as for all of Hindemith's stage works, was denied them. But the transition was there, the formal possibility identified.

Among the moderns Kurt Weill achieved the first significant success in one-act opera with his *Protagonist.* Here the problem was finally solved; the musical arrangement, the arioso style of the choral parts, and the unerring sureness of the excellent libretto by Georg Kaiser were suggestive and convincing in their effect. Weill then pushed the genre further. *Royal Palace* initially met a somewhat lukewarm reception, but it cleverly and very fruitfully transferred the devices of the revue into the area of opera. The counterpart to *Protagonist* came in *Der Zar läßt sich photographieren.* And that was a success.

In the meantime, Baden-Baden recognized the problem and addressed it: Hindemith, Milhaud, Toch, and Weill each presented an operatic epigram in the summer of 1927. Weill achieved the strongest effect with his choral play *Mahagonny* (with Bert Brecht). The ice had been broken: the form arrived at eminent perfection in the next few years.

Following the worldwide success of *Jonny* (in which, incidentally, the arrangement of short scenes reminiscent of the revue should be noted), Ernst Krenek wrote three one-act operas that have just met with triumph in Wiesbaden. Most noteworthy in these works is their relation to Puccini, who incidentally crowned his life's work with the overwhelmingly splendid and inspired *Gianni Schicchi*—a one-act opera.

The young French composers, headed by Milhaud, are discussing new types of short operas. Short ballets, most recently Wilhelm Grosz's *Baby in der Bar,* are becoming increasingly popular.

IV

Has the effect of the traditional long opera been exhausted? There is some truth to this assumption, in particular the somewhat questionable success Strauss achieved with *Ägyptische Helena.* Musical arrangements have also been transformed. The young composers of our time appear unable to bear endlessly symphonic treatments. Perhaps it is no accident that gramophone records, with their limited playing time of a maximum of six minutes, established themselves so surprisingly. Musical accompaniments to film, with an average length of two minutes, also conform to the modern principle of compression.

A theoretical problem arises, that of musical time. Music is capable of lengthening or shortening the duration of a minute in our perception. But an investigation of the extent to which musical time plays a conscious role in modern compositions must be attempted another time.

One thing is certain: the short opera in one act has won a place for itself; the modern listener has pronounced it good.

Theatrical directors will have to revise their prejudices.

242

KURT WEILL

Correspondence about *The Threepenny Opera*

First published as "Korrespondenz über Dreigroschenoper," *Musikblätter des Anbruch*, no. 11 (January 11, 1929), 24–25.

Dear Mr. Weill:

The sensational success of *The Threepenny Opera,* which allows a work of totally novel style that points to the future to become suddenly a box-office hit, most gratifyingly confirms the prophecies that were repeatedly expressed in these pages. The new popular opera-operetta, which draws the proper inference from the artistic and social assumptions of the present, has succeeded in this beautiful, exemplary model. You have the advantage of practical results and demonstrated success over our sociological and aesthetic speculations, may we ask you to comment theoretically in these pages about the course that has been traveled.

The editor of Anbruch

Dear *Anbruch:*

Thank you for your letter and I confess to you that it is not entirely easy for me to provide a theoretical basis for what I have done in *The Threepenny Opera*. But I will gladly say something about the path that we, Brecht and I, followed in this work and along which we contemplate continuing.

In your letter you allude to the sociological significance of *The Threepenny Opera*. Indeed, the success of our play proves that the creation and success of this new genre came not only at the correct moment for the artistic situation but also that the public almost seemed to be waiting for a renewal of a privileged theatrical genre. I do not know if our genre will now replace operetta. Since even Goethe has now appeared on earth again through the medium of an operetta tenor, why should a further succession of historical or at least princely personalities not utter their tragic outcry at the conclusion of the second act? That is easily settled: I do not believe that this is an opening that is worth filling. More important for all of us is the fact that here a breakthrough into a consumer industry, which until now had been reserved for a completely different type of composer or writer, has been accomplished for the first time. With *The Threepenny Opera* we addressed a public that either did not know us at all or denied us the capability of interesting a circle of listeners that far exceeded the boundaries of the musical and operatic audience.

Seen from this standpoint, *The Threepenny Opera* appears to join a movement which today touches almost every young musician. The problem of the art-for-art's-sake standpoint, the renunciation of individualistic artistic principles, the film-music ideas, the connection with the youth-music movement, all those that stand together for the simplification of the means of musical expression—those are all steps along the same path.

Only opera remains in its "splendid isolation." The operatic audience still represents a closed group of people who seemingly stand apart from the larger theatrical audience. Opera and theater are still treated as two entirely distinct concepts. In new operas a dramatic technique is still employed, a language is still spoken, and subjects are still treated that would be completely unthinkable in the contemporary theater. Again and again one must hear: "Maybe that is possible in theater, but not in opera!" Opera was established as an aristocratic genre, and everything called the "tradition of opera" emphasizes that basic, socially exclusive nature of this genre. But even today in the whole world there is no artistic form of a more pronounced socially exclusive bearing. The theater in particular has decisively turned in a direction that one can characterize accurately as socially formative. If the frame of opera does not bear an approximation of that kind to the contemporary theater, quite certainly that framework must be exploded.

Only in this way can one understand that the fundamental character of almost all genuinely worthwhile operatic endeavors of recent years has been purely destructive. A reconstruction was possible in *The Threepenny Opera* since the possibility existed to start fresh here. What we wished to make was the prototype of opera. The question emerges anew with each musical stage work: how is music, above all, how is song possible in the theater at all? This question was resolved here in the most primitive manner. I had a realistic plot. Therefore I had to set the music against it, since I reject the notion that music has any possibility of realistic effect. Thus either the action was interrupted in order to make music, or it was led deliberately to a certain point where it simply had to be sung. Moreover this piece offered us the opportunity to posit the concept of opera as the theme of a theatrical evening. Right at the beginning of the play this was made clear to the audience: "This evening you will see an opera for beggars. Because this opera was conceived so splendidly, as only beggars would imagine it, and because it still had to be so cheap that beggars could afford it, it is called *The Threepenny Opera.*" Therefore, the last "Dreigro- schenfinale" is by no means a parody; rather, here the concept of opera was applied directly to the resolution of conflict, that is, as an action-structuring element. Therefore it had to be constructed in its purest, most fundamental form.

This reversion to a primitive operatic form brought with it a far-reaching simplification of musical language. It was a question of writing music that could be sung by actors, that is, by musical amateurs. But what appeared initially to be a limitation proved to be a huge enrichment in the course of the work. Only the realization of a comprehensible, palpable melodic structure made possible what was achieved in *The Threepenny Opera,* the creation of a new genre of musical theater.

Yours truly,
Kurt Weill

243

PAUL HINDEMITH AND WALTER GROPIUS

For the Renewal of Opera

First published as "Für die Erneuerung der Oper," *Berliner Börsen-Courier* (February 19, 1929).

PAUL HINDEMITH: *THE NECESSITY OF EXPERIMENTATION*

Klemperer and his theater are indispensible to us. Our musical life, which is not bursting with health, needs a place where attempts to create a new foundation for opera can be carried out. Musicians need a theater like this one, which, like no other theater in the world, offers them the guarantee that their pieces will be performed just as they want them to be. Never before has the will of large masses been responsible for creating a new style. Early Italian operatic theater and the orchestra of the Mannheim school—the foundations of our contemporary operatic and symphonic music—were *experimental institutions.* In this regard they were similar to today's Russian state theaters, to whose productions, insofar as one has had the opportunity of seeing them here, even reactionary viewers can scarcely object. The campaign against Klemperer and his theater should not be taken too seriously. Naturally what is attempted there violates the taste of many; but one occasionally sees performances there—like Stravinsky's *Oedipus*—for which it would have been worthwhile to travel from America to Berlin. Klemperer should be given time and the opportunity to attempt what is important for us today or could become important for us tomorrow. Short-sightedness will surely exact its price: if Klemperer goes today, tomorrow in an ambitious provincial city a theater will be established that undertakes the same experiments and in three years we will welcome them here in Berlin as a great innovation.

WALTER GROPIUS: *ANTI-DEVELOPMENTAL FORCES*

I recently had the experience of seeing how the petit-bourgeois public in a provincial city, with the stubborn persistance of stupidity, drove an important orchestral conductor from his position because he took pains *to introduce his listeners to pieces by living composers* alongside classical works of music. The blame for the disgraceful persecution thus lay with the usual spiritual indolence of small minds, which the authorities were not able to overcome.

What happened at the Staatsoper am Platz der Republik? For the same reasons as in that provincial city, people attempted to drive out Otto Klemperer, the important conductor and great representative of intelligent Germany.

This indolence, always resistant to the unsettling nature of the vital, must be accepted as a natural factor that remains constant given the average weakness of human beings, and so it is in Berlin as well. Critical for the intellectual life of a city, however, is whether the responsible cultural and political leaders overcome or support the indolence of the majority. We are at present experiencing a wave of cultural reaction that is dangerous because a system is concealed behind it. One hopes that the authorities and the intellectual elite of Berlin, whose task above all it is to see that contemporary works in addition to the classics are presented in the public theaters, will be able to protect the State Opera from these regressive forces.

244

HANNS GUTMAN

Music for Use

First published as "Gebrauchsmusik," *Melos* 8 (1929), 74–78.

The frequent use of this apt catchword suffices to expose a questionable state of affairs. For to speak of utilitarian music as a particular type is to presuppose the existence of another kind of music, the characteristic of which is that it cannot be used. And so it goes. But it should not be so.

We will not touch upon the difficult question of whether it is permissible for art to be devoted to a purpose. The penetration of politics into the artistic sphere, evidenced by Erwin Piscator and his admittedly fascinating directorial accomplishments, has lent the question a heightened relevance in Germany. Nevertheless it is indisputable that to call an artwork useless is to condemn it. Purpose thus appears to be a criterion after all. And anyone who looks back into past epochs notes that the purpose, even the external occasion, of a work has frequently played a role in artistic creation. Very often the occasion was extremely concrete, one obviously related to the problem of the minimum living wage.

For the image of the divine artist working in isolation, who for no obvious reason is suddenly overcome by a spirit dictating a symphony to him—the oleograph of a genius wrestling with the stars—is an invention of the nineteenth century. Earlier one composed upon receiving a commission. Whoever had talent was always inspired. The commission supplied the creator with a stimulus. If he had none, or did not at least see a possibility of having his work financed, then he did not write it. And, as one expected a cobbler would punctually deliver the shoes he had been charged with repairing, the commissioner of a violin sonata could justifiably expect the composer to finish his manuscript by the appointed date—as long as he was not a cobbler. J. S. Bach, with the conscientiousness of a respectable artisan, wrote his works in conformity with the requirements of the ecclesiastical year. And even in Mozart's time the idea of composing a piece out of the blue without any occasion for it would have been completely absurd. One can read in his letters how long he cherished the desire of working on a large-scale opera without ever fulfilling it, because he saw no chance of it being performed. He once explained to Baron Dalberg: "As for your opera, I assure you that I would sincerely like to set it to music. But indeed I could not undertake this work for 25 louis d'or, as you yourself would admit; for it, calculated quite modestly, is twice as much work as a monodrama . . ." Such were the restrictive circumstances from which the music of the eighteenth century emerged. It was not the worse for that reason.

The revolution—like so many transformations—occurs in the person of Beethoven. As stylistically he at first speaks the language of his environment, so is he bound to it sociologically as a young man. He receives commissions and carries them out. Soon enough, however, he throws off the customary fetters; he composes whenever and as long as he desires. Concern with the possibility of execution and the probability of performance no longer burdens him. His statement that he could waste thought on a single miserable violin when the spirit came over him is well known. The development quickly progresses in Beethoven himself. Since he wants to express his extremely individual ego in music, he becomes self-willed to the point of incomprehensibility. The later works, the last sonatas and quartets, have lost nearly all contact with their contemporary public; no one plays them at all because they are considered absurd. He cannot change; he writes as he must. If no one understands him today, then someone will tomorrow.

That is quite obviously the point at which the unhappy distinction between artistic music and utilitarian music sets in. One is justified in claiming that no such separation existed previously. Palestrina's masses, [J. S.] Bach's cantatas, Mozart's sonatas are utilitarian music without therefore being any less artistic. One need not burden Beethoven with the consequences of what he set in motion and with the nonsense that has since been perpetrated in his name about the musician's personality and its individualistic megalomania. However, and this cannot be changed, he was the first to set foot in the domain of musical abstraction. Those who preach the arrogant doctrine that genius is that which no one understands have flourished on the strength of his last quartets. The quartet in C-sharp minor, for example, no longer had any utilitarian value for the listener of 1836; there was, speaking crudely, simply no use for it, because it offered no basis for communication between the author and the public. One derided such works, to the extent that they were known at all, as the misguided speculations of a peculiar man; to listen to them was a senseless bother, since he was only speaking with himself. (With which nothing is said about or, certainly, against the intellectual value of the works.)

This process of alienation between the creators and consumers of art advanced steadily, if in part subterraneously, during the whole of the 1800s, ultimately entering a critical stage around the turn of this century. Impressionism was expressly *l'art pour l'art*. And that which must be termed expressionism until a better designation is found was only the last attempt at self-justification undertaken by an individualism pushed to the point of absurdity. It signaled the collapse of the last pillars of that fragile bridge barely connecting naïve but willing art lovers to esoteric art. And how could the universality of an artwork be possible in an age when every creator believes that the world revolves around him? Finally even the plaintive cry, "Oh, my brother," vainly directed at the whole world as a conciliatory greeting, became nothing more than the artist's pathetic self-address.

The universal crisis of art (as Adolf Weissmann puts it) also severely affected music. What followed was chaos. Old values were overthrown without anyone being able to name new ones. For a while it appeared as if the negation of the past was a sufficient foundation for the present. Romanticism, as the typical expressive form of the preceding generations, fell victim to the hateful rejection of a new breed of composers, who—plunging from one extreme to the next—sought to rid music of any emotion. The parody came into its own, the farce, no less so. And jazz, freshly imported from America, perpetrated the uncalled-for excess of scornfully sharing the romantic melody between the saxophone and trumpet.

Overthrows are always radical. But, once the revolution had ebbed, the search was still made in the rubbish heap of dashed ideals for whatever usable values might be found. Musicians too, after a few years of nihilism, began to seek footholds in the past. Allegedly dispensable tonality regained respect within certain limits. Forms and types of an older musical practice were taken up anew. Yet no one has the right to reproach composers with desertion or remorse: in itself the development was thoroughly grounded. And however much the early radicalism of the new music might have dissipated over time, one judgment—indeed, the most important one—remained untouched: no artwork can be justified in isolation; artistic music is vital only to the extent that it once again becomes utilitarian.

The retort will no doubt be made that in the most recent works none of this is to be noted. For it is precisely the victory of the abstruse, the intentionally unintelligible that they celebrate. Yet the case is scarcely so simple, so unequivocal, even if there is some evidence for the objection, above all on the level of appearance. Such rejoinders usually issue from the mouths of those who have had a typical experience with modern music. At some time, presumably when the confusion was at its height, they came across a composer and felt violated by his aggressive cacophony. To quote Freud, the traumatic experience remained with them; and since they refuse the only possible therapy, namely repeated confrontations with the new, they fail to see how much has changed in the meantime. They do not want to see it because it is so pleasant to feel justified in scorning one's contemporaries. On the contrary, it must be conceded that though the goals are more clearly defined today, the solutions offered are not yet in any way definitive. At least the reconciliation between listeners and creators has become part of the program. The sins of a century cannot be made good in a decade.

That the music of this last decade has also frequently wandered off along speculative paths which are not congenial to the public cannot be denied by anyone who has followed its development since 1918 with open eyes and ears. However ruinous it had proved to be in the prewar period, the principle of *l'art pour l'art* continued to be respected on the whole, if somewhat less openly. Proceeding with extreme consistency, Arnold Schoenberg (whose intellectual achievement towers over whatever ill will it might inspire), removed himself as a creative individualist so far from the common disposition that the lack of resonance in his work becomes comprehensible. (And precisely this example illuminates with utmost clarity how little the absolute validity of a work, in certain circumstances, needs to be proved in relation to a listener. Given the state of things today, what is more desirable, validity or universal validity?—that, of course, remains the question.) As great therefore as Schoenberg's personal validity might be, he is just as little capable of achieving his effects in breadth. Within the highly diversified circle of his students, Anton von Webern offers the most doctrinaire renunciation of that which the lay person calls "musical sensibility." Just recently it became apparent at the music festival in Siena how the unbroken instinct of a romantic audience rebels against such eccentricity. And, just to name an example from another part of the musical landscape, Alois Haba has been stuck for years in the same spot with his speculative introduction of quarter tones because he obviously cannot demonstrate the utilitarian value of his invention.

Juxtaposed against these are a large number of works that clearly express the intention of providing music with a broader appeal. In Germany Hindemith has been able to find the most secure balance between an individual tonal language and the general intelligibility music cannot do without. His work for the Youth Movement as well as his efforts in film and mechanical music prove this; but even his contributions to so-called artistic music bear witness to his refusal to confine himself to a secret cell of esoterics. A new opera, with a text by Marcellus Schiffer, will mark another step along this path. Stravinsky, particularly with his ballets, has enjoyed the greatest international success since Richard Strauss. Under his influence, as well as that of Erik Satie, a group of musicians is currently active in France to whom the audience is no longer a secondary concern. They, [Darius] Milhaud, [Georges] Auric, and [Francis] Poulenc, were immediately reproached for having too anxious an eye on the public. Perhaps so, but that is in any case better than staring into the romantic depths. And even if the much-reviled _Jonny_ by Ernst Krenek is certainly no stroke of genius, it undoubtedly betrays the same tendency. The operas by Kurt Weill, the numerous and highly playable piano and chamber pieces, and the ballets, which are attracting renewed interest, are all united in trying to reclaim listeners rather than arrogantly dismissing them.

The gramophone and radio have intensified the situation quite expediently. These world-encompassing technical apparatuses offer the best criterion for the utilitarian value of music. They automatically dismiss anything that exceeds a large audience's capacity for understanding. That gives composers a strong incentive to realize the theoretical insight that music need not be inferior to be popular. It is truly possible to identify experiments in how ingenuity and good craftsmanship can be used to elevate lower types of art. One need only consider the minor but in their own way consummate revues by [Friedrich] Hollaender and [Mischa] Spoliansky to find confirmation for this claim. Dance has liberated jazz to the extent that it has not degenerated back into a routine from the tedious model of tonic and dominant, from the stupefying monotony of a four-four beat. And Weill drew on everything vital on the streets today to write a score for Brecht's _The Threepenny Opera_ that is quite listenable—moreover, it is listened to by thousands. To their joy, it proves to them that modern music does not have to be the dead issue of the brain.

In the mutual interpenetration of what used to be strictly distinguished as artistic and utilitarian music lies the future potential of contemporary music. It will take some time for it to be adequately realized. In the meanwhile it would be fitting for everyone to admit finally that good utilitarian music is still more valuable than bad artistic music.

245

ALBAN BERG

On My *Wozzeck*

First published as "Alban Berg über seinen *Wozzeck*," *Der Scheinwerfer* 4 (November 1929), 3–4.

It is now ten years since I started to compose *Wozzeck;* already so much has been written about it that I can hardly say anything without plagiarizing my critics. I should like, however, to correct an error that arose in 1925 soon after it was produced and that has spread widely since.

I have never entertained the idea of reforming the structure of opera through *Wozzeck*. Neither when I started nor when I completed the work did I consider it a model for further efforts by any other composer. I never assumed or expected that *Wozzeck* should become the basis of a school.

I simply wanted to compose good music; to develop musically the contents of Georg Büchner's immortal drama; to translate his poetic language into music. Other than that, when I decided to write an opera my only intention, as related to the technique of composition, was to give the theater what belongs to the theater. The music was to be so formed that at each moment it would fulfill its duty of serving the action. Even more, the music was to be prepared to furnish whatever the action needed for transformation into reality on the stage. The function of a composer is to solve the problems of an ideal stage director. Nevertheless this objective should not prejudice the development of the music as an entity, absolute, and purely musical. No externals should interfere with its individual existence.

That I accomplished these purposes by a use of musical forms more or less ancient (considered by critics as one of the most important of my ostensible reforms of the opera) was a natural consequence of my method. It was first necessary to make a selection from Büchner's twenty-five loosely constructed, partly fragmentary scenes for the libretto. Repetitions not lending themselves to musical variation were avoided. Finally, the scenes were brought together, arranged, and grouped into acts. The problem therefore became more musical than literary, and had to be solved by the laws of musical structure rather than by the rules of dramaturgy.

It was impossible to shape the fifteen scenes I selected in different manners so that each would retain its musical coherence and individuality and at the same time follow the customary method of development appropriate to the literary content. No matter how rich structurally, no matter how aptly it might fit the dramatic events, after a number of scenes so composed the music would inevitably create monotony. The effect would become boring with a series of a dozen or more formally composed entr'actes which offered nothing but this type of illustrative music, and boredom, of course, is the last thing one should experience in the theater.

I obeyed the necessity of giving each scene and each accompanying piece of entr'acte music—prelude, postlude, connecting link or interlude—an unmistakable aspect, a rounded off and finished character. It was imperative to use everything essential for the creation of individualizing characteristics on the one hand, and coherence on the other. Hence the much discussed utilization of both old and new musical forms and their application in an absolute music.

The appearance of these forms in opera was to some degree unusual, even new. Nevertheless novelty, path breaking, was not my conscious intention. I must reject the claim of being a reformer of the opera through such innovations, although I do not wish to depreciate my work thereby, since others who do not know it so well can do that much better.

What I do consider my particular accomplishment is this. No one in the audience, no matter how aware he may be of the musical forms contained in the framework of the opera, of the precision and logic with which it has been worked out, no one, from the moment the curtain parts until it closes for the last time, pays any attention to the various fugues, inventions, suites, sonata movements, variations, and passacaglias about which so much has been written. No one gives heed to anything but the vast social implications of the work which by far transcend the personal destiny of Wozzeck. This, I believe, is my achievement.

246

ARNOLD SCHOENBERG

My Public

First published as "Mein Publikum," *Der Querschnitt* 10, vol. 4 (April 1930), 222–224.

Called upon to say something about my public, I have to confess: I do not believe I have one.

At the start of my career, when to the annoyance of my opponents a noticeable part of the audience did not hiss but applauded, and when the hissers did not succeed in carrying the day against the majority, although hisses sound more striking than applause, then these opponents of mine alleged that those bestowing their approval were my friends and had only applauded out of friendship and not because they liked the piece. My poor friends: as true as few. They were indeed thought depraved enough to be my friends and yet not so depraved as to enjoy my music.

Whether I then had a public—that I cannot judge.

But after the upheaval, there were in every major city those certain few hundred young people with just no idea what to do with themselves. They therefore tried hard to put it on record that they had a philosophy—by supporting all lost causes. About then, when that great variable, their philosophy, included even me—blameless party that I was— optimists asserted that I now had a public. I challenged this; I did not see how people could suddenly have come to understand me overnight. (My works had not, after all, become any more stupid or shallow overnight.) The rapid decline of the radicals—still not knowing what to do with themselves but finding other things to meddle with—justified my view: I had not written anything shallow.

There are many reasons why the great public makes little contact with me. Above all, the generals, who today still occupy the music directorates, are mostly moving along lines that my line does not fit, or else they are afraid to put before the public something they do not themselves understand. Some of them (even though when they admit it they politely look regretful) really regard not understanding me as a virtue. Granted even that is their greatest virtue, I still had to feel surprised the first time a Viennese conductor made it known to me that he could not perform my *Kammersymphonie* because he did not understand it. I was amused, though; why did he have to pick on me in this sudden burst of wanting to understand and not on the classical works he blithely conducted year in, year out? But seriously, I must say that it is, after all, no honor for a musician not to understand a score, but a matter for shame—many even of my opponents will admit this today, as regards my *Kammersymphonie.*

Apart from these conductors, those who get between me and the public are the many musicians who do not conduct but know other ways to mislead. I have seen countless times that, as regards the main point, it was not the public who hissed: it was a small but active "expert" minority. The public's behavior is either friendly or indifferent, unless they are intimidated because their spiritual leaders are protesting. As a whole they are always rather inclined to enjoy something they have devoted time and money to. They come less to judge than to enjoy, and can to some extent sense whether the person appearing before them is entitled to do so. What they are not interested in doing is using their more or less correct judgment in order to display themselves in a better light. This is partly because no single member stands to gain or lose anything (he will either be outnumbered or be swallowed up in the majority); and partly because among the public there are after all people who count for something, even without first having to shine by their artistic judgments, and who, without losing prestige, may keep their impressions to themselves, unassessed. One may keep anything to oneself, except expert judgment—for what is expert judgment unless one shows it off? For this reason, I also take it to have been the expert judges, not the art lovers, who received my *Pierrot Lunaire* with such hostility when I performed it in Italy. I was indeed honored that Puccini, not an expert judge but a practical expert, already ill, made a six-hour journey to get to know my work, and afterwards said some very friendly things to me; that was good, strange though my music may have remained to him. Nevertheless it was characteristic that the loudest disturber of the concert was identified as the director of a conservatoire. It was also he who proved unable at the end to bridle his truly Mediterranean temperament—who could not refrain from exclaiming: "If there had been just one single honest triad in the whole piece!" Obviously his teaching activities gave him too little opportunity to hear such honest triads, and he had come hoping to find them in my *Pierrot.* Am I to blame for his disappointment?

I have to think it possible that the Italian public did not know what to make of my music. But the image of a concert where there was hissing—in twenty-five years I have seen it so often that I may be believed—was always as follows: in the front third of the hall, roughly, there was little applause and little hissing; most people sat unconcerned, many stood looking around in amazement or amusement toward the parts of the hall farther back where things were livelier. There the applauders were in the majority—there were fewer unconcerned, and a few hissers. But the most noise, both applause and hisses, always came from the standing space at the back and from the galleries. It was there that the people instructed or influenced by the expert judges went into battle against those who were impressed.

And yet I never had the impression that the number of people hissing was particularly great. It never sounded full, like a chord of solid applause entering with precision, but more like an ad hoc group of ill-assorted soloists, the extent of whose ensemble was limited to the fact that their noises told one the direction they were approaching from.

That was how I saw the public and in no other way except when, as today with my older works, they applauded. But besides a number of very pleasant letters I receive now and then, I also know the public from another side. Perhaps I may end by relating a few pleasing little experiences. When just drafted to a reserve company during the war, I, the conscript who had had many a bad time, once found myself treated with striking mildness by a newly arrived sergeant. When he addressed me after we had drilled, I hoped I was going to be praised for my progress in all things military. There followed a blow to my soldierly keenness; surprisingly, the tribute was to my music. The sergeant, a tailor's assistant in civil life, had recognized me, knew my career and many of my works, and so gave me still more pleasure than by praising my drill (even though I was not a little proud of that!). There were two other such meetings in Vienna: once when I had missed a train and had to spend the night in a hotel, and again when a taxi was taking me to a hotel. I was recognized the first time by the *night porter,* the other time by the *taxi driver,* from the name on the label of my luggage. Both assured me enthusiastically that they had heard *Gurrelieder.* Another time in a hotel in Amsterdam, a hired man addressed me, saying that he was a long-standing admirer of my art; he had sung in the choir in *Gurrelieder* when I conducted them in Leipzig. But the prettiest story last: a short while back, again in a hotel, the elevator attendant asked me whether it was I who had written *Pierrot.*

247

ERNST KRENEK

New Humanity and Old Objectivity

First published as "Neue Humanität und alte Sachlichkeit," *Neue Schweizer Rundschau* 24 (April 1931), 244–258.

Attempts have recently been made, and more will be made in the future, to create an art, particularly an art of the musical theater, which will fit the enlarged society as earlier art fitted the limited society—in other words, to find a basis for an art that the general public could enter into and assimilate. In this connection I must mention my own efforts. They consisted mainly of including some parts of the rhythmic and harmonic elements of jazz in my works. The motives that led me to this now strike me as twofold. Firstly I thought that by using the jazz elements I might hit on an atmosphere that would fit the collective feeling of the age. As jazz music in practice enjoyed undisputed mastery and general validity, it seemed conceivable that from it one might derive an artistic means that after all belonged to the sphere of music, and so was capable of the most serious and intellectual development, while at the same time having a natural place in the life of modern man. This, I felt, might give me the possibility of saying something generally valid.

The second consideration was an internal musical one. As must be fairly well known, there has been a complete disruption of musical systems of organization along with the democratic opening up of the conventions of life. At first atonality, which tried to replace these systems, extended the range of musical means to infinity, theoretically at least, so that today there is really nothing that is musically impossible. Every conceivable harmonic combination can be produced at any time, without special preparation, and a new organization from this quarter is not to be hoped for. So far atonality has not proved particularly suitable for versatile dramatic presentation and in the circumstances jazz, with its stereotyped harmonic and rhythmic elements, seemed an effective protection against the ineffectual ubiquity of all musical possibilities, because it offered a sort of new convention. But there was never any idea, least of all in my mind, of its being a complete substitute for every other kind of expressive world; only if that were successfully achieved would the product really deserve the name of "jazz opera." In my attempt, as in all the others I know of, jazz was only alluded to at the points demanded by the action; apart from this the harmony was colored by its elements, thus guaranteeing the homogeneity of the whole and justifying the way I had deliberately limited the means—a protection against atonality.

Looking back on the results, one is bound to be aware that works of this kind were only connected with the general public "atmospherically"—that is, by being reminiscent of the familiar pop-style—while their real artistic value remained irrelevant and obscure. Nevertheless it must be admitted that in this sphere the good is still usually more successful than the inferior, while just the reverse seems to be true of operetta, for example. The amazement and agitation I caused by showing a station and having somebody telephone on the stage have since died down, and there is not much point now in going into the programmatic interpretations people read into these things. There have always been naturalistic operas, and the props, if they are no more than that, are probably the least important symptoms of an attitude of mind. From any moderately reasonable point of view, my *Jonny spielt auf* is one of the unhappiest examples to quote in connection with New Objectivity, for although new objects occur in it they do so only as objects surrounding present-day people, without proclaiming any positive attitude concerning them. Nobody prays to the engine or lauds the virtues of the telephone; these things merely play a subordinate, functional role as props needed by the action, and there is no more reason why a present-day work should do without them than why a drama taking place in the past should do without the modern props of that age.

But there are other efforts along these lines which must be taken much more seriously; in them the essential thing is not just using daily objects for personal reasons, as in *Jonny spielt auf,* but assenting to everyday aims as such. Of course it is true that anything can be made into artistic material, but it is essential that the object should stand in a dynamic relationship to man. The object must release a feeling; to apply this to the complicated conditions of a theatrical process, the object must be an obvious vehicle of dramatic movement within the course of an emotional pattern translated into action. For example, the fact that there is a telephone means absolutely nothing artistically; however intensely the instrument is accepted, as it may be by many people, this cannot give any occasion for artistic creation. For even if you wanted to address a poem to the telephone you would have no choice but to gear it to man's use of the machine, its position in man's life; and to get the emotional content needed for the poem you would have to examine whether and how the fact of telephoning plays a part in the expression of man's inner life. Description alone is not enough, and even a list of all the component parts of an aeroplane would not add up to a Homeric epic.

On the stage the telephone can only be used as a prop, a characteristic feature of a milieu, as stage-coaches, distaffs, shepherds' crooks, spears, and swords were features of other milieus, and no one milieu is a priori better than another. Nothing further can be derived from this—no theory, no aesthetic position, no dogma, nothing to gladden the heart of the philistine thirsting for knowledge. But the New Objectivity I have criticized puts the prop in the center of the picture and so reflects the situation described above—the fact that the technical devices created by man have long since become ends in themselves and have reduced their erstwhile masters to servitude. Instead of machines serving us silently and exactly, and setting us free to find ourselves more quickly and easily, they get in our way and themselves become the monuments they have destroyed, for which we have such an ineradicable taste. The divine in man has been replaced by the fact that he can travel faster than a bird flies; and in the advertisements, the inventor of a new kind of engine rivals the creator of the world.

We now have the "rhythm of the age" and so know all the less about the rhythms of music; we are bored to death with the "tempo of the age," but nobody is allowed to fall behind. Now I conceive of a work of art as the intellectual form of an emotional content, and so can see little point in an art that rejects emotion as too human and not mechanical enough and intellect as too exhausting. However, the easiness of an object is one of the first conditions of its intrinsic value in this age. As I indicated, we are dealing with a race of overworked and distracted consumers. Since in art, as in everything else, they are more concerned with quantity than with intensity, each individual work must be striking and sensational so as to be noticed at all, but at the same time easy and quick to consume, fileted and easy to digest so that nothing is left and there is plenty of room for the next pleasure. Both characteristics are to be found in the daily tidbits which, as I have shown, the press serves up to the public in such large quantities. The social note is considered particularly effective and contemporary, but in reality it only produces scantiness and sensationalism. I quite agree that no material is impossible in itself, but however fine a social tendency is, it cannot compensate for a lack of artistic shaping.

248

THEODOR W. ADORNO

Mahagonny

First published as "Mahagonny," *Musikblätter des Anbruch* 14 (February-March 1932), 12–15.

The city of Mahagonny is a representation of the social world in which we live, projected from the bird's-eye perspective of an already liberated society. Not a symbol of demonic greed or a dream of desperate fantasy, absolutely nothing that might signify anything other than itself: it is instead the precise projection of present-day circumstances onto the untouched white surface of things as they should be in the image of translucent banners. Mahagonny does not present a classless society as a positive standard against which to compare the depraved present; instead, from time to time this society shimmers through just barely—as unclear as a movie projection over which another has been superimposed—in accordance with a recognition that is capable, with the force exerted by the future, of splitting the darkness of the present with beams of light, but which has not been authorized to paint out a picture of that future. The power of the future is revealed, on the contrary, in the constellation of the present. Just as in Kafka's novels the commonplace bourgeois world appears absurd and displaced in that it is viewed from the hidden perspective of redemption, the bourgeois world is unmasked in Mahagonny as absurd when measured against a socialist world that itself remains concealed. Its absurdity is actual and not symbolic. The present system, with its order, rights, and mores, is exposed as anarchy; we ourselves live in Mahagonny, where everything is permitted save one thing: having no money. In order to represent this convincingly it is necessary to transcend the closed world of bourgeois consciousness which considers bourgeois social reality to be immutable. Outside of this framework, however, there is no position to take—at least for the German consciousness, there is no site that is noncapitalist. Paradoxically, therefore, transcendence must take place within the framework of that which is. What the steady gaze cannot achieve can perhaps be achieved through the oblique gaze of the child, to whom the trousers of the adult he is looking up at seem like mountains, with the face as its distant peak. The oblique infantile perspective, which feeds on American Indian tales and stories of adventure on the sea, becomes a means for the disenchantment of the capitalist order, whose courtyards are transformed into the plains of Colorado, whose crises have turned into hurricanes, whose apparatuses of power have assumed the form of cocked revolvers. In Mahagonny, the Wild West (as children understand it in the context of their play) is revealed as the immanent fable of capitalism. The projection of reality through the medium of the child's perspective alters it to such an extent that its basis is revealed; it does not, however, transfigure this reality into metaphor but grasps it simultaneously in its unmediated historical tangibility. The anarchy of commodity production, which Marxism has analyzed, is projected as the anarchy of consumption, abbreviated to the point of a crass horror that could not be rendered by an economic analysis. The reification of interpersonal relationships is evidenced in the image of prostitution, and whatever love may exist here can only burst forth from the smoking rubble of adolescent fantasies of sexual power. The absurdity of class privilege is demonstrated (very much as it is in Kafka) through the plot structure of a trial at which the district attorney sells the tickets as his own doorman. Everything has been subjected to an evenly displaced optical perspective that distorts the surface forms of bourgeois life into the grimaces of a reality that is otherwise hidden by ideologies.

But the mechanism of displacement which is at work here is not the same as the blind displacement that occurs in dreams; rather it proceeds precisely in accordance with the knowledge which forces the comparison of the Wild West and the world of exchange value. It is the knowledge of violence as the foundation of the present order and of the ambiguity in which this order and power confront each other. The representative symbols of mythic power and mythic justice are frightened up out of the stone masses of the metropolis. Brecht names their paradoxical simultaneity. During the powerful parody of the national constitution when the city is founded, the procuress Leokadja Begbick bestows her infernal blessing upon it: "But this entire city of Mahagonny exists only because everything is so bad, because there is no peace and no harmony, and because there is nothing anyone can believe in." Jimmy Mahonney, who urges on the latent anarchy that devours him along with the city, later is angry with her, and his anger is expressed through the same curse in opposite terms: "Ah, no one will ever be happy throughout your Mahagonny because there is too much peace and too much harmony, and because there is too much in which one can believe." Both of them are saying the same thing—because there is nothing to really believe in, because blind instinct is dominant, there is therefore too much to believe in: justice and moral codes, they share the same origin; therefore Mahagonny (or the metropolis) must collapse. This is expressed at one crystal-clear moment: "We are still inside it, we haven't enjoyed anything. We vanish all of a sudden, and they slowly disappear as well."

The representation of capitalism is more precisely that of its surrender to the dialectics of the anarchy that is inherent within it. This dialectic does not unfold smoothly in accordance with an idealistic schema; rather it has intermittent elements that cannot be dissolved in the process, just as the opera as a whole evades a rational solution—the images of the dominant horror which it projects are brought forth in accordance with its own logic only to be collapsed again at the end into the social reality whose origins they contain.

These intermittent elements are of two types. On the one hand, nature, the amorphous entity that underlies society, plays its role. It intersects with the social process and pushes it forward. There is a hurricane, a natural phenomenon, indicated on the map as a kind of bogeyman, and in the face of his fear of death, the hero—this "Jim"—discovers "the laws of human happiness" whose victim he becomes. The turning point, which grotesquely tears the historical dialectic from the context of nature which until then had exerted an effect, is magnificent: the hurricane curves around the city and continues on its course just as history continues on its course once it has found it. What occurs during the night of the hurricane, however—what explodes and, in the bewildered entanglement of anarchy, refers beyond it—is spontaneous improvisation: the boisterous songs in which human freedom is announced ("We don't need a hurricane, we don't need a typhoon") and the antinomical theology of "You make your bed and you lie in it" ("Wie man sich bettet, so liegt man"). Thus intentions of freedom rise up, oblique and concealed, within capitalism and especially during its periods of crisis, and it is within these intentions alone that a possible future is announced.

The form this announcement takes is that of intoxication. The central positive scene in Mahagonny is the scene of drunken revelry in which Jim and his friends construct a sailboat from a pool table and a curtain rod and sail the South Sea during a stormy night towards an Alaska that borders on the South Sea; for this, they sing the song of the mariner's lot (*Seemannslos*), the immortal catastrophe of kitsch which serves as a polar star for their wobbling seasickness, and they set the sails of their dream journey for a sunny polar-bear paradise. Quite correctly, the mechanism that brings about the ending is brought into the vision of this scene; anarchy runs aground on the improvisation it engenders and which exceeds it. Jim can be forgiven for murder, bloodshed, and seduction, all of which can be paid off in terms of law, justice, and money, but he cannot escape the curtain rod and the three glasses of whiskey for which he cannot pay and which, within this context, can never be paid for at all because the dream function which they have assumed through him can no longer be expressed in terms of any exchange value. This Jimmy Mahonney is a subject without subjectivity, a dialectical Chaplin. Just as Chaplin eats his shoes, Jimmy wants to eat his hat because he is so bored once anarchy has been regulated; he follows to the letter the law of human happiness which allows anything until he strays into the net that has been intricately woven by a mixture of anarchy and order and to which Mahagonny actually owes its name as the "city of nets" (*Netzestadt*). He is afraid before his death and would like to prevent the day from breaking so that he would not have to die, but when he finally is confronted with the electric chair (which, more than any images of the Wild West called up from childhood, is a naked emblem of its culture) he sings "Don't let yourself be seduced" ("*Laßt euch nicht verführen*") as an open protest on the part of the oppressed class to which he belongs because of the fact that he cannot pay his debt. He had bought himself a woman and, to make things easier for himself, had requested that she not wear any underwear. He asks her forgiveness before he dies—"don't think badly of me," he begs—and her contemptuous reply—"What for?"—contains a greater degree of radiant reconciliation than all the novelists of noble resignation put together could ever come up with. He is no hero to the same extent that *Mahagonny* is no tragedy: he is a bundle of impulses and meanings that intersect, a human being in all the scattered diffusion of his drives. He is by no means a revolutionary, but he is also not a proper bourgeois or man of the Wild West. Rather he is a fragment of productive power who recognizes and exposes anarchy and must therefore die; a person, perhaps, who doesn't enter into social relations but shakes them all up. With his death Mahagonny must die, and little hope remains: the hurricane has been eluded, but salvation comes too late.

The aesthetic form of the opera is that of its construction, and nothing would be more incorrect than to read into it an opposition between its political intention, which is directed towards reality, and a procedural method in which that same reality is not mirrored naturalistically, for the transformation process to which reality is thereby subjected is demanded by the political desire to decipher what exists. Simply referring to epic theater doesn't tell us much about *Mahagonny*. It takes the position of replacing a closed bourgeois totality with the fragmented conglomerate of its debris in order to take possession of the fable which is immanent in the hollow spaces between the debris, and to destroy it at close range by dint of its own infantile gold-digging passion. The form within which a disintegrated reality is captured without a better one having been realized is itself not permitted to take on the appearance of a totality.

Moreover, the instance of intermittence which profoundly determines the dialectic of *Mahagonny* can only be achieved through interruptions. It appears, for example, in the *Moralität* of the second act where, after having been saved from the hurricane, the dark bliss of anarchy is referred to in four allegorical images (those of eating, sex, boxing, and alcohol), representations of happiness that eventually must be paid for with an unreconciled death. But the intermittent form at work here is not that of reportage, as is the case in the mania for paragraphs which can be found in the plays of the new naturalism; rather it is more that of montage. The debris of the disintegrating organic reality is constructively contextualized. The beginning and end points of this construct lie in empirical reality— between them, it is autonomous, stretched around the prototypical images of capitalism. Ultimately it shows us that these prototypes are totally contemporary and thus definitely force open the aesthetic continuum. I am reminded of the moment in Wagner in which the Dutchman emerges beneath and, as it were, out of his portrait—this same logic is at work in *Mahagonny*'s finale. When in the same "Benares Song" the earth trembles for the newspaper readers, it comes to a halt after Jimmy's death, and God appears in Mahagonny, an equivocal demiurge, whom they obey down to the last "no" which resounds from the hell into which he has brought them, and against which the demiurgical power meets its limits. The woman who has been banished to the lowest level of this hell of "instinctual relations" (*Naturzusammenhänge*) finally expresses this "no," and the demonstrations moving away from the burning Mahagonny, which erase the scene, begin.

More fundamentally than through all of the montage and any intermittently interspersed songs, bourgeois immanence is threatened by the forms of language and phantasy which individually recreate the oblique and frightening perspective of the child. Mahagonny is the first surrealistic opera. The bourgeois world is presented as being already necrotic through the moment of its horror, and it is demolished in the scandal in which its past is manifested. One instance which represents this kind of shock is the hurricane, a natural phenomenon that develops and then disappears for no reason; another is the blurred exaggeration of the eating scene of Mr. Schmidt, whose real name is Jack O'Brien and who eats two calves and consequently dies, whereupon a veterans' association sings the dirge. The chalky photographic color of this scene is that of the wedding photographs of Henri Rousseau; in their magnesium light the astral bodies of their previous underworld existence visibly attach themselves to the bourgeoisie. Or there is the scene in the "Here You Are Allowed To" tavern "under a big sky" which hangs above it like a glass roof, on which the cloud of a gentle madness moves back and forth. The wild men of Mahagonny dreamily follow this image, which rises with the anxious certainty of memory. If nature alone, in the form of the hurricane or the newspaper earthquake, appears as catastrophic, it is because the instinct-bound, blind bourgeois world, to which the typhoon belongs in the same uncanny way as the crises, can only be illuminated and rendered alterable through the shock of catastrophe. The surrealistic intentions of *Mahagonny* are borne out by the music, which, from the first note to the last, is dedicated to the shock that the sudden representation of the disintegrated bourgeois world engenders. First of all, it clarifies the gloriously misunderstood *Threepenny Opera,* which exists as a paragon between the first version of *Mahagonny* and its definitive form, and shows how little the easily comprehended melodies ultimately have to do with successful entertainment and rousing vitality—these qualities, certainly present in Weill's music, are only a means for carrying through in the consciousness of man the horror of the acknowledged demonology. Except for a few polyphonic moments such as the introduction and a couple ensemble phrases, the music economizes with the most primitive means; more correctly, it drags the worn-out, shabby furniture of the bourgeois drawing room to a children's playground where the undersides of these old commodities disseminate horror as totem figures. This music, pieced together from triads and off-notes with the good beat of old music-hall songs that we hardly recognize anymore but are nonetheless remembered as an heirloom, is hammered and glued together with the fetid mucilage of a soggy potpourri of operas. This music, made up of the debris of past music, is completely contemporary. Its surrealism is radically different from any New Objectivity or new classicism. Its intention is not to restore a ruined bourgeois music, to "bring it back to life," as people love to put it nowadays, or to freshen up the preterit with recourse to the pluperfect. Rather its construction, its montage of the dead renders it evident as dead and illusory and extracts from the horror that emanates from it the power of a manifesto. Its improvisational, rambling, homeless élan originates in this power. This conglomeration of broken shards (which have been revealed as such), like only the most advanced music of a material-specific dialectic—that of Schoenberg—deviates from the space of bourgeois music, and whoever might be seeking in it a collective experience like that to be found in the youth movement will certainly take offense at it, even if all the songs from it run through his head over and over.

Therefore the music is allowed to make use of triads because it does not believe in them; rather it destroys them through the very manner in which they are used. This becomes apparent on the level of the music itself in the metrics, which distorts and obliterates symmetrical relationships as they are fixed in the tonal chords, since the triads have lost their power and are no longer able to construct a form—the form is, to a much greater extent, assembled from them from without. The form of the harmonics itself corresponds to this principle, a harmonics that hardly recognizes the principle of progression anymore, or the tension of a leading tone, or the function of cadence, but instead lets go of the last trace of communication between the chords which were the hallmark of the later chromatics, so that the results of the chromatic interaction now are released from any function. In all of this, *Mahagonny* far exceeds the stage music for *The Threepenny Opera*: the music no longer serves a function, but itself is dominant, continuously set (*durchkomponiert*) throughout the opera, and evolves in accordance with its infernal measure. It has its modulations in both the insignificant and the substantial at once. This is evident above all in the expressionless, puzzling music of the duets between Jimmy and Jenny, captured in a song; it is present in the billiards ensemble, and at the grandly conceived finale when the "Alabama Song," with its "We've lost our dear old mama," appears as a gentle *cantus firmus* and, with the greatest scenic effect, is revealed as the lament of the creature in the face of its isolation. The "Alabama Song" is certainly one of the strangest pieces in *Mahagonny,* and never has music been better suited to the archaic power of the memory of the singing that once existed, was forgotten, and then recognized in wretched bars of melody as in this song, whose stupid repetitions in the introduction also redeem it from the realm of dementia. If the satanic kitsch of the nineteenth century, the "lot of the mariner" and "a prayer to the virgin," are intentionally cited and paraphrased, this is not done as a literary joke; rather, it delineates the borderline of a music that makes its way through a region, even without naming it, and which only in caesurae speaks the name of that which no longer has any power over it.

[Gustav] Mahler is strangely present throughout the opera, in its fairy tales, its ostinato, its gloomy major-minor keys. As in Mahler, it makes use of the explosive force of the lower elements to destroy those of the middle range in order to participate in the higher ones. It tears down the images that are present in it not to proceed into emptiness but to redeem the spoils for the banners of its own undertaking.

24
New Mass Media: Radio and Gramophone

ON THE EVENING OF OCTOBER 29, 1923, after four years of technical experimentation and one year of legal wrangling over control of the airwaves, the Vox record company in Berlin broadcast the first German radio program. About two hundred listeners tuned in with wireless boxes, huge earphones, and heavy antennae. As radio technology improved, the number of subscribers also dramatically increased: one-hundred thousand in 1924, one million in 1926, two million in 1928, and over four million in 1932. Half of all households had a "wireless" when Hitler came to power in 1933. Justly concerned about the potential for political misuse and commercialization of this newest and most potent instrument of mass communication, the German government took measures from the very start to regulate the airwaves. As early as 1922, radio in Germany became state controlled (under the postal ministry) to prevent any single political party or private enterprise from owning a radio station. Whereas privatization in the United States had by 1922 created over two hundred radio stations, all supported by advertising, in Germany the government insisted upon state ownership and supervision not only for the protection of German culture but also of democracy—with the ironic effect, of course, that radio under the Nazi dictatorship became the most powerful propaganda tool of the state. Criticism of censorship and of biased political reporting accompanied the development of state-supervised radio from its beginnings.

Brecht, whose play *A Man's a Man* (*Mann ist Mann*) was successfully adapted for radio in 1927, recognized the inherent political power of the apparatus if it were used as a public communication system to inform and educate the growing mass of listeners in political as well as cultural matters. Radio ultimately seemed capable of bringing high art down from its rarefied and isolated realm to the common people; the sheer prospect of being able to transmit new music by Schoenberg or a play by Brecht to millions of listeners caused immense excitement among artists. At the same time, conservative cultural critics voiced concern about a further trivialization of culture. The idea of receiving opera at home the same way one received gas and water was still shocking to many. In addition, some feared that radio broadcasts which simultaneously reached millions of individuals were bound to invade the private sphere and collectivize experience. Others objected to the commercial misuse of repeatedly playing (and thereby publicly advertising) selected hit songs. The power of radio to manipulate public taste in everything from music to literature was seen early on, for any message that instantaneously reached several million listeners was practically an advertisement in itself. Thanks to the radio, catchy tunes became hit songs overnight; thanks to the radio, jazz fever spread across the republic like wildfire.

Radio became a catalyst in the debates about the democratization, even socialization, of culture. The first radio broadcast consisted of classical music played live by an orchestra performing in a studio. Radio programs expanded to include operas (beginning with Mozart's *The Magic Flute* in 1924), chamber music, poetry recitals, lectures and readings from novels and plays, raising the inevitable question of whether radio could become art itself rather than merely disseminating it. In the spirit of New Objectivity, O. A. Palitzsch argued for the use of live radio reportage to record public events as they unfold. He also called for an original, medium-specific genre, the radio play, an acoustic collage of real-life sounds that would convey a sense of place to the listener and reproduce reality in a radio-specific manner. The most avant-garde broadcasting station in the republic, Radio Frankfurt, under the directorship of Hans Flesch and (from 1929–1933) Ernst Schoen, promoted programs featuring new music by Hindemith and Krenek with introductory lectures by Adorno, radio plays and features by Brecht and Walter Benjamin, and reportages by Paul Laven, who pioneered live sports event coverage. Radio also became a major source of income for writers and intellectuals.

The creation of a specific radio genre, the *Hörspiel*—a literary text composed exclusively for radio—became a much-debated issue in the 1920s. At a conference on literature and radio held at the Prussian Academy of the Arts in the fall of 1929, the future of the radio play was discussed, but another discourse already interfered with a purely aesthetic assessment of the new art form. Arnolt Bronnen, playwright and radio play author, espoused a nationalistic agenda that prefigured his later involvement with the Nazi regime. His intervention also serves as a reminder of how openly right-wing politics infiltrated the cultural sphere in the last years of the republic.

The 1920s also saw the commercial breakthrough of the gramophone. Recordings of popular hits, dance music and jazz, as well as classical and new music became increasingly affordable and popular. Even writers used the modern technology to record their voices; we can still listen, for instance, to Brecht singing songs from *The Threepenny Opera*. Musicians' fears that the masses would rather buy records than go to concerts were not unjustified. In his 1926 overview of the debate about "mechanical" music (meaning music recorded by machines), H. H. Stuckenschmidt discusses the technical, aesthetic, and social consequences of technology's inroads into music. Adorno's similar but more theoretical reflections about the relationship between original music and its mechanical reproduction introduce issues of authenticity, technology, and ideology that he would later explore more fully.

249

KURT WEILL

Dance Music

First published as "Tanzmusik," *Der Deutsche Rundfunk* 4 (March 14, 1926), 732–733.

A branch of musical programing which is a part of the existing institutions in all radio broadcasting stations of the entire world has never before been appreciated in its full significance here. Like all large European broadcasting stations, the Berlin Radio Station also broadcasts dance music every evening after the conclusion of its evening programs. For metropolitan people of our time dance is one of those few things that can lift them above daily routine; naturally, dance music achieves a significance that it did not possess in earlier times. On the one hand this has led to an artistically alienating industrialization of the light-music business: the carefree gypsy life of dance musicians of earlier times has yielded to blatant commercialization. But on the other hand a certain branch of dance music so completely expresses the spirit of our times that it has even been able to achieve a temporary influence over a certain part of serious art music. The rhythm of our time is jazz.

The Americanization of our whole external life, which is happening slowly but surely, finds its most peculiar outcome here. Unlike art music, dance music does not reflect the sense of towering personalities who stand above time, but rather reflects the instinct of the masses. And a glance into the dance halls of all continents demonstrates that jazz is just as precisely the outward expression of our time as the waltz was of the outgoing nineteenth century. Even inveterate opponents of this "spirit of the time" must concede that in an institution that broadcasts dance music every evening the shimmy must occupy by far the predominant part. But jazz music is not created by merely playing a syncopated 2/2 bar. Negro music, which constitutes the source of the jazz band, is full of complex rhythm, harmonic precision, and auditory and modulatory richness which our dance bands simply cannot achieve. Every night for a week now we have heard an actual jazz band on the radio: the jazz symphonists of Erno Rapée. If one measures it against the splendid jazz bands of the Negro revue, this ensemble is also lacking in subtle balance. But it already exhibits that stomping confusion of saxophones, jazz drums, and muted trumpets, that liberated rhythm and improvised humor which make the jazz band uniquely tolerable.

250

H. H. STUCKENSCHMIDT

Mechanical Music

First published as "Mechanische Musik," *Der Kreis* 3, no. 11 (November 1926), 506–508.

A bitter fight has erupted. Some believe the sacred rights of music have been infringed upon and proclaim the end of the world. Individualism rises up in final, desperate resistance.

I dared to publish a report in a leading music journal about mechanical music, and to predict the end of the era of musical interpreters. Had I suspected the sort of reactions the essay would unleash, how rigorously some would attempt to discredit my beliefs, how elementally the hatred of the new would be turned against me—even from the camp of the most-up-to-date—I would have waited ten years.

The mechanization of music, albeit in the most primitive beginnings of its development, is today a fact.

The phonograph, pneumatic piano, and orchestrion are increasingly becoming the actual sources from which the masses of the people satisfy their musical needs.

It is not a matter of utopias; the problem is too important for that.

Art today has become a luxury, a privilege of the wealthy, and the artist leads a parasitic existence. The moment the state, city, and private supporter perceive a vital need for their money elsewhere, theater and the symphonic orchestra are condemned to death.

Theoretically this moment has long since arrived. Concerts are poorly attended and budget deficits grow from year to year.

The general level of musical performance is visibly declining. Only the flattest, least challenging music enjoys success. Savings must be made at the expense of the performance of significant works.

Meanwhile, composers continue to work undisturbed. Scores become increasingly complex, demands ascend into the immeasurable, musicians fall into despair.

There are already works of modern music that are unperformable; that is, works in which, at least in places, the intentions of the composer exceed human capacities of interpretation.

Instrumental music of the last hundred years quite clearly suggests the necessity of replacing the musician, whose technical capacities are obviously restricted by a thousand physical and psychological deficiencies, by something less limited.

And here the dominion of the machine necessarily begins. The phonograph, the most universal, radical, and cheapest musical apparatus, still suffers from considerable weaknesses despite the numerous improvements introduced in recent years. The sound is never entirely free of static; the sonorous range is minimal. But the probability exists that this unfortunate state will be overcome the moment the instrument is taken beyond its current job of providing entertainment to become a requirement of culture.

A new system in which a magnetic process causes the membrane to vibrate appears incidentally to have completely remedied the problem of static. If so, then at least the qualitative problem will have been solved.

As for increasing the tonal range quantitatively, it has been my long-standing recommendation and that of others that several records and membranes be employed simultaneously.

The primary objection of those who have accepted everything up to this point will be the following: Without the human interpreter, the phonograph is inconceivable! To produce a record, the work has to be played.

Until today, that has certainly been necessary. But:

First of all, for the production of a record only a single performance is necessary. One recording made, for example, in New York can supply the whole globe.

Second, parts of the score that are so difficult they exceed human capacities can be recorded at a slower tempo. (The change in pitch that accompanies the process will, of course, be taken into account!)

Third, there is the possibility of producing a record graphically, like an etching, without involving a human interpreter. For various reasons nothing more can be said here about the practical execution of this proposal, which is no longer merely hypothetical.

Aside from the phonograph there are perhaps other, more perfected systems.

[Ferruccio] Busoni, in his "Outline of a New Aesthetic in the Musical Arts," makes reference to a dynamophone, built by a Dr. Thaddeus Cahill, which produces all conceivable timbres with any desired pitch, tempo, and arrangement by means of electrical vibrations.

Americans working on this basis have built machines that more closely approximate perfection; they not only totally replace the orchestra, voice, and each individual instrument, but in richness of nuance surpass them in every respect.

Only one mechanical instrument has so far been created that achieves complete artistic perfection: the pneumatic piano. [. . .]

Whoever has listened to a Busoni roll played on this instrument will no longer be able to speak of "dead mechanics," "soulless automats," and similar bits of foolishness.

The mechanical piano has delivered the proof that a machine can replace musical interpreters with absolutely equal results.

Further development will show that it can surpass them. [. . .]

Ten more or less trained fingers set the keys in motion. The type of movement is dictated by the spirit of the pianist. At the moment, however, that the movement is decided upon, it ceases to be spirit and soul. It is now mechanical. Controllable. Concrete. It can be recorded, catalogued, cinematographed. It will not be easy for anyone to identify a soul in it. Naturally, the spirit of the pianist is contained in it. But the spirit has been transformed, has become matter. The critical point is that it also remains in the music once the movement has been mechanized!

That, however, is the greatness, the metaphysical problem, the actual substance of the machine, that it can reproduce the effect of a single spiritual achievement a thousandfold.

What needs to be proved appears therefore to have been proved. Every expressive nuance the pianist produces by manipulating the keyboard can be achieved and fixed by mechanical means. Beyond this, however, certain types of fingering are possible on a machine that a human hand could never accomplish.

To name just a few examples: playing tied chords in fast tempo; performing vibrato in fast tempo; simultaneous playing in several timbres with one hand; etc.

There remain as the final argument the pedagogical advantages of mechanical instruments. It is well known that phonographs are used in the gymnasium for language instruction. And teachers employ records for music classes in school.

It will not be long before the voice recording machine is introduced into music instruction as a whole, with particular relevance, for example, to instrumentation.

For someone studying music, perhaps a young choir director, there could be no more instructive practice than to listen repeatedly to an orchestral work with the score in hand and thus to master every nuance of orchestration and enunciation more completely than would be possible with a single concert performance.

Naturally these arguments will be refused by all reproducing (and, unfortunately, many producing) musical artists. For one thing, because there is no more conservative mentality, none more disinclined to innovation, than the musician's. In such ideas they see a betrayal of sacrosanct traditions, vain decadence, and brazen iconoclasm.

But, then, they are not wrong in fearing a violation of their interests. The moment concerts played with mechanical instruments become generally accepted thousands of musicians will be deprived of their daily bread. Once everyone has realized that the machine gives better lessons than a human, students will cease paying fees to a teacher.

To my honored colleagues, however, who were so little capable of containing their rage toward me, a small consolation: a good fifty years will pass before things come to that point.

251

OTTO ALFRED PALITZSCH

Broadcast Literature

First published as "Gefunkte Literatur," *Der Kreis* 1, no. 4 (January 1927), 6–10.

Radio crept up on us under cover of silence. It belongs today to the inventory of a household like a fancy wardrobe and potted plants. Seemingly uninvolved, obscured by spools, wires, and hard rubber disks, the magical boxes sit in their corners. You adjust the steel ring, and charming melodies suddenly resound. A violin hums, an older gentleman sings "In the Month of May," a farmer speaks of synthetic manure. The world is vast and its tones are manifold.

Technology, not unjustly decried as miraculous and gargantuan, lies quiet as a house cat in the parlor. Clever, able, and persevering, twentieth-century dwellers have succeeded in taming it, at least partially, and coaching it to do many strange things. It is only a question of whether they also know how to turn these services to a proper end.

Every so-called bit of progress has the single purpose of making people stronger, happier, and cheerier. It might be the construction of a new boxing arena, the introduction of synchronized traffic lights, or the invention of the singing film. The radio belongs to this as well: it first of all brings home the stock market reports free of charge; second, replaces the piano player at private balls; and third, fills the family's long evening hours with stimulation and instruction. Besides this, it makes it possible for every human being graced with reason to be present simultaneously on the Grindelallee in Hamburg and the Cathedral Square in Cologne. That people nowadays have not yet gone crazy in the face of such paradoxes testifies to the vigor of their constitution.

Radio broadcasting, which serious men maintained just two years ago was not practically realizable, has developed rapidly. No one knows where this development, now beginning in the area of television, will lead. The main thing is this: not to let the reins slip from the hand and rush blindly into the future. The danger is always present these days that the organization of the human spirit lags woefully behind technical advance.

A very respected writer of the previous generation has recently said that all the antennae could be destroyed for all he cares. Such cases of unrealistic sentimental eccentricity are not rare in Europe. It is not intended here to sing hymn number one-thousand-and-one in praise of America; it is only to be soberly established that American vitality seizes strongly and clearly upon every new technological advance and harnesses it without sentimentality to the energy of daily life. Here in the old and correspondingly suspicious world all the protest of the intellectuals comes first. Precisely the same intellectuals maintained for such a long time that film was not art until *The Last Laugh, The Goldrush* and *Potemkin* proved otherwise. We Germans especially find a favorite occupation in protesting. The gatherings which are convened solely for this purpose run into the hundreds every year.

In reference to radio, the preferred choice over protest is the gentler form of passive resistance. Certain circles, among whom culture is passed around like a waiting-room magazine, keep delicately to themselves. To the voice of the facts they turn a willfully deaf ear. But once a German broadcast area comes to encompass 200,000 subscribers, it proves itself to have become a cultural factor whose significance should not be underestimated. When one further considers that radio eschews politics, that therefore there is no question of competition with the daily newspapers, then one must concede on purely objective grounds that radio will accomplish enormous amounts in the special areas of art and science, or at least that much could be accomplished.

It is obvious that the vast power of the broadcaster carries with it an equally great responsibility. Orchestral concerts and lectures on vegetable-washing techniques, the care of infants and Goethe's last love obviously fall short of the mark. The comforts of technology easily seduce one to indolence and irresolution. Whatever can be spoken can also be blasted through a microphone. It seems for that reason obvious to turn a radio station into a hodgepodge of university, lecture hall, and cabaret, and otherwise to sit twiddling one's thumbs. There is surely no lack of subjects, and presumably every East Elbian Junker and every Bavarian milkmaid has a burning interest in learning more details about the life of Hölderlin.

But what of the particular potential unique to radio? Transmissions of music, lectures, and recitations are all very nice. The foundation is set. But what more? Once one has conjured the genie who flies obediently through the air into every possible speaker, one must assign it somewhat more original tasks. On-the-spot reporting, first of all, suggests the direction such tasks might take. Let us take an especially well-known case as an example: the transmission from the Cologne Cathedral on January 31, 1926 of the Rhineland commemoration of liberation. Hundreds of thousands in the most distant provinces took part in this festival with its speeches, the rumbling confusion of voices, the echo of the city astir, and the chimes of the German bells upon the Rhine. A singular event, a piece of history, was captured by the radio and transmitted just as it proceeded in reality. Or one sits in a German country inn on New Year's Eve and hears Big Ben strike twelve in London. Or a broadcast from Berlin of one hour of the Six-Day Race in the Palace of Sports. These are examples, stirring, emotion-filled, or sensational, depending on the subject, of exciting radio reportage. Hans Bodenstedt, the enthusiastic and imaginative director of the Norddeutscher Rundfunk, has already gone further in this direction. He has made a reality of the idea of interviewing people in the particular atmosphere of their lives. A zookeeper, a diver from the bottom of the sea (through a telephone on board). Seen from such perspectives, radio reveals it own unique magic. No doubt radio will undergo a development similar to that of film. Film too was unaware of its own capacities at the beginning—until it discovered that its own true setting is the world, the world, always growing and changing, as it lies before us—it clung to tedious little tricks. Only once the world became the set did the camera become the eye through which the millions observe the world. And thus will the microphone become the ear through which they listen to it.

To the musical and verbal content of the program is added, as a newcomer from previously undiscovered regions, radio reportage, which is legitimated as a cultural factor to the extent that it strengthens the network of relationships among peoples. While film reports on the side visual level, from which the masses learn what it looks like in London, Cairo, and Madrid—radio broadcasting develops on the acoustical level. But what is its artistic status? More precisely, in regard to the particular art form of radio? With transmissions of opera, concerts, and musicals, as well as recitations and lectures, the soil of art can be thoroughly tilled without special pains. The voices of the rarest tenors penetrate to the most distant coal-miners' huts, and the most celebrated actors flood entire provinces with the joys and sorrows of the heart. The popularization of the high and highest arts will be promoted to an inconceivable degree. Whether it is to their benefit remains, admittedly, to be seen.

Once again, the parallels to film are evident. In one of the earliest stages of its development, film threw itself voraciously upon literature. It swallowed Dante and Ibsen, Shakespeare and Rudolf Herzog without discrimination, and when everything in sight appeared to have been consumed, it threw itself with its last energy upon the Ten Commandments. But the more it swallowed the hungrier it became, and, since it ultimately had to become aware of this remarkable result, it came ever so gradually to accept that it might expect a wholesome diet only from the fruits it harvested on its own. Through this labor the film writer was born. Radio finds itself today in a similar situation, if somewhat less dramatically expressed. According to the principle, "He who gives much will give something to everyone," it rushes currents of dead and living literature through the microphone. The thought that the rector of the university, a haberdasher, a circus rider, and the madame chair of the morals society are all listening at the same moment can baffle even a broadcast director with nerves of steel. Thus the unavoidable character of compromise in all radio programming.

But compromise alone will not do. The lever of development must be positioned somewhere. My most urgent recommendation for attention falls in the category, radio play. The overwhelmingly popular method of today—to present plays, proven attractions or those sanctified with age, just as they are before the microphone—is honorable but not especially original. Exhumations often end in utter failure. A bad play will not be improved for having been trumpeted to the heavens; nor indeed will a good one. The world of visual appearance, which belongs to stagecraft like shine to silver, cannot be excluded without loss. It never happens that a theatrical play is broadcast without some amputation.

A radio writer is therefore necessary. Just as a few have learned after many difficult experiments to produce film as art according to its own essential laws, so will others learn to populate the auditory world of the radio with original works of art. I unfortunately am not yet familiar with Bodenstedt's *Herr der Erde,* which represents an effort in this direction. In any case it is important as a symptom of an incipient movement. The attempt is to create a pure radio play that is not somehow carried by a choir or geared to voices and music but is integrated into an acoustical atmosphere in which the hooting of the automobile and the bray of a donkey are able to find their place, just like the whistle of the wind and the chiming of devotional bells in a village church. In the place of colored sets come tonal ones. Only in this fashion can radio convey the sense of place that is indispensable to the dramatic movement of plot.

Alongside the radio play, the radio story will develop. The function of the storyteller is of extreme significance precisely in this connection, for broadcasters are immediately connected to that lost epoch when the people's hunger for fables was stilled by itinerant singers and chroniclers. Just as those vagabond artists of old came to the most distant settlements as the only messengers of the wide world, so it is today with the voice from the microphone. This voice may narrate more immediately than the novelist, who carefully forms and smooths his material at the desk. Through improvisation, changes of tempo, and the use of musical or other acoustical incidents, it can strive for effects that belong only to radio. Such supplements to the voice of the narrator would correspond to the harp chords of the traveling chroniclers. They should produce a tonal atmosphere, no more and no less.

All of those who, like old cavalry horses, attend only to established signals, to the signals of a culture handed down, will reject such experiments outright. But radio is here and will develop at so rapid a speed as to dizzy the uncalled protectors of the past. Today the theme of this essay can only be touched upon; tomorrow it will be carried forth from New York to Tokyo, from Königsberg to Buenos Aires.

252

KURT TUCHOLSKY

Radio Censorship

First published under the name Ignaz Wrobel as "Rundfunkzensur," *Die Weltbühne* 24, no. 16 (April 17, 1928), 590–593.

Not a word can be spoken on the radio that has not been understood and approved by a host of uncontrollable, irresponsible, and nearly surreptitious bureaucrats and independent reactionaries, average citizens, and obedient little shopkeepers. Consequently radio can never surpass a certain average standard, which would not be all that bad except for the fact that it robs large segments of the population of the chance to lend expression to their ways of life, their political demands, their ideals, desires, and views—as must be possible in any republic that propagates democracy. The censors conceal their true goals behind two excuses: first, that radio should not be political; second, that listeners complain about statements that are too flagrant and radical.

There cannot be an apolitical radio because absolutely nothing in the world is apolitical. The apolitical can no more exist than a person, for example, can be unmedical—everyone is subject to the laws of nature, anatomy, and biochemistry; even Goethe and Stefan George and Thomas Edison. A reasonable view of the world requires that the observer not perceive all areas of life in a single glance. If someone therefore investigates Schopenhauer's lifework, he can quite properly adduce the philosopher's economic circumstances as one of the explanations of his work, but he cannot rest content with that; he will have to leave the economic data aside for particular aspects of the investigation. In so doing he does not remove it from existence. Nor does radio remove its political foundation from existence by apparently ignoring it. It remains.

It remains, in fact, so clearly that radio, far from being politically neutral, as it obviously imagines itself, is thoroughly partisan. The faint note of *revanche*, the hint of imperial history, the world views of property owners, former officers, current judges, and industrialists, their moral and ethical convictions—they are granted a hearing on the radio with such matter-of-factness that it simply shows to which class the censors belong. If a free thinker, a radical worker, or a proponent of abortion attempts to express views, which are every bit as self-evident to us as their own views are to others, they can be certain of being censored. That is an ugly injustice.

The censors' second pretext is that listeners do not want to hear such statements. Now here—just as in regard to the cinema—the German people are sorely in need of a type of education they so evidently lack: an education in tolerance. There are only two possibilities. Either a ruling caste exercises a clear and avowed dictatorship recognized by everybody—in which case all is well. Or we live in a democracy.

In such a democracy, everyone has the duty to let opponents act and allow arguments to exert what force they will given the cleverness of the arguers, general conditions, the power of propaganda—and all must be given an equal start. I consider films that glorify war to be a crime; as long as the wholly inadequate and criminal penal code that the republic is acquiring does not recognize the offense, I have no right to hinder the presentation of such films by force. I can protest the presentation, and I certainly do; I can criticize the film, expose it for what it is, work against it—but I may not hinder its presentation. If pacifists do not want to see a war film—then they should not attend it.

But it is exactly the same in reverse. If someone does not want to hear what he holds sacred ridiculed on the radio, he should turn it off; he has no right to impose his views by force. A broadcast administration that accommodates the obstreperous philistines, indeed accommodates them gladly, is not unpolitical, is not even politically neutral; rather it is simply the representative of the ruling class and its moral views. This censorship must be completely abolished. And that is not done by allowing people from the German Writers' Defense League to sit on the commissions; nor by having the Writers' Academy, which remains remarkably impotent, redress this or that abuse; nor by giving a bad writer like Wolfgang Goetz, who is no doubt as pure and honest as can be intellectually, the occasional chance to prevent particularly grievous cuts at the censor's office. Censorship of radio and film must be eliminated.

The artistic consequences of censorship in radio and film are equally marked.

Since it is impossible to broadcast what the average listener describes in his complaint letters as "eccentric" on the air, and because it is quite possible to have a book printed for eight hundred people, but not possible to make a film for eight hundred viewers (except in rare cases of patronage), the cinema and radio remain mired in mediocrity. Such an exceptional person as Chaplin might be able to develop his genius on the basis of universal accessibility, but that simply represents a rare individual case. When years ago Hans Siemsen was the first to call for genuine and cultivated film criticism, one could only agree; he will meanwhile have discovered the limits of cinematic art himself. They are not located where, as might be thought, the viewer's imagination fails but where the producer's does: it does not appear on the screen if General Director [Ludwig] Klitzsch does not understand it, and that is how it comes out looking in the end. The artists involved endeavor to raise the level of the film, but they are not able to lift the foundation on which it rests. (The counterexample is *Potemkin*.)

Film therefore lacks nearly all of the refinements one finds by the thousands in literature. Radio therefore lacks virtually all varieties of new, colorful, sensitive, and razor-sharp experimentation; it emits scarcely a sound that reaches the heights. Completely aside from the fact that aural perception, when it is not a matter of music, is cruder and above all slower than visual, a radio censor must accept the unusual to be able to sleep well at night: he permits the works of Stefan George to be read, because "one" knows him—but he would never let a younger Stefan George on the air, which is logical and welcome. As it is, radio represents an intellectual steerage deck.

Radio censorship is a weapon of reaction in the worst sense. All those commissions, boards, appeals panels, and offices are superfluous because—like a large part of the German civil service—they do not accomplish any productive work but merely hinder the work of others. Radio censorship lowers the intellectual level of the people, similar in this respect to a portion of the press: the blusterings of both distract from the essential. Radio censorship must be abolished.

253

THEODOR W. ADORNO
The Curves of the Needle

First published as "Nadelkurven," *Musikblätter des Anbruch* 10 (February 1928), 47–50.

Talking machines and phonograph records seem to have suffered the same historical fate as that which once befell photographs: the transition from artisanal to industrial production transforms not only the technology of distribution but also that which is distributed. As the recordings become more perfect in terms of plasticity and volume, the subtlety of color and the authenticity of vocal sound declines as if the singer were being distanced more and more from the apparatus. The records, now fabricated out of a different mixture of materials, wear out faster than the old ones. The incidental noises, which have disappeared, nevertheless survive in the more shrill tone of the instruments and the singing. In a similar fashion history drove out of photographs the shy relation to the speechless object that still reigned in daguerreotypes, replacing it with a photographic sovereignty borrowed from lifeless psychological painting to which, furthermore, it remains inferior. Artisanal compensations for the substantive loss of quality are at odds with the real economic situation. In their early phases these technologies had the power to penetrate rationally the reigning artistic practice. The moment one attempts to improve these early technologies through an emphasis on concrete fidelity, the exactness one has ascribed to them is exposed as an illusion by the very technology itself. The positive tendency of consolidated technology to present objects themselves in as unadorned a fashion as possible is, however, traversed by the ideological need of the ruling society, which demands subjective reconciliation with these objects—with the reproduced voice as such, for example. In the aesthetic form of technological reproduction, these objects no longer possess their traditional reality. The ambiguity of the results of forward-moving technology—which does not tolerate any constraint—confirms the ambiguity of the process of forward-moving rationality as such.

The relevance of the talking machines is debatable. The spatially limited effect of every such apparatus makes it into a utensil of the private life that regulates the consumption of art in the nineteenth century. It is the bourgeois family that gathers around the gramophone in order to enjoy the music that it itself—as was already the case in the feudal household—is unable to perform. The fact that the public music of that time—or at least the arioso works of the first half of the nineteenth century—was absorbed into the record repertoire testifies to its private character, which had been masked by its social presentation. For the time being, Beethoven defies the gramophone. The diffuse and atmospheric comfort of the small but bright gramophone sound corresponds to the humming gaslight and is not entirely foreign to the whistling teakettle of bygone literature. The gramophone belongs to the pregnant stillness of individuals.

If one were to be thoroughly rigorous, the expression "mechanical music" is hardly appropriate to talking machines. The mechanism of the gramophone effects only the reduced transmission, adapted to domestic needs, of pre-existing works. The work and its interpretation are accommodated but not disturbed or merged into each other: in its relative dimensions the work is retained and the obedient machine—which in no way dictates any formal principles of its own—follows the interpreter in patient imitation of every nuance. This sort of practice simply assumes the unproblematic existence of the works themselves as well as the interpreter's right to that freedom, which the machine accompanies with devout whirring. Yet both of these are in decline. Neither the works (which are dying out) nor the interpreters (who are growing silent) obey the private apparatus any more. Interpretations whose subjective aspect had been eliminated—as is virtually the case in works by Stravinsky—do not require any further reproduction; the works that in themselves are in need of free interpretation begin to become unreproducible. The archival character of records is readily apparent: just in time, the shrinking sounds are provided with herbaria that endure for ends that are admittedly unknown. The relevance of the talking machines is debatable.

The transformation of the piano from a musical instrument into a piece of bourgeois furniture—which Max Weber accurately perceived—is recurring in the case of the gramophone but in an extraordinarily more rapid fashion. The fate of the gramophone horns marks this development in a striking manner. In their brassness, they initially projected the mechanical being of the machines onto the surface. In better social circles, however, they were quickly muffled into colored masses or wood chalices. But they proceeded to make their way into private apartments, these fanfares of the street, loud-speakers and shrouds of the emptiness that people usually prefer to enshroud within themselves. In Max Beckmann's postwar paintings, these drastic symbols are still recorded. The stabilization subsequently excises these disturbers of the peace with a gentle hand; the last ones still drone out of bordello bars. In the functional salon, the gramophone stands innocuously as a little mahogany cabinet on little rococo legs. Its cover provides a space for the artistic photograph of the divorced wife with the baby. Through discrete cracks comes the singing of the Revelers, all of whom have a soul; baby remains quiet. Meanwhile, the downtrodden gramophone horns reassert themselves as proletarian loudspeakers.

With its movable horn and its solid spring housing, the gramophone's social position is that of a border marker between two periods of musical practice. It is in front of the gramophone that both types of bourgeois music lovers encounter each other. While the expert examines all the needles and chooses the best one, the consumer just drops in his dime—and the sound that responds to both may well be the same.

In Nice, on the other side far away from the big hotels, there is a locale where, with considerable effort, one extracts some publicity from the gramophone whose private character is conserved in French fashion. There along the walls in sealed glass cases, one finds twenty gramophones lined up one next to another, each of which doggedly services one record. The gramophones are operated automatically by inserting a token. In order to hear something, one has to put on a pair of headphones: those who don't pay hear nothing. And yet, one after another, everyone hears. In this manner the use of radio technology penetrates the tenaciously preserved sphere of the gramophone and explodes it from within. Audience and object alike are petit-bourgeois girls, most of them underage. The big attractions are a screeching record by Mistinguett and the lewd chansons of a baritone who rhymes the impotent Siméon with his large pantalons. Both text and music hang on the wall above. The girls wait for someone to approach them.

The dog on records listening to his master's voice off of records through the gramo-phone horn is the right emblem for the primordial affect which the gramophone stimulated and which perhaps even gave rise to the gramophone in the first place. What the gramophone listener actually wants to hear is himself, and the artist merely offers him a substitute for the sounding image of his own person, which he would like to safeguard as a possession. The only reason that he accords the record such value is because he himself could also be just as well preserved. Most of the time records are virtual photographs of their owners, flattering photographs—ideologies.

The mirror function of the gramophone arises out of its technology. What is best reproduced gramophonically is the singing voice. Here, "best" means most faithful to the natural ur-image and not at all most appropriate to the mechanical from the outset. But good records want, above all, to be similar.

Male voices can be reproduced better than female voices. The female voice easily sounds shrill—but not because the gramophone is incapable of conveying high tones, as is demonstrated by its adequate reproduction of the flute. Rather, in order to become unfettered, the female voice requires the physical appearance of the body that carries it. But it is just this body that the gramophone eliminates, thereby giving every female voice a sound that is needy and incomplete. Only there where the body itself resonates, where the self to which the gramophone refers is identical with its sound, only there does the gramophone have its legitimate realm of validity: thus Caruso's uncontested dominance. Wherever sound is separated from the body—as with instruments—or wherever it requires the body as a complement—as is the case with the female voice—gramophonic reproduction becomes problematic.

With the advent of the gramophone absolute pitch runs into difficulties. It is almost impossible to guess the actual pitch if it deviates from the original one. In that case, the original pitch becomes confused with that of the phonographic reproduction. For as a whole, the sound of the gramophone has become so much more abstract than the original sound that again and again it needs to be complemented by specific sensory qualities of the object it is reproducing and on which it depends in order to remain at all related to that object. Its abstraction presupposes the full concreteness of its object, if it is to become in any way graspable, thereby circumscribing the domain of what can be reproduced. Phonographic technology calls for a natural object. If the natural substance of the object is itself already permeated by intentionality or mechanically fractured, then the record is no longer capable of grasping it. Once again the historical limits of the talking machines are inscribed upon them.

The turntable of the talking machines is comparable to the potter's wheel: a tone-mass (*Ton-Masse*) is formed upon them both, and for each the material is preexisting. But the finished tone/clay container that is produced in this manner remains empty. It is only filled by the hearer.

There is only one point at which the gramophone interferes with both the work and the interpretation. This occurs when the mechanical spring wears out. At this point the sound droops in chromatic weakness and the music bleakly plays itself out. Only when gramophonic reproduction breaks down are its objects transformed. Or else one removes the records and lets the spring run out in the dark.

254

FRANK WARSCHAUER

The Future of Opera on the Radio

First published as "Die Zukunft der Oper im Rundfunk," *Musikblätter des Anbruch* 11, no. 6 (June 1929), 274–276.

The public will be involved in determining the future of opera. The composition of a given public is the result of social processes of stratification and technical development, which are decisive and irrefutable factors in breaking down traditional forms. The future of opera essentially depends on the fate of the technical means of its dissemination.

This simple observation, however, is oddly unfamiliar in considerations of opera today and tomorrow. It is rare that reference is made to these facts; at most general tendencies in this direction are known.

Already today opera is, as a purely musical form, an affair of the broad masses. At least it is presented on the radio in multiple repetitions to that dark, indefinite multitude of people. Whether the latter affirms or rejects it will one day become clear.

Radio is the most powerful disintegrator of the old opera public that had a mind set, or at least the preconditions for one, produced by definite educational and temperamental prerequisites. With radio, opera is broadcast across all such boundaries. It marks a definitive end to attempts to use the work to shape and consolidate a public, as was manifest most obviously and powerfully in the artistic will of Richard Wagner. Radio and with it the other technical means of musical dissemination are first of all energizing factors, and only after their function in this sense has been fulfilled will they proceed to assist in the initiation of new forces of group formation, a formative process that will henceforth act upon the total public of the world.

Consider that tomorrow opera in its entirety will be delivered to residential dwellings like gas and water. Far removed from all cheap triumphs, what glorious progress we have made; far removed from an infantile *à tout prix* optimism in regard to technology, it must nevertheless be said that with the realization of television, already at the point of technical utilization, a startling novelty in the history of culture will make its appearance: opera as an everyday event in one's own home. This is contrary to the whole idea of festival performances: opera with beer and house slippers. The opera of the solitary auditor, with which the famous Ludwig [King Ludwig II], ordering performances for himself alone in Munich, receives a remarkable retrospective confirmation.

What technical form will this take? Television divides the continual optical event into individual images and then decomposes the latter into tiny particles, which are extremely rapidly recomposed at the point of reception. A simultaneous film, so to speak, is made of the visible reality (without, of course, fixing it on celluloid), and this is broadcast through the air. On the receiving apparatus (now usually with a viewing field of eight to twelve inches circumference) one sees what is happening in the same instant at the broadcast point. This is perceived in individual images following in rapid succession, which for the present flutter rather considerably and are also otherwise not terribly clear.

"But this will never . . ."—with such an expression the artistically literate Central European begins his reaction. For he is fond of saying that. Nor does he allow it to disconcert him that he is repeatedly proven wrong. "And what has that to do with opera . . . ? Do you really believe . . . ?"

I do not merely believe, I know it—without any further claims to divine omniscience. One small technical step farther and it will all proceed as follows: the receiver projects its image like a home cinema on a large surface suited to the purpose; there one beholds, just as in film, the events viewed from afar, for example those on an opera stage—and, indeed, with depth and in their natural colors (as the English inventor [John Logie] Baird has already achieved). Simultaneously one hears the acoustical events, as previously on a wireless telephone, so that one gains an overall impression scarcely diminished by technological deficiencies. The separation of the various sense impressions, as they have been previously available on the radio and phonograph records, will cease, and out of them the totality will be recomposed. [. . .]

Radio already has its own stage, if only for the purpose of broadcasting. Once television has been introduced, there will someday emerge a great broadcast theater whose performances will be designed like those of contemporary opera houses for the attending public, like those for the radio audience. It will be the future's most substantial and powerful opera stage.

Radio makes opera a reality for everyone. It will undermine the aristocratic prerequisites of the opera and thereby pose the question of its fate, a question that has so far received no better answer than the other problems of this age of denial and of the transcendence of existing relations.

255

ARNO SCHIROKAUER

Art and Politics in Radio

First published as "Kunst-Politik im Rundfunk," *Die literarische Welt* 5, no. 35 (August 30, 1929), 1.

On three million receivers three million families listen to the radio—that is, approximately nine million people. The public nature of art has reached a degree that can no longer be surpassed. Art has been socialized. From private ownership it has become everyone's possession. The artist is a public figure just as much as the statesman. His productions no longer belong to the single person who commissions, orders, or consumes them but to the nine million listeners. The artist's unique production becomes a good belonging to all through the ingenious mechanism of reproduction.

For 450 years people have been printing books, which is nothing other than the multiple reproduction of thoughts and their effect. They print music and distribute it to the multitude in editions of a hundred thousand phonograph records. They make prints of paintings and magically transfer Cézanne's works from private possession to the apartment walls of thousands. But only through radio has the socialization of art been completed. Radio art must therefore assume a character different from the one art had as long as it was private. The public nature of this type of art presents it with new and particular tasks. There was a courtly art for the court, the poetry of master singers for the rich artisans of the cities, a bourgeois art for the bourgeoisie—now there will have to be an art for nine million.

The ten German broadcasting companies operate with a budget of thirty million (after the forty million due the national postal system has been deducted). The economic potential of each of the ten broadcasters exceeds that of a couple dozen of the larger theaters.

Each German broadcaster can spend nearly ten thousand marks a day. There are no supporters of the arts, no public cultural institutions, that could ever have enjoyed similar opportunities. With these means colossal things can be accomplished, or, to put it negatively, colossal things can be prevented from happening. With these means cultural development, a new attitude toward art, can be accelerated, inhibited, suppressed, or diverted. This influence over the production of art is art politics. Art politics is integrally involved in the sphere of tasks allotted to radio.

Even the most well disposed cannot say that radio has so far been pursuing a clear and conscious cultural policy. Controlled by postal officials, structured internally in the bureaucratic likeness of the national postal system, it in no way distinguishes itself from a massive concert office with subdivisions devoted to traveling theaters and institutions of popular higher education.

In earlier times culture was the affair of a privileged caste. Artists were the private employees of someone with an interest in art. There was only artistic production, but no reproduction. The man who ordered palaces to be built, minnesongs composed, passion plays performed, chivalrous epics written—*he* was the public, the user and consumer of art. There was scarcely any art that was not produced first hand for a first-hand audience. The artist was responsible only to the person who fed and employed him. The invention of the printing press changed the situation. Thousands of hands reached for the work of a single person. The artist was no longer a private person, his work no longer private. He was no longer responsible to a *single person* for everything he did, but to a multitude. He "published"! What he "brought out," he delivered into the hands of all.

But what is the public nature of the book, even of the daily press, compared to the public nature of the radio!

Naturally the people at the broadcasting stations did not immediately understand what an instrument and what potential had been placed in their hands. They ended up in broadcasting by accident; they wanted to do business with it, and they have become no more honorable for having succeeded in doing business. In the sixth year of radio broadcasting, it has become a common practice to seek the assistance of theater administrators, directors, and music educators so that programs, until now the result of what happened to be available, could be organized according to plan. The artistic organization of the programs is taken care of in monthly conferences of all the broadcast managers and the permanent programming officer from the National Radio Company. The structuring of an organic program according to plan cannot content itself with looking through unsolicited manuscripts but makes suggestions of its own, makes assignments to the specific artists best suited for specific tasks. This active programming, however, is nothing other than cultural politics.

256

ARNOLT BRONNEN

Radio Play or Literature?

First published as "Hörspiel oder Literatur?" *Deutsche Allgemeine Zeitung,* no. 457 (October 1929).

I am encouraged by the particular subject matter of this conference not to content myself with simply examining the practical issues of the radio play. A conference on "Literature and Radio Broadcasting" obviously does not wish to claim that literature and radio are the same. With the focus on what distinguishes the two, the aim of the conference should be to address the challenges issued by literature to radio and by radio to literature. We have heard few such challenges made here. And if we did hear any at all, they were strictly of a material nature. We have heard people who espouse the unfortunate view that radio broadcasting is an institution existing for the support and maintenance of pensioned-off literary writers. In reality, radio is not there for writers but for the nation. It is not interested in what the individual creates, it views the writer only as a medium for the nation's thoughts and ideas.

Quite naturally every new technology stimulates a desire for specialization. Radio, excluding the visual from its domain, attracted a great number of people who did not possess a creative eye and who threw themselves into the arms of a supposedly new art form. But this art form was not created out of the limitation inherent in this new media; rather it was created from the writer's erroneous disposition toward radio which does not recognize or take advantage of either its limitations or its possibilities.

In contrast, it must be quite firmly articulated that specialization—on any level of human endeavor—cannot be anything but limited in its life span. The fate of the silent film now unreeling before our eyes ought to serve as a lesson that the intellect is insufficient to stop developments that are dictated by the instincts.

Every artistic development, however, conjures up the memory of the collective gestalt. The present state of affairs proves nothing but the total anarchy of our artistic will. This anarchy is still the best we have compared with the ludicrous and contemptible state of the various art forms. And it does not say much for the honesty of today's creative artistic producers that they do not even recognize this fact.

The radio play voraciously eats its way into today's drama productions. The latest manuscripts sit and molder. In radio broadcasting the dramatic advisor takes a close look at these radio plays and asks in amazement: why did he not write a theatrical play? And the dramatist examining these plays asks in amazement: why did he even write this? The answer he hears is: because the opportunity was there. Literature disengaged from its inner instincts reaches for external ones.

One often hears that a golden age prevailed when the wealthy, the nobility, or public institutions supplied artists with commissions, thus spurring them on to brilliant achievements. Without a doubt the radio play developed along such lines of art-by-commission and accordingly, given radio's increasing authority and significance, we should have to turn our attention to the marvelous development of the radio play. A belief such as this is lethal because the view underlying it is a lethal one. It is deadly, however, because it does not know what its own fundamental principles are.

Every art form must derive its impetus from the infinite. Responsibility, more than ability, is what we expect from the artist, and more than responsibility we expect a sense of inner vocation. Can this role be filled by institutions? Can the medium of radio inspire an author to write (even if it is a radio play), an author who is aware that he is quite removed from any divine powers? The institutions point to the past and say: it can. But that is the decisive point; in the past, those in power mandated their commissions with such a strong cultural will that even the most godless artist felt inspired by heavenly powers, whereas contemporary institutions expressly impose limits on their commissions. Broadcasting asks for a radio play and gets one; but would it not be better to demand literature and get it, even though the result would be a novella instead of a radio play? Only an institution's cultural will entitles it to commission a work, which is then to be systematically carried out. Whoever orders a commission must first have one to execute.

Radio wields the greatest power today in the verbal arts. This power is empty and without substance, a phantom that propagates itself via the airwaves. This power needs to be imbued with a radiating spirit, inspired by a people that welcomes it. In a time of total confusion, in a country upon which a shameless gang of irresponsible literary writers has imposed itself, a gang alienated from its people and bound to its own milieu, let men who animate this power from the inside outward take a stand: in service to the nation!

257

W. E.

The Writer Speaks and Sings on Gramophone Records

First published as "Der Dichter spricht und singt auf Grammophonplatten," *Die literarische Welt,* no. 41 (October 11, 1929), 1–2.

Records of poets speaking and singing, as are now being produced by Deutsche Grammophon and Orchestrola in a very fortunate experiment, represent a primary and long since forgotten category of literary effects. They are strictly distinguished from an actor's rendition of a literary work as well as from the common practice of readings by poets, which usually are simply boring.

The speaking and singing poet came earlier than the writing and printed poet. The former enjoyed artistic possibilities that were maintained by writing and printing, but, so to speak, on a steeply declining developmental path until they became nothing but received customs lacking nearly completely in inner vitality. Today, the speaking and singing poet has the chance to reanimate deadened worlds. [. . .]

Bert Brecht sings a few songs from *The Threepenny Opera.* Of course, some actors can do it better; but here we have the same breaths and heartbeats from which the rhythm of the songs originally derived, the cooperation of ear and larynx, the hearing of the sounds at the moment of conception, the first humming of the notes. The indissoluble reality of the physiological and intellectual oneness comes to living expression on this record. It is not important that Brecht, like every other amateur, specifies the points of execution to a certain extent only as directives, to a certain extent only to suggest his opinion; the simple fact of these directives themselves is important. Their effect on the listener lingers because the elemental intention is more powerful than the effect that would be available from an actor's perfect delivery of the same song. Still more important is the hint of medieval Bavaria in his vocal chords, since a particular vowel sounds right like this, a consonant has to sound like that, because it belongs to the concept of the whole. [. . .]

The truth is that such authenticity as this suggests perhaps the only way for the vitality of poetry and certain adjacent activities to be maintained. The more print lays claim to the eye of the reader, the more one-sidedly the visual sense develops toward abstract sensory associations; it *sees* less nowadays the more it *reads.* The *ear,* whose function in the field of art has almost always been restricted to listening to music, can also be trained to *see* the physical dimensions of language in their actual contours.

The most difficult task is selection. It is necessary neither to have only the best poets speak nor to have them read only their best works. The sole deciding factor must be the unquantifiable, nearly physiological correspondence between a particular poet and his particular work, so that those contours toward which the listener is to be trained become acoustical facts. The confessional nature, the essential privacy of poetry, is condemned these days as uncontemporary, as asocial. This privacy, conveyed by the essential privacy of the untrained voice of the poet, is strangely transcended through the dialectic of an apparent doubling. Precisely the most private poem read by the most private voice has the most general, the most dimensional, the roundest, and most cohesive effect.

258

M. M. GEHRKE AND RUDOLF ARNHEIM
The End of the Private Sphere

First published as "Das Ende der privaten Sphäre," *Die Weltbühne* 26, no. 2 (January 7, 1930), 61–64.

M. M. GEHRKE

The Great War, like all wars, transcended isolation and raised the masses to a hitherto unimaginable level of importance. The importance remained as the war ended; the masses have recognized their weight and become active. Soviet Russia is only the most complete example of collectivism; the great trend is everywhere the same.

We are not experiencing today the first reaction of history to individualism, we are not experiencing for the first time the preponderance of the masses; but for the first time a parallel development provides a previously unimaginable and unprecedented support: the development of technology.

Prior to the existence of cities, isolation and, as its internal form and consequence, individualism were facts of nature. The more people came together in dense concentrations, the stronger became the external preconditions of collectivism. Almost every new technical invention also signified and signifies a more intense concentration of people. One recalls the distinction between workshop and factory; one imagines what it means to travel in a sedan chair, on a horse, and certainly in a carriage, or instead in a train of twenty cars—immediate examples that anyone might supplement at will. Such were the developments before 1914. Since the end of the war the technologization of life has proceeded with bewildering speed. There is radio, through which it is no longer just a few hundred or thousand theater-goers who share the same experience, but which day-by-day, night-by-night, forces the same program upon the ears of tens of thousands, hundreds of thousands of listeners.

Forces? But it is hardly the case that anyone is forced to take out a radio subscription! Certainly not. But—disregarding entirely the imponderable influence of mass phenomena in themselves—the neighbor down the street has a radio, and the one across the hall, the one below, above, and next door. All of them have speakers, all of them open their windows well into the autumn, and if they are closed in the winter, the speakers, so very good at reproductions, penetrate the walls of old and new buildings alike into the home that was once my castle. I am steadfastly a pirate listener, although it was not in the least my intention to become one. If the radio is silent, then the gramophone resounds; there is no apartment house in which it would not be represented in numbers, no homeowner who lacks the altruistic need of allowing everyone around to take part in the perfection of his recordings. For collectivism has one of its most distinct effects in the contemporary form of entertainment. Before, entertainment and sociability were always mutually determined for the majority of people; is it an accident that in today's fairgrounds and dance halls there are social classes represented from which in previous times only the men, at most, would be present, and then only secretly. Is it an accident that everyone today expects the understanding participation of the whole street in the sounds of his entertainment, and that in such streets there no longer exists the odd individual who takes the speakers and gramophones, the barking of a dog and the clatter of a running engine for an invasion of the private sphere? An accident that he, as the single individual, lacks the courage to invoke for his own benefit what few civil prohibitions there are? A majority, however, that feels itself bothered and proceeds in solidarity against the disturbers of the peace—that tellingly does not exist.

It would be foolish to speak of the end of the private sphere were there no further evidence than a collective reaction to an individualistic century. It is only the parallel development of technology that justifies the concern, and, in light of the most recent developments, now more than ever. The problem of the telephone is all but completely solved; now we are at work on television. There is no question that here, too, we are very near a practical solution. A General Union of German Televisers has already been founded for the purpose of "promoting television and representing all interests associated with it." It will achieve its goal, and humanity will be one wonderful invention the richer. But will it be possible to deploy this invention in such a way that it serves the general public without disturbing the sphere of the individual?

It will hardly be possible—if only for the reason that there will be scarcely any, and certainly too few, individuals who feel this disturbance to be just that. That no one will be forced to acquire a television, and, once one has one, will always be able to turn it off? But who can guarantee that airwaves will not be discovered and machines invented that subordinate the viewer's will to that of the broadcasters against which the viewer has as little defense as a church steeple has against being observed by someone with binoculars? Utopia? After the events of the last century, that word is no longer valid.

Defense measures? They have no chance of success, since there is no will for defense in general. Conclusions? No conclusions should be drawn. The attempt has merely been made to offer evidence, not for the sake of argument but because we all, each in his own way, must come to terms with that evidence.

RUDOLF ARNHEIM RESPONDS

M. M. Gehrke stresses her forbearance from taking a position, claiming only to establish the facts. But she speaks only of unpleasantries, only of the noise of terriers, pigeons, and exhaust pipes unleashed on the individual by dear neighbors in an era of the collectivism of engineers. As if there were not also more worthy sounds pressed by one person upon the other. She steps into our times like someone who has long been sheltered from a pouring rain; raising her umbrella, she fears in the future that this meager defense will be taken away as well.

Collectivism is a dangerous concept because it is an unstable one. Collectivism is not a product of technology nor of life together in cities. It is much more to be found in it purest form in the first beginnings of culture, among primitive peoples and animals. The development and specialization of intellectual work among humans, the increasing division of labor, the disintegration of community into classes of various educational and income levels—these developments destroyed collectivism. It was precisely the factory work mentioned by Gehrke, which, seen from without in comparison to the artisans' workshops, began the formation of great masses and overthrew a genuine collectivism, a collaboration that was self-evident at the time of the guilds.

Collectivism is not the equivalent of massing together. Big-city dwellers, packed together body and soul, lead no more a life of community than do sardines in a can. They do not live together; they bother one another. That is not collectivism; collectivism would simply be the nicest and most efficient way of coming to terms with the nuisances.

More powerful attacks on private life than cheap modern walls and automobile horns are currently underway. Here one would have to speak of the general concentration of cultural production, of the standardization of utensils and diet, of the entertainment monopoly of radio and television concerns, against which one will need not only, as Gehrke stresses, defend oneself, but upon which one will become dependent. Who knows whether twenty years from now there will not be but a single play to be heard each evening in all the apartments of the nation (unless, that is, a captain of industry invites his friends to his private theater). How to come to terms with that?

The conflict between the individual and the collective did eventually find its resolution, one of much benefit to our work, but which brought with it an impoverishment of life. Papered walls and a bank account offered sufficient protection for those inquiries that thrived magnificently in greenhouses, that led science and art to the pinnacle. But the majority of people will live without education and culture until precisely the same economic system that brought forth illiteracy tears down the walls by making needs equivalent and leading the whole of the people—perhaps to culture, perhaps to vulgarity. Those who until now have indulged themselves in all the peacefulness of privacy with the good things of life, now see themselves being forced to take into consideration the needs of the general public because the individual sources of supply are slowly drying up. And they see themselves referring not to self-interest but to an altruism that can be exceedingly useful. For now that the same bread is being baked for all, it is in their own interest to contrive to improve that which is offered and to refine the tastes of the masses so that the general fare they purchase with their greater income might also be palatable. This necessity will admittedly cause enormous harm to the work of culture for a long time to come, and it is no pleasure to see what barbarism and crudity the Soviet system, for example, is introducing into art and science. But the present necessity, seen from the egoistic standpoint of the individual, simultaneously awakens the crippled joy of life in the community, of helping, of exchange. It will vouchsafe to the productive the pleasure of teaching, of giving, a welcome bonus to the fanaticism that the loneliness of the study so often involves. And it will, as is so evident in our contemporaries, tempt one to betray the intellect and in the protection of cozy, lulling comradeship give oneself over to the pleasures upon which the masses still depend today but which signal depravity in the cultivated. A useful disturbance: the all too solid position of the pampered will be shaken; in difficult circumstances they will have to rearm themselves to become fruitful, not only for the object of their attentions, but for their fellow men as well. And onto the groat-strewn pond where the teeming mass lives its life will fall sunshine and the stimulating fragrance of new-fashioned, dangerous feed. The discontent is worth it.

259

BERTOLT BRECHT

The Radio as an Apparatus of Communication

First published as "Der Rundfunk als Kommunikationsapparat. Aus einem Referat," *Blätter des Hessischen Landestheaters,* no. 16 (July 1932), 181–184.

In our society one can invent and perfect discoveries that still have to conquer their market and justify their existence; in other words discoveries that have not been called for. Thus there was a moment when technology was advanced enough to produce the radio and society was not yet advanced enough to accept it. The radio was then in its first phase of being a substitute: a substitute for theater, opera, concerts, lectures, café music, local newspapers and so forth. This was the patient's period of halcyon youth. I am not sure if it is finished yet, but if so then this stripling who needed no certificate of competence to be born will have to start looking retrospectively for an object in life. Just as a man will begin asking at a certain age, when his first innocence has been lost, what he is supposed to be doing in the world.

As for the radio's object, I don't think it can consist merely in prettifying public life. Nor is radio in my view an adequate means of bringing back coziness to the home and making family life bearable again. But quite apart from the dubiousness of its functions, radio is one-sided when it should be two. It is purely an apparatus for distribution, for mere sharing out. So here is a positive suggestion: change this apparatus over from distribution to communication. The radio would be the finest possible communication apparatus in public life, a vast network of pipes. That is to say, it would be if it knew how to receive as well as to transmit, how to let the listener speak as well as hear, how to bring him into a relationship instead of isolating him. On this principle the radio should step out of the supply business and organize its listeners as suppliers. Any attempt by the radio to give a truly public character to public occasions is a step in the right direction.

Whatever the radio sets out to do it must strive to combat that lack of consequences which makes such asses of almost all our public institutions. We have a literature without consequences, which not only itself sets out to lead nowhere, but does all it can to neutralize its readers by depicting each object and situation stripped of the consequences to which they lead. We have educational establishments without consequences, working frantically to hand on an education that leads nowhere and has come from nothing.

The slightest advance in this direction is bound to succeed far more spectacularly than any performance of a culinary kind. As for the technique that needs to be developed for all such operations, it must follow the prime objective of turning the audience not only into pupils but into teachers. It is the radio's formal task to give these educational operations an interesting turn, i.e. to ensure that these interests interest people. Such an attempt by the radio to put its instruction into an artistic form would link up with the efforts of modern artists to give art an instructive character.

25
Cinema from Expressionism to Social Realism

OFTEN CALLED THE GOLDEN AGE of German cinema, the Weimar Republic was an era of unprecedented innovation and experimentation in the short history of film since 1895. The expressionist style, typified by Robert Wiene's *The Cabinet of Dr. Caligari* (1920), Paul Wegener's *The Golem* (1920), F. W. Murnau's *Nosferatu* (1922), and Fritz Lang's *Metropolis* (1927), revolutionized the emerging language of film and established German cinema in the 1920s as a major force of high art in world cinema. German filmmakers were eager to overcome the stigma of the medium's plebeian origins: coming from the fairgrounds, catering to the entertainment needs of the lower classes, and relying on electricity and machines to depict the world—how could cinema ever become art? From early on, debates centered around the issue of cinema's artistic potential, and most of the classical films of the Weimar Republic were in fact attempts to prove to the educated middle class that cinema could indeed be art. By luring actors, directors, and set designers away from the established and highly respected theater, German cinema attained an artistic standard in the 1920s that, in Fritz Lang's view, surpassed the products of Hollywood.

Voraciously borrowing from the traditional arts (painting, architecture, dance, and theater), German expressionist cinema emphasized stylization, abstraction, and theatricality over Hollywood's realism; mise-en-scène and atmosphere over narrative and suspense; camera movement and composition over montage; and character gaze over action. Weimar film became known as a highbrow alternative to Hollywood movies—a simplified opposition, of course, because most of the three hundred to four hundred films produced in Germany each year between 1919 and 1929 were far from highbrow. In popular film production, adventure serials, thrillers, horror films, and even German Westerns catered to the entertainment needs of large urban masses. Emil Jannings describes the impetus behind the popular crime film: a romantic longing for adventure and danger in the midst of modern rationality. Still the best escapist fare came from Hollywood, which after 1924 flooded the German market with comedies and action pictures. Charlie Chaplin was the best-known and best-loved actor—he was treated like royalty when he visited Berlin in 1932—alongside Mary Pickford, Buster Keaton, and Douglas Fairbanks. For many German intellectuals, American cinema was the essence of what cinema was supposed to be: nonliterary, action-packed, fast-paced fun.

Film in the Weimar Republic epitomized modernity: speed, motion, simultaneity, and the predominance of the visual. A product both of science and the imagination, film was the site of an uneasy symbiosis between technology and magic. Not surprisingly, many early films featured mad scientists and inventors as well as artificial creations and robots that rebel against their creators. Allusions to hypnotism, hallucination, somnambulism, black magic, and occultism in such films as *The Cabinet of Dr. Caligari, Dr. Mabuse,* and *Metropolis* referred to the uncanny effects of the film medium itself while the interest in ghost-like shadows, machines, and projections thematized the cinematic apparatus. In 1920 *The Cabinet of Dr. Caligari* was considered a modernist breakthrough in its narrative multiperspectivism, distorted mise-en-scène, and stylized acting. Although the film did not find many imitators, *Caligarisme* was perceived as a touchstone for those who believed in the artistic potential of film.

Still, modern writers were not easily persuaded to write screenplays, not even after sound was introduced in 1929–30. Brecht, for instance, was hesitant to involve himself in a process in which he was unable to control the end product; his experiences with G. W. Pabst's 1931 film adaptation of his *Threepenny Opera* confirmed his fears. Brecht's only film, *Kuhle Wampe,* a narrative about the effects of unemployment, was produced with a minimal budget by a proletarian-revolutionary company in 1932. It applied principles of Epic Theater to film and used montage effects in the manner of Sergei Eisenstein's *Battleship Potemkin,* which was shown in Germany in 1926 after various censorship battles. Walter Benjamin used *Potemkin* to illustrate his theory of revolutionary-collectivist art in general.

The expressionist films, with their preponderance of golems, vampires, and doppelgängers, were supplanted by the mid-1920s by films of the New Objectivity which ventured out into the streets to capture social reality. Fritz Lang's *Metropolis,* the most expensive film production at the time, occupies a curious stylistic and ideological middle position between expressionism (the revolt against machines and instrumental rationality) and New Objectivity (the fascination with machines and Americanism). *Metropolis* translated this admittedly ambiguous but complex position, which was often harshly criticized by contemporaries, into fantastic images that still thrill science-fiction film fans.

Most films of the late 1920s and early 1930s, however, dealt with pressing issues of urban life and espoused an unambiguous social-critical message while retaining stylistic elements of expressionism. Siegfried Kracauer's 1930 review of Josef von Sternberg's *The Blue Angel,* one of the first sound films, faulted the film for precisely the lack of such a message; *The Blue Angel,* he maintained, simply ignored the contemporary reality in Germany. On the other hand, Lang's film *M* (1930), which dramatized the search for the serial murderer Peter Kürten, was criticized for its calculated topicality: the film's premiere fell within a few days of Kürten's sentencing. Many topical films made by the left ran into problems with the censors who in the last years of the republic became increasingly unpredictable and arrogant. Films that instead appealed to national sentiments by expressing the collective wish for a national rebirth, such as the series of highly popular Fridericus Rex films between 1922 and 1930, were praised and promoted by the state.

The strong sociological orientation of Germany's film criticism found programmatic expression in Kracauer's reflections on the tasks of the film critic. Kracauer, who reviewed films for the influential *Frankfurter Zeitung* from 1924 to 1933, developed a style of analytical film criticism that judges film's social functions. It was no coincidence that he would later establish underlying affinities between Weimar cinema's power-crazed protagonists and the fascist mentality in his book *From Caligari to Hitler: A Psychological History of German Cinema* (1947). He wrote this polemical study in exile—a fate he shared with over two thousand others who had worked in Weimar's dynamic film industry. German cinema never recovered from this loss.

260

HERBERT JHERING

An Expressionist Film

First published as "Ein expressionistischer Film," *Berliner Börsen-Courier* (February 29, 1920).

Expressionism and film have always played off each other in a challenging way. Film demanded exaggerated and rhythmic gestures while expressionism required the possibilities of acting and variation inherent in the movies. Specifically for the actor, film forced a highly expressive acting style which corresponded to the tendencies of the new stagecraft. If one had recognized at the right time the supernaturalistic requirements of the photoplay, the cinema could have—despite the artistic demoralization brought to bear by the pressures of the industry—contributed to the development of a precise, mimetic art that was fantastic through objectivity. But conceptions remained so retrograde and captive to subject matter that the expressionist film, which should have been an organic development, is regarded today as a sensational experiment.

It is telling that Carl Mayer and Hans Janowitz rendered their photoplay *The Cabinet of Dr. Caligari* expressionistically only because it is set in an insane asylum. It opposes the notion of a sick unreality to the notion of a healthy reality. In other words, impressionism concerns the arena in which one remains accountable, expressionism the arena in which one is unaccountable. In other words, insanity becomes the excuse for an artistic idea. But we want to assume that in his next film the risk of expressionism will appear less frightful to Robert Wiene, leaving him able to laugh at the motivation underlying his initial attempt, because expressionism is the precondition and the rule for the kind of performance that overpowers the subject matter. The quality of a film does not depend on how it deceptively compensates for the necessary absence of the word but on the extent to which film can communicate without language at all. The rhythm of soundlessness, which transcends language through gestures, should be the end and the goal.

In its particulars, *The Cabinet of Dr. Caligari* strives toward this end but does not always achieve it. When a sturdy, naturalistic bed sits in a setting where all of the visual lines cut across one another, the rhythm is annulled. When actors act without energy and definition in landscapes and rooms whose formal qualities cause them to strain beyond themselves, the continuation of the principle into the realm of bodily expression is lost. When performers made up rigidly like masks alternate with others done up naturalistically, the style obliterates itself. Elements that should work to intensify each other reciprocally get in each other's way. Leaving the minor roles aside, Fritz Feher performs the same old kitsch of an inflated film mime; and Lil Dagover is sweet talentlessness itself, unacceptable everywhere with her expressionless gloss, but here truly impossible. Expressionism unmasks. It cannot be indulgent in the selection of actors.

Conrad Veidt was born to play the role of the sleepwalker, transcending as he did his body's own limitations, while Werner Krauss, as Dr. Caligari, was simply phenomenal. But it is strange: Krauss who on stage draws from the uncanny intensity of his body every accent without resort to belittling nuance, is in the film, where the expressive power of his body must achieve the ultimate intensification, often unsettled, relying on overdone props which he otherwise eschews.

As for the rest: this film represents an advance in its painterly design (thanks to Hermann Warm, Walter Reimann and Walter Röhrig); as to direction, it shows promise.

To fulfill that promise, however, compromises must be rejected. In the ending the conventional rushings about, the obligatory chase scenes, and the banal groupings of actors must be eliminated. Then the film will be able to press beyond the technical mastery represented by [Ernst] Lubitsch to a freer rhythm and thereby to the intellectuality it demands.

261

CURT ROSENBERG

Fridericus Rex

First published as *"Fridericus Rex," Die Weltbühne* 19 (July 5, 1923), 13–14.

Anyone wishing to gain some insight into the state of the German national psyche is urgently advised to view this presentation, which is extremely informative. The large UFA-Palast, with several thousand seats, is always sold out, although the price of a ticket is rather high. The audience comes primarily from the middle class. It watches with rapt attention.

What is responsible for the power of this film? It is a depiction of the Seven Years' War as conceived in the patriotic legends. These legends are actually old hat; no one is really interested in them any more and no one knows them properly. The attraction for the public is threefold: the splendor of the military past; the analogy to the present; and the appearance of the great king, who is the primal image of the strong man for whom so many long today.

This weakness for the splendor of weapons, for military spectacles, and for inflammatory marches must be in the people's blood. Before the war it could get such sensations at the Kaiser's parades, of which there are none today. The film offers a substitute, and, due to its daily repetition, works its effect on substantially broader masses. As soon as Frederick the Great's helmeted batallions march in behind their waving flags, the applause breaks out—which is otherwise rare in the cinema. And it is not to be denied that there is something stirring about such things, however critically one's intellect might behave.

But more important than this general stimulation of the military disposition are the parallels to the history of the very recent past. Propaganda is being made in the most effective fashion for the nationalist conception of the German past. The origins of the Seven Years' War are in fact quite similar to those of the World War. At the beginning of the Seven Years' War, too, Prussia appears as the aggressor, but contends that the war was forced upon it by the opposing coalition.

Battle is the centerpiece of *Fridericus Rex.* It depicts all the splendor, all the fire, and all the terror of war. First the famous address to the generals: "Scoundrels all, who are not for Fritz." Then the charge into battle with marching music and waving flags. Thundering applause. The competition among the generals for the most dangerous assignments, courage in the face of death, cavalry charges. The public indulges an orgy of excitation. It thinks: ah, could not we too do this again, and finally take revenge?!

What can we learn from all this? How deeply rooted in the people is the feeling for the military, for glorious history, and for heroes! How dangerous these instincts are, and how ineradicable! It is insanity to humiliate a people possessed of such traditions to the point that they scream for revenge. The French amused themselves after 1870 with their revues in Longchamps, applauded their dragoons, and thought of revenge—the Germans are applauding *Fridericus Rex* and thinking of the same. Is it supposed to continue like this in eternal alternation until everything ends in mutual annihilation? The danger is very real, and one should attend to its omens.

262

FRITZ LANG

The Future of the Feature Film in Germany

First published as "Wege des großen Spielfilms in Deutschland," *Die literarische Welt* 2 (October 1, 1926), 3, 6.

There has perhaps never before been a time so determined as ours in its search for new forms of expression. Fundamental revolutions in painting, sculpture, architecture, and music speak eloquently of the fact that people of today are seeking and finding their own means of lending artistic form to their sentiments. Film has an advantage over all other expressive forms: its freedom from space, time, and place. What makes it richer than the others is the natural expressiveness inherent in its formal means. I maintain that film has barely risen above the first rung on the ladder of its development, and that it will become the more personal, the stronger, and more artistic the sooner it renounces all transmitted or borrowed expressive forms and throws itself into the unlimited possibilities of the purely filmic.

The speed with which film has developed in the last five years makes all predictions about it appear dangerous, for it will probably exceed each one by leaps and bounds. Film knows no rest. What was invented yesterday is already obsolete today. This uninterrupted drive for new modes of expression, this intellectual experimentation, along with the joy Germans characteristically take in overexertion, appear to me to fortify my contention that film as art will first find its form in Germany. For it is not to be found in the absence of a desire to experiment, nor in the absence of a drive toward incessant formal invention (however trustworthy and fruitful the old remains), nor most especially in the absence of uninterrupted overexertion in the name of results, which can only be achieved with that particularly German kind of stamina and imagination, of those who become obsessed with the work from the first idea on.

Germany has never had, and never will have, the gigantic human and financial reserves of the American film industry at its disposal. To its good fortune. For that is exactly what forces us to compensate a purely material imbalance through an intellectual superiority.

From among the thousands of examples that support my theory, I wish to single out only one.

American cinematic photography is regarded, thanks to its as yet unparalleled recording equipment, its film stock and the brilliant work of its technicians, as the best photography in the world. But the Americans have still not understood how to use their magnificent equipment to elevate the miracle of photography into the realm of the spirit; that means, for example, that the concepts of light and shade are not to be made mere transporters of mood but factors that contribute to plot. I recently had the opportunity of showing an American technician a few scenes from *Metropolis,* in which the beam of an electric flashlight illumined the pursuit of a young girl through the catacombs of Metropolis. This beam of light pierced the hunted creature like the sharp claws of an animal, refused to release her from its grasp, drove her unremittingly forward to the point of utter panic. It brought the amiable American to a naive confession, "We can't do that!" Of course they could. But the idea never occurs to them. For them, the *thing* remains without essence, unanimated, soulless. I, on the contrary, believe that the great German dramatic film of the future will have the *thing* play just as important a role as *the human character*. Actors will no longer occupy a space that they appear to have entered by accident; rather the space will be constructed in such a way that the characters' experiences appear possible only in it, appear logical only on account of it. An expressionism of the most subtle variety will make surroundings, properties, and plot conform to one another, just as I believe in general that German film technique will develop along lines that not only raises it to the level of an optical expression of the characters' actions but also elevate the particular performer's environment to the status of a carrier of the action in its own right and, most important, of the character's soul! We are already trying to photograph *thoughts,* that is, render them visually; we are no longer trying to convey the plot complex of an event but to make visual the *ideational* content of the experience seen from the perspective of the one who experiences it.

The first important gift for which we have film to thank was in a certain sense *the rediscovery of the human face*. Film has revealed to us the human face with unexampled clarity in its tragic as well as grotesque, threatening as as well as blessed expression.

The second gift is that of visual empathy: in the purest sense the expressionistic representation of thought processes. No longer will we take part purely externally in the workings of the soul of the characters in film. We will no longer limit ourselves to seeing the effects of feelings, but will experience them in our own souls, from the instant of their inception on, from the first flash of a thought through to the logical last conclusion of the idea.

If earlier performers satisfied themselves with being pretty, pleasant, or dangerous, funny or repulsive, film will propel new German actors and actresses from carriers of the plot to *carriers of an idea*. To become preachers of every creed that has people since they left their abode in the trees.

The internationalism of filmic language will become the strongest instrument available for the mutual understanding of peoples, who otherwise have such difficulty understanding each other in all too many languages. To bestow upon film the double gift of ideas and soul is the task that lies before us.

We will realize it!

263
WILLY HAAS
Metropolis

First published as *"Metropolis," Film-Kurier*, no. 9 (January 11, 1927).

Rumors were already circulating a year and a half ago that a marvel of film technology was in the works. And the reality surpasses even our wildest expectations. What has been achieved in this German film leaves all the American accomplishments in cinematography in the dust, and is unique in the history of cinema. Not only with regard to the artistic craftsmanship—in many scenes the technical aspects vanish behind the lyrical and symphonic images. The technology responds to the subtle wishes and touches of such an extraordinary master of the art of kinetic composition as Fritz Lang. Take, for example, Maria's escape through the catacombs, continually tracked by the spotlight cast by a small electrical flashlight—a mouse trapped by a minute, gliding spot of light; or the spectral strobes of light and eerie phantoms that skim across the screen, providing a visionary backdrop as Freder collapses and falls into a faint. This alone made the weeks spent filming with sophisticated cameras well worth the effort. The list of these accomplishments goes on and on—for example, the wonderfully light, spirited tempo of *Metropolis*'s visionary mise-en-scène, the airplanes smoothly swimming across the skies, the automobiles that practically hover in the air as they glide across hugh steel girders—with this, the industry of luxury that has been cultivated to the point of silent discretion is heard in a refined voice. And so on.

I am sorting out the commendable aspects of the film. The massive scope—naturally above all the scale, if you will. Gigantic is hardly the word for it. One is rendered speechless. The spectacular set design of *Ben Hur,* for example, looks like a poor relation, a simple little production measured against such prodigious displays. The Tower of Babel is shown once in a quick episode, a moment surpassed architecturally twenty times over. No wonder that Jehovah became truly enraged and so confused the language spoken by the film's creators that they could no longer understand each other.

At this juncture, it is only reluctantly that one decides to continue. Fritz Lang worked for over a year with superhuman energy and tenacity. The detailed technical work accomplished here is, in its scope alone, so absolutely astounding that I would not contradict someone who told me that this film had been five, six years in the making. In fact, it sounds unbelievable that this incredibly detailed, prodigious work was really accomplished within the span of a year or a year and a half—which is usually an enormous amount of time for a film.

But this should not be the last or even the most decisive word on a film of such enormous scale and ostentation.

What may, indeed must, be expected when for a year and a half the following are mobilized: 36,000 extras, 1,100 extras with shorn heads, 750 children, 100 Negroes, 3,500 pairs of shoes, 75 wigs, 50 futuristic automobiles, 500 to 600 seventy-story skyscrapers, a few thousand utopian internal-combustion engines, 2,034,120 feet of negative film and 4,265,091 feet of positive film and above all, above everything else, the intelligence of a director concentrated to a superhuman degree.

Not much. Please do not laugh, dear reader. [. . .]

Taking well-measured doses of world history and mixing them together as allusion and allegory is not the way to do it: a bit of Christianity with its concept of the mediator, the religious service in the catacombs, the holy mother Maria ("Let the children come unto me"—standing in for the absent son); a bit of socialism with its shiny new cult of the machine, the enslavement of the soulless proletariat, and the fully actualized "accumulation of capital," to speak in Marxist terms, which makes a single human being the unseen master of the world; then throw in a dash of Nietzscheanism with the deification of the ruling class. Everything is so carefully blended together that any other more cohesive idea slips past by a hair's breadth. And heaven forbid that the film should have any meaningful currency of ideas. [. . .] But that is exactly the curse of the large-scale production, that is the reason why nine-tenths of the enormous set design of every such film seems empty and superfluous: because it is precisely the large-scale production, the spectacle, that carefully calculates its appeal to everyone, that avoids offending anyone, is evasive and gives plenty of nothing. For the philosopher or for the artist the plate is full; but the gourmet must resign himself to a small plate of hors d'oeuvres.

Everything else follows from the basic precept.

The profound lack of inner form. Take a hyper-American, utopian, urban mechanism from, let's say, A.D. 3000 and put into that setting fragile, guileless souls, an artificially constructed *femme machine* ("Edison's Eve of the Future" by Villiers d'Isle Adam). But, still, there is not a single creatively conceived, lifelike human being in this mechanized world from which we are so removed in spirit. It has been projected so far into the future that its inner life, perhaps also its no less ludicrous physique, is completely incomprehensible to us. This is something [H. G.] Wells so often attempted to do, although also without any compelling creativity. And added to that once again is the romance of the medieval church—right in the midst of incredible dynamos, turbines, airplanes, and automobiles. But it is not just all of the above that makes every cultivated person who is sensitive to form nervous—it is symptomatic of something more objectionable. It is the noncommittal attitude of belles-lettres that so desperately requires tomorrow and yesterday in order to escape from today. What sort of obscure humor is at work when, in the midst of this wild oscillation between a romantic yesterday and a romantic tomorrow, the barest trace of a down-to-earth here and now pops up by coincidence? For example, the young hero reads a copy of *Apokalypse* that was published by the Avalon Press in Hellerau a few years ago. I could well imagine that one of these dead chess-piece figures indeed was able to read a book that I too have in my library. The entire precision machinery of this calculated world comes to a standstill because it is not compatible with anything that reminds us of a real, tangible, distinct, and empirically grounded life . . . because it simply is not like life, neither the life of yesterday nor of tomorrow; real life could never be so disavowed.

[. . .] Rather, and I beg a thousand pardons, real life could be disavowed by the mundane romanticism of the fair sex. It is always the same, a genre that does not even want to tackle the bitter and the sweet aspects of life, the real concerns, the real longings, the really burning existential questions. [. . .]

Only one symbol of a more deeply perceived nature makes itself felt, although it is certainly one not desired or even intended by the author: it is a kind of poignant version of the female doppelgänger motif in which the unleashed hell of the senses and the virgin's most tender virtues are physically identical . . . but this is really getting far afield!

Especially if you like and admire Fritz Lang, especially if you esteem Thea von Harbou's talents as a screenwriter, then you have to speak bluntly, even though quite honestly you say it with a heavy heart. One and a half years of nerve-wracking work! A thousand wonderfully conceived and executed, thoroughly worked-out details! By and large it is a matchless technical marvel. And yet . . . it would be a great fault to keep silent on the matter.

264

WALTER BENJAMIN

A Discussion of Russian Filmic Art and Collectivist Art in General

First published as "Eine Diskussion über russische Filmkunst and kollektivistische Kunst überhaupt," *Die literarische Welt* 3 (March 11, 1927), 7–8.

What is the point of lamenting the deflowering of art by politics while one looks for all the sublimations, libidinal remnants, and complexes in the artistic production of two millennia? How long is art to remain the privileged daughter who, even though she is supposed to know her way around the most disreputable back alleys, is to refrain from knowing anything about politics? That political tendencies are inherent to every work of art and every artistic epoch—since they are historical products of consciousness—goes without saying. But just as the deeper layers of a stone come to light only at the site of a fissure so does the deeper formation, the "tendency," appear to the eye only in the fissures of art history (and artworks). Revolutions in technology—these are the fissures in art's development in which the tendencies bit by bit (having been, so to speak, exposed) make their appearance. In every new revolution of technology, this tendency that is there in a hidden way becomes, as if by itself, a manifest element of art. Which brings us, finally, to the question of film.

One of the most violent fissures in artistic formations is film. With film there truly arises *a new region of consciousness*. It is, succinctly put, the only prism in which the immediate environment—the spaces in which he lives, goes about his business, and takes his pleasures—reveals itself intelligibly, sensibly, and passionately to the contemporary observer. In themselves these offices, furnished rooms, bars, city streets, train stations, and factories are ugly, unintelligible, and hopelessly sad. (Rather they were and they appeared to be that way until the advent of film. Having discovered the dynamite of tenths of a second, film exploded this old world of incarceration, leading us into adventurous journeys among the scattered ruins.) The compass of a house or a room suddenly contains dozens of the most surprising points of arrival, the strangest of station names. It is not so much the continuous changing of the images but the sudden switch of perspectives that overpowers a milieu, ruling out any disclosure but its own and forcing from a petit-bourgeois apartment the same beauty one admires in an Alfa Romeo.

So far, so good. Difficulties appear only once the "plot" comes into play. Satisfactory answers to the question of a meaningful film plot are just as rare as solutions to the abstract problems of form that arise from the new technique. And this equation proves one thing above all: the important, elementary moments of progress in art are novelties neither of content nor of form; the revolution in technique precedes both. That film technique however, has found neither the form nor the content adequate to its fundamental nature is no accident at all. On the contrary, it proves that playing with questions of form and plot in the absence of a specific tendency require that the questions be posed anew for every individual case. The superiority of Russian films of revolution, just like those of American farce, derives from the fact that both in their own way have taken for their respective bases a tendency to which they constantly, consistently return. That is to say, the farcical film is also tendentious, albeit in a less evident fashion. Its peaks take aim against technique. Such a film is comical, after all, only in that the laughter it inspires hovers over the abyss of horror. The reverse of a ridiculously unrestrained technique is the mortal precision of a fleet of naval vessels on maneuver, relentlessly captured in *Potemkin*.

The film of the international bourgeoisie has not been able to find a consistent, ideological schema. That is one of the causes of its crises. (For the conspiracy between film technique and milieu, the most genuine of the crises' reproaches, does not tolerate the glorification of the bourgeois.) The proletariat is the hero of those adventurous spaces to which, heart pounding, the bourgeois gives himself over in the cinema, because he must enjoy the "beautiful" precisely there where it speaks to him of the destruction of his class. The proletariat is, however, a collective as these spaces are spaces of the collective. And it is only here at the point of the human collective that film can complete the prismatic work that it began with milieu. (*Potemkin* has the effect of an epic precisely because this work has never before been so accessible to recognition.) For the first time the mass movement has that wholly architectonic yet so completely unmonumental (read: UFA-) character that constitutes the first proof of its right to be recorded on film. No other medium could reproduce this collective in motion; more precisely, no other could communicate such beauty as well as the movement of its terror, its panic. Since *Potemkin* such scenes are the inalienable possession of Russian cinematic art. As in *Potemkin* during the shelling of Odessa, so too in the newer film, Vsevolod Pudovkin's *Mother,* a pogrom against the factory workers portrays the sufferings of the urban masses as if inscribed into the asphalt-paved streets.

Potemkin was made consistently with a sense of collectivism. The leader of the revolt, Lieutenant Schmidt, one of the legendary figures of revolutionary Russia, does not appear in the film. That is, if you like, a falsification of history, but it has nothing whatever to say concerning an evaluation of the film's achievement. Why then, in any case, should the actions of the collective be unfree and those of the individual free? This abstruse sport of determinism remains every bit as unfathomable in itself as in its significance for the debate.

The antagonist must of course conform to the collective character of the mutinous masses. It would have made absolutely no sense to have juxtaposed it to differentiated individuals. The ship's doctor and the captain must be typical characters. They must be types drawn from the bourgeoisie. Let us call them types of sadists whom an evil, dangerous system calls to the pinnacles of power. With that we have arrived once again at a political formulation. It is not to be avoided because it is true. Nothing is more helpless than the appeal to individual cases. The individual may be a singularity; the unchecked consequences of his evil deeds are not. They lie instead in the nature of the imperialistic state and, within certain limits, of any state as such. Certainly many facts exist which only obtain their meaning, their contours, if they are recovered from isolated observation. These are the facts with which statistics deal. That a Mr. X takes his own life in March rather than April may be of little consequence in terms of his individual fate. But it would be extraordinarily interesting if one were to learn that the annual suicide curve attains its maximum in that month. So perhaps the acts of sadism on the part of the ship doctor are merely individual instances in his life; perhaps he slept badly or got a rotten egg for breakfast. The case becomes interesting only when one factors in the relation between the doctor's position and the power of the state. More than one investigator was able to conduct extremely precise studies of this matter for the last years of World War I, and the wretched sadist of *Potemkin* can only inspire sympathy when one compares his deed and the just punishment he received to the hangman's atrocities thousands of his colleagues performed for the General Staff—without penalty—in the last few years.

Potemkin is a film of rare greatness. To single it out for critical protest already bespeaks a mood of desperation. There exists otherwise enough bad tendentious art, including bad socialist tendentiousness. Such things are determined by their effects, depend on worn-out reflexes, used-up models. But this film is ideologically sturdy, correctly calculated in all details like the arch of a bridge. The more powerfully the blows rain down upon it, the more beautifully it hums. Only those who tap upon it with their little fingers in gloves hear and move nothing.

265

BÉLA BALÁZS

Writers and Film

First published as "Dichter und Film," in *Film-Photos wie noch nie,* ed. Edmund Bucher and Albrecht Kindt (Giessen: Kindt & Bucher Verlag, 1929), 18.

Has anyone ever asked about him? Has anyone noted the name of any film writer? Actors and directors have become famous—the performers too. But *what* they performed seems to be a matter of complete indifference.

Is that unfair? Actually it is not. For this "what" seems, in film, not to be there at all. In the theater we are always perceiving a double thing: the drama and its performance. They appear nearly independently of each other, always as a duality. There is a play in and for itself, which the actors and director only interpret. But it is possible for us to consider whether they have done this correctly or incorrectly. For we hear the text, the words of the writer, and can judge whether the performance corresponds. The original always remains accessible to us.

With film it is different. We cannot perceive an independent play behind the performance and judge it independently of the given presentation. The film's audience is unable to check whether the director and the actors have performed the work of the writer well or poorly, for they never see the original work. The performance has fully absorbed the text. It is no longer there in film. What we see is *only* the work of the performers, the director, and the photographer. *They* are the writers of the film. Who cares about another one?

But it was once so in the theater as well. We know that there was theater before there was a dramatic literature. In theater too people began by improvising, simply acting on the basis of some situation described in very general terms. The commedia dell'arte was also the original form of the theater. Actors and directors were around long before there were writers. It marked a critical stage of development when performers put themselves in the service of a definite, indeed predetermined, idea, in the service of an already-formed work of art. And that occurred once the childlike joy in simple play-acting no longer sufficed, once it began asking after the meaning underlying the play, which the actors were supposed to reproduce as accurately as possible. That was where the play emerged from play-acting. It was a sign of maturity. Perhaps the loss of an innocence. Nevertheless with the question of deeper meaning came the cry for the writer.

Film appears to be entering this critical stage of development. Everywhere there are complaints about kitschy, banal, shallow manuscripts. Does that mean they used to be better? But who asked about them then? There was so much joy to be had in the direct visual phenomenon of the acting, in the beauty of a woman, the horsemanship of a man, in the speed of a racing automobile, in the visual effect of an interesting shot, or in the emotional expression of an actor's face that it was completely sufficient in itself, especially since there was always something new and surprising to see. Just a few years ago the audience was still applauding an interesting and beautiful shot. No longer. For good photography has become so general today, has become so self-evident, the *sine qua non* of filmmaking, that its effects are no longer surprising. The director's techniques for manipulating mood have also reached such a level in general (and for the time being have remained on that level) that there are no particular surprises to sustain our interest. After the play-acting, the time for the play has come.

In the beginning we were overjoyed by the new technology, then by the discovery of the visible world, then by the purely objective. This now appears to have been exhausted for a time. Merely naïve visual desires have been satisfied. Now we are asking for meaning and challenging the writers. Have we perhaps matured?

266

EMIL JANNINGS

Romanticizing the Criminal in Film

First published as "Kriminal-Romantik im Film," *Film-Photos wie noch nie,* ed. Edmund Bucher and Albrecht Kindt (Giessen: Kindt und Bucher Verlag, 1929), 13–14.

The world of respectable people becomes less and less romantic. But what did we call romantic? The unusual, the colorful, the distant, and the adventurous. Our world grows smaller everyday. Increasingly we hear from people in other parts of the world; science and the press inform us quickly and thoroughly, and finally film too offers us some visual instruction. Therefore what before appeared colorful, strange, adventurous—in a word, romantic—has today been brought within easy reach and lost the charm of the distant.

But a romanticism still remains, and it is not of this world. It is the romanticism of the underworld. We still believe in this one, and thus arise the fables of the dark individuals with almost preternatural talents. There we still believe in people who are disdainful of death, in those who fight with an army of policemen, or in daring lads who rob a bank in broad daylight, and so on and so forth.

It is certainly not to everyone's taste. But if we want to understand our times correctly, we may not pass over the dark side of human society. If for this reason alone, crime films would be effective and important.

Mauritz Stiller never directed a single crime film in his whole life. And it was my belief that he would never have consented to film that sort of subject, filled exclusively with evil people and degenerates. When, however, he once got some such material in his hand calling for a humane understanding of this world of characters driven by criminal instinct and seduced by horror, he appeared to undergo a transformation. He said: if there is anything at all like romanticism today, then we will find it among the dregs of human society.

The film he then shot, with me in the leading role, depicted a criminal who was *also* a "human being." We are accustomed to seeing inferior beings in the antipodes of good morality, and it is well known that some criminologists regard criminals as sick. Certainly the great bulk of wrongdoers is recruited from inferior subjects. But the heads of the underworld are leaders by nature, just as in the bourgeois order. There too we find vision, genius, cleverness, culture, and all the personal virtues like self-sacrifice, courage, and loyalty.

These people, however, find themselves engaged in a constant struggle against the society from which they have been excluded—whether with or without their complicity is not at issue here. This struggle creates moments of suspense everyday. The great criminal is always on the lookout for the police; he is not secure in his life for a second, and must wager his life in every one of these seconds. I believe that if our great leaders of the overworld had to act just as constantly at the risk of their lives—our ministers, bank directors, industrial magnates, newspaper editors—they would not cut a very good figure.

Struggle is the criminal's element.

267

SIEGFRIED KRACAUER

The Blue Angel

First published as "*Der blaue Engel*," *Die neue Rundschau* 41, no. 6 (June 1930), 861–863.

It often happens in German public life that something appears on the scene that has been excellently made and has only one fault; namely that it is really nothing at all. It could not be more artistically put together but its trappings are mere ornament. Such empty showpieces are typical of our public life today. The concealed reason for this is that there is nothing behind it.

A prime example of this lack of substance, which it would be worthwhile to analyze, is the film that has been so much praised in the press—*The Blue Angel*. It contains details that could not be better; it is built up and cut with undeniable skill. It must be admitted that it is an outstanding achievement; that the alternation between dialogue scenes and silent scenes confers on the film a special power that has never before been so penetratingly realized; that some scenes (e.g., that of the headmaster in the classroom or of the wedding breakfast) are extraordinarily conspicuous; that Jannings with the assurance of a well-seasoned actor extracts every conceivable effect from anything that could possibly provide one; and that there is a pleasing harmony between Marlene Dietrich's vocal organs and beautiful legs. All this is admitted, but to what purpose the legs, the effects, the technique, the gigantic theater?

For a private tragedy that in this version and today concerns no one very much. The fact that Heinrich Mann's novel is misused is not a decisive factor here. More important is the fact that this prewar book has been chosen at all as a basis. What interest led the film producers, who could equally well have chosen Mann's *Der Untertan*, to the dark psyche of Professor Unrat and his relations with the singer Lola? It was this: the subjects that are nowadays considered to be of interest betray the fact that they are not real subjects at all. The selection that is made of themes and structures may be conscious or unconscious, but nevertheless the aim is, as *The Blue Angel* testifies, to forget reality and to conceal it. The personal fate of Unrat is not an end in itself—much more than this it is just a means to an end—i.e., escape from reality, and in this respect is like the painting on the theater curtain which gives the illusion of the play. Unfortunately the public never notices that the curtain is never raised.

But do individual destinies and psychology not exist now after the war as they did before? Certainly, and there would be nothing against their legitimate representation. Only our film has nothing to do with the suitable unfolding of its theme. If it were to concern itself with that and nothing else the characters would then form part of a wider society; in fact the conditions which bring the grammar-school teacher and the *chanteuse* together would of themselves come into the foreground. For if we have learned anything at all from the recent past it is this: that individual destinies where they seem undetermined are in fact determined by the contemporary economic and social situation. This film, however, avoids, with an assiduity that must have been exhausting, any reference that could move us to include present social conditions. It suppresses the social environment that would force itself upon the naive spectator of Unrat's catastrophe, it tears the performers out of any social context in which they would have gained contemporary significance and places them in a vacuum. Neither Lola nor Unrat has enough air to breathe, which confirms the claim that it is less the reality of their existence that is to be demonstrated, than the existence of reality that is to be veiled.

So what seems to be questioned is not in question at all. But more than this; this futile shadow boxing is inflated to colossal significance. In this too *The Blue Angel* keeps to the rule that is valid here for most public events. One seeks through the use of monumental architecture to raise the illusion that the content which this architecture surrounds is indeed content. One places decorative walls in front of subjects that are only pretexts and claims that they are real subjects. With the same din with which savages drive away evil spirits, people here want to stifle unpleasant realizations, i.e., realizations which make us conscious of that reality from which we are fleeing.

Whilst in truth Professor Unrat should disintegrate noiselessly, in the film he perishes with a great flourish. The spiritual events, which today more than ever seem to belong in a transparent casing, are dragged into the open and with visual and acoustic close-ups are turned into the main outward events: this has its justifications. If the outer conditions of our existence are to move out of our consciousness then the inner life must rush to fill out the external world, and develop into an ostentatious facade behind which the real exterior can disappear unnoticed. An inverted glove—the inside becomes the outside so that the outside is made invisible, and Jannings can crow as loudly as he likes. The appearance of lost inwardness which otherwise would serve no purpose is here just right as the substitute for outer reality.

Fortunately this reversal of the normal order of things avenges itself. Compared with the broad school scenes, Unrat plunges downwards too suddenly and abruptly. This is what happens when one uses spiritual events as decoration: their continuity is not always transferable. Also the intent desire of the artificial harbor street to be expressive long after expressionism is deceiving. It subjects itself freely to psychic invasion: it is reduced to the level of decor. And finally the screeching and clattering; the sadism and the battle cries at the end: what a hopeless comparison between hullabaloo and meaning is set up here. But the hullabaloo is required to conceal the lack of meaning.

The success of *The Blue Angel* in covering up our situation by thundering over it, and thus escaping it, is in itself a characteristic of this situation. For those strata that determine the face of German public life there is nothing left but to cloud reality. They have no vital perceptions with which to counter attacks from the opposition. They find themselves, as I have pointed out in my book, *White-Collar Workers*, ideologically on the defensive. Therefore in their own interests they cannot permit public debate about the fundamentals of the existing situation. How the dangers of such debate are exorcized is shown by the exemplary case of *The Blue Angel*. It shows too that in the long run all attempts to escape are in vain as they lead to a gaping void.

268

ERICH POMMER

Writers and the Sound Film

First published as "Dichter und Tonfilm," *Der Querschnitt* 11, no. 1 (January 1931), 46.

Film production was always based on collectivism, on a colorful multitude of components coming together from opposing directions. By pushing this principle to the extreme, the sound film rearranged all the relations among those involved in the production, who felt the ground beneath their feet wobble under the initial onslaught. Now the tasks have once again become clear. The screenplay writer, who requires extreme dramatic and technical precision in the sound (in silent films the occasional error could be corrected later in the editing), gained considerably in significance. Dialogue authors were brought in for the first time. There was no lack of material. The central question in sound films as well as silent is, primarily, how?

It remains desirable for *writers* to devote themselves to film production. They should not be put off by the fact that film production has already had rather bad experiences with writers. Outstanding writers have sometimes been capable of giving nothing to film because they regarded the matter as complete once they had lent their names to it, the exploitation of which seemed to them to be the point. So when they went to work on the black-and-white art, they did not bring to it the same creative energy they accepted as self-evident in their literary activity. Film will belong to writers once they give themselves to it without reservation.

269

GABRIELE TERGIT

Fritz Lang's M: Filmed Sadism

First published as "Der Fritz Lang–Film: Der Film des Sadismus," *Die Weltbühne* 27, no. 23 (June 9, 1931), 834–835.

The murder film *M* is the swiftest opportunism. The beast was just in court, and already on the screen!

In this film there is everything the censor otherwise cuts even in the most harmless varieties: the murderer reaches in his pocket, whets the knife—a scene cannot be any more sadistic.

The state is mocked; the mobsters are heroized [. . .] A hymn of praise to the asocial; a hymn of praise to the violent. Romanticized criminality of the worst sort! Vigilante justice is represented as true justice. The police are dismissed with a wave, the detective photographed from below like the Soviet people photographed [Alexander] Kerensky or old tsarist generals.

The murderer tries to flee the secret mobster court sitting in judgment over him. He is stopped by four strapping fellows. It is a typical lynch scene. At the premiere a lady in the back screamed: "The guy ought to be quartered!"

That is how it stimulates the rawest instincts, the cruelty slumbering everywhere.

But otherwise as well: Never was a bloody Wild West film in the outlying cinemas any more tasteless. Because things get really evil only when raw and uncivilized sentiments are mixed with the most refined and highly civilized ability!

Perhaps already the name [Peter] Kürten no longer inspires horror enough, Kürten who did not shrink from cannibalism. But imagine someone presenting the deeds of the butcher [and serial killer Karl] Denke complete with a clownish frame!

There is also a humor of horror, a humor incidentally that is typically northern German, the humor of Holbein and Dürer, Cranach and Bruegel, but also the humor of Munch and Kubin, a humor that is crazy and cosmic at once. One could imagine a murder film by Stroheim drawn according to the fantasies of E. T. A. Hoffmann, a passing nightmare: "Humanity is at its best when it shivers." But this is a case of the flattest burlesque humor! [. . .]

Alongside the silliness, there is sentimentality. In *Film Reporter*, Buster Keaton in his greatest scene politely lifts the knife that the cruel Chinese dropped as he was trying to do Keaton in. It is touching, because it is grotesque and no more than a symbol. Everyone feels that all tender, good, and unknowing creatures likewise hand the knife to their executioners. But here naturalism is made of the grotesque, and when the little child bends to give his murderer the knife, it is nothing but a thick coat of sentimentality.

The film as a whole is neither touching nor gruesome. Rather it is tastelessly calculated to please instincts that favor trashy criminal fiction and sadistic tales, and for which an execution was a popular festival fifty years ago.

When Peter Lorre depicts the murderer's drivenness, the bestial fear, the horrific power of a degenerate species, in a nearly poetic, in any case superbly acted, outburst and one of the exalted mobsters calls out, "Guy must wanna claim Paragraph 51, we know what dat is," enthusiastic applause erupts from the premiere audience. Every killer an expert on the ethics of murder. Every member of the Berlin underground the stuff of myth! Is it all just a farce, what mankind dreams of in the way of noble humanity, and what was later established scientifically through precise research into the human psyche? Are the insane also guilty, as was thought two hundred years ago? Paragraph 51 accounts only for mental insanity; it does not yet recognize the spiritual variety. It all depends on this "yet."

Human beings are so constituted that they are habitually quick to rest, quick to seek a victim. Scratch a bit and you find a Tartar. There were many Tartars in the UFA-Palast at the premiere. There would not be so much to say about this film if Lang were not regarded as the leading representative of German film and were this not the standard by which German creativity is judged.

This film is certain to have the effect of skilled tastelessness everywhere. The most shocking thing for us, is that, three weeks after the Kürten trial, Lang and Thea von Harbou have made themselves party to the exploitation of the horror for the sake of the box office. They have brought Satan himself into the business calculation and, lacking in all respect and seriousness, minted little pennies of success out of the need of mothers robbed of their children, out of the terror of an entire city.

Will anyone dare to show this film in Düsseldorf as well? Will Fritz Lang in his smoking jacket and Thea von Harbou in her white dress take a bow there too?

270

SIEGFRIED KRACAUER
The Task of the Film Critic

First published as "Über die Aufgabe des Filmkritikers," *Frankfurter Zeitung* (May 23, 1932).

The convention of photoplay theater owners in Frankfurt offers me a good occasion to say something of a general nature about the tasks of independent film criticism, about the sort of film criticism we have been seeking to cultivate for years in the *Frankfurter Zeitung.*

Film in a capitalist economy is one commodity among others. With the exception of a small number of outsiders, producers make films neither in the interest of art nor to enlighten the masses but for the sake of the profits they promise to yield. This observation applies, in any case, to the great majority of films that the critic reviews.

How should he treat them? These films are arranged now better, now worse, and made with greater or lesser effort depending on the investment of resources and talent. It is obvious that the review, especially the review in the daily papers, must take such differences into account. But in doing so some critics in their appreciation of this or that film confine themselves to calling attention to all possible details that either do or do not correspond to their own taste.

A treatment of this sort, which moreover usually departs from completely undeclared sensitivities, can in no way exhaust the task of the critic in relation to mainstream productions. For, though mainstream achievements might not demand evaluation as works of art, they are hardly indifferent commodities adequately treated by judgments drawn purely according to taste. It is much more the case that they exercise extraordinarily important social functions that no film critic deserving of the name is justified in neglecting.

In fact, the poorer the majority of musical and military films, dramatic entertainments, etc. are in holding their own against strict aesthetic judgment, the weightier becomes their social significance, which can by no means be overestimated. Today the smallest village has a cinema, and every halfway passable film passes through one of a thousand channels to the masses in city and countryside alike. What do these films convey to their mass public and in what sense do they influence it? These are the cardinal questions, the ones that any responsible observer must ask of mainstream products.

One could object here that some films do indeed promote explicitly political and social tendencies but that most aim merely at elevated entertainment or cheap diversion. The objection is both correct and incorrect. Certainly the typical film, more than any other, appears to strive for the absence of any identifiable tendency; but that in no way denies that it does not represent specific social interests indirectly. And this is how it has to be because, for one thing, the producers, anchored as they are in the dominant economic system, cannot change their spots, and for another they depend, for the sake of higher ticket sales, on satisfying the desires and needs of those strata of the population which are still more or less in a position to pay. That is to say, they depend on consumers whose fate is by and large tied to the preservation of the social status quo.

The task of the adequate film critic consists, in my opinion, in extrapolating from mainstream films other social intentions that often assert themselves very inconspicuously, and in granting them the kind of publicity they usually shun. He has to point out, for example, the image of society that innumerable films promote by raising a modest employee to unimagined heights or by representing some lordly gentleman as not only rich but full of feeling as well. Further, he has to compare the illusory world portrayed in such films with social reality; he must reveal the extent to which the former falsifies the latter. Briefly stated, the film critic of note is conceivable only as a social critic. His mission is to unveil the social images and ideologies hidden in mainstream films and through this unveiling to undermine the influence of the films themselves wherever necessary.

I have intentionally dealt with the necessary critical orientation only in relation to mainstream productions. Films of real substance have been and are rare. In their cases, it is unjustified to place the sole emphasis on the sociological, but rather the latter must be integrated into an immanent aesthetic analysis. However the difficulties of such an integration exceed the scope of this essay.

Ringl + Pit, "Eckstein with Lipstick," 1931. (Collection of the J. Paul Getty Museum, Malibu, California. Print courtesy of the Museum. Copyright © Ringl + Pit, Courtesy of Robert Mann Gallery.) Amateur dancers from Hertha Feist's Laban School, in the Berlin Stadium, 1923. (Courtesy of Dance Books, London. Copyright © Valerie Preston-Dunlop.)

26
Visual Culture: Illustrated Press and Photography

THE FIGURES ARE STAGGERING: over four thousand titles, comprising daily newspapers, tabloids, weeklies, journals, illustrated press and magazines, were published on a regular basis in Germany in the mid-1920s. Berlin alone had forty-five morning papers (the most famous ones being *Berliner Tageblatt, Die Vossische Zeitung, Berliner Lokal-Anzeiger, Berliner Morgenpost, Berliner Börsen-Courier*); two lunchtime papers (the most popular was *B. Z. am Mittag*); and fourteen evening papers (among them *8 Uhr-Abendblatt* and the tabloid, *Tempo*). The respected *Frankfurter Zeitung,* which had a Berlin office, was also widely read in the capital. In addition, each of the major political parties had its own newspaper (with its own regional editions): the Communist *Die Rote Fahne,* the National Socialist *Völkischer Beobachter,* the Social Democratic *Vorwärts,* and the right-wing, nationalist *Die Deutsche Allgemeine Zeitung.*

Some of the weeklies, such as the *Berliner Illustrirte Zeitung* (also known as *BIZ*) or *Die grüne Post,* reached circulations of over a million each. Both were published by the immensely influential and commercially astute Ullstein Press. Ullstein also published *Uhu* and *Die Dame,* monthly periodicals devoted to defining (and, in fact, actively shaping) the image of the New Woman. In addition, *Der Querschnitt,* Ullstein's answer to *The New Yorker,* with its modern eclecticism (that freely mixed high and low culture) promoted a new cosmopolitan outlook and sophisticated lifestyle. In addition to the liberal Ullstein Press, four other major media empires, all named after their founders, controlled public opinion in Berlin and much of the Reich: on the liberal side Rudolf Mosse and August Scherl; on the conservative side Alfred Hugenberg, who also owned a news agency and (after 1927) the largest German film studio, Universal Film A.G., or UFA; and on the communist end of the spectrum, Willi Münzenberg, an entrepreneur who single-handedly built up a huge multimedia conglomerate of magazines, party-affiliated newspapers, brochures, and books, in addition to a socialist film production company.

Hundreds of illustrated papers and magazines, some of them short-lived, catered to audiences with special interests. There were, for example, various fashion journals (among others, a German edition of *Vogue*); lifestyle magazines (*Der Junggeselle, Garçonne, Die Freundin, Ullstein's Blatt der Hausfrau*); sports papers (*Arena, Sport und Gesundheit*); magazines promoting health and nudism; several occultist magazines; and monthlies for auto enthusiasts. Every political and cultural subgroup—and they certainly were abundant in the Weimar Republic—seems to have had its own illustrated publication, often featuring well-known contributors.

All these magazines relied on photography for illustration, reportage, and a sense of immediacy. Becoming less and less dependent on accompanying text, pictures began to tell stories in their own medium, gradually undermining the authority of the written word. The emphasis on visual communication that pervaded modern urban life found expression in the mushrooming number of photo-illustrated magazines. As a pioneer in this field, the large-format *BIZ* introduced the photo essay, a new journalistic form in which several pages of photographs were devoted to a single topic. For *BIZ* editor Kurt Korff, only pictures gave a strong and complete sense of an event; journalists, he thought, needed to be capable of "seeing life in pictures." Exiled in 1933, Korff became an adviser to Henry Luce's *Life* magazine, which first appeared in 1936. *BIZ* and *Life* shared the conviction that the image, not the explanatory text, leaves a more lasting impression. Photojournalism was also aided by the introduction in 1926 of the first 35mm camera, a small lightweight Leica, and by the rapid growth of amateur photography. Many thought that only photography was able to capture the quick pace of modern life in a fraction of a second. In general, the Weimar Republic developed a passion for the new visual culture as evidenced by the internationally renowned "Film und Foto" exhibitions in 1920, 1925, and 1929; the flood of magazines, journals, and books about photography; the attention given to the medium in art periodicals; and above all the era's talented photographers themselves.

Two photographers typify different stylistic trends: August Sander's documentary, direct approach depicts German men and women in their social and professional environments; Albert Renger-Patzsch's style of objective realism opposes pictorial elements and painterly abstractions, and instead, in the spirit of New Objectivity, emphasizes those characteristics that belong exclusively to photography. There were many others: Erich Salomon whose stylish snapshots of public figures lifted photojournalism to new heights; Werner Gräff who argued for a programmatic violation of all photographic laws and aesthetic norms; and several famous women photographers—Lotte Jacobi, Aenne Biermann, Marianne Breslauer—who specialized in portraits. Grete Stern and Ellen Auerbach ran the famous Studio Ringl & Pit, which became known for its innovative and often surrealistic commercial photography. The Bauhaus also played a large role in the promotion of photography, using aesthetic experiments (such as Laszlo Moholy-Nagy's photograms, i.e., exposures without camera) for commercial purposes in advertising layout, posters, and typography. Generally speaking, photography was seen as applied art, playing an essential part in commodity production, distribution, and consumption.

The structural affinities between the tenets of New Objectivity and the laws of photography in terms of objectivity, matter-of-factness, and realism were well recognized by most photographers throughout the Weimar Republic. Renger-Patzsch's highly polished close-ups of gleaming faucets, cogs, and pipes added an aesthetic dimension to technology; machine parts are made to look like flower stems and leaves. His book *The World Is Beautiful* drew much attention from the literary intellectuals of the period as an example of the new objective attitude vis-à-vis social reality. It was advertised as follows: "The enjoyment of looking has been reawakened in our impoverished Germany. That is an enjoyment that can be shared by everyone, poor or rich alike. Only the sensibility for it has to be awakened. The best guide for it is *The World Is Beautiful: One Hundred Pictures by Albert Renger-Patzsch.*"

A radically different and politically activist role was assigned to photography in Münzenberg's weekly *Arbeiter Illustrierte Zeitung* (or *AIZ*), which at the end of the 1920s had a circulation of 450,000. John Heartfield gave this illustrated workers' paper a unique profile with his critical photomontages that exposed hidden agendas in politics and commerce by juxtaposing seemingly unrelated images. Dating back to dadaist experiments, photomontage was widely used for book designs and advertising as well as for political propaganda. In the case of dada-inspired artists (such as Raoul Hausmann and Hannah Höch) photomontages became a new art form that corresponded to the "explosion of viewpoints" typical of urban perception.

271

EDLEF KÖPPEN

The Magazine as a Sign of the Times

First published as "Das Magazin als Zeichen der Zeit," *Der Hellweg* 5, no. 24 (June 17, 1925), 457.

The mark of our age is haste, hurry, nervousness. People have no time, indeed they flee the calm of contemplation; they reel recklessly through the streets with no intention of catching hold. The rhythm of life pounds short and hard: further—further! The consequence is in many respects superficiality.

This haste also appears in areas that by nature must really expect more: the domains of art. The enjoyment of art presupposes, alongside an intuitive grasp, a tranquil and concentrated focus, a surrender, a release of the self to be conducted beyond the borders of the palpable. (The creation of art presupposes the same measure of inner composure.)

But the preconditions are lacking. And if there is one thing right now that could be taken to be symbolic of this, then it is the appearance of all the magazines that have been flooding Germany for just about a year. One finds them everywhere, in every bookstore, even the good ones, in most reading halls, often even in very serious ones. They are spreading like pestilence. One publisher started, a few dozen followed and continue to follow suit. The magazine has become a concentrated sign of our times.

The father of the idea is America and England. Magazines have existed there for a quarter of a century. And from there Germany took over the schematic model.

What is their content?

Nearly all contemporary magazines print a rich abundance of illustrated material. The whole visual complex of the popular revue, the sort that all the larger theaters feel obliged to offer to their audiences at least once a year, reappears here either in cruder form or in a more blatant presentation. Legs or bosoms of naked girls play just as inexhaustible a role as the dress of an elegant woman, the cut of a so-called gentleman's suit. Images of famous contemporaries, photographs of boxers, horse races, domestic and foreign abnormalities join in the parade. The accompanying texts are "designed" with great skill; filled with more or less witty remarks, magazines of this sort supply up-to-date commentaries on the milieu and thus contribute to the public's "general education."—Yet, not satisfied with that, somewhere in the distance floats something like literary status as the final goal. The short story is celebrated. Three or four pages are devoted to novelistic sketches filled with suspense, once again lent a kind of palatability by proxy for the public through copious illustrations reminiscent of cinema placards. Amusing features, that is, playgrounds for wit and witticisms, and puzzles—oh, crosswords!—of all sorts strewn in. Short and sweet, the recipe is apparently borrowed directly from the *vox populi:* "Please Take One," already thoroughly typical, is the way the magazine is put together to gratify the widest-possible array of readers.

There might be nothing as such to object to here. What remains somewhat questionable, however, is the level of this gratification and its impressive generalization. It is doubtless in the nature of every periodical phenomenon—every "period"ical—to feature topics of the most complex sort, to which a frequently scanty discussion is attached. Nevertheless a serious publication proceeds with a certain skepticism in the selection and combination of appropriate material. The magazine—and not a single one can be completely excepted—pursues complexity with such an emphatic single-mindedness that it cannot but appear suspect: what is being cultivated here is nothing but exceedingly banal entertainment through the deployment of the crudest conceivable means. The motto here is to be informed about everything, but know nothing thoroughly. Every type of "literature" is to be represented; meaning, however, that they are noted only in their crudest instances and then graced with nothing but platitudes. One leafs through a magazine and doubtless comes upon so-called names among the contributors. One reads, and can really do nothing but conclude with astonishment and regret that the possessors of these names—and it has to be conscious on their part—have lowered the level of their work for the sake of the magazine business and a mass of readers who reject every good effort as boring. Exceptions must be admitted, but they are usually translations. Germans are apparently incapable of mastering the short story as, for example, a Kipling, a Bret Harte, and an O. Henry can; pithiness and artistic compression are replaced by flippancy, superficiality, and sloppiness.

Objections of a practical nature are finally coming from booksellers' circles. It is believed that there has been a noticeable decline in book sales since magazines made their appearance. There is something to that no doubt. For one mark—the usual price of a magazine—a good book cannot be produced; besides, the public is obviously being drawn suggestively into that *multa non multum* and supported in an unfortunate view: when I can buy so much variety for so little money, then I would not be satisfied with so little (for example, one book with "only one work in it"). This view has recently taken on greater import since one publisher filled the columns of every one of its issues, alongside all the rest, with a complete novel.

Thus is the magazine a sign—and, as has been shown, a dubious sign—of our times.

272

AUGUST SANDER

Remarks on My Exhibition at the Cologne Art Union

First published as "Erläuterung zu meiner Ausstellung im Kölnischen Kunstverein" (November 1927).

PEOPLE OF THE TWENTIETH CENTURY:
A CULTURAL HISTORY IN PHOTOGRAPHS

Divided into seven groups, arranged by cities, comprising about forty-five portfolios.

I am often asked what gave me the idea of creating this work, "Seeing, Observing, and Thinking," and the question is answered.

Nothing seems better suited than photography to give an absolutely faithful historical picture of our time.

We find illustrated writings and books from every period of history, but photography has given us new possibilities and tasks that are different from those of painting. It can render things with magnificent beauty but also with terrifying truthfulness; and it can also be extraordinarily deceptive.

We must be able to bear the sight of the truth, but above all we must transmit it to our fellow men and to posterity, regardless of whether this truth is favorable to us or not.

Now if I, as a healthy person, am so immodest as to see things as they are and not as they should or might be, I hope I will be forgiven, but I can do no differently.

I have been a photographer for thirty years and have taken photography very seriously; I have followed good and bad paths and have recognized my mistakes.

The exhibition in the Cologne Art Union is the result of my search, and I hope to be on the right path. There is nothing I hate more than sugar-glazed photography with gimmicks, poses, and fancy effects.

Therefore let me honestly tell the truth about our age and people.

273

KURT KORFF

The Illustrated Magazine

First published as "Die illustrierte Zeitschrift," *Fünfzig Jahre Ullstein (1877–1927)* (Berlin: Ullstein, 1927), 279–303.

It was the change in the public's attitude toward life that worked to the benefit of the illustrated magazines. The magazines of earlier decades essentially published more or less comprehensive texts that were illustrated by pictures. Sometimes it was also vice versa: an explanatory text was written for an existing picture. But only when seeing life "through the eye" began to play a more significant role did the need for visual observation become so pressing that it was possible to make the transition to the picture itself as the report.

The shift signified a completely new attitude toward pictures. It is no accident that the development of the cinema and the development of the *Berlin Illustrated Newspaper* [BIZ] run roughly parallel. To the extent that life became more hectic, and the individual was less prepared to leaf through a magazine in a quiet moment, to that extent it became necessary to find a sharper, more efficient form of visual representation, one which did not lose its impact on the reader even if he only glanced fleetingly at the magazine page by page.

The public grew increasingly accustomed to receiving a stronger impression of world events from pictures than from written reports. The report was admittedly faster, but the event in its full dimensions, in its total effect—only the picture offered that to the reader. Without a picture the things going on in the world were reproduced incompletely, often implausibly; the picture conveyed the strongest and most lasting impression.

The *BIZ* recognized this changed attitude toward pictures early and consciously developed it. This new standpoint had to make itself felt at the early stage of selecting the pictures, for not every picture alone conveyed an impression of the desired intensity. The picture has to have the most intense possible concentration, has to capture a situation at its climax; when it does, it occasionally achieves an effect that remains out of reach of even the most eloquent text.

The *BIZ* adopted the editorial principle that all events should be presented in pictures with an eye to the visually dramatic and excluding everything that is visually uninteresting. It was not the importance of the material that determined the selection and acceptance of pictures, but solely the allure of the photo itself. This reorientation is responsible for the change charted by the *BIZ* in the appearance of illustrated papers, which are no longer directed by text editors but by those who are capable, like film writers and directors, of seeing life in pictures.

The editorial staff of *BIZ* was quite likely also the first to invite an artistic advisor into the editorial offices; that is, someone with the eye of an artist who was responsible for seeking out the strongest and best pictorial solutions—not only for individual pictures, but also in the grouping of pictures among themselves and in their relation to the text, etc. The present-day form of the illustrated newspaper—with its arrangement of pictures, its distribution of text, captions, etc.—appears effortless and obvious. But if one looks through the old volumes, it becomes apparent how much experimentation was necessary in this area before satisfying results were achieved.

274

ALBERT RENGER-PATZSCH

Joy before the Object

First published as "Die Freude am Gegenstand," *Das Kunstblatt* 12, no. 1 (January 1928), 19.

Photography has existed for nearly a hundred years. The country-fair magicians have become serious professionals.

Through films and illustrated magazines, photography exerts a tremendous influence on the masses. The photographic industry is developing at an American tempo and we are in possession of a splendid tool.

It strikes us as all the more peculiar, then, that so-called "artistic photography" still lies slumbering like Sleeping Beauty, and that pictures in the style of an 1890 *Gartenlaube*[1] are still accorded the highest recognition at the great international exhibitions.

Due to its mechanical processes, photography is without doubt the most refractory artistic medium; and at a time when photography was technically still very unfinished, the most obvious course of action was to compete with painting and to produce photos in which one tried to feign "art," ruining one's own technique with an alien method.

To a photographer who remains within the limits prescribed for photographic technique, the mechanical procedure of his medium, the swiftness of its execution, the objectivity of its representations, and the possibility of arresting static moments of fast and even the fastest movements—these represent the greatest and most obvious advantages over every other medium of expression.

The rigid adherence of "artist-photographers" to the model provided by painting has always been damaging to photographic achievement. There is an urgent need to examine old opinions and look at things from a new vantage point. There must be an increase in the joy one takes in an object, and the photographer should become fully conscious of the splendid fidelity of reproduction made possible by his technique.

Nature, after all, is not so poor that it requires constant improvement. There is still room within that rectangle of shining bromide paper for new spatial and planar effects; many things still await the one who will recognize their beauty.

1. *Die Gartenlaube* was a popular magazine aimed at a middle-class audience and known for its sentimental illustrations.

275

JOHANNES MOLZAHN

Stop Reading! Look!

First published as "Nicht mehr lesen! Sehen!" *Das Kunstblatt* 12, no. 3 (March 1928), 78–82.

A piece of paper, in the hand a pencil, and on the table the object—the looking eye; otherwise, a wrist and the tedious work of many, many hours.

One-hundredth of a second through the highly sensitive eye of your camera and the picture of the object there on the table is captured on the thin coating of emulsion on the film.

It is the pictorial telegram that you might already be holding in your hand tomorrow. Chaplin, Harold Lloyd, Buster Keaton, whose utter immediacy captivated you yesterday evening in the visual-kinetic pictorial succession on the screen. The newspaper that informs you just a few hours later of everything that happened on earth. The illustrated book, magazine—not yet today but tomorrow. They all are ruled by the same principle. Photography! This greatest of the physical-chemical-technical wonders of the present— this triumph of tremendous consequence! One of the more important tools for elucidating current problems, for recreating the harmony between the processes of work and life. It is the photo that continually informs us and suggests the new phenomena of contemporary work through the penetrating language of the image. The photo is the pacesetter for the tempo of time and development; the multitude and arrangement of visual sensations forces the uninterrupted work of assimilation on the eye and the psyche. Every new form rapidly becomes a reality and is superseded; one day—and this day is not very far off—we will have absorbed not only the image but also the spirit of these new contours of the age, and this spirit will inform our action.

Yes, this genuinely visual present will necessarily produce its greatest effects through visual means. The image will become one of the more effective weapons against intellectualism and against the mechanization of the spirit. "Stop reading! Look!" will be the motto in education. "Stop reading! Look!" will be the guiding developmental principle of daily newspapers—already today newspaper illustrations are claiming more space. But only the shift to the photographic principle in production processes will inaugurate the final revolution. Only once "phototype" has matured into a reliable instrument can the whole of book printing be integrated into the economy of contemporary production. Then there will be nothing left of today's typesetter but the name; he will shoot type and image through the objective of his phototype machine and with a simple adjustment of the dimension lever obtain whatever variation he needs. No longer will the layout of a newspaper page be composed of many thousands of characters and leads laboriously put together by hand. It will be a homogenous whole—one operation—that feeds directly into the offset press, exploiting for the first time the latter's full, effective rationality.

The eye of the draftsman is replaced by the eye of the camera, not because it is somehow more pleasing that way but because it is the more economical and therefore the only way.

Complete mechanization! That need not necessarily signify the atrophy of labor power. Energies have been released that impatiently await transformation. The technical functions of traditional handicrafts may well have been taken over by industrialization—not, however, the motivating forces on the intellectual plane; they must be transferred as well. The confusing chatter to which people are still resorting today must finally be overcome and forgotten. The point is not to have to do everything laboriously. The faculty for performing manual work must perfect itself anew in the all-consuming work to which we must finally apply ourselves. The laws that necessarily form the basis of all labor, of every one of our achievements, dictate that we reinvent validity; the effort must be made to return to our work the fertile soil that it requires to flourish. [. . .]

The photography expert of the past, in imitating painting, chose the wrong point of departure for the development of the phototype; the displays still found today in the photography ateliers evidence this attempt—but it achieves no more than a lamentable surrogate for painting. The formal consequences of accomplished technological facts always leave the experts behind. [. . .]

In short, the new visual orientation of modern people results from the unique tempo and disorientation characteristic of our anxious times and will lead to the elaboration of new forms to foster the quickest possible orientation and to take the transformation of physical nature and its psychology into account. Traditions of all sorts are slipping from our hands, for good or ill! We cannot oppose the effects of physical law. We will not be able to stave off these effects, until ultimately the most trifling aspect of work and the last remnant of our previous way of life, the last gesture of the human hand, is permeated by the new spirit.

276

WERNER GRÄFF

Foreword to *Here Comes the New Photographer!*

First published as "Vorwort," *Es kommt der neue Fotograf!* (Berlin: H. Reckendorf, 1929), 1.

The purpose of this book is to break down barriers, not create them. Useful though manuals of photography are, so long as they describe the technique of the negative and positive process, they are positively harmful when they set limits based on aesthetic or artistic rules as these are generally presented. The style of "picture criticism" in specialized periodicals, and the majority of photographic exhibitions, show clearly the extraordinary influence of the maxims constantly impressed on the photographer: the pundits have succeeded in closely circumscribing the art of photography, and only seldom do photographers dare to overstep the bounds set by them. Rules that stem from bygone eras of painting are set up as iron laws, though they can easily be shown to be untenable.

Given the insistence on these rules, it is not surprising that industry has almost completely concentrated on the type of camera necessary for "regular" pictures, and this again makes it harder for the photographer to stray from the preordained path. It is time, therefore, to make industry aware of modern needs.

In what follows we are only concerned with photographic technique in so far as it relates to equipment and methods for producing unusual photographs. This is not a book about the technical elements of the photographic art. The fact that unconventional photographs predominate should not be misunderstood: we have nothing against ordinary ones. In a great many cases, a successful shot of the ordinary kind will no doubt best serve the purpose. All we are concerned with is that it should not be regarded as the only right and possible one in every case. For it is equally certain that the most telling effect can sometimes be achieved with shots that are completely contrary to the "rules of the art" and are therefore condemned by its official masters.

Right. We hope you are now convinced that you should treat with great suspicion and refuse to accept any kind of restriction on the way in which you take photographs. Rules based on painting cannot be applied to photography without further ado, and even in painting the rules in question are completely out of date.

Photography is a free, independent art. It must not be subjected to alien, antiquated laws, nor should it be enslaved to nature (does this surprise you?).

We can of course use photography to produce as good a "likeness" of nature as we please. But it is not, as one might suppose, the first purpose of photography to produce lifelike pictures.

On the contrary, we are well aware of its shortcomings for this purpose—first and foremost, the fact that it is not in color. There are many cases in which this makes it sadly inadequate, and it is to be hoped that color photography will soon advance from its present crudeness and garishness to a state of greater refinement. But let us meanwhile use photography as it is.

Have you noticed on moonlit nights how uncannily expressive black-and-white scenery can be? This is not just the effect of unfamiliarity. The shapes of hills, trees, and stones speak a language of their own, which is all the more distinct when they are devoid of color.

But, even though photographs are in black and white, how few of them convey this eloquent language to us!

The reason is that they try to be too close to nature. Yet one can make objects speak in any number of different ways by extracting fresh values from their forms.

The most impressive posters are made with the help of the new photography.

When will the postcard industry start to use its help? When shall we see the last of the usual boring scenes?

A cautious beginning is being made with air and night photography, and there are already some photographic advertising cards.

Other developments will follow. This is a wide field for the photographer.

277

WILLI WARSTAT

Photography in Advertising

First published as "Die Photographie in der Werbekunst," *Deutscher Kamera-Almanach 1930*, vol. 20 (Berlin: Roth & Co., 1930), 85–98.

The enormous significance of photography as an advertising tool was recognized relatively late, at least here in Europe. Only in the last several years have industry and commerce taken significant steps toward making use of photography to commend their wares in advertisements, posters, catalogues, and other printed forms. And this awakening interest on the part of dominant economic forces has recently led to an almost violent intensification in the development of photographic advertising techniques, or, let us simply say, in the development of the photographic advertising arts such that it has become worthwhile to investigate and illuminate them in context. For the development is by no means at an end.

On the contrary, photographic applications can expect such a promising future along so many paths that it seems appropriate to discuss it with specific reference to the limitations to which professional photography has obviously been subjected in other areas, in portrait photography above all.

The belated appreciation of photography as an advertising tool is less understandable, since the *qualities* that predestine it to technical advertising applications have been known and, in other contexts—particularly the sciences—emphasized and exploited for a long time. Among these qualities, the most immediate is its *objectivity* in the *representation of things.* Photography creates an image of things (in reference to advertising technique, of products) with such perfect fidelity and precision, and it is capable of reproducing all the details of the design structure and surface with such perfection that no other technique, least of all that of the graphic artist, can surpass it. In this connection incidentally it becomes immediately clear that it is not the "artistic printing processes" striving for the dissolution of the surface, the unfocused softness of reproduction and refined pictorial composition, that will find favor in advertising photography, but the simple (and currently most perfected) photographic-printing process, the simple contact print with enlargement geared to maximum sharpness and precision. [. . .]

The second quality that makes photography appear particularly suited to technical advertising applications is of more psychological than technical significance. Photography is generally regarded—whether rightly or wrongly is a matter of complete indifference in this context—as possessing the highest conceivable, nearly *documentary fidelity in the representation of objects.* And this general attitude toward photographic representation is of tremendous significance in terms of the *psychology of advertising.* The public simply believes without reservation that the *photographic* representation of an object is truer and more real than any artist's graphic representation. And that is the decisive factor in this context. For manufacturers or merchants who want to commend their products to the public and who use images for this purpose (since they can scarcely put the product itself into the hand of every reader of an advertisement or poster) have to be interested primarily in the trust the image inspires in the reader. For precisely this reason, they *must* choose photography—because it appears to the public as the most faithful reproduction and because, by virtue of this psychological fact, it alone can be regarded as the most *effective* form of advertising representation.

278

RAOUL HAUSMANN

Photomontage

First published as "Fotomontage," *a bis z* (May 1931), 61–62.

In the battle of opinions it is often claimed that photomontage is practicable in only two forms, political propaganda and commercial advertising. The first photomonteurs, the dadaists, began from a point of view incontestable for them: that the painting of the war period, post-futurist expressionism, had failed because it was nonrepresentational and it lacked convictions; and that not only painting but all the arts and their techniques required a revolutionary transformation in order to remain relevant to the life of their times. The members of the Club Dada, who all held more or less left-wing political views, were naturally not interested in setting up new aesthetic rules for making art. On the contrary, they at first had almost no interest in art, but were all the more concerned with materially giving new forms of expression to new contents. Dada, which was a kind of cultural criticism, stopped at nothing. It is a fact that many of the early photomontages attacked the political events of the day with biting sarcasm. But just as revolutionary as the content of photomontage was its form—photography and printed texts combined and transformed into a kind of static film. The dadaists, who had "invented" the static, the simultaneous, and the purely phonetic poem, applied these same principles to pictorial expression. They were the first to use the material of photography to combine heterogeneous, often contradictory structures, figurative and spatial, into a new whole that was in effect a mirror image wrenched from the chaos of war and revolution, as new to the eye as it was to the mind. And they knew that great propagandistic power inhered in their method, and that contemporary life was not courageous enough to develop and absorb it.

Things have changed a great deal since then. The current exhibition at the Art Library shows the importance of photomontage as a means of propaganda in Russia. And every movie program—be it *The Melody of the World,* Chaplin, Buster Keaton, *Mother Krausen's Journey to Happiness,* or *Africa Speaks*—proves that the business world has largely recognized the value of this propagandistic effect. The advertisements for these films are unimaginable without photomontage, as though it were an unwritten law.

Today, however, some people argue that in our period of New Objectivity, photomontage is already outdated and unlikely to develop further. One could reply that photography is even older, and that nevertheless there are always new men who, through their photographic lenses, find new visual approaches to the world surrounding us. The number of modern photographers is large and growing daily, and no one would think of calling Renger-Patzsch's objective photography outdated because of Sander's exact photography, or of pronouncing the styles of Lerski or Bernatzik more modern or less modern.

The realm of photography, silent film, and photomontage lends itself to as many possibilities as there are changes in the environment, its social structure, and resultant psychological superstructures; and the environment is changing every day. Photomontage has not reached the end of its development any more than silent film has. The formal means of both media need to be disciplined, and their respective realms of expression need sifting and reviewing.

If photomontage in its primitive form was an explosion of viewpoints and a whirling confusion of picture planes more radical in its complexity than futuristic painting, it has since then undergone an evolution one could call constructive. There has been a general recognition of the great versatility of the optical element in pictorial expression. Photomontage in particular, with its opposing structures and dimensions (such as rough versus smooth, aerial view versus close-up, perspective versus flat plane), allows the greatest technical diversity or the clearest working out of the dialectical problems of form. Over time the technique of photomontage has undergone considerable simplification, forced upon it by the opportunities for application that spontaneously presented themselves. As I mentioned previously, these applications are primarily those of political or commercial propaganda. The necessity for clarity in political and commercial slogans will influence photomontage to abandon more and more its initial individualistic playfulness. The ability to weigh and balance the most violent oppositions—in short, the dialectical dynamics of form that are inherent in photomontage—will assure it a long survival and ample opportunities for development.

In the photomontage of the future the exactness of the material, the clear particularity of objects, and the precision of plastic concepts will play the greatest role, despite or because of their mutual juxtaposition. A new form worth mentioning is statistical photomontage—apparently no one has thought of it yet. One might say that like photography and the silent film, photomontage can contribute a great deal to the education of our vision, to our knowledge of optical, psychological, and social structures; it can do so thanks to the clarity of its means, in which content and form, meaning and design, become one.

279

ALFRED KEMÉNYI

Photomontage as a Weapon in Class Struggle

First published under the name Durus as "Fotomontage als Waffe im Klassenkampf," *Der Arbeiter-Fotograf* 6, no. 3 (1932), 55–57.

The bourgeois conception of photomontage can be summarized in the following remark made by a well-known bourgeois art critic: "Montage means that the artist and the craftsman are replaced by the engineer. Pieces of photographs are pasted together the way parts of machines are joined together with screws." Is this the actual state of affairs? Has the engineer actually taken the place of the artist? Are pieces of photographs installed like parts of machines? Not at all. The photo "monteur" is an artist—not an engineer. And the photo "montage" is a work of art—not just a machine. A work of art that offers completely new opportunities—with regard to content, not just form—for uncovering relationships, oppositions, transitions, and intersections of social reality. Only when the photomonteur makes use of these opportunities does his photomontage become a truly revolutionary weapon in the class struggle.

We must emphasize: In a class society there can be no "classless-revolutionary" photomontage. Like all art forms before the classless society, photomontage is determined by social class. The nonrepresentational stance of formalist photomontage—playing with light effects, superimpositions, overexposures, strange angles "without content"—merely veils the bourgeois contents, the dead-end perspective of rootless bourgeois artists. In this as in any other field, the revolutionary working class does not separate theory from practice—it sets a high value on photomontage as an extraordinarily effective propagandistic and organizational weapon in the class struggle.

It is becoming increasingly obvious that the cognitive value of photomontage is inseparable from its role in the class struggle. Could the development of photomontage take place outside the context of class struggle? Certainly not. Why did formalist photomontage grind to a halt after a few superficially interesting experiments? Because it operated in a vacuum, divorced from the decisive social conflicts of our era; because it could not carry out its essential purpose: to reveal the truth. Why did proletarian-revolutionary photomontage attain such a high level in the Soviet Union and Germany? Because not only did it not oppose the revolutionary development of humanity, but it developed in close conjunction with the revolutionary workers' movement.

And we can see that while in response to the intensified economic crisis the bourgeois advertising industry is dispensing with more and more of its most artistically and technically expert photomonteurs, our publishing houses and our magazines require an ever-greater number of qualified photomonteurs. One need only look at the display windows of our bookstores: invariably one's eye is caught by interesting, original, and thought-provoking photomontages on the covers of books and brochures.

The very first dadaist works using paste and photographs (by Heartfield, George Grosz, Hausmann, and [Johannes] Baader) set the course for the development of a consciously political proletarian photomontage—despite the anarchist-individualist philosophy of their creators. But the rising line of German proletarian-revolutionary photomontage is most intimately associated with the epoch-making work of the brilliant monteur John Heartfield.

His works can already be considered classic. He pioneered the use of photomontage for book jackets and in the design of political picture books. He always focused the aesthetically effective elements of photography's "gray-scale structures," of planar division, of combinations of script and photography, on maximizing the political content. All traces of "beautiful, self-contained form" have been ruthlessly swept away. In place of a bourgeois aesthetic we have the sharpest, strongest, most penetrating political militancy of a no longer neutral art. Faced with the powers of inertia and habitual rigidity, Heartfield never took the path of least resistance. After years of stubborn and consistent work, he won the adoption of the line that he considered the most appropriate for the proletarian liberation struggle.

As a creator of satirical photomontages, he is unsurpassed. His satirical contributions to *AIZ*—the "Tiger," the "Cabbage Head," "Solar Eclipse on the 'Liberated' Rhine," "Six Million Nazi Voters: Fodder for a Big Mouth," to mention just a few—are among the most significant satirical creations of our time.

Today the ranks of revolutionary photomonteurs are increasing considerably in Germany. The best photomontages by the members of the League of Revolutionary Artists, who use this art form as a weapon in the daily practice of class struggle, are by no means simple imitations of Heartfield. [. . .] Naturally, as with many other problems awaiting our solution, proletarian photomontage experiences occasional setbacks. Sometimes the work being turned out is politically shallow and the products are frequently slipshod, particularly the designs for magazine covers.

27
Visions of Plenty: Mass Consumption, Fashion, and Advertising

AFTER THE GERMAN ECONOMY stabilized in 1924, higher labor productivity and a new emphasis on technological efficiency created conditions that promised an end to scarcity and privation. The mass production of consumer goods from cars to cosmetics required mass markets that needed first to be created by advertising. This powerful nexus of mass production, mass consumption, and advertising revolutionized the culture of everyday life in the Weimar Republic. Popular culture, fashion magazines, and illustrated press actively propagated a new lifestyle that was easy, forward-looking, and fun-filled. The German tragic sense of life, often evoked by cultural critics and idealist philosophers, seemed powerless against the lure of luxury. (Hitler, in contrast, would later appeal to the ideals of self-sacrifice and spiritual mission, which in his view distinguished the German people.)

Fashion, traditionally centered in Paris, became caught in an interesting double-bind in 1923 when the French occupation of the Ruhr raised the question of whether the world of fashion could be immune to politics. In a passionate plea for a political boycott of French fashion, the Association of the German Fashion Industry defended its resolution to place national pride higher than the acknowledged dependency on Paris. The close relationship between politics and fashion was also observed in the fall of 1929 when the turn to the political right in the wake of economic collapse coincided with the return of the formal dress. If rising hemlines during the 1920s signaled women's freedom, as Stephanie Kaul claimed, then the return to longer-length dresses may have augured a reversal of this newly won freedom. Already in 1925, the weekly *Berliner Illustrirte Zeitung* (*BIZ*), one of the most widely read illustrated papers and a major trendsetter in matters of style, found fault with the new flappers who wore men's clothes and, after having bobbed their hair, began to sport a men's hairstyle: sleek and brushed straight back. The masculinization of the woman in the mid-1920s became an outward sign of changing relations between the sexes. However, by the end of the 1920s in the wake of the widespread reaction against the modernism of New Objectivity in the arts, the ideal of the emancipated New Woman was soon denounced. "Women," Kaul wrote in 1930, "wanted once again to be genuine women."

In the same vein, Liselotte de Booy, the first Miss Germany, contemplated the superficiality and futility of fashion, balls, dances, and—men.

If Germany looked to France for fashion, it followed the United States in matters of lifestyle and advertising. Words such as *sex appeal* found their way into the German language because they were perceived as modern and fashionable; but as an article in the satirical magazine *Uhu* pointed out, such Anglo-American terms named already familiar things. The sheer linguistic attraction of such foreign words as *jazz, flirt,* and *sex appeal* illustrated the magic of America as an emblem of modernity. Throughout the period of relative stabilization from 1924 to 1929, America's consumerist, "happy" lifestyle infiltrated the traditional bastions of German values and challenged calcified thinking patterns as pitifully premodern or simply old-fashioned. Images of a modern lifestyle proliferated in the Weimar Republic and influenced fashion, manners, beauty, sexual mores, leisure, and entertainment. American movies in particular celebrated the ideal of consumption and trumpeted promises of material abundance. They created images and fantasies about the New World that were crucial in shaping the German assessment of modernity. Vicki Baum, author of the bestseller *Menschen im Hotel* (1929; its 1931 film version, *Grand Hotel,* featured Greta Garbo), gives an ironic and richly detailed account of the new modern woman who is driven to (admittedly slight) despair by her pursuit of happiness.

Advertising in the 1920s promoted not only commodities but also a certain outlook on life. It created desires for products charged with symbolic value. For example, the international success of chewing gum—Wrigley's Spearmint Gum Company opened a factory in Frankfurt in 1925—was due to effective advertising. Chewing gum, said Ernst Lorsy, "is the cheapest way to Americanize oneself." New magazines sprang up to promote commodities such as automobiles as signs of a lifestyle that conferred distinction on the owner. Precariously situated between industry and culture, advertising utilized (some would say vampirized) all of the arts—creatively and often shamelessly enlisting literature, painting, photography, and design in its service. In turn, advertising was deemed capable of rejuvenating and modernizing the traditional arts. The International Advertising Congress in Berlin in 1929 occasioned numerous reflections on the impact of advertising on literature (see Döblin's *Berlin Alexanderplatz*), film (advertising films were almost always experimental), and the other arts. Indeed, advertisements became, as Hans Siemsen claimed, the new literature for nonreaders.

As a new art form under the aegis of consumer culture, advertising targeted women, who were viewed as little more than mindless shoppers. Enticements to consume confronted the shopper at every turn; from the venerable Berlin department stores (dating back to the 1890s) with their elaborate window displays and elegant fashion shows, to the ever more sumptuous ads in the illustrated press and the alluring billboard images—all of which signified plenitude and pleasure. As technological inventions and mass production gradually lowered the price of consumer products, a modern consumption-oriented lifestyle began to expand, slowly but surely, across the social classes.

280

Boycott of French Fashion Goods

First published as "Boykott französischer Modewaren," *Styl. Blätter des Verbandes der deutschen Modeindustrie* 2, no. 1 (February 1923), 52–53.

The daily and professional press has made it widely known that the German fashion industry has decided to speak out for a boycott of French fashion goods. This decision is frequently misunderstood, and it is therefore best that a few words be said about it.

We in fashion are fully aware of our dependence on Paris to provide us with the taste of worldwide fashion. It is better to say these things directly than to talk around the issue. We also know that we harm ourselves in multiple ways if we do not travel to Paris. The exporting businesses clearly suffer disadvantages from this step; likewise the fashion salons with foreign retail customers will have to sacrifice this or that sale, for among their customers quite a few specifically want to see patterns from Paris.

In order not to increase damage to ourselves, the Association has no objection if someone wants to travel to Holland, Switzerland, or Vienna to view fashion developments and perhaps purchase copies from houses that were in Paris so that we might supplement our collections with what we would otherwise have lacked. It should be noted here that in these countries too the purchase of original patterns from Paris or any sort of fashion goods originally from France is not permitted.

It was not easy for the men whose inspiration it was to recommend this resolution. It has been seriously and amply considered. Political circumstances were more powerful than any more reasonable considerations and, as so often happens these days, action must be taken under the force of these circumstances.

It is not a question of advantage and disadvantage, not a question of the interests, greater or smaller, of individuals, and not in this case a question of the interests of the industry involved. Rather this time it is a question of the whole, a matter of life and death. We took this step aware that it will put us at a disadvantage, thus we have made a willing sacrifice. We would have found it abominable if fashion representatives had traveled to Paris and made purchases there in a moment when our countrymen in the Ruhr valley, from the simplest workers to the largest industrialists and highest officials, are being harassed and mistreated to the point of bloodshed. It was no longer possible for us to turn our eyes from the fact that the French are doing absolutely everything conceivable to ruin us. In such a moment it is not a question of business, but for everyone who still possesses a spark of national feeling or a spark of the feeling of self-respect there is something natural in self-defense against such humiliation. Those who have no feeling for this have relinquished their right to demand to be respected as a German inside the country or out; neither can they have retained any self-respect, for they betray their national and personal honor for the sake of material interest.

For a long time now, one can say since 1914, our enemies have become so excessive in their behavior, which is condemned the world over in the hearts of the people, that we are seeing sympathies for us slowly rise once again. Since the beginning of the occupation of the Ruhr valley it has been our passive resistance—something only people with firmly clenched jaws and with character can accomplish—that has again created a new respect in the world for us as Germans. Who would want to stand idly by such a development?

Let us make no secret of our position. Let us say openly to our customers in and outside of Germany: we were not in Paris; have a look at our things and judge whether they are good or bad. And we will see that our customers will also understand us. Most countries possess enough national feeling of their own that they will respect those who say they were not in Paris.

Inside Germany everyone must help us to put the resolution completely and thoroughly into practice and lend to the spirit of the resolution their most emphatic support.

281

Enough is Enough! Against the Masculinization of Women

First published as "Nun aber genug! Gegen die Vermännlichung der Frau," *Berliner Illustrirte Zeitung* (March 29, 1925), 389.

What started as a playful game in women's fashion is gradually becoming a distressing aberration. At first it was like a charming novelty: that gentle, delicate women cut their long tresses and bobbed their hair; that the dresses they wore hung down in an almost perfectly straight line, denying the contours of the female body, the curve of the hips; that they shortened their skirts, exposing their slender legs up to calf level. Even the most traditional of men were not scandalized by this. A creature like this could have been warmly greeted with the now obsolete pet name *my angel*—for angels are asexual, yet they have always been represented in a pre-adolescent female form, even the archangel Gabriel. But the male sensibility began to take offense at this as the fashion that was so becoming to young girls and their delicate figures was adopted by all women. It did an aesthetic disservice to stately and full-figured women. But the trend went even further; women no longer wanted to appear asexual; rather fashion was increasingly calculated to make women's outward appearance more masculine. The practice of wearing men's nightclothes became increasingly widespread among women, even to the point of wearing them whenever possible for daytime lounging.

And we observe more often now that the bobbed haircut with its curls is disappearing, to be replaced by the modern, masculine hairstyle: sleek and brushed straight back. The new fashion in women's coats is also decidedly masculine: it would scarcely be noticed this spring if a woman absentmindedly put on her husband's coat. Fashion is like a pendulum swinging back and forth. With the hoop skirt the dictates of fashion brought the accentuation of the female form to an extreme, and now things are moving in the completely opposite direction. It is high time that sound male judgment take a stand against these odious fashions, the excesses of which have been transplanted here from America. In the theater we might enjoy, one time, seeing an actress playing a man's part if she is suitable for the role; but not every woman should venture to display herself in pants or shorts, be it on stage or at sporting events. And the masculinization of the female face replaces its natural allure with, at best, an unnatural one: the look of a sickeningly sweet boy is detested by every real boy or man.

282

HANNS KROPFF

Women as Shoppers

First published as "Frauen als Käuferinnen," *Die Reklame. Zeitschrift des Verbandes deutscher Reklamefachleute* (July 1926), 649–650.

Seventy-five percent of all things are bought by women. Women buy for themselves, for their children, for their homes, and also very often for their husbands. Most money spent passes through the hands of women. For this reason you should check carefully whether your goods are not also purchased by women. The tie that a man buys because his wife likes it has in reality been purchased by her.

Women tend to think in strongly personal terms. Nevertheless they are easy to influence. Their first question will always be: is there a use or advantage in it for me? They relate everything directly to their appearance, their happiness, their sympathies. General facts, logical reasons, abstract considerations, and technical details do not say much to them. Statistics and politics leave them cold in the moment of a purchase. They demand instead that their smaller desires be understood. They are pleased by easily understood explanations of the use of an item or about the reasons it is better.

Women love a simple and personal language, however modern they might be in their professions and progressive in their opinions. With things that touch them personally, they are first of all women. And, once again, that is the reason they perceive everything personally.

Only in the rarest of cases will women analyze their feelings or actions. Their sensations, decisions, affections, and rejections are thoroughly emotional and irrevocable.

The majority of marketers find it very difficult to write advertisements for women. They think in terms that are too complicated, too masculine. The love they have for the products they sell is colored by their own perspective. They frequently use expressions that mean something entirely different to women, that lead to misunderstandings, indeed, that often offend them. An idea that is good in itself is often spoiled by an incorrect expression.

Consider the fact that women love their homes, be they ever so simple, and that they are proud of certain pieces of furniture and keepsakes. Do not insult them with sarcastic disparagement. Never use ridicule in your texts and never be skeptical. You might cause a few to laugh, but many will be irritated.

Shopping is a serious matter for all people, but most especially for women. Do not attempt to make advertisements humorous, for firstly there are only a few really humorous ads and secondly to women humor is neither generally understood, nor congenial, nor persuasive.

Women regard life as a shockingly serious business which must be endured if necessary with clenched teeth. They wash, they iron, they sweep, they cook, they sew, they attend to the children, they make the beds . . . a woman's work is never done. Not only do they have their own language in which they think and discuss these things, but they also have a whole set of very particular feelings for them, which an advertiser must know and may never overlook.

Consider the fact that women are experienced in the care and treatment of children. If you give them advice in this area, then do so in a way that does not offend the views they learned from their mothers. Women are generally conservative. They find sudden innovations unpleasant—with the exception of those in fashion. Their education in new thoughts must proceed slowly and carefully. Convince the women that your offerings represent an easily understood advantage for them or their children and half the battle is already won.

Speak to housewives of the "small amenities of the item," of the work it saves. Give her suggestions on how to procure and prepare meals with less trouble. Speak with her about new methods for simplifying housework. Inform mothers of new advances in the area of hygiene and nutrition.

Do not speak of slavery but offer the woman a hand to gain more time for herself. She will be grateful to you.

The woman with a profession, unburdened by crude household worries and in possession of more money that she can dispose of freely, wants simply to be a woman in her leisure time. She does not think so much of the price if you convince her that your goods will make her life easier, more pleasant, and nicer. Like the housewife her first question in regard to a fashion advertisement is: does it become me? And like the former, she is interested only in the one pictured, and not in the dozen presented in the text. She strives for new knowledge in order to advance herself, but learning by being entertained is most congenial to her. Women politicians and parliamentarians are captivated by a pretty and skillful speech, even if the calculation is wrong, even if the statistical figures do not add up and even if after the third word all the men are already shaking their heads. In short, having a profession has not changed her in her heart of hearts. She remains a woman.

You see that it is not easy for men to write texts for women. It is even harder to illustrate such texts. Give your drafts, pictures, and texts to women to evaluate—not your wife or your daughter or a lady who knows what is at issue but a complete outsider. A woman's judgment is quickly influenced when she knows why she is supposed to give it.

Everything that has been said already applies to an even greater extent to illustrations. If a good picture is worth a thousand words, then ten thousand good words will not induce any woman to look at an ugly or false picture. The effect of the ad stands and falls with the picture. They look first of all at the picture, and if it appeals to them, they read the text. Something incorrect in fashion, a badly arranged kitchen, or a false step in the care of the children, everything that is ridiculous, impossible, or horrible to women occasions them to pass over the ad immediately in scorn and irritation.

Without a doubt the majority of women would rather look at a pretty, appetizing girl than an ugly one. But the ever-cheerful "sweet girl" performing the dirty chores in the public toilet wearing elegant evening gloves is even more ridiculous for women than for men.

Pure text ads, be they ever so clear and aesthetically pleasing, do not interest women. Mere text is too cold and structural for them. Not even trimmings and borders help matters. On the other hand, many women, out of curiosity and the desire for sensation, read the personal ads and the announcements of weddings and engagements, carefully. A clever ad in close proximity to these generally succeeds.

Let us summarize: ads for women must be as personal as possible. They must take into account the typical female characteristic: to agree without reservation, or to repudiate absolutely. Women see things with their eyes—nothing can move them to read an ad that, for some reason or other, does not appeal to them on first sight.

The young women of the postwar period distinguish themselves in some things very clearly from their sisters of 1914. Their bodies, freed from the corset, reasonably dressed, and athletically trained, have become more natural and prettier. Their minds, steeled by need and the worries of war and sharpened by the business of work, are freer and clearer.

Their demeanor, although more tomboyish, is easier and less forced than it was in the times when it was thought that the solution to the problem of the erotic was solved by hushing it up. The fellowship of young men and women, often slandered and abused, has become a fact in many parts of Europe.

A new race of women is growing up in Europe, consciously demanding the rights from which they have been barred by the slavery to convention of earlier times.

283

ERNST LORSY

The Hour of Chewing Gum

First published as "Die Stunde des Kaugummis," *Das Tagebuch*, no. 26 (June 26, 1926), 913–915.

When the great [William] Wrigley opened his chewing gum factory in Frankfurt am Main in 1925, some predicted failure. Granted there had always been chewing gum in Germany, but it could never become a proper item of mass consumption. And now, after one year, it is apparent that the battle will be won. Divided in the popular referenda, the Germans appear to want to become for Wrigley a united nation of gum chewers. Perhaps no other item enjoyed such a rapid increase in turnover during the stabilization crisis as chewing gum. The Fordson tractor lags far behind Wrigley's Spearmint. Chewing gum is the cheapest way to Americanize oneself, and that is why the Germans of today, who harbor an intense yearning for America, have chosen it. That is, they have been selected and effectively dealt with by the lord of chewing gum as a predestined people. And today they are ripe for chewing gum.

That a shelf-warmer could become a fashion item, that a quiet little sect sticking inconspicuously to its old habits could grow into a mass movement convinced of the novelty of its rite, testifies more than anything else to the power of advertising. The history of chewing gum is the history of its publicity and presents the most compelling example of the way needs are inspired by advertising. For the moment it likely remains true that no one who does not want to has to chew gum. Nevertheless in America the number of people who can help themselves from chewing gum is already small. Just wait until the German chewing gum advertisements, today still in the infancy of half-finished texts from across the sea, reach the level of the American ads, not in their insane scale but quite likely in their sense of certainty and their ability to enforce conformity: then it will be hard not to chew gum.

The path by which chewing gum makes its inexorable advance on the soul of the modern masses took its cue from strategy in the World War: enormous, purely quantitative accumulation. Long before Joffre, the Broadway strategists of the illuminated billboard knew of the irresistible effect of a barrage from which there is no escape. The big city becomes a battleground on which the public, with its necessarily weakened nerves, succumbs in accord with the proven expectation of the billboard Hindenburgs. The big-city dweller has had to become accustomed to a few things, his temptation threshold continues to rise visibly, but he will never become as dulled as the little Wrigley man who has no nerves at all. The little Wrigley man, whose sly, gnomish gaze has confronted Americans for years now, is a nocturnal acrobat on the lighted roofs of their avenues. A stroller drops his eyes from one of them, and his comrade springs into view. The number of little Wrigley men amounts to a battalion ready for war, and the master of these troops, the man Wrigley, is a powerful commander.

It was not Wrigley who invented chewing gum. If he had, he would perhaps be the genius the humorists credit him with being. He did, however, invent the gigantic chewing gum advertisement, and ultimately what is most essential about chewing gum is the advertisement, with Wrigley now exercising an influence over the American people through his ads as few since Lincoln have. If the citizens of the States want to visit Capitol Hill in their nation's capital, then they have first to pass by a little Wrigley man. At night the Capitol is dark, and broad Pennsylvania Avenue, which leads directly to it, is thoroughly dominated by an oversized little Wrigley man blinking away in a yellowish glow. The little Wrigley man actually consists of those thick arrows that are the Wrigley's trademark. Chomping excitedly, it persuades America that it must chew Wrigley's gum to calm itself. "Pleasant and refreshing," says the illuminated ad, "the aroma lingers," it proclaims, "perfumes your breath," it screams, "aids digestion," it bellows, "preserves your teeth," it puffs, "chew it after every meal," it advises, admonishes, orders, threatens, extorts. America cowers and chews.

In a sensational trial it recently was made known that Wrigley invests fifty percent of his pure profits year after year in advertising; it is worth it. Wrigley's fortune is estimated at 140,000,000 dollars. His business tower on Lake Michigan is a Chicago landmark. He competed with the powers of fate to help shape the face of America and the faces of Americans. He boasts that he brought the famous hardness to that face, which happily occupies the midpoint between a profile of Caesar and that of a ruminant, and the possession of which is thought by the average American to be an honor. [Leon] Trotsky credits Wrigley with yet another world-historical service. By teaching the workers of America to chew gum, he and his competitors erected a barrier in the path of proletarian revolution. Due to the continual movement of the jaw, they never got to thinking, to contemplating their class position, the regulation of work, or the goal of life. Wrigley must, when he reads these sentences, do something that all American multimillionaires are inclined to do: he must consider himself a benefactor to mankind.

284

HANS SIEMSEN

The Literature of Nonreaders

First published as "Die Literatur der Nichtleser," *Die literarische Welt* 2, no. 37 (September 10, 1926), 4.

Literature is not nearly as important as we sometimes imagine. At least not that which we usually understand as literature.

We read Hamsun, Döblin, Proust, or Leskov. But we are few. The others read Rudolf Herzog. And the others are many more than we. But we and the others together are an invisibly small group in comparison to those who read no books at all, or as good as none.

But those who read no books also have their literature. They read the newspaper, especially the columns. They go to the cinema. For the cinema is the *biblia pauperum* of our time, to a much, much greater degree than the actual "picture bible" was four hundred years ago. And they read the ad pillars and the billboards on buildings, roofs, and streetcars.

Who knows Pascal? Everyone knows Odol.[1] No doctrine in the world is as widespread as this one: "Shave in the dark!" And no sentence in all of world literature is read as often and by so many as the one on that little, inconspicuous sign: "Patrons are requested to attend to their clothing before exiting."

This, the literature of nonreaders, is the most widely read literature in the world. Its history has not yet been written. Nor do I feel quite up to the task myself. I would simply like to make reference to one of its branches: poetry. For the literature of nonreaders, like "our" own, has a special category for poetry.

Every couple of weeks there is a survey: "Who is the most beloved poet of the year?" Every time, the question is answered incorrectly. The ones we know are not even considered. Neither Rilke nor Cäsar Flaischlen, not Goethe and not Gottfried Benn. Rather: Fritz Grünbaum ("When You Can't, Let Me Do It!"), [Rudolf] Schanzer and [Ernst] Welisch ("If You See My Aunt"), Beda ("It Had To Be Bananas"), Dr. Robert Katscher ("Madonna, You Are More Beautiful than the Sunshine")—and who else? A lot more—before Flaischlen, Rilke, and Benn come up.

"The 222 Newest Hits"—that is the most popular poetry anthology of all. The contents are revised and expanded every two months. And the whole thing costs just ten cents.

Here there is only one geniune type of poem: the love poem. Girls, women, females— other topics are not favored. [. . .]

"Art to the People!"

Why? They have what they need. For all situations. Practical, cheap, useful. Are verses like "The day will come" or "You are mine, I long for you" not truly beautiful? "Our" literature will have to try very hard if it wants to keep pace with the literature of nonreaders.

285

VICKI BAUM

People of Today

First published as "Leute von heute," *Die Dame* (November 27, 1927), 17–32.

May I introduce you to Ypsi, the small, very modern woman whom you have certainly seen a thousand times, at premieres, races, boxing matches, and celebrities' funerals. So, this is Ypsi (unfortunately, she doesn't look her best today for the Lindbergh-style hat doesn't become her, but, my God, dear lady, one does have to follow fashion, no?), and here is Ypsi's husband, Peter, and Ypsi's friend, Renatus, and Ypsi's girlfriend, Alexandra, also called Sonya or Sasha. And, now, to begin at the beginning. Naturally, Ypsi's name is not Ypsi, but Caroline. I know that accidentally because she went to school with me, saddled by that vulgar name Caroline Shoemaker. That utterly chic Ypsi is a recent creation, born by cutting the tail off a racy "ypsilon," just like a terrier. Original, no? No, unfortunately, not entirely original, but produced on the model of the famous film diva Ypsi Lona. And unfortunately no registered trademark, for since Ypsi Lona's last great success, there are

---

1. A brand of mouthwash.

dozens, even hundreds of Ypsi's running around the world, to Ypsi the Second's burning remorse, running around that world, that is, which is also Ypsi's. Ypsi's husband, by the way, was not named Peter but Wolfgang; a perfectly nice name, indeed, but not one really suited to a husband. Husbands are usually called Peter now; there is something of a commitment to broad-shouldered amiability and somewhat self-effacing good-fellowness in the name Peter. And Peter, shrugging his horsehair-upholstered shoulders, does what he can to adopt the look, name, and being of all husbands of the given season. But neither does Renatus, meant by nature to be modest Gustav, have it easy. The touch of the esthete, the blasé man of the world, which Yspi is justified in demanding from an up-to-date friend, he funneled into his inner and outer being only with difficulty. Faux pas do happen and are regrettable. As for the girlfriend, Alexandra (Sasha, Sonya), however, she is a dumb and scarcely pretty piece of woman born to drift along in will-less dependence, a foil to the prettier one. Recently Ypsi had the hair on this harmless unhappy being cut and induced her to wear a man's hat, stiff white tie, and a smoking jacket. A riding crop, a present from Ypsi, opens the door to wicked thoughts. It is—you know this, dear lady?—the latest thing to have a girlfriend who looks like this, or similar. Mia Huber and Lia Meier, if you please, have such girlfriends too.

Now it is time to tell who Ypsi really is. Ypsi is, to put it briefly, a copyist. No, don't be shocked, she in no way belongs to that anemic and regrettable species that sits over a typewriter and copies files or manuscripts, always seven carbons at once, twenty cents a page. She is still spending her life in badly heated galleries painting four hundred times, one after the other, a lute-playing angel by Carpaccio. She is a copyist by fate. She imitates. She copies. What does she copy, you ask, dear lady? Well, simply everything. From her haircut to her lap dog, from her liqueur glasses to her marital conflicts, from her earrings to her dreams, everything is second-hand, everything imitated, everything a copy. Incidentally, about those dreams, they come from the fashion of having oneself psychoanalyzed. Naturally Ypsi participates in the fashion, and since she began she has been dreaming what others have already dreamed for her.

Ypsi has a great desire: she would like to be original. And a great fear: she could come off unmodern.

These two things struggle heroically and painfully in Ypsi's small, ash-blonde soul. Not because they are opposed to each other but the contrary, because the one is like the other to the point of self-annihilation. That is, it is modern to be original. In consequence, all modern women are original. In consequence, and since all of them are equally original, not a single one of them is. I hope, dear lady, you can follow this bewilderingly simple logic.

For example: on that great day (a long time ago) when Ypsi, pale with excitement, had her hair cut, every one of the Ypsis had her hair cut. An act of boldness became a fashion, which went, more or less, with the face but which in any case had to be followed. Oh, these whispering consultations in the fragrant box of the beauty salon to create something original out of the uniform of bobbed hair. Cut it, cut it still shorter, cut it down to the skin, let it grow, comb it off the forehead, lay it down across the forehead, flatten it, crimp it into African curls, stand it up, turn it under, in front of the ear, behind the ear—everything original, but, oh! everything modern and done by hundreds of thousands. Color it gold-blonde, color it henna-red, color it coal-black—oh! Ypsi first thinks of it after everyone else has already thought of it and the parquet at the premieres looks like a flower bed planted full of gold-blonde, henna-red, or coal-black fashion heads. There would only be one way to be truly original: if Ypsi let her hair grow long, ash-blonde and somewhat needy, just as God created it. But that is exactly where Ypsi lacks the courage, the expanse of soul, the push of the heroic. That is the tragedy in Ypsi's nature.

Peter, Renatus, and Sonya, this phalanx surrounds her and honestly wants to smooth her way, to make her life easier. But there are crises and black days anyway. There is, for example, the press ball that comes every year. Ypsi would give body and soul if she could once, just one single time at this great festival of representation, stand out properly, make a wholly and thoroughly original impression. Already in September the shadows begin closing in on her soul and formless ideas of dresses, hairstyles, and jewelry float through her imagination. She flips through magazines, stares intently at social dramas in the cinema, and becomes feverish as the stars parade the newest models on the stage at premieres; she dashes to fashion teas and conducts long, deep discussions with the tender, ephebic young man who is her tailor.

The result is very tight, very short, and completely aglitter in gold spangles, with a white wig and many expensive artificial pearls. Peter and Renatus go in together to get her the many expensive artificial pearls. Ypsi buys herself a monocle to crown the original idea and has herself operated on to do away with her soft, unmodern, and utterly unoriginal bustline.

And oh! Ypsi's rage, pain, and desperation as eighty percent of the ladies at the press ball appear very tight, very short, completely aglitter in gold spangles, with monocle, artificial pearls, white wigs, and no bust! You saw Ypsi on that evening, dear lady, but you do not remember her? No, she was not dressed to her advantage, even if Peter, Renatus, and Alexandra (poor things) swore a thousand oaths that Ypsi caused a stir. But so is it always. Blue wigs, gold wigs, décolleté in the front, décolleté in the back, no décolleté at all, nothing but décolleté. Narrow skirt to the knees, broad, long, stylish dress with a train—everything very pretty, everything modern, but everything such a washed-out already-was. The truth is Ypsi is always doing things that aren't really her. The truth is she is always wearing things that do not become her. The truth is that in the deepest, most secret little corners of her self she is still Caroline Shoemaker with the ash-blonde pigtail. One has to admire how much she takes on herself. Adultery, cocaine, operations, uncomfortable chairs made of aluminum in her strictly au courant apartment, riding with a man's saddle (devilishly painful around the bottom), plucking her eyebrows, reading boring books, shoes too small, hats too small, undergarments too thin in winter, tennis matches in ninety-degree heat in July, no children and stomach complaints, nicotine poisoning and slimming diets. And then there is Renatus, who bores her most next to Alexandra-Sonya-Sasha, who gets terrifically on her nerves. Everything, everything that she puts up with just to be up to date, just so someone turns to look at her on the street and says: what an original woman!

By the way, dear lady, do you know the latest? You will not believe it, but it is certain: round is becoming modern again. Feminine lines are making a comeback. Ypsi's masseuse told her so, the beautician and the tailor confirmed it. It has also already appeared in an American magazine. Pills are available which supposedly powerfully reinforce this transformation to a beautiful figure. The masseuse said so and Ypsi knows it for certain! The great Ypsi Lona takes six everyday. Mia Huber and Lia Meier too. And Ypsi, our Ypsi—she eats them now too, shuddering at the consequences and pale with anxiety over the boldness of her experiment. Shall we bet, dear lady, that on the first evening Ypsi appears at the ball, round as a baroque cherub, the hall will be full with four thousand fattened, Rubenesque Ypsis?

Poor Yspi! Poor martyr of today, always fleeing yesterday without ever catching tomorrow.

286

Auto-Magazin

Editorial Statement

First published as "Zum Geleit," *Auto-Magazin*, no. 1 (January 1928), 1.

With the enormous upswing that automobilism in Germany has experienced in recent years, the desire for a magazine devoted, alongside the technical periodicals, to the automobile grew as well. There is scarcely any industry that is faster growing than the automobile industry. The young people of today already possess an educational background in automotive technology. Girls and women understand something about the automobile, and fathers are able in the long run to ignore the expertise their families have acquired just as little as they can escape the slow but sure arrival of the day when they purchase an automobile. In Germany today there are approximately three-quarters of a million automobiles on the streets. In just a few years this number will have doubled, so the need for an automobile magazine is obvious. Our task is to report about the automobile here at home and abroad, to illustrate innovations, to report on sporting events, to show automobile fashions just as much as to publish the latest photographs of automobile races, to convey data, ideas, and expert advice, to depict automobile travel, and to collect automotive caricatures from all over the world—in short, to unreel month by month the entire repertoire conjured by the magical word *automobile*.

The *Auto-Magazin* will do justice to all of these desires. Every month in these pages interest in the automobile will be reinvigorated in amusing form, and soon there will not be a single automobilist who can do without the *Auto-Magazin*. This, in a few brief words, is the goal we have set ourselves. To achieve it we need the cooperation of our readers—in particular we would like to receive abundant photographic material.

287

ANITA

Sex Appeal: A New Catchword for an Old Thing

First published as "Sex Appeal. Ein neues Schlagwort für eine alte Sache," *Uhu* 5 (October 1928), 72–77.

Every generation has a catchword for the ideal of its time. Once the formula has been found it spreads like wildfire, for then the idea will be discussed, analyzed, and enthusiastically defended—until it is worn out.

This time no German word was found for the new ideal. Apparently there are things between heaven and earth for which only one solitary language can completely capture the deepest meaning and which are therefore taken over into the vocabulary of the world untranslated.

To internationally valid terms like five o'clock, flirt, dancing, and cocktail, a new, extremely important one has been added: sex appeal. For years one called it "that certain something." What was meant was that magic that emanates from a being that cannot be simply subsumed under the rubric of beauty.

And suddenly it came from America like an illumination—what it was is sex appeal.

Until recently the question about a woman was simply: does she have pretty legs? Now the burning question is: does she have sex appeal?

To give the etymology of this word one can only resort to pictures and show those who have "it." But what do they have? That is where the difficulty of explanation begins.

"Une belle laide," say the French. "She's got something," in the vernacular. "Not pretty, something more than that." All of these are rewrites for sex appeal.

It is the perfect incarnation of the sex, whether male or female—for, although one thinks in this connection almost exclusively of women, the idea of sex appeal has to be valid for men too. One simply speaks less of the man—perhaps because successful men by definition have sex appeal. With women other factors, beauty, elegance, gracefulness, etc., still have their special meanings.

Every generation has the ambition to take out a new patent on its catchword. Later, with longer use, it becomes evident that exactly the same meaning has been registered under several other names.

Sex appeal existed, of course, in times when no one yet spoke English. And in the Middle Ages people were simply burned for having too much sex appeal—in those times it was called witchcraft. . . .

When a very beautiful woman also has sex appeal—that is when earth-shattering things occur. At the least she will become a film star, the subject of dreams on five continents and the cause of complexes for an entire generation.

Our objective era searches for and finds the technical expression and the objective explanation for everything until it comes upon a point where, for the time being, it can go no further. That point is called atom, radio wave, sex appeal.

288

WOLF ZUCKER

Art and Advertising

First published as "Kunst und Reklame. Zum Weltreklamekongreß in Berlin," *Die literarische Welt* 5, no. 32 (August 9, 1929), 1.

Advertising experts from all over the world are currently gathered in Berlin for a major congress, which they have organized as befits their profession, like a crusade. They have employed the tools of their trade to seek and win the attention of the world. Congress participants discuss issues of professional training and the protection of their interests and copyrights; they listen to addresses on the psychology, sociology, and the metaphysics of advertising, and meanwhile one completely forgets that all this is really only concerned with the best means for earning the most money. Instead it begins to seem to be a congress devoted to questions of philosophy or aesthetics. So it makes a certain sense to discuss it in these pages. For it may indeed be maintained that no phenomenon of modern culture has a more substantial relation, objective as well as ideal, to art than advertising.

In discussing materials first of all one may easily say that the institution of advertising has done more for the maintenance and advancement of art than all the cultural-support organizations together. Consider film, for example: advertisements have been more daring and definitive in the elaboration of a non-naturalistic way of seeing than most dramatic films. And the short advertising films that run in an only semidarkened room prior to the actual feature presentation are more interesting, as well as artistically more fertile, than the film itself. There are such outstanding examples of editing, trick shots, and fades to be seen in these short films that the subsequent feature presentation leaves one sitting there bored, resisting the reversion to the conventional visual style. Advertising gave many brave young experimental photographers, letterers, and graphic artists a chance to place their work before the public, and it also sustained them materially.

Precisely this example is quite characteristic. The world of pure art, with its exhibitions and very limited chances for display and publication, is an affair of a small and dwindling elite; these artists are blessed by material success only in exceptional cases. There will never be a purely private commission for an absolute film. But that is where advertising comes in; during the eternal search for something new, for that which has not yet been, it discovered the youth and gave them commissions, so to speak, in the most modern of the arts and crafts. Hundreds of organizations devoted to the salvation of handicrafts, to finding allegedly necessary gainful employment for artists, have gone bankrupt after losing significant amounts of money without having helped either artists or art. Advertising offers not charity but practical assignments. Artists were invited to try their hand, and it is not the worst of them who heeded the call. Clear goals were set—"Eat More Fish" or "Buy Ready-Made Clothes"—and the effect of such slogans in images or words was always the best.

Naturally it would be nonsense to see the tasks of art solely in the attainment of practical goals. But in those places where these objective assignments have contributed to the development of style, to the training of people to see and hear in new ways—they are more welcome than the artistic conservation of the social type of romantically alienated artist. The shortage of apartments was the best and most effective stimulus to the new architectural style. In exactly the same way, advertising has relegated to the arts, not least among them the verbal arts, the task of achieving the greatest possible effect with the simplest devices. Advertising thereby possesses the merit that it must constantly change and renew the devices it employs. Nowhere is a phrase, a conventional verbal effect, as quickly exhausted as in advertising technique. And that is what I mean: writers too could learn considerably from this applied art. How many lead articles would be less boring if their writers knew how to lend more-diverse expression to that which they want to say, which they want to commend to the public. How many newspapers would be more lively, surprising, and exciting if the editors were inclined to learn some tricks from advertising experts.

Advertising, especially the language of advertising, should be seen as belonging to the arts and crafts; it concerns the possibilities of expression in the service of utterly concrete goals. A well-written advertising prospectus is more valuable than the average feuilleton. And it should not be forgotten that many literary masterpieces owe their inception to a kind of advertising commission. And thus does the World Advertising Congress signify to us an event that with other means and in other areas pursues the same tasks that we do: constructive work on expression, on language, on art.

289

FRANZ HESSEL

On Fashion

First published as "Von der Mode" in *Spazieren in Berlin* (Vienna and Leipzig: Epstein, 1929), 33–39.

Berlin's big department stores are not bewildering bazaars overflowing with goods but clearly arranged sites of great organization. And they spoil the shopper with their high level of comfort. One might be purchasing a yard of pink rubber-band from a rotating stand of gleaming brass, but, waiting for the items to be entered on the sales slip, one's gaze rests on marble or glides along mirrors and over the shining parquet. In lighted courtyards and winter gardens we sit on granite benches, our packages on our laps. Exhibits of art, which extend into the refreshment room, separate the toys from the section devoted to swimming needs. Under decorative canopies of velvet and silk we wander over to soaps and toothbrushes. It is remarkable how little the taste for kitsch is satisfied in these department stores dedicated to the broad masses. Most things offered for sale are almost plain and simple. "Respectable"—the adjective that taste cannot resist. Only in the handicraft section and at the novelty goods do more questionable thoughts arise. The items one sees in the clothing department are exclusively dignified and unostentatious, clothes that approximate the fashionable with a certain hesitation and resistance, seeking more to hush it up than make concessions. [. . .]

Berlin, seen from the standpoint of society, remains small, the elegance of the ladies a second-hand affair. But there is already appearing a new type of woman who is carrying the day against those whose tailors and cleaning ladies live in Tiergarten—the young avant-garde, the postwar woman of Berlin. Around 1920 there must have been a couple of very good years for births. They produced girls with subtly athletic shoulders. They walk so prettily, weightlessly, in their dresses; splendid is their skin, which their make-up seems only to have illuminated; refreshing their smiles around healthy teeth, and the self-confidence with which they push in pairs through the afternoon bustle of Tauentzienstraße and the Kurfürstendamm. No, *push* is the wrong word. They do the crawl while others swim the breaststroke. Sharply and smoothly they steer over to the display windows. Just where did they get those pretty dresses, those hats and coats? Aside from the few large stores that have already spread this far, in the Bavarian Quarter, around Kurfürstenstraße, on the side streets of the Kurfürstendamm, is a whole bunch of small fashion shops. A first name frequently suffices on the sign. They likely have one, two Parisian models. *Vogue* and *Femina* stand out, *Harper's Bazaar, Art, Goût et Beauté*. The owner of the shop has a light touch and her customers an exact knowledge of their own figures, and both find fun in the interplay of fantasy and precision. These young shoppers are beginning to find a style equally distant from the snobbism of the "trademark" and indifference, which makes do with retail goods. Is it already true, what people are beginning to assert ever more loudly and generally, that the women of Berlin can measure their elegance against the best of the Europeans? Why check too fussily how that really stands? It should be enough for us to see these bevies of young and still-younger girls, this *défilé* of youth and freshness in short, tight-fitting skirts with a hat (and a curl peeking out from under), the springy step of long legs, to become convinced that Berlin is well on its way to becoming an elegant city.

290

STEPHANIE KAUL

Whose Fault Is the Long Dress?

First published as "Wer ist eigentlich an den langen Kleidern schuld?" *Uhu* 7 (October 1931), 32–36.

The new long dress is one of the more brilliant surprise attacks in the history of fashion. A few writers and journalists in Germany and England would have us believe that women are filled with indignation and disgust and are ready to join a protest strike against the new fashion. And even while they were screaming about this betrayal—about how the point of the long dresses is to rob women of their newly won freedoms behind their backs and make those athletically trained, comradely disposed women who have been hardened in the daily struggle once again into poor, slavish creatures, dependent and subordinate to men—they were themselves already wearing the long dress.

The fashion of short, very revealing dresses is only to be understood historically. In the years from 1914 to 1921, the force of living conditions caused women to become increasingly masculine. Amid the general storm of destruction, a voracious striving after the pleasures of life came into play. The shortage of money for elegant pleasures effected a simplification of dresses and a shortening of skirts so that dresses finally became the symbol of women's freedom.

A shortage of food created an artificial thinness on the part of women, who were raised to the status of idols and remained so even after it was no longer necessary. Burst illusions, the failing foundations of life, and the effacement of social distinctions allowed to a greater extent than ever before the difference between men and women to grow ever fainter.

Women believed it necessary to demonstrate their new freedom; some of them styled themselves according to a female type, which became known as the *garçonne*.

At first men may have been pleased that women approached them so directly. This approach in *camaraderie,* this approach in fashion, did away with any and all distance.

But the excess of fellowship eventually got on their nerves. Wherever one looked or listened there was objectivity. Objectivity in the home, objectivity in the construction of buildings, objectivity in the conduct of life. Above all, objective women who wanted to conquer and demolish the whole world in objective speech. Ultimately one could find a bit of romance or a bit of beauty only in the theater and in film. But somewhere deep inside, now perhaps carefully veiled with Europe's American objectivity, there remained that small remnant of desire for tenderness, elegance, and affection, for beauty. Somewhere in man, there remained the desire for a feminine woman, a feminine companion. Fashion, the most sensitive barometer of all currents streaming through the world and the experience of the world, sensed this. Tired by so much masculinity, women once again wanted to be pretty, once again wanted to be genuine women. And the fashion designers called attention to this turning point. They gave women a new exterior form that corresponded to their own will.

Women quickly understood what a great new chance they were being offered. They recognized how advantageously the long dress reshaped them: how they appeared taller and thinner; how much more elegant, graceful, and ladylike they looked. They recognized that by dressing in this new way for men, their clothes would once again carry a new element of attraction.

291

LISELOTTE DE BOOY [MISS GERMANY 1932]

Wasted Evenings

First published as "Herausgeschmissene Nächte," *Der Querschnitt* 12, no. 1 (1932), 285–289.

In school we all had to write essays, whether we wanted to or not, and we did so too without considering whether what we were writing was not the purest nonsense. But when one writes an essay for the public, then one has a somewhat greater feeling of responsibility. I cannot stand senseless scribbling—just to have written something—any more than I can stand dancing or idling away half the evening, or even the entire evening. Earlier, girls had nothing to do but try on dresses and make themselves pretty for the balls. At that time the balls were also much nicer and a greater event for everyone. Nowadays one usually goes to the ball just out of habit or to gape at the celebrities. And the next morning one has a terrible hangover. For those with a profession it is even worse, for they cannot rest properly and are scarcely able to accomplish what they must.

Is it not much nicer, when one wants entertainment or distraction, to go to a good theater or to one of the rare good films? Often there are lectures on literature, art, history, and all manner of subjects: everyone can find something that especially pleases him. People explain their lack of interest in such things by saying that they have so many worries and stresses all day long and they want a little distraction in the evening. Certainly it is nice to dance and laugh in pleasant company once in a while, but, because no one does anything else, this kind of socializing has become routine and monotonous. One has nothing whatever to say and, just to fill up the hours, turns to card games.

How would it be, however, if people, instead of allowing themselves to be brought down by their daily worries and seeking a change in inferior things, would turn to higher ones and let themselves be carried away from daily misery by great art and great thoughts. It is only because demands in general are not high enough that the average level of films and many modern theatrical plays is so low. Light entertainment—no one appears to want anything more. I said appears, for I am convinced that if film and theater directors did not orient themselves entirely according to what draws a big audience but would more often present something as well with sense and understanding, then the viewers would orient themselves to that and notice that great art distracts one much better from worries than light entertainment does. And at the same time, it would raise the level of social entertainment.

The people, especially the men, whom one meets at dinners these days all wear a mask. Everyone tries as much as possible to hide his personality and one is amazed at what superficial and dull neighbors one has at the table. Without the social masks, however, one can have an interesting—often even intelligent—conversation with many men. But in the long run almost all of them fall back into the same old banalities with us young girls.

The average person of today, especially the urban person, is, to be honest, irresponsibly superficial. There is scarcely any relationship between his daily life and world events and the divine. And he also lacks a proper relation to nature. How distant we are from the true meaning of life!

28
The Cult of the Body: *Lebensreform,* Sports, and Dance

IN THE LATE NINETEENTH CENTURY, in response to industrialization and urbanization, radical reformers sprang up across Germany advocating a new relationship to the body and a return to nature. Clothing reform, improved personal hygiene, dietary reform, sunbathing, and gymnastics promised to free the body from the restrictions of modern industrialization and city living. *Körperkultur* ("culture of the body") became a means of self-fulfillment and a compensation for unsanitary living conditions. From 1890 to 1910 a large variety of alternative groups and religious sects came into existence, ranging from youth culture organizations such as the *Wandervogel* movement (whose membership had dwindled to thirty thousand in 1929) to *Lebensreform* (life reform) groups propagating vegetarianism and nudism; from land commune dwellers and theosophists to German Buddhists. Despite the potential for progressive criticism of hectic, inhuman modernization, most of these groups followed a reactionary course in their longing for the utopia of a premodern world. The futile search for purity, for example, led some to propagate rabid racism (spouting forth theories about the superiority of an Aryan race) and anti-Semitism; others, in their contempt for materialism and bourgeois values, prefigured the hippie culture of the 1960s. Then there were the followers of Rudolf Steiner's anthroposophy, which espoused an eclectic mixture of ideas taken from reform pedagogy, mysticism, and Goethean humanism. The youth movement itself split into numerous groups and associations, spanning the entire political spectrum from Communism to National Socialism. Hitler began to recruit members for the Hitler Youth as early as 1922.

The uncertainty of the postwar period generated a large number of preachers, political demagogues, and half-crazed philosophers. Traveling from town to town with small entourages of followers, they usually cast contemporary problems in terms of conspiracies to which they offered global solutions. Hitler may have been seen by many in the mid-1920s as just one more of these zealous but harmless doomsday prophets. Virtually all of these movements, in which critical and reactionary motifs were inextricably mixed, continued to flourish until 1933, when they found themselves absorbed into the eclectic jumble of ideas that composed the Third Reich's *Weltanschauung.*

The call for a return to nature sometimes took curiously literal forms. In 1923 Adolf Koch, a teacher in Berlin's working-class district, began conducting gymnastics classes in the nude, justifying it on the lofty ground that nudity made everyone equal, including the worker. After being charged with the corruption of minors, Koch founded a private gymnastics school in Berlin and became a tireless promoter of *Freikörperkultur* (or FKK, "free body culture"), writing voluminous books that traced nudism back to its Hellenic roots. Nudism also meant liberation from traditional bourgeois restrictions and taboos, from a grim housing situation and oppressive working conditions as well as a general sense of alienation in the urban environment. As represented in the 1920s, nudism promised to reclaim the body that was being mercilessly pressed into service at the assembly line and functionalized by the industrial process. It also promised, according to Hans Surén's immensely popular book *Man and Sunlight,* a feeling of national and racial superiority.

The native German gymnastic movement could indeed look back at a long tradition. Friedrich Ludwig Jahn founded the first gymnastics club (*Turnverein*), in 1811 with the aim of hardening German youth in the struggle against the French occupiers. Sports in the Weimar Republic still played a major role in the schools' curricula and in the recreational activities of political organizations. In 1920 Dr. Carl Diem, who would later be in charge of the 1936 Berlin Olympic Games, took over the organization of that city's sports; in 1932 he founded a university for gymnastics and orchestrated citywide sports events such as the highly popular relay races and gymnastic competitions. Germany had enormous sports organizations that were divided, as everything else was in the Weimar Republic, along political lines: thus the nationalistic *Deutsche Turnerschaft* coexisted with the workers' *Turn- und Sportbund,* which had over one million members and which even staged special workers' olympic games. In 1926 Fritz Wildung wrote that workers' sports activities had a political dimension insofar as workers were delivered from a state of exploitation and alienation into a state of dignity. The unusually heavy emphasis on athletics in the Weimar Republic was claimed also for the good of the German nation, echoing the original goals of Jahn's physical culture movement whose aim was to promote military preparedness, discipline, racial superiority, and national survival.

Sports stood at the intersection of nationalism, popular culture, and self-development, functioning as a discursive metaphor on many levels. Numerous intellectuals of the Weimar Republic, for instance, preferred boxing to other sports precisely because it represented not only toughness and hard-boiled Americanism but also a new body consciousness. Brecht was especially proud of his friendship with professional boxers Paul Samson Körner and Hans Breitensträter. Max Schmeling, who became the first German to win the world heavyweight championship in New York in 1930 (which he then lost in 1932), mingled freely with Berlin's intelligentsia. The magazine *Der*

Querschnitt, ever alert to the latest trend, made a point of promoting boxing as the most noble of all sports, and the respected theater critic Herbert Jhering praised it for its refreshing anti-intellectualism.

Sports and a new sense of the body (*Körpersinn*) re-energized German life by the mid-1920s, and even a cursory glance at the illustrated press finds numerous examples of people depicted in various forms of motion such as jumping, running, flying through the air, dancing, and doing gymnastics.

This energy had also been the inspiration for the "new dance." Created by Rudolf von Laban, it had emerged out of the *Lebensreform* movement as a romantic celebration of pure physicality and creative self-expression. It was no coincidence that Laban developed the new dance at the Monte Verità commune in Ascona where writers, naturists, anthroposophists, artists, and philosophers gathered in the prewar years to search for an alternative way of life that was close to nature. Mary Wigman, Laban's most prominent student, carried on the tradition of the new dance, incorporating it into gymnastics, while Valeska Gert pioneered a type of dance that was expressionistic in its grotesque distortions. The 1924 documentary film *Ways to Strength and Beauty* presented an astoundingly rich parade of dancers and gymnasts, *Lebensreform* philosophers, and promoters of body culture. One of the dancers in this film was Leni Riefenstahl who ten years later would make *Triumph of the Will,* the official documentary film of the Party rally at Nuremberg, which shows masses of bodies in constant motion.

292

ADOLF KOCH

The Truth about the Berlin Nudist Groups

First published as "Die Wahrheit über die Berliner Gruppen für Freie Körperkultur," *Junge Menschen,* no. 5 (August 1924).

Two and a half years ago I became acquainted with a circle of friends (all the parents of workers) who were seriously attempting to do something for their deteriorating bodies and, in particular, to create a rational way of life for their children. This little group became the foundation in June 1925 of the nudist groups, who conceived the following guidelines for their work:

1. The urgency of the times in which we live, the monotony of work, and the world war and its results have caused a disturbance in our spiritual and physical dispositions. Religion taught that flesh was sin. We forgot our bodies and failed to see that a healthy spirit requires a proud and free body. The human being we aspire to be should not as previously be either a mind or muscle person. We strive for the unity of body and soul.

2. From an early age our children should feel at home with this conception. One way to accomplish this is to have pride in one's own body. In our nudist associations we seek ways to cultivate a natural nakedness and a free feeling for the body. Joy in speaking and singing as well as joy in color, expressiveness, and movement, are parts of this work. A healthy body is the goal. Working against tuberculosis, dipsomania, venereal diseases, etc., is an obvious extension of the cultivation of the body.

3. "No more war" should not be a mere empty phrase but represent an unalterable belief, based on respect for the body of the other, that war has become impossible. Our life should be built on love for others, on the principle of mutual aid and mutual understanding. Human existence must be affirmed. Among humanity's parasites are market speculators, exploiters of labor power, representatives of the alcohol business, and pedagogical reactionaries. The sharpest struggle must be waged against these drones and brutes.

4. We need people who do not merely want to mend the past but who believe they are working on a new world. We want the new religious person to act on the basis of his own experience. "You should" must become "I want" (I want because I can do no other). We do not assess values exclusively according to economic standards; the struggle for culture is our highest priority. Culture is rooted in love, therefore it counts love as its most vital force in all its expressions and accomplishments. The most important cultural issues of our time are, among others, training in work and in school; cultivating youth and the general welfare; the women's and mothers' movements; the right and duty to work; protection of nature and the wanderer movement (*Wanderbewegung*).

293

FELIX HOLLAENDER

Ways to Strength and Beauty

First published in *"Wege zur Kraft und Schönheit,"* Programmheft. Ein Film über moderne Körperkultur (n.p., 1924), 5–10.

Ways to Strength and Beauty is the name of the newest film from UFA's cultural department. Its creators were justified in giving it this proud name. Their goal was to conjure up on the screen a brilliant, colorful image of current endeavors in physical education and sports, departing from the pedagogical principles of Greek gymnastics and the sophisticated body culture of the Romans.

Mens sana in corpore sano [a sound mind in a sound body] is the leitmotif of this film, and it is brought to life in a plenitude of examples.

One could also interpret the phrase to mean that the training and care of the human body intensifies the feeling of life, that physical exercises also have a critical effect on the development of mental capacities.

This film might awaken an idea of the connection between body and soul in even the simplest viewer—and there might be no stronger indication of success in this regard than that the sight of the naked bodies of man and woman, as it appears here on the basis of a careful selection of materials, stimulates no impure sensations, but only feelings of joy and admiration in the aesthetic and human sense.

What was created was meant to be a hymn to endeavors aimed equally at awakening the sense of beauty and contributing to recovering the nation's health. It sought to show with what vigor our maligned era has seized upon and developed the issue of body culture—the extent to which it has been able to approximate the Greek ideal of beauty. [. . .]

This film seeks to indicate the kind of forces now at work that would make a rebirth of the body in the spirit of antiquity possible. And even if it accepts its task with great seriousness and a nearly philosophical meticulousness, it does not, within certain limits, shy from bitter sarcasm and satirical critique.

It shows the philistine in all his shadings, shows him looking at classical works of art, whose unalloyed nudism is not to be denied, and it parades the poor, exploited fellow who is pitifully stunted in modern office environs and who, less out of inertia than the unfavorable conditions of his life, is unable to come up with a free hour for a bit of exercise.

In contrast to the image of languishing youth, the representatives of a new generation appear here, for whom the care of their bodies is synonymous with existence and who are educated in the ways and means of keeping themselves strong and healthy. It may be that they take advantage of light, air, and water, or they might steel and train their bodies by marching, engaging in gymnastics, boxing, playing catch, or rowing. [. . .]

This film from UFA therefore does not stop short at individual athletic accomplishments but inquires into the system of physical fitness, allowing entire schools of dance to demonstrate the results of their artistic work in having discovered the methods and expressive forms of rhythmic gymnastics.

294

HANS SURÉN

Man and Sunlight

First published in *Der Mensch und die Sonne* (Stuttgart: Dieck & Coin Verlag, 1925).

PREFACE TO THE FIRST EDITION

This book arose from my desire to call attention to the fundamental facts of national existence and development. If physical strength is allowed to decay, even the highest achievements of the spirit and the most profound scientific knowledge will not avert national decline and death. Using every means possible with unflagging energy, a nation should be united in the will to promote the strength of its people. Moral fortification and the strengthening of character is closely tied to this, as I have briefly outlined in this book.

Physical exercise will only make its true, noble, physical, and spiritual influences felt when it is practiced in the form of gymnastics. Young people should not regard their goal to be breaking records but the power of the health and beauty of their own fully trained bodies. The photographs in this book display people as symbols of strength and health. Their bodies, governed by firm character, assure a better future. It is the duty of those with high aspirations to steel and train their bodies in such manner.

Nakedness and habituation to nature are necessary means to this end. Training in the nude with members of one's own sex must be recognized as essential. This is in contrast to nudism among both sexes—only the right kind of people should assemble for such purpose lest pure motives be misunderstood and sullied. I am well aware that co-ed nudism is not suitable for the general public; nonetheless, I have endeavored to bring some degree of clarity to this pressing question, since it is now a subject of great discussion.

PREFACE TO THE 61ST EDITION:

The astonishing success of my book shows how aptly it reflects the aspirations of the true German race. As is noted in reviews and commentaries, the book has opened up new paths, particularly toward a new conception of gymnastics, sports, and training. I take this opportunity to thank the countless correspondents who have written from all German-speaking countries and even from German settlements overseas. They encourage me to continue my efforts. [. . .] My fundamental views and doctrines concerning education are now complete, with the exception of a few special areas; during the past few years I have been able almost to perfect the system. My pamphlets on gymnastics (with and without equipment), my various instructional booklets, and my book, *German Gymnastics,* should suffice to guide all those who aspire to health and strength. It is everyone's sacred duty to help in this great enterprise by active individual hygienics: for the benefit of the race and of humanity. Active hygienics requires gymnastics, air, and sunlight.

ODE TO LIGHT

Hail to all of you who love nature and sunlight! Joyfully you wander through field and meadow, over hill and vale. Barefoot in your linen smocks open at the neck, your knapsack on your back, you wander happily whether the skies be blue or storms rage. The straw in the barn or the noble temple of the forest itself is your resting place at night. Evenings around the campfire, sacred nature stirs you in the depths of your soul. But the joy of being is even more deeply felt when you have cast off your clothing by the bank of a stream or lake to bathe in sunlight and water. A marvelous feeling of freedom flows through you, and you exalt in your work. Now you experience yourself, you experience your body! Most people do not know their own bodies; it is for them only a necessary, often burdensome, machine of existence. Even many wanderers are strangers to their own bodies, first attaining true knowledge thereof only in the midst of nature, their nakedness clothed in light. There is a purity, a sacredness, in our natural nakedness. We experience a marvelous revelation in the beauty and strength of the naked body, transfigured by godlike purity shining from the clear and open eye that mirrors the entire depth of a noble and questing soul. Placed in the bright frame of exalted nature, the human body finds its most ideal manifestation.

Therefore hail to all who love the sun in natural and healthy nakedness. One single bond unites us children of sunlight—equally, regardless of who or what we are. Friends of the Sun! Courageously you threw off the shackles of a false upbringing, and have won many hard fights against antiquated ideas and prudery. You are seekers of new paths to a happier being, and seekers are those who sincerely strive, whether young or old. How many there are who must painfully hide from the knowledge of their fellow men their quest for the sun and their longing to know their own bodies! Yet there can be no turning back to the falseness and pathology of today's ideas and customs, since in truth, all who follow the path see as their bright goal the radiant sun of a purer, happier humanity. So fight, you sun-lovers, a hard yet joyous battle for your happiness, and many a glad day of sunshine shall give strength for the many days of hard labor! Be patient in the difficult times of your captivity. In the inner circle of light are many who are distinguished by the sorrow and the scars enjoined upon them in the sun-battle, in the fight for light in the face of misunderstanding and outlived traditions. Let all followers of light joyfully hail these pioneers!

295

ARTUR MICHEL

Flying Man

First published as "Der fliegende Mensch," *Uhu* 2 (February 1926), 22–26.

A new joy in movement has come over the people. The big-city dweller has realized that he has been neglecting in his life in the parlor, the office and the factory the foundation of his humanity, his breathing, blood-circulating body. A new youth has grown up with a love for movement. Sport has been newly discovered in all its forms. Its goal and meaning is not merely the strengthening of the muscles, the steeling of the body, which has indeed been the concern of German calisthenics since Father Jahn. The goal and meaning of sport (insofar as it does not strive for record-book achievements) and of all exercise is primarily the expression of joy in a newly discovered body, the pleasure in bodily movement, which finally has, as it did in the American "body culture," gripped our people as well. Thus the demand enjoyed by all suppliers of the most modern gymnastic equipment. Thus, too, the eagerness with which men and women rush to the motion choirs called into being by Rudolf von Laban and his youths.

The joy in movement on the part of the lay person, that is, the working people who were unable to choose dance or gymnastics as their profession, finds its strongest and most vital gratification in such motion choirs. For in them this joy finds an outlet in festive, expressive exercise similar to dance and challenging for the whole being, body and soul.

The highest and most splendid expression of the new joy in movement, however, is to be found in artistic dance. For genuine dance is intensified motion. At the same time it is the release of tensions which grip the entire personality of the dancer—the ability to experience which makes up the essence of all dancers and distinguishes them from the average person, however great the latter's own joy in movement. But to be able genuinely to release such high tensions within the successive movements of the dance, the dancer requires an incomparable program of physical training. The creator of modern dance, Rudolf von Laban, along with his brilliant student, Mary Wigman, provide personal models of fitness and have also developed a training program requiring years of the most strenuous exertion. Only those who have their bodies fully within their control, who have learned to lend each dancerly impulse a distinct, immediately intelligible form in movement, are capable of expressing in dance what moves them.

This also means that modern dance does not, like the art of ballet, aspire to be a charming play of bodies in graceful motion. It aspires to make the body a representational tool for all that excites and moves a person most deeply. Artistic dance is—like a poem, a play, a piece of music—an expressive system. For this reason in the modern art of dance the solo retreats in favor of the group dance. The dance troupe, as an orchestra of thoroughly trained dancers, performs the work of art created by the dance poet. In this way the dancer, the person moving through space, has gained a whole new breadth of movement possibilities. They range from the tragically dark through measured seriousness to boundless passion and to illuminating cheerfulness, from the charmingly lyrical to the dreadfully wild. So it is that in dance the joyfully striding, heavily creeping, cravenly crawling, blessedly soaring person also becomes the flying man. For flight and pursuit, the rapid burst of happiness, and frenetic jubilation, just as sudden fear and hellish dread, happily seek expression in leaps and series of leaps, whether harmoniously pretty or disharmoniously grotesque, and can further intensify the character of flight through contrasting movements before and after or through the harmonious movements in contrast to the other dancers on the stage.

The circus acrobat or the athletically trained professional jumper might occasionally, through his one-sided training to break the record, accomplish a higher leap than the dancer, for whom the leap is one among many of the expressive tools of dance. The photographs (most of which will appear soon in Rudolf von Laban's new book, *Exercise and Dance*) might manage to illustrate the difference, to the extent that photographs are at all capable of capturing the flow and swing of fleeting movement.

296

FRITZ WILDUNG

Sport is the Will to Culture

First published as "Sport ist Kulturwille," *Kulturwille* 3, no. 5 (May 1926), 85.

There have been many attempts, until now all in vain, to supply a clear definition for the term *sport.* A leading bourgeois sports figure, Carl Diem, coined the phrase "Sport is battle!" But this formulation is very one-sided and applies only to actual competitions. Competition meanwhile is only one of sport's methods, and definitely not the essential one. Sport in Germany is incidentally still too new and too little rooted in the character of the German people to make it possible to point to a definition that has grown organically from the German way of life. In any case, the opinion represented by Diem, among others, that a physical exercise is to be designated a sport only when it is carried out as a battle or competitive exercise, should be regarded as outmoded. The people speak of every seriously undertaken physical exercise as sport and it is incumbent upon the expert to accept this judgment.

It seems to us that one comes much closer to the essence of sport when it is derived from the natural human drive to play. We know the play drive of children and the extreme variety of ways it is expressed, but play is always an activity of people who are in the process of becoming whole. We do not know of games of a strictly physical or strictly mental sort in children, for to the child games represent a simultaneously physical, mental, and psychological occupation: work. People never lose this drive to play; it only changes its forms of expression with the growth of their physical and mental powers and the differentiation of their psychological life. Young men experience that pleasure through competition, whereas mature men find that same pleasure in creative desires, that is, in work. That is why adolescents favor athletic competition and games whereas the more mature man turns to the more contemplative forms of sport. Women of all ages are inclined much more than men to rhythmic exercises. The expressive forms assumed by the play drive are moreover definitively influenced by the role occupied by both young and mature people in the process of production. Normally the work performed by people is meant to satisfy their play drive at the highest level of its development. In work people find the purpose of their existence fulfilled; it is a means by which they express their creative, formative powers and a practice field for all of their aptitudes and talents. Therefore it represents play in the higher sense at the same time, and people derive from it the peace of mind that lends harmony to their lives. So it should be. But how diametrically opposed to this ideal is today's wage labor for manual and mental workers! Only a very few people are able to select their life's occupation according to their wishes, inclinations, and talents. How rarely are desire and inclination decisive in the selection of an apprenticeship. In the majority of cases either accident or the desire for immediate earnings determines the trade to be pursued, and those so affected are weighed down with a poorly chosen occupation their whole lives. This is to say nothing of the host of those with no occupation at all, which, with the increasing division of labor, is growing daily.

Meanwhile the progression of the division of labor causes the labor process to become more monotonous, undifferentiated, and soulless for the majority of working people. The creative impulse is given scarcely any room for development, and the body becomes an automaton, whose movements are strictly prescribed by the particular nature of the work.

We can scarcely speak of a gratification of the natural play drive, for the physical and psychological processes of work are obligatory and render the individualized self-cultivation of the worker impossible. To all of this is added the workers' miserable pay, the uninterrupted struggle for wages, and the low standard of living that stands in such blatant contradiction to the high level of mental development of today's workers. From this coincidence just briefly sketched here of physical and mental need on the part of the majority of people today arises the enormous degree of dissatisfaction and inner strife characteristic of our capitalist era. If this development is not stopped, it will doubtless lead to the decline of civilization.

What is the relationship between sport and these symptoms of decay in capitalist society? Does it signify a flight from a bleak reality into an illusory world, or is it a sign of self-assertion against the ominous decline of the race? It is both, and much more. Make no mistake: *panem et circenses* [bread and circuses] applies to our time as well. But the modern proletarian is not comparable to the lumpenproletarian of ancient Rome. He possesses the force of the self-conscious rebel who does not resign himself to his fate. He bursts his confines and seeks a way out. Sport is a rebellion against the threat of decay, an expression of the will to live. Young life does not want to be crushed on the treadmill of the economic system but strives to raise itself to higher forms. That is why it seeks the movement necessary to life and psychological balance in a kind of work that it recognizes as struggle and play and therefore a source of joy and well-being. Seen in this way sport is a playful form of work and thereby a necessary correlate of today's production processes. On the mental, physical, and psychological plane, it gives young people what contemporary work, thanks to its degeneration into modern slave labor, cannot: the movement vital to life! That is the deepest meaning of sport.

But—this is the question of concerned people—does it not also contain the danger of a turn away from the intellectual world and the idea of socialism? Yes and no! It depends on whether we place sport at the service of socialism by leading young people to recognize that sport is uncreative if it does not go hand-in-hand with the social struggle for improving the conditions against which it signifies a protest. Sport necessarily perishes when people lack time and nourishment to such a degree that engaging in it is impossible. A sick race cannot cultivate sport; it is forced to exhaust itself in its concern for healing its sores. We have to hammer into young people that production cannot be developed through a return to ancestral methods but that the division of labor must be further developed if an increase in production, which is a precondition of socialism, is to be achieved. This recognition then yields the practical lesson that salvation is only to be had from a considerable reduction in soulless labor and therefore a gain in leisure time sufficient for vital activities in all areas of life. Influenced by such thoughts, sport can become a powerful factor in favor of socialism, particularly in arousing parts of the population that we can reach only with great difficulty with our purely intellectual weapons.

I bring this discussion to a close with the affirmation that sport, in its best and strongest sense, is the will to culture. Let us see to it that the liberating act will be the product of this will.

297

ERNST PREISS

Physical Fitness—A National Necessity

First published as "Die Körperausbildung—eine Volksnotwendigkeit," in *Neue Wege der Körperkultur* (Stuttgart: Dieck, 1926).

That the German people have suffered a significant decline in their vital energies over the last two decades has been proven repeatedly. This decline manifests the influences of agricultural and industrial occupations on the human body.

The gradation in the "fitness ratio" identified among the various German racial groupings from the southeast to the northwest (from 49 percent to 46 percent) is to be regarded as a result of the advance of urban, industrial ways of life, so that one may speak of a geographical and temporal law of cultural effects.

In the face of this threat to our national body, adequate social-hygienic measures must be implemented to reinvigorate our endangered common vitality.

For this purpose, and aside from proper nutrition, the general promotion of a healthy practice of personal hygiene and physical exercise must be undertaken in addition to the provision of maternal counseling, infant care, suitable dwellings and recreational opportunities, and the endeavors of the housing movement.

In this way the individual will gain the necessary foundation for a creative life in a healthy body, and the entirety of the people the support columns for a new ascent.

298

WOLFGANG GRAESER

Body Sense: Gymnastics, Dance, Sport

First published in *Körpersinn. Gymnastik, Tanz, Sport* (Munich: C.H. Beck'sche Verlagsbuchhandlung, 1927), 7–11.

Something new has appeared. It could be called a movement, a wave, a fashion, a passion, a new feeling for life; this is a reality that has inundated, pursued, inspired, reformed and influenced millions of people.

It came from the unknown, from the unconscious, it came almost out of nothingness; it spread like wildfire and caught on like a flame. It fought aggressively and was joined in battle by its hundreds of apostles. And it had the strength within itself to triumph in a world of malcontents and skeptics, to assert itself against the defenses erected by a narrow moral order that over the course of a century had become calcified and limited. This tidal wave washed over and washed away attitudes cherished for generations.

No one knew from whence this new tendency came. It seeped through almost unnoticed, and its pervasive presence was like an unstemmable tide. It had no name but was called by a hundred old names and a hundred new ones, and ultimately the old expressions were unable to capture the new sensibility:

Body culture, gymnastics, dance, cult dances, the new corporeality, the new physicality, the revival of the ideals of antiquity, the new gymnastics, physical exercise and hygiene, sport in all its incarnations such as those played in the nude, nudism, life reform, functional gymnastics, physical education, rhythmical exercise with all its countless expressions, and so on.

These are a few of the descriptive names for the new phenomenon. In this regard one might consider how the intellectual world is at a loss when confronted by this new development, the immediate reality of which is lived and experienced by thousands of people.

The entire Western world and its sphere of influence has been transformed by this strange new sensibility and way of life—from America to Australia, from Europe to Japan. The individual manifestations may be different, but essentially it is always the same thing.

Do we not see the change in the streets, in every slender young woman who carries herself with great self-assurance, is it not evident in men's suntanned faces? Don't we see it in our homes, our clothing, our hairstyles, our customs?

Has not literature, art, and society come to feel its influence? Where is the fussy ornamentation of yesteryear? Where is the confinement, the fear of light and air prevalent in the days when the body was encased in tight corsets, draped with enough fabric to fill a store, when one sat on olive-green, dusty velour sofas while knitting wool stockings?

Is not the entire wasteland of a diseased and decaying middle-class way of thinking disappearing? And how does this new sensibility manifest itself? In a true hunger for light. Sober clarity in form and content, objectivity, tempo, air and sunlight—these are all desirable things.

One seeks and finds health, strength, beauty, versatility, and security. The anxious separation of the sexes has disappeared. Fresh air, a more self-confident and responsible spirit seems to have spread across the land. Our attitudes have changed: toward life, spirituality and the body, toward what is decent and indecent, sensual and abstract, toward religion and sex. We see the past and we see history with new eyes. And everything that is new is connected, either directly or indirectly, with the new corporeality.

The way of life spawned by the new corporeality must always be taken into consideration in interpreting any of these phenomena correctly.

Where did all this come from? What caused such an internal and external revolution? Can the outward impetus for this change be found?

It was the Great War; it opened up an unbridgeable, yawning abyss between then and now, drew a dividing line between old and new. It abruptly severed all ties with the past and obliterated with a bloodstained paintbrush the plethora of forms and shapes that had determined life in earlier times. The war stirred the soul of the people at its most elemental level and reopened the floodgates of the dark, chaotic unconscious.

The people of yesteryear experienced a grim awakening from a self-satisfied dream of world domination and world peace; they had to look in the face of the nerve-rending nothingness of dark primal forces that emerged from incomprehensible depths. Like a volcanic explosion, seething barbaric life broke through the ossified crust and raged for four years among the people.

In the fierce intoxification of the war, victor and vanquished alike whipped themselves into a state of frenzy and exhaustion; wind, rain, and blood washed away the illusions of ideology. People returned to their homes, their apartments, their old schools and over the doorways were inscribed the sayings of long ago.

But then the time came to once again put on the (now unaccustomed) constricting clothing, to tread once more the (formerly abandoned) paths of middle-class life—it was then that everything disintegrated into a meaningless and leaderless chaos. The old order consisted of nothing more than hollow remnants, but there was nothing there to replace it. Without a feasible goal, without stability, without a unified will, people swung back and forth between political and spiritual extremes, until years later, after struggling in despair, each nation found a way to express these experiences and life's new sensibility.

Russia finally escaped from its ties to the Orient. The fundamental elements of the modern syndicalist state developed in Italy, the land of Roman clarity of form. In a Germany that had been torn to pieces, and from which a feeling for external form had always emanated, the experience had a profound effect. A new, influential metaphysics developed. The external façade was shattered and decayed, at which point a self-discovery process began, a search for a physical and spiritual unity. The entire world longed to hear the heartbeat of the living.

The murderous war had become the creator of this new life. To those who died it was a great liberator and we must sanction it as such. What have been discussed here are the symptoms of a new way of life characteristic of the postwar population. Bolshevism, fascism, sports, body culture, and the New Objectivity are all interrelated.

The development of forms in the West had not yet reached its true maturity, its apogee; otherwise it would perhaps have been totally destroyed by the ravages of war. But these forms still retained some of their power and thus were able to resurrect themselves and infuse life with new blood, fortifying and strengthening it. Russia was ripe for decline; but we have the destiny of a thousand-year-old culture to fulfill. The clarified spirit of the Western world has emerged from a catastrophe.

The materialism and rationalism of the nineteenth century have finally been vanquished. Of course, many people do not want to admit what is happening; they let themselves be led astray by the clamorous events of the day. They are unable to discern out of this din deeper tones and resounding vibrations, they do not see what kind of truly barbaric fanaticism is behind the economic and industrial leaders as they fight for power amongst themselves. Whoever does not believe this should take a look at what is happening in Italy, which is the most interesting phenomenon in Europe today. He would see how in just a few years a mordant economy came to life in the truest sense of the word, becoming a living function of the national organism rather than a self-contained unit. Whoever does not believe this should consider how the Soviet Union wasted millions and millions on revolutionary propaganda at the same time as the country was in bitter misery, not for any kind of intellectual or materialistic goals but rather out of zealous fanaticism.

In all realms and walks of life, blood, new impulses, and intuition are rising up once more against mere reason, will, and the intellect.

299

MARY WIGMAN

Dance and Gymnastics

First published as "Tanz und Gymnastik," *Der Tanz,* no. 2 (November 1927), 6–7.

The flourishing of the dance in Germany as the vital expression of an entire generation is a fact we can no longer ignore today.

We dancers have to realize that we owe the lively effect of our work primarily to German youth, who have a wholly different orientation than their counterparts in other

European nations. Both athletic and artistic dance is known outside Germany, but only ballet in a more or less revuelike guise is recognized as such. The great common denominator we have in Germany is gymnastics.

Gymnastics is neither sport nor athletic dance. These two classes of movement, independent of any evaluation of their final and actual meaning, are necessarily maximum performances. What we know as gymnastics contains both athletic and dancelike elements. Gymnastics is athletic insofar as it involves the strengthening and cultivation of the body and its capacity for performance, that is, body culture. It is dancelike because it is simultaneously an expression inspired by the soul. This peculiar compound form presumably leaves the Latins nonplussed. But for us it is thoroughly natural, and all of our youth marches under its banner.

Gymnastics can never be and has absolutely no desire to be art. If the confusion occasionally arises, it is regrettable but not important.

We are justified in saying that the idea of gymnastics is maintained primarily by female youth, and with an emphasis on its dancelike aspect. There is certainly no better body training for a woman. Comparisons with young women's bodies in other countries are already yielding results favorable to our German girls trained in gymnastics.

Dance begins where gymnastics leaves off. To mark the boundary with absolute precision is impossible. The decisive factor is neither the type nor the style of the gesture but something that cannot actually be seen or said. Precisely this invisible and neverthelessperceptible feature, this mysterious binding agent, that which exists between the lines transforms gymnastics into dance and distinguishes dancers from gymnasts. Our dance cannot live without gymnastics. It is the basis upon which the dance stands, the actual point of its departure. But the meaning of course is different. Gymnastics in every form should and must pursue its own independent goal. It makes no difference if the emphasis is purely hygienic or more or less dancelike. The human body is at stake! By no means developed to the full extent of its purely physical potential, it has not expanded to the full range of its immediate capacities for experience and expression. For dancers the body can never be a goal in this sense. Like the gymnast, they must experience the physical, come to know and master it. Yet they will never simply accept the body as such, but will reach beyond to form it into an instrument of dance. Only when the body becomes an instrument does dance begin to distinguish itself from gymnastics. Only when psychological expression is refined into a clear formal language can one speak of dance.

There are many people with expressive talent who consider themselves dancers but who are not and never will be. For dance exists in people as a gift, as a fatelike predetermination, no matter when it might surface and no matter where it might lead.

Gymnastics is instead much more a matter of disposition and is thoroughly conditioned by ethical and social considerations. At this point, the sphere of gymnastic effects is still that of dance's potential. Though it seems incomprehensible, it is nevertheless a fact that dance and gymnastics occasionally succumb to a relation of mutual hostility. Confusion arises in both areas, the result of their common foundation! On the one hand, the dancer looks down in arrogance at gymnastic exercises, forgetting that that is where he himself began and has usually not surpassed them as much as he thinks. The gymnast, on the other hand, often mistakes his attempts at expression for dance and therefore places impossible demands on himself.

The necessary clarification cannot be achieved from one day to the next and then codified. We must not forget that the one as well as the other concerns a human good. Just as the common foundation emerges and develops organically so must the process of distinguishing between them be an organic and not a forced one. And there will be borderline cases, just as there are in every area of human expression.

300

HERBERT JHERING

Boxing

First published as "Boxen," *Das Tagebuch* 8 (1927), 587–589.

There is nothing funnier than the struggle going on today for and against sports. Against: whatever else, they can be seen as a distraction from intellectual and political passions. For: how can anyone fire off polemical phrases for something that has long since become the matter-of-fact property of hundreds of thousands? Reading some sports reporting one might think that boxing and six-day races are just as problematic and crisis-ridden as school, theater, church, and socialism.

Attempts are underway to remove sports from among the immediate interests of the public. Slowly and zealously, through pathetic observations, sports are being robbed of the advantage they have above all other public proceedings. There is no audience as naïve and justified as the sports public. It reacts instinctively to every blow in a boxing match, to all the pursuit in a six-day race. It is impressed solely by achievement. A favorite is booed the moment he fails, like Franz Diener. A Frenchman will be elevated above a German when he is superior in battle, like Kid Nitram. As for the brutish public, it casts off its chains in the sport palaces and only in the sports palaces. Terrible, transported by the moment, whistling and stomping, yelling and rocking. And this healthily involved, this robustly surrendered, this passionately enthused public is now to be transformed by critical education into a multitude of individual experts. From the naive, stirred-up masses, proudly judicious individuals are to be made intellectual authorities.

That profiteering in the operation of sports has been discovered goes without saying. But if the point of the polemic is to educate the boxing public so that it places more value on matches that end in a draw than on those that end with a knockout, then that is a misunderstanding of what attracts the public to sporting events. The people make their way to the arena to see victors and vanquished. They want to experience results. Cheated out of decisions in their occupational lives, with no prospect of a sudden turn or surprise in their work, they come here to get their excitement and suspense. An aesthetically beautiful athletic game means nothing to them. Tens of thousands react simultaneously to the most incredible competitors and the most elegant tactics. Captivated, they take in the mobile boxing style of Domgörgen, every shift of the hips, every extension of the left arm, the dance of every defensive and offensive posture. But they are excited by the most fascinating strategic variations only because without knowing it they are looking to them for the decisive end. Every duck, every attack means nothing to the public as a movement in itself. It senses only the momentary advantages and disadvantages of the opponents. The crowd wants to experience the up and down of a real battle; it wants to experience the *risk*. And only in this context is it interested in the aesthetic appeal of the individual rounds.

To reprimand the sports public—as sometimes happens because it boos, attacks the judgment of the referee, has sympathies and antipathies, or does not agree with the model of academic boxing—remains a mistake. It is precisely the excitability of the public that sports, particularly boxing, has above all other public events. The people's desire to see decisions should not be driven out of them for the contrary purpose of rendering them useful for intellectual and political processes. Sport is lively. It fulfills a need. Its enemies can change none of that, and its friends, only if they turn boxing into an abstract athletic science so that the public is no longer present at battles but at podium discussions.

The liveliness of sports has already enriched language. High German, intellectualized and burdened with culture, has gained in imagery and activity from the speech of engineering and the inroads of sports. A different kind of person, a different way of expressing himself. Opponents and spectators are forced into an objective style of seeing. The sort of comparisons involved lead back into more naïve times. Paolino versus Breitensträter, "Basque lumberjack versus German oak"—that might sound funny, but it has striking force. That is how people talk; it is their jargon.

That boxing influences the language is good. It would be terrible only if, vice versa, an artificial, aesthetic terminology pounced upon sport, if the vocabulary of theater criticism made its way into soccer and sports commentaries: the affectation of a cultivated German versus naïvely practical, cool athletes. An awful literary vocabulary versus a healthy, brutally naïve public. The German language has already repelled many attacks; it will defend itself against this mélange as well. Centuries ago it struggled with the French invasion. That it was locked up inside Latin and French syntactical structures for a long time only made it hardy and strong. The penetration of the English–American jargon of the sports dialect will do a proper service to the German language. An enrichment will remain once the barren shop talk, once the annoying use of the aesthetic vocabulary has ceased.

301

MARIELUISE FLEISSER

The Athletic Spirit and Contemporary Art: An Essay on the Modern Type

First published as "Sportgeist und Zeitkunst. Essay über den modernen Menschentyp," *Germania* (September 12, 1929).

When people today are asked to name the type of person they consider the representative of the specifically modern sentiment, those in the know name the athlete. The facts justify the claim. Yet it would be sad if this judgment of the culture of our time were to remain conclusive in its one-sided limitation to the physical. Considered precisely, the essence of the athlete is that which distinguishes him from a well-drilled recruit: his athletic spirit and his competitive orientation toward life. If it is true that this athletic spirit, in its resolute and deliberate activity, comprises the peak of contemporary sentiments, no reason remains for confining its effects one-sidedly to the body. Perhaps the person devoted to mental work can learn from the methods applied by the athlete.

We were otherwise accustomed to thinking that the formal expression of the general will to life was the task of artistic production. That is what lent legitimacy to the life of the artist. Is the artist today supposed to have lost this function? That thought arises when one sees how the masses stream to athletic contests while evincing little interest in artistic events. Physical accomplishments are more easily transformed into something understandable in the view of the masses. That alone is not enough to condemn art to extinction. There remain the ambitious, those who want to continue learning and taste the finer things of life, because the struggles and triumphs of the spirit are what make our complex world that much more vital. But they come away empty-handed. The art with which they are presented fails to supply their natural fanaticism with the kind of content that would affect them strongly enough to brighten suddenly their dark instincts and take on a leading role in their attitude toward life. So they would rather stay away. That is a judgment. Art seems to have distanced itself, in form and content, from that which concerns the youth of the nation. [. . .]

What is the athletic spirit? Genuine athletic spirit is the aggressive orientation of an individual toward his own body, whereby, given the prospect of certain difficult accomplishments, he attempts to repress his body's natural reluctance through an exercise of will. Once gained, an athletic achievement is not something that simply remains; rather, it constantly must be reasserted against the body's own unwelcome laws of inertia, against its tendency to let up. The neural pathways by which will is translated into physical movement are trained until they react to the slightest impulse. The result is determination. Tendons, muscles, nerves, and bones are accustomed to delivering force and accustomed to cold-bloodedness, control, speed, endurance, intensification, coiled concentrations of will, and those sudden explosions that go into a spurt. Yet once the highest form has been achieved, the will is not the only effective force responsible for exceptional accomplishments. The body, drawing on the very last of its reserves, seems suddenly to have been seized by an alien power, permeated with fantastic abilities that make the accomplishment visible. The athlete enters, so to speak, into a temporary chemical compound with a being of a different dimension. This blending can be achieved by a body operating in top form, like the flash of lightning attracted by a rod. It is the highest natural form of activity known in man. It is the business of athletes to approximate as nearly as possible the flash through the energy in their bodies. To drive oneself toward the flash, to conjure the tension required, is the passion that makes up the driving nerve of the modern human type.

Sports arenas have, through their mere existence (which is inseparable from the contemporary feel of life) posed a challenge to us. Let us accept it! If in our case we put mind in the place of body, then we will become in our minds athletically tough with ourselves. Literature is living in an unacknowledged epoch of world-weariness. We are burdened by the idea that we are a race cast out of the chaos. That it confronts overwhelming powers, however, is no reason for an organism to allow its energies to subside. Hardness toward ourselves is imperative. The forces suffocating in world-weariness must be freed for a determined accomplishment. We must begin with ourselves to make this body, which we are, bigger. We are dependent once and for all on this limited but viable body, and we must draw out of it what can possibly be drawn. It no longer suffices to depict conditions and their presumably shattering senselessness. The point is to sow the seeds of will, which will awaken an energetic race responsible for driving itself forward, thus creating for itself a conscience.

302

VALESKA GERT

Dancing

First published as "Tanzen," *Schrifttanz* 4, no. 1 (June 1931), 5–7.

What position does modern dance occupy in the contemporary history of the arts? Modern dance represents the transition from old to new theater. The modern dancer had to liberate himself from old theatrical ways and he had to become independent. He did not concern himself with tradition: he was without the constraints of old theatrical conventions. In total naïvete he gave visible expression to his innermost feelings. The directness of expression in modern dance is similar to that of conventional theater (but not to that of the ballet). The dissociation from everything superficial and the restriction to essentials created the most intense movement and the most intensive expression possible: the dance. The dancer of our time, if he does not want to stagnate, has to be articulate about his intentions. His only mission is to be the link between the old and the new theater. His need for expression frequently pushes him to use masks. He wants to say something, and as he is unable to do so by means of his body alone he uses a mask. Our time strives for the absolute, the typical, the nonpersonal, hence the mask.

But the mask alone is not enough. The dancer must express his feelings with so much intensity that the body itself becomes the absolute, the typical: the mask. The theatrical modern dance is not, as often assumed, a modern version of classical ballet but it is a modern development of the theater, a dramatized moving presentation of modern man.

Now I will talk about my own dances. How I create them varies. Usually I am possessed by a certain tension that can last for days. This tension disturbs me. I try out various movements. If they release the tension, then they are good. I often deliberately make the tension last in order to create the amount of new forms I need. Sometimes I achieve this without effort and in a very short time, but sometimes I cannot find movements that release the tension and I work over and over again in my search for them. This tension has become very real to me and I can recreate it whenever I like. Once a piece is made I do not give up until it is perfected, if I believe at all in its development. Some dances remain of interest to me for a long time, some even at the peak of their creation no longer excite me and I abandon them. Often I hear from the audience, "why don't you do your *Tango* or *Circus* or *Cabaret*," or one of the others, but if these dances are dead and finished for me I cannot ever repeat them.

My favorite dance is the one I can change the most. What is permanent and never changes is the basic structure of steps and movements. Each time the same steps follow each other in the same order: what is changing, however, is the emotion out of which the dance grows. I experience the dance anew each time. In *Kanaille* a different destiny is presented every time but it is always the destiny of a prostitute. One day this girl enjoys her work, another day she despises it, yet on another day she does her work out of desperation or indifference, or even out of spite. As there is a different emotion behind the dance each time it is performed, the character of the steps changes as well. This makes them appear improvised, the same steps that yesterday were performed with hesitation and resentment the next time are performed quickly and with enjoyment. The climax of this dance is the surrender. In my dance *Der Tod* I always repeat the same phrases: from walking slowly to shouting aloud in fear of death until I gradually let go of life and its anguish and give up peacefully. Only every time my death is different, sometimes my fear is greater, sometimes I surrender more easily. The climax of the dance is my anguish. I am not interested in presenting a particularly artistic arrangement of movements. I only use the most basic and easiest of steps. If one takes the body and its own laws as a starting point, the result will be a dance in which the actions have grown out of each other. However, if one wants to create from the depths of one's spirit and soul, one should not simply develop one movement out of another. Also, I do not believe that by simply devising a skilful sequence of movement one can reveal one's soul. Art shies away from the deliberately artistic. It happens so often that dances are created according to recipes, although even in an activity as functional as cooking the most beautiful dishes can only be created through an intuitive approach. I believe that art is sorcery; if the spell is successful then the body will follow the mind without resistance.

303

CARL DIEM

The German Academy for Gymnastics

First published in *Die deutsche Hochschule für Leibesübungen* (Hannover: Continental, 1932), 5–9.

Our academy is a child of Germany's distress and anguish but also of Germany's strength in this situation. The idea for this school originated in the inner circles of the sports movement; the need for it arose and was created out of unbound forces. Truly, there are few institutions of this type that are so rooted in pure idealism and willing self-sacrifice. Up until now its strongest pillar of support has been the voluntary collaboration of leaders in the fields of gymnastics and sports, and in the sciences.

The inspiration for an independent educational facility for gymnastics grew as a consequence of the heavy loss of human life suffered in the world war, the victims of which were, of course, precisely the ones who had been the leaders of the gymnastics clubs and sports leagues. They were all healthy, well-trained, ready for action, and accustomed to physical exertion and to danger. It was no wonder that they stood, and fell, on the front lines of battle. [. . .] In addition to so few men returning from the battlefield with peacetime experience in the supervision of gymnastics and sports, because of the almost complete suspension of gymnastic club activities there was also a shortage of new, trained directors. A tradition had abruptly ceased to be. The urgent need for directors became that much more tangible as young people turned to the sports clubs in droves. In addition, economic conditions made it difficult for the unsalaried directors to work in the gymnastics and sports clubs. Where there was a shortage of volunteers, professionals had to be found for the job. It was thus necessary to train posthaste such professional teachers of gymnastics and, in addition, gradually to provide the unsalaried, inexperienced instructors with professional training.

That was the immediate reason for establishing this academy. Public institutions were unable adequately to attend to the concerns of the sports leagues; they had more than enough to do with regard to training gymnastics teachers in the public schools.

The inner reason for founding this academy went deeper, however. At that time in Germany, as now, healthy life forces fought the convulsions caused by the calamity of war and its aftermath and battled the constraints imposed by the enemy. These healthy instincts, lying dormant in the general populace, aspired to build a new house out of the ruins. Healthy, strong-willed people were needed for this task. Gymnastics was by no means in last place among the numerous methods used to try to improve the health of the population and to strengthen its will power. Sports and gymnastics were appropriate for once again allowing the development of people who were steadfast, well-balanced, and full of zest for living, people willing to work and used to physical exertion. A force within the populace led it to pay increased attention to the value of physical training. People looked for the newest and best forms of training; sports, refereed by well-trained professionals, would become something for everyone to engage in. Exercising the body was viewed as a restorative practice.

These energies, spurring on the population's inner development, cried out for a place of learning that would at the same time work to promote itself. The new doctrine was to have its own apostles as it forged its spiritual armor. High-minded youths did not want sports to be simply a leisure activity but rather a part of a new culture. No mere gymnastics class could carry out this task; for that a place for independent learning, creative activity, and research was needed; nothing less than an academy would do. But how was this to come into being? It was certainly no coincidence that scientists from the University of Berlin met with the intellectual leaders of sport associations to undertake a new venture together.

Up until now our upbringing, in fact our entire culture, has been governed by the dictates of rationality. In terms of education, the body was a barely acknowledged servant to whom attention was paid only in sickness. The German population, as healthy as it was before the war, could allow itself this; the heritage bequeathed by strong ancestors seemed indestructible. At a crucial age young men schooled their bodies in the mighty German army. Great success in research and technology made intellectual endeavors worthwhile. Doctors and educators, in fact, men of all professions, had surely always warned against one-sided intellectualism. But it took the powerful shock of the World War for it to become evident that the mysterious interdependence of body, reason, and soul would not in the long run allow itself to be violated for the benefit of one side alone without exacting punishment. This realization originated, of necessity, in the natural sciences. Thus, it was neither philosophers nor educators but medical doctors who perceived and acknowledged the need for a research institute dedicated to the field of gymnastics, volunteering their services and making their workplaces available to the cause.

The substance of the new academy was thus established. [. . .] From the beginning it was clear that while in substance our academy would have the same intellectual freedom as other institutions of higher learning, in other ways it would take on a different cast. It was easy to predict that the purely intellectually oriented scholars and their imitators would view our academy with mistrust, for it was only with great difficulty that they had been able in the past to come to terms with the idea of a "technical" institute. In their view, the fact that in our case the experts were in part nonacademics, and that some of our students with great physical aptitude had no higher education damaged the character of the higher-learning institutions, while this fact was for us a confirmation of the school's character. It was not the fact that some of its members were recipients of advanced degrees that made the new academy part of the system of higher education, but rather that each person could, in academic freedom, do his very best in his chosen field.

29
Sexuality: Private Rights versus Social Norms

WHEN MAGNUS HIRSCHFELD opened his Institute of Sexual Science in Berlin in 1919, his twenty-five years of work on behalf of sexual reform and education had finally found an institutional home. Devoted to all aspects of sexuality, the institute along with its specialized library was used for premarital consultation and instruction as well as for legal and medical research. Uppermost on the agenda was the campaign against Paragraph 175, the law in Germany's penal code against male homosexuality. Since 1895 Hirschfeld had been a pioneer in the struggle for the rights of the Third Sex, as he originally called homosexuals, publishing such periodicals as *Annals of Sexual Intermediacy* (1900–1923) and the *Journal of Sexual Science* (1908); serving as consultant for such film productions as Richard Oswald's 1919 film, *Different from the Others;* and testifying in court cases involving sexual deviance. Hirschfeld also founded the World League for Sexual Reform on a Scientific Basis, which held five international congresses from 1911 to 1932. At the Third Sexual Reform Congress held in London in 1929, he mapped out the ground plans for the now respectable field of sexology. According to Christopher Isherwood's vivid autobiographical account of his visit to the institute in 1929, Hirschfeld had three strikes against him: he was a homosexual, a Jew, and a Communist sympathizer. (In 1917 the Communist Party had declared all forms of sexual activity between consenting adults a private matter.) He was twice assaulted by right-wing groups while lecturing in Munich, and in 1933 his institute was destroyed by the Nazis. Two years later Hirschfeld died in Paris.

Hirschfeld was not alone in his commitment to achieve equality for sexual minorities. Kurt Hiller presented legal arguments for it in many articles, and Kurt Tucholsky openly opposed the attacks against the National Socialist Ernst Röhm because they dealt with his sexual preference, not his politics. Besides the large male homosexual subculture in Berlin, there was an active lesbian community. It too was organized around favorite bars and clubs as well as magazines, books, and films, the most famous of which is Leontine Sagan's *Mädchen in Uniform* (1931). Although their policy favored separatism, gay women and men sometimes joined forces to protest a legal system that criminalized sexual deviance.

Against the background of a general revolution of sexual mores, the institution of marriage also came under scrutiny in the 1920s. Was it modern to be married? Was it appropriate to cling to an institution that offered an illusion of permanence at a time when everything else seemed to be in transition? How was it possible for the New Woman to work in an office or factory and fulfill her traditional roles as housewife and mother? In 1925 almost 11.5 million women—more than a third of the total labor force—worked for a living; about a third of them were married. It was the task of the Sex Reform movement, which consisted of doctors, social workers, working-class activists, family planners, and sexologists, to help women cope with contradictory claims and expectations. The "Guidelines of the German Association for the Protection of Mothers and Sexual Reform," published in the Sex Reform periodical *The New Generation* in 1922, afford a glimpse of the aims of one such reform group. Questions of birth control and procreation, motherhood, love, marriage, sexuality, leisure, work, and family were intensely debated in all major periodicals and newspapers of the Weimar Republic. In 1929 Helene Stöcker, pioneer in the Sexual Reform movement since 1905, founder of the International League for the Protection of Mothers and Sexual Reform, as well as editor of *The New Generation,* presented an authoritative account of the state of marriage as an institution. After surveying various alternatives to the traditional marriage—trial marriage, companionate marriage (*Kameradschaftsehe*), three-party marriage or "universal sexual love"—she concluded that no reform proposals could compete with the moral responsibility and love between individuals. Such sentiments reflected a general mood of retrenchment at the end of the Weimar Republic which could also be found in other documents. Grete Ujhely's plea for "sexual tolerance," for instance, referred to the right of the individual woman to refuse sex even though social pressure would make such refusal seem unfashionable. This meant in essence a caution against libertinage, which was also the focus of Lola Landau's critique of companionate marriage as it had been proposed by Ben Lindsey, an American juvenile court judge. Lindsey's book, which appeared in German translation in 1926, had stirred up controversy with its suggestion that young people ought to enter a trial marriage without, however, procreating.

Consciously or not, the debates about sex reform and marriage redirected the new freedom that the New Woman exhibited in matters of sexuality back into the mainstream of marriage and motherhood. It seemed important to a male-dominated society with a visibly declining birthrate that women not forsake their place in the home as wives and mothers. One of the unspoken goals of the Sex Reform movement consisted then in providing education about modern sexual practices and techniques while simultaneously upholding the ideal of a traditional marriage. It was therefore no coincidence that the first semi-scientific sex manual, Theodor H. Van de Velde's *The Ideal*

Marriage published in 1926, became an instant bestseller in the Weimar Republic, with over forty printings by 1931.

The preoccupation with sexuality and the confines of bourgeois marriage was not new to the Weimar Republic. Theodor Fontane and Frank Wedekind had dramatized the tensions between private desires and public order even before the turn of the century. What was arguably new in the Weimar Republic was the widespread public attempt to deal with sexuality in a de-eroticized, sober, and matter-of-fact way rather than to demonize it as mysterious and dangerous. To describe sexual activity in terms of sports, as Alfred Döblin did, would have been hard to imagine around 1900. And a common-sense discussion of birth control as a man's responsibility, as Walter von Hollander suggested, would have fallen on deaf ears in earlier times. In the Weimar Republic the discussion of birth control was part of a vociferous debate about abortion and its legal status. In 1931, for example, an estimated one million abortions, mostly illegal, were performed, of which about ten to twelve thousand ended in the woman's death. Such figures illuminate a dark area where sexuality intersected with economy, religion, politics, medical practice, and the law.

304

KURT HILLER

The Law and Sexual Minorities

First published as "Recht und sexuelle Minderheiten," *Das Tagebuch* 47, no. 2 (November 19, 1921), 1400–1401, 1435.

The extreme brevity of the time I have at my disposal permits no argumentation, only a statement of the thesis. I ask, however, that it be believed that I am able to prove what I am going to assert—to the extent at least that proof is possible at all in the area of ethical and legal–political values.

Two things seem to me necessary to assume: a basic fact and a basic claim.

The basic fact is that there are typical variations between people not only in regard to somatic–racial and characterological features, but also in regard to sexuality. That means there are typical variations not only in skin, eye, and hair color; in cranial shape and facial and body form; in language, style, taste, temperament, talents, and ethical character but also in the direction of the sexual drive. These variations, regardless of how one tries to explain them, are empirically demonstrable and must be registered as such, not subsumed under a moral category. If they seem to represent anomalies or deviations from a norm, then they do so only in the sense that in principle the norm is not a statement of value, but rather of *frequency:* that from the outset the typological deviation is valid not as a *disqualification* but merely as a *disquantification.* To determine a variation, a variant, a deviation from the average case or the rule is not to bring a moral judgment; in the concept of the abnormal, of the irregular, however, there is a bit of valuation—which is why it is not to be wondered that the abnormal and the irregular are so often confounded with the pathological and the unhealthy. A red-haired person is as such abnormal, not pathological. For the invert the same is true. That abnormality and pathology occur cumulatively, even quite frequently, is an issue in its own right—and justifies a confusion of the two concepts all the less since precisely this confusion is responsible for the frequent coincidence of the two phenomena. How understandable that a healthy abnormal person becomes psychically ill, if society reacts to him as if he were sick . . . or worse!

The fundamental claim we must assume here is a claim on the state. The state is a human tool designed for the benefit of humanity, not an absolute with metaphysical status nor an end in itself to which the person gives himself as a means or as a sacrifice offered in humility. The state may not interfere with the individuals within its compass in the expression of their particularity, in the manifestation of their individuality. It may not interfere with them in the shaping of their lives nor in their activities and arrangements even in cases of extreme deviation from the "norm"—unless the activity of the individual collides with the interests of another individual, a grouping of other individuals, or perhaps of the whole, the society.

Let every one of us regard man-to-man romantic relations in whatever personal, aesthetic light desired; their decontrol is a pressing humanitarian and libertarian need of our time. Decontrol will not promote the inversion of a normal person any more than punishment has succeeded in making an inverted person normal. Supposing that homosexual relations were penalized because they damaged interests (they do not), then it would still not be expedient to penalize them: for the punishment would never accomplish its necessary goal, to better and to improve. Yes, if it were a matter of a bad habit, of a vice, of habitual behavior subject to correction through energetic self-cultivation, of something subject to remedy, something unnatural. But it is a matter of *nature*. "*Naturam expelles furca, tamen usque recurret*" ("You may drive out nature with a pitchfork, but she always comes back," Horace).

Worse, however, than the technical futility of this *furca* penalty is its moral and political groundlessness. For the sake of an act, by which only individual pleasure is produced and not a fly in the cosmos is harmed, the state martyrs productive citizens; it shatters flourishing existences—and this does not even take the effects of blackmail into consideration.

A German Kaiser, whom the Republicans would not deny the respect due a liberal and benevolent man, called anti-Semitism the scourge of his century. But when in Germany were the Jews ever so persecuted as the homosexuals? Does the criminal code contain any regulation against that racial minority like the infamous regulation against this sexual minority? The scourge of this century is Paragraph 175.

305

Guidelines of the German Association for the Protection of Mothers

First published as "Richtlinien des Deutschen Bundes für Mutterschutz," *Neue Generation*, nos. 9–10 (November–December 1922), 383–386.

1. CONTENT AND GOAL OF THE MOVEMENT

The movement for the protection of mothers and for sexual reform grows out of a joyous, life-affirming worldview. It springs from the conviction of the highest value, the sanctity and inviolability of human life.

It is from this basis that our movement seeks to make life between man and woman, between parents and children, among all people, as rich and fruitful as possible.

Therefore, it is our task to unmask the offensive social conditions and ethical views which tolerate and promote prostitution and venereal diseases, sexual hypocrisy and compulsory abstinence, and to carry this insight to ever-widening circles.

The confusion of prevalent moral judgments and their resulting personal suffering and social evils cry out for help. However, this cry cannot be answered by eliminating symptoms but only by the radical extermination of the real causes.

But our movement should not only eradicate evils but also promote the progress of individual and social life. It will support and improve life and foster joy in living.

To protect life at its source, to let it develop pure and strong: to protect mothers; to recognize human sexuality as a powerful instrument, not only for propagation but also for the progressive development of a joy in living, i.e., sexual reform, which is the content and final goal of our aspirations.

2. THE GENERAL PRINCIPLE OF MORALITY

The first precondition for the improvement of human and sexual relationships is the absolute break with those moral views that base their commandments either on allegedly supernatural arrangements or on arbitrary human laws or simply on tradition. The laws of morality should also be founded on the insights gained by progressive science. What was true in other times and circumstances or served only the interests of the ruling classes must not be allowed to continue thoughtlessly as the moral command of today. The hallmark of our morality should be its suitability for enriching human life—the social cooperation among people—of making it more harmonious and freeing it from evils!

Therefore, we reject the idea that the human body and mind oppose each other. We do not want natural sexual attraction to be branded as sin, sensuality fought as something degrading or animalistic, or the overcoming of carnality raised to a matter of moralistic principle. Rather, to us, the human is a sensual emotional being whose intellectual and physical traits have the same right to a healthy and progressive development. [. . .]

3. SEXUAL MORALS

We regard legally recognized monogamy as the highest and most desirable form of human sexual relationship, as best suited to guarantee a permanent regulation of sexual inter-course, the healthy development of the family, the preservation of the human community. But we do not fail to recognize that a lifelong, strictly monogamous marriage has existed, and still exists, only as an ideal attainable by a very few. The larger part of sexual life does occur before and outside marriage. For emotional and economic reasons the legal marriage is incapable of absorbing all possibilities of justified love relationships, that is, of turning them into permanent monogamy in all cases.

Accordingly, we favor:

1. Preservation of the legally recognized monogamous marriage on the basis of real equality of the sexes; the furtherance of the economic possibilities of marriage, but also the emotional possibilities through education for marriage and parenthood as well as through coeducation and other suitable methods for a better and deeper "learning to know each other" of the sexes.

2. Liberalization of divorce laws when the conditions which led to marriage no longer exist; also, if the marriage can no longer fulfill the purpose of a lasting relationship.

3. Moral and legal recognition for relationships in which the partners are aware of their responsibility to fulfill their obligations and have demonstrated their intention to do so—even if the legal formalities are not preserved.

4. The fight against prostitution by sanitary measures as well as by intellectual and economic means for eliminating its causes.

306

HUGO BETTAUER

The Erotic Revolution

First published as "Die erotische Revolution," *Er und Sie* 1 (1924), 1–2.

Social contradictions have never been sharper, the direst housing shortage, the impov-erishment of entire social strata through monetary devaluation, hate between races and nations, Germany's struggle for existence, social upheaval, tax pogroms, capitalist self-assertion and the strivings of the lower classes not to lose what they have gained, and, meanwhile, tremendous technological progress—these are the things that occupy the world, that fill the newspapers, that are the center of all discussions. Upon closer inspection they are only transitory problems, merely affairs of tomorrow and the day after, inessential compared to the eternal questions on which the development of humanity and the happiness of the coming generations depend.

So confused and benumbed are we by these daily concerns, these minor and major sensations, that we utterly fail to realize, to feel, that we are living in the midst of the most powerful and fateful revolutions of all time. Without leaders and partisan debates, without the exertion of force and demagogy, a revolution is pursuing its inexorable course, which, more than the political one, will necessarily change the lives of those to come.

It is the erotic revolution!

Since the triumph of Christianity all the institutions in Europe that dealt directly or indirectly with sexual questions have remained stable and unchanged. Their fundamental principle: the erotic drives had to be restrained to only what was necessary. The adult male was to choose his life companion, who was to remain erotically linked with him until death. With this chosen companion he was to satisfy his erotic lust, with her he was to conceive children, wither, become unfruitful, and die. Every departure from this fundamental principle was more or less punishable, avenged by social ostracism, and accursed in its consequences. Adultery was a crime, the illegitimate child condemned, the girl who gave herself to a man outside of wedlock despised, or, when bitter need arose, the whore existed outside the law and without rights. [. . .]

The fundamental principle, that the erotic belongs to marriage, was created by men and takes no consideration of the woman. The woman is simply an object, a thing to marry; she exists up until marriage in subjection to the parents, then to the husband. If her erotic drive is stronger than her husband's, then she necessarily goes psychologically and phys-ically to ruin; if she fails to find a husband, she is deprived of all erotic activity and turns into a horrid, withered being suffering scorn and ridicule as an old virgin because she followed the fundamental principle established by men instead of circumventing it. If, however, she circumvents it in public, then she ceases being a member of society, becomes a whore whom people are allowed to spit upon and persecute. Only a clandestine circumvention of the fundamental principle is allowed. As in erotic matters altogether, only hypocrisy, lies, and betrayal are permitted, as the whole of public life, insofar as sexual questions are concerned, is built upon hypocrisy, lies, and betrayal.

In changing times the fundamental principal has remained triumphant, and officially the relationship between man and woman has scarcely changed. As always, the man is allowed to choose the woman, but the woman cannot choose the man; as always she must adapt her erotic nature to his; as always, the man is allowed to turn the single woman into a whore, with the whore having no claim to human rights; as always, the man has access to free love through secret means whereas for the woman there is only subjection. Only one thing has changed, and that fundamentally: with the advancing industrialization of the world the woman has been dragged out of the harem, the bower, the woman's quarters, the weaving, sewing, and children's rooms and into life, into the factory, the sweatshop, and the office. And, in unavoidable consequence, the woman could not be deprived of an apparent equality of rights. An apparent one. For if the woman can also ride, drive a car, go out alone, or travel; if she is permitted to become a doctor or legislator; if she is permitted, indeed compelled, to toil and slave like a man, she remains nonetheless his subject, dependent on him in her most exquisite and vitally important functions, and is vilified and condemned if she violates the fundamental principle.

Things are not better now for the woman but worse than they were a hundred years ago. Back then in seclusion she learned contentment and discharged her eroticism as a childbearer. Today she is sexually stimulated, can move around freely for hours in an alcohol and a nicotine haze, but only as far as a clearly drawn limit, a limit drawn by the man for purely egotistical reasons. [. . .]

Woman has become a beast of burden, like the man. This has not, however, won her her sexual freedom. [. . .] For the fundamental principle remains in force.

Or remained in force. For the erotic revolution is underway; it is not to be stopped, despite all manner of ostrich policies. For two, perhaps three years now, things erotic are beginning to be rearranged, with the young starting to assail the fundamental principle. The *working, producing people have begun,* have taken the axe to an ancient system of hypocrisy and duplicity in the creation of which the name of the savior was misused. Whoever has open eyes, whoever is not so dumb as to believe that the occupation of the Ruhr and "broadcasting" are the most important things in the world, can see how the erotic revolution advances day by day. The erotic revolution that wants to create free, happy people. For it is simply the case, and no one can change it, that *everything existing is based on eroticism,* everything that is beautiful, good, and lovely on earth is bound up inseparably with eroticism. The flower in the meadow, the butterfly floating above it, the singing of the birds, the chirping of the crickets, the rustling of the trees, and the ripening of the fruit—erotic symbols, erotic purpose, erotic will. It was reserved to the greed, selfishness, stupidity, and maliciousness of people to brand the god Eros a criminal, to sully erotic play with filth.

This magazine, which has arisen under the sign of the erotic revolution, wants to join the struggle and to speak openly about things that the blinkered philistines continue to pass over. It will not shrink from discussing the most ticklish, delicate problems of life and will not be stopped from revealing open wounds that others want to veil in hypocrisy and lies.

307

MAGNUS HIRSCHFELD

Sexual Catastrophes

First published in *Sexual-Katastrophen. Bilder aus dem modernen Geschlechts- und Eheleben* (Leipzig: A.H. Payne, 1926), 40–42.

There is a reluctance to speak about the fact of homosexuality. To understand it requires serious consideration, which means intellectual exertion. So some plead that the topic is not respectable enough for them. Understanding homosexuality presupposes a psychological reorientation, a self-liberation from the tutelage of the legislator who ignorantly subsumes homosexuality and depravity under the same concept.

What is homosexuality? The sexual inclination of men to male, women to female persons. There have been decades of fruitless controversy as to whether homosexuality is endogenous—that is, inborn—or acquired through training, habit, seduction, etc.

Modern research, based on the biological law that the opposite sex is latent in every individual, has elaborated the following formula:

In every living being born of the union of two sexes, the characteristics of one sex are to be identified to varying degrees alongside those of the other.

The key to this formula derives from a fact discovered by embryological science in the previous century: unisexuality is a later development subsequent to an original bisexuality. This is to be observed in plants but also in animals, such as snails.

It is therefore a fact that homosexuality is an inborn condition, that is, a matter of constitution. Typical initial symptoms are demonstrable in homosexuals as early as the seventh and eighth, indeed, even in the third and fourth year of life.

If one carries this thought process through to the conclusion that homosexuality is a natural, in-born disposition, then the moral condemnation of homosexuality can only be regarded as an injustice and Paragraph 175 of the criminal code as a remnant of medieval conceptions.

The criminal prosecution of homosexuality is based on the fundamental juridical principle that legitimate interests are to be defended against violation. But what interests are violated by a homosexual act? Salacious (to use the technical term) sexual involvement with children is already punishable by a prison sentence on the basis of other articles in the criminal code. The age at which children are no longer protected could also be appropriately raised. The homosexual rape of adults, on the other hand, is inconceivable; mutual consent is a necessary condition of homosexual activity, which takes place in private without violating the interests of third parties.

Only one out of every hundred thousand infractions is ultimately subject to criminal prosecution, and that only accidentally; the law exists solely on paper. In the Reichstag, [August] Bebel once justifiably said of Paragraph 175 that, if an article in the criminal code can only be applied as an exception, the question arises as to whether it is possible to enforce it at all. Bebel may be quoted again in reference to the actual impossibility of enforcement. He said on January 13, 1898, in the Reichstag: "If the Berlin police—I want to speak now only of Berlin—were to do its duty and completely fulfill its obligation in this area, there would be a scandal that would make the Panama Scandal and Dreyfus Affair look like child's play." Perhaps that is one of the reasons why the police are so extraordinarily lax about enforcing precisely this criminal offense.

The world war has become a barometer of the health of peoples. In France, Belgium, Italy, Japan, Turkey, etc. homosexuality is not prosecuted. Has this had a noticeable effect on their populations?

Once, however, the essence of homosexuality has been recognized, it is the obligation of every fair-minded person to speak out for the elimination of an injustice that already produces more victims and claims by the hour.

308

LOLA LANDAU

The Companionate Marriage

First published as "Kameradschaftsehe," in *Die Tat* 20, 11 (February, 1929), 831–835.

Marriage, as the cell of collective life, has always possessed a social significance that raises it far above the happiness of two individuals or the purely expedient consideration of protecting the interests of descendants. That is how marriage as a model in miniature of human community acquired its ethical idea. It became the primal basis of the larger cellular structure and the source of fruitful and constructive forces. [. . .]

By the end of the previous century the bourgeois marriage had evolved into an economic institution; the family had become a small trust with the earnings and operation of capital. The magnetic attraction of monetary accumulation, however, led increasingly to marriage for money, which suppressed its original sense of ethical community.

While a hypocritical social morality artificially maintained the old forms and symbols, they had long since rigidified into dead formulas. Venerable words like fidelity, home, and family lost their incantatory power since their content had become merely apparent. Meanwhile, however, the elemental life force of youth pressed onward under the thin veneer of convention, rooting out new paths for itself. Unnoticed, a mighty revolution in ways of life had already been completed in reality when people first began to discuss openly the crisis in marriage.

At the center of these fermenting forces is the woman of our day. As an autonomous person economically and intellectually independent from the man, the new woman shattered the old morality. The compulsory celibacy of the young woman and the indissolubility of marriage were invalidated by the straightforward reality of life. The independent woman of today, just as much as the man, assumes for herself the right to a love life before marriage, the more so since marital togetherness for the woman can signify nothing but a faint future possibility given the current numerical deficiency of men.

In this way, the psychological attitude of women toward marriage changed fundamentally. Women no longer wait for marriage, frequently not even desiring such a tie for themselves, which they fear might hinder their free development. While in previous times the life of a young woman was little more than a period of preparation for marriage, which she then took on as a full-time occupation, the woman of today is scarcely capable of accepting marriage as her life's work. Back then household activities and the never-ending work of motherhood taxed a woman's energies to the utmost. Today there is some relief to be had in the private household from modern conveniences, and birth control, a matter of utter economic necessity, either shelters women from motherhood or interrupts it with long breaks. Certainly, by being able to prevent conception, the woman has escaped from the slavery of her own body; but at the same time she is deprived of the elemental happiness of fulfilled tranquility. The woman—whose natural maternal energies, through no fault of her own, have to lay fallow today, who, just like the man is forced at an early age into the work-a-day grind—searches for a substitute experience of her vitality and finds it in fruitful employment, usually outside the home. The occupational independence thus gained signifies as well a looser psychological tie to the man. The home is no longer the fortified garden of profound and happy rest. Family life is also subject to the effects of the transformation; it is already being replaced, in part, by the self-tutelage of the young, by group life that takes the children out of their parents' house.

Who would want to deny that this reorganization unsettles certain essential emotional values, that it silences a kind of gentle atmospheric music! But development marches to a relentless beat. No wishful romanticism can force woman back to her earlier way of being. The bourgeois woman has also become a worker. Her face, too, is chiseled by the hard mechanism of our time; she too is subject to the depersonalization and leveling of our age. And she too will slowly have to assume the shape of the new female personality in order to stand beside the man as an equal and complementary companion.

If, however, the man of today continues to seek the woman of yesterday, his creature, the pliant helpmate, he will be bitterly disappointed not to find her anymore.

Marriage and its value as the cell of community is threatened with crisis. For new ideas of marriage have not yet caught on. What is permitted today? Nearly everything. But what is truly good? What is bad? The warning signals of inhibition no longer function. Everywhere, however, one notes the confusion, the aimlessness, a tortured seeking, and in between, the impotent smile of flippancy.

In his book, *Companionate Marriage,* Ben Lindsey, the American juvenile-court judge, has attempted to save marriage from this chaos by lending it a new form. As impossible as it is simply to transpose his reform proposals into our European conditions, he nevertheless offers fruitful suggestions from his socially critical point of view. Lindsey would like to introduce, alongside permanent marriage, the companionate marriage as a second legal form of marriage. Companionate marriage in his sense denotes the lawful tie between two young people who, in the first years, use birth control to avoid having children, so that they can check carefully whether their respective characters will match harmoniously in the long run.

If the first rush of love has passed and the young people have been disappointed in their expectations, then the companionate marriage can be dissolved quite easily. All that is required for divorce is a simple, mutual agreement. Nor is there any obligation of support, since they have no responsibility for children and the wife has continued in her occupation. If, however, the two people live happily with each other, then after a certain trial period they can change their companionate marriage into a family marriage and fulfill their desires for children. [. . .]

The marriage of the future will perhaps be the companionate marriage, but in a much broader sense than Lindsey's. It will mean not only a childless trial marriage for young people but the ever-maturing challenge to live a full life. It will reestablish in another form its original idea of community and grow into a fruitful cell in the overall cellular state. It will unite the woman, with her informed views and matured heart, to the man as a comrade, and two free personalities will march along the same path toward a great goal, allowing the uniform beat of their steps to blend into a single rhythm.

309

LEAGUE FOR HUMAN RIGHTS
Appeal to All Homosexual Women

First published as "Aufruf an alle gleichgeschlechtlich liebenden Frauen," *Die Freundin* 12, no. 5 (September 18, 1929).

All of you women who love the same sex are derided and ridiculed by heterosexuals because of your preference just as much as homosexual men are. For ten years the latter have been active in the League for Human Rights in the struggle not only against social ostracism but above all against Paragraph 175. The struggle has not been in vain. Much has been accomplished, much more must be accomplished. To achieve complete victory across the board, the LHR needs the assistance of all homosexual women who feel their disparagement by others to be unjust and humiliating.

Women, do you not feel the burden of humiliation weighing on yourselves and your names on account of your innocent preference?

Do you not feel the humiliation of your situation, of having to hide your lovers in the shadows and keep your love secret from other people?

Those of you who do not feel the injustice and humiliation to which you are continuously subjected have no self-respect.

Dances and social events will not suffice to bring you equal rights. If you want to be esteemed and respected, it is also necessary to struggle.

The eagerness to struggle must fill your hearts and shine from your eyes. Become members of Violetta, your alliance within the League for Human Rights.

Your leader, Lotte Hahn, is working together with the executive committee of the LHR for your welfare, and nowhere else are your interests so expertly and energetically represented.

Rid your ranks of all misanthropy. Boycott all events sponsored by so-called ladies' clubs that agitate against the LHR and your special organization, Violetta.

The homosexual men of Germany have unanimously joined the LHR and its associated alliances. So must it be in the future for all homosexual women as well.

Only the LHR represents the entire, serious-minded homosexual movement in Germany, of which you are also a part.

On the occasion of the tenth anniversary of the LHR, major events have been organized September 20–23, and every homosexual woman is obligated to participate in them for her own sake.

Your organization, Violetta, will take part in the general demonstration on Friday, September 20, at the former Gentlemen's Club, Leipzigstraße 3.

On Saturday, September 21, there will be a huge celebration, for women only, with a rich artistic program and ball in the American Dance Palace (Magic Flute). Gentlemen's festivities will be restricted to the second- and third-floor meeting rooms ("Florida" and "Oriental Casino").

On Sunday, September 22, a ball will be held—women only in the lower hall, men on the second floor.

For Monday, September 23, a large, public, women's meeting is planned for the lower hall, at which the well-known writer Elsbeth Killmer will speak on equal rights for homosexual women.

Homosexual women, show that you are not merely to be tolerated but are also prepared to fight for your freedom.

Come en masse to the events announced above.

League for Human Rights
Berlin S14, Neue Jakobstraße 9
Executive Committee

310

HELENE STÖCKER

Marriage as a Psychological Problem

First published in *Sexual Reform Congress* (London, September 8–14, 1929), ed. Norman Haire (London: Kegan Paul, 1930), 604–605.

If one compares the present Congress for Sexual Reform with Sexual Reform work twenty or twenty-five years ago it is possible to note some progress. When twenty-five years ago we began the *Mutterschutz* movement, and when in 1911 we held the first Congress for Sexual Reform in Dresden, we had to have two separate congresses. One was concerned with sexual reform in the narrower sense, while birth control had to be dealt with separately.

Today it has at least become clear that these problems are intimately related. But most of the problems are still unsolved, and it requires all our energy and mental integrity, all our enthusiasm for the higher development of civilization, to solve them.

It is out of the question that the institutions that have arisen from the absolute sexual dominance of men in former times should continue to exist unchanged amid the changed political, cultural, and economic conditions of today. This being an age of transition, there are peculiar difficulties and conflicts, and proposals have been made to deal with these by new forms of marriage. Thus we have proposals for trial marriage; for companionate marriage; for three-party marriage; even four-party marriage. Another proposes marriage in youth, another marriage for a term. A seventh would like to embrace the whole world in love. The German-American Ruedebusch proposes erotic relations with unlimited numbers. But beyond all these reformers we have the groups who differ widely from one another but agree in regarding every divorce as the destruction of the true ideal of marriage.

I venture to ask a question that will no doubt be regarded as heretical in this assembly. Are not all these proposals for changes in the form of marriage, or for increasing facilities for divorce, no matter how instructive and valuable they may be—are not all these proposals, in the last analysis, *unimportant?*

The important question is: What is the nature of the human being who is to live in marriage? How does he try to play his part in marriage? Whatever reforms and changes we suggest we must always come to a point when the individual has to impose a limit on his own desires, either for his own sake or for the sake of another. And is it not better to do this before we have eliminated from life all profound ethical values and moral responsibility?

No sort of marriage reform will ever comfort the broken heart or reconcile human beings who have real emotions to giving up the intimate contact, the feeling of unity with another person, which is a world in itself. Marriage for three is conceivable as an exceptional arrangement for exceptional people and ethically tolerable. Goethe's "Stella" is a picture of such an arrangement. But if marriage stands for love, for an intimate physical and spiritual contact, then it does not seem to me that there is much to be expected from this sort of reform in the way of an improvement of human life or an increase in happiness.

The demand for polygamy, as in the three-party marriage proposal, or in Ruedebusch's universal sexual love, is based on a recognition of the fact that sexual desire is promiscuous, but this is a long way from love in the real sense.

Georges Anquetil (a French author) is responsible for the three-party marriage proposal, but his book rests on an idea which is psychologically superficial. It is a grotesque fact that even in the Orient, in Russia, and in Turkey, polygamy is regarded as out of date; and now Western Europeans propose to introduce it again! What psychological and ethical differences there are between people living in the same country at the same time!

[...]

The progress towards a final understanding between man and woman is very slow because it is only in very recent times that women themselves have begun to take any part in the study of sex problems. Fortunately even the blindest can see today that a change is taking place in the distribution of power between the sexes. In literature and science we still find that many men cannot get rid of the limitations of sex in themselves although in politics and daily life these have already disappeared. But science has known for some time that male and female exist in all of us in varying degrees, and that in actual life there is no such thing as the theoretical types *man* and *woman*.

Thus from recent discoveries in biology and sociology, and with a more profound and objective psychology of sexual differences and with a clearer knowledge of the mind, we can build up a higher ethic for the creative transformation of our lives. Out of the fleeting temporary intoxication of the senses, out of passion, we can make an enduring relation between man and woman. We wish to get beyond mere nature. We wish to attain civilization, we wish to attain a permanent union, in which all human faculties, sensual, mental, and spiritual, will be united in a higher synthesis.

One point, which in my opinion is of very great importance in relation to happiness in marriage, is often ignored. Every age has its marriage problem. Discussions of marriage during recent decades usually give the impression that it is only young people who are concerned in the solution of sexual problems. All problems are problems of puberty. It is a welcome and important step in the direction of human maturity that at last the young people are being allowed what is necessary for their healthy sexual development. The young people will certainly not allow the enlightenment they have won to be taken from them again. But, in addition to the other revolutions which we have witnessed in recent years—the revolt of women, the revolt of youth, the revolt of the workers—there is another revolution which is essential for the increase in human happiness and achievement. This is revolution of the middle-aged. A revolt is necessary against the deplorable convention that imposes a premature sexual death on human beings. At present human beings unfortunately accept this with the same patience as they do the penalty of death inflicted undeservedly and foolishly by war. We must fight against the convention, which is part of the double standard of morality, that human beings, especially if they are women, are regarded as dead, as no longer fit for life and love, when they are only at the middle of their lives. Has anyone ever tried to calculate how much vital energy, how much joy of life, is destroyed or injured or made impossible in this way? How much creative power is wasted? How many voluntary deaths, how much of the premature senility of admirable human beings is to be credited to this barbaric superstition?

The marriage problem for young people is comparatively simple. Young people have already, by actual practice, and with the support of modern sexologists such as Judge Lindsey, Alexandra Kollontai and others of our movement, created, so to speak, a system of companionate marriage.

Life is still before the young people. If a love union or marriage is broken up, this is naturally much easier to bear than it is in cases where there is nothing before the individual but a slow progress towards the grave. The advice of the French philosopher not to waste the years of love is fortunately usually followed. But we must learn to accept without prejudice the epoch-making discovery of psychoanalysis which is fundamentally a platitude: namely, that the need for love and the capacity for love—which indeed are a part of the instinct for life itself—accompany us from the cradle to the grave and require fulfillment if the character is to be adequately adjusted.

As we try to be fair to young people we must also try and be fair towards those who are no longer young. Many desirable changes have already taken place. Not only has the span of life been increased but also the span of love. This change must go further in proportion as care of her body, satisfaction in a vocation which she has chosen for herself, and increase in mental and economic independence make woman into a personality centered in herself. Such a woman can spread pleasure and attraction around her like a man of creative capacity. This development will depend also on the extent to which men learn to love the whole personality of women and not merely their sex.

We find around us today marriages and permanent love relationships between men and women in which, in spite of suffering, disappointments and temporary difficulties, such as are always likely to occur, love is in no way diminished by age; certainly not by middle-age. The sexual embrace is only *one* expression of love.

Wherever the spirit remains alive, where the soul is in love, where the character is still developing, then there is no reason why love should come to an end. There may be changes in externals; there may be changes in degree but not in kind. In the later years there may be a gradual decline in the intense passion. But tenderness and spiritual unity grow. Wherever we have genuine and great love, only death can separate the lovers.

An important part of our great work of Sexual Reform on a Scientific Basis consists in bringing home to the consciousness of men that love is omnipresent. It is as essential to life as breathing. It is intimately bound up in the whole of lives from the cradle to the grave. Anyone who helps in any way to do this is with us and we welcome him as a co-worker. It is perhaps even more necessary to see this fact given practical recognition in the lives of women than in the lives of men. For the dominant position that man has had hitherto, and the victorious sense of his capacity and readiness for love, have already given it to him.

Many men, even today, still accept the idea that only youth is worthy of love. This idea belongs to a more primitive conception of sexuality and is responsible for the destruction of happiness in marriage. It causes many a hell of loneliness. "Many married women are cloistered nuns," said [Gerhart] Hauptmann.

Much bitterness, despair and unhappiness would be avoided and the joy of life would be increased if the purely sexual idea of love were replaced by a more developed conception. This higher conception of love seeks to increase man's capacity for love and make love an ever more complete expression of the whole personality. "Die and grow" is true for both sexes. But when growing means self-development, as it does for all intelligent human beings, then we have perpetual youth, which, as Schleiermacher taught us, is always capable of love and always worthy of being loved.

Since the outbreak of the war many of us have had to face the terrible problem: How is it possible for peoples who are supposed to be civilized to waste so much human life and happiness and to inflict such misery on each other? It seems to us that one of our great tasks is to stamp out this shameful thing.

I have not time now to go into the connection between repressed sexuality and cruelty. But I may say this much: If we devote our energies to suppressing war, and to movements for sexual reform, if we go on as we have for the last twenty-five years, then we shall realize what our great teacher, Nietzsche, once expressed so beautifully:

"Since men have existed men have had too little joy. That, O my brothers, is the original sin. Let us learn better how to be joyous and then we will best unlearn how to cause pain."

It is our task, it is the task of sexual reform of sexual science, to teach people how best to enjoy life.

311

MAGNUS HIRSCHFELD

The Development and Scope of Sexology

First published as "Presidential Address to the Third International Congress for Sexual Reform on a Scientific Basis" in *Sexual Reform Congress* (London, September 8–14, 1929), ed. Norman Haire (London: Kegan Paul, 1930), xii–xv.

Sexology has acquired the dignity of an independent science only since the beginning of the present century. Its development was stimulated by the publication somewhere about 1900 of a number of comprehensive books on sex life. The three most deserving of mention are *Studies in the Psychology of Sex,* by Havelock Ellis, *The Sexual Question,* by August Forel, and *Sexual Life of our Time,* by Iwan Bloch. It was a fact of some significance, but one which had certain unfortunate consequences later, that the author of one of these books was a psychiatrist and another a specialist in venereal disease. But many other departments of science besides these have made contributions to sexology. I may mention genetics, embryology, endocrinology, gynecology, psychoanalysis, as well as general psychology, ethnology and sociology.

It gradually became clear that the whole body of sexology could be conveniently divided into four departments: (1) sexual biology; (2) sexual pathology; (3) sexual ethnology; and (4) sexual sociology.

The basis of sexual biology is sexual anatomy. This is concerned with the structure of the actual sexual apparatus and also with all anatomical differences between the sexes from the sperm and ovum up to every organ on the body. Closely related to it we have sexual physiology, which has for its subject all the sexual functions and processes in the body. An important branch is sexual chemistry, dealing with the effect of the ductless glands on sexual processes. Another part of sexual biology is sexual psychology. This has to deal not only with the afferent and efferent nervous impulses relating to sex but also with the many complicated relations between the sexual life and the mental life. [. . .]

The more deeply we study the physiology of love the better we are able to judge what things should be regarded as advantageous and what are disadvantageous, what are harmful and what are not. This leads us to another department, that of sexual hygiene. This is a subject which is in urgent need of revision, for we cannot fail to see that much that has been written on the subject (and there is a great deal) is not scientifically sound. An important branch of sexual hygiene is the prevention of venereal disease, sexual prophylaxis in the narrower sense of the word. Another branch is eugenics which, although historically derived from genetics, is closely related to sexology. It is necessary to refer only to "sexual advisory bureaus," which can only do sound work, whether they are concerned with marriage or birth control, if those directing them have a sound knowledge of sexual hygiene.

Persons whose impulse departs very widely from the normal must be regarded as unsuited either for marriage or for reproduction. Marriage is not a cure-all. It is apt to be so regarded. The physician who recommends it as such does more harm than he realizes, especially to the other party to the marriage; this brings us to the next great branch of sexology, which is that of sexual pathology.

Sexology would be incomplete as a science if it failed to study those individuals whose sexual life is abnormal. But we should not allow ourselves to be led into overemphasizing this department of the subject by the circumstance that it has been more extensively written about than any other department since [Richard von] Krafft-Ebing's pioneer work *Psychopathia Sexualis*. This has been due partly to the public interest aroused by certain sensational criminal trials. The importance of sexual abnormalities should not be exaggerated nor should it be underestimated. Above all sexual abnormalities should not be ignored in a conspiracy of silence. Even sexual minorities have certain rights.

Leaving aside venereal disease, which is a study in itself, sexual pathology is concerned essentially with anomalies in the sexual impulse. Firstly, we have those of strength (deficiency or excess); then come the abnormal sexual constitutions, of which the infantile and the intersexual are the most important.

It is often difficult to decide, and indeed no definite objective principle can be laid down, as to whether sexual abnormalities should be regarded as pathological or as biological variations. Opinions on the subject vary with the individual, indeed they vary almost as extensively as do the abnormalities in question. It can however be stated as certain that between the normal and pathological type there is a range of borderline cases which must be regarded as biological variations. The dividing line may be drawn so as to make this class very extensive or very limited. I believe that we should extend our idea of the range of biological variations and limit the conception of pathological cases. In this matter I follow Mantegazza rather than [Cesare] Lombroso.

One's view as to what is pathological and what is not, as to whether a sexual abnormality is merely a variation or a sign of degeneracy is important both from the therapeutic standpoint and from that of the criminal law. This is seen in medical practice. Some practitioners try to "cure," others to help; some try to adjust the individual to society, others to adapt life to the individual. But the attitude of the legislator is still more dependent on the point of view taken in the matter. Both a historical survey of the laws prevailing at different times in one society and a geographical survey of those prevailing in different societies at any one time show a degree of variety which proves that no objective principles have as yet been established in this matter. Many sexual offenses were punishable with death up to the Age of Enlightenment at the end of the eighteenth century. After the French Revolution they ceased to be regarded as offenses at all. The Council of Trent actually condemned all acts of sexual intercourse other than those between parties who had been married in church.

The third great department of sexology is sexual ethnology. This deals with the sexual life of the human race from prehistoric times up to our own. Such a study teaches us that in spite of all the restraints imposed upon it, sex has everywhere and at all times been the central fact around which the life of the individual and the community and all cultural life has been built. But the laws which have existed at different times and in different places vary extraordinarily and are often contradictory. This applies both to written and to unwritten laws, to customs and to ideas of morality. To find some fundamental principle in this chaos is the task of the sexual sociologist. Morality should not be dependent on accidents of time and place nor should it be based on supernatural considerations. It should be based on what nature teaches; and the mouthpiece of nature is science. A sexual ethics based on science is the only sound system of ethics.

Sexual ethics and sexual criminal law are two branches of sexual sociology. A third is sexual statesmanship. This involves the provision of a sexual code dealing not only with marriage and divorce but all sexual relations, including those of unmarried persons, the difficult problem of prostitution, and above all the scientific regulation of birth.

Such then is the scope of sexology. We rejoice that this congress is being held in a country in which many of the pioneers of sexology have lived and worked. We may mention among many [Thomas] Malthus (the founder of Malthusianism), Josephine Butler (the pioneer of abolitionism), Charles Darwin, and Francis Galton (the founder of eugenics). What distinguished all of these great pioneers was their strong sense of responsibility, their knowledge, and their serious purpose. These are still the essential qualities for the student of sexology, which has now become a broad stream from the confluence of its many tributaries.

312

GRETE UJHELY

A Call for Sexual Tolerance

First published as "Aufruf zu sexueller Toleranz," *Der Querschnitt* 10, no. 3 (1930), 185–186.

In those circles that consider themselves the leading ones, the ones confirmed in this superiority by curiosity, anecdotal obsession, and imitation, a prescriptive notion of sexuality has come into being which in its rigidity and severity yields nothing to the moral system of the Middle Ages but whose punitive sanctions are crueler than ever. It therefore appears to us that the time has once again come to break a lance for the sexual freedom of individuals and in particular of women, to break that lance which through all the social reshufflings of history has managed to keep itself, if only metaphorically, unbroken.

The days when the revolutionary was revolutionary are over in Europe (at least in the area of sexuality), and demands have turned into dogmas with amazing speed. Our courageous grandmothers fought for women's participation in sexual pleasure, the essential component of which (probably because they did not know van de Velde) they recognized as the temporary renewal of their partner. Their granddaughters and grandsons, however, began, in their philosophical naiveté, to confuse right with duty.

With melancholy I recall a clever and attractive friend of my youth who once in the heat of a discussion contended that it belonged among the most sacred of human rights to engage, free of moral hypocrisy and police surveillance, and if such were the need, by the light of the day in the middle of the street, in that activity which nature has placed prior to the having of children. He expressed himself, by the way, more colloquially. But as his partner in the discussion (let us assume it was I) . . . as I faint-heartedly objected, "But if I don't have the need at all—must I then?" . . . he then responded with the gentle insight of the true prophet, affectionately and soothingly, "No, my child. If you don't want to, you don't have to."

Today, however, we have to. I do not mean exactly on the street, but in general. A girl or a woman who, for example, wishes to be faithful to her friend, or even to her husband, or who, for example in winter, is simply not in an erotic mood, or who for any other private reason whatever completely or temporarily wants to live chastely—she becomes with absolute certainty ridiculous. For a time, perhaps with wounding regret and occasional offensive remarks concerning her provincial origins, her deficient temperament, or her lack of erotic talent, she will be left in peace. But soon enough, society (understood in the broader sense as composed of intimates) hangs upon her its severest penalty: ridicule.

How comparatively easy it was to endure the expressions of intolerance of past decades: the whispering of envious girlfriends; dramatic scenes with the husband; the decline in invitations from the wife of the postmaster; parental curses; and heightened impudence among the gentlemen! Expressions in which recognition, even envy was too clearly betrayed for them to have been capable of serious offense.

But not only society—those twenty people with whom one by turn drinks tea, dances, and discusses problems—but literally everyone lays claim to the damning judgment of the unhappy woman who does not want to. Have you ever said no to one of the lords of creation? (Of course you have!) The result is a popular lecture for the next half hour from the angle of psychoanalysis, with primary emphasis on that nice, handy word *inhibitions*. When that stratagem comes to nothing, the man in his fine logical security concludes that you are either frigid or stupid. Usually both. The conclusion, which despite everything remains possible, that his nose perhaps does not appeal to you, has yet to be drawn. (I know, the man can come to no such judgment, once again because of [Alfred] Adler's competition principle, because it is out of the question that he cultivate in himself an inferiority complex. But in us, he may!)

A resolution as follows would therefore be timely, necessary, and liberating:

1. Every woman has the right, but none the duty.
2. If she declines, it is not a personal insult.
3. This does not mean that she is either a ninny or neuter or a lesbian. (*Very important!*)
4. Chastity suggests neither insult nor derision; it is rather a somewhat old-fashioned expression denoting a condition not subject to further objection.

313

ALFRED DÖBLIN

Sexuality as Sport

First published as "Sexualität als Sport," *Der Querschnitt* no. 11 (1931), 760–762.

I am supposed to say if sexuality is overestimated or underestimated. I have but a single certainty, garnered from observation, that the old saying is true: the world is driven by hunger and love. And by love I understand sexual love—love stemming from a sexual source. Therefore one cannot possibly overestimate sexuality. It is—according to the old saying—the second axis about which our existence turns. And perhaps our existence turns only about a single axis, and hunger and love belong together like nourishment and growth.

But you say, that is not what I want to know. You cannot do business with philosophy and I want to know practically: Do not the people of today make too much fuss over naked sexuality? Should one not say openly that love is much more important than naked sexuality, this wicked drive, this base, mercilessly organic scourge of humanity from which, as a clever man has already remarked, one is only freed by age (and, incidentally, not even then, as some instances attest)?

So, the topic concerns "naked" sexuality, "organic" sexuality, and I recall that there is a scholarly distinction to be drawn between such naked, organic sexuality and one not naked but veiled—from the combination of an organic sexuality with another feeling: the detumescence drive (in plain words, shrinking drive) and the contrectation drive (that is probably a drive for intimacy or love). Certainly one can draw such a scholarly distinction. But it seems to me that these things do not occur in such a way on their own. They are bound together from the very start. Nature was so clever, so ingenious, so humane, that it did not create a dumb, blind sexual drive, or detumescence drive at all, but immediately supplemented it with an unbelievably hard-working selection apparatus. Here and there it is probably possible for the one to make itself independent and go into battle on its own; there are countless variations of occasional, unorderly independence in such a system, usually either driven by need or pathological. But that is not the rule and in principle one should believe neither in Platonic love nor in sexuality without love. A little love and a little sensuality are always present.

Now if people argued in earlier times—how was it with Goethe and Mrs. von Stein? and what do you say about Casanova?—is that true love? No, such a question does not interest me in the slightest and now people are often much more modern. They say: of course love is nonsense, really a thing for grandmothers, but one should not make so much of sexuality, it is all really quite worthless; love and hunger really do belong together. They are natural needs, yet one eats and drinks and that is the end of it; on the other hand. . . . You understand. So it is like this: one should neither overvalue nor undervalue sexuality plus or minus love, rather not value it very much at all, just accept it; it belongs to existence and one should not make a big hullabaloo about it; it is all just clamor from the hothouse of old appetites; half a taste is as good as a whole. A general indifference in things of love and sex has been gaining ground. Love has received a kick in the pants; it has become a fusty, old-fashioned matter (which it really was—that can be proved). And thus it is that we see the virgin boys and girls of all ages behaving today: they do not overestimate the matter nor do they underestimate it; neither from head to toe nor in the other direction are they focused on love; but they play tennis, drive cars, dance, go on the dole, engage in politics and love, and (let us use for once the proper word) they play sex as sport.

What do I have to say about it? In general, this trivialization of love exists, is also good, and was finally necessary. Active and half-militarized times like the present cannot busy themselves with love and perfume like others have. But meanwhile people are loving all over the place. It has decidedly taken on a healthier color. As to its objective nature. . . . I do not believe in objective love—I mean among these boy and girl virgins. One should not be deceived by their grand gesture. It goes superbly with a technological, economic era. It belongs to the style of this era not to love, but simply to . . . You have the word on the tip of your tongue. But there is something wrong about it. What? You must not ask me that. I am simply establishing the fact: something is wrong with it; more precisely, it does not exist, it is simply maintained for polemical purposes. You must know, ladies and gentlemen, dear listeners, readers, skeptics of both sexes: the human is a complete organism and no machine, and a very old animal, if not quite as old as a glance in our boring daily papers might suggest; humans have loved with all the accessories through millennia, and a small difference in timbre brought about by the economy and technology changes little or only superficially. We know all about this. Look it up, how all of Greece rose like a single man to conquer Troy because of Helen; those old Greeks knew no more rational motive for making war. It does not seem to me that the newer motives are any more rational. And as the worthy men of Troy on the city's walls caught sight of the lady, meanwhile long since deceased but ever again reborn, passing by, then they were happy and the war could take its course all the way through to Wilson's Fourteen Points or, respectively, the fall of Hector. (Excuse me for a moment. It is pouring rain and I must close the window.)

I read through, after the digression at the window, what I have written, and it could appear as if I had broken a charming, knightly lance, a spear for the high and lofty, sweet love, with or without accessories, which I attribute to the happy garçons and garçon muses of today. I am not of that opinion, nor have I even given myself permission to advance it. Rather I see myself obligated to establish emphatically against all potential intrigues that the whole is neither to be held in contempt nor may it be held in contempt in a criminal sense. Love extends neither to the fabrication of children nor to marriage; sexuality belongs to that. And that is to be maintained seriously with a manly and womanly word. Sexuality without love is a cursedly impoverished thing. It appears among individuals of stunted development; the one lacks love, the other potency (the refrain of a popular song). But love without sexuality is a perfect abomination. Where it appears (if it appears), one should salute and break camp. Where it is affirmed in marriages one should predict a bad end. Something is wrong and tomorrow the courts will be served up with false reasons. The whole, however wonderful and extremely edifying in union with the hunger, maintains the drive of the world. When the hunger subsides, love is there alone, and when it becomes powerful, then love has nothing to complain about. So it is today. One plays it as sport.

314

KURT TUCHOLSKY

Röhm

First published as "Röhm," *Die Weltbühne*, no. 17 (April 26, 1932), 641.

For awhile now accusations, jokes, and insults against Captain Röhm, an employee of the Hitler movement, have been making their way through the radical left press. The ridiculous titles Hitler bestows on his people should never be used; just as the categories defined by the Nazis should not be adopted. Many Germans are vulnerable to their foolish suggestions and busy themselves with such things as if Hitler had assigned it as homework. We are not in school, and the titles, distinctions, praise, and blame distributed by that house painter mean nothing to us.

So Röhm is a homosexual.

The commotion about Röhm got its start from items published in the *Munich Post,* which revealed this fact.

Then a letter was published that Röhm wrote to a friend concerning his inclination—the document could just as easily have appeared in any *Psychopathia Sexualis,* and the letter was not even uncongenial.

I consider these attacks against the man improper. Anything is good enough to use against Hitler and his people. Whoever treats others so mercilessly has no claim to mercy—Let him have it! Nor would I shrink from details of the private lives of those involved in the Hitler movement—Never relent! But in this case it has gone too far—it has gone too far for our own sake.

First of all, one should not seek out one's enemy in bed.

The only thing that would be acceptable would be to refer to remarks Nazis have made in which they deal with the "oriental vices" of the postwar period, as if the Russians invented homosexuality, lesbianism, and the like and introduced them to the pure German people. If a Nazi says some such, then but only then may one say, in your own movement there are homosexuals who acknowledge their inclination and are even proud of it—so shut your mouth.

But I am unable to find the jokes about Röhm appetizing. His inclination does nothing to undermine the man. He can be thoroughly respectable as long as he is not abusing his position to drag people onto his couch, and there is not the slightest proof of that. We oppose the disgraceful Paragraph 175 wherever we can; therefore we may not join voices with the chorus that would condemn a man because he is a homosexual. Did Röhm commit a public scandal? No. Has he abused young boys? No. Has he consciously transmitted venereal diseases? No. Such and only such can justify public criticism—everything else is his affair.

A curious zeal has attended the discussion of the important fact of whether this man will continue to be employed by Hitler. Are we the caretakers of his private army? As far as we are concerned, Hitler can employ burglars.

If Goebbels screeches or Hitler thunders about the moral decay of modern times, then it should be pointed out that there are obviously homosexuals among the Nazi troops.

Otherwise, however, Röhm's emotional life concerns us just as little as Hitler's patriotism.

315

WALTER VON HOLLANDER

Birth Control —A Man's Business!

First published as "Geburtenregelung Männersache!" *Die Weltbühne* 28, no. 48 (November 29, 1932), 805–808.

The question of progeny lies squarely at the intersection between the personal and the social. It is the only question in which every person is indirectly or directly interested, and usually both, as an individual and as a member of society.

This fact alone explains why the struggle over Paragraph 218 is capable at any time of igniting a popular movement in which the concepts of the state, the individual, and the collective can be fundamentally recast. It also explains, however, why this is a movement for and against the freedom of the individual, for and against the interference of the state in the life of the family, for and against the interference of the individual in a process of nature, and why it is being conducted with such different goals and from such various points of departure. That is why one participant in the movement can fight against Paragraph 218 for the freedom of the individual, another for the emancipation of a class from social pressures, one against the overextension of the concept of the collective, and another for planning in the area of human reproduction.

All of this fits naturally into the same popular movement. But it does not serve to clarify the movement. It does not strengthen the movement. It does make for the participation of muddle-headed sorts. And it makes for politicians reaching decisions in this important matter not according to insight but according to specific partisan perspectives. It makes for the superficial casting to and fro of half-baked scientific concepts like eugenics, race, and social indices—and for the scientific proof, now one way, now the other, of things that are scientifically unprovable, like the question of whether pregnancy or the interruption of pregnancy is more harmful to the woman or the question of whether this or that means of contraception is harmful or not harmful.

What tomorrow will be self-evident is today still heresy: that every social question terminates in an individual question and, ultimately and quite naturally, is to be answered only by the individual (an irreversible principle, for there are numerous individual questions that do not terminate in social questions). It is also true that the confusion surrounding Paragraph 218 can only be cleared up once the question is freed of all legal and social baggage and directed back to its origins in individuals. It will very quickly become obvious that the legal and social treatment of this issue is far more certain of success if left to the people, rather than judged from the perspective of the social organism.

It remains to be said as a preliminary that until now the state has only sown confusion by dictating things that it can neither oversee nor answer for in their consequences when it attempts to substitute regulations for what it was not capable of achieving through education. From the standpoint of *raison d'état,* one can therefore only support the repeal of Paragraph 218. From the standpoint of population policy and of social policy, however one can only be for a reduction in population given the domination of industry by the machine. Even from the standpoint of imperialist power politics there is no longer any reason in the age of machine wars for producing the maximum number of children. And the famous question of the quality of children born to older parents—among which there have naturally been found a few geniuses, but understandably as well a host of unwanted, joyless, badly raised, and poorly nourished children—has so far not been a question of science but one of faith. Those who believe that geniuses are blown into the world by accidental winds and would not be born if the wind should change have to accept the whole pile of actually accidental children for the sake of a couple of potential geniuses. They have to support the completely random production of children.

We others believe that trusting in the accidental, bending to it, and accepting its fruits has no chance to improve the posterity of the race.

So much for the general, from which the individual could already draw sufficient lessons. In individual marriages things are generally such that the man is outraged by the suggestion of legislation while in the majority of cases the worry as to whether children are on the way or not is left to the woman. It could therefore also happen that the types of contraception used by men will fall farther and farther into the background and those for the woman will take the leading role in research and the chemical industry. And it could happen that, following the failure of contraception, the question of abortion and therefore of Paragraph 218 will be increasingly discussed.

The primary question is this: how does one teach the man that he alone has the responsibility for the question of whether children are to be conceived or not? How does one assign responsibility?

Looked at logically, the matter could not be simpler. Why should the evil be combatted after it has already run its course, when it can be defeated at the source? Looked at naturally, however, it appears that the worries of all the women are superfluous, the worries of all the men superfluous, the chemical contraceptives superfluous, and of course abortion with all its misery just as superfluous as the unwanted children, if . . .

Yes, if a single tiny thing were accomplished. If the man were educated. If the man, who so fondly parades himself as the superior protector, finally learns to take the lead in at least this one area where everything depends on him.

We are, of course, not well enough educated to speak about these natural things in natural words. So all that can be said here is that an enormous amount of knowledge is available on the mastery of the sexual act by the man. Ethnologists, researchers of earlier cultures, and cultural historians of primitive societies all report that sexually mature young men are required to have gained absolute mastery of the sexual act through manifold exercises and tests before they are allowed to approach a woman, and that nowhere where promiscuity or premarital sex is prevalent does the question of unwanted progeny arise. [. . .]

With this, the conflict over Paragraph 218 has been referred back to where it belongs: to the man. The man bears responsibility, because he has the possibility of mastery. The extent to which the woman has the same possibility I do not know. Some old cultures maintain that they do, and in all probability correctly so. The women should concern themselves with that. It is clear that a large part of overall education is contained within this self-education. It is clear that when one masters fate in this area, one can overcome it elsewhere as well. It is clear that the social questions are in part resolved by individual education, and clear, finally, that this mastery is only the first lesson in the general knowledge of love and the knowledge of procreation as a whole.

But at least it is a beginning. Responsibility is unambiguously determined and is the basis upon which all who are involved with the education of the human race can agree—in our case, that is, socialists, communists, and the believers in all religions. And even the nonbelievers can learn their part: namely, that the power of man reaches farther than he himself thought.

30

On the Margins of the Law: Vice, Crime, and the Social Order

"Cocaine or cards?" a shady character asks the undercover detective in Fritz Lang's 1922 film, *Dr. Mabuse, the Gambler.* The choice of vices was plentiful in the Weimar Republic. Drugs, especially cocaine and opium, were easily obtainable, gambling widespread, and prostitution common, particularly in Berlin. For many, the experience of war, revolution, inflation, and famine as well as the frenzied pursuit of pleasure in the chaotic postwar period had sanctioned moral corruption and fostered a pervasive sense of nihilism and cynicism. A swift decline in moral standards and values seemed to parallel the rapid currency devaluation. A society known for its authoritarian discipline and oppressive adherence to tradition was coming unglued. To those who survived the horrors of war, all legal and bureaucratic restrictions, rules and regulations appeared petty and irrelevant. Drugs, gambling, and illicit nightlife proliferated, and vice laws were only selectively enforced and huge profits were made by catering to those seeking escape or distraction from economic despair. Acknowledging widespread use of cocaine, an advertisement for Pitigrilli's 1927 best-selling novel, *Kokain,* suggested: "Don't use coke! Read Pitigrilli!" No less secret than drug use was the astounding prevalence of prostitution in Berlin—about 100,000 prostitutes were counted in 1926. Their stories were dishearteningly similar: from the provinces to prostitution. Employment as domestic servants in large cities such as Berlin often yielded more than just a meager paycheck. Many of the young women, finding themselves pregnant by their employer, were summarily dismissed and, without legal recourse, ended up on the streets. Though often associated with glamorous decadence and titillating depravity, Weimar's common prostitution in fact bespeaks the republic's severe underlying economic and juridical inequalities for women.

Crime was rampant—and bold—in the Weimar Republic. Across the entire spectrum of Weimar media, accounts of bigger-than-life criminals joined reports of mayhem to exploit the public's perception that criminality was on the rise. Clever bank robbers such as the Saas brothers, heinously sadistic serial killers such as Fritz Haarmann (see Theodor Lessing's study, *Haarmann,* of 1925), successful con men such as Harry Domela (see his autobiography, *Der falsche Prinz,* 1927) or the clairvoyant Erik Jan Hanussen

(*Meine Lebenslinie,* 1930), monopolized headlines and captured the imagination of millions of Germans who became aware for the first time that the terrifying anonymity of the metropolis meant that no one was immune to the threat of crime. Not surprisingly, the various sensational crimes committed in the 1920s found their way into literature and film. The series "Outsiders of Society: The Crimes of Today" devoted book-length studies to the psychology and court trials of prominent criminals. The authors of this reportage series, inspired by the tenets of New Objectivity, included Alfred Döblin, E. E. Kisch, Ivan Goll, Theodor Lessing, and Joseph Roth. Fritz Lang's two-part film about *Dr. Mabuse,* which shows a criminal mastermind's pursuit of wealth and power against the background of hyperinflation, would later inspire a sequel in 1932, *The Testament of Dr. Mabuse.* Lang's renowned 1931 film, *M,* dramatized and commented on the case of Peter Kürten, the Düsseldorf child murderer caught in 1930 and sentenced to death shortly before the film opened. In *Berlin Alexanderplatz,* Alfred Döblin featured Franz Biberkopf, an ex-prisoner whose efforts to reform himself are doomed by an urban milieu that seems to scoff at human decency.

Berlin's underworld was tightly organized along petit-bourgeois lines and often camouflaged itself as professional sports clubs (so-called *Ringvereine*) complete with membership dues, mandatory weekly attendance, and penalties for infractions of statutes and rules. Organized crime, which was part of the often romanticized underworld (as in Brecht and Weill's *The Threepenny Opera*), needs to be distinguished from criminals who were, as in Fritz Lang's *M,* psychopathic, unpredictable, and thus more dangerous to the social fabric than "professional" bank robbers. Detective novels—Edgar Wallace was widely read in translation—and thriller films used crime to explore the disintegrating consensus about law, order, and justice. As a site of friction between the individual and the state, between transgressive desires and social regimentation, and between private rights and the public good, criminality both fascinated and perturbed the Weimar public. The period's obsession with crime reflected a preoccupation with a disappearing sense of security and a rekindled desire for law and order.

The Weimar Republic also witnessed intense debates regarding more humane treatment of criminals. The question of the state's right to invoke the death penalty was discussed with renewed urgency in the wake of world-wide demonstrations against the controversial execution in 1927 of Sacco and Vanzetti. Franz Alexander and Hugo Staub issued an appeal from psychoanalytic circles for a new concept of criminal justice that would refer to a deeper understanding of a criminal's motives when determining a court sentence. (The number of executions in Germany declined drastically from twenty-eight in 1921 to four in 1932.) One of the most effective pleas for a more compassionate treatment of criminals, Georg Fuchs's chronicle of his four years in jail, *We Prisoners: Memories of Inmate No. 2911,* exposed the cruelty of prison life in Germany. His status as a political prisoner prompted numerous public figures (including Sigmund Freud and Oswald Spengler) to provide wildly diverging responses to his book.

Trying to explain the increase in murder and manslaughter in the last years of the republic, Siegfried Kracauer drew connections between urban violence and the growing number of unemployed living without welfare on the margins of society. By 1931, as five million were economically disenfranchised and expelled from mainstream society, many lost sight of accustomed norms of behavior. If the social and cultural transformation brought on by modernization had left many Germans deeply disoriented, confused, and resentful, poverty and despair blunted their sense of right and wrong. Shock waves from the collapse of the old order reverberated throughout Weimar society, causing widespread feelings of insecurity and instability. A sense of powerlessness paralyzed the democratic forces of the Weimar Republic in the face of increasing violence that frequently was racially and politically motivated. Kracauer explored the nexus of criminality, unemployment, and the dislocations caused by modernization, and concluded with a statement that—in light of what supplanted the Weimar Republic—resonates prophetically: "Until the new contours have become solidified, our path will continue to be marked by blood and tears."

316

THOMAS WEHRLING

Berlin Is Becoming a Whore

First published as "Die Verhurung Berlins," *Das Tage-Buch* 1 (November 6, 1920), 1381–1383.

I do not speak lovingly of the poor streetwalkers. Only those who have lost all sense of taste and memory of the natural beauty of the human body can report on the nature and morality of the street girls of Berlin. The prostitutes in Paris and Naples also inspire terror. But there they exist mainly for the ugliest and therefore most shunned of men, for the cripples, the alcoholics, and the *dégénéré*. The healthy adult male does not need them. Consorting with prostitutes demeans the Latins. In Berlin, however, I saw men who were from all appearances good, strong, and in their own way capable of loving arm-in-arm with ghastly females.

But it was not of the proletarian merchants of love that I wanted to speak. What we all perceive wide-eyed and everyday anew is the *corruption of the bourgeois woman,* the young girls from so-called good families who are turning into whores. Countless marriages have become a façade for the most wanton sexual chaos. "Do any still exist," I recently heard a young woman from Berlin asked a few months ago, "twenty-year-olds who are not having an affair?" Twenty-year-olds? She could have said seventeen, perhaps even fifteen. A generation of females has grown up that has nothing but the merchandising of their physical charms in mind. They sit in the parlors, of which there are a dozen new ones every week; they go to the cinema in the evenings, wear skirts that end above the knees, buy *Elegant World* and the film magazines. They populate Garmisch-Partenkirchen, Saarow-Pieskow, the winter hotels in Thüringen, the Harz, and the seaside resorts. The display windows in the delicatessens are filled for these females; they buy furs and shoes at the most-extravagant prices and stream in herds down the Kurfürstendamm on Sunday mornings. For a long time now there has been more than merely a single caste of the *demimondaine*. The young bourgeois woman and the bourgeois daughter have joined the competition. Corrosive moral decay has eaten deeply into the middle-class family. Fathers and husbands close their eyes to it because they lack the force, the courage, or the sense of security to resist the wanton corrosion. Here the doctor's wife, five years ago still an upright lady, knows many bachelor apartments; there the merchant's daughter gets away with slipping into her own bed three times a week as morning nears.

What am I calling the overrunning of Berlin by whores? There are two aspects of the process. First, the financing of sexuality. Institutions such as previously flourished only in Budapest, houses with albums of photographs and prices for women waiting on call, have established themselves in Berlin, and, since the provincial cities do not want to miss out on progress, they will soon have branches in Leipzig, Hannover, and Breslau. Board a train traveling from Berlin to Frankfurt and you will find a quick connection in nearly every second-class compartment. But I have no desire to slander. There are many beginners who still bashfully avoid discussing the price. Nevertheless, the corrosion has set in. Every woman who has lost her memory for the experiences of her lower body—and this is the second, deeper feature—has fallen victim to the sexual corruption. Once the internal unity between psychic and sexual experience was broken, once the isolation of sexual experience became the norm, Berlin arrived at a Hellenism of its own. It celebrates its festivals in the dark rooms adjoining every dance hall.

How to explain the overrunning of Berlin by whores?

It appeared in every Western city as a result of the long period of war. The men had been gone four or even five years. An oversupply of females confronted a very sporadic demand. The competition for the men remaining behind slackened the females' reserve. The men, however, who remained here were not the most manly but the craftiest and the most corrupt, people who were accustomed to profiteering and getting what they wanted for a price. It is obvious that the profiteers who had no time to enlist and take part in the fighting ended up trafficking in women as well.

And to that was added the material need of the bourgeois family. A university professor earns less than a streetcar conductor, but the scholar's daughter was used to wearing silk stockings. It is no accident that the nude dancer Celly de Rheidt is the wife of a former Prussian officer. Thousands of bourgeois families are now being forced, if they want to live uprightly on their budget, to leave their six-room apartments and adopt a vegetarian diet. This impoverishment of the bourgeoisie is necessarily bound up with the women accustomed to luxury turning into whores.

The collapse of the Prussian-Kantian social order ultimately has not demonstrated any new faith in the bourgeoisie (as it did in the revolutionary proletariat). A dissolute nihilism proliferates on the rubble of yesterday's worldview. The impoverished noblewoman becomes a bar maid; the discharged navy officer makes films; the daughter of the provincial justice cannot expect her father to make a present of her winter clothes.

In this devastated world a type like Othmar Strauß emerges as victor. More precisely, the fat, pleasure-hungry businessman, who came upon his money easily and will just as easily lose it again. Connoisseurs of the time should wander one evening through the parlors and fancy eating establishments—everywhere, in every lousy corner you will smack up against the same plump face of the pot-bellied profiteers of war and peace. Othmar Strauß became the Tristan of this era of whores.

Woman, however, forms herself according to the will of the man. Otto Weininger divided the female species into mothers and whores. Many a poor, young streetwalker belongs, despite all the external devastation, to the species of mother, and the clairvoyant would place many a well-bathed, nicely dressed mother of three reluctantly conceived offspring into the other category. An overwhelming majority, however, belongs in the middle and vacillates between whoredom and motherhood. If a fortunate fate smiles upon her so that such a vacillating creature acquires the strong, protective, shaping love of an unspoiled man, then motherhood will release her from the drive to prostitution.

But where are these strong, sustaining men? A lamentable fear of woman's mother-hood lives not only among the females but in the big-city man as well. Never has there been such an extraordinary consumption of anti-impregnation devices as now. And whatever the short-sighted social calculus might say in favor of contraceptives, this is clear: the daily use of devices to prevent pregnancy leads inexorably to whoredom on the part of woman. She learns to enjoy but she forgets how to have a destiny. These preventatives lead to the inner debasement of the sacred act. It becomes insignificant and pleasant, like champagne guzzling and warm baths. A putrid craving for pleasure is written on her face. Woman no longer has a female destiny, and in exchange she acquires a routine that debases her.

The late Robert Hessen, not one to cower and no despiser of pleasure, once wrote that an age is to be judged by how it perceives the symbol of the mother and child. If so, then we are mired, from the bourgeoisie to the proletariat, in the swamp of the most hopeless degeneration. Ask any one of these short-skirted, silk-stockinged females what she makes of the thought of carrying and bearing a child. She turns away from the possibility with an amused shudder. There has never been less reverence for the madonna and child.

317

CARL LUDWIG SCHLEICH

Cocaineism

First published as "Kokainismus," *Das Tagebuch* 43, no. 2 (October 29, 1921), 1,311–1,315.

In the mobility mania that seized the whole of our modern culture before the war there is an ecstatic longing for intensification. This law of the yearning for heightened stimuli is nowhere as alive as in our nerve fibers. Our ganglia are tiny, sensing, butterfly feelers in search of blood and stimuli. Externally, happy events quicken our pace, while internally the rush of blood heightens our emotions. In both cases the instinctive longing for intensified stimuli as well as a heightened sense of joy and well-being lead to a psychic disposition shading into the demonic–pathological, to addictions. The pleasure of the moment, like the dove of God, does not always descend on the one with whom He is pleased, and it is not only the human being who has invented substitute pleasures that either imitate lucky events or create the possibility of experiencing them more constantly: Gambling! Gambling for antes of all denominations, from chips and gold pieces on up to life itself in sport and prize-fights. The gambler yearns for the feeling of an accelerated rhythm, and not always solely for the sake of vile profit. No, also solely for the exultation of being smiled on by a fate who finds favor in risk—that is the psychology of the kind of gambling that begins in the animal realm: the passion for gambling is a yearning for lucky events.

This accelerated rhythm and the search for it, however, can also be produced, as we have seen, in a purely physical way through the enjoyment of stimulating narcotics: alcohol, nicotine, tea, coffee, morphine, opium, hashish, chloral hydrate, and a host of soporifics. Among these promoters of artificial well-being (euphoria) via the blood, among the stimulants of natural operating juices (hormones), belongs cocaine as well, a substance coming to us from South America. [. . .]

The eyes shine—pupils enlarge, cheeks glow, lips quiver, hands tremble and churn, light and free as if in roses and curls; breath comes like a blessed floating, and the pulse glides fast and unrestrained through the veins.

Can one really hold it against those afflicted with toil and burdens, the failed and the broken, the hopeless pariahs of this earth, if they fall victim to this nirvana? Let them seek here and perhaps find a kind of beautiful death, a euthanasia, let them commit suicide on the path of pleasure. It is perhaps a pity for many. But woe to them who, driven perhaps just one time to play with danger, venture into this whirlpool! In the grip of the pleasure of cocaine they sink almost irretrievably into the gurgling depths. It is infinitely harder to withdraw from cocaine than, for example, from morphine, and possible only with incomparably more torment. The cocaine demon has its victim gripped too tightly in its vampire claws; the longing for intensified stimuli attains an enormous level of tension and torment, and does so very quickly. If even one-time use produces a not inconsiderable depression, and the beautiful delirium is often interrupted by attacks of frenzy, rage, and cramps, then the vital energies of chronic cocaine sinners sink in an unbelievably short time to zero. A greenish-brown shadow surrounds hollow eyes, now bereft of shine and with the haze of death wandering fleetingly over their surface. The enormous unrest, trembling limbs, quivering, drooling lips, twitching chin, fits of yawning, the head sunk helplessly on the chest, complete rhythmic and motivational enervation—that all comes with such horrifying rapidity, such gripping certainty, that an observer is inevitably seized by a profound shudder on viewing the unfortunate victim who has drunk for the first time of this poisonous cup. But it is the enormous danger of all demons that their secret priests are always searching for comrades in their hellish cult, that every vice seeks cohorts at the devil's altar; they form clubs and associations devoted to their clandestine thrills, wishing to organize their fellowships and lodges as a sort of conventional guild of outlaws. Today, as in all revolutionary times, when the existence of the individual trembles to the roots, when life and death are separated by a hair, the ecstasy of delirium and dance sprouts up as if in search of mass narcosis. The present hullabaloo caused a cocaine fellowship, a cult of the poisonous drug to float to the surface, which is quite likely unprecedented in the cultural history of humanity. If supply and demand determine the price of a commodity, how strong the yearning for cocaine must be in Berlin, where a kilo of cocaine, which cost sixteen marks before the war, is now offered at 17,000. That speaks volumes about cocaine addiction in our Sodom!

318

ERNST ENGELBRECHT AND LEO HELLER

Night Figures of the City

First published in "Nachtgestalten der Großstadt," in *Kinder der Nacht. Bilder aus dem Verbrecherleben* (Berlin: Hermann Paetel Verlag, 1926), 21–25.

The people of the provinces already lie in the arms of Morpheus and the streets and squares have become empty and lonely, but a lively commotion still reigns in the streets of the metropolis Berlin. Cars and buses pass by and sleepy carriages rock down the streets at an easy trot. Crowds often jam the sidewalks of the thoroughfares, people gently pushing their way through. No one is hurried and no one thinks of going home to bed. Amusement is in order, something to experience, for the nightlife of Berlin has begun.

"A respectable establishment," whispers a doubtful-looking gentlemen from a doorway as we pass. And as he sees that he has gotten our attention, he quickly completes the invitation. "Respectable, strictly respectable and tip-top. Lady dancers, too, good sirs." With which he wants the "respectable" to refer only to the prices and otherwise does not want to put any narrow limits on the respectability of his joint. Some thirty steps farther on there is another who comes on more boldly with his invitation. "Naked dancers, gentlemen, but first class!" he tempts us. And so it is that we regularly meet such charming gentlemen in the employ of one wild nightclub or another, seeking out guests. Barkers these fellows are called. They extend their invitations and then transfer the offerings of the takers to a panderer standing nearby, who then conducts the former into the club. These clubs are only in the rarest of cases to be found in licensed establishments. Usually they have been thrown together in some kind of rented apartment, in a shop or cellar—for this purpose not even the usual junk or coal cellar is disdained. It is precisely the unusual, the weird that holds a particular attraction for this kind of audience. That in such establishments, which are well secured against sudden surprises from the side of the police through one or several bouncers, the public is taken advantage of, severely diddled, is understood. For the many—and truly not too shabby—paychecks for the barkers, bouncers, waiters, dancers, etc. must of course be paid by the business, and above all the profits to the owner, who does not want to come up short in view of the large risks of the enterprise. Customers must always pay handsomely and only in the rarest cases do they get anything respectable to drink in return. And the other pleasures promised are inferior too. In so far as one can even speak of pleasure! For to watch a dancer—four decades already behind her and with depraved eyes and common features which immediately betray her true calling as a free priestess to the goddess Venus—to watch her disrobe and show her "charms" can only be a very doubtful pleasure. And other dangers lurk here as well. Criminal types await their mark; a drunken guest who, either in the club itself or on the street on the way home, will make easy prey. Thus has many a wanderer in the night had to pay for such an excursion to a club with the loss of his coin purse, wallet, pocketwatch, and other valuables.

Just as dangerous are the wild gambling clubs to which friendly gents issue their invitations well into the early morning hours. Here, too, there are really always all kinds of scoundrels who become friendly with inexperienced guests and rob them and steal from them, not to mention that these wild gambling enterprises are greatly favored by sharps, among both the managers and the guests. In these wild gambling clubs, just as often as in the nightclubs, we find lots of "ladies" who have settled there for reasons of business, when they do not prefer strolling up and down the streets asking for love. Either alone or in herds, these girls make their way down the nighttime streets until early morning, or lie in wait for their moneyed prey on one or another corner. Their pimps are often discharging a kind of watch or security service nearby. And woe to the poor fellow who is unable to come to an agreement with the girl! The scoundrel is on the spot in a moment to ambush the victim and often enough to set things right with force.

In the doorways of buildings or on the corners of the lively streets, the sausage seller has set up shop, peddling a couple of steaming sausages—"pure pork," he guarantees—for a few pennies to the wanderers of the night. And it seems he always finds a substantial clientele. Around him gather idle prostitutes for a bit of chat. The sausage seller sells not only his sausage treats but offers his customers the chance for other, forbidden pleasures as well. For on the side he also does a booming retail trade in cocaine, the poisonous white powder, and in this connection his clientele might well be much more extensive and loyal. One has no idea how quickly the vice of cocaine has made its home in Germany; broad groups of the population have fallen hopelessly into its clutches. One can estimate that thirty percent of all prostitutes, gamblers, and pederasts are cocaine users, and in other callings as well, in particular among artists, cocaine has found its loyal slaves.

The many cigarette sellers constantly crossing our path, calling after us their typical "cigarettes, cigarettes!" are also often engaged in the distribution of cocaine. And when they do not sell it themselves, it is certain that they know where some can be obtained within the next five minutes. The severe penalties for cocaine dealers, which, in view of the all-around dangerousness of their activity and damage to the life of the German people, can hardly be made severe enough, have recently caused a noticeable abatement in their business. The scourge of cocaine has spread to other lands, too, to Russia, Poland, and to the Latin countries, apparently to a still greater degree than in Germany.

On a street corner a man approaches us hesitantly. Would we like to see some interesting pictures? And then, all the while looking anxiously about, he leads us into a doorway to show us all sorts of forbidden books and obscene photographs. If there is no more business to be found on the streets, then he seeks out customers in the nightclubs. He is often welcome enough as a visitor there. All kinds of questionable figures confront us as they saunter slowly down the street; their keen looks size us up, exhort us to caution. And this caution is necessary. For the night is the workday for the criminal whose design is favored by darkness and the isolation of the street. He goes to work in the night, dares a promising-looking burglary of a business, an apartment break-in, even a sidewalk robbery.

The harmless citizen who must pass on the streets at night notices little of the dangers lurking around him. The nightlife and its activities often seem harmless to him. And nonetheless does the night in the metropolis continually demand its sacrificial victims. Thus is many an existence morally and physically destroyed. Thus does many a swindler and counterfeiter have just one such big-city night to thank for his crime, and thus is many a careless passerby subjected to the loss of cash and steady damage to his health.

319

ERNST ENGELBRECHT AND LEO HELLER

Opium Dens

First published as "Opiumhöhlen," in *Kinder der Nacht. Bilder aus dem Verbrecherleben* (Berlin: Hermann Paetel Verlag, 1926), 26–30.

Thirty-odd years ago any Chinese or Japanese person who let himself be seen in a German city was regarded as a kind of fantastic animal. Troops of children trailed along behind and never tired of looking at his slanted eyes or even his ponytail! How that has all changed in the meantime! With the suppression of the Boxer uprising in 1900 and 1901, China too began to come closer to the West, a move which its little Mongolian brother, Japan, had undertaken several decades previously. Today Chinese trade ships are to be found in the larger German harbors, and even its warships honor us occasionally with more or less welcome visits. These Chinese trade ships are manned almost exclusively by Chinese and Malays, and only in rare cases does a Japanese or European belong to the crew.

The Chinese has generally sacrificed his ponytail to civilization, but in his customs he has generally remained very conservative. This is to be seen, if nowhere else, in the Chinese restaurants, which Hamburg, like all of the larger port cities, displays in abundance. The fork is strictly forbidden, and instead the Chinese eats with chopsticks and enjoys his favorite native dishes, the ingredients and preparation of which often occasions a certain disgust on the part of Europeans. Enterprising Chinese have leased dance clubs and cafés in Hamburg, where they offer entertainment of all sorts to their fellow countrymen streaming into the harbor. To insure that the Chinese and Malay seamen do not suffer other deprivations—that is seen to by the masses of German and foreign prostitutes who throw themselves shamelessly upon the (not exactly clean) Mongolian sailing crews. With the growth of Chinese ship traffic, their bad habits and vices have also gained a foothold in the port cities.

The enjoyment of opium is probably the most widespread of the Chinese vices, one to which large numbers in China have hopelessly succumbed. Morphine, ether, and cocaine have declined significantly as intoxicants. The opium scourge is slowly making its way into the life of the German people. And the foreign sailing crews have introduced two other narcotics into Hamburg: marijuana and heroin, two drugs that ultimately seem to be of Spanish or South American origin. Just as cocaine is obtained on the black market under the names "cement," "coke," or "cacao," heroin is widely known in the St. Pauli neighborhoods favored by criminals and sailors as "H." Opium, like the other drugs just mentioned, is extremely harmful to the human body. A single indulgence in opium can result in terrible diseases of the nervous system; and frequent use leads in general in a very short time to the complete ruin of the body and to chronic infirmity.

It is seen to that the seafaring Chinese do not have to do without their opium. Resourceful Chinese have seized the occasion to set up opium salons in out-of-the-way cellars on the most notorious streets of St. Pauli. These Chinese opium dens are visited generally only by Chinese and Malays, and otherwise kept strictly secret. A European requires cunning and quite an expenditure of energy to gain entry into such an "original Chinese opium den." Since operations in opium bars always proceed calmly so that even a next-door neighbor knows nothing of it, it is especially difficult for the police to discover them. All of the Chinese opium dens are probably located in St. Pauli, and within St. Pauli, in the area of highest concentration of the Chinese and Malay element. Just as the nightclubs in Berlin, and incidentally in Hamburg too, have all manner of barkers, panderers, and bouncers, the dealer in opium resorts to such aids as well. These barkers, panderers, and bouncers are, however, all Chinese themselves in this case, and they have acquired the ability through long years of practice to identify immediately those among their race who desire opium. With the greatest caution, they inquire of them whether they are not looking for a "pipe of opium." The panderer brings the customer to the building where the bouncer conducts him to the well-hidden opium den.

Just now at midnight the Chinese bouncer has allowed a European visitor into the building. Next the visitor enters a dimly lit antechamber where the money changes hands and where coat, umbrella, cane, and, if necessary, weapons must be checked. Then a large, red-carpeted cellar room is opened to him. In very dim red light he sees a number of couches on which a few guests are already tossing restlessly in their deep dreams. A sickeningly sweet atmosphere envelops him. The host makes a low bow and brings the opium pipe, puts a small pebble of opium in the bowl, and indicates a couch. Quietly, almost without a sound, the old Chinese slinks away, but not without first having cast a glance about at his other guests. The calm resumes, broken only by the occasional sound of one of the guests muttering in a foreign language, or the gesticulations of another, arms and hands moving in the wild desire of the dream. Cautiously the guest takes a puff from the pipe, and then after a brief pause another. Then he continues to smoke discreetly. He looks curiously at his sleepy neighbors, counts eight, nine Chinese, and a clean-shaven white face twisted by the dream into a laughing grimace and saying, "oh, yes," "oh . . . oh," a long, drawn-out "oh . . . yes." Soon enough the new guest is immersed in wonderful dreams; he feels himself released from all earthly matters and lets himself be washed over with erotic pleasure. One, two, three hours he lies there in sleep, then suddenly starts. First he has to concentrate and consider where he is and how he got there. Only with difficulty does he regain the memory. His watch says 5:00 AM. Already the old Chinese is standing before him. With a smile on his face, he again bows deeply and offers his guest a paper-thin porcelain cup with something hot to drink. The guest takes it and brings the cup carefully to his lips. It is scarcely to be said what it tastes like, so strong and bitter is the tea. He slowly rises; a faint headache is the cost of the unaccustomed pleasure. His neighbors in sleep are also awake, except for two Chinese, who, thanks to the greater quantity of opium, still lie immersed in dream. Once again he looks over his surroundings, and a boundless loathing comes over him, for the room and the events of his opium night. He leaves the opium den in the greatest hurry.

"Come once more very soon!" calls the Chinese bouncer as he leaves, "You make such pretty dreams."

320

MARGOT KLAGES-STANGE

Prostitution

First published as "Prostitution," *Die Weltbühne* 22, no. 15 (April 13, 1926), 579–580.

Discussing prostitution in public is still a ticklish affair in Germany. In other countries, particularly in Scandinavia, a freer and healthier view of things is manifest. Public health reaps the benefits of this popular enlightenment, for the fact is that prostitution and venereal diseases are not to be separated from each other.

Comprehensive documentation about those who "go out onto the street" still does not exist today, cannot exist, because only professional prostitutes are included in the statistics. These are either women whose behavior has attracted the attention of the vice squad or women who have submitted, voluntarily and unceremoniously, to supervision. Much larger, of course, is the number of prostitutes that constantly eludes the arm of the law, however vigilant it might be. In Berlin at present there are approximately nine thousand prostitutes under supervision; the total number, including surreptitious streetwalkers, is estimated at about 100,000. These naked figures are proof enough of how matters stand concerning prostitution.

The bulk of the professional women under supervision come from the class of domestic servants. The girl from the country—and most of those employed in the home do not come from the city itself—have quite naïve views on sexuality. They are threatened by venereal infections, and in many cases they have lost their positions as a consequence. Transplantation from the country into the city, moreover, entails a thorough change in accustomed habits and circumstances. Frequently the girl has no one in whom she can confide, and the need for support leads her astray. Wages are just barely sufficient to satisfy the heightened desire for finery, and the financial deficiency is made up "in other ways." On average, one is justified in assuming that the majority of prostitutes come from the lower social strata.

Among female workers, those lacking in skills represent the largest proportion. Singers, dancers, and barmaids are in the main dependent on side earnings from the outset, because they cannot possibly live on their wages. Things are similar in the clothing trade. In slack periods, when the firm's budgetary measures compel a reduction in staff, the contingent of prostitutes grows. Many girls then fail to find their way back to work; but the number of those who are eager to go back on the labor market as conditions improve is larger.

The next category—which admittedly only represents a small fraction of professional prostitutes—are sales girls and stenotypists. Their professional life takes them out of their parents' home. Moreover, due to the economic competition between the sexes, the woman often develops the view, "what the man wants is fine with me," and so sees extramarital relations as her natural right. That is the case far beyond the bounds of actual prostitution. Virginity maintained until marriage has ceased to exist in the big cities. This development has advanced rapidly since the war, since the number of girls who find a husband has sharply declined. Before the war there were for every 1,000 men in Germany 1,024 women. After the war the ratio was 1,000 to 1,084, and in the most important age groups, from fifteen to twenty, as much as 1,000 to 1,116. Thus are nearly 2.5 million women condemned to remain single and therefore to seek extramarital relations. The great danger in this is the increase in venereal diseases, determined by the growing number of women who occasionally engage in prostitution.

321

E. M. MUNGENAST
The Murderer and the State

First published in *Der Mörder und der Staat. Die Todesstrafe im Urteil hervorragender Zeitgenossen* (Stuttgart: Walter Hädecke, 1928), 19, 27–32.

The death penalty can only be judged a *remnant* of past times. It contradicts all principles and experience, all the demands and emotional maxims of a modern civilized state, and, not least, precisely the raison d'état in which the proponents and adherents of the death penalty sometimes garb their opinion. Even the slightest qualification of the recognition of an individual's absolute right to life denotes a concession to its denial. The contemporary state therefore cannot for reasons of state privilege the killing of one individual without at the same time subjecting the life of every single citizen to a kind of sabotage.

History proves that the life of an individual counted least in those ages in which the most and the most gruesome executions were carried out. When the death penalty was repealed for crimes of theft, its proponents anticipated a flood of burglaries and thefts. The opposite occurred.

One cannot help feeling that human society never pronounces a more severe judgment than when it allows or even demands the killing of one of its members. It destroys the member that it is itself responsible for producing, thereby denying him all possibility of making reparations for his misdeed. At the same time, however—and this is the essence of the matter—it condemns itself in that, rather than seeking to alter the *conditions* from which the murderer came in an effort to prevent future occurrences, it simply does not want to see and believe what it is lacking.

The murderer can be rehabilitated. The adherents of the death penalty have never yet been able to prove the contrary.

The case of Sacco and Vanzetti caused an uproar the world over. America suffered a severe moral defeat. The fate of the two insignificant Italians stirred the deepest feelings in millions of grown men and women in all countries. They were wounded to the core both by the possibility of a judicial error and by the fact that the two men were executed after the unheard-of torment of seven years imprisonment. They all experienced it as a slap in the face of humanity. They felt themselves to have been deeply insulted personally and cried out—what a disastrous effect of the death penalty!—curses against the judges which, as they affirmed themselves afterward, they had never spoken before and which had been utterly alien to them until that time. Peacefully working men and women were suddenly transformed into blood-thirsty masses with the single thought of wiping out the offenders against humanity. There were voices that attempted to justify the execution by reference to the dictate of *raison d'état*. The representatives of *this raison d'état* declare reason to be either idiotic or divine, according to their need or preference.

The execution of Sacco and Vanzetti spurred increased discussion of the expediency and permissibility of the death penalty. The majority of people suddenly recognized the senselessness of the absolute penalty and determined that it was not at all the solution one believed to have come from a wise and just lawgiver, indeed that the lawgiver could not even have been so wise and just as one had simply believed before. One suddenly had the feeling of being cast in a distorted and false light, of being ominously insulted and just as ominously threatened. [. . .]

Appeals Court Justice E. Dosenheimer correctly refers, in his essay "The Causes of Crime and Their Remedy" to the problem of human will—Dosenheimer subscribes to Spinoza's belief in the unfreedom of the human will—which is conditioned by three factors: predisposition, upbringing and individual conditions. Incest, alcoholism, mental illness, poor upbringing and deficient and one-sided schooling make for an inexhaustible source of misery and crime; and then there are external circumstances:

> For everyone who has a heart for the people, who considers the possibility of bridging or at least mitigating the gap between the haves and the have-nots, there can be only one position. The first line of attack must be the elimination of the harms and excesses of capitalism and the creation of a truly social state. Articles 151, 155, and 163 of the constitution cannot be allowed to remain mere promises but must take on life and form. If the state and society, on the basis of these constitutional requirements, guarantees to every citizen a dignified existence, a healthy dwelling, and a livelihood through work, then the primary social question will be essentially solved, then the causes of crime will be largely overcome. [. . .]

In an extensive description in the *Catholic Newsletter* (Berlin, December 11, 1927), Dr. Karl Sonnenschein considers the metropolis Berlin. Among other things, he writes:

> No! From the Roman Café to Luna Park! That is not a cross-section of Berlin: not the oriental colorfulness of Friedrichstraße! . . . If you please! Berlin is elsewhere! The city of 4.2 million! One-tenth of Prussia! Two-thirds of Bavaria! Four-fifths of Saxony! In population figures! . . . If you please! In the last three weeks we have put the numbers together! Then we were on the telephone for three days! Police! Cemeteries! Doctor's offices! Prison! Courts! Each one gave us information: many thanks!

There then follow seven images of Berlin in figures. Only a few have been selected, and these severely abridged:

> Third, shelter. . . . Urban shelter: Fröbelstraße! Berlin NE 55! The homeless call it the "Palms." . . . Occupancy, December 6, 1927: 2,073 men, 164 women, 72 youths!

2,309 people! Added to that from the Schnitter House book: on the same night, 51 women and 71 children. On December 6 it was nearly 800 more: 3,095 homeless! For whom their little money was not enough for the Salvation Army, the City Mission, St. John's House. Completely homeless! . . .

Fourth: the youth. Youth Welfare cares for 21,000 crippled children, 53,000 wards, 16,000 day-nursery children, 9,000 welfare pupils, 16,000 foster children. That makes 115,000 people. A big German city! Buer near Dortmund has that many. Of the 53,000 wards, 50,000 are illegitimate. A mass choir of misery! A mass choir of indictment! . . . The city counts 8,000 completed criminal proceedings against young people. From January to November. In this year alone! 8,000 youth before the court! . . .

Sixth: the war. The city cares for 44,000 war invalids! Of these, 19,000 are severely disabled! In addition, 88,700 survivors of war dead. Of these, 3,400 complete orphans, 48,000 half orphans, 2,300 parent couples, 35,000 widows! A choir of women by the tomb at Susa. Odes of smoldering pain! Behind the women, the orchestra of war invalids! Around them, groups of orphan children and abandoned parents! The whole a metropolis of mourning!

Seventh: prison. The number is scribbled quickly on the board. The gates are opened daily. Of the jail! Of the penitentiary! Of the remand prison! Every day 300 people walk through these gates! . . . Convict welfare looks after 40 to 50 in the summer, 70 to 80 in the winter. The rest go their way alone. To their parents? To a bride? To a new life? That is 110,000 a year! The German army is made up of 100,000! An army that streams through Berlin's gates into the country! 300 every day! . . .

Images in numbers! This is Berlin! . . . The film that Karl Freund is shooting for the American company Fox is called *Symphony of a Big City*. Behind the symphony is the atonal world! Is the storm of need!

Build a dam around it and just leave it to rage? Hold it in check with blood and iron? With the weight of authority? To which the satiated so fondly appeal. And which, perhaps, is only an old car on an old track.

For a modern, Christian, civilized state, it is absolutely impossible to maintain within its body an army of millions whose relation to the whole is unstable and which can undermine it, thus plunging decades of development and cultural work yet deeper into misery with it. How can the social order insist on an authority that fires a gas grenade in the face of the authority of reason, of responsibility, of conscience, of Christianity, of humanity and humaneness? That punishes the unfortunate because it has rendered them so! That destroys the miserable because the sight of misery gets on its nerves! That destroys the miserable because they dared to have nerves! That hacks off the head of the miserable because they were so wanton as to take on its airs! That pursues the unfortunate because they dared to document their misfortune! That, should Christ return today, would crucify him again come evening! And would speak with the Romans: "I wash my hands in innocence."

Alfred Döblin once turned with great passion somewhere against the execution of youth in particular, demanding that when a young person becomes a criminal he be taken firmly in hand and called to account, above all to himself. No stone in the youth's whole environment should be left unturned. But to calmly kill him and then leave everything

like it was before, that was the absolute worst of the worst, a horrifying idea, a disgraceful
convenience.

322

ARTUR LANDSBERGER

The Berlin Underworld

First published in *Die Unterwelt von Berlin* (Berlin: Paul Stegemann, 1929), 9–10, 15–18, 20, 22–24.

The tempo of development in Berlin is breathtaking. First came the inflation, then the radio
broadcast tower, the police exhibition, later the Iron Gustav, the London gas explosion in
Tempelhof . . . but the final touch was still lacking. Then—at last—on the first day of
the year 1929 Berlin became a metropolis: the slums of Chicago and the gangsters of New
York were pushed into the shadows by—the underworld of Berlin.

To be sure, fifteen thousand people were already disappearing without a trace in
Berlin annually; fifty thousand complaints were registered with the police: on account of
burglaries and pickpocketings, on account of forgery and bond swindles, on account of
counterfeiting and more delicate things. The police were busy, the courts were busy,
district attorneys were pleading their cases on an assembly line. And at Alexanderplatz,
our first-rate Scotland Yard, fingerprints were diligently being collected (a half a million
are already on file). And the mugshot album displayed, not without pride, forty thousand
portraits.

Horrifying numbers? Now Berlin has meanwhile absorbed four and a half million
inhabitants; the times of the famous stilt-house village in the woods are unfortunately past
and not everyone is bedded on roses. All kinds of things are happening. Murders and
manslaughter, one every three days; uproars and cocaine are the sociological comforts of
the metropolis. [. . .]

The antithesis between the bourgeoisie and the proletariat is manifest, to deny it would
be a pointless venture. Individuals slip out of both classes, lose the connection to their class,
and become—in the sense of the state—asocial. When the well-situated bourgeois child
slips out, he becomes a bohemian or, if he musters enough courage, a swindler, an insurance
or loan embezzler, a counterfeit prince, or a hotel thief. If the proletarian slips out of his
class, he is forced to commit break-ins or skip out on checks, to become a pickpocket or
a vagrant. He lacks the necessary education for the "higher" crimes.

Between the criminality of the bourgeoisie and that of the proletariat is an intermediary
stratum of people unable to embrace either their class or criminality. They lack will in all
respects: these are the passive elements who fail to find the strength to maintain themselves
in their classes, who are too weak to commit a "proper" crime. From among these people
the bohemians are recruited, the gigolos, pimps, and prostitutes. They live on with the
longing for "higher things" in their hearts—higher things appear to them as the well-
tended order of the bourgeoisie. They do not distinguish what is to be valued from what
is to be despised in bourgeois institutions. They fall for appearances, which are most
accessible to their desires: the Bacchanalian rituals of students, solidarity, flags and insignia
tablecloths, association meetings, and first-class funerals with music.

Since it is evident to them that membership in the Blue-Red Tennis Club or Wannsee Golf and Country Club is out of their reach, they found their own associations.

Their associational life is in no way to be distinguished from that of a men's singing group or ex-servicemen's association, as is demonstrated by the following statutes:

1.

1. The association bears the name "Ever-True Sport Club of 1921" and has its seat in Berlin.
2. Political and religious endeavors are prohibited.

2.

The goal of the association is to be achieved:

1. Through the promotion of friendship and conviviality among the members;
2. through support to be rendered in case of illness and special emergencies;
3. through support upon occasions of death. [. . .]

17.

1. The association considers it its supreme duty to bury every deceased member as is fitting to the honor and dignity of the Ever-True Association.
2. Should the treasury find itself in such a weakened condition that it cannot cover the costs, a collection must be made to acquire the necessary funds.

18.

1. Every member will receive a signet ring upon completing five years of membership.

In Berlin there are approximately a dozen such associations. One could never characterize the membership as a whole as criminals or pimps. There are certain to be honorable cigarette wholesalers among them, modest handicraft workers, people who have only once been convicted of a petty triviality and are no longer fully recognized by the rigorous citizenry (for in this regard the class-conscious proletariat is also a citizen). Here in their association they feel at ease, are people among people; they do not have to fear skeptical glances and pointed remarks. Here as well the sense of group honor develops, which is much more sensitive than the personal sort. And many among them have never been sentenced.

Even if they are also linked to many similar associations in the country through the cartel of "the ring," it is nevertheless wrong to represent them as dangerous. On the contrary, insofar as they lend moral encouragement to their members, infuse them with their good and strict bourgeois code of honor, they do good. Since these associations have existed (the first was founded nearly fifty years ago and membership during the war was mainly non-political deserters who could not, like the bohemians, go to Switzerland) surveillance of criminality has been made much easier: the police easily find the intermediate stratum all gathered together. They are likely reluctant for that reason to dissolve the associations. Who wants to make his work harder for no reason? Moreover, the ring associations are thoroughly apolitical. They could not care less whether Hitler or Thälmann, Seeckt or Scheidemann declares the dictatorship. They have better things to do: tending to the life of the association.

And when the associations hold their celebrations, solemnly carrying the banner into the decorated hall to the sound of drums and call of bugles, then just try coming and saying it is all a farce. It is deadly earnest to them, true to their motto: The Good, the True, the Beautiful.

323

FRANZ ALEXANDER AND HUGO STAUB
The Criminal and His Judges

First published in *Der Verbrecher und seine Richter. Ein psychoanalytischer Einblick in die Welt der Paragraphen* (Vienna: Internationaler Psychoanalytischer Verlag, 1929), xvii–xix.

It is no longer necessary to try to justify the claims psychoanalysis makes in understanding the mentally sick and in extending to them therapeutic help.

Yet not so many centuries ago hysteria still belonged to a domain other than medicine; it was a phenomenon on which only the law courts were supposed to be competent to pass judgment. The woman suffering from hysteria was called a witch and she was punished as such; the punishment was severe, more severe than the one meted out today to a murderer. It is not improbable that our treatment of the criminal will undergo a similar change in the future. The very fact that in "doubtful" cases today a medical expert (i.e., a psychiatrist) is usually asked by the court for an opinion is the first step in this direction. A deeper knowledge of the psychology of the criminal would considerably increase the number of such "doubtful" cases. Yet our plea for a better understanding of the criminal seems to require some justification. Is not the criminal a public menace? Should not the interest we have in him be limited to an attempt to render him harmless and to make the punishment imposed upon him serve as an example to others? Thus, a deeper study of the criminal personality might at first appear as nothing but a luxury, a manner of squandering one's scientific zeal. Is it not true that *tout comprendre c'est tout pardonner?* Is it not true that the psychologist who strives to understand the criminal must at first put himself in the criminal's place, or as we say in psychoanalysis, he must identify himself with the criminal? One might even become suspicious that such a psychologist seeks to help the criminal rather than society; thus the psychologist becomes open to suspicion of disloyalty to society.

The authors hope that in the course of this study they will succeed in clearing themselves of any such suspicion; they wish, however, to try to prove in the beginning that a psychological understanding of the criminal does not primarily help the criminal but, on the contrary, serves the interests of society. In order to do this we will have to deviate from our main line of thought, but this deviation will furnish us incidentally with some basic ideas that will prove the need for a psychoanalytical criminology.

We are justified, we believe, in assuming that a sentence on a criminal which is generally perceived as just presupposes the psychological understanding of the person responsible for the act judged; in other words, it presupposes a knowledge of motives underlying the given act. One and the same act may be approved or condemned, depending upon the motives underlying it. We praise the killing of the enemy in war; we condone a murder committed in self-defense; we sometimes forgive the killing of a person when it is done in a state of understandable affect, but the murderer who kills to rob is unanimously condemned. As far as the act itself is concerned, it is identical in all cases cited; our judgment on it seems to depend merely upon the various conscious aims it has and its various emotional motivations. Without the knowledge of these motivations one is unable to form any attitude toward a given act. The main question whether or not a given act is to be considered criminal depends entirely upon the psychological diagnosis we make. This paramount importance of psychology by which the judge is guided will be considered in detail later. It is mentioned here only in order to establish definitely that the feeling that a given court sentence is just is closely bound with the proper evaluation of the motives which lead to a given act.

Yet this reason alone does not appear sufficiently to justify a too zealous search for the psychological understanding of the criminal from whom society seeks to protect itself. We may say, of course, that our intention to study the psychic life of the criminal in detail is justified because we want to assure the criminal a just judgment of the law. But why this intense need of a theoretical justice in cases of frankly antisocial individuals? It might almost seem that we are trying to find a way to protect the criminal from society and not society from the criminal. Thus, our previous assertion that we seek to serve the interests of society appears unwarranted. This apparent contradiction might disappear only if it could be definitely proved that the judgment pronounced upon the criminal, which we perceive as just, really serves the interests of society. Hence, for the purpose of clarity we are ready to submit to cross-examination by the Solicitor General of Society, who might want to bring the authors of these pages to account and say:

"Why this wish to understand the criminal at any cost? It is much more important to seize him and free society of his presence. Why not turn your psychological ardor toward the understanding of more worthy objects? Despite all you say, your great ardor does appear to me nothing but an attempt to help the criminal."

No, our chief aim is not this. We want to understand the criminal in order to be able to judge him correctly, so that our judgment may be just beyond question. Our assertion that our clear understanding of the criminal serves the interests of society is based on the fact that the sense of justice belongs to the most fundamental factors of human social organization; any disturbance of the common sense of justice has a destructive effect upon society. When the sense of justice is disturbed, then that part of our ego which was called by Freud the superego and which is yet in a rather weak state of organization, loses its power over the asocial impulses of the average individual.

324

WILLI PRÖGER

Sites of Berlin Prostitution

First published under the name of Weka in *Stätten der Berliner Prostitution* (Berlin: Auffenburg Verlagsgesellschaft, 1930), 41–44.

We continue our tour now to the north, toward Alexanderplatz. It is early evening. Colossal traffic.

Frankfurter Allee. Suddenly there's a tug from somewhere on my coattails. "Hey man!" A boy grabs me by the sleeve. Ten, twelve years-old, fresh, insolent face. From underneath the saucy cap, abundant long hair. "Hey man, ain't ya got a sec?" The boy stops and gives me a conspiratorial look. "Whyn't ya come for a blink in the hall there." Robbery would not seem a danger, so we go "for a blink in the hall." "I might have somethin' for ya, ya got a sec or two, somethin maybe's not bad." Having become curious, I confirm I have the time. "What I got's a sister, what's not bad, I'm tellin ya." "I'm quite ready to believe you, that you have a sister, but why make a point of it here in the hall?" The boy grins and twists congenially on the button on my coat. "Come on, don't gotta make it tough. She's real top stuff, I'm tellin ya." I protest once more my incomprehension and finally learn that I'm supposed to "love" her, the sister. Apparently, she's simply "ace," "cheap," "but ain't just no snap-to-it either." That is approximately what one gets by way of technical information from a twelve-year-old boy in a hall on Frankfurter Allee. It tempts me to find out more about the circumstances of his middleman business, so I go with him. "Ya see there," said my guide, "knowed it from the top, you's one what knows what's what . . . !"

We stopped in front of a big apartment block on Breslauer Strasse. "So, here's where we stayin'. Ya also got a nickel or so for me for my work? I take quarters too." After the "commission" was paid, business took its course. A lighted building in the front led to a totally dark courtyard filled with ash cans. Three, four flights of wobbly stairs, and at the top a Lilliputian kerosene lamp. My leader opened a door and we found ourselves in a kitchen. It smelled of cabbage and herring. The boy asked me to wait, disappeared through a door, presumably into the only other room in the apartment, and returned with his "sister." A conservative estimate puts her at 36 to 38 years old; she could be therefore, if she is related to the boy at all, his mother. But otherwise cleanly dressed and not even without her appeal for one with modest expectations. The boy had already taken off, and I carefully explained to the woman that my curiosity about this kind of customer touting had brought me there, which, however, did not imply any pecuniary loss to her. The woman led me into the other room, simply and cleanly furnished, with red-paper lampshades to give it a "cozy" atmosphere. I sensed the presence of a folded-down bed behind a curtain. . . . The woman smoked and told her story. "Good Lord, you have to live. . . . I used to walk the streets . . . but the competition is too tough. . . . My husband's been dead eight years . . . I'm not about to marry misery again. . . . The boy is my stepchild—he came with my husband. . . . You have to make the men curious . . . then they're more likely to come. . . . Now we just get by. . . . What do you want? . . . My two girlfriends even send their husbands off pimping. . . ." I leave the apartment and make my slow way back. On the Frankfurter Allee I see the boy again. He is just tugging on a man's sleeve. "Hey man . . . !"

325

GEORG FUCHS

We Prisoners: Memories of Inmate No. 2911

First published in *Wir Zuchthäusler. Erinnerungen des Zellengefangenen Nr. 2911* (Munich: Albert Langen, 1931), 2–3.

Crime is a threat to every individual, whoever he may be; anyone, whoever he may be, can at any moment become a victim of a terrible crime. Every person, whoever he may be, is therefore immensely interested in the question of whether the danger that constantly threatens his life, health, property, honor, and wife and children is being effectively opposed. This danger is increased by the criminal's improper treatment in prison. While the correct treatment can never totally do away with the threat of danger, it can certainly diminish it to an extent never before thought possible.

The world has entered an era of crisis similar to the one experienced by the world of antiquity in the year zero (calculated by the Gregorian calendar). From both sides of the ocean, voices are increasingly heard which attribute the seemingly insurmountable global crisis to the fact that a world economic system based one-sidedly on technology—and capital–intensive industrialism has exhausted itself. Another reason has to do with an assumption that arose in conjunction with the enormous initial successes enjoyed by technology and industry in the preceding century. The expectation was that the development of technology and capital-intensive industrialism would be unlimited, giving rise to boundless improvements in living standards. This has proven to be erroneous. Today's global crisis compels us to recognize that, as with everything in nature and in world affairs, technology, industry, and mechanization take on their own forms of existence with strict and well-ordered boundaries, which, as soon as they are overstepped, necessarily have a destructive effect. Instead of increased well-being and prosperity, they bring world wars and global crises to mankind; instead of creative personal fulfillment, unemployment; instead of moral refinement, a rise in criminality; instead of vigorous art, a desolate business that speculates with "names" and "success"; instead of increased fertility, a decline in the birth rate. Where one would expect a higher level of culture this decline is accompanied by an ever more rapidly approaching extinction of civilized populations that are being overrun by a devitalized, spiritually bankrupt chaos, by members of the human race who are incapable of civilization.

Accordingly we see today that technical and organizational methods do not bring us any further in the battle against criminality, that here as well the currently existing system has exhausted itself. It is precisely in the United States that criminality has shockingly and clearly proven to be an expression, albeit an exceptional one, of the present global crisis. Thus we are no longer dealing with a special legal question but with a basic problem that affects all of humanity!

War, the death penalty, prison: these are the three moral issues of today, and even more of tomorrow! But basically these are one and the same problem: does the general public have the right to deprive another human being of his life? Are there certain values in the defense of which the officially sanctioned killing of a fellow human being can, in good conscience, be deemed legitimate or even be simply tolerated by the cultured person of today? The prisoner, whether serving a life sentence or a long-term one, is also deprived of his life, cannot live his life, is buried alive. Walled up in the tomblike prison, he is compelled to experience consciously what others killed by official sanction in war, on the gallows, in the electric chair are spared: his own death and burial.

But the conscience of humanity has already been galvanized! Ghastly events in the prisons of the United States have shaken it up; but above all there are also the works of the most famous authors of our time, whose words are rightly and attentively heard by the entire civilized world! [Fyodor] Dostoyevsky's memoirs, *The House of the Dead,* Paul Verlaine's *Mes Prisons,* Oscar Wilde's *Ballad of Reading Gaol,* the extremely moving novel by the Danish author Mathilda von Wrede—all these stir the soul. And whoever has read Jakob Wassermann's novel *The Case of Mauritius,* Alfred Döblin's *Berlin Alexanderplatz,* Gerhart Hauptmann's *Dorothea Angermann,* Thomas Mann's *Tonio Kröger,* Ferdinand Bruckner's *The Criminals* will feel, given that he is a human being and not a monster, a tormenting thorn in his soul, whenever he hears the word *prison.*

326

SIGMUND FREUD AND OSWALD SPENGLER

[Responses to Fuchs, *We Prisoners*]

First published in *Wir Zuchthäusler. Erinnerungen des Zellengefangenen Nr. 2911* (Munich: Albert Langen, 1931), x–xi, xiii–xiv.

SIGMUND FREUD

The wave of a most intense sympathy felt after reading your letter was broken at once by two considerations: an internal obstacle and an external hindrance. A sentence from your own preface gave expression to the former: "There are certainly those people who hold contemporary civilization in such low esteem that they dispute the existence of a universal conscience." I believe that I count myself as one of those people. I could not, for example, subscribe to the view that the treatment of prisoners is a disgrace to our civilization. On the contrary, a voice would tell me: it is completely consonant with our civilization, a necessary expression of the brutality and the lack of judgment that govern our civilization today. And if miraculously the conviction were suddenly to arise that the reform of the criminal-justice system was to be our civilization's next and most urgent task, what other result would ensue but that capitalist society would not have the means to pay for this reform's requisite expenditures! The recognition of the other, external obstacle came at the point in your letter where you extol me as a recognized intellectual leader and cultural trailblazer, attributing to me a privileged position where the attentiveness of the civilized world is concerned. My dear sir, I wish that it were so; then I would not refuse you your wish. But it seems to me that I am *persona ingrata,* if not *ingratissima,* to the German people, to the learned and the unlearned alike. I certainly hope that you do not believe that I have been greatly offended by these expressions of disapproval. I have not acted so childishly in decades; and compared with your example, it would be too absurd. I mention these trivialities only to confirm that I am not the advocate you desire for a book that aims to rouse the vast reading public's sympathy for a good cause. Your book is otherwise quite moving, excellent, intelligent and good!

OSWALD SPENGLER

In my opinion, the problem raised by punishment in general must be distinguished from the very real fact of the prosecution of political activities. The latter belongs to the political struggle, the tendencies and forms of which are not legitimately applicable to questions of law and punishment. The political struggle is also a kind of war in which the participants must accept the consequences just as they do in every war—to the death and with no lamenting. But with regard to the so-called problem of criminal law, which has recently become a problem in revolutionary Germany, it is characteristic of every revolution to have a sentimental feeling of sympathy for the murderer rather than for the one who has been murdered. At present we cannot help but observe this phenomenon all around us, to the point of disgust. These disorderly ways are quite rightly made fun of abroad. And in the final analysis, this disorder can be traced back to the fact that there is no difference in moral values among revolutionaries, criminals, and the literati, not to mention their other differences. The German justice system, which before the war was unsurpassed in its incorruptibility and dignity, is now subverted, made into an object of contempt, and has become the concern of political parties with the result that respectable people's trust in the justice system is on the verge of disappearing. In light of this fact I consider a crime every assault on the remaining legal penalties that still have some authority and I would welcome and support, sight unseen, every stringent reformulation of the law that is conceivable. If after suspension of the death sentence the prison sentence is also dropped, then we run the risk of total anarchy; in light of this danger I strongly advocate the stringent reformulation of the laws now in force.

The following should be noted: the reform movement calling for a reformulation of criminal law and the execution of sentences is nowhere in Europe as fervent as in revolutionary Germany and Austria. But as concerns the civilized world outside Europe—the consciousness in the United States is much greater (due to the horrifying rise in criminality) that the prevailing methods used to fight crime and also those of pronouncing sentence are completely inadequate. The activities of the American Prison Association in all the states in the Union have shown that a change in the system is one of today's crucial issues. And now this tremendous upsurge in criminality that is starting to develop from the worldwide unemployment crisis! One observes, almost paralyzed in horror, how even now in the United States, in Germany, in Italy, and elsewhere it is not only unemployed, demoralized youth but often the hard-working and respectable men of mature years who, under the curse of not being able to work, lose all means of support (indeed there is no alternative). In despairing rage at their situation they join the constantly swelling ranks of the criminal class, whose army of members already numbers in the millions. They usually do so in the hope that they will be able to extricate themselves when "things get back to normal" and they once again find employment. Does one want to condemn categorically these men *ex officio* to a life of crime by stigmatizing them as convicts? Or will the means be sought which will help those get back on their feet whom, through no fault of their own, the rational-mechanization process has excluded and made into hapless outcasts? In truth if there is to be any salvation from the sense of helplessness brought about by the continuing state of crisis in the world that is driving the members of this now faltering but highly technologized civilization toward chaos, then the first problem to be solved will be that of purging the populace of its criminal elements and along with that the prison question!

327

SIEGFRIED KRACAUER

Murder Trials and Society

First published as "Mordprozeß und Gesellschaft," *Die neue Rundschau* 42 (March 1931), 431–432.

Murders in Berlin and elsewhere in Germany are on the increase. I am not thinking just of political murders—those street shootings and meeting-hall slaughters reported without interruption in the daily press. A striking number of bloody crimes are being committed by persons other than the National Socialists and the communists. Life has recently become cheap.

A careful observation of the Ulbrich murder trial yields some of the reasons for widespread unstable behavior in regard to the fundamentals of life and death. This case gains symptomatic significance in that the three youths involved are average people who cannot be essentially differentiated from others in their circles. I grant the inferiority of the perpetrators; still, Stolpe's brutality, Benziger's weak will, and the girl's erratic nature do not suffice to distinguish the three within their environment. An additional noteworthy factor is that they stumbled into the crime without any genuinely personal motivation. They were driven neither by the passion of lovers nor hate nor insatiable greed. In short, they did not really commit the murder, but simply happened upon it unexpectedly. Normal people are slipping toward atrocity without noticing their slide.

It is important to know that the perpetrators come from the milieu of the unemployed. Unemployment, which now affects approximately five million Germans, has long since ceased to be an individual fate. It has become the permanent condition of masses of Germans, and doubtless an immediate cause of the desperate, thoughtless games being played with life. For those who are cast out of the social order and condemned to a backstairs existence also lose sight of the accustomed rules of behavior. And the hopeless wait for a change cannot but render them utterly insensitive to the laws responsible for the preservation of order. I do not know of a single place in which waiting could be more demoralizing than in the Unemployment Office. Completely aside from the fact that in these stagnant times there is no manifest goal, what is lacking above all is the magic. Neither outrage is permitted to raise its voice here, nor can the enforced idleness be devoted to anything else. On the contrary, doing nothing can only take place in the shadows and must do without the title of nobility that is otherwise its due. Still there would be much to conjure, for in these rooms poverty has nothing to look at but itself. Abandoned to merely unmitigated presence together, the waiting these people suffer is doubly burdensome. The older ones perhaps befriend it like a comrade, but for the youthful unemployed it is a poison slowly working its way through their veins.

To the ominous lack of routine in which people without work are compelled to live is added the difficulty altogether of gaining a footing in current social conditions. It is exceedingly telling that Stolpe complained that he was verbally abused by the officers during his incarceration. (The judge's obvious reminder of Stolpe's own crime obviously did not really penetrate his consciousness.) In the letters of Lieschen Neumann as well, emphasis fell randomly on trivial and significant details. This remarkable deadening of the capacity to distinguish necessarily leads to particularly severe excesses in times of need; for if the murderer is vexed by a few rude words, then the murder he commits will seem to him nothing more than rudeness. Would that the perpetrators were still pathological in nature, but their normality marks the prevailing confusion of standards among them as the sign of a more general disposition. Certainly they went a step farther than most other, more inhibited people: but what made their crime possible was their loss of a doctrine to orient them in daily life. This is the other side of the German temperament and German philosophy—and it is not by accident that it becomes so plainly evident today: that it has opened the nation's daily life to all kinds of attacks and insinuations. In France, for example, there are still certain traditions that extend all the way from top to bottom, encompassing individuals relatively independently of social status, to enforce on all a specific attitude toward the basic facts of existence. Here, on the contrary, all things that go without saying are dying out one by one; our ethical foundations are being shaken along with the economic, and new points of stability are in the meantime wanting.

We live in a state of confusion which is recognizable by various signs. It is not the least betrayed by the disappearance of social hierarchy. The upper stratum has long since ceased to offer a true model for the so-called lower orders, however much property might still be desired and fashions imitated. At present it is neither capable of lending its ideological superstructure the force of ideas, nor does it influence the masses through its behavior. In a series of investigations that appeared several years ago in the *Frankfurter Zeitung,* "The Little Shop Girls Go to the Movies," I analyzed various exemplary social films, teasing from them a few truths that they are all too eager to conceal. It turned out, and this is easily demonstrated in the most recent films as well (for example, the sound film *The Private Secretary*), that though all of these productions endeavor to actualize the daydreams of the public through enticing depictions of high society, they in fact continually discredit the very same society. The suppression of binding social obligations is also intensified by the neutrality of important public expressions of opinion. This may in part be a result of domestic political tensions—but the other part undoubtedly signals a failure. Dominating the radio and ruling over the fake variety of juxtapositions in many big newspapers, neutrality expands to every area it possibly can to inspire the impression of plenitude—a neutrality that is the precise opposite of wisdom and attests to nothing more than the absence of any guiding principles. The lack of substantive consensus necessarily endangers the suffering masses the most. For Lieschen Neumann and her unemployed comrades, the insecurity of society in regard to all critical matters has become their doom.

The exceptional degree of this insecurity is what characterizes the overwhelming process of social transformation that has been our lot since the end of the world war. Until the new contours have become solidified, our path will continue to be marked by blood and tears.

Biographies

The following biographies seek to provide a context for understanding an author's background. Despite our best efforts, many lives could not be traced. Although we emphasize in the biographies the authors' contributions to the intellectual life of the Weimar Republic, we could not help being captivated with their fate after 1933. More than half of those women and men whom we consider to be the most representative of Weimar's astounding energy and spirit of innovation emigrated to the United States, especially to Los Angeles, which among emigrés was often jokingly referred to as "Weimar am Pazifik."

Adorno, Theodor W. (1903–1969), began his career as music and theater critic in Frankfurt. In 1930 he joined the Institut für Sozialforschung, later known as the Frankfurt School. Emigrated to New York in 1937, where he taught at Columbia; he moved to Los Angeles in 1941. Co-author with Max Horkheimer of *Dialectic of Enlightenment* (1947); co-author of *The Authoritarian Personality* (1950), an empirical study of prejudice and fascism. After 1950, professor for social philosophy at the University of Frankfurt. Concerned with avant-garde art and modernity; relentless critic of mass culture as manipulation.

Alexander, Franz (1891–1964), born in Budapest, became M.D. in 1913. A member of the neo-Freudian school of psychoanalysis, he was among the first to practice psychosomatic medicine in the late 1930s.

Arendt, Hannah (1906–1975), studied philosophy with Husserl and Jaspers; her writings also reflect Heidegger's influence. In 1933 she fled to France, then US, naturalized citizen in 1950. After working in various Jewish organizations, she became professor of political philosophy at the University of Chicago and the New School for Social Research. Author of *Origins of Totalitarianism* (1950) and *Eichmann in Jerusalem* (1961).

Arnheim, Rudolf (1904–), frequent contributor as film critic to *Die Weltbühne* during the late 1920s. His influential *Film as Art* (1932) addresses film as a creative interpretation (rather than mechanical recording) of the world. Emigrated to US in 1933, became citizen in 1946. Taught psychology of art at the University of Michigan.

Balázs, Béla [Herbert Bauer] (1884–1949), from a German-Hungarian family, came to Germany in 1926. Film director, screenplay writer, and journalist. His theoretical writings conceive an aesthetic for cinema based on its ability to perceive the world anew through close-up and montage (*Der sichtbare Mensch,* 1924; *Der Geist des Films,* 1930). After 1945, he worked to restore the Hungarian film industry.

Bartels, Adolf (1862–1945), a freelance writer and author of fiercely nationalistic and anti-Semitic German literary histories, which were widely read in the 1920s. Founded Deutscher Schillerbund in Weimar in 1907. An advocate and representative of *Heimatkunst* and an ardent Nazi (*Der Nationalsozialismus. Deutschlands Rettung,* 1924).

Bauer, Otto (1881–1938), born in Austria. Editor of the socialist *Arbeiter-Zeitung* and leader of the Austrian Marxists. Austrian Foreign Secretary in 1918–19. Emigrated in 1934 to Czechoslovakia, then France.

Bäumer, Gertrud (1873–1954), novelist and leading figure of the German women's movement. Co-editor (with Helene Lange) of periodical *Die Frau* (1893–1944), also editor of *Handbuch der Frauenbewegung* (5 vols.). Advisor to the Ministry of the Interior from 1919–33. Her cultural-historical texts focus on the position of women in modern society (*The War and Woman*, 1914).

Baum, Vicki (1888–1960), born in Vienna. Worked for the Ullstein publishing house. In 1919 she began to write light novels and stories set in contemporary urban contexts which dealt with social and economic issues, as well as the New Woman. In 1931 the most successful, *Menschen im Hotel* (1929), was filmed as *Grand Hotel* in Hollywood. Went to US in 1931, became US citizen.

Becher, Johannes R. (1891–1958), writer and activist. Member of Spartacus League and Communist Party. A deputy in the Reichstag, he was charged with treason for his poetry (*Der Leichnam auf dem Thron*, 1925) and novel (*Levisite*, 1926). While his early work displayed expressionist sensibilities, he later advocated socialist realism. Co-founded the Bund Proletarisch-Revolutionärer Schriftsteller, a communist writers' association, in 1928. Emigrated to USSR in 1934. Became Minister of Culture in the German Democratic Republic after the war.

Beckmann, Max (1884–1950), painter and graphic artist. Met Edvard Munch in 1906. Although initially trained as an impressionist, he adopted expressionist style and thematics, as seen in "The Night" (1918) and his self-portraits. After 1933, his works were judged "degenerate" by the Nazis. Went to Paris in 1937, to Amsterdam in 1938; he eventually settled in the US and taught art at Washington University in St. Louis.

Behne, Adolf (1885–1948), author, journalist, and art critic. Contributed to numerous newspapers and periodicals in the 1920s, including *Die Weltbühne*.

Benjamin, Walter (1892–1940), cultural critic and literary journalist in Berlin. Influenced by both Marxist theory and Jewish mystical tradition, he was associated with Adorno and Gershom Scholem; he was also a friend of Brecht. Concerned with topics of mass culture ("The Work of Art in the Age of Mechanical Reproduction"), high culture (*Origin of German Tragic Drama*), and modernity (*The Arcades Project*). In 1933, settled in Paris. Committed suicide on the Spanish border while attempting to reach the US.

Benn, Gottfried (1886–1956), expressionist poet (*Morgue*, 1912), and a military doctor during World War I. Throughout the 1920s, his poems and essays sought to situate literature outside of history. He retreated into "inner emigration" after a brief infatuation with the fascist worldview. After World War II, hailed as a major literary figure in the Federal Republic of Germany.

Berg, Alban (1885–1935), born in Vienna, trained under Schoenberg. Influenced by Debussy and Mahler. Wrote *Three Orchestral Pieces* in 1914–15, which only was performed after the success of his atonal opera *Wozzeck* in 1925. His opera *Lulu*, based on Frank Wedekind's plays, remained unfinished.

Bettauer, Hugo (1872–1925), prolific Austrian writer whose novel, *The Joyless Street*, was filmed by G. W. Pabst in 1925. Author of *Stadt ohne Juden* (1924). Murdered by an anti-Semitic fanatic.

Biha, Otto [Bihalji] (1900–n.d.), born in Yugoslavia. After 1929 literary critic and editor at the Communist literary periodical *Die Linkskurve* in Berlin. Emigrated to Paris in 1933. Returned to Belgrade in 1945.

Bloch, Ernst (1885–1977), Marxist philosopher and essayist. Friend of Lukács, Benjamin, Adorno, Brecht. His early works (*Spirit of Utopia,* 1918; *Thomas Münzer,* 1921; *Heritage of Our Times,* 1935) reflect both an expressionistic rebellion against his industrialized hometown of Ludwigshafen and a rejection of patriotism and nationalism in favor of a utopian ideal. Emigrated in 1933 to Czechoslovakia, in 1938 to US. Wrote *The Principle of Hope* (3 vols) in American exile but did not publish it until 1959. From 1945–57 professor of philosophy at the University of Leipzig. Left East Germany in 1961, taught in Tübingen.

Brecht, Bertolt (1898–1956), born in Augsburg. Quit medical school and pursued a career writing poetry and drama. In 1922 received the Kleist Prize for *Trommeln in der Nacht*; moved to Berlin in 1924, directed for Max Reinhardt, and learned Marxist theory from Karl Korsch and Fritz Sternberg. With Kurt Weill he wrote *The Threepenny Opera* in 1928, which embodied his paradigm of "epic theater." Emigrated to Scandanavia in 1937 and to US in 1941. Worked with Fritz Lang on *Hangmen also Die* (1943). Was investigated by the Anti-Communist "House Un-American Activities Committee." Returned to East Germany in 1949 and co-founded the Berliner Ensemble.

Breuer, Marcel (1902–1981), born in Hungary. Studied architecture and design at the Bauhaus from 1920–25. Was appointed master of carpentry and joinery. His furniture designs, including the tubular chair, reflect modernist principles of technology and space. Emigrated to US in 1937, taught at Harvard University with Gropius until 1946.

Brockdorff-Rantzau, Count Ulrich von (1859–1928), trained in law, entered diplomatic service in 1894, envoy to Denmark, 1912–18. Supported the October Revolution in czarist Russia, but sought to prevent a similar revolution in Germany. Foreign Minister in Scheidemann's cabinet. Led the German delegation to Versailles. From 1922–28 ambassador to USSR.

Brod, Max (1884–1968), born in Prague, civil servant, and a theater and music critic. Friend and supporter of Kafka, he edited and published works like *The Castle* and *America* after the author's death. His own writings reflect his Zionist affiliations, and are infused with a religious world view (*Tycho Brahes Weg zu Gott,* 1916). Emigrated to Palestine in 1939.

Bronnen, Arnolt (1895–1959), expressionist playwright, novelist, and author of radio plays; friend of Brecht in the early 1920s. Although his play *Vatermord* (1913) caused a scandal due to its radical anti-authoritarian, leftist stance, he shifted his political allegiance to National Socialism by the mid-twenties. Forbidden to write in 1937 and expelled from the Party in 1940. Joined a communist resistance movement.

Buber, Martin (1878–1965), born in Vienna, studied philosophy and art history. Became a Zionist in 1898, but rejected the exclusiveness of the political branch of the movement. Worked at Frankfurt Lehrhaus with Franz Rosenzweig, translated the Hebrew Bible into German (1925–38), and wrote on Hassidic culture. *I and Thou* (1927) articulates a dialogical form of spirituality. Emigrated in 1938 to Palestine and taught at the Hebrew University.

Bülow, Prince Bernhard von (1849–1929), diplomat after his service in war of 1871. A skillful negotiator, in 1897 he became Foreign Secretary and chancellor of the Empire from 1900–1909.

Darré, R[ichard] W[alter] (1895–1953), born in Belgrano near Buenos Aires; attended German colonial school. Volunteer in German army during World War I. Diplomas in colonial economics and agronomy. In 1928 consultant to the German embassy in Riga. In

1928 published *The Peasantry as the Life Source of the Nordic Race*. Affiliated with Nazis after 1930, close to Himmler. In 1933 became Minister of Agriculture.

Diem, Carl (1882–1962), leader of various governmental sports bureaus. Organized the 1936 Olympics in Berlin. From 1938–45, head of the International Olympic Institute in Berlin.

Döblin, Alfred (1878–1957), novelist and political journalist. Served as army doctor in war. Member of expressionist circles in Berlin, published his first stories in 1913. A socialist who practiced medicine in the Berlin slums, he was also a proponent of the modernist novel with its rejection of realism in favor of montage, stream-of-consciousness, and urban setting (*Berlin Alexanderplatz,* 1929). In 1933, fled to France, then California, converted from Judaism to Catholicism. Returned to Germany in 1945 as a reeducation officer. Emigrated to Paris in 1949.

Eich, Günter (1907–1972), lyrical poet; worked with Klaus Mann on the *Anthologie jüngster Lyrik* (1927), while a student of Chinese and law. Went into "inner emigration" and concentrated on radio plays and poetry. An American POW, he became a major figure of postwar literature in West Germany.

Einstein, Albert (1879–1955), theoretical physicist. His early work on relativity, Brownian motion, and the photoelectric effect (for which he received the Nobel Prize in 1922) affected both the scientific and the intellectual communities through its reconceptualization of the relationship between time and space. Promoted Franco-German relations; by 1933, he advocated complete disarmament. Emigrated in 1932, took US citizenship, and taught at Princeton. Although aware of the inherent dangers, he supported the development of atomic weapons, but returned to pacifism after Hiroshima and Nagasaki.

Einstein, Carl (1885–1940), an art critic, editor, and dramatist, he was an early member of expressionist and dadaist circles in Berlin. After serving in Brussels during the war, he became a Spartacist. He was charged with blasphemy for his play *Die schlimme Botschaft*. Fought in Spanish Civil War in 1936, interned in 1940 at Bordeaux. He committed suicide when the Nazis invaded France.

Eisler, Hanns (1898–1962), studied with Schoenberg after serving in war. A member of the KPD from 1926, he composed music for Communist choirs and agit-prop shows. Collaborated with Brecht, and wrote *Composing for the Film* (1947) with Adorno. Emigrated in 1933 to USSR, and in 1938 to US. Deported after House Un-American Activities Committee hearing, he settled in East Berlin. He composed the national anthem of the GDR.

Engelbrecht, Ernst (1884–n.d.), a police superintendant in Berlin. Author of fictional and nonfictional books on urban criminality, as well as film scripts for crime thrillers.

Feuchtwanger, Lion (1884–1958), playwright and internationally recognized novelist. His stories often employ historical settings to comment on the position of Jews in Germany. His bestseller *Jud Süß* (1925) was later appropriated by the Nazis for a propaganda film. Friend and supporter of Brecht. Expatriated in 1933, interned by Vichy government, but escaped to US. Lived near Thomas Mann in Pacific Palisades after 1941. Co-editor of exile periodical *Das Wort*.

Finckh, Ludwig (1876–1964), born in Swabia, studied medicine and law, doctor during World War I. His poetry and prose are intimately connected to Swabian landscape and history. Prolific author of texts on genealogy and race favored by the Nazis.

Fleißer, Marieluise (1901–1974), playwright and novelist. While studying in Munich, she became acquainted with Feuchtwanger and Brecht, who negotiated a Berlin production of her play, *Fegefeuer in Ingolstadt* in 1926. Her work thematizes the encounter with the metropolis, sexuality, and women's experiences, while her consciously barren style reflects the influence of Brecht and the popularity of the *Volksstück*. Left Berlin after friendship with Brecht ended. Forbidden to write under the Nazis.

Freud, Sigmund (1856–1939), doctor in Vienna and father of psychoanalysis, studied medicine, specialization in neurology, trained under Charcot in Paris. His *Studies of Hysteria* (with Breuer) (1895) and *The Interpretation of Dreams* (1900) mark the beginnings of modern psychoanalysis. In the 1920s his focus shifted from individual cases studies to the examination of larger social phenomena including religious belief (*The Future of an Illusion,* 1928) and culture (*Civilization and its Discontents,* 1930). His books were among the first burned by the Nazis. After the annexation of Austria he moved to London.

Freyer, Hans (1887–1969), professor of sociology in Kiel and Leipzig. Theoretical writings on rationality and the state (*Der Staat,* 1925; *Revolution von rechts,* 1931).

Frisch, Efraim (1873–1942), born in Austria, studied law, philosophy, art history, and literature. A consultant to publishing houses in Berlin, dramaturg at the Deutsches Theater and teacher at the Reinhardt School. Medical orderly in army from 1915–18. Continued as theater critic, novelist, and translator after the war. In 1933 he emigrated to Switzerland.

Fuchs, Georg (1868–1949), initiator of Munich Künstlertheater. Participated in separatist movement in Bavaria. In 1923 sentenced to twelve years in prison for high treason, released in 1927. In *Wir Zuchthäusler* he wrote about prison reform.

Gehrke, M[artha] M[aria] (1904–n.d.), studied literature. Journalist and author of popular self-help novels and radio plays throughout the 1920s.

Geiger, Theodor Julius (1891–1952), studied law. His sociological studies of the metropolis and industrial society focus upon group formation, social classes, and legal sociology.

Georg, Hanns [Erwin Schoettle] (1899–1976), member of the SPD, active in politics. Editor of Social Democratic paper, he advocated solidarity with the KPD against National Socialism. Fled to England in 1939 and was interned. Returned to Germany in 1946.

Georg, Manfred (1893–1965), correspondent, feuilleton editor, and theater critic in Berlin. Author of novels, short stories, and biographies. In 1933 emigrated to Prague and established the *Jüdische Revue.* In 1938 exile in the US. Founded the German Jewish newspaper, *Aufbau.*

Gert, Valeska [Gertrud Anderson] (1892–1978), expressionist dancer whose comic-grotesque dance and pantomime provoked scandal in Berlin. Performed in left-wing cabarets and on stage. Also acted under Pabst's direction in *Joyless Streets* (1925), *Diary of a Lost Girl* (1929), and *The Threepenny Opera* (1931). Fled to Britain, naturalized citizen in 1936. Emigrated to New York in 1938. Later returned to West Germany.

Goebbels, Paul Joseph (1897–1945), Nazi Minister of Propaganda. Catholic, son of an accountant, unable to serve in war due to lameness. Received Ph.D. in literature in 1922. Author of novel *Michael* (1929). Interested in modernism. Initially, more leftist member of the Nazi Party, in 1926 became party head in Berlin, major campaign organizer, and orator for Hitler. Spearheaded the book burnings and Kristallnacht in 1938. He controlled artistic production and the media during the Third Reich. Advocated total mobilization of war after 1943. Following Hitler's suicide, he and his family ended their lives with poison.

Goll, Ivan [Isaac Lang], (1891–1950), German citizen, bilingual in French and German. A pacifist, he spent the war in Switzerland. Best known in Germany for his lyric poetry, which shifted from an expressionist to a surrealist style under the influence of Joyce and Apollinaire. From 1919 worked as foreign correspondent for German newspapers in Paris. Emigrated to New York in 1939. Returned to Paris in 1947.

Gottl-Ottilienfeld, Friedrich von (1868–1958), born in Vienna, from 1926 professor of political economy in Berlin. His hotly debated theoretical writings, heavily influenced by Dilthey, united economic theory, history, and sociology (*Fordismus,* 1924), and developed a cultural theory of economy.

Gräff, Werner Friedrich (1901–1978), studied art and photography in Berlin until 1920 and then under Oskar Schlemmer at the Bauhaus. Freelance photographer; worked with Hans Richter on films. Emigrated in 1934 to Spain and 1936 to Locarno. Returned to Berlin in 1947.

Graeser, Wolfgang (1906–1928), born in Zurich, grew up in Naples and Munich. Something of a boy genius, he exhibited paintings in Munich in 1919 when he was twelve. Studied mathematics, physics, and Asian languages. Published study of Bach (*Kunst der Fuge*) in same year as *Körpersinn,* which was influenced by—and dedicated to—Spengler. After severe nervous breakdown, committed suicide at twenty-one.

Gropius, Walter (1883–1969), studied with architect Peter Behrens. Sought to reform European society through radical groups like the Novembergruppe and the Arbeitsrat für Kunst. Founded the Bauhaus in 1919 as reorganization of the Weimar School of Arts and Crafts. Designer of the Dessau Bauhaus (1925) and the Fagus Shoe-Last factory, which illustrate principles of space and flexibility through use of glass and steel. The target of violent right-wing opposition, he left Germany in 1934, moving first to England, then to US, where he taught at Harvard University and became a US citizen.

Grosz, George[e] (1893–1959), painter and member of Berlin Dada group; anglicized his first name out of protest against German militarism. Relentless critic of German bourgeoisie. Due to the political nature of his work, he was charged several times with blasphemy and treason. Co-authored *Die Kunst ist in Gefahr* in 1925, advocating the service of art to politics. Emigrated to New York in 1933 to teach art. Died in an accident after returning to Berlin.

Gumbel, Emil Julius (1891–1966), studied mathematics and economics, volunteered in World War I, became a pacifist in 1915. A republican and advocate of reconciliation with France, he made many right-wing enemies, who later forced his discharge from the University of Heidelberg in 1932. Emigration to France, then to US in 1940, where he taught at the New School for Social Research in New York.

Haas, Willy (1891–1973), born in Prague, friends with Kafka and Brod. Established *Die literarische Welt,* a literary journal as forum for the younger generation, in 1925. In 1939 emigrated to India and wrote screenplays. After returning to Hamburg in 1947, he worked as a literary critic at *Die Welt.* Edited Kafka's letters and collections of Tucholsky's essays.

Halfeld, Adolf (1898–1955), conservative cultural critic. Published on relationship of Germany to US (*Kulturen und Revolution,* 1924; *Amerika und Amerikanismus,* 1928).

Hartlaub, Gustav Friedrich (1884–1963), art historian and author, from 1923–33 he was director of the Kunsthalle Mannheim. He was the first to exhibit paintings from the anti-expressionist school of the New Objectivity.

Hausenstein, Wilhelm (1882–1957), art historian and radical Social Democrat. Served as the Federal Republic's first ambassador to France from 1953–55.

Hauser, Henrich (1901–1955), wrote travel literature and stories. Also authored polemics against Hitler. Emigrated to US in 1938.

Hausmann, Raoul (1886–1971), born in Vienna, taught himself photography. Associated with *Der Sturm* and *Die Aktion,* later co-founded Club Dada. Pioneer of the photomontage and organizer of first Dada Exhibition in 1919 with Grosz and Heartfield. Emigrated 1933 to Spain, 1939 to France.

Heartfield, John [Helmut Herzfeld] (1891–1968), anglicized his name in 1915 as protest against anti-British propaganda. Developed his collage technique within expressionist and dadaist circles in Berlin with Grosz. Designer at the communist Malik publishing house, and for Reinhardt's and Piscator's theaters. A member of KPD from 1919. His photomontages graphically attacked nationalism and imperialism and celebrated Soviet communism. Emigrated to Prague in 1933, then London. Returned to East Germany in 1950.

Heidegger, Martin (1889–1976), a Jesuit novice, doctorate in philosophy, in 1915 lecturer at Freiburg under Husserl. His rejection of technology and modernization echoes throughout *Sein and Zeit* (1927) which struggles with questions of existence. Was appointed rector by the Nazis in 1933, but resigned in 1934. Dismissed in 1945 due to initial enthusiasm for Nazis, but reinstated in 1951.

Heller, Leo (1876–1949), writer and editor in Berlin. Wrote stories about the city and crime (*Rund um den Alex,* 1924). Co-authored *Berliner Razzien* (1924) and *Kinder der Nacht* (1926) with Engelbrecht.

Hellpach, Willy Hugo (1877–1955), neurologist. Authored *Die geopsychischen Erscheinungen* (1923) which posited a relationship between geological conditions and mental health. During the war, became interested in physiognomy of German races and in politics. After a series of political offices in Baden-Württemberg, nominated as candidate for president in 1925 by German Democratic Party (DDP).

Hesse, Hermann (1877–1962), novelist and poet. Grew up in Basel, lived in Germany, and resumed Swiss citizenship in 1923. Influenced by Pietist traditions, he studied theology before becoming a writer. In 1911 he traveled to India, and from 1916 underwent psychoanalysis. His works in the 1920s coincide with cultural interest in spirituality, mysticism, the Romantic tradition (*Märchen,* 1919), Eastern religion (*Siddharta,* 1922), and adolescence. Received Nobel Prize in 1946.

Hessel, Franz (1880–1941), born in Poland, essayist and reader at Rowohlt Verlag from 1919–33. Translator of French texts by Balzac, Stendahl. Collaborated with Benjamin on translation of Proust's *Remembrance of Things Past* (1926). Emigrated in 1938 to Paris. Interned in French concentration camp in 1940.

Heuss, Theodor (1884–1963), studied art history and political economy, editor of *Die Hilfe* from 1905–1912. A member of the liberal German Democratic Party (DDP), twice elected to parliament. From 1920–1933 he taught at the Hochschule für Politik in Berlin. Although banned from writing by the Nazis, continued to do so under the pseudonym Brackenheim. Elected the first president of the Federal Republic in 1949 and again in 1954 under the banner of the Free Democratic party.

Hilferding, Rudolf (1877–1944), doctor in Austro-Hungarian army. An active socialist, he edited numerous journals including *Vorwärts,* and the USPD organ, *Die Freiheit*. In 1910 he published *Das Finanzkapital,* linking war and imperialism. After taking German citizenship in 1919, joined the SPD, served as Finance Minister in 1923 (and introduced the Reichsmark), and again in 1928–29. Emigrated to Switzerland in 1933, then to Paris. He was arrested after France capitulated, and later found hanged in cell.

Hiller, Kurt (1885–1972), student of law, enamored with expressionism, he founded the Neuer Klub and the cabaret "Gnu," where the activists protested the authoritarianism of the empire. Developed a theory of "Logokratie" in which "Geist" would rule. With Helene Stöcker, he was active in pacifist movement; early spokesman for gay rights. Released after a year in Oranienburg, in 1934 went to Prague, then London. Returned to Hamburg in 1955.

Hindemith, Paul (1895–1963), studied, performed, and composed music from an early age. His work is satirical and iconoclastic in theme, dissonant and yet tonal. Conceptualized *Gebrauchsmusik* and became a leader of the avantgarde. After his anti-authoritarian opera, *Mathis der Maler* (1935), forbidden to teach or perform. Exile in Turkey, Switzerland, then US, where he taught at Yale until 1953.

Hindenburg, Paul von Beneckendorff und von (1847–1934), served in Franco-Prussian war. In World War I gained reputation as victor at Tannenburg (1914), became a field marshal and advocated all-out war. His memoirs (*Aus meinem Leben,* 1920) supported the stab-in-the-back legend. Elected president of Weimar Republic in 1925, he named Hitler chancellor in 1933.

Hirschfeld, Magnus (1868–1935), Berlin doctor. Advanced a theory of a gender continuum and worked for social acceptance and decriminalization of homosexuality. Founded the internationally recognized Institute of Sexology in 1919 and the first marriage counseling facility, which were destroyed by Nazi students in 1933. Moved to Paris and founded the Institute des Sciences Sexologiques.

Hitler, Adolf (1889–1945), son of Austrian customs officer, decorated as soldier in Bavarian Army during World War I, failed artist. Co-founder of NSDAP (Nationalsozialistische Deutsche Arbeiterpartei) in 1920. After a failed coup attempt in 1923, he was imprisoned and wrote *Mein Kampf* (published in 1925), which details his anti-Semitic, totalitarian concept of politics. After his release (after serving only a few months) he sought to gain power by parliamentary means. Acquired German citizenship in 1932, and on January 30, 1933 he was named chancellor. Suicide in 1945 in Berlin.

Hofmannsthal, Hugo von (1874–1929), Austrian poet and playwright, influenced by impressionism and symbolism. His fin-de-siècle works attracted the attention of Arthur Schnitzler and Stefan George. The "Chandos Letter" (1902) characterizes the artist's alienation in the modern world as a rift between language and reality. Collaborated with composer Richard Strauss (*Der Rosenkavalier,* 1911); they co-founded the Salzburg Festival in 1920 with Max Reinhardt. His interwar writings focus on the preservation and rejuvenation of European culture.

Hollaender, Felix (1867–1931), after working at the Deutsches Theater with Reinhardt from 1908–13, headed the Großes Schauspielhaus from 1920–1931. Introduced Shaw and Strindberg to Germany. Wrote socialist novels in the style of naturalism.

Hollaender, Friedrich (1896–1976), born in London. Composed for orchestra and cabaret, and for Reinhardt's theatrical productions. Also wrote numerous film scores, including for *The Blue Angel.* Opened the Tingeltangel Theater in 1931. In 1933 he emigrated to the US.

Hollander, Walther von (1892–1973), served in World War I. From 1918 to 1920 editor and theater critic in Bavaria, afterwards bookseller and left-wing critic in Berlin. Member of Gruppe 25, a support group of young authors in Berlin.

Horkheimer, Max (1895–1973), Marxist philosopher. Member of the Frankfurt Institut für Sozialforschung, he became director in 1930. Articulated the basic principles of the Frankfurt School's critique of technological and industrial society, which interpreted cultural phenomena in light of the interdependence of political and economic factors. In 1933 he moved to US, returning to Frankfurt in 1950 to teach at the University and re-establish the Institut.

Huelsenbeck, Richard (1892–1974), writer and critic, co-founder of Dada, carried the movement from Zurich to Berlin. In 1936 he emigrated to US and practiced psychiatry in New York. Returned to Switzerland in 1970.

Jacobsohn, Siegfried (1881–1926), influential theater critic, established and edited journal *Die Schaubühne* after 1905. The scope of the journal expanded during war, becoming more politically engaged; it changed its name in 1918 to *Die Weltbühne.* Friendship with Ossietzky, Tucholsky, Jhering, Feuchtwanger, Polgar.

Jannings, Emil (1884–1950), theater and film actor; worked in theater after 1900, under Max Reinhardt from 1915. Major film roles: the porter in *The Last Laugh* and Professor Rath in *The Blue Angel.* Known for his physiognomy and comic talent, he worked with Josef von Sternberg in Hollywood from 1926–29. Won an Oscar for best actor. Returned to Germany in 1929 when sound film arrived. Continued career under Nazis.

Jaspers, Karl (1883–1969), psychiatrist who, thanks to Max Weber, became professor of philosophy in 1921, but as an adamant critic of totalitarian government was dismissed in 1933. Settled in Basel in 1948. His existentialism relies on the definition of the "limit situation" as a moment of self-discovery, and the experience of transcendence through failure. After 1945, opposed development of atomic weapons (*Die Atombombe und die Zukunft der Menschen,* 1957).

Jessner, Leopold (1878–1945), theater manager and director in Hamburg, assumed leadership of Berlin Staatstheater in 1919. Politicized classical plays, replacing fable with the *idea* of fable through use of symbolism. Due to public outcry against his parodic and anti-monarchist *Hamlet* in 1926, stepped down as director but continued to direct until 1933. Emigrated to Palestine, then Hollywood.

Jhering, Herbert (1888–1977), theater and film critic in Berlin, then dramaturg and director in Vienna, returned to Berlin in 1918. Strong supporter of Brecht and advocate of plays of New Objectivity. Film criticism meant for him social criticism.

Johst, Hanns (1890–1978), expressionist playwright and novelist. After serving in the war, he wrote plays and novels with nationalistic tendencies. A member of the NSDAP, he authored the widely acclaimed nationalistic play *Schlageter* (1933). From 1935–45, president of the Nazi literary academy, SS brigade leader, and personal friend of Hitler and Himmler. After 1945, interned for war crimes.

Jung, Edgar Julius (1894–1934), journalist and contributor to conservative papers. Was lieutenant in war, member of Freikorps, and after 1923 lawyer in Munich. A member of several right-wing groups and advisor to Papen, he was critical of the Hitler regime. Arrested in 1934 and shot.

Jünger, Ernst (1895–), joined Foreign Legion at eighteen, enlisted in 1914, wounded seven times, decorated with Pour le Mérite. His early writings glorify and aestheticize his war experiences (*In Stahlgewittern*, 1920). As a journalist for conservative papers he propagated an authoritarian society based on a new technologized warrior class (*Der Arbeiter*, 1932). Criticized vulgarity of Nazis in the novel *Auf den Marmorklippen* (1939).

Kalveram, Wilhelm (1882–1951), taught political science at Frankfurt. His work focuses on the relationship between banking and other branches of the economy.

Kästner, Erich (1899–1974), poet and journalist; moved to Berlin in 1927. His satirical cabaret chansons, witty poetry and prose engaged contemporary political events and urban life (*Fabian*, 1931), employing the style of New Objectivity. Also wrote successful children's books, e.g. *Emil und die Detektive*, 1927.

Kaus, Gina (1894–1985), Austrian essayist, playwright, and novelist (*Die Verliebten*, 1928), acquainted with Broch, Werfel, Musil, and Kraus in Vienna. In Berlin she established the periodical *Die Mutter* and a women's counseling center. Her works thematize love relationships and her protagonists are usually women. In 1938 she emigrated to Hollywood where she wrote screenplays. Contact with Brecht, Eisler, and Baum.

Kayser, Rudolf (1889–1964), professor of literature and publisher of *Die neue Rundschau*. His writings extend from literary expressionism to biographies (Lenin, Bismarck) and cultural critiques (*Die Zeit ohne Mythos*, 1923). In 1933 he emigrated to Holland and then to the US. Taught at Brandeis University from 1951 to 1957.

Keményi, Alfred (1895–1945), studied art history in Budapest. Supported the Hungarian Soviet Republic in 1919 and joined the KPD in 1923. Editor of *Die Rote Fahne* in Berlin, he wrote on Marxist aesthetics and belonged to Herwarth Walden's Sturm group.

Kessler, Count Harry (1868–1937), born in Paris of German and English parents, cosmopolitan upbringing. Friends with Hofmannsthal, Munch, Strauss. As diplomat in London, contested allied presence on Rhine in 1923. Founding member of the German Democratic Party (DDP) and pacifist. After illness in 1926–27 withdrew from political arena to follow career as man of letters. Exile in Paris from 1933.

Keyserling, Count Hermann (1880–1946), writer and sharp observer of life in Berlin in the 1920s. Born in Russia, he studied sciences and combined philosophy, cultural history, and personal experience in his diaries on foreign cultures (*Reisetagebuch eines Philosophen,* 1919), the interwar period, and America. Founded Society for Free Philosophy in 1920, and promoted Franco-German relations.

Kienle, Else (1900–1970), gynecologist. In 1928 she established her own practice in Stuttgart and headed sexual counseling center. Fought Paragraph 218, was arrested in 1931 with Friedrich Wolf for performing illegal abortions. Wrote *Frauen. Aus dem Tagebuch einer Ärztin* (1932) while in prison.

Kisch, Egon Erwin (1885–1948), born in Prague. Journalist and travel writer. After serving in war, he moved to Berlin in 1921 and was active in several Communist organizations. Through his journalistic reportage and travel books he advocated a politically engaged literature. Arrested after Reichstag fire, released, emigrated to Paris in 1933, lived in Mexico from 1940–46. Returned to Prague.

Kleist-Schmenzin, Ewald von (1890–1945), officer in war. A staunch conservative, he contested the Weimar Republic as "ungodly," but also rejected National Socialism, and warned against its racism and imperialism. In 1938 traveled to London to secure support against Hitler. In 1945 he was arrested and executed for plotting against Hitler.

Knauf, Erich (1895–1944), son of a worker, politically active in left wing of SPD. From 1922–27, cultural and literary critic for workers' presses. Known for his reportage-style novel about the Kapp Putsch, *Ça ira* (1930). Hanged by Nazis for subversive activities.

Koch, Adolf (1897–1970), socialist teacher in Berlin until dismissed for advocating and practicing nudism. He believed that nudism would improve the alienated and unnatural condition of the working class and eliminate class barriers. Opened numerous body culture schools (closed by the Nazis) which offered gymnastics, sexual consultation, and therapy. Prolific writer on nudism and physical education, for example, *Wir sind nackt und nennen uns Du* (1932).

Köppen, Edlef (1893–1939), editor in Verlag Gustav Kiepenheuer from 1921. Worked in radio from 1925. Was dismissed in 1933. Author of the anti-war novel, *Heeresbericht* (1930).

Korff, Kurt (1876–1938), editor-in-chief of *Berliner Illustrirte* from 1905, and *Die Dame* from 1911, he re-oriented the papers to focus on topical issues and to use more illustrations and photographs. In 1933 he emigrated to Vienna, then to US in 1935, where he worked as an advisor to *Life* magazine.

Korsch, Karl (1886–1961), 1912 member of SPD; 1919 USPD, 1923 KPD. Also in 1923 became professor of law in Jena. *Marxism and Philosophy* (1923) argues for a restitution of Hegelian Marxian ideas (against Leninist orthodoxy). Left KPD in 1926. Teacher of Brecht. Emigrated to England in 1933, and to US in 1936.

Kortner, Fritz (1892–1970), actor on stage and in film. Born in Vienna, studied acting, and became member of Reinhardt's Deutsches Theater. After being boycotted by Nazis, emigrated to Austria, England, and US in 1937. Called before the House Un-American Activities Committee to testify in Brecht hearing. Returned to Germany in 1947.

Kracauer, Siegfried (1889–1966), studied architecture, philosophy, and sociology. Worked as an architect until 1921 when he became a literary and film critic for the *Frankfurter*

Zeitung. In close contact with Löwenthal, Adorno, Bloch, and Benjamin, he wrote social critiques that were influenced by Marxism. After his dismissal in 1933, he spent eight years in Paris before moving to New York. In 1947 published *From Caligari to Hitler* which argues that tyrannical figures in expressionist films prefigure Hitler and his regime. Research at Columbia University. In 1960 published *Theory of Film: The Redemption of Physical Reality*.

Krenek, Ernst (1900–1992), composer known for his Jazz opera, *Jonny spielt auf* (1927). After 1932 adopted and further developed Schoenberg's twelve tone system. In 1938 emigrated to US and taught at University of California.

Landau, Lola [Leonore] (1892–n.d.), author, poet, and journalist in Berlin until 1933, when she emigrated to Palestine.

Landsberger, Artur (1876–1933), author whose novels are set in the milieu of Berlin (*Das Ghettobuch*, 1914; *Berlin ohne Juden*, 1925). Also was interested in satanism.

Lang, Fritz (1890–1976), born in Vienna, studied art and architecture, served in war. In 1918 moved to Berlin to work as screenwriter and director. Highly stylized, his films embrace the mythical past (*Die Nibelungen*, 1924) and the dystopian future (*Metropolis*, 1926/27); they address the experiences and fears of the urban dweller (*M*, 1931). Rejecting Goebbels' offer of the leadership of the German film industry, he emigrated to Paris in 1933 and Hollywood in 1934 and continued a highly successful career as director. Returned briefly to Germany after the war but died in Los Angeles.

Lessing, Theodor (1872–1933), social and cultural critic. Wrote aggressive polemics against Hindenburg. Murdered by Nazis in 1933 after emigration to Czechoslovakia.

Lihotzky, Grete [Schütte-Lihotzky] (1897–), Austrian architect; studied applied art with Heinrich Tessenow in Vienna. From 1921 to 1925 collaboration with Adolf Loos. Housing design with Ernst May from 1926–30, including famous "Frankfurt Kitchen." Constructed new cities in Soviet Union from 1930–37. Imprisoned from 1941–45 for anti-Nazi activity in Austria. Architect in Vienna after 1947.

Löwenthal, Leo (1900–1993), after brief military service in 1918, from 1923–26 editor of various Jewish publications in Frankfurt. Member of the Institut für Sozialforschung from 1926–49, he concentrated on literary sociology and analysis of mass culture. Emigrated to US in 1934. Director of research for Voice of America, 1949–54. Professor of sociology at the University of California at Berkeley.

Lüders, Marie-Elisabeth (1878–1966), studied economics, first woman in Germany to receive Ph.D. Member of German Democratic Party in 1918, supported acceptance of Treaty of Versailles. Member of Reichstag in 1920–21 and 1924–30. Fought for the reform of the rights of women and children, and of the penal system. Arrested briefly in 1934 by Nazis. After war, active in Berlin politics.

Lukács, Georg (1885–1971), born in Budapest, converted to communism in 1918, active in Hungarian politics after the war. His *History and Class Consciousness* (1923) was founding text of Hegelian Marxism. Studies of literature influenced the development of Socialist Realism. Active in Berlin in building up a writers' association that was close to Moscow. As participant in the expressionism debate of 1933–34, he attacked Brecht's aesthetics of distantiation as "non-realist." Emigration to Moscow in 1933. Returned to Budapest in 1944. After the Hungarian Revolution in 1956, became private scholar.

Luxemburg, Rosa (1870–1919), political writer and radical socialist. Born in Poland, studied economics in Zurich and wrote for the SPD organ. Imprisoned for anti-war propaganda in Germany where she wrote the "Junius Pamphlet." Also authored *The Accumulation of Capital*; co-founder of the Spartacus League and the KPD, and advocate of socialist revolution in Germany. In January 1919 she and Karl Liebknecht were arrested and shot by Freikorps troops in Berlin.

Mann, Heinrich (1871–1950), born in Lübeck. His savagely satirical portraits of Wilhelmine Germany culminated in his novel of 1905, *Professor Unrat*, filmed as *The Blue Angel* in 1930. A humanist, democrat and pacifist, he attacked brother Thomas's nationalistic response to the war. Ran for president of Germany in 1925. Advocated Franco-German reconciliation, and lived in France until 1940, when Feuchtwanger aided his escape to California. In 1949, elected president of new Academy of Arts in the GDR, but died before return.

Mann, Thomas (1875–1955), born in Lübeck. His first major novel, *Buddenbrooks* (1900), earned him the Nobel Prize for Literature in 1929. After book-length essay, *Reflections of an Unpolitical Man* (1918) in which he argued for a conservative, anti-Western "German" agenda, he tirelessly spoke out in defense of the democratic forces of the Republic. His novel *The Magic Mountain* appeared in 1924. Emigration to US in 1938, naturalized American citizen in 1942, returned to Switzerland in 1952.

Mannheim, Karl (1893–1947), born in Budapest, part of Lukács circle. Studied sociology under Alfred Weber. *Ideology and Utopia* (1929) reflects the influence of Marxist critiques of ideology, neo-Kantianism, and phenomenology. Professor in France 1930–33 and after 1933 in England at London School of Economics.

Meinecke, Friedrich (1862–1954), son of Prussian civil servant, student of Dilthey, became professor of history in 1901. During World War I advocated constitutional reform. Became a *Vernunftrepublikaner* and co-founded German Democratic Party with Weber and Troeltsch. Indebted to German Idealism and secular Christianity, he combined intellectual and political history (*Machiavellism*, 1924). After World War II he co-founded Free University in Berlin.

Mendelsohn, Erich (1887–1953), architect who worked with Gropius and Mies van der Rohe. Worked in concrete and steel, as reflected in his Einstein Tower (1920) and the Universum Cinema in Berlin (1928). In 1933 emigrated to London, Palestine, and then San Francisco, where he designed public buildings.

Meyer, Hannes (1889–1954), born in Basel, architect who sought to resolve urban problems through city planning. He was director of the Bauhaus from 1928–30, after which he emigrated first to the USSR and then to Mexico in 1939.

Michel, Artur (1883–1946), dance critic. Emigrated to New York.

Mies van der Rohe, Ludwig (1889–1969), modernist architect who worked with glass and steel. His furniture and building designs were influenced by neo-classical structures. Director of Bauhaus from 1930–33, which he closed in protest of Nazi regime. Briefly attracted to Nazism, but emigrated to US in 1937, and headed the Illinois Institute of

Technology. Designed landmark Barcelona Pavilion (1929) and buildings in New York and Chicago.

Moeller van den Bruck, Arthur (1876–1925), after bohemian existence as a young man, during war developed thesis of Germany's central position between East and West. Became an active right-wing intellectual and head of the conservative Juniklub. Although not based upon racial ideology, *Das Dritte Reich* (1923) deeply influenced Hitler with its anti-Marxist, antiliberal views. Committed suicide shortly after nervous breakdown in 1924.

Molzahn, Johannes (1892–1965), trained as artist and photographer. Served on Eastern front from 1915–18. Exhibited his early work at the Sturm Gallery. Member of the Novembergruppe and the Bauhaus. Emigrated to US in 1938, and returned to West Germany in 1959.

Moreck, Curt [Konrad Haemmerling] (1888–1957), a freelance writer in Berlin, he authored texts on cinema (*Sittengeschichte des Kinos,* 1926), guides to Berlin (*Führer durch das "lasterhafte" Berlin,* 1931), and aesthetics. Forbidden to publish by Nazis.

Mungenast, E[rnst] M[oritz] (1898–1964), gave up medical studies due to war wounds. Authored books on crime and the state (*Der Mörder und der Staat,* 1928), as well as a biography of Hindenburg for children in 1934.

Münzenberg, Willi (1889–1940), his early engagement in socialist youth activities led to the establishment of the Communist Youth International. KPD delegate in Reichstag, master of propaganda and supporter of Soviet Union. Following Reichstag fire, fled to Paris, and after Hitler-Stalin pact, rejected Soviet Russia. Interned in 1940 near Lyon as antifascist.

Neckarsulmer, Ernst (1877–1931), editor of the right-wing *National Zeitung* and *Standarte.* Wrote short stories.

Nicolson, Sir Harold George (1886–1968), historian and diplomat. Married to Victoria Sackville-West. Diplomat from 1909–1929, British envoy to Berlin. Throughout the 1920s he wrote literary biographies and kept a diary. Member of Labor Party from 1947, he was ennobled in 1953.

Niekisch, Ernst (1889–1967), friend of Ernst Toller, he took part in Räterepublik in Munich in 1918–19. His newspaper, *Der Widerstand* (1926–34), criticized the Weimar Republic for its orientation towards the West and advocated National Bolshevism. A vocal opponent of the Nazis, in 1937 he was arrested and received a life sentence. Politician in East Germany from 1945, but left the Party after criticizing the East German government policies in 1953.

Orend, Misch (1896–1976), historian of Saxony's Siebenbürgen region. Director of folklore department at the Bruckenthal Museum in Hermannstadt from 1928–43.

Ossietzky, Carl von (1889–1938), a radical pacifist after World War I. As a journalist in Berlin, he worked with Tucholsky at the *Berliner Vokszeitung* and for *Das Tagebuch.* As editor of *Die Weltbühne,* in 1932 sentenced to eighteen months in prison for an article which opposed the covert rearmament of Germany. In 1933 incarcerated at Sonnenburg, amnestied after being awarded Nobel Peace Prize in 1935. Died of tuberculosis in Berlin.

Ostwald, Hans (1873–1940), wrote cultural-historical studies of Berlin (*Berlin und die Berlinerin,* 1911), which is also the milieu of his novels.

Palitzsch, Otto Alfred (1896–1944), journalist, theater critic, and playwright. Belonged to a circle of intellectuals which sought to promote and establish radio plays as literature.

Papen, Franz von (1879–1969), general staff officer in Far East, after the war, representative of conservative, monarchist wing of Center Party. With Hindenburg's support, became chancellor for short time in 1932 and aided Nazi take-over. After Röhm putsch in 1934, left the Hitler government and served as diplomat. Found innocent at Nuremberg, but served three years in a work camp.

Pfemfert, Franz (1879–1954), worked on anarchist paper *Kampf* from 1904. In 1911 he established the socialist revolutionary periodical, *Die Aktion,* which was the mouthpiece for the expressionist movement. After the war, opposed both Weimar democracy and later Stalinism. In 1940 emigrated to Mexico.

Pinthus, Kurt (1886–1975), worked for Kurt Wolff Verlag until 1925, edited the first collection of film scripts (*Kinobuch,* 1914) and the definitive anthology of expressionist verse (*Menschheitsdämmerung,* 1919). Moved to Berlin, dramaturg for Reinhardt, worked in radio. Continued career as film and literary critic until 1933, when he emigrated to New York. Taught at Columbia until 1960.

Piscator, Erwin (1893–1966), experimental theater director. Soldier in war, joined Spartacists in 1919. His anti-Aristotelian political theater radicalized theatrical presentation through multi-media spectacle. He directed the Proletarian Theater from 1924–27, and headed the International Association of Revolutionary Theaters in Russian from 1931–36, when he emigrated to Paris and New York. Taught at the New School for Social Research. Returned to West Berlin, became head of Freie Volksbühne in 1962.

Polgar, Alfred (1873–1955), born in Vienna. Political reporter who became a drama critic for *Die Weltbühne* in 1925; also wrote satires about cultural trends. In 1933 fled to Vienna, and in 1938 to New York.

Pommer, Erich (1889–1966), film producer, in 1915 he co-founded Decla film company which merged with Universal Film AG (UFA) in 1921. Headed UFA 1921–26; went to Hollywood in 1927, returned to Berlin 1928–33. He produced some of the most important early German films including *The Cabinet of Dr. Caligari, Metropolis,* and *The Blue Angel.* Worked in Hollywood from 1933–36 and 1940–46. From 1946–49 he was film production control officer in Germany for the American military government.

Radek, Karl (1885–1939), born in Lemberg, joined Social Democratic Party in Poland, worked as foreign correspondent in Berlin. Spent war in Switzerland where he met Lenin, followed him to Russia in 1917. Joined Bosheviks, and served as a delegate at Brest-Litovsk, returned to Germany to help expand the KPD. Close to Trotsky, he lost favor in Moscow in 1927, and was arrested during Stalin's purges.

Reich, Wilhelm (1897–1957), born in Austria, psychologist whose interest in the intersection of psychoanalysis and Marxism is reflected in his thesis that society oppresses through sexual guilt. In 1928 became member of Austrian Communist Party, and established sexual hygiene clinics. In 1930 founded Sexpol (German Society of Proletarian Sexual Politics) in Berlin. Fled in 1933 to Norway and US. Experienced political persecution during McCarthy Era.

Reinhardt, Max [orig. Goldmann] (1873–1943), born in Austria, directed Deutsches Theater from 1905. In 1924 he assumed leadership of Theater in der Josefstadt in Vienna. His contributions to theater lie in his innovative use of lighting and staging, including the revolving stage. Forced to resign in 1933, he emigrated to US in 1937.

Reissner, Larissa Michailovna (1895–1926), born in Lublin. Her early writings were influenced by the symbolists. An active revolutionary whose travels formed the basis of her writings (*Berlin in 1923*, 1925).

Renger-Patzsch, Albert (1897–1966), an independent photographer with strong affinities to New Objectivity. Published *Die Welt ist schön* (1928), a book of photographs about inanimate objects. Atelier in Folkwang-Museum Essen from 1928–1944.

Roh, Franz (1890–1965), art historian and writer; taught contemporary art history in Munich.

Rosenberg, Alfred (1893–1946), born in Estonia, studied architecture in Riga and Moscow. In 1918 he moved to Munich, where he met Hitler. His early writings are anti-Semitic, anti-Communist, and anti-Christian. Later focused on the creation of a neo-Germanic culture (*Der Mythos des Zwanzigsten Jahrhunderts,* 1930). An active Nazi, he edited the *Völkischer Beobachter,* founded the Kampfbund für deutsche Kultur, and served as Foreign Minister under Hitler. In 1946, sentenced to death at Nuremberg.

Rosenzweig, Franz (1886–1929), Jewish theologian. Studied history and philosophy with Meinecke. *Der Stern der Erlösung* (1920) was written on postcards while he served on the Macedonian front. Conceived of a "new thought" in which language and time play decisive roles in the constitution of reality. Translated part of Bible with Buber.

Roth, Joseph (1894–1939), born in Austria of Jewish parents. After volunteering in war, worked as journalist in Berlin, Vienna, and Frankfurt. A self-styled "European," after an initial engagement with socialism, became more reactionary, and many of his novels reflect his nostalgia for the stability of the Habsburg empire (*Radetzkymarsch,* 1932). Emigrated to Paris in 1933, died an alcoholic.

Rühle, Otto (1874–1943), teacher, in 1902 fired for his political affiliations with the SPD. A member of the Reichstag, he voted against war credits in 1915. With Liebknecht, founded the Spartacus League and then the KPD, eventually establishing the Communist Workers' Party (KAP). Emigration in 1932 to Prague, then to Mexico where he served as consultant to Ministry of Education.

Rühle-Gerstel, Alice (1894–1943), born in Prague, in 1921 she received a Ph.D. in psychology and married Otto Rühle. Author of texts on Marxism and individual psychology as well as the position of women in capitalism. In 1935 she emigrated to Mexico and came into close contact with Trotsky. Committed suicide.

Salomon, Ernst von (1902–1972), a member of the Freikorps from 1919–1921, imprisoned for his part in Rathenau's assassination in 1922. His autobiographical novels (*Die Geächteten,* 1931; *Die Stadt,* 1932) register his distaste for the Weimar Republic. Wrote propaganda films, and was interned by the Americans at the end of World War II.

Sander, August (1876–1964), studied painting, became portrait photographer in 1909. His encyclopedic photo project, "Men of the Twentieth Century," is based on tenets of the New Objectivity and documented cultural figures like Paul Hindemith and Hans Poelzig.

During the Third Reich, turned to landscape photography. Produced portfolio of imprisoned opponents of National Socialism and a portrait series of persecuted Jews.

Schairer, Erich (1887–1956), after training as pastor, left the church and became a journalist. Founded his own weekly paper in 1920, which, although not affiliated with any political party, opposed nationalism, rearmament, clericalism, and the NSDAP. Resigned in 1932, publication forbidden in 1937. Established the *Stuttgarter Zeitung* in 1946.

Schirokauer, Arno (1899–1954), professor of literature and author, participated in the promotion of literature through radio. Authored numerous experimental radio plays and theoretical articles on radio. Fled in 1933, interned in concentration camp. Emigrated to US in 1939, where he taught at Johns Hopkins.

Schleich, Carl Ludwig (1859–1922), doctor and surgeon. Head of a surgical-gynecological private clinic in Berlin; during World War I, he served in a military hospital. In addition to medical texts, he wrote philosophical essays and biographical sketches.

Schmitt, Carl (1888–1985), professor of law and social philosopher, antiliberal and authoritarian, a critic of parliamentarism and pluralism, became member of and theorist for NSDAP. Author of *Political Romanticism* (1923) and *The Concept of the Political* (1928). In 1936–37 forced to leave public office.

Schoenberg, Arnold (1874–1951), modernist composer, broke with tonality. With Berg and Webern, created New Vienna School. Developed controversial twelve-tone system of serial composition which exploded traditional forms of musical expression (*Moses and Aron,* 1932). Professor in Berlin from 1926–1933; emigration to US where he taught at UCLA.

Scholem, [Gerhard] Gershom (1897–1982), born in Germany, joined the Hebrew University in Jerusalem in 1923 and taught Jewish mysticism. Published major works on Judaism and the Kabbalah. Lifelong close friendship from 1915–40 with Walter Benjamin. Author of *Sabbatai Sevi* (1973).

Schröder, Fritz (1891–1937?), a trade union official, he wrote articles for *Die Arbeit* and *Vorwärts* promoting legislation to improve working conditions. Member of Reichstag in 1933. Emigrated to the Netherlands, but returned to Germany illegally in 1937 and was arrested.

Schultze-Naumburg, Paul (1869–1949), architect and author, from 1930 director of the Weimar Kunsthochschule. His designs reflect his affiliations with *Heimatkunst* and his belief in the national renewal of art.

Seiwert, Franz Wilhelm (1894–1933), artist and writer. Attended School of Applied Arts in Cologne. Participated in "Gruppe progressiver Künstler" and "Die Aktion." From 1929–33 edited the journal *A bis Z*. Relocated to Vienna in 1932.

Sieburg, Friedrich (1893–1964), pilot in war, became journalist in Frankfurt in 1924, foreign correspondent in 1926. Cultural critic in 1920s, famous for his book *Gott in Frankreich? Ein Versuch* (1929). After war, editor of *Die Gegenwart,* and head of literature section of *Frankfurter Allgemeine Zeitung* from 1956.

Siemsen, Hans (1891–1969), journalist and staff member of *Die Weltbühne,* an advocate of jazz as early as 1921. *Rußland, ja und nein* (1931) was banned by Nazis. Fled to Paris in 1934, later to US where he worked as a radio broadcaster. Returned to Germany in 1948.

Simmel, Ernst (1882–1947), born in Poland, studied pharmacy and medicine, MD in 1908. From 1908–14 practiced in poor communities. Served as army doctor and in 1916 headed hospital for war neuroses. Associate of Freud and founder of first psychoanalytic sanitarium. Emigrated to England in 1933, to US in 1934, and became naturalized citizen in 1940.

Spengler, Oswald (1880–1936), studied mathematics, science, philosophy, and history. Volume I of *Decline of the West* appeared at the end of the war. Conceiving historical periods as cyclical, he predicated the destruction of Faustian or Western culture (*Kultur*) upon the rise of non-white races and as a result of civilization (*Zivilisation*), embodied by technology and industrialization. Rejected the Weimar Republic in favor of military dictatorship, but skeptical of Nazis, he refused professorship in 1933.

Stapel, Wilhelm (1882–1954), journalist and editor; turned to *völkisch* ideology during the war. Opposed Weimar Republic and joined conservative Juniklub around Moeller van den Bruck. Editor of *Deutsches Volkstum* from 1919–38, an organ of the new nationalism. Never a member of the NSDAP, was attacked in 1933.

Starke, Margot [Berta Hollweg] (1892–1970), studied music. Taught piano until 1917 when she began to write stories and poetry. Emigrated in 1933 to England and Spain, and to US in 1937. Returned to West Germany in 1952.

Stöcker, Helene (1869–1943), in 1901 received Ph.D in Bern. Organizer and writer for women's movement in Berlin from 1902. Radical feminist who co-founded the Bund für Mutterschutz and Sexualreform in 1905. Advocate of pacifism during World War I. Wrote on issues of love, marriage, and morality. Emigrated to New York in 1933.

Stössinger, Felix (1889–1954), born in Prague. Member of the SPD and editor of *Sozialistische Monatshefte* in Berlin. During the war, advocated French-German reconciliation. After 1917, joined the USPD and published *Die Freiheit,* but left the party in 1922. Worked as a translator, essayist, and music critic for radio. Interned for illegal entry into Switzerland in 1942.

Stuckenschmidt, H[ans] H[einz] (1901–1988), studied music in Paris after the war, in 1920 became a freelance composer. Promoted the music of Berg, Webern, Hindemith. From 1931–33 studied with Schoenberg. In 1941 drafted into German Army as an interpreter. Later imprisoned by the Americans. Subsequent career as composer and music critic.

Surén, Hans (1885–1972), born into a military family, 1905 lieutenant. Sports instructor in military school, soon responsible for reform of German army's sports and physical education program. In 1924 published *Der Mensch und die Sonne,* a book about nudism, which sold 250,000 copies. Writer and propagator of the FKK (*Freikörperkultur*) movement. Joined Nazi party in May 1933.

Taut, Bruno (1880–1938), architect of Deutsche Gartenstadtgesellschaft, worked with his brother, Max Taut, and Gropius. A leader in the socialist Novembergruppe and Arbeitsrat für Kunst. Propagated role of architecture in the creation of a utopian socialist society (*Die Stadtkrone,* 1919). His buildings include the Glass Pavilion in Cologne (1914) and Berlin workers' housing projects. Responsible for the "Glass Chain" correspondence among young architects. Traveled to Japan, USSR, and Turkey in 1930s. Died in Istanbul.

Tergit, Gabriele [Elise Reifenburg] (1894–1982), journalist on numerous Berlin papers, from 1925–33 editor of the *Berliner Tageblatt,* known for her semi-literary court reporting. In 1931 published novel *Käsebier erobert den Kurfürstendamm.* In 1933 emigrated to Palestine, in 1938 to London.

Thälmann, Ernst (1886–1944), from petit-bourgeoisie, member of SPD, soldier on the Western front, deserted in 1918 and joined USPD. A member of KPD from 1920, he occupied increasingly important political positions, from parliamentary representative to head of the KPD and candidate for president. Arrested in 1933. Died in Buchenwald.

Tillich, Paul (1886–1965), professor of theology and philosophy, took position in Frankfurt in 1929. An active socialist, he came into contact with Adorno and Horkheimer. Emigrated to US in 1933 and taught at Harvard University and University of Chicago.

Traven, B. (?–1969), possibly Otto Feige (born 1882 in East Prussia), he wrote under the pseudonyms Ret Marut and Richard Maurhut. Published the journal *Der Ziegelbrenner* from 1917–1921 in Munich, and participated in the revolution of 1919. Sought refuge in Mexico, and adopted the name Traven Torsvan, becoming a citizen in 1951. His concern for the oppressed surfaces in his novels, and his tendency toward exoticism is reflected in his self-created legend.

Troeltsch, Ernst (1865–1923), Protestant theologian. Supported constitutional reform and moderate war goals. Co-founder of German Democratic Party with Max Weber and defender of the Weimar Republic. Advocate of liberal Protestant theology, he used sociological and historical methods to analyze modern culture (*Historical Relativism and its Problems,* 1922). Author of *Spektatorbriefe.* Was suggested as candidate for president of Republic.

Tucholsky, Kurt (1890–1935), after serving on Eastern front, moved to Berlin in 1918 where he wrote satirical pieces for cabarets and worked as a journalist at *Die Weltbühne.* Briefly a member of the USPD. He continued his searing cultural and literary critiques of German militarism, nationalism, and the emergent Nazism from Paris between 1924 and 1928, and Sweden 1929–1932, when he ceased to publish. Expatriated in 1933. Took his own life.

Wagenführ, Rolf (1905–n.d.), statistician and economist. Developed system of economic and social statistics based on Marxist reproduction theory.

Wagner, Martin (1885–1957), architect who worked with Mies van der Rohe, Taut, Gropius, and Poelzig. From 1926–33 served as city planning advisor in Berlin. Traveled to Moscow in 1930. Emigrated to US and taught at Harvard from 1936–50. Naturalized US citizen in 1944. Died in Cambridge, Massachusetts.

Walter, Hilde (1895–1976), a journalist who worked at the *Berliner Tageblatt* and *Die Weltbühne* from 1929–33. Took in Ossietzky's family during his imprisonment, and helped effect his being awarded the Nobel Prize. Emigration in 1941 to New York. Returned to West Germany in 1952.

Weber, Alfred (1868–1958), bourgeois liberal *Vernunftrepublikaner,* co-founder of DDP with brother Max. A professor of economics, he concentrated on the economic and political effects of the war and formulated a "sociology of freedom." Author of *Die Krise des modernen Staatsgedankens in Europa* (1925).

Weber, Marianne (1870–1954), activist in the women's movement from 1898, married to Max Weber. From 1919–23 chair of the Bund Deutscher Frauenvereine.

Weber, Max (1864–1920), professor of sociology. His studies focus upon relationships between the individual and authority, bureaucracy, charisma and economic history (*The Protestant Ethic and the Spirit of Capitalism,* 1920). After the capitulation, he supported constitutional reform toward the establishment of a parliamentary monarchy. Member of the peace delegation to Versailles in 1919.

Wedderkop, Hermann von (1876–n.d.), editor of the magazine *Der Querschnitt* from 1923–31. Propagated in his magazine the new style of New Objectivity and flirted with mass culture, including boxing.

Weill, Kurt (1900–1950), son of synagogue cantor, studied with Engelbert Humperdinck and Ferruccio Busoni. Composed for theater and worked with Georg Kaiser before collaborating with Brecht on *The Threepenny Opera* (1928) and *Mahagonny* (1930). Using musical styles from jazz to operetta, he practiced political critique while maintaining a mass appeal. Emigrated to France and US, where he wrote for Broadway.

Westheim, Paul (1886–1963), soldier during war. From 1917–33 editor of *Das Kunstblatt,* art critic for various newspapers and radio talk shows. His sociological interpretation of art and his preference for expressionism made him a chief supporter of what the Nazis later called "degenerate art." Emigrated to France in 1933, where he was interned in concentration camp. Emigrated to Mexico in 1941 and took citizenship in 1953.

Wigman, Mary [Marie Wiegmann] (1886–1973), studied with Jacques Dalcroze, was head dancer for Rudolf von Laban, in 1920 opened her own schools of modern and free dance, performing in world-wide tours. Choreographer of "absolute dance," which combined dynamic movement with music composed specifically for a particular dance.

Wolf, Friedrich (1888–1953), medical doctor in Stuttgart. A member of KPD, he wrote a controversial play condemning illegality of abortion as bourgeois (*Cyancali,* 1929). In 1931 arrested for violating Paragraph 218. Emigrated to USSR in 1941, but returned to East Berlin in 1945.

Wolfradt, Willi (1892–n.d.), art historian who wrote on sculpture and on Caspar David Friedrich.

Zehrer, Hans (1899–1966), political publicist, from 1923 editor of the *Vossische Zeitung,* becoming foreign editor from 1925–31. In 1933 editor of the conservative periodical, *Die Tat.*

Zucker, Wolf (1905–n.d.), literary and film critic for *Die Literarische Welt.* Collaborated with Benjamin on radio plays. Emigrated to US in 1949, naturalized citizen in 1956.

Zuckmayer, Carl (1896–1977), served in war, worked as assistant theater producer in Berlin, Kiel, and Munich. His early expressionist style (*Kreuzweg,* 1921) gave way to the more popular Volksstück (*Katharina Knie,* 1925; *Der Hauptmann von Köpenick,* 1931). Wrote screenplay for *The Blue Angel.* An outspoken opponent of Nazis, emigrated to Austria in 1933, then US. Returned as American military government official in 1946.

Zweig, Arnold (1887–1968), soldier at Verdun. Wrote *Der Streit um den Sergeanten Grischa* (1927), the first war novel from a pacifist point of view and participated in the general cultural debate about the interpretation of the war. Other writings focus on the position of Jews in the twentieth century. Emigrated to Palestine in 1933, but returned to East Berlin in 1948.

Zweig, Stefan (1881–1942) born in Vienna, he traveled extensively through America, Asia, and Europe. Friends with Romain Rolland, he moved to Zurich to give voice to his pacifism (*Jeremias,* 1916). Freud's influence is evident in his biographical essays and miniatures. In 1934 fled to London, and in 1940 to Brazil, where he took his own life.

Political Chronology

Oct. 28	Sailors mutiny in Kiel.
Nov. 8	Independent Socialist Kurt Eisner proclaims a republic in Bavaria. Chancellor Max von Baden calls for Kaiser Wilhelm II to abdicate. German armistice commission under Center Party member Matthias Erzberger begins negotiations with Allies.
Nov. 9	Social Democrat Philipp Scheidemann proclaims a republic after the Kaiser abdicates. Social Democrat Friedrich Ebert becomes Chancellor. Provisional government of Social Democrats (SPD) and Independent Socialists (USPD) formed. Workers' and Soldiers' Councils formed by the Spartacists.
Nov. 10	Wilhelm II flees to Holland. General Wilhelm Groener puts army at Ebert's disposal in exchange for support in maintaining order within the armed forces.
Nov. 11	Armistice with Allies signed at Compiègne.
Dec. 16–20	National Congress of Workers' and Soldiers' Councils in Berlin.
Dec. 18	German People's Party (DVP) formed.
Dec. 25.	Reactionary Stahlhelm Bund founded under Franz Seldte.
Dec. 27	Provisional government dissolved after Independent Socialists walk out.
Dec. 30	German Communist Party (KPD) founded.

1919

Jan. 5–12	General strike and Spartacus uprising in Berlin. Social Democrat Gustav Noske enters Berlin on Jan. 11 aided by Freikorps troops. German Worker's Party (DAP) founded.
Jan. 15	Spartacists Rosa Luxemburg and Karl Liebknecht murdered by Freikorps in Berlin.
Jan. 19	Election for deputies to National Assembly. The SPD emerges the majority party.
Feb. 9	National Assembly opens in Weimar.
Feb. 11	Ebert elected president.
Feb. 13	Scheidemann forms a coalition government of SPD, German Democratic Party (DDP), and Center Party.
Feb. 21	Kurt Eisner murdered by nationalist, Count Arco-Valley.

March/April	Fighting in Berlin, the Ruhr, and central Germany.
April 7–May 1	Soviet Republic (Räterepublik) formed in Munich but crushed on May 2 by Prussian and Wurttemberg troops and the Freikorps.
June 20	Scheidemann government resigns.
June 21	New cabinet formed under Social Democratic Gustav Bauer.
June 28	New peace delegation, headed by Foreign Minister Hermann Müller, a Social Democrat, signs the Treaty of Versailles which imposes heavy reparations, requires reduction of the German army, forbids a German-Austrian *Anschluß*, and insists upon German acceptance of the "war guilt clause."
July 7	General Hindenburg steps down. General officer staff dissolved.
July 31	Weimar Assembly adopts the proposed constitution which provides for a strong president who, under Article 48, can govern alone in a state of emergency.
Aug. 11	President Ebert signs Weimar constitution.
Aug. 14	Weimar constitution becomes law.

1920

Feb. 24	German Workers' Party founded, renamed the National Socialist Workers' Party (NSDAP) in August. First mass meeting at the Hofbräuhaus in Munich. Adolf Hitler announces the party program.
March 13–17	Dr. Wolfgang Kapp and General Erich Ludendorff lead a putsch in Berlin for the restoration of the monarchy. The government flees to Dresden. Putsch defeated through a general strike.
March/April	Communist uprising in Ruhr and central Germany. The Red Army defeated by the Reichswehr.
June 6	National elections for Reichstag. Support for right-wing parties increases.

1921

Jan. 24–25	At Paris Conference, German reparations set at 269 billion gold marks, payable over 42 years.
March 23	Communists lead uprisings in Saxony and Hamburg.
May 10	Center Party member Joseph Wirth forms new government.
July 29	Hitler made first chairman of NSDAP.
Aug. 18	550 marks = 1 dollar.
Aug. 24–25	United States signs peace treaties with Germany and Austria.
Aug. 26	Matthias Erzberger, held responsible for the Treaty of Versailles, is

assassinated by right-wing "Organization Consul." State of emergency declared until Dec. 16.

Oct. 16	Independent Socialists vote to merge with the Communist Party.
Nov. 4	SA (Sturmabteilung: Brown Shirts) established.
mid-Nov.	German currency begins to fall.

1922

Jan. 31	Chancellor Wirth names Walther Rathenau foreign minister.
April 16	Rathenau concludes the Treaty of Rapallo with USSR, which cancels the countries' reciprocal war debts and establishes diplomatic and economic relations.
July 21	Law protecting the republic against antirepublican attacks on the government and its symbols enacted.
June 24	Walther Rathenau assassinated by anti-Semitic monarchists who object to his international views.
July 29	Secret agreement signed between Germany and USSR in Berlin.
Nov. 14	Chancellor Wirth resigns.
Nov. 22	Shipping magnate Wilhelm Cuno becomes chancellor. Count Ulrich von Brockdorff-Rantzau becomes the Weimar Republic's first ambassador to Moscow.
Dec. 26	Allied Reparations Commission threatens sanctions against Germany because of failure to meet obligations.

1923

Jan. 11	French and Belgian troops, including colonial forces, occupy the Ruhr to operate the mining industries for the victors.
Jan. 13	Policy of passive resistance to occupation announced.
Jan. 27–28	Communist Party forms action committees against fascism. First Nazi party rally in Munich.
May 24	54,300 marks = 1 dollar.
May 26	Execution of Leo Schlageter as a saboteur by French occupation forces in Ruhr.
Aug. 11	Cuno resigns as chancellor. Stresemann forms new government.
Sept. 3	A ticket on a Berlin streetcar now costs 400,000 marks.
Sept. 26	Stresemann government gives up policy of passive resistance to the occupation of the Ruhr. Martial law declared in Bavaria and a state of emergency in Germany.

Oct. 12   4 billion marks = 1 dollar.

Oct. 19   Berlin stockmarket shuts down. Conflict between Bavaria and Weimar Republic (continues until Feb. 2, 1924).

Oct. 21   Separatist movements arise in the Rhineland.

Oct. 22–23   Communists attempt an uprising in Hamburg.

Oct. 29   Government acts against Social Democratic and Communist parties in Saxony.

Nov. 8   Beer Hall Putsch in Munich is led by Adolf Hitler, Hermann Göring, and General Ludendorff.

Nov. 11   Hitler arrested and held in Landsberg fortress.

Nov. 15   New currency introduced to end inflation. (1 Rentenmark = 1 billion marks.)

Nov. 20   4.2 Rentenmarks (4,200 billion marks) = 1 dollar. The mark stabilizes.

Nov. 22   Communist Party banned until March 1, 1924.

Nov. 23   Social Democrats overthrow Stresemann cabinet due to its leniency toward right-wing militants. Center Party member Wilhelm Marx becomes chancellor.

1924

April 1   Hitler sentenced to 5 years in prison for participation in Putsch.

May 4   Reichstag elections: Nazis win 6.4 percent of the vote.

July 16   Allies meet in London to discuss the Dawes Plan which proposes evacuation of the Ruhr, the reduction of reparations, and loans to Germany.

Aug.   German delegates sent to London to meet with the Allies.

Sept. 1   Dawes Plan enacted.

Dec. 7   Reichstag elections show right-wing parties losing strength. A period of relative stability begins.

Dec. 17   Hitler released from prison after serving less than nine months of his sentence.

1925

Feb. 24   NSDAP re-established.

Feb. 28   Friedrich Ebert dies.

April 26   General Field Marshal Paul von Hindenburg elected president of the Weimar Republic.

Oct. 12   Commercial treaty between Germany and USSR signed.

Nov. 9	The Nazi paramilitary organization, the SS (Schutzstaffel: Black Shirts) formed.
Dec. 1	Treaty of Locarno, signed by France, Great Britain, Belgium, Italy, and Germany, recognizes the western, but not the eastern, borders of Germany.
Dec. 8	First volume of Hitler's *Mein Kampf* is published.

1926

Jan. 20	Social Democrat Hans Luther becomes chancellor.
April 24	Treaty of Berlin promising friendship and neutrality between Germany and USSR signed.
May 17	Wilhelm Marx becomes chancellor. Hindenburg assents to red-white-black flag.
June 20	Plebiscite to extend the expropriation of princes throughout Germany fails.
Sept. 8	Germany becomes a member of the League of Nations.
Oct. 9	General Hans von Seeckt forced to resign as head of army; civilian rule asserted over military.
Dec. 10	French Foreign Minister Aristide Briand and Stresemann receive Nobel Peace Prize for their efforts to secure peace in Europe.

1927

Jan. 29	Marx resumes chancellorship.
July 7	Law providing for unemployment support for everyone passes.
Aug. 19	Nazis hold first Nuremberg party rally: march of 30,000 Brown Shirts.

1928

May 20	Reichstag elections: Nazis win 2.5% of the vote.
June 28	Hermann Müller forms a cabinet primarily of Social Democrats.
Aug. 28	The Grand Coalition of SPD, Center, DDP, and DVP is formed under Chancellor Müller as the Weimar Republic's sixteenth government.
Dec. 22	Allies form delegation to examine Germany's ability to pay reparations.

1929

| May 1 | Communists stage uprising in Berlin. |
| June 7 | Dawes Plan revised under the Young Plan Conference. |

June 9	Industrialist Alfred Hugenberg, Hitler, and Seldte unite to oppose the Young Plan.
June 8–15	Communists denounce Social Democratic party as "social-fascist."
Aug. 2	NSDAP rally held in Nuremberg with 150,000 participants.
Aug. 6–13	Young Plan accepted, according to which reparations are drastically reduced and Germany is accorded full responsibility over its finances. Denounced by Hitler and Hugenberg (DNVP).
Oct. 3	Foreign Minister Stresemann dies, and is followed by Julius Curtius, also a member of DVP.
Oct. 24	"Black Friday": The stock market crash on Wall Street touches off worldwide economic crisis and the withdrawal of loans to Germany.

1930

Jan. 23	National Socialist Wilhelm Frick made Minister of the Interior in Thuringia.
Feb. 23	Nazi Horst Wessel shot in Berlin during a street fight.
March 27	Müller cabinet resigns over the financing of unemployment benefits.
March 30	Center Party delegate Heinrich Brüning forms a minority government.
June 30	Allied troops withdraw from the Rhineland.
July 16	Chancellor Brüning invokes Article 48, thereby dissolving the Reichstag.
Sept. 14	Turn-out for national elections is heavy. Social Democrats maintain their majority, but the Nazis increase their number of seats from 12 to 107 (18% of the vote).

1931

Jan.	Five million are unemployed.
March 28	State of Emergency declared.
July 13	The Dresdener Bank collapses. Government closes all banks and stock exchanges until Aug. 5.
Oct. 11	Harzburg Conference establishes a "national front" against Bolshevism. Participants include the NSDAP, the German National People's party (DNVP), the Stahlhelm, and representatives of right-wing economic and financial circles.
Oct. 12	The National Socialist student organization gains the majority in the German students' union.

1932

| Jan. | Over 6 million are unemployed. |
| Jan. 22 | Hitler, seeking support from industry, speaks before the Industry Club. |

April 10	Hindenburg is re-elected President.
April 13	Nazi paramilitary organizations, the SS and the SA, are banned.
May 12	Defense Minister General Groener forced to resign.
May 30	Advised by General Kurt von Schleicher, President Hindenburg dismisses the Brüning cabinet. Reactionary Center Party member Franz von Papen becomes chancellor.
June 1	Von Papen creates a cabinet of right-wing aristocrats and industrialists aptly dubbed the "cabinet of barons."
June 4	Hindenburg dissolves the Reichstag.
June 14	Hindenburg rescinds the ban on the SA and the SS.
July 20	Von Papen seizes the Prussian government from the Social Democrats and governs as "Commissioner of the Reich."
July 31	Elections end in victory for the Nazi Party with 37.8% of the vote and 230 seats. After a failed attempt at a coalition—Hitler demands to be named chancellor—von Papen calls for new elections.
Aug. 11	New elections show a loss of support for the Nazis.
Aug. 30	New Reichstag opened by Communist Clara Zetkin. Nazi delegates wear their uniforms.
Sept. 12	Von Papen dissolves the Reichstag.
Sept. 14	Germany walks out of first Hague Disarmament Conference.
Nov. 3	Berlin transport goes on strike.
Nov. 6	Elections held with Nazis losing two million votes and thirty-four seats. Despite Communist gains, the NSDAP remains the strongest party in the Reichstag.
Nov. 17	Von Papen resigns as chancellor. Von Schleicher becomes chancellor on Dec. 3.

1933

Jan. 28	Von Schleicher resigns as Chancellor.
Jan. 30	Hindenburg names Hitler chancellor, and von Papen his deputy.

Selected Bibliography

General Works on the Weimar Republic

Abelshauser, Werner, Anselm Faust, and Dietmar Petzina, eds. *Deutsche Sozialgeschichte 1914–1945. Ein historisches Lesebuch*. Munich: C.H. Beck, 1985.

Benz, Wolfgang, and Hermann Graml, eds. *Biographisches Lexikon zur Weimarer Republik*. Munich: C.H. Beck, 1988.

Bracher, Karl Dietrich, et al. *Die Weimarer Republik, 1918–1933. Politik, Wirtschaft, Gesellschaft*. Düsseldorf: Droste, 1987.

Bullivant, Keith, ed. *Culture and Society in the Weimar Republic*. Manchester: Manchester University Press, 1978.

Elefanten Press, ed. *Die wilden Zwanziger: Weimar und die Welt 1919–1933. Ein Bilder-Lese-Buch*. Reinbek: Rowohlt, 1986.

Erdmann, Karl Dietrich, and Hagen Schulze, eds. *Weimar: Selbstpreisgabe einer Demokratie. Eine Bilanz heute*. Düsseldorf: Droste, 1980.

Eyck, Erich. *A History of the Weimar Republic,* trans. Harlan P. Hanson and Robert G.L. Waite, 2 vols. Cambridge: Harvard University Press, 1962–1963.

Friedrich, Otto. *Before the Deluge: A Portrait of Berlin in the 1920's*. New York: Harper and Row, 1972.

Halperin, S. William. *Germany Tried Democracy: A Political History of the Reich from 1918 to 1933*. New York: Norton, 1965.

Hermand, Jost, and Frank Trommler. *Die Kultur der Weimarer Republik*. Munich: Nymphenburger, 1978.

Gay, Peter. *Weimar Culture: The Outsider as Insider*. New York: Harper and Row, 1968.

Grimm, Reinhold, and Jost Hermand, eds. *Die sogenannten Zwanziger Jahre*. First Wisconsin Workshop. Bad Homburg: Gehlen, 1970.

Grube, Frank. *Die Weimarer Republik*. Hamburg: Hoffmann and Campe, 1983.

Jonge, Alex de. *The Weimar Chronicle: Prelude to Hitler*. New York: New American Library, 1978.

Kaes, Anton, ed. *Weimarer Republik. Manifeste und Dokumente zur deutschen Literatur 1918–1933*. Stuttgart: J.B. Metzler, 1983.

Kolb, Eberhard. *The Weimar Republic,* trans. P.S. Fall. Boston: Unwin Hyman, 1988.

Kühnl, Reinhard. *Die Weimarer Republik. Errichtung, Machtstruktur und Zerstörung einer Demokratie*. Reinbek: Rowohlt, 1985.

Kunstamt Kreuzberg, ed. *Weimarer Republik*. Berlin: Elefanten Press, 1977.

Lambsdorff, Hans Georg. *Die Weimarer Republik. Krisen, Konflikte, Katastrophen*. Frankfurt a.M.: Peter Lang, 1990.

Laqueur, Walter. *Weimar: A Cultural History, 1918–1933*. New York: G. Putnam's, 1974.

Longerich, Peter, ed. *Die erste Republik. Dokumente zur Geschichte des Weimarer Staats*. Munich: Piper, 1992.

Mönch, Walter. *Weimar. Gesellschaft, Politik, Kultur in der ersten deutschen Republik*. Frankfurt a.M.: Peter Lang, 1988.

Michalka, Wolfgang, and Gottfried Niedhart, eds. *Die ungeliebte Republik. Dokumente zur Innen- und Außenpolitik Weimars 1918–1933*. Munich: dtv, 1981.

Neebe, Reinhard, ed. *Die Republik von Weimar 1918–1933: Demokratie ohne Demokraten?* Stuttgart: E. Klett, 1987.

Pachter, Henry. *Weimar Etudes.* New York: Columbia University Press, 1982.

Peukert, Detlev J.K. *The Weimar Republic: The Crisis of Classical Modernity,* trans. Richard Deveson. New York: Hill and Wang, 1992.

Pross, Harry, ed. *Die Zerstörung der deutschen Politik. Dokumente 1871–1933.* Frankfurt a.M.: Fischer, 1983.

Rosenberg, Arthur. *A History of the German Republic.* London: Methuen, 1936.

Ruge, Wolfgang. *Weimar. Republik auf Zeit.* Berlin: Deutscher Verlag der Wissenschaften, 1982.

Schrader, Bärbel, and Jürgen Schebera. *The "Golden" Twenties: Art and Literature in the Weimar Republic,* trans. Katherine Vanovitch. New Haven: Yale University Press, 1988.

Schulze, Hagen. *Weimar. Deutschland 1917–1933.* 2nd ed. Berlin: Siedler, 1982.

Snyder, Louis L. *The Weimar Republic: A History of Germany from Ebert to Hitler.* Princeton, N.J.: Van Nostrand, 1966.

Stachura, Peter D. *The Weimar Era and Hitler, 1918–1933: A Critical Bibliography.* Oxford: Clio Press, 1977.

Stürmer, Michael, ed. *Die Weimarer Republik. Belagerte Civitas.* Königstein: Athenäum, 1985.

Werner, Bruno E. *Die Zwanziger Jahre.* Munich: F. Bruckmann, 1962.

Willett, John. *Art and Politics in the Weimar Period: The New Sobriety 1917–1933.* New York: Pantheon, 1978.

———. *The Weimar Years: A Culture Cut Short.* London: Thames and Hudson, 1984.

A New Democracy in Crisis

Abraham, David. *The Collapse of the Weimar Republic: Political Economy and Crisis.* New York: Holmes and Meier, 2d ed., 1986.

Angress, Werner T. *Stillborn Revolution: The Communist Bid for Power in Germany, 1921–1923.* Princeton, N.J.: Princeton University Press, 1963.

Bessel, Richard, and E.J. Feuchtwanger, eds. *Social Change and Political Development in Weimar Germany.* London: Croon Helm, 1981.

Bracher, Karl Dietrich. *Die Auflösung der Weimarer Republik. Eine Studie zum Problem des Machtzerfalls in der Demokratie.* Stuttgart: Ring Verlag, 1957.

Breitman, Richard. *German Socialism and Weimar Democracy.* Chapel Hill, N.C.: University of North Carolina Press, 1981.

Broszat, Martin. *Hitler and the Collapse of Weimar Germany,* trans. V.R. Berghahn. New York: St. Martin's Press, 1987.

Carsten, F.L. *The Reichswehr and Politics, 1918–1933.* Oxford: Oxford University Press, 1966.

———. *Revolution in Central Europe 1918–1919.* Berkeley and Los Angeles: University of California Press, 1972.

Diehl, James. *Paramilitary Organizations and the Weimar Republic: The Militarization of German Politics, 1919–1930.* Bloomington, Ind.: Indiana University Press, 1977.

Dobkowski, Michael N., and Isidor Wallimann, eds. *Towards the Holocaust: The Social and Economic Collapse of the Weimar Republic.* Westport, Conn.: Greenwood Press, 1983.

Dorpalen, Andreas. *Hindenburg and the Politics of the Weimar Republic.* Princeton, N.J.: Princeton University Press, 1964.

Eksteins, Modris. *Theodor Heuss und die Weimarer Republik. Ein Beitrag zur Geschichte des deutschen Liberalismus.* Stuttgart: E. Klett, 1969.

————. *The Limits of Reason: The German Democratic Press and the Collapse of Weimar Democracy.* London: Croom-Helm, 1975.

Epstein, Klaus. *Matthias Erzberger and the Dilemma of German Democracy.* Princeton, N.J.: Princeton University Press, 1959.

Eschenburg, Theodor. *Die improvisierte Demokratie. Gesammelte Aufsätze zur Weimarer Republik.* Munich: R. Piper Verlag, 1964.

Evans, Richard, and Dick Geary, eds. *The German Unemployed: Experiences and Consequences of Mass Unemployment from the Weimar Republic to the Third Reich.* New York: St. Martin's Press, 1987.

Feldman, Gerald D. *Iron and Steel in the German Inflation, 1916–1923.* Princeton, N.J.: Princeton U. Press, 1977.

————, et al., eds. *The German Inflation Reconsidered: A Preliminary Balance.* Berlin: De Gruyter, 1982.

————, ed. *Die Nachwirkungen der Inflation auf die deutsche Geschichte 1924–1933.* Munich: R. Oldenburg, 1985.

————, et al., eds. *Konsequenzen der Inflation.* Berlin: Colloquium Verlag, 1989.

Felix, David. *Walter Rathenau and the Weimar Republic: The Politics of Reparations.* Baltimore: Johns Hopkins University Press, 1971.

Flechtheim, Ossip. *Die Kommunistische Partei Deutschlands in der Weimarer Republik.* Frankfurt a.M.: Europäische Verlagsanstalt, 1969.

Fowkes, Ben. *Communism in Germany under the Weimar Republic.* New York: St. Martin's Press, 1984.

Freyburg, Thomas von. *Industrielle Rationalisierung in der Weimarer Republik: Untersuchung an Beispielen aus dem Maschinenbau und der Elektroindustrie.* Frankfurt a.M.: Campus Verlag, 1989.

Gatzke, Hans. *Stresemann and the Rearmament of Germany.* Baltimore: Johns Hopkins University Press, 1954.

Gessner, Dieter. *Das Ende der Weimarer Republik. Fragen, Methoden und Ergebnisse interdisziplinärer Forschung.* Darmstadt: Wissenschaftliche Buchgesellschaft, 1988.

Gordon, Harold J. *The Reichswehr and the German Republic, 1919–1926.* Princeton, N.J.: Princeton University Press, 1957.

Gusy, Christoph. *Weimar, die wehrlose Republik? Verfassungsrecht und Verfassungsschutz in der Weimarer Republik.* Tübingen: Mohr, 1991.

Hallgarten, Georg F.W. *Hitler, Reichswehr und Industrie. Zur Geschichte der Jahre 1918–1933.* Frankfurt a.M: Europäische Verlagsanstalt, 1955.

Holtferich, Carl-Ludwig. *The German Inflation, 1914–1923*, trans. Theo Balderston. New York: De Gruyter, 1986.

Ihlau, Olaf. *Die roten Kämpfer. Ein Beitrag zur Geschichte der Arbeiterbewegung in der Weimarer Republik und im Dritten Reich.* Meisenheim am Glan: A. Hain, 1969.

Kahn-Freund, Otto. *Labor Law and Politics in the Weimar Republic,* trans. Jon Clark. Oxford: Blackwell, 1981.

Kaufmann, Walter H. *Monarchism in the Weimar Republic.* New York: Bookman Associates, 1953.

Kershaw, Ian, ed. *Weimar: Why Did German Democracy Fail?* New York: St. Martin's Press, 1990.

Kruedener, Jürgen, Freiherr von. *Economic Crisis and Political Collapse: The Weimar Republic, 1924–1933*. New York: St. Martin's Press, 1990.

Kruger, Peter. *Die Außenpolitik der Republik von Weimar*. Darmstadt: Wissenschaftliche Buchgesellschaft, 1985.

Lang, Jochen von. *Und willst du nicht mein Bruder sein—Der Terror in der Weimarer Republik*. Vienna: P. Zsolnay, 1989.

Leopold, John A. *Alfred Hugenberg: The Radical Nationalist Campaign against the Weimar Republic*. New Haven: Yale University Press, 1977.

Matthias, Erich, and Rudolf Morsey, eds. *Das Ende der Parteien 1933. Darstellungen und Dokumente*. Düsseldorf: Droste Verlag, 1979.

Mitchell, Alan. *Revolution in Bavaria 1918–1919: The Eisner Regime and the Soviet Republic*. Princeton, N.J.: Princeton University Press, 1965.

McNeil, William C. *American Money and the Weimar Republic: Economics and Politics on the Eve of the Great Depression*. New York: Columbia University Press, 1986.

Neumann, Sigmund. *Die Parteien der Weimarer Republik*. Stuttgart: W. Kohlhammer, 1965.

Nuss, Karl. *Militär und Wiederaufrüstung in der Weimarer Republik*. Berlin: Militärverlag der DDR, 1977.

Petzina, Dietmar. *Die deutsche Wirtschaft in der Zwischenkriegszeit*. Wiesbaden: Steiner, 1977.

Schneider, Werner. *Die Deutsche Demokratische Partei in der Weimarer Republik. 1924–1930*. Munich: Fink, 1978.

Stern, Fritz, ed. *The Path to Dictatorship, 1918–1933*. Garden City, N.Y.: Doubleday Anchor, 1966.

Schulz, Gerhard. *Zwischen Demokratie und Diktatur. Verfassungspolitik und Reichsreform in der Weimarer Republik*. Berlin: De Gruyter, 1987.

Stachura, Peter D. ed. *Unemployment and the Great Depression in Weimar Germany*. New York: St. Martin's Press, 1986.

———. *Political Leaders in Weimar Germany: A Biographical Study*. New York: Harvester Wheatsheaf, 1993.

Stürmer, Michael. *Koalition und Opposition in der Weimarer Republik, 1924–1928*. Düsseldorf, Droste, 1967.

Turner, Henry Ashby. *Stresemann and the Politics of the Weimar Republic*. Princeton, N.J.: Princeton University Press, 1963.

———. *German Big Business and the Rise of Hitler*. New York: Oxford University Press, 1985.

Waite, Robert G.L. *Vanguard of Nazism: The Free Corps Movement in Postwar Germany, 1918–1923*. Cambridge, Mass.: Harvard University Press, 1952.

Waldman, Eric. *The Spartacist Uprising of 1919 and the Crisis of the German Socialist Movement*. Milwaukee: Marquette University Press, 1958.

Pressure Points of Social Life

Abelshauser, Werner, ed. *Die Weimarer Republik als Wohlfahrtsstaat. Zum Verhältnis von Wirtschafts- und Sozialpolitik in der Industriegesellschaft*. Stuttgart: F. Steiner, 1987.

Bering, Dietz. *The Stigma of Names: Anti-Semitism in German Daily Life, 1812–1933*, trans. Neville Plaice. Ann Arbor: University of Michigan Press, 1992.

Bock, Hans Manfred. *Syndikalismus und Linkskommunismus von 1918–1923*. Meisenheim am Glan: A. Hain, 1969.

Boesch, Hermann. *Jugend in der Weimarer Republik. Erlebte Zeitgeschichte*. Melle: E. Knoth, 1989.

Braunthal, Gerard. *Socialist Labor and Politics in Weimar Germany: The General Federation of German Trade Unions*. Hamden, Conn.: Archon Books, 1978.

Bridenthal, Renate, Atina Grossmann, and Marion Kaplan, eds. *When Biology Became Destiny: Women in Weimar and Nazi Germany*. New York: Monthly Review Press, 1984.

Evans, Richard. *The Feminist Movement in Germany (1894–1933)*. Beverly Hills: Sage Publications, 1976.

Frauengruppe Faschismusforschung, ed. *Mutterkreuz und Arbeitsbuch. Zur Geschichte der Frauen in der Weimarer Republik und im Nationalsozialismus*. Frankfurt a.M.: Fischer, 1981.

Frevert, Ute. *Women in German History. From Bourgeois Emancipation to Sexual Liberation*, trans. Stuart McKinnon-Evans et al. Oxford: Berg, 1989.

Friedrich, Gerhard. *Proletarische Literatur und politische Organisation. Die Literaturpolitik der KPD in der Weimarer Republik und die proletarisch-revolutionäre Literatur*. Frankfurt a.M: Lang, 1981.

Geisel, Eike, ed. *Im Scheunenviertel. Bilder, Texte und Dokumente*. Berlin: Severin und Siedler, 1981.

Grab, Walter, and Julius H. Schoeps, eds. *Juden in der Weimarer Republik*. Stuttgart: Burg, 1986.

Hagemann, Karen. *Frauenalltag und Männerpolitik. Alltagsleben und gesellschaftliches Handeln von Arbeiterfrauen in der Weimarer Republik*. Bonn: Dietz, 1990.

Hermand, Jost, and Gert Mattenklott, eds. *Jüdische Intelligenz in Deutschland*. Hamburg: Argument, 1988.

Hoffmann, Ludwig, and Daniel Hoffman-Ostwald. *Deutsches Arbeitertheater, 1918–1944*. 2 vols. Munich: Rogner & Bernhard, 1972.

Kater, Michael H. *Studentenschaft und Rechtsradikalismus in Deutschland 1918–1933*. Hamburg: Hoffmann und Campe, 1975.

Klatt, Gudrun. *Arbeiterklasse und Theater. Agitprop–Tradition, Theater im Exil, Sozialistisches Theater*. Berlin: Akademie Verlag, 1975.

Klein, Alfred. *Im Auftrag ihrer Klasse. Weg und Leistung der deutschen Arbeiterschriftsteller 1918 bis 1933*. Berlin: Aufbau-Verlag, 1975.

Knütter, Hans-Helmuth. *Die Juden und die deutsche Linke in der Weimarer Republik 1918–1933*. Düsseldorf: Droste Verlag, 1971.

Kontos, Silvia. *Die Partei kämpft wie ein Mann. Frauenpolitik der KPD in der Weimarer Republik*. Basel: Stroemfeld Verlag, 1979.

Koonz, Claudia. *Mothers in the Fatherland*. New York: St. Martin's Press, 1987.

Lewek, Peter. *Arbeitslosigkeit und Arbeitslosenversicherung in der Weimarer Republik, 1918–1927*. Stuttgart: F. Steiner, 1992.

Liptzin, Solomon. *Germany's Stepchildren*. Philadelphia: Jewish Publication Society of America, 1944.

Lorenz, Ina Susanne, ed. *Die Juden in Hamburg zur Zeit der Weimarer Republik. Eine Dokumentation*. Hamburg: H. Christians, 1987.

Luthardt, Wolfgang, ed. *Sozialdemokratische Arbeiterbewegung und Weimarer Republik*. 2 vols. Frankfurt a.M.: Suhrkamp, 1978.

Michaelis, Herbert, ed. *Ursachen und Folgen. Vom deutschen Zusammenbruch 1919 bis zur staatlichen Neuordnung Deutschlands in der Gegenwart*. Berlin: Dokumenten-Verlag, 1958.

Mommsen, Hans. *From Weimar to Auschwitz,* trans. Philip O'Connor. Princeton, N.J.: Princeton University Press, 1991.

Mosse, George L. *Fallen Soldiers: Reshaping the Memory of the World Wars*. New York: Oxford, 1990.

Mosse, Werner E., and Arnold Paucker, eds. *Deutsches Judentum in Krieg und Revolution 1916–1923*. Tübingen: J.C.B. Mohr, 1971.

———, eds. *Entscheidungsjahr 1932. Zur Judenfrage in der Endphase der Weimarer Republik*. Tübingen: J.C.B. Mohr, 1966.

Niewyk, Donald L. *Socialist, Anti-Semite, and Jew: German Social Democracy Confronts the Problem of Anti-Semitism, 1918–1933*. Baton Rouge: LSU Press, 1971.

———. *The Jews in Weimar Germany*. Baton Rouge: LSU Press, 1980.

Noakes, Jeremy, and Geoffrey Pridham, eds. *Nazism: A History in Documents and Eyewitness Accounts, 1919–1945*. New York: Schocken, 1990.

Orfali, Stephanie. *A Jewish Girl in the Weimar Republic*. Berkeley: Ronin, 1987.

Patch, William L., Jr. *The Christian Trade Unions in the Weimar Republic, 1919–1933: The Failure of Corporate Pluralism*. New Haven: Yale University Press, 1985.

Paucker, Arnold. *Der jüdische Abwehrkampf gegen Antisemitismus und Nationalsozialismus in den letzten Jahren der Weimarer Republik*. Hamburg: Leibniz Verlag, 1968.

Pregardier, Elisabeth, and Anne Mohr. *Politik als Aufgabe. Engagement christlicher Frauen in der Weimarer Republik*. Annweiler/Essen: Ploger, 1990.

Reicke, Ilse. *Die großen Frauen der Weimarer Republik. Erlebnisse im 'Berliner Frühling'* Freiburg i.B.: Herder, 1984.

Saatz, Ursula. *Paragraph 218, das Recht der Frau ist unteilbar. Über die Auswirkungen des Paragraphs 218 und die Bewegung gegen die Abtreibungsgesetzgebung zur Zeit der Weimarer Republik*. Münster: Votum, 1991.

Soden, Kristine, and Maruta Schmidt, eds. *Neue Frauen. Die zwanziger Jahre*. Berlin: Elefanten Press, 1988.

Showalter, Dennis E. *Little Man, What Now?* Der Stürmer *in the Weimar Republic*. Hamden, Conn.: Archon Books, 1982.

Stachura, Peter D. *Nazi Youth in the Weimar Republic*. Santa Barbara, Ca.: Clio Books, 1975.

———. *The Weimar Republic and the Younger Proletariat: An Economic and Social Analysis*. Houndsmill: Macmillan, 1989.

Unterstell, Rembert. *Mittelstand in der Weimarer Republik. Die soziale Entwicklung und politische Orientierung von Handwerk, Kleinhandel und Hausbesitz 1919–1933. Ein Überblick*. Frankfurt a.M.: P. Lang, 1989.

Usborn, Cornelie. *The Politics of the Body in Weimar Germany: Women's Reproductive Rights and Duties*. Ann Arbor: University of Michigan Press, 1993.

Vollmer-Heitmann, Hanna. *Wir sind von Kopf bis Fuß auf Liebe eingestellt. Die Zwanziger Jahre*. Hamburg: Kabel, 1993.

Weber, Richard. *Proletarisches Theater der revolutionären Arbeiterbewegung 1918 bis 1925*. Cologne: Gaehme, Henke, 1976.

Will, Wilfried van der, and Rob Burns, eds. *Arbeiterkulturbewegung in der Weimarer Republik. Texte, Dokumente, Bilder*. Frankfurt a.M.: Ullstein, 1982.

Winkler, Heinrich August. *Mittelstand, Demokratie und Nationalsozialismus. Die politische Entwicklung von Handwerk und Kleinhandel in der Weimarer Republik*. Cologne: Kiepenheuer and Witsch, 1972.

—————. *Von der Revolution zur Stabilisierung. Arbeiter und Arbeiterbewegung in der Weimarer Republik, 1918 bis 1924*. Berlin: J.H.W. Dietz, 1984.

—————. *Der Schein der Normalität. Arbeiter und Arbeiterbewegung in der Weimarer Republik, 1924 bis 1930*. Berlin: J.H.W. Dietz, 1985.

—————. *Der Weg in die Katastrophe. Arbeiter und Arbeiterbewegung in der Weimarer Republik, 1930 bis 1933*. Berlin: J.H.W. Dietz, 1987.

Intellectuals and the Ideologies of the Age

Bance, Alan, ed. *Weimar Germany: Writers and Politics*. Edinburgh: Scottish Academic Press, 1982.

Barnouw, Dagmar. *Weimar Intellectuals and the Threat of Modernity*. Bloomington, Ind.: Indiana University Press, 1988.

Bendersky, Joseph W. *Carl Schmitt: Theorist for the Reich*. Princeton, N.J.: Princeton University Press, 1983.

Bering, Dietz. *Die Intellektuellen. Geschichte eines Schimpfwortes*. Stuttgart: Klett-Cotta, 1978.

Berking, Helmuth. *Masse und Geist. Studien zur Soziologie in der Weimarer Republik*. Berlin: Wissenschaftlicher Autoren-Verlag, 1984.

Berle, Waltraud. *Heinrich Mann und die Weimarer Republik. Zur Entwicklung eines politischen Schriftstellers in Deutschland*. Bonn: Bouvier, 1983.

Bowen, Ralph. *German Theories of the Corporatist State*. New York: Russell and Russell, 1947.

Bronner, Stephen Eric, and Douglas Kellner, eds. *Passion and Rebellion: The Expressionist Heritage*. New York: J.F. Bergin, 1983.

Clemens, Gabriele. *Martin Spahn und der Rechtskatholizismus in der Weimarer Republik*. Mainz: Grünewald, 1983.

Deak, Istvan. *Weimar Germany's Left-wing Intellectuals: A Political History of the Weltbühne and its Circle*. Berkeley and Los Angeles: University of California Press, 1968.

Frisby, David. *Fragments of Modernity: Theories of Modernity in the Work of Simmel, Kracauer and Benjamin*. Cambridge, Mass.: MIT Press, 1986.

Herf, Jeffrey. *Reactionary Modernism: Technology, Culture, and Politics in Weimar and the Third Reich*. New York: Cambridge University Press, 1984.

Jay, Martin. *The Dialectical Imagination: A History of the Frankfurt School and the Institute of Social Research, 1923–1950*. Boston: Little, Brown, 1973.

Klemperer, Klemens von. *Germany's New Conservatism: Its History and Dilemma in the Twentieth Century*. Princeton, N.J.: Princeton University Press, 1957.

Krockow, Christian Graf von. *Die Entscheidung. Eine Untersuchung über Ernst Jünger, Carl Schmitt, Martin Heidegger*. Stuttgart: Ferdinand Enke, 1958.

Lebovics, Herman. *Social Conservatism and the Middle Classes in Germany, 1914–1933*. Princeton, N.J.: Princeton University Press, 1969.

Löwy, Michael. *Redemption and Utopia: Jewish Libertarian Thought in Central Europe: A Study in Elective Affinity*, trans. Hope Heaney. Stanford: Stanford University Press, 1992.

Lunn, Eugene. *Prophet of Community: The Romantic Socialism of Gustav Landauer*. Berkeley: University of California Press, 1973.

Lunn, Eugene. *Marxism and Modernism: An Historical Study of Lukács, Brecht, Benjamin and Adorno*. Berkeley and Los Angeles: University of California Press, 1982.

Luthardt, Wolfgang. *Sozialdemokratische Verfassungstheorie in der Weimarer Republik*. Opladen: Westdeutscher Verlag, 1986.

Mohler, Armin. *Die Konservative Revolution in Deutschland, 1918–1932. Grundriß ihrer Weltanschauungen*. Stuttgart: Vorwek, 1950.

Mosse, George L. *The Crisis of German Ideology: Intellectual Origins of the Third Reich*. New York: Grosset and Dunlap, 1964.

————. *Germans and Jews: The Right, the Left and the Search for a "Third Force" in Pre-Nazi Germany*. New York: Grosset and Dunlap, 1970.

Müller, Hans-Harald. *Intellektueller Linksradikalismus in der Weimarer Republik. Seine Entstehung, Geschichte und Literatur*. Kronberg/Ts.: Scriptor, 1977.

Muller, Jerry Z. *The Other God That Failed: Hans Freyer and the Deradicalization of German Conservatism*. Princeton, N.J.: Princeton University Press, 1987.

Petzold, Joachim. *Konservative Theoretiker des deutschen Faschismus. Jungkonservative Ideologen in der Weimarer Republik als geistige Wegbereiter der faschistischen Diktatur*. Berlin: Deutscher Verlag der Wissenschaften, 1982.

Anthony Phelan, ed. *The Weimar Dilemma: Intellectuals in the Weimar Republic*. Manchester: Manchester University Press, 1985.

Raulet, Gérard, ed. *Weimar ou l'explosion de la modernité*. Paris: Anthropos, 1984.

Ringer, Fritz K. *The Decline of the German Mandarins: The German Academic Community, 1890–1933*. Cambridge, Mass.: Harvard University Press, 1969.

Rudolph, Hermann. *Kulturkritik und konservative Revolution*. Tübingen: Niemeyer, 1971.

Schivelbusch, Wolfgang. *Intellektuellendämmerung. Zur Lage der Frankfurter Intelligenz in den zwanziger Jahren*. Frankfurt a.M.: Suhrkamp, 1985.

Schluchter, Wolfgang. *Entscheidung für den sozialen Rechtstaat. Hermann Heller und die staatstheoretische Diskussion in der Weimarer Republik*. Baden-Baden: Nomos, 1983.

Schüddekopf, Otto Ernst. *Linke Leute von Rechts. Die National-revolutionären Minderheiten und der Kommunismus in der Weimarer Republik*. Stuttgart: Kohlhammer, 1960.

Schürgers, Norbert J. *Politische Philosophie in der Weimarer Republik. Staatsverständnis zwischen Führerdemokratie und bürokratischem Sozialismus*. Stuttgart: J.B. Metzler, 1989.

Smith, Gary, ed. *On Walter Benjamin: Critical Essays and Reflections*. Cambridge: MIT Press, 1988.

Sontheimer, Kurt. *Antidemokratisches Denken in der Weimarer Republik. Die politischen Ideen des deutschen Nationalismus zwischen 1918 und 1933*. Munich: Nymphenburger, 1968.

Stark, Gary D. *Entrepreneurs of Ideology: Neoconservative Publishers in Germany, 1890–1933*. Chapel Hill: University of North Carolina Press, 1981.

Stark, Michael, ed. *Deutsche Intellektuelle 1910–1933. Aufrufe, Pamphlete, Betrachtungen*. Heidelberg: Lambert Schneider, 1984.

Stern, Fritz. *The Politics of Cultural Despair: A Study in the Rise of the Germanic Ideology*. Garden City, N.Y.: Doubleday Anchor, 1965.

Stölting, Erhard. *Akademische Soziologie in der Weimarer Republik*. Berlin: Duncker und Humblot, 1986.

Struve, Walter. *Elites against Democracy: Leadership Ideals in Bourgeois Political Thought in Germany, 1890–1933*. Princeton, N.J.: Princeton University Press, 1973.

Walter, Franz. *Nationale Romantik und revolutionärer Mythos. Politik und Lebensweisen im frühen Weimarer Jungsozialismus*. Berlin: Europäische Perspektiven, 1986.

Witte, Bernd. *Walter Benjamin: An Intellectual Biography,* trans. James Rolleston. Detroit: Wayne State University Press, 1991.

Zimmerman, Michael. *Heidegger's Confrontation with Modernity: Technology, Politics, Art.* Bloomington, Ind.: Indiana University Press, 1990.

The Challenge of Modernity

Ades, Dawn. *Photomontage.* London: Thames and Hudson, 1976.

Banham, Reyner. *Theory and Design in the First Machine Age.* Cambridge: MIT Press, 1980.

————. *A Concrete Atlantis: U.S. Industrial Building and European Modern Architecture.* Cambridge: MIT Press, 1986.

Benjamin, Walter. *Reflections: Essays, Aphorisms, Autobiographical Writings,* ed. Peter Demetz, trans. Edmund Jephcott. New York: Harcourt Brace Jovanovich, 1978.

Bergius, Hanne. *Das Lachen Dadas.* Gießen: Anabas, 1989.

Bloch, Ernst. *Heritage of Our Times,* trans. Stephen and Neville Plaice. Berkeley and Los Angeles: University of California Press, 1991.

Boberg, Jochen, Tilman Fichter, and Eckhart Gillen, eds. *Die Metropole. Industriekultur in Berlin im 20. Jahrhunderts.* Munich: Beck, 1986.

Clair, Jean, ed. *The 1920s: Age of the Metropolis.* Montreal: The Montreal Museum of Fine Arts, 1991.

Dal Co, Francesco. *Figures of Architecture and Thought: German Architecture Culture 1880–1920,* trans. Stephen Sartarelli. New York: Rizzoli, 1990.

Elderfield, John. *Kurt Schwitters.* London: Thames and Hudson, 1985.

Fischer, Wend, ed. *Zwischen Kunst und Industrie. Der Deutsche Werkbund.* Stuttgart: Deutsche Verlags-Anstalt, 1987.

Flavell, M. Kay. *George Grosz: A Biography.* New Haven: Yale University Press, 1988.

Fraser, James, ed. *The Malik Verlag 1916–1947: Berlin, Prague, New York.* New York: Goethe House, 1984.

Friedrich, Thomas. *Berlin between the Wars.* New York: The Vendome Press, 1991.

Harrison, Charles, and Paul Wood, eds. *Art in Theory: An Anthology of Changing Ideas.* Oxford and Cambridge, Mass.: Blackwell, 1992.

Haxthausen, Charles W., and Heidrun Suhr, eds. *Berlin: Culture and Metropolis.* Minneapolis: University of Minnesota Press, 1991.

Hays, K. Michael. *Modernism and the Posthumanist Subject: The Architecture of Hannes Meyer and Ludwig Hilberseimer.* Cambridge: MIT Press, 1992.

Herzogenrath, Wulf, and Johann-Karl Schmid, eds. *Otto Dix. Zum 100. Geburtstag 1891– 1991.* Stuttgart and Berlin: Gallerie der Stadt Stuttgart, Verlag G. Hatje, Staatliche Museen Preußischer Kulturbesitz, 1991.

Hirdina, Heinz, ed. *Neues Bauen Neues Gestalten. Das neue Frankfurt/Die neue Stadt. Eine Zeitschrift zwischen 1926 und 1923.* Berlin: Elefanten Press, 1984.

Huse, Norbert. *Neues Bauen 1918–1933. Moderne Architektur in der Weimarer Republik.* 2d ed. Berlin: Ernst, 1985.

Isaacs, Reginald. *Gropius: An Illustrated Biography of the Creator of the Bauhaus.* Boston: Little Brown, 1991.

Joachimides, Christos M., Norman Rosenthal, and Wieland Schmied, eds. *German Art in the 20th Century.* New York: Prestel Verlag, 1985.

Kändler, Klaus, ed. *Berliner Begegnungen. Ausländische Künstler in Berlin 1918 bis 1933.* Berlin: Dietz Verlag, 1987.

Kandinsky: Russian and Bauhaus Years. New York: Solomon R. Guggenheim Museum, 1983.

Kracauer, Siegfried. *The Mass Ornament,* trans. Thomas Levin. Cambridge: Harvard University Press, forthcoming.

Lane, Barbara Miller. *Architecture and Politics in Germany, 1918–1945*. Cambridge: Harvard University Press, 1968.

Lange, Annemarie. *Berlin in der Weimarer Republik*. Berlin: Dietz Verlag, 1987.

Lavin, Maud. *Cut with the Kitchen Knife: The Weimar Photomontages of Hannah Höch*. New Haven: Yale University Press, 1993.

Lees, Andrew. *Cities Perceived: Urban Society in European and American Thought, 1820–1940*. Manchester: Manchester University Press, 1985.

Lewis, Beth Irwin. *George Grosz: Art and Politics in the Weimar Republic*. Madison: University of Wisconsin Press, 1971.

Lloyd, Jill. *German Expressionism: Primitivism and Modernity*. New Haven: Yale University Press, 1991.

Neumann, Eckhard, ed. *Bauhaus and Bauhaus People*. New York: Van Nostrand Reinhold, 2d ed., 1993.

Neumeyer, Fritz, ed. *The Artless Word: Mies van der Rohe on the Building Art*. trans. Mark Jarzombek. Cambridge: MIT Press, 1991.

Pachnicke, Peter, and Klaus Honnef, eds. *John Heartfield*. New York: Harry N. Abrams, 1992.

Paris–Berlin 1900–33. Paris: Centre Georges Pompidou, 1978.

Pehnt, Wolfgang. *Expressionist Architecture*. London: Thames and Hudson, 1973.

PEM. *Heimweh nach dem Kurfürstendamm. Aus Berlins glanzvollsten Tagen und Nächten*. Berlin: Lothar Blanvalet Verlag, 1962.

Pommer, Richard, and Christian F. Otto. *Weissenhof 1927 and the Modern Movement in Architecture*. Chicago: University of Chicago Press, 1991.

Rabinbach, Anson. *The Human Motor: Energy, Fatigue, and the Origins of Modernity*. New York: Basic Books, 1990.

Richter, Hans. *Dada: Art and Anti-Art*, trans. David Britt. New York: Harry N. Abrams, 1965.

Rogoff, Irit, ed. *The Divided Heritage: Themes and Problems in German Modernism*. Cambridge: Cambridge University Press, 1991.

Roters, Eberhard, ed. *Berlin 1910–1933,* trans. Marguerite Mounier. New York: Rizzoli, 1982.

Schmied, Wieland. *Neue Sachlichkeit und magischer Realismus in Deutschland 1918–1933*. Hannover: Fackelträger Verlag, 1969.

Schneede, Uwe M., ed. *Die Zwanziger Jahre. Manifeste und Dokumente deutscher Künstler*. Cologne: DuMont, 1979.

Schulz-Hoffmann, Carla, and Judith C. Weiss, eds. *Max Beckmann Retrospective*. Saint Louis, Missouri and Munich: Saint Louis Art Museum and Prestel Verlag, 1984.

Schulze, Franz. *Mies van der Rohe: A Critical Biography*. Chicago: University of Chicago Press, 1985.

Stölzl, Christoph, ed. *Die Zwanziger Jahre in München. Katalog zur Ausstellung im Münchner Stadtmuseum*. Munich: Münchner Stadtmuseum, 1979.

Tower, Beeke Sell, ed. *Envisioning America: Prints, Drawings, and Photographs by George Grosz and his Contemporaries*. Cambridge: Busch-Reisinger Museum of Harvard University, 1990.

Wagner, Martin, ed. *Das neue Berlin. Großstadt-Probleme*. Basel: Birkhäuser Verlag, 1988.

Weinstein, Joan. *The End of Expressionism: Art and the November Revolution in Germany, 1918–1919*. Chicago: University of Chicago Press, 1990.

Whyte, Iain Boyd. *Bruno Taut and the Architecture of Activism*. Cambridge, England: Cambridge University Press, 1982.

Wiedenhoeft, Roland. *Berlin's Housing Revolution: German Reform in the 1920s*. Ann Arbor: UMI Research Press, 1985.

Wingler, Hans M. ed. *The Bauhaus: Weimar, Dessau, Berlin, Chicago*, trans. Wolfgang Jabs and Basil Gilbert. Cambridge: MIT Press, 1969.

Changing Configurations of Culture

Arnheim, Rudolf. *Film as Art*. Berkeley and Los Angeles: University of California Press, 1967.

Bach, Steven. *Marlene Dietrich: Life and Legend*. New York: Morrow, 1992.

Barlow, John D. *German Expressionist Film*. Boston: Twayne, 1982.

Bemmann, Helga. *Berliner Musenkinder-Memoiren*. Berlin: Lied der Zeit-Musikverlag, 1987.

Bienert, Michael. *Die eingebildete Metropole. Berlin im Feuilleton der Weimarer Republik*. Stuttgart: Metzler, 1992.

Buache, Freddy. *Le cinéma Allemand. 1918–1933*. Paris: Hatier, 1984.

Budzinski, Klaus. *Das Kabarett. 100 Jahre literarische Zeitkritik*. Düsseldorf: Econ, 1985.

Bullivant, Keith, ed. *Das literarische Leben in der Weimarer Republik*. Königstein/Ts.: Scriptor, 1978.

Coke, Van Deren. *Avantgarde Photography in Germany 1919–1939*. New York: Pantheon, 1982.

Cook, Susan C. *Opera for a New Republic: The 'Zeitopern' of Krenek, Weill, and Hindemith*. Ann Arbor, MI: UMI Research Press, 1988.

Curjel, Hans. *Experiment Krolloper 1927–1931*. Munich: Prestel, 1975.

Danzi, Michael, and Rainer E. Lotz. *American Musician in Germany, 1924–1939: Memoirs of the Jazz, Entertainment, and Movie World of Berlin during the Weimar Republic and the Nazi Era, and in the United States*. Schmitten: N. Ruecker, 1986.

Drew, David. *Kurt Weill: A Handbook*. Berkeley and Los Angeles: University of California Press, 1987.

Eisner, Lotte H. *The Haunted Screen*. Berkeley and Los Angeles: University of California Press, 1969.

―――. *Fritz Lang*. New York: Oxford University Press, 1977.

Güttinger, Fritz. *Kein Tag ohne Kino. Schriftsteller über den Stummfilm*. Frankfurt a.M.: Deutsches Filmmuseum, 1984.

Hay, Gerhard, ed. *Literatur und Rundfunk 1923–1933*. Hildesheim: Gerstenberg, 1975.

Heller, Heinz B. *Literarische Intelligenz und Film. Zu Veränderungen der ästhetischen Theorie und Praxis unter dem Eindruck des Films 1910–1930 in Deutschland*. Tübingen: Niemeyer, 1985.

Hepp, Michael. *Kurt Tucholsky. Biographische Annäherungen*. Reinbek: Rowohlt, 1993.

Hertling, Viktoria. *Quer durch, von Dwinger bis Kisch: Berichte und Reportagen über die Sowjetunion aus der Epoche der Weimarer Republik*. Königstein/Ts.: Scriptor, 1982.

Hickethier, Knut, ed. *Grenzgänger zwischen Theater und Kino. Schauspielerporträts aus dem Berlin der Zwanziger Jahre*. Berlin: Ästhetik und Kommunikation, 1986.

Hinton, Stephen. *The Idea of Gebrauchsmusik: A Study of Musical Aesthetics in the Weimar Republic (1919–1933) with Particular Reference to the Works of Paul Hindemith.* New York: Garland, 1989.

Hörburger, Christian. *Das Hörspiel der Weimarer Republik. Versuch einer kritischen Analyse.* Stuttgart: Heinz, 1975.

Huyssen, Andreas, and David Bathrick, eds. *Modernity and the Text: Revisions of German Modernism.* New York: Columbia University Press, 1989.

Innes, C.D. *Erwin Piscator's Political Theater.* London: Cambridge University Press, 1972.

Jansen, Wolfgang. *Glanzrevuen der zwanziger Jahre.* Berlin: Edition Hentrich, 1987.

Jensen, Paul M. *The Cinema of Fritz Lang.* New York: A.S. Barnes and Co., 1969.

Jung, Uli, and Walter Schatzberg, eds. *Filmkultur zur Zeit der Weimarer Republik.* Munich/New York: K.G. Saur, 1992.

Kaes, Anton, ed. *Kino-Debatte. Texte zum Verhältnis von Literatur und Film 1909–1929.* Tübingen: Max Niemeyer Verlag, 1978.

Klein, Alfred, ed. *Zur Tradition der deutschen Sozialistischen Literatur. Eine Auswahl von Dokumenten, 1926–1935.* Berlin and Weimar: Aufbau-Verlag, 1979.

Klooss, Reinhard, and Thomas Reuter. *Körperbilder—Menschenornamente in Revuetheater und Revuefilm.* Frankfurt a.M.: Syndikat, 1980.

Knellessen, F.W. *Agitation auf der Bühne. Das politische Theater der Weimarer Republik.* Emsdetten: Lechte, 1976.

Korte, Helmut, ed. *Film und Realität in der Weimarer Republik.* Munich: Hanser, 1978.

Kowalke, Kim H. *Kurt Weill in Europe.* Ann Arbor: UMI Research Press 1979.

Kracauer, Siegfried. *From Caligari to Hitler: A Psychological History of the German Film.* Princeton: Princeton University Press, 1947.

———. *Kino. Essays, Studien, Glossen zum Film.* Frankfurt a.M.: Suhrkamp, 1974.

Kreimeier, Klaus. *Die Ufa-Story. Geschichte eines Filmkonzerns.* Munich: Hanser, 1992.

Kühn, Gertraude, et al., eds. *Film und revolutionäre Arbeiterbewegung in Deutschland 1918–1932.* 2 vols. Berlin: Hochschule für Film und Fernsehen der DDR, 1975.

Kurtz, Rudolf. *Expressionismus und Film.* Berlin: Wolffsohn, 1926 (repr. 1965).

Lerg, Winfried B. *Rundfunkpolitik in der Weimarer Republik.* Munich: dtv, 1980.

Lethen, Helmut. *Neue Sachlichkeit 1924–1932. Studien zur Literatur des "Weißen Sozialismus."* Stuttgart: J.B. Metzler, 1975.

Manning, Susan A. *Ecstasy and the Demon. Feminism and Nationalism in the Dances of Mary Wigman.* Berkeley and Los Angeles: University of California Press, 1993.

Mellor, David, ed. *Germany: The New Photography 1927–33.* London: Arts Council of Great Britain, 1978.

Mendelsohn, Peter de. *Zeitungsstadt Berlin.* Berlin: Ullstein, 1959.

Mierau, Fritz, ed. *Russen in Berlin. Literatur, Malerei, Theater, Film 1918–1933.* Leipzig: Reclam, 1987.

Mörchen, Helmut. *Schriftsteller in der Massengesellschaft.* Stuttgart: J.B. Metzler, 1973.

Monaco, Paul. *Cinema and Society: France and Germany during the Twenties.* New York: Elsevier, 1976.

Murray, Bruce. *Film and the German Left in the Weimar Republic.* Austin: University of Texas Press, 1990.

Ott, Frederick W. *The Films of Fritz Lang.* Secaucus: The Citadel Press, 1979.

Petersen, Klaus. *Literatur und Justiz in der Weimarer Republik.* Stuttgart: J.B. Metzler, 1988.

Petrie, Graham. *Hollywood Destinies: European Directors in America, 1922–1931*. London: Routledge & Kegan Paul, 1985.

Petro, Patrice. *Joyless Streets: Women and Melodramatic Representation in Weimar Germany*. Princeton, N.J.: Princeton University Press, 1989.

Phillips, Christopher, ed. *Photography in the Modern Era. European Documents and Critical Writings, 1913–1940*. New York: The Metropolitan Museum of Art/Aperture, 1989.

Plummer, Thomas, et al., eds. *Film and Politics in the Weimar Republic*. New York: Holmes and Meier, 1982.

Prawer, S.S. *Caligari's Children: The Film as Tale of Terror*. New York: Da Capo, 1980.

Preston-Dunlop, Valerie, and Susanne Lahusen, eds. *Schrifttanz: A View of German Dance in the Weimar Republic*. London: Dance Books, 1990.

Reich, Willi. *The Life and Works of Alban Berg*. London: Thames and Hudson, 1965.

Reinhardt, Stephan, ed. *Lesebuch Weimarer Republik: Deutsche Schriftsteller und ihr Staat von 1918 bis 1933*. Berlin: Wagenbach, 1982.

Rothe, Wolfgang, ed. *Die deutsche Literatur in der Weimarer Republik*. Stuttgart: Reclam, 1974.

Rühle, Günther, ed. *Theater für die Republik. 1917–1933 im Spiegel der Kritik*. 2 vols. Berlin: Henschelverlag, 1988.

Sander, August. *Photographs of an Epoch*. New York: Aperture, 1980.

Schebera, Jürgen. *Damals im Romanischen Café. Künstler und ihre Lokale im Berlin der zwanziger Jahre*. Frankfurt a.M.: Büchergilde Gutenberg, 1988.

Schneider, Irmela, ed. *Radio-Kultur in der Weimarer Republik*. Tübingen: Gunter Narr, 1984.

Schrader, Bärbel, and Jürgen Schebera, eds. *Kunstmetropole Berlin 1918–1933*. Berlin and Weimar: Aufbau-Verlag, 1987.

Schütz, Erhard. *Romane der Weimarer Republik*. Munich: W. Fink, 1986.

Schutte, Sabine. *Ich will aber gerade vom Leben singen . . . Über populäre Musik vom ausgehenden 19. Jahrhundert bis zum Ende der Weimarer Republik*. Reinbek: Rowohlt, 1987.

Seidenstücker, Friedrich. *Von Weimar bis zum Ende. Fotografien aus bewegter Zeit*. Dortmund: Harenberg, 1980.

Sloterdijk, Peter. *Literatur und Organisation von Lebenserfahrung. Autobiographien der Zwanziger Jahre*. Munich: Hanser 1978.

———. *Critique of Cynical Reason,* trans. Michael Eldred. Minneapolis: University of Minnesota Press, 1987.

Stern, Dietrich, ed. *Angewandte Musik. 20er Jahre*. Berlin: Argument-Verlag, 1977.

Stewart, John L. *Ernst Krenek: The Man and His Music*. Berkeley and Los Angeles: University of California Press, 1991.

Voigts, Manfred, ed. *100 Texte zu Brecht. Materialien aus der Weimarer Republik*. Munich: W. Fink, 1980.

Willett, John, ed. and trans. *Brecht on Theatre. The Development of an Aesthetic*. New York: Hill and Wang, 1964.

———. *The Theatre of the Weimar Republic*. New York: Holmes & Meier, 1988.

The Transformation of Everyday Life

Andritzky, Michael, and Thomas Rautenberg, eds. *Wir sind nackt und nennen uns du. Eine Geschichte der Freikörperkultur*. Gießen: Anabas, 1990.

Bollé, Michael, ed. *Eldorado. Homosexuelle Frauen und Männer in Berlin 1850–1950. Geschichte, Alltag und Kultur.* Berlin: Frölich & Kaufmann, 1984.

Eckardt, Wolf von, and Sander L. Gilman. *Bertolt Brecht's Berlin: A Scrapbook of the Twenties.* Garden City, NY: Anchor Press, Doubleday, 1975.

Eichstedt, Astrid, and Bernd Polster. *Wie die Wilden. Tänze auf der Höhe ihrer Zeit.* Berlin: Rotbuch, 1985.

Eissler, W.U. *Arbeiterparteien und Homosexuellenfrage. Zur Sexualpolitik von SPD und KPD in der Weimarer Republik.* Berlin: Verlag rosa Winkel, 1980.

Evans, Richard, ed. *The German Underworld: Deviants and Outcasts in German History.* London/New York: Routledge, 1988.

Fischer, Lothar. *Tanz zwischen Rausch und Tod. Anita Berber, 1918–28 in Berlin.* Berlin: Haude und Spener, 1984.

Hirschfeld, Magnus, and Andreas Gaspar. *Sittengeschichte des Weltkrieges.* 2 vols. Leipzig: Verlag für Sexualwissenschaft—Schneider & Co., 1930.

Hohmann, Joachim S. *Sexualforschung und -Aufklärung in der Weimarer Republik.* Frankfurt a.M.: Foerster, 1985.

Isherwood, Christopher. *Christopher and His Kind, 1929–39.* New York: Farrar, Straus, and Giroux, 1976.

Kähler, Hermann. *Berlin-Asphalt und Licht. Die große Stadt in der Literatur der Weimarer Republik.* Berlin: deb, 1986.

Kern, Elga. *Wie sie dazu kamen. Lebensfragmente bordellierter Mädchen.* Darmstadt: Luchterhand, 1985 (repr. of 1928).

Koebner, Thomas, et al., eds. *"Mit uns zieht die neue Zeit." Der Mythos Jugend.* Frankfurt a.M.: Suhrkamp, 1985.

Köhn, Eckhard. *Straßenrausch. Flanerie und kleine Form. Versuch zur Literaturgeschichte des Flaneurs bis 1933.* Berlin: Das Arsenal, 1989.

Kreutzahler, Birgit. *Das Bild des Verbrechers im Roman der Weimarer Republik.* Frankfurt/ Bern/New York: Lang, 1976.

Kunstgewerbemuseum Berlin, ed. *Metropolen machen Mode. Haute Couture der Zwanziger Jahre.* Berlin: D. Reimer, 1977.

Kuczynski, Jürgen. *Geschichte des Alltags des deutschen Volkes (1918–1945).* Berlin: Akademie-Verlag 1982.

Liang, Hsi-Huey. *The Berlin Police Force in the Weimar Republic.* Berkeley and Los Angeles: University of California Press, 1970.

Moreck, Curt. *Führer durch das "lasterhafte" Berlin.* Leipzig: Verlag moderner Stadführer, 1931.

Müller, Hedwig, and Patricia Stöckemann. *"...jeder Mensch ist ein Tänzer": Ausdruckstanz in Deutschland zwischen 1900 und 1945.* Gießen: Anabas-Verlag, 1993.

Ostwald, Hans. *Sittengeschichte der Inflation.* Berlin: Neufeld & Henius, 1931.

Plant, Richard. *The Pink Triangle: The Nazi War against Homosexuals.* New York: Henry Holt and Co., 1986.

Richard, Lionel. *La vie quotidienne sous la Republique de Weimar (1919–1933).* Paris: Hachette, 1983.

Schlör, Joachim. *Nachts in der großen Stadt. Paris-Berlin-London 1840–1930.* Munich: Artemis & Winkler, 1991.

Schrader, Bärbel, and Jürgen Schebera. *Kunstmetropole Berlin 1918–1933.* Berlin and Weimar: Aufbau, 1987.

Schulte, Regina. *Sperrbezirke. Tugendhaftigkeit und Prostitution in der bürgerlichen Welt*. Frankfurt a.M.: Syndikat, 1979.

Schwerk, Ekkehard. *Die Meisterdiebe von Berlin*. Kreuzberger Hefte 5. Berlin: Nishen-Verlag, 1984.

Spiess, Volker, ed. *Gauner, Künstler, Originale. Die 20er Jahre in Berlin*. Berlin: Haude & Spener, 1988.

Steakley, James. *The Homosexual Emancipation Movement in Germany*. New York: Arno, 1975.

Strohmeyer, Klaus. *Warenhäuser. Geschichte, Blüte und Untergang im Warenmeer*. Berlin: Wagenbach, 1980.

Tergit, Gabriele. *Blüten der Zwanziger Jahre*. Berlin: Rotation Verlag, 1984.

Theweleit, Klaus. *Male Fantasies,* trans. Stephen Conway. 2 vols. Minneapolis: University of Minnesota Press, 1987.

Westphal, Uwe. *Berliner Konfektion und Mode. 1836–1939. Die Zerstörung einer Tradition*. Berlin: Edition Hentrich, 1986.

Wigman, Mary. *The Mary Wigman Book. Her Writings*, ed. Walter Sorell. Middletown: Wesleyan University Press, 1975.

Wittig, Bernd. *Männerbünde und Massen. Zur Krise männlicher Identität in der Literatur der Moderne*. Opladen: Westdeutscher Verlag, 1992.

Wulffen, Erich. *Woman as a Sexual Criminal*, trans. David Berger. New York: American Ethnological Press, 1934.

Acknowledgments

Unless otherwise noted below, all translations are by Don Reneau.

3. From Alma Luckau, *The German Delegation at the Paris Peace Conference* (New York: Columbia University Press, 1941). Reprinted by permission of Columbia University Press. Translated by the author. 8. Ernst Jünger, *Sämtliche Werke, Band 8*. Copyright © 1980 by Ernst Klett Verlag für Wissen und Bildung GmbH, Stuttgart. 9. Reprinted with permission of Rowohlt Verlag. Copyright © 1960 by Rowohlt Verlag GmbH, Reinbek bei Hamburg. 10. Carl Zuckmayer, *Aufruf zum Leben*. Copyright © 1976 by S. Fischer Verlag Gmbh, Frankfurt a.M. 11. Translated by Bruce Campbell. 12. Copyright © 1933 by International Institute of Intellectual Co-operation, League of Nations, Paris. Translated by Stuart Gilbert. 13. From *The New York Times*, November 29, 1918. 14. Copyright © by Aufbau Verlag, Berlin. 15. From *Rosa Luxemburg Speaks*, edited by Mary-Alice Waters. Reprinted by permission of Pathfinder Press. Copyright © 1970 by Pathfinder Press, New York. Translated by Eden and Cedar Paul. 16. From *Documents of German History*, edited by Louis Snyder, Copyright © 1958 by Rutgers University Press. Translated by the editor. 17. From *In The Twenties: The Diaries of Harry Kessler*. English translation copyright © 1971 by Weidenfeld and Nicolson, London. Translated by Charles Kessler. 20. *Memoirs of Prince von Bülow, III: The World War and Germany's Collapse*, (Boston: Little, Brown, and Company, 1932). Translated by Geoffrey Dunlop. 25. Copyright © Dr. Peter Milford. Reprinted by permission of Dr. Peter Milford and Tom Bottomore. Translated by Patrick Goode. 32. From *Living Age*, vol. 344, no. 4398 (March 1933), 27–38. 35. From Max Weber, *Selections in Translation*, edited by W.G. Runciman. Copyright © 1978 by Cambridge University Press. Reprinted with the permission of Cambridge University Press. Translated by Eric Matthews. 36. Reprinted with the permission of Rowohlt Verlag. Copyright © 1960 by Rowohlt Verlag. 39. From Thomas Mann, *Order of the Day*, translated by H.T. Lowe-Porter. Copyright © 1942 and renewed 1970 by Alfred A. Knopf, Inc. Reprinted by permission of Alfred A. Knopf and S. Fischer Verlag. 41. Copyright © by Aufbau Verlag. 44. Reprinted with the permission of Rowohlt Verlag. Copyright © 1960 by Rowohlt Verlag GmbH. 45, 48, 50. Reprinted from *Nazi Ideology Before 1933*, introduced and translated by Barbara Miller Lane and Leila J. Rupp, copyright © 1978. Reprinted by permission of the authors and the University of Texas Press. 47. From *National Socialism*, edited by Raymond Murphy. English translation by E.T.S. Dugdale (United States Department of State, Publication 1864, Washington, 1943). 49. From *Mein Kampf* by Adolf Hitler, Copyright © 1943, renewed 1971 by Houghton Mifflin Company. Reprinted by permission of Houghton Mifflin Company, Boston and Hutchinson, London. All rights reserved. Translated by Ralph Mannheim. 51. From *Documents of German History,* edited by Louis Snyder. Copyright © 1958 by Rutgers University Press. Translated by the editor. 52. From *Adolf Hitler: My New Order,* edited with a commentary by Raoul de Roussy de Sales (New York: Reynal & Hitchcock, 1941). 53. From Simon Taylor, *Germany 1918–1933* (London: Gerald Duckworth and Company, 1983). Copyright © 1983 by Simon Taylor. Reprinted by permission of Duckworth. Translated by the author.

55. From *In the Twenties: The Diaries of Harry Kessler*. English translation copyright © 1971 by Weidenfeld and Nicolson, London. Translated by Charles Kessler. **56.** From Ernst Bloch, *Heritage of Our Times* (Berkeley and Los Angeles: University of California Press, 1990). Copyright © 1962 by Suhrkamp Verlag, Frankfurt a.M. Translated by Neville and Stephen Plaice. **57.** From Thomas Mann, *Order of the Day,* translated by H.T. Lowe-Porter. Copyright © 1942 and renewed 1970 by Alfred A. Knopf and S. Fischer Verlag. Reprinted by permission of the publishers. **58.** English translation copyright © 1979 by Jerold Wikoff. Reprinted with permission of *New German Critique*. German text copyright © 1972 by Suhrkamp Verlag. Reprinted with permission of Suhrkamp Verlag and Harvard University Press. **59.** Copyright © by Aufbau Verlag. **62.** From *Joseph Roth Werke, Band III-Das Journalistische Werk, 1929–1939*, published by Verlag Kiepenheuer & Witsch, Köln. Copyright © 1991 by Verlag Kiepenheuer and Witsch, Köln, and Allert de Lange, Amsterdam. Used with permission. **64.** From *The Long Generation: Germany from Ruin to Empire, 1913–1945*, edited by Henry Cord Meyer (New York: Harper and Row, 1973). Copyright © 1973 by Henry Cord Meyer. Reprinted with permission of HarperCollins publishers. Translated by the editor. **70.** From Siegfried Kracauer, *Die Angestellten*, Suhrkamp Verlag, Copyright © 1971 by Suhrkamp Verlag. **83.** Copyright © by Suhrkamp Verlag. Reprinted with permission of the publisher. **87.** From Larissa Reissner, *Hamburg at the Barricades*, translated from the Russian and edited by Richard Chappell (London: Pluto Press, 1977). Copyright © 1977 by Pluto Press. **90.** Translated by Susan Buck-Morss. Translation Copyright © 1973 Susan Buck-Morss. Reprinted with permission of Harvard University Press and Suhrkamp Verlag. Copyright © 1969 by Suhrkamp Verlag. **94.** From Hanns Eisler, *A Rebel in Music: Selected Writings*, edited with an introduction by Manfred Grabs (New York: International Publishers, 1978). Copyright © by 1976 VEB Deutscher Verlag für Musik, Leipzig. All rights reserved. English translation © Copyright Seven Seas Books, Berlin, 1978, published with permission of VEB Deutscher Verlag. Translated by Marjorie Meyer. **95.** From Georg Lukács, *Essays on Realism*, edited by Rodney Livingstone, translated by David Fernbach (Cambridge: MIT Press, 1981). Copyright © Ferenc Jánossy. English-language edition copyright © 1980 by Lawrence and Wishart, London. **98.** From Martin Buber, *Israel and the World* (New York: Schocken Books, 1948). Reprinted with permission of the Estate of Martin Buber. Translated by O. Marx. **103.** From *Franz Rosenzweig: His Life and Thought*, edited by N.N. Glatzer (New York: Schocken Books, 1953). Copyright © 1953 Schocken Books Inc. Reprinted by permission of Schocken Books, published by Pantheon Books, a division of Random House, Inc. Translated by Francis C. Golffing. **105.** From Joseph Roth, *Werke Band IV-Das Journalistische Werk, 1924–1928*, published by Verlag Kiepenheuer & Witsch, copyright © 1989 by Verlag Kiepenheuer & Witsch and Allert de Lange. Used with permission. **106.** Used with permission of Matthes & Seitz Verlag, Munich. **107.** From Gershom Scholem, *The Messianic Idea in Judaism* (New York: Schocken Books, 1971). Copyright © 1971 by Schocken Books. Reprinted by permission of Pantheon Books, a division of Random House, Inc. **109.** English translation from *The Menorah Journal*, 26, 1 (January–March 1938), 105–113. German text copyright © Aufbau Verlag. **111.** Copyright © by Walter-Verlag, Solothurn. Used with permission. **115.** From Karl Mannheim, *Ideology and Utopia*, translated by Louis Wirth and Edward Shils (New York: Harcourt Brace Jovanovich, 1955). Reprinted by permission of Harcourt Brace Jovanovich, Inc. and Routledge, London. **116.** Used with permission of Lotte Kohler. Copyright © by Hannah Arendt Literary Trust. **118.** English translation by Ben Brewster, originally published in *Screen* volume 14, number 2, 1974. Translation copyright © 1974 by *Screen*. German text copyright © by Suhrkamp Verlag. Reprinted with permission of

Suhrkamp Verlag and Harvard University Press. **119**. Copyright © 1977 by Suhrkamp Verlag. **121**. From Karl Korsch, *Marxism and Philosophy*, translated with an introduction by Fred Halliday (London: NLB, 1970), Copyright © 1970 by NLB. Reprinted by permission of Monthly Review Foundation. **122**. From Max Horkheimer, *Dawn and Decline: Notes 1926–1931 and 1950–1969* (New York: Continuum, 1978). English translation copyright © 1978 by The Continuum Publishing Company. Reprinted by permission of the publisher. Translated by Michael Shaw. **123**. From *Critical Theory and Society*, edited by Stephen Bronner and Douglas Kellner (New York: Routledge, 1989). Reprinted by permission of Routledge, Chapman and Hall, Inc. and MIT Press. Translated by Peter Wagner. **124**. From Wilhelm Reich, *Sex-Pol Essays: 1929–1934*, edited by Lee Baxandall. Copyright © 1966, 1971, 1972 by Lee Baxandall. Reprinted by permission of Random House, Inc. Translated by Anna Bostock, Tom DuBose, and Lee Baxandall. **125**. From Leo Löwenthal, *Literature and Mass Culture: Communication and Society*, volume 1 (New Brunswick: Transaction Books, 1989). Copyright © 1989 by Transaction Books. Reprinted by permission of the publisher. Translated by Susanne Hoppmann-Löwenthal. **128**. From Arthur Moeller van den Bruck, *Germany's Third Empire* (London: George Allen and Unwin, 1934). Translated by E.O. Lorimer. **129**. From Carl Schmitt, *The Crisis of Parliamentary Democracy* (Cambridge: MIT Press, 1985). Copyright © 1985 by Massachusetts Institute of Technology. Translated by Ellen Kennedy. **132**. Used with permission of S. Fischer Verlag. **133**. From Carl Schmitt, *The Concept of the Political*, Copyright © 1976 by Rutgers, The State University. Translated by George Schwab. **138**. From *The Decline of the West* by Oswald Spengler. Copyright © 1926 by Alfred A. Knopf, Inc. Reprinted by permission of the publisher. Translated by Charles Francis Atkinson. **141**. From "Kunst des Müβiggangs" copyright © 1973 by Suhrkamp Verlag. Used with permission of the publisher. **142**. From Martin Heidegger, *Being and Time*, Copyright © 1962 by SCM Press Ltd. Reprinted by permission of HarperCollins publishers. Translated by John Macquarie and Edward Robinson. **143**. First published in Berlin, 1931. Copyright © 1991 by Ernst Klett Verlag für Wissen und Bildung GmbH. **144**. From Karl Jaspers, *Man in the Modern Age* (New York: Routledge and Kegan Paul, 1951). Reprinted with permission of the publisher. Translated by Eden and Cedar Paul. **145**. From Ernst Jünger, *Sämtliche Werke Band 8: Der Arbeiter*. Copyright © 1981 by Ernst Klett Verlag für Wissen und Bildung GmbH, Stuttgart. Used with permission of Ernst Klett Verlag and State University of New York Press, Albany. **147**. From Gottfried Benn, *Prose, Essays, Poems*, edited by Volkmar Sander. Copyright © 1987 by The Continuum Publishing Company. Reprinted by permission of The Continuum Publishing Company. Translated by Joel Agee. **149**. Used with permission of Walter-Verlag, Solothurn. **154**. From Siegfried Kracauer, *The Mass Ornament* (Cambridge: Harvard University Press, forthcoming). Reprinted by permission of Harvard University Press. Translated by Thomas Levin. **160**. Used with permission of Rowohlt Verlag. Copyright © 1960 by Rowohlt Verlag GmbH. **162**. Translated by Edward Dimendberg. Used with permission of Aufbau-Verlag. **165**. English translation copyright © by Thomas Sheehan. **166, 167, 186**. From *Programs and Manifestoes on 20th-Century Architecture*, edited by Ulrich Conrads. English translation copyright © 1970 by Lund Humphries, London, and the Massachusetts Institute of Technology, Cambridge, Massachusetts. Gropius text translated by Wolfgang Jabs and Basil Gilbert. Taut and Work Council texts translated by Michael Bullock. **172**. Used with permission of Professor Rudolf Arnheim. **173**. Used with permission of Mrs. Esther Mendelsohn Joseph. **188**. Used with permission of Marthe Prévot. **189**. Translated by Charles W. Haxthausen. Reprinted by permission of the Estate of George Grosz/VAGA, New York, 1993. **191**. Copyright © 1993 by ARS, New York/VG Bild-Kunst, Bonn. **193**. Copyright © by Fannei & Walz Verlag, Berlin. Used with permission of the publisher. **195**. Translated by Edward Dimendberg. **198**. Reprinted by permission of the Estate of George Grosz/VAGA, New York, 1993. **201**. Reprinted with permission of Aufbau Verlag. **202**. From Walter Benjamin, *Reflections: Essays, Aphorisms, Autobiographical Writings*, Copyright © 1955 by Suhrkamp Verlag, English translation copyright © 1978 by Harcourt Brace and Company, reprinted by Harcourt Brace and Company. Translated by Edmund Jephcott. **203**. Copyright © by Walter-Verlag. Used with permission of the publisher. **208**. Reprinted with permission of Aufbau-Verlag. **210**. From Gottfried Benn, *Primal Vision*, edited by E.B. Ashton, Copyright © 1971 by New Directions Publishing Corporation. All rights reserved. Reprinted by permission of New Directions Publishing Company. Translated by Eugene Jolas. **217, 222**. From *Brecht As They Knew Him*, edited by Hubert Witt (New York: International Publishers, 1974). Copyright © 1974 by International Publishers. Reprinted by permission of the publisher. Translated by John Peet. **219, 221**. From *Brecht on Theatre* by Bertolt Brecht. Translation copyright © 1964 by John Willet. Reprinted by permission of Hill and Wang, a division of Farrar, Straus, and Giroux, Inc. and Reed International Books, London. Translated by John Willet. **224**. From Erwin Piscator, *The Political Theatre: A History 1914–1929*, translated with chapter introductions and notes by Hugh Rorrison (New York: Avon Books, 1978). Copyright © 1963 by Rowohlt Verlag. Used with permission of the publisher. **237**. Copyright © Suhrkamp Verlag. Reprinted by permission. **240, 242**. From *Kurt Weill in Europe*, edited and translated by Kim Kowalke (Ann Arbor: UMI Research Press, 1979). Copyright © The Kurt Weill Foundation for Music, Inc. Reprinted by permission. **243**. Used with Permission of Foundation Hindemith. **245**. From *Writings of German Composers*, edited by Jost Hermand and James Steakley. Copyright © 1984 by The Continuum Publishing Company. Translated by Willi Reich. **246**. From Arnold Schoenberg, *Style and Idea: Selected Writings of Arnold Schoenberg*, edited by Leonard Stein and translated by Leo Black (London: Faber and Faber Ltd., 1975). **247**. From Ernst Krenek, *Exploring Music*, translated by Margaret Shenfield (London: Calder and Boyars, 1966). **248**. From Theodor W. Adorno, *Gesammelte Schriften*, volume 19 edited by Rolf Tiedemann. Copyright © 1984 by Suhrkamp Verlag, Frankfurt am Main. English translation copyright © by Jamie Owen Daniel. **249**. From *Kurt Weill in Europe*, edited and translated by Kim Kowalke (Ann Arbor: UMI Research Press, 1979). Copyright © by The Kurt Weill Foundation for Music, Inc. Reprinted by permission. **252**. Used with permission of Rowohlt Verlag. Copyright © 1960 by Rowohlt Verlag. **253**. From Theodor W. Adorno, *Gesammelte Schriften*, volume 19 edited by Rolf Tiedemann. Copyright © 1984 by Suhrkamp Verlag, Frankfurt am Main. Translated by Thomas Levin. English translation copyright © Thomas Levin. **258**. Used with permission of Professor Rudolf Arnheim. **259**. From *Brecht on Theatre* by Bertolt Brecht, translated by John Willett (New York: Hill and Wang, 1964). Translation copyright © 1964 by John Willett. Reprinted by permission of Hill and Wang, a division of Farrar, Straus, and Giroux, Inc. and Reed International Books. **264**. Copyright © 1977 by Suhrkamp Verlag. **267**. From Siegfried Kracauer, *Schriften* 2, copyright © 1990 by Suhrkamp Verlag. English translation from *Joseph von Sternberg*, edited by Peter Baxter (London: British Film Institute, 1980). Copyright © by British Film Institute. Translated by Jill Dimmock. **270**. From Siegfried Kracauer, *Kino: Essays, Studien, Glossen zum Film* copyright © 1974 by Suhrkamp Verlag. **272**. From *Photography in the Modern Era: European Documents and Critical Writings, 1913–1940*, edited with an introduction by Christopher Phillips (New York: Metropolitan Museum of Art/Aperture, 1989). Original German text copyright © by August Sander

Archive. English translation by Joel Agee copyright © 1989 by Metropolitan Museum of Art. **274**. From *Photography in the Modern Era: European Documents and Critical Writings, 1913–1940*. Original German text copyright © Albert Renger-Patzsch Archiv c/o Ann and Jürgen Wilde, Zülpich. English translation by Joel Agee copyright © 1989 by Metropolitan Museum of Art. **276**. From *Germany: The New Photography 1927–33, Documents Selected and Edited by David Mellor* (London: Arts Council, 1976). Original German text copyright © by VG-H. English translation by P.S. Falla copyright © by Arts Council of Great Britain. **278**. From *Photography in the Modern Era: European Documents and Critical Writings, 1913–1940*. Original German text copyright © by Marthe Prévot. English translation by Joel Agee copyright © 1989 by the Metropolitan Museum of Art. **279**. From *Photography in the Modern Era: European Documents and Critical Writings, 1913–1940*. English translation by Joel Agee, copyright © 1989 by The Metropolitan Museum of Art. **298**. Translated by Leslie A. Pahl. **302**. From *Schrifttanz*, edited and translated by Valerie Preston-Dunlop and Susanne Lahusen (London: Dance Books, 1990). Translated by the editors. Copyright © by Valerie Preston-Dunlop. **313**. Used with permission of Walter-Verlag. Copyright © by Walter Verlag. **314**. Used with permission of Rowohlt Verlag. Copyright © 1960 by Rowohlt Verlag. **323**. Reprinted with the permission of The Free Press, a Division of Macmillan, Inc., from *The Criminal, The Judge, and the Public: A Psychological Analysis*, Revised Edition, by Franz Alexander, M.D. and Hugo Staub. Copyright © 1956 by The Free Press. Copyright © 1931 by the Macmillan Company. Translated by Gregory Zilboorg. **327**. Copyright © by Suhrkamp Verlag. Reprinted by permission.

The editors and publisher are grateful to the above copyright owners for permission to republish material in this book. Despite great efforts, it has not been possible in every case to locate all rights holders and estates. The editors and publisher apologize in advance for any unintended errors and omissions, which they will seek to correct in future printings. Please address inquiries to: University of California Press, 405 Hilgard Avenue, Los Angeles, California 90024.

Index

Page numbers in italic indicate a document that is authored by that individual or group.

Designer: Sandy Drooker
Compositor: Braun-Brumfield, Inc.
Text: 10/12 Granjon
Display: Kable, Futura
Printer: Braun-Brumfield, Inc.
Binder: Braun-Brumfield, Inc.